Gleim Publications, Inc., offers five study manuals of objective questions and explanations:

REVIEWERS AND CONTRIBUTORS

Grady M. Irwin, J.D., University of Florida, has taught in the University of Florida College of Business. Mr. Irwin provided many answer explanations and extensive editorial assistance throughout.

Karen A. Louviere, B.A., University of Florida, reviewed the manuscript and provided production assistance throughout the project.

Travis Moore, M.B.A., University of Florida, is our production coordinator. Mr. Moore coordinated and supervised the production staff and reviewed the entire manuscript.

Nancy Raughley, B.A., Tift College, is our editor. Ms. Raughley reviewed the manuscript and assisted in all phases of production.

John F. Rebstock, CIA, is a graduate of the Fisher School of Accounting at the University of Florida. He has passed the CIA and CPA exams, and is a CMA candidate. Mr. Rebstock prepared the page layout for the entire edition.

A PERSONAL THANKS

This manual would not have been possible without the extraordinary effort and dedication of Terry Hall, Gail Luparello, and Rhonda Powell, who typed the entire manuscript and all revisions as well as prepared the camera-ready pages.

We appreciate the production and editorial assistance of Chad Houghton, Katandra Littles, Jennifer Menge, Shana Robbins, and Lisa Saltz.

Finally, we appreciate the encouragement and tolerance of our families throughout the project.

Visit our Internet site (www.gleim.com/updates.html) for the latest updates and information on all of our products.

Seventh Edition

FINANCIAL ACCOUNTING

Objective Questions and Explanations

by

Irvin N. Gleim, Ph.D., CPA, CIA, CMA

and

William A. Collins, Ph.D., CPA

ABOUT THE AUTHORS

Irvin N. Gleim is Professor Emeritus in the Fisher School of Accounting at the University of Florida and is a member of the American Accounting Association, American Business Law Association, American Institute of Certified Public Accountants, Association of Government Accountants, Florida Institute of Certified Public Accountants, The Institute of Internal Auditors, Institute of Management Accountants, and the National Association of Accountants. He has had articles published in the *Journal of Accountancy, The Accounting Review,* and *The American Business Law Journal* and is author/coauthor of numerous accounting and aviation books and CPE courses.

William A. Collins is Professor and Department of Accounting Head at the Joseph M. Bryan School of Business and Economics, University of North Carolina at Greensboro. He is a member of the American Accounting Association, the American Institute of Certified Public Accountants, and the Florida Institute of Certified Public Accountants. He has authored and coauthored articles that have been published in the *Journal of Accountancy, The Accounting Review, Journal of Accounting Research,* and *Internal Auditor.* Monographs coauthored by him have been published by the Financial Accounting Standards Board and the Institute of Internal Auditors. Professor Collins also annually authors and presents continuing education seminars dealing with the authoritative accounting and reporting standards.

iv

Gleim Publications, Inc.
P.O. Box 12848
University Station
Gainesville, Florida 32604
(352) 375-0772
(800) 87-GLEIM
FAX: (352) 375-6940
Internet: www.gleim.com
E-mail: admin@gleim.com

ISSN: 1091-451X

ISBN 0-917539-66-4

This is the first printing of the seventh edition of *Financial Accounting, Objective Questions and Explanations*. Please e-mail update@gleim.com with FIN OQE 7-1 as the subject or text. You will receive our current update as a reply.

EXAMPLE:

To: update@gleim.com
From: your e-mail address
Subject: FIN OQE 7-1

ACKNOWLEDGMENTS

Material from Uniform Certified Public Accountant Examination questions and unofficial answers, Copyright © 1972-1995 by the American Institute of Certified Public Accountants, Inc. is reprinted and/or adapted with permission.

The authors also appreciate and thank The Institute of Internal Auditors, Inc. for permission to use The Institute's Certified Internal Auditor Examination questions, copyright © 1975-1995 by The Institute of Internal Auditors, Inc.

The authors also appreciate and thank the Institute of Certified Management Accountants for permission to use questions from past CMA examinations, copyright © 1972-1995 by the Institute of Management Accountants.

The authors also acknowledge the Florida State Board of Accountancy and its written professional examination as a source of questions.

This publication is designed to provide accurate and authoritative information with regard to the subject matter covered. It is sold with the understanding that the publisher is not engaged in rendering legal, accounting, or other professional service.

If legal advice or other expert assistance is required, the services of a competent professional person should be sought.

(From a declaration of principles jointly adopted by a Committee of the American Bar Association and a Committee of Publishers.)

PREFACE FOR ACCOUNTING STUDENTS

The purpose of this study manual is to help you understand financial accounting principles and procedures, and their applications. In turn, these skills will enable you to perform better on your undergraduate examinations, as well as look ahead to (and prepare for) professional examinations.

One of the major benefits of this study manual is comprehensive coverage of financial accounting topics. Accordingly, when you use this study manual to help prepare for financial accounting courses and examinations, you are assured of covering virtually all topics that could reasonably be expected to be studied in typical college or university intermediate and advanced financial accounting courses.

The question-and-answer format is designed and presented to facilitate effective study. Students should be careful not to misuse this text by referring to the answers before independently answering each question.

The majority of the questions are from past CIA, CMA, and CPA examinations. Although a citation for the source of each question is provided, a substantial number have been modified to accommodate changes in professional pronouncements, to clarify questions, and/or to emphasize a financial accounting concept or its application. In addition, hundreds of publisher-written questions test areas covered in current textbooks but not directly tested on accounting certification examinations. Finally, we are pleased to be using questions submitted by accounting professors.

Note that this study manual should not be relied upon to prepare for the professional examinations. You should use review manuals specifically developed for each examination. *CIA Review, CMA Review,* and *CPA Review* are up to date and comprehensively cover all material necessary for successful completion of these examinations. An order form for these and other Gleim books is provided at the back of this book.

Thank you for your interest in this study manual. We deeply appreciate the many letters and suggestions received from accounting students and educators during the past years, as well as from CIA, CMA, and CPA candidates. Please send us your suggestions, comments, and corrections concerning this edition. The last page of this book has been designed to help you note corrections and suggestions throughout your study process. Please photocopy it or tear it out and mail it to us with your suggestions.

Please read the first three chapters carefully. They are very short but nonetheless very important.

Good Luck on Your Exams,

Irvin N. Gleim
William A. Collins

December 1996

PREFACE FOR ACCOUNTING PRACTITIONERS

The first purpose of this study manual is to permit you to assess your technical proficiency concerning financial accounting standards and special skills. The second purpose is to facilitate your review and update of financial accounting standards and techniques with our compendium of objective questions. The third purpose is to provide CPE credit for your self-assessment and review/update study effort in conjunction with the Gleim CPE program.

This approach to CPE is both motivating and intense. You should be continually challenged to answer each question correctly. When you answer a question incorrectly or have difficulty, you should pursue a complete understanding by reading the answer explanation and consulting reference sources as necessary.

Most of the questions in *Financial Accounting Objective Questions and Explanations* were taken from various professional examinations, but many have been revised, adapted, etc., to provide broader, up-to-date coverage of the financial accounting body of technical knowledge. While many are from the CPA exam, others are from the CIA and CMA exams. Thus, you have an opportunity to consider the appropriateness of pursuing these other accounting certifications. In addition, hundreds of publisher questions cover material not directly tested on the accounting certification examinations.

Chapters One and Two of *Financial Accounting Objective Questions and Explanations* are directed primarily to accounting and auditing students. Those practitioners interested in multiple certification, however, may find the discussion of the CIA and CMA certification programs in Chapter 3 to be useful. If, as you work through this study book and take the open-book CPE final exams, you find you need to refer to a current textbook, Chapter One contains a list of current titles. You should be sure to read carefully "Introduction: How to Use This CPE Program" in the accompanying CPE book.

Finally, we ask for any supplemental comments, reactions, suggestions, etc., that you may have as you complete our CPE program. The last page of this study book has been designed to help you note corrections and suggestions throughout your study process. Please attach it to the Course Evaluation form included with your CPE program. An order form and further descriptions of our CPE programs are provided at the back of this book.

Thank you for your interest, and we look forward to hearing from you.

Best Wishes in Your CPE Endeavors,

Irvin N. Gleim
William A. Collins
December 1996

CONTRIBUTING PROFESSORS

We are especially grateful to the following professors who submitted questions for this and previous editions. Their participation has made *Financial Accounting Objective Questions and Explanations* truly a community project. We welcome further submissions of questions either for the Eighth Edition of *Financial Accounting Objective Questions and Explanations* or for future editions of our other objective questions and explanations books.

Barnhart, James R. . . . . Ball State University
Bayes, Paul E. . . . . East Tennessee State University
Boze, Ken M. . . . . University of Alaska, Anchorage
Bradley, David B. . . . . Lyndon State College
Broome, O. Whitfield, Jr. . . . . University of Virginia
Bruno, Joan D. . . . . University of Houston
Bush, H. Francis . . . . Bradley University
Byrd, Sandra . . . . Southwest Missouri State University
Cerepak, John . . . . Fairleigh Dickinson University
Derstine, Robert P. . . . . Villanova University
Dugopolski, Christiana . . . . University of Missouri at St. Louis
Emig, James M. . . . . Villanova University
Flesher, D.L. . . . . University of Mississippi
Garfinkle, Caryn . . . . Brooklyn College - CUNY
Hall, Connie . . . . East Central University
Hall, J.O. . . . . Western Kentucky University
Helling, Alene G. . . . . Stark Technical College
Higley, Wayne M. . . . . Siebens Forum
Hora, Judith A. . . . . University of Hawaii at Hilo
Kame, Donald G. . . . . Stark Technical College
Krueger, LaVern E. University of Missouri - Kansas City
Lockett, Pete . . . . Cal State LA
Mantooth, J.W. . . . . University of Science and Arts of Oklahoma
McBrayer, Phil . . . . High Point College
McKenna, John N. . . . . Pace University
Miller, Tim . . . . Murray State University
Oddo, Alfonso R. . . . . Niagara University
O'Keefe, Ruth R. . . . . Jacksonville University
Phillips, T.J., Jr. . . . . Louisiana Tech University
Posey, Roderick B. . . . . University of Southern Mississippi
Putnam, Karl . . . . University of Texas at El Paso
Richter, Marshal . . . . Brooklyn College - CUNY
Ried, G. . . . . University of Toledo
Rubin, Steven . . . . Brooklyn College - CUNY
Schultz, Sally . . . . SUNY College at New Paltz
Skender, C.J. . . . . North Carolina State University
Spede, Edward C. . . . . Virginia Commonwealth University
Sperry, John B. . . . . Virginia Commonwealth University
Trebby, James P. . . . . Marquette University
Venkateswar, Sankaran . . . . Trinity University
Welton, Ralph . . . . Clemson University
Westmoreland, G. Florida State University, Panama City

TABLE OF CONTENTS

CHAPTER ONE
HOW TO USE THIS BOOK

This chapter explains how and why this study manual was written. More importantly, it describes how to use it efficiently and effectively.

The format and content of this study manual are innovative in the accounting text market. The first purpose is to provide accounting students with a well-organized, comprehensive compendium of objective questions covering the topics taught in typical intermediate and advanced financial undergraduate accounting courses. The second purpose is to provide accounting professionals with a comprehensive presentation of diagnostic objective questions for self-diagnostic use and/or review of intermediate and advanced level accounting standards and procedures.

This study manual consists solely of objective questions and answer explanations, with the exception of the first three chapters:

1. How to Use This Book
2. How to Study for Success
3. The CIA, CMA, CPA, and Other Certification Programs

The Gleim objective questions and explanations books really work! You can pretest yourself before class to see if you are strong or weak in the assigned area. You can retest after class to see if you really understand the material. The questions in these books cover **all** topics in your related courses, so you will encounter few questions on your exams for which you will not be well prepared.

The chapter titles and organization of Chapters 4 through 34 are based on the current intermediate financial and advanced financial textbooks listed in Appendix A. Some textbooks may have been inadvertently omitted, for which we apologize. Appendix A contains the table of contents of each of these books with cross-references to chapters and modules in this book.

OUR USE OF MODULES

Each chapter of this book is divided into subtopics to assist your study program. We call these subtopics "modules." Modules permit broad and perhaps overwhelming topics to be divided into more manageable study components.

Choosing modules and arranging questions within these subtopics was difficult. The number of questions is large enough for comprehensive coverage but does not present an insurmountable task. We have defined each module narrowly enough to cover a single topic but broadly enough to prevent questions from being repetitious.

Within each module, the multiple-choice questions are presented in a sequence moving from the general to the specific, elementary to advanced, etc., to provide an effective learning sequence. Duplicate questions and redundant explanations have been kept to a minimum.

SOURCES OF OBJECTIVE QUESTIONS

Past CIA, CMA, and CPA examinations are the primary sources of questions in this study manual. In addition, your authors have prepared questions (identified in this text as *Publisher*) based upon the content of intermediate and advanced financial accounting textbooks (listed in Appendix A), APB Opinions, FASB pronouncements, etc. These *Publisher* questions were developed to review topics not adequately covered by questions from the other sources. Also, professors from schools around the country have contributed questions. See page vii for a list of their names and school affiliations.

IDENTIFICATION OF THE SOURCE OF EACH QUESTION

The source of each question appears in the first line of its answer explanation, in the column to the right of the question. Summary of source codes:

CIA	Certified Internal Auditor Examination
CMA	Certified Management Accountant Examination
CPA	Uniform Certified Public Accountant Examination
Publisher	Your authors
Professor Name	Name of professor who submitted the question

After each source code (except Publisher or a professor's name), codes for the following information are given:

Month and year (e.g., 592, which signifies a May 1992 exam date)
Exam part (See below.)
Question number (See below.)

Roman numerals signify the parts of the CIA exam, e.g., I, II, III, IV. Arabic numerals signify the parts of the CMA exam, e.g., 1, 2, 3, 4. The parts of the CPA exam covered in this book are coded as follows:

Pre-1994	1994 and after
L -- Business Law	*L* -- Business Law
A -- Auditing	*A* -- Auditing
I -- Practice I	*TMG* -- TAX-MAN-GOV
II -- Practice II	*F* -- Financial
T -- Theory	

Below are examples of codes and their meaning:

(CIA 591 I-17)	CIA exam, May 1991, Part I, question 17
(CMA 1290 4-11)	CMA exam, December 1990, Part 4, question 11
(CPA 590 II-1)	CPA exam, May 1990, Practice II section, question 1
(Publisher)	Prepared by your authors
(P. McBrayer)	Prepared by Professor Phil McBrayer

UNIQUENESS OF OBJECTIVE QUESTIONS

The major advantage of objective questions is the ability to cover (for study or test purposes) a large number of topics with little time and effort when compared to essay questions and computational problems.

A multiple-choice question is actually a series of four or five statements, of which all but one are incorrect given the facts of the question. The advantage of multiple-choice questions over true-false questions is that they require more analysis and result in a lower score for those with little or no knowledge. Random guessing on questions with four answer choices results in an expected grade of 25%. Guessing on a true-false test results in an expected grade of 50%.

Students and practitioners both like multiple-choice questions. Because they present alternative answers from which only one needs to be selected, students find them relatively easy to answer. Professors like objective questions because they are easy to grade and because much more material can be tested in the same period of time.

ANSWER EXPLANATIONS ALONGSIDE THE QUESTIONS

Our more efficient format presents questions and answer explanations side by side. The answer explanations appear to the right of each question. The example below is financial question number 8 of the May 1994 CPA Examination.

8. At December 31, 1992 and 1993, Apex Co. had 3,000 shares of $100 par, 5% cumulative preferred stock outstanding. No dividends were in arrears as of December 31, 1991. Apex did not declare a dividend during 1992. During 1993, Apex paid a cash dividend of $10,000 on its preferred stock. Apex should report dividends in arrears in its 1993 financial statements as a(n)

A.   Accrued liability of $15,000.

B.   Disclosure of $15,000.

C.   Accrued liability of $20,000.

D.   Disclosure of $20,000.

The correct answer is (D). *(CPA 594 F-8)*
REQUIRED: The amount and means of reporting preferred dividends in arrears.
DISCUSSION: Dividends in arrears on preferred stock are not an obligation of the company and are not recognized in the financial statements. However, the aggregate and per share amounts of arrearages in cumulative preferred dividends should be disclosed on the face of the balance sheet or in the notes (APB 10). The aggregate amount in arrears is $20,000 [(2 years x 5% x $100 par x 3,000 shares) – $10,000 paid in 1993].
Answers (A) and (C) are incorrect because dividends in arrears do not meet recognition criteria. Answer (B) is incorrect because $15,000 is the arrearage for 1 year.

The format in this study manual (illustrated above) is designed to facilitate your study of objective questions, their answers, and the answer explanations. The intent is to save you the time, effort, and aggravation of turning pages back and forth from questions to answers.

Be careful, however. You must avoid consulting the answers before you have answered the questions. Misuse of the readily available answers will give you a false sense of security and result in poor performance on examinations and decreased benefit from your studies. The best way to use this study manual is to cover the answer explanations with a sheet of paper as you read and answer each question. As a crucial part of the learning process, you must honestly commit yourself to an answer before looking at the answer explanation. Whether you are right or wrong, your memory of the correct answer will be reinforced by this process.

GLEIM HOME PAGE (www.gleim.com): FREE UPDATES, SOFTWARE, AND SUPPORT

Our extensive web page is updated regularly to provide convenient, up-to-date information. Some of the features include

- Free Demonstration Versions of Our Software
- Updates and Corrections for Gleim Books and Software
- Listings of Bookstores That Carry Gleim's *CPA Review*

- Technical Support Request Form
- Links to Other Helpful Sites
- Information about Other Gleim Products
- Order Forms

CITATIONS TO AUTHORITATIVE ACCOUNTING PRONOUNCEMENTS

Throughout the book, we refer to authoritative accounting pronouncements by the following abbreviations:

ARB - Accounting Research Bulletins were issued by the AICPA Committee on Accounting Procedure from 1939 to 1959. A total of 51 ARBs were issued. ARB 43, issued in 1953, is a codification of the first 42 ARBs and consists of numerous chapters. References to ARB 43 indicate the pertinent chapter number.

APB - APB Opinions were issued by the AICPA Accounting Principles Board from 1959 to 1973. A total of 30 opinions were issued.

APB Statements - APB Statements, also issued by the Accounting Principles Board, were only advisory in nature. They have effectively been replaced by the FASB's Statements of Financial Accounting Concepts.

SFAS - Statements of Financial Accounting Standards are issued by the Financial Accounting Standards Board (FASB), which was established in 1973. As of March 1994, 117 SFASs had been issued. Many SFASs supersede prior SFASs, APB Opinions, and Accounting Research Bulletins.

FASB Interpretations - Financial Accounting Standards Board Interpretations interpret existing pronouncements rather than establish new, superseding, or amending positions. (41 Interpretations had been issued as of April 1995.)

SFAC - FASB Statements of Financial Accounting Concepts establish financial accounting and reporting objectives and concepts, not rules; i.e., they do not constitute GAAP. They were designed for use by the FASB in developing their other authoritative pronouncements. (Six SFACs had been issued as of June 1993.)

SOP - AICPA Statements of Position are issued by the Accounting Standards Executive Committee of the AICPA. SOPs were originally set forth by the AICPA to provide accounting practitioners with guidance on unusual and specialized topics. SOPs are included in category (b) of the GAAP hierarchy for financial statements of nongovernmental entities. In the future, AICPA SOPs will only be issued in areas not appropriate for FASB pronouncements, e.g., personal financial statements.

The number following each acronym is the number of the pronouncement. The first time an authoritative pronouncement is cited, its complete title is given in italics. When the pronouncement is referred to again in the related series of questions, the title is usually omitted.

COVERAGE OF AUTHORITATIVE PRONOUNCEMENTS

Most of the authoritative pronouncements from the AICPA and the FASB currently in effect are covered in this book. The following listing of Chapters 4 through 34 indicates where coverage of each pronouncement can be found:

Chapter 4 - Basic Concepts
      ARB 43-1A, 3A
      APB Statement No. 4
      SFAC 1, 2, 5, 6

Chapter 5 - The Accounting Process

Chapter 6 - Income Statements
      ARB 43-2A
      APB 9, 12, 13, 30
      SFAS 16

Chapter 7 - Present Values and Future Values
      APB 21

Chapter 8 - Current Asset Except Inventory
      ARB 43-1A
      APB 6, 12
      SFAS 115, 125

Chapter 9 - Inventory
      ARB 43-4
      SFAS 48, 49

Chapter 10 - Property, Plant, and Equipment
      APB 6, 29
      SFAS 34, 42, 58, 62, 121
      FASB Interpretation No. 30

Chapter 11 - Depreciation and Depletion
      ARB 43-9
      APB 6, 12

Chapter 12 - Intangible Assets
      APB 17
      SFAS 2, 45, 68, 86, 121
      FASB Interpretation No. 6

Chapter 13 - Investments in Debt and Equity Securities
      APB 18
      SFAS 91, 115
      FASB Interpretation No. 35

Chapter 14 - Current Liabilities and Contingencies
      ARB 43-3A
      SFAS 5, 6, 43, 49, 78
      FASB Interpretation No. 8, 14, 34

Chapter 15 - Long-Term Liabilities
      APB 14, 21, 26
      SFAS 4, 15, 47, 64, 84, 114, 118, 125

Chapter 16 - Pensions, Other Postretirement Benefits, and Postemployment Benefits
      AICPA SOP 76-3
      SFAS 35, 75, 87, 88, 106, 110, 112

Chapter 17 - Leases
      SFAS 13, 22, 23, 27, 28, 29, 98
      FASB Interpretation No. 19, 23, 24, 26, 27

ARB, APB, AND FASB PRONOUNCEMENT CROSS-REFERENCE

The following listing of pronouncements directs you to the chapter in this study manual related to the coverage of each pronouncement listed. The chapter number follows the pronouncement title. Most pronouncements are covered by at least two multiple-choice questions. The index can also be helpful in locating questions on specific topics.

Pronounce-ment	Gleim Chapter(s)	Accounting Research Bulletins
ARB 43		
1A	4 and 8	Rules Adopted by Membership
1B	18	Profits or Losses on Treasury Stock
2A	6	Comparative Financial Statements
3A	4, 8, and 14	Current Assets and Current Liabilities
4	9	Inventory Pricing
7A	18	Quasi-Reorganization
7B	18	Stock Dividends and Stock Splits
9	11	Depreciation
10A	6	Real and Personal Property Taxes
11	6	Government Contracts
13B	18	Stock Option Compensation Plans
ARB 45	25	Long-Term Construction Contracts
ARB 46	18	Discontinuance of Dating Retained Earnings
ARB 51	28	Consolidated Financial Statements

		Accounting Principles Board Opinions
APB 2 & 4	20	Accounting for the Investment Credit
APB 6	8, 10, 11, 18, and 28	Status of Accounting Research Bulletins
APB 9	6	Reporting the Results of Operations
APB 10	18 and 25	Omnibus Opinion-1966
APB 12	6, 8, 11, and 16	Omnibus Opinion-1967
APB 13	6	Amending Paragraph 6 of APB 9, Application to Commercial Banks
APB 14	15 and 18	Convertible Debt and Debt Issued with Stock Purchase Warrants
APB 15	19	Earnings Per Share
APB 16	28	Business Combinations
APB 17	12	Intangible Assets
APB 18	13	Equity Method for Investments in Common Stock
APB 20	21	Accounting Changes
APB 21	7 and 15	Interest on Receivables and Payables
APB 22	24	Disclosure of Accounting Policies
APB 23	20	Accounting for Income Taxes-Special Areas
APB 25	18	Accounting for Stock Issued to Employees
APB 26	15	Early Extinguishment of Debt
APB 28	29	Interim Financial Reporting
APB 29	10 and 18	Accounting for Nonmonetary Transactions
APB 30	6	Reporting the Results of Operations

Pronounce-ment	Gleim Chapter(s)	Statements of Financial Accounting Standards
SFAS 2	12	Accounting for Research and Development Costs
SFAS 3	29	Reporting Accounting Changes in Interim Financial Statements
SFAS 4	15	Reporting Gains and Losses from Extinguishment of Debt
SFAS 5	14	Accounting for Contingencies
SFAS 6	14	Classification of Short-Term Obligations Expected to be Refinanced
SFAS 7	24	Accounting and Reporting by Development Stage Enterprises
SFAS 10	28	Extension of "Grandfather" Provisions for Business Combinations
SFAS 13	17	Accounting for Leases
SFAS 14	30	Financial Reporting for Segments of a Business Enterprise
SFAS 15	15	Accounting by Debtors and Creditors for Troubled Debt Restructurings
SFAS 16	6, 21, and 29	Prior Period Adjustments
SFAS 18	30	Financial Reporting for Segments of a Business Enterprise - Interim Financial Statements
SFAS 19	34	Financial Accounting and Reporting by Oil and Gas Producing Companies
SFAS 21	19, 24, and 30	Suspension of the Reporting of Earnings Per Share and Segment Information by Nonpublic Enterprises
SFAS 22	17	Changes in the Provisions of Lease Agreements Resulting from Refundings of Tax-Exempt Debt
SFAS 23	17	Inception of the Lease
SFAS 24	30	Reporting Segment Information in Financial Statements that Are Presented in Another Enterprise's Financial Report
SFAS 25	34	Suspension of Certain Accounting Requirements for Oil and Gas Producing Companies
SFAS 27	17	Classification of Renewals or Extensions of Existing Sales-Type or Direct Financing Leases
SFAS 28	17	Accounting for Sales with Leasebacks
SFAS 29	17	Determining Contingent Rentals
SFAS 30	28 and 30	Disclosure of Information About Major Customers
SFAS 34	10	Capitalization of Interest Cost
SFAS 35	16	Accounting and Reporting by Defined Benefit Pension Plans
SFAS 38	28	Accounting for Preacquisition Contingencies of Purchased Enterprises
SFAS 42	10	Determining Materiality for Capitalization of Interest Cost
SFAS 43	14	Accounting for Compensated Absences
SFAS 44	34	Accounting for Intangible Assets of Motor Carriers
SFAS 45	12	Accounting for Franchise Fee Revenue
SFAS 47	15	Disclosure of Long-Term Obligations
SFAS 48	9	Revenue Recognition When Right of Return Exists
SFAS 49	9 and 14	Accounting for Product Financing Arrangements
SFAS 50	34	Financial Reporting in the Record and Music Industry
SFAS 51	34	Financial Reporting by Cable Television Companies
SFAS 52	31	Foreign Currency Translation
SFAS 53	34	Financial Reporting by Producers and Distributors of Motion Picture Films
SFAS 57	24	Related Party Disclosures
SFAS 58	10	Capitalization of Interest Cost in Financial Statements that Include Investments Accounted for by the Equity Method
SFAS 60	34	Accounting and Reporting by Insurance Enterprises
SFAS 61	34	Accounting for Title Plant
SFAS 62	10	Capitalization of Interest Cost in Situations Involving Certain Tax-Exempt Borrowings and Certain Gifts and Grants
SFAS 63	34	Financial Reporting by Broadcasters
SFAS 64	15	Extinguishments of Debt Made to Satisfy Sinking-Fund Requirements
SFAS 65	34	Accounting for Certain Mortgage Banking Activities
SFAS 66	34	Accounting for Sales of Real Estate
SFAS 67	34	Accounting for Costs and Initial Rental Operations of Real Estate Projects
SFAS 68	12	Research and Development Arrangements
SFAS 69	34	Disclosures about Oil and Gas Producing Activities
SFAS 71	34	Accounting for the Effects of Certain Types of Regulation
SFAS 72	28	Accounting for Certain Acquisitions of Banking or Thrift Institutions
SFAS 73	21	Reporting a Change in Accounting for Railroad Track Structures
SFAS 75	16	Deferral of the Effective Date of Certain Accounting Requirements for Pension Plans of State and Local Governmental Units

Pronounce-ment	Gleim Chapter(s)	Statements of Financial Accounting Standards
SFAS 78	14	Classification of Obligations That Are Callable by the Creditor
SFAS 79	28	Elimination of Certain Disclosures for Business Combinations by Nonpublic Enterprises
SFAS 80	34	Accounting for Futures Contracts
SFAS 84	15	Induced Conversions of Convertible Debt
SFAS 85	19	Yield Test for Determining Whether a Convertible Security Is a Common Stock Equivalent
SFAS 86	12	Accounting for the Costs of Computer Software to Be Sold, Leased, or Otherwise Marketed
SFAS 87	16	Employers' Accounting for Pensions
SFAS 88	16	Employers' Accounting for Settlements and Curtailments of Defined Benefit Pension Plans and for Termination Benefits
SFAS 89	23	Financial Reporting and Changing Prices
SFAS 90	34	Regulated Enterprises - Accounting for Phase-in Plans, Abandonments, and Disallowances of Plant Costs
SFAS 91	17	Accounting for Nonrefundable Fees and Costs Associated With Originating and Acquiring Loans
SFAS 92	34	Regulated Enterprises - Accounting for Phase-in Plans
SFAS 93	33	Recognition of Depreciation by Not-for-Profit Organizations
SFAS 94	28	Consolidation of All Majority-Owned Subsidiaries
SFAS 95	22	Statement of Cash Flows
SFAS 97	34	Accounting and Reporting by Insurance Enterprises for Certain Long-Duration Contracts and for Realized Gains and Losses from the Sale of Investments
SFAS 98	17	Accounting for Leases - Sale-Leaseback Transactions Involving Real Estate; Sales-Type Leases of Real Estate; Definition of the Lease Term; Initial Direct Costs of Direct Financing Leases
SFAS 101	34	Regulated Enterprises - Accounting for the Discontinuation of Application of FASB Statement No. 71
SFAS 102	22	Statement of Cash Flows - Exemption of Certain Enterprises and Classification of Cash Flows from Certain Securities Acquired for Resale
SFAS 104	22	Statement of Cash Flows - Net Reporting of Certain Cash Receipts and Cash Payments and Classification of Cash Flows from Hedging Transactions
SFAS 105	24	Disclosures of Information about Financial Instruments with Off-Balance-Sheet Risk and Financial Instruments with Concentrations of Credit Risk
SFAS 106	16	Employers' Accounting for Postretirement Benefits Other than Pensions - Not effective for some entities until fiscal years beginning after 12/15/94
SFAS 107	24	Disclosures about Fair Value of Financial Statements
SFAS 109	20	Accounting for Income Taxes
SFAS 110	16	Reporting by Defined Benefit Pension Plans of Investment Contracts
SFAS 111	21	Revision of FASB Statement No. 32 and Technical Corrections
SFAS 112	16	Employers' Accounting for Postemployment Benefits
SFAS 113	34	Accounting and Reporting for Reissuance of Short-Duration and Long-Duration Contracts
SFAS 114	15	Accounting by Creditors for Impairment of a Loan
SFAS 115	8 and 13	Accounting for Certain Investments in Debt and Equity Securities
SFAS 116	33	Accounting for Contributions Received and Contributions Made
SFAS 117	33	Financial Statements of Not-for-Profit Organizations
SFAS 118	15	Accounting by Creditors for Impairment of a Loan-Income Recognition and Disclosures
SFAS 119	24	Disclosure about Derivative Financial Instruments and Fair Value of Financial Instruments
SFAS 120	34	Accounting and Reporting by Mutual Life Insurance Enterprises and by Insurance Enterprises for Certain Long-Duration Participating Contracts
SFAS 121	10 and 12	Accounting for the Impairment of Long-Lived Assets and for Long-Lived Assets to Be Disposed Of
SFAS 122	34	Accounting for Mortgage Servicing Rights
SFAS 123	18	Accounting for Stock-Based Compensation
SFAS 124	33	Accounting for Certain Investments Held by Not-for-Profit Organizations
SFAS 125	8 and 15	Accounting for Transfers and Servicing of Financial Assets and Extinguishments of Liabilities (Effective for transactions after December 31, 1996)

Pronounce-ment	Gleim Chapter(s)	FASB Interpretations
No. 1	21	Accounting Changes Related to the Cost of Inventory
No. 4	28	Applicability of SFAS 2 to Business Combinations Accounted for by the Purchase Method
No. 6	12	Applicability of SFAS 2 to Computer Software
No. 7	24	Applying SFAS 7 in Financial Statements of Established Operating Enterprises
No. 8	14	Classification of a Short-Term Obligation Repaid Prior to Being Replaced by a Long-Term Security
No. 9	28	Applying APB 16 and 17 When a Savings and Loan Association or Similar Institution is Acquired in a Business Combination Accounted for by the Purchase Method
No. 14	14	Reasonable Estimation of the Amount of Loss
No. 18	29	Accounting for Income Taxes in Interim Periods
No. 19	17	Lessee Guarantee of the Residual Value of Leased Property
No. 20	21	Reporting Accounting Changes under AICPA Statements of Position
No. 21	28	Accounting for Leases in a Business Combination
No. 23	17	Leases of Certain Property Owned by a Governmental Unit or Authority
No. 24	17	Leases Involving only Part of a Building
No. 26	17	Accounting for Purchase of a Leased Asset by the Lessee during the Term of the Lease
No. 27	17	Accounting for a Loss on a Sublease
No. 28	18	Accounting for Stock Appreciation Rights and Other Variable Stock Option or Award Plans
No. 30	10	Accounting for Involuntary Conversions of Nonmonetary Assets to Monetary Assets
No. 31	19	Treatment of Stock Compensation Plans in EPS Computations
No. 33	34	Applying SFAS 34 to Oil and Gas Producing Operations Accounted for by the Full Cost Method
No. 34	14	Disclosure of Indirect Guarantees of Indebtedness of Others
No. 35	13	Criteria for Applying the Equity Method of Accounting for Investments in Common Stock
No. 36	34	Accounting for Exploratory Wells in Progress at the End of a Period
No. 37	31	Accounting for Translation Adjustments upon Sale of Part of an Investment in a Foreign Entity
No. 38	18	Determining the Measurement Date for Stock Option, Purchase, and Award Plans Involving Junior Stock
No. 39	24	Offsetting of Amounts Related to Certain Contracts (Effective for financial statements issued for periods beginning after 12/15/93)
No. 40	34	Applicability of GAAP to Mutual Life Insurance and Other Enterprises (Effective for financial statements issued for fiscal years beginning after 12/15/94, but the disclosure provisions are effective for annual statements for fiscal years beginning after 12/15/92)
No. 41	24	Offsetting of Amounts Related to Certain Repurchase and Reverse Repurchase Agreements
No. 42	33	Accounting for Transfers of Assets in Which a Not-for-Profit Organization is Granted Variance Power

		Statements of Financial Accounting Concepts
SFAC 1	4	Objectives of Financial Reporting by Business Enterprises
SFAC 2	4	Qualitative Characteristics: Criteria for Selecting and Evaluating Financial Accounting and Reporting Policies
SFAC 4	33	Objectives of Financial Reporting by Nonbusiness Organizations
SFAC 5	4	Recognition and Measurement in Financial Statements of Business Enterprises
SFAC 6	4	Elements of Financial Statements

CHAPTER TWO
HOW TO STUDY FOR SUCCESS

The central theme of this chapter is control: establish plans, perform effectively, evaluate your performance, understand shortcomings, and follow through with improved performance. It is an executive approach that will work for you, especially if you aspire to be an executive. You should, because you will have the opportunity.

PLANNING YOUR CURRICULUM

Begin by chronologically listing all of your courses to date by semester (quarter). Put credits and grades to the right. Underneath this listing, organize a desirable schedule of remaining courses and credits. After spending 10 minutes on this exercise, consult your university catalog, college and departmental advisement sheets, and any other relevant materials. Make sure you will meet all the requirements to graduate. Have you planned your courses in the proper sequence in terms of prerequisites? After you have thought through your schedule, review it with an appropriate administrator or counselor. Confirm that it satisfies the requirements for your graduation.

What is your objective? Presumably, it is to earn a degree in accounting. Why? The prospects of employment are good and starting salaries are high. What then? What will you be doing in 5 years? 10 years? 15 years? No one knows, but to the extent that you improve your study program, i.e., learn more and become more qualified, you will brighten your prospects.

Thus, you want to train not only to be a professional accountant but also to be able to go on to "bigger and better opportunities."

IMPORTANCE OF GRADES

Grades are important. What grade point average (GPA) is required? Usually, a "B" average is necessary to enter graduate and/or law school. Some CPA firms and other employers restrict their hiring to individuals with a "B" average or better. Conversely, many students with "C" or "C+" GPAs are extremely successful once out of school. If your GPA is currently below a "B" average, this discussion is particularly relevant to you. Note that average grades vary from school to school. You should use your best GPA on your resume: cumulative, upper division, accounting courses, etc.

You must do your best in each course, especially those relevant to your career. Other required courses are important because they affect your overall GPA and serve to make you a better-rounded human being. Your employers will be interested in you as a whole person, not just as an accounting technician.

YOUR COGNITIVE PROCESSES[1]

Which mental processes do you use for learning? How do you internalize assignments? How do you process facts, concepts, etc., to complete assignments and take tests?

Your objective is to better understand how you "study" and how you can be both more efficient and more effective. If, as a result of this introspection, you improve your study processes 20%, you can change 80% grades to 96% grades and reduce 40 hours in class and at the library to 32 hours.

Your Learning Process

Learning in the broad sense is the change in behavior or knowledge as a result of experience, practice, effort, etc. We are interested in the narrower definition, i.e., knowledge (accounting related), in contrast to other behaviors and skills, like riding a bicycle, or vocational skills, like cutting hair.

In other words, psychologists have defined many categories of learning, such as classical conditioning, trial-and-error learning, sensorimotor learning, verbal learning, concept learning, and rule learning (Wingfield, p. 8). We are interested in concept learning and rule learning.

Wingfield (p. 25)[1] sets forth a learning model consisting of three major stages: input, storage, and retrieval. Furthermore, he distinguishes between short-term and long-term memory as diagrammed on the next page.

---

[1]Two texts relied on in preparing the following discussion are Bloom's *Taxonomy of Educational Objectives*, copyright © 1956 by David McKay Company, Inc., and Arthur Wingfield, *Human Learning and Memory: An Introduction*, copyright © 1979 by Harper & Row.

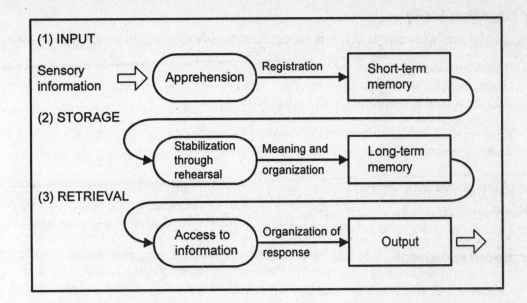

While this illustration is very useful, it is an oversimplification because it does not focus on the multidimensionality of knowledge. The multidimensionality of knowledge is how meaning and organization are added to information.

Most accounting and business concepts are multidimensional. Just as more can be learned about an automobile by walking around it and looking at it from all sides (and getting into it, opening the hood, etc.) versus studying a picture of the automobile, accounting and business concepts can be better understood by examining their multiple aspects. For example, a financial accounting transaction may be viewed in light of

1. Journal entry(ies) required
2. Impact on the financial statements
3. Consequences of the transaction for the business
4. Motivation of all parties to enter into the transaction
5. Behavioral implications to employees, customers, competitors, etc.

This multidimensionality describes understanding, i.e., relating many concepts, rules, relationships. The above list is incomplete; take a few minutes to pencil in a few additional dimensions in the margin.

Train yourself to ask what the implications of the underlying business transactions might be for all accounting procedures you study, e.g., impact on

- Purchasing power
- Cash flows
- Financial ratios

Levels of Cognitive Ability

In ascending order of complexity, one categorization (Bloom) of the levels of knowledge is

1. Recall knowledge
2. Understanding to interpret
3. Application of knowledge to solve problems
4. Analytical skills
5. Synthesis
6. Ability to evaluate

Each of the above is discussed briefly. Multiple levels of knowledge exist above recall and tend to be cumulative. They constitute "building blocks" of cognitive processes. To interpret, you need some recall knowledge; to solve problems, you must understand to interpret, etc.

1. **Recall knowledge.** The first level is recall knowledge, e.g., definitions of technical terms and sources of information. Objective questions often test this kind of knowledge, which is the most fundamental since it entails basic memorization.

   EXAMPLE: According to Statement on Financial Accounting Concepts No. 2, the two primary decision-specific qualitative characteristics of accounting information are reliability and relevance. Gaining knowledge of these characteristics requires little mental processing beyond simple recall.

2. **Understanding to interpret.** The second level of knowledge is the understanding and interpretation of written and quantitative data. Questions at this level test understanding of concepts, including interrelationships within data. This level of knowledge is also called comprehension.

   EXAMPLE: SFAC 2 defines reliability as the "quality of information that provides assurance that the information is reasonably free from error and bias and faithfully represents what it purports to represent." What does this mean? Do you understand? Can you explain it to someone else? The ability to explain it to someone else is a very good indicator of your comprehension.

3. **Application of knowledge to solve problems.** The third level of knowledge is problem solving. Questions at this level examine practical applications of concepts to solve a problem. Unfortunately, some problem solving is based only on recall knowledge.

   EXAMPLE: Memorizing the cost of goods sold formula (CGS = BI + Pur - EI) is mere recall. **Instead** you should understand that CGS equals purchases adjusted for the change in inventory. For example, an increase in inventory means that not all of purchases were sold. Conversely, a decrease in inventory means all of purchases plus some inventory were sold.

   Given BI, Pur, and EI, most students can solve for CGS by plugging numbers into the formula. But an interpretive understanding of the relationship of the change in inventory level to CGS permits solving of more complex problems, e.g., effect of inventory errors.

4. **Analytical skills.** The fourth level of knowledge is analytical ability, including identification of cause-and-effect relationships, internal inconsistencies or consistencies, relevant and irrelevant items, and underlying assumptions. The following question requires analysis and interrelation of a number of variables to reach a conclusion.

   EXAMPLE: Would you accept a customer's order at a lower-than-usual price? Variables to consider include contribution margin generated, available production capacity, and psychological and economic effects on other customers.

5. **Synthesis.** The fifth level is the ability to put parts together to form a new whole.

   EXAMPLE: The development of the FASB's major pension pronouncement (SFAS 87, *Employers' Accounting for Pensions*) illustrates the synthesis of existing elements. It retains such aspects of prior pension accounting as delayed recognition of certain events, reporting net cost, and offsetting liabilities and assets. SFAS 87 combines them with applications of the existing principles of accrual accounting, full disclosure, and comparability to develop a new approach to pension accounting.

6. **Ability to evaluate.** The sixth level is evaluative ability. What is the best (most effective) method (alternative)? Evaluation has in common with analysis and synthesis the consideration of qualitative as well as quantitative variables. Qualitative variables are usually multidimensional and thus cannot be meaningfully quantified or measured. For example, multiple-choice questions consist of a series of either true or false statements with one exception (the correct answer); if the question is evaluative, all of the answer choices will be true or false, but one answer will be better than the others. Questions of this kind usually require the best reason, least valid answer, etc.

   EXAMPLE: "The most important nonfinancial issue that a company should consider is..." requires evaluation of qualitative variables.

Undergraduate accounting courses generally emphasize the first three levels: recall, interpretation, and problem solving. Your career in professional accounting, however, will require and emphasize the last three levels: analysis, synthesis, and evaluation.

Put another way, the first three levels are required to prepare financial data. The second three are necessary to use financial data and exercise professional judgment. How does accounting differ from bookkeeping? Professional judgment.

Yes, in **your** study of accounting, **you** must go well beyond recall and memorization. Many accountants move on to executive positions after beginning their professional career as an "accountant." Even those who remain in accounting exercise more and more judgment and rely less and less on rote memory as they take on and exercise more responsibility.

PREPARING FOR EXAM SUCCESS

The Preparation Process. In order to be successful on examinations, you need to undertake the following steps:

1. **Understand the exam, including coverage, content, format, administration, and grading.** The better you understand the examination process from beginning to end, the better you will perform. Ask your professor for clarification of the exam process publicly in class and privately in his/her office, talk to former students, and attempt to review your professor's exams from prior terms.

   Virtually all certification programs, admission tests, and other "established" exams have information books developed by those responsible for the examination. Review manuals and "test prep" books usually also exist to help you become conversant with the exam.

2. **Learn and understand the subject matter tested.** Confirm text and chapter coverage with your professor. Also, to what extent are class lectures, examples, handouts, etc., tested? Confirm coverage by looking at past examinations (if available).

3. **Practice answering questions to perfect your exam answering techniques.**
    Answering questions helps you understand the standards to which you will be held. It
    also helps you learn and understand the material tested -- see "Using Objective
    Questions to Study" in this chapter.

4. **Plan and practice exam execution.** Anticipate the exam environment and prepare
    yourself with a plan: When will you arrive? How dressed? With which exam supplies?
    How many questions and what format? Order of answering questions? Time to spend
    on each question?

    Expect the unexpected and adjust! Remember that your sole objective when taking an
    examination is to maximize your score. Most examinations are "curved," and you must
    out-perform your peers.

5. Most importantly, develop confidence and assure success with a controlled preparation
    program followed by **confident execution** during the examination.

Control. You have to be in control to be successful during exam preparation and execution.
Perhaps more importantly, control can also contribute greatly to your personal and other
professional goals.

What is control? Control is a process whereby you

1. Develop expectations, standards, budgets, and plans.

2. Undertake activity, production, study, and learning.

3. Measure the activity, production, output, and knowledge.

4. Compare actual activity with what was expected or budgeted.

5. Modify the activity, behavior, or production to better achieve the expected or desired
    outcome.

6. Revise expectations and standards in light of actual experience.

7. Continue the process.

The objective is to improve performance as well as be confident that the best possible results
are achieved. Most accountants follow this process in relation to standard costs; i.e., they
establish cost standards and compute cost variances.

Every day you rely on control systems implicitly. For example, when you comb, brush, and/or
fix your hair, you use a control system. You have expectations about the desired appearance of
your hair and the time required to style it. Implicitly you monitor your progress and make
adjustments as appropriate.

The point is that either you have and enforce standards or you do not, or you are somewhere
in between. In all of your endeavors, you do or do not exercise control, implicitly or explicitly.
However, the results of most activities will improve with explicit control. This is particularly true of
certification examinations.

1. Practice your question answering techniques (and develop control) as you prepare
    question solutions during your study program.

2. Develop an explicit control system over your study program (restudy this chapter).

3. Think about using more explicit control systems over any and all of your endeavors.

STUDY SUGGESTIONS

The emphasis in the next few pages is on developing strategies, approaches, and procedures to help you learn and understand better, in less time. We begin with the "where" and the "when," and then move on to the "how."

Where to Study

Study where you study best. Some study best at home. Others study best at the library. Some prefer to study at different locations at various times in the day and/or on different days. Still others study at only one location.

The issue is effective study. You must seek out the study locations that provide you with the most effective environment for concentration, which means avoiding or blocking out distractions, which are most often produced by people you know. Try out-of-the-way places where other accounting majors/friends do not study, e.g., the English library or the fine arts library.

When to Study

Study on a regular basis, 7 days a week to the extent possible. Do **not** study to catch up before exams and assignment due dates. Trying to catch up emphasizes rote memorization, which does **not** result in learning and understanding. You will improve your grade point average and increase the amount learned by investing several hours on each class at the very beginning of each term (see the next section, "Course Overview").

Are you a morning person? Do you study effectively first thing in the morning? Others study better at night. Experiment with different study times to determine when you are most effective, and schedule your time accordingly.

Remember, the important point is that you must **study regularly** to stay ahead. Class lectures and discussion are much more meaningful and beneficial when you have studied the assignment prior to attending class. A good rule to follow is, **"You are behind if you are not ahead."** Stay ahead of all of your classes by following a regular study schedule.

Course Overview

At the very beginning of the term, as soon as you have your text and syllabus, you should obtain an executive overview of each course. **Begin by writing down the chapter titles.** What is the course about? How does its content relate to courses you have already taken? To courses you plan to take in the future?

Given this brief chapter listing and perhaps also a course description provided in the syllabus, you are in a position to survey the individual chapters in the text. You began with a one-line listing of chapters. Now **skim each chapter,** reading the introduction and summary/conclusion. Your objective is to gain more insight into each chapter's content and approach than that provided by the chapter title. **Document your effort** with a short paragraph and/or summary outline of each chapter.

After you have completed your chapter-by-chapter analysis, examine the entire course overview. Has your executive overview of the course changed and become more focused as a result of your chapter-by-chapter analysis? The entire process will probably take 2 to 4 hours. Spend half a day at the library and do a thorough job for each course.

At this point, you have a basis for understanding how the chapters and their parts fit into the overall course. Now you will be able to put individual definitions and concepts into the context of the entire course.

How to Study a Chapter

Before reading a chapter, gain a general understanding of the chapter contents. The following seven steps should precede actual study:

1. **Skim through the chapter.** What is it about?

2. **Read the chapter summary.**

3. **Try to answer the discussion questions** at the back of the chapter to see if you can provide answers based upon your present knowledge and common sense.

4. **Look at the requirements** of the exercises and problems to see what is expected.

5. Each Gleim *Objective Questions and Explanations* book contains tables cross-referencing the chapters of most related textbooks to the modules in

   - *MANAGERIAL ACCOUNTING Objective Questions and Explanations with Study Outlines*
   - *AUDITING & SYSTEMS Objective Questions and Explanations*
   - *BUSINESS LAW/LEGAL STUDIES Objective Questions and Explanations*
   - *FEDERAL TAX Objective Questions and Explanations*
   - *FINANCIAL ACCOUNTING Objective Questions and Explanations*

   Turn to the module(s) listed for the chapter you are studying, and answer five to 10 questions to determine the standards to which you will be held. This process will help motivate you to study the chapter more carefully.

6. **Outline the chapter** based on the centerheadings and sideheadings. Rewrite them in your own words.

   - **Do not** recopy words from the textbook. Put concepts into your own words so you understand, rather than memorize, words.

7. Now that you have an overview of the chapter and have thought about what is in it, you can **begin studying, NOT reading.** Studying means understanding. What is(are) the author(s) saying? Do you agree? How does each concept fit into the chapter?

Remember, the objective is **not** to read the chapter and complete an assignment. The objective **is** to understand the material well enough to be able to explain it to someone else. To this end, you need to be sufficiently conversant with the material in each chapter so that you can confidently discuss it, question it, and/or critique it with your professor.

We wish to donate a copy of each of our objective questions and explanations books to the library reserve room at each college/university where the books are recommended by one or more professors or are used as a source of exam questions. If these books are being used as described but are not on reserve at your school, call (800) 87-GLEIM to give us the name and address of the school's library reserve room and the name and telephone number of the person responsible for the reserve room. Also, include the course number and the name of the professor who is recommending the books or using them as a source of exam questions.

Ask at least one question during each class session. There is not enough time for everyone to ask questions in class, but do not use that as an excuse for your failure to participate. Engage your professor in discussion about a topic, procedure, or principle that you do not understand. Many accounting students are introverts and do not like to participate in class. While introverts are frequently attracted to accounting, practicing accountants are expected to be extroverts. Accountants are in the communication business and are expected to be good communicators.

Many students sit passively in class and only receive information. This approach is inefficient because these students simply write down formulas, definitions, etc., for later regurgitation without understanding the concepts.

Stay ahead of your professor, answering all questions asked (usually to yourself) and looking ahead during his/her lectures. Try to anticipate what will be next. This process requires preclass preparation but permits you to learn the material in class. The poor alternative (both inefficient and ineffective) is to play "catch-up," i.e., attempt to memorize lists, definitions, etc., out of context after class is over.

Attempt to relate your current course material to that covered in previous courses. Gaining a thorough understanding of the material in previous courses makes it feasible to tie the contents of all your courses together. One of the major weaknesses of undergraduate accounting programs is that one course is taken at a time, without the integration of the individual courses into an entire program that usually occurs in graduate programs.

As you study, make notes in the margins of your books. Books are to be written in. They are your study vehicle. Just as you should ask questions and discuss topics with your professor, you need to understand the author(s) of your text. Critique your text as you study! Write notes in the margins on how it could be improved. How would you organize and present the material?

Highlighters and underlining: Do **not** become dependent on them! Using highlighters or underlining to isolate the key points in the author's text encourages memorizing, not learning and understanding. Yes, most students highlight and underline, but most students use short-term memory to become familiar with the concepts, facts, and definitions to complete courses. **You** are in school to learn and understand with the objective of a successful career, **not** just to get a sheet of paper (a diploma).

How to Complete Homework Assignments

Most accounting course assignments consist of computational problems. They are largely similar to the examples and illustrations in your chapters. Thus, most of your homework problems are susceptible to "cookbooking" or copying from the chapter illustration, step-by-step. Barely more than rote memorization is required to achieve false success. **Do not cookbook!**

Work your homework assignments under **exam conditions**. This means time pressure and no reference back to the chapter. As you approach exercises and problem assignments, scan the exercise or problem and set a 5-, 10-, or 15-minute time limit. With a watch before you, see how much you can accomplish in 5, 10, or 15 minutes. As you get each problem under control, note the issues (questions) you need to research after you have substantially completed the problem. Put yourself in a frame of mind to be highly productive during homework preparation. Do your best! No one can ask for more.

Develop and use your question answering techniques (discussed later in this chapter) on each homework assignment. These should be systematic methods of problem solving that is executive in nature. Before you start, determine what has to be done, how it has to be done, the sequence of procedures, etc. It is the same general approach recommended for course overviews, studying a chapter, taking an exam, etc.

Using Objective Questions to Study

Experts on testing increasingly favor multiple-choice questions as a valid means of examining various levels of knowledge. Using objective questions to study for undergraduate examinations is an important tool not only for obtaining good grades, but also for long-range preparation for certification and other examinations. The following suggestions can help you study in conjunction with each of our objective questions and explanations books (see our order form at the back of this book):

1. Locate the chapter and module that contain questions on the topic you are currently studying. Each *Objective Questions and Explanations* book contains cross-references to the tables of contents of most textbooks.

2. Work through a series of questions, one or more modules at a time.

    a. Cover the answers and explanations as you work the questions.
    b. Circle the answer you think is correct.
    c. Check your answer.

3. **Do not consult the answer or answer explanations on the right side of each page until after you have chosen and written down an answer.**

    It is crucial that you cover the answer explanations and intellectually commit yourself to an answer. This method will help you understand the concept much better, even if you answered the question incorrectly.

4. Study the explanations to each question you answered incorrectly. In addition to learning and understanding the concept tested, analyze **why** you missed the question. Did you misread the question? Misread the requirement? Make a computational error? Not know the concept tested? Identify your weaknesses in answering multiple-choice questions and take corrective action (before you take a test).

    Studying the important concepts that we provide in our answer explanations will help you understand the principles to the point that you can answer that question (or any other like it) successfully.

5. Prepare a summary analysis of your work on each module (topic). It will show your weaknesses (areas needing more study) and also your strengths (areas of improvement). You can improve your performance on objective questions both by increasing your percentage of correct answers and by decreasing the time spent per question. Here are sample column headings for the summary analysis:

Date	Module	Time to Complete	Number of Questions	Minutes per Question	Number Correct	Percent Correct

Multiple-Choice Question Answering Technique

You need a personalized control system **(technique)** for answering multiple-choice questions, essay questions, and computational problems. The objective is to obtain complete, correct, and well-presented answers.

The following series of steps is suggested for answering multiple-choice questions. The important point is that you need to devote attention to and develop **the technique that works for you**. Personalize and practice your multiple-choice question answering technique on questions in this study manual. Modify the following suggested steps to suit your individual skills and ability. For example, you will need to cover the readily available answer explanations at the right of each question. There will be none of these on your exam! Begin now, and develop **your** control system.

Budget your time. We make this point with emphasis. Just as you would fill up your gas tank prior to reaching empty, so too should you finish your exam before time expires.

1. Calculate the time allowed for each multiple-choice question after you have allocated time to the other questions (OOFs, essays) on the exam; e.g., if one overall question consists of 20 individual multiple-choice items and is allocated 40 minutes on your exam, you should spend a little under 2 minutes per item (always budget extra time for transferring answers to answer sheets, interruptions, etc.).

2. Before beginning a series of multiple-choice questions, write the starting time on the exam near the first question.

3. As you work through the individual questions, check your time. Assuming a time allocation of 120 minutes for 60 questions, if you have worked five questions in 9 minutes, you are fine, but, if you have spent 11 minutes on five questions, you need to speed up. Remember that your goal is to answer all questions and achieve the maximum score possible.

Answer the questions in numerical order.

1.   Do **not** agonize over any one item. Stay within your time budget.

2.   Mark any unanswered question with a big "?" and return to it later if time allows.

3.   Never leave a multiple-choice question unanswered if you will not be penalized for guessing.

For each multiple-choice question, follow the steps below:

1.   **Cover up the answer choices** with your hand or a piece of scratch paper. Do not allow the answer choices to affect your reading of the question.

    a.   If four answer choices are presented, three of them are incorrect. They are called **distractors** for good reason.

2.   **Read the question** stem (the part of the question that precedes the answer choices) carefully to determine the precise requirement.

    a.   You may wish to underline or circle key language or data used in the stem.

    b.   Focusing on what is required enables you to ignore extraneous information and to proceed directly to determining the correct answer.

        1)   Be especially careful to note when the requirement is an **exception**; e.g., "Which of the following accounts is **not** used in a perpetual inventory system?"

3.   **Determine the correct answer** before looking at the answer choices.

    a.   By adhering to the steps above, you know what is required and which are the relevant facts.

    b.   However, some multiple-choice questions are structured so that the answer cannot be determined from the stem alone.

4.   **Read the answer choices** carefully.

    a.   Even if answer (A) appears to be the correct choice, do **not** skip the remaining answer choices. Answer (B), (C), or (D) may be even better.

    b.   Treat each answer choice as a true-false question. Consider marking a "T" or an "F" next to each answer choice as you analyze it.

5.   **Select the best answer.** Circle the most likely or best answer choice on the question booklet. If you are uncertain, guess intelligently. Do not give up your 25% chance of getting the correct answer.

After you have answered all of the questions, **transfer your answers to the objective answer sheet**, if one is provided.

1.   Make sure you are within your time budget so you will be able to perform this vital step in an unhurried manner.

2.   Do not wait to transfer answers until the very end of the exam session because you may run out of time.

3.   Double-check that you have transferred the answers correctly; e.g., recheck every fifth or tenth answer from your test paper to your answer sheet to ensure that you have not fallen out of sequence.

Other Objective Format (OOF) Questions

Other objective format (OOF) questions are, literally, questions that are not four-answer multiple-choice questions but that can be graded with an optical scanner. The OOF-type question is being used more frequently by professors and the governing bodies of professional certification programs because it is an alternative to the traditional essay question or computational problem. Thus, OOFs reduce the time and cost of grading essay and computational questions, and also provide an objective (i.e., unbiased) method of grading.

Many OOFs are matching questions which contain a list of numbered questions that you associate with a list of possible answers. A variation of the matching question may be to match a list of questions to two lists of answers, e.g., a set of questions concerning variance analysis with one list of numeric answers and one list containing three choices: favorable, unfavorable, no effect.

Other OOFs may be of the free-response type. For example, a series of facts is followed by a number of questions asking you to compute answers. The numeric answers are to be written or bubbled in on a specifically designed answer sheet. You will encounter many different types of OOF questions throughout your studies because of the various approaches the authors of each OOF will take.

1. If it is a free-response computational question, work it as you would any other computational question.

    a. Computational questions are discussed in *CIA Review*, *CMA Review*, and *CPA Review*.

    b. OOF computational questions may be either free-response, for which you blacken the answer digits, or a correct answer selection from a list of possible answers.

2. A matching question can be considered a variation of a multiple-choice question. Note the following:

    a. The number of stems (i.e., items) that have the same answer choices
    b. The number of answer choices, which may vary from 2 to 15 or more

        1) Two are usually true/false, increase/decrease, favorable/unfavorable.
        2) Three are usually true/false/not enough information.
        3) Five or more make it more difficult to guess.

    c. Most matching questions will permit answers to be used once, more than once, or not at all.

        1) This makes each stem independent.
        2) Answer each stem as if it were a separate multiple-choice question.

    d. For each item,

        1) Do not be distracted by answer choices (cover them).
        2) Understand the requirement -- read the item carefully.
        3) Determine the correct answer independent of the answer choices.
        4) Mark the best answer choice in your question booklet.

            a) Most often items are numbered and answers are lettered. Write the correct answer letter next to the item number.

If You Don't Know the Answer

Assuming the exam you are taking does not penalize incorrect answers, you should guess; but make it an educated guess, which means select the best answer. First, rule out answers that you feel are incorrect. Second, speculate on what the examiner is looking for and/or the rationale behind the question. This may lead you to the correct answer. Third, select the best answer, or guess between equally appealing answers. Mark the question with a "?" in case you have time to return to it for further analysis.

If you cannot make an educated guess, read the item and each answer, and pick the best or most intuitive answer. It's just a guess!

Do **not** look at the previous answer to try to detect an answer. Answers are usually random, and it is possible to have four or more consecutive questions with the same answer letter, e.g., answer B.

NOTE: Do not waste time beyond the amount you budgeted for each question. Move forward and stay on or ahead of schedule.

Preparing for Essay Questions and Computational Problems

Do not overemphasize studying objective questions to the extent of underemphasizing essay questions and computational problems. Remember that most exams, including professional certification exams, contain essay questions and/or computational problems. Thus, a complete study program must include working essay questions and computational problems as well as objective questions under exam conditions.

When working intermediate or advanced financial essay questions and/or computational problems, survey the question/problem and set a time budget, e.g., 10, 15, or 20 minutes. Then complete the question or problem in the budgeted time. Question/problem answering strategies for essay questions and computational problems are discussed and illustrated in Gleim's professional certification review books: *CIA Review*, *CMA Review*, and *CPA Review*.

CHAPTER THREE
THE CIA, CMA, CPA, AND
OTHER CERTIFICATION PROGRAMS

The purpose of this chapter is to describe the three primary accounting certification examinations and the CIA, CMA, and CPA designations. You should become conversant with these programs and their requirements very early in your accounting career so you can "look ahead" to all three accounting examinations. The best time to prepare for these exams is now. A secondary benefit will be good grades; i.e., the high standards of these examinations will force you to work hard, learn much, and do well in your courses. If you are a practitioner, you should consider these examinations as professional development opportunities rather than examinations or tests.

See page 27 for the addresses to use to get application and registration forms and additional information for the CIA and CMA programs. While all are nationally uniform examinations, application for the CPA exam must be made through your individual state board of accountancy. The addresses of the 54 state boards of accountancy (one for each state plus the District of Columbia, Guam, Puerto Rico, and the U.S. Virgin Islands) appear on page 35.

OVERVIEW OF ACCOUNTING CERTIFICATION PROGRAMS

The CPA (Certified Public Accountant) exam is the grandparent of all the professional accounting examinations. Its origin was in the 1896 public accounting legislation of New York. In 1917 the American Institute of CPAs (AICPA) began to prepare and grade a uniform CPA exam. It is currently used to measure the technical competence of those applying to be licensed as CPAs in all 50 states, Guam, Puerto Rico, the Virgin Islands, and the District of Columbia. More than 60,000 candidates sit for each CPA exam which is given twice a year in May and November.

The CIA (Certified Internal Auditor), CMA (Certified Management Accountant), and CFM (Corporate Financial Management) examinations are relatively new certification programs compared to the CPA. The CMA exam was first administered in 1972, and the first CIA exam in 1974. The CFM exam will be administered beginning December 1, 1996. Why were these certification programs begun? Generally, the requirements of the CPA designation instituted by the boards of accountancy, especially the necessity for public accounting experience, led to the development of the CIA, CMA, and CFM programs.

Certification is important to professional accountants because it provides

1. Participation in a recognized professional group
2. An improved professional training program arising out of the certification program
3. Recognition among peers for attaining the professional designation
4. An extra credential for the employment market/career ladder
5. The personal satisfaction of attaining a recognized degree of competency

These reasons hold particularly true in the accounting field due to wide recognition of the CPA designation. Accountants and accounting students are often asked if they are CPAs when people learn they are accountants. Thus, there is considerable pressure for accountants to become *certified*.

A new development is multiple certifications, which is important for the same reasons as initial certification. Accounting students and recent graduates should look ahead and obtain multiple certifications. Obtaining multiple certifications will help to broaden your career opportunities. The table of selected CIA, CMA, CFM, and CPA examination data on page 27 provides an overview of these accounting examinations.

RATIONALE FOR ACCOUNTING CERTIFICATION PROGRAMS

The primary purpose of the CIA, CMA, CFM, and CPA examinations is to measure the technical competence of candidates. Competence includes technical knowledge, ability to apply such knowledge with good judgment, and comprehension of professional responsibility. Additionally, the nature of these examinations (low pass rate, broad and rigorous coverage, etc.) has several very important effects.

1. Candidates are forced to learn all of the material that should have been presented and learned in a good accounting educational program.

2. Relatedly, candidates must integrate the topics and concepts that are presented in individual courses in accounting education programs.

3. The content of each examination provides direction to accounting education programs; i.e., what is tested on the examinations will be taught to accounting students.

EXAMINATION CONTENT

The content of these examinations is specified by their governing boards with lists of topics to be tested. In the Gleim review manuals -- *CIA Review, CMA Review, CFM Review,* and *CPA Review* -- the material tested is divided into subtopics called study units. A study unit is a more manageable undertaking than an overall part of each exam. The listings of topics on pages 28 through 30 provide an overview of the content of these three exams.

CIA, CMA/CFM, CPA EXAMINATION SUMMARY

	CIA	CMA/CFM[1]	CPA
Sponsoring Organization	Institute of Internal Auditors 249 Maitland Avenue Altamonte Springs, FL 32701 (407) 830-7600	Institute of Certified Management Accountants 10 Paragon Drive Montvale, NJ 07645-1759 (201) 573-9000 (800) 638-4427	American Institute of Certified Public Accountants Harborside Financial Center 201 Plaza III Jersey City, NJ 07311-3881 (201) 938-3419
Passing Score	75%	70%	75%
Average Pass Rate by Exam Part	45%	40%	33%
Cost	$300 (50% student discount)	$240 (50% student discount; requires IMA membership)	$35-315 (Varies by state)
Year Examination Was First Administered	1974	1972	1916
Major Exam Sections and Length	I. Internal Audit Process (3½ hours)	1. Economics, Finance, and Management (4 hours)	1. Business Law & Professional Responsibilities (3 hours)
	II. Internal Audit Skills (3½ hours)	2. Financial Accounting and Reporting (4 hours) 2CFM. Corporate Financial Management (3 hours)[1]	2. Auditing (4½ hours)
	III. Management Control and Information Tech. (3½ hours)	3. Management Reporting, Analysis, and Behavioral Issues (4 hours)	3. Accounting & Reporting -- Taxation, Managerial, & Governmental and Not-for-Profit Organizations (3½ hours)
	IV. The Audit Environment (3½ hours)	4. Decision Analysis and Information Systems (4 hours)	4. Financial Accounting & Reporting -- Business Enterprises (4½ hours)
Length of Exam	14 hours	16 hours (CMA) 15 hours (CFM)	15½ hours
When Administered	2 weeks after CPA Wed, Thur	2nd week of June, Dec Wed, Thur	1st week of May, Nov Wed, Thur
Candidates Sitting for Exam:	Total number of candidates sitting for two examinations; many are repeaters.		
1990	4,363	4,839	143,572
1991	4,597	6,404	140,042
1992	4,961	7,464	136,541
1993	5,103	7,879	140,100
1994	4,557	8,259	131,000
1995	4,649	8,675	126,000

[1] On December 1, 1996, the ICMA will administer Part 2CFM at Sylvan Learning Centers in a computerized multiple-choice question format. Passing this Part 2CFM allows persons who have also passed Parts 1, 3, and 4 of the CMA exam to obtain the CFM designation. Please visit our Internet site (www.gleim.com) or call (800) 87-GLEIM for details.

Other professional accounting-related designations include: CBA (Certified Bank Auditor), CDP (Certificate in Data Processing), CFA (Chartered Financial Analyst), CFE (Certified Fraud Examiner), CISA (Certified Information Systems Auditor), Enrolled Agent (one enrolled to practice before the IRS).

CIA REVIEW
Use Gleim's *CIA Review* for exam success.

Part I: Internal Audit Process
   Auditing (65-75%)
     · *Nature of Internal Auditing in Profit,*
      Not-for-Profit, and Governmental Entities
     · *Internal Control Concepts*
     · *Administration of the Internal Auditing*
      Assignment
     · *Auditing the Activities of Organizations*
     · *Auditing the Efficiency of Operations and*
      Programs
     · *Audit Evidence*
     · *EDP Auditing*
   Professionalism (10-20%)
     · *Professional Standards*
     · *The IIA Code of Ethics*
   Fraud (10-20%)

From the CIA Content Specification Outline

Part II: Internal Audit Skills
   Problem Solving Skills (30-40%)
   Communication Skills (30-40%)
   Behavioral Skills (10-20%)
   Statistics (10-20%)

Part III: Management Control and Information Tech.
   Organizations and Management (35-45%)
   Information Technology (35-45%)
   Managerial Accounting (10-20%)
   Quantitative Methods (0-10%)

Part IV: The Audit Environment
   Financial Accounting (35-45%)
   Finance (35-45%)
   Economics (5-15%)
   International/Government (5-10%)
   Tax (0-5%)
   Marketing (5-10%)

Each of the four parts is 3½ hours in length (8:30 - 12:00 and 1:30 - 5:00).

> Part I: 70% objective (70 items) and 30% essays (1-2 questions)
> Part II: 50% objective (50 items) and 50% essays (2-3 questions)
> Part III: 100% objective (100 items)
> Part IV: 100% multiple-choice (80 items)

The first two parts of the CIA exam focus on the theory and practice of internal auditing. The body of knowledge of internal auditing and the auditing skills to be tested consist of

1. The typical undergraduate auditing class (as represented by auditing texts, e.g., Arens and Loebbecke, Taylor and Glezen, etc.)

2. Internal auditing textbooks (e.g., Sawyer and Sumners, *The Practice of Modern Internal Auditing,* and Atkisson, Brink, and Witt, *Modern Internal Auditing*)

3. Various IIA (Institute of Internal Auditors) pronouncements (e.g., The IIA Code of Ethics, Standards for the Professional Practice of Internal Auditing, and Statement of Responsibilities of Internal Auditing)

4. Communications and problem-solving skills, and dealing with auditees within an audit context (i.e., the questions will cover audit topics, but test audit skills)

The remaining 50% of the exam covers 10 topics: Parts III and IV.

1. Management cannot personally observe the functioning of all officers, employees, and specialized functions (finance, marketing, operations, etc.). Each has a unique perspective. Only internal auditing is in a position to take a total company point of view.

2. Thus, Parts III and IV of the CIA exam assure that internal auditors are conversant with topics, methodologies, and techniques ranging from individual and organizational behavior to economics.

CMA and CFM REVIEW

Use Gleim's *CMA/CFM Review* for exam success.

Part 1: Economics, Finance, and Management
- Microeconomics
- Macroeconomics
- International Economics
- Institutional Environment of Business
- Working Capital Finance
- Capital Structure Finance
- Organization Theory
- Motivation and the Directing Process
- Communication
- Ethics and the Management Accountant

Part 2: Financial Accounting and Reporting*
- Financial Accounting: Development of Theory and Practice
- Financial Statement Presentation
- Special Financial Reporting Problems
- SEC Reporting Requirements
- Ratio and Accounts Analysis
- Internal Control
- External Auditing
- Income Taxes

*Persons who have passed the CPA exam are not required to take Part 2 of the CMA exam.

**CMAs in good standing need only pass this part to earn the CFM designation.

Part 2CFM: Certified in Financial Management**
- Financial Statements and Annual Reports
- Financial Statements: Special Topics
- Long-Term Capital Financing
- Financial Markets and Interest Rates
- Investment Banking and Commercial Banking
- Financial Statement Analysis
- Business Combinations and Restructurings
- Risk Management
- External Financial Environment
- Accounting Standard Setting

Part 3: Management Reporting, Analysis, and Behavioral Issues
- Process and Job Order Costing
- Variable and Absorption Costing
- Planning
- Budgeting
- The Controlling Process
- Standard Costs and Variance Analysis
- Responsibility Accounting

Part 4: Decision Analysis and Information Systems
- Incremental Costing
- Cost-Volume-Profit Analysis
- Capital Budgeting
- Decision Making Under Uncertainty
- Inventory Models
- Quantitative Methods
- Information Systems
- Internal and Operational Auditing

Each part of the CMA exam is 4 hours in length (8:00 - 12:00 and 1:30 - 5:30). Part 2CFM is 3 hours in length.

These exams have broader coverage than the CPA exam in several areas. For example,

1. The management information systems area of EDP is tested more extensively on the CMA exam.

2. SEC Financial Reporting Releases and Cost Accounting Standards Board pronouncements are covered on the CMA exam but not on the CPA exam.

3. Topics like economics, finance, and management on Part 1 and Part 2CFM are covered lightly, if at all, on the CPA exam.

4. The CMA exam tests internal auditing to a far greater degree than does the CPA exam.

5. The CMA exam tests business ethics, but not business law.

CMA questions are generally more analysis oriented than CPA questions. On the CPA exam, the typical requirement is the solution of an accounting problem, e.g., consolidated worksheet, funds statement, etc. The CMA exam generally has an additional requirement to analyze the impact of the data in the accounting presentation or to explain how the accounting data are used.

Each of the four CMA-only parts consists of 30 multiple-choice questions (1 hour, 25% of grade) and six essay/computational questions (3 hours, 75% of grade). Part 2CFM consists of 120 multiple-choice questions. Each part of the CMA will be 120 multiple-choice, computer-administered questions in December 1997.

CPA REVIEW

Use Gleim's *CPA Review* for exam success.

Business Law & Professional Responsibilities

   I. Professional and Legal Responsibilities
  II. Business Organizations
 III. Contracts
 IV. Debtor-Creditor Relationships
  V. Government Regulation of Business
 VI. Uniform Commercial Code
VII. Property

Auditing

   I. Evaluate the prospective client and engagement, decide whether to accept or continue the client and the engagement, enter into an agreement with the client, and plan the engagement.
  II. Obtain and document information to form a basis for conclusions.
 III. Review the engagement to provide reasonable assurance that objectives are achieved and evaluate information obtained to reach and to document engagement conclusions.
 IV. Prepare communications to satisfy engagement objectives.

Accounting & Reporting -- TAX-MAN-GOV

   I. Federal Taxation -- Individuals
  II. Federal Taxation -- Corporations
 III. Federal Taxation -- Partnerships
 IV. Estates and Trusts, Exempt Organizations, and Preparers' Responsibilities
  V. Governmental and Not-for-Profit Organizations
 VI. Managerial Accounting

Financial Accounting & Reporting

   I. Concepts/Standards
  II. Typical Items in Financial Statements
 III. Specific Types of Transactions/Events

From the AICPA Content Specification Outlines

---

1. The table below presents the CPA exam schedule and exam composition by question type.

Section	Day	Time	Objective		Essay/Problem
			MC	Other	
Business Law	Wednesday	9:00-12:00	50-60%	20-30%	20-30%
Auditing	Wednesday	1:30-6:00	50-60%	20-30%	20-30%
TAX-MAN-GOV	Thursday	8:30-12:00	50-60%	40-50%	0
Financial	Thursday	1:30-6:00	50-60%	20-30%	20-30%

2. The "other objective question format" (OOF) is any question that can be answered on an answer sheet that can be optically scanned, except four-answer multiple-choice.

3. Essay questions will be graded for writing skills.

4. Calculators will be provided for both Thursday sessions (Sharp Model EL-231C).

5. Every aspect of the CPA examination is explained, illustrated, and analyzed in *CPA Review: A System for Success*. Accounting faculty and student accounting organizations should order this free booklet in bulk for distribution to senior accounting students.

EXAMINATION SCHEDULES AND FUTURE DATES

The CPA exam is given during the first week of May and November on Wednesday and Thursday. The CIA exam is given on a Wednesday and Thursday 1 or 2 weeks after the CPA examination. The CMA exam is offered in the first or second week of June and December.

Note that all four examinations can be taken within a 6-week period, which is ideal owing to the great amount of overlap of the material tested. The formats of the exams are very similar, contributing to the synergy of preparing for and taking all three exams together.

	1996		1997		1998	
CPA EXAM	May 8, 9	Nov. 6, 7	May 7, 8	Nov. 5, 6	May 6, 7	Nov. 4, 5
CIA EXAM	May 15, 16	Nov. 20, 21	May 14, 15	Nov. 19, 20	May 13, 14	Nov. 18, 19
CMA EXAM	June 12, 13	Dec. 11, 12	June 11, 12	Computer-Based/On-Demand		
CFM EXAM	Computer-Based/On-Demand		Computer-Based/On-Demand		Computer-Based/On-Demand	

When to Sit for the Exams

Sit for all four examinations as soon as you can. The CIA, CMA, and CFM exams can be taken in your last undergraduate quarter or semester, and offer a 50% reduction in fees to full-time students. In many states you may also take the CPA exam in your last quarter or semester. If you are graduating in May, consider taking the CPA exam the first week of May, the CIA exam 1 or 2 weeks thereafter, and the CMA or CFM exam in early June. Your preparation program for these exams is synergistic and not appreciably more work than preparing for just the CPA exam.

EXAMINATION PASS RATES

The pass rates on the CIA and CMA exams are somewhat higher than the CPA exam. Nationally, the pass rate on the CPA exam is about 33% on each of the four parts. The pass rates on the CIA and CMA exams average 40%-45% per part (see the tables on pages 32 and 33).

Unfortunately, a great deal of confusion surrounds CPA exam pass rates. There is considerable variation in the pass rate from state to state, even though the national rate is fairly constant. Approximately 20% of all candidates sitting for each CPA exam successfully complete the exam (this includes those passing the entire exam on one sitting and those passing their final parts for successful completion). Over 80% of *serious* CPA candidates eventually complete the CPA exam.

There is confusion between CPA pass rates and condition rates. While 75% is the passing grade for each part, *conditional* status is assigned to candidates who pass some, but not all, parts. The combined pass and condition rate is therefore higher than the pass rate. Relatedly, the qualifications and the requirements of conditional status vary from state to state.

Many schools and CPA review courses advertise the quality of their programs by reporting pass rates. Obviously, the best rates are emphasized. Thus, the reported percentage may be that for first-time candidates, all candidates, candidates passing a specific section of the examination, candidates completing the examination, or even candidates successfully completing the exam after a specified number of sittings.

Reasons for the Low Pass Rates

Although a very high percentage of serious candidates successfully complete each of the examinations, the 33% CPA pass rate and the 40% - 45% CIA and CMA pass rates warrant an explanation. First, the pass rates are low (relative to bar and medical exams) because these examinations reflect the high standards of the accounting profession, which contribute greatly to the profession's reputation and also attract persons with both competence and aspiration.

Second, the pass rates are low because most accounting educational programs are at the undergraduate rather than graduate level. (See the table on page 35 and look under the 150-Hr. Requirement column.) Undergraduate students are generally less career-oriented than graduate students. Undergraduates may look on their program as a number of individual courses required for graduation rather than as an integrated program to prepare them for professional practice. We encourage accounting undergraduates to take accounting seriously by helping them look ahead to professional practice and the CIA, CMA, and CPA exams.

Third, the pass rates are low because accounting programs and curricula at most colleges and universities are not given the budgetary priority they deserve. Accounting faculties are often understaffed for the number of accounting majors, the number and nature of accounting courses (problem-oriented vs. descriptive), etc., relative to other faculties. However, you cannot use this as an excuse or reason for not achieving your personal goals. You must do your best to improve your control systems and study resources.

		PART I		PART II		PART III		PART IV	
MO/YR	**TOTAL SITTING**	**No.**	**%**	**No.**	**%**	**No.**	**%**	**No.**	**%**
5/90	2,069	1,227	43.3%	1,248	42.1%	1,036	43.2%	1,036	42.1%
11/90	2,294	1,426	43.4%	1,410	42.8%	1,139	42.7%	1,102	40.0%
5/91	2,244	1,301	42.4%	1,293	42.8%	1,129	42.5%	1,094	41.4%
11/91	2,303	1,355	42.7%	1,331	44.0%	1,214	45.2%	1,120	45.5%
5/92	2,428	1,400	44.9%	1,372	46.2%	1,190	42.9%	1,137	46.4%
11/92	2,533	1,501	43.1%	1,479	45.0%	1,262	47.1%	1,186	46.6%
5/93	2,558	1,488	46.2%	1,464	43.2%	1,248	46.4%	1,225	47.5%
11/93	2,545	1,396	42.2%	1,413	44.2%	1,315	49.0%	1,296	45.3%
5/94	2,266	1,092	46.5%	1,403	47.3%	1,168	45.5%	1,176	43.8%
11/94	2,291	1,212	47.9%	1,369	48.5%	1,157	47.7%	1,172	45.3%
5/95	2,254	1,215	44.9	1,393	44.7%	1,063	49.9%	1,106	45.1%
11/95	2,395	1,400	44.4	1,484	44.1%	1,099	43.7%	1,188	43.9%

NUMBER OF CIA CANDIDATES AND PASSING PERCENTAGE BY PART

PASS RATES ON THE CMA EXAMINATION*										
	June 1991	Dec. 1991	June 1992	Dec. 1992	June 1993	Dec. 1993	June 1994	Dec. 1994	June 1995	Dec. 1995
Part 1 • Economics, Finance, and Management	41%	44%	40%	37%	38%	44%	38%	39%	37%	40%
Part 2 • Financial Accounting and Reporting	38%	43%	31%	31%	42%	36%	38%	36%	36%	40%
Part 3 • Management Reporting, Analysis, and Behavioral Issues	39%	39%	42%	34%	39%	44%	41%	41%	45%	38%
Part 4 • Decision Analysis and Information Systems	46%	40%	38%	40%	37%	38%	45%	44%	46%	46%
Weighted average for entire examination	41%	42%	39%	36%	39%	41%	41%	40%	42%	41%
All parts passed in one sitting	14%	14%	12%	13%	13%	13%	13%	13%	16%	13%
Number of candidates sitting	3,104	3,311	3,718	3,746	3,982	3,897	4,038	4,221	4,327	4,348

*Information on Part 2CFM pass rates will be available on our Internet site (www.gleim.com) soon.

COST TO OBTAIN AND MAINTAIN PROFESSIONAL CERTIFICATION

The cost to take the CIA exam is a $60 registration fee plus $60-per-part examination fee, which totals $300 (assuming you pass all parts the first time you take them). Full-time students save 50%. A $20-per-year record-keeping fee is charged to maintain CPE records for nonmembers of The Institute of Internal Auditors (The IIA). Membership in The IIA is not required.

The cost to take the CMA/CFM exam is $60 for each of the parts plus the Institute of Management Accountants (IMA) membership fee, which varies from $20 for students to $120 for regular members. Membership in the IMA is required. Students may take the examination once at a reduced fee of $30 per part.

The cost of the CPA exam varies by state. The table on page 35 lists the examination fee in each state. Additionally, most states require an annual fee to maintain the CPA certificate and/or license.

WHERE TO TAKE THE CPA EXAM

If you are not going to practice public accounting, you may wish to become certified in a state that

1. Issues a CPA certificate separate from a license to practice
2. Does **not** require experience to receive a CPA certificate
3. Does **not** require continuing professional education of CPA certificate holders
4. Does **not** require residency to sit for the CPA exam

You may also be concerned with the 150-hour requirement to sit for the CPA exam. Consult the table on page 35. This topic and more specific recommendations are presented in Chapter 1 of *CPA Review: A System for Success.*

STATE BOARDS OF ACCOUNTANCY

All 50 states (and the District of Columbia, Guam, Puerto Rico, and the Virgin Islands) have an administrative agency that administers the laws and rules which regulate the practice of public accounting in each state. Each of these 54 jurisdictions contracts with the AICPA to use the AICPA's Uniform CPA Examination.

While the 54 jurisdictions agree on using the same examination, the rules and procedures for applying to take the exam and becoming licensed to practice public accounting vary considerably. You should call or write to your state board for a CPA exam application form. With the form you will receive that board's rules, regulations, and directions to you as a candidate.

The opposite page contains a list of the state boards, their addresses, phone numbers, and the following information relevant to most CPA candidates.

CPA REQUIREMENTS BY STATE (next page)

Residency: Some states have in-state guidelines to meet in order to sit for the CPA exam: R = residency, E = employment, O = office (business). A "C" means U.S. citizenship is required.

150-hour requirement: As of May 1996, 35 states have legislated the requirement for 150 semester hours to take the CPA exam, which is generally a baccalaureate plus 30 hours. The effective dates of this requirement are listed on the table on the opposite page. Contact individual boards for exact information.

Education beyond high school (in years) required to take exam/apply for certificate: B = bachelor's; A = emphasis in accounting; + = hours in excess of bachelor's. The slashes are used to separate various levels of education, which affect the amount of experience required to practice (see Experience, below).

Experience (in public accounting) required to practice: Years of experience correspond to education which is listed in the column just to the left. Varying education requirements and varying experience requirements are separated by slashes. For example, Alaska permits persons to take the CPA exam if one of the following requirements is met:

1. A bachelor's degree not in accounting
2. A bachelor's degree with an accounting major

After passing the CPA exam, either 3 or 2 years' experience is required before a CPA certificate is issued.

1. Three years if the exam was taken with a bachelor's degree not in accounting
2. Two years if the exam was taken with a bachelor's degree in accounting

Exam application deadline -- first time: New candidates

Exam application deadline -- re-exam: For candidates with conditional status (see below)

Exam conditioning requirements: Number of parts to pass, or P for practice, followed by minimum grade on other parts, if any

Exam fee: For all four parts, usually less if conditioned

Ethics test: An E indicates a separate ethics test is given (not during the CPA exam). A dash indicates no ethics test. A pound sign (#) means the ethics test is required at the time of certification.

CPA certificate issued separately from a license to practice: Indicated by a "Y"

CPA REQUIREMENTS BY STATE
as of July 1996

NOTE: Each State Board is currently updating requirements to accommodate the 1996 changes in the CPA exam. Contact your State Board for complete up-to-date information.

STATE BOARD • Address	Telephone #	Residency	150-Hr. Requirement	Education	Experience	Application Deadline First Time	Application Deadline Re-Exam	Condition Requirements	Exam Fee	Ethics	Separate Certificate
AK P.O. Box 110806 • Juneau, AK • 99811	(907) 465-2580	--	1997	B/BA	3/2	60 days	60 days	2, 50	$100	E	--
AL 770 Washington Ave., Ste. 236 • Montgomery, AL • 36130	(334) 242-5700	C	1995	B+	2/5	2/28; 8/31	3/31; 9/30	2, 50	$190	--	Y
AR 101 East Capitol, Ste. 430 • Little Rock, AR • 72201	(501) 682-1520	R/E	1998	BA/+	2/1	60 days	30 days	2, 50	$160	--	Y
AZ 3110 N. 19th Avenue • Suite 140 • Phoenix, AZ • 85015	(602) 255-3648	O		BA/+	2/1	2/28; 8/31	2/28; 8/31	2, 50	$175	#	--
CA 2000 Evergreen Street • Suite 250 • Sacramento, CA • 95815	(916) 263-3673	--		B/BA	3/2	3/1; 9/1	3/1; 9/1	2	$160	E	--
*CO 1560 Broadway, Suite 1370 • Denver, CO • 80202	(303) 894-7800	R/E		BA/+	3/2	60 days	60 days	2, 50	$200	#	--
*CT 30 Trinity Street • Hartford, CT • 06106	(203) 566-8272	R/E	2000	BA/+	3/2	60 days	60 days	2, 50	$220	#	--
DC P.O. Box 37200 • Washington, DC • 20013-7200	(202) 727-7468	--	2000	BA	2	90 days	60 days	2, 50	$120		Y
*DE Cannon Bldg., Ste 203 • P.O. Box 1401 • Dover, DE • 19903	(302) 739-4522	--		2/BA/+	4/2/1	3/1; 9/1	3/1; 9/1	2, 50	$195	#	Y
FL 2610 NW 43rd St. • Suite 1-A • Gainesville, FL • 32606	(352) 955-2165	--	1983	BA+	0	2/1; 8/1	3/1; 9/1	2, 50	$175	E	--
*GA 166 Pryor Street, S.W. • Atlanta, GA • 30303	(404) 656-2281	--	1998	BA	2	2/1; 8/1	3/1; 9/1	2, 50	$200		--
GU P.O. Box P • Agana, GU • 96910	(671) 475-2672	C/R/E/O	2000	BA/+	2/1	60 days	60 days	2, 50	$ 35		--
*HI P.O. Box 3469 • Honolulu, HI • 96801	(808) 586-2694	--	1978	BA+	2	3/1; 9/1	3/1; 9/1	2, 50	$270		Y
*IA 1918 SE Hulsizer Ave. • Ankeny, IA • 50021	(515) 281-4126	R/E/O	2001	0/BA/+	3/2/0	2/28; 8/31	2/28; 8/31	2, 50	$210	E	Y
ID 1109 Main Street • Suite 470 • Boise, ID • 83720-0002	(208) 334-2490	R	2000	BA/+	2/2	3/1; 9/1	3/1; 9/1	2, 50	$150	E	--
IL 320 W. Washington St., 3rd Floor • Springfield, IL • 62786	(217) 785-0800	--	2001	BA	1	3/1; 9/1	3/1; 9/1	2, 50	$180		Y
*IN 302 West Washington St., E034 • Indianapolis, IN • 46204	(317) 232-3935	R	2000	BA/+	3/2	3/1; 9/1	3/1; 9/1	2, 50	$160		--
KS 900 S.W. Jackson St., Ste. 556 • Topeka, KS • 66612	(913) 296-2162	R/E/O	1997	BA/+	2/2	3/15; 9/15	3/15; 9/15	2, 50	$150	E	Y
KY 322 W. Broadway • Suite 310 • Louisville, KY • 40202	(502) 595-3037	--	2000	BA/+	2/1	3/1; 9/1	3/15; 9/15	2, 50	$140	#	--
*LA 601 Poydras St. • Suite 1770 • New Orleans, LA • 70130	(504) 566-1244	R	1996	BA/+	2/1	3/1; 9/1	3/1; 9/1	2, 50	$190		Y
*MA 100 Cambridge St. • Room 1315 • Boston, MA • 02202	(617) 727-1806	--		BA	3/2	3/15; 9/15	3/15; 9/15	2, 50	$215		--
MD 501 St. Paul Place • Room 902 • Baltimore, MD • 21202	(410) 333-6322	--	1999	BA	0	60 days	60 days	2, 50	$ 98	E	--
*ME 35 State House Station • Augusta, ME • 04333	(207) 624-8603	R/E		B/+	2/1	3/1; 9/1	3/1; 9/1	2	$180		Y
MI P.O. Box 30018 • Lansing, MI • 48909-0018	(517) 373-0682	R/E/O		BA/+	2/1	60 days	60 days	2, 50	$120		--
MN 85 East 7th Place, Room 125 • St. Paul, MN • 55101	(612) 296-7937	R/E/O		0/2/B/BA/+	6/5/3/2/1	3/1; 9/1	3/1; 9/1	2, 50	$150	E	Y
*MO P.O. Box 613 • Jefferson City, MO • 65102	(573) 751-0012	R/E/O	1999	BA	2	3/1; 9/1	3/1; 9/1	2, 50	$200	#	Y
MS 653 North State Street • Jackson, MS • 39202-3304	(601) 354-7320	R/O	1995	BA+	2/3	3/15; 9/15	3/15; 9/15	2, 45	$150		Y
MT 111 N. Jackson • P.O. Box 200513 • Helena, MT • 59620	(406) 444-3739	--	1997	B/BA	2/1	3/15; 9/15	3/15; 9/15	2, 50	$130	#	Y
NC P.O. Box 12827 • Raleigh, NC • 27605	(919) 733-4222	C		2/B/BA/+	4/2/2/1	1/31; 7/31	2/28; 8/31	2, 50	$150	E	--
ND 2701 S. Columbia Rd. • Grand Forks, ND • 58201	(800) 532-5904	R	2000	0/BA	4/0	3/15; 9/15	3/15; 9/15	2, 40	$140	E	Y
NE P.O. Box 94725 • Lincoln, NE • 68509	(402) 471-3595	R/E/O	1998	B	2	3/31; 9/30	3/31; 9/30	2, 50	$160	#	Y
NH 57 Regional Drive • Concord, NH • 03301	(603) 271-3286	--		4/+	2/1	3/15; 9/15	3/15; 9/15	2, 50	$225	--	--
*NJ P.O. Box 4500 • Newark, NJ • 07101	(201) 504-6380	--	2000	BA	2	3/1; 8/1	3/1; 9/1	2, 50	$290		--
NM 1650 University NE, Ste. 400A • Albuquerque, NM • 87102	(505) 841-9108	R/O		B/BA	3/1	3/1; 9/1	3/1; 9/1	2, 50	$125	E	Y
NV 200 South Virginia Street, #670 • Reno, NV • 89501	(702) 786-0231	--	2001	BA	2	3/1; 9/1	3/1; 9/1	2, 50	$150	#	--
*NY Cultural Ed. Center • Room 3013 • Albany, NY • 12230	(518) 474-3836	--		0/BA/+	15/2/1	2/1; 8/1	3/1; 9/1	2	$225		--
*OH 77 S. High St., 18th Fl. • Ste. 222 • Columbus, OH • 43266	(614) 466-4135	R/E/O	2000	BA/+	2/1	3/1; 9/1	3/1; 9/1	2, 50	$225	E	--
OK 4545 Lincoln Blvd., Ste. 165 • Ok. City, OK • 73105	(405) 521-2397	R		0/BA	3/0	60 days	60 days	2	$100		--
OR 3218 Pringle Rd., SE • #110 • Salem, OR • 97302	(503) 378-4181	--		0/BA/+	4/2/1	3/1; 9/1	3/1; 9/1	2, 50	$150		--
PA P.O. Box 2649 • Harrisburg, PA • 17105	(717) 783-1404	R/E		BA/+	2/1	2/15; 8/15	3/1; 9/1	2	$103.75		--
*PR P.O. Box 3271 • San Juan, PR • 00904	(809) 754-1959	C/R/E/O	2000	0/B/BA	6/4/0	3/1; 9/1	60 days	2	$250		--
*RI 233 Richmond St., Ste. 236 • Providence, RI • 02903	(401) 277-3185	R/E	1999	BA/+	2/1	3/15; 9/15	3/15; 9/15	2	$235	#	--
SC 800 Dutch Square Blvd • Ste. 260 • Columbia, SC • 29210	(803) 731-1677	--	1997	BA	2	3/15; 9/15	3/15; 9/15	2, 40	$185		Y
SD 301 E. 14th St., Ste. 200 • Sioux Falls, SD • 57104	(605) 367-5770	--	1998	2A/BA/+	2/2/1	3/1; 9/1	3/1; 9/1	2, 50	$200	E	Y
*TN 500 J. Robertson Pkwy, 2nd Fl. • Nashville, TN • 37243-1141	(615) 741-2550	R/E	1993	BA+	2	3/1; 9/1	3/1; 9/1	2, 50	$200	E	Y
TX 333 Guadalupe Tower III • Suite 900 • Austin, TX • 78701	(512) 505-5580	--	1997	B/BA/+	4/2/1	2/28; 8/31	2/28; 8/31	2, 50	$200	#	--
UT 160 E. 300 South • Box 45805 • Salt Lake City, UT • 84145	(801) 530-6628	--	1994	BA+	3/1	60 days	60 days	2, 50	$165	E	Y
*VA 3600 West Broad Street • Richmond, VA • 23230	(804) 367-8505	--		4A/BA/+	2/2/1	3/1; 9/6	60 days	2, 50	$162	E	Y
VI 1-B King St. • Christiansted, St. Croix • VI • 00820	(809) 773-0096	R/E/O		0/B/BA	6/3/2	3/15; 9/15	3/15; 9/15	2	$150		--
*VT 109 State Street • Montpelier, VT • 05609	(802) 828-2837	--		0/2A	2/2	3/15; 9/15	3/15; 9/15	2, 50	$315	E	--
*WA P.O. Box 9131 • Olympia, WA • 98507-9131	(360) 753-2585	--	2000	BA	1	3/1; 9/1	3/1; 9/1	2, 50	$200	#	Y
WI P.O. Box 8935 • Madison, WI • 53708	(608) 266-1397	--		BA	3	3/1; 9/1	3/1; 9/1	2, 50	$123	E	--
WV 201 L&S Bldg. • 812 Quarrier St. • Charleston, WV • 25301	(304) 558-3557	R/O	2000	BA	2	2/15; 8/15	2/15; 8/15	2	$140	E	--
WY 2020 Corey • Suite 100 • Cheyenne, WY • 82002	(307) 777-7551	R/E/O	2000	BA	2	3/1; 9/1	3/1; 9/1	2	$175	E	Y

* CPA Examination Services, a division of the National Association of State Boards of Accountancy, administers the CPA exam including exam application in these 20 states. Call (800) CPA-EXAM.

CONTINUING PROFESSIONAL EDUCATION (CPE) REQUIREMENTS

The IIA, ICMA, most State Boards of Accountancy, and the AICPA have CPE requirements. The IIA refers to CPE as CPD (continuing professional development). The purpose is to promote the development and maintenance of accounting and auditing proficiency for those who have passed initial certification examinations. For CIAs wishing to have a current CPD listing, The IIA requires 100 CPD hours every 3 years, including at least 10 hours each year. The ICMA requires 90 hours every 3 years and annual reporting in July. CPE requirements for CPAs are mandated by individual state boards, which generally require documentation and restrict the nature of the courses allowed. See the table on page 35.

Gleim Publications, Inc. offers a variety of self-study CPE programs in both book and computer diskette form. Call or write to obtain our latest CPE brochure order form.

OTHER CERTIFICATION PROGRAMS

Certificate in Data Processing (CDP). The CDP program is administered by the Institute for Certification of Computer Professionals (ICCP). The ICCP represents a number of professional computer-related societies, of which the Data Processing Management Association (DPMA) is probably the most closely aligned to the CDP program.

The CDP exam is organized into five 1-hour sections. The topics tested are

1. Data Processing Equipment
2. Computer Programming and Software
3. Principles of Management
4. Accounting and Quantitative Methods
5. Systems Analysis and Design

Write to the ICCP for information and an application form:

> Institute for Certification of Computer Professionals
> 35 East Wacker Drive
> Chicago, IL 60601
> (312) 782-9437

Certified Information Systems Auditor (CISA). In 1976 the EDP Auditors Association (EDPAA) formed the EDP Auditors Foundation to support research and educational activities. The organization is now known as the Information Systems Audit and Control Association (ISACA). The first CISA examination was administered in 1981. The objective of the CISA examination is to evaluate an individual's competence in conducting information systems audits.

The CISA exam is 5 hours in length and consists of 250 multiple-choice questions. It is offered on a Saturday in June from 8:30 a.m. to 1:30 p.m. It is administered at over 100 locations worldwide and is offered in French, Hebrew, Japanese, and Spanish, in addition to English. The fee is $250, with an additional $75 U.S. registration fee for non-ISACA members.

The test covers eight topics (domains):

1. Auditing Standards, Procedures, and Techniques 12%
2. Organization and Management 13%
3. Information Processing Facility Operations 12%
4. Logical Access, Physical Access, and Environmental Controls 14%
5. Continuity of Operations 12%
6. Operating Systems Software Development, Acquisition, and Maintenance 12%
7. Application Software Development, Acquisition, and Maintenance 13%
8. Application Systems 12%

100%

Call or write the ISACA for more information:

Manager of Certification
Information Systems Audit and Control Association
P.O. Box 88180
Carol Stream, IL 60188-0180
(708) 682-1200

Other professional accounting-related designations include **CBA (Chartered Bank Auditor)**, **CFA (Chartered Financial Analyst)**, and **Enrolled Agent** (one enrolled to practice before the IRS).

HOW TO OBTAIN *CIA REVIEW*, *CMA REVIEW*, AND *CPA REVIEW*

Every aspect of the CPA examination is explained, illustrated, and analyzed in *CPA Review: A System for Success*. The Gleim *CPA Review* series consists of *CPA Review: A System for Success* and the four companion volumes, one for each section of the exam:

CPA Review: Business Law   *CPA Review: TAX-MAN-GOV*
CPA Review: Auditing   *CPA Review: Financial*

Each of these volumes is organized according to the AICPA Content Specification Outlines. The Gleim study outlines and the AICPA questions/answers are packaged into 18 to 21 study units, which cover identifiable topics and are conveniently sized to maximize your learning and understanding. Each study unit contains study outlines covering the subject matter of that study unit as well as recent CPA questions and answer explanations on the subject matter.

CIA Review and *CMA Review* have similar formats and approaches. Each has four important introductory chapters:

1. The CIA or CMA Program: An Overview
2. CIA or CMA Exam: Preparation, Administration, and Grading
3. Preparing to Pass the CIA or CMA Exam
4. Writing the CIA or CMA Examination

Each text then has a chapter for each part of that exam, and each chapter is subdivided into four to nine study units or subtopics. Each study unit in Volume I (23 in *CIA Review* and 33 in *CMA Review*) contains a comprehensive, easy-to-study outline of the subject matter.

Volume II for each manual is divided into those same study units and contains

1. Multiple-choice questions from recent examinations

2. Essay questions/computational problems from recent examinations

3. The IIA or ICMA answers for the multiple-choice questions

4. One- or two-paragraph explanations of the multiple-choice questions and answers

5. The IIA or ICMA suggested solution for each essay question/computational problem, following a one- or two-paragraph commentary on the question answering technique

The Seventh Edition of *CIA Review* (Volumes I and II) is now available. This new edition contains questions, answers, and answer explanations from the 1996 CIA exam, as well as updated outlines. *CMA Review* is in the Seventh Edition and is current and up-to-date for the 1996 and 1997 exams.

Each review manual is a multi-volume set of 8½- x 11-inch paperbacks, presented in easy-to-read type styles and spacing. They may be used with or without any other study materials or review courses. The primary objective of each is to provide you with a complete, efficient, inexpensive, and effective study program. Each set is all you should need to obtain the knowledge and the confidence to pass the CPA, CIA, or CMA examination.

Order *CPA Review*, *CIA Review*, and/or *CMA Review* directly from Gleim Publications, Inc. in Gainesville, Florida. Please submit requests to your school's and/or your employer's librarian to acquire these texts. Orders from individuals must be prepaid. Gleim Publications guarantees immediate, complete refund on all mail orders if a resalable text is returned within 30 days. An order form is provided at the back of this book.

GLEIM'S *TEST PREP* SOFTWARE

As you prepare for the CIA, CMA, and/or CPA, improve your study process and test yourself in an interactive environment with actual CIA, CMA, or CPA questions. You can customize study and test sessions and receive diagnostic and performance analysis feedback.

In the test mode, the Gleim software provides a controlled testing environment which accurately and quickly assesses your knowledge level. In the study mode, you receive immediate feedback and explanations on each response which facilitates learning and understanding.

GLEIM PRODUCT MULTIPLE-CHOICE QUESTION COUNTS

CIA	Part I	Part II	Part III	Part IV	TOTAL
Books	754	408	671	626	2,459
Software	928	609	975	993	3,505
CMA	Part 1	Part 2	Part 3	Part 4	TOTAL
Books	437	395	236	343	1,411
Software	754	793	768	822	3,137
CPA	LAW	AUD	TMG	FIN	TOTAL
Books	619	646	707	646	2,618
Software	1,253	1,393	1,222	1,327	5,195

CHAPTER FOUR
BASIC CONCEPTS

The conceptual framework is a coherent set of interrelated objectives and fundamentals established by the Financial Accounting Standards Board. This framework is contained in the Statements of Financial Accounting Concepts (see page 10 for a listing of SFACs). These statements do not themselves establish the accounting and reporting requirements for particular items and events. Instead, the purpose of the SFACs is to describe concepts and relationships that will lead to and underlie the establishment of a consistent set of standards that will prescribe and establish the accounting and reporting requirements.

4.1 Objectives

1. The information provided by financial reporting pertains to

A. Individual business enterprises, rather than to industries or an economy as a whole or to members of society as consumers.

B. Individual business enterprises and industries, rather than to an economy as a whole or to members of society as consumers.

C. Individual business enterprises and an economy as a whole, rather than to industries or to members of society as consumers.

D. Individual business enterprises, industries, and an economy as a whole, rather than to members of society as consumers.

The correct answer is (A). (CPA 1181 T-2)
REQUIRED: The economic level(s) to which the information provided by financial reporting pertains.
DISCUSSION: According to SFAC 1, *Objectives of Financial Reporting by Business Enterprises*, financial reporting pertains essentially to individual business enterprises. Information about industries and economies in which an industry operates is usually provided only to the extent necessary for understanding the individual business enterprise.
Answers (B), (C), and (D) are incorrect because financial reporting pertains to individual business enterprises only, not to industries, the economy as a whole, or members of society as consumers.

2. During a period when an enterprise is under the direction of a particular management, its financial statements will directly provide information about

A. Both enterprise performance and management performance.

B. Management performance but not directly provide information about enterprise performance.

C. Enterprise performance but not directly provide information about management performance.

D. Neither enterprise performance nor management performance.

The correct answer is (C). (CPA 594 F-4)
REQUIRED: The information directly provided by financial statements.
DISCUSSION: Financial reporting provides information about an enterprise's performance during a period when it was under the direction of a particular management but does not directly provide information about that management's performance. Financial reporting does not try to separate the impact of a particular management's performance from the effects of prior management actions, general economic conditions, the supply and demand for an enterprise's inputs and outputs, price changes, and other events.
Answers (A), (B), and (D) are incorrect because financial statements will directly provide information about enterprise performance but not about management performance.

3. What are the Statements of Financial Accounting Concepts intended to establish?

A. Generally accepted accounting principles in financial reporting by business enterprises.

B. The meaning of "present fairly in accordance with generally accepted accounting principles."

C. The objectives and concepts for use in developing standards of financial accounting and reporting.

D. The hierarchy of sources of generally accepted accounting principles.

The correct answer is (C). *(CPA 594 F-2)*
REQUIRED: The purpose of the SFACs.
DISCUSSION: SFACs set the objectives, qualitative characteristics, and other concepts that guide the FASB in developing sound accounting principles. They are not established GAAP and therefore are not covered by Conduct Rule 203, which pertains to established accounting principles and departures therefrom.

Answer (A) is incorrect because SFACs are intended to guide the development of promulgated GAAP. Answer (B) is incorrect because AU 411 (SAS 69) clarifies the meaning of "present fairly in accordance with generally accepted accounting principles." Answer (D) is incorrect because AU 411 establishes the hierarchy of sources of GAAP.

4. According to the FASB conceptual framework, the objectives of financial reporting for business enterprises are based on

A. The need for conservatism.

B. Reporting on management's stewardship.

C. Generally accepted accounting principles.

D. The needs of the users of the information.

The correct answer is (D). *(CPA 1193 T-5)*
REQUIRED: The objectives of financial reporting for business enterprises.
DISCUSSION: SFAC 1 states that one objective of financial reporting is to provide information that is useful to present and potential investors, creditors, and other users in making rational investment, credit, and similar decisions.

Answer (A) is incorrect because conservatism is a qualitative characteristic. Answer (B) is incorrect because financial reporting provides information that is helpful in evaluating management's stewardship but does not directly provide information about that performance. Answer (C) is incorrect because GAAP governs how to account for items in the financial statements.

5. Which of the following statements reflects the basic purposes of financial reporting?

A. The primary focus of financial reporting is information about an enterprise's resources.

B. The best indication of an enterprise's ability to generate favorable cash flow is information based on previous cash receipts and payments.

C. Financial accounting is expressly designed to measure directly the value of a business enterprise.

D. Investment and credit decisions often are based, at least in part, on evaluations of the past performance of an enterprise.

The correct answer is (D). *(Publisher)*
REQUIRED: The correct statement about the basic purposes of financial reporting.
DISCUSSION: SFAC 1 states that, although investment and credit decisions reflect investors' and creditors' expectations about future enterprise performance, those expectations are commonly based, at least in part, on evaluations of past enterprise performance.

Answer (A) is incorrect because the primary focus of financial reporting is information about earnings and its components (not resources). Answer (B) is incorrect because the best indication of an enterprise's present and continuing ability to generate favorable cash flow is information about enterprise earnings based on accrual (not cash basis) accounting. Answer (C) is incorrect because financial accounting is not designed to measure the value of a business enterprise directly, but the information provided may be helpful to those who wish to estimate its value.

6. The best indication of an enterprise's present and continuing ability to generate favorable cash flows is information about enterprise earnings based on which of the following?

- A. Cash accounting basis.
- B. Modified cash accounting basis.
- C. Accrual accounting basis.
- D. Tax accounting basis.

The correct answer is (C). *(Publisher)*
REQUIRED: The basis that best indicates an enterprise's ability to generate favorable cash flows.
DISCUSSION: SFAC 1 states that information about enterprise earnings based on accrual accounting generally provides a better indication of the enterprise's present and continuing ability to generate favorable cash flows than would information limited to the financial effects of cash receipts and payments. Accrual accounting attempts to record the financial effects on an enterprise of transactions and other events and circumstances that have cash consequences in the periods in which those transactions, events, and circumstances occur, rather than only in the periods in which cash is received or paid by the enterprise.

Answers (A), (B), and (D) are incorrect because the accrual basis best indicates an enterprise's ability to generate favorable cash flows.

7. Which of the following statements about accrual accounting is not correct?

- A. Accrual accounting is concerned with the process by which cash expended on resources and activities is returned as more (or perhaps less) cash to the enterprise, not just with the beginning and end of that process.
- B. Accrual accounting recognizes that buying, producing, selling, and other operations of an enterprise during a period often do not coincide with the cash receipts and payments of the period.
- C. Accrual accounting attempts to record the financial effects on an enterprise of transactions and other events and circumstances that have cash consequences for an enterprise.
- D. Accrual accounting is primarily concerned with the cash receipts and cash payments of an enterprise.

The correct answer is (D). *(Publisher)*
REQUIRED: The false statement about accrual accounting.
DISCUSSION: Accrual accounting attempts to record the financial effects on an enterprise of transactions and other events and circumstances that have cash consequences in the periods in which those transactions, events, and circumstances occur, rather than only in the periods in which cash is received or paid by the enterprise. Thus, the focus of accrual accounting is not primarily on the actual cash receipts and cash payments. It is concerned with the process by which cash expended on resources is returned as more (or perhaps less) cash to the enterprise, not just with the beginning and end of the process.

Answers (A), (B), and (C) are incorrect because each is a true statement about accrual accounting.

8. FASB's conceptual framework explains both financial and physical capital maintenance concepts. Which capital maintenance concept is applied to currently reported net income, and which is applied to comprehensive income?

	Currently Reported Net Income	Comprehensive Income
A.	Financial capital	Physical capital
B.	Physical capital	Physical capital
C.	Financial capital	Financial capital
D.	Physical capital	Financial capital

The correct answer is (C). *(CPA 1191 T-1)*
REQUIRED: The capital maintenance concepts applicable to currently reported net income and comprehensive income.
DISCUSSION: The financial capital maintenance concept is the traditional basis of financial statements as well as the full set of financial statements, including comprehensive income, discussed in the conceptual framework. Under this concept, a return on investment (defined in terms of financial capital) results only if the financial amount of net assets at the end of the period exceeds the amount at the beginning after excluding the effects of transactions with owners. Under a physical capital concept, a return on investment (in terms of physical capital) results only if the physical productive capacity (or the resources needed to achieve that capacity) at the end of the period exceeds the capacity at the beginning after excluding the effects of transactions with owners. The latter concept requires many assets to be measured at current (replacement) cost.

Answers (A), (B), and (D) are incorrect because comprehensive income and currently reported net income are based on financial capital.

9. The primary current source of generally accepted accounting principles for nongovernment operations rests with the

    A. Securities and Exchange Commission.

    B. New York Stock Exchange.

    C. Financial Accounting Standards Board.

    D. American Institute of Certified Public Accountants.

The correct answer is (C). *(Publisher)*

    REQUIRED: The institution primarily responsible for the establishment of generally accepted accounting principles.

    DISCUSSION: In 1973, the Financial Accounting Standards Board was created as a seven-member, full-time autonomous board with the responsibility of establishing financial accounting standards. The Board is charged to be responsive to the needs and viewpoints of the entire economic community, not just the public accounting profession, and it operates in full view of the public through a due process system.

    Answers (A), (B), and (D) are incorrect because, while these bodies are influential in the establishment of generally accepted accounting principles, none is the primary source.

10. In the hierarchy of generally accepted accounting principles, APB Opinions have the same authority as AICPA

    A. Statements of Position.

    B. Industry Audit and Accounting Guides.

    C. Issues Papers.

    D. Accounting Research Bulletins.

The correct answer is (D). *(CPA 1194 F-2)*

    REQUIRED: The AICPA pronouncement with the same authority as APB Opinions.

    DISCUSSION: In the GAAP hierarchy established by SAS 69, *The Meaning of "Present Fairly in Conformity with Generally Accepted Accounting Principles" in an Independent Auditor's Report*, the highest category consists of pronouncements of established accounting principles by a body designated by the AICPA to establish such principles pursuant to the AICPA's Code of Professional Conduct. This category of established accounting principles includes FASB Statements (SFASs) and Interpretations, APB Opinions, and ARBs.

    Answers (A), (B), and (C) are incorrect because SOPs and Industry Audit and Accounting Guides are in a lower category of established accounting principles, and Issues Papers are considered other accounting literature.

11. FASB Interpretations of Statements of Financial Accounting Standards have the same authority as the FASB

    A. Statements of Financial Accounting Concepts.

    B. Emerging Issues Task Force Consensus.

    C. Technical Bulletins.

    D. Statements of Financial Accounting Standards.

The correct answer is (D). *(CPA 592 T-1)*

    REQUIRED: The pronouncement having the same authority as FASB Interpretations of FASB Statements of Financial Accounting Standards.

    DISCUSSION: SAS 69 establishes the hierarchy of generally accepted accounting practices. The highest category includes FASB Statements and Interpretations, APB Opinions, and AICPA Accounting Research Bulletins. The second highest category includes FASB Technical Bulletins, AICPA Industry Audit and Accounting Guides, and AICPA Statements of Position. The third highest category includes consensus positions of the FASB Emerging Issues Task Force and AICPA Practice Bulletins. The fourth highest category includes AICPA Accounting Interpretations, questions and answers published by the FASB staff, and industry practices widely recognized and prevalent. The fifth category includes other accounting literature.

    Answer (A) is incorrect because it is included in the lowest category. Answer (B) is incorrect because it is included in the third highest category. Answer (C) is incorrect because it is included in the second highest category.

12. The operating cycle of a business is that span of time that

A. Coincides with the economy's business cycle, which runs from one trough of the economy's business activity to the next.

B. Corresponds with its natural business year, which runs from one trough of the particular firm's business activity to the next.

C. Is set by the industry's trade association, usually on an average length of time for all firms that are members of the association.

D. Runs from cash disbursement for items of inventory through their sale to the realization of cash from sale.

The correct answer is (D). *(CPA 1174 T-12)*
REQUIRED: The definition of the operating cycle of a business.
DISCUSSION: As stated in ARB 43, Chapter 3A, *Current Assets and Current Liabilities*, the average amount of time from cash disbursement to the realization of cash from sale is the operating cycle of the business.
Answer (A) is incorrect because financial reporting is geared toward a business enterprise's business cycle, not the economy's. Answer (B) is incorrect because it defines the firm's fiscal year rather than its operating cycle. One operating cycle may last 12 months or more, although usually the fiscal year of the business includes a number of operating cycles. Answer (C) is incorrect because the operating cycle of a business is determined by the firm's transactions, not by reference to an industry trade association estimate.

13. The business reason usually given for a firm to select a fiscal year different from the calendar year is

A. The firm's owners may have a personal preference.

B. Tax laws favor firms which employ a fiscal year other than the calendar year.

C. The fiscal year-end is selected to coincide with the low points in sales, production, and inventories, which may occur at some period other than the calendar year-end.

D. Public accounting firms might not be able to handle the workload if all their clients were to report on a calendar-year basis.

The correct answer is (C). *(CMA 680 4-12)*
REQUIRED: The most common reason for selecting a fiscal year different from the calendar year.
DISCUSSION: A fiscal year is a 12-month period that ends at a date other than December 31. The business's natural business year is normally chosen. A natural year runs from one low point in a firm's business activity to the same low point 12 months later.
Answers (A), (B), and (D) are incorrect because, even though they sometimes affect the selection of a fiscal year, they are not the usual justification given. From a theoretical viewpoint, the best justification is based upon the natural year concept.

14. The primary purpose of the Statement of Financial Position is to reflect

A. The market value of the firm's assets at some point in time.

B. The status of the firm's assets in case of forced liquidation of the firm.

C. The firm's potential for growth in stock values in the stock market.

D. Items of value, debts, and net worth.

The correct answer is (D). *(CMA 680 4-15)*
REQUIRED: The primary purpose of the Statement of Financial Position (balance sheet).
DISCUSSION: In conformity with GAAP, the Statement of Financial Position or balance sheet presents three major financial accounting elements: assets (items of value), liabilities (debts), and owners' equity (net worth). According to SFAC 6, *Elements of Financial Statements*, assets are probable future economic benefits resulting from past transactions or events. Liabilities are probable future sacrifices of economic benefits arising from present obligations as a result of past transactions or events. Equity is the residual interest in the assets after deduction of liabilities.
Answer (A) is incorrect because the balance sheet reflects different attributes of assets rather than their market value. Answer (B) is incorrect because the balance sheet usually does not report forced liquidation values. Answer (C) is incorrect because the future value of a company's stock is more dependent upon future operations and investors' expectations than on the data found in the balance sheet.

15. What is the purpose of information presented in notes to the financial statements?

  A. To provide disclosures required by generally accepted accounting principles.

  B. To correct improper presentation in the financial statements.

  C. To provide recognition of amounts not included in the totals of the financial statements.

  D. To present management's responses to auditor comments.

The correct answer is (A). *(CPA 594 F-6)*
  REQUIRED: The purpose of information presented in notes to the financial statements.
  DISCUSSION: Footnotes are an integral part of the basic financial statements. Footnotes provide information essential to understanding the financial statements, including disclosures required by GAAP (SFAC 5).
  Answer (B) is incorrect because footnotes may not be used to rectify an improper presentation. Answer (C) is incorrect because disclosure in footnotes is not a substitute for recognition in financial statements for items that meet recognition criteria. Answer (D) is incorrect because management's responses to auditor comments are not an appropriate subject of financial reporting.

4.2 Qualitative Characteristics

16. SFAC 2, *Qualitative Characteristics of Accounting Information*, identifies the two primary qualities that make accounting information useful for decision making as

  A. Neutral and verifiable.

  B. Fair and precise.

  C. Relevant and reliable.

  D. Consistent and comparable.

The correct answer is (C). *(J. Cerepak)*
  REQUIRED: The two primary qualities that make accounting information useful.
  DISCUSSION: SFAC 2 identifies relevance and reliability as the two primary qualities that make accounting information useful for decision making. Relevance is the capacity of information to make a difference in the user's decision. Reliability provides assurance that the information is reasonably free from error and bias and that it represents what it purports to represent.
  Answer (A) is incorrect because neutrality and verifiability are ingredients of reliability. Answer (B) is incorrect because, while accounting information should be fairly presented, precision is not always possible when estimates are necessary. Answer (D) is incorrect because consistency and comparability are secondary qualities that interact with the two primary qualities to contribute to usefulness.

17. According to Statements of Financial Accounting Concepts, neutrality is an ingredient of

	Reliability	Relevance
A.	Yes	Yes
B.	Yes	No
C.	No	Yes
D.	No	No

The correct answer is (B). *(CPA 1194 F-1)*
  REQUIRED: The quality of which neutrality is an ingredient.
  DISCUSSION: The primary quality of reliability assures that information is reasonably free from error and bias and faithfully represents what it purports to represent. Its ingredients are representational faithfulness, verifiability, and neutrality. Neutrality is the absence of bias intended to reach a predetermined result or induce a certain behavior.
  Answers (A), (C), and (D) are incorrect because neutrality is an element of reliability, not relevance. The ingredients of relevance are feedback value, predictive value, and timeliness.

18. According to SFAC 2, materiality is a pervasive concept that relates to

	Relevance	Reliability
A.	No	No
B.	Yes	No
C.	No	Yes
D.	Yes	Yes

The correct answer is (D). *(Publisher)*
  REQUIRED: The relationship of materiality to relevance and reliability.
  DISCUSSION: In accordance with SFAC 2, materiality is a pervasive concept that relates to both of the primary decision-specific qualities: relevance and reliability.
  Answers (A), (B), and (C) are incorrect because materiality relates to both relevance and reliability.

19. Which of the following is considered a pervasive constraint by SFAC 2?

    A. Benefits/costs.

    B. Conservatism.

    C. Timeliness.

    D. Verifiability.

The correct answer is (A). *(CPA 582 T-14)*

REQUIRED: The accounting quality that is a pervasive constraint.

DISCUSSION: All accounting information is subject to two quantitative constraints: materiality and cost/benefit. If a reasonable person relying on the information would not have changed his/her judgment as a result of an omission or misstatement, it is not considered material. The constraint of benefits/costs states that the benefits of information must exceed the cost of obtaining it.

Answer (B) is incorrect because conservatism is defined as a prudent reaction to uncertainty. Answer (C) is incorrect because timeliness is an ingredient of relevance. Answer (D) is incorrect because verifiability is an ingredient of reliability.

20. Materiality is one of the pervasive concepts discussed in SFAC 2. Which of the following statements is true with regard to materiality?

    A. Materiality judgments generally may be based solely on the magnitude of the item.

    B. The nature and magnitude of an item as well as the circumstances in which the judgment has to be made are integral aspects of a materiality judgment.

    C. Relevant items are always material.

    D. Materiality judgments generally may be made without consideration of the magnitude of the item involved.

The correct answer is (B). *(Publisher)*

REQUIRED: The true statement with regard to materiality.

DISCUSSION: In accordance with SFAC 2, the basis for a materiality judgment is generally not sufficient unless the nature of the item, the circumstances in which the judgment has to be made, and the magnitude of the item are all considered.

Answers (A) and (D) are incorrect because the magnitude of the item is only one aspect of a materiality judgment. Answer (C) is incorrect because materiality is a pervasive concept that relates to the qualitative characteristic of relevance. Information may be relevant because it can make a difference in a single investment decision, but it may be too small (immaterial) to make that difference matter over the year.

21. Under SFAC 2, the ability through consensus among measurers to ensure that information represents what it purports to represent is the definition of the concept of

    A. Relevance.

    B. Verifiability.

    C. Comparability.

    D. Feedback value.

The correct answer is (B). *(CPA 1182 T-1)*

REQUIRED: The term that describes the ability to ensure that information represents what it purports to represent.

DISCUSSION: Verifiability is defined as the ability through consensus among measurers to ensure that information represents what it purports to represent. It is easily confused with representational faithfulness, which refers to the agreement between a description and that which it purports to measure. However, representational faithfulness refers to the validity of the measurement, while verifiability refers to the application of the measurement rule.

Answer (A) is incorrect because relevance (a primary decision-specific quality) is the capacity of the information to make a difference in a decision. Answer (C) is incorrect because comparability (a secondary interactive quality) refers to the quality of information that enables users to identify similarities in and differences between two sets of data. Answer (D) is incorrect because feedback value (an ingredient of relevance) is the quality of information that enables users to confirm or correct prior expectations.

22. According to the FASB conceptual framework, which of the following situations violates the concept of reliability?

    A.   Financial statements were issued 9 months late.

    B.   Data on segments having the same expected risks and growth rates are reported to analysts estimating future profits.

    C.   Financial statements included property with a carrying amount increased to management's estimate of market value.

    D.   Management reports to stockholders regularly refer to new projects undertaken, but the financial statements never report project results.

The correct answer is (C). *(CPA 593 T-1)*
    REQUIRED: The situation violating the concept of reliability.
    DISCUSSION: Reliability is defined as the quality of information that provides assurance that the information is reasonably free from error and bias and faithfully represents what it purports to represent. In accordance with GAAP, the carrying amount of property should not be increased to market value. If it is reported at markup value, it is misrepresented, which violates the concept of reliability.
    Answers (A), (B), and (D) are incorrect because they relate to the concept of relevance, the capacity of information to make a difference in a decision.

23. Factors that might influence a decision maker's judgment as to what accounting information is useful include

    A.   The decision to be made.

    B.   The information already possessed.

    C.   The decision maker's capacity to process the information.

    D.   All of the answers are correct.

The correct answer is (D). *(Publisher)*
    REQUIRED: The factors that influence a decision maker's judgment as to the usefulness of accounting information.
    DISCUSSION: The judgment by a decision maker as to what accounting information can be useful includes

1. The type of decision to be made;
2. The methods by which the decision would be made;
3. The information already possessed or attainable from other sources; and
4. The decision maker's capacity, either alone or with professional help, to process the information. See SFAC 2.

    Answers (A), (B), and (C) are incorrect because all three are factors that influence a decision maker's judgment as to the usefulness of accounting information.

24. Accounting information that enables decision makers to confirm or correct prior expectations is said to have

    A.   Predictive value.

    B.   Representational faithfulness.

    C.   Feedback value.

    D.   Comparability.

The correct answer is (C). *(CMA 1294 2-1)*
    REQUIRED: The characteristic of accounting information enabling confirmation or correction of prior expectations.
    DISCUSSION: The primary quality of relevance is the capacity of information to make a difference in a decision. It is composed of (1) predictive value, (2) feedback value, and (3) timeliness. Feedback value is the quality of information that permits users to confirm or correct prior expectations.
    Answer (A) is incorrect because predictive value enables users to predict the outcome of future events. Answer (B) is incorrect because representational faithfulness is the agreement between a measure or description and the phenomenon that it purports to represent. Answer (D) is incorrect because comparability enables users to identify similarities in and differences between two sets of economic phenomena.

25. According to the FASB conceptual framework, which of the following relates to both relevance and reliability?

- A. Comparability.
- B. Feedback value.
- C. Verifiability.
- D. Timeliness.

The correct answer is (A). *(CPA 1192 T-2)*
REQUIRED: The item that relates to both relevance and reliability.
DISCUSSION: Comparability (a secondary interactive quality) refers to the quality of information that enables users to identify similarities in and differences between two sets of data. Comparability interacts with relevance and reliability to contribute to the usefulness of information (SFAC 2).
Answer (B) is incorrect because feedback value is an ingredient of the primary quality of relevance but not of reliability. Answer (C) is incorrect because verifiability is an ingredient of the primary quality of reliability but not of relevance. Answer (D) is incorrect because timeliness is an ingredient of the primary quality of relevance but not of reliability.

26. According to SFAC 2, an interim earnings report is expected to have which of the following?

	Predictive Value	Feedback Value
A.	No	No
B.	Yes	Yes
C.	Yes	No
D.	No	Yes

The correct answer is (B). *(CPA 582 T-15)*
REQUIRED: The qualitative value(s) expected in an interim earnings report.
DISCUSSION: According to SFAC 2, an interim earnings report gives feedback on past performance as well as providing a basis for predicting annual earnings before the year-end. Feedback value is the quality of information that permits users to confirm or correct prior expectations. An interim earnings report enables a user to match its information with the prior predictions of the firm's earnings capacity. Predictive value is the quality of information that permits users to increase the probability of making correct forecasts. An interim earnings report has predictive value as well as feedback value because it serves to enhance a forecast of annual earnings.
Answers (A), (C), and (D) are incorrect because an interim earnings report is expected to have both predictive and feedback value.

27. Consolidated financial statements are prepared when a parent-subsidiary relationship exists in recognition of the accounting concept of

- A. Materiality.
- B. Entity.
- C. Verifiability.
- D. Going concern.

The correct answer is (B). *(CPA 579 T-17)*
REQUIRED: The accounting concept recognized in consolidated financial statements.
DISCUSSION: Consolidated financial statements should reflect the economic activities of a business enterprise measured without regard to the boundaries of the legal entity. Accounting information pertains to a business enterprise, the boundaries of which are not necessarily those of the legal entity. For instance, a parent and subsidiary are legally separate but are treated as a single business enterprise in consolidated statements.
Answer (A) is incorrect because materiality requires reporting of information that has a value significant enough to affect decisions of those using the financial statements. Answer (C) is incorrect because verifiability means having an existence independent of the observer. Answer (D) is incorrect because the going concern concept assumes that the business entity will continue to operate in the absence of evidence to the contrary, but it is not a reason for preparing consolidated statements.

28. During the lifetime of an entity, accountants produce financial statements at arbitrary moments in time in accordance with which basic accounting concept?

A. Verifiability.

B. Periodicity.

C. Conservatism.

D. Matching.

The correct answer is (B). *(CPA 1178 T-6)*
REQUIRED: The basic accounting concept requiring financial statements to be issued at arbitrary moments in time.
DISCUSSION: A basic feature of the financial accounting process is that information about the economic activities of the business enterprise should be issued at regular intervals. These time periods should be of equal length to facilitate comparability. They should also be of relatively short duration, e.g., 1 year, to provide business information useful for decision making.
Answer (A) is incorrect because verifiability is a qualitative characteristic, not a concept of the timing of financial statements. Answer (C) is incorrect because conservatism requires accountants to choose the less optimistic estimate if two estimates are equally probable. Answer (D) is incorrect because matching (another term for associating cause and effect) requires costs to be recognized as expenses on the basis of their direct association with specific revenues to the extent possible.

29. The basic accounting equation (assets – liabilities = owners' equity) reflects the

A. Entity point of view.

B. Fund theory.

C. Proprietary point of view.

D. Enterprise theory.

The correct answer is (C). *(CMA 684 3-13)*
REQUIRED: The concept on which the basic accounting equation is based.
DISCUSSION: The equation is based on the proprietary theory: The owners' interest in an enterprise (residual equity) is what remains after the economic obligations of the enterprise are deducted from its economic resources.
Answer (A) is incorrect because the entity concept limits accounting information to that related to a specific entity (possibly not the same as the legal entity). Answer (B) is incorrect because fund theory stresses that assets equal obligations (owners' equity and liabilities are sources of assets). Answer (D) is incorrect because the enterprise concept stresses ownership of the assets; that is, the emphasis is on the credit side of the balance sheet.

30. When a company makes a change in accounting principle, prior-year financial statements are not generally restated to reflect the change. The Accounting Principles Board decided that this procedure would prevent a dilution of public confidence in financial statements but recognized that this procedure conflicts with the accounting concept of

A. Materiality.

B. Conservatism.

C. Verifiability.

D. Comparability.

The correct answer is (D). *(CPA 1178 T-5)*
REQUIRED: The accounting concept which conflicts with the general accounting procedure for changes in accounting principle.
DISCUSSION: APB 20, *Accounting Changes*, requires that most changes in accounting principle be recognized by including the cumulative effect of the change in net income of the period of the change, i.e., no restatement of prior-period financial statements. This procedure conflicts with the concept of consistency or comparability, which requires that similar events be accounted for similarly in successive periods, i.e., requiring restatement of prior-year statements for accounting changes.
Answer (A) is incorrect because the materiality concept states that accounting information may be ignored if it is not significant enough to affect users' decisions. Answer (B) is incorrect because conservatism is a modifying convention which requires the use of the less optimistic estimate when two or more estimates are equally probable. Answer (C) is incorrect because verifiability is a qualitative ingredient of reliability not related to consistency of financial statements.

31. Continuation of an accounting entity in the absence of evidence to the contrary is an example of the basic concept of

    A. Accounting entity.

    B. Consistency.

    C. Going concern.

    D. Substance over form.

The correct answer is (C). *(CPA 1179 T-27)*
    REQUIRED: The concept regarding the continuation of a business entity.
    DISCUSSION: A basic feature of financial accounting is that the business entity is assumed to be a going concern in the absence of evidence to the contrary. The going concern concept is based on the empirical observation that many enterprises have an indefinite life.
    Answer (A) is incorrect because the accounting entity concept refers to the business enterprise, which may or may not be synonymous with the legal entity. The emphasis is also on the separation of the entity from its ownership. Answer (B) is incorrect because the consistency principle requires that similar events be accounted for similarly in succeeding accounting periods to facilitate comparability between periods. Answer (D) is incorrect because the concept of substance over form requires accounting treatment to be based upon the economic substance of events rather than upon the legal form.

32. The accounting measurement that is not consistent with the "going concern" concept is

    A. Historical cost.

    B. Realization.

    C. The transaction approach.

    D. Liquidation value.

The correct answer is (D). *(CMA 684 4-3)*
    REQUIRED: The accounting measurement inconsistent with the going concern concept.
    DISCUSSION: Financial accounting principles assume that a business entity is a going concern in the absence of evidence to the contrary. The concept justifies the use of depreciation and amortization schedules, and the recording of assets and liabilities at attributes other than liquidation value.
    Answers (A), (B), and (C) are incorrect because each is part of the basic structure of accrual accounting.

33. The concept of consistency is sacrificed in the accounting for which of the following income statement items?

    A. Discontinued operations.

    B. Loss on disposal of a segment of a business.

    C. Extraordinary items.

    D. Cumulative effect of change in accounting principle.

The correct answer is (D). *(CPA 1180 T-6)*
    REQUIRED: The income statement item which does not follow the concept of consistency.
    DISCUSSION: Changes in accounting principles generally are accounted for by means of a cumulative effect adjustment in the year of change with no restatement of prior-year statements. Therefore, a break in consistency will have occurred because similar events are not accounted for in the same way in succeeding accounting periods.
    Answers (A), (B), and (C) are incorrect because, even though each event is unusual, as long as the same accounting treatment is applied whenever the event occurs, no consistency violation occurs.

34. Uncertainty and risks inherent in business situations should be adequately considered in financial reporting. This statement is an example of the concept of

- A. Conservatism.
- B. Completeness.
- C. Neutrality.
- D. Representational faithfulness.

The correct answer is (A). *(CPA 582 T-16)*
REQUIRED: The accounting concept promoted by adequately considering uncertainty and risks.
DISCUSSION: SFAC 2 defines conservatism as a prudent reaction to uncertainty to try to ensure that uncertainty and risks inherent in business are adequately considered. Conservatism is generally construed to mean a preference for that course which would be least likely to overstate net assets or income when there is genuine doubt as to the accuracy of an estimate, the outcome of a transaction, etc.
Answer (B) is incorrect because completeness (an ingredient of reliability) requires the inclusion in reported accounting information of everything material that is needed for adequate representation. Answer (C) is incorrect because neutrality is that ingredient of reliability which implies an absence of bias. Answer (D) is incorrect because representational faithfulness means that the accounting information represents what it purports to represent.

35. Which of the following accounting concepts states that an accounting transaction should be supported by sufficient evidence to allow two or more qualified individuals to arrive at essentially similar measures and conclusions?

- A. Matching.
- B. Verifiability.
- C. Periodicity.
- D. Stable monetary unit.

The correct answer is (B). *(CPA 581 T-5)*
REQUIRED: The accounting concept described by having sufficient evidence so that measures and conclusions can be arrived at independently.
DISCUSSION: The essence of reliability is that accounting measures represent what they purport to represent. The measurements of financial accounting transactions must be able to be corroborated by outside or independent persons; i.e., accounting information is verifiable if it is capable of independent replication.
Answer (A) is incorrect because matching involves recognizing costs as expenses on the basis of direct association with revenues, e.g., cost of goods sold. Answer (C) is incorrect because periodicity requires accounting information to be reported at regular intervals to foster comparability, and at relatively short intervals to provide useful information. Answer (D) is incorrect because the stable monetary unit concept assumes that the unit of measure (e.g., the U.S. dollar) does not fluctuate.

36. The concept of verifiability is complied with when an accounting transaction occurs that

- A. Involves an arm's-length transaction between two independent interests.
- B. Furthers the objectives of the company.
- C. Is promptly recorded in a fixed amount of dollars.
- D. Allocates revenues or expense items in a rational and systematic manner.

The correct answer is (A). *(CPA 578 T-1)*
REQUIRED: The situation that complies with the concept of verifiability.
DISCUSSION: Verifiability is an ingredient of reliability of accounting information (SFAC 2). The essence of verifiability is that a measurement of accounting information should be capable of independent replication. The existence of an arm's-length transaction between independent interests suggests that the requisite reliability is present in the transaction.
Answer (B) is incorrect because verifiability relates to the reliability of accounting measurement, not to the particular objectives of any company. Answer (C) is incorrect because recording at a fixed dollar amount does not guarantee the reliability of the measurement. Answer (D) is incorrect because rational and systematic allocation is a specific means of expense recognition. Systematic and rational allocation of expenses is undertaken when a direct means of associating cause and effect (expense and revenue) is lacking.

4.3 Elements

37. Under SFAC 6, *Elements of Financial Statements*, interrelated elements of financial statements that are directly related to measuring the performance and status of an enterprise include

	Distribution to Owners	Notes to Financial Statements
A.	Yes	Yes
B.	Yes	No
C.	No	Yes
D.	No	No

The correct answer is (B). *(CPA 583 T-3)*

REQUIRED: The financial statement element(s) directly related to measuring status and performance of an entity.

DISCUSSION: The elements of financial statements directly related to measuring the performance and status of both business enterprises and not-for-profit organizations are assets, liabilities, equity of a business, or net assets of a not-for-profit organization, revenues, expenses, gains, and losses. Three elements of financial statements of business enterprises only are investments by owners, distribution to owners, and comprehensive income. Information disclosed in footnotes or parenthetically on the face of financial statements amplifies or explains information recognized in the financial statements.

Answers (A), (C), and (D) are incorrect because only distribution to owners is directly related to measuring the performance and status of an enterprise. The notes to financial statements supplement and amplify the information contained in the statements.

38. According to the FASB conceptual framework, which of the following is an essential characteristic of an asset?

A. The claims to an asset's benefits are legally enforceable.

B. An asset is tangible.

C. An asset is obtained at a cost.

D. An asset provides future benefits.

The correct answer is (D). *(CPA 592 T-2)*

REQUIRED: The essential characteristic of an asset.

DISCUSSION: One of the three essential characteristics of an asset is that the transaction or event giving rise to the enterprise's right to or control of its assets has already occurred; i.e., it is not expected to occur in the future. A second essential characteristic of an asset is that an enterprise can obtain the benefits of, and control others' access to, the asset. The third essential characteristic is that an asset must embody a probable future benefit that involves a capacity to contribute to future net cash inflows. (SFAC 6)

Answer (A) is incorrect because claims to an asset's benefits may not be legally enforceable, for example, in the case of goodwill. Answer (B) is incorrect because some assets are intangible. Answer (C) is incorrect because assets may be obtained through donations or investments by owners.

39. Which of the following is an essential characteristic of a liability?

A. Liabilities must require the obligated enterprise to pay cash to a recipient entity.

B. Liabilities must be legally enforceable.

C. The identity of the recipient entity must be known to the obligated entity before the time of settlement.

D. Liabilities represent an obligation that has arisen as the result of a previous transaction.

The correct answer is (D). *(Publisher)*

REQUIRED: The characteristic that is essential to the existence of a liability.

DISCUSSION: SFAC 6 defines three essential characteristics of a liability: (1) It represents an obligation that requires settlement by probable future transfer or use of assets; (2) the enterprise has little or no discretion to avoid the obligation; and (3) the transaction or other event giving rise to the obligation has already occurred.

Answer (A) is incorrect because, while liabilities often require the payment of cash, they could also be satisfied through the use of other assets or the provision of services. Answer (B) is incorrect because, while liabilities are usually legally enforceable, that is not an essential characteristic. Answer (C) is incorrect because the identity of the recipient must be known only by the time of settlement, not before.

40. According to the FASB's conceptual framework, asset valuation accounts are

   A. Assets.

   B. Neither assets nor liabilities.

   C. Part of shareholders' equity.

   D. Liabilities.

The correct answer is (B). *(CPA 1188 T-1)*
   REQUIRED: The conceptual framework's definition of asset valuation accounts.
   DISCUSSION: Asset valuation accounts are separate items sometimes found in financial statements that reduce or increase the carrying amount of an asset. The conceptual framework considers asset valuation accounts to be part of the related asset account. They are not considered to be assets or liabilities in their own right (SFAC 6).
   Answers (A), (C), and (D) are incorrect because asset valuation accounts are part of the related asset accounts but are not assets, liabilities, or part of shareholders' equity.

41. Which of the following best describes the distinction between expenses and losses?

   A. Losses are reported net of related tax effect, whereas expenses are not reported net of tax.

   B. Losses are extraordinary charges, whereas expenses are ordinary charges.

   C. Losses are material items, whereas expenses are immaterial items.

   D. Losses result from peripheral or incidental transactions, whereas expenses result from ongoing major or central operations of the entity.

The correct answer is (D). *(CIA 1188 IV-38)*
   REQUIRED: The distinction between expenses and losses.
   DISCUSSION: SFAC 6 defines expenses as "outflows or other using up of assets or incurrences of liabilities (or a combination of both) from delivering or producing goods, rendering services, or carrying out other activities that constitute the entity's ongoing major or central operations." Losses are defined as "decreases in equity (net assets) from peripheral or incidental transactions of an entity and from all other transactions and other events and circumstances affecting the entity except those that result from expenses or distributions to owners."
   Answers (A), (B), and (C) are incorrect because, while expenses result from ongoing operations, losses result from peripheral transactions.

42. According to the FASB conceptual framework, an entity's revenue may result from

   A. A decrease in an asset from primary operations.

   B. An increase in an asset from incidental transactions.

   C. An increase in a liability from incidental transactions.

   D. A decrease in a liability from primary operations.

The correct answer is (D). *(CPA 1192 T-3)*
   REQUIRED: The possible source of revenue.
   DISCUSSION: According to SFAC 6, revenues are inflows or other enhancements of assets or settlements of liabilities from activities that constitute the entity's ongoing major or central operations. Thus, a revenue may result from a decrease in a liability from primary operations, for example, by delivering goods that were paid for in advance.
   Answer (A) is incorrect because a decrease in an asset from primary operations results in an expense. Answer (B) is incorrect because an increase in an asset from incidental transactions results in a gain. Answer (C) is incorrect because an increase in a liability from incidental transactions results in a loss.

43. A stated purpose of SFAC 6, *Elements of Financial Statements*, is to

- A. Define three classes of net assets for businesses.

- B. Define the elements necessary for presentation of financial statements of both business and not-for-profit organizations.

- C. Apply the comprehensive income concept to not-for-profit organizations.

- D. Apply its principles to reporting by state and local governmental units.

The correct answer is (B). *(Publisher)*
REQUIRED: The stated purpose of SFAC 6, *Elements of Financial Statements*.
DISCUSSION: SFAC 6 extends SFAC 3 to cover not-for-profit entities. It defines 10 interrelated elements of financial statements that are directly related to measuring the performance and status of an entity. Of these, seven are found in statements of both business and not-for-profit entities: assets, liabilities, equity or net assets, revenues, expenses, gains, and losses. Investments by owners, distributions to owners, and comprehensive income are elements of financial statements of business enterprises only.
Answer (A) is incorrect because SFAC 6 defines three classes of net assets of not-for-profit entities and the changes therein during the period. Answer (C) is incorrect because the comprehensive income concept is not applicable to not-for-profit organizations. Answer (D) is incorrect because SFAC 6 does not apply its principles to reporting by state and local governmental units.

44. Which of the following correctly defines an element directly related to measuring the performance and status of a business entity?

- A. Revenues are inflows from peripheral or incidental transactions as well as the entity's ongoing major operations.

- B. Investments by owners are limited to receipts of assets and satisfaction or conversion of liabilities.

- C. Equity is a residual interest.

- D. Gains are increases in equity from transactions and other events and circumstances that result from revenues or investments by owners.

The correct answer is (C). *(Publisher)*
REQUIRED: The definition of an element of financial statements.
DISCUSSION: Equity in a business enterprise is the residual interest in the assets of the entity. It is the ownership interest (assets minus liabilities). In a not-for-profit entity, net assets is the residual interest in assets that remains after deducting liabilities.
Answer (A) is incorrect because revenues are inflows or other enhancements of assets or settlements of liabilities from the major or central operations of the entity. Answer (B) is incorrect because investments by owners may be in the form of services. Answer (D) is incorrect because gains do not result from investments by owners and transactions producing revenues.

4.4 Recognition and Measurement

45. According to the FASB conceptual framework, the process of reporting an item in the financial statements of an entity is

- A. Allocation.

- B. Matching.

- C. Realization.

- D. Recognition.

The correct answer is (D). *(CPA 594 F-1)*
REQUIRED: The process of reporting an item in an entity's financial statements.
DISCUSSION: Recognition is the process of formally recording or incorporating an item in the financial statements of an entity.
Answer (A) is incorrect because allocation is the process of assigning or distributing an amount according to a plan or formula. Answer (B) is incorrect because matching is the simultaneous recognition of the revenues and expenses that result directly and jointly from the same transactions or events. Answer (C) is incorrect because realization is the identification of revenues or gains or losses on assets sold.

46. Recognition is the process of formally incorporating an item into the financial statements of an entity as an asset, liability, revenue, or expense. Recognition criteria include all of the following except

- A. Measurability with sufficient reliability.
- B. Definitions of elements of financial statements.
- C. Decision usefulness.
- D. Relevance.

The correct answer is (C). *(CMA 1290 2-18)*
REQUIRED: The item not included in the recognition criteria.
DISCUSSION: SFAC 5 states that an item and information about the item should be recognized when the following four fundamental recognition criteria are met: (1) The item meets the definition of an element of financial statements; (2) it has a relevant attribute measurable with sufficient reliability (measurability); (3) the information about the item is capable of making a difference in user decisions (relevance); and (4) the information is representationally faithful, verifiable, and neutral (reliability). Decision usefulness is the most important quality in the hierarchy of accounting qualities given in SFAC 2, not a specific recognition criterion.
Answers (A), (B), and (D) are incorrect because they are included among the recognition criteria.

47. According to the FASB conceptual framework, which of the following statements conforms to the realization concept?

- A. Equipment depreciation was assigned to a production department and then to product unit costs.
- B. Depreciated equipment was sold in exchange for a note receivable.
- C. Cash was collected on accounts receivable.
- D. Product unit costs were assigned to cost of goods sold when the units were sold.

The correct answer is (B). *(CPA 1193 T-6)*
REQUIRED: The statement that conforms to the realization concept.
DISCUSSION: The term "realization" is used most precisely in accounting and financial reporting with regard to sales of assets for cash or claims to cash. According to SFACs 5 and 6, the terms "realized" and "unrealized" identify revenues or gains and losses on assets sold and unsold, respectively. Thus, the sale of depreciated equipment falls under the realization concept.
Answers (A) and (D) are incorrect because assigning costs to products is allocation, not realization. Answer (C) is incorrect because realization occurred when the accounts receivable (claims to cash) were recognized.

48. Revenues of an entity are usually measured by the exchange values of the assets or liabilities involved. Recognition of revenue does not occur until

- A. The revenue is realizable.
- B. The revenue is realized and earned.
- C. Products or services are exchanged for cash or claims to cash.
- D. The entity has substantially accomplished what it agreed to do.

The correct answer is (B). *(CMA 1290 2-20)*
REQUIRED: The appropriate timing of the recognition of revenue.
DISCUSSION: In accordance with SFAC 5, revenues should be recognized when they are realized or realizable and earned. Revenues are realized when products, merchandise, or other assets are exchanged for cash or claims to cash. Revenues are realizable when related assets received or held are readily convertible to known amounts of cash or claims to cash. Revenues are earned when the entity has substantially accomplished what it must do to be entitled to the benefits represented by the revenues.
Answers (A), (C), and (D) are incorrect because none is a complete statement of the criteria for revenue recognition.

49. The ABC Company operates a catering service specializing in business luncheons for large corporations. ABC requires customers to place their orders 2 weeks in advance of the scheduled events. ABC bills its customers on the tenth day of the month following the date of service and requires that payment be made within 30 days of the billing date. Conceptually, ABC should recognize revenue from its catering services at the date when a

A. Customer places an order.

B. Luncheon is served.

C. Billing is mailed.

D. Customer's payment is received.

The correct answer is (B). *(CIA 590 IV-26)*
REQUIRED: The date at which a catering service should recognize revenue.
DISCUSSION: Revenues should be recognized when they are realized or realizable and earned. The most common time at which these two conditions are met is when the product or merchandise is delivered or services are rendered to customers.
Answers (A), (C), and (D) are incorrect because the time at which the luncheon is served represents the moment at which the revenue is realized and earned.

50. For $50 a month, Rawl Co. visits its customers' premises and performs insect control services. If customers experience problems between regularly scheduled visits, Rawl makes service calls at no additional charge. Instead of paying monthly, customers may pay an annual fee of $540 in advance. For a customer who pays the annual fee in advance, Rawl should recognize the related revenue

A. When the cash is collected.

B. At the end of the fiscal year.

C. At the end of the contract year after all of the services have been performed.

D. Evenly over the contract year as the services are performed.

The correct answer is (D). *(CPA 1194 F-21)*
REQUIRED: The timing of recognition of revenue.
DISCUSSION: Accrual-based revenue should be recognized when realized or realizable and earned. When the earnings process involves service, these conditions are usually met when the services are rendered. Because these services entail monthly visits, the annual payment should be recognized evenly over the period in which the services are performed.
Answer (A) is incorrect because recognition when cash is collected is appropriate when the cash basis is used. Answers (B) and (C) are incorrect because the revenue should be recognized evenly over the contract year.

51. Citizen Metals Corporation produces precious metals from its mining activities. The selling price for its product is reasonably assured, the units are interchangeable, and the costs of selling and distributing the product are insignificant. In order for Citizen to recognize revenue as early in the revenue cycle as is permitted by generally accepted accounting principles, the revenue recognition method that Citizen should use is the

A. Cash method.

B. Production method.

C. Percentage-of-completion method.

D. Cost recovery method.

The correct answer is (B). *(CMA 685 4-33)*
REQUIRED: The revenue recognition method allowing proper recognition of revenue prior to the sale of the merchandise.
DISCUSSION: Revenue is to be recognized when the conditions of "realized or realizable" and "earned" are met. If products or other assets are readily realizable because they are salable at reliably determinable prices without significant effort, revenues may be recognized at completion of production or when prices of the asset change.
Answers (A), (C), and (D) are incorrect because, while each represents a point at which revenues are realized or realizable and earned in certain instances, none fulfills the criteria for earliest recognition in the incident described.

52. An acceptable method for recognizing profit when the collection of cash is in doubt is the

A. Percentage-of-completion method.

B. Installment method.

C. Completed-contract method.

D. Consignment method.

The correct answer is (B). *(CMA 685 4-35)*
REQUIRED: The acceptable method of recognizing profit when the collection of cash is in doubt.
DISCUSSION: Revenue is to be recognized when it is realized or realizable and earned. If the collectibility of assets to be received for products, services, or other assets is doubtful, revenues and gains may be recognized on the basis of cash received, as in the installment method.
Answers (A), (C), and (D) are incorrect because they are not acceptable methods for recognizing profit when the collection of cash is in doubt.

53. Under a royalty agreement with another enterprise, a company will receive royalties from the assignment of a patent for 3 years. The royalties received should be reported as revenue

A. At the date of the royalty agreement.

B. In the period earned.

C. In the period received.

D. Evenly over the life of the royalty agreement.

The correct answer is (B). *(CPA 592 T-46)*

REQUIRED: The timing of recognition of royalty revenue.

DISCUSSION: In accordance with SFAC 5, revenues should be recognized when they are realized or realizable and earned. Revenues are realized when products, merchandise, or other assets are exchanged for cash or claims to cash. Revenues are realizable when related assets received or held are readily convertible to known amounts of cash or claims to cash. Revenues are earned when the entity has substantially accomplished what it must do to be entitled to the benefits represented by the revenues. Earning embraces the activities that give rise to revenue, for example, allowing other entities to use enterprise assets (such as patents) or the occurrence of an event specified in a contract (such as production using the patented technology).

Answers (A), (C), and (D) are incorrect because revenue should be recognized when it is realized or realizable and earned.

54. Determining periodic earnings and financial position depends on measuring economic resources and obligations and changes in them as these changes occur. This explanation pertains to

A. Disclosure.

B. Accrual accounting.

C. Materiality.

D. The matching concept.

The correct answer is (B). *(CPA 576 T-3)*

REQUIRED: The accounting concept described by the measurement of economic resources and obligations as they change.

DISCUSSION: A basic feature of financial accounting is that it is an accrual system, under which the determination of periodic earnings and financial position is dependent upon the measurement of all economic resources and obligations (e.g., receivables and payables) and changes in them as the changes occur.

Answer (A) is incorrect because disclosure pertains to the requirement that the user of financial statements be provided with sufficient information to avoid being misled. Answer (C) is incorrect because materiality pertains to accounting data being sufficiently significant to be included in the accounting system. Answer (D) is incorrect because the matching concept concerns the association of cause and effect, i.e., costs with revenues.

55. Which of the following is not a theoretical basis for the allocation of expenses?

A. Systematic allocation.

B. Cause and effect.

C. Profit maximization.

D. Immediate recognition.

The correct answer is (C). *(CPA 1177 T-2)*

REQUIRED: The accounting concept that is not a theoretical basis for allocation of expenses.

DISCUSSION: Profit maximization is not a theoretical basis for the allocation of expense. The allocation of expenses on such a basis would subvert the purpose of GAAP to fairly present the results of operations and financial position because expenses would not be reported.

Answer (A) is incorrect because expenses are to be allocated by a systematic and rational allocation in the absence of a direct means of associating cause and effect for cost and revenue. Answer (B) is incorrect because expenses should be recognized in a particular period if they have a direct association with specific revenues recognized in that period. Answer (D) is incorrect because immediate recognition is appropriate when costs have no discernible future benefits or there is no other theoretically sound basis for allocation of the expenses.

56. Costs that can be reasonably associated with specific revenues but not with specific products should be

A. Charged to expense in the period incurred.

B. Allocated to specific products based on the best estimate of the production processing time.

C. Expensed in the period in which the related revenue is recognized.

D. Capitalized and then amortized over a period not to exceed 60 months.

The correct answer is (C). *(CPA 575 T-15)*
REQUIRED: The time to recognize costs that can be reasonably associated with specific revenues but not with specific products.
DISCUSSION: The expense recognition principle of "associating cause and effect" or "matching" applies when a direct cause and effect relationship can be demonstrated between costs and particular revenues. A typical example of expenses recognized by the association of cause and effect is cost of goods sold. Association of costs with revenues can also be applied to services. Association of costs with specific products is not necessary.

Answer (A) is incorrect because immediate recognition is permitted only if no cause and effect relationship can be demonstrated and there is no other basis on which to expense the costs. Answers (B) and (D) are incorrect because a systematic and rational allocation of costs (based on processing time or length of asset service) is made if only a general (not direct) cause and effect relationship exists between costs and revenues.

57. Some costs cannot be directly related to particular revenues but are incurred to obtain benefits that are exhausted in the period in which the costs are incurred. An example of such a cost is

A. Salespersons' monthly salaries.

B. Salespersons' commissions.

C. Transportation to customers.

D. Prepaid insurance.

The correct answer is (A). *(CPA 585 T-2)*
REQUIRED: The costs not directly related to particular revenues but incurred to obtain benefits exhausted in the same period in which they are incurred.
DISCUSSION: Expenses should be recognized when there is a consumption of benefit. The consumption of benefit may occur when the expenses are matched with the revenues, when they are allocated on a systematic and rational basis to the periods in which the related assets are expected to provide benefits, or when the cash is spent or liabilities are incurred for goods and services that are used up either simultaneously with the acquisition or soon after. An example of a cost that cannot be directly related to particular revenues but which is incurred to obtain benefits that are exhausted in the same period in which the cost is incurred is salespersons' monthly salaries.

Answers (B) and (C) are incorrect because these costs are recognized upon recognition of revenues that result directly and jointly from the same transaction or other events as the cost. Answer (D) is incorrect because prepaid insurance would benefit a number of accounting periods. Its cost should thus be allocated on a systematic and rational basis to the accounting periods benefited.

58. The concept underlying the matching principle is that

- A. Net income should be reported on an annual basis.
- B. All transactions must refer to a statement of the Accounting Principles Board (APB) or Financial Accounting Standards Board (FASB).
- C. All cash receipts for a period should be related to the cash disbursements for the period.
- D. If possible, the expenses to be included in the income statement were directly incurred to produce the revenues.

The correct answer is (D). *(CMA 678 4-22)*
REQUIRED: The best description of the matching principle.
DISCUSSION: SFAC 6 defines matching as "simultaneous or combined recognition of the revenues and expenses that result directly and jointly from the same transactions or other events." To the extent possible, expenses are matched with revenues. If expenses are not directly associated with revenues, an attempt is made to expense them in a systematic and rational manner. Costs that can neither be matched nor be systematically and rationally allocated are immediately expensed.
Answer (A) is incorrect because the accounting concept underlying annual reporting of income is periodicity. Answer (B) is incorrect because generally accepted accounting principles have been developed through standard usage and experience, as well as through the pronouncements of the FASB, APB, and other authoritative bodies. Answer (C) is incorrect because the relation of cash receipts to disbursements is cash-basis accounting.

59. When bad debt expense is estimated on the basis of the percentage of past actual losses from bad debts to past net credit sales, and this percentage is adjusted for anticipated conditions, the accounting concept of

- A. Matching is being followed.
- B. Matching is not being followed.
- C. Substance over form is being followed.
- D. Going concern is not being followed.

The correct answer is (A). *(CPA 1180 T-12)*
REQUIRED: The item describing bad debt expense estimated based on past and expected future experience.
DISCUSSION: When bad debt expense is estimated on the basis of net credit sales, a cost (bad debt expense) is being directly associated with a revenue of the period (net credit sales). This is the expense recognition principle of "associating cause and effect," also known as matching.
Answer (B) is incorrect because matching is being followed. Answer (C) is incorrect because substance over form refers to that feature of financial accounting that emphasizes the economic substance of a transaction rather than its legal form; e.g., a lease may actually be a purchase. Answer (D) is incorrect because the going concern concept refers to the assumption that the enterprise is going to continue in operation and liquidation values do not have to be used.

60. Why are certain costs of doing business capitalized when incurred and then depreciated or amortized over subsequent accounting cycles?

- A. To reduce the federal income tax liability.
- B. To aid management in the decision-making process.
- C. To match the costs of production with revenues as earned.
- D. To adhere to the accounting concept of conservatism.

The correct answer is (C). *(CPA 578 T-5)*
REQUIRED: The reason certain costs are capitalized and then depreciated or amortized.
DISCUSSION: If costs benefit more than one accounting period, they should be systematically and rationally allocated to all periods benefited. This is done by capitalizing the costs and depreciating or amortizing them over the periods in which the asset helps generate revenue. The term "matching" is most narrowly defined as the expense recognition principle of associating cause and effect, but it is sometimes used more broadly (as here) to apply to the entire process of expense recognition or even of income determination.
Answer (A) is incorrect because capitalization and depreciation of costs on the financial statements have no effect on federal income tax liability. Answer (B) is incorrect because expense recognition principles are applied to benefit all users of financial statements, not merely management. Answer (D) is incorrect because the more conservative approach would be to recognize all costs immediately.

61. Which of the following is an example of the expense recognition principle of associating cause and effect?

    A. Allocation of insurance cost.

    B. Sales commissions.

    C. Depreciation of fixed assets.

    D. Officers' salaries.

The correct answer is (B). *(CPA 581 T-3)*

    REQUIRED: The example of associating cause and effect for expense recognition.

    DISCUSSION: If a direct cause and effect relationship can be established between costs and revenues, the costs should be recognized as expenses when the related revenue is recognized. Costs of products sold or services provided and sales commissions are examples of costs that can be associated with specific revenues.

    Answers (A) and (C) are incorrect because allocation of insurance cost and depreciation are examples of allocating costs among several periods on a systematic and rational basis. Answer (D) is incorrect because officers' salaries are examples of expenses that are immediately recognized because they provide no discernible future benefits and there is no other more useful basis of allocation.

62. Which of the following principles best describes the conceptual rationale for the methods of relating depreciation expense to revenues?

    A. Associating cause and effect.

    B. Systematic and rational allocation.

    C. Immediate recognition.

    D. Partial recognition.

The correct answer is (B). *(CPA 578 T-18)*

    REQUIRED: The accounting principle underlying the methods of relating depreciation expense to revenues.

    DISCUSSION: A direct cause and effect relationship between depreciation expense and specific revenues usually cannot be demonstrated. Such costs, however, are capable of being related to specific accounting periods on the basis of a systematic and rational allocation among the periods benefited. The depreciation of a fixed asset, for example, benefits (helps generate revenue in) the accounting periods over its useful life. Thus, a systematic and rational method of allocating the expense among the benefited periods is appropriate.

    Answer (A) is incorrect because association of depreciation expense with particular revenues is usually not feasible. Answer (C) is incorrect because depreciation expense relates to assets that by definition have a useful life of more than 1 year. Answer (D) is incorrect because partial recognition of depreciation expense is a nonsense phrase.

63. Which of the following is an application of the principle of systematic and rational allocation?

    A. Amortization of intangible assets.

    B. Sales commissions.

    C. Research and development costs.

    D. Officers' salaries.

The correct answer is (A). *(CPA 1181 T-3)*

    REQUIRED: The application of the concept of systematic and rational allocation.

    DISCUSSION: The expense recognition principle of systematic and rational allocation is applied to the amortization of intangible assets because of the absence of a direct means of associating cause and effect. The costs benefit a number of periods (i.e., they generate revenue in those periods) and should be systematically and rationally allocated.

    Answer (B) is incorrect because sales commissions directly relate to particular revenues and should be recognized as an expense when the related revenues are recognized. Answers (C) and (D) are incorrect because each is expensed in the period incurred.

64. A patent, purchased in 1996 and amortized over a 10-year life, was determined to be worthless in 2001. The write-off of the asset in 2001 is an example of which of the following principles?

A. Associating cause and effect.

B. Immediate recognition.

C. Systematic and rational allocation.

D. Objectivity.

The correct answer is (B). *(CPA 584 T-3)*
REQUIRED: The accounting principle of which the write-off of a patent is an example.
DISCUSSION: The patent was being amortized in a systematic and rational manner. When it was determined that the costs associated with the patent (recorded as an asset) no longer provided discernible benefits, the remaining unamortized costs were written off; i.e., the loss was recognized immediately.
Answers (A) and (C) are incorrect because each is a method of deferring costs to future periods which is not appropriate when a cost has no discernible future benefit. Answer (D) is incorrect because objectivity is a quality of accounting information rather than an accounting principle.

65. Which of the following is not a basis for the immediate recognition of a cost during a period?

A. The cost provides no discernible future benefit.

B. The cost recorded in a prior period no longer produces discernible benefits.

C. The federal income tax savings using the immediate write-off method exceed the savings obtained by allocating the cost to several periods.

D. Allocation of the cost on the basis of association with revenue or among several accounting periods is considered to serve no useful purpose.

The correct answer is (C). *(CPA 578 T-25)*
REQUIRED: The item that should not be immediately recognized as an expense.
DISCUSSION: In applying the principles of expense recognition, costs are analyzed to determine whether they can be associated with revenue on a cause and effect basis, e.g., cost of goods sold. If not, a systematic and rational allocation should be attempted, e.g., depreciation. If neither principle is applicable, only then are costs recognized as expenses in the period incurred or in which a loss is discerned. Accordingly, even though federal income tax savings could be obtained by the immediate write-off method, GAAP might require another treatment of the expense.
Answers (A), (B), and (D) are incorrect because each is a basis for immediate recognition of a cost.

66. Items reported in financial statements are measured by different attributes. The unit of measurement is money unadjusted for changes in purchasing power over time. According to SFAC 5,

A. Units of constant general purchasing power should replace nominal units of money.

B. A single attribute should be selected for measuring all assets and liabilities.

C. The use of different measurement attributes should continue.

D. Present practice is based on a single attribute with several major exceptions.

The correct answer is (C). *(Publisher)*
REQUIRED: The approach of SFAC 5 to measurement attributes and the unit of measurement.
DISCUSSION: SFAC 5 characterizes current practice as based on different attributes: historical cost (historical proceeds), current cost, current market value, net realizable (settlement) value, and present (or discounted) value of future cash flows. SFAC 5 suggests that use of different attributes will continue.
Answer (A) is incorrect because, unless inflation increases to an intolerable level, nominal units of money will continue to be used. Answers (B) and (D) are incorrect because use of different attributes will continue.

67. SFAC 5 states that items currently reported in financial statements are measured by different attributes. The amount of cash or its equivalent that would have to be paid if the same or an equivalent asset were acquired currently defines the attribute of

- A. Historical cost.
- B. Current cost.
- C. Current market value.
- D. Net realizable value.

The correct answer is (B). *(Publisher)*
REQUIRED: The measurement attribute defined by SFAC 5.
DISCUSSION: The amount of cash or its equivalent that would have to be paid if the same or an equivalent asset were acquired currently is the definition of the measurement attribute current (replacement) cost. Some inventories are reported in accordance with this attribute.
Answer (A) is incorrect because historical cost is the amount of cash or its equivalent paid to acquire an asset. Answer (C) is incorrect because current market value is the amount of cash or its equivalent that could be obtained by selling an asset in orderly liquidation. Answer (D) is incorrect because net realizable value is the nondiscounted amount of cash or its equivalent into which an asset is expected to be converted in due course of business less direct cost, if any, necessary to make that conversion.

68. According to SFAC 5, *Recognition and Measurement in Financial Statements of Business Enterprises*, the appropriate attribute to use when measuring long-term payables is

- A. Historical cost.
- B. Current cost.
- C. Net realizable value.
- D. Present value of future cash flows.

The correct answer is (D). *(CMA 691 2-16)*
REQUIRED: The appropriate attribute to use when measuring long-term payables.
DISCUSSION: According to SFAC 5, the appropriate measurement attribute for long-term liabilities is "the present or discounted value of future cash outflows expected to be required to satisfy the liability in due course of business."
Answer (A) is incorrect because historical cost is an attribute of assets, not liabilities. Answer (B) is incorrect because current cost is an attribute of assets, not liabilities. Answer (C) is incorrect because net realizable value is an attribute of assets, not liabilities.

69. According to SFAC 5, *Recognition and Measurement in Financial Statements of Business Enterprises*, the appropriate attribute to use when measuring land currently used in the business is

- A. Historical cost.
- B. Current cost.
- C. Net realizable value.
- D. Present value of future cash flows.

The correct answer is (A). *(CMA 691 2-18)*
REQUIRED: The attribute to use when measuring land currently used in the business.
DISCUSSION: According to SFAC 5, land used in the business should be valued at its historical cost. "Property, plant, and equipment and most inventories are reported at their historical cost, which is the amount of cash, or its equivalent, paid to acquire an asset, commonly adjusted after acquisition for amortization or other allocations."
Answers (B), (C), and (D) are incorrect because land currently used in the business is recorded at historical cost.

70. Reporting inventory at the lower of cost or market is a departure from the accounting principle of

- A. Historical cost.
- B. Consistency.
- C. Conservatism.
- D. Full disclosure.

The correct answer is (A). *(CPA 594 F-3)*
REQUIRED: The principle from which reporting inventory at the lower of cost or market is a departure.
DISCUSSION: Historical cost is the amount of cash, or its equivalent, paid to acquire an asset. Thus, the LCM rule departs from the historical cost principle when the utility of the inventory is judged no longer to be as great as its cost.
Answer (B) is incorrect because LCM does not violate the consistency principle as long as it is consistently applied. Answer (C) is incorrect because LCM yields a conservative inventory valuation. Answer (D) is incorrect because, as long as the basis of stating inventories is disclosed, LCM does not violate the full disclosure principle.

CHAPTER FIVE
THE ACCOUNTING PROCESS

This chapter reviews the basic bookkeeping process: recording, classifying, summarizing, and reporting. The adjusting process (deferrals and accruals) is emphasized.

5.1 Definitions

1. The correct order of the following steps of the accounting cycle is

A. Posting, closing, adjusting, reversing.

B. Posting, adjusting, closing, reversing.

C. Posting, reversing, adjusting, closing.

D. Adjusting, posting, closing, reversing.

The correct answer is (B). *(CIA 1195 IV-3)*

REQUIRED: The proper sequence of steps in the accounting cycle.

DISCUSSION: The order of the steps in the accounting cycle is identification and measurement of transactions and other events required to be recognized, journalization, posting from the journals to the ledgers, the development of a trial balance, adjustments to produce an adjusted trial balance, statement presentation, closing, taking a postclosing trial balance (optional), and making reversing entries (optional).

Answer (A) is incorrect because adjusting entries are made prior to closing. Answer (C) is incorrect because reversing entries are made after adjustments and closing entries. Answer (D) is incorrect because posting is done prior to adjusting.

2. A chart of accounts is

A. A flowchart of all transactions.

B. An accounting procedures manual.

C. A journal.

D. A list of names of all account titles.

The correct answer is (D). *(Publisher)*

REQUIRED: The definition of a chart of accounts.

DISCUSSION: A chart of accounts is a listing of all account titles used within an accounting system. Business transactions that affect these accounts are initially recorded by journal entries, and then posted to the individual accounts which are maintained in the ledger.

Answer (A) is incorrect because actual transactions are not flowcharted. Flowcharts of accounting procedures are developed by auditors and systems analysts (but are not called charts of accounts). Answer (B) is incorrect because an accounting procedures manual explains how to use the chart of accounts, e.g., whether to make adjusting entries, reversing entries, etc. Answer (C) is incorrect because a journal contains the initial recording of the transactions that affect the accounts contained in the chart of accounts.

3. As generally used, the term "net assets" represents

   A. Retained earnings of a corporation.

   B. Current assets less current liabilities.

   C. Total paid-in capital of a corporation.

   D. Total assets less total liabilities.

The correct answer is (D). *(CPA 1174 T-1)*
   REQUIRED: The definition of "net assets."
   DISCUSSION: Net assets is equal to total assets less total liabilities. This is synonymous with the net worth of a company as expressed in the balance sheet equation, assets – liabilities = owners' equity.
   Answer (A) is incorrect because retained earnings is the cumulative income earned by a corporation less amounts declared as dividends. Answer (B) is incorrect because current assets less current liabilities is working capital. Answer (C) is incorrect because total paid-in capital of a corporation is the sum of all money and property received from investors. In addition to total paid-in capital, net assets includes retained earnings.

4. What function do general ledgers serve in the accounting process?

   A. Reporting.

   B. Summarizing.

   C. Classifying.

   D. Recording.

The correct answer is (C). *(Publisher)*
   REQUIRED: The function of general ledgers in the accounting process.
   DISCUSSION: General ledgers serve to classify accounting data. Transactions that have been recorded in the journals are posted to the general ledger accounts where they are classified as to the accounts that have been affected.
   Answer (A) is incorrect because accounting data are reported in the financial statements. Answer (B) is incorrect because data are summarized during the adjusting and closing process. Answer (D) is incorrect because transactions are recorded in the journals.

5. A subsidiary ledger is

   A. A listing of the components of account balances.

   B. A backup system to protect against record destruction.

   C. A listing of account balances just before closing entries are prepared.

   D. All accounts of a subsidiary.

The correct answer is (A). *(Publisher)*
   REQUIRED: The definition of a subsidiary ledger.
   DISCUSSION: A general or controlling ledger contains the balance for each asset, liability, and owners' equity account. A subsidiary ledger consists of the detail of a general ledger account, e.g., the individual receivables making up accounts receivable in the aggregate.
   Answer (B) is incorrect because a subsidiary ledger does not comprise a supplementary accounting system. Answer (C) is incorrect because a listing of account balances just before closing entries are prepared is the definition of a trial balance. Answer (D) is incorrect because the term "subsidiary ledger" relates to a specific general ledger account, not the accounting systems of a subsidiary company.

6. What is the purpose of nominal accounts?

   A. To provide temporary accumulations of certain account balances for a meaningful period of time.

   B. To facilitate accounting for small amounts.

   C. To correct errors as they are detected.

   D. To record all transactions initially.

The correct answer is (A). *(Publisher)*
   REQUIRED: The purpose of nominal accounts.
   DISCUSSION: The primary focus of financial reporting is to account for earnings. To facilitate the calculation of earnings, nominal revenue and expense accounts are created to temporarily accumulate the components of earnings during an accounting period. At the end of the period, they are usually aggregated to determine net income. Each nominal account is reduced to a zero balance by closing it to the balance sheet account, retained earnings.
   Answer (B) is incorrect because small amounts are recorded in real as well as nominal accounts. Answer (C) is incorrect because errors are corrected wherever they are found, e.g., in real accounts, nominal accounts, ledgers, journals, etc. Answer (D) is incorrect because all transactions are initially recorded in the books of original entry called journals.

7. An example of a nominal account is

   A. Customer deposits.

   B. Capital stock.

   C. Petty cash.

   D. Sales returns.

The correct answer is (D). *(Publisher)*

REQUIRED: The item that is an example of a nominal account.

DISCUSSION: Sales returns is a nominal account because it is used to accumulate the amount of sales returns for a given period. At the end of the period, the balance of sales returns is brought to zero; i.e., the account is closed at the end of the year. Nominal accounts usually are closed to retained earnings. They exist for an accounting period for the purpose of determining the net effect on owners' equity, i.e., net income.

Answers (A), (B), and (C) are incorrect because each is a real account (balance sheet account) and is not closed at the end of an accounting period. The nonzero balances in real accounts at the end of one accounting period become the beginning balances of the next period.

8. The term "double entry system" refers to

   A. The use of real and nominal accounts.

   B. The recording of each transaction in two parts.

   C. The use of two journals.

   D. The use of a journal and a ledger.

The correct answer is (B). *(Publisher)*

REQUIRED: The meaning of the term "double entry system."

DISCUSSION: In the double entry system, each transaction is composed of two parts, debits and credits. The debits must equal the credits, and the sum of all debits for all transactions in a double entry system must equal the sum of all credits.

Answer (A) is incorrect because the distinction between real and nominal accounts is based on the relative permanence of accounts rather than the double entry, self-balancing attribute of accounting systems. Answer (C) is incorrect because many journals may be used, e.g., general journal, sales journal, cash receipts journal, cash payments journal, etc. Answer (D) is incorrect because even though journals and ledgers are parts of all double entry systems, they have nothing to do with the term "double entry."

9. In the equation, assets + expenses = liabilities + revenue + capital, the expenses and revenues are

   A. Contra asset and contra liability accounts, respectively, that assist analysis of the financial progress of the firm.

   B. Incorrectly stated because their signs are reversed; i.e., both are contra items that should have negative signs in the formula.

   C. Adjustments to capital that are postponed until the end of a specific accounting period to determine their net effect on capital for that period.

   D. Incorrectly included in the formula because assets = liabilities + capital.

The correct answer is (C). *(Publisher)*

REQUIRED: The status of expenses and revenues in the basic accounting equation.

DISCUSSION: Expenses and revenues are adjustments to the capital or retained earnings account that are not made immediately upon their occurrence but, instead, are postponed until the end of a specific accounting period to determine their net effect on capital for that period, i.e., at the time of computation of net income. They are initially recorded in nominal accounts.

Answer (A) is incorrect because contra asset and contra liability accounts reduce the related accounts; e.g., accumulated depreciation offsets the related asset account. Answer (B) is incorrect because expenses are debits and thus positive on the left-hand side of the equation; revenues are credits and thus positive on the right-hand side of the equation. Answer (D) is incorrect because, while A = L + C, the equation A + E = L + R + C is also correct.

10. What are real accounts?

    A. Nonfictitious accounts.

    B. Accounts in existence.

    C. Balance sheet accounts.

    D. Income statement accounts.

The correct answer is (C). *(Publisher)*

REQUIRED: The definition of the term "real accounts."

DISCUSSION: Real accounts are not closed at the end of the year and can carry forward nonzero balances from one accounting period to the next. Real accounts are typically balance sheet accounts and are also called permanent accounts.

Answer (A) is incorrect because "nonfictitious accounts" has no accounting meaning. Answer (B) is incorrect because nominal accounts can also exist. Answer (D) is incorrect because income statement accounts are nominal accounts.

11. Why are adjusting entries necessary?

    A. To record revenues and expenses.

    B. To make debits equal credits.

    C. To close nominal accounts at year-end.

    D. To correct erroneous balances in accounts.

The correct answer is (A). *(Publisher)*

REQUIRED: The rationale for adjusting entries.

DISCUSSION: Adjusting entries are used to adjust expenses (and the related asset or liability accounts) or revenues (and the related asset or liability accounts) to year-end amounts. Adjusting entries are needed to properly reflect revenues recognized when they are realized or realizable and earned and expenses recognized in accordance with the expense recognition principles. Accrual adjusting entries are made when the expense or revenue is recognized prior to the payment or receipt of cash. Deferral adjusting entries are necessary when the expense or revenue is recognized after the payment or receipt of cash.

Answer (B) is incorrect because all transactions result in equal debits and credits, and the cumulative balances of debits and credits are always equal. Answer (C) is incorrect because it relates to closing entries. Answer (D) is incorrect because it relates to correcting entries.

12. Which of the following statements is a correct description of reversing entries?

    A. The recording of reversing entries is a mandatory step in the accounting cycle.

    B. Reversing entries are made at the end of the next accounting period, after recording regular transactions of the period.

    C. Reversing entries are identical to the adjusting entries made in the previous period.

    D. Reversing entries are the exact opposite of the adjustments made in the previous period.

The correct answer is (D). *(CIA 1195 IV-4)*

REQUIRED: The best description of reversing entries.

DISCUSSION: Reversing entries are made at the beginning of a period to reverse the effects of adjusting entries made at the end of the preceding period. They are optional entries made for the sake of convenience in recording the transactions of the period. In order for reversing entries to reverse the prior adjustments, they must be the exact opposite of the adjustments made in the previous period.

Answer (A) is incorrect because reversing entries are optional. Answer (B) is incorrect because reversing entries are made at the beginning of the next accounting period. Answer (C) is incorrect because reversing entries are the exact opposite of the adjustments made in the previous period.

13. Closing entries

    A. Transfer the balances in all of the nominal accounts to the capital account.

    B. Must be made after the reversing entries but before the adjusting entries.

    C. Close out all of the accounts in the general ledger.

    D. Must be followed by reversing entries.

The correct answer is (A). *(Publisher)*

REQUIRED: The correct statement about closing entries.

DISCUSSION: Closing entries transfer the balances in all the nominal accounts to the capital or retained earnings account. This is usually done by closing amounts to the income summary account and then to the capital account.

Answer (B) is incorrect because closing entries are made after adjusting entries and before reversing entries. Answer (C) is incorrect because closing entries close only nominal accounts. Answer (D) is incorrect because reversing entries are not required. They merely facilitate accounting for certain transactions in the next accounting period.

14. Compared with the accrual basis of accounting, the cash basis of accounting understates income by the net decrease during the accounting period of

	Accounts Receivable	Accrued Expenses
A.	Yes	Yes
B.	Yes	No
C.	No	No
D.	No	Yes

The correct answer is (D). *(CPA 594 F-42)*

REQUIRED: The cash-basis item(s), if any, the net decrease of which understates income compared with accrual-basis accounting.

DISCUSSION: A net decrease in accounts receivable indicates that cash collected exceeded accrual-basis revenue from receivables in the current period. A net decrease in accrued expenses indicates that cash paid for expenses exceeded the current period's accrual-basis expenses. Thus, a net decrease in receivables results in an overstatement of cash-basis income compared with accrual-basis income, and a net decrease in accrued expenses results in an understatement.

Answers (A), (B), and (C) are incorrect because the net decrease in accrued expenses but not accounts receivable understates cash-basis compared with accrual-basis income.

Question 15 is based on the following information. On January 1, a new landscaping firm acquired a fleet of vehicles, all the necessary tools and equipment, and a parking and storage facility. It began operations immediately. It is now the end of the first year of operations, and the first set of year-end financial statements are being prepared. Certain decisions have to be made regarding the appropriate accounting and reporting practices for this company. Relevant information for these decisions is described below:

In order to promote sales for the coming year, maintenance contracts were sold in December at very reasonable prices, provided that the customers paid cash.

During the first year of operations, the company experienced a 5% bad debt rate on credit sales. None of the bad debts are expected to be recovered, since this is the industry average level of bad debts. Total credit sales for the year were $400,000. The year-end balance of accounts receivable, which includes uncollected overdue accounts, is $100,000. Half of the uncollected overdue amounts are estimated to be uncollectible.

---

15. The company will recognize revenue from the December sale of the maintenance contracts in the <List A> year if it selects <List B> basis reporting.

	List A	List B
A.	First	Cash
B.	First	Accrual
C.	Second	Cash
D.	Third	Accrual

The correct answer is (A). *(CIA 1194 IV-25)*

REQUIRED: The year in which revenue from maintenance contracts is recognized.

DISCUSSION: Under the cash basis of accounting, revenue is recognized when the cash is received. Because the customers paid cash for the maintenance contracts in the first year, that is the year in which the revenue should be recognized.

Answer (B) is incorrect because, if the accrual basis is used, revenue received for the maintenance contracts is recognized after the first year. The services are provided and the revenue is earned after year one. Answer (C) is incorrect because using cash-basis accounting, the revenue received in the first year is recognized in the first year. Answer (D) is incorrect because accrual-basis accounting recognizes the revenue in year two. Services will be provided in year two.

---

16. To calculate net sales, <List A> must be <List B> cash receipts from customers.

	List A	List B
A.	An increase in net accounts receivable	Added to
B.	An increase in net accounts receivable	Subtracted from
C.	An increase in net accounts payable	Added to
D.	An increase in net accounts payable	Subtracted from

The correct answer is (A). *(CIA 595 IV-1)*

REQUIRED: The calculation of net sales.

DISCUSSION: To convert from the cash basis (cash receipts) to the accrual basis (net sales), the increase in net accounts receivable must be added to cash receipts from customers.

Answer (B) is incorrect because a decrease in receivables would be subtracted from cash receipts. Answers (C) and (D) are incorrect because changes in accounts payable are not included in the calculation of net sales.

17. On April 1, 1996, Ivy began operating a service proprietorship with an initial cash investment of $1,000. The proprietorship provided $3,200 of services in April and received full payment in May. The proprietorship incurred expenses of $1,500 in April that were paid in June. During May, Ivy drew $500 against her capital account. What was the proprietorship's income for the 2 months ended May 31, 1996 under the following methods of accounting?

	Cash-Basis	Accrual-Basis
A.	$1,200	$1,200
B.	$1,700	$1,700
C.	$2,700	$1,200
D.	$3,200	$1,700

The correct answer is (D). *(CPA 1193 I-43)*
REQUIRED: The income for a proprietorship under the cash basis and accrual basis.
DISCUSSION: Under the cash basis, $3,200 of income is recognized for the payments received in May for the services rendered in April. The $1,500 of expenses is not recognized until June. Under the accrual basis, the $3,200 of income and the $1,500 of expenses incurred in April but not paid until June are recognized. The net income is $1,700 under the accrual basis. The cash investment and capital withdrawal are ignored because they do not affect net income.
Answer (A) is incorrect because the $500 withdrawal should not be recognized in the computation of net income under either method, and the $1,500 of expenses should not be recognized under the cash basis. Answer (B) is incorrect because the cash basis does not recognize the $1,500 in expenses until June. Answer (C) is incorrect because the $500 withdrawal should not be recognized in the computation of net income under either method.

18. In financial statements prepared on the income tax basis, how should the nondeductible portion of expenses such as meals and entertainment be reported?

A. Included in the expense category in the determination of income.

B. Included in a separate category in the determination of income.

C. Excluded from the determination of income but included in the determination of retained earnings.

D. Excluded from the financial statements.

The correct answer is (A). *(CPA 1195 F-56)*
REQUIRED: The treatment of nondeductible expenses in financial statements prepared on the income tax basis.
DISCUSSION: When financial statements are prepared on the income tax basis, permanent difference items, e.g., nondeductible expenses, are included as revenues or expenses in the income statement. They are not required to be presented in a special category of the income statement.
Answer (B) is incorrect because there is no special requirement to report these expenses in a separate category of the income statement. Answers (C) and (D) are incorrect because permanent tax difference items are reported in the income statement.

5.2 Deferrals and Accruals

19. How would the proceeds received from the advance sale of nonrefundable tickets for a theatrical performance be reported in the seller's financial statements before the performance?

A. Revenue for the entire proceeds.

B. Revenue to the extent of related costs expended.

C. Unearned revenue to the extent of related costs expended.

D. Unearned revenue for the entire proceeds.

The correct answer is (D). *(CPA 1191 T-19)*
REQUIRED: The reporting of the proceeds received from the advance sale of nonrefundable tickets.
DISCUSSION: Revenue is recognized when it is realized or realizable and earned. The entire proceeds should be credited to an unearned revenue account because the earning process will not be complete until the performance has been given even though the tickets are not refundable. "Revenues are considered to have been earned when the entity has substantially accomplished what it must do to be entitled to the benefits represented by the revenues" (SFAC 5).
Answers (A) and (B) are incorrect because revenue is recognized when it is realized or realizable and earned. Answer (C) is incorrect because the entire proceeds should be credited to unearned revenue.

20. An adjusting entry that records the earned portion of unearned revenue previously recorded always includes a

- A. Debit to an account in the asset category.
- B. Credit to an account in the asset category.
- C. Credit to an account in the owners' equity category.
- D. Credit to an account in the liability category.

The correct answer is (C). *(CMA 1284 4-8)*
REQUIRED: The effect of an adjusting entry that records the earned portion of unearned revenue previously recorded.
DISCUSSION: When cash from customers is collected in advance, a credit is made to the unearned revenue account. When the revenue is earned, usually on the basis of production and delivery, the unearned revenue account must then be debited, with a corresponding credit to a revenue account (an owners' equity account).
Answers (A), (B), and (D) are incorrect because the recognition of the earned portion of unearned revenues previously recorded requires a credit to a revenue account.

21. A company that sprays chemicals in residences to eliminate or prevent infestation of insects requires that customers prepay for 3 months' service at the beginning of each new quarter. Select the term that appropriately describes this situation from the viewpoint of the exterminating company.

- A. Unearned revenue.
- B. Earned revenue
- C. Accrued revenue
- D. Prepaid expense.

The correct answer is (A). *(CIA 1193 IV-30)*
REQUIRED: The classification of collected fees that pertain to a future period.
DISCUSSION: Under the revenue recognition principle, revenue is recognized (reported as revenue) in the period in which it is earned; therefore, when it is received in advance of its being earned, the amount applicable to future periods is deferred. The amount unearned (received in advance) is considered a liability because it represents an obligation to perform a service in the future arising from a past transaction. Unearned revenue is revenue that has been received but not earned.
Answer (B) is incorrect because the revenue is not earned. The exterminator has not performed the related services for the customer. Answer (C) is incorrect because accrued revenue is revenue that has been earned but not received. The exterminator has revenue that has been received but not earned. Answer (D) is incorrect because the customer has a prepaid expense (expense paid but not incurred); the exterminator has unearned revenue (revenue received but not earned).

22. An accrued expense can best be described as an amount

- A. Paid and currently matched with earnings.
- B. Paid and not currently matched with earnings.
- C. Not paid and not currently matched with earnings.
- D. Not paid and currently matched with earnings.

The correct answer is (D). *(CPA 578 T-17)*
REQUIRED: The best description of an accrued expense.
DISCUSSION: An accrued expense is one that has been incurred but not paid. Thus, it should be charged (matched) against revenue in the current period and recorded as a liability.
Answer (A) is incorrect because an expense paid in the same period in which it is incurred is not accrued and does not require an adjusting entry. Answer (B) is incorrect because it describes a deferral of expense. Answer (C) is incorrect because an amount neither paid nor incurred requires no original entry and no adjusting entry.

23. On November 1, 1996, Key Co. paid $3,600 to renew its insurance policy for 3 years. On December 31, 1996, Key's unadjusted trial balance showed a balance of $90 for prepaid insurance and $4,410 for insurance expense. What amounts should be reported for prepaid insurance and insurance expense in Key's December 31, 1996 financial statements?

	Prepaid Insurance	Insurance Expense
A.	$3,300	$1,200
B.	$3,400	$1,200
C.	$3,400	$1,100
D.	$3,490	$1,010

The correct answer is (C). *(CPA 592 I-23)*

REQUIRED: The amounts reported for prepaid insurance and insurance expense.

DISCUSSION: The entry to record the insurance renewal included a debit to insurance expense for $3,600, and the balance in prepaid insurance has expired. At year-end, the expense and prepaid insurance accounts should be adjusted to reflect the expired amounts. The 3-year prepayment is amortized at $100 per month ($3,600 ÷ 36 months), or $200 for 1996. Consequently, insurance expense for the year should be $1,100 [$90 prepaid insurance balance + ($4,410 − $3,400 unexpired amount of the November 1 prepayment)]. The $3,400 unexpired amount should be debited to prepaid insurance.

Answer (A) is incorrect because an asset balance of $3,300 and an expense of $1,200 assume the renewed policy has been in effect for 3 months. Answer (B) is incorrect because an expense of $1,200 assumes the renewed policy has been in effect for 3 months. Answer (D) is incorrect because the unadjusted prepaid insurance balance ($90) represents an expired amount.

24. An analysis of Thrift Corp.'s unadjusted prepaid expense account at December 31, 1996 revealed the following:

- An opening balance at $1,500 for Thrift's comprehensive insurance policy. Thrift had paid an annual premium of $3,000 on July 1, 1995.
- A $3,200 annual insurance premium payment made July 1, 1996.
- A $2,000 advance rental payment for a warehouse Thrift leased for 1 year beginning January 1, 1997.

In its December 31, 1996 balance sheet, what amount should Thrift report as prepaid expenses?

A. $5,200

B. $3,600

C. $2,000

D. $1,600

The correct answer is (B). *(CPA 593 I-27)*

REQUIRED: The amount reported for prepaid expenses.

DISCUSSION: The $1,500 beginning balance of prepaid insurance expired on 6/30/96, leaving a $0 balance. The $3,200 annual insurance premium paid on 7/1/96 should be allocated equally to 1996 and 1997, leaving a $1,600 prepaid insurance balance. The $2,000 advance rental payment is an expense that is wholly deferred until 1997. Consequently, the total of prepaid expenses at year-end is $3,600 ($1,600 + $2,000).

Answer (A) is incorrect because half of the $3,200 of prepaid insurance should be expensed in 1996. Answer (C) is incorrect because half of the $3,200 of prepaid insurance should not be expensed in 1996. Answer (D) is incorrect because the prepaid rent is deferred until 1997.

25. On February 12, 1996, VIP Publishing, Inc. purchased the copyright to a book for $15,000 and agreed to pay royalties equal to 10% of book sales, with a guaranteed minimum royalty of $60,000. VIP had book sales of $800,000 in 1996. In its 1996 income statement, what amount should VIP report as royalty expense?

A. $60,000

B. $75,000

C. $80,000

D. $95,000

The correct answer is (C). *(CPA 593 I-50)*

REQUIRED: The royalty expense for the year.

DISCUSSION: The 1996 royalty expense is equal to 10% of book sales, with a guaranteed minimum royalty of $60,000. Thus, 1996 royalty expense is $80,000 (10% x $800,000 book sales).

Answer (A) is incorrect because $60,000 is the guaranteed minimum royalty. Answer (B) is incorrect because $75,000 equals the guaranteed minimum royalty plus the copyright purchase price, which is not included in royalty expense. Answer (D) is incorrect because the copyright purchase price is not included in royalty expense.

26. Seldin Co. owns a royalty interest in an oil well. The contract stipulates that Seldin will receive royalty payments semiannually on January 31 and July 31. The January 31 payment will be for 20% of the oil sold to jobbers between the previous June 1 and November 30, and the July 31 payment will be for oil sold between the previous December 1 and May 31. Royalty receipts for 1996 amounted to $80,000 and $100,000 on January 31 and July 31, respectively. On December 31, 1995, accrued royalty revenue receivable amounted to $15,000. Production reports show the following oil sales:

June 1, 1995 - November 30, 1995	$400,000
December 1, 1995 - May 31, 1996	500,000
June 1, 1996 - November 30, 1996	425,000
December 1, 1996 - December 31, 1996	70,000

What amount should Seldin report as royalty revenue for 1996?

   A. $179,000

   B. $180,000

   C. $184,000

   D. $194,000

The correct answer is (C). *(CPA 1191 I-49)*
   REQUIRED: The royalty revenue for 1996.
   DISCUSSION: The royalty revenue for 1996 is 20% of 1996 oil sales. We are given that 12/1/95 - 5/31/96 oil sales are $500,000. We know that last year's accrued royalty for December was $15,000. Thus, oil sales for December must be $75,000 ($15,000 accrued ÷ 20%). Hence, oil sales from 1996 are $920,000 [($500,000 − $75,000) + $425,000 + $70,000]. Thus, royalty revenue for 1996 is $184,000 (20% x $920,000).
   Answer (A) is incorrect because $179,000 incorrectly computes part of the revenue with the sales from 6/1/95 - 11/30/95 instead of 1/1/95 - 5/31/96. Answer (B) is incorrect because $180,000 is the royalty payments received in 1996. Answer (D) is incorrect because $194,000 is the royalty payments received in 1996, plus 20% of December 1996's sales.

27. The following information pertains to Eagle Co.'s 1996 sales:

Cash sales

Gross	$ 80,000
Returns and allowances	4,000

Credit sales

Gross	120,000
Discounts	6,000

On January 1, 1996, customers owed Eagle $40,000. On December 31, 1996, customers owed Eagle $30,000. Eagle uses the direct write-off method for bad debts. No bad debts were recorded in 1996. Under the cash basis of accounting, what amount of net revenue should Eagle report for 1996?

   A. $76,000

   B. $170,000

   C. $190,000

   D. $200,000

The correct answer is (D). *(CPA 1194 F-58)*
   REQUIRED: The revenue under the cash basis of accounting.
   DISCUSSION: Under the cash basis of accounting, revenue is recognized when cash is received. Eagle had $76,000 ($80,000 − $4,000) in net cash sales and $114,000 ($120,000 − $6,000) in net credit sales. Given that accounts receivable decreased, cash collections thereon must have exceeded net credit sales by $10,000 ($40,000 − $30,000). No adjustment for bad debts is needed because no bad debts were recorded. Accordingly, net revenue is $200,000 ($76,000 + $114,000 + $10,000).
   Answer (A) is incorrect because $76,000 equals net cash sales. Answer (B) is incorrect because $170,000 equals total gross sales minus ending accounts receivable. Answer (C) is incorrect because $190,000 does not reflect an adjustment for the change in receivables.

28. Kemp Co. must determine the December 31, 1996 year-end accruals for advertising and rent expenses. A $500 advertising bill was received January 7, 1997. It related to costs of $375 for advertisements in December 1996 issues and $125 for advertisements in January 1997 issues of the newspaper. A store lease, effective December 16, 1995, calls for fixed rent of $1,200 per month, payable 1 month from the effective date and monthly thereafter. In addition, rent equal to 5% of net sales over $300,000 per calendar year is payable on January 31 of the following year. Net sales for 1996 were $550,000. In its December 31, 1996 balance sheet, Kemp should report accrued liabilities of

A. $12,500

B. $12,875

C. $13,100

D. $13,475

The correct answer is (D). *(CPA 591 I-37)*
REQUIRED: The accrued liabilities reported at year-end.
DISCUSSION: The $375 of advertising expense should be accrued in 1996 because this amount can be directly related to events in that period. The $125 amount is related to events in 1997 and should not be accrued in 1996. The fixed rental is due at mid-month. Thus, the fixed rental for the last half month of 1996 ($1,200 ÷ 2 = $600) and the rental based on annual sales [5% x ($550,000 – $300,000) = $12,500] should also be accrued, for a total of $13,475 ($375 + $600 + $12,500).

Answer (A) is incorrect because $12,500 omits the half-month of the fixed rental and the advertising bill for December. Answer (B) is incorrect because $12,875 omits the half-month of the fixed rental. Answer (C) is incorrect because $13,100 excludes the advertising bill for December.

29. Zach Corp. pays commissions to its sales staff at the rate of 3% of net sales. Sales staff are not paid salaries but are given monthly advances of $15,000. Advances are charged to commission expense, and reconciliations against commissions are prepared quarterly. Net sales for the year ended March 31, 1996 were $15,000,000. The unadjusted balance in the commissions expense account on March 31, 1996 was $400,000. March advances were paid on April 3, 1996. In its income statement for the year ended March 31, 1996, what amount should Zach report as commission expense?

A. $465,000

B. $450,000

C. $415,000

D. $400,000

The correct answer is (B). *(CPA 593 I-49)*
REQUIRED: The commission expense for the year.
DISCUSSION: Sales commissions should be recognized as an expense when the related revenues are earned. Given that Zach pays commissions at a rate of 3% of net sales, commission expense is $450,000 (3% x $15,000,000 net sales).

Answer (A) is incorrect because $465,000 is the sum of commission expense and one monthly advance. Answer (C) is incorrect because $415,000 equals the unadjusted balance in commissions expense plus one monthly advance. Answer (D) is incorrect because $400,000 is the unadjusted balance in commissions expense.

30. Wren Corp.'s trademark was licensed to Mont Co. for royalties of 15% of sales of the trade-marked items. Royalties are payable semiannually on March 15 for sales in July through December of the prior year, and on September 15 for sales in January through June of the same year. Wren received the following royalties from Mont:

	March 15	September 15
1995	$10,000	$15,000
1996	12,000	17,000

Mont estimated that sales of the trademarked items would total $60,000 for July through December 1996. In Wren's 1996 income statement, the royalty revenue should be

A. $26,000

B. $29,000

C. $38,000

D. $41,000

The correct answer is (A). *(CPA 1194 F-40)*
REQUIRED: The amount of royalty revenue to be reported.
DISCUSSION: The royalty revenue for 1996 is $26,000 [$17,000 received in September 1996 + ($60,000 x 15%) to be received in March 1997 for sales in 1996].

Answer (B) is incorrect because $29,000 includes $12,000 that was received in March 1996 but was applicable to 1995 sales and leaves out the $9,000 ($60,000 x 15%) attributable to sales for July through December 1996. Answer (C) is incorrect because $38,000 includes $12,000 that was received in March 1996 but was applicable to 1995 sales. Answer (D) is incorrect because $41,000 includes $15,000 that was received in September 1995 and was applicable to 1995 sales.

31. Pak Co.'s professional fees expense account had a balance of $82,000 at December 31, 1996, before considering year-end adjustments relating to the following:

- Consultants were hired for a special project at a total fee not to exceed $65,000. Pak has recorded $55,000 of this fee based on billings for work performed in 1996.
- The attorney's letter requested by the auditors, dated January 28, 1997, indicated that legal fees of $6,000 were billed on January 15, 1997 for work performed in November 1996 and that unbilled fees for December 1996 were $7,000.

What amount should Pak report for professional fees expense for the year ended December 31, 1996?

    A. $105,000

    B. $95,000

    C. $88,000

    D. $82,000

The correct answer is (B). *(CPA 592 I-48)*
    REQUIRED: The professional fees expense for the year.
    DISCUSSION: Pak should recognize an expense only for the work done by the consultants and attorneys in 1996. Thus, no adjustment is necessary for the consulting fees, but the legal fees, billed and unbilled, for November and December 1996 should be debited to the account. The professional fees expense for the year is therefore $95,000 ($82,000 + $6,000 + $7,000).
    Answer (A) is incorrect because $105,000 includes the maximum fee that may be payable to the consultants. Answer (C) is incorrect because $88,000 excludes the attorneys' fees for December. Answer (D) is incorrect because $82,000 excludes the attorneys' fees for November and December.

32. Winn Company sells subscriptions to a specialized directory that is published semiannually and shipped to subscribers on April 15 and October 15. Subscriptions received after the March 31 and September 30 cutoff dates are held for the next publication. Cash from subscribers is received evenly during the year and is credited to deferred revenues from subscriptions. Data relating to 1996 are as follows:

Deferred revenues from subscriptions,
   balance 12/31/95 $1,500,000
Cash receipts from subscribers   7,200,000

In its December 31, 1996 balance sheet, Winn should report deferred revenues from subscriptions of

    A. $1,800,000

    B. $3,300,000

    C. $3,600,000

    D. $5,400,000

The correct answer is (A). *(CPA 1191 I-29)*
    REQUIRED: The balance to be reported as deferred revenues from subscriptions at year-end.
    DISCUSSION: The deferred revenues from subscriptions account records subscription fees received that have not been earned. The balance in this account in the 12/31/96 balance sheet should reflect the subscription fees received after the September 30 cutoff date. Because cash from subscribers is received evenly during the year, $1,800,000 ($7,200,000 x 3/12 of the year) should be reported as deferred revenues from subscriptions.
    Answer (B) is incorrect because $3,300,000 is the sum of the existing deferred revenues balance and the fees received after the September 30 cutoff. Answer (C) is incorrect because $3,600,000 equals 6 months of fees. Answer (D) is incorrect because $5,400,000 equals 9 months of fees.

33. On December 1, 1996, Clark Company leased office space for 5 years at a monthly rental of $60,000. On that date, Clark paid the lessor the following amounts:

First month's rent $ 60,000
Last month's rent   60,000
Security deposit (refundable at
   lease expiration)   80,000
Installation of new walls and offices   360,000

Clark's December 1996 expense relating to its use of this office space is

    A. $60,000

    B. $66,000

    C. $126,000

    D. $200,000

The correct answer is (B). *(CPA 1192 I-56)*
    REQUIRED: The lessee's expense relating to an operating lease.
    DISCUSSION: During 1996, this operating lease was effective only for the month of December. The 1996 expenses therefore include the $60,000 monthly rent plus the $360,000 cost of the installation of the new walls and offices allocated over the 60 months of the rental agreement. Thus, the total December expense equals $66,000 [$60,000 + ($360,000 ÷ 60 months)].
    Answer (A) is incorrect because $60,000 omits the allocation of the leasehold improvements. Answer (C) is incorrect because $126,000 includes the last month's rent. Answer (D) is incorrect because $200,000 includes the last month's rent and the security deposit and omits the allocation of the cost of the leasehold improvements.

34. Clark Co.'s advertising expense account had a balance of $146,000 at December 31, 1996, before any necessary year-end adjustment relating to the following:

- Included in the $146,000 is the $15,000 cost of printing catalogs for a sales promotional campaign in January 1997.
- Radio advertisements broadcast during December 1996 were billed to Clark on January 2, 1997. Clark paid the $9,000 invoice on January 11, 1997.

What amount should Clark report as advertising expense in its income statement for the year ended December 31, 1996?

- A. $122,000
- B. $131,000
- C. $140,000
- D. $155,000

The correct answer is (C). *(CPA 1194 F-47)*

REQUIRED: The amount to be reported as advertising expense.

DISCUSSION: Advertising expense should be recognized when the promotions occur. It should include the $9,000 for radio advertisements broadcast in December. The $15,000 cost of printing catalogs should not be included because the expense relates to 1997 income. Hence, 1996 advertising expense is $140,000 ($146,000 – $15,000 + $9,000).

Answer (A) is incorrect because $122,000 results from subtracting the radio and catalog expenses. Answer (B) is incorrect because $131,000 results from subtracting the catalog expenses and not including the radio expenses. Answer (D) is incorrect because $155,000 results from adding the radio advertising and not subtracting the catalog expenses.

35. Based on 1996 sales of music recorded by an artist under a contract with Bain Co., the artist earned $100,000 after an adjustment of $8,000 for anticipated returns. In addition, Bain paid the artist $75,000 in 1996 as a reasonable estimate of the amount recoverable from future royalties to be earned by the artist. What amount should Bain report in its 1996 income statement for royalty expense?

- A. $100,000
- B. $108,000
- C. $175,000
- D. $183,000

The correct answer is (A). *(CPA 591 I-56)*

REQUIRED: The royalty expense.

DISCUSSION: Income is earned by the artist and an expense is incurred by Bain based on net sales (sales – returns). Amounts paid in advance and recoverable from future royalties are classified as prepaid expenses. Thus, Bain should report royalty expense of $100,000.

Answer (B) is incorrect because $108,000 includes the adjustment of $8,000 for anticipated returns. Answer (C) is incorrect because $175,000 includes the prepayment. Answer (D) is incorrect because $183,000 includes the prepayment and the adjustment of $8,000 for anticipated returns.

36. Ann's Video Mart sells 1- and 2-year mail order subscriptions for its video-of-the-month business. Subscriptions are collected in advance and credited to sales. An analysis of the recorded sales activity revealed the following:

	1995	1996
Sales	$420,000	$500,000
Minus cancellations	20,000	30,000
Net sales	$400,000	$470,000

Subscriptions expirations:

1995	$120,000	
1996	155,000	$130,000
1997	125,000	200,000
1998		140,000
	$400,000	$470,000

In Ann's December 31, 1996 balance sheet, the balance for unearned subscription revenue should be

- A. $470,000
- B. $465,000
- C. $400,000
- D. $340,000

The correct answer is (B). *(CPA 591 I-43)*

REQUIRED: The balance for unearned subscription revenue.

DISCUSSION: The earning process for subscription revenue is complete upon production and delivery. The balance for unearned subscription revenue should reflect the advance collections for which production and delivery have not yet occurred. Thus, the unexpired subscriptions as of 12/31/96 total $465,000 ($125,000 + $200,000 + $140,000), which is the balance for unearned subscription revenue.

Answer (A) is incorrect because $470,000 equals net sales for 1996. Answer (C) is incorrect because $400,000 equals net sales for 1995. Answer (D) is incorrect because $340,000 omits the 1995 sales of subscriptions that will expire in 1997.

37. In its 1996 financial statements, Cris Co. reported interest expense of $85,000 in its income statement and cash paid for interest of $68,000 in its cash flow statement. There was no prepaid interest or interest capitalization at either the beginning or the end of 1996. Accrued interest at December 31, 1995 was $15,000. What amount should Cris report as accrued interest payable in its December 31, 1996 balance sheet?

A. $2,000

B. $15,000

C. $17,000

D. $32,000

The correct answer is (D). *(CPA 1194 F-18)*
REQUIRED: The accrued interest payable at year-end.
DISCUSSION: The cash paid for interest was $68,000, including $15,000 of interest paid for 1995. Consequently, $53,000 ($68,000 – $15,000) of the cash paid for interest related to 1996. Interest payable is therefore $32,000 ($85,000 – $53,000).

Answer (A) is incorrect because $2,000 results from adding the $15,000 to $68,000 and subtracting that sum from the $85,000 interest expense. Answer (B) is incorrect because $15,000 is the interest paid for 1995. Answer (C) is incorrect because $17,000 is the difference between the interest expense and cash paid out.

38. Dana Co.'s officers' compensation expense account had a balance of $490,000 at December 31, 1996 before any appropriate year-end adjustment relating to the following:

• No salary accrual was made for the week of December 25-31, 1996. Officers' salaries for this period totaled $18,000 and were paid on January 5, 1997.

• Bonuses to officers for 1996 were paid on January 31, 1997 in the total amount of $175,000.

The adjusted balance for officers' compensation expense for the year ended December 31, 1996 should be

A. $683,000

B. $665,000

C. $508,000

D. $490,000

The correct answer is (A). *(CPA 593 I-52)*
REQUIRED: The adjusted balance in the officers' compensation expense account.
DISCUSSION: The officers' compensation expense account should include the entire compensation expense incurred in 1996. Accordingly, it should include the $490,000 previously recorded in the account, the $18,000 of accrued salaries, and the $175,000 of accrued bonuses. The adjusted balance should therefore be $683,000 ($490,000 + $18,000 + $175,000).

Answer (B) is incorrect because $665,000 does not include salaries accrued at year-end. Answer (C) is incorrect because $508,000 does not include the bonuses. Answer (D) is incorrect because $490,000 does not include the bonuses and the accrued salaries.

39. On August 1, 1996, Metro, Inc. leased a luxury apartment unit to Klum. The parties signed a 1-year lease beginning September 1, 1996 for a $1,000 monthly rent payable on the first day of the month. At the August 1 signing date, Metro collected $540 as a nonrefundable fee for allowing Klum to sign a 1-year lease (the normal lease term is 3 years) and $1,000 rent for September. Klum has made timely payments each month, but prepaid January's rent on December 20. In Metro's 1996 income statement, rent revenue should be reported as

A. $4,000

B. $4,180

C. $4,540

D. $5,180

The correct answer is (B). *(CPA 1191 I-58)*
REQUIRED: The proper reporting of rent revenue.
DISCUSSION: Under the accrual method of accounting, revenue is recognized when it is realizable and earned. In addition to the $1,000 monthly rent, the $540 nonrefundable fee must be allocated on a systematic and rational basis over the 1-year lease term. Thus, rent revenue is increased by $45 per month ($540 fee ÷ 12 months). The rent revenue includes the rent received to cover the rent for September through December, plus the $45 per month fee allocation. Thus, the rent revenue equals $4,180 ($1,045 x 4 months).

Answer (A) is incorrect because $4,000 excludes the allocation of the nonrefundable fee. Answer (C) is incorrect because $4,540 fails to allocate the fee over the entire lease term. Answer (D) is incorrect because $5,180 incorrectly includes January's prepaid rent which has not yet been earned.

40. Toddler Care Co. offers three payment plans on its 12-month contracts. Information on the three plans and the number of children enrolled in each plan for the September 1, 1996 through August 31, 1997 contract year follows:

Plan	Initial Payment per Child	Monthly Fees per Child	Number of Children
#1	$500	$ --	15
#2	200	30	12
#3	--	50	9
			36

Toddler received $9,900 of initial payments on September 1, 1996 and $3,240 of monthly fees during the period September 1 through December 31, 1996. In its December 31, 1996 balance sheet, what amount should Toddler report as deferred revenues?

A. $3,240

B. $3,300

C. $6,600

D. $9,900

The correct answer is (C). *(CPA 1192 I-29)*

REQUIRED: The amount reported as deferred revenues.

DISCUSSION: Unearned (deferred) revenues relate to the portion of the contracts for which services have not been performed (the earning process has not been completed). At 12/31/96, deferred revenues should equal $6,600 ($9,900 prepayments received x 8/12 months remaining).

Answer (A) is incorrect because $3,240 is the total of monthly fees collected in 1996. Answer (B) is incorrect because $3,300 is the portion of prepayments earned in 1996. Answer (D) is incorrect because $9,900 equals the total prepayments.

41. Under East Co.'s accounting system, all insurance premiums paid are debited to prepaid insurance. For interim financial reports, East makes monthly estimated charges to insurance expense with credits to prepaid insurance. Additional information for the year ended December 31, 1996 is as follows:

Prepaid insurance at December 31, 1995	$105,000
Charges to insurance expense during 1996 (including a year-end adjustment of $17,500)	437,500
Prepaid insurance at December 31, 1996	122,500

What was the total amount of insurance premiums paid by East during 1996?

A. $332,500

B. $420,000

C. $437,500

D. $455,000

The correct answer is (D). *(CPA 591 I-30)*

REQUIRED: The total amount of insurance premiums paid.

DISCUSSION: The company debits prepaid insurance for all insurance premiums paid and credits the account when it charges insurance expense. Thus, total debits equal insurance premiums paid. The asset account had total credits (charges to expense) of $437,500 and increased by $17,500 ($122,500 ending balance – $105,000 beginning balance). Consequently, total debits (premiums paid) must have been $455,000 ($437,500 total charges to insurance expense + $17,500 increase in the asset account).

Answer (A) is incorrect because $332,500 equals total credits minus the beginning balance. Answer (B) is incorrect because $420,000 results from subtracting, not adding, the difference between the beginning and ending balances. Answer (C) is incorrect because $437,500 equals total credits to the account.

42. Tara Co. owns an office building and leases the offices under a variety of rental agreements involving rent paid in advance monthly or annually. Not all tenants make timely payments of their rent. Tara's balance sheets contained the following data:

	1995	1996
Rentals receivable	$ 9,600	$12,400
Unearned rentals	32,000	24,000

During 1996, Tara received $80,000 cash from tenants. What amount of rental revenue should Tara record for 1996?

A. $90,800

B. $85,400

C. $72,000

D. $66,600

The correct answer is (A). *(CPA 591 I-53)*
REQUIRED: The rental revenue for the current year.
DISCUSSION: The ending balance in the rental receivable was $2,800 higher than the beginning balance ($12,400 – $9,600). Thus, revenues exceeded cash receipts. The ending balance in unearned rent was $8,000 less than the beginning balance ($32,000 – $24,000). Again, revenues exceeded cash receipts. Rental revenue is $90,800 ($80,000 + $2,800 + $8,000).

Answer (B) is incorrect because $85,400 is [$80,000 + ½($2,800 + $8,000)]. Answer (C) is incorrect because $72,000 is [$80,000 – ($32,000 – $24,000)]. Answer (D) is incorrect because $66,600 is [$80,000 – ($32,000 – $24,000) – ½($2,800 + $8,000)].

43. Dunne Co. sells equipment service contracts that cover a 2-year period. The sales price of each contract is $600. Dunne's past experience is that, of the total dollars spent for repairs on service contracts, 40% is incurred evenly during the first contract year and 60% evenly during the second contract year. Dunne sold 1,000 contracts evenly throughout 1996. In its December 31, 1996 balance sheet, what amount should Dunne report as deferred service contract revenue?

A. $540,000

B. $480,000

C. $360,000

D. $300,000

The correct answer is (B). *(CPA 1193 I-38)*
REQUIRED: The amount of deferred service contract revenue reported on the balance sheet.
DISCUSSION: Revenue should be recognized when it is realized or realizable and earned. Service contract revenue should be recognized as the services are provided. Assuming that services are provided in proportion to the incurrence of expenses, 40% of revenue should be recognized in the first year of a service contract. Given that expenses are incurred evenly throughout the year, revenue will also be recognized evenly. Moreover, given that Dunne sold 1,000 contracts evenly throughout 1996, total revenue will be $600,000 (1,000 x $600), and the average contract must have been sold at mid-year. Thus, the elapsed time of the average contract must be half a year, and revenue earned in 1996 must equal $120,000 (40% x $600,000 total revenue x .5 year). Deferred revenue at year-end will equal $480,000 ($600,000 – $120,000).

Answer (A) is incorrect because $540,000 assumes the average contract has been outstanding for 3 months. Answer (C) is incorrect because $360,000 equals the second year's revenue for all contracts. Answer (D) is incorrect because $300,000 is the amount deferred if 50% of expenses are expected to be incurred each year and the average contract has been outstanding for 1 year.

44. Delect Co. provides repair services for the AZ195 TV set. Customers prepay the fee on the standard 1-year service contract. The 1995 and 1996 contracts were identical, and the number of contracts outstanding was substantially the same at the end of each year. However, Delect's December 31, 1996 deferred revenue balance on unperformed service contracts was significantly less than the balance at December 31, 1995. Which of the following situations might account for this reduction in the deferred revenue balance?

- A. Most 1996 contracts were signed later in the calendar year than were the 1995 contracts.

- B. Most 1996 contracts were signed earlier in the calendar year than were the 1995 contracts.

- C. The 1996 contract contribution margin was greater than the 1995 contract contribution margin.

- D. The 1996 contribution margin was less than the 1995 contract contribution margin.

The correct answer is (B). *(CPA 593 T-40)*
REQUIRED: The situation that might explain the reduction in the deferred revenue balance.
DISCUSSION: Revenue should be recognized when it is realized or realizable and earned. Service contract fees are not earned until the services are provided. Thus, the fees collected in advance should be reported as unearned (deferred) revenue in the liability section of the balance sheet until the services are provided. The earlier a service contract is signed, the longer the time to provide the service and earn the revenue. Completion of the earning process reduces the deferred revenue balance. Thus, if most contracts outstanding on 12/31/96 were signed earlier in the period than those outstanding a year earlier, the deferred revenue balance should have decreased.
Answer (A) is incorrect because, if most 1996 contracts were signed later in the calendar year than were the 1995 contracts, the deferred revenue balance would have increased. Answers (C) and (D) are incorrect because the contribution margin relates to profit, not revenue.

5.3 Journal Entries

45. In reviewing a set of journal entries, you encounter an entry composed of a debit to interest expense and a credit to interest payable. The purpose of this journal entry is to record

- A. An accrued expense.
- B. A deferred expense.
- C. A contingent liability.
- D. An unexpired cost.

The correct answer is (A). *(CIA 588 IV-32)*
REQUIRED: The purpose of a journal entry that debits an expense and credits a payable.
DISCUSSION: An accrued expense is one that has been incurred in the current period but has not yet been paid. The journal entry to record an accrued expense requires a debit to an expense account and a credit to a payable account.
Answer (B) is incorrect because a deferred expense is a prepayment and is recorded as an asset. Answer (C) is incorrect because interest expense is not a contingent liability. Answer (D) is incorrect because an unexpired cost is an asset.

46. In performing an audit, you encounter an adjusting journal entry recorded at year-end that contains a debit to rental revenue and a credit to unearned rental revenue. The purpose of this journal entry is to record

- A. An accrued revenue.
- B. An unexpired cost.
- C. An expired cost.
- D. A deferred revenue.

The correct answer is (D). *(CIA 590 IV-28)*
REQUIRED: The purpose of a journal entry that debits rental revenue and credits unearned rental revenue.
DISCUSSION: Revenues should be recognized when realized or realizable and earned. If rental fees are collected before the revenue is earned and a credit is made to rental revenue, an adjusting entry may be necessary at year-end. The purpose of the journal entry is to adjust both rental revenue and unearned rental revenue to reflect the rental fees collected that had not been earned during this accounting period.
Answer (A) is incorrect because an accrued revenue is reflected as a receivable. Answer (B) is incorrect because an unexpired cost is recorded as an asset. Answer (C) is incorrect because an expired cost is charged to expense.

47. On December 1, 1996, a company sold services to a customer and accepted a note in exchange with a $120,000 face value and an interest rate of 10%. The note requires that both the principal and interest be paid at the maturity date, December 1, 1997. The company's accounting period is the calendar year. What adjusting entry (related to this note) will be required at December 31, 1996 on the company's books?

A. Deferred interest income $1,000
   Interest receivable $1,000

B. Interest income $1,000
   Interest receivable $1,000

C. Interest receivable $1,000
   Deferred interest income $1,000

D. Interest receivable $1,000
   Interest income $1,000

The correct answer is (D). *(CIA 591 IV-32)*
REQUIRED: The adjusting entry related to a note receivable.
DISCUSSION: Interest receivable should be debited and interest income credited for the interest on the note accrued (earned but not paid) at year-end [(10% x $120,000) x 1/12 = $1,000].
Answers (A), (B), and (C) are incorrect because interest receivable should be debited and interest income credited. Furthermore, deferred interest income is not affected because the interest income is recognized as it accrues.

48. What is the purpose of the following entry?

Supplies XXXX
   Supplies expense XXXX

A. To recognize supplies used, if purchases of supplies are recorded in supplies.

B. To recognize supplies on hand, if purchases of supplies are recorded in supplies expense.

C. To record the purchase of supplies during or at the end of the period.

D. To close the expense account for supplies at the end of the period.

The correct answer is (B). *(CIA 592 IV-31)*
REQUIRED: The purpose of the given entry.
DISCUSSION: The debit to supplies and credit to supplies expense is an end-of-period adjusting entry. Assuming the acquisition of supplies was debited to expense, an adjusting entry is needed to record the supplies on hand and to recognize the correct amount of expense.
Answer (A) is incorrect because, if purchases are initially recorded in a real account, the entry to record use of supplies is

Supplies expense
   Supplies

Answer (C) is incorrect because the correct entry to record the purchase of supplies is

Supplies or Supplies expense
   Cash or Accounts payable

Answer (D) is incorrect because the entry to close supplies expense is

Income summary
   Supplies expense

49. On December 31, earned but unpaid wages amounted to $10,300. What reversing entry could be made on January 1?

A. Wages expense $10,300
   Wages payable $10,300

B. Prepaid wages $10,300
   Wages expense $10,300

C. Wages expense $10,300
   Prepaid wages $10,300

D. Wages payable $10,300
   Wages expense $10,300

The correct answer is (D). *(Publisher)*
REQUIRED: The reversing entry for an accrual of wages expense.
DISCUSSION: The accrual of an expense requires a debit to expense and a credit to a liability. Accordingly, the reversing entry is to debit the liability and credit expense. The purpose of reversing this accrual of expense is to avoid having to apportion the first cash disbursement in the next period between the liability and expense accounts.
Answer (A) is incorrect because it is the adjusting rather than the reversing entry. Answer (B) is incorrect because it reflects an adjusting entry when wages have been prepaid and the original debit was to an expense account (which is not frequently found in practice). Answer (C) is incorrect because it is the reversing entry for an adjusting entry that occurs when wages have been prepaid and the original debit was to an expense account.

50. A 2-year insurance policy was purchased on July 1 for $3,000, and prepaid insurance was debited. Assuming a December 31 year-end, what is the reversing entry at the beginning of the next period?

A. None is required.

B. Cash $3,000
        Prepaid insurance $3,000

C. Prepaid insurance $2,250
        Insurance expense $2,250

D. Insurance expense $750
        Prepaid insurance $750

The correct answer is (A). *(Publisher)*
REQUIRED: The reversing entry when a prepaid expense was debited to an asset account.
DISCUSSION: Since the original entry recorded the prepaid insurance as an asset, the adjusting entry will debit expense and credit the asset for the amount of insurance that has expired. Accordingly, at the beginning of the year, the unexpired insurance will be in an asset account, as was the case in the previous year; i.e., no reversing entry is required.
Answer (B) is incorrect because it is the opposite (not a reversing entry) of the entry which was made to record the purchase of the 2-year insurance policy. Answer (C) is incorrect because it is the correct adjusting entry if the original entry had debited insurance expense rather than prepaid insurance. Answer (D) is incorrect because it is the correct adjusting entry (which requires no reversing entry).

51. Given a periodic inventory system, and beginning inventory of $30,000, ending inventory of $34,000, and purchases of $450,000, what is the net debit to cost of goods sold?

A. $450,000

B. $30,000

C. $34,000

D. $446,000

The correct answer is (D). *(Publisher)*
REQUIRED: The net debit to cost of goods sold.
DISCUSSION: The entry to record cost of goods sold will be

Cost of goods sold $446,000
Ending inventory   34,000
    Purchases $450,000
    Beginning inventory   30,000

Note that the debit to cost of goods sold often is made directly to an income summary account.
Answer (A) is incorrect because $450,000 is the amount of purchases. Answer (B) is incorrect because $30,000 is the beginning inventory. Answer (C) is incorrect because $34,000 is the ending inventory.

Questions 52 and 53 are based on the following information. RAR Enterprises prepares monthly financial statements. The clerical staff is paid every 2 weeks on the Monday following the end of the 2-week (10 working days) pay period ending on the prior Friday. The last pay period ended on Friday, November 19. The next payday is Monday, December 6 for the pay period ending December 3. The total clerical payroll for a 2-week period is $30,000, income tax withholding averages 15%, and Social Security taxes amount to 6.5%. None of the clerical staff's earnings will exceed the maximum limit for Social Security taxes.

52. The adjusting entry required to accrue the payroll as of November 30 is to

A. Debit wage expense for $21,000 and credit wages payable for $21,000.

B. Debit wage expense for $30,000, credit payroll tax expense for $1,950, and credit wages payable for $28,050.

C. Debit wage expense for $21,000, credit income tax withholding payable for $3,150, credit payroll taxes payable for $1,365, and credit wages payable for $16,485.

D. Debit wage expense for $30,000, credit income tax withholding payable for $4,500, credit payroll taxes payable for $1,950, and credit wages payable for $23,550.

The correct answer is (C). *(CMA 1282 4-5)*
REQUIRED: The adjusting entry necessary to accrue the payroll.
DISCUSSION: The 7 days included in the period from November 20 through November 30 represents 70% of the 10 working days in a 2-week pay period. Thus, $21,000 in wages expense should be accrued ($30,000 x 70%). Of this amount, $3,150 ($21,000 x 15%) must be credited to tax withholding payable, $1,365 ($21,000 x 6.5%) to payroll tax payable, and the remainder, $16,485, to wages payable.
Answer (A) is incorrect because wages payable must be reduced by income tax withholding and Social Security. Answers (B) and (D) are incorrect because the period from November 20 - 30 includes only 7 working days, not the full 2-week period.

53. RAR Enterprises would also be required to record an accrual for the company's obligation for payroll tax expenses. This adjusting entry should be to

A. Debit payroll tax expense for $1,955 and credit payroll taxes payable for $1,955.

B. Debit payroll tax expense for $1,365 and credit payroll taxes payable for $1,365.

C. Debit payroll tax expense for $6,450 and credit payroll taxes payable for $6,450.

D. Debit payroll tax expense for $4,515 and credit payroll taxes payable for $4,515.

The correct answer is (B). *(CMA 1282 4-6)*
REQUIRED: The adjusting entry necessary to accrue the company's obligation for Social Security taxes.
DISCUSSION: In addition to the Social Security taxes that must be withheld from employees' wages and remitted to the tax collection agency, the employer must also accrue and remit an equivalent amount as the employer's share. Thus, an additional expense of $1,365 must be accrued.
Answers (A), (C), and (D) are incorrect because only the employer's share of Social Security is an expense to the employer.

54. Howard Company sublet a portion of its warehouse for 5 years at an annual rental of $18,000, beginning on May 1. The tenant paid 1 year's rent in advance, which Howard recorded as a credit to unearned rental income. Howard reports on a calendar-year basis. The adjustment on December 31 of the first year should be

A. No entry.

B. Unearned rental income $6,000
   Rental income $6,000

C. Rental income $6,000
   Unearned rental income $6,000

D. Unearned rental income $12,000
   Rental income $12,000

The correct answer is (D). *(CPA 581 II-38)*
REQUIRED: The adjusting entry at year-end for unearned rental income.
DISCUSSION: Since Howard originally recorded the $18,000 received as a credit to a liability account, the adjusting entry is to debit the liability account and credit revenue for the revenue earned, which would be $1,500 a month ($12,000) for 8 months.
Answer (A) is incorrect because an adjusting entry is needed for all deferrals and accruals. Answers (B) and (C) are incorrect because the rental income to be recognized is for 8 months at $1,500 a month, not for 4 months. Also, answer (C) is incorrect because the debit and credit entries are switched.

55. Nichols Corporation renewed an insurance policy for 3 years beginning September 1, 1996 and recorded the $81,000 premium in the prepaid insurance account. The $81,000 premium represents an increase of $23,400 from the $57,600 premium charged 3 years ago. Assuming Nichols records its insurance adjustments only at the end of the calendar year, the adjusting entry required to reflect the proper balances in the insurance accounts at December 31, 1996, Nichols' year-end, would be to

A. Debit insurance expense for $9,000 and credit prepaid insurance for $9,000.

B. Debit prepaid insurance for $9,000 and credit insurance expense for $9,000.

C. Debit insurance expense for $72,000 and credit prepaid insurance for $72,000.

D. Debit insurance expense for $21,800 and credit prepaid insurance for $21,800.

The correct answer is (D). *(CMA 1293 2-9)*
REQUIRED: The entry to adjust the prepaid insurance account assuming annual adjustments.
DISCUSSION: The $57,600 premium paid 3 years ago would have been at the rate of $1,600 per month ($57,600 ÷ 36 months). On 1/1/96, the prepaid insurance account would have had a balance of $12,800 ($1,600 x 8 months). On September 1, the prepaid insurance account would have been debited for an additional $81,000 covering the next 36 months at a monthly rate of $2,250 ($81,000 ÷ 36 months). The expense for 1996 is therefore $21,800 [$12,800 + (4 months x $2,250)]. The adjusting entry is to debit insurance expense and credit prepaid insurance for $21,800.
Answer (A) is incorrect because $9,000 is the expense for only 4 months. Answer (B) is incorrect because, if the initial payment is debited to a real account, the adjustment requires a debit to a nominal account and a credit to the real account. Answer (C) is incorrect because $72,000 is the ending balance in prepaid insurance.

56. After a successful drive aimed at members of a specific national association, Gorham Publishing Company received a total of $90,000 for 3-year subscriptions beginning April 1, 1996, and recorded this amount in the unearned revenue account. Assuming Gorham only records adjustments at the end of the calendar year, the adjusting entry required to reflect the proper balances in the accounts at December 31, 1996, would be to

A. Debit subscription revenue for $67,500 and credit unearned revenue for $67,500.

B. Debit unearned revenue for $67,500 and credit subscription revenue for $67,500.

C. Debit subscription revenue for $22,500 and credit unearned revenue for $22,500.

D. Debit unearned revenue for $22,500 and credit subscription revenue for $22,500.

The correct answer is (D). *(CMA 695 2-14)*
REQUIRED: The year-end adjusting entry.
DISCUSSION: The company initially debited cash and credited unearned revenue, a liability account, for $90,000. Subscriptions revenue should be recognized when it is realized or realizable and the earning process is substantially complete. Because 25% (9 months ÷ 36 months) of the subscription period has expired, 25% of the realized but unearned revenue should be recognized. Thus, the adjusting entry is to debit unearned revenue and credit subscription revenue for $22,500.
Answer (A) is incorrect because $67,500 would be the debit to the revenue account if it had been credited initially. Answer (B) is incorrect because a $67,500 debit to the unearned revenue account would be appropriate if 75% of the subscription period had elapsed. Answer (C) is incorrect because $22,500 would be the debit to the revenue account if it had been credited initially and if 75% of the subscription period had elapsed.

57. A machine costing $27,000 with a residual value of $2,000 is to be depreciated on a straight-line basis over 10 years. What is the year-end adjusting entry?

A. Depreciation expense $2,500
     Machine $2,500

B. Depreciation expense $2,500
     Cash $2,500

C. Machine $27,000
     Cash $22,500
     Depreciation expense   2,500
     Residual value   2,000

D. Depreciation expense $2,500
     Accumulated depreciation $2,500

The correct answer is (D). *(Publisher)*
REQUIRED: The year-end adjusting entry to depreciate a machine.
DISCUSSION: At year-end, depreciation expense is debited, and accumulated depreciation (a contra asset account) is credited. The amount of depreciation is one-tenth of the depreciation base of $25,000 ($27,000 machine cost – $2,000 residual value).
Answer (A) is incorrect because the credit is not made directly to the asset but to the contra account, accumulated depreciation. Answer (B) is incorrect because cash is expended when the machine is purchased, not each year when depreciation is recorded. Answer (C) is incorrect because $27,000 was the machine cost; depreciation expense is a debit rather than a credit; and residual value is not separately recorded.

58. Ron Company issued 1,000 shares of common stock of the company for $35,000. Par value of the stock is $15 per share. What is the entry to record this sale?

A. Cash $35,000
    Common stock $35,000

B. Cash $35,000
    Common stock $15,000
    Paid-in capital
      in excess of par 20,000

C. Cash $35,000
    Paid-in capital $35,000

D. Cash $15,000
    Common stock $15,000

The correct answer is (B). *(Publisher)*
REQUIRED: The entry to record an issuance of common stock.
DISCUSSION: When par value stock is issued, common stock is credited for the par value of the stock. Cash is debited and the difference, i.e., the excess of amount received over par, is credited to paid-in capital in excess of par.
Answer (A) is incorrect because it is the correct entry to record issuance of 1,000 shares of $35 par value stock or 1,000 shares of no par stock. Answer (C) is incorrect because common stock is credited for the entire amount received only if it is no par stock. Answer (D) is incorrect because it is a journal entry to record a sale at par value.

59. Select the best explanation for the following adjusting, closing, or reversing journal entry:

Income summary $29,000
    Operating expense $17,000
    Administrative expense 10,000
    Interest expense 2,000

A. Closing entry to close the expenses at year-end. No reversing entry is made.

B. Closing entry to close the expenses at year-end. A reversing entry is required at the beginning of the next accounting period.

C. Adjusting entry for operating expenses, administrative expenses, and interest expenses.

D. Reversing entry at the beginning of an accounting period to facilitate entries to expense accounts during the period.

The correct answer is (A). *(Publisher)*
REQUIRED: The best explanation of the journal entry presented.
DISCUSSION: The debit to income summary and credits to expense accounts close the balances in the expense accounts to the income summary (profit and loss) account. A closing entry such as this is made at year-end to summarize profit and loss and to give the expense accounts zero balances at the beginning of the next year. It cannot be reversed because income of the next period would be misstated.
Answers (B) and (D) are incorrect because a reversing entry may not be made for a closing entry. Reversing entries apply only to adjusting entries (generally all accruals and deferrals that are recorded in nominal accounts when cash is received or paid). Answer (C) is incorrect because all adjusting entries affect at least one nominal account and one real account. All the accounts in the closing entry are nominal accounts.

60. A consulting firm started and completed a project for a client in December 1996. The project has not been recorded on the consulting firm's books, and the firm will not receive payment from the client until February 1997. The adjusting entry that should be made on the books of the consulting firm on December 31, 1996, the last day of the firm's fiscal year, is

A. Cash in transit XXX
    Consulting revenue XXX

B. Consulting revenue receivable XXX
    Consulting revenue XXX

C. Unearned consulting revenue XXX
    Consulting revenue XXX

D. Consulting revenue receivable XXX
    Unearned consulting revenue XXX

The correct answer is (B). *(CMA 1284 4-6)*
REQUIRED: The adjusting entry necessary to record consulting revenue.
DISCUSSION: Revenues should be recognized when they are realized or realizable and earned. Consulting revenue is realized and earned when the consulting service has been performed. Therefore, for a consulting project that has been started and completed during 1996, an adjusting entry should be made at year-end to record both a receivable and the revenue. The journal entry is a debit to consulting revenue receivable and a credit to consulting revenue.
Answer (A) is incorrect because cash in transit is not an account. Answer (C) is incorrect because the unearned revenue account is used only if the client prepays. Answer (D) is incorrect because the revenue was earned during the period.

CHAPTER SIX
INCOME STATEMENTS

This chapter contains questions on the format of income statements. By contrast, questions concerning the principles of income recognition appear in virtually every chapter. For example, the recognition of gains and losses on nonmonetary exchanges is covered in Chapter 10, Property, Plant, and Equipment. Only three questions are presented here on the cumulative effect of accounting changes because Chapter 21, Accounting Changes and Error Corrections, emphasizes accounting for changes in accounting principles.

At December 1, 1996, the FASB had a Proposed Statement of Financial Accounting Standards, *Reporting Comprehensive Income*, outstanding. If and when issued as a final statement, it will require entities, other than not-for-profit entities, that present a complete set of general purpose financial statements to include the following in these statements: (1) comprehensive income, both in the aggregate and by components, in either a separate statement of comprehensive income or in a combined statement of net income and other comprehensive income; (2) comprehensive income per share (if presenting per-share information); and (3) accumulated other comprehensive income as a separate component of equity in the statement of financial position.

Only a few questions relate to the statement of retained earnings because of its relative simplicity compared to the income statement and statement of cash flows (the latter is the subject of Chapter 22). Questions on the balance sheet, *per se*, are not presented. Many questions throughout the book, however, cover the correct presentation of various accounts in the balance sheet.

6.1 General Concepts

1. Under GAAP, comparative financial statements are

A. Required for at least the current and the prior year.

B. Required for at least the current and the prior 2 years.

C. Recommended for at least the current and the prior year.

D. Neither required nor recommended.

The correct answer is (C). *(S. Rubin)*

REQUIRED: The position of GAAP concerning comparative financial statements.

DISCUSSION: ARB 43, Ch. 2A, states that in any 1 year it is ordinarily desirable that financial statements of two or more periods be presented. This position is generally understood to be a recommendation rather than a requirement.

Answers (A) and (B) are incorrect because comparative financial statements are not required. Answer (D) is incorrect because comparative financial statements are recommended.

2. Which of the following should be reflected, net of applicable income taxes, in the statement of stock-holders' equity as an adjustment of the opening balance in retained earnings?

A. Correction of an error in previously issued financial statements.

B. Cumulative effect of a change in depreciation method.

C. Loss on disposal of a segment of a business.

D. Extraordinary item.

The correct answer is (A). *(CPA 584 T-22)*
REQUIRED: The item treated as an adjustment to beginning retained earnings.
DISCUSSION: According to SFAS 16, *Prior Period Adjustments*, the correction of an error occurring in a prior period should be accounted for as a prior-period adjust-ment. It should be charged or credited net of tax to retained earnings and reported as an adjustment in the statement of stockholders' equity. It is not included in net income for the current period.
Answers (B), (C), and (D) are incorrect because each is an income statement item.

3. What are the disclosure requirements with respect to changes in capital accounts other than retained earnings and changes in other owners' equity data?

A. When the income statement and balance sheet are presented, all changes in the capital accounts and changes in the number of shares of equity securities must be disclosed.

B. When the balance sheet is presented, all changes in the capital accounts must be disclosed.

C. When the income statement is presented, all changes in the capital accounts and changes in the number of shares of equity securities must be disclosed.

D. Changes in the number of shares of equity securities must be disclosed when a balance sheet is presented, but there is no specific disclosure requirement with respect to the capital accounts other than retained earnings.

The correct answer is (A). *(Publisher)*
REQUIRED: The disclosure requirements with respect to changes in capital accounts other than retained earnings and changes in other owners' equity data.
DISCUSSION: APB 12, *Omnibus Opinion-1967*, requires disclosure both of changes in the separate accounts appearing in stockholders' equity (in addition to retained earnings) and of changes in the number of shares of equity securities when both the balance sheet and the income state-ment are presented. This disclosure may be in separate statements, the basic financial statements, or the footnotes.
Answers (B) and (C) are incorrect because the require-ment applies only when both the balance sheet and the income statement are presented. Answer (D) is incorrect because there is a specific disclosure requirement with respect to the changes in the capital accounts.

4. The major segments of the statement of retained earnings for a period are

A. Dividends declared, prior-period adjustments, and changes due to treasury stock transactions.

B. Prior-period adjustments, before tax income or loss, income tax, and dividends paid.

C. Net income or loss from operations, dividends paid, and extraordinary gains and losses.

D. Net income or loss, prior-period adjustments, and dividends paid and/or declared.

The correct answer is (D). *(CMA 687 4-4)*
REQUIRED: The major segments of the statement of retained earnings.
DISCUSSION: The statement of retained earnings is a basic financial statement. APB 9, *Reporting the Results of Operations*, states that the income statement and the statement of retained earnings (presented separately or combined) are designed to broadly reflect the "results of operations." The statement of retained earnings consists of beginning retained earnings adjusted for any prior-period adjustments (net of tax), with further adjustments for net income (loss), dividends paid and/or declared, and certain other rare adjustments, e.g., quasi-reorganizations and certain treasury stock transactions. The final figure is ending retained earnings.
Answer (A) is incorrect because net income (loss) is a major segment of the retained earnings statement. Treasury stock transactions result in changes in retained earnings only in limited circumstances. Answer (B) is incorrect because after-tax net income is reflected in the statement of retained earnings. Answer (C) is incorrect because operating income and extraordinary gains and losses should be included in the determination of after-tax net income.

5. The major distinction made between the multiple-step and single-step income statement formats is the separation of

    A. Operating and nonoperating data.

    B. Income tax expense and administrative expenses.

    C. Cost of goods sold expense and administrative expenses.

    D. The effect on income taxes due to extraordinary items and the effect on income taxes due to income before extraordinary items.

The correct answer is (A). *(CIA 590 IV-32)*

REQUIRED: The major distinction between the multiple-step and single-step income statement formats.

DISCUSSION: Within the income from continuing operations classification, the single-step income statement provides one grouping for revenue items and one for expense items. The single-step is the one subtraction necessary to arrive at income from continuing operations prior to the effect of income taxes. In contrast, the multiple-step income statement matches operating revenues and expenses separately from nonoperating items. This format emphasizes subtotals such as gross margin, operating income, and nonoperating income within the presentation of income from continuing operations.

Answers (B), (C), and (D) are incorrect because none is the major distinction between multiple-step and single-step income statements.

---

6. In Baer Food Co.'s 1996 single-step income statement, the section titled *Revenues* consisted of the following:

Net sales revenue		$187,000
Results from discontinued operations:		
Loss from operations of segment		
(net of $1,200 tax effect)	$(2,400)	
Gain on disposal of segment		
(net of $7,200 tax effect)	14,400	12,000
Interest revenue		10,200
Gain on sale of equipment		4,700
Cumulative change in 1994 and		
1995 income due to change in		
depreciation method		
(net of $750 tax effect)		1,500
Total revenues		$215,400

In the revenues section of the 1996 income statement, Baer Food should have reported total revenues of

    A. $216,300

    B. $215,400

    C. $203,700

    D. $201,900

The correct answer is (D). *(CPA 591 I-3)*

REQUIRED: The total revenues that should have been reported.

DISCUSSION: Revenue is a component of income from continuing operations. Results of discontinued operations and the cumulative effect of a change in accounting principle are classifications in the income statement separate from continuing operations. Hence, total revenues were $201,900 ($215,400 – $12,000 results from discontinued operations – $1,500 cumulative-effect type change).

Answer (A) is incorrect because $216,300 equals $215,400 reported total revenues, plus the $2,400 loss from operations of the segment, minus the $1,500 cumulative-effect type change. Answer (B) is incorrect because $215,400 reflects no adjustment for results from discontinued operations and the cumulative-effect type change. Answer (C) is incorrect because $203,700 improperly subtracts interest revenue and does not adjust for the results from discontinued operations.

---

7. A company has a 50% gross margin, general and administrative expenses of $50, interest expense of $20, and net income of $10 for the year just ended. If the corporate tax rate is 50%, the level of sales revenue for the year just ended was

    A. $90

    B. $135

    C. $150

    D. $180

The correct answer is (D). *(CIA 1194 IV-16)*

REQUIRED: The sales revenue for the year.

DISCUSSION: Net income before taxes is $20 [$10 NI ÷ (1.0 – .5 tax rate)]. Hence, the gross margin (sales – cost of sales) is $90 ($20 NI before taxes + $20 interest + $50 G&A expenses). Sales must then be $180 ($90 gross margin ÷ 50% gross margin ratio).

Answer (A) is incorrect because $90 is the cost of goods sold. Answer (B) is incorrect because $135 is calculated by adding the 50% gross margin to 1 and multiplying the resulting 1.5 by the $90 cost of goods sold. Answer (C) is incorrect because $150 results from calculating earnings before tax as .5 times net income instead of 2 times net income.

8. Select the best order for the following items appearing in income statements:

1. Cumulative effect of change in accounting principle
2. Extraordinary items
3. Income from continuing operations
4. Discontinued operations
5. Prior-period adjustments
6. Taxes on income from continuing operations
7. Dividends
8. Net income
9. Revenues
10. Expenses
11. Income from continuing operations before income tax

   A.   9 - 10 - 8 - 7 - 6 - 2 - 4

   B.   8 - 6 - 7 - 1 - 2 - 5

   C.   9 - 10 - 8 - 6 - 3 - 2 - 1 - 4

   D.   9 - 10 - 11 - 6 - 3 - 4 - 2 - 1 - 8

The correct answer is (D). *(Publisher)*
   REQUIRED: The order of items appearing in income statements.
   DISCUSSION: The order of appearance in income statements of the items is

9. Revenues
10. Expenses
11. Income from continuing operations before income tax
6. Taxes on income from continuing operations
3. Income from continuing operations
4. Discontinued operations
2. Extraordinary items
1. Cumulative effect of change in accounting principle
8. Net income

Prior-period adjustments (5) and dividends (7) appear only in retained earnings statements.
   Answers (A), (B), and (C) are incorrect because net income is the final amount presented, and dividends and prior-period adjustments are not included in the income statement. Moreover, certain items are in the wrong order and some are missing.

9. On December 31, 1996, Salo Corp.'s balance sheet accounts increased by the following amounts compared with those at the end of the prior year:

Assets	$178,000
Liabilities	54,000
Capital stock	120,000
Additional paid-in capital	12,000

The only charge to retained earnings during 1996 was for a dividend payment of $26,000. Net income for 1996 amounted to

   A. $34,000

   B. $26,000

   C. $18,000

   D. $8,000

The correct answer is (C). *(CPA 1191 II-4)*
   REQUIRED: The net income for the year given the increases in assets, liabilities, and paid-in capital.
   DISCUSSION: To calculate net income, add back the dividend payment ($26,000) to the increase in assets ($178,000). The excess of this sum ($204,000) over the increase in liabilities ($54,000) gives the total increase in owners' equity ($150,000). The excess of this amount over the combined increases in the capital accounts ($132,000) equals the increase in retained earnings ($18,000) arising from net income.
   Answer (A) is incorrect because $34,000 equals the dividend payment plus the excess of the sum of the increases in liabilities, capital stock, and additional paid-in capital over the increase in assets. Answer (B) is incorrect because $26,000 is the dividend payment. Answer (D) is incorrect because $8,000 is the excess of the sum of the increases in liabilities, capital stock, and additional paid-in capital over the increase in assets.

6.2 Income from Continuing Operations

10. APB 9, *Reporting the Results of Operations*, concludes that the all-inclusive income statement concept

A. Is synonymous with the current operating concept, and that both are acceptable per GAAP.

B. Is generally more appropriate than the current operating concept.

C. Is not appropriate. The current operating concept is appropriate per GAAP.

D. Produces an interactive income statement which avoids the problems associated with the changing value of currencies.

The correct answer is (B). *(Publisher)*
REQUIRED: The correct statement about the all-inclusive income statement concept.
DISCUSSION: In the calculation of net income, the all-inclusive concept of income includes all income transactions that either increase or decrease owners' equity during the current period. The current operating concept includes only the ordinary, normal, recurring operations in the net income of the current period. Other items are direct adjustments to retained earnings. APB 9 follows the all-inclusive concept except for the rare transaction treated as a prior-period adjustment. The all-inclusive concept has been strengthened by SFAS 16, which limits prior-period adjustments in most instances to corrections of errors. As a result, most revenue, expense, gain, and loss items are continuing operation items in the income statement.
Answers (A) and (C) are incorrect because the current operating concept is generally not appropriate per APB 9. Answer (D) is incorrect because an "interactive income statement" does not exist in financial accounting.

11. Brock Corp. reports operating expenses in two categories: (1) selling and (2) general and adminis-trative. The adjusted trial balance at December 31, 1996 included the following expense and loss accounts:

Accounting and legal fees	$120,000
Advertising	150,000
Freight out	80,000
Interest	70,000
Loss on sale of long-term investment	30,000
Officers' salaries	225,000
Rent for office space	220,000
Sales salaries and commissions	140,000

One-half of the rented premises is occupied by the sales department. Brock's total selling expenses for 1996 are

A. $480,000

B. $400,000

C. $370,000

D. $360,000

The correct answer is (A). *(CPA 1190 I-40)*
REQUIRED: The total selling expenses.
DISCUSSION: Within the categories of expenses presented, the $150,000 of advertising, the $80,000 of freight out, 50% of the $220,000 rent for office space, and the $140,000 of sales salaries and commissions should be classified as selling expenses. Total selling expenses are therefore $480,000.
Answer (B) is incorrect because $400,000 excludes the freight-out expense. Answer (C) is incorrect because $370,000 excludes 50% of the rent for office space. Answer (D) is incorrect because $360,000 excludes the advertising and freight-out expenses and includes the entire rent for the office.

12. On January 1, 1996, Brecon Co. installed cabinets to display its merchandise in customers' stores. Brecon expects to use these cabinets for 5 years. Brecon's 1996 multi-step income statement should include

A. One-fifth of the cabinet costs in cost of goods sold.

B. One-fifth of the cabinet costs in selling expenses.

C. All of the cabinet costs in cost of goods sold.

D. All of the cabinet costs in selling expenses.

The correct answer is (B). *(CPA 592 T-17)*
REQUIRED: The cabinet costs included in the determination of current net income.
DISCUSSION: The cost of the cabinets is a selling expense. However, because the cabinets will provide benefits over a 5-year period, their cost should be allocated systematically and rationally over that period, for example, by the straight-line method. In effect, periodic depreciation of the cabinets should be recognized as a selling expense.
Answers (A) and (C) are incorrect because selling costs are not inventoried. Answer (D) is incorrect because the cost should be allocated to the periods benefited.

13. An income statement for a business prepared under the current operating performance concept includes only the recurring earnings from its normal operations and

    A. No other items.

    B. Any extraordinary items.

    C. Any prior-period adjustments.

    D. Any gains or losses from extinguishment of debt.

The correct answer is (A). *(CMA 684 3-15)*
   REQUIRED: The items included in a current operating performance income statement.
   DISCUSSION: According to APB 9, the current operating performance concept emphasizes the ordinary, normal, recurring operations of the entity during the current period. Inclusion of extraordinary items or prior-period adjustments might impair the significance of net income. This viewpoint has been rejected, however, in favor of the all-inclusive concept.
   Answers (B) and (C) are incorrect because each would be excluded under the current operating performance concept. Answer (D) is incorrect because such gains and losses are extraordinary.

14. When APB 9, *Reporting the Results of Operations*, was issued, an AICPA committee was in the process of recommending an income statement format for commercial banks. As a result, the applicability of APB 9 to commercial banks was deferred. What is the current status of APB 9 with respect to commercial banks?

    A. APB 13 has been issued, which concluded that APB 9 is applicable to banks.

    B. Commercial banks continue to be exempt from APB 9.

    C. Banks issue a statement of condition rather than an income statement.

    D. The controller of the currency specifies the detailed format of commercial bank income statements.

The correct answer is (A). *(Publisher)*
   REQUIRED: The applicability of APB 9 to commercial banks.
   DISCUSSION: APB 9 now applies to income statements of all profit-oriented entities. The amendment by APB 13 made APB 9 applicable to financial statements issued by commercial banks. The deferral of APB 9's applicability for a few years was simply a courtesy extended by the APB to an AICPA committee that was studying financial reporting by banks.
   Answers (B) and (D) are incorrect because APB 9 governs income statements of commercial banks issued for public reporting purposes. Answer (C) is incorrect because a statement of condition is a bank's balance sheet, not its income statement.

15. The effect of a material transaction that is infrequent in occurrence but not unusual in nature should be presented separately as a component of income from continuing operations when the transaction results in a

	Gain	Loss
A.	Yes	Yes
B.	Yes	No
C.	No	No
D.	No	Yes

The correct answer is (A). *(CPA 594 F-40)*
   REQUIRED: The circumstances in which an infrequent but not unusual transaction is shown as a separate component of income from continuing operations.
   DISCUSSION: In order to be classified as an extraordinary item, a transaction must be both unusual in nature and infrequent in occurrence within the environment in which the business operates. If an item meets one but not both of these criteria, it should be presented separately as a component of income from continuing operations. Whether the transaction results in a gain or a loss does not affect this presentation.
   Answers (B), (C), and (D) are incorrect because a gain or loss from an infrequent but not unusual transaction should be presented as a component of income from continuing operations.

16. Thorpe Co.'s income statement for the year ended December 31, 1996 reported net income of $74,100. The auditor raised questions about the following amounts that had been included in net income:

Unrealized holding loss on available-for-sale securities	$ (5,400)
Gain on early retirement of bonds payable (net of $11,000 tax effect)	22,000
Adjustment to profits of prior years for errors in depreciation (net of $3,750 tax effect)	(7,500)
Loss from fire (net of $7,000 tax effect)	(14,000)

The loss from the fire was an infrequent but not unusual occurrence in Thorpe's line of business. Thorpe's December 31, 1996 income statement should report net income of

- A. $65,000
- B. $66,100
- C. $81,600
- D. $87,000

The correct answer is (D). *(CPA 591 I-5)*

REQUIRED: The net income.

DISCUSSION: The unrealized holding loss on available-for-sale securities should have been debited to a stockholders' equity account, not included in the determination of net income (SFAS 115, *Accounting by Debtors and Creditors for Troubled Debt Restructurings*). The gain on early retirement of bonds payable, however, was properly included as an extraordinary gain (SFAS 4, *Reporting Gains and Losses from Extinguishment of Debt*). The fire loss was also properly included as an ordinary loss, but the adjustment for depreciation errors should have been charged directly to retained earnings as a prior-period adjustment (SFAS 16, *Prior-Period Adjustments*). Thus, reported net income should have been $87,000 ($74,100 + $5,400 + $7,500).

Answer (A) is incorrect because $65,000 improperly excludes the gain on early retirement of bonds. Answer (B) is incorrect because $66,100 results from subtracting the gain on early retirement of bonds and adding back the fire loss. Answer (C) is incorrect because $81,600 fails to adjust for improper recognition of the unrealized holding loss on the available-for-sale securities.

6.3 Discontinued Operations

17. In accordance with APB 30, which of the following qualifies as a disposal of a segment of a business?

- A. Super B Drugs, operator of a chain of discount drug stores, reaches an agreement to sell its Summittville location to a competitor.

- B. Treadrite, a shoe manufacturer, has decided to discontinue its line of work boots. Treadrite's operations are concentrated in a single plant.

- C. Petro, Inc. supplies its own service stations and independent operators from its refineries. Petro decides to discontinue marketing to independents.

- D. Blue Lake, Inc., producer of bottled artesian spring waters and soft drinks, discontinues production of its bottled artesian spring water. This operation is self-contained.

The correct answer is (D). *(R. Welton)*

REQUIRED: The situation that qualifies as a disposal of a segment.

DISCUSSION: APB 30 defines a segment as a component of an entity whose activities represent a separate major product line or class of customer and whose assets, results of operations, and activities can be physically and operationally distinguished from the remainder of the entity for financial reporting purposes. The discontinued spring water operation thus qualifies as disposal of a segment.

Answer (A) is incorrect because one outlet of a multi-location enterprise does not qualify as a separate line or class of customer. Answers (B) and (C) are incorrect because, in either case, the entity is not disposing of separately identifiable assets that can be physically distinguished from the remainder of the entity.

18. A loss from the disposal of a segment of a business enterprise should be reported separately as a component of income

- A. After cumulative effect of accounting changes and before extraordinary items.

- B. Before cumulative effect of accounting changes and after extraordinary items.

- C. After extraordinary items and cumulative effect of accounting changes.

- D. Before extraordinary items and cumulative effect of accounting changes.

The correct answer is (D). *(CPA 1181 T-30)*

REQUIRED: The proper reporting of a loss from disposal of a segment of a business.

DISCUSSION: The results of operations of a segment that has been or will be discontinued, together with any gain or loss on disposal, should be reported separately as a component of income before extraordinary items and the cumulative effect of accounting changes. Income from discontinued operations and the gain or loss on disposal should each be disclosed net of tax.

Answers (A), (B), and (C) are incorrect because a loss on disposal of a segment should be reported before extraordinary items and the cumulative effect of accounting changes.

19. The gain or loss from disposal of a segment

A. Includes the operating gain or loss realized by the segment from the beginning of the fiscal year to the disposal date.

B. Is reported as an addition or subtraction for the beginning balance of retained earnings on the statement of retained earnings.

C. Is reported as an extraordinary item on the income statement.

D. Is reported as a component of net income and distinguished from the operating gain or loss realized by the segment prior to the measurement date.

The correct answer is (D). *(CMA 693 2-22)*
REQUIRED: The true statement about the gain or loss from disposal of a segment.
DISCUSSION: Discontinued operations should be presented as two subcategories. The first is operating income or loss of the segment prior to the measurement date. The second is the gain or loss on disposal. The gain or loss on disposal includes estimated operating income or loss of the segment from the measurement date to the disposal date and any disposal costs incurred during the phaseout period, plus the estimated gain or loss on the actual disposal.
Answer (A) is incorrect because the operating gain or loss for the partial period is not combined with the gain or loss on disposal. Answer (B) is incorrect because gain or loss on disposal is reported on the income statement, not the retained earnings statement. Answer (C) is incorrect because gain or loss on disposal is reported in a discontinued operations section prior to extraordinary items.

20. On November 1, 1996, Smith Co. contracted to dispose of an industry segment on February 28, 1997. Throughout 1996, the segment had operating losses. These losses were expected to continue until the segment's disposition. If a loss is anticipated on final disposition, how much of the operating losses should be included in the loss on disposal reported in Smith's 1996 income statements?

I. Operating losses for the period January 1 to October 31, 1996
II. Operating losses for the period November 1 to December 31, 1996
III. Estimated operating losses for the period January 1 to February 28, 1997

A. II only.

B. II and III only.

C. I and III only.

D. I and II only.

The correct answer is (B). *(CPA 1193 T-18)*
REQUIRED: The amount of operating losses included in the loss on disposal reported in the income statement.
DISCUSSION: APB 30 requires that an estimated loss on disposal be recognized as of the measurement date. The measurement date is 11/1/96. The loss recognized should include any estimated operating losses during the phaseout period (11/1/96 to 2/28/97), disposal costs incurred during the phaseout period, and any estimated loss on the disposal itself. Thus, the loss on disposal should include the operating losses for the period 11/1/96 to 12/31/96, and estimated operating losses for the period 1/1/97 to 2/28/97.
Answer (A) is incorrect because estimated operating losses for 1/1/97 to 2/28/97 should also be reported. Answers (C) and (D) are incorrect because operating losses for the entire phaseout period but not for the period prior to the measurement date are included in the determination of income.

21. On December 1, 1996, Shine Co. agreed to sell a business segment on March 1, 1997. Throughout 1996, the segment had operating losses that were expected to continue until the segment's disposition. However, the gain on disposition was expected to exceed the segment's total operating losses in 1996 and 1997. The amount of estimated net gain from disposal recognized in 1996 equals

A. Zero.

B. The entire estimated net gain.

C. All of the segment's 1996 operating losses.

D. The segment's December 1996 operating losses.

The correct answer is (A). *(CPA 591 T-24)*
REQUIRED: The amount of estimated net gain from disposal recognized in 1996.
DISCUSSION: An estimated loss from the disposal of a segment is recognized at the measurement date (APB 30). A net gain from the disposal of a segment, however, is recognized only when realized, ordinarily at the disposal date. Because the disposal will occur in 1997, the gain has not been realized at the balance sheet date and cannot be recognized at that time.
Answer (B) is incorrect because no unrealized gain on disposal is recognized in 1996. Answer (C) is incorrect because the first 11 months of losses would be recognized separately as operating loss from discontinued operations in 1996. Answer (D) is incorrect because the December 1996 losses would be deferred and become a contra gain in 1997, the year of the sale.

22. Trent Company had net income of $700,000 for the year ended December 31, 1996, after giving effect to the following events which occurred during the year:

- The decision was made January 2 to discontinue the plastics manufacturing segment.

- The plastics manufacturing segment was sold June 30.

- Operating loss from January 1 to June 30 for the plastics manufacturing segment amounted to $60,000 before tax benefit.

- Plastics manufacturing equipment with a book value of $350,000 was sold for $200,000.

Trent's tax rate was 40% for 1996. For the year ended December 31, 1996, Trent's after-tax income from continuing operations was

- A. $574,000

- B. $700,000

- C. $784,000

- D. $826,000

The correct answer is (D). *(CPA 585 I-48)*
 REQUIRED: The after-tax income from continuing operations.
 DISCUSSION: The gain or loss from discontinued operations included the $60,000 operating losses from the measurement date (January 1) to the disposal date (June 30), plus the loss on the actual disposal of the asset of $150,000 ($350,000 – $200,000). The loss on disposal was

Operating loss	$ (60,000)
Sale of assets	(150,000)
Loss on disposal	$(210,000)

Hence, the net-of-tax loss was $126,000 [$210,000 x (1.0 – .40)].

The net income of $700,000 included the loss from discontinued operations of $126,000 and the income from continuing operations. Thus, income from continuing operations was $826,000.

Income from continuing operations	$826,000
Loss from discontinued operations	(126,000)
Net income	$700,000

Answer (A) is incorrect because $574,000 results from subtracting the $126,000 loss from net income. Answer (B) is incorrect because $700,000 equals net income. Answer (C) is incorrect because $784,000 adds the tax benefit from the disposal to net income.

23. On December 31, 1996, Greer Co. entered into an agreement to sell its Hart segment's assets. On that date, Greer estimated the gain from the disposition of the assets in 1997 would be $700,000 and Hart's 1997 operating losses would be $200,000. Hart's actual operating losses were $300,000 in both 1996 and 1997, and the actual gain on disposition of Hart's assets in 1997 was $650,000. Disregarding income taxes, what net gain (loss) should be reported for discontinued operations in Greer's comparative 1997 and 1996 income statements?

	1997	1996
A.	$50,000	$(300,000)
B.	$0	$50,000
C.	$350,000	$(300,000)
D.	$(150,000)	$200,000

The correct answer is (C). *(CPA 592 I-57)*
 REQUIRED: The net gain (loss) reported for discontinued operations in comparative income statements.
 DISCUSSION: Greer should report the $300,000 actual operating loss of the segment for the period up to the measurement date (12/31/96) as discontinued operations in the 1996 income statement. Because Greer estimated a net gain from disposal ($700,000 gain from asset disposition – $200,000 phaseout period operating loss = $500,000 gain) at the measurement date, no gain or loss on disposal is recognized in the 1996 income statement. In the 1997 income statement, Greer should recognize the actual realized gain on disposal of $350,000 ($650,000 gain on disposition of assets – $300,000 operating loss during the phaseout period).

Answers (A) and (B) are incorrect because $50,000 is the excess of the actual gain on disposition of the assets over the segment's operating losses for 1996 and 1997. Answer (D) is incorrect because reporting a $150,000 loss for 1997 and a $200,000 gain for 1996 assumes that the unrealized estimated net gain on disposal is recognized on the measurement date, and the adjustment for the difference between the estimated and actual results is treated as a change in estimate.

24. On October 1, 1996, Mann Company approved a formal plan to sell Mill Division, considered a segment of the business. The sale will occur on March 31, 1997. The division had operating income of $500,000 for the quarter ended December 31, 1996, but expects to incur an operating loss of $100,000 for the first quarter of 1997. Mann also estimates that it will incur a loss of $750,000 on the sale of the division's assets. Mann's tax rate for 1996 is 40%. In its income statement for the year ended December 31, 1996, how much gain or loss should Mann report on disposal of Mill Division?

A. $210,000 loss.

B. $300,000 gain.

C. $350,000 loss.

D. $500,000 gain.

The correct answer is (A). *(CPA 586 I-59)*
REQUIRED: The amount to be reported as gain or loss on disposal of a segment.
DISCUSSION: If a loss is expected from the disposal of a segment, the loss should be provided for at the measurement date (October 1). The estimate should take into account any operating losses estimated to be incurred between the measurement date and the disposal date.

Operating income (10/1 - 12/31)	$ 500,000
Estimated operating loss (1/1 - 3/31)	(100,000)
Estimated loss on asset sale	(750,000)
Estimated loss on disposal	$(350,000)

The estimated loss of $350,000 net of the 40% tax rate amounts to a $210,000 loss on disposal.
Answer (B) is incorrect because $300,000 is the after-tax operating income from the measurement date to year-end. Answer (C) is incorrect because $350,000 is the estimated pretax loss on disposal. Answer (D) is incorrect because $500,000 is the pretax operating income from the measurement date to year-end.

25. On July 1, 1996, Tyler Corporation approved a formal plan to sell its plastics division, considered a segment of the business. The sale will occur in the first 3 months of 1997. The division had an operating loss of $400,000 for the 6 months ended December 31, 1996, and expects to incur a loss of $200,000 for the first quarter of 1997. The sales price is $22,000,000, and the carrying value at the date of sale should be $20,000,000. Tyler's effective tax rate for 1996 is 40%. At year-end, December 31, 1996, how much gain should Tyler report on disposal of the plastics division?

A. $0

B. $840,000

C. $1,080,000

D. $1,200,000

The correct answer is (A). *(CPA 584 I-44)*
REQUIRED: The year-end gain reported for disposal of a segment.
DISCUSSION: The gain or loss on disposal should include not only the gain or loss on disposal of the assets but also any income or loss from operations during the phaseout period. If a net loss is expected, it should be provided for at the measurement date (7/1/96). If a net gain is expected, it should be recognized when realized, which is usually the disposal date (1997). Accordingly, the $2,000,000 ($22,000,000 – $20,000,000) expected gain from the sale of assets in 1997 offsets the $400,000 loss from operating the segment from the measurement date to the end of 1996 and the $200,000 loss from the beginning of 1997 to the disposal date. The net gain of $1,400,000 ($2,000,000 – $400,000 – $200,000) will be recognized when realized in 1997. Thus, no gain or loss should be recognized in 1996.
Answer (B) is incorrect because $840,000 is the estimated net-of-tax gain to be reported in 1997. Answer (C) is incorrect because $1,080,000 is the estimated net-of-tax gain to be reported in 1997, excluding the operating loss from the measurement date to year-end. Answer (D) is incorrect because $1,200,000 is the estimated net-of-tax gain on the actual disposal of the assets.

Questions 26 and 27 are based on the following information. On December 31, 1996, the board of directors of Maxx Manufacturing, Inc. committed to a plan to discontinue the operations of its Alpha Division in 1997. Maxx estimated that Alpha's 1997 operating loss would be $500,000 and that Alpha's facilities would be sold for $300,000 less than their carrying amounts. Alpha's 1996 operating loss was $1,400,000. Maxx's effective tax rate is 30%.

26. In its 1996 income statement, what amount should Maxx report as loss from discontinued operations?

A. $980,000

B. $1,330,000

C. $1,400,000

D. $1,900,000

The correct answer is (A). *(CPA 593 I-57)*

REQUIRED: The loss from discontinued operations at year-end.

DISCUSSION: The results of operations of a segment that has been or will be discontinued, together with any gain or loss on disposal, should be reported separately as a component of income before extraordinary items and the cumulative effect of accounting changes. Income or loss from discontinued operations and the gain or loss on disposal should each be disclosed net of tax. Accordingly, the loss from discontinued operations, net of tax effect, is $980,000 [$1,400,000 loss prior to the 12/31/96 measurement date x (1.0 – 30% tax rate)].

Answer (B) is incorrect because $1,330,000 equals the after-tax 1996 loss from discontinued operations, plus the estimated after-tax operating loss for 1997. Answer (C) is incorrect because $1,400,000 is the pretax 1996 loss from discontinued operations. Answer (D) is incorrect because $1,900,000 equals the pretax 1996 loss from discontinued operations, plus the estimated pretax operating loss for 1997.

27. In its 1996 income statement, what amount should Maxx report as loss on disposal of discontinued operations?

A. $210,000

B. $300,000

C. $560,000

D. $800,000

The correct answer is (C). *(CPA 593 I-58)*

REQUIRED: The loss on disposal of discontinued operations reported on the income statement.

DISCUSSION: The gain or loss on disposal should include not only the gain or loss on disposal of the assets but also any income or loss from operations during the phaseout period. If a net loss is expected, it should be provided for at the measurement date (12/31/96). Thus, loss on disposal of discontinued operations, net of taxes, is $560,000 [($500,000 expected operating loss + $300,000 estimated loss on asset sale) x (1 – 30%)].

Answer (A) is incorrect because $210,000 does not include the expected operating loss. Answer (B) is incorrect because $300,000 is a pretax amount that does not include the expected operating loss. Answer (D) is incorrect because the loss on disposal of discontinued operations should be reported net of tax.

28. Munn Corp.'s income statements for the years ended December 31, 1996 and 1995 included the following, before adjustments:

	1996	1995
Operating income	$ 800,000	$600,000
Gain on sale of division	450,000	--
	1,250,000	600,000
Provision for income taxes	375,000	180,000
Net income	$ 875,000	$420,000

On January 1, 1996, Munn agreed to sell the assets and product line of one of its operating divisions for $1,600,000. The sale was consummated on December 31, 1996, and resulted in a gain on disposition of $450,000. This division's net losses were $320,000 in 1996 and $250,000 in 1995. The income tax rate for both years was 30%. In preparing revised comparative income statements, Munn should report which of the following amounts of gain (loss) from discontinued operations?

	1996	1995
A.	$130,000	$0
B.	$130,000	$(250,000)
C.	$91,000	$0
D.	$91,000	$(175,000)

29. On October 1, 1996, Host Co. approved a plan to dispose of a segment of its business. Host expected that the sale would occur on April 1, 1997, at an estimated gain of $350,000. The segment had actual and estimated operating losses as follows:

1/1/96 to 9/30/96	$(300,000)
10/1/96 to 12/31/96	(200,000)
1/1/97 to 3/31/97	(400,000)

In its 1996 income statement, what should Host report as a loss on disposal of the segment before income taxes?

A. $200,000

B. $250,000

C. $500,000

D. $600,000

The correct answer is (D). *(CPA 1191 I-45)*
REQUIRED: The amounts reported under discontinued operations for 1996 and 1995.
DISCUSSION: Both the measurement date (January 1) and the disposal date (December 31) fall in 1996. Thus, discontinued operations for 1996 will include only a gain or loss on disposal. This gain or loss equals the $320,000 operating loss from the measurement date to the disposal date, plus the $450,000 gain on disposition. The pretax gain on disposal is therefore $130,000 ($450,000 – $320,000). The after-tax amount is $91,000 [$130,000 x (1.0 – .3)]. Because 1995 was prior to the measurement date, the $250,000 of operating losses would have been reported under income from continuing operations in the 1995 income statement as originally issued. This loss is now attributable to discontinued operations, and the 1995 financial statements presented for comparative purposes must be reclassified. In the reclassified 1995 income statement, the $250,000 pretax loss should be shown as a $175,000 [$250,000 x (1 – .3)] loss from discontinued operations prior to the measurement date.
Answer (A) is incorrect because $130,000 is the pretax gain on disposal for 1996. Moreover, the company must now report a 1995 loss from discontinued operations. Answer (B) is incorrect because $130,000 is the pretax gain on disposal for 1996, and $(250,000) is the pretax loss on discontinued operations for 1995. Answer (C) is incorrect because the company must now report a 1995 loss from discontinued operations.

The correct answer is (B). *(CPA 595 F-44)*
REQUIRED: The loss on disposal.
DISCUSSION: A gain or loss on disposal includes not only the gain or loss on the actual sale (disposal) of the segment but also any income or loss from operations during the phaseout period (10/1/96 to 3/31/97). Thus, the loss on disposal equals $250,000 ($350,000 expected gain minus $200,000 operating losses from 10/1/96 to 12/31/96 minus $400,000 expected operating losses from 1/1/97 to 3/31/97). Since a net loss is expected, it should be provided for at the measurement date (10/1/96) and thus be included in the 1996 income statement.
Answer (A) is incorrect because $200,000 is the operating loss from 10/1/96 to 12/31/96. Answer (C) is incorrect because $500,000 is the operating loss for 1996. Answer (D) is incorrect because the $600,000 loss does not include the $350,000 gain on sale.

Questions 30 and 31 are based on the following information. Marvel Construction Co., Inc. had a net income of $600,000 for the year ended December 31 after inclusion of the following special events that occurred during the year:

- The decision was made on January 2 to discontinue the cinder block manufacturing segment.

- The cinder block manufacturing segment was actually sold on July 1.

- Operating income from January 1 to June 30 for the cinder block manufacturing segment amounted to $90,000 before taxes.

- Cinder block manufacturing equipment with a book value of $250,000 was sold for $100,000.

- Marvel was subject to a 40% income tax rate.

30. Marvel's after-tax income from continuing operations for the year ended December 31 was

A. $360,000

B. $564,000

C. $600,000

D. $636,000

The correct answer is (D). *(CPA 581 II-39)*
REQUIRED: The after-tax income from continuing operations.
DISCUSSION: If net income was $600,000 and the assumed tax rate was 40%, the pretax income was $1,000,000. After adding back the net loss on disposal of the discontinued operations (the operating income of $90,000 matched against the loss on the sale of the assets of $150,000), and after deducting a 40% tax, the after-tax income from continuing operations is $636,000.

Net income	$ 600,000
Add back tax	400,000
Net income before taxes	$1,000,000
Add back loss on disposal	60,000
	$1,060,000
Minus 40% tax	(424,000)
Income from continuing operations	$ 636,000

Answer (A) is incorrect because $360,000 equals after-tax net income assuming pretax net income was $600,000. Answer (B) is incorrect because $564,000 results from subtracting the $36,000 net after-tax loss on disposal from net income. Answer (C) is incorrect because $600,000 is net income.

31. Marvel's aggregate income tax expense for the year ended December 31 should be

A. $216,000

B. $240,000

C. $400,000

D. $424,000

The correct answer is (C). *(CPA 581 II-40)*
REQUIRED: The aggregate income tax expense for the year ended December 31.
DISCUSSION: Marvel's net income for the year was $600,000. If $600,000 is 60% of the pretax income, the pretax income was $1,000,000 and the aggregate income tax was $400,000. As computed in the preceding question, the tax on the income from continuing operations was $424,000, which was mitigated by the tax savings from the $60,000 loss on discontinued operations. The tax savings reduced the taxes by $24,000 to $400,000.

Answer (A) is incorrect because $216,000 is the tax expense assuming $540,000 ($600,000 − $60,000 loss on disposal) is the pretax net income. Answer (B) is incorrect because $240,000 is the tax expense assuming $600,000 is the pretax net income. Answer (D) is incorrect because $424,000 is the tax on income from continuing operations.

6.4 Extraordinary Items

32. In 1996, Teller Co. incurred losses arising from its guilty plea in its first antitrust action and from a substantial increase in production costs caused when a major supplier's workers went on strike. Which of these losses should be reported as an extraordinary item?

	Antitrust Action	Production Costs
A.	No	No
B.	No	Yes
C.	Yes	No
D.	Yes	Yes

The correct answer is (C). *(CPA 1191 T-23)*
REQUIRED: The loss(es), if any, reported as an extraordinary item.
DISCUSSION: APB 30 specifically states that the effects of a strike are not extraordinary. However, a loss from the company's first antitrust action is clearly infrequent and most likely unusual, that is, abnormal and of a type unrelated to the typical activities of the entity, in the environment in which it operates.
Answers (A), (B), and (D) are incorrect because the litigation loss is extraordinary, but the effects of the strike are not.

33. In open market transactions, Gold Corp. simultaneously sold its long-term investment in Iron Corp. bonds and purchased its own outstanding bonds. The broker remitted the net cash from the two transactions. Gold's gain on the purchase of its own bonds exceeded its loss on the sale of the Iron bonds. Gold should report the

A. Net effect of the two transactions as an extraordinary gain.

B. Net effect of the two transactions in income before extraordinary items.

C. Effect of its own bond transaction gain in income before extraordinary items and report the Iron bond transaction as an extraordinary loss.

D. Effect of its own bond transaction as an extraordinary gain and report the Iron bond transaction loss in income before extraordinary items.

The correct answer is (D). *(CPA 1195 F-41)*
REQUIRED: The reporting of the sale of a long-term investment in bonds and an extinguishment of debt.
DISCUSSION: APB 26 requires that differences between the reacquisition prices and the net carrying amounts of extinguished debt be recognized currently as gains or losses in income of the period of extinguishment. SFAS 4 requires that such gains or losses be aggregated and, if material, classified as extraordinary items, net of related income tax effect. An exception is provided by SFAS 64 for gains or losses from extinguishments of debt that satisfy sinking fund requirements that must be met within 1 year. Other transactions are presumed to be ordinary and usual unless a pronouncement specifically states otherwise or the evidence clearly supports classification as extraordinary. The sale of securities is not clearly infrequent and unusual in the environment in which the entity operates. Thus, the loss on the sale of bonds should be reported in income before extraordinary items.
Answers (A), (B), and (C) are incorrect because the extinguishment resulted in an extraordinary gain and the sale of securities in an ordinary loss.

34. Which one of the following material events would be classified as an extraordinary item on an income statement?

    A. A write-down of inventories.

    B. A loss due to the effects of a strike against a major supplier.

    C. A gain or loss from the extinguishment of debt.

    D. A gain or loss from the exchange of foreign currency due to a major devaluation.

The correct answer is (C). *(CMA 694 2-29)*
    REQUIRED: The event that would be classified as an extraordinary item on the income statement.
    DISCUSSION: APB 30 gives examples of certain transactions that are not to be considered extraordinary items. These include write-downs of receivables and inventories, translation of foreign exchange, disposal of a business segment, disposal of productive assets, the effects of strikes, and the adjustments of accruals on long-term contracts. A gain or loss on the early extinguishment of debt is to be shown as an extraordinary item under the provisions of SFAS 4.
    Answers (A), (B), and (D) are incorrect because APB 30 specifically excludes a write-down of inventories, a loss due to the effects of a strike against a major supplier, and a gain or loss from the exchange of foreign currency due to a major devaluation from the definition of extraordinary items.

35. A transaction that is unusual in nature and infrequent in occurrence should be reported separately as a component of income

    A. After cumulative effect of accounting changes and before discontinued operations of a segment of a business.

    B. After cumulative effect of accounting changes and after discontinued operations of a segment of a business.

    C. Before cumulative effect of accounting changes and before discontinued operations of a segment of a business.

    D. Before cumulative effect of accounting changes and after discontinued operations of a segment of a business.

The correct answer is (D). *(CPA 1194 F-53)*
    REQUIRED: The reporting of a transaction that is unusual in nature and infrequent in occurrence.
    DISCUSSION: A transaction that is unusual in nature and infrequent in occurrence in the environment in which the entity operates is classified as an extraordinary item. The following is the order of items to be reported separately in the income statement: income from continuing operations, discontinued operations, extraordinary items, cumulative effect of changes in accounting principle, net income.
    Answers (A), (B), and (C) are incorrect because an extraordinary item should be reported after discontinued operations and before cumulative effect of accounting changes.

36. An extraordinary item should be reported separately on the income statement as a component of income

	Net of Income Taxes	Before Discontinued Operations of a Segment of a Business
A.	Yes	Yes
B.	Yes	No
C.	No	No
D.	No	Yes

The correct answer is (B). *(CPA 594 F-48)*
    REQUIRED: The presentation of an extraordinary item.
    DISCUSSION: Extraordinary items should be shown separately in the income statement, net of tax, after results of discontinued operations but before the cumulative effect of a change in accounting principle.
    Answers (A), (C), and (D) are incorrect because an extraordinary item is presented net of tax after discontinued operations.

37. APB 30, *Reporting the Results of Operations*, recommends which of the following policies regarding extraordinary items?

   A. Earnings per share data should be presented in a separate schedule.

   B. Extraordinary items should always be presented as an aggregate amount.

   C. Income taxes applicable to extraordinary items should be presented in a separate schedule.

   D. Earnings per share data should be presented on the face of the income statement.

The correct answer is (D). *(Publisher)*
   REQUIRED: The policy recommended by APB 30 regarding extraordinary items.
   DISCUSSION: Paragraph 9 of APB 30 requires that EPS data for income from continuing operations and for net income, computed under APB 15, *Earnings Per Share*, be presented on the face of the income statement.
   Answer (A) is incorrect because EPS data should be presented on the face of the income statements. EPS data for the results of discontinued operations and for gain or loss from disposal of a segment may be presented in a related note if not on the face of the income statement. Answer (B) is incorrect because extraordinary items should be presented individually, rather than in the aggregate, and on the face of the income statement, if practicable; otherwise, disclosure in related footnotes is acceptable. Answer (C) is incorrect because extraordinary item income tax data should be presented on the face of the income statement or in a related note.

38. Kent Co. incurred the following infrequent losses during 1996:

- A $300,000 loss was incurred on disposal of one of four dissimilar factories.

- A major currency devaluation caused a $120,000 exchange loss on an amount remitted by a foreign customer.

- Inventory valued at $190,000 was made worthless by a competitor's unexpected product innovation.

In its 1996 income statement, what amount should Kent report as losses that are not considered extraordinary?

   A. $610,000

   B. $490,000

   C. $420,000

   D. $310,000

The correct answer is (A). *(CPA 592 I-54)*
   REQUIRED: The amount of losses not considered extraordinary.
   DISCUSSION: To be classified as an extraordinary item, a transaction must be both unusual in nature and infrequent in occurrence in the environment in which the business operates. APB 30 specifies six items that are not considered extraordinary. These items include gains and losses on disposal of a segment; foreign exchange gains and losses, including those resulting from major devaluations and revaluations; and write-downs of receivables and inventories. Hence, the amount of ordinary losses is $610,000 ($300,000 + $120,000 + $190,000).
   Answer (B) is incorrect because $490,000 omits the foreign exchange loss. Answer (C) is incorrect because $420,000 omits the inventory write-off. Answer (D) is incorrect because $310,000 omits the loss on disposal of the factory.

39. In 1996, hail damaged several of Toncan Co.'s vans. Hailstorms had frequently inflicted similar damage to Toncan's vans. Over the years, Toncan had saved money by not buying hail insurance and either paying for repairs, or selling damaged vans and then replacing them. In 1996, the damaged vans were sold for less than their carrying amount. How should the hail damage cost be reported in Toncan's 1996 financial statements?

   A. The actual 1996 hail damage loss as an extraordinary loss, net of income taxes.

   B. The actual 1996 hail damage loss in continuing operations, with no separate disclosure.

   C. The expected average hail damage loss in continuing operations, with no separate disclosure.

   D. The expected average hail damage loss in continuing operations, with separate disclosure.

The correct answer is (B). *(CPA 593 T-35)*
   REQUIRED: The reporting of hail damage costs when a company is uninsured and sells the damaged item for a loss.
   DISCUSSION: Because Toncan sold its damaged vans for less than their carrying amount, the company suffered a loss. Since this occurrence is not unusual or infrequent, the actual loss should be included in continuous operations with no separate disclosure.
   Answer (A) is incorrect because a frequent occurrence does not meet the definition of an extraordinary item. Answer (C) is incorrect because Toncan should report the actual loss incurred in 1996. Answer (D) is incorrect because Toncan should report the actual loss, and a separate disclosure is not needed.

40. Fuqua Steel Co. had the following unusual financial events occur during 1996:

- Bonds payable were retired 5 years before their scheduled maturity, resulting in a $260,000 gain. Fuqua has frequently retired bonds early when interest rates declined significantly.

- A steel forming segment suffered $255,000 in losses from hurricane damage. This was the fourth similar loss sustained in a 5-year period at that location.

- A segment of Fuqua's operations, steel transportation, was sold at a net loss of $350,000. This was Fuqua's first divestiture of one of its operating segments.

Before income taxes, what amount should be disclosed as the gain (loss) from extraordinary items in 1996?

- A. $260,000

- B. $5,000

- C. $(90,000)

- D. $(350,000)

The correct answer is (A). *(CPA 1191 I-51)*
   REQUIRED: The amount disclosed as the gain (loss) from extraordinary items.
   DISCUSSION: SFAS 4 requires material gains related to the reacquisition and retirement of bonds (an extinguishment of debt) to be classified as extraordinary. Thus, the bond retirement results in a $260,000 extraordinary gain. The divestiture is reported as a discontinued operation. The hurricane damage, which is unusual but not infrequent, is reported separately as a component of income from continuing operations.
   Answer (B) is incorrect because $5,000 is the net of the extraordinary gain and the $255,000 loss reported in continuing operations. Answer (C) is incorrect because $(90,000) is the net of the loss from discontinued operations and the extinguishment gain. Answer (D) is incorrect because $(350,000) is the loss from discontinued operations.

41. During 1996, both Raim Co. and Cane Co. suffered losses due to the flooding of the Mississippi River. Raim is located 2 miles from the river and sustains flood losses every 2 to 3 years. Cane, which has been located 50 miles from the river for the past 20 years, has never before had flood losses. How should the flood losses be reported in each company's 1996 income statement?

	Raim	Cane
A.	As a component of income from continuing operations	As an extraordinary item
B.	As a component of income from continuing operations	As a component of income from continuing operations
C.	As an extraordinary item	As a component of income from continuing operations
D.	As an extraordinary item	As an extraordinary item

The correct answer is (A). *(CPA 1195 F-42)*
   REQUIRED: The reporting of flood losses in the income statement.
   DISCUSSION: For Raim, flood losses are neither unusual nor infrequent in the environment in which it operates. Thus, they should be classified as a component of income from continuing operations, not as an extraordinary item. For Cane, the flood losses meet the criteria of an extraordinary item because they are unusual and infrequent: Cane had never before suffered food losses.
   Answers (B), (C), and (D) are incorrect because Raim should report the flood losses as a component of income from continuing operations, and Cane should report them as an extraordinary item.

6.5 Cumulative Effect of a Change in Accounting Principle

42. On December 31, 1996, Kerr, Inc. appropriately changed its inventory valuation method to FIFO cost from weighted-average cost for financial statement and income tax purposes. The change will result in a $700,000 increase in the beginning inventory on January 1, 1996. Assume a 30% income tax rate. The cumulative effect of this accounting change reported for the year ended December 31, 1996 is

A. $0

B. $210,000

C. $490,000

D. $700,000

The correct answer is (C). *(CPA 1189 I-51)*
REQUIRED: The cumulative effect of a change in accounting principle.
DISCUSSION: The change from the weighted-average cost inventory valuation method to FIFO cost is a change from one generally accepted accounting principle to another. It should be reported as a cumulative effect-type adjustment in the income statement. The cumulative effect is the adjustment to the beginning balance of retained earnings based on a retroactive computation. It equals the $700,000 increase in beginning inventory, net of the 30% income tax rate. Accordingly, the cumulative effect is $490,000 [$700,000 x (1 − 30%)].
Answer (A) is incorrect because the cumulative effect of an accounting change should be included in the determination of net income. Answer (B) is incorrect because $210,000 is the increase in tax expense associated with the $700,000 increase in beginning inventory. Answer (D) is incorrect because $700,000 is the pretax change.

43. A company changes its method of accounting for depreciation during the current year. In its income statement for the year, the cumulative, retroactive effect of the change is

A. Not disclosed.

B. Included with current depreciation charges.

C. Disclosed as a separate type of depreciation expense, directly following depreciation expense for the current year.

D. Disclosed, net of tax, as a separate item directly following extraordinary items.

The correct answer is (D). *(CIA 595 IV-21)*
REQUIRED: The treatment of a change in depreciation methods.
DISCUSSION: A change in depreciation methods is properly reported as a cumulative effect adjustment. In the year of change, the cumulative effect of the change on beginning retained earnings is included, net of tax effect, in the determination of net income. It is presented directly following extraordinary items on the income statement.
Answer (A) is incorrect because changes in accounting principles are reflected in the financial statements for the period. Answers (B) and (C) are incorrect because the cumulative effect of a change in depreciation methods is shown in a separate caption on the income statement after extraordinary items.

44. Pro forma effects of retroactive application would usually be reported on the face of the income statement for a change

A. In the service lives of depreciable assets.

B. In the salvage value of a depreciable asset.

C. From the straight-line method of depreciation to the double-declining-balance method.

D. From presenting statements for individual companies to presenting consolidated statements.

The correct answer is (C). *(CPA 582 T-24)*
REQUIRED: The situation requiring disclosure of pro forma effects of retroactive application of a change in accounting principle.
DISCUSSION: A change in depreciation methods from straight-line to double-declining-balance is a change in accounting principle that, under APB 20, *Accounting Changes,* does not permit restatement of the actual financial statements of prior periods. Rather, pro forma effects of retroactive application should be shown on the face of the income statement for all periods presented as if the newly adopted principle had been applied during the affected periods.
Answers (A) and (B) are incorrect because each is a change in accounting estimate which does not require restatement of amounts previously reported or reporting of pro forma effects on prior periods. Answer (D) is incorrect because it is a change in the reporting entity and requires restatement of the actual financial statements of all prior periods presented.

CHAPTER SEVEN
PRESENT VALUES AND FUTURE VALUES

This chapter contains questions on interest concepts, i.e., present values (PV) and future values (FV). Further accounting applications appear in Chapter 16, Pensions, Other Postretirement Benefits, and Postemployment Benefits; Chapter 17, Leases; and Chapter 13, Investments in Debt and Equity Securities.

7.1 Present Value

1. What is the time value of money?

A. Interest.

B. Present value.

C. Future value.

D. Annuity.

The correct answer is (A). *(Publisher)*
REQUIRED: The meaning of time value of money.
DISCUSSION: Time value of money means that, because of the interest factor, money held today is worth more than the same amount of money to be received in the future. Interest is paid for the use of money, i.e., on debts, in a normal business transaction. This payment compensates the lender for not being able to use the money for current consumption.
Answer (B) is incorrect because present value is the value today, net of the interest factor, of one or more payments to be made in the future. Answer (C) is incorrect because future value is the value some time in the future of a deposit today or of a series of deposits. Answer (D) is incorrect because an annuity is generally a series of equal payments at equal intervals of time.

2. Which of the following is a series of equal payments at equal intervals of time with each payment made (received) at the beginning of each time period?

A. Ordinary annuity.

B. Annuity in arrears.

C. Annuity due.

D. Payments in advance.

The correct answer is (C). *(Publisher)*
REQUIRED: The type of annuity in which the payment is made (received) at the beginning of each period.
DISCUSSION: An annuity is a series of equal payments made (or received) at equal intervals of time. An annuity due, also known as an annuity in advance, is a series of equal payments at equal intervals of time occurring at the beginning of each time period involved.
Answers (A) and (B) are incorrect because an ordinary annuity (also known as an annuity in arrears) is an annuity in which payments are made at the end, rather than at the beginning, of the time periods involved. The difference for present value calculations is that, in an annuity due, no interest is computed on the first payment. In future value computations, interest is earned on a deposit made at the beginning of the first period for an annuity due in contrast with a deposit made at the end of the first period (ordinary annuity). Answer (D) is incorrect because payments may or may not be equal in amount.

3. On July 1, 1996, Cody Company obtained a $2,000,000, 180-day bank loan at an annual rate of 12%. The loan agreement requires Cody to maintain a $400,000 compensating balance in its checking account at the lending bank. Cody would otherwise maintain a balance of only $200,000 in this account. The checking account earns interest at an annual rate of 6%. Based on a 360-day year, the effective interest rate on the borrowing is

A. 12%

B. 12.67%

C. 13.33%

D. 13.5%

The correct answer is (B). *(CPA 587 I-32)*
REQUIRED: The annual effective interest rate on a loan requiring a compensating balance.
DISCUSSION: The effective interest rate on the 180-day borrowing is equal to the net interest cost divided by the net available proceeds of $1,800,000 ($2,000,000 loan – $200,000 increase in the compensating balance). The net interest cost is equal to the gross interest cost minus the incremental interest revenue. The gross interest cost is $120,000 ($2,000,000 x 12% x 6/12). Because the incremental interest revenue is $6,000 ($200,000 x 6% x 6/12), the net interest cost is $114,000 ($120,000 – $6,000). The 6-month effective interest rate is therefore 6.33% ($114,000 ÷ $1,800,000). The annual effective interest rate is 12.67% (6.33% x 2).
Answer (A) is incorrect because 12% is the annual rate. Answers (C) and (D) are incorrect because the interest revenue from the checking account must be included in the calculations.

4. The relationship between the present value of a future sum and the future value of a present sum can be expressed in terms of their respective interest factors. If the present value of $100,000 due at the end of 8 years, at 10%, is $46,650, what is the approximate future value of $100,000 invested for the same length of time and at the same rate?

A. $46,650

B. $100,000

C. $146,650

D. $214,360

The correct answer is (D). *(CIA 592 IV-53)*
REQUIRED: The approximate future value of an amount.
DISCUSSION: The interest factor for the future value of a present sum is equal to the reciprocal of the interest factor for the present value of a future sum. Thus, the future value is $214,362 [($100,000 ÷ $46,650) x $100,000].
Answer (A) is incorrect because $46,650 is the present value of $100,000 to be received in 8 years. Answer (B) is incorrect because $100,000 is the present value, not the future value, of $100,000 invested today. Answer (C) is incorrect because the addition of the present and future values has no accounting meaning.

5. A company purchased some large machinery on a deferred payment plan. The contract calls for $20,000 down on January 1st and $20,000 at the beginning of each of the next 4 years. There is no stated interest rate in the contract, and there is no established exchange price for the machinery. What should be recorded as the cost of the machinery?

A. $100,000

B. $100,000 plus the added implicit interest.

C. Future value of an annuity due for 5 years at an imputed interest rate.

D. Present value of an annuity due for 5 years at an imputed interest rate.

The correct answer is (D). *(CIA 584 IV-13)*
REQUIRED: The cost of machinery acquired under a deferred payment plan.
DISCUSSION: The contract calls for an annuity due because the first annuity payment is due immediately. In an ordinary annuity (annuity in arrears), each payment is due at the end of the period. According to APB 21, *Interest on Receivables and Payables*, an interest rate must be imputed in the given circumstances to arrive at the present value of the machinery.
Answers (A) and (B) are incorrect because the implicit interest should be subtracted from the $100,000 in total payments. Answer (C) is incorrect because the present value, not the future value, is the appropriate concept.

6. On November 1, 1994, a company purchased a new machine that it does not have to pay for until November 1, 1996. The total payment on November 1, 1996 will include both principal and interest. Assuming interest at a 10% rate, the cost of the machine will be the total payment multiplied by what time value of money factor?

A. Present value of annuity of $1.

B. Present value of $1.

C. Future amount of annuity of $1.

D. Future amount of $1.

The correct answer is (B). *(CPA 1190 T-46)*
  REQUIRED: The time value of money factor to compute current cost when payment is to be made in a lump sum at a future date.
  DISCUSSION: The cost of the machine to the company on 11/1/94 is the present value of the payment to be made on 11/1/96. To obtain the present value, i.e., today's price, the future payment is multiplied by the present value of $1 for two periods at 10%.
  Answer (A) is incorrect because the present value of an annuity determines the value today of a series of future payments (not merely one payment). Answer (C) is incorrect because the future value of an annuity determines the amount available at a specified time in the future after a series of deposits (investments). Answer (D) is incorrect because the future value of a dollar determines how much will be available at a specified time in the future based on the single investment (deposit) today.

7. The computation of the current value of an asset using the present value of future cash flows method does not include the

A. Cost of alternate uses of funds given up.

B. Productive life of the asset.

C. Applicable interest rate.

D. Future amounts of cash receipts or cash savings.

The correct answer is (A). *(CPA 1180 T-7)*
  REQUIRED: The information not used in computing current value by the present value of future cash flows method.
  DISCUSSION: The present value of future cash flows is one technique for computing current value of an asset. To calculate the current value of an asset (using the "present value" method) requires (1) the discount period (the productive life of the asset), (2) the discount rate (the applicable interest rate), and (3) the future values (the future amounts of cash receipts or cash savings). This method does not take into account opportunity costs (costs of giving up alternate uses of funds).
  Answers (B), (C), and (D) are incorrect because each is included in the current value computation.

8. On May 1, a company sold some machinery to another company. The two companies entered into an installment sales contract at a predetermined interest rate. The contract required five equal annual payments with the first payment due on May 1, the date of sale. What present value concept is appropriate for this situation?

A. Present value of an annuity due of $1 for five periods.

B. Present value of an ordinary annuity of $1 for five periods.

C. Future amount of an annuity of $1 for five periods.

D. Future amount of $1 for five periods.

The correct answer is (A). *(CPA 1179 T-39)*
  REQUIRED: The present value concept appropriate for an installment sale with the first payment due immediately.
  DISCUSSION: The contract calls for five equal annual payments with the first due immediately. Ordinary annuity tables assume the first payment occurs at the end of the first time period. An annuity in which the first payment occurs at the beginning of the first period is called an "annuity due" or an "annuity in advance."
  The number of payments earning interest in an annuity due is one less than the number earning interest in an ordinary annuity because there is no interest on the first payment. Accordingly, the present value of an annuity due of $1 for five periods can be calculated by taking the present value of an ordinary annuity of $1 for four periods and adding $1. Hence, a special table for an annuity due or the method described above can be used in this situation.
  Answer (B) is incorrect because the question describes an annuity due (not an ordinary annuity) for five periods. Answers (C) and (D) are incorrect because a present value computation is required.

9. In the determination of a present value, which of the following relationships is correct?

    A. The lower the discount rate and the shorter the discount period, the lower the present value.

    B. The lower the future cash flow and the shorter the discount period, the lower the present value.

    C. The higher the discount rate and the longer the discount period, the lower the present value.

    D. The higher the future cash flow and the longer the discount period, the lower the present value.

The correct answer is (C). *(Publisher)*
    REQUIRED: The correct relationship between the discount period, discount rate, and present value.
    DISCUSSION: As the discount rate increases, the present value decreases. Also, as the discount period increases, the present value decreases.
    Answers (A) and (B) are incorrect because as the discount period decreases, the present value increases. Answer (D) is incorrect because increased future cash flows increase the present value.

10. The figure .9423 is taken from the column marked 2% and the row marked three periods in a certain interest table. From what interest table is this figure taken?

    A. Amount of $1.

    B. Amount of annuity of $1.

    C. Present value of $1.

    D. Present value of annuity of $1.

The correct answer is (C). *(CPA 1176 T-35)*
    REQUIRED: The interest table from which the figure was taken given the interest rate and number of time periods.
    DISCUSSION: This question is best answered by process of elimination as explained below. The present value of $1 is the value today of $1 to be paid in the future. Thus, $1 discounted at 2% for three periods has a present value of something over $.94 because there is a 2% discount in each of the three periods. Although $1 discounts to $.94, the 2% interest each year compounds; i.e., interest earned in prior periods earns interest in subsequent periods. The exact interest factor is .9423 $[1 \div (1 + .02)^3]$.
    Answer (A) is incorrect because if the table were for an amount of $1, the figure would be in excess of $1. Answer (B) is incorrect because the amount of an annuity of $1 would be in excess of $3 as it is the future value of a series of three payments plus compounded interest. Answer (D) is incorrect because the present value of an annuity of $1 for three periods would be less than $3, but more than $1.

11. For which of the following transactions would the use of the present value of an annuity due concept be appropriate in calculating the present value of the asset obtained or liability owed at the date of incurrence?

    A. A capital lease is entered into with the initial lease payment due 1 month subsequent to the signing of the lease agreement.

    B. A capital lease is entered into with the initial lease payment due upon the signing of the lease agreement.

    C. A 10-year 8% bond is issued on January 2 with interest payable semiannually on July 1 and January 1 yielding 7%.

    D. A 10-year 8% bond is issued on January 2 with interest payable semiannually on July 1 and January 1 yielding 9%.

The correct answer is (B). *(CPA 582 T-4)*
    REQUIRED: The transaction for which the present value of an annuity due concept would be appropriate.
    DISCUSSION: In an annuity due, the first payment is made at the beginning of the first period and is therefore not discounted. In an ordinary annuity, the first payment is made at the end of the first period and therefore is discounted. For annuities due, the first payment is included in the computation at its face value.
    Answers (A), (C), and (D) are incorrect because in each case the initial payment is not due immediately.

12. An accountant wishes to find the present value of an annuity of $1 payable at the beginning of each period at 10% for eight periods. He has only one present value table which shows the present value of an annuity of $1 payable at the end of each period. To compute the present value factor he needs, the accountant would use the present value factor in the 10% column for

A. Seven periods.

B. Seven periods and add $1.

C. Eight periods.

D. Nine periods and subtract $1.

13. An office equipment representative has a machine for sale or lease. If you buy the machine, the cost is $7,596. If you lease the machine, you will have to sign a noncancelable lease and make five payments of $2,000 each. The first payment will be paid on the first day of the lease. At the time of the last payment, you will receive title to the machine. The present value of an ordinary annuity of $1 is as follows:

No. of Periods	Present Value		
	10%	12%	16%
1	0.909	0.893	0.862
2	1.736	1.690	1.605
3	2.487	2.402	2.246
4	3.170	3.037	2.798
5	3.791	3.605	3.274

The interest rate implicit in this lease is approximately

A. 10%

B. 12%

C. Between 10% and 12%.

D. 16%

The correct answer is (B). *(CPA 576 T-29)*
REQUIRED: The method to compute the present value of an annuity due using the present value of an ordinary annuity table.
DISCUSSION: An annuity payable at the start of each period for eight periods is an ordinary annuity for seven periods plus the first payment. The present value of the first payment is its face value since it is paid immediately and therefore not discounted. To compute the interest factor, use the factor in the ordinary annuity table in the 10% column for seven periods and add $1.
Answer (A) is incorrect because it ignores the down payment. Answer (C) is incorrect because it assumes an annuity due is an ordinary annuity. Answer (D) is incorrect because it is the adjustment that would be made to convert the future value of an ordinary annuity to the future value of an annuity due.

The correct answer is (D). *(CPA 1178 I-39)*
REQUIRED: The interest rate implicit in a lease.
DISCUSSION: Present value tables can be used to determine the interest rate if the present value is already known. Divide the present value by the periodic amount to find the interest factor. Find the interest factor in the present value of an ordinary annuity table by looking in the row corresponding to the number of periods over which the annuity is payable.
In this question, the series of payments is an annuity due, and an adjustment must be made before using the ordinary annuity table. The first payment is due immediately, so its present value (face amount) of $2,000 is deducted from the given present value of the annuity. The row for n – 1 periods (4) should then be used.

Present value	$ 7,596
Less first payment	(2,000)
	$ 5,596
Divided by annuity amount	÷2,000
Present value factor	2.798

The present value factor of 2.798 is found under 16% in the row for four periods.
Answers (A), (B), and (C) are incorrect because the present value factor used falls under 16%.

14. A businessman wants to withdraw $3,000 (including principal) from an investment fund at the end of each year for 5 years. How should he compute his required initial investment at the beginning of the first year if the fund earns 6% compounded annually?

A. $3,000 times the amount of an annuity of $1 at 6% at the end of each year for 5 years.

B. $3,000 divided by the amount of an annuity of $1 at 6% at the end of each year for 5 years.

C. $3,000 times the present value of an annuity of $1 at 6% at the end of each year for 5 years.

D. $3,000 divided by the present value of an annuity of $1 at 6% at the end of each year for 5 years.

The correct answer is (C). *(CPA 1176 T-36)*
REQUIRED: The computation for the initial investment required to permit withdrawal of $3,000 at the end of each of 5 years given 6% interest.
DISCUSSION: The question requires a present value rather than a future value, i.e., today's equivalent of $3,000 at the end of each of the next 5 years. Use the present value of an ordinary annuity of $1 table. The interest factor corresponding to 6% for five periods is multiplied by $3,000 to provide the answer.
Answers (A) and (B) are incorrect because the question requires a present value rather than a future value calculation. "Amount of an annuity" is synonymous with future value of an annuity. Answer (D) is incorrect because $3,000 must be multiplied (rather than divided) by the present value of an ordinary annuity of $1 for 6% and five periods.

15. A company bought Machine 1 on March 5, 1995 for $5,000 cash. The estimated salvage was $200 and the estimated life was 11 years. On March 5, 1996, the company learned that it could purchase a different machine for $8,000 cash. It would save the company an estimated $250 per year. The new machine would have no estimated salvage and an estimated life of 10 years. The company could get $3,000 for Machine 1 on March 5, 1996. Ignoring income taxes, which of the following calculations would best assist the company in deciding whether to purchase the new machine?

A. (Present value of an annuity of $250) + $3,000 − $8,000

B. (Present value of an annuity of $250) − $8,000

C. (Present value of an annuity of $250) + $3,000 − $8,000 − $5,000

D. (Present value of an annuity of $250) + $3,000 − $8,000 − $4,800

The correct answer is (A). *(CPA 1175 I-30)*
REQUIRED: The calculation that would best assist the company in deciding whether to purchase the new machine.
DISCUSSION: The sale of the first machine for $3,000 and the purchase of the new machine for $8,000 on 3/5/96 would create an incremental cost to the company of $5,000. If the present value of the future savings from the second machine exceeds $5,000 [the formula presented in answer (A)], the company should purchase the new machine. Note that the remaining estimated useful life of the first machine is the same as that of the second. Note also that the cost of Machine 1 should be ignored because it is a sunk cost.
Answer (B) is incorrect because it fails to take into account the resale value of Machine 1 on 3/5/96. Answers (C) and (D) are incorrect because they improperly take into account the sunk cost of Machine 1.

16. On July 1, 1996, Hart signed an agreement to operate as a franchisee of Ace Printers for an initial franchise fee of $120,000. On the same date, Hart paid $40,000 and agreed to pay the balance in four equal annual payments of $20,000 beginning July 1, 1997. The down payment is not refundable and no future services are required of the franchisor. Hart can borrow at 14% for a loan of this type.

Present value of $1 at 14% for 4 periods	0.59
Future amount of $1 at 14% for 4 periods	1.69
Present value of an ordinary annuity of $1 at 14% for 4 periods	2.91

Hart should record the acquisition cost of the franchise on July 1, 1996 at

    A. $135,200

    B. $120,000

    C. $98,200

    D. $87,200

The correct answer is (C). *(CPA 587 I-10)*
    REQUIRED: The acquisition cost of a franchise to be paid for in installments.
    DISCUSSION: The acquisition cost would be recorded at $120,000 if this amount of cash was paid immediately. Since the $120,000 is to be paid in installments, the acquisition cost is equal to the down payment of $40,000 plus the present value of the series of four annuity payments beginning 1 year after the date of purchase. The proper interest factor to be employed is the present value of an ordinary annuity of $1 at 14% for four periods, or 2.91.

$$\begin{array}{r} \$\ 20,000 \\ \underline{\times\quad 2.91} \\ \$\ 58,200 \\ \underline{+40,000} \\ \underline{\$\ 98,200} \end{array}$$

    Answers (A), (B), and (D) are incorrect because the factor that should be used is the present value of an ordinary annuity of $1 at 14% for four periods.

17. On January 1, 1996, Orr Company bought a building with an assessed value of $220,000 on the date of purchase. Orr gave as consideration a $400,000 noninterest-bearing note due on January 1, 1999. There was no established exchange price for the building, and the note had no ready market. The prevailing rate of interest for a note of this type at January 1, 1996 was 10%. The present value of $1 at 10% for three periods is 0.75. What amount of interest expense should be included in Orr's 1996 income statement?

    A. $22,000

    B. $30,000

    C. $33,333

    D. $40,000

The correct answer is (B). *(CPA 1185 I-38)*
    REQUIRED: The interest expense on a noninterest-bearing note.
    DISCUSSION: The purchase of a building without an established exchange price should be recorded at the fair market value of the consideration given. A noninterest-bearing note should be recorded at its fair market value or present value of the future cash flows discounted at the prevailing rate of interest. Orr's note and building should therefore be recorded at $300,000 ($400,000 x 0.75). The amount of interest expense for the first year is $30,000 [the carrying value of the note ($300,000) times the 10% interest rate prevailing at the date of issuance of the note].
    Answer (A) is incorrect because $22,000 results from applying the interest rate to the assessment value of the building. Answer (C) is incorrect because $33,333 is a nonsense number. Answer (D) is incorrect because $40,000 fails to consider the present value of the note.

18. On January 1, 1995, Tone Company exchanged equipment for a $200,000 noninterest-bearing note due on January 1, 1998. The prevailing rate of interest for a note of this type at January 1, 1995 was 10%. The present value of $1 at 10% for three periods is 0.75. What amount of interest revenue should be included in Tone's 1996 income statement?

    A. $7,500

    B. $15,000

    C. $16,500

    D. $20,000

The correct answer is (C). *(CPA 589 I-59)*
    REQUIRED: The interest revenue for a noninterest-bearing note in the second year.
    DISCUSSION: A noninterest-bearing note should be recorded at its fair value, which is the present value of the future cash flows discounted at the prevailing rate of interest. Tone Company's note should therefore be recorded at $150,000 ($200,000 x 0.75) on 1/1/95. Interest revenue for 1995 is $15,000 ($150,000 beginning balance x 10% interest rate). This note is noninterest-bearing; hence, there are no periodic cash (interest) payments. Accordingly, the $15,000 of interest should be added to the $150,000 1/1/95 balance to determine the $165,000 1/1/96 balance. Interest revenue for 1996 is $16,500 ($165,000 x 10%).
    Answer (A) is incorrect because $7,500 is one-half of the first year's interest. Answer (B) is incorrect because $15,000 fails to add the 1995 interest to determine the balance on 1/1/96. Answer (D) is incorrect because $20,000 fails to consider the present value of the note.

19. A company plans to purchase a machine with the following conditions:

- Purchase price = $300,000.
- The down payment = 10% of purchase price with remainder financed at an annual interest rate of 16%.
- The financing period is 8 years with equal annual payments made every year.
- The present value of an annuity of $1 per year for 8 years at 16% is 4.3436.
- The present value of $1 due at the end of 8 years at 16% is .3050.

The annual payment (rounded to the nearest dollar) is

A. $39,150

B. $43,200

C. $62,160

D. $82,350

The correct answer is (C). *(CIA 1192 IV-55)*
REQUIRED: The annual payment (rounded to the nearest dollar).
DISCUSSION: The periodic payment is found by dividing the amount to be accumulated ($300,000 price – $30,000 down payment = $270,000) by the interest factor for the present value of an ordinary annuity for 8 years at 16%. Consequently, the payment is $62,160 ($270,000 ÷ 4.3436).

Answer (A) is incorrect because $39,150 is based on dividing ($270,000 x 1.16) by 8 (years). Answer (B) is incorrect because $43,200 is 16% of $270,000. Answer (D) is incorrect because $82,350 reflects multiplication by the present value of a sum due (.305) instead of dividing by the present value of an annuity (4.3436).

20. On December 30, 1996, Bart, Inc. purchased a machine from Fell Corp. in exchange for a noninterest-bearing note requiring eight payments of $20,000. The first payment was made on December 30, 1996, and the others are due annually on December 30. At date of issuance, the prevailing rate of interest for this type of note was 11%. Present value factors are as follows:

Period	Present Value of Ordinary Annuity of 1 at 11%	Present Value of Annuity in Advance of 1 at 11%
7	4.712	5.231
8	5.146	5.712

On Bart's December 31, 1996 balance sheet, the note payable to Fell was

A. $94,240

B. $102,920

C. $104,620

D. $114,240

The correct answer is (A). *(CPA 590 I-29)*
REQUIRED: The carrying value of a noninterest-bearing note payable at the date of issuance.
DISCUSSION: The payment terms of this purchase agreement provide for a $20,000 initial payment and seven equal payments of $20,000 to be received at the end of each of the next 7 years. The note payable, however, should reflect only the present value of the seven future payments. The present value factor to be used is the present value of an ordinary annuity for seven periods at 11%, or 4.712. The note payable should be recorded at $94,240 ($20,000 x 4.712).

Answer (B) is incorrect because $102,920 uses the factor for eight periods rather than seven. Answer (C) is incorrect because the factor for an ordinary annuity should be used. Answer (D) is incorrect because the factor used should be for an ordinary annuity of seven periods, not an annuity in advance for eight periods.

21. A corporation is contemplating the purchase of a new piece of equipment with a purchase price of $500,000. It plans to make a 10% down payment and will receive a loan for 25 years at 10% interest. The present value interest factor for an annuity of $1 per year for 25 years at 10% is 9.8226. The annual payment (to the nearest dollar) required on the loan will be

A. $18,000

B. $45,813

C. $45,000

D. $50,903

The correct answer is (B). *(CIA 1188 IV-55)*

REQUIRED: The annual payment required on the loan.

DISCUSSION: The corporation plans a 10% down payment on equipment with a purchase price of $500,000. The amount of the loan will therefore equal $450,000. Because the loan will be financed at 10% for 25 years, the annual payments can be calculated by dividing the amount of the initial loan by the present value interest factor for an annuity of $1 per year for 25 years at 10%. The annual payment required is equal to $45,813 ($450,000 ÷ 9.8226).

Answer (A) is incorrect because $18,000 results from allocating the $450,000 equally over 25 years. Answer (C) is incorrect because $45,000 results from multiplying $450,000 by the 10% interest. Answer (D) is incorrect because $50,903 results if the $50,000 down payment is not removed before the annual payment is calculated.

22. Filmore is planning a project that will cost $22,000. The annual cash inflow, net of income taxes, will be $5,000 a year for 7 years. The present value of $1 at 12% is as follows:

Period	Present Value of $1 at 12%
1	.893
2	.797
3	.712
4	.636
5	.567
6	.507
7	.452

Using a rate of return of 12%, what is the present value of the cash flow generated by this project?

A. $22,600

B. $22,820

C. $34,180

D. $35,000

The correct answer is (B). *(CPA 1177 I-23)*

REQUIRED: The present value of the cash flow generated by the project.

DISCUSSION: If the cash inflow, net of taxes, at the end of each of 7 years is $5,000, and if the discount rate is 12%, the present value of this series of cash flows will be equal to the present value of an ordinary annuity of $5,000 for 7 years at 12%. The interest factor for the present value of an ordinary annuity is equal to the sum of the interest factors for the present value of $1 for the same period. The interest factor for an ordinary annuity of $5,000 for seven periods is 4.564. The present value is $22,820 ($5,000 x 4.564).

The alternative is to calculate the present value of each $5,000 cash flow using the interest factor for the present value of $1 at 12% for each of the periods one through seven. The sum of these products is equal to the present value of an ordinary annuity of $5,000 for seven periods at 12%.

$$
\begin{array}{rll}
\$5,000 \times & .893 = & \$ \ 4,465 \\
5,000 \times & .797 = & 3,985 \\
5,000 \times & .712 = & 3,560 \\
5,000 \times & .636 = & 3,180 \\
5,000 \times & .567 = & 2,835 \\
5,000 \times & .507 = & 2,535 \\
5,000 \times & \underline{.452} = & \underline{2,260} \\
5,000 \times & 4.564 = & \underline{\$22,820}
\end{array}
$$

Answers (A), (C), and (D) are incorrect because the present value of the cash flow is equal to the annual inflow times the sum of the present value factors.

23. Based on 8% interest compounded annually from day of deposit to day of withdrawal, what is the present value today of $4,000 to be received 6 years from today?

Periods	Present Value of $1 Discounted at 8% per Period
1	.926
2	.857
3	.794
4	.735
5	.681

A. $4,000 x 0.926 x 6

B. $4,000 x 0.794 x 2

C. $4,000 x 0.681 x 0.926

D. Cannot be determined from the information given.

The correct answer is (C). *(CPA 1174 T-26)*
   REQUIRED: The present value today of $4,000 to be received 6 years from today.
   DISCUSSION: To calculate the present value of an amount to be received 6 years from today when present value factors for only five periods are available, multiply $4,000 by the present value of $1 factor for five periods. This discounts the $4,000 back 5 years. This new product should then be discounted back one additional year, i.e., multiplied by the present value factor for one period.
   Answers (A) and (B) are incorrect because the $4,000 should first be discounted for 5 years; then that amount should be discounted for 1 additional year. Answer (D) is incorrect because the present value can be determined from the information given.

7.2 Future Value

24. Which of the following tables should be used to calculate the amount of the equal periodic payments that would be equivalent to an outlay of $3,000 at the time of the last payment?

A. Amount of $1.

B. Amount of an annuity of $1.

C. Present value of an annuity of $1.

D. Present value of $1.

The correct answer is (B). *(CPA 573 T-33)*
   REQUIRED: The appropriate table to calculate the amount of an equal periodic payment equivalent to an amount in the future.
   DISCUSSION: The question relates to a series of equal periodic payments; i.e., an annuity table is required. The annuity is to be equal to $3,000 at some point in the future. Thus, a FV rather than a PV table is required. The term "amount of an annuity of $1" is synonymous with "future value of an annuity."
   Answers (A), (C), and (D) are incorrect because the future value table for an annuity, or amount of an annuity, should be used.

25. Jarvis wants to invest equal semiannual payments in order to have $10,000 at the end of 20 years. Assuming that Jarvis will earn interest at an annual rate of 6% compounded semiannually, how would the periodic payment be calculated?

A. $10,000 divided by the future amount of an ordinary annuity of 40 payments of $1 each at an interest rate of 3% per period.

B. $10,000 divided by the present value of an ordinary annuity of 40 payments of $1 each at an interest rate of 3% per period.

C. The future amount of an ordinary annuity of 20 payments of $1 each at an interest rate of 6% per period divided into $10,000.

D. The present value of an ordinary annuity of 40 payments of $1 each at an interest rate of 3% per period divided by $10,000.

The correct answer is (A). *(CPA 577 I-34)*
   REQUIRED: The method of calculating the periodic payment to accumulate a known future amount.
   DISCUSSION: The question involves future value because it requires computation of the periodic amount of an annuity that must be invested to produce a given future amount. Accordingly, the appropriate factor reflecting the compound interest effect will be derived from the formula for the future value of an ordinary annuity of $1. This factor multiplied by the periodic payment is equal to the desired future value. If the payment is unknown, it may be calculated by dividing the known future amount ($10,000) by the appropriate factor derived from the future amount of an ordinary annuity formula. If the payments are to be made semiannually for 20 years, 40 compounding periods are involved. If the interest rate is 6% per annum, the semiannual interest rate is 3%.
   Answers (B) and (D) are incorrect because the question calls for a future value computation. Answer (C) is incorrect because 40 semiannual payments are to be made at an interest rate of 3% per period (not 20 payments at 6%).

26. Which of the following tables would show the largest value for an interest rate of 5% for six periods?

   A. Amount of $1 at compound interest.

   B. Present value of $1 at compound interest.

   C. Amount of annuity of $1 per period.

   D. Present value of annuity of $1 per period.

The correct answer is (C). *(CPA 574 T-13)*
   REQUIRED: The table that would show the largest value for an interest rate of 5% for six periods.
   DISCUSSION: The amount of an annuity of $1 per period would show the largest value. The value would be in excess of six, reflecting the sum of six individual payments of $1 plus compound interest earned.
   Answer (A) is incorrect because the table for the amount of $1 at compound interest would reflect only a value of $1 plus the interest earned over the six periods at 5%. With interest, the amount would be less than two. Answer (B) is incorrect because the value would be less than $1. Answer (D) is incorrect because it would be less than six since the payments would be discounted at 5%.

27. On March 15, 1996, Ashe Corp. adopted a plan to accumulate $1,000,000 by September 1, 2000. Ashe plans to make four equal annual deposits to a fund that will earn interest at 10% compounded annually. Ashe made the first deposit on September 1, 1996. Future value and future amount factors are as follows:

Future value of $1 at 10% for four periods   1.46

Future amount of ordinary annuity of $1 at
  10% for four periods   4.64

Future amount of annuity in advance of $1 at
  10% for four periods   5.11

Ashe should make four annual deposits (rounded) of

   A. $250,000

   B. $215,500

   C. $195,700

   D. $146,000

The correct answer is (C). *(CPA 1191 I-9)*
   REQUIRED: The amount of an annuity in advance that would generate a future sum.
   DISCUSSION: Ashe Corp. wishes to have $1,000,000 at the end of a 4-year period (9/1/96 to 9/1/00). The amount will be generated from four equal annual payments (an annuity) to be made starting at the beginning of the 4-year period. The annual payment for this annuity in advance is obtained by dividing the desired future amount of $1,000,000 by the factor for the future amount of an annuity in advance of $1 at 10% for four periods. Each annual deposit should therefore equal $195,700 ($1,000,000 ÷ 5.11).
   Answers (A), (B), and (D) are incorrect because the factor for the future amount of an annuity in advance of $1 at 10% for four periods should be divided into the future amount needed to determine the amount of each deposit.

28. An individual is to receive $137,350 in 4 years. Using the correct factor, determine the current investment if interest of 10% is assumed.

Periods	FVIF	PVIF	FVIFA	PVIFA
1	1.1000	.9091	1.0000	.9091
2	1.2100	.8264	2.1000	1.7355
3	1.3310	.7513	3.2781	2.4869
4	1.4641	.6830	4.5731	3.1699
5	1.6105	.6029	5.9847	3.7908

   A. $30,034.33

   B. $43,329.44

   C. $93,810.05

   D. $201,094.14

The correct answer is (C). *(CIA 1190 III-44)*
   REQUIRED: The current investment required to receive a future amount of money at a given interest rate.
   DISCUSSION: The current investment is the present value of the given future amount. It equals the future amount multiplied by the factor for the present value of $1 for four periods at 10%. Accordingly, the current investment is $93,810.05 ($137,350 x .6830).
   Answers (A), (B), and (D) are incorrect because the PVIF for four periods should be used.

29. A pension fund is projecting the amount necessary today to fund a retiree's pension benefits. The retiree's first annual pension check will be in 10 years. Payments are expected to last for a total of 20 annual payments. Which of the following best describes the computation of the amount needed today to fund the retiree's annuity?

A. Present value of $1 for 10 periods, times the present value of an ordinary annuity of 20 payments, times the annual annuity payment.

B. Present value of $1 for nine periods, times the present value of an ordinary annuity of 20 payments, times the annual annuity payment.

C. Future value of $1 for 10 periods, times the present value of an ordinary annuity of 20 payments, times the annual annuity payment.

D. Future value of $1 for nine periods, times the present value of an ordinary annuity of 20 payments, times the annual annuity payment.

The correct answer is (B). *(CIA 1193 IV-40)*
REQUIRED: The formula to compute the amount needed today to fund a pension that will begin in the future.
DISCUSSION: Multiplying the annual annuity pension payment times the present value of an ordinary annuity of 20 payments factor results in a present value determination 1 year prior to the start of the payments, or 9 years hence. Multiplying the present value of ordinary annuity pension payments by a present value of $1 factor for 9 years results in the amount needed today to fund the retiree's annuity.
Answers (A), (C), and (D) are incorrect because the present value factor for nine periods should be used to determine the amount needed to fund the pension plan.

30. An actuary has determined that a company should have $90,000,000 accumulated in its pension fund 20 years from now in order for the fund to be able to meet its obligations. An interest rate of 8% is considered appropriate for all pension fund calculations involving an interest component. The company wishes to calculate how much it should contribute to the pension fund at the end of each of the next 20 years in order for the pension fund to have its required balance in 20 years. Assume you are given the following two factors from present value and future value tables:

1) Factor for present value of an ordinary annuity for n=20, i=8%
2) Factor for future value of an ordinary annuity for n=20, i=8%

Which of the following sets of instructions correctly describes the procedures necessary to compute the annual amount the company should contribute to the fund?

A. Divide $90,000,000 by the factor for present value of an ordinary annuity for n=20, i=8%.

B. Multiply $90,000,000 by the factor for present value of an ordinary annuity for n=20, i=8%.

C. Divide $90,000,000 by the factor for future value of an ordinary annuity for n=20, i=8%.

D. Multiply $90,000,000 by the factor for future value of an ordinary annuity for n=20, i=8%.

The correct answer is (C). *(CIA 1192 IV-39)*
REQUIRED: The set of instructions that correctly describes the procedures necessary to compute the annual amount the company should contribute to the fund.
DISCUSSION: The future value of an annuity equals the appropriate interest factor (for n periods at an interest rate of i), which is derived from standard tables, times the periodic payment. The $90,000,000 amount is the future value of the funding payments. The amount of each funding payment can be calculated by dividing the future value of the funding payments by the interest factor for future value of an ordinary annuity for n equals 20 and i equals 8%.
Answer (A) is incorrect because the $90,000,000 is a future value figure. The interest factor to be used for the division process should be a future value factor, not a present value factor. Answer (B) is incorrect because the $90,000,000 is a future value figure. The factor to be used should be a future value factor. That factor should be used in a division, rather than a multiplication, process. Answer (D) is incorrect because the $90,000,000 should be divided by the appropriate interest factor.

31. A loan is to be repaid in eight annual installments of $1,875. The interest rate is 10%. The
present value of an ordinary annuity for eight periods
at 10% is 5.33. Identify the computation that approximates the outstanding loan balance at the end of the
first year.

A. $1,875 x 5.33 = $9,994

B. $1,875 x 5.33 = $9,994;
   $9,994 – $1,875 = $8,119

C. $1,875 x 5.33 = $9,994;
   $1,875 – $999 = $876;
   $9,994 – $876 = $9,118

D. $1,875 x 8 = $15,000;
   $15,000 – ($1,875 – $1,500) = $14,625

The correct answer is (C). *(CIA 582 IV-6)*
   REQUIRED: The computation approximating the
outstanding loan balance at the end of year one.
   DISCUSSION: If the present value of an ordinary annuity
of $1 for eight periods at 10% is 5.33, then the present value
for $1,875 is $9,994 (5.33 x $1,875). This figure is the original
amount of the loan. If the interest rate is 10%, the interest on
the principal for year one will be approximately $999.
Accordingly, the first installment will have an interest
component of $999 and a principal component of $876
($1,875 – $999 interest). The first payment will therefore
reduce the principal balance of $9,994 by $876 to $9,118.
   Answer (A) is incorrect because it gives the present value
of the annuity, not the loan balance at the end of year one.
Answer (B) is incorrect because it improperly deducts both
principal and interest for year one in arriving at the principal
balance. Answer (D) is incorrect because it does not take
into account the time value of money.

Questions 32 and 33 are based on the following
information. Present value, amount of $1, and
ordinary annuity information are presented in the
next column. All values are for four periods with
an interest rate of 8%.

Amount of $1	1.36
Present value of $1	0.74
Amount of an ordinary annuity of $1	4.51
Present value of an ordinary annuity of $1	3.31

---

32. Jim Green decides to create a fund to earn 8%
compounded annually that will enable him to withdraw $5,000 per year each June 30, beginning in
2001 and continuing through 2004. Jim wishes to
make equal contributions on June 30 of each of the
years 1997 through 2000. Which equation would be
used to compute the balance which must be in the
fund on June 30, 2000 for Jim to satisfy his
objective?

A. $X = $5,000 x 3.31

B. $X = $5,000 x (3.31 + 1.00)

C. $X = $5,000 x 1.36

D. $X = $5,000 x 4.51

The correct answer is (A). *(CIA 582 IV-4)*
   REQUIRED: The equation to compute the balance in the
fund on 6/30/00 to permit withdrawals of $5,000 on each
June 30 for the next 4 years.
   DISCUSSION: The fund balance on 6/30/00 should be
equal to the present value of four equal annual payments of
$5,000 each discounted at a rate of 8%. If the factor for the
present value of an ordinary annuity of $1 for four periods at
8% is 3.31, the present value of an ordinary annuity of $5,000
for four periods discounted at 8% is $5,000 x 3.31.
   Answer (B) is incorrect because it gives the present value
of an annuity due for five periods. Answer (C) is incorrect
because it gives the future value in four periods of $5,000
invested today. Answer (D) is incorrect because it is the
future value of an annuity of four annual deposits of $5,000.

33. Jones wants to accumulate $50,000 by making
equal contributions at the end of each of 4 succeeding years. Which equation would be used to
compute Jones's annual contribution to achieve the
$50,000 goal at the end of the fourth year?

A. $X = $50,000 ÷ 4.51

B. $X = $50,000 ÷ 4.00

C. $X = $12,500 ÷ 1.36

D. $X = $50,000 ÷ 3.31

The correct answer is (A). *(CIA 582 IV-5)*
   REQUIRED: The equation to compute the annual year-
end payment necessary to accumulate $50,000 at the end of
4 years.
   DISCUSSION: Use the factor for the amount of an
ordinary annuity of $1 for four periods at 8% (4.51). If an
investment of $1 at 8% at the end of each of four periods
would generate a future amount of 4.51, an investment of $X
per period for four periods at 8% would generate the
necessary $50,000. The required annual payment is equal to
$50,000 ÷ 4.51.
   Answer (B) is incorrect because it does not take into
account interest to be earned. Answer (C) is incorrect
because it gives the present value of $12,500 to be received
four periods hence. Answer (D) is incorrect because it gives
the amount of the periodic payment needed to produce an
ordinary annuity with a present value of $50,000.

CHAPTER EIGHT
CURRENT ASSETS, CASH, ACCOUNTS RECEIVABLE, AND SHORT-TERM NOTES RECEIVABLE

This chapter covers current assets and working capital. It also covers cash, accounts receivable, and short-term notes receivable -- assets included in current assets and working capital. Other assets included in current assets and working capital, such as inventory and short-term investments, are covered in other chapters -- inventory in Chapter 9, Inventory, and short-term investments in Chapter 13, Investments in Debt and Equity Securities.

8.1 Current Assets

1. On Merf's April 30, 1996 balance sheet, a note receivable was reported as a noncurrent asset, and its accrued interest for 8 months was reported as a current asset. Which of the following terms would fit Merf's note receivable?

A. Both principal and interest amounts are payable on August 31, 1996 and 1997.

B. Principal and interest are due December 31, 1996.

C. Both principal and interest amounts are payable on December 31, 1996 and 1997.

D. Principal is due August 31, 1997, and interest is due August 31, 1996 and 1997.

The correct answer is (D). (CPA 593 T-24)
REQUIRED: The terms explaining classification of a note receivable as a noncurrent asset and its accrued interest as a current asset.
DISCUSSION: A noncurrent note receivable is not expected to be converted into cash within 1 year or one operating cycle, whichever is longer. Because the principal is due more than 1 year from the balance sheet date, it must be regarded as noncurrent. However, the accrued interest is a current asset because it is due in 4 months.
Answers (A), (B), and (C) are incorrect because principal amounts due in less than 1 year are current assets.

2. Brown Company is a leading producer of finely cured korapte. From the time the korapte seeds are planted until the crop is cured and sold, a period of 3 years will have passed. The basis for the segregation of current assets will be

A. Assets that may be immediately realized.

B. Assets that may be realized in cash within 1 year.

C. Assets that are directly used in the seeding and curing of korapte.

D. Assets that are realized in cash, sold, or consumed during the 3-year period from seeding to sale of the crop.

The correct answer is (D). (Publisher)
REQUIRED: The proper basis for classifying assets as current.
DISCUSSION: ARB 43, Chapter 3A, Current Assets and Current Liabilities, defines current assets as those reasonably expected to be realized in cash, sold, or consumed during the operating cycle of the business or within 1 year, whichever is longer. The operating cycle is the time between the acquisition of materials or services and the final cash realization from the earning process. Brown's operating cycle is 3 years, and the assets realized in cash, sold, or consumed during the 3-year period should be categorized as current.
Answers (A) and (B) are incorrect because neither is based on the appropriate time period: the longer of 1 year or the operating cycle. Answer (C) is incorrect because the 1-year or operating-cycle rule applies to all assets of the enterprise.

3. At October 31, 1996, Dingo, Inc. had cash accounts at three different banks. One account balance is segregated solely for a November 15, 1996 payment into a bond sinking fund. A second account, used for branch operations, is overdrawn. The third account, used for regular corporate operations, has a positive balance. How should these accounts be reported in Dingo's October 31, 1996 classified balance sheet?

A.   The segregated account should be reported as a noncurrent asset, the regular account should be reported as a current asset, and the overdraft should be reported as a current liability.

B.   The segregated and regular accounts should be reported as current assets, and the overdraft should be reported as a current liability.

C.   The segregated account should be reported as a noncurrent asset, and the regular account should be reported as a current asset net of the overdraft.

D.   The segregated and regular accounts should be reported as current assets net of the overdraft.

4. The following is Gold Corp.'s June 30, 1996 trial balance:

Cash overdraft		$ 10,000
Accounts receivable, net	$ 35,000	
Inventory	58,000	
Prepaid expenses	12,000	
Land held for resale	100,000	
Property, plant, and equipment, net	95,000	
Accounts payable and accrued expenses		32,000
Common stock		25,000
Additional paid-in capital		150,000
Retained earnings		83,000
	$300,000	$300,000

Additional information:

• Checks amounting to $30,000 were written to vendors and recorded on June 29, 1996, resulting in a cash overdraft of $10,000. The checks were mailed on July 9, 1996.

• Land held for resale was sold for cash on July 15, 1996.

• Gold issued its financial statements on July 31, 1996.

In its June 30, 1996 balance sheet, what amount should Gold report as current assets?

A. $225,000

B. $205,000

C. $195,000

D. $125,000

The correct answer is (A). *(CPA 1192 T-13)*
REQUIRED: The proper reporting of three cash accounts.
DISCUSSION: Current assets include cash available for current operations and items that are the equivalent of cash. Hence, the account used for regular operations is current. Cash that is restricted to use for other than current operations, designated for the acquisition or construction of noncurrent assets, or segregated for the liquidation of long-term debts is noncurrent. "Even though not actually set aside in special accounts, funds that are clearly to be used in the near future for the liquidation of long-term debts, payments to sinking funds, or for other similar purposes should also, under this concept, be excluded from current assets" (ARB 43, Chapter 3A). The overdraft should be treated as a current liability and not netted against the other cash balances. If the company had another account in the same bank with a positive balance, netting would be appropriate because the bank would have a right of offset.
   Answers (B) and (D) are incorrect because the segregated account is noncurrent. Answers (C) and (D) are incorrect because the overdraft should not be netted.

The correct answer is (A). *(CPA 593 I-1)*
REQUIRED: The amount reported for current assets on the balance sheet.
DISCUSSION: Current assets include cash, inventory, receivables, trading securities, certain held-to-maturity and available-for-sale securities, and prepaid expenses, such as insurance, interest, rent, and taxes that are reasonably expected to be realized in cash, sold, or consumed within 1 year, or the normal operating cycle of the business, whichever is longer. Thus, Gold's current assets include $20,000 of cash ($30,000 of checks mailed in the next period but prematurely recorded – $10,000 overdraft), net accounts receivable ($35,000), inventory ($58,000), prepaid expenses ($12,000), and the land held for resale (treated as a current asset because it was held for immediate sale). The total is $225,000.
   Answer (B) is incorrect because $205,000 does not include the $20,000 in cash. Answer (C) is incorrect because $195,000 reflects the $30,000 of checks not mailed at 6/30/96. Answer (D) is incorrect because $125,000 does not include the land held for resale, which was realized in cash after the balance sheet date.

Question 5 is based on the following information. The following trial balance of Trey Co. at December 31, 1996 has been adjusted except for income tax expense.

	Dr.	Cr.
Cash	$ 550,000	
Accounts receivable, net	1,650,000	
Prepaid taxes	300,000	
Accounts payable		$ 120,000
Common stock		500,000
Additional paid-in capital		680,000
Retained earnings		630,000
Foreign currency translation adjustment	430,000	
Revenues		3,600,000
Expenses	2,600,000	
	$5,530,000	$5,530,000

Additional Information

• During 1996, estimated tax payments of $300,000 were charged to prepaid taxes. Trey has not yet recorded income tax expense. There were no differences between financial statement and income tax income, and Trey's tax rate is 30%.

• Included in accounts receivable is $500,000 due from a customer. Special terms granted to this customer require payment in equal semiannual installments of $125,000 every April 1 and October 1.

5. In Trey's December 31, 1996 balance sheet, what amount should be reported as total current assets?

A. $1,950,000

B. $2,200,000

C. $2,250,000

D. $2,500,000

The correct answer is (A). *(CPA 1194 F-8)*

REQUIRED: The total current assets.

DISCUSSION: Trey's current assets include cash, accounts receivable, and prepaid taxes. However, income tax expense is $300,000 [30% x ($3,600,000 revenues – $2,600,000 expenses)]. After recording income tax expense, prepaid taxes equal $0. In addition, $250,000 of the receivables is due in 1998 and therefore is noncurrent. Thus, total current assets equal $1,950,000 [$550,000 cash + ($1,650,000 – $250,000 noncurrent A/R)].

Answer (B) is incorrect because $2,200,000 includes the noncurrent accounts receivable. Answer (C) is incorrect because $2,250,000 includes $300,000 of prepaid taxes. Answer (D) is incorrect because $2,500,000 includes $300,000 of prepaid taxes and the noncurrent accounts receivable.

8.2 Working Capital

6. A characteristic of all assets and liabilities included in working capital is that they are

A. Cash equivalents.

B. Current.

C. Monetary.

D. Marketable.

The correct answer is (B). *(CPA 1180 T-4)*

REQUIRED: The characteristic of all assets and liabilities included in working capital.

DISCUSSION: Working capital is defined by ARB 43, Chapter 3A, as the excess of current assets over current liabilities. Working capital identifies the relatively liquid portion of the capital of the enterprise available for meeting obligations within the operating cycle of the firm.

Answers (A), (C), and (D) are incorrect because, whereas assets and liabilities may be any combination of monetary, marketable, or cash equivalents in addition to cash, they must be current to be part of working capital.

7. Current liabilities are best defined as those obligations

A. The liquidation of which will require the use of resources properly classifiable as current assets within the next operating cycle or 1 year, whichever is longer.

B. The liquidation of which will require the use of cash or increase current liabilities within the next operating cycle or 1 year, whichever is longer.

C. The liquidation of which is reasonably expected to require the use of current assets or the creation of other current liabilities within the next operating cycle or 1 year, whichever is longer.

D. Involving commitments made within the next operating cycle or 1 year, whichever is longer.

The correct answer is (C). *(Publisher)*
REQUIRED: The correct description of current liabilities.
DISCUSSION: ARB 43, Chapter 3A, defines current liabilities as obligations the liquidation of which is reasonably expected to require the use of existing resources properly classifiable as current assets or the creation of other current liabilities during the next operating cycle or year, whichever is longer. SFAS 78, *Classification of Obligations That Are Callable by the Creditor*, amends ARB 43 to include as current liabilities (1) obligations that by their terms are or will be due on demand within 1 year (or the operating cycle, if longer) and (2) obligations that are or will be callable by the creditor because of a violation of a debt covenant at the balance sheet date.

Answer (A) is incorrect because liabilities are also current if their liquidation requires creation of other current liabilities. Answer (B) is incorrect because liabilities are current if they are settled with any current assets, not just cash. Answer (D) is incorrect because commitments made during the longer of the next year or the operating cycle may not even be liabilities at the balance sheet date.

8. Which of the following items enter into the determination of working capital?

A. Inventory of finished products that as of the balance sheet date has been held by a manufacturer for 1 year of a 3-year aging cycle.

B. Cash value of life insurance policies pledged as collateral against 90-day bank notes.

C. Cash held by an investment banker to be used to acquire in the open market an additional 25% of a 55%-owned subsidiary.

D. U.S. Treasury bills maturing 60 days after the balance sheet date, the proceeds of which, by direction of the board of directors, will be used to retire long-term debts.

The correct answer is (A). *(Publisher)*
REQUIRED: The item that is considered part of working capital.
DISCUSSION: Working capital is the excess of current assets over current liabilities. An asset is current if it is reasonably expected to be realized in cash, sold, or consumed during the longer of 1 year or the normal operating cycle of the business. The operating cycle is the average time elapsing between the acquisition of materials or services entering into the earning process and the final cash realization. If a manufacturer's inventory must undergo a 3-year aging process before it can be sold, the inventory must be classified as a current asset because it will be sold during the operating cycle.

Answer (B) is incorrect because the cash surrender value of life insurance policies is a long-term investment. Answers (C) and (D) are incorrect because cash and Treasury bills are not current assets if they are restricted to purchase noncurrent assets or pay long-term debts.

9. The following transactions occurred during a company's first year of operations:

I. Purchased a delivery van for cash
II. Borrowed money by issuance of short-term debt
III. Purchased treasury stock

Which of the items above caused a change in the amount of working capital?

A. I only.

B. II and III only.

C. I and III only.

D. I, II, and III.

The correct answer is (C). *(CIA 593 IV-28)*
REQUIRED: The items that caused a change in the amount of working capital.
DISCUSSION: Working capital is computed by deducting total current liabilities from total current assets. The purchase of a delivery van for cash reduces current assets and has no effect on current liabilities. The borrowing of cash by incurring short-term debt increases current assets by the same amount as it increases current liabilities; hence, it will have no effect on working capital. The purchase of treasury stock decreases current assets but has no effect on current liabilities. Thus, the purchases of the van and treasury stock affect working capital.

Answers (A), (B), and (D) are incorrect because the purchases of the van and treasury stock but not the issuance of short-term debt affect working capital.

10. A service company's working capital at the beginning of January 1996 was $70,000. The following transactions occurred during January:

Performed services on account	$30,000
Purchased supplies on account	5,000
Consumed supplies	4,000
Purchased office equipment for cash	2,000
Paid short-term bank loan	6,500
Paid salaries	10,000
Accrued salaries	3,500

What is the amount of working capital at the end of January?

A. $80,500

B. $78,500

C. $50,500

D. $47,500

The correct answer is (A). *(CIA 1193 IV-36)*

REQUIRED: The amount of working capital.

DISCUSSION: Working capital is the excess of total current assets (CA) over total current liabilities (CL). Thus, working capital at the end of January equals $80,500 computed as follows:

		CA*	CL*
Beginning working capital	$70,000		
Performed services on account	30,000	I	N
Purchased supplies on account	-0-	I	I
Consumed supplies	(4,000)	D	N
Purchased office equipment	(2,000)	D	N
Paid short-term bank loan	-0-	D	D
Paid salaries	(10,000)	D	N
Accrued salaries	(3,500)	N	I
Working capital, end of January	$80,500		

* N = no effect; I = increase; D = decrease

Answer (B) is incorrect because $78,500 does not include the consumed supplies, the cash purchase of office equipment, and the accrued salaries, and includes the supplies purchased on account and the repayment of the short-term bank loan. Answer (C) is incorrect because $50,500 does not include the services performed on account. Answer (D) is incorrect because $47,500 does not include the services performed on account and accrued salaries and includes the repayment of short-term loan.

11. Comparative balance sheets for a company are presented below:

Assets	12/31/96	12/31/95
Cash	$ 35,000	$ 30,000
Accounts receivable	80,000	75,000
Inventory	230,000	240,000
Equipment	620,000	600,000
Accumulated depreciation	(220,000)	(200,000)
Intangibles	150,000	140,000
Total assets	$895,000	$885,000
Liabilities and equity		
Accounts payable	$ 50,000	$ 60,000
Taxes payable	30,000	25,000
Salaries payable	55,000	70,000
Bonds payable (due 1999)	400,000	400,000
Discount on bonds payable	(4,000)	(5,000)
Common stock	270,000	250,000
Retained earnings	94,000	85,000
Total liabilities and equity	$895,000	$885,000

What is the increase in working capital for the year ended December 31, 1996?

A. $5,000

B. $10,000

C. $20,000

D. $29,000

The correct answer is (C). *(CIA 589 IV-28)*

REQUIRED: The increase in working capital for the current year.

DISCUSSION: Working capital is the excess of current assets over current liabilities. The change in working capital is equal to the aggregate change in those accounts classified as current assets and current liabilities. Increases in current assets and decreases in current liabilities increase (are sources of) working capital. Decreases in current assets and increases in current liabilities decrease (are uses of) working capital. The change in working capital for the year is presented below:

Working Capital Accounts	Increase (Decrease)
Cash	$ 5,000
Accounts receivable	5,000
Inventory	(10,000)
Accounts payable	10,000
Taxes payable	(5,000)
Salaries payable	15,000
Increase in working capital	$20,000

Answer (A) is incorrect because $5,000 does not include the change in salaries payable. Answer (B) is incorrect because $10,000 is the increase in total assets. Answer (D) is incorrect because $29,000 is the increase in working capital plus the increase in retained earnings.

12. Bal Corp. declared a $25,000 cash dividend on May 8, 1996 to shareholders of record on May 23, 1996, payable on June 3, 1996. As a result of this cash dividend, working capital

A. Was not affected.

B. Decreased on June 3.

C. Decreased on May 23.

D. Decreased on May 8.

The correct answer is (D). *(CPA 592 II-3)*
REQUIRED: The effect of a cash dividend on working capital.
DISCUSSION: On May 8, the date of declaration, retained earnings is debited and dividends payable credited. The declaration decreases working capital because a current liability is increased.
Answer (A) is incorrect because working capital was decreased on May 8. Answer (B) is incorrect because, when payment is made, both a current liability (dividends payable) and a current asset (cash) are decreased, which has no net effect on working capital. Answer (C) is incorrect because no entry is made on the record date.

8.3 Cash

13. Microchip Corp. has supplied you with the following list of its bank accounts and cash at December 31:

Checking account (compensating balance of $10,000 with no restriction)	$ 32,000
Savings account, 5.25%	20,000
Certificate of deposit, 6 months, 10%	40,000
Money market (30-day certificate), current rate, 9.25%	25,000
Payroll checking account	2,000
Certificate of deposit, 2 years, 12%	50,000
Petty cash	1,000
	$170,000

The amount reported as "cash on hand" as of December 31 should be

A. $55,000

B. $170,000

C. $95,000

D. $75,000

The correct answer is (A). *(C. Garfinkle)*
REQUIRED: The amount of cash on hand at year-end.
DISCUSSION: The cash account on the balance sheet should include coin and currency on hand, deposits in checking and savings accounts, and near-cash assets such as undeposited checks. To be classified as cash, an asset must be readily available for use by the business; i.e., its use should not be restricted. The money market account and the certificates of deposit are not considered readily available and should be classified as investments. The cash on hand thus equals $55,000 ($32,000 checking + $20,000 savings + $2,000 payroll + $1,000 petty cash). The $10,000 compensating balance is unrestricted and available.
Answer (B) is incorrect because $170,000 includes the money market account and certificates of deposit. Answer (C) is incorrect because $95,000 includes the 6-month certificate of deposit. Answer (D) is incorrect because $75,000 is the sum of the money market account and the 2-year certificate of deposit.

14. The objective of a petty cash system is to

A. Facilitate office payment of small, miscellaneous items.

B. Cash checks for employees.

C. Account for cash sales.

D. Account for all cash receipts and disbursements.

The correct answer is (A). *(Publisher)*
REQUIRED: The objective of a petty cash system.
DISCUSSION: In an imprest petty cash system, a specific amount of money, e.g., $100, is set aside in the care of a petty cash custodian to pay office expenses that are too small to pay by check or to record in the accounting system as they occur. The entry is to debit petty cash and to credit cash. Periodically, the fund is reimbursed for all expenditures based on expense receipts, and journal entries are made to reflect the transactions. However, entries are made to the petty cash account only to establish the fund, to change its amount, or to adjust the balance if it has not been reimbursed at year-end.
Answer (B) is incorrect because, if necessary, a separate check cashing fund should be established with daily bank deposits of checks cashed. Answers (C) and (D) are incorrect because petty cash systems are for cash disbursements, not cash receipts.

15. On January 1, a company establishes a petty cash account and designates one employee as petty cash custodian. The original amount included in the petty cash fund is $500, and it will be used to make small cash disbursements. The fund will be replenished on the first of each month, after the petty cash custodian presents receipts for disbursements to the general cashier. The following disbursements are made in January:

Office supplies	$173
Postage	112
Entertainment	42

The balance in the petty cash box at the end of January is $163.

The entry required at the end of January is

A.
Office supplies expense	$173	
Postage expense	112	
Entertainment expense	42	
Cash		$327

B.
Office supplies expense	$173	
Postage expense	112	
Entertainment expense	42	
Petty cash		$327

C.
Office supplies expense	$173	
Postage expense	112	
Entertainment expense	42	
Cash over and short	10	
Cash		$337

D.
Office supplies expense	$173	
Postage expense	112	
Entertainment expense	42	
Cash		$317
Cash over and short		10

The correct answer is (C). *(CIA 594 IV-10)*
REQUIRED: The entry for petty cash fund disbursements.
DISCUSSION: Each expense item is recognized, cash is credited for the total expenditures plus the cash shortage ($173 + $112 + $42 + $10 = $337), and the discrepancy is debited to the cash over and short account. The discrepancy is the original balance of the fund, minus total documented expenditures, minus the ending balance of the fund ($500 – $327 – $163 = $10).
Answer (A) is incorrect because this entry does not recognize that $10 is missing from the petty cash fund. Answer (B) is incorrect because this entry credits petty cash rather than cash and does not recognize that $10 is missing from the petty cash fund. Answer (D) is incorrect because this entry credits the cash account for the wrong amount ($317 rather than $337) and credits the cash over and short account rather than debiting it.

16. Usually, if the petty cash fund is not reimbursed just prior to year-end and an appropriate adjusting entry is not made,

A. A complete audit is necessary.

B. The petty cash account should be returned to the company cashier.

C. Expenses will be overstated and cash will be understated.

D. Cash will be overstated and expenses understated.

The correct answer is (D). *(Publisher)*
REQUIRED: The effect of not reimbursing the petty cash fund prior to year-end and not making the appropriate adjusting entry.
DISCUSSION: When the petty cash fund is established, petty cash is debited and cash credited. As monies are expended, expense receipts are obtained. The petty cash fund consists of the cash and expense receipts. Upon reimbursement of the petty cash fund, the various expenses are debited and cash is credited.
If the petty cash fund is not reimbursed at year-end and an adjusting entry debiting expenses and crediting cash is not made, the cash account will be overstated and expenses understated because petty cash is a component of the cash account.
Answer (A) is incorrect because complete audits are usually undertaken only if fraud is suspected. Petty cash is ordinarily not material. Answer (B) is incorrect because the petty cash cannot be returned to the cashier. At least some of the cash will usually have been expended. Answer (C) is incorrect because expenses will be understated and cash overstated.

17. Davis Corporation had the following transactions in its first year of operations:

Sales (90% collected in first year)	$1,500,000
Bad debt write-offs	60,000
Disbursements for costs and expenses	1,200,000
Disbursements for income taxes	90,000
Purchases of fixed assets	400,000
Depreciation on fixed assets	80,000
Proceeds from issuance of common stock	500,000
Proceeds from short-term borrowings	100,000
Payments on short-term borrowings	50,000

What is the cash balance at December 31 of the first year?

A. $150,000

B. $170,000

C. $210,000

D. $280,000

The correct answer is (C). *(CPA 577 I-22)*
REQUIRED: The cash balance at year-end.
DISCUSSION: The cash balance may be determined by setting up a T-account and appropriately debiting or crediting the account for each of the transactions listed. The beginning balance is $0 for the first year of operations. The sales collections give rise to a debit of $1,350,000 (.9 x $1,500,000). The bad debt write-offs and depreciation on fixed assets are not cash transactions. The disbursements for costs and expenses, taxes, fixed assets, and debt service are all credits. The proceeds from stock and short-term borrowings are debits. At December 31, therefore, the account has a debit balance of $210,000.

Cash (in 000's)			
Sales	$1,350	Disburse.	$1,200
Stock	500	Taxes	90
Loan	100	FA	400
		Loan	50
	$ 210		

Answer (A) is incorrect because $150,000 results from a credit to the cash account for the bad debt write-offs. Answer (B) is incorrect because $170,000 results from a debit to cash for 100% (instead of 90%) of sales and credits bad debt and depreciation but not the loan payment. Answer (D) is incorrect because $280,000 incorrectly debits cash for 100% of sales for the year and credits cash for depreciation on fixed assets.

18. Bank reconciliations are usually prepared on a monthly basis upon receipt of the bank statement to identify either bank errors or items that need to be adjusted on the depositor's books. The adjustments should be made for

A. Deposits in transit and outstanding checks.

B. All items except deposits in transit, outstanding checks, and bank errors.

C. Deposits in transit, outstanding checks, and bank errors.

D. All items except bank errors, NSF checks, outstanding checks, and deposits in transit.

The correct answer is (B). *(Publisher)*
REQUIRED: The adjustments made as a result of a bank reconciliation.
DISCUSSION: Deposits in transit and outstanding checks are reconciling items that have no effect on the correctness of either the depositor's or the bank's accounting records. They reflect a timing difference between the two sets of books as to when cash receipts and disbursements are recognized. Thus, they require no adjustment by the bank or the depositor. Bank errors must be corrected by the bank, not the depositor. All other items must be adjusted on the depositor's books.
Answers (A) and (C) are incorrect because deposits in transit and outstanding checks do not require adjustment on either the bank's or depositor's books. Answer (D) is incorrect because NSF checks require a debit to a receivable and a credit to cash on the depositor's books.

19. A proof of cash, also known as a four-column bank reconciliation, is

A. A reconciliation of beginning balances, deposits-receipts, checks-disbursements, and ending balances.

B. Bank reconciliations for four selected periods.

C. Reconciliation of beginning balances, receipts, and disbursements, usually for 1 month.

D. Reconciliation of the beginning account balance and the ending account balance, taking into account deposits in transit, outstanding checks, and other reconciling items.

The correct answer is (A). *(Publisher)*
REQUIRED: The description of a proof of cash.
DISCUSSION: The proof of cash adds a time dimension to a bank reconciliation. Instead of reconciling a balance per bank and a balance per depositor at a given date, the proof of cash reconciles the beginning balance, receipts, disbursements, and the ending balance for a period according to the bank statement with the respective amounts according to the books. The proof of cash actually includes four reconciliations.
Answer (B) is incorrect because a proof of cash contains only two bank reconciliations (for the beginning and ending balances). Answer (C) is incorrect because the ending balance is also reconciled. Answer (D) is incorrect because it describes a bank reconciliation.

20. The following information is shown in the accounting records of a company:

<u>Balances as of January 1, 19X6</u>

Cash	$62,000
Merchandise inventory	86,000
Accounts receivable	67,000
Accounts payable	53,000

<u>Balances as of December 31, 19X6</u>

Merchandise inventory	$78,000
Accounts receivable	91,000
Accounts payable	48,000

Total sales and cost of goods sold for 19X6 were $798,000 and $583,000, respectively. All sales and all merchandise purchases were made on credit. Various operating expenses of $107,000 were paid in cash. Assume that there were no other pertinent transactions. The cash balance on December 31, 19X6 would be

A. $108,000

B. $149,000

C. $256,000

D. $305,000

The correct answer is (B). *(CIA 587 IV-12)*

REQUIRED: The cash balance at year-end.

DISCUSSION: Cash collected from customers equals $774,000 ($798,000 credit sales – $24,000 increase in A/R). The amount of purchases is $575,000 ($583,000 CGS – $8,000 decrease in inventory). Disbursements to suppliers totaled $580,000 ($575,000 Pur. + $5,000 decrease in A/P). The cash collected is added to the beginning balance in the cash account. The disbursements to suppliers and for operating expenses are subtracted to arrive at an ending cash balance of $149,000.

Accounts Receivable			
	$ 67,000		
Sales	798,000	Collections	$774,000
	<u>$ 91,000</u>		

Merchandise Inventory			
	$ 86,000		
Purchases	575,000	CGS	$583,000
	<u>$ 78,000</u>		

Accounts Payable			
			$ 53,000
Disburse.	$580,000	Purchases	575,000
			<u>$ 48,000</u>

Cash			
	$ 62,000		
Collections	774,000	Disburse.	$580,000
		Disburse.	107,000
	<u>$149,000</u>		

Answer (A) is incorrect because $108,000 is the excess of total sales over cost of goods sold and operating expenses. Answer (C) is incorrect because $256,000 does not include a credit to cash for the operating expenses. Answer (D) is incorrect because $305,000 appears to be a random number.

21. George Company maintains two checking accounts. A special account is used for the weekly payroll only, and the general account is used for all other disbursements. Every week, a check in the amount of the net payroll is drawn on the general account and deposited in the payroll account. The company maintains a $5,000 minimum balance in the payroll account. On a monthly bank reconciliation, the payroll account should

A. Show a zero balance per the bank statement.

B. Show a $5,000 balance per the bank statement.

C. Reconcile to $5,000.

D. Be reconciled jointly with the general account in a single reconciliation.

The correct answer is (C). *(CPA 1174 II-1)*

REQUIRED: The correct statement concerning the monthly bank reconciliation of the payroll account.

DISCUSSION: Because a minimum balance of $5,000 is maintained, the check drawn on the general account is deposited to the special account before any payroll checks are written. The balance in the special account recorded by the bank, minus any outstanding checks, plus any bank charges not yet recorded on the company's books should equal $5,000.

Answers (A) and (B) are incorrect because the balance per bank statement should be equal to $5,000, plus the amount of any outstanding checks, minus any bank charges not recorded by George Company. Answer (D) is incorrect because each checking account reflected in the formal accounting system should be separately reconciled with the related bank statement.

22. An organization is reconciling its bank statement with internal records. The cash balance per the bank statement is $10,000 while the cash balance per the organization's books is $9,000. There are $1,000 of bank charges not yet recorded, $1,500 of outstanding checks, $2,500 of deposits in transit, and $3,000 of bank credits and collections not yet recorded in the organization's books. If there are no bank or book errors, what is the organization's correct cash balance?

A. $10,000

B. $11,000

C. $12,000

D. $14,500

The correct answer is (B). *(CIA 1195 IV-8)*
REQUIRED: The cash balance given no bank or book errors.
DISCUSSION: The balance per bank is $10,000, which includes the bank charges, credits, and collections not recorded on the books. Adding deposits in transit and subtracting outstanding checks results in a correct cash balance of $11,000 ($10,000 + $2,500 – $1,500).

Answer (A) is incorrect because $10,000 is the balance per bank. Answer (C) is incorrect because $12,000 equals the balance per bank, plus bank credits and collections, minus bank charges. Answer (D) is incorrect because $14,500 results from adding the desposits in transit to the balance per bank.

23. Ral Corp.'s checkbook balance on December 31, 1996 was $5,000. In addition, Ral held the following items in its safe on that date:

Check payable to Ral Corp., dated January 2, 1997, in payment of a sale made in December 1996, not included in December 31 checkbook balance $2,000

Check payable to Ral Corp., deposited December 15 and included in December 31 checkbook balance, but returned by Bank on December 30 stamped "NSF." The check was redeposited on January 2, 1997 and cleared on January 9.   500

Check drawn on Ral Corp.'s account, payable to a vendor, dated and recorded in Ral's books on December 31 but not mailed until January 10, 1997   300

The proper amount to be shown as cash on Ral's balance sheet at December 31, 1996 is

A. $4,800

B. $5,300

C. $6,500

D. $6,800

The correct answer is (A). *(CPA 1189 II-1)*
REQUIRED: The amount to be recorded as cash on the year-end balance sheet.
DISCUSSION: The December 31 checkbook balance is $5,000. The $2,000 check dated 1/2/97 is properly not included in this balance because it is not negotiable at year-end. The $500 NSF check should not be included in cash because it is a receivable. The $300 check that was not mailed until January 10 should be added to the balance. This predated check is still within the control of the company and should not decrease the cash account. Consequently, the cash balance to be reported on the 12/31/96 balance sheet is $4,800.

Balance per checkbook	$5,000
Add: Predated check	300
Deduct: NSF check	(500)
Cash balance 12/31/96	$4,800

Answer (B) is incorrect because $5,300 does not include the deduction for the NSF check. Answer (C) is incorrect because $6,500 incorrectly includes the postdated check and does not include the predated check. Answer (D) is incorrect because $6,800 incorrectly includes the postdated check.

24. A company shows a cash balance of $35,000 on its bank statement dated November 1. As of November 1, there are $11,000 of outstanding checks and $7,500 of deposits in transit. The correct cash balance on the company books as of November 1 would be

A. $24,000

B. $31,500

C. $42,500

D. $53,500

The correct answer is (B). *(CIA 596 IV-6)*
REQUIRED: The cash balance on the company books.
DISCUSSION: The $35,000 cash balance on the November 1 bank statement does not reflect either the $11,000 of outstanding checks or the $7,500 of deposits in transit. Adding the deposits in transit and subtracting the outstanding checks result in a cash balance per books of $31,500 ($35,000 + $7,500 – $11,000).

Answer (A) is incorrect because $24,000 does not include the $7,500 of deposits in transit. Answer (C) is incorrect because $42,500 does not include the $11,000 of outstanding checks. Answer (D) is incorrect because $53,500 results from adding the $11,000 of outstanding checks and the $7,500 of deposits in transit.

25. In preparing its bank reconciliation at December 31, 1996, Case Company has available the following data:

Balance per bank statement, 12/31/96	$38,075
Deposit in transit, 12/31/96	5,200
Outstanding checks, 12/31/96	6,750
Amount erroneously credited by bank to Case's account, 12/28/96	400
Bank service charges for December	75

Case's adjusted cash in bank balance at December 31, 1996 is

A. $36,525

B. $36,450

C. $36,125

D. $36,050

The correct answer is (C). *(CPA 588 I-12)*
REQUIRED: The adjusted cash in bank balance at year-end.
DISCUSSION: The balance per bank statement at December 31 is $38,075. As indicated below, the $5,200 deposit in transit should be added to this amount. The $6,750 in outstanding checks and the $400 that was erroneously credited by the bank to Case's account should be deducted. The $75 bank service charges are already included in the December 31 bank statement balance. The adjusted cash in bank balance at December 31 is therefore $36,125.

Balance per statement	$38,075
Add: Deposit in transit	5,200
Deduct: Outstanding checks	(6,750)
Bank error	(400)
Adjusted cash in bank	$36,125

Answer (A) is incorrect because $36,525 does not include the deduction for the bank error. Answer (B) is incorrect because $36,450 does not include the deduction for the bank error and incorrectly includes the bank service charges. Answer (D) is incorrect because $36,050 incorrectly includes the deduction for bank service charges.

8.4 Accounts Receivable

26. Which of the following statements is not valid in determining balance sheet disclosure of accounts receivable?

A. Accounts receivable should be identified on the balance sheet as pledged if they are used as security for a loan even though the loan is shown on the same balance sheet as a liability.

B. That portion of installment accounts receivable from customers coming due more than 12 months from the balance sheet date usually would be excluded from current assets.

C. Allowances may be deducted from the accounts receivable for discounts, returns, and adjustments to be made in the future on accounts shown in the current balance sheet.

D. Trade receivables are best shown separately from nontrade receivables when amounts of each are material.

The correct answer is (B). *(CPA 1174 T-27)*
REQUIRED: The invalid statement concerning balance sheet disclosure of accounts receivable.
DISCUSSION: Current assets are reasonably expected to be realized in cash or to be sold or consumed within 12 months or the operating cycle of the business, whichever is longer. If the ordinary trade receivables of the business fall due more than 12 months from the balance sheet date, the operating cycle is clearly longer than 12 months, and the trade receivables should be included in current assets.

Answer (A) is incorrect because accounts receivable pledged or used as security for a loan should be presented with relevant information disclosed in a footnote or in a parenthetical explanation. Answer (C) is incorrect because various allowance or valuation accounts may be set up as contra accounts to receivables to arrive at the net realizable value of receivables in the balance sheet. Allowances may be made for discounts granted to customers, returned merchandise, collection expenses, and uncollectible accounts. Answer (D) is incorrect because, if the different categories of receivables are material in amount, they should be segregated in the balance sheet.

27. On a balance sheet, what is the preferable presentation of notes or accounts receivable from officers, employees, or affiliated companies?

A. As trade notes and accounts receivable if they otherwise qualify as current assets.

B. As assets but separately from other receivables.

C. As offsets to capital.

D. By means of notes or footnotes.

The correct answer is (B). *(CPA 574 T-10)*

REQUIRED: The preferable balance sheet presentation of receivables from officers, employees, or affiliated companies.

DISCUSSION: The general rule is that, if the different categories of receivables are material in amount, they should be presented separately in the balance sheet. Receivables from officers, employees, or affiliated companies are assets and should be presented in the balance sheet as such, but, if material, they should be segregated from other classifications of receivables. See ARB 43, Chapter 1A, *Rules Adopted by Membership*.

Answer (A) is incorrect because such receivables, if material, should be separately classified even though they qualify as current assets. Answer (C) is incorrect because such receivables are assets and should not be presented in the owners' equity section. Answer (D) is incorrect because such receivables are assets that should be included in the body of the balance sheet. Footnote presentation would understate financial position.

Questions 28 and 29 are based on the following information. EGC Company recorded two sales on March 1 of $20,000 and $30,000 under credit terms of 3/10, n/30. Payment for the $20,000 sale was received March 10. Payment for the $30,000 sale was received on March 25.

---

28. Under the gross method and the net method, net sales in the March income statement should appear as which of the following amounts?

	Gross Method	Net Method
A.	$48,500	$48,500
B.	$48,500	$49,400
C.	$49,400	$48,500
D.	$49,400	$49,400

The correct answer is (C). *(Publisher)*

REQUIRED: The correct amounts of net sales under the gross and the net methods.

DISCUSSION: The gross method accounts for receivables at their face value. If a discount is taken, a sales discount is recorded and classified as an offset to sales in the income statement to yield net sales.

The expression "3/10, n/30" means that a 3% discount can be taken if payment is made within 10 days of the invoice. The $20,000 payment was received during this period. The $30,000 payment was not. Under the gross method, a $600 sales discount offsets the $50,000 of gross sales to give net sales of $49,400.

The net method records receivables net of the applicable discount. If the payment is not received during the discount period, an interest revenue account such as sales discounts forfeited is credited at the end of the discount period or when the payment is received. Consequently, both sales would be recorded net of discount ($48,500), and $900 (3% of $30,000) would be recorded as an interest income item.

The income effect of both methods is the same. The difference is in how the items are presented in the income statement.

Answer (A) is incorrect because the gross method net sales of $48,500 includes the $900 discount lost. Answer (B) is incorrect because the net sales amounts should be reversed. Answer (D) is incorrect because the net method records receivables net of all applicable discounts.

29. What would gross sales be for the month of March?

	Gross Method	Net Method
A.	$50,000	$50,000
B.	$50,000	$48,500
C.	$49,400	$48,500
D.	$48,500	$50,000

The correct answer is (B). *(Publisher)*
REQUIRED: The gross sales for the month under the gross method and the net method.
DISCUSSION: The gross method records March sales at the gross amount ($50,000). Because the $20,000 receivable was paid within the discount period, sales discount is debited for $600 at the payment date.
The net method records March sales at the net amount ($48,500, or $50,000 minus 3% of $50,000). The $30,000 receivable was not paid within the discount period, and the following entry must also be made:

Accounts receivable	$900	
Sales discounts forfeited		$900

Answer (A) is incorrect because the net method records sales at the net amount. Answer (C) is incorrect because the gross method records sales at the gross amount. Answer (D) is incorrect because the gross sales amounts should be reversed.

30. Fenn Stores, Inc. had sales of $1,000,000 during December 1996. Experience has shown that merchandise equalling 7% of sales will be returned within 30 days and an additional 3% will be returned within 90 days. Returned merchandise is readily resalable. In addition, merchandise equaling 15% of sales will be exchanged for merchandise of equal or greater value. What amount should Fenn report for net sales in its income statement for the month of December 1996?

A. $900,000

B. $850,000

C. $780,000

D. $750,000

The correct answer is (A). *(CPA 593 I-37)*
REQUIRED: The amount of net sales.
DISCUSSION: Net sales equal gross sales minus net returns and allowances. No adjustments are made for anticipated exchanges for merchandise of equal or greater value. Hence, net sales equal $900,000 [$1,000,000 − (10% x $1,000,000)].
Answer (B) is incorrect because $850,000 equals sales minus 15% of sales. Answer (C) is incorrect because $780,000 equals sales, minus 15% of sales, minus 7% of sales. Answer (D) is incorrect because $750,000 equals net sales minus 15% of sales.

31. Delta, Inc. sells to wholesalers on terms of 2/15, net 30. Delta has no cash sales but 50% of Delta's customers take advantage of the discount. Delta uses the gross method of recording sales and trade receivables. An analysis of Delta's trade receivables balances at December 31, 1996 revealed the following:

Age	Amount	Collectible
0-15 days	$100,000	100%
16-30 days	60,000	95%
31-60 days	5,000	90%
Over 60 days	2,500	$500
	$167,500	

In its December 31, 1996, balance sheet, what amount should Delta report for allowance for discounts?

A. $1,000

B. $1,620

C. $1,675

D. $2,000

The correct answer is (A). *(CPA 594 F-15)*
REQUIRED: The amount to be reported as an allowance for discounts.
DISCUSSION: The allowance for discounts should include an estimate of the expected discount based on the eligible receivables. According to the analysis, receivables equal to $100,000 are still eligible. Based on past experience, 50% of the customers take advantage of the discount. Thus, the allowance should be $1,000 [$100,000 x 50% x 2% (the discount percentage)].
Answer (B) is incorrect because $1,620 assumes that 50% of all collectible amounts are eligible for the discount. Answer (C) is incorrect because $1,675 assumes that 50% of the total gross receivables are eligible for the discount. Answer (D) is incorrect because $2,000 assumes 100% of eligible customers will take the discount.

32. Ward Company's usual sales terms are net 60 days, FOB shipping point. Sales, net of returns and allowances, totaled $2,300,000 for the year ended December 31, 1996, before year-end adjustment. Additional data are as follows:

- On December 27, 1996, Ward authorized a customer to return, for full credit, goods shipped and billed at $50,000 on December 15, 1996. The returned goods were received by Ward on January 4, 1997, and a $50,000 credit memo was issued on the same date.

- Goods with an invoice amount of $80,000 were billed to a customer on January 3, 1997. The goods were shipped on December 31, 1996.

- On January 5, 1997, a customer notified Ward that goods billed and shipped on December 23, 1996 were lost in transit. The invoice amount was $100,000.

Ward's adjusted net sales for 1996 should be

A. $2,330,000

B. $2,280,000

C. $2,250,000

D. $2,230,000

The correct answer is (A). *(CPA 1185 I-27)*
REQUIRED: The adjusted net sales for the year.
DISCUSSION: Prior to adjustment, sales net of returns and allowances were $2,300,000. The goods returned ($50,000) should be recorded in the year in which the return was authorized (1996) rather than the year in which the credit memo was issued (1997). The $80,000 item billed in January should be added to the December sales because the shipment occurred in December. The company's terms are FOB shipping point, which means title normally passes to the buyer at the time and place of shipment. For this reason, the goods lost in transit are not an adjustment to sales because the buyer held title and bore the risk of loss at the point of shipment. Thus, Ward's adjusted net sales for 1996 should be $2,330,000 ($2,300,000 − $50,000 + $80,000).

Answer (B) is incorrect because $2,280,000 incorrectly deducts the $100,000 of goods lost in transit and does not include the deduction for the returned goods. Answer (C) is incorrect because $2,250,000 does not include the $80,000 item shipped in December. Answer (D) is incorrect because $2,230,000 incorrectly deducts the $100,000 of goods lost in transit and does not deduct the $50,000 of goods returned.

33. Which of the following is a method to generate cash from accounts receivable?

	Assignment	Factoring
A.	Yes	No
B.	Yes	Yes
C.	No	Yes
D.	No	No

The correct answer is (B). *(CPA 589 T-2)*
REQUIRED: The method(s) of generating cash from accounts receivable.
DISCUSSION: Methods of generating cash from accounts receivable include both assignment and factoring. Assignment occurs when specifically named accounts receivable are pledged as collateral for a loan. The accounts receivable remain those of the assignor. However, when cash is collected from these accounts receivable, the cash must be remitted to the assignee. Accounts receivable are factored when they are sold outright to a third party. This sale may be with or without recourse.

Answer (A) is incorrect because factoring is a way to generate cash from accounts receivable. Answer (C) is incorrect because assignment is a way to generate cash from accounts receivable. Answer (D) is incorrect because both assignment and factoring are ways to generate cash from accounts receivable.

34. On January 1, Garfield College assigned $500,000 of accounts receivable to the Scholastic Finance Company. Garfield gave a 14% note for $450,000 representing 90% of the assigned accounts and received proceeds of $432,000 after deduction of a 4% fee. On February 1, Garfield remitted $80,000 to Scholastic, including interest for 1 month on the unpaid balance. As a result of this $80,000 remittance, accounts receivable assigned and notes payable will be decreased by what amounts?

	A/R Assigned	Notes Payable
A.	$80,000	$74,750
B.	$80,000	$80,000
C.	$72,000	$74,750
D.	$74,750	$80,000

The correct answer is (A). *(A.G. Helling)*
REQUIRED: The decrease in assigned accounts receivable and notes payable when cash is collected and remitted to the assignor.
DISCUSSION: When assigned accounts receivable are collected, the cash should be remitted to the assignee. The accounts receivable assigned account should be decreased for the amount collected ($80,000), and the note should be decreased by the amount remitted ($80,000) minus interest ($450,000 x 14% x 1/12 = $5,250).
Answer (B) is incorrect because notes payable should be decreased by the amount remitted. Answer (C) is incorrect because accounts receivable should be decreased by the amount collected. Answer (D) is incorrect because notes payable should be decreased by the amount remitted, and the accounts receivable should be decreased by the amount collected.

35. In accounting for the transfer of financial assets, which of the following is the approach underlying the accounting prescribed by SFAS 125, *Accounting for Transfers and Servicing of Financial Assets and Extinguishments of Liabilities*?

A. Financial components approach.
B. The risks and rewards approach.
C. Inseparable unit approach.
D. Linked presentation approach.

The correct answer is (A). *(Publisher)*
REQUIRED: The conceptual approach underlying the accounting for transfers of financial assets prescribed by SFAS 125.
DISCUSSION: The accounting for the transfer of financial assets prescribed by SFAS 125 follows the financial-components approach. Under this approach, a transfer of financial assets is disaggregated into its component assets and liabilities. Each party to the transaction then recognizes the component assets and liabilities controlled and derecognizes the component assets and liabilities surrendered or extinguished.
Answers (B), (C), and (D) are incorrect because these approaches were rejected. These approaches are consistent with viewing each financial asset as a total unit.

36. First Municipal Bank makes a large loan to a major borrower and then transfers an undivided interest in this loan to Third Union Bank. This transfer is on a nonrecourse basis, and First Municipal will continue to service the loan. Third Union is not a major competitor of First Municipal. First Municipal should account for this transfer as a secured borrowing if the participation agreement

A. Allows Third Union Bank to pledge its participation interest.
B. Does not grant First Municipal the right of first refusal on the sale of Third Union's participation interest.
C. Does not allow Third Union to sell its participation interest.
D. Prohibits Third Union from selling its participation interest to banks which are direct, major competitors of First Municipal.

The correct answer is (C). *(Publisher)*
REQUIRED: The condition under which a loan participation should be accounted for as a secured borrowing.
DISCUSSION: A transfer of financial assets, such as a loan participation agreement, should be accounted for as a sale if the transferor (originating lender) surrenders control over the participation interest transferred to the transferee (participating bank). If control is not surrendered, the transfer should be accounted for as a secured borrowing. Control is not surrendered if the participation agreement constrains the participating bank from pledging or exchanging its participation interest.
Answer (A) is incorrect because the right to exchange or pledge participation interests is consistent with the relinquishment of control. Answers (B) and (D) are incorrect because, while limitations on the rights of the participating bank, they are not presumed to prevent this bank from exchanging or pledging its interest.

37. Simpson Corporation sells an 80% pro rata interest in a $1,000,000 note receivable to Bruns Company for $960,000. The note was originally issued at face value. Future benefits and costs of servicing the note are immaterial. If the provisions of SFAS 125 are followed, the amount of gain or loss Simpson should recognize on this transfer of a partial interest is

A. ($40,000)

B. $0

C. $160,000

D. $200,000

The correct answer is (C). *(Publisher)*
REQUIRED: The amount of gain or loss to be recognized on a transfer of partial interest in a loan.
DISCUSSION: The fair value of the note is $1,200,000 ($960,000 divided by 80%). The book value is $1,000,000. There is no servicing asset or liability. Therefore, Simpson should record the receipt of the $960,000 as cash, reduce the carrying amount of the note receivable by $800,000 ($1,000,000 × 80%), and recognize a $160,000 ($960,000 − $800,000) gain.
Answer (A) is incorrect because a loss of $40,000 is equal to the $960,000 cash received less the $1,000,000 carrying value of the note. Answer (B) is incorrect because a gain should be recognized equal to the pro rata (80%) difference between the fair value and the carrying value of the note. Answer (D) is incorrect because $200,000 is equal to 100% of the difference between the fair value and the carrying value of the note.

8.5 Allowance for Uncollectible Accounts/Bad Debt Expense

38. When may an asset valuation allowance, such as the allowance for bad debts, be shown on the credit side of the balance sheet?

A. Never.

B. When they have to be repaid.

C. In the airline industry.

D. When it exceeds 10% of the accounts receivable balance.

The correct answer is (A). *(Publisher)*
REQUIRED: The circumstances in which asset valuation and allowance accounts may be shown on the credit side of the balance sheet.
DISCUSSION: APB 12, *Omnibus Opinion - 1967*, indicates that all allowance accounts must be shown contra to the related asset accounts (in all industries).
Answer (B) is incorrect because valuation accounts for bad debts are not repaid. Answer (C) is incorrect because there are no industry exceptions. Answer (D) is incorrect because the materiality of the account does not affect its classification as a contra asset account.

39. A method of estimating uncollectible accounts that emphasizes asset valuation rather than income measurement is the allowance method based on

A. Aging the receivables.

B. Direct write-offs.

C. Gross sales.

D. Credit sales minus returns and allowances.

The correct answer is (A). *(CPA 1189 T-7)*
REQUIRED: The method of estimating uncollectible accounts that emphasizes asset valuation.
DISCUSSION: Under the allowance method, accounts are estimated in two ways. One emphasizes asset valuation. The other emphasizes income measurement. The method that emphasizes asset valuation is based on an aging of the receivables to determine the balance in the allowance for uncollectible accounts. Bad debt expense is the amount necessary to adjust the allowance account to this estimated balance. The method emphasizing the income statement recognizes bad debt expense as a percentage of sales. The corresponding credit is to the allowance for uncollectible accounts.
Answer (B) is incorrect because the direct write-off method is not a means of estimation. Answers (C) and (D) are incorrect because an estimate based on these figures focuses on the income measurement.

40. When the allowance method of recognizing uncollectible accounts is used, the entries at the time of collection of a small account previously written off would

A. Increase the allowance for uncollectible accounts.

B. Increase net income.

C. Decrease the allowance for uncollectible accounts.

D. Have no effect on the allowance for uncollectible accounts.

The correct answer is (A). *(CPA 592 T-47)*
REQUIRED: The effect of the collection of an account previously written off.
DISCUSSION: When an account receivable is written off, both accounts receivable and the allowance for uncollectible accounts are decreased. When an account previously written off is collected, the account must be reinstated by increasing both accounts receivable and the allowance. The account receivable is then decreased by the amount of cash collected.
Answer (B) is incorrect because neither write-off nor reinstatement and collection affects bad debt expense or net income. Answers (C) and (D) are incorrect because the allowance is increased.

41. When the allowance method of recognizing uncollectible accounts is used, the entry to record the write-off of a specific account

A. Decreases both accounts receivable and the allowance for uncollectible accounts.

B. Decreases accounts receivable and increases the allowance for uncollectible accounts.

C. Increases the allowance for uncollectible accounts and decreases net income.

D. Decreases both accounts receivable and net income.

The correct answer is (A). *(CPA 1194 F-12)*
REQUIRED: The effect of the write-off of a specific uncollectible account.
DISCUSSION: The entry to record bad debt expense under the allowance method is to debit bad debt expense and credit the allowance account. When a specific account is then written off, the allowance is debited and accounts receivable credited. Net income is affected when bad debt expense is recognized, not at the time of the write-off. Because accounts receivable and the allowance account are decreased by the same amount, a write-off of an account also has no effect on the net amount of accounts receivable.
Answer (B) is incorrect because the allowance for uncollectible accounts decreases. Answer (C) is incorrect because the allowance for uncollectible accounts decreases, and net income is not affected. Answer (D) is incorrect because net income is not affected.

42. Which method of recording uncollectible accounts expense is consistent with accrual accounting?

	Allowance	Direct Write-Off
A.	Yes	Yes
B.	Yes	No
C.	No	Yes
D.	No	No

The correct answer is (B). *(CPA 595 F-35)*
REQUIRED: The method(s) of recording uncollectible accounts expense consistent with accrual accounting.
DISCUSSION: Under the allowance method, accounts are estimated in two ways. One emphasizes asset valuation. The other emphasizes income measurement. The method that emphasizes asset valuation is based on an aging of the receivables to determine the balance in the allowance for uncollectible accounts. Bad debt expense is the amount necessary to adjust the allowance account to this estimated balance. The method emphasizing the income statement recognizes bad debt expense as a percentage of sales. The corresponding credit is to the allowance for uncollectible accounts. Either method is acceptable under GAAP. The direct write-off method debits expense and credits accounts receivable at the time uncollectibility is established. It is not acceptable under GAAP and may only be used when the results of applying this method do not differ materially from the allowance method.
Answers (A), (C), and (D) are incorrect because the allowance method is consistent with accrual accounting. The direct write-off method is not.

43. Inge Co. determined that the net value of its accounts receivable at December 31, 1996, based on an aging of the receivables, was $325,000. Additional information is as follows:

Allowance for uncollectible accounts -- 1/1/96	$ 30,000
Uncollectible accounts written off during 1996	18,000
Uncollectible accounts recovered during 1996	2,000
Accounts receivable at 12/31/96	350,000

For 1996, what would be Inge's uncollectible accounts expense?

A. $5,000

B. $11,000

C. $15,000

D. $21,000

The correct answer is (B). *(CPA 1194 F-45)*
   REQUIRED: The uncollectible accounts expense.
   DISCUSSION: The allowance for uncollectible accounts before year-end adjustment is $14,000 ($30,000 beginning balance − $18,000 write-offs + $2,000 recovered). The balance should be $25,000 ($350,000 year-end A/R − $325,000 net value based on aging). Thus, the allowance account should be credited and uncollectible accounts expense debited for $11,000 ($25,000 desired balance − $14,000).
   Answer (A) is incorrect because $5,000 is the difference between gross and net accounts receivable ($25,000) and the balance in the allowance account at the beginning of the year ($30,000). Answer (C) is incorrect because $15,000 equals $25,000 minus the difference between the $30,000 allowance and the $18,000 written off, reduced by the $2,000 recovered. Answer (D) is incorrect because $21,000 equals $30,000 allowance, plus $18,000 written off, reduced by $2,000 recovered, minus $25,000.

44. Ward Co. estimates its uncollectible accounts expense to be 2% of credit sales. Ward's credit sales for 1996 were $1,000,000. During 1996, Ward wrote off $18,000 of uncollectible accounts. Ward's allowance for uncollectible accounts had a $15,000 balance on January 1, 1996. In its December 31, 1996 income statement, what amount should Ward report as uncollectible accounts expense?

A. $23,000

B. $20,000

C. $18,000

D. $17,000

The correct answer is (B). *(CPA 593 I-51)*
   REQUIRED: The uncollectible accounts expense as a percentage of sales.
   DISCUSSION: When bad debt expense is estimated on the basis of net credit sales, a cost (bad debt expense) is being directly associated with a revenue of the period (net credit sales). Thus, uncollectible accounts expense is $20,000 (2% x $1,000,000 credit sales).
   Answer (A) is incorrect because $23,000 assumes that $20,000 is the required ending balance in the allowance account (expense = write-offs + the change in the allowance). Answer (C) is incorrect because $18,000 equals the write-offs for 1996. Answer (D) is incorrect because $17,000 is the ending balance in the allowance account.

45. The following information relates to Jay Co.'s accounts receivable for 1996:

Accounts receivable, 1/1/96	$ 650,000
Credit sales for 1996	2,700,000
Sales returns for 1996	75,000
Accounts written off during 1996	40,000
Collections from customers during 1996	2,150,000
Estimated future sales returns at 12/31/96	50,000
Estimated uncollectible accounts at 12/31/96	110,000

What amount should Jay report for accounts receivable, before allowances for sales returns and uncollectible accounts, at December 31, 1996?

A. $1,200,000

B. $1,125,000

C. $1,085,000

D. $925,000

The correct answer is (C). *(CPA 593 I-12)*
   REQUIRED: The year-end balance in accounts receivable.
   DISCUSSION: The $1,085,000 ending balance in accounts receivable is equal to the $650,000 beginning debit balance, plus debits for $2,700,000 of credit sales, minus credits for $2,150,000 of collections, $40,000 of accounts written off, and $75,000 of sales returns. The $110,000 of estimated uncollectible receivables and the $50,000 of estimated sales returns are not relevant because they affect the allowance accounts but not gross accounts receivable.

Accounts Receivable (in 000's)			
1/1/96	$ 650	75	Sales returns
Credit sales	2,700	$2,150	Collections
		40	Write-off
	$1,085		

Answer (A) is incorrect because $1,200,000 does not subtract write-offs and sales returns from accounts receivable. Answer (B) is incorrect because $1,125,000 does not subtract write-offs from accounts receivable. Answer (D) is incorrect because estimated future sales returns and uncollectible accounts affect their respective allowance accounts, not gross accounts receivable.

46. The following information pertains to Tara Co.'s accounts receivable at December 31, 1996:

Days Outstanding	Amount	Estimated % Uncollectible
0 - 60	$120,000	1%
61 - 120	90,000	2%
Over 120	100,000	6%
	$310,000	

During 1996, Tara wrote off $7,000 in receivables and recovered $4,000 that had been written off in prior years. Tara's December 31, 1995 allowance for uncollectible accounts was $22,000. Under the aging method, what amount of allowance for uncollectible accounts should Tara report at December 31, 1996?

- A. $9,000
- B. $10,000
- C. $13,000
- D. $19,000

The correct answer is (A). *(CPA 593 I-17)*
REQUIRED: The allowance for uncollectible accounts under the aging method.
DISCUSSION: The aging schedule determines the allowance for uncollectible accounts based on year-end A/R balances, their age, and estimated collectibility. This year-end amount is $9,000 [(1% x $120,000) + (2% x $90,000) + (6% x $100,000)].
Answer (B) is incorrect because $10,000 equals the beginning balance, plus the recovery, minus write-offs, minus the amount determined by the aging schedule ($22,000 – $4,000 – $7,000 – $9,000). Answer (C) is incorrect because $13,000 equals the beginning balance minus the amount determined by the aging schedule ($22,000 – $9,000). Answer (D) is incorrect because $19,000 equals the beginning balance, plus the recovery, minus write-offs ($22,000 – $4,000 – $7,000).

47. An analysis and aging of Jay Company's accounts receivable at December 31, 1996 disclosed the following:

Accounts receivable	$900,000
Allowance for uncollectible accounts per books	50,000
Amounts deemed uncollectible	64,000

The net realizable value of the accounts receivable at December 31 should be

- A. $886,000
- B. $850,000
- C. $836,000
- D. $786,000

The correct answer is (C). *(CPA 1186 II-16)*
REQUIRED: The net realizable value of accounts receivable.
DISCUSSION: The net realizable value of accounts receivable is equal to the $900,000 gross accounts receivable minus the $64,000 estimate of the accounts estimated to be uncollectible. The $50,000 balance in the allowance account is not used because it is an unadjusted balance.
Answer (A) is incorrect because $886,000 is the gross accounts receivable account, minus the amount deemed uncollectible, plus the allowance for uncollectible accounts. Answer (B) is incorrect because $850,000 is the gross accounts receivable account minus the allowance for uncollectible accounts. Answer (D) is incorrect because $786,000 is the gross accounts receivable account minus the allowance for uncollectible accounts and the amount deemed uncollectible.

48. The following accounts were abstracted from Roxy Co.'s unadjusted trial balance at December 31, 1996:

	Debit	Credit
Accounts receivable	$1,000,000	
Allowance for uncollectible accounts		8,000
Net credit sales		$3,000,000

Roxy estimates that 3% of the gross accounts receivable will become uncollectible. After adjustment at December 31, 1996, the allowance for uncollectible accounts should have a credit balance of

A. $90,000

B. $82,000

C. $38,000

D. $30,000

The correct answer is (D). *(CPA 590 I-9)*

REQUIRED: The ending balance in the allowance for uncollectible accounts.

DISCUSSION: The allowance for uncollectible accounts at year-end should have a credit balance of $30,000. This amount is equal to the $1,000,000 of accounts receivable multiplied by the 3% that is estimated to become uncollectible.

Answer (A) is incorrect because $90,000 is equal to 3% of net credit sales less the unadjusted balance in the allowance account. Answer (B) is incorrect because $82,000 is equal to 3% of accounts receivable plus the unadjusted balance in the allowance account. Answer (C) is incorrect because $38,000 is equal to 3% of accounts receivable.

8.6 Notes Receivable

49. How should unearned discounts, finance charges, and unearned interest included in the face amount of notes receivables be presented in the balance sheet?

A. As a deferred credit.

B. As a deduction from the related receivables.

C. In the footnotes.

D. As a current liability.

The correct answer is (B). *(Publisher)*

REQUIRED: The proper presentation of unearned discounts, finance charges, and unearned interest in the balance sheet.

DISCUSSION: APB 6, *Status of Accounting Research Bulletins*, states that unearned discounts, finance charges, and unearned interest included in the face amount of notes receivable should be shown as contra items to the face amounts of the related receivables in the balance sheet. Thus, a note should be recorded at its net amount, that is, as a debit for the face amount and a credit for the unearned discount, finance charge, or unearned interest.

Answers (A), (C), and (D) are incorrect because each is an incorrect balance sheet presentation.

50. Frame Co. has an 8% note receivable dated June 30, 1994 in the original amount of $150,000. Payments of $50,000 in principal plus accrued interest are due annually on July 1, 1995, 1996, and 1997. In its June 30, 1996 balance sheet, what amount should Frame report as a current asset for interest on the note receivable?

A. $0

B. $4,000

C. $8,000

D. $12,000

The correct answer is (C). *(CPA 1193 I-17)*

REQUIRED: The amount reported as a current asset for interest on a note receivable.

DISCUSSION: Current assets are those reasonably expected to be realized in cash, sold, or consumed during the longer of the operating cycle of a business or 1 year. Given that the date of the balance sheet is 6/30/96, the interest to be paid on the next day, 7/1/96, should be classified as a current asset.

Answer (A) is incorrect because $8,000 of interest is reported as a current asset. Answer (B) is incorrect because $4,000 is the interest to be earned in 1997. Answer (D) is incorrect because $12,000 is the interest earned in 1995.

51. A 90-day, 15% interest-bearing note receivable is sold to a bank after being held for 30 days. The proceeds are calculated using an 18% interest rate. The note receivable has been

	Discounted	Pledged
A.	No	Yes
B.	No	No
C.	Yes	No
D.	Yes	Yes

The correct answer is (C). (CPA 584 T-7)

REQUIRED: The proper description of the sale of a note receivable.

DISCUSSION: A note receivable sold before maturity has been discounted. A pledge is a security transaction in which the collateral to secure a debt is held by the secured party. No security has been given in this case.

Answer (A) is incorrect because the note has been discounted but not pledged. Answer (B) is incorrect because the note has been discounted. Answer (D) is incorrect because the note has not been pledged.

52. On November 1, 1996, Davis Co. discounted with recourse at 10% a 1-year, noninterest-bearing, $20,500 note receivable maturing on January 31, 1997. What amount of contingent liability for this note must Davis disclose in its financial statements for the year ended December 31, 1996?

A. $0

B. $20,000

C. $20,333

D. $20,500

The correct answer is (D). (CPA 1193 I-41)

REQUIRED: The amount to be disclosed in the financial statements for a contingent liability.

DISCUSSION: When a note receivable is discounted with recourse, the discounting firm is responsible for the full amount of the note ($20,500) if the receivables are not paid. Consequently, this amount should be disclosed in the footnotes.

Answer (A) is incorrect because a footnote should disclose the full potential liability. Answers (B) and (C) are incorrect because Davis may be responsible for the full amount of the note ($20,500).

53. Rand, Inc. accepted from a customer a $40,000, 90-day, 12% interest-bearing note dated August 31, 1996. On September 30, 1996, Rand discounted the note at the Apex State Bank at 15%. However, the proceeds were not received until October 1, 1996. In Rand's September 30, 1996 balance sheet, the amount receivable from the bank, based on a 360-day year, includes accrued interest revenue of

A. $170

B. $200

C. $300

D. $400

The correct answer is (A). (CPA 590 I-12)

REQUIRED: The accrued interest revenue recognized when a note is discounted.

DISCUSSION: As determined below, the interest received by Rand if it had held the 90-day note to maturity would have been $1,200. The discount fee charged on a note with a maturity value of $41,200 ($40,000 face + $1,200 interest) discounted at 15% for 60 days is $1,030. The difference of $170 ($1,200 interest − $1,030 discount fee) should be reflected as accrued interest revenue at the balance sheet date because the cash proceeds were not received until the next period.

$40,000 x 12% x 90/360 = $1,200 interest
$41,200 x 15% x 60/360 = (1,030) discount fee
Accrued interest revenue $ 170

Answers (B), (C), and (D) are incorrect because the accrued interest revenue is the difference between the interest on the note if held to maturity minus the discounted value of the note.

54. Brook Corp. discounted its own $50,000, 1-year note at a bank, at a discount rate of 12%, when the prime rate was 10%. In reporting the note on Brook's balance sheet prior to the note's maturity, what rate should Brook use for the accrual of interest?

A. 10.0%

B. 10.7%

C. 12.0%

D. 13.6%

The correct answer is (D). (CPA 586 II-14)

REQUIRED: The effective rate of interest on a discounted note.

DISCUSSION: The note had a face value of $50,000. The proceeds from discounting the note were $44,000 [$50,000 − ($50,000 x .12 x 1 year)]. Thus, Brook paid $6,000 interest ($50,000 − $44,000) on $44,000 for 1 year. The effective interest rate was thus 13.6% ($6,000 ÷ $44,000).

Answers (A), (B), and (C) are incorrect because the rate used for the accrual of interest is the effective interest rate.

55. Roth, Inc. received from a customer a 1-year, $500,000 note bearing annual interest of 8%. After holding the note for 6 months, Roth discounted the note at Regional Bank at an effective interest rate of 10%. What amount of cash did Roth receive from the bank?

A. $540,000

B. $528,400

C. $513,000

D. $486,000

The correct answer is (C). *(CPA 1193 I-15)*

REQUIRED: The amount of cash received when a note is discounted.

DISCUSSION: The maturity value of the note is $540,000 [$500,000 face value + (8% x $500,000)]. The discount is $27,000 [10% x $540,000 x (6/12)]. Consequently, the proceeds equal $513,000 ($540,000 – $27,000).

Answer (A) is incorrect because $540,000 is the maturity value. Answer (B) is incorrect because $528,400 assumes a nominal rate of 10% and a discount rate of 8%. Answer (D) is incorrect because $486,000 results from discounting the note for 1 year.

56. On August 1, 1996, Vann Corp.'s $500,000 1-year, noninterest-bearing note due July 31, 1997, was discounted at Homestead Bank at 10.8%. Vann uses the straight-line method of amortizing bond discount. What carrying value should Vann report for notes payable in its December 31, 1996 balance sheet?

A. $500,000

B. $477,500

C. $468,500

D. $446,000

The correct answer is (C). *(CPA 1192 I-22)*

REQUIRED: The carrying value reported for notes payable.

DISCUSSION: The discount is $54,000 (10.8% x $500,000). Hence, the carrying amount on August 1 was $446,000. Given straight-line amortization of the discount, the carrying amount at year-end is $468,500 {$500,000 – [$54,000 – ($54,000 x 5/12)]}.

Answer (A) is incorrect because $500,000 is the face amount of the note payable. Answer (B) is incorrect because $477,500 will be the carrying amount after 7 months. Answer (D) is incorrect because $446,000 was the carrying amount on August 1.

57. Leaf Co. purchased from Oak Co. a $20,000, 8%, 5-year note that required five equal annual year-end payments of $5,009. The note was discounted to yield a 9% rate to Leaf. At the date of purchase, Leaf recorded the note at its present value of $19,485. What should be the total interest revenue earned by Leaf over the life of this note?

A. $5,045

B. $5,560

C. $8,000

D. $9,000

The correct answer is (B). *(CPA 1194 F-38)*

REQUIRED: The total interest revenue earned on a discounted note receivable.

DISCUSSION: Leaf Co. will receive cash of $25,045 (5 x $5,009). Hence, interest revenue is $5,560 ($25,045 – $19,485 present value).

Answer (A) is incorrect because $5,045 does not include the discount amortization. Answer (C) is incorrect because $8,000 equals $20,000 times 8% nominal interest for 5 years. Answer (D) is incorrect because $9,000 equals $20,000 times the 9% yield rate for 5 years.

58. Platt Co. has been forced into bankruptcy and liquidated. Unsecured claims will be paid at the rate of $.50 on the dollar. Maga Co. holds a noninterest-bearing note receivable from Platt in the amount of $50,000, collateralized by machinery with a liquidation value of $10,000. The total amount to be realized by Maga on this note receivable is

A. $35,000

B. $30,000

C. $25,000

D. $10,000

The correct answer is (B). *(CPA 1185 II-17)*

REQUIRED: The amount to be realized from a liquidation claim.

DISCUSSION: The $50,000 note receivable is secured to the extent of $10,000. The remaining $40,000 is unsecured, and Maga will be paid on this claim at the rate of $.50 on the dollar.

Secured claim	$10,000
Unsecured ($40,000 x .5)	20,000
	$30,000

Answer (A) is incorrect because $35,000 is the note receivable applied to the liquidation rate plus the liquidation value of the collateral [($50,000 x .5) + $10,000]. Answer (C) is incorrect because $25,000 is the amount that would be realized if no collateral had been pledged (.5 x $50,000). Answer (D) is incorrect because $10,000 is the liquidation value of the collateral.

CHAPTER NINE
INVENTORY

This chapter includes questions on inventory record keeping procedures and valuation methods and their impact on accounting income. Long-term construction contracts are covered in Chapter 25, Long-Term Contracts, Consignments, and Installment Sales.

9.1 General Concepts

1. Inventory is defined as those goods held for sale in the ordinary course of business, in the process of production for such sale, and to be consumed in the production of goods or services available for sale. Which item would not be properly classified as inventory?

A. Manufacturing supplies.

B. Raw materials.

C. Office supplies.

D. Work-in-process.

The correct answer is (C). *(Publisher)*
REQUIRED: The item that is not properly classified as inventory.
DISCUSSION: Office supplies are neither held for sale nor consumed in the production of goods or services available for sale.
Answer (A) is incorrect because manufacturing supplies are consumed in the production of goods and may be classified as inventory. Answers (B) and (D) are incorrect because finished goods, raw materials, and work-in-process are the traditional components of inventory of a manufacturing entity.

2. According to the net method, which of the following items should be included in the cost of inventory?

	Freight Costs	Purchase Discounts Not Taken
A.	Yes	No
B.	Yes	Yes
C.	No	Yes
D.	No	No

The correct answer is (A). *(CPA 1188 T-6)*
REQUIRED: The items that should be included as inventoriable cost.
DISCUSSION: ARB 43, Chap. 4, *Inventory Pricing*, states that cost is "the sum of the applicable expenditures and charges directly or indirectly incurred in bringing an article to its existing condition and location." Freight costs are therefore an inventoriable cost. Under the net method, purchase discounts are treated as reductions in the invoice prices of specific purchases. Accordingly, goods available for sale reflect the purchase price net of the discount, and a purchase discount not taken is recognized as an item of interest expense.
Answer (B) is incorrect because, under the net method, purchase discounts not taken are an interest expense. Answer (C) is incorrect because freight costs are part of inventory costs, but purchase discounts not taken under the net method are not inventory costs. Answer (D) is incorrect because freight costs are included in the cost of inventory.

3. Inventories can be valued using different costing methods. All of the following methods of inventory valuation are acceptable for financial reporting purposes except

A.   Dollar-value LIFO method.

B.   Full absorption cost method.

C.   Weighted-average cost method.

D.   Base-stock method.

The correct answer is (D). *(CMA 688 4-27)*
REQUIRED: The inventory valuation method not acceptable in accordance with GAAP.
DISCUSSION: The acceptable methods of inventory valuation specified in ARB 43 include FIFO, LIFO, weighted average, retail inventory, and weighted moving average. ARB 43 also requires the use of the absorption method of inventory valuation. The base-stock method is not acceptable under GAAP. It is also not an acceptable method for tax purposes. The base-stock method assumes that a minimum amount of inventory is always required. Accordingly, the inventory base or minimum amount is considered a long-term investment to be recorded at its original cost. Last-in, first-out (LIFO) has the same effect if base levels of inventory are not sold.
Answers (A), (B), and (C) are incorrect because each is an inventory valuation method acceptable for financial reporting purposes under GAAP.

4. In pricing inventory, cost may be determined under any one of several assumptions as to the flow of cost factors. The major objective in selecting a method should be to choose the one that, under the circumstances, most clearly reflects the

A.   Current value of the inventory.

B.   Periodic income.

C.   Future utility of the inventory.

D.   Conservative accounting assumption.

The correct answer is (B). *(Publisher)*
REQUIRED: The principal reason for choosing from among the various inventory cost flow assumptions.
DISCUSSION: ARB 43, Chap. 4, *Inventory Pricing*, states that the inventory cost flow method used by a firm should be the one that most clearly reflects periodic income. Periodic income is best reflected when costs are recognized in the same period as the related revenues.
Answers (A), (C), and (D) are incorrect because, although each is an objective of inventory pricing, the major objective is to reflect income clearly.

5. All of the following should be disclosed when reporting inventories except

A.   The use of the lower of cost or market method, if applicable.

B.   Classifications of inventory items.

C.   The method(s) used for determining the cost.

D.   An estimated amount of obsolete inventory included in the total inventory valuation.

The correct answer is (D). *(CMA 693 2-28)*
REQUIRED: The item not a required disclosure when reporting inventories.
DISCUSSION: ARB 43 states the required disclosures regarding inventories: the basis of stating inventories (e.g., lower of cost or market) and, if a significant change is made, the nature of the change and the effect on income; any goods stated above cost; and accrued net losses on firm purchase commitments. Moreover, APB 22 states that disclosures required regarding accounting policies include those relating to inventory pricing and composition (classification) of inventories.
Answers (A), (B), and (C) are incorrect because disclosures should include the use of the LCM method, classifications based on the types of inventory, the method of determining inventory cost, and any changes in determining inventory cost.

6. The following information applied to Fenn, Inc. for 1996:

Merchandise purchased for resale	$400,000
Freight-in	10,000
Freight-out	5,000
Purchase returns	2,000

Fenn's 1996 inventoriable cost was

A. $400,000

B. $403,000

C. $408,000

D. $413,000

The correct answer is (C). *(CPA 1190 I-7)*

REQUIRED: The amount of inventoriable cost for the year.

DISCUSSION: Inventoriable cost is the sum of the applicable expenditures and charges directly or indirectly incurred in bringing all items of inventory to their existing condition and location. Thus, inventoriable cost includes the $400,000 cost of the merchandise purchased, plus the $10,000 of freight-in, minus the $2,000 of purchase returns. Freight-out is not a cost incurred in bringing the inventory to a salable condition. Consequently, the inventoriable cost for Fenn during 1996 was $408,000 ($400,000 + $10,000 – $2,000).

Answer (A) is incorrect because $400,000 is the amount of gross purchases. Answer (B) is incorrect because $403,000 incorrectly includes freight-out as a cost instead of freight-in. Answer (D) is incorrect because $413,000 incorrectly includes freight-out.

7. The following costs were incurred by Griff Co., a manufacturer, during 1996:

Accounting and legal fees	$ 25,000
Freight-in	175,000
Freight-out	160,000
Officers' salaries	150,000
Insurance	85,000
Sales representatives' salaries	215,000

What amount of these costs should be reported as general and administrative expenses for 1996?

A. $260,000

B. $550,000

C. $635,000

D. $810,000

The correct answer is (A). *(CPA 1193 I-52)*

REQUIRED: The amount to be reported as general and administrative expenses for the year.

DISCUSSION: General and administrative expenses are incurred for the direction of the enterprise as a whole and are not related wholly to a specific function, e.g., selling or manufacturing. They include accounting, legal, and other fees for professional services; officers' salaries; insurance; wages of office staff; miscellaneous supplies; utilities' costs; and office occupancy costs. Thus, the general and administrative expenses for Griff equaled $260,000 ($25,000 + $150,000 + $85,000).

Answer (B) is incorrect because $550,000 does not include insurance and incorrectly includes the sales representatives' salaries and freight-out (selling costs). Answer (C) is incorrect because freight-out costs and sales representatives' salaries are included. Answer (D) is incorrect because freight costs and sales representatives' salaries are not considered general and administrative costs.

8. Herc Co.'s inventory at December 31, 1996 was $1,500,000 based on a physical count priced at cost and before any necessary adjustment for the following:

- Merchandise costing $90,000, shipped FOB shipping point from a vendor on December 30, 1996, was received and recorded on January 5, 1997.

- Goods in the shipping area were excluded from inventory although shipment was not made until January 4, 1997. The goods, billed to the customer FOB shipping point on December 30, 1996, had a cost of $120,000.

What amount should Herc report as inventory in its December 31, 1996 balance sheet?

A. $1,500,000

B. $1,590,000

C. $1,620,000

D. $1,710,000

The correct answer is (D). *(CPA 1194 F-13)*

REQUIRED: The year-end inventory.

DISCUSSION: The inventory balance prior to adjustments was $1,500,000. The merchandise shipped FOB shipping point to Herc should be included because title passed when the goods were shipped. The goods in the shipping area should be included because title did not pass until the goods were shipped on January 4, 1997, even though the customer was billed in 1996. Thus, the inventory should be $1,710,000 ($1,500,000 + $90,000 + $120,000).

Answer (A) is incorrect because $1,500,000 excludes the $90,000 of goods shipped by a vendor and the $120,000 of goods not shipped until January 4. Answer (B) is incorrect because $1,590,000 results from failing to include the $120,000 of goods not shipped until January 4. Answer (C) is incorrect because $1,620,000 does not include the $90,000 of goods shipped by a vendor FOB shipping point.

9. In theory, the cash discounts allowed on purchased merchandise (purchase discounts) in a periodic inventory system should be

- A. Deducted from purchases in determination of goods available for sale.

- B. Deducted from cost of goods sold in the income statement.

- C. Shown as other income in an income statement.

- D. Deducted from inventory on the balance sheet at year-end.

The correct answer is (A). *(D.G. Kame)*
REQUIRED: The theoretically correct treatment of cash discounts earned on the purchase of merchandise.
DISCUSSION: In theory, cash discounts on purchases should be treated as reductions in the invoiced prices of specific purchases so that goods available for sale reflects the purchase price net of the discounts. It is consistent with this approach to record any purchase discounts not taken as a financial expense in the income statement.
Answers (B), (C), and (D) are incorrect because the purchase discounts should be reflected in goods available for sale, which is allocated to either cost of goods sold or ending inventory.

10. On July 1, the BJD Company recorded purchases of inventory of $40,000 and $50,000 under credit terms of 2/15, net 30. The payment due on the $40,000 purchase was remitted on July 14. The payment due on the $50,000 purchase was remitted on July 25. Under the net method and the gross method, these purchases should be included at what respective net amounts in the determination of cost of goods available for sale?

	Net Method	Gross Method
A.	$90,000	$90,000
B.	$89,200	$88,200
C.	$88,200	$89,200
D.	$88,200	$88,200

The correct answer is (C). *(Publisher)*
REQUIRED: The amounts at which net purchases should be valued under the net and gross methods for the determination of cost of goods available for sale.
DISCUSSION: The 2/15, net 30 credit phrase indicates that a 2% discount may be taken if payment is made within 15 days of the invoice date and that payment is overdue if not made within 30 days.
Under the net method, purchases are recorded net of any discount. Purchase discounts not taken are reflected as an expense in purchase discounts lost. The $90,000 in purchases should be recorded net of the 2% discount at $88,200 ($39,200 + $49,000) to determine cost of goods available for sale.
Under the gross method, purchases are recorded at their gross amount and offset by a purchase discounts account for discounts taken. Net purchases included in the determination of cost of goods available for sale are equal to the gross purchase amount of $90,000 less the $800 ($40,000 x 2%) discount taken. Net purchases equal $89,200 under the gross method.
Answers (A), (B), and (D) are incorrect because the net method records purchases as if the discounts were taken, and the gross method records purchases to reflect the actual discounts taken.

11. West Retailers purchased merchandise with a list price of $20,000, subject to trade discounts of 20% and 10%, with no cash discounts allowable. West should record the cost of this merchandise as

- A. $14,000

- B. $14,400

- C. $15,600

- D. $20,000

The correct answer is (B). *(CPA 590 I-14)*
REQUIRED: The amount to be recorded as cost of inventory subject to trade discounts.
DISCUSSION: When inventory is subject to cash discounts, the purchases may be reflected either net of these discounts or at the gross prices. However, purchases should always be recorded net of trade discounts. A chain discount is the application of more than one trade discount to a list price. Chain discounts should be applied in steps as indicated below.

List price	$20,000
20% discount	(4,000)
	$16,000
10% discount	(1,600)
Cost of merchandise	$14,400

Answer (A) is incorrect because $14,000 applies both discounts to the retail price. Answer (C) is incorrect because $15,600 assumes the 10% discount is applied to the 20% discount. Answer (D) is incorrect because $20,000 is the list price, and it fails to reflect the discounts.

12. On December 28, 1996, Kerr Manufacturing Co. purchased goods costing $50,000. The terms were FOB destination. Some costs incurred in connection with the sale and delivery of the goods were

Packaging for shipment	$1,000
Shipping	1,500
Special handling charges	2,000

These goods were received on December 31, 1996. In Kerr's December 31, 1996 balance sheet, what amount of cost should be included in inventory?

   A. $54,500

   B. $53,500

   C. $52,000

   D. $50,000

The correct answer is (D). *(CPA 1191 I-12)*
   REQUIRED: The amount of cost for goods included in inventory.
   DISCUSSION: FOB destination means that title passes upon delivery at the destination, the seller bears the risk of loss, and the seller is responsible for the expense of delivering the goods to the designated point. Consequently, the packaging, shipping, and handling costs are not included in the inventory. The amount that should be included is therefore the purchase price of $50,000.
   Answer (A) is incorrect because the packaging, shipping, and handling costs should not be included. Answer (B) is incorrect because the shipping and handling costs should not be included. Answer (C) is incorrect because the handling costs should not be included.

13. On June 1, 1996, Pitt Corp. sold merchandise with a list price of $5,000 to Burr on account. Pitt allowed trade discounts of 30% and 20%. Credit terms were 2/15, n/40, and the sale was made FOB shipping point. Pitt prepaid $200 of delivery costs for Burr as an accommodation. On June 12, 1996, Pitt received from Burr a remittance in full payment amounting to

   A. $2,744

   B. $2,940

   C. $2,944

   D. $3,140

The correct answer is (C). *(CPA 590 I-10)*
   REQUIRED: The amount received as a remittance in full payment.
   DISCUSSION: Inventory sold should always be invoiced net of trade discounts. Remittances paid during the cash or purchase discount period should be net of these discounts. When goods are shipped FOB shipping point, they become the purchaser's inventory at the time of shipment. Thus, the purchaser is responsible for the payment of delivery costs. As indicated below, the remittance received by Pitt should amount to $2,944.

List price	$5,000
30% trade discount	(1,500)
	$3,500
20% trade discount	(700)
	$2,800
2% cash discount	(56)
	$2,744
Delivery costs	200
	$2,944

   Answer (A) is incorrect because $2,744 excludes the delivery costs. Answer (B) is incorrect because $2,940 includes a 2% cash discount on the delivery costs. Answer (D) is incorrect because $3,140 includes a 2% discount on the delivery costs and double counts the delivery costs.

14. Inventory may properly be stated above cost

   A. When its market value or its net realizable value exceeds its cost.

   B. When cost is determined under the first-in, first-out method.

   C. When cost is determined under the last-in, first-out method.

   D. Only in exceptional cases.

The correct answer is (D). *(CMA 685 3-28)*
   REQUIRED: The justification for stating inventory above cost.
   DISCUSSION: ARB 43, Chap. 4, *Inventory Pricing*, states that only in exceptional cases may inventories be stated above cost. Examples are precious metals that have a fixed monetary value with no additional cost of marketing, and fungible (interchangeable) agricultural, mineral, and other products that have an immediate marketability at quoted prices and for which it may be difficult to obtain appropriate costs.
   Answer (A) is incorrect because inventory may be stated at market value or net realizable value (sales price – costs of completion and disposal) when these amounts are less (not more) than cost in accordance with the lower of cost or market rule. Answers (B) and (C) are incorrect because FIFO and LIFO are based on cost flow assumptions. They reflect cost, not amounts above cost.

15. The following information pertains to Deal Corp.'s 1996 cost of goods sold:

Inventory, 12/31/95	$ 90,000
1996 purchases	124,000
1996 write-off of obsolete inventory	34,000
Inventory, 12/31/96	30,000

The inventory written off became obsolete because of an unexpected and unusual technological advance by a competitor. In its 1996 income statement, what amount should Deal report as cost of goods sold?

  A. $218,000

  B. $184,000

  C. $150,000

  D. $124,000

The correct answer is (C). *(CPA 593 I-48)*
  REQUIRED: The cost of goods sold for the year.
  DISCUSSION: As indicated in the T-account analysis below, cost of goods sold equals purchases plus any decrease in inventory or minus any increase in inventory (purchases minus the change in inventory). The write-off of obsolete inventory is a loss, not a component of CGS. Thus, cost of goods sold is $150,000.

Inventory

12/31/95	$ 90,000	$ 34,000	obsolescence
Purchases	124,000	150,000	CGS
	$ 30,000		

  Answer (A) is incorrect because $218,000 results from adding obsolete inventory to, not subtracting it from, beginning inventory. Answer (B) is incorrect because $184,000 includes the obsolete inventory in CGS. Answer (D) is incorrect because $124,000 equals purchases.

16. King Corp.'s trial balance for the year ended December 31, 1996 included the following:

	Debit	Credit
Sales		$300,000
Cost of sales	$120,000	
Administrative expenses	30,000	
Loss on sale of equipment	18,000	
Sales commissions	20,000	
Interest revenue		10,000
Freight-out	6,000	
Loss on early retirement of long-term debt	20,000	
Bad debt expense	6,000	
Totals	$220,000	$310,000

Other Information

Finished goods inventory:

January 1, 1996	$200,000
December 31, 1996	180,000

In King's 1996 multiple-step income statement, the cost of goods manufactured was

  A. $100,000

  B. $106,000

  C. $140,000

  D. $146,000

The correct answer is (A). *(CPA 1191 I-2)*
  REQUIRED: The cost of goods manufactured.
  DISCUSSION: Cost of goods sold equals beginning finished goods inventory, plus cost of goods manufactured, minus ending finished goods inventory. Rearranging this equation, we get cost of goods manufactured equals cost of goods sold, plus ending finished goods inventory, minus beginning finished goods inventory, or $100,000 ($120,000 cost of goods sold + $180,000 ending finished goods inventory – $200,000 beginning finished goods inventory).
  Answer (B) is incorrect because $106,000 includes the freight-out. Answer (C) is incorrect because $140,000 subtracts ending finished goods and adds beginning finished goods. Answer (D) is incorrect because $146,000 subtracts ending finished goods inventory and adds beginning finished goods. It also includes the freight-out.

17. When a company sells its products and gives the buyer the right to return the product, revenue from the sale should be recognized at the time of sale only if certain criteria are met. According to SFAS 48, *Revenue Recognition When Right of Return Exists*, which one of the following is not a criterion?

A. The seller does not have significant obligations for future performance to directly bring about the resale of the product by the buyer.

B. The buyer acquiring the product for resale has economic substance apart from that provided by the seller.

C. The buyer's obligation to the seller would not be changed in the event of physical destruction of the product.

D. The seller's price to the buyer is contingent upon the ultimate selling price received when the product is resold.

The correct answer is (D). *(CMA 692 2-17)*

REQUIRED: The item not a criterion for the recognition of a sale when the right of return exists.

DISCUSSION: SFAS 48 states that revenue may be recognized at the time of sale if all of the following conditions are met:

1. The seller's price is substantially fixed or determinable.
2. The buyer has paid the seller, or the buyer is obligated to pay, and the obligation is not contingent on resale.
3. The buyer's obligation to the seller is unchanged by damage to or theft of or destruction of the product.
4. The buyer has economic substance apart from the seller.
5. The seller does not have any significant obligations regarding resale of the product by the buyer.
6. The amount of future returns can be reasonably estimated.

Thus, the seller's price must not be contingent on the resale price; the seller's price must be substantially fixed or determinable.

Answer (A) is incorrect because the seller may not have significant future obligations. Answer (B) is incorrect because the buyer must have economic substance apart from the seller. Answer (C) is incorrect because risk of loss must reside with the buyer.

18. A sponsoring enterprise enters into an agreement whereby it sells a product to another enterprise and agrees to repurchase that product at specified prices at later dates. If the specified prices fluctuate solely because of changes in purchasing, financing, and holding costs, the transaction should be treated as which of the following?

A. A borrowing.

B. A consignment.

C. A sale and repurchase.

D. Not recorded.

The correct answer is (A). *(Publisher)*

REQUIRED: The correct accounting treatment of a product financing arrangement.

DISCUSSION: According to SFAS 49, *Accounting for Product Financing Arrangements*, such an arrangement "is a transaction in which an enterprise sells and agrees to repurchase inventory with the repurchase price equal to the original price plus carrying and financing costs, or other similar transactions." It should be treated as a borrowing if the specified prices do not fluctuate except to cover changes in purchasing, financing, and holding costs.

Answer (B) is incorrect because a consignment is the consigner's inventory physically located at the consignee's place of operations. Answer (C) is incorrect because a sale and repurchase describes the form of the transaction, not the substance. Answer (D) is incorrect because liabilities must be recorded.

19. Brad Corp. has unconditional purchase obligations associated with product financing arrangements. These obligations are reported as liabilities on Brad's balance sheet, with the related assets also recognized. In the notes to Brad's financial statements, the aggregate amount of payments for these obligations should be disclosed for each of how many years following the date of the latest balance sheet?

A. 0

B. 1

C. 5

D. 10

The correct answer is (C). *(CPA 1192 II-51)*

REQUIRED: The proper reporting for unconditional purchase obligations associated with product financing arrangements.

DISCUSSION: The standards specify that the aggregate amount of payments for an unconditional purchase obligation associated with a product financing arrangement must be disclosed for 5 years after the date of latest balance sheet.

Answers (A), (B), and (D) are incorrect because the standards require disclosure for 5 years.

20. On July 1, 1996, Link Development Company purchased a tract of land for $900,000. Additional costs of $150,000 were incurred in subdividing the land during July through December 1996. Of the tract acreage, 70% was subdivided into residential lots, as shown below, and 30% was conveyed to the city for roads and a park.

Lot Class	Number of Lots	Sales Price per Lot
A	100	$12,000
B	100	8,000
C	200	5,000

Under the relative sales value method, the cost allocated to each Class A lot should be

A. $2,625

B. $2,940

C. $3,600

D. $4,200

The correct answer is (D). *(CPA 587 I-17)*
REQUIRED: The cost to be allocated to each Class A lot under the relative sales value method.
DISCUSSION: SFAS 67, *Accounting for Costs and Initial Rental Operations of Real Estate Projects*, states that real estate donated to municipalities or other governmental agencies for uses that will benefit the project shall be allocated as a common cost of the project. Thus, none of the costs of the project should be allocated to the land donated to the city. The total cost of acquiring the land ($900,000 + $150,000 = $1,050,000) should be allocated to the lots that will generate revenue. Using the relative sales value method as indicated below, 40% of the total cost, or $420,000 (40% x $1,050,000), should be allocated to the Class A lots. The amount per lot will be $4,200 ($420,000 ÷ 100).

Lot Class	Number of Lots	Sales Price	Sales Value	Relative Value
A	100	$12,000	$1,200,000	40%
B	100	8,000	800,000	26 2/3%
C	200	5,000	1,000,000	33 1/3%
			$3,000,000	100%

Answer (A) is incorrect because $2,625 results from the relative value based on the number of lots per lot class. Answer (B) is incorrect because $2,940 incorrectly allocates only 70% of the total costs to the residential lots. Answer (C) is incorrect because $3,600 excludes the cost of subdividing the land.

9.2 FIFO, LIFO, Weighted Average

21. The weighted average for the year inventory cost flow method is applicable to which of the following inventory systems?

	Periodic	Perpetual
A.	Yes	Yes
B.	Yes	No
C.	No	Yes
D.	No	No

The correct answer is (B). *(CPA 586 T-11)*
REQUIRED: The applicability of the weighted-average cost flow method to periodic and perpetual inventory systems.
DISCUSSION: The weighted-average method determines an average cost only once (at the end of the period) and is therefore applicable only to a periodic system. In contrast, the weighted moving average method requires determination of a new weighted-average cost after each purchase and thus applies only to a perpetual system.
Answers (A), (C), and (D) are incorrect because the weighted average applies only to the periodic inventory system.

22. The LIFO inventory cost flow method may be applied to which of the following inventory systems?

	Periodic	Perpetual
A.	No	No
B.	No	Yes
C.	Yes	Yes
D.	Yes	No

The correct answer is (C). *(CPA 1182 T-6)*
REQUIRED: The applicability of LIFO to periodic and perpetual inventory systems.
DISCUSSION: In a periodic system, a purchases account is used, and the beginning inventory remains unchanged during the accounting period. Cost of goods sold is determined only at year-end and is the difference between the goods available for sale (beginning inventory + purchases) and ending inventory.
In a perpetual system, purchases are directly recorded in the inventory account, and cost of goods sold is determined as the goods are sold. LIFO may be applied to both a periodic and a perpetual system, but the amount of cost of goods sold may vary with the system chosen.
Answers (A), (B), and (D) are incorrect because LIFO may be used under both a periodic and a perpetual inventory system.

Questions 23 through 27 are based on the following information. Addison Hardware began the month of November with 150 large brass switchplates on hand at a cost of $4.00 each. These switchplates sell for $7.00 each. The following schedule presents the sales and purchases of this item during the month of November.

| Date of Transaction | Purchases | | |
	Quantity Received	Unit Cost	Units Sold
November 5			100
November 7	200	$4.20	
November 9			150
November 11	200	4.40	
November 17			220
November 22	250	4.80	
November 29			100

23. If Addison uses FIFO inventory pricing, the value of the inventory on November 30 would be

A. $936

B. $1,012

C. $1,046

D. $1,104

The correct answer is (D). *(CMA 1292 2-25)*
REQUIRED: The value of the ending inventory using the FIFO method of inventory costing.
DISCUSSION: Under FIFO, the ending inventory consists of the most recent inventory purchased. The beginning inventory included 150 units and purchases totaled 650 units, a total of 800 units. Sales equaled 570 units (100 + 150 + 220 + 100). Thus, ending inventory was 230 units (800 – 570). Under FIFO, these units are valued at the cost of the most recent 230 units purchased, or $4.80. Ending inventory is therefore $1,104 (230 x $4.80).
Answer (A) is incorrect because $936 is based on periodic LIFO. Answer (B) is incorrect because $1,012 is based on the weighted-average unit cost of $4.40, not $4.80. Answer (C) is incorrect because $1,046 is the ending inventory under perpetual LIFO.

24. If Addison uses perpetual moving average inventory pricing, the sale of 220 items on November 17 will be recorded at a unit cost of

A. $4.00

B. $4.16

C. $4.20

D. $4.32

The correct answer is (D). *(CMA 1292 2-26)*
REQUIRED: The unit cost of the items sold on November 17 under the perpetual moving-average method.
DISCUSSION: The beginning inventory consisted of 150 units at $4.00 each. Following the November 5 sale, the inventory valuation was $200 (50 units x $4). The November 7 purchase added 200 units at $4.20, after which the moving average unit cost was $4.16 {[[$200 + (200 units x $4.20)] ÷ (50 units + 200 units)}. The November 9 sale of 150 units left 100 units at $4.16. Adding $416 (100 units x $4.16) to the $880 purchase on November 11 brought the total inventory to 300 units with a total cost of $1,296, or $4.32 each. Thus, $4.32 was the unit cost of items sold on November 17.
Answer (A) is incorrect because $4.00 was the cost of the beginning inventory. Answer (B) is incorrect because $4.16 was the unit cost of the items sold on November 9. Answer (C) is incorrect because $4.20 would have been the cost if the perpetual LIFO method had been used for the November 9 sale.

25. Please refer to the information preceding question 23. If Addison uses weighted-average inventory pricing, the gross profit for November will be

   A. $1,046

   B. $1,482

   C. $1,516

   D. $1,528

The correct answer is (B). *(CMA 1292 2-27)*

   REQUIRED: The gross profit if the weighted-average method is used.

   DISCUSSION: The value of the total goods available for sale is determined as follows:

Beginning inventory	150 × $4.00 =	$ 600.00
Nov. 7 purchase	200 × $4.20 =	840.00
Nov. 11 purchase	200 × $4.40 =	880.00
Nov. 22 purchase	250 × $4.80 =	1,200.00
Total available	800	$3,520.00

   The weighted-average unit cost is $4.40 ($3,520 ÷ 800 units available). The cost of goods sold and total sales are therefore $2,508 ($4.40 x 570 units sold) and $3,990 ($7 x 570 units), respectively. Consequently, gross profit is $1,482 ($3,990 – $2,508).

   Answer (A) is incorrect because $1,046 is the ending inventory under perpetual LIFO. Answer (C) is incorrect because $1,516 is based on perpetual LIFO. Answer (D) is incorrect because $1,528 is based on the moving-average method.

26. Please refer to the information preceding question 23. If Addison uses periodic LIFO inventory pricing, the cost of goods sold for November will be

   A. $2,416

   B. $2,444

   C. $2,474

   D. $2,584

The correct answer is (D). *(CMA 1292 2-28)*

   REQUIRED: The cost of goods sold using periodic LIFO.

   DISCUSSION: The value of the goods available for sale is as follows:

Beginning inventory	150 × $4.00 =	$ 600.00
Nov. 7 purchase	200 × $4.20 =	840.00
Nov. 11 purchase	200 × $4.40 =	880.00
Nov. 22 purchase	250 × $4.80 =	1,200.00
Total available	800	$3,520.00

   The ending inventory consists of 230 units. Under periodic LIFO, these are costed at the prices paid for the earliest 230 units purchased, or 150 units at $4.00 and 80 units at $4.20, a total of $936. Hence, cost of goods sold is $2,584 ($3,520 goods available – $936 EI).

   Answer (A) is incorrect because $2,416 is based on the FIFO method. Answer (B) is incorrect because $2,444 is based on the moving-average method. Answer (C) is incorrect because $2,474 is based on perpetual LIFO.

27. Please refer to the information preceding question 23. If Addison uses perpetual LIFO inventory pricing, the value of the inventory at November 30 will be

A. $936

B. $1,012

C. $1,046

D. $1,076

The correct answer is (C). *(CMA 1292 2-29)*

REQUIRED: The value of the inventory using the perpetual LIFO inventory pricing method.

DISCUSSION: Under perpetual LIFO, the inventory valuation is recalculated as follows after every purchase and sale. The 230 units in ending inventory consist of 150 units at $4.80 each, 30 units at $4.20 each, and 50 units from the beginning inventory at $4.00 each.

Date	Receipts	Sales	Ending Inventory
11-1	150 @ $4.00 = $600		$ 600.00
11-5		100 @ $4.00 = $400	200.00
11-7	200 @ $4.20 = $840		1,040.00
11-9		150 @ $4.20 = $630	410.00
11-11	200 @ $4.40 = $880		1,290.00
11-17		200 @ $4.40 = $880	
		20 @ $4.20 = $ 84	326.00
11-22	250 @ $4.80 = $1,200		1,526.00
11-29		100 @ $4.80 = $480	1,046.00

Answer (A) is incorrect because $936 is based on periodic LIFO. Answer (B) is incorrect because $1,012 is based on the weighted-average method. Answer (D) is incorrect because $1,076 is based on the moving-average method.

28. The cost of materials has risen steadily over the year. Which of the following methods of estimating the ending balance of the materials inventory account will result in the highest net income, assuming all other variables remain constant?

A. Last-in, first-out (LIFO).

B. First-in, first-out (FIFO).

C. Weighted average.

D. Specific identification.

The correct answer is (B). *(CIA 596 IV-11)*

REQUIRED: The inventory flow assumption yielding the highest net income given rising prices.

DISCUSSION: Net income will be higher when cost of goods sold is lower, other factors held constant. Cost of goods sold equals beginning inventory, plus purchases, minus ending inventory. Accordingly, cost of goods sold will be lowest when the ending inventory is highest. Ending inventory is highest under FIFO because the older, less expensive items are deemed to have been sold, leaving the more expensive items in the ending inventory.

Answer (A) is incorrect because LIFO yields the lowest net income. Answer (C) is incorrect because weighted average averages inventory, so it results in a lower net income than FIFO. Answer (D) is incorrect because, under specific identification, the newest (most expensive) items are sold first, resulting in a higher cost of goods sold and lower income.

29. The operations of a firm may be viewed as a continual series of transactions or as a series of separate ventures. The inventory valuation method that views a firm as a series of separate ventures is

A. First-in, first-out.

B. Last-in, first-out.

C. Weighted average.

D. Specific identification.

The correct answer is (D). *(CMA 684 3-14)*

REQUIRED: The inventory valuation method that views a firm as a series of separate ventures.

DISCUSSION: When specific inventory is clearly identified from the time of purchase through the time of sale and is costed on that basis, the firm's operations may be viewed as a series of separate ventures or transactions. Much business activity, however, involves goods whose identity is lost between the time of acquisition and the time of sale. Moreover, if items of inventory are interchangeable, the use of specific identification may not result in the most useful financial information. For these reasons, other inventory cost flow assumptions essentially view the firm as a continual series of transactions.

Answers (A), (B), and (C) are incorrect because each views the firm's activities as a continual series of transactions.

30. During periods of rising prices, when the FIFO inventory method is used, a perpetual inventory system results in an ending inventory cost that is

   A. The same as in a periodic inventory system.

   B. Higher than in a periodic inventory system.

   C. Lower than in a periodic inventory system.

   D. Higher or lower than in a periodic inventory system, depending on whether physical quantities have increased or decreased.

The correct answer is (A). *(CPA 592 T-24)*

REQUIRED: The difference (if any) between periodic and perpetual FIFO during inflation.

DISCUSSION: FIFO (first-in, first-out) assumes that the earliest purchased goods are sold first. Thus, under both a periodic and a perpetual FIFO, ending inventory will always be the same regardless of inflation.

Answers (B), (C), and (D) are incorrect because FIFO ending inventory will always be the same regardless of whether a perpetual or a periodic system is used and whether prices are constant, increasing, or decreasing.

31. A company had 1,000 units of opening inventory that cost $10 per unit. On May 1, 1,000 units were purchased at a cost of $11 each, and on September 1, another 1,000 units were purchased at a cost of $12 each. If 2,000 units were sold during the year, the company will report cost of goods sold of <List A> if the <List B> method of inventory valuation is used.

	List A	List B
A.	$22,000	LIFO
B.	$23,000	Weighted average
C.	$21,000	FIFO
D.	$22,000	FIFO

The correct answer is (C). *(CIA 595 IV-13)*

REQUIRED: The proper match of cost of goods sold and inventory valuation method.

DISCUSSION: Under FIFO, the first items purchased are presumed to be the first sold. Given that 3,000 units were available and 2,000 units were sold, FIFO cost of goods sold equals $21,000 [(1,000 x $10) BI + (1,000 x $11) May 1 purchase].

Answer (A) is incorrect because cost of goods sold is $22,000 under the weighted-average method. Under LIFO, cost of goods sold is $23,000 ($12,000 + $11,000). The 2,000 most recently purchased units are presumed to have been sold. Answer (B) is incorrect because the weighted-average unit cost of all items available for sale is $11 [($10,000 + $11,000 + $12,000) ÷ 3,000]. Given that 2,000 units were sold, cost of goods sold is $22,000 (2,000 x $11) under this method. Answer (D) is incorrect because FIFO cost of goods sold is $21,000. Under the weighted-average method, cost of goods sold is $22,000.

32. Ordinarily, which inventory costing method approximates most closely the current cost for each of the following?

	Cost of Goods Sold	Ending Inventory
A.	LIFO	FIFO
B.	LIFO	LIFO
C.	FIFO	FIFO
D.	FIFO	LIFO

The correct answer is (A). *(CPA 1191 T-7)*

REQUIRED: The inventory costing method that approximates most closely the current cost of cost of goods sold and ending inventory.

DISCUSSION: The LIFO basis assumes that the most recently purchased items are the first to be sold. Thus, LIFO is a better approximation of current cost of goods sold than FIFO. According to SFAS 89, if "turnover is rapid and material amounts of depreciation are not allocated to inventory, cost of goods sold measured on a LIFO basis may provide an acceptable approximation of cost of goods sold, measured at current cost, provided that the effect of any LIFO inventory liquidations (that is, decreases in earlier years' LIFO layers) is excluded." However, the FIFO basis more closely approximates the current cost of ending inventory because it assumes the most recent purchases are the last to be sold.

Answers (B), (C), and (D) are incorrect because current cost of goods sold and current cost of ending inventory are most closely approximated by LIFO and FIFO, respectively.

33. Which of the following factors would not be considered in the selection of LIFO as an inventory costing method?

A. Tax benefits.

B. Matching.

C. Physical flow.

D. Improved cash flow.

The correct answer is (C). *(Publisher)*
REQUIRED: The factor that would not be considered in selecting LIFO as an inventory costing method.
DISCUSSION: Inventory costing methods are based on cost flow assumptions, not physical flow assumptions. If a LIFO physical flow were actually followed, the first goods purchased might never be sold. In most cases, they would deteriorate from damage, obsolescence, etc.
Answer (A) is incorrect because tax benefits do arise from LIFO. Less taxable income is reported in periods of rising prices. Answer (B) is incorrect because LIFO permits the matching of current costs (the most recent inventory purchases) with current revenues. Answer (D) is incorrect because the tax benefits arising from LIFO in periods of rising prices improve cash flow relative to FIFO.

34. In a periodic inventory system that uses the weighted-average cost flow method, the beginning inventory is the

A. Net purchases minus the ending inventory.

B. Net purchases minus the cost of goods sold.

C. Total goods available for sale minus the net purchases.

D. Total goods available for sale minus the cost of goods sold.

The correct answer is (C). *(CPA 1188 T-26)*
REQUIRED: The beginning inventory in a periodic system using weighted-average cost.
DISCUSSION: In a periodic system, beginning inventory is equal to the total goods available for sale minus net purchases, regardless of the cost flow method used.
Answer (A) is incorrect because it states the difference between the beginning inventory and the cost of goods sold. Answer (B) is incorrect because this difference is the change in inventory valuation during the period. Answer (D) is incorrect because goods available minus cost of sales equals ending inventory.

35. The acquisition cost of a heavily used raw material changes frequently. The book value of the inventory of this material at year-end will be the same if perpetual records are kept as it would be under a periodic inventory method only if the book value is computed under the

A. Weighted-average method.

B. First-in, first-out method.

C. Last-in, first-out method.

D. Base-stock method.

The correct answer is (B). *(CPA 1172 T-6)*
REQUIRED: The cost flow assumption giving the same year-end book value under both perpetual and periodic inventory systems.
DISCUSSION: Under FIFO, the oldest goods are assumed to have been sold first, and it would not matter whether the cost of goods sold was determined at the point of sale (perpetual) or at year-end (periodic).
Answers (A), (C), and (D) are incorrect because, under each method, different goods are assumed to be sold if the determination is made at the time of sale (perpetual) rather than at year-end (periodic).

36. Drew Co. uses the average cost inventory method for internal reporting purposes and LIFO for financial statement and income tax reporting. At December 31, 1996, the inventory was $375,000 using average cost and $320,000 using LIFO. The unadjusted credit balance in the LIFO reserve account on December 31, 1996 was $35,000. What adjusting entry should Drew record to adjust from average cost to LIFO at December 31, 1996?

		Debit	Credit
A.	Cost of goods sold	$55,000	
	Inventory		$55,000
B.	Cost of goods sold	$55,000	
	LIFO reserve		$55,000
C.	Cost of goods sold	$20,000	
	Inventory		$20,000
D.	Cost of goods sold	$20,000	
	LIFO reserve		$20,000

The correct answer is (D). *(CPA 1193 I-19)*
REQUIRED: The journal entry to adjust from average cost to LIFO.
DISCUSSION: The LIFO reserve account is an allowance that adjusts the inventory balance stated according to the method used for internal reporting purposes to the LIFO amount appropriate for external reporting. If the LIFO effect is $55,000 ($375,000 average cost – $320,000 LIFO cost) and the account has a $35,000 credit balance, it must be credited for $20,000, with a corresponding debit to cost of goods sold.
Answer (A) is incorrect because the balance in the reserve account should equal $55,000, and inventory should not be adjusted. Answer (B) is incorrect because the balance in the reserve account should be $55,000. Answer (C) is incorrect because inventory should not be adjusted.

37. Which of the following is not valid as it applies to inventory costing methods?

   A. If inventory quantities are to be maintained, part of the earnings must be invested (plowed back) in inventories when FIFO is used during a period of rising prices.

   B. LIFO tends to smooth out the net income pattern because it matches current cost of goods sold with current revenue, if inventories remain at constant quantities.

   C. When a firm using the LIFO method fails to maintain its usual inventory position (reduces stock on hand below customary levels), there may be a matching of old costs with current revenue.

   D. FIFO, but not LIFO, permits some control by management over the amount of net income for a period through controlled purchases.

The correct answer is (D). *(CPA 1174 T-22)*
   REQUIRED: The invalid statement concerning inventory valuation.
   DISCUSSION: Under LIFO, the most recent purchases are included in cost of goods sold. Management could affect net income with an end-of-period purchase that would immediately alter cost of goods sold. A last-minute FIFO purchase included in the ending inventory would have no such effect.
   Answer (A) is incorrect because maintenance of inventory quantities results in an increased dollar investment in inventory when FIFO is used during inflationary times. Answer (B) is incorrect because LIFO smoothes income in a period of rising prices. The inflated current costs are matched with current sales prices. Answer (C) is incorrect because LIFO results in matching old, lower costs with current revenues when inventory is liquidated. If sales exceed purchases, a firm liquidates earlier, lower-priced LIFO layers.

38. The Hastings Company began operations on January 1 of the year before last and uses the FIFO method in costing its raw material inventory. Management is contemplating a change to the LIFO method and is interested in determining what effect such a change will have on net income. Accordingly, the following information has been developed:

Final Inventory	Year 1	Year 2
FIFO	$240,000	$270,000
LIFO	200,000	210,000
Net Income (per FIFO)	$120,000	$170,000

Based upon the above information, a change to the LIFO method in Year 2 would result in net income for Year 2 of

   A. $110,000

   B. $150,000

   C. $170,000

   D. $230,000

The correct answer is (A). *(CPA 578 II-7)*
   REQUIRED: The second-year net income after a change from FIFO to LIFO in the second year of operations.
   DISCUSSION: In the first year of operations, beginning inventory is the same under FIFO and LIFO. The amount of purchases in any year is also the same. The difference in the first year was that FIFO ending inventory was $40,000 greater ($240,000 FIFO – $200,000 LIFO). Thus, FIFO net income was also $40,000 greater. The difference in income in the second year is equal to the $20,000 difference between the FIFO inventory change and the LIFO inventory change (FIFO: $270,000 – $240,000 = $30,000 change; LIFO: $210,000 – $200,000 = $10,000 change; $30,000 – $10,000 = $20,000 difference). Because a change from FIFO to LIFO will be treated as a cumulative effect-type accounting change, the $170,000 FIFO net income will decrease by $60,000 ($40,000 cumulative effect on beginning retained earnings + $20,000). Net LIFO income will therefore be $110,000 ($170,000 – $60,000). In some cases, the cumulative effect on beginning retained earnings of a change from FIFO to LIFO may not be included in the calculation of net income. The reason is that the cumulative effect may not be determinable (APB 20, *Accounting Changes*). For Hastings Company, however, this concern does not arise.
   Answer (B) is incorrect because $150,000 incorrectly adds the difference from Year 1 to the net income under LIFO for Year 2. Answer (C) is incorrect because $170,000 is the income for Year 2 under FIFO. Answer (D) is incorrect because $230,000 incorrectly adds the difference between LIFO and FIFO to FIFO net income, instead of subtracting the difference from FIFO net income.

9.3 Lower of Cost or Market

39. Which of the following statement(s) is(are) correct when a company applying the lower-of-cost-or-market method reports its inventory at replacement cost?

I. The original cost is less than replacement cost.
II. The net realizable value is equal to or greater than replacement cost.

    A. I only.

    B. II only.

    C. Both I and II.

    D. Neither I nor II.

The correct answer is (B). *(CPA 1194 F-14)*
   REQUIRED: The value of inventory under the lower-of-cost-or-market rule.
   DISCUSSION: ARB 43, Chap. 4, *Inventory Pricing*, defines market as current replacement cost subject to maximum and minimum values. The maximum is net realizable value; the minimum is net realizable value minus normal profit. When replacement cost is within this range, it is used as the market value. Consequently, only statement II is correct.
   Answers (A) and (C) are incorrect because replacement cost must be lower than original cost. Answer (D) is incorrect because replacement cost must not exceed net realizable value.

40. The lower-of-cost-or-market rule for inventories may be applied to total inventory, to groups of similar items, or to each item. Which application usually results in the lowest inventory amount?

    A. All applications result in the same amount.

    B. Total inventory.

    C. Groups of similar items.

    D. Separately to each item.

The correct answer is (D). *(CPA 1193 T-4)*
   REQUIRED: The application of the LCM rule that usually results in the lowest amount.
   DISCUSSION: Applying the LCM rule to each item of inventory produces the lowest valuation for each item and therefore the lowest and most conservative valuation for the total inventory. The reason is that aggregating items results in the inclusion of some items at amounts greater than LCM. For example, if item A (cost $2, market $1) and item B (cost $3, market $4) are aggregated for LCM purposes, the inventory valuation is $5. If the rule is applied separately to A and B, the LCM valuation is $4.
   Answer (A) is incorrect because each application results in a different amount. Answers (B) and (C) are incorrect because grouping all or some items results in a higher valuation than applying the LCM rule to individual items.

41. Thread Co. is selecting its inventory system in preparation for its first year of operations. Thread intends to use either the periodic weighted-average method or the perpetual moving-average method, and to apply the lower-of-cost-or-market rule either to individual items or to the total inventory. Inventory prices are expected to generally increase throughout 1996, although a few individual prices will decrease. What inventory system should Thread select if it wants to maximize the inventory carrying amount at December 31, 1996?

	Inventory Method	Cost or Market Application
A.	Perpetual	Total inventory
B.	Perpetual	Individual Item
C.	Periodic	Total inventory
D.	Periodic	Individual item

The correct answer is (A). *(CPA 1191 T-27)*
   REQUIRED: The inventory system that maximizes the inventory carrying amount at year-end.
   DISCUSSION: The weighted-average inventory pricing system is applicable to a periodic inventory system. The weighted-average unit cost is equal to the total cost of goods available for sale divided by the number of units available for sale. The moving-average system is applicable only to perpetual inventories. It requires that a new weighted average be computed after every purchase. This moving average is based on remaining inventory held and the new inventory purchased. In a period of rising prices, the moving-average method results in a higher unit and total ending inventory because the most recent purchases are given greater weight in the calculation. ARB 43, Chap. 4, *Inventory Pricing*, permits application of the lower-of-cost-or-market rule either to each item in the inventory or to the inventory as a whole. Applying the LCM rule to the total inventory will maximize the carrying amount because the reduction in the inventory will equal only the excess of aggregate cost over aggregate market. LCM applied on an individual item basis recognizes all of the inventory declines but none of the gains.
   Answers (B), (C), and (D) are incorrect because the moving-average method and applying the LCM rule to the total inventory result in a higher ending inventory.

42. The replacement cost of an inventory item is below the net realizable value and above the net realizable value minus the normal profit margin. The original cost of the inventory item is below the net realizable value minus the normal profit margin. Under the lower-of-cost-or-market method, the inventory item should be valued at

A. Net realizable value.

B. Net realizable value minus the normal profit margin.

C. Original cost.

D. Replacement cost.

The correct answer is (C). *(CPA 1190 T-17)*
REQUIRED: The value for an inventory item under the lower-of-cost-or-market method.
DISCUSSION: When replacement cost is below the NRV and above the NRV minus the normal profit margin, replacement cost should be used as the market value. Given that the original cost of the inventory item is below market, the original cost should be used to value the inventory item under the lower-of-cost-or-market method.
Answers (A) and (B) are incorrect because the replacement cost, given the circumstances, is designated as market. Answer (D) is incorrect because cost is below market.

43. The original cost of an inventory item is below both replacement cost and net realizable value. The net realizable value minus normal profit margin is below the original cost. Under the lower of cost of market method, the inventory item should be valued at

A. Replacement cost.

B. Net realizable value.

C. Net realizable value minus normal profit margin.

D. Original cost.

The correct answer is (D). *(CPA 1192 T-14)*
REQUIRED: The value of inventory under the lower of cost or market method.
DISCUSSION: ARB 43, Chap. 4, *Inventory Pricing*, defines market as current replacement cost subject to maximum and minimum values. The maximum is net realizable value, and the minimum is net realizable value minus normal profit. When replacement cost is within this range, it is used as the market value. The original cost is above the NRV minus normal profit margin but below the NRV and the replacement cost. Thus, market must be the NRV (if it is less than replacement cost) or the replacement cost (which is greater than NRV minus normal profit), and LCM is equal to original cost.
Answers (A) and (B) are incorrect because replacement cost and the NRV are greater than original cost. Answer (C) is incorrect because net realizable value minus normal profit margin is less than original cost.

44. Morse Co. has determined its December 31, 1996 inventory on a FIFO basis to be $400,000. Information pertaining to that inventory follows:

Estimated selling price	$408,000
Estimated cost of disposal	20,000
Normal profit margin	60,000
Current replacement cost	360,000

Morse records losses that result from applying the lower-of-cost-or-market rule. At December 31, 1996, what should be the net carrying value of Morse's inventory?

A. $400,000

B. $388,000

C. $360,000

D. $328,000

The correct answer is (C). *(CPA 593 I-21)*
REQUIRED: The net carrying value of Morse's inventory.
DISCUSSION: Under the lower-of-cost-or-market method, market is current replacement cost subject to a maximum (ceiling) equal to net realizable value and a minimum (floor) equal to net realizable value minus a normal profit. NRV equals selling price minus costs of completion and disposal. Here, original cost equals $400,000 and replacement cost equals $360,000. The lower-of-cost-or-market method uses the lower of the two, $360,000, to value its inventory. However, the inventory cannot be valued higher than the NRV of $388,000 ($408,000 selling price – $20,000 cost of disposal). Furthermore, the inventory cannot be valued lower than NRV minus normal profit or $328,000 ($388,000 NRV – $60,000 normal profit). Since the lower of cost or market ($360,000) is between $388,000 (ceiling) and $328,000 (floor), the net carrying value of inventory is $360,000.
Answer (A) is incorrect because $400,000 is the original cost. Answer (B) is incorrect because $388,000 is the NRV (ceiling). Answer (D) is incorrect because $328,000 is the NRV minus normal profit (floor).

Per Unit	Skis	Boots	Parkas
Historical cost	$190.00	$106.00	$53.00
Selling price	217.00	145.00	73.75
Cost to distribute	19.00	8.00	2.50
Current replacement cost	203.00	105.00	51.00
Normal profit margin	32.00	29.00	21.25

Questions 45 through 47 are based on the following information. The data in the opposite column concerns items in Sportaway Co.'s inventory.

45. The limits to the market value (i.e., the ceiling and the floor) that should be used in the lower-of-cost-or-market comparison of skis are

A. $217 and $198.

B. $217 and $185.

C. $198 and $166.

D. $185 and $166.

The correct answer is (C). *(CMA 694 2-22)*
REQUIRED: The limits of market value for skis.
DISCUSSION: ARB 43, Chap. 4, *Inventory Pricing*, defines market as current replacement cost subject to a maximum equal to net realizable value and a minimum equal to net realizable value minus a normal profit. Net realizable value is equal to selling price minus costs of completion and disposal. For Sportaway's Skis, the net realizable value is $198 ($217 selling price – $19 distribution cost). Net realizable value minus normal profit is $166 ($198 net realizable value – $32 normal profit).
Answer (A) is incorrect because $217 is the selling price, and $198 is the NRV. Answer (B) is incorrect because $217 is the selling price, and $185 is the selling price minus normal profit. Answer (D) is incorrect because the ceiling equals the net realizable value, not selling price minus normal profit.

46. The cost amount that should be used in the lower of cost or market comparison of ski boots is

A. $105

B. $106

C. $108

D. $137

The correct answer is (B). *(CMA 694 2-23)*
REQUIRED: The cost amount for ski boots.
DISCUSSION: The cost amount used in the lower-of-cost-or-market comparison is the historical cost of an item. Thus, for ski boots, the historical cost of $106 is compared with the market figure.
Answer (A) is incorrect because $105 is the current replacement cost, not the historical cost. Answer (C) is incorrect because $108 is the net realizable value less the normal profit margin, not the historical cost. Answer (D) is incorrect because net realizable value ($137) is not used in the calculation of historical cost.

47. The market amount that should be used to value the parkas on the basis of lower of cost or market is

A. $51.00

B. $53.00

C. $50.00

D. $71.25

The correct answer is (A). *(CMA 694 2-24)*
REQUIRED: The market amount for parkas.
DISCUSSION: Net realizable value for parkas is $71.25 ($73.75 selling price – $2.50 distribution cost). The net realizable value minus normal profit is $50 ($71.25 net realizable value – $21.25 normal profit margin). The $51 replacement cost falls between the $71.25 ceiling and the $50 floor and is the appropriate market value. Because the $51 market value is lower than the $53 historical cost, it should be the basis of valuation for the parkas.
Answer (B) is incorrect because $53 is the historical cost. Answer (C) is incorrect because $50 is the floor. It is used only if replacement cost is lower. Answer (D) is incorrect because $71.25 is the net realizable value. It is used as the market amount only if replacement cost is greater.

48. Based on a physical inventory taken on December 31, 1996, Chewy Co. determined its chocolate inventory on a FIFO basis at $26,000 with a replacement cost of $20,000. Chewy estimated that, after further processing costs of $12,000, the chocolate could be sold as finished candy bars for $40,000. Chewy's normal profit margin is 10% of sales. Under the lower-of-cost-or-market rule, what amount should Chewy report as chocolate inventory in its December 31, 1996 balance sheet?

A. $28,000

B. $26,000

C. $24,000

D. $20,000

The correct answer is (C). *(CPA 1193 I-21)*

REQUIRED: The amount reported for inventory under the lower-of-cost-or-market rule.

DISCUSSION: ARB 43, Chap. 4, *Inventory Pricing*, defines market as current replacement cost subject to maximum and minimum values. The maximum is net realizable value, and the minimum is net realizable value minus normal profit. When replacement cost is within this range, it is used as the market value. Cost is given as $26,000. Net realizable value is $28,000 ($40,000 selling price – $12,000 additional processing costs), and net realizable value minus a normal profit equals $24,000 [$28,000 – (10% x $40,000)]. Because the lowest value in the range ($24,000) exceeds replacement cost ($20,000), it is used as the market value. Because market value ($24,000) is less than cost ($26,000), it is also the inventory valuation.

Answer (A) is incorrect because $28,000 is the NRV.
Answer (B) is incorrect because $26,000 is the cost.
Answer (D) is incorrect because $20,000 is the replacement cost.

9.4 Gross Margin Ratio

49. Which of the following methods of inventory valuation is allowable at interim dates but not at year-end?

A. Weighted average.

B. Estimated gross profit rates.

C. Retail method.

D. Specific identification.

The correct answer is (B). *(CPA 579 T-3)*

REQUIRED: The inventory valuation method permitted at interim dates but not at year-end.

DISCUSSION: APB 28, *Interim Financial Reporting*, permits using the estimated gross profit method to determine inventory for interim statements provided that adequate disclosure is made of reconciliations with the annual physical inventory at year-end. Any method allowable at year-end is also allowable at an interim date.

Answers (A), (C), and (D) are incorrect because each is allowable at year-end according to GAAP.

50. Zeno Menswear, Inc. maintains a markup of 60% based on cost. The company's selling and administrative expenses average 30% of sales. Annual sales amounted to $960,000. Zeno's cost of goods sold and operating profit for the year are

	Cost of Goods Sold	Operating Profit
A.	$576,000	$96,000
B.	$576,000	$288,000
C.	$600,000	$72,000
D.	$600,000	$288,000

The correct answer is (C). *(CPA 1185 I-37)*

REQUIRED: The estimated cost of goods sold and operating profit.

DISCUSSION: A markup of 60% based on cost is equal to the fraction 60% markup ÷ 100% cost. Because retail is equal to markup plus cost, a markup on retail is equal to the 60% markup divided by the total of the 100% cost plus the 60% markup. Zeno's markup on retail is therefore 37.5% [60% ÷ (100% + 60%)]. If the markup on retail is 37.5%, cost of goods sold must be 62.5% (1 – .375) of sales. Thus, cost of goods sold must be $600,000 ($960,000 sales x 62.5%). Selling and administrative expenses average 30% of sales and are estimated to be $288,000 ($960,000 sales x 30%). Accordingly, operating profit is $72,000 ($960,000 sales – $600,000 CGS – $288,000 S&A expenses).

Answer (A) is incorrect because cost of goods sold is based on a 60% markup from cost, not sales, and the $96,000 operating profit is based on the incorrect cost of goods sold. Answer (B) is incorrect because cost of goods sold is based on a 60% markup from cost, not sales, and the $288,000 is the selling and administrative expenses. Answer (D) is incorrect because $288,000 is the selling and administrative expenses.

51. The following information is available for Cooke Company for its most recent year:

Net sales	$1,800,000
Freight-in	45,000
Purchase discounts	25,000
Ending inventory	120,000

The gross margin is 40% of net sales. What is the cost of goods available for sale?

A. $840,000

B. $960,000

C. $1,200,000

D. $1,220,000

The correct answer is (C). *(CPA 582 II-13)*
REQUIRED: The amount of cost of goods available for sale.
DISCUSSION: Because the gross margin equals 40% of net sales, cost of goods sold equals 60% of net sales, or $1,080,000. Cost of goods available for sale equals the cost of goods sold plus the cost of the goods in ending inventory. Hence, cost of goods available for sale equals $1,080,000 plus $120,000, or $1,200,000 (BI + PUR = GAFS* = CGS + EI). Freight-in and purchase discounts are not used to estimate CGS or GAFS in the gross margin approach.

Ending inventory	$ 120,000
Cost of goods sold	1,080,000
Goods available for sale*	$1,200,000

Answer (A) is incorrect because $840,000 is gross margin plus ending inventory. Answer (B) is incorrect because $960,000 is cost of goods sold minus ending inventory. Answer (D) is incorrect because $1,220,000 is cost of goods available for sale plus freight-in and minus purchase discounts.

52. The following information is available for the Silver Company for the 3 months ended March 31 of this year:

Merchandise inventory, January 1 of this year	$ 900,000
Purchases	3,400,000
Freight-in	200,000
Sales	4,800,000

The gross margin recorded was 25% of sales. What should be the merchandise inventory at March 31?

A. $700,000

B. $900,000

C. $1,125,000

D. $1,200,000

The correct answer is (B). *(CPA 1180 II-11)*
REQUIRED: The estimated ending inventory using the gross profit method.
DISCUSSION: If the gross profit margin is 25% of sales, cost of goods sold equals 75% of sales. Ending inventory is equal to goods available for sale minus cost of goods sold.

Beginning inventory	$ 900,000
Purchases	3,400,000
Freight-in	200,000
Goods available for sale	$4,500,000
CGS (1 – .25) x ($4,800,000)	(3,600,000)
Ending inventory	$ 900,000

Answer (A) is incorrect because $700,000 excludes freight-in. Answer (C) is incorrect because ending inventory is goods available for sale minus cost of goods sold. Answer (D) is incorrect because $1,200,000 is the gross margin.

53. A store uses the gross profit method to estimate inventory and cost of goods sold for interim reporting purposes. Past experience indicates that the average gross profit rate is 25% of sales. The following data relate to the month of March:

Inventory cost, March 1	$25,000
Purchases during the month at cost	67,000
Sales	84,000
Sales returns	3,000

Using the data above, what is the estimated ending inventory at March 31?

A. $20,250

B. $21,000

C. $29,000

D. $31,250

The correct answer is (D). *(CIA 1185 IV-14)*
REQUIRED: The estimated ending inventory value based on a 25% gross margin ratio.
DISCUSSION: The gross profit rate is 25% of sales. Thus, estimated cost of goods sold is 75% (1 – .25) of sales. Subtracting estimated cost of goods sold from total goods available for sale leaves an estimated ending inventory figure of $31,250.

Beginning inventory	$25,000
Purchases	67,000
Goods available for sale	$92,000
Estimated CGS (1 – .25) x ($84,000 – $3,000)	(60,750)
Estimated ending inventory	$31,250

Answer (A) is incorrect because $20,250 is the gross margin. Answer (B) is incorrect because $21,000 is the gross margin without considering sales returns. Answer (C) is incorrect because $29,000 fails to consider sales returns.

54. Q Co. prepares monthly income statements. A physical inventory is taken only at year-end; hence, month-end inventories must be estimated. All sales are made on account. The rate of markup on cost is 50%. The following information relates to the month of June:

Accounts receivable, June 1	$10,000
Accounts receivable, June 30	15,000
Collection of accounts receivable during June	25,000
Inventory, June 1	18,000
Purchases of inventory during June	16,000

The estimated cost of the June 30 inventory is

A. $12,000

B. $14,000

C. $19,000

D. $22,000

The correct answer is (B). *(CPA 1173 I-10)*

REQUIRED: The estimated cost of ending inventory assuming a 50% markup on cost.

DISCUSSION: To determine inventory cost, cost of sales must be determined. Sales can be derived from a T-account analysis of accounts receivable; that is, the beginning balance ($10,000) plus credit sales equals the collections ($25,000) plus the ending balance ($15,000). Thus, sales equal $30,000 ($25,000 + $15,000 – $10,000). Because sales equal cost of sales plus the 50% markup on cost, sales equal 150% of cost. Cost of sales therefore equals sales ($30,000) divided by 1.5, or $20,000. Cost of sales deducted from the cost of goods available for sale equals the ending inventory.

Beginning inventory	$18,000
Purchases	16,000
Goods available for sale	$34,000
Cost of goods sold	(20,000)
Ending inventory	$14,000

Answers (A) and (D) are incorrect because they incorrectly compute sales. Answer (C) is incorrect because $19,000 incorrectly uses a markup based on sales instead of cost.

55. Dart Company's accounting records indicated the following information:

Inventory, 1/1/96	$ 500,000
Purchases during 1996	2,500,000
Sales during 1996	3,200,000

A physical inventory taken on December 31, 1996, resulted in an ending inventory of $575,000. Dart's gross profit on sales has remained constant at 25% in recent years. Dart suspects some inventory may have been taken by a new employee. At December 31, 1996, what is the estimated cost of missing inventory?

A. $25,000

B. $100,000

C. $175,000

D. $225,000

The correct answer is (A). *(CPA 1187 I-9)*

REQUIRED: The missing inventory estimated based on a gross margin ratio.

DISCUSSION: To estimate the missing inventory, the estimated cost of goods sold is subtracted from the cost of goods available for sale to estimate the amount of inventory that should be on hand. Given that the gross margin is 25% of sales, 75% of sales, or $2,400,000, is the estimated cost of goods sold.

1/1/96 balance	$ 500,000
Purchases	2,500,000
Cost of goods available	$3,000,000
Estimated cost of goods sold [$3,200,000 sales x (1 – .25)]	(2,400,000)
Estimated 12/31/96 balance	$ 600,000
Physical inventory 12/31/96	(575,000)
Estimated theft loss	$ 25,000

Answer (B) is incorrect because $100,000 is the difference between estimated ending inventory and actual beginning inventory. Answer (C) is incorrect because $175,000 is the ending physical inventory minus beginning inventory, plus purchases, minus cost of goods sold. Answer (D) is incorrect because $225,000 is the gross margin minus actual ending inventory.

56. A division experienced a 1996 fire, which destroyed all but $6,000 of inventory (at cost). Data available are below:

	1995	1996 (to Date of Fire)
Sales	$100,000	$40,000
Purchases	70,000	35,000
Cost of goods sold	60,000	
Ending inventory	10,000	

What is the approximate inventory lost to the fire?

   A. $10,000

   B. $15,000

   C. $16,000

   D. $21,000

The correct answer is (B). *(CIA 1190 IV-47)*

REQUIRED: The approximate inventory lost to fire.

DISCUSSION: Based on the 1995 figures, the ratio of cost of goods sold to sales is 60% ($60,000 ÷ $100,000). This ratio can be used to approximate 1996 cost of goods sold (60% x $40,000 1996 sales = $24,000). As indicated below, this estimate is deducted from goods available to determine estimated inventory at the time of the fire ($21,000). Given actual remaining inventory of $6,000, the inventory lost to fire is $15,000.

Beginning inventory	$10,000
Purchases	35,000
Cost of goods available	$45,000
Estimated cost of goods sold	(24,000)
Estimated inventory	$21,000
Actual inventory	(6,000)
Approximate inventory destroyed	$15,000

Answer (A) is incorrect because $10,000 is the ending inventory in 1995 and the beginning inventory in 1996. Answer (C) is incorrect because $16,000 is the 1996 beginning inventory plus the 1996 ending inventory of $6,000. Answer (D) is incorrect because $21,000 is the estimated ending inventory for 1996.

9.5 Retail Inventory Methods

57. The retail inventory method is characterized by

   A. The recording of sales at cost.

   B. The recording of purchases at selling price.

   C. The reporting of year-end inventory at retail in the financial statements.

   D. The recording of markups at retail and markdowns at cost.

The correct answer is (B). *(CIA 578 IV-2)*

REQUIRED: The characteristic of the retail inventory method.

DISCUSSION: In the retail inventory method, records of the beginning inventory and net purchases are maintained at both cost and retail. Sales at retail are deducted from the sum of beginning inventory and purchases at retail to provide ending inventory at retail. This figure is adjusted to cost using a cost-to-price (retail) ratio.

Answer (A) is incorrect because sales are not recorded at cost. Answer (C) is incorrect because inventory must be reported at cost per GAAP. Answer (D) is incorrect because both markups and markdowns should be recorded at retail.

58. With regard to the retail inventory method, which of the following is the most accurate statement?

   A. Accountants usually ignore net markups and net markdowns in computing the cost-price percentage.

   B. Accountants usually include both net markups and net markdowns in computing the cost-price percentage.

   C. This method results in a lower ending inventory cost if net markups are included but net markdowns are excluded in computing the cost-price percentage.

   D. It is not adaptable to LIFO costing.

The correct answer is (C). *(CPA 1174 T-28)*

REQUIRED: The most accurate statement concerning the retail inventory method.

DISCUSSION: The cost-retail ratio is lower if retail (the denominator) is increased. Excluding markdowns increases the denominator, thus decreasing the ratio applied to ending inventory stated at retail, and also decreasing ending inventory stated at cost. Excluding markdowns approximates lower of cost or market and is characteristic of the conventional retail method.

Answers (A) and (B) are incorrect because accountants usually include net markups but not net markdowns in computing the denominator of the cost-retail ratio. Answer (D) is incorrect because the retail method is adaptable to FIFO, LIFO, average cost, or lower of cost or market.

59. Under the retail inventory method, freight-in would be included in the calculation of the goods available for sale for which of the following?

	Cost	Retail
A.	No	No
B.	No	Yes
C.	Yes	No
D.	Yes	Yes

The correct answer is (C). *(CPA 1182 T-7)*
REQUIRED: The calculation that includes freight-in when determining goods available for sale.
DISCUSSION: In the retail inventory method, records of the components of net purchases (purchases, freight-in, and purchase returns and allowances) are kept at cost and are included with beginning inventory in the calculation of the goods available for sale at cost. Records are kept at retail only for net purchases, not its components, because retail prices are usually set to cover a variety of costs, such as freight-in. Consequently, freight-in, a component of net purchases, is explicitly and directly included only in the calculation of goods available for sale at cost.
Answers (A), (B), and (D) are incorrect because freight-in is used in the calculation of cost, and it is not used in the calculation of retail.

60. The retail inventory method includes which of the following in the calculation of both cost and retail amounts of goods available for sale?

A. Purchase returns.

B. Sales returns.

C. Net markups.

D. Freight-in.

The correct answer is (A). *(CPA 1190 T-16)*
REQUIRED: The element common to calculation of goods available for sale at cost and at retail.
DISCUSSION: In the retail inventory method, records are kept of beginning inventory and net purchases at both cost and retail. Purchase returns are deducted in the calculation of net purchases at both cost and retail because the return of goods reduces both total cost and the total sales price of the purchased goods.
Answer (B) is incorrect because sales returns is an element of retail only. Answer (C) is incorrect because markups and markdowns affect only retail. Answer (D) is incorrect because freight-in is an element of cost; there is no retail counterpart.

61. If the retail method is used to approximate a lower of average cost or market valuation, which of the following describes the proper treatment of net additional markups and markdowns in the cost-retail ratio calculation?

A. Net additional markups should be included in the ratio; net markdowns should be excluded.

B. Net additional markups should be excluded from the ratio; net markdowns should be included.

C. Both net additional markups and markdowns should be included in the ratio calculation.

D. Both net additional markups and markdowns should be excluded from the ratio calculation.

The correct answer is (A). *(S. Venkateswar)*
REQUIRED: The treatment of markups and markdowns in computing the cost-retail ratio under a lower of average cost or market approach.
DISCUSSION: The cost-retail ratio based on a lower of average cost or market valuation approach should include net additional markups but not net markdowns. Including net additional markups and excluding net markdowns approximates lower of cost or market. The reason is that increasing the denominator of the ratio (BI at retail + Pur at retail + Markups) while holding the numerator (BI at cost + Pur at cost) constant gives a more conservative (a lower) valuation.
Answers (B), (C), and (D) are incorrect because, when approximating LCM, net additional markups are included in the cost-retail ratio; net markdowns are excluded.

62. In the retail inventory method, when computing the cost-retail ratio, under what flow assumption(s) is beginning inventory excluded from both cost and retail?

A. FIFO.

B. LIFO.

C. Weighted-average cost or weighted-average lower of cost or market.

D. (A) and (B) only.

The correct answer is (D). *(Publisher)*
REQUIRED: The flow assumption(s) requiring that beginning inventory be excluded in determining the cost-retail ratio.
DISCUSSION: Under both FIFO and LIFO, the cost-retail ratio must be computed for purchases, not goods available for sale. For FIFO, beginning inventory is excluded because ending inventory includes only goods from current purchases. For LIFO, the layers of goods from the purchases of separate accounting periods must be considered separately.
Answers (A) and (B) are incorrect because each answer excludes the other, and both FIFO and LIFO exclude beginning inventory in determining the cost-retail ratio. Answer (C) is incorrect because weighted average includes beginning inventory as well as purchases.

63. Using the retail inventory method, when is the cost-retail ratio based only on the cost and retail values of beginning inventory?

A. When FIFO is used and sales exceed purchases at retail.

B. When FIFO is used and sales are less than purchases at retail.

C. When LIFO is used and sales exceed purchases at retail.

D. When LIFO is used and sales are less than purchases at retail.

The correct answer is (C). *(Publisher)*
REQUIRED: The circumstances in which the cost-retail ratio is based only upon beginning inventory cost and retail values.
DISCUSSION: If LIFO is used and sales exceed purchases at retail, the ending inventory will be less than beginning inventory. Ending inventory will consist entirely of values from beginning inventory and should be converted from retail to cost using the cost-retail ratio that existed in the beginning inventory.
Answers (A) and (B) are incorrect because, under FIFO, ending inventory includes goods purchased during the period. Answer (D) is incorrect because, under LIFO, when sales are less than purchases at retail, the ending inventory will include beginning inventory plus a layer of goods purchased during the period.

64. The accounting records of The Sarah Boutique contain the following amounts on November 30, 1996, the end of its fiscal year:

	Cost	Retail
Beginning inventory	$ 68,000	$100,000
Purchases	262,000	400,000
Net markups		50,000
Net markdowns		110,000
Sales		360,000

The Sarah Boutique's ending inventory as of November 30, 1996, computed by the conventional retail method, is:

A. $80,000

B. $60,000

C. $54,400

D. $48,000

The correct answer is (D). *(CMA 1292 2-30)*
REQUIRED: The ending inventory under the conventional retail method.
DISCUSSION: The lower-of-cost-or-market retail method includes net markups but not net markdowns in the determination of goods available for sale. The approximate LCM (conventional) retail method is a weighted-average method. Accordingly, the numerator of the cost-retail ratio is the sum of the beginning inventory at cost plus purchases at cost, and the denominator is the sum of beginning inventory at retail, purchases at retail, and net markups.

	Cost	Retail
Beginning inventory	$ 68,000	$100,000
Purchases	262,000	400,000
Markups, net		50,000
Goods available	$330,000	$550,000
Sales		(360,000)
Markdowns, net		(110,000)
Ending inventory -- retail		$ 80,000
Cost-retail ratio ($330 ÷ $550)		x 60%
Ending inventory at cost		$ 48,000

Answer (A) is incorrect because $80,000 is ending inventory at retail. Answer (B) is incorrect because $60,000 incorrectly uses a 75% cost-retail ratio. Answer (C) is incorrect because $54,400 incorrectly uses a 68% cost-retail ratio.

65. Hutch, Inc. uses the conventional retail inventory method to account for inventory. The following information relates to 1996 operations:

	Average	
	Cost	Retail
Beginning inventory and purchases	$600,000	$920,000
Net markups		40,000
Net markdowns		60,000
Sales		780,000

What amount should be reported as cost of sales for 1996?

A. $480,000

B. $487,500

C. $520,000

D. $525,000

The correct answer is (D). *(CPA 592 I-49)*

REQUIRED: The cost of sales based on the conventional retail inventory method.

DISCUSSION: The lower-of-cost-or-market retail method includes net markups but not net markdowns in the determination of goods available for sale. The approximate LCM (conventional) retail method is a weighted-average method. Accordingly, the numerator of the cost-retail ratio is the sum of the beginning inventory at cost plus purchases at cost, and the denominator is the sum of beginning inventory at retail, purchases at retail, and net markups. The numerator of the ratio (goods available at cost) is given as $600,000, and the denominator (goods available at retail) is $960,000 ($920,000 BI and purchases + $40,000 net markups). Ending inventory at retail is $120,000 ($960,000 goods available at retail – $60,000 net markdowns – $780,000 sales). Hence, ending inventory at cost is $75,000 [$120,000 EI at retail x ($600,000 ÷ $960,000) cost-retail ratio], and cost of sales must be $525,000 ($600,000 BI and purchases at cost – $75,000 EI at cost).

Answer (A) is incorrect because $480,000 results from subtracting ending inventory at retail from the sum of beginning inventory and purchases at cost. Answer (B) is incorrect because $487,500 omits net markdowns from the computation. Answer (C) is incorrect because $520,000 assumes net markdowns are deducted in determining the cost-retail ratio.

66. The Good Trader Company values its inventory by using the retail method (FIFO basis, lower of cost or market). The following information is available for the year just ended:

	Cost	Retail
Beginning inventory	$ 80,000	$140,000
Purchases	297,000	420,000
Freight-in	4,000	--
Shortages	--	8,000
Markups (net)	--	10,000
Markdowns (net)	--	2,000
Sales	--	400,000

At what amount would The Good Trader Company report its ending inventory?

A. $112,000

B. $113,400

C. $117,600

D. $119,000

The correct answer is (A). *(CPA 1179 II-9)*

REQUIRED: The ending inventory at cost using the retail method (FIFO basis, LCM).

DISCUSSION: Under FIFO, ending inventory is composed of the latest purchases. Thus, in calculating the cost-retail ratio, only current purchases are included. To approximate the lower of cost or market, the denominator of the ratio includes net markups but not net markdowns.

	Cost	Retail
Purchases	$297,000	$420,000
Freight-in	4,000	
Net markups		10,000
Adjusted purchases	$301,000	$430,000
Beginning inventory	80,000	140,000
Goods available	$381,000	$570,000
Net markdowns		(2,000)
Shortages		(8,000)
Sales		(400,000)
Ending inventory - retail		$160,000
Cost-retail ratio ($301,000 ÷ $430,000)		x .7
Ending inventory		$112,000

Answer (B) is incorrect because $113,400 fails to consider net markdowns in retail ending inventory. Answer (C) is incorrect because $117,600 ignores the effects of shortages in retail ending inventory. Answer (D) is incorrect because $119,000 incorrectly includes net markups in retail ending inventory.

67. The Frozen Tundra department store uses a calendar year and the LIFO retail inventory method (assuming stable prices). Information relating to the computation of the inventory at December 31 is as follows:

	Cost	Retail
Beginning inventory	$ 150	$ 300
Purchases (net)	1,650	4,860
Net markups		830
Net markdowns		970
Sales		4,180

What should be the ending inventory at cost at December 31 using the LIFO retail inventory method?

A. $252

B. $333

C. $339

D. $840

The correct answer is (C). *(K. Boze)*

REQUIRED: The ending inventory at cost using the LIFO retail inventory method.

DISCUSSION: Under the LIFO retail method (assuming stable prices), markups and markdowns are included in the calculation of the cost-retail ratio because the lower of cost or market is not being approximated. The markups and markdowns are usually assumed to apply only to purchases, and the ratio applies only to the LIFO layer added from the current purchases. Hence, the cost-retail ratio excludes beginning inventory and includes only purchases, markups, and markdowns. As indicated below, this ratio is 35%. The ending inventory will consist of a layer at 35% and a layer at the previous year's ratio.

	Cost	Retail
Purchases	$1,650	$4,860
Markups		830
Markdowns		(970)
Adjusted purchases	$1,650	$4,720
Beginning inventory	150	300
Goods available	1,800	$5,020
Sales		(4,180)
Ending inventory - retail		$ 840

Current cost-retail ratio ($1,650 ÷ $4,720) = .35

BI layer at cost	$ 150
Current layer at cost = ($840 – $300) x .35	189
Ending inventory at cost	$ 339

Answer (A) is incorrect because $252 is the ending inventory based on the conventional retail method. Answer (B) is incorrect because $333 results from using a cost-retail ratio equal to purchases at cost divided by purchases at retail. Answer (D) is incorrect because $840 is the retail ending inventory.

68. Union Corp. uses the first-in, first-out retail method of inventory valuation. The following information is available:

	Cost	Retail
Beginning inventory	$12,000	$ 30,000
Purchases	60,000	110,000
Net additional markups		10,000
Net markdowns		20,000
Sales revenue		90,000

If the lower-of-cost-or-market rule is disregarded, what would be the estimated cost of the ending inventory?

A. $24,000

B. $20,800

C. $20,000

D. $19,200

The correct answer is (A). *(CPA 590 I-13)*

REQUIRED: The ending inventory using the FIFO version of the retail inventory method.

DISCUSSION: Under FIFO, ending inventory consists of purchases because beginning inventory is assumed to be sold first. Both markdowns and markups are used to calculate the cost-retail ratio because lower of cost or market is not being approximated.

	Cost	Retail
Purchases	$60,000	$110,000
Markups		10,000
Markdowns		(20,000)
Adjusted purchases	$60,000	$100,000
Beg. inv. 1/1	12,000	30,000
Goods available	$72,000	$130,000
Sales		(90,000)
Ending inventory - retail		$ 40,000
Cost-retail ratio ($60,000 ÷ $100,000)		x .6
Ending inventory - FIFO		$ 24,000

Answer (B) is incorrect because $20,800 incorrectly uses a 52% cost-retail ratio. Answer (C) is incorrect because $20,000 incorrectly uses a 50% cost-retail ratio. Answer (D) is incorrect because $19,200 incorrectly uses a 48% cost-retail ratio.

9.6 Dollar-Value LIFO

69. Estimates of price-level changes for specific inventories are required for which of the following inventory methods?

A. Conventional retail.

B. Dollar-value LIFO.

C. Weighted-average cost.

D. Average cost retail.

The correct answer is (B). *(CPA 1193 T-3)*
REQUIRED: The inventory method for which estimates of price-level changes for specific inventories are required.
DISCUSSION: Dollar-value LIFO accumulates inventoriable costs of similar (not identical) items. These items should be similar in the sense of being interchangeable, having similar uses, belonging to the same product line, or constituting the raw materials for a given product. Dollar-value LIFO determines changes in ending inventory in terms of dollars of constant purchasing power rather than units of physical inventory. This calculation uses a specific price index for each year. The ending inventory is deflated by the current-year index to arrive at base-year cost. This amount is then compared to the beginning inventory stated at base-year cost to determine what layers are to be in the ending inventory. Each layer is then inflated by the relevant price index for the year it was created to determine the aggregate ending inventory valuation.
Answers (A) and (D) are incorrect because retail inventory methods calculate ending inventory at retail and then adjust it to cost by applying a cost-retail ratio. Answer (C) is incorrect because weighted-average cost method computes ending inventory based on an average cost determined at year-end.

70. The double-extension method and the link-chain method are two variations of which of the following inventory cost flow methods?

A. Moving average.

B. FIFO.

C. Dollar-value LIFO.

D. Conventional (lower-of-cost-or-market) retail.

The correct answer is (C). *(CPA 1183 T-10)*
REQUIRED: The inventory cost flow method of which the double-extension method and the link-chain method are variations.
DISCUSSION: The double-extension method and the link-chain method are variations of dollar-value LIFO. In dollar-value LIFO, similar (rather than identical) dollar-value pools of inventory are accumulated. Each layer of inventory is stated in dollar-value terms based on the price index for the relevant year. The link-chain version uses beginning-of-the-year costs as the denominator of the index for each year after the base year. Each successive year's index is multiplied by the cumulative index. The double-extension version uses the base-year prices in the annual index. The two methods are mutually exclusive.
Answers (A), (B), and (D) are incorrect because none of these methods uses variations with the double-extension method and the link-chain method.

71. Which of the following inventory cost flow methods could use dollar-value pools?

A. Conventional (lower-of-cost-or-market) retail.

B. Weighted average.

C. FIFO.

D. LIFO.

The correct answer is (D). *(CPA 1180 T-18)*
REQUIRED: The cost flow assumption using dollar-value pools.
DISCUSSION: A modification of LIFO may be employed to account for dollar-value pools of similar items rather than identical items. This method overcomes a difficulty with traditional LIFO: Some items may be liquidated below the LIFO base while the value of similar items may increase. Dollar-value LIFO prevents the loss of the advantages of LIFO when the mixture of similar items changes.
Answers (A), (B), and (C) are incorrect because the dollar-value pool approach has been used only with LIFO.

72. When the double-extension approach to the dollar-value LIFO inventory method is used, the inventory layer added in the current year is multiplied by an index number. Which of the following correctly states how components are used in the calculation of this index number?

A. In the numerator, the average of the ending inventory at base-year cost and at current-year cost.

B. In the numerator, the ending inventory at current-year cost, and, in the denominator, the ending inventory at base-year cost.

C. In the numerator, the ending inventory at base-year cost, and, in the denominator, the ending inventory at current-year cost.

D. In the denominator, the average of the ending inventory at base-year cost and at current-year cost.

The correct answer is (B). *(CPA 1191 T-28)*
REQUIRED: The true statement of how components are used in the calculation of an index number under the double-extension method.
DISCUSSION: An enterprise applying dollar-value LIFO may calculate price indexes rather than use externally determined numbers. The double-extension approach states ending inventory at current-year cost and then divides that amount by the base-year cost to determine the index for the current year. Hence, this method extends the quantity of the inventory at both current-year and base-year unit cost. The indexes determined in this way are then multiplied by the appropriate inventory layers stated at base-year cost.
Answer (A) is incorrect because the numerator is the current-year cost. Answer (C) is incorrect because the numerator is the current-year cost and the denominator is the base-year cost. Answer (D) is incorrect because the denominator is the base-year cost.

73. The dollar-value LIFO inventory cost flow method involves computations based on

	Inventory Pools of Similar Items	A Specific Price Index for Each Year
A.	No	Yes
B.	No	No
C.	Yes	No
D.	Yes	Yes

The correct answer is (D). *(CPA 1186 T-6)*
REQUIRED: The computations required for dollar-value LIFO inventory.
DISCUSSION: Dollar-value LIFO accumulates inventoriable costs of similar (not identical) items. These items should be similar in the sense of being interchangeable, having similar uses, belonging to the same product line, or constituting the raw materials for a given product. Dollar-value LIFO determines changes in ending inventory in terms of dollars of constant purchasing power rather than units of physical inventory. This calculation uses a specific price index for each year. The ending inventory is deflated by the current-year index to arrive at base-year cost. This amount is then compared to the beginning inventory stated at base-year cost to determine what layers are to be in the ending inventory. Each layer is then inflated by the relevant price index for the year it was created to determine the aggregate ending inventory valuation.
Answer (A) is incorrect because dollar-value LIFO uses inventory pools of similar items. Answer (B) is incorrect because dollar-value LIFO uses inventory pools and a price index. Answer (C) is incorrect because this method uses a price index.

74. Dollar-value LIFO is used to minimize the problem of LIFO liquidation caused by technological change. When technological change occurs and a new or improved product is added, a reconstructed cost must be established. Which price would not be used as a reconstructed cost?

A. The price of the product at the base date of the inventory.

B. The price to the firm if no prior costs can be determined.

C. The price at the item's first availability if it did not exist at the inventory base date.

D. The price of the item at the end of the year in which it is added to the company inventory.

The correct answer is (D). *(Publisher)*
REQUIRED: The price that would not be used as a reconstructed cost for dollar-value LIFO.
DISCUSSION: Reconstructed cost problems arise when technological change alters the nature of inventory accounted for under dollar-value LIFO. A good example is the change from black and white to color television sets. Under dollar-value LIFO, the price used for the new product is either the price in effect when LIFO was adopted by the company, the price at the product's first availability, or, if those prices are not available, the price which the company first paid for the goods. Use of the year-end price would be consistent with the FIFO rather than the LIFO flow assumption.
Answers (A), (B), and (C) are incorrect because each may be used as a reconstructed cost.

Questions 75 and 76 are based on the following information. Wright Hardware adopted the dollar-value last-in, first-out (LIFO) method of inventory valuation at December 31, 1994. Inventory balances and price indices are shown below.

December 31	Ending Inventory at End-of-Year Prices	Price Index at December 31
1994	$240,000	100
1995	275,000	110
1996	300,000	120

75. Wright Hardware's ending inventory as of December 31, 1995 computed by the dollar-value LIFO method was

A. $240,000

B. $250,000

C. $251,000

D. $275,000

The correct answer is (C). *(CMA 1291 2-29)*
   REQUIRED: The dollar-value LIFO inventory for 1995.
   DISCUSSION: The first step is to convert the 1995 ending inventory into base-year prices. Dividing by the price index for 1995 results in an inventory value of $250,000 ($275,000 ÷ 1.1). This amount consists of two layers: $240,000 purchased during the base year (1994) and $10,000 acquired in the current year (1995). The latter amount must be converted back into year-end prices because this merchandise was not purchased during the base year. The 1995 increment therefore has a dollar-value LIFO valuation of $11,000 ($10,000 x 1.1). Total inventory is $251,000 ($240,000 + $11,000).
   Answer (A) is incorrect because $240,000 does not include the 1995 layer. Answer (B) is incorrect because $250,000 includes the 1995 layer at base-year prices. Answer (D) is incorrect because $275,000 is the ending inventory at end-of-year prices.

76. Wright Hardware's ending inventory as of December 31, 1996, computed by the dollar-value LIFO method would be

A. $240,000

B. $250,000

C. $251,000

D. $300,000

The correct answer is (C). *(CMA 1291 2-30)*
   REQUIRED: The dollar-value LIFO inventory for 1996.
   DISCUSSION: The first step is to convert the 1996 ending inventory at year-end prices into base-year prices. Dividing by the price index for 1996 results in an inventory value at base-year prices of $250,000 ($300,000 ÷ 1.2). This figure is exactly the same as that for 1995 (see previous question). Thus, no increment was added during 1996, and the dollar-value LIFO ending inventory for 1996 is the same as at the end of 1995 ($251,000). This amount consists of a $240,000 layer purchased in 1994 and an $11,000 layer purchased in 1995. Under LIFO, the assumption is that nothing is still on hand from 1996 purchases because the inventory stated in base-year prices is the same as at the end of the preceding year.
   Answer (A) is incorrect because $240,000 does not include the 1995 layer. Answer (B) is incorrect because $250,000 includes the 1995 layer at base-year prices. Answer (D) is incorrect because $300,000 is the ending inventory at end-of-year prices.

77. Which of the following is an advantage of the dollar-value LIFO method over the specific-goods LIFO method?

    A. The dollar-value LIFO method may be used only for identical inventory items.

    B. Under dollar-value LIFO, new inventory items are entered into the inventory pool at their entry year cost.

    C. Under dollar-value LIFO, a given inventory item may experience a unit count decrease, but no liquidation need be recorded.

    D. Under dollar-value LIFO, updating of the cost basis of old inventory items is facilitated.

The correct answer is (C). *(D.L. Flesher)*

  REQUIRED: The advantage of the dollar-value LIFO method.

  DISCUSSION: The dollar-value LIFO method is applicable to pools of similar but not identical inventory items. The method deals with layers of inventory, not with individual inventory items. Thus, when a given inventory item experiences a unit count decrease, but the overall pool of inventory does not decrease, no liquidation is recorded.

  Answer (A) is incorrect because dollar-value LIFO is used for inventory pools composed of similar but not identical items. Answer (B) is incorrect because new inventory items are placed in the pool at the substituted item's base-year price. Answer (D) is incorrect because no LIFO method permits an updating of old inventory items.

9.7 Purchase Commitments

78. Net losses on firm purchase commitments for goods for inventory result from a contract price that exceeds the current market price. If a firm expects that losses will occur when the purchase is effected, expected losses, if material,

    A. Should be recognized in the accounts and separately disclosed as losses on the income statement of the period during which the decline in price takes place.

    B. Should be recognized in the accounts and separately disclosed as net unrealized losses on the balance sheet at the end of the period during which the decline in price takes place.

    C. Should be recognized in the accounts and separately disclosed as net unrealized losses on the balance sheet at the end of the period during which the contract is executed.

    D. Should not be recognized in the accounts until the contract is executed and need not be separately disclosed in the financial statements.

The correct answer is (A). *(CMA 685 3-26)*

  REQUIRED: The accounting treatment of losses arising from a firm (noncancelable) purchase commitment not yet exercised.

  DISCUSSION: ARB 43, Chap. 4, *Inventory Pricing*, requires the accrual of a loss in the current year's income statement on goods subject to a firm purchase commitment if the market price of these goods declines below the commitment price. This loss should be measured in the same manner as inventory losses. Disclosure of the loss is also required.

  Answers (B) and (C) are incorrect because the losses should be recognized in the determination of net income. Answer (D) is incorrect because, if a loss arises out of a firm, noncancelable, and unhedged commitment, it should be recognized in the current year.

79. On January 1, 1996, Card Corp. signed a 3-year, noncancelable purchase contract, which allows Card to purchase up to 500,000 units of a computer part annually from Hart Supply Co. at $.10 per unit and guarantees a minimum annual purchase of 100,000 units. During 1996, the part unexpectedly became obsolete. Card had 250,000 units of this inventory at December 31, 1996 and believes these parts can be sold as scrap for $.02 per unit. What amount of probable loss from the purchase commitment should Card report in its 1996 income statement?

A. $24,000

B. $20,000

C. $16,000

D. $8,000

The correct answer is (C). *(CPA 593 II-20)*

REQUIRED: The amount of probable loss from the purchase commitment.

DISCUSSION: ARB 43, Chap. 4, *Inventory Pricing*, requires the accrual of a loss in the current year's income statement on goods subject to a firm purchase commitment if the market price of these goods declines below the commitment price. This loss should be measured in the same manner as inventory losses. Disclosure of the loss is also required. Consequently, given that 200,000 units must be purchased over the next 2 years for $20,000 (200,000 x $.10) and the parts can be sold as scrap for $4,000 (200,000 x $.02), the amount of probable loss from the purchase commitment for 1996 is $16,000 ($20,000 – $4,000).

Answer (A) is incorrect because $24,000 includes the purchase commitment for the current year. Answer (B) is incorrect because $20,000 excludes the net realizable value of the parts from the calculation. Answer (D) is incorrect because $8,000 excludes the probable loss expected in the last year of the purchase commitment.

80. During the year, the Guileman Manufacturing Company signed a noncancelable contract to purchase 1,000 lbs. of a raw material at $32 per lb. during the forthcoming year. On December 31, the market price of the raw material is $26 per lb., and the selling price of the finished product is expected to decline accordingly. The financial statements prepared for the year should report

A. An appropriation of retained earnings for $6,000.

B. Nothing regarding this matter.

C. A footnote describing the expected loss on the purchase commitment.

D. A loss of $6,000 in the income statement.

The correct answer is (D). *(Publisher)*

REQUIRED: The proper financial statement treatment of a loss on inventory that the firm is committed to purchase.

DISCUSSION: ARB 43, Chap. 4, requires recognition in the income statement of a material loss on a purchase commitment as if the inventory were already owned. Losses on firm purchase commitments are measured in the same way as inventory losses. If the cost is $32,000 and the market price is $26,000, a $6,000 loss should be disclosed.

Answers (A), (B), and (C) are incorrect because net income is to be charged for purchase commitment losses in the year market prices decline below commitment prices. Appropriating retained earnings does not affect net income.

9.8 Inventory Errors

81. On December 31, 1996, Occident, Inc. shipped merchandise with a list price of $90,000 to Plaza Company. The goods were sold on account with terms of net 30 days, F.O.B. shipping point. Due to an oversight, the sale was not recorded until January 1997, and the merchandise, which was sold at a 25% markup, was included in Occident's perpetual inventory on December 31, 1996. As a result, Occident's income before taxes for the year ended December 31, 1996 was understated by

A. $90,000

B. $72,000

C. $67,500

D. $18,000

The correct answer is (D). *(CMA 1293 2-11)*

REQUIRED: The amount by which pretax income was understated because of failure to record a sale.

DISCUSSION: Given that terms were FOB shipping point, the title passed to the buyer at the time and place of shipment, i.e., on December 31. Thus, the sale should have been recorded and the inventory should not have been shown on Occident's financial statements. The failure to record the sale understated revenues by $90,000. Cost of goods sold would also have been understated by the cost of the inventory. Because the goods were sold at a 25% markup (125% of cost), cost must have been $72,000 ($90,000 ÷ 125%). The net effect on income is $18,000 ($90,000 – $72,000 CGS).

Answer (A) is incorrect because $90,000 is the effect on sales. Answer (B) is incorrect because $72,000 is the effect on cost of goods sold. Answer (C) is incorrect because $67,500 is the cost based on a 25% markup on sales.

82. Bren Co.'s beginning inventory at January 1, 1996 was understated by $26,000, and its ending inventory was overstated by $52,000. As a result, Bren's cost of goods sold for 1996 was

A. Understated by $26,000.

B. Overstated by $26,000.

C. Understated by $78,000.

D. Overstated by $78,000.

83. If ending inventory is underestimated due to an error in the physical count of items on hand, then cost of goods sold for the period will be <List A> and net earnings will be <List B>.

	List A	List B
A.	Underestimated	Underestimated
B.	Underestimated	Overestimated
C.	Overestimated	Underestimated
D.	Overestimated	Overestimated

84. The following inventory valuation errors have been discovered for Knox Corporation:

• The 1994 year-end inventory was overstated by $23,000.

• The 1995 year-end inventory was understated by $61,000.

• The 1996 year-end inventory was understated by $17,000.

The reported income before taxes for Knox was

Year	Income before Taxes
1994	$138,000
1995	254,000
1996	168,000

Reported income before taxes for 1994, 1995, and 1996, respectively, should have been

A. $161,000, $170,000, and $212,000.

B. $115,000, $338,000, and $124,000.

C. $161,000, $338,000, and $90,000.

D. $115,000, $338,000, and $212,000.

The correct answer is (C). *(CPA 1194 F-43)*
REQUIRED: The misstatement of cost of goods sold.
DISCUSSION: When beginning inventory is understated, cost of goods sold will be understated. When ending inventory is overstated, cost of goods sold will be understated. Thus, Bren Co.'s inventory is understated by $78,000 ($26,000 + $52,000).
Answer (A) is incorrect because the overstatement of ending inventory also understates cost of goods sold. Answers (B) and (D) are incorrect because both errors understate cost of goods sold.

The correct answer is (C). *(CIA 1194 IV-10)*
REQUIRED: The effect on cost of goods sold and net earnings of an error in counting inventory.
DISCUSSION: Cost of goods sold equals beginning inventory, plus purchases, minus ending inventory. If the ending inventory is underestimated, the cost of goods sold will be overestimated. If cost of goods sold is overestimated, net earnings will be underestimated.
Answers (A), (B), and (D) are incorrect because, if the ending inventory is underestimated, the cost of goods sold will be overestimated. If cost of goods sold is overestimated, net earnings will be underestimated.

The correct answer is (B). *(CMA 694 2-5)*
REQUIRED: The reported income after correction of inventory errors.
DISCUSSION: Cost of sales equals beginning inventory, plus purchases or cost of goods manufactured, minus ending inventory. Hence, over (under) statement of inventory affects cost of sales and income. The 1994 pretax income was affected by the $23,000 1994 overstatement of year-end inventory. This error understated 1994 cost of sales and overstated pretax income. The corrected income is $115,000 ($138,000 – $23,000). The same $23,000 error caused 1995 income to be understated by overstating beginning inventory. In addition, the $61,000 understatement of 1995 year-end inventory also caused 1995 income to be understated. Thus, the corrected 1995 pretax income is $338,000 ($254,000 + $23,000 + $61,000). The $61,000 understatement at the end of 1995 caused 1996 income to be overstated by understating beginning inventory. Income for 1996 is understated by the $17,000 of year-end inventory understatement. Accordingly, the corrected income is $124,000 ($168,000 – $61,000 + $17,000).
Answer (A) is incorrect because 1994 income of $161,000 results from adding, not subtracting, the $23,000 overstatement of ending inventory. Similarly, 1995 income of $170,000 results from subtracting, not adding, the $23,000 overstatement of beginning inventory and the $61,000 understatement of ending inventory. Finally, 1996 income of $212,000 results from adding, not subtracting, the $61,000 understatement of beginning inventory and subtracting, not adding, the understatement of ending inventory. Answer (C) is incorrect because 1996 income of $90,000 results from subtracting, not adding, the $17,000 understatement of ending inventory. Answer (D) is incorrect because 1996 pretax income should be $124,000.

9.9 Direct Costing

85. Direct costing refers to inventory that includes

A.   Prime costs only.

B.   Variable costs only.

C.   Variable overhead costs only.

D.   Prime and fixed overhead costs only.

The correct answer is (B). *(Publisher)*
REQUIRED: The costs included in inventory in a direct costing system.
DISCUSSION: Inventory based on direct costing includes variable costs only. They include direct materials, direct labor, and variable overhead. These product costs are deferred to future periods to the extent the inventory is not sold. However, all fixed overhead costs are expensed when they are incurred.
    Answer (A) is incorrect because prime costs include direct materials and direct labor costs only. Answer (C) is incorrect because it does not include direct materials and direct labor costs. Answer (D) is incorrect because direct cost inventory includes variable (not fixed) overhead costs.

86. Absorption costing income exceeds direct costing income

A.   When production exceeds sales.

B.   When sales exceed production.

C.   When production equals sales.

D.   Always.

The correct answer is (A). *(Publisher)*
REQUIRED: The situation in which absorption costing income exceeds direct costing income.
DISCUSSION: Under direct costing, fixed overhead is expensed immediately as a period expense. Under absorption costing, fixed overhead is allocated to the units produced as a product (inventory) cost and is expensed when the goods are sold. When production exceeds sales, some fixed costs are not expensed under absorption costing.
    Answer (B) is incorrect because, when sales exceed production, direct costing income exceeds absorption costing income. Answer (C) is incorrect because, when production equals sales, absorption costing income equals direct costing income. Answer (D) is incorrect because absorption costing income will only exceed direct costing income when production exceeds sales.

CHAPTER TEN
PROPERTY, PLANT, AND EQUIPMENT

This chapter covers accounting for the acquisition and disposal of property, plant, and equipment, including subsequent expenditures and nonmonetary exchanges. The tax aspects are covered in Chapter 20, Income Tax Allocation. Chapter 11 deals with depreciation and depletion.

10.1 Acquisition Cost

1. Property, plant, and equipment are conventionally presented in the balance sheet at

A. Replacement cost minus accumulated depreciation.

B. Historical cost minus salvage value.

C. Original cost adjusted for general price-level changes.

D. Historical cost minus depreciated portion thereof.

The correct answer is (D). *(CPA 1174 T-21)*
REQUIRED: The conventional balance sheet presentation of property, plant, and equipment.
DISCUSSION: Property, plant, and equipment are recorded at their acquisition cost. They are then measured in accordance with SFAC 5 at their historical cost attribute. When property, plant, and equipment are used in normal operations, this historical cost must be allocated (depreciated) on a systematic and rational basis to the accounting periods in which they are used. Land is an exception because it is not depreciated.
Answer (A) is incorrect because historical cost rather than replacement cost is the attribute at which property, plant, and equipment are measured. Answer (B) is incorrect because assets appear in the balance sheet at historical cost with an offset for accumulated depreciation (not salvage value). Answer (C) is incorrect because the basic financial statements are not adjusted for price-level changes.

2. A donated plant asset for which the fair value has been determined, and for which incidental costs were incurred in acceptance of the asset, should be recorded at an amount equal to its

A. Incidental costs incurred.

B. Fair value and incidental costs incurred.

C. Book value on books of donor and incidental costs incurred.

D. Book value on books of donor.

The correct answer is (B). *(CPA 585 T-9)*
REQUIRED: The amount at which donated plant assets should be recorded.
DISCUSSION: A donated plant asset should be recorded at its fair value plus any incidental costs necessary to make the asset ready for its intended use. Donated capital should be credited for the fair value.
Answers (A), (C), and (D) are incorrect because any plant asset, including a donated plant asset, should be recorded at fair value plus costs necessary to render the asset operational.

3. Charging the cost of ordinary repairs to the machinery and equipment asset account during the current year would

- A. Understate net income for the current year.

- B. Understate shareholders' equity at the end of the current year.

- C. Not affect the total assets at the end of the current year.

- D. Not affect the total liabilities at the end of the current year.

The correct answer is (D). *(CMA 685 4-9)*
REQUIRED: The effect of charging the cost of ordinary repairs to the machinery and equipment asset account.
DISCUSSION: When an asset is acquired, the expenses of maintaining the asset are expenses of the period in which the ordinary repairs are rendered. To charge such ordinary repairs to the machinery and equipment asset account would overstate total assets, the current year's net income, and shareholders' equity. Liabilities, however, would not be affected.
Answers (A) and (B) are incorrect because net income and shareholders' equity would be overstated (not understated). Answer (C) is incorrect because assets are overstated.

4. When fixed assets are self-constructed, which costs should be expensed in the period of construction?

- A. Excess of construction costs over third-party selling price.

- B. Fixed and variable overhead costs.

- C. Fees paid to outside consultants.

- D. Cost of safety devices required by government agencies.

The correct answer is (A). *(Publisher)*
REQUIRED: The costs of self-constructed fixed assets that should be expensed in the period of construction.
DISCUSSION: An asset should not be recorded in excess of its fair value. Thus, a self-constructed fixed asset should not be capitalized at an amount greater than that at which the asset could be purchased from a third party. Any excess cost is a loss that should not be deferred to future periods and should be expensed.
Answer (B) is incorrect because some fixed costs may be expensed rather than capitalized when the construction reduces normal production. Answers (C) and (D) are incorrect because expenditures directly related to the construction of fixed assets should be capitalized.

5. According to current authoritative literature, write-ups of property, plant, and equipment to reflect current appraisals are

- A. Permissible only during times of rapidly increasing prices.

- B. Permissible provided current value evidence is sufficiently objective.

- C. Usually not acceptable in financial statements.

- D. Permitted in statements of unconsolidated United States domestic subsidiaries.

The correct answer is (C). *(Publisher)*
REQUIRED: The permissibility of write-ups of property, plant, and equipment to reflect current appraisals.
DISCUSSION: APB 6, *Status of Accounting Research Bulletins*, states that property, plant, and equipment should not be written up by an entity to reflect appraisal, market, or current values that are above cost to the business. The exceptions to this rule are minor.
Answers (A) and (D) are incorrect because write-ups to reflect current appraisals are usually not permissible. Answer (B) is incorrect because APB 6 makes no exception for circumstances in which evidence of current value is sufficiently objective.

6. On January 2, 1996, Parke Corp. replaced its boiler with a more efficient one. The following information was available on that date:

Purchase price of new boiler	$60,000
Carrying amount of old boiler	5,000
Fair value of old boiler	2,000
Installation cost of new boiler	8,000

The old boiler was sold for $2,000. What amount should Parke capitalize as the cost of the new boiler?

- A. $68,000

- B. $66,000

- C. $63,000

- D. $60,000

The correct answer is (A). *(CPA 1191 I-15)*
REQUIRED: The amount to be capitalized as the cost of the replacement asset.
DISCUSSION: When a fixed asset is replaced, the new asset should be recorded at its purchase price plus any incidental costs necessary to make the asset ready for its intended use. Consequently, the replacement boiler should be recorded at $68,000 ($60,000 purchase price + $8,000 installation cost). In addition, the $5,000 carrying amount of the old boiler should be removed from the accounts, and a loss of $3,000 ($2,000 proceeds – $5,000 carrying amount) should be recognized.
Answer (B) is incorrect because $66,000 improperly deducts the fair value of the old boiler. Answer (C) is incorrect because $63,000 results from deducting the carrying amount of the old boiler. Answer (D) is incorrect because $60,000 does not consider the installation costs.

7. A machine with an original estimated useful life of 10 years is moved to another location in the factory after it has been in service for 3 years. The efficiency of the machine is increased for its remaining useful life. The reinstallation costs should be capitalized if the remaining useful life of the machine is

	5 Years	10 Years
A.	No	No
B.	No	Yes
C.	Yes	No
D.	Yes	Yes

The correct answer is (D). *(CPA 584 T-11)*
REQUIRED: The proper treatment of reinstallation costs that increase a machine's efficiency.
DISCUSSION: Costs that significantly improve the future service potential of an asset by increasing the quality or quantity of its output should be capitalized even though the machine's useful life is not extended. The reinstallation cost should be capitalized whether the remaining useful life is 5 or 10 years.
Answers (A), (B), and (C) are incorrect because the reinstallation costs should be capitalized whether the remaining useful life is 5 or 10 years.

8. Derby Co. incurred costs to modify its building and to rearrange its production line. As a result, an overall reduction in production costs is expected. However, the modifications did not increase the building's market value, and the rearrangement did not extend the production line's life. Should the building modification costs and the production line rearrangement costs be capitalized?

	Building Modification Costs	Production Line Rearrangement Costs
A.	Yes	No
B.	Yes	Yes
C.	No	No
D.	No	Yes

The correct answer is (B). *(CPA 592 T-11)*
REQUIRED: The accounting for building modification costs and production line rearrangement costs.
DISCUSSION: A rearrangement is the movement of existing assets to provide greater efficiency or to reduce production costs. If the rearrangement expenditure benefits future periods, it should be capitalized. If the building modification costs likewise improve future service potential, they too should be capitalized.
Answer (A) is incorrect because the production line rearrangement costs should be capitalized. Answer (C) is incorrect because the building modification costs and production line rearrangement costs should be capitalized. Answer (D) is incorrect because the building modification costs should be capitalized.

9. A building suffered uninsured fire damage. The damaged portion of the building was refurbished with higher quality materials. The cost and related accumulated depreciation of the damaged portion are identifiable. To account for these events, the owner should

A. Reduce accumulated depreciation equal to the cost of refurbishing.

B. Record a loss in the current period equal to the sum of the cost of refurbishing and the carrying amount of the damaged portion of the building.

C. Capitalize the cost of refurbishing and record a loss in the current period equal to the carrying amount of the damaged portion of the building.

D. Capitalize the cost of refurbishing by adding the cost to the carrying amount of the building.

The correct answer is (C). *(CPA 593 T-26)*
REQUIRED: The proper accounting for a substitution.
DISCUSSION: When a substantial portion of a productive asset is replaced and the cost and related accumulated depreciation associated with the old component are identifiable, the substitution method of accounting is used. Under this approach, the asset account and accumulated depreciation should be reduced by the appropriate amounts and a gain or loss recognized. In this instance, the damages were uninsured, and a loss equal to the carrying amount of the damaged portion of the building should be recognized. In addition, the cost of refurbishing should be capitalized in the asset account.
Answers (A), (B), and (D) are incorrect because the cost of refurbishing should be capitalized, and a loss equal to the carrying amount of the damaged portion of the building should be recognized.

10. During 1996, a company spent $2,700,000 to rearrange and $1,200,000 to reinstall the assembly line at one of its plants in order to convert the plant over to the manufacture of a new company product beginning in 1997. The $1,200,000 in reinstallation costs were charged to the related machinery and equipment, which has an average remaining useful life of 15 years. The new product has an expected life of 9 years. The $2,700,000 in rearrangement costs should be charged in 1996 to

A. A deferred expense account and expensed at a rate of $300,000 per year beginning in 1997.

B. A deferred expense account which is never amortized.

C. An expense account.

D. Factory machinery and equipment and depreciated over 15 years.

The correct answer is (A). *(CIA 587 IV-33)*
REQUIRED: The proper accounting for rearrangement costs.
DISCUSSION: Costs that significantly improve the future service potential of an asset by increasing the quality or quantity of its output should be capitalized. Because the rearrangement and reinstallation costs were incurred to increase the productivity of the assembly line, both costs should be capitalized as part of the related machinery and equipment. These capitalized costs should then be amortized over the expected 9-year life of the new product. Thus, the $2,700,000 in rearrangement costs should be debited to either the asset account or a deferred expense account and then expensed over the 9 years at a rate of $300,000 per year.
Answer (B) is incorrect because the rearrangement costs should be capitalized and amortized over 9 years. Answer (C) is incorrect because the rearrangement costs increase the quality or quantity of output so the costs should not be treated as an expense. Answer (D) is incorrect, because the rearrangement costs benefit the new product which has an expected life of 9 years; therefore, the cost should not be amortized over 15 years (the life of the old equipment).

11. An expenditure subsequent to acquisition of assembly-line manufacturing equipment benefits future periods. The expenditure should be capitalized if it is a

	Betterment	Rearrangement
A.	No	No
B.	No	Yes
C.	Yes	No
D.	Yes	Yes

The correct answer is (D). *(CPA 1186 T-8)*
REQUIRED: The type(s) of expenditure that should be capitalized.
DISCUSSION: A betterment occurs when a replacement asset is substituted for an existing asset, and the result is increased productivity, capacity, or expected useful life. A rearrangement is the movement of existing assets to provide greater efficiency or to reduce production costs. If the betterment or rearrangement expenditure benefits future periods, it should be capitalized.
Answers (A), (B), and (C) are incorrect because betterments and rearrangements which benefit future periods should be capitalized.

12. During 1996, Fox Company made the following expenditures relating to plant machinery and equipment:

• Renovation of a group of machines at a cost of $50,000 to secure greater efficiency in production over their remaining 5-year useful lives. The project was completed on December 31, 1996.

• Continuing, frequent, and low-cost repairs at a cost of $35,000.

• Replacement of a broken gear on a machine at a cost of $5,000.

What total amount should be charged to repairs and maintenance in 1996?

A. $35,000

B. $40,000

C. $85,000

D. $90,000

The correct answer is (B). *(CPA 588 I-23)*
REQUIRED: The amount to be charged to repair and maintenance expense.
DISCUSSION: Repair and maintenance costs are incurred to maintain plant assets in operating condition. The continuing, frequent, and low-cost repairs and the replacement of a broken gear meet the definition of repairs and maintenance expense. Accordingly, the amount that should be charged to repairs and maintenance is $40,000 ($35,000 + $5,000). The renovation cost increased the quality of production during the expected useful life of the group of machines. Hence, this $50,000 cost should be capitalized.
Answer (A) is incorrect because the cost of a broken gear should also be charged to repairs and maintenance. Answer (C) is incorrect because the renovation of machines should not be charged to repairs and maintenance; it should be capitalized. The broken gear should be included in repairs and maintenance. Answer (D) is incorrect because the renovation of machines should be capitalized, not charged to repairs and maintenance.

13. On June 18, 1996, Dell Printing Co. incurred the following costs for one of its printing presses:

Purchase of collating and stapling attachment	$84,000
Installation of attachment	36,000
Replacement parts for overhaul of press	26,000
Labor and overhead in connection with overhaul	14,000

The overhaul resulted in a significant increase in production. Neither the attachment nor the overhaul increased the estimated useful life of the press. What amount of the above costs should be capitalized?

    A. $0

    B. $84,000

    C. $120,000

    D. $160,000

The correct answer is (D). *(CPA 590 I-16)*

    REQUIRED: The amount of costs to be capitalized.

    DISCUSSION: Expenditures that increase the quality or quantity of a machine's output should be capitalized whether or not its useful life is extended. Thus, the amount of the cost to be capitalized equals $160,000 ($84,000 + $36,000 + $26,000 + $14,000).

    Answer (A) is incorrect because $160,000 of costs should be capitalized. Answer (B) is incorrect because all of the costs associated with the purchase of the parts and the overhaul should be capitalized. Answer (C) is incorrect because the cost of replacement parts and labor and overhead should also be capitalized.

14. Merry Co. purchased a machine costing $125,000 for its manufacturing operations and paid shipping costs of $20,000. Merry spent an additional $10,000 testing and preparing the machine for use. What amount should Merry record as the cost of the machine?

    A. $155,000

    B. $145,000

    C. $135,000

    D. $125,000

The correct answer is (A). *(CPA 1193 I-22)*

    REQUIRED: The amount to be recorded as the acquisition cost of the machine.

    DISCUSSION: The amount to be recorded as the acquisition cost of a machine includes all costs necessary to prepare it for its intended use. Thus, the cost of a machine used in the manufacturing operations of a company includes the cost of testing and preparing the machine for use and the shipping costs. The acquisition cost is $155,000 ($125,000 + $20,000 + $10,000).

    Answer (B) is incorrect because $145,000 does not include the $10,000 cost of testing and preparation. Answer (C) is incorrect because $135,000 does not include the shipping costs. Answer (D) is incorrect because $125,000 does not include the shipping, testing, and preparation costs.

15. On July 1, 1996, Conway Company sells land with a carrying value of $75,000 to Stratton Company in exchange for $50,000 in cash and a note calling for five annual $10,000 payments beginning on June 30, 1997, and ending on June 30, 2001. The fair value of the land is uncertain, and Stratton can borrow long-term funds at 11%. What should be the amount capitalized as acquisition cost of the land to Stratton Company? (The present value of $1 for five periods at 11% is 0.59345, and the present value of an ordinary annuity of $1 for five periods at 11% is 3.6959.)

    A. $55,935

    B. $75,000

    C. $86,959

    D. $100,000

The correct answer is (C). *(S. Schultz)*

    REQUIRED: The cost at which an asset should be capitalized when acquired under a financing agreement.

    DISCUSSION: The acquisition of land should be recorded at fair value. When the fair value of the asset received is uncertain, the fair value of the assets transferred is used. The assets transferred included $50,000 in cash and a note. Given that Stratton can borrow long-term funds at 11%, the market value of the note can be approximated by imputing an 11% rate and using it to calculate the present value of the five equal annual payments. The present value of this ordinary annuity is $36,959 ($10,000 payment x 3.6959), and the land should be recorded at $86,959 ($50,000 + $36,959).

    Answer (A) is incorrect because $55,935 is the $50,000 in cash plus the present value of $10,000 to be received in 5 years. Answer (B) is incorrect because $75,000 is Conway Company's carrying value of the land. Answer (D) is incorrect because $100,000 is the $50,000 in cash plus $50,000 of payments which should have been calculated at present value.

16. Land was purchased to be used as the site for the construction of a plant. A building on the property was sold and removed by the buyer so that construction on the plant could begin. The proceeds from the sale of the building should be

- A. Classified as other income.
- B. Deducted from the cost of the land.
- C. Netted against the costs to clear the land and expensed as incurred.
- D. Netted against the costs to clear the land and amortized over the life of the plant.

The correct answer is (B). *(CPA 592 T-12)*
REQUIRED: The treatment of proceeds from the sale of a building removed to prepare for construction.
DISCUSSION: Land obtained as a plant site should be recorded at its acquisition cost. This cost includes the purchase price of the land and any additional expenses such as legal fees, title insurance, recording fees, assumption of encumbrances on the property, and any other costs incurred in preparing the property for its intended use. Because the intended use of the land was as a site for the construction of a plant, the proceeds from the sale of the building removed to prepare the land for construction should be deducted from the cost of the land.
Answers (A), (C), and (D) are incorrect because the proceeds affect the cost of the land. They do not affect income.

17. On December 1, 1996, East Co. purchased a tract of land as a factory site for $300,000. The old building on the property was razed, and salvaged materials resulting from demolition were sold. Additional costs incurred and salvage proceeds realized during December 1996 were as follows:

Cost to raze old building	$25,000
Legal fees for purchase contract and to record ownership	5,000
Title guarantee insurance	6,000
Proceeds from sale of salvaged materials	4,000

In East's December 31, 1996 balance sheet, what amount should be reported as land?

- A. $311,000
- B. $321,000
- C. $332,000
- D. $336,000

The correct answer is (C). *(CPA 592 I-22)*
REQUIRED: The amount to be reported as the cost of land.
DISCUSSION: When land is acquired as a factory site, the cost of the land should include the purchase price of the land and such additional expenses as legal fees, title insurance, recording fees, subsequent assumption of encumbrances on the property, and the costs incurred in preparing the property for its intended use. Because the land was purchased as a factory site, the cost of razing the old building, minus any proceeds received from the sale of salvaged materials, should be capitalized as part of the land account. Thus, the amount to be reported as land is $332,000 ($300,000 + $5,000 + $6,000 + $25,000 − $4,000).
Answer (A) is incorrect because $311,000 excludes the net cost of razing the old building. Answer (B) is incorrect because $321,000 excludes the legal fees and title insurance. Answer (D) is incorrect because $336,000 excludes the proceeds of razing the old building.

18. During 1996, Burr Co. had the following transactions pertaining to its new office building:

Purchase price of land	$ 60,000
Legal fees for contracts to purchase land	2,000
Architects' fees	8,000
Demolition of the old building on site	5,000
Sale of scrap from old building	3,000
Construction cost of new building (fully completed)	350,000

In Burr's December 31, 1996, balance sheet, what amounts should be reported as the cost of land and cost of building?

	Land	Building
A.	$60,000	$360,000
B.	$62,000	$360,000
C.	$64,000	$358,000
D.	$65,000	$362,000

The correct answer is (C). *(CPA 591 I-24)*
REQUIRED: The amounts reported as the cost of land and cost of building.
DISCUSSION: The cost of the land should include the purchase price of the land and such additional expenses as legal fees, title insurance, recording fees, subsequent assumption of encumbrances on the property, and the costs incurred in preparing the property for its intended use. Because the land was purchased as the site of an office building, the cost of razing the old building, minus any proceeds received from the sale of salvaged materials, should be capitalized as part of the land account. Thus, land should be reported as $64,000 ($60,000 + $2,000 + $5,000 − $3,000). The architect's fees are included in the cost of the building, which should be reported as $358,000 ($350,000 + $8,000).
Answer (A) is incorrect because a $60,000 land cost omits the legal fees and the net demolition cost, and a $360,000 building cost improperly includes the legal fees. Answer (B) is incorrect because a $62,000 land cost omits the legal fees or the net demolition cost, and a $360,000 building cost improperly includes the legal fees. Answer (D) is incorrect because a $65,000 land cost includes the gross demolition cost but not the legal fees. A $362,000 building cost includes the legal fees and the net demolition cost.

19. On April 1, 1996, ABC Company exchanged 10,000 shares of its common stock with a total par value of $20,000 for a piece of land owned by XYZ Company. The shares of stock were treasury shares that were purchased years earlier by ABC for a total of $35,000 and that had a market value of $44,000 on April 1, 1996. The land had a recorded value on XYZ's books of $28,000. What amount should be recorded as the cost of the land by ABC Company?

A. $20,000

B. $28,000

C. $35,000

D. $44,000

The correct answer is (D). *(CIA 1191 IV-28)*
REQUIRED: The amount that should be recorded as the cost of the land.
DISCUSSION: If the fair values of the assets involved in a nonmonetary exchange are reasonably determinable and the exchange is the culmination of an earning process, accounting for the transaction should be based upon the fair value of the asset relinquished or of the asset obtained, whichever is more clearly determinable (APB 29). This transaction culminated an earning process because it involved dissimilar assets. Accounting for the exchange should be based on the fair value of the asset surrendered ($44,000) because it is more clearly determinable than the fair value of the asset obtained.
Answer (A) is incorrect because $20,000 is the par value of the stock. Answer (B) is incorrect because $28,000 is the recorded value of the land. Answer (C) is incorrect because $35,000 is the cost of the treasury stock.

20. On July 1, 1996, Casa Development Co. purchased a tract of land for $1,200,000. Casa incurred additional costs of $300,000 during the remainder of 1996 in preparing the land for sale. The tract was subdivided into residential lots as follows:

Lot Class	Number of Lots	Sales Price per Lot
A	100	$24,000
B	100	16,000
C	200	10,000

Using the relative sales value method, what amount of costs should be allocated to the Class A lots?

A. $300,000

B. $375,000

C. $600,000

D. $720,000

The correct answer is (C). *(CPA 595 F-10)*
REQUIRED: The amount of costs allocated using the relative sales value method.
DISCUSSION: The relative sales value method allocates cost based on the relative value of assets in a group. The total sales value of the lots is $6,000,000 [($24,000 x 100) + ($16,000 x 100) + ($10,000 x 200)]. Class A represents 40% of the total value ($2,400,000 ÷ $6,000,000). Total costs equal $1,500,000 ($1,200,000 + $300,000). Thus, the amount of costs allocated to Class A is $600,000 ($1,500,000 x .40).
Answer (A) is incorrect because $300,000 equals the additional costs incurred. Answer (B) is incorrect because $375,000 equals 25% of the total cost. Class A represents 25% of the lots but 40% of the total value. Answer (D) is incorrect because $720,000 equals 48% of the total cost. Class A's sales price per lot is 48% of the sum of the unit sales prices of Classes A, B, and C.

10.2 Capitalization of Interest

21. According to SFAS 34, *Capitalization of Interest Costs*, interest should be capitalized for assets that are

A. In use or ready for their intended use in the earning activities of the enterprise.

B. Being constructed or otherwise being produced as discrete projects for an enterprise's own use.

C. Not being used in the earning activities of the enterprise and not undergoing the activities necessary to get them ready for use.

D. Routinely produced.

The correct answer is (B). *(CMA 1292 2-21)*
REQUIRED: The types of assets for which interest should be capitalized.
DISCUSSION: SFAS 34 requires capitalization of material interest costs for assets constructed for internal use and those constructed for sale or lease as discrete projects. It does not apply to products routinely produced for inventory, assets in use or ready for use, assets not being used or being prepared for use, and idle land.
Answer (A) is incorrect because interest is not capitalized for assets in use or ready for use. Answer (C) is incorrect because assets not being used and being prepared for use are not subject to interest capitalization rules. Answer (D) is incorrect because capitalized interest should not be added to routinely produced inventory.

22. During 1996, Bay Co. constructed machinery for its own use and for sale to customers. Bank loans financed these assets both during construction and after construction was complete. How much of the interest incurred should be reported as interest expense in the 1996 income statement?

	Interest Incurred for Machinery for Bay's Own Use	Interest Incurred for Machinery Held for Sale
A.	All interest incurred	All interest incurred
B.	All interest incurred	Interest incurred after completion
C.	Interest incurred after completion	Interest incurred after completion
D.	Interest incurred after completion	All interest incurred

The correct answer is (D). *(CPA 591 T-23)*
REQUIRED: The interest incurred reported as interest expense.
DISCUSSION: In accordance with SFAS 34, interest should be capitalized for two types of assets: those constructed or otherwise produced for an enterprise's own use, including those constructed or produced by others; and those intended for sale or lease that are constructed or produced as discrete products (e.g., ships). SFAS 58, *Capitalization of Interest Cost in Financial Statements That Include Investments Accounted for by the Equity Method*, adds equity based investments to the list of qualifying assets. Machinery constructed for a company's own use qualifies for capitalization of interest if relevant expenditures have been made, activities necessary to prepare the asset for its intended use are in progress, and interest is being incurred. Machinery routinely constructed for sale to others does not qualify. Thus, interest incurred for machinery held for sale and interest incurred after an asset has been completed should be expensed.
Answers (A), (B), and (C) are incorrect because all interest incurred for machinery held for sale and interest incurred for machinery for Bay's own use after completion should be expensed.

23. Which one of the following ways of determining an interest rate should be used when the average accumulated expenditures for the constructed asset exceed the amounts of specific new borrowings associated with the asset?

A. Average rate of return on equity for the last 5 years.

B. Cost of capital rate for the company.

C. Prime interest rate.

D. Weighted average of the interest rates applicable to the other borrowings of the company.

The correct answer is (D). *(CMA 1280 3-25)*
REQUIRED: The method of determining the interest rate used to capitalize interest costs.
DISCUSSION: The actual interest rate on specific new borrowings is used to capitalize construction expenditures to the extent of the new borrowings. When average accumulated construction expenditures for the period exceed the specific new borrowings related to the construction, interest on other borrowings must be capitalized. SFAS 34 requires a weighted-average interest rate to be used to capitalize interest costs on accumulated construction expenditures in excess of the specific new borrowings associated with the asset.
Answers (A), (B), and (C) are incorrect because none is specified by SFAS 34.

24. During the second quarter of a calendar-year company, the following expenditures were made relative to a qualifying asset on which interest is to be capitalized: $80,000 on April 1, $90,000 on May 1, and $100,000 incurred uniformly during the period. What was the average amount of accumulated expenditures for this quarterly accounting period?

A. $180,000

B. $190,000

C. $240,000

D. $270,000

The correct answer is (B). *(Publisher)*
REQUIRED: The average accumulated expenditures during a quarterly accounting period.
DISCUSSION: To determine the average accumulated expenditures on which interest is to be capitalized, the expenditures must be weighted by the portion of the accounting period for which they were incurred. The $80,000 expended on April 1 was incurred during the entire period. The $90,000 expended on May 1 was incurred for two-thirds of the period. The $100,000 incurred uniformly throughout is equivalent to an expenditure of $50,000 for the whole period. The average amount of accumulated expenditures is equal to $190,000 [($80,000 x 1) + ($90,000 x 2/3) + ($100,000 x ½)].
Answer (A) is incorrect because $180,000 assumes the whole $100,000 is included and none of the $90,000. Answer (C) is incorrect because $240,000 assumes that the whole $100,000 is included. Answer (D) is incorrect because $270,000 is not the average amount of accumulated expenditures; it is the sum of the three interest expenditures.

25. Cole Co. began constructing a building for its own use in January 1996. During 1996, Cole incurred interest of $50,000 on specific construction debt, and $20,000 on other borrowings. Interest computed on the weighted-average amount of accumulated expenditures for the building during 1996 was $40,000. What amount of interest cost should Cole capitalize?

   A. $20,000

   B. $40,000

   C. $50,000

   D. $70,000

The correct answer is (B). *(CPA 594 F-17)*
   REQUIRED: The amount of interest capitalized.
   DISCUSSION: Material interest costs incurred for the construction of certain assets for internal use are capitalized. The interest to be capitalized is determined by applying an appropriate rate to the average qualifying expenditures accumulated during a given period. Thus, $40,000 of the interest incurred on the construction is capitalized.
   Answer (A) is incorrect because $20,000 equals interest on other borrowings. Answer (C) is incorrect because $50,000 equals the total interest on specific construction debt. Answer (D) is incorrect because $70,000 equals the sum of interest on other borrowings and the total interest on specific construction debt.

26. Which of the following is not an accurate statement of a criterion that must be met before interest is required to be capitalized in accordance with the provisions of SFAS 34?

   A. Expenditures relative to a qualifying asset have been made.

   B. Activities necessary to prepare the asset for its intended use are in progress.

   C. Interest cost is incurred on borrowings.

   D. Debt is incurred for the project.

The correct answer is (D). *(Publisher)*
   REQUIRED: The criterion not required by SFAS 34 for the capitalization of interest.
   DISCUSSION: Capitalization of interest for a qualifying asset is required when expenditures have been made, activities are in progress to ready the asset for its intended use, and interest cost is being incurred. The mere incurrence of debt is not sufficient. Capitalized interest is limited to interest on borrowings. Accordingly, the incurrence of debt, such as trade payables, upon which no interest cost is being incurred, is not sufficient to meet the required criteria, even if qualifying expenditures have been made and the appropriate activities are in progress.
   Answers (A), (B), and (C) are incorrect because each is one of the three criteria required by SFAS 34. Interest should be capitalized when all three are met.

27. Which of the following items should not have been capitalized?

   A. The cost of reinstalling or rearranging equipment to facilitate more efficient future production.

   B. The cost of removing an old building from land that was purchased with the intent of constructing a new office building on the site.

   C. The estimated cost of equity capital during the construction period of a new office building.

   D. The cost of a new hospital wing.

The correct answer is (C). *(CIA 582 IV-3)*
   REQUIRED: The item that should not have been capitalized.
   DISCUSSION: SFAS 34 requires the capitalization of interest on debt incurred as a cost of acquiring an asset during the period in which an asset is being constructed for the company's own use. Imputed interest on equity capital is not capitalized. The view of the FASB is that recognizing the cost of equity capital would not conform to the current accounting framework.
   Answer (A) is incorrect because such a cost will benefit future periods and thus should be capitalized. Answer (B) is incorrect because the removal cost is associated with preparing land for its intended use and therefore should be capitalized. Answer (D) is incorrect because a new hospital wing is an addition and should be capitalized.

28. SFAS 62, *Capitalization of Interest Cost in Situations Involving Certain Tax-Exempt Borrowings and Certain Gifts and Grants*, amends SFAS 34 to require the offsetting of related interest income and interest expense in situations involving acquisition of qualifying assets financed with the proceeds of tax-exempt borrowings

A. And similarly applies to assets acquired with gifts and grants which are restricted by the donor or grantor to the acquisition of particular assets to the extent funds are available.

B. When those funds are externally restricted to the financing of specific qualifying assets.

C. Only if the funds are used for nonqualifying assets.

D. If the interest earned is less than 50% of the related interest expense.

The correct answer is (B). *(Publisher)*
REQUIRED: The condition under which interest income from funds raised by tax-exempt borrowings and not yet expended for qualifying assets can offset capitalizable interest expense.
DISCUSSION: Ordinarily, interest income earned should not be offset against interest costs in determining the amount of interest to be capitalized. The exception, provided by SFAS 62, is when qualifying assets are financed with the proceeds of tax-exempt borrowings and the funds are externally restricted to the acquisition of specified qualifying assets or to the servicing of the debt related to those assets.
Answer (A) is incorrect because the interest earned from investments of gifts and grants is considered an addition to the gift or grant per SFAS 62. Answer (C) is incorrect because the funds must be used for qualifying assets (as specified in SFAS 62). Answer (D) is incorrect because no limits exist on the amount of interest income that can offset interest expense.

29. SFAS 42, *Determining Materiality for Capitalization of Interest Cost*, amended SFAS 34 in which of the following ways?

A. It set new materiality standards based on the remote, reasonably possible, and probable standards.

B. It constituted a minor wording change to avoid new tests of materiality for interest capitalization.

C. It provided a detailed cost benefit formula to determine if interest cost needs to be capitalized.

D. It concluded that interest cost does not need to be capitalized if the rollover effect occurring from amortizing previously capitalized interest approximates interest costs planned in the future.

The correct answer is (B). *(Publisher)*
REQUIRED: The correct statement regarding the effect of SFAS 42 on capitalization of interest costs.
DISCUSSION: SFAS 34 implies that interest may not have to be capitalized when the net income over a series of years is approximately the same whether interest is capitalized or expensed. This could occur when amortization equals the annual interest expense. SFAS 42 corrects this implication and requires interest to be capitalized on qualifying assets when the usual materiality considerations are met.
Answer (A) is incorrect because SFAS 42 reaffirms that SFAS 34 does not establish new tests of materiality. Answers (C) and (D) are incorrect because SFAS 34 requires interest cost on certain qualifying assets to be capitalized regardless of cost-benefit analysis or the effect on net income.

30. SFAS 58, *Capitalization of Interest Cost in Financial Statements That Include Investments Accounted for by the Equity Method*, amends SFAS 34 to clarify when interest may be capitalized on equity method investments and other assets. SFAS 58 concludes that interest may be capitalized on

A. Equity method investments in activities in progress necessary to the commencement of the planned principal operations when the activities include the use of funds to acquire qualifying assets.

B. Assets that are not included in the consolidated balance sheet of a parent company with consolidated subsidiaries.

C. Investments accounted for by the equity method after the planned principal operations of the investee begin.

D. Investments in regulated investees that are capitalizing the cost of both debt and equity capital.

The correct answer is (A). *(Publisher)*
REQUIRED: The qualifying assets on which interest may be capitalized under SFAS 58.
DISCUSSION: SFAS 58 applies to investments in joint ventures, unconsolidated subsidiaries, and investees accounted for under the equity method. If these investees are in the process of commencing planned principal operations and they are using funds to acquire qualifying assets for their operations, interest may be capitalized as part of the investment.
Answers (B), (C), and (D) are incorrect because each is an example of assets for which interest cannot be capitalized per SFAS 58.

10.3 Gains and Losses on Disposal

31. On July 1, 1996, one of Rudd Co.'s delivery vans was destroyed in an accident. On that date, the van's carrying value was $2,500. On July 15, 1996, Rudd received and recorded a $700 invoice for a new engine installed in the van in May 1996, and another $500 invoice for various repairs. In August, Rudd received $3,500 under its insurance policy on the van, which it plans to use to replace the van. What amount should Rudd report as gain (loss) on disposal of the van in its 1996 income statement?

A. $1,000

B. $300

C. $0

D. $(200)

The correct answer is (B). *(CPA 592 I-45)*
REQUIRED: The gain (loss) on disposal of the van.
DISCUSSION: Gain (loss) is recognized on an involuntary conversion equal to the difference between the proceeds and the carrying amount. The carrying amount includes the carrying value at July 1 ($2,500) plus the capitalizable cost ($700) of the engine installed in May. This cost increased the carrying amount because it improved the future service potential of the asset. Ordinary repairs, however, are expensed. Consequently, the gain is $300 [$3,500 – ($2,500 + $700)].
Answer (A) is incorrect because $1,000 results from expensing the cost of the engine. Answer (C) is incorrect because gain (loss) is recognized on an involuntary conversion. Answer (D) is incorrect because $(200) assumes the cost of repairs increased the carrying amount.

32. Lano Corp.'s forest land was condemned for use as a national park. Compensation for the condemnation exceeded the forest land's carrying amount. Lano purchased similar, but larger, replacement forest land for an amount greater than the condemnation award. As a result of the condemnation and replacement, what is the net effect on the carrying amount of forest land reported in Lano's balance sheet?

A. The amount is increased by the excess of the replacement forest land's cost over the condemned forest land's carrying amount.

B. The amount is increased by the excess of the replacement forest land's cost over the condemnation award.

C. The amount is increased by the excess of the condemnation award over the condemned forest land's carrying amount.

D. No effect, because the condemned forest land's carrying amount is used as the replacement forest land's carrying amount.

The correct answer is (A). *(CPA 592 T-13)*
REQUIRED: The net effect on the carrying amount of forest land reported in the balance sheet.
DISCUSSION: The forced sale of property was an involuntary conversion of a nonmonetary asset to monetary assets. FASB Interpretation No. 30, *Accounting for Involuntary Conversions of Nonmonetary Assets to Monetary Assets*, requires that gain or loss be recognized even though an enterprise reinvests or is obligated to reinvest the monetary assets in replacement nonmonetary assets. Hence, the condemned land carrying value should be credited and a gain recognized. The replacement property should be recorded at its cost.
Answer (B) is incorrect because the increase in the carrying amount is not reduced by the gain (condemnation award – former carrying amount). Answer (C) is incorrect because the condemnation award is not a reported cost of the new asset. Answer (D) is incorrect because the condemnation and replacement are separate transactions. Hence, a gain must be recognized, and the new asset should be recorded at its cost.

33. A state government condemned Cory Co.'s parcel of real estate. Cory will receive $750,000 for this property, which has a carrying amount of $575,000. Cory incurred the following costs as a result of the condemnation:

Appraisal fees to support a $750,000 value	$2,500
Attorney fees for the closing with the state	3,500
Attorney fees to review contract to acquire replacement property	3,000
Title insurance on replacement property	4,000

What amount of cost should Cory use to determine the gain on the condemnation?

A. $581,000

B. $582,000

C. $584,000

D. $588,000

The correct answer is (A). *(CPA 1191 I-19)*
REQUIRED: The amount of cost used to determine the gain on the condemnation.
DISCUSSION: FASB Interpretation No. 30, *Accounting for Involuntary Conversions of Nonmonetary Assets to Monetary Assets*, requires that gain or loss be recognized on an involuntary conversion. The determination of the gain is based on the carrying amount ($575,000) and the costs incurred as a direct result of the condemnation ($2,500 appraisal fees and $3,500 attorney fees), a total of $581,000. Because the recipient is not obligated to reinvest the condemnation proceeds in other nonmonetary assets, the costs associated with the acquisition of the replacement property (attorney fees and title insurance) should be treated as part of the consideration paid for that property.
Answer (B) is incorrect because $582,000 includes the costs associated with the replacement property but not the costs incurred as a direct result of the condemnation. Answer (C) is incorrect because $584,000 includes the attorney fees associated with the replacement property. Answer (D) is incorrect because $588,000 includes the costs associated with the replacement property.

34. SFAS 121, *Accounting for the Impairment of Long-Lived Assets and for Long-Lived Assets to Be Disposed Of*, requires the review for possible impairment of long-lived assets that an entity expects to hold and use in their future operations

A. At each interim and annual balance sheet date.

B. At annual balance sheet dates only.

C. Periodically.

D. Whenever events or changes in circumstances indicate that the recorded value of an asset may not be recoverable.

The correct answer is (D). *(Publisher)*
REQUIRED: The appropriate time required to review for impairment of long-lived assets to be held and used in operations.
DISCUSSION: For long-lived assets an entity expects to hold and use in future operations, SFAS 121 requires a review of possible impairment whenever events or changes in circumstances indicate that the sum of undiscounted expected future cash flows may be less than the carrying value of an asset. At this time, the value of an asset may not be recoverable.
Answers (A), (B), and (C) are incorrect because review of possible impairment is required only when events or changes in circumstances indicate that the carrying value of an asset may not be recoverable.

35. Triad Machine Shop uses a special machine to fill certain customer needs. This machine is used only to produce a specific product which differs from that produced by other machines. In addition, the customers served generally do not order other products from Triad. Since the opening of a competitive machine shop that uses more modern equipment, orders for the product produced by this machine have materially decreased. Because of this, Triad has gathered the following information to determine whether to recognize an impairment loss:

Carrying value	Undiscounted future cash flows	Discounted future cash flows	Fair value
$525,000	$450,000	$245,000	$295,000

What amount of impairment loss should Triad recognize?

A. $0

B. $75,000

C. $230,000

D. $280,000

The correct answer is (C). *(Publisher)*
REQUIRED: The impairment loss to be recognized.
DISCUSSION: For a long-lived asset that is to be held and used in future operations, an impairment loss should be considered when events or changes in circumstances indicate that future cash flows may not be sufficient to recover the carrying value of the asset. An impairment loss shall be recognized only if the sum of the undiscounted expected future cash flows is less than the carrying amount of the asset. The impairment loss recognized is equal to the amount by which the carrying amount of the asset exceeds the asset's fair value. Since the undiscounted expected future cash flows ($450,000) are less than the carrying amount ($525,000) of the machine, Triad should recognize an impairment loss of $230,000 ($525,000 carrying amount less $295,000 fair value).
Answer (A) is incorrect because an impairment loss should be recognized. Answer (B) is incorrect because $75,000 is equal to the carrying amount less the undiscounted expected future cash flows. Answer (D) is incorrect because $280,000 is equal to the carrying amount less the discounted expected future cash flows.

10.4 Coinsurance

36. When an insurance policy has a coinsurance clause, the minimum amount recoverable by the insured is never limited by

A. The insured's loss.

B. The coinsurance requirement.

C. The face amount of the policy.

D. The book value of the asset.

The correct answer is (D). *(Publisher)*
REQUIRED: The response which is not a limitation on amounts recoverable under a coinsurance clause.
DISCUSSION: A coinsurance clause requires the insured to have at least a specified percentage of the value of the property insured or the insurance company will pay only a proportionate part of a partial loss. The amount that can be recovered on a partial loss when an insurance policy has a coinsurance clause is the lowest of three amounts: the insured's loss, the coinsurance requirement, or the face amount of the policy. The book value of the asset determines only the accounting gain or loss on the insurance settlement.
Answers (A), (B), and (C) are incorrect because each is a limitation on recovery under a policy with a coinsurance clause.

37. Ignito Corporation carries a $50,000 fire insurance policy on its office building in downtown Pyroville. The policy has an 80% coinsurance clause. The building, having a book value of $50,000 and a fair market value of $75,000, sustained $30,000 of fire damage last year. How much can Ignito collect on the insurance policy?

A. $20,000

B. $36,000

C. $30,000

D. $25,000

The correct answer is (D). *(C. Dugopolski)*
REQUIRED: The amount collectible under a fire insurance policy with a coinsurance clause.
DISCUSSION: Under an 80% coinsurance clause, the property must be insured for at least 80% of its fair market value (insurable value). If a lesser amount is carried, the insured becomes a coinsurer. The insurance company is thus liable for only a proportionate amount of any partial loss. Here, Ignito can collect $25,000 from its insurance company.

$$\frac{\$50,000 \text{ } face \text{ } value}{80\% \times \$75,000 \text{ } FMV} \times \$30,000 \text{ } loss = \$25,000$$

Answer (A) is incorrect because $20,000 is the difference between the amount of insurance carried and the cost of the damage. Answer (B) is incorrect because $36,000 is more than the cost of the damage. Answer (C) is incorrect because $30,000 is the full amount of the damage which should be prorated since Ignito is subject to coinsurance.

38. On July 1, a fire destroyed $200,000 of Lane Company's $600,000 inventory (fair market values). Lane carried a $240,000 fire insurance policy with an 80% coinsurance clause. What is the maximum amount of insurance that Lane can collect as a result of this loss?

A. $200,000

B. $192,000

C. $160,000

D. $100,000

The correct answer is (D). *(CPA 1185 I-13)*

REQUIRED: The amount recoverable when the insurance carried does not meet the coinsurance requirement.

DISCUSSION: Under a coinsurance agreement, the amount recoverable on a loss is the ratio of the face value of the insurance policy to the coinsurance requirement (i.e., to the percentage of insurance required times the fair market value of the insured assets), all times the amount of the loss. Lane Company can collect a maximum of $100,000.

$$\frac{\$240,000 \; face \; value}{80\% \times \$600,000 \; FMV} \times \$200,000 \; loss = \$100,000$$

The amount recoverable is limited to the lowest of (1) the coinsurance requirement, (2) the face value of the policy, or (3) the amount of the casualty loss.

Answer (A) is incorrect because $200,000 is the total cost of damages which is subject to the coinsurance clause. Answer (B) is incorrect because $192,000 is 80% of the $240,000 face amount of the policy. Answer (C) is incorrect because $160,000 is 80% of the $200,000 in damage.

39. If four separate carriers have written fire insurance policies totaling $60,000 on a single property with a cash value of $100,000, what fraction of a loss of $20,000 would be collectible from a carrier whose $30,000 policy contains a 90% coinsurance clause?

A. 60/90

B. 30/90

C. 30/60

D. 20/100

The correct answer is (B). *(CPA 1172 T-16)*

REQUIRED: The fraction of a loss collectible from a carrier whose policy contains a 90% coinsurance clause.

DISCUSSION: If two or more insurers have insured the same asset, and the various policies have different coinsurance percentages, the amount recoverable from each policy is determined by multiplying the loss by a percentage equal to the face value of the policy divided by the greater of the coinsurance amount or the aggregate face value of all the policies.

The property had an insurable value of $100,000, but the fire insurance policies totaled only $60,000. Since the policy in question had a 90% coinsurance clause, the percentage collectible from that carrier is $30,000 (the face amount of the policy) divided by $90,000 (the greater of the coinsurance requirement or the total value of all the policies).

Answer (A) is incorrect because 60/90 is the total amount of coverage over the coinsurance requirement. Answer (C) is incorrect because 30/60 is the face amount of one of the policies over the total amount of coverage from all of the carriers. Answer (D) is incorrect because 20/100 is the amount of loss over the fair value of the insured property.

10.5 Exchange of Nonmonetary Assets

40. Departures from the use of fair values in accounting for nonmonetary transactions are acceptable when

A. Nonmonetary assets are exchanged and the exchange represents the culmination of an earning process.

B. Similar productive assets are exchanged.

C. A nonmonetary asset is received in a nonreciprocal transfer.

D. Any nonreciprocal transfer of nonmonetary assets is made to an owner.

The correct answer is (B). *(Publisher)*
REQUIRED: The appropriate departure from fair values in accounting for nonmonetary transactions.
DISCUSSION: According to APB 29, *Accounting for Nonmonetary Transactions*, nonmonetary transactions should usually be based on the fair values of the assets or services involved. If the fair values are not determinable or if an exchange is not the culmination of an earning process, the transactions should not be based on fair value. A nonmonetary transaction involving similar productive assets or inventory is not the culmination of an earning process and should be recorded at the book value of the assets given up.
Answers (A) and (C) are incorrect because each should be accounted for at fair value. Answer (D) is incorrect because nonreciprocal transfers of nonmonetary assets made to owners (property dividends) should be accounted for at the fair value of the assets transferred unless the transaction is a form of reorganization.

41. Accounting for an exchange of nonmonetary assets between an enterprise and another entity should be based on

A. The recorded amount of the asset relinquished if the exchange is essentially the culmination of an earning process.

B. The recorded amount of the asset relinquished if the exchange is not essentially the culmination of an earning process.

C. The fair value of the asset relinquished if the exchange is not essentially the culmination of an earning process.

D. The fair value of the asset relinquished, if determinable, whether or not the exchange is the culmination of an earning process.

The correct answer is (B). *(Publisher)*
REQUIRED: The proper accounting for an exchange of nonmonetary assets between two enterprises.
DISCUSSION: If the fair values of the assets are reasonably determinable and the exchange is the culmination of an earning process, accounting for the transaction should be based upon the fair value of the asset relinquished or of the asset obtained, whichever is more clearly determinable (APB 29). The exchange of similar productive assets or similar items of inventory is not the culmination of an earning process and should be recorded at the book value of the assets given up.
Answer (A) is incorrect because, if the transaction culminates an earning process, accounting should be based upon the fair value of the asset relinquished, not book value. Answers (C) and (D) are incorrect because, if the exchange does not culminate an earning process, accounting should be based upon the book value of the asset relinquished.

42. Vik Auto and King Clothier exchanged goods, held for resale, with equal fair values. Each will use the other's goods to promote its own products. The retail price of the car that Vik gave up is less than the retail price of the clothes received. What gain should Vik recognize on the nonmonetary exchange?

A. A gain is not recognized.

B. A gain equal to the difference between the retail prices of the clothes received and the car.

C. A gain equal to the difference between the retail price and the cost of the car.

D. A gain equal to the difference between the fair value and the cost of the car.

The correct answer is (D). *(CPA 1192 T-24)*
REQUIRED: The gain recognized on the nonmonetary exchange.
DISCUSSION: An exchange of dissimilar assets is considered the culmination of an earning process. Thus, the transaction should be recorded at the fair value of the assets surrendered or of the assets received, whichever is more clearly evident. Hence, Vik's gain is the difference between the fair value, which is the same for the two assets, and the cost (carrying amount) of the asset surrendered.
Answer (A) is incorrect because a gain is recognized. The exchange culminates an earning process. Answers (B) and (C) are incorrect because fair value, not retail price, is the basis of the accounting.

43. May Co. and Sty Co. exchanged nonmonetary assets. The exchange did not culminate an earning process for either May or Sty. May paid cash to Sty in connection with the exchange. To the extent that the amount of cash exceeds a proportionate share of the carrying amount of the asset surrendered, a realized gain on the exchange should be recognized by

	May	Sty
A.	Yes	Yes
B.	Yes	No
C.	No	Yes
D.	No	No

The correct answer is (C). *(CPA 591 T-35)*
REQUIRED: The party(ies) that should recognize a realized gain on a nonmonetary exchange involving boot but not culminating an earning process.
DISCUSSION: Both parties should usually account for an exchange of nonmonetary assets that does not culminate an earning process based on the book values of the assets transferred. For such transactions, gain or loss should not be recognized. However, if partial monetary consideration (boot) is involved, a partial sale is considered to have taken place, and a proportionate amount of gain should be recognized by the recipient of the boot. The entity paying the boot should not recognize gain but should record the asset received at the sum of the boot plus the book value of the nonmonetary asset transferred. The recipient of boot should recognize a gain on the exchange to the extent that the amount of the boot exceeds a proportionate share of the recorded amount of the asset surrendered. The gain recognized equals the total potential gain times the ratio of the boot to the sum of the boot and the fair value of the asset received.
Answers (A), (B), and (D) are incorrect because only the party receiving the cash in a nonmonetary exchange recognizes a gain.

44. Bensol Co. and Sable Co. exchanged similar trucks with fair values in excess of carrying amounts. In addition, Bensol paid Sable to compensate for the difference in truck values. As a consequence of the exchange, Sable recognizes

A. A gain equal to the difference between the fair value and carrying amount of the truck given up.

B. A gain determined by the proportion of the cash received to the total consideration.

C. A loss determined by the proportion of cash received to the total consideration.

D. Neither a gain nor a loss.

The correct answer is (B). *(CPA 1193 T-37)*
REQUIRED: The consequences of exchanging similar nonmonetary assets when boot is given.
DISCUSSION: The receipt of boot is considered a partial culmination of an earning process requiring recognition of a partial gain. A gain is realized because the carrying value of Sable's truck was less than its fair value, and the total consideration received apparently equaled the fair value. The recognized gain equals the realized gain times the ratio of boot to total consideration received.
Answer (A) is incorrect because the amount of gain recognized is in proportion to the amount of boot (cash) received. Answer (C) is incorrect because a gain should be recognized. Answer (D) is incorrect because Sable recognizes a gain.

45. In an exchange of similar assets, Transit Co. received equipment with a fair value equal to the carrying amount of equipment given up. Transit also contributed cash. As a result of the exchange, Transit recognized

A. A loss equal to the cash given up.

B. A loss determined by the proportion of cash paid to the total transaction value.

C. A gain determined by the proportion of cash paid to the total transaction value.

D. Neither gain nor loss.

The correct answer is (A). *(CPA 593 T-16)*
REQUIRED: The gain or loss, if any, on the exchange of similar assets if cash is given.
DISCUSSION: In an exchange of similar assets involving boot, the party giving the boot normally records the asset acquired at the sum of the boot given plus the book value of the asset surrendered. However, when this amount exceeds the fair value of the asset received, the latter should be recorded at its fair value, with the difference recognized as a loss.
Answer (B) is incorrect because the entire indicated loss should be recognized. Answers (C) and (D) are incorrect because a loss equal to the cash given up should be recognized.

46. Wall and Star are two independent companies involved in the home building business. Each owns a tract of land being held for development; however, each would prefer to build on the other's land. Accordingly, the companies agree to exchange their land. An appraiser was hired, and from the appraisal report and the companies' records, the following information was obtained:

	Wall's Land	Star's Land
Cost and book value	$ 80,000	$50,000
Fair value based		
upon appraisal	100,000	85,000

Given this information, the land parcels were exchanged and, based on the difference in appraised fair values, Star paid $15,000 to Wall. At what amount should Star record the land received on its books?

A. $100,000

B. $85,000

C. $65,000

D. $50,000

The correct answer is (C). *(W. Higley)*
REQUIRED: The accounting for an exchange of similar productive assets when boot is given.
DISCUSSION: When a nonmonetary asset is acquired in an exchange of similar productive assets, the exchange is not considered the culmination of an earning process. When cash (boot) is given in the exchange, the party paying the cash should not recognize gain. The asset should be recorded at the book value of the asset given plus the amount of the cash paid. Star should therefore record the land received as $65,000 ($50,000 + $15,000).
Answer (A) is incorrect because $100,000 is the fair value of the land Star received. Answer (B) is incorrect because $85,000 is the fair value of the land Star exchanged. Answer (D) is incorrect because $50,000 is the book value of the land Star exchanged. The cash Star paid should be added to this amount to determine the amount recorded for the new land.

47. Minor Baseball Company had a player contract with Doe that was recorded in its accounting records at $145,000. Better Baseball Company had a player contract with Smith that was recorded in its accounting records at $140,000. Minor traded Doe to Better for Smith by exchanging the players' contracts. The fair value of each contract was $150,000. What amount should be shown in the accounting records after the exchange of player contracts?

	Minor	Better
A.	$140,000	$140,000
B.	$140,000	$145,000
C.	$145,000	$140,000
D.	$150,000	$150,000

The correct answer is (C). *(CPA 1183 I-40)*
REQUIRED: The accounting for a nonmonetary exchange of baseball players' contracts.
DISCUSSION: A nonmonetary transaction that involves only similar productive assets does not represent the completion of the earning process. The asset acquired must therefore be recorded at the book value of the asset given up (APB 29). Minor gave up an asset with a book value of $145,000 to obtain Smith. Minor should thus record Smith's contract at $145,000. Better relinquished an asset with a book value of $140,000 to acquire Doe. Better should thus record Doe's contract at $140,000.
Answers (A), (B), and (D) are incorrect because a nonmonetary exchange of similar assets is not the culmination of an earnings process and should be recorded at the book values of the assets given up.

48. During 1996, Beam Co. paid $1,000 cash and traded inventory, which had a carrying amount of $20,000 and a fair value of $21,000, for other inventory in the same line of business with a fair value of $22,000. What amount of gain (loss) should Beam record related to the inventory exchange?

A. $2,000

B. $1,000

C. $0

D. $(1,000)

The correct answer is (C). *(CPA 593 II-9)*
REQUIRED: The amount of gain (loss) recorded relating to the inventory exchange.
DISCUSSION: The exchange of similar productive assets or inventory is not the culmination of an earning process and should be recorded at the book value of the assets given up. A loss is recognized if the fair value of the asset received is less than the book value of the asset(s) transferred. No gain is recognized unless boot is received. The book value of the assets relinquished is $21,000 ($20,000 + $1,000). The amount of gain (loss) is $0.
Answer (A) is incorrect because $2,000 equals the fair value of the inventory acquired minus the book value of the inventory transferred. Answer (B) is incorrect because $1,000 equals the fair value of the inventory acquired minus the book value of the inventory transferred and the $1,000 paid. Answer (D) is incorrect because a $1,000 loss assumes that the fair value of the inventory acquired is less than the book value of the inventory transferred plus the cash.

49. Yola Co. and Zaro Co. are fuel oil distributors. To facilitate the delivery of oil to their customers, Yola and Zaro exchanged ownership of 1,200 barrels of oil without physically moving the oil. Yola paid Zaro $30,000 to compensate for a difference in the grade of oil. On the date of the exchange, cost and market values of the oil were as follows:

	Yola Co.	Zaro Co.
Cost	$100,000	$126,000
Market values	120,000	150,000

In Zaro's income statement, what amount of gain should be reported from the exchange of the oil?

A. $0

B. $4,800

C. $24,000

D. $30,000

The correct answer is (B). *(CPA 592 II-11)*
REQUIRED: The amount of gain reported from the exchange of inventory.
DISCUSSION: A nonmonetary transaction involving similar productive assets or inventory is not the culmination of an earning process and should be recorded at the book value of the assets given up. However, if partial monetary consideration (boot) is received, a partial sale is considered to have taken place, and a proportionate amount of gain should be recognized by the recipient of the boot. The gain recognized equals the total potential gain times the ratio of the boot to the sum of the boot and the fair value of the asset received. The total potential gain is $24,000 [($30,000 cash + $120,000 market value received) − $126,000 book value given up], and the gain recognized is $4,800 {[($30,000 ÷ ($30,000 + $120,000)] x $24,000}.
Answer (A) is incorrect because a gain should be recognized. Answer (C) is incorrect because $24,000 is the total potential gain. Answer (D) is incorrect because $30,000 is the boot.

50. On July 1, 1996, Balt Co. exchanged a truck for 25 shares of Ace Corp.'s common stock. On that date, the truck's carrying amount was $2,500, and its fair value was $3,000. Also, the book value of Ace's stock was $60 per share. On December 31, 1996, Ace had 250 shares of common stock outstanding and its book value per share was $50. What amount should Balt report in its December 31, 1996 balance sheet as investment in Ace?

A. $3,000

B. $2,500

C. $1,500

D. $1,250

The correct answer is (A). *(CPA 1192 I-20)*
REQUIRED: The amount reported for stock received in exchange for a nonmonetary asset.
DISCUSSION: Accounting for nonmonetary transactions should usually be based on the fair values of the assets or services involved (APB 29). The principal exceptions are when the transaction is not the culmination of an earning process, or when the fair value of neither the asset relinquished nor the asset received is clearly evident. An exchange of dissimilar nonmonetary assets culminates an earning process, and the fair value of the asset relinquished is clearly evident. Hence, Balt should report the investment in Ace as $3,000, the fair value of the asset relinquished.
Answer (B) is incorrect because $2,500 is the truck's carrying amount, not its fair value. Answer (C) is incorrect because $1,500 was the book value of 25 shares of Ace's stock on July 1. Answer (D) is incorrect because $1,250 is the book value of 25 shares of Ace's stock on December 31.

51. Amble, Inc., exchanged a truck with a carrying amount of $12,000 and a fair value of $20,000 for a truck and $5,000 cash. The fair value of the truck received was $15,000. At what amount should Amble record the truck received in the exchange?

A. $7,000

B. $9,000

C. $12,000

D. $15,000

The correct answer is (B). *(CPA 593 II-10)*

REQUIRED: The amount recorded for a nonmonetary asset obtained in an exchange if boot is received.

DISCUSSION: Amble has a potential gain of $8,000 ($15,000 fair value of truck received + $5,000 cash – $12,000 carrying amount of truck given up). Because the exchange did not give rise to a loss and is also not considered the culmination of an earning process (similar productive assets were exchanged), the transaction should be accounted for at book value (APB 29). The receipt of boot, however, is considered a partial culmination of an earning process requiring recognition of a partial gain. The recognized gain is determined by the ratio of boot to total consideration received. Boot was $5,000 and total consideration received was $20,000. Thus, boot was 25% of total consideration received. The gain to be reported is $2,000 (25% x $8,000 potential gain). Accordingly, the entry is to credit the carrying amount of the truck given up ($12,000), credit a partial gain of $2,000, debit cash for the $5,000 received, and debit the truck received for $9,000.

Answer (A) is incorrect because $7,000 results from recognizing no gain. Answer (C) is incorrect because $12,000 is the carrying amount of the asset given up. Answer (D) is incorrect because $15,000 is the amount that would be recorded for the asset received if the exchange had been of dissimilar productive assets.

52. An entity disposes of a nonmonetary asset in a nonreciprocal transfer. A gain or loss should be recognized on the disposition of the asset when the fair value of the asset transferred is determinable and the nonreciprocal transfer is to

	Another Entity	A Shareholder of the Entity
A.	No	Yes
B.	No	No
C.	Yes	No
D.	Yes	Yes

The correct answer is (D). *(CPA 1188 T-36)*

REQUIRED: The circumstances under which gain or loss should be recorded in a nonreciprocal transfer.

DISCUSSION: A nonreciprocal transfer is a transfer of assets or services in one direction. APB 29 states that a nonreciprocal transfer of a nonmonetary asset to a shareholder or to another entity should be recorded at the fair value of the asset transferred, and a gain or loss should be recognized on the transfer. However, an exception to this general rule is provided for distributions of nonmonetary assets to owners in a spin-off or other form of reorganization or liquidation or in a plan that is in substance the rescission of a prior business combination.

Answers (A), (B), and (C) are incorrect because a gain or loss ordinarily should be recognized when nonmonetary assets are disposed of in a nonreciprocal transfer to another entity or a shareholder of the entity.

53. Doe Corporation owned 1,000 shares of Spun Corporation. These shares were purchased for $9,000. On September 15, Doe declared a property dividend of one share of Spun for every ten shares of Doe held by a shareholder. On that date, when the market price of Spun was $14 per share, there were 9,000 shares of Doe outstanding. What gain and net reduction in retained earnings would result from this property dividend?

	Gain	Net Reduction in Retained Earnings
A.	$0	$8,100
B.	$0	$12,600
C.	$4,500	$3,600
D.	$4,500	$8,100

The correct answer is (D). *(CPA 1181 II-19)*
REQUIRED: The gain and net reduction in retained earnings from a property dividend.
DISCUSSION: The Spun shares had a carrying value of $9 per share ($9,000 ÷ 1,000 shares). Because 900 shares were distributed by Doe as a property dividend (9,000 shares ÷ 10), the shares used as a property dividend had an aggregate carrying value of $8,100. The fair value of the 900 shares on the date of declaration was $12,600 (900 shares x $14 per share).

A nonreciprocal transfer of a nonmonetary asset to a shareholder should be recorded at the fair value of the asset transferred, and a gain or loss should be recognized on the disposition (APB 29). The gain is $4,500 ($12,600 fair value – $8,100 carrying value). The net reduction in retained earnings is $8,100 ($12,600 dividend less $4,500 gain). The journal entries are

Retained earnings	$12,600	
Property dividend payable		$12,600

Property dividend payable	$12,600	
Investment in Spun		$8,100
Gain on Spun disposition		4,500

Answers (A) and (B) are incorrect because a gain must be recognized when a shareholder receives a nonreciprocal transfer of a nonmonetary asset, and retained earnings should be reduced. Answer (C) is incorrect because $3,600 is the gain if the full amount of the $9,000 in Spun Corporation stock were subtracted from the $12,600 dividend.

54. Pine City owned a vacant plot of land zoned for industrial use. Pine gave this land to Medi Corp. solely as an incentive for Medi to build a factory on the site. The land had a fair value of $300,000 at the date of the gift. This nonmonetary transaction should be reported by Medi as

A. Extraordinary income.

B. Additional paid-in capital.

C. A credit to retained earnings.

D. A memorandum entry.

The correct answer is (B). *(CPA 1191 II-9)*
REQUIRED: The accounting for a donated asset.
DISCUSSION: In general, a nonmonetary asset received in a nonreciprocal transfer should be recorded at the fair value of the asset received. An exception to this general rule is provided for distributions of nonmonetary assets to owners in a spin-off or other form of reorganization or liquidation or in a plan that is in substance the rescission of a prior business combination (APB 29). A donated fixed asset represents capital contributed to the enterprise other than for the issuance of stock. Thus, the credit should be to an additional paid-in capital account such as additional paid-in capital from donated assets.

Answer (A) is incorrect because a donation is neither income nor an extraordinary item, but rather contributed capital. Answer (C) is incorrect because a donation is not part of earnings. Answer (D) is incorrect because a donation should be recognized in the accounts.

CHAPTER ELEVEN
DEPRECIATION AND DEPLETION

This chapter covers the depreciation of fixed assets and the general concepts of depletion. Specific industry applications of depletion, e.g., oil and gas, are dealt with in Chapter 34, Specialized Industry Accounting. Also, amortization of intangibles is covered in Chapter 12, Intangible Assets.

11.1 Theory

1. Depreciation of a plant asset is the process of

A. Asset valuation for statement of financial position purposes.

B. Allocating the cost of the asset to the periods of use.

C. Accumulating a fund for the replacement of the asset.

D. Asset valuation based on current replacement cost data.

The correct answer is (B). *(CMA 689 4-6)*
REQUIRED: The purpose of depreciation of fixed assets.
DISCUSSION: In accounting, depreciation is the systematic and rational allocation of the cost of the productive capacity of a fixed asset to the accounting periods the asset benefits. The asset's historical cost minus expected salvage value is the basis for the allocation.
Answers (A) and (D) are incorrect because depreciation is a process of cost allocation, not valuation. Answer (C) is incorrect because depreciation allocates cost; it does not provide for replacement.

2. On January 1, 1992, Crater, Inc. purchased equipment having an estimated salvage value equal to 20% of its original cost at the end of a 10-year life. The equipment was sold December 31, 1996 for 50% of its original cost. If the equipment's disposition resulted in a reported loss, which of the following depreciation methods did Crater use?

A. Double-declining-balance.

B. Sum-of-the-years'-digits.

C. Straight-line.

D. Composite.

The correct answer is (C). *(CPA 593 T-27)*
REQUIRED: The method that would result in a reported loss upon disposition.
DISCUSSION: The straight-line method of depreciation yields the lowest amount of depreciation for the early part of the depreciable life of the asset. Because only 50% of the original cost was received and straight-line accumulated depreciation equaled 40% of cost {[(100% − 20%) ÷ 10 years] x 5 years} at the time of sale, a 10% loss [50% − (100% − 40%)] results.
Answer (A) is incorrect because the DDB method results in 5-year accumulated depreciation that is greater than 50% of cost. Answer (B) is incorrect because the SYD method results in 5-year accumulated depreciation that is greater than 50% of cost. Answer (D) is incorrect because the composite method of depreciation applies to the weighted average of multiple useful lives of assets, whereas only one asset is mentioned in this question. Moreover, it recognizes no gain or loss on disposition.

3. Net income is understated if, in the first year, estimated salvage value is excluded from the depreciation computation when using the

	Straight-Line Method	Production or Use Method
A.	Yes	No
B.	Yes	Yes
C.	No	No
D.	No	Yes

The correct answer is (B). *(CPA 590 T-21)*
REQUIRED: The depreciation method(s) that understate(s) net income if estimated salvage value is excluded from the computation.
DISCUSSION: Under the straight-line method, the depreciable base of an asset is allocated uniformly over the time periods of the estimated use of the asset. Under the production or use method, the depreciable base is allocated as a constant per-unit amount as goods are produced. For both methods, the depreciable base is equal to the original cost minus the salvage value. Thus, if the estimated salvage value is excluded from the depreciable base calculated using either method, the amount of depreciation will be overstated. The result will be an understatement of net income.
Answers (A), (C), and (D) are incorrect because, under both the straight-line and production or use depreciation methods, excluding the salvage value from the depreciable base overstates depreciation expense and understates net income.

4. Depreciation is computed on the original cost minus estimated salvage value under which of the following depreciation methods?

	Double-Declining-Balance	Productive-Output
A.	No	No
B.	No	Yes
C.	Yes	Yes
D.	Yes	No

The correct answer is (B). *(CPA 588 T-25)*
REQUIRED: The method(s) under which depreciation is computed on original cost minus estimated salvage value.
DISCUSSION: Under the productive-output method, depreciation is determined by allocating the original cost minus the estimated salvage value to the projected units of output during the expected life of the asset. Under the double-declining-balance method, depreciation is determined by multiplying the book value at the beginning of each period by a constant rate that is equal to twice the straight-line rate of depreciation. Each year the book value of the asset decreases by the depreciation expense recognized. The double-declining-balance calculation does not include salvage value in calculating depreciation. However, the asset may not be depreciated below the amount of the estimated salvage value.
Answers (A), (C), and (D) are incorrect because the productive-output method uses a depreciable base equal to original cost minus salvage value, but the DDB method excludes the salvage value from the depreciable base.

5. An organization purchased a computer on January 1, 1996 for $108,000. It was estimated to have a 4-year useful life and a salvage value of $18,000. The double-declining-balance method is to be used. The amount of depreciation to be reported for the year ending December 31, 1996 is

A. ($108,000 – $18,000)(25% x 2)

B. ($108,000 – $18,000)(25% x ½)

C. ($108,000)(25% x 2)

D. ($108,000)(25% x ½)

The correct answer is (C). *(CIA 593 IV-30)*
REQUIRED: The computation to calculate the amount of depreciation under the double-declining-balance method.
DISCUSSION: When using a declining-balance method, a constant rate is applied to the changing carrying value of the asset. The carrying value for the first period's calculation is the acquisition cost ($108,000). The constant rate for the double-declining-balance method is twice the straight-line rate [(100% ÷ 4 years) x 2].
Answer (A) is incorrect because the salvage value is ignored in computing depreciation by use of a declining-balance method until the later years of the life. The asset should not be depreciated below its residual value.
Answer (B) is incorrect because the salvage value is ignored. Furthermore, the rate used should be twice the straight-line rate. Answer (D) is incorrect because the rate used should be twice the straight-line rate.

6. On January 1, 1996, Howell Corporation purchased equipment costing $200,000 with a salvage value of $40,000. Depreciation expense for 1996 was $80,000. If Howell Corporation uses the double-declining-balance method of depreciation, what is the estimated useful life of the asset?

    A. 5

    B. 4

    C. 2.5

    D. 2

The correct answer is (A). *(J. Hora)*

    REQUIRED: The estimated useful life of an asset being depreciated using the double-declining-balance method.

    DISCUSSION: DDB uses a depreciation rate that is twice the straight-line rate. In the first year of this equipment's life, the DDB depreciation rate is 40% ($80,000 ÷ $200,000). The straight-line rate is therefore 20% (40% ÷ 2). Accordingly, the expected useful life of the asset is 5 years.

    Answer (B) is incorrect because 4 years assumes salvage value is subtracted from the cost to determine the depreciable base used to calculate DDB depreciation. Answer (C) is incorrect because 2.5 years is equivalent to a straight-line rate of 40% and a DDB rate of 80%. Hence, DDB depreciation would be $160,000 (80% x $200,000). Answer (D) is incorrect because, if the useful life were 2 years, the depreciation expense would be $160,000 [(100% x $200,000 cost) – $40,000 salvage].

7. An organization uses the sum-of-the-year's-digits method of depreciation. In the third year of use of an asset with a 4-year estimated useful life, the portion of the depreciation cost for the asset that the organization will expense is

    A. 10%

    B. 20%

    C. 30%

    D. 33.33%

The correct answer is (B). *(CIA 1195 IV-19)*

    REQUIRED: The SYD depreciation in the third year.

    DISCUSSION: The SYD fraction (remaining years of the useful life at the beginning of the year ÷ the sum of the years of the useful life) is applied to the constant depreciable base (cost – salvage). For the third year of use of an asset with a 4-year life, the percentage of the depreciable base to be recognized is 20% [2 years ÷ (1 + 2 + 3 + 4)].

    Answer (A) is incorrect because 10% results from calculating the portion of depreciable cost to expense in any given year using the end of the current year in the numerator. Answer (C) is incorrect because 30% uses the digit of the current year in the numerator. Answer (D) is incorrect because 33.33% calculates the denominator as the sum of the years up to the end of the current year.

8. A machine with a 5-year estimated useful life and an estimated 10% salvage value was acquired on January 1, 1993. On December 31, 1996, accumulated depreciation using the sum-of-the-years'-digits method is

    A. (Original cost minus salvage value) multiplied by 1/15.

    B. (Original cost minus salvage value) multiplied by 14/15.

    C. Original cost multiplied by 14/15.

    D. Original cost multiplied by 1/15.

The correct answer is (B). *(CPA 592 T-16)*

    REQUIRED: The accumulated depreciation at the end of 4 years under the SYD method.

    DISCUSSION: SYD depreciation is calculated on a constant depreciable base equal to the original cost minus the salvage value, multiplied by the SYD fraction. The SYD fraction's numerator is the number of years of remaining useful life of the asset. The denominator is the sum of the digits of the total years of the expected useful life. In this case, the denominator is 15 (1 + 2 + 3 + 4 + 5). Thus, the accumulated depreciation at the end of the fourth year is the sum of the depreciation calculated in each of the 4 years, or 14/15 (5/15 + 4/15 + 3/15 + 2/15) times the depreciable base, which is the original cost minus the salvage value.

    Answer (A) is incorrect because (original cost minus salvage value) multiplied by 1/15 is the depreciation for year 5. Answer (C) is incorrect because original cost multiplied by 14/15 is the depreciation on 12/31/96 assuming no salvage value. Answer (D) is incorrect because original cost multiplied by 1/15 is the depreciation for year 5 assuming no salvage value.

9. Which of the following uses the straight-line depreciation method?

	Group Depreciation	Composite Depreciation
A.	No	No
B.	Yes	No
C.	Yes	Yes
D.	No	Yes

The correct answer is (C). *(CPA 593 T-28)*
REQUIRED: The method(s) using straight-line depreciation.
DISCUSSION: Both composite and group depreciation use the straight-line method. Both methods aggregate groups of assets. The composite method is used for a collection of dissimilar assets with varying useful lives, whereas the group method deals with similar assets. Each method involves the calculation of a total depreciable cost for all the assets included in one account and of a weighted-average estimated useful life.
Answers (A), (B), and (D) are incorrect because both methods use the straight-line method of depreciation.

10. A company using the composite depreciation method for its fleet of trucks, cars, and campers retired one of its trucks and received cash from a salvage company. The net carrying amount of these composite asset accounts was decreased by the

A. Cash proceeds received and original cost of the truck.

B. Cash proceeds received.

C. Original cost of the truck minus the cash proceeds.

D. Original cost of the truck.

The correct answer is (B). *(CPA 588 T-9)*
REQUIRED: The effect of a retirement on the net carrying amount of a composite asset account.
DISCUSSION: Because both composite and group methods use weighted averages of useful lives and depreciation rates, early and late retirements are expected to offset each other. Consequently, gains and losses on retirements of single assets are treated as adjustments of accumulated depreciation. The entry is to credit the asset at cost, debit cash for any proceeds received, and debit accumulated depreciation for the difference. Thus, the net book value of the composite asset accounts is decreased by the amount of cash received. The net book value of total assets is unchanged.
Answers (A), (C), and (D) are incorrect because the net carrying amount of the composite asset accounts is decreased only by the cash proceeds received.

11. When depreciation is calculated for similar articles of small value, either the retirement or the replacement system may be utilized. Under which of these two systems would the cost of the replacement assets purchased be capitalized?

	Retirement	Replacement
A.	Yes	Yes
B.	Yes	No
C.	No	Yes
D.	No	No

The correct answer is (B). *(Publisher)*
REQUIRED: The system(s) under which the cost of replacement assets is capitalized.
DISCUSSION: Both retirement and replacement systems are used when depreciation must be calculated for similar articles of small value. These systems are principally used by public utilities for such assets as poles and telephones.
Under the retirement system, the cost of the replacement assets is capitalized in the asset account. The cost of the assets retired minus their salvage value is charged to depreciation expense as they are retired.
Under the replacement system, the cost of the old assets is maintained in the asset account. The cost of the newly acquired assets minus the salvage value of the replaced assets is charged to depreciation expense.
Answers (A), (C), and (D) are incorrect because the cost of the replacement assets purchased are capitalized under the retirement method, not the replacement method.

12. The inventory (appraisal) method of depreciation computes depreciation as

A. A means of valuing fixed assets at current replacement cost.

B. Systematic and rational.

C. The difference between the value at the beginning of the year, plus additions, and the inventory at the end of the year.

D. Usually requiring the use of an accumulated depreciation account.

The correct answer is (C). *(Publisher)*
REQUIRED: The correct statement about the inventory (appraisal) method of depreciation.
DISCUSSION: The inventory depreciation method is a means of accounting for numerous small items such as hand tools. Depreciation in any one year is the carrying value at the beginning of the year, plus acquisitions, minus the amount on hand at the end of the year. This method is similar to the periodic system of accounting for merchandise inventory.
Answer (A) is incorrect because depreciation methods are used to allocate cost not to value assets. Answer (B) is incorrect because the inventory method is not a systematic and rational amortization of cost over several periods. Answer (D) is incorrect because an accumulated depreciation account is ordinarily not used.

13. Under which of the following depreciation methods is it possible for depreciation expense to be higher in the later years of an asset's useful life?

A. Straight-line.

B. Activity method based on units of production.

C. Sum-of-the-years'-digits.

D. Declining-balance.

The correct answer is (B). *(CIA 594 IV-19)*
REQUIRED: The depreciation method under which higher depreciation is possible later in an asset's useful life.
DISCUSSION: Under the activity method, depreciation is a function of use, not the passage of time. If the estimated activity level (stated, for example, in units of production) is higher in the later years of the asset's useful life, depreciation expense will be higher.
Answer (A) is incorrect because the straight-line method results in a constant depreciation expense. Answers (C) and (D) are incorrect because depreciation expense diminishes over time when an accelerated method, e.g., SYD or declining-balance method, is used.

14. In which of the following situations is the units-of-production method of depreciation most appropriate?

A. An asset's service potential declines with use.

B. An asset's service potential declines with the passage of time.

C. An asset is subject to rapid obsolescence.

D. An asset incurs increasing repairs and maintenance with use.

The correct answer is (A). *(CPA 1193 T-34)*
REQUIRED: The situation in which the units-of-production method of depreciation is most appropriate.
DISCUSSION: The units-of-production depreciation method allocates asset cost based on the level of production. As production varies, so will the credit to accumulated depreciation. Consequently, when an asset's service potential declines with use, the units-of-production method is the most appropriate method.
Answer (B) is incorrect because the straight-line method is appropriate when an asset's service potential declines with the passage of time. Answer (C) is incorrect because an accelerated method is best when an asset is subject to rapid obsolescence. Answer (D) is incorrect because the units-of-production method does not allow for increasing repairs and maintenance.

15. A depreciable asset has an estimated 15% salvage value. At the end of its estimated useful life, the accumulated depreciation will equal the original cost of the asset under which of the following depreciation methods?

	Straight-Line	Productive-Output
A.	Yes	No
B.	Yes	Yes
C.	No	Yes
D.	No	No

The correct answer is (D). *(CPA 589 T-4)*
REQUIRED: The method(s) under which accumulated depreciation will equal cost at the end of a salvageable asset's useful life.
DISCUSSION: The straight-line and productive-output depreciation methods both deduct estimated salvage value from the original cost to determine the depreciable base. At the end of the asset's estimated useful life, the accumulated depreciation will equal the cost minus the salvage value under each of these methods. The net book value (cost − accumulated depreciation) will equal the salvage value.
Answers (A), (B), and (C) are incorrect because neither the straight-line nor the productive-output method depreciates an asset beyond its salvage value.

16. An organization acquired a fixed asset with an estimated useful life of 5 years and no salvage value for $15,000 at the beginning of 1995. For financial statement purposes, how would the depreciation expense calculated using the double-declining-balance method compare with that calculated using the sum-of-the-years'-digits method in 1995 and 1996, respectively?

	1995	1996
A.	Lower	Lower
B.	Lower	Higher
C.	Higher	Lower
D.	Higher	Higher

The correct answer is (C). *(CIA 592 IV-27)*

REQUIRED: The comparison for 2 years of DDB and SYD depreciation expense.

DISCUSSION: DDB is an accelerated depreciation method that determines periodic depreciation expense by multiplying the book value at the beginning of each period by a constant rate that is equal to twice the straight-line rate of depreciation. Each year the book value of the asset decreases by the depreciation expense recognized. Salvage value is ignored in determining the book value except as a floor beneath which the asset may not be depreciated. SYD depreciation multiplies a constant depreciable base (cost minus salvage value) by the SYD fraction. The SYD fraction's numerator is the number of years of remaining useful life (n). The formula to compute the denominator in the SYD method is

$$n \; \frac{(n + 1)}{2}$$

For a 5-year estimated useful life, the denominator of the fraction is 15 [5(5 + 1) ÷ 2].

DDB: Year 1995 = $15,000(.4) = $6,000
          Year 1996 = $9,000(.4) = $3,600

SYD: Year 1995 = $15,000(5/15) = $5,000
          Year 1996 = $15,000(4/15) = $4,000

Answer (A) is incorrect because DDB depreciation is higher in 1995. Answer (B) is incorrect because DDB depreciation is higher in 1995 and lower in 1996. Answer (D) is incorrect because DDB depreciation is lower in 1996.

17. The JME Company purchased a stretch limo for $45,000. The estimated useful life of the limo is 5 years or 80,000 miles, and the salvage value is $5,000. Actual mileage driven in the first year was 20,000 miles. Which of the following methods will result in the highest depreciation for the first year?

A. Straight-line.

B. Productive-output.

C. Sum-of-the-years'-digits.

D. Double-declining-balance.

The correct answer is (D). *(J. Emig)*

REQUIRED: The method that will result in the highest depreciation for the first year.

DISCUSSION: Under the straight-line, productive-output, and SYD methods, the depreciable base is $40,000 ($45,000 original cost – $5,000 estimated salvage value). Under the straight-line method, this base is allocated equally to the 5 years, resulting in a depreciation expense of $8,000. Under the units-of-output method, the $40,000 is allocated evenly across the estimated mileage to produce a depreciation charge of $.50 per mile. Thus, first-year depreciation expense is $10,000 ($.50 x 20,000 miles). Under SYD, the depreciable base is multiplied by the SYD factor (years remaining at the beginning of the year ÷ the sum of the digits). SYD depreciation expense in the first year is therefore $13,333 [$40,000 x (5/15)]. Under the DDB method, the $45,000 original cost is multiplied by a rate that is equal to twice the straight-line rate (2 x 20% = 40%). The result is a depreciation expense of $18,000 (40% x $45,000) in the first year.

Answer (A) is incorrect because straight-line depreciation is $8,000. Answer (B) is incorrect because productive-output depreciation is $10,000. Answer (C) is incorrect because SYD depreciation is $13,333.

18. According to current authoritative literature, all of the following disclosures should be made in the financial statements or notes thereto regarding depreciable assets and their corresponding methods of depreciation except

A. Balances of major classes of depreciable assets, by nature or function at the balance sheet date.

B. Accumulated depreciation, either by major classes of depreciable assets or in total, at the balance sheet date.

C. A general description of the method or methods used in computing depreciation with respect to major classes of depreciable assets.

D. The depreciation lives by major class of assets used in computing depreciation expense.

The correct answer is (D). *(Publisher)*
REQUIRED: The disclosure not required in the financial statements or notes thereto regarding depreciable assets and their corresponding depreciation methods.
DISCUSSION: APB 12 requires disclosure of

1) Depreciation expense for the period
2) Balances of major classes of depreciable assets at the financial statement date
3) Amount of accumulated depreciation as of the financial statement date
4) General description of methods used in computing depreciation

APB 12 does not require disclosure of the estimated useful lives employed in depreciation calculations.
Answers (A), (B), and (C) are incorrect because each states a disclosure required by APB 12.

19. The objective of annuity and sinking-fund depreciation methods is to

A. Provide the necessary funds for asset replacement.

B. Provide a constant return on book value.

C. Require funds to be set aside for replacement of assets.

D. Quantify the cost of using assets.

The correct answer is (B). *(Publisher)*
REQUIRED: The objective of the annuity and sinking-fund depreciation methods.
DISCUSSION: For most depreciation methods, the periodic credit to accumulated depreciation either remains constant or decreases over time while the book value of the asset decreases. Assuming the asset generates a constant income stream, the rate of return on the asset increases (the difference between constant income and the increase in accumulated depreciation divided by the decreasing book value).
Compound-interest depreciation methods were designed to provide a constant return on book value. Under these methods, the credit to accumulated depreciation increases each year so the rate of return remains constant.
Answers (A) and (C) are incorrect because compound-interest methods are based on historical cost. They do not set aside funds or require funds to be set aside for asset replacement. Answer (D) is incorrect because the objective of annuity and sinking-fund depreciation methods is to provide a constant return on book value.

20. APB 6, *Status of Accounting Research Bulletins*, reaffirms that property, plant, and equipment normally should not be written up to appraisal, market, or current value. However, in those situations in which appreciation has been recorded, APB 6 states that which of the following is true?

A. Depreciation should be based on the appreciated amounts.

B. Depreciation should be based on the historical cost.

C. Depreciation, if taken on written-up assets, should be charged directly to the appraisal capital account and not flow through the income account.

D. Depreciation cannot be charged on write-ups unless there is verifiable objective evidence (e.g., a formal property appraisal report) that the asset's value has changed significantly from its historical cost.

The correct answer is (A). *(Publisher)*
REQUIRED: The correct statement about depreciation relative to property, plant, and equipment that has been written up to appraisal, market, or current value.
DISCUSSION: When appreciation on an asset has been recorded, APB 6, *Status of Accounting Research Bulletins*, states that depreciation should be based on the appreciated value rather than on the historical cost.
Answer (B) is incorrect because the depreciation should be based on the appreciated value. Answer (C) is incorrect because the depreciation expense should flow through the income statement and not be charged directly to shareholders' equity. Answer (D) is incorrect because the depreciation on the written-up value should be recorded regardless of any formal property appraisal reports.

11.2 Depreciation Calculations

21. On January 2, 1996, Lem Corp. bought machinery under a contract that required a down payment of $10,000, plus 24 monthly payments of $5,000 each, for total cash payments of $130,000. The cash equivalent price of the machinery was $110,000. The machinery has an estimated useful life of 10 years and estimated salvage value of $5,000. Lem uses straight-line depreciation. In its 1996 income statement, what amount should Lem report as depreciation for this machinery?

   A. $10,500

   B. $11,000

   C. $12,500

   D. $13,000

The correct answer is (A). *(CPA 594 F-45)*
   REQUIRED: The depreciation on the machinery.
   DISCUSSION: The cash equivalent price of the machinery (present value), reduced by the salvage value, equals the depreciable base. The excess of the total cash to be paid over the cash equivalent price of the machinery will be recognized as interest expense, not depreciation. Accordingly, 1996 straight-line depreciation is $10,500 [($110,000 cash equivalent price – $5,000 salvage value) ÷ 10 years].
   Answer (B) is incorrect because $11,000 does not allow for the salvage value. Answer (C) is incorrect because $12,500 is based on the total cash payments minus salvage value. Answer (D) is incorrect because $13,000 is based on the total cash payments with no allowance for salvage value.

22. On May 1, a company purchased a new piece of equipment on an installment payment plan. A down payment of $5,000 was made, and four monthly installments of $5,000 each were to be made beginning June 1. The cash equivalent price of the equipment was $24,400. In addition to the down payment, the company paid $700 on May 1 for installation charges for the equipment. The equipment is estimated to have a service life of 5 years and no salvage value. What is the depreciable cost of this asset?

   A. $24,400

   B. $25,000

   C. $25,100

   D. $25,700

The correct answer is (C). *(CIA 1189 IV-38)*
   REQUIRED: The depreciable cost of an asset.
   DISCUSSION: The equipment should be recorded at the cash equivalent price of acquiring the asset and preparing it for its intended use. The cash equivalent price of the equipment was $24,400, and $700 additional installation costs were incurred. Consequently, the depreciable cost should be $25,100 ($24,400 + $700).
   Answer (A) is incorrect because $24,400 excludes the installation costs. Answer (B) is incorrect because $25,000 does not take into account the effect of either the time value of money or the installation costs. Answer (D) is incorrect because $25,700 does not take into account the effect of the time value of money.

23. On January 2, 1993, Reed Co. purchased a machine for $800,000 and established an annual depreciation charge of $100,000 over an 8-year life. During 1996, after issuing its 1995 financial statements, Reed concluded that (1) the machine suffered permanent impairment of its operational value, and (2) $200,000 is a reasonable estimate of the amount expected to be recovered through use of the machine for the period January 1, 1996 through December 31, 2000. In Reed's December 31, 1996 balance sheet, the machine should be reported at a carrying amount of

   A. $0

   B. $100,000

   C. $160,000

   D. $400,000

The correct answer is (C). *(CPA 593 I-24)*
   REQUIRED: The carrying amount of an asset following a permanent impairment of its value.
   DISCUSSION: Because the asset suffered permanent impairment of its operational value, it should be written down to its recoverable value of $200,000. Reed should recognize a loss of $300,000 [($800,000 cost – $300,000 accumulated depreciation) – $200,000 carrying value at the date of permanent impairment]. Depreciation for the remaining useful life of 5 years is $40,000 per year ($200,000 ÷ 5). Accordingly, the machine should be reported at a carrying amount of $160,000 ($200,000 – $40,000 depreciation) on 12/31/96.
   Answer (A) is incorrect because the machine still has a recoverable value. Answer (B) is incorrect because $100,000 results from deducting the originally computed annual depreciation from the new recoverable amount. Answer (D) is incorrect because $400,000 assumes no impairment.

	Total Cost	Estimated Salvage Value	Estimated Life in Years
Questions 24 through 26 are based on the following information. At the start of his business, Lester decided to use the composite method of depreciation and prepared the schedule of machinery owned presented in the opposite column.	Machine X $550,000	$50,000	20
	Machine Y 200,000	20,000	15
	Machine Z 40,000	--	5

24. Lester computes depreciation on the straight-line method. Based upon the information presented, the composite life of these assets (in years) should be

A. 13.3

B. 16.0

C. 17.6

D. 20.0

The correct answer is (B). *(CPA 1177 II-5)*
REQUIRED: The composite life of the assets in years.
DISCUSSION: The composite or average useful life of the assets is essentially a weighted average. As illustrated below, the annual straight-line depreciation for each asset should be calculated. The total cost, estimated salvage value, and depreciable base of the assets should then be computed. Dividing the composite depreciable base ($720) by the total annual straight-line depreciation ($45) gives the composite life (16 years) of these assets.

	Total Cost	Salvage Value	Dep. Base	Est. Life	Annual S/L Dep.
X	$550	$50	$500	20	$25
Y	200	20	180	15	12
Z	40	0	40	5	8
	$790	$70	$720		$45

Answer (A) is incorrect because 13.3 is the average useful life of the three assets. Answer (C) is incorrect because 17.6 ignores salvage value. Answer (D) is incorrect because 20 is the estimated life of asset X.

25. At the start of the fifth year of operations, Lester sold Machine Z for $10,000. Determine the depreciation expense and the ending balance in the accumulated depreciation account that should be recorded for year five.

A. $45,000 and $225,000.

B. $45,000 and $195,000.

C. $42,500 and $222,500.

D. $42,500 and $192,500.

The correct answer is (D). *(Publisher)*
REQUIRED: The calculation of depreciation expense and accumulated depreciation under the composite method when an asset is sold.
DISCUSSION: The straight-line depreciation rate is 6.25% ($45,000 ÷ $720,000). When an asset included in a composite group is sold, the original cost of that asset minus the amount received for it is debited to the accumulated depreciation account. No gain or loss is recorded. The depreciation rate is multiplied by the depreciable base of the remaining assets to determine the depreciation expense.
The depreciation expense for the fifth year is equal to $42,500 [($720,000 – $40,000) x 6.25%]. The accumulated depreciation at the start of year five ($180,000) is increased by the $42,500 depreciation expense and decreased by $30,000 ($40,000 original cost – $10,000 cash received), leaving a year-end balance of $192,500.
Answer (A) is incorrect because $45,000 is the annual straight-line depreciation, and $225,000 is the accumulated depreciation if the machine is not sold. Answer (B) is incorrect because $45,000 is the original annual depreciation, and $195,000 equals the accumulated depreciation after 4 years, plus the original annual depreciation, minus $30,000 ($40,000 cost of Z – $10,000 sale price). Answer (C) is incorrect because $222,500 reflects a failure to deduct the accumulated depreciation associated with machine Z.

26. Refer to the information preceding question 24. Assume that, in addition to the sale of Machine Z for $10,000 at the start of year five, Lester purchased Machine W for $60,000 to replace the machine that was sold. Machine W is expected to last 5 years with an expected salvage value of $10,000. If Machine W is included in the composite asset group, the depreciation expense for the fifth year should be equal to which of the following amounts?

A. $42,500

B. $45,000

C. $45,625

D. $46,250

The correct answer is (C). *(Publisher)*

REQUIRED: The depreciation expense under the composite method when a new asset is added.

DISCUSSION: When Machine Z was sold, the depreciable base of the composite group was decreased from $720,000 to $680,000. The purchase of Machine W adds $50,000 to the depreciable base. This increase is the original cost ($60,000) minus the salvage value ($10,000). The new depreciable base ($730,000) is multiplied by the straight-line depreciation rate (6.25%), resulting in year five depreciation of $45,625. Once a composite rate has been set, it continues to be used unless there are significant changes in the estimated lives or the composition of the assets through additions and retirements.

Answer (A) is incorrect because $42,500 is the depreciation expense excluding the new asset. Answer (B) is incorrect because $45,000 fails to consider the effects of both the sale of Z and the purchase of W. Answer (D) is incorrect because $46,250 fails to exclude the salvage value from the new asset's depreciable base.

27. Gei Co. determined that, because of obsolescence, equipment with an original cost of $900,000 and accumulated depreciation on January 1, 1996 of $420,000 had suffered permanent impairment and, as a result, should have a carrying value of only $300,000 as of the beginning of the year. In addition, the remaining useful life of the equipment was reduced from 8 years to 3. In its December 31, 1996 balance sheet, what amount should Gei report as accumulated depreciation?

A. $100,000

B. $520,000

C. $600,000

D. $700,000

The correct answer is (D). *(CPA 1193 I-24)*

REQUIRED: The amount of accumulated depreciation reported given a change in estimate.

DISCUSSION: The carrying value of the equipment before the permanent impairment was $480,000 ($900,000 – $420,000). After the impairment, the carrying value should be $300,000; therefore, $180,000 ($480,000 – $300,000) of additional accumulated depreciation should be recorded. In addition, the depreciation for 1996 should be $100,000 ($300,000 ÷ 3). Hence, the accumulated depreciation in the balance sheet on 12/31/96 is $700,000 ($420,000 + $180,000 to decrease carrying value + $100,000 depreciation for the year).

Answer (A) is incorrect because $100,000 is the depreciation in 1996. Answer (B) is incorrect because $520,000 is the sum of the accumulated depreciation on 1/1/96 and the revised 1996 depreciation. Answer (C) is incorrect because $600,000 is the accumulated depreciation before adjusting the useful life and claiming 1996 depreciation.

28. A company has just purchased a machine for $100,000 that has a five-year estimated useful life and a zero estimated salvage value. It is expected to be used to produce 250,000 units of output, and 75,000 of those units are expected to be produced in the first year. Which of the following depreciation methods will result in the greatest amount of depreciation expense for this machine in its first year?

A. Straight-line.

B. Activity method based on units of production.

C. Sum-of-the-years'-digits.

D. Declining-balance method with a 30% depreciation rate.

The correct answer is (C). *(CIA 594 IV-20)*

REQUIRED: The method that will result in the greatest depreciation expense.

DISCUSSION: SYD depreciation is based on a constant depreciable base equal to the original cost minus the salvage value, multiplied by the SYD fraction. The SYD fraction's numerator is the number of years of remaining useful life of the asset. The denominator is the sum of the digits of the total years of the expected useful life. Thus, first year SYD depreciation is $33,333 [($100,000 – $0) x (5 years ÷ 15)].

Answer (A) is incorrect because straight-line depreciation expense is $20,000 ($100,000 ÷ 5 years). Answer (B) is incorrect because the units-of-production method results in depreciation expense of $30,000 ($100,000 x 75,000/250,000). Answer (D) is incorrect because a 30% declining-balance depreciation is $30,000 ($100,000 x 30%).

29. A company is depreciating an asset with a 5-year useful life. It cost $100,000 and has no salvage value. If the <List A> method is used, depreciation expense in the second year will be <List B>.

List A	List B
A. Sum-of-years'-digits	$20,000
B. Sum-of-years'-digits	$40,000
C. Double-declining-balance	$16,000
D. Double-declining-balance	$24,000

The correct answer is (D). *(CIA 595 IV-15)*

REQUIRED: The proper match of depreciation expense and method.

DISCUSSION: The DDB method uses twice the straight-line rate. In the first year of the asset's life, depreciation expense was $40,000 ($100,000 x 20% x 2). In the second year, the depreciation base is reduced by the amount of depreciation expense already taken in the first year, so depreciation expense in year two is $24,000 [2 x 20% x ($100,000 – $40,000)].

Answer (A) is incorrect because depreciation in year two will be $20,000 under the straight-line method of depreciation. Under the SYD method, it is $26,667 [(4 ÷ 15) x $100,000]. Answer (B) is incorrect because SYD depreciation in the second year is $26,667. Answer (C) is incorrect because $16,000 assumes the declining-balance method is used with the straight-line rate.

30. Frey, Inc. purchased a machine for $450,000 on January 2, 1995. The machine has an estimated useful life of 4 years and a salvage value of $50,000. The machine is being depreciated using the sum-of-the-years'-digits method. The December 31, 1996 asset balance, net of accumulated depreciation, should be

A. $290,000

B. $270,000

C. $170,000

D. $90,000

The correct answer is (C). *(CPA 589 I-26)*

REQUIRED: The carrying value of an asset at the end of the second year under the SYD method.

DISCUSSION: For SYD, the depreciable base of the machine is $400,000 ($450,000 purchase price – $50,000 salvage value). Each year, this constant base is multiplied by a declining fraction that is equal to the remaining years in the useful life at the beginning of the year divided by the sum of the years' digits. As indicated below, the depreciation expense for 1995 is $160,000. For 1996, the depreciation expense is $120,000. Hence, accumulated depreciation at the end of 1996 is $280,000. The $450,000 asset cost net of the $280,000 of accumulated depreciation is $170,000.

1995: ($450,000 – $50,000) × 4/10 =	$160,000
1996: ($450,000 – $50,000) × 3/10 =	120,000
	$280,000

Answer (A) is incorrect because $290,000 is the asset's carrying value after the first year. Answer (B) is incorrect because $270,000 is the carrying value after the first year assuming no salvage value. Answer (D) is incorrect because $90,000 is the carrying value after 3 years.

Questions 31 and 32 are based on the following information. Patterson Company has the following information on one of its vehicles purchased on January 1, 1992:

Vehicle cost	$ 50,000
Useful life, years, estimated	5
Useful life, miles, estimated	100,000
Salvage value, estimated	$ 10,000
Actual miles driven, 1992	30,000
1993	20,000
1994	15,000
1995	25,000
1996	12,000

No estimates were changed during the life of the asset.

31. The 1994 depreciation expense for the vehicle using the sum-of-the-years'-digits (SYD) method was

A. $6,000

B. $8,000

C. $10,000

D. $16,000

The correct answer is (B). *(CMA 695 2-4)*
REQUIRED: The 1994 depreciation expense under the SYD method.
DISCUSSION: Under the SYD method, the amount to be depreciated is $40,000 ($50,000 original cost – $10,000 salvage). The portion expensed each year is based on a fraction, the denominator of which is the summation of the years of life of the asset being depreciated. For an asset with a 5-year life, the denominator is 15 (5 + 4 + 3 + 2 + 1). The numerator equals the years remaining. For 1994, the fraction is 3 ÷ 15, and depreciation expense is $8,000 [$40,000 × (3 ÷ 15)].
Answer (A) is incorrect because $6,000 is based on the units-of-production method. Answer (C) is incorrect because $10,000 omits the vehicle's salvage value from the calculation. Answer (D) is incorrect because $16,000 is the double-declining-balance method depreciation for 1992 if the salvage value is subtracted from the cost.

32. Using the units-of-production method, what was the 1996 depreciation expense?

A. $4,000

B. $4,800

C. $5,000

D. $6,000

The correct answer is (A). *(CMA 695 2-6)*
REQUIRED: The depreciation expense for 1996 under the units-of-production method.
DISCUSSION: Under the units-of-production method, periodic depreciation is based on the proportion of expected total production that occurred. For the years 1992 through 1995, the total depreciation was $36,000 {($50,000 – $10,000) × [(30,000 + 20,000 + 15,000 + 25,000) ÷ 100,000]}. Hence, the remaining depreciable base was $4,000 ($50,000 cost – $10,000 salvage – $36,000). Given that the 12,000 miles driven in 1996 exceeded the remaining estimated production of 10,000 miles (100,000 – 30,000 – 20,000 – 15,000 – 25,000), only the $4,000 of the remaining depreciable base should be recognized in 1996.
Answer (B) is incorrect because $4,800 is based on a 1996 rate of 12% (12,000 miles ÷ 100,000 miles of estimated usage). It ignores the effects of depreciation expense deducted in prior years. Answer (C) is incorrect because $5,000 assumes that depreciation is based on original cost without regard to salvage value. Answer (D) is incorrect because $6,000 is based on a 12% rate and ignores salvage value.

33. Aston Company acquired a new machine at a cost of $200,000 and incurred costs of $2,000 to have the machine shipped to its factory. Aston also paid $4,500 to construct and prepare a site for the new machine and $3,500 to install the necessary electrical connections. Aston estimates that the useful life of this new machine will be 5 years and that it will have a salvage value of $15,000 at the end of that period. Assuming that Aston acquired the machine on January 1 and will take a full year's depreciation, the proper amount of depreciation expense to be recorded by Aston if it uses the double-declining-balance method is

A. $74,000

B. $84,000

C. $80,000

D. $80,800

34. South Co. purchased a machine that was installed and placed in service on January 1, 1995 at a cost of $240,000. Salvage value was estimated at $40,000. The machine is being depreciated over 10 years by the double-declining-balance method. For the year ended December 31, 1996, what amount should South report as depreciation expense?

A. $48,000

B. $38,400

C. $32,000

D. $30,720

35. Turtle Co. purchased equipment on January 2, 1994 for $50,000. The equipment had an estimated 5-year service life. Turtle's policy for 5-year assets is to use the 200% double-declining-balance depreciation method for the first 2 years of the asset's life and then switch to the straight-line depreciation method. In its December 31, 1996 balance sheet, what amount should Turtle report as accumulated depreciation for equipment?

A. $30,000

B. $38,000

C. $39,200

D. $42,000

The correct answer is (B). *(CMA 1292 2-5)*
REQUIRED: The proper amount of depreciation under the double-declining-balance (DDB) method.
DISCUSSION: The acquisition cost of the machine includes all costs necessary to prepare it for its intended use. Hence, the depreciable cost is $210,000 ($200,000 invoice price + $2,000 delivery expense + $4,500 site preparation + $3,500 electrical work). Under the DDB method, salvage value is ignored at the beginning. Thus, the full $210,000 will be subject to depreciation. Given a 5-year life, the annual straight-line rate is 20%, and the DDB rate is 40%. Depreciation for the first year is therefore $84,000 (40% x $210,000).
Answer (A) is incorrect because $74,000 assumes that the depreciable cost is the invoice price minus salvage value. Answer (C) is incorrect because the depreciable cost of the machine was $210,000, not the $200,000 invoice price. Answer (D) is incorrect because $80,800 assumes a depreciable cost of $202,000, which does not include the site preparation and electrical costs.

The correct answer is (B). *(CPA 592 I-50)*
REQUIRED: The DDB depreciation expense reported in the second year.
DISCUSSION: DDB is an accelerated depreciation method that determines periodic depreciation expense by multiplying the book value at the beginning of each period by a constant rate that is equal to twice the straight-line rate of depreciation. Since this machine has a 10-year useful life, the DDB rate is 20%. Each year the book value of the asset decreases by the depreciation expense recognized. Salvage value is ignored in determining the book value except as a floor beneath which the asset may not be depreciated. The book value at the end of the first year was $192,000 [(100% – 20%) x $240,000 cost]. Thus, second-year depreciation is $38,400 (20% x $192,000).
Answer (A) is incorrect because $48,000 was the first-year depreciation. Answer (C) is incorrect because $32,000 assumes that salvage value is included in the calculation. Answer (D) is incorrect because $30,720 will be the third-year depreciation.

The correct answer is (B). *(CPA 594 F-18)*
REQUIRED: The amount of accumulated depreciation to be reported in the balance sheet.
DISCUSSION: Under the DDB method, the assets are depreciated at a constant rate of 40% (200% x 20% straight-line rate). This rate is applied in each of the first 2 years. For year 3, straight-line is used based on the remaining book value. The calculation is as follows:

1994: $50,000 × 40%	$20,000
1995: ($50,000 – $20,000) × 40%	12,000
1996: ($50,000 – $20,000 – $12,000) ÷ 3	6,000
	$38,000

Answer (A) is incorrect because $30,000 equals the accumulated straight-line depreciation. Answer (C) is incorrect because $39,200 equals DDB depreciation for 3 years. Answer (D) is incorrect because $42,000 includes third-year straight-line depreciation calculated without regard to DDB depreciation previously taken.

36. Weir Co. uses straight-line depreciation for its property, plant, and equipment, which, stated at cost, consisted of the following:

	12/31/96	12/31/95
Land	$ 25,000	$ 25,000
Buildings	195,000	195,000
Machinery and equipment	695,000	650,000
	$915,000	$870,000
Minus accumulated depreciation	400,000	370,000
	$515,000	$500,000

Weir's depreciation expense for 1996 and 1995 was $55,000 and $50,000, respectively. What amount was debited to accumulated depreciation during 1996 because of property, plant, and equipment retirements?

A. $40,000

B. $25,000

C. $20,000

D. $10,000

The correct answer is (B). *(CPA 1193 I-23)*
REQUIRED: The amount that was debited to accumulated depreciation because of retirements.
DISCUSSION: When an asset is depreciated, a debit is made to depreciation expense and a credit to accumulated depreciation. An equipment retirement results in a debit to accumulated depreciation. During 1996, accumulated depreciation increased by $30,000 despite recognition of a $55,000 expense (a credit). Consequently, a $25,000 ($55,000 – $30,000) debit must have been made to the accumulated depreciation account.
Answer (A) is incorrect because $40,000 is equal to $55,000 minus the $15,000 increase in net property, plant, and equipment. Answer (C) is incorrect because $20,000 is the difference between 1995 depreciation ($50,000) and the $30,000 increase in accumulated depreciation. Answer (D) is incorrect because $10,000 is equal to $55,000 minus the $45,000 increase in the gross property, plant, and equipment.

Questions 37 through 39 are based on the following information. Since 1993, Lane Steel Company has replaced all of its major manufacturing equipment and now has the following equipment recorded in the appropriate accounts. Lane uses a calendar year as its fiscal year.

- A forge purchased January 1, 1993 for $100,000. Installation costs were $20,000, and the forge has an estimated 5-year life with a salvage value of $10,000.
- A grinding machine costing $45,000 purchased January 1, 1994. The machine has an estimated 5-year life with a salvage value of $5,000.
- A lathe purchased January 1, 1996 for $60,000. The lathe has an estimated 5-year life with a salvage value of $7,000.

---

37. Using the straight-line depreciation method, Lane's 1996 depreciation expense is

A. $45,000

B. $40,334

C. $40,600

D. $40,848

The correct answer is (C). *(CMA 1293 2-6)*
REQUIRED: The 1996 depreciation expense under the straight-line method.
DISCUSSION: The straight-line method allocates the depreciation evenly over the estimated useful life of an asset. The depreciable cost equals cost minus salvage value for each asset, and dividing that amount by the life of the asset gives the periodic depreciation as follows:

Asset	Cost	Salvage	C - S	Life	Expense
Forge	$120,000	$10,000	$110,000	5	$22,000
Grind	45,000	5,000	40,000	5	8,000
Lathe	60,000	7,000	53,000	5	10,600
Total					$40,600

Answer (A) is incorrect because $45,000 fails to consider the deduction for salvage value. Answer (B) is incorrect because $40,334 is based on the sum-of-the-years'-digits method. Answer (D) is incorrect because $40,848 is based on the double-declining-balance method.

38. Using the double-declining-balance method, Lane's 1996 depreciation expense is

A. $36,464

B. $40,334

C. $40,600

D. $40,848

The correct answer is (D). *(CMA 1293 2-7)*

REQUIRED: The 1996 depreciation expense under the double-declining-balance method.

DISCUSSION: The DDB method allocates a series of decreasing depreciation charges over an asset's life. A percentage that is double the straight-line rate is multiplied each year times an asset's remaining book value at the beginning of the year. Given that each asset has a 5-year life, the straight-line rate is 20%. The DDB rate is therefore 40%. The forge was purchased in 1993 at a total cost of $120,000. The depreciation for each year is calculated as follows:

Year	Book Value	%	Expense
1993	$120,000	40%	$48,000
1994	72,000	40%	28,800
1995	43,200	40%	17,280
1996	25,920	40%	10,368

For the grinding machine, the calculations are

Year	Book Value	%	Expense
1994	$45,000	40%	$18,000
1995	27,000	40%	10,800
1996	16,200	40%	6,480

The 1996 calculation for the new lathe requires multiplying the $60,000 cost times 40% to yield a $24,000 expense. Adding the 1996 expense for each of the three machines ($10,368 + $6,480 + $24,000) produces total depreciation of $40,848.

Answer (A) is incorrect because $36,464 is based on the double-declining-balance method but with salvage value deducted from the initial depreciable base. Answer (B) is incorrect because $40,334 is based on the sum-of-the-years'-digits method. Answer (C) is incorrect because $40,600 is based on the straight-line method.

39. Using the sum-of-the-years'-digits method, Lane's 1996 depreciation expense (rounded to the nearest dollar) is

A. $36,464

B. $40,334

C. $40,600

D. $40,848

The correct answer is (B). *(CMA 1293 2-8)*

REQUIRED: The 1996 depreciation under the sum-of-the-years'-digits method.

DISCUSSION: The SYD method is an accelerated depreciation method. The depreciation base (cost – salvage value) is allocated based on a fraction. The numerator of the fraction equals the years remaining in the asset's life. The denominator is the sum of all of the years in the asset's life. For an asset with a 5-year life, the denominator is 15 (5 + 4 + 3 + 2 + 1). For the first year, the numerator is five, for the second year the numerator is four, etc. The calculations for 1996 are

Asset	Cost	Salvage	C - S	Fraction	Expense
Forge	$120,000	$10,000	$110,000	2/15	$14,667
Grind	45,000	5,000	40,000	3/15	8,000
Lathe	60,000	7,000	53,000	5/15	17,667
Total					$40,334

Answer (A) is incorrect because $36,464 is based on the double-declining-balance method but with salvage value deducted from the initial depreciable base. Answer (C) is incorrect because $40,600 is based on the straight-line method. Answer (D) is incorrect because $40,848 is based on the double-declining balance method.

Questions 40 through 42 are based on the following information. Vorst Corporation's schedule of depreciable assets at December 31, 1995 is shown in the next column. Vorst takes a full year's depreciation expense in the year of an asset's acquisition, and no depreciation expense in the year of an asset's disposition. The estimated useful life of each depreciable asset is 5 years.

Asset	Cost	Accumulated Depreciation	Acquisition Date	Salvage Value
A	$100,000	$ 64,000	1994	$20,000
B	55,000	36,000	1993	10,000
C	70,000	33,600	1993	14,000
	$225,000	$133,600		$44,000

40. Vorst depreciates asset A on the double-declining-balance method. How much depreciation expense should Vorst record in 1996 for asset A?

A. $32,000

B. $24,000

C. $14,400

D. $1,600

The correct answer is (C). *(CPA 583 II-31)*
REQUIRED: The current depreciation expense for asset A using the DDB method.
DISCUSSION: DDB depreciation equals book value at the beginning of the year times twice the straight-line rate. Salvage value is considered only as the floor beneath which the book value may not be reduced. Asset A has a useful life of 5 years; therefore, the S/L rate is 20%. The DDB rate is 40% (2 x 20%). Book value is $36,000 ($100,000 cost – $64,000 accumulated depreciation). Annual depreciation expense for year three is thus $14,400 (.4 x $36,000).
Answer (A) is incorrect because $32,000 is first-year depreciation after subtracting salvage value from the depreciable base. Answer (B) is incorrect because $24,000 was the 1995 depreciation. Answer (D) is incorrect because $1,600 will be the difference between the 12/31/96 book value and the salvage value that will be the 1997 depreciation.

41. Using the same depreciation method as used in 1993, 1994, and 1995, how much depreciation expense should Vorst record in 1996 for asset B?

A. $6,000

B. $9,000

C. $12,000

D. $15,000

The correct answer is (A). *(CPA 583 II-32)*
REQUIRED: The current depreciation expense for asset B under the depreciation method previously used.
DISCUSSION: The cost of asset B was $55,000, and the depreciation accumulated after 3 years of its 5-year life is $36,000. Under the straight-line method, depreciation would have totaled $27,000 [3 x .2 x ($55,000 – $10,000 salvage value)]. DDB depreciation would have been $43,120 (40% of a declining book value each year). The SYD method multiplies a fraction (the years remaining ÷ the SYD) times a constant depreciable base (cost – salvage). The SYD is 15 [n(n + 1) ÷ 2 = 5(5 + 1) ÷ 2]. Total SYD depreciation after 3 years is $36,000. Thus, 1996 depreciation is $6,000 [(2/15) x $45,000].

1993: 5/15 × ($55,000 – $10,000) =		$15,000
1994: 4/15 × ($55,000 – $10,000) =		12,000
1995: 3/15 × ($55,000 – $10,000) =		9,000
		$36,000

Answer (B) is incorrect because $9,000 was the third-year SYD depreciation. Answer (C) is incorrect because $12,000 was the depreciation for the second year. Answer (D) is incorrect because $15,000 was the depreciation for the first year.

42. Vorst depreciates asset C by the straight-line method. On June 30, 1996, Vorst sold asset C for $28,000 cash. How much gain or (loss) should Vorst record in 1996 on the disposal of asset C?

    A. $2,800

    B. $(2,800)

    C. $(5,600)

    D. $(8,400)

The correct answer is (D). *(CPA 583 II-33)*

    REQUIRED: The gain (loss) on disposal of asset C.

    DISCUSSION: Asset C had a book value at the time of its disposition of $36,400 ($70,000 cost – $33,600 accumulated depreciation), given that no depreciation was recognized in the year of sale. The loss on the transaction was $8,400 ($36,400 book value – $28,000 cash received).

    Answer (A) is incorrect because $2,800 assumes that a year's depreciation was taken in 1996. Answer (B) is incorrect because $(2,800) assumes depreciation was taken for the first half of the year. Answer (C) is incorrect because $(5,600) equals the accumulated depreciation balance less the cash received.

11.3 Depletion

43. Miller Mining, a calendar-year corporation, purchased the rights to a copper mine on July 1, 1996. Of the total purchase price, $2,800,000 was appropriately allocable to the copper. Estimated reserves were 800,000 tons of copper. Miller expects to extract and sell 10,000 tons of copper per month. Production began immediately. The selling price is $25 per ton. Miller uses percentage depletion (15%) for tax purposes. To aid production, Miller also purchased some new equipment on July 1, 1996. The equipment cost $76,000 and had an estimated useful life of 8 years. After all the copper is removed from this mine, however, the equipment will be of no use to Miller and will be sold for an estimated $4,000. If sales and production conform to expectations, what is Miller's depletion expense on this mine for financial accounting purposes for the calendar year 1996?

    A. $105,000

    B. $210,000

    C. $215,400

    D. $420,000

The correct answer is (B). *(CPA 575 I-1)*

    REQUIRED: The 1996 depletion expense for financial accounting purposes assuming accurate estimates of sales and production.

    DISCUSSION: Depletion expense is based on the units-of-production method. Assuming total reserves of 800,000 tons at a price of $2,800,000, the depletion charge per ton is $3.50. If 10,000 tons are extracted in each of the last 6 months of 1996 (60,000 tons), the depletion charge should be $210,000. The equipment cost is not included in the depletion base and is depreciated separately.

    Answer (A) is incorrect because $105,000 is the depletion expense for 3 months. Answer (C) is incorrect because $215,400 includes depreciation of the equipment based on the units-of-production method. Answer (D) is incorrect because $420,000 is the 15% tax depletion.

44. Crowder Company acquired a tract of land containing an extractable natural resource. Crowder is required by the purchase contract to restore the land to a condition suitable for recreational use after it has extracted the natural resource. Geological surveys estimate that the recoverable reserves will be 5,000,000 tons and that the land will have a value of $1,000,000 after restoration. Relevant cost information follows:

Land	$9,000,000
Estimated restoration costs	1,500,000

If Crowder maintains no inventories of extracted material, what should be the charge to depletion expense per ton of extracted material?

    A. $2.10

    B. $1.90

    C. $1.80

    D. $1.60

The correct answer is (B). *(CPA 1183 I-35)*

    REQUIRED: The depletion expense per ton of extracted material.

    DISCUSSION: The depletion base ($9,500,000) is the purchase price of the land ($9,000,000), minus the value of the land after restoration ($1,000,000), plus the costs of restoration ($1,500,000). Given that 5,000,000 tons can be extracted, the charge to depletion expense per ton is $1.90 if no inventories are maintained.

    Answer (A) is incorrect because $2.10 fails to exclude the land's value after restoration from the depreciable base. Answer (C) is incorrect because $1.80 includes only the purchase price in the depreciable base. Answer (D) is incorrect because $1.60 excludes the estimated restoration costs from the depreciable base.

45. In January 1996, Vorst Co. purchased a mineral mine for $2,640,000 with removable ore estimated at 1,200,000 tons. After it has extracted all the ore, Vorst will be required by law to restore the land to its original condition at an estimated cost of $180,000. Vorst believes it will be able to sell the property afterwards for $300,000. During 1996, Vorst incurred $360,000 of development costs preparing the mine for production and removed and sold 60,000 tons of ore. In its 1996 income statement, what amount should Vorst report as depletion?

A. $135,000

B. $144,000

C. $150,000

D. $159,000

The correct answer is (B). *(CPA 595 F-36)*

REQUIRED: The amount of depletion to be reported.

DISCUSSION: The depletion base is the purchase price of the land ($2,640,000), minus the value of the land after restoration ($300,000 − $180,000 = $120,000), plus any costs necessary to prepare the property for the extraction of ore ($360,000). This depletion base must be allocated over the 1,200,000 tons of ore that the land is estimated to yield. Accordingly, Vorst's depletion charge per ton is $2.40 [($2,640,000 − $120,000 + $360,000) ÷ 1,200,000]. Vorst should report $144,000 ($2.40 x 60,000 tons sold) as depletion in its 1996 income statement.

Answer (A) is incorrect because $135,000 does not include the $180,000 restoration costs. Answer (C) is incorrect because $150,000 does not consider the restoration costs and the residual value of the land. Answer (D) is incorrect because $159,000 adds the $180,000 restoration cost instead of deducting the $120,000 net residual value of the land.

CHAPTER TWELVE
INTANGIBLE ASSETS

This chapter covers intangible assets but not mineral exploration rights, development stage companies, and other similar topics, which are covered in Chapter 34, Specialized Industry Accounting. Cash surrender value appears in Chapter 13, Investments in Debt and Equity Securities. Property insurance, including coinsurance, is treated in Chapter 10, Property, Plant, and Equipment. Additional questions on goodwill arising from business combinations are in Chapter 28, Business Combinations, Consolidations, and Branch Accounting.

12.1 Intangible Assets

1. Which of the following intangible assets is considered an unidentifiable intangible asset?

   A. Trademark.

   B. Goodwill.

   C. Franchise.

   D. Copyright.

The correct answer is (B). *(Publisher)*
   REQUIRED: The unidentifiable intangible asset.
   DISCUSSION: APB 17, *Intangible Assets*, states that a primary difference between identifiable and unidentifiable intangible assets is that the latter cannot be acquired singly. Goodwill, the excess of the cost of an acquired company over the sum of the fair values of the company's identifiable net assets, is the most common unidentifiable intangible asset.
   Answers (A), (C), and (D) are incorrect because individual trademarks, franchises, and copyrights are identifiable with respect to specified assets and can be acquired singly.

2. Amortization of intangible assets, such as copyrights or patents, is the accounting process of

   A. Determining the cash flow from operations for the current period.

   B. Systematically allocating the cost of the intangible asset to the periods of use.

   C. Accumulating a fund for the replacement of the asset at the end of its useful life.

   D. Systematically reflecting the change in general price levels over the current period.

The correct answer is (B). *(CMA 691 2-10)*
   REQUIRED: The meaning of amortization.
   DISCUSSION: Amortization is a means of allocating an initial cost to the periods that benefit from that cost. It is similar to depreciation, a term associated with long-lived tangible assets, and depletion, which is associated with natural resources.
   Answer (A) is incorrect because amortization is an allocation process that is not cash-based. Answer (C) is incorrect because no funding is associated with amortization. Answer (D) is incorrect because amortization has nothing to do with changes in price levels.

3. How are intangible assets different from deferred charges?

    A. They are noncurrent assets.

    B. They represent costs deferred to future periods.

    C. They are disclosed in the footnotes rather than presented in the balance sheet.

    D. They represent a well-defined group of items with specific financial reporting guidelines.

The correct answer is (D). *(Publisher)*
REQUIRED: The difference between intangible assets and deferred charges.
DISCUSSION: Intangible assets are property rights, e.g., patents and copyrights, which are not tangible personal or real property. APB 17, *Intangible Assets*, prescribes the proper accounting treatment for them. By contrast, deferred charges are a collection of noncurrent assets that are not property, plant, and equipment; investments; or intangible assets. Deferred charges are usually not classifiable elsewhere, and no authoritative pronouncements deal with the general topic of deferred charges.
    Answers (A) and (B) are incorrect because each is a characteristic of both intangible assets and deferred charges. Answer (C) is incorrect because both intangible assets and deferred charges are presented in the balance sheet.

4. A material amount of legal fees and other costs incurred by a holder of a copyright in successfully defending a copyright suit should be

    A. Capitalized as part of the cost of the copyright and amortized over the remaining estimated useful life of the copyright, not to exceed 40 years.

    B. Charged to an expense account in the period incurred.

    C. Charged to a loss account in the period incurred.

    D. Capitalized in a separate asset account and amortized over 40 years.

The correct answer is (A). *(CIA 591 IV-35)*
REQUIRED: The accounting for material legal fees and other costs incurred in defending a copyright suit.
DISCUSSION: The accounting for copyrights is similar to the accounting for patents. Legal fees and other costs incurred in successfully defending a suit are to be charged to the patent account because the suit establishes the legal rights of the holder. The same guideline can be applied to accounting for the costs of successfully defending a copyright suit. The balance in the copyright account is then amortized over the remaining estimated useful life of the copyright. The total amortization period for any intangible asset should not exceed 40 years, even though the legal life and useful life may be greater. The duration of a copyright is the life of the author plus 50 years.
    Answers (B) and (C) are incorrect because the costs should be capitalized and amortized over the remaining useful life of the copyright. The total amortization period should not exceed 40 years. Answer (D) is incorrect because the costs should be charged to the copyright account and amortized over the remaining useful life of the copyright. The total amortization period should not exceed 40 years.

5. Which of the following assets acquired this year are amortizable?

	Goodwill	Trademarks
A.	No	No
B.	No	Yes
C.	Yes	Yes
D.	Yes	No

The correct answer is (C). *(CPA 583 T-18)*
REQUIRED: The currently acquired assets that are amortizable.
DISCUSSION: The cost of goodwill and other intangible assets acquired from others, including trademarks, patents, etc., should be recorded as an asset and amortized by systematic charges over the period estimated to be benefited. The period of amortization may not exceed 40 years.
    Answers (A), (B), and (D) are incorrect because goodwill and trademarks are both amortizable.

6. Intangible assets acquired singly from other enterprises or individuals should be recorded at cost at date of acquisition. Cost may not be measured by which of the following?

    A. Net book value of the previous owner.

    B. Amount of cash disbursed.

    C. Present value of amounts to be paid for liabilities incurred.

    D. Fair value of other assets distributed.

The correct answer is (A). *(Publisher)*
    REQUIRED: The method not allowed to measure cost of intangible assets.
    DISCUSSION: Intangibles acquired singly should be recorded at their cost of acquisition (APB 17). Cost may be measured by the amount of cash disbursed, the fair value of other assets distributed, the present value of amounts to be paid for liabilities incurred, or the fair value of the consideration received for stock issued as described in APB 16, *Business Combinations*. Book value of the previous owner is not a proper measurement of cost.
    Answers (B), (C), and (D) are incorrect because each is an allowable measurement of cost depending on the consideration used.

7. In accordance with generally accepted accounting principles, which of the following methods of amortization is normally recommended for intangible assets?

    A. Sum-of-the-years'-digits.

    B. Straight-line.

    C. Units-of-production.

    D. Double-declining-balance.

The correct answer is (B). *(CPA 578 T-12)*
    REQUIRED: The normal method of amortization of intangible assets.
    DISCUSSION: The recommended method of amortization of intangible assets is the straight-line method unless another systematic method is demonstrated by the reporting entity to be more appropriate. Disclosure of the method used and the period of amortization is required.
    Answers (A), (C), and (D) are incorrect because each may be used only if demonstrated as being more appropriate than the straight-line method.

8. Which of the following is not a consideration in determining the useful life of an intangible asset?

    A. Legal, regulatory, or contractual provisions.

    B. Provisions for renewal or extension.

    C. Expected actions of competitors.

    D. Initial cost.

The correct answer is (D). *(CPA 1180 T-15)*
    REQUIRED: The consideration not used in determining the useful life of an intangible.
    DISCUSSION: APB 17 lists seven criteria that should be considered in estimating the useful lives of intangible assets. Initial cost is not one of them because it has no causal connection with the receipt of benefits from the intangible asset in future periods.
    Answers (A), (B), and (C) are incorrect because each is one of the criteria listed by APB 17. The other four are

1) Life expectancies of certain employees
2) Effect of obsolescence
3) Apparent indefinite life
4) A composite of many individual factors

9. Jud Co. bought a trademark from Krug Corp. on January 1, 1996 for $224,000. Jud retained an independent consultant who estimated the trademark's remaining useful life to be 50 years. Its unamortized cost on Krug's accounting records was $112,000. Jud decided to amortize the trademark over the maximum period allowed. In Jud's December 31, 1996 balance sheet, what amount should be reported as accumulated amortization?

    A. $5,600

    B. $4,480

    C. $2,800

    D. $2,240

The correct answer is (A). *(CPA 1193 I-25)*
    REQUIRED: The amount reported as accumulated amortization.
    DISCUSSION: An intangible asset acquired externally should be recorded as an asset in an amount equal to its acquisition cost. This cost should usually be amortized by the straight-line method over the shorter of the period estimated to be benefited or 40 years. Because 40 years is the shorter, the $224,000 cost should be amortized at the rate of $5,600 ($224,000 ÷ 40 years) per year.
    Answer (B) is incorrect because $4,480 is based on a 50-year amortization period. Answer (C) is incorrect because $2,800 is based on the cost recorded on Krug's books. Answer (D) is incorrect because $2,240 is based on the cost recorded on Krug's books and a 50-year amortization period.

10. When should leaseholds and leasehold improvements be amortized over different periods?

   A. When the useful life of the leasehold improvement is less than the term of the leasehold.

   B. When the term of the leasehold exceeds 40 years.

   C. When the term of the leasehold is less than the useful life of the leasehold improvement.

   D. If the company is in the development stage.

The correct answer is (A). *(Publisher)*
   REQUIRED: The appropriate time for amortization periods of leaseholds and leasehold improvements to differ.
   DISCUSSION: A leasehold refers to the property under lease. Leasehold improvements should be amortized over their useful life if it is less than the term of the lease. But if the useful life is greater than the term of the lease, the improvement should be amortized over the life of the lease because the property will revert to the lessor at the end of the lease. If an option exists for renewal of the lease and the lessee intends to renew, the leasehold improvements should be amortized over the option period as well, but not to exceed their useful life.
   Answer (B) is incorrect because a leasehold should be amortized in the same way as other similar property. There is no minimum or maximum period. Answer (C) is incorrect because, when the term of the lease is less than the improvement's useful life, amortization should occur over the shorter period. Answer (D) is incorrect because SFAS 7, *Accounting and Reporting by Development Stage Enterprises*, requires the same amortization by development stage companies as by established operating companies.

11. How does amortization of intangibles differ from amortization of fixed assets, e.g., property, plant, and equipment?

   A. Intangibles are always expensed in the period expenditures are made.

   B. Intangibles must be amortized on an accelerated basis.

   C. Depreciation expense generally is recorded in a contra asset account, accumulated depreciation, and amortization expense generally is credited directly to the intangible account.

   D. Intangible assets are frequently not amortized.

The correct answer is (C). *(Publisher)*
   REQUIRED: The difference between amortizing intangibles and fixed assets.
   DISCUSSION: Intangible assets normally do not have a separate allowance for amortization account. Rather, the credit arising from the debit to amortization expense is taken directly to the asset account.
   Answer (A) is incorrect because the cost of intangible assets (except internally developed R&D) and the cost of fixed assets are capitalized and allocated to the periods benefited. Answer (B) is incorrect because intangibles should be amortized on a straight-line basis (unless another method is shown to be more appropriate). Answer (D) is incorrect because intangible assets are generally capitalized and amortized, with the exception of internally developed R&D costs.

12. Which of the following legal fees should be capitalized?

	Legal Fees to Obtain a Franchise	Legal Fees to Successfully Defend a Trademark
A.	No	No
B.	No	Yes
C.	Yes	Yes
D.	Yes	No

The correct answer is (C). *(CPA 1188 T-9)*
   REQUIRED: The legal fees that should be capitalized.
   DISCUSSION: An intangible asset acquired externally should be recorded as an asset at the amount equal to its acquisition cost. The acquisition cost includes legal fees. Legal fees incurred in the successful defense of an intangible asset also should be capitalized as part of its cost. A franchise is a contract right acquired by the franchisee from the franchisor to distribute certain products or services or an entire business concept in a particular territory. A trademark is a device, such as a word, that identifies the origin or ownership of a product and that is legally reserved to the exclusive use of the owner. Franchises and trademarks are therefore intangible assets. Accordingly, both the legal fees to obtain a franchise and the legal fees to successfully defend a trademark should be capitalized.
   Answers (A), (B), and (D) are incorrect because both legal fees to obtain a franchise and legal fees to successfully defend a trademark should be capitalized.

13. According to current authoritative literature relating to intangible assets acquired or developed subsequent to 1970,

    A. Costs of developing and maintaining intangible assets which are inherent in a continuing business and related to the enterprise as a whole should be amortized over a period not to exceed 40 years.

    B. If the indeterminate lives of some intangible assets are likely to exceed 40 years, the costs of those assets may be amortized over any period not to exceed 40 years.

    C. The financial statements should disclose the method and period of amortization of intangible assets.

    D. The straight-line method of amortizing the costs of intangible assets should be used at all times.

The correct answer is (C). *(Publisher)*
    REQUIRED: The correct statement concerning intangible assets acquired or developed subsequent to 1970.
    DISCUSSION: APB 17 is effective for intangible assets acquired after October 31, 1970. APB 17 requires amortization of the cost of each intangible asset acquired on the basis of its estimated useful life (not to exceed 40 years). The straight-line method should be used unless a company demonstrates that another systematic method is more appropriate. Financial statement disclosure is required concerning the method and the period of amortization.
    Answer (A) is incorrect because these costs (such as to create goodwill) should be deducted from income when incurred. Answer (B) is incorrect because, if the life of an intangible asset is likely to exceed 40 years or is indeterminate, the cost of the asset must be amortized over a 40-year period. Answer (D) is incorrect because APB 17 permits the use of any other systematic method that is more appropriate than straight-line.

12.2 Goodwill

14. Which of the following costs of goodwill should be capitalized and amortized?

	Maintaining Goodwill	Developing Goodwill
A.	Yes	No
B.	No	No
C.	Yes	Yes
D.	No	Yes

The correct answer is (B). *(CPA 1193 T-10)*
    REQUIRED: The costs of goodwill that should be capitalized and amortized.
    DISCUSSION: APB 16, *Business Combinations*, requires that the cost of goodwill arising from a business combination accounted for as a purchase be capitalized and amortized over its estimated useful life. In contrast, the cost of developing, maintaining, or restoring intangible assets that are inherent in a continuing business and related to an enterprise as a whole should be expensed as incurred.
    Answers (A), (C), and (D) are incorrect because costs of maintaining and developing goodwill should not be capitalized.

15. The owners of the Zoot Suit Clothing Store are contemplating selling the business to new interests. The cumulative earnings for the past 5 years amounted to $450,000 including extraordinary gains of $10,000. The annual earnings based on an average rate of return on investment for this industry would have been $76,000. If excess earnings are to be capitalized at 10%, implied goodwill should be

    A. $120,000

    B. $140,000

    C. $440,000

    D. $450,000

The correct answer is (A). *(CPA 1178 II-7)*
    REQUIRED: The amount of implied goodwill if excess earnings are capitalized at 10%.
    DISCUSSION: One method of computing goodwill is to deduct the fair values of the tangible net assets and the identifiable intangible assets from the purchase price of the business. This method is applied for accounting purposes. A second method is to compute goodwill by capitalizing excess earnings. The latter method is used to value a business rather than to account for it. Past earnings provide estimates of future earnings; thus, the extraordinary gains of $10,000 should be excluded. Given ordinary earnings of $440,000 over the past 5 years, the average annual earnings were $88,000. Given also that annual earnings based on an average industry rate of return were $76,000, the excess earnings were $12,000. Implied goodwill capitalized at 10% is $120,000 ($12,000 ÷ 10%).
    Answer (B) is incorrect because $140,000 results from including the $10,000 extraordinary gain in earnings for the past 5 years. Answer (C) is incorrect because $440,000 equals the past 5 years' earnings minus extraordinary gains. Answer (D) is incorrect because $450,000 equals the cumulative earnings for the past 5 years.

16. A business broker is attempting to value the ABC fast food franchise. Average earnings over the last 6 years have been $66,000 and are relatively stable. The original investment was $240,000, and the current fair value of the net identifiable assets is $410,000. What is the amount of implied goodwill if the average earnings rate in this industry is 10% of investment?

A. $66,000

B. $240,000

C. $250,000

D. $660,000

The correct answer is (C). *(Publisher)*

REQUIRED: The implied goodwill given average annual earnings and the average rate of return.

DISCUSSION: Given that the industry average earnings rate is 10% and average earnings are $66,000, the overall value of the food franchise is $660,000 ($66,000 ÷ 10%). Because the fair value of the net identifiable assets is $410,000, the value of the franchise includes $250,000 of implied goodwill ($660,000 − $410,000).

Answer (A) is incorrect because $66,000 equals the average earnings. Answer (B) is incorrect because $240,000 equals the original investment. Answer (D) is incorrect because $660,000 is the overall value of the franchise.

17. On June 30, 1996, Union, Inc. purchased goodwill of $125,000 when it acquired the net assets of Apex Corp. During 1996, Union incurred additional costs of developing goodwill by training Apex employees ($50,000) and hiring additional Apex employees ($25,000). Before amortization of goodwill, Union's December 31, 1996 balance sheet should report goodwill of

A. $200,000

B. $175,000

C. $150,000

D. $125,000

The correct answer is (D). *(CPA 591 I-28)*

REQUIRED: The goodwill reported before amortization.

DISCUSSION: Goodwill is recorded only when it arises from a business combination accounted for as a purchase. The cost of developing, maintaining, or restoring goodwill inherent in a continuing business and related to an enterprise as a whole should be expensed as incurred. Thus, the goodwill reported before amortization is $125,000.

Answer (A) is incorrect because $200,000 includes the cost of developing goodwill by training employees and hiring new employees. Answer (B) is incorrect because $175,000 includes the cost of developing goodwill by training new employees. Answer (C) is incorrect because $150,000 includes the cost of developing goodwill by hiring new employees.

18. When a business is acquired, the purchasing company calculates goodwill associated with the acquisition as the difference between the purchase price and the

A. Book value of the identifiable net assets acquired.

B. Fair value of the identifiable net assets acquired.

C. Book value of the net tangible assets acquired.

D. Fair value of the net tangible assets acquired.

The correct answer is (B). *(CIA 1195 IV-31)*

REQUIRED: The calculation of goodwill.

DISCUSSION: In a business combination accounted for as a purchase, goodwill is recorded as the difference between the purchase price and the fair value of the identifiable net assets acquired.

Answers (A), (C), and (D) are incorrect because goodwill is the difference between the purchase price and the fair value of the identifiable net assets acquired, whether tangible or intangible.

19. What is the proper treatment of the recorded goodwill when an entity disposes of a large segment of its business?

A. All of the goodwill should be considered as part of the cost of the assets sold.

B. An appropriate portion of the goodwill should be considered as part of the cost of the assets sold.

C. Goodwill cannot be considered sold; it should be written off as a loss.

D. Goodwill cannot be sold; it should be amortized over its original useful life.

The correct answer is (B). *(Publisher)*
REQUIRED: The correct statement about goodwill when a segment of a business is sold.
DISCUSSION: When goodwill is recorded on the books of an entity that disposes of a substantial portion of its assets, APB 17 requires that any unamortized goodwill, recognized when those assets were acquired, be included in the cost of the assets sold.
Answers (A), (C), and (D) are incorrect because an appropriate portion of the goodwill should be considered as sold.

12.3 Patents

20. A purchased patent has a remaining legal life of 15 years. It should be

A. Expensed in the year of acquisition.

B. Amortized over 15 years regardless of its useful life.

C. Amortized over its useful life if less than 15 years.

D. Amortized over 40 years.

The correct answer is (C). *(CPA 1183 T-12)*
REQUIRED: The period over which a patent should be amortized.
DISCUSSION: A U.S. patent is valid and legally enforceable for 17 years, and its cost should be amortized over its remaining legal life or useful life, whichever is shorter.
Answer (A) is incorrect because an intangible asset acquired from another should be recorded as an asset. Answer (B) is incorrect because the amortization period is not to exceed the useful life. Answer (D) is incorrect because the remaining legal life of the patent is only 15 years.

21. Legal fees incurred by a company in defending its patent rights should be capitalized when the outcome of litigation is

	Successful	Unsuccessful
A.	Yes	Yes
B.	Yes	No
C.	No	No
D.	No	Yes

The correct answer is (B). *(CPA 1187 T-9)*
REQUIRED: The condition for capitalizing legal fees incurred in defending a patent.
DISCUSSION: Legal fees incurred in the successful defense of a patent should be capitalized as part of the cost of the patent and then amortized over its remaining useful life. Legal fees incurred in an unsuccessful defense should be expensed as the costs are incurred.
Answers (A), (C), and (D) are incorrect because legal fees incurred should be capitalized as part of the cost of the patent only if the outcome of litigation is successful.

22. Hy Corp. bought Patent A for $40,000 and Patent B for $60,000. Hy also paid acquisition costs of $5,000 for Patent A and $7,000 for Patent B. Both patents were challenged in legal actions. Hy paid $20,000 in legal fees for a successful defense of Patent A and $30,000 in legal fees for an unsuccessful defense of Patent B. What amounts should Hy capitalize for patents?

    A. $162,000

    B. $112,000

    C. $65,000

    D. $45,000

The correct answer is (C). *(CPA 592 I-20)*
    REQUIRED: The amount capitalized for patents.
    DISCUSSION: When an intangible asset is acquired externally, it should be recorded at its cost at the date of acquisition. Cost is measured by the cash paid, the fair value of other assets distributed, the present value of amounts to be paid for liabilities incurred, or the fair value of consideration received for stock issued (APB 17). Legal fees incurred in the successful defense of a patent should be capitalized as part of the cost of the patent and then amortized over its remaining useful life. Legal fees incurred in an unsuccessful defense should be expensed as the costs are incurred. Hence, the cost of Patent A ($40,000 + $5,000) and the legal fees for its successful defense ($20,000) should be capitalized in the amount of $65,000. The costs associated with Patent B should be written off immediately because its unsuccessful defense suggests that no asset exists.
    Answer (A) is incorrect because $162,000 includes all costs associated with Patent B. Answer (B) is incorrect because $112,000 equals the total acquisition costs for Patents A and B but excludes legal fees. Answer (D) is incorrect because $45,000 excludes the legal fees for a successful defense of Patent A.

23. On January 2, 1993, Lava, Inc. purchased a patent for a new consumer product for $90,000. At the time of purchase, the patent was valid for 15 years; however, the patent's useful life was estimated to be only 10 years due to the competitive nature of the product. On December 31, 1996, the product was permanently withdrawn from sale under governmental order because of a potential health hazard in the product. What amount should Lava charge against income during 1996, assuming amortization is recorded at the end of each year?

    A. $9,000

    B. $54,000

    C. $63,000

    D. $72,000

The correct answer is (C). *(CPA 1193 I-54)*
    REQUIRED: The amount charged against income when a product is permanently withdrawn from sale.
    DISCUSSION: Since the patent was written off at the end of the year, the amount charged against income is equal to amortization expense plus the carrying value of the asset at the time of the write-off. Amortization expense is $9,000 ($90,000 cost ÷ 10 years useful life). The carrying value of the asset is $54,000 ($90,000 cost − 4 years of amortization expense). Thus, the amount charged against income is $63,000 ($9,000 + $54,000).
    Answer (A) is incorrect because $9,000 includes only amortization expense. Answer (B) is incorrect because $54,000 includes only the carrying value of the asset at the time of write-off. Answer (D) is incorrect because $72,000 bases amortization on 15 years.

24. Malden, Inc. has two patents that have allegedly been infringed by competitors. After investigation, legal counsel informed Malden that it had a weak case for patent A34 and a strong case for patent B19. Malden incurred additional legal fees to stop infringement on B19. Both patents have a remaining legal life of 8 years. How should Malden account for these legal costs incurred relating to the two patents?

    A. Expense costs for A34 and capitalize costs for B19.

    B. Expense costs for both A34 and B19.

    C. Capitalize costs for both A34 and B19.

    D. Capitalize costs for A34 and expense costs for B19.

The correct answer is (A). *(CPA 1192 T-29)*
    REQUIRED: The accounting for legal costs incurred.
    DISCUSSION: Legal fees incurred in a successful defense of a patent should be capitalized and amortized. Legal fees incurred in an unsuccessful defense should be expensed as incurred. Hence, Malden should expense costs for A34 and capitalize costs for B19.
    Answer (B) is incorrect because Malden should capitalize costs for B19. Answer (C) is incorrect because Malden should expense costs for A34. Answer (D) is incorrect because Malden should expense costs for A34 and capitalize costs for B19.

12.4 Organization Costs

25. The costs of organizing a business, including fees of attorneys and accountants, should be

- A. Capitalized, but not amortized, because of the indefinite life of the business.

- B. Not recorded because they are an expense of the organizer.

- C. Capitalized and amortized over their useful life, not to exceed 40 years.

- D. Capitalized and deferred until liquidation of the business.

The correct answer is (C). *(CIA 593 IV-32)*
REQUIRED: The proper accounting treatment of the costs of organizing a business.
DISCUSSION: Organization costs are usually classified as an intangible asset. All intangible assets are to be amortized over their useful lives, but the amortization period is not to exceed 40 years. Organization costs are associated with the formation of a business, including costs incurred for the initial sale of stocks and bonds, legal fees, accounting fees, promotion costs, and incorporation fees.
Answers (A) and (D) are incorrect because the organization costs should be amortized for no more than 40 years. Answer (B) is incorrect because organization costs are incurred by the organization.

26. Fay, Inc. was organized late in 1995 and began operations on January 1, 1996. Prior to the start of operations, the following costs were incurred:

Attorney's fees for incorporating	$6,000
State incorporation filing fees	4,000

Fay amortizes organization costs over the maximum period allowable under GAAP. How much amortization should Fay record for the year ended December 31, 1996?

- A. $100

- B. $150

- C. $250

- D. $2,000

The correct answer is (C). *(CPA 587 I-44)*
REQUIRED: The organization costs amortized for the first year of operation.
DISCUSSION: Costs incurred in the formation of a business entity should be capitalized and amortized over the period of their expected useful life, not to exceed 40 years. Organization costs include both the $6,000 attorney's fees and the $4,000 incorporation filing fees. If they are amortized over the maximum period, amortization will be $250 ($10,000 ÷ 40 years) per year.
Answer (A) is incorrect because $100 is the amortization of the filing fees only. Answer (B) is incorrect because $150 is the amortization of the attorney's fees only. Answer (D) is incorrect because $2,000 is the difference between the attorney's fees and the filing fees.

12.5 Franchises

27. On January 2, 1996, Rafa Co. purchased a franchise with a useful life of 10 years for $50,000. An additional franchise fee of 3% of franchise operation revenues must be paid each year to the franchisor. Revenues from franchise operations amounted to $400,000 during 1996. In its December 31, 1996 balance sheet, what amount should Rafa report as an intangible asset-franchise?

- A. $33,000

- B. $43,800

- C. $45,000

- D. $50,000

The correct answer is (C). *(CPA 594 F-20)*
REQUIRED: The amount of the intangible asset that is recorded for a franchise.
DISCUSSION: Franchise fees are capitalized and amortized over the shorter of 40 years or the useful life. The capitalizable amount includes the initial fee and other expenditures necessary to acquire the franchise. Future franchise fees are expensed as incurred. Thus, the amount that should be reported as an intangible asset is $45,000 [$50,000 − ($50,000 ÷ 10)].
Answer (A) is incorrect because $33,000 results from subtracting the additional franchise fee. Answer (B) is incorrect because $43,800 includes amortization of the additional franchise fee. Answer (D) is incorrect because $50,000 is the unamortized initial fee.

28. Mark Co. bought a franchise from Fred Co. on January 1, 1996 for $204,000. An independent consultant retained by Mark estimated that the remaining useful life of the franchise was 50 years. Its unamortized cost on Fred's books on January 1, 1996 was $68,000. Mark has decided to amortize the franchise over the maximum period allowed. What amount should be amortized for the year ended December 31, 1996?

- A. $5,100
- B. $4,080
- C. $3,400
- D. $1,700

The correct answer is (A). *(CPA 1189 I-13)*
REQUIRED: The first-year amortization expense of the cost of a franchise.
DISCUSSION: A franchise is an intangible asset. The acquisition cost of an intangible asset should be amortized over the useful life of the asset, or 40 years, whichever is the shorter. The cost of the franchise should therefore be amortized over 40 years even though the useful life was estimated to be 50 years. Annual amortization is $5,100 ($204,000 ÷ 40 years) per year under the straight-line method.
Answer (B) is incorrect because $4,080 is based on a 50-year period. Answer (C) is incorrect because $3,400 is the difference between the $204,000 franchise price and Fred's $68,000 unamortized cost, divided by 40 years. Answer (D) is incorrect because $1,700 equals the unamortized cost on Fred's books amortized over 40 years.

29. On December 31, 1996, Rice, Inc. authorized Graf to operate as a franchisee for an initial franchise fee of $150,000. Of this amount, $60,000 was received upon signing the agreement, and the balance, represented by a note, is due in three annual payments of $30,000 each beginning December 31, 1997. The present value on December 31, 1996 of the three annual payments appropriately discounted is $72,000. According to the agreement, the nonrefundable down payment represents a fair measure of the services already performed by Rice; however, substantial future services are required of Rice. Collectibility of the note is reasonably certain. In Rice's December 31, 1996 balance sheet, unearned franchise fees from Graf's franchise should be reported as

- A. $150,000
- B. $132,000
- C. $90,000
- D. $72,000

The correct answer is (D). *(CPA 591 I-40)*
REQUIRED: The amount at which the franchisor should report unearned franchise fees.
DISCUSSION: SFAS 45, *Accounting for Franchise Fee Revenue*, states that franchise fee revenue should ordinarily be recognized at the earliest time when the franchisor has substantially performed or satisfied all material services or conditions relating to the franchise sale. The earliest time usually is the commencement of operations by the franchisee unless it can be demonstrated that substantial performance of all obligations occurred previously. Hence, Rice should recognize $60,000 of revenue. The note is a long-term receivable that should be reported at its present value. However, this amount ($72,000) should be recorded as unearned revenue because the franchisor has not substantially performed (completed the earning process).
Answer (A) is incorrect because $150,000 is the total initial fee. Answer (B) is incorrect because $132,000 includes $60,000 for services already performed. Answer (C) is incorrect because $90,000 is the undiscounted total of the annual payments.

30. Each of Potter Pie Co.'s 21 new franchisees contracted to pay an initial franchise fee of $30,000. By December 31, 1996, each franchisee had paid a nonrefundable $10,000 fee and signed a note to pay $10,000 principal plus the market rate of interest on December 31, 1997, and December 31, 1998. Experience indicates that one franchisee will default on the additional payments. Services for the initial fee will be performed in 1997. What amount of net unearned franchise fees would Potter report at December 31, 1996?

- A. $400,000
- B. $600,000
- C. $610,000
- D. $630,000

The correct answer is (C). *(CPA 1191 I-27)*
REQUIRED: The net unearned franchise fees reported at year-end by the franchisor.
DISCUSSION: SFAS 45, *Accounting for Franchise Fee Revenue*, states that franchise fee revenue should ordinarily be recognized at the earliest time when the franchisor has substantially performed or satisfied all material services or conditions relating to the franchise sale. Potter should not recognize revenue from initial franchise fees because the related services will not be performed until 1997, and the earning process is therefore not complete. The franchisor should recognize the cash received (21 x $10,000 = $210,000), a net receivable for the principal amounts estimated to be collected (20 x $20,000 = $400,000), and unearned franchise fees ($210,000 + $400,000 = $610,000).
Answer (A) is incorrect because $400,000 is the principal amount that the franchisor estimates will be collected. Answer (B) is incorrect because $600,000 omits the nonrefundable fee paid by one franchisee. Answer (D) is incorrect because $630,000 is based on the assumption that all franchisees will pay in full.

31. Which of the following should be expensed as incurred by the franchisee for a franchise with an estimated useful life of 10 years?

    A. Amount paid to the franchisor for the franchise.

    B. Periodic payments to a company, other than the franchisor, for that company's franchise.

    C. Legal fees paid to the franchisee's lawyers to obtain the franchise.

    D. Periodic payments to the franchisor based on the franchisee's revenues.

The correct answer is (D). *(CPA 1185 T-7)*
    REQUIRED: The payment that should be expensed as incurred by the franchisee.
    DISCUSSION: Payments under a franchise agreement made to a franchisor based on the franchisee's revenues do not create benefits in future periods and should not be treated as an asset. These payments should be treated as operating expenses in the period in which incurred.
    Answers (A), (B), and (C) are incorrect because each represents a cost of acquiring the franchise. These costs benefit future periods and should therefore be capitalized and amortized over the useful life of the franchise, but not to exceed 40 years.

12.6 Research and Development Costs

32. SFAS 2, *Accounting for Research and Development Costs*, differentiates research and development activities from activities not considered research and development. Which one of the following is not considered a research and development activity?

    A. Laboratory research intended for the discovery of a new product.

    B. Testing in search of product processing alternatives.

    C. Modification of the design of a process.

    D. Periodic design changes to existing products.

The correct answer is (D). *(CMA 695 2-24)*
    REQUIRED: The item not considered an R&D activity.
    DISCUSSION: SFAS 2 requires that R&D costs be expensed as incurred. Research is planned search or critical investigation aimed at discovery of new knowledge with the hope that such knowledge will be useful in developing a new product or service or a new process or technique or in bringing about a significant improvement in an existing product or process. Development is the translation of research findings or other knowledge into a plan or design for a new product or process or for a significant improvement in an existing product or process whether intended for sale or use. Seasonal or other periodic design changes in existing products do not meet either of these definitions.
    Answers (A), (B), and (C) are incorrect because laboratory research aimed at discovery of new knowledge, testing in search of product or process alternatives, and modification of the formulation or design of a product or process are R&D activities.

33. West, Inc. made the following expenditures relating to Product Y:

- Legal costs to file a patent on Product Y -- $10,000. Production of the finished product would not have been undertaken without the patent.

- Special equipment to be used solely for development of Product Y -- $60,000. The equipment has no other use and has an estimated useful life of 4 years.

- Labor and material costs incurred in producing a prototype model -- $200,000.

- Cost of testing the prototype -- $80,000.

What is the total amount of costs that will be expensed when incurred?

    A. $280,000

    B. $295,000

    C. $340,000

    D. $350,000

The correct answer is (C). *(CPA 592 I-51)*
    REQUIRED: The total amount of costs that will be expensed when incurred.
    DISCUSSION: R&D costs are expensed as incurred. SFAS 2 specifically excludes legal work in connection with patent applications or litigation and the sale or licensing of patents from the definition of R&D. Thus, the legal costs of filing a patent should be capitalized. West's R&D costs include the cost of equipment used solely for a specific project and those incurred for the design, construction, and testing of preproduction prototypes. Thus, the total amount of costs that will be expensed when incurred is $340,000 ($60,000 + $200,000 + $80,000).
    Answer (A) is incorrect because $280,000 omits the cost of the special equipment. Answer (B) is incorrect because $295,000 includes 1 year's straight-line depreciation on the special equipment instead of the full cost. Answer (D) is incorrect because $350,000 includes the legal costs of filing a patent.

34. During 1996, Orr Co. incurred the following costs:

Research and development services performed by Key Corp. for Orr	$150,000
Design, construction, and testing of preproduction prototypes and models	200,000
Testing in search for new products of process alternatives	175,000

In its 1996 income statement, what should Orr report as research and development expense?

    A. $150,000

    B. $200,000

    C. $350,000

    D. $525,000

The correct answer is (D). *(CPA 1194 F-44)*
    REQUIRED: The R&D expense.
    DISCUSSION: Research is planned search or critical investigation aimed at discovery of new knowledge useful in developing a new product, service, process, or technique, or in bringing about a significant improvement to an existing product, etc. Development is translation of research findings or other knowledge into a plan or design for a new or improved product or process. R&D expenses include R&D performed under contract by others; design, construction, and testing of prototypes; and testing in search for new products (SFAS 2). Thus, R&D expense of $525,000 ($150,000 + $200,000 + $175,000) should be recognized.
    Answer (A) is incorrect because $150,000 does not include design, construction, and testing of preproduction prototypes or testing in search of new products. Answer (B) is incorrect because $200,000 does not include R&D performed under contract by others or testing in search for new products. Answer (C) is incorrect because $350,000 does not include testing in search for new products.

35. In 1996, Ball Labs incurred the following costs:

Direct costs of doing contract research and development work for the government to be reimbursed by governmental unit	$400,000

Research and development costs not included above were

Depreciation	$300,000
Salaries	700,000
Indirect costs appropriately allocated	200,000
Materials	180,000

What was Ball's total research and development expense in 1996?

    A. $1,080,000

    B. $1,380,000

    C. $1,580,000

    D. $1,780,000

The correct answer is (B). *(CPA 1191 I-47)*
    REQUIRED: The total research and development expense.
    DISCUSSION: Under SFAS 2, materials used in R&D, compensation costs of personnel, and indirect costs appropriately allocated are R&D costs that should be expensed immediately. The costs of equipment and facilities that are used for R&D activities and have alternative future uses, whether for other R&D projects or otherwise, are to be capitalized as tangible assets when acquired or constructed. Depreciation on this equipment is to be expensed as R&D expense. However, SFAS 2 does not apply to R&D activities conducted for others. Hence, the reimbursable costs are not expensed. Ball's total R&D expense is therefore $1,380,000 ($300,000 + $700,000 + $200,000 + $180,000).
    Answer (A) is incorrect because $1,080,000 omits the depreciation. Answer (C) is incorrect because $1,580,000 includes the reimbursable costs of R&D conducted for others but omits the indirect costs. Answer (D) is incorrect because $1,780,000 includes the reimbursable costs of R&D conducted for others.

36. Brill Co. made the following expenditures during 1996:

Costs to develop computer software for internal use in Brill's general management information system	$100,000
Costs of market research activities	75,000

What amount of these expenditures should Brill report in its 1996 income statement as research and development expenses?

    A. $175,000

    B. $100,000

    C. $75,000

    D. $0

The correct answer is (D). *(CPA 1193 I-56)*
    REQUIRED: The amount of research and development expenses.
    DISCUSSION: SFAS 2 states that costs of market research are not R&D costs. FASB Interpretation No. 6, *Applicability of FASB No. 2 to Computer Software*, states that costs to develop software for the company's own general management information system are also not R&D costs.
    Answer (A) is incorrect because R&D expenses do not include costs to develop software for internal use in a general management information system or the costs of market research. Answer (B) is incorrect because R&D costs do not include costs to develop software for internal use in a general management information system. Answer (C) is incorrect because R&D costs do not include market research costs.

37. On December 31, 1995, Bit Co. had capitalized costs for a new computer software product with an economic life of 5 years. Sales for 1996 were 30% of expected total sales of the software. At December 31, 1996, the software had a net realizable value equal to 90% of the capitalized cost. What percentage of the original capitalized cost should be reported as the net amount on Bit's December 31, 1996 balance sheet?

- A. 70%

- B. 72%

- C. 80%

- D. 90%

The correct answer is (A). *(CPA 592 T-14)*
REQUIRED: The percentage of the original capitalized cost reported as the net amount on the balance sheet.
DISCUSSION: SFAS 86, *Accounting for the Costs of Computer Software to Be Sold, Leased, or Otherwise Marketed*, states that, after technological feasibility has been established for a software product, all software production costs incurred until the product is available for general release to customers shall be capitalized and subsequently reported at the lower of unamortized cost or net realizable value. The capitalized cost should be amortized based on the ratio that current gross revenues for the product bear to the total of current and anticipated future gross revenues for that product. However, the annual minimum must at least equal the straight-line amortization over the remaining estimated economic life of the product. Amortization for 1996 should equal the 30% ratio of current to total gross revenues, not the 20% straight-line rate based on a 5-year life. Accordingly, the percentage of the original capitalized cost reported as the net amount on the balance sheet should be 70%, which is the lower of unamortized cost or NRV (90%).

Answer (B) is incorrect because 72% assumes a write-down to NRV and amortization of that amount at the 20% straight-line rate. Answer (C) is incorrect because 80% assumes amortization at the 20% straight-line rate. Answer (D) is incorrect because 90% is the NRV.

Questions 38 and 39 are based on the following information. During 1996, Pitt Corp. incurred costs to develop and produce a routine, low-risk computer software product, as described in the next column.	
Completion of detail program design	$13,000
Costs incurred for coding and testing to establish technological feasibility	10,000
Other coding costs after establishment of technological feasibility	24,000
Other testing costs after establishment of technological feasibility	20,000
Costs of producing product masters for training materials	15,000
Duplication of computer software and training materials from product masters (1,000 units)	25,000
Packaging product (500 units)	9,000

38. In Pitt's December 31, 1996 balance sheet, what amount should be reported in inventory?

A. $25,000

B. $34,000

C. $40,000

D. $49,000

The correct answer is (B). *(CPA 591 I-21)*

REQUIRED: The amount reported in inventory.

DISCUSSION: SFAS 86 states that costs incurred internally in creating a computer software product shall be charged to expense when incurred as R&D until technological feasibility has been established. Thereafter, all software production costs incurred until the product is available for general release to customers shall be capitalized and amortized. The costs of duplicating the software, documentation, and training materials from the product masters and of physically packaging the product for distribution are capitalized as inventory. Hence, inventory should be reported at $34,000 ($25,000 duplication costs + $9,000 packaging costs).

Answer (A) is incorrect because $25,000 excludes packaging costs. Answer (C) is incorrect because $40,000 excludes packaging costs but includes costs of producing product masters. Answer (D) is incorrect because $49,000 includes costs of producing product masters.

39. In Pitt's December 31, 1996 balance sheet, what amount should be capitalized as software cost subject to amortization?

A. $54,000

B. $57,000

C. $59,000

D. $69,000

The correct answer is (C). *(CPA 591 I-22)*

REQUIRED: The amount capitalized as software cost subject to amortization.

DISCUSSION: SFAS 86 specifies that costs incurred internally in creating a computer software product shall be charged to expense when incurred as research and development until technological feasibility has been established for the product. Thereafter, all software production costs incurred until the product is available for general release to customers shall be capitalized and subsequently reported at the lower of unamortized cost or net realizable value. Hence, the costs of completing the detail program design and establishing technological feasibility are expensed, the costs of duplicating software and training materials and packaging the product are inventoried, and the costs of coding and other testing after establishing technological feasibility and the costs of producing product masters are capitalized and amortized. The amount capitalized as software cost subject to amortization is therefore $59,000 ($24,000 + $20,000 + $15,000).

Answer (A) is incorrect because $54,000 equals inventoriable costs plus the other testing costs. Answer (B) is incorrect because $57,000 is the sum of the costs expensed and the costs inventoried. Answer (D) is incorrect because $69,000 assumes the costs of coding and testing to establish feasibility are capitalized and amortized.

40. During 1996, Lyle Co. incurred $204,000 of research and development costs in its laboratory to develop a patent that was granted on July 1, 1996. Legal fees and other costs associated with registration of the patent totaled $41,000. The estimated economic life of the patent is 10 years. What amount should Lyle capitalize for the patent on July 1, 1996?

A. $0

B. $41,000

C. $204,000

D. $245,000

The correct answer is (B). *(CPA 593 I-23)*

REQUIRED: The amount to be capitalized for an internally developed patent.

DISCUSSION: SFAS 2 requires that R&D costs be expensed as they are incurred. Legal fees and registration fees are excluded from the definition of R&D by SFAS 2. Thus, the $41,000 in legal fees and other costs associated with the registration of the patent should be capitalized. The $204,000 in R&D costs should be expensed.

Answer (A) is incorrect because legal fees and other costs associated with the registration of the patent should be capitalized. Answer (C) is incorrect because legal fees and other costs associated with the registration of the patent should be capitalized, whereas R&D costs must be expensed as incurred. Answer (D) is incorrect because R&D costs must be expensed as incurred.

41. If a company constructs a laboratory building to be used as a research and development facility, the cost of the laboratory building is matched against earnings as

A. Research and development expense in the period(s) of construction.

B. Depreciation deducted as part of research and development costs.

C. Depreciation or immediate write-off depending on company policy.

D. An expense at such time as productive research and development has been obtained from the facility.

The correct answer is (B). *(CPA 1177 T-12)*

REQUIRED: The proper treatment of the cost of a laboratory building used as an R&D facility.

DISCUSSION: The costs of equipment and facilities that are used for R&D activities and have alternative future uses, whether for other R&D projects or otherwise, are to be capitalized as tangible assets when acquired or constructed. The depreciation of a facility such as a laboratory building used for R&D is an R&D expense.

Answer (A) is incorrect because the cost should be matched against earnings in the period of construction only if the building is usable for a particular research project and has no alternative use. Answers (C) and (D) are incorrect because a company has no discretion regarding R&D costs.

42. On January 1, 1996, Jambon purchased equipment for use in developing a new product. Jambon uses the straight-line depreciation method. The equipment could provide benefits over a 10-year period. However, the new product development is expected to take 5 years, and the equipment can be used only for this project. Jambon's 1996 expense equals

A. The total cost of the equipment.

B. One-fifth of the cost of the equipment.

C. One-tenth of the cost of the equipment.

D. Zero.

The correct answer is (A). *(CPA 1191 T-32)*

REQUIRED: The expense for equipment usable only for developing a new product.

DISCUSSION: The costs of materials, equipment, or facilities that are acquired or constructed for a particular R&D project and that have no alternative future uses and therefore no separate economic values are R&D costs when incurred. R&D costs are expensed in full when incurred.

Answers (B), (C), and (D) are incorrect because the total cost of the equipment should be expensed in 1996.

Questions 43 and 44 are based on the following information. Partnership A advances $1,000,000 to Corporation B to perform research and development. The terms of the agreement specify that B must repay the funds upon successful completion of the project.

43. Corporation B accounts for the $1,000,000 as

   A. A liability.

   B. Income from operations.

   C. Deferred contract revenue.

   D. Shareholders' equity.

The correct answer is (C). *(E. Spede/J. Sperry)*
REQUIRED: The classification of an R&D advance in the accounts of the recipient.
DISCUSSION: SFAS 68, *Research and Development Arrangements*, indicates how a company is to treat R&D advances. If the enterprise is obligated to repay any of the funds provided by the other party regardless of the outcome of the project, the enterprise recognizes a liability. If repayment depends solely on the results of the R&D having future economic benefit, the enterprise accounts for its obligation as a contract to perform R&D for others. Given that B must repay only on successful completion of the project, the advance should be recorded as deferred contract revenue.

Answer (A) is incorrect because the enterprise is not obligated to repay if the R&D has no future economic benefit. Answer (B) is incorrect because no services have yet been performed. Answer (D) is incorrect because the transaction is a contract to perform services, not an investment by Partnership A.

44. Partnership A accounts for the $1,000,000 as

   A. Accounts receivable.

   B. Research and development expense.

   C. Deferred research and development costs.

   D. Advances on contract.

The correct answer is (B). *(E. Spede/J. Sperry)*
REQUIRED: The classification of the advance in the accounts of the lender.
DISCUSSION: If repayment to the enterprise of any advance to other parties depends solely on the results of the R&D having future economic benefits, the advance is accounted for as a cost incurred by the enterprise. Furthermore, the costs are charged to R&D expense. B's repayment depends solely on the successful completion of the R&D, and Partnership A should treat the advance as R&D expense.

Answer (A) is incorrect because Corporation B does not have an unconditional obligation to repay the advance. Answers (C) and (D) are incorrect because, when repayment depends solely on the results of the R&D having future economic benefits, the advance must be expensed.

CHAPTER THIRTEEN
INVESTMENTS IN DEBT AND EQUITY SECURITIES

This chapter covers investments in debt and equity securities. It also includes coverage of impairments of loans. A module on the cash surrender value of life insurance is also included. Chapter 28, Business Combinations, Consolidations, and Branch Accounting, contains additional questions related to the equity method of accounting for investees.

13.1 Investments in Debt and Equity Securities

1. Investments in equity securities that have readily determinable fair values may be classified as

I.   Available-for-sale securities
II. Held-to-maturity securities
III. Trading securities

   A. I only.

   B. I and II only.

   C. I and III only.

   D. I, II, and III.

The correct answer is (C). *(Publisher)*
   REQUIRED: The possible classification(s) of equity securities.
   DISCUSSION: SFAS 115, *Certain Investments in Debt and Equity Securities*, applies to equity securities with readily determinable fair values. Equity securities held principally for sale in the near term are classified as trading securities. Equity securities not classified as trading securities are classified as available-for-sale securities. Held-to-maturity securities include debt securities only.
   Answers (A), (B), and (D) are incorrect because equity securities are classified as trading or available-for-sale.

2. Investments in debt securities should be classified as held-to-maturity securities if the reporting entity has the

	Ability to Hold to Maturity	Intent to Hold to Maturity
A.	Yes	Yes
B.	Yes	No
C.	No	Yes
D.	No	No

The correct answer is (A). *(Publisher)*
   REQUIRED: The condition(s) necessary for classifying debt securities as held-to-maturity.
   DISCUSSION: Under SFAS 115, a reporting enterprise must have both the positive intent and the ability to hold debt securities until maturity to classify them as held-to-maturity.
   Answers (B), (C), and (D) are incorrect because SFAS 115 requires that both conditions be met to classify debt securities as held-to-maturity.

3. Investment in trading securities should be valued on the statement of financial position at

A. Acquisition cost.

B. Lower of cost or market for the portfolio.

C. Lower of cost or market for individual securities.

D. Fair value.

The correct answer is (D). *(CMA 1293 2-3)*
REQUIRED: The valuation of trading securities on the balance sheet.
DISCUSSION: Trading securities are those held principally for sale in the near term. They are classified as current and consist of debt securities and equity securities with readily determinable fair values. Unrealized holding gains and losses on trading securities are reported in earnings. On a statement of financial position, these securities are reported at fair value, which is "the amount at which a financial instrument could be exchanged in a current transaction between willing parties, other than in a forced or liquidation sale."
Answers (A), (B), and (C) are incorrect because the proper valuation is fair value.

4. Investments in available-for-sale securities should be valued on the statement of financial position at

A. Acquisition cost.

B. Lower of cost or market for the portfolio.

C. Lower of cost or market for individual securities.

D. Fair value.

The correct answer is (D). *(CMA 1293 2-4)*
REQUIRED: The valuation of available-for-sale securities on the balance sheet.
DISCUSSION: Available-for-sale securities are investments in debt securities that are not classified as held-to-maturity or trading securities and in equity securities with readily determinable fair values that are not classified as trading securities. They are measured at fair value in the balance sheet.
Answers (A), (B), and (C) are incorrect because the proper valuation is fair value.

5. Investments in debt securities classified as held-to-maturity securities should be valued at

A. Acquisition cost.

B. Amortized cost.

C. Lower of cost or market.

D. Fair value.

The correct answer is (B). *(Publisher)*
REQUIRED: The attribute for measuring held-to-maturity securities.
DISCUSSION: SFAS 115 requires that debt securities classified as held-to-maturity be valued at amortized cost. In this respect, SFAS 115 does not depart from prior practice.
Answer (A) is incorrect because the acquisition cost of held-to-maturity securities is adjusted for amortization. Answer (C) is incorrect because held-to-maturity securities are written down below amortized cost only when a decline in fair value below amortized cost is other than temporary. Answer (D) is incorrect because debt securities classified as held-to-maturity are reported at amortized cost.

6. A decline in the value of an available-for-sale security below cost that is deemed to be other than temporary should

A. Be accumulated in a valuation allowance.

B. Be treated as a realized loss and included in the determination of net income for the period.

C. Not be realized until the security is sold.

D. Be treated as an unrealized loss and included in the equity section of the balance sheet as a separate item.

The correct answer is (B). *(CMA 693 2-17)*
REQUIRED: The proper accounting treatment of an other-than-temporary impairment of an available-for-sale security.
DISCUSSION: Any other-than-temporary decline in the value of available-for-sale securities should be considered a realized loss. The cost basis should be written down to fair value, thus establishing a new cost basis. This new cost basis would not be adjusted for cost recoveries. Realized gains and losses should be included in income in the period in which they occur.
Answer (A) is incorrect because no valuation allowance is recognized. Answer (C) is incorrect because a permanent decline in value of an available-for-sale security is recognized as a realized loss without regard to whether the investment has been sold. Answer (D) is incorrect because a permanent decline in value is to be considered a realized loss. However, a subsequent recovery would be credited to a separate component of equity.

7. When the fair value of investments in debt securities exceeds their carrying amounts, held-to-maturity securities and available-for-sale securities should be reported at the end of the year at

	Held-to-Maturity Securities	Available-for-Sale Securities
A.	Fair value	Amortized cost
B.	Amortized cost	Fair value
C.	Amortized cost	Amortized cost
D.	Fair value	Fair value

The correct answer is (B). *(CPA 593 T-22)*
REQUIRED: The proper reporting of held-to-maturity and available-for-sale debt securities.
DISCUSSION: Held-to-maturity securities should be reported at their amortized cost and available-for-sale and trading securities should be reported at fair value.
Answers (A), (C), and (D) are incorrect because held-to-maturity securities are reported at amortized cost, and available-for-sale securities are reported at fair value.

8. The amount by which the fair value of an equity security exceeds its cost should be accounted for as a separate component of shareholders' equity when the security is classified as

	Trading	Available-for-Sale
A.	No	No
B.	No	Yes
C.	Yes	Yes
D.	Yes	No

The correct answer is (B). *(CPA 588 T-5)*
REQUIRED: The accounting for the excess of fair value over cost.
DISCUSSION: SFAS 115 requires recognition in earnings of unrealized holding gains and losses on trading securities. Unrealized holding gains and losses on available-for-sale securities are recognized as a net amount in a separate component of shareholders' equity until realized.
Answers (A), (C), and (D) are incorrect because unrealized holding gains and losses on available-for-sale securities are recognized as a separate component of shareholders' equity.

9. Nola Co. has adopted SFAS 115, *Accounting for Certain Investments in Debt and Equity Securities*. Nola has a portfolio of marketable equity securities that it does not intend to sell in the near term. How should Nola classify these securities, and how should it report unrealized gains and losses from these securities?

	Classify as	Report as a
A.	Trading securities	Component of income from continuing operations
B.	Available-for-sale securities	Separate component of shareholders' equity
C.	Trading securities	Separate component of shareholders' equity.
D.	Available-for-sale securities	Component of income from continuing operations

The correct answer is (B). *(CPA 594 F-14)*
REQUIRED: The proper classification of certain marketable equity securities and the reporting of unrealized gains and losses.
DISCUSSION: Marketable equity securities may be classified as either trading or available-for-sale. Equity securities that are not expected to be sold in the near term should be classified as available-for-sale. These securities should be reported at fair value, with unrealized holding gains and losses excluded from earnings and reported in a separate component of shareholders' equity.
Answers (A), (C), and (D) are incorrect because equity securities that are not expected to be sold in the near term are classified as available-for-sale securities, and related unrealized gains and losses are reported as a separate component of shareholders' equity.

10. On December 31, 1996, Ott Co. had investments in trading securities as follows:

	Cost	Fair Value
Man Co.	$10,000	$ 8,000
Kemo, Inc.	9,000	11,000
Fenn Corp.	11,000	9,000
	$30,000	$28,000

Ott's December 31, 1996 balance sheet should report the trading securities as

A. $26,000

B. $28,000

C. $29,000

D. $30,000

The correct answer is (B). *(CPA 1191 I-8)*
   REQUIRED: The amount at which the trading securities should be reported.
   DISCUSSION: Trading securities are reported at fair value, and unrealized holding gains and losses are included in earnings. Consequently, the securities should be reported as $28,000.
   Answer (A) is incorrect because $26,000 is the lower of cost or fair value determined on an individual security basis. Answer (C) is incorrect because $29,000 is the average of the aggregate cost and aggregate fair value. Answer (D) is incorrect because $30,000 is the aggregate cost.

11. Zinc Co.'s adjusted trial balance at December 31, 1996, includes the following account balances:

Common stock, $3 par	$600,000
Additional paid-in capital	800,000
Treasury stock, at cost	50,000
Net unrealized loss on available-for-sale equity securities	20,000
Retained earnings: appropriated for uninsured earthquake losses	150,000
Retained earnings: unappropriated	200,000

What amount should Zinc report as total shareholders' equity in its December 31, 1996 balance sheet?

A. $1,680,000

B. $1,720,000

C. $1,780,000

D. $1,820,000

The correct answer is (A). *(CPA 592 I-5)*
   REQUIRED: The total shareholders' equity.
   DISCUSSION: Total credits to shareholders' equity equal $1,750,000 ($600,000 common stock at par + $800,000 additional paid-in capital + $350,000 retained earnings). Total debits equal $70,000 ($50,000 cost of treasury stock + $20,000 unrealized loss on available-for-sale securities). Thus, total shareholders' equity equals $1,680,000.
   Answer (B) is incorrect because $1,720,000 treats the unrealized loss as a credit. Answer (C) is incorrect because $1,780,000 treats the treasury stock as a credit. Answer (D) is incorrect because $1,820,000 treats the treasury stock and the unrealized loss as credits.

12. On January 2, 1995, Adam Co. purchased as a long-term investment 10,000 shares of Mill Corp.'s common stock for $40 a share. These securities were properly classified as available for sale. On December 31, 1995, the market price of Mill's stock was $35 a share, reflecting a temporary decline in market price. On January 28, 1996, Adam sold 8,000 shares of Mill stock for $30 a share. For the year ended December 31, 1996, Adam should report a realized loss on disposal of a long-term investment of

A. $100,000

B. $80,000

C. $60,000

D. $40,000

The correct answer is (B). *(CPA 591 I-58)*
   REQUIRED: The loss on disposal of a long-term investment.
   DISCUSSION: A realized loss or gain is recognized when an individual security is sold or otherwise disposed of. The investment was acquired for $40 per share. Because the shares were purchased as a long-term investment, they should be classified as available-for-sale securities. Thus, the temporary decline in fair value at 12/31/95 was debited to a separate component of shareholders' equity and was not included in earnings. Accordingly, the realized loss included in earnings at 12/31/96 was $80,000 [8,000 shares x ($40 – $30)].
   Answer (A) is incorrect because $100,000 assumes disposal of 10,000 shares. Answer (C) is incorrect because $60,000 is the fair value of the remaining shares. Answer (D) is incorrect because $40,000 was the amount of the temporary decline in value of 8,000 shares at 12/31/95.

13. The following information was extracted from Gil Co.'s December 31, 1996 balance sheet:

Noncurrent assets:
Long-term investments in available-for-
sale equity securities (at fair value) $96,450
Shareholders' equity:
Net unrealized loss on long-term
investments in available-for-sale
equity securities   (19,800)

Historical cost of the long-term investments in available-for-sale equity securities was

     A. $63,595

     B. $76,650

     C. $96,450

     D. $116,250

The correct answer is (D). *(CPA 591 II-18)*
     REQUIRED: The historical cost of the available-for-sale securities.
     DISCUSSION: The existence of a shareholders' equity account with a debit balance signifies that the available-for-sale securities are reported at fair value that is less than historical cost. The difference is the net unrealized loss balance. Hence, historical cost must have been $116,250 ($96,450 available-for-sale securities at fair value + $19,800 net unrealized loss).
     Answer (A) is incorrect because $63,595 is a nonsense figure. Answer (B) is incorrect because $76,650 results from subtracting the unrealized loss instead of adding. Answer (C) is incorrect because $96,450 ignores the unrealized loss balance.

14. On January 10, 1996, Box, Inc. purchased equity securities of Knox, Inc. and Scot, Inc. Box classified both securities as noncurrent and available-for-sale. At December 31, 1996, the cost of each investment was greater than its fair value. The loss on the Knox investment was considered permanent and that on Scot was considered temporary. How should Box report the effects of these investing activities in its 1996 income statement?

I. Excess of cost of Knox stock over its market value
II. Excess of cost of Scot stock over its market value

     A.   An unrealized loss equal to I plus II.

     B.   An unrealized loss equal to I only.

     C.   A realized loss equal to I only.

     D.   No income statement effect.

The correct answer is (C). *(CPA 1193 T-7)*
     REQUIRED: The income statement effects of permanent and temporary declines in value of available-for-sale securities.
     DISCUSSION: If a decline in fair value of an available-for-sale security is other than temporary, its cost basis is written down to fair value. The write-down is a realized loss and is included in the determination of earnings. A temporary decline in the fair value of available-for-sale securities is treated as an unrealized holding loss. It is excluded from the determination of earnings and debited to a separate component of shareholder's equity until realized.
     Answers (A), (B), and (D) are incorrect because the loss on Knox securities is permanent and therefore a realized loss that is included in the determination of earnings.

15. Data regarding Ball Corp.'s available-for-sale securities follow:

	Cost	Fair Value
December 31, 1995	$150,000	$130,000
December 31, 1996	150,000	160,000

Differences between cost and fair values are considered temporary. The decline in fair value was properly accounted for at December 31, 1995. Ball's 1996 statement of changes in shareholders' equity would report an increase of

     A. $30,000

     B. $20,000

     C. $10,000

     D. $0

The correct answer is (A). *(CPA 591 I-18)*
     REQUIRED: The increase reported in the statement of changes in shareholders' equity because of a change in the fair value of available-for-sale securities.
     DISCUSSION: Unrealized holding gains and losses on available-for-sale securities classified as temporary are excluded from earnings. They are reported as a net amount in a separate component of shareholders' equity. At 12/31/96, the fair value was greater than the cost. Consequently, the net amount reported (an unrealized net holding gain) is a credit of $10,000 ($160,000 fair value – $150,000 cost). At 12/31/95, the separate component of shareholders' equity would have had a debit balance of $20,000 ($150,000 cost – $130,000 fair value). Thus, the change from a debit of $20,000 to a credit of $10,000 increases total shareholders' equity by $30,000.
     Answer (B) is incorrect because $20,000 is the excess of cost over fair value on December 31, 1995. Answer (C) is incorrect because $10,000 is the excess of fair value over cost on 12/31/96. Answer (D) is incorrect because shareholders' equity increases when the unrealized holding gain or loss account is credited.

16. On December 1, 1996, Wall Company purchased equity securities and properly classified them as trading securities. Pertinent data are as follows:

Security	Cost	Fair Value at 12/31/96
A	$39,000	$36,000
B	50,000	55,000
C	96,000	85,000

On December 31, 1996, Wall reclassified its investment in security C from trading to available-for-sale because Wall intends to retain security C. What net loss on its securities should be included in Wall's income statement for the year ended December 31, 1996?

A. $0

B. $9,000

C. $11,000

D. $14,000

The correct answer is (B). *(CPA 588 I-18)*
REQUIRED: The net loss to be included in net income when a trading security is reclassified.
DISCUSSION: Unrealized holding gains and losses on trading securities are included in earnings, and reclassification is at fair value. Furthermore, "for a security transferred from the trading category, the unrealized holding gain or loss at the date of transfer will have already been recognized in earnings and shall not be reversed" (SFAS 115). Thus, the net unrealized holding loss at 12/31/96 is $9,000 ($3,000 loss on A – $5,000 gain on B + $11,000 loss on C).
Answer (A) is incorrect because $0 ignores the unrealized losses. Answer (C) is incorrect because $11,000 ignores the loss on A and the gain on B. Answer (D) is incorrect because $14,000 ignores the gain on B.

17. Cap Corp. reported accrued investment interest receivable of $38,000 and $46,500 at January 1 and December 31, 1996, respectively. During 1996, cash collections from the investments included the following:

Capital gains distributions	$145,000
Interest	152,000

What amount should Cap report as interest revenue from investments for 1996?

A. $160,500

B. $153,500

C. $152,000

D. $143,500

The correct answer is (A). *(CPA 1191 I-42)*
REQUIRED: The interest revenue from investments.
DISCUSSION: When a receivable increases, revenue exceeds collections. Since the accrued interest receivable balance increased by $8,500 ($46,500 – $38,000), and interest collected equaled $152,000, interest revenue equals $160,500 ($152,000 + $8,500). Capital gains distributions do not affect interest.
Answer (B) is incorrect because $153,500 equals capital gains plus the increase in accrued interest receivable. Answer (C) is incorrect because $152,000 equals collections. Answer (D) is incorrect because $143,500 equals collections of interest minus the increase in accrued interest receivable.

13.2 Bonds

18. When bond interest payments are sent to the owner of the bonds by the debtor, the bonds are called

A. Participating bonds.

B. Coupon bonds.

C. Registered bonds.

D. Debenture bonds.

The correct answer is (C). *(Publisher)*
REQUIRED: The bonds on which interest payments are sent to the owner by the debtor.
DISCUSSION: Registered bonds are issued in the name of the owner. Thus, interest payments are sent directly to the owner. When the owner sells registered bonds, the bond certificates must be surrendered and new certificates issued. They differ from coupon (bearer) bonds, which can be freely transferred and have a detachable coupon for each interest payment.
Answer (A) is incorrect because such bonds participate in excess earnings of the debtor as defined in the contractual agreement. Answer (B) is incorrect because the debtor does not keep records of the owners of coupon (bearer) bonds. Answer (D) is incorrect because debentures are unsecured as opposed to secured bonds.

19. On January 1, Welling Company purchased 100 of the $1,000 face value, 8%, 10-year bonds of Mann, Inc. The bonds mature on January 1 in 10 years, and pay interest annually on January 1. Welling purchased the bonds to yield 10% interest.

Present value of $1 at 8% for 10 periods	0.4632
Present value of $1 at 10% for 10 periods	0.3855
Present value of an annuity of $1 at 8% for 10 periods	6.7101
Present value of an annuity of $1 at 10% for 10 periods	6.1446

How much did Welling pay for the bonds?

A. $87,707

B. $92,230

C. $95,477

D. $100,000

The correct answer is (A). *(CPA 581 I-31)*
REQUIRED: The present value to the investor (price paid) of an investment in long-term bonds.
DISCUSSION: An investment in a bond should be recorded at its fair market value, i.e., the present value of its cash flow discounted at the market (yield) rate of interest. The present value of the investment has two components: the value of the periodic cash interest payments and the value of the bond proceeds at maturity. The interest payment at 8% on each bond will be $80 per year for 10 years. Applying a present value factor of 6.1446 (annuity, 10 periods, 10%) gives a present value of the periodic interest payments of $491.57. The proceeds of each bond at maturity of $1,000 are multiplied by a factor of .3855 (10%, 10 periods) for a present value of $385.50. The resulting total price per bond of $877.07 ($491.57 + $385.50) multiplied by 100 bonds gives a total payment of $87,707.

Answer (B) is incorrect because $92,230 is based on a present value of an annuity factor of 6.7101. Answer (C) is incorrect because $95,477 results from using a present value factor of .4632. Answer (D) is incorrect because $100,000 is the face value of the bonds, which were purchased at a discount.

20. Bonds that investors may present for payment prior to maturity are

A. Callable bonds.

B. Redeemable bonds.

C. Convertible bonds.

D. Income bonds.

The correct answer is (B). *(Publisher)*
REQUIRED: The type of bond that may be presented for payment prior to maturity.
DISCUSSION: Redeemable bonds may be presented for payment by the creditor prior to the maturity date. The bonds usually are redeemable only after a specified period of time.

Answer (A) is incorrect because callable bonds are the opposite; the debtor may call the bonds for redemption. Answer (C) is incorrect because convertible bonds may be exchanged, usually at the option of the creditor, for common stock or other equity securities. Answer (D) is incorrect because the distinctive feature of income bonds is that interest is paid only if income is earned by the debtor.

21. On September 1, the Consul Company acquired $10,000 face value, 8% bonds of Envoy Corporation at 104. The bonds were dated May 1, and mature in 5 years on April 30, with interest payable each October 31 and April 30. What entry should Consul make to record the purchase of the bonds?

A.	Investment in bonds	$10,400	
	Interest receivable	266	
	Cash		$10,666
B.	Investment in bonds	$10,666	
	Cash		$10,666
C.	Investment in bonds	$10,666	
	Accrued interest receivable		$ 266
	Cash		10,400
D.	Investment in bonds	$10,000	
	Premium on bonds	666	
	Cash		$10,666

The correct answer is (A). *(CPA 1176 II-11)*
REQUIRED: The entry to record a bond purchased at a premium with accrued interest.
DISCUSSION: At 104, the price paid for the bonds would be $10,400 in the absence of any accrued interest. Because the bonds were purchased between interest dates, cash interest accrued for the 4 months from May 1 to September 1 (date of purchase) must be computed and included in the purchase price. The interest for 4 months at 8% is $266.67 (4/12 x 8% x $10,000), which is recorded as interest receivable and added to the $10,400 purchase price for a total amount paid of $10,666. When interest is received on October 31, the $266 in interest receivable will be credited.

Answers (B) and (C) are incorrect because interest receivable should be debited for $266. Answer (D) is incorrect because the premium paid was $400. The interest receivable of $266 should be recorded separately from bond premium.

22. Loan origination fees are charged to the borrower in connection with originating, refinancing, or restructuring a loan (e.g., points, lending fees, etc.). Loan origination fees should be

A. Recognized in income when collected.

B. Recognized in income on a straight-line basis during the life of the loan but over no more than 5 years.

C. Deferred and recognized in income over the life of the loan using the straight-line method.

D. Deferred and recognized in income over the life of the loan by the interest method.

The correct answer is (D). *(Publisher)*
   REQUIRED: The lender accounting procedure for loan origination fees.
   DISCUSSION: SFAS 91, *Accounting for Nonrefundable Fees and Costs Associated With Originating and Acquiring Loans*, requires that loan origination fees be recognized in income over the life of the loan using the interest method. The objective is to achieve a constant effective yield over the life of the loan.
   Answer (A) is incorrect because the fees are deferred, not recognized immediately. Answers (B) and (C) are incorrect because the effective interest method is used, not straight-line amortization.

23. An investor purchased a bond classified as a long-term investment between interest dates at a discount. At the purchase date, the carrying amount of the bond is more than the

	Cash Paid to Seller	Face Amount of Bond
A.	No	Yes
B.	No	No
C.	Yes	No
D.	Yes	Yes

The correct answer is (B). *(CPA 591 T-4)*
   REQUIRED: The carrying amount of a bond purchased at a discount between interest dates.
   DISCUSSION: At the date of purchase, the carrying amount of the bond equals its face value minus the discount. The cash paid equals the initial carrying amount plus accrued interest. Hence, the initial carrying amount is less than the cash paid by the amount of the accrued interest and less than the face amount by the amount of the discount.
   Answers (A), (C), and (D) are incorrect because the carrying amount is less than either the face value or the cash paid.

24. On March 1, 1996, Clark Co. issued bonds at a discount. Clark incorrectly used the straight-line method instead of the effective interest method to amortize the discount. How were the following amounts, as of December 31, 1996, affected by the error?

	Bond Carrying Amount	Retained Earnings
A.	Overstated	Overstated
B.	Understated	Understated
C.	Overstated	Understated
D.	Understated	Overstated

The correct answer is (C). *(CPA 591 T-6)*
   REQUIRED: The effects of the error on the bond carrying amount and retained earnings.
   DISCUSSION: The straight-line method records the same amount of expense (cash interest paid + proportionate share of discount amortization) for each period. The effective interest method applies a constant rate to an increasing bond carrying amount (face value − discount + accumulated discount amortization), resulting in an increasing amortization of discount and increasing interest expense. Accordingly, in the first 10 months of the life of the bond, since straight-line amortization of discount is greater than under the interest method, interest expense is also greater. The effects are an understatement of unamortized discount, an overstatement of the carrying amount of the bonds, an understatement of net income, and an understatement of retained earnings.
   Answer (A) is incorrect because the error understates retained earnings. Answer (B) is incorrect because the error overstates the carrying amount. Answer (D) is incorrect because the error overstates the carrying amount and understates retained earnings.

25. On July 1, 1996, York Co. purchased as a long-term investment $1,000,000 of Park, Inc.'s 8% bonds for $946,000, including accrued interest of $40,000. The bonds were purchased to yield 10% interest and were properly classified as held-to-maturity securities. The bonds mature on January 1, 2003 and pay interest annually on January 1. York uses the effective interest method of amortization. In its December 31, 1996 balance sheet, what amount should York report as investment in bonds?

- A. $911,300
- B. $916,600
- C. $953,300
- D. $960,600

The correct answer is (A). *(CPA 593 I-15)*
REQUIRED: The amount reported as bond investment at year-end.
DISCUSSION: The bond investment's original balance was $906,000 ($946,000 price – $40,000 accrued interest) because the carrying value does not include accrued interest. Under the effective interest method, interest income equals the yield or effective interest rate times the carrying value of the bonds at the beginning of the interest period. The amortization of premium or discount is the difference between this interest income and the periodic cash payments. For the period 7/1 to 12/31/96, interest income is $45,300 (6/12 x 10% x $906,000), and the actual interest is $40,000 (6/12 x 8% x $1,000,000). Hence, the carrying value at year-end is $911,300 [$906,000 + ($45,300 – $40,000)].
Answer (B) is incorrect because $916,600 amortizes the discount for 12 months. Answer (C) is incorrect because $953,300 includes the accrued interest. Answer (D) is incorrect because $960,600 includes the accrued interest and amortizes the discount for 12 months.

26. On July 1, 1996, Pell Co. purchased Green Corp. 10-year, 8% bonds with a face amount of $500,000 for $420,000. The bonds mature on June 30, 2004 and pay interest semiannually on June 30 and December 31. Using the interest method, Pell recorded bond discount amortization of $1,800 for the 6 months ended December 31, 1996. From this long-term investment, Pell should report 1996 revenue of

- A. $16,800
- B. $18,200
- C. $20,000
- D. $21,800

The correct answer is (D). *(CPA 590 I-46)*
REQUIRED: The interest revenue when amortization of bond discount is known.
DISCUSSION: Interest income for a bond issued at a discount is equal to the sum of the periodic cash flows and the amount of bond discount amortized during the interest period. The periodic cash flows are equal to $20,000 ($500,000 face amount x 8% coupon rate x 1/2 year). The discount amortization is given as $1,800. Thus, revenue for the 6-month period from 7/1 to 12/31/96 is $21,800 ($20,000 + $1,800).
Answer (A) is incorrect because $16,800 is 50% of 8% of $420,000. Answer (B) is incorrect because $18,200 equals the cash flow minus discount amortization. Answer (C) is incorrect because $20,000 equals the cash flow.

27. On July 1, 1996, Cody Co. paid $1,198,000 for 10%, 20-year bonds with a face amount of $1,000,000. Interest is paid on December 31 and June 30. The bonds were purchased to yield 8%. Cody uses the effective interest rate method to recognize interest income from this investment. The bonds are properly classified as held-to-maturity. What should be reported as the carrying amount of the bonds in Cody's December 31, 1996 balance sheet?

- A. $1,207,900
- B. $1,198,000
- C. $1,195,920
- D. $1,193,050

The correct answer is (C). *(CPA 592 I-12)*
REQUIRED: The amount reported as bond investment at year-end.
DISCUSSION: Under the effective interest method, interest income equals the yield or effective interest rate times the carrying value of the bonds at the beginning of the interest period. The amortization of premium or discount is the difference between this interest income and the periodic cash payments. For 1996, interest income is $47,920 (6/12 x 8% x $1,198,000), and interest received is $50,000 (6/12 x 10% x $1,000,000). Hence, the carrying value at year-end is $1,195,920 [$1,198,000 – ($50,000 – $47,920)].
Answer (A) is incorrect because $1,207,900 equals the investment if interest income is determined using a 10% rate, and the difference between actual interest and interest income is added to the carrying value. Answer (B) is incorrect because $1,198,000 is the carrying value before adjustment for the premium amortization. Answer (D) is incorrect because $1,193,050 assumes that interest income is based on a 10% rate and that the bonds have been outstanding for 3 months.

28. In 1996, Lee Co. acquired, at a premium, Enfield, Inc. 10-year bonds as a long-term investment. At December 31, 1996, Enfield's bonds were quoted at a small discount. Which of the following situations is the most likely cause of the decline in the bonds' fair value?

A. Enfield issued a stock dividend.

B. Enfield is expected to call the bonds at a premium, which is less than Lee's carrying amount.

C. Interest rates have declined since Lee purchased the bonds.

D. Interest rates have increased since Lee purchased the bonds.

The correct answer is (D). *(CPA 593 T-11)*
    REQUIRED: The most likely cause of a decline in a bond's fair value.
    DISCUSSION: Bonds selling at a premium have a nominal rate in excess of the market rate. Bonds selling at a discount have a nominal rate less than the market rate. Thus, interest rates in the market must have increased in order for a bond originally acquired at a premium to be currently quoted at a discount.
    Answer (A) is incorrect because a stock dividend has no effect on quoted fair values of bonds. Answer (B) is incorrect because bonds expected to be called at a premium would not be quoted at a discount. Answer (C) is incorrect because, if interest rates decline below the stated rate, the bonds will be quoted at a higher premium.

29. When bonds with detachable stock warrants are purchased, the price should be allocated between the warrants and the bonds based upon their relative market values at issuance. The amount debited to investment in stock warrants relative to the total amount paid

A. Increases the premium on the investment in bonds.

B. Increases the discount on investment in bonds.

C. Increases either any premium on the bonds or any discount on the bonds.

D. Has no effect on the investment of bond premium or discount as the warrants are purchased separately.

The correct answer is (B). *(Publisher)*
    REQUIRED: The effect on the carrying value of bonds of debiting investment in stock warrants.
    DISCUSSION: The portion of the price allocated to the detachable stock warrants decreases the allocation to investment in bonds. Thus, amounts debited to investment in stock warrants increase the discount or decrease the premium recorded for the investment in bonds.
    Answers (A), (C), and (D) are incorrect because the allocation to detachable stock warrants decreases the premium or increases any discount.

13.3 Equity Method

30. X Company owns 15% of the voting stock of Y Co., and it owns 25% of the voting stock of Z Co. Under what circumstances should X account for each investment using the equity method?

	Investment in Y	Investment in Z
A.	In all cases	In all cases
B.	Never	In all cases
C.	Never	Only if X has the ability to exercise significant influence over Z
D.	Only if X has the ability to exercise significant influence over Y	Only if X has the ability to exercise significant influence over Z

The correct answer is (D). *(S. Rubin)*
    REQUIRED: The circumstances in which the equity method of accounting for a stock investment should be used.
    DISCUSSION: APB 18, *Equity Method for Investments in Common Stock*, prescribes the equity method when an investee has the ability to exercise significant influence. An investment of 20% or more of the voting stock of an investee leads to a presumption that an investor has the ability to exercise significant influence. An investment of less than 20% leads to a presumption that an investor does not have such ability. However, those presumptions can be overcome by predominant evidence to the contrary. See FASB Interpretation No. 35, *Criteria for Applying the Equity Method of Accounting for Investments in Common Stock*.
    Answers (A), (B), and (C) are incorrect because the equity method should be used only if X Company has the ability to exercise significant influence over Y and/or Z.

31. Current authoritative literature states that the equity method of accounting for investments in common stock

A. Should be used in accounting for investments in common stock of corporate joint ventures.

B. Should be used only for investments in common stock of unconsolidated domestic subsidiaries reported in consolidated financial statements.

C. Is a valid substitute for consolidation.

D. May not be used when accounting for an investment of less than 25% of the voting stock of an investee.

The correct answer is (A). *(WPE 1076-18)*
REQUIRED: The correct statement about the equity method.
DISCUSSION: Investors should account for investments in common stock of corporate joint ventures by the equity method because it best enables them to reflect the underlying nature of their investments. Usually, the investors have the ability to exert significant influence on the operation of the joint venture.
Answer (B) is incorrect because investments in which the investor has significant influence must be accounted for by the equity method whether the unconsolidated subsidiaries are domestic or foreign. Answer (C) is incorrect because APB 18 specifically states that application of the equity method is not a valid substitute for consolidation. Answer (D) is incorrect because the equity method would most likely be used if ownership were 20% or greater.

32. When an investor uses the equity method to account for investments in common stock, the investment account will be increased when the investor recognizes

A. A proportionate interest in the net income of the investee.

B. A cash dividend received from the investee.

C. Periodic amortization of the goodwill related to the purchase.

D. Depreciation related to the excess of market value over book value of the investee's depreciable assets at the date of purchase by the investor.

The correct answer is (A). *(CPA 583 T-13)*
REQUIRED: The basis for increasing the investment account when the investor uses the equity method.
DISCUSSION: Under the equity method, the investor's share of the investee's net income is accounted for as an addition to, and losses and dividends are reflected as reductions of, the carrying value of the investment on the investor's books.
Answers (B), (C), and (D) are incorrect because each reduces the carrying value.

33. When the equity method is used to account for investments in common stock, which of the following affects the investor's reported investment income?

	Goodwill Amortization Related to the Purchase	Cash Dividends from Investee
A.	Yes	Yes
B.	No	Yes
C.	No	No
D.	Yes	No

The correct answer is (D). *(CPA 1191 T-14)*
REQUIRED: The transaction(s) affecting the investor's reported investment income when the equity method is used.
DISCUSSION: The difference between the cost of an investment and the investee's underlying equity should be assigned first to any undervalued or overvalued assets, with the remainder allocated to goodwill and amortized over a period not to exceed 40 years. Subsequent amortization of goodwill related to the purchase reduces investment income. The receipt of a cash dividend from the investee does not affect equity-based earnings.
Answers (A), (B), and (C) are incorrect because goodwill amortization related to the purchase but not cash dividends affect investment income.

34. In its financial statements, Pulham Corp. uses the equity method of accounting for its 30% ownership of Angles Corp. At December 31, 1996, Pulham has a receivable from Angles. How should the receivable be reported in Pulham's 1996 financial statements?

A. None of the receivable should be reported, but the entire receivable should be offset against Angles' payment to Pulham.

B. 70% of the receivable should be separately reported, with the balance offset against 30% of Angles' payment to Pulham.

C. The total receivable should be disclosed separately.

D. The total receivable should be included as part of the investment in Angles, without separate disclosure.

The correct answer is (C). *(CPA 592 T-41)*
REQUIRED: The method of reporting a receivable from a 30%-owned company.
DISCUSSION: According to SFAS 57, *Related Party Disclosures*, related parties include an enterprise and its equity-based investees. A receivable from a related party should be separately disclosed in full. Indeed, nontrade receivables generally are subject to separate treatment.
Answers (A) and (B) are incorrect because elimination of intercompany transactions is inappropriate except in the case of combined or consolidated statements. Moreover, a general principle of accounting is that assets and liabilities should not be offset in the balance sheet unless a right of offset exists (APB 10, *Omnibus Opinion -- 1966*). Answer (D) is incorrect because the investment balance equals cost plus the investor's share of earnings and losses, minus any return of the investment. Also, separate disclosure is required.

35. FASB Interpretation No. 35 restated the criterion of APB 18 for applying the equity method of accounting for investments of 50% or less. The criterion is the ability to exercise significant influence over the investee. A 20% or greater ownership is a presumptive indication of that ability. Which example below does not indicate an inability to exercise significant influence over an investee even though the investor owns 30% of the common stock of the investee?

A. The investor and investee sign an agreement under which the investor surrenders significant rights.

B. The investor tries and fails to obtain representation on the investee's board of directors.

C. Opposition by the investee, such as litigation or complaints to governmental regulatory authorities, challenges the investor's exercise of significant influence.

D. The majority ownership of the investee is spread among a large group of shareholders who have objectives with respect to the investee that differ from those of the investor.

The correct answer is (D). *(Publisher)*
REQUIRED: The situation that indicates ability to exercise significant influence.
DISCUSSION: If the investor owns 20% to 50% of an investee and the remainder of the ownership is spread among a large group of shareholders, the investee will be able to exert significant influence even though most of the other owners have objectives contrary to those of the investor. The presumption of significant influence could be overcome by evidence that majority ownership is held by a small number of shareholders who operate the investee without regard to the investor's views.
Answers (A), (B), and (C) are incorrect because each is a specific example given in FASB Interpretation No. 35 of an inability to exercise significant influence over an investee.

36. On January 2, 1996, Well Co. purchased 10% of Rea, Inc.'s outstanding common shares for $400,000. Well is the largest single shareholder in Rea, and Well's officers are a majority on Rea's board of directors. Rea reported net income of $500,000 for 1996, and paid dividends of $150,000. In its December 31, 1996 balance sheet, what amount should Well report as investment in Rea?

A. $450,000

B. $435,000

C. $400,000

D. $385,000

The correct answer is (B). *(CPA 1194 F-16)*
REQUIRED: The amount reported in the investment account.
DISCUSSION: The equity method should be used because Well Co. exercises significant influence over Rea. The investment in Rea equals $435,000 [$400,000 investment + (10% x $500,000 net income) − (10% x $150,000 of dividends)].
Answer (A) is incorrect because $450,000 does not deduct Well's dividends. Answer (C) is incorrect because $400,000 does not include Well's share of net income or deduct Well's dividends. Answer (D) is incorrect because $385,000 does not include Well's share of net income.

37. An investor uses the equity method to account for an investment in common stock. After the date of acquisition, the investment account of the investor is

A. Not affected by its share of the earnings or losses of the investee.

B. Not affected by its share of the earnings of the investee but is decreased by its share of the losses of the investee.

C. Increased by its share of the earnings of the investee but is not affected by its share of the losses of the investee.

D. Increased by its share of the earnings of the investee and is decreased by its share of the losses of the investee.

The correct answer is (D). *(CPA 1188 T-5)*
REQUIRED: The effect(s) on an equity-based investment in common stock of investee earnings and losses.
DISCUSSION: After the date of acquisition, an equity-based investment in common stock account of an investor is increased by its share of the earnings of the investee, decreased by its share of the losses of the investee, and decreased by its share of cash dividends received from the investee.
Answers (A), (B), and (C) are incorrect because the investment account is affected by the investor's share of both earnings and losses of the investee.

38. The investor's accounting procedure under the equity method is to debit the investment account to record investee income and credit the investment account to record investee dividends. In substance, the net effect is to

A. Recognize only distributed income of the investee.

B. Not consider distributed income of the investee as income.

C. Increase the investment account for investee distributed income.

D. Recognize both distributed and undistributed income of the investee.

The correct answer is (D). *(Publisher)*
REQUIRED: The substance of the entries to record investee income and dividends under the equity method.
DISCUSSION: The traditional journal entries for the equity method are

Investment in investee	$XXX	
Investment income		$XXX
Cash	XXX	
Investment in investee		XXX

If they are compounded into a single entry, the net effect is to debit the investment account for undistributed income, to debit cash for distributed income, and to credit investment income for total income.
Answer (A) is incorrect because it describes the cost method. Answer (B) is incorrect because both distributed and undistributed income are recognized by the investor. Answer (C) is incorrect because the investment account is increased for all investee income, not just distributed income.

39. Which procedure mentioned below is a requirement in the application of the equity method of accounting for investments?

A. The investor's share of extraordinary items should be classified in a similar manner, if material, in the income statement of the investor.

B. The difference between the cost of an investment and the amount of the underlying equity in net assets of the investee should be permanently capitalized in the balance sheet of the investor.

C. Even if the percentage ownership of the investee's common stock held by the investor falls below the level needed to exercise significant influence, the equity method should still be employed.

D. The investor should continue using the equity method even when the investee's losses are large enough to cause the investment account to be reduced below a zero balance.

The correct answer is (A). *(WPE 879 II-55)*
   REQUIRED: The proper procedure in applying the equity method.
   DISCUSSION: The income statement of an investor reflects investment income resulting from the investor's share of the earnings of the investee company. APB 18 specifies that the investor's share of the investee's extraordinary items should be reported as extraordinary items in the investor's income statement.
   Answer (B) is incorrect because the difference between the cost of an investment and the investee's underlying equity should be assigned first to any undervalued or overvalued assets, with the remainder allocated to goodwill and amortized over a period not to exceed 40 years. Answer (C) is incorrect because, if an investment falls below the level needed to exert significant influence, the investor should discontinue use of the equity method and change to the cost method. Answer (D) is incorrect because, when the investment account is reduced to zero by the losses of the investee, the investor should discontinue using the equity method.

40. In accordance with APB 18, which of the following is incorrect?

A. Company A owns 19% of Company B's voting common stock and acquires 1% more. Company A's investment, results of operations (current and prior periods presented), and retained earnings should be adjusted retroactively.

B. Depending on the circumstances, an investor may account for an investment under the cost method even though he owns more than 20% of the voting common stock.

C. Company A owns 20% of Company B's voting common stock and sells 1%. Company A's investment, results of operations (current and prior periods presented), and retained earnings should be adjusted retroactively.

D. One of the disclosures necessary under the equity method of accounting for investments is the difference, if any, between the amount at which an investment is carried and the amount of underlying equity in net assets and the accounting treatment of the difference.

The correct answer is (C). *(WPE 974 O-57)*
   REQUIRED: The false statement regarding the equity method of investment accounting.
   DISCUSSION: When an investor accounts for an investment by the equity method (at a level of 20% ownership or greater) and subsequently sells shares such that significant influence can no longer be presumed to be exerted over the investee, the change to the cost basis is accounted for on a prospective basis; i.e., no retroactive adjustment is made. The carrying value of the investment is unchanged, and subsequent dividends are accounted for using the cost method.
   Answer (A) is incorrect because achieving a level of significant influence subsequent to the initial purchase of an investment requires retroactive application of the equity method. Answer (B) is incorrect because, when significant influence cannot be exerted over the investee despite 20% or greater ownership, the cost method should be used. Answer (D) is incorrect because APB 18 specifically requires disclosure of the difference, if any, between the amount in the investment account and the underlying equity in the net assets of the investee and the method by which the difference is being amortized.

41. Peel Co. received a cash dividend from a common stock investment. Should Peel report an increase in the investment account if it uses the cost method or the equity method of accounting?

	Cost	Equity
A.	No	No
B.	Yes	Yes
C.	Yes	No
D.	No	Yes

The correct answer is (A). *(CPA 1193 T-9)*

REQUIRED: The effect of a cash dividend on the investment account under the cost and equity methods.

DISCUSSION: Under the cost method, dividends from an investee should be accounted for by the investor as dividend income unless a liquidating dividend is received. Thus, assuming that the dividend is not liquidating, it has no effect on the investment account under the cost method. Under the equity method, cash dividends decrease the investment account because the dividend is considered to be a return of investment.

Answers (B), (C), and (D) are incorrect because a cash dividend does not result in an increase in the investment account under either the cost or the equity method.

42. Shani Company has gradually purchased stock in Astro Company (a nonsubsidiary). At the beginning of the year, its ownership interest in Astro totaled 18%; purchases throughout the year put total ownership up to 23%. Which of the following statements best expresses how this investment should be reflected and accounted for after the last purchase?

A. The equity method is not appropriate in this case, as all holdings were not purchased at the same time to meet the 20% test.

B. The purchase should be recorded at cost, and the equity method should be used to account for earnings from the purchase date forward.

C. The investment should be adjusted to 20% of the shareholders' equity of the investee on the date of the last purchase; any difference between original cost and adjusted basis should be treated as goodwill.

D. The investment, results of operations, and retained earnings should be adjusted retroactively in a manner consistent with the accounting for a step-by-step acquisition of a subsidiary using the equity method.

The correct answer is (D). *(WPE 975 O-19)*

REQUIRED: The correct accounting for an investment when the level of ownership has increased from 18% to 23%.

DISCUSSION: When ownership of an investee reaches the level of significant influence (20%), the investor must adopt the equity method. The investor must retroactively adjust the carrying amount of the investment, results of operations, and retained earnings as if the equity method had been in effect during all of the previous periods in which any percentage was held (even though less than 20% was owned in the previous periods).

Answer (A) is incorrect because the requisite ownership interest need not be acquired at one time for the equity method to apply; i.e., the equity method should be used when ownership reaches 20%. Answer (B) is incorrect because the equity method is not appropriate until the second purchase, and then it must be applied retroactively. Answer (C) is incorrect because it excludes determination of the excess of purchase price over underlying equity at the date of the initial purchase, and the accumulated amortization of that excess from the purchase date forward. Furthermore, the investment should be adjusted for 23% of the equity, not just 20%.

43. On January 1, 1996, Point, Inc. purchased 10% of Iona Co.'s common stock. Point purchased additional shares bringing its ownership up to 40% of Iona's common stock outstanding on August 1, 1996. During October 1996, Iona declared and paid a cash dividend on all of its outstanding common stock. How much income from the Iona investment should Point's 1996 income statement report?

A. 10% of Iona's income for January 1 to July 31, 1996 plus 40% of Iona's income for August 1 to December 31, 1996.

B. 40% of Iona's income for August 1 to December 31, 1996 only.

C. 40% of Iona's 1996 income.

D. Amount equal to dividends received from Iona.

The correct answer is (A). *(CPA 1193 T-8)*

REQUIRED: The income from an investment that has increased from less than 20% to more than 20% during the period.

DISCUSSION: Once the ownership percentage increased from 10% to 40%, Point was presumed to exercise significant influence over Iona; therefore, the investment should be accounted for retroactively under the equity method. Given that Point held 10% of Iona's common stock for the first 7 months of the year, it should recognize in earnings 10% of Iona's income for that period. It should recognize 40% of Iona's income for the balance of the year. Point's share of the dividend is credited to the investment account and is not included in earnings.

Answer (B) is incorrect because adoption of the equity method is retroactive to the acquisition of the first shares of stock of the investee. Answer (C) is incorrect because Point held only 10% of Iona's stock for the January-July period. Answer (D) is incorrect because Iona's dividends do not affect Point's net income.

44. A corporation that uses the equity method of accounting for its investment in a 40%-owned investee that earned $20,000 and paid $5,000 in dividends made the following entries:

Investment in subsidiary	$8,000	
Equity in earnings of subsidiary		$8,000
Cash	$2,000	
Dividend revenue		$2,000

What effect will these entries have on the parent's statement of financial position?

A. Investment understated, retained earnings understated.

B. Investment overstated, retained earnings overstated.

C. Investment overstated, retained earnings understated.

D. Financial position will be fairly stated.

The correct answer is (B). *(CPA 1180 T-20)*
REQUIRED: The effect of an error in recording investment income and/or dividends received.
DISCUSSION: In the case of 40% ownership, the equity method of accounting for the investment in the investor's books should be applied. The 40% share of the investee's $20,000 net income ($8,000) is correctly recorded.
Dividends received from an investee must be recorded in the books of the investor as a decrease in the carrying value of the investment and an increase in assets (cash). Hence, dividend revenue was incorrectly credited with the $2,000 dividend resulting in an overstatement of retained earnings. The investment account should have been credited for $2,000. Thus, the effect on the investment account is also an overstatement.
Answers (A), (C), and (D) are incorrect because the investment should be credited for $2,000 of dividend revenue. Thus, investment and retained earnings are overstated.

45. Moss Corp. owns 20% of Dubro Corp.'s preferred stock and 80% of its common stock. Dubro's stock outstanding at December 31, 1996 is as follows:

10% cumulative preferred stock	$100,000
Common stock	700,000

Dubro reported net income of $60,000 for the year ended December 31, 1996. What amount should Moss record as equity in earnings of Dubro for the year ended December 31, 1996?

A. $42,000

B. $48,000

C. $48,400

D. $50,000

The correct answer is (A). *(CPA 1194 F-15)*
REQUIRED: The equity of a parent in the earnings of a subsidiary.
DISCUSSION: The equity method requires Moss to record its share of Dubro's earnings available to common shareholders. When an investee has outstanding cumulative preferred stock, the investor should calculate its share of the investee's net income after deducting the preferred dividends, whether or not declared (APB 18). Thus, the equity of Moss in Dubro's earnings available to common shareholders is $40,000 {80% x [$60,000 – (10% x $100,000)]}. Moss is also entitled to preferred dividends of $2,000 (20% x 10% x $100,000). The total equity in the earnings of Dubro is therefore $42,000 ($40,000 + $2,000).
Answer (B) is incorrect because $48,000 equals 80% of Dubro's net income. Answer (C) is incorrect because $48,400 equals 80% of Dubro's net income plus 20% of a 20% share of the preferred dividends. Answer (D) is incorrect because $50,000 equals Dubro's net income minus the preferred dividends.

46. Park Co. uses the equity method to account for its January 1, 1996 purchase of Tun, Inc.'s common stock. On January 1, 1996, the fair values of Tun's FIFO inventory and land exceeded their carrying amounts. How do these excesses of fair values over carrying amounts affect Park's reported equity in Tun's 1996 earnings?

	Inventory Excess	Land Excess
A.	Decrease	Decrease
B.	Decrease	No effect
C.	Increase	Increase
D.	Increase	No effect

The correct answer is (B). *(CPA 591 T-20)*
REQUIRED: The effect on equity in investee earnings of the excess of the fair values of the investee's FIFO inventory and land over their book values.
DISCUSSION: The equity method of accounting requires the investor's proportionate share of the investee's reported net income for the difference at acquisition between the fair value and carrying value of inventory acquired when that inventory is sold. A similar adjustment for land would be required when that land was sold. Assuming that the FIFO inventory was sold in 1996 and the land was not, Park's proportionate share of Tun's reported net income would be decreased by the inventory differential allocated at the date of acquisition.
Answers (A), (C), and (D) are incorrect because the inventory excess decreases equity in the investee's earnings, but the land excess has no effect.

47. On January 2, 1996, Kean Co. purchased a 30% interest in Pod Co. for $250,000. On this date, Pod's shareholders' equity was $500,000. The carrying amounts of Pod's identifiable net assets approximated their fair values, except for land, whose fair value exceeded its carrying amount by $200,000. Pod reported net income of $100,000 for 1996 and paid no dividends. Kean accounts for this investment using the equity method and amortizes goodwill over 10 years. In its December 31, 1996 balance sheet, what amount should Kean report as investment in subsidiary?

    A. $210,000

    B. $220,000

    C. $270,000

    D. $276,000

The correct answer is (D). *(CPA 594 F-19)*
  REQUIRED: The amount reported as investment in subsidiary under the equity method.
  DISCUSSION: The equity method requires the purchase price to be allocated to the fair value of the identifiable net assets acquired with the remainder allocated to goodwill. The fair value of Kean's 30% interest in Pod's identifiable net assets is $210,000 [30% x ($500,000 + $200,000)]. Goodwill is $40,000 ($250,000 – $210,000). The equity method further requires the investor's share of subsequent net income reported by the investee to be adjusted for the difference at acquisition between the fair value and the carrying value of the investee's identifiable net assets and for any goodwill when the net assets and goodwill are sold or consumed in operations. The land is assumed not to be sold. The goodwill is amortized (consumed) at $4,000 ($40,000 ÷ 10 years) per year. Thus, Kean's share of Pod's net income is $26,000 [(30% x $100,000 declared income) – $4,000] and the investment account at year-end is $276,000 ($250,000 acquisition balance + $26,000 investment income).
  Answer (A) is incorrect because $210,000 equals the fair value of the identifiable net assets acquired. Answer (B) is incorrect because $220,000 equals the price minus Kean's equity in Pod's net income. Answer (C) is incorrect because $270,000 assumes a 4-year amortization period.

48. Sage, Inc. bought 40% of Adams Corp.'s outstanding common stock on January 2, 1996 for $400,000. The carrying amount of Adams' net assets at the purchase date totaled $900,000. Fair values and carrying amounts were the same for all items except for plant and inventory, for which fair values exceeded their carrying amounts by $90,000 and $10,000, respectively. The plant has an 18-year life. All inventory was sold during 1996. Goodwill, if any, is to be amortized over 40 years. During 1996, Adams reported net income of $120,000 and paid a $20,000 cash dividend. What amount should Sage report in its income statement from its investment in Adams for the year ended December 31, 1996?

    A. $48,000

    B. $42,000

    C. $36,000

    D. $32,000

The correct answer is (B). *(CPA 592 I-40)*
  REQUIRED: The amount reported as investment income.
  DISCUSSION: Sage holds 40% of the investee's stock and is assumed to exercise significant influence. It should therefore account for the investment on the equity basis by recognizing its proportionate share of the investee's net income. To determine the amount of investment income the investor should report, the investee's net income of $120,000 should be adjusted for the $10,000 excess of fair value over the carrying value of the inventory acquired because this inventory was sold. The investee's reported net income should also be adjusted for the share of the difference between the fair value and carrying value of the plant that has been consumed (depreciated). This amounts to $5,000 ($90,000 difference ÷ 18 years). No adjustment for goodwill is necessary since the $400,000 purchase price equals a proportionate share of the fair value of the identifiable net assets {[40% x ($900,000 + $90,000 + $10,000)] = $400,000}. Thus, Sage should report investment income of $42,000 [40% x ($120,000 – $10,000 – $5,000)].
  Answer (A) is incorrect because $48,000 equals the proportionate share of the investee's reported net income. Answer (C) is incorrect because $36,000 adjusts the reported net income for the dividend disclosed and does not adjust for the plant depreciation. Answer (D) is incorrect because $32,000 includes a $10,000 adjustment for goodwill amortization.

49. Green Corp. owns 30% of the outstanding common stock and 100% of the outstanding noncumulative nonvoting preferred stock of Axel Corp. In 1996, Axel declared dividends of $100,000 on its common stock and $60,000 on its preferred stock. Green exercises significant influence over Axel's operations. What amount of dividend revenue should Green report in its income statement for the year ended December 31, 1996?

A. $0

B. $30,000

C. $60,000

D. $90,000

The correct answer is (C). *(CPA 592 I-42)*

REQUIRED: The dividend revenue reported given declaration of common and preferred dividends by an investee.

DISCUSSION: An investment in common stock enabling the investor to exercise significant influence over the operations and management of the investee should be accounted for by the equity method rather than the cost method. A 20% or greater ownership is presumed to permit such influence. Under the equity method, the receipt of a cash dividend from the investee should be credited to the investment account. It is a return of, not a return on, the investment. However, the equity method is not applicable to preferred stock. Thus, Green should report $60,000 of revenue when the preferred dividends are declared.

Answer (A) is incorrect because the preferred dividends should be credited to revenue. Answers (B) and (D) are incorrect because the cash dividends on common stock should be credited to the investment account.

50. On January 1, 1995, Mega Corp. acquired 10% of the outstanding voting stock of Penny, Inc. On January 2, 1996, Mega gained the ability to exercise significant influence over financial and operating control of Penny by acquiring an additional 20% of Penny's outstanding stock. The two purchases were made at prices proportionate to the value assigned to Penny's net assets, which equaled their carrying amounts. For the years ended December 31, 1995 and 1996, Penny reported the following:

	1995	1996
Dividends paid	$200,000	$300,000
Net income	600,000	650,000

In 1996, what amounts should Mega report as current-year investment income and as an adjustment, before income taxes, to 1995 investment income?

	1996 Investment Income	Adjustment to 1995 Investment Income
A.	$195,000	$160,000
B.	$195,000	$120,000
C.	$195,000	$40,000
D.	$105,000	$40,000

The correct answer is (C). *(CPA 1191 I-41)*

REQUIRED: The amounts reported as current-year investment income and as an adjustment, before income taxes, to the previous year's investment income.

DISCUSSION: When ownership of an investee reaches the level of significant influence, the investor must adopt the equity method. The investor must also retroactively adjust the carrying amount of the investment, results of operations, and retained earnings as if the equity method had been in effect during all of the previous periods in which any percentage was held. Consequently, Mega should report 1996 investment income before taxes equal to $195,000 (30% x $650,000 net income reported by Penny for 1996). Ignoring taxes, it should retroactively adjust 1995 investment income by $40,000 [(10% interest held in 1995 x $600,000 investee net income in 1995) – (10% x $200,000 dividends paid by investee in 1995)].

Answer (A) is incorrect because $160,000 equals 30% of Penny's 1995 net income minus 10% of Penny's 1995 dividends. Answer (B) is incorrect because $120,000 equals 30% of Penny's 1995 net income minus 30% of Penny's 1995 dividends. Answer (D) is incorrect because $105,000 equals Mega's share of 1996 net income minus its share of dividends.

51. Pare, Inc. purchased 10% of Tot Co.'s 100,000 outstanding shares of common stock on January 2, 1996 for $50,000. On December 31, 1996, Pare purchased an additional 20,000 shares of Tot for $150,000. There was no goodwill as a result of either acquisition, and Tot had not issued any additional stock during 1996. Tot reported earnings of $300,000 for 1996. What amount should Pare report in its December 31, 1996 balance sheet as investment in Tot?

  A. $170,000

  B. $200,000

  C. $230,000

  D. $290,000

The correct answer is (C). *(CPA 1193 I-14)*
REQUIRED: The amount reported in the investment account.
DISCUSSION: Since Pare owned 30% of Tot at year-end, Pare can presumably exercise significant influence. Therefore, the equity method should be used. Although, Pare held 20% or greater ownership only on the last day of 1996, the adoption of the equity method must be retroactive. However, the retroactive effect is based on the percentage of ownership held prior to the adoption of the equity method. Consequently, Pare should recognize its equity in the earnings of Tot as if the equity method had been in effect since 1/2/96. Accordingly, its share of Tot's 1996 earnings will be $30,000 (10% x $300,000), and the investment account balance at year-end will be $230,000 ($150,000 + $50,000 + $30,000).
  Answer (A) is incorrect because $170,000 results from subtracting the equity in Tot's earnings. Answer (B) is incorrect because $200,000 ignores the equity in Tot's earnings. Answer (D) is incorrect because $290,000 assumes Pare held a 30% interest throughout the year.

52. On July 1, 1996, Denver Corp. purchased 3,000 shares of Eagle Co.'s 10,000 outstanding shares of common stock for $20 per share. On December 15, 1996, Eagle paid $40,000 in dividends to its common shareholders. Eagle's net income for the year ended December 31, 1996 was $120,000, earned evenly throughout the year. In its 1996 income statement, what amount of income from this investment should Denver report?

  A. $36,000

  B. $18,000

  C. $12,000

  D. $6,000

The correct answer is (B). *(CPA 593 I-43)*
REQUIRED: The income reported from an investment in common stock.
DISCUSSION: Denver Corp's purchase of 30% of Eagle presumably allows it to exercise significant influence. Hence, it should apply the equity method. The investor's share of the investee's income is a function of the percentage of ownership and the length of time the investment was held. The income from this investment was therefore $18,000 ($120,000 x .30 x 6/12).
  Answer (A) is incorrect because $36,000 assumes Denver owned the stock for the full year. Answer (C) is incorrect because $12,000 equals 30% of the dividend. Dividends do not affect income under the equity method. Answer (D) is incorrect because $6,000 equals 50% of 30% of the dividends.

53. Pear Co.'s income statement for the year ended December 31, 1996, as prepared by Pear's controller, reported income before taxes of $125,000. The auditor questioned the following amounts that had been included in income before taxes:

Equity in earnings of Cinn Co.	$40,000
Dividends received from Cinn	8,000
Adjustments to profits of prior years for arithmetical errors in depreciation	(35,000)

Pear owns 40% of Cinn's common stock. Pear's December 31, 1996 income statement should report income before taxes of

  A. $85,000

  B. $117,000

  C. $120,000

  D. $152,000

The correct answer is (D). *(CPA 593 I-5)*
REQUIRED: The amount reported as income before taxes on the income statement.
DISCUSSION: Under the equity method, the investor's share of the investee's net income is accounted for as an addition to, and losses and dividends are reflected as reductions of, the carrying value of the investment. Consequently, the equity in earnings of Cinn Co. was correctly included in income, but the dividends received should have been excluded. In addition, error corrections related to earlier periods are treated as prior-period adjustments and are not included in net income. Thus, income before taxes should have been $152,000 ($125,000 – $8,000 dividends + $35,000 depreciation error).
  Answer (A) is incorrect because $85,000 subtracts the equity in earnings of Cinn Co. and includes the dividends and the effects of the prior-period adjustment. Answer (B) is incorrect because $117,000 includes the prior-period adjustment. Answer (C) is incorrect because $120,000 equals the computed income, minus the equity in the earnings of Cinn, plus the depreciation error.

54. In 1996, Neil Co. held the following investments in common stock:

- 25,000 shares of B&K, Inc.'s 100,000 outstanding shares. Neil's level of ownership gives it the ability to exercise significant influence over the financial and operating policies of B&K.

- 6,000 shares of Amal Corp.'s 309,000 outstanding shares.

During 1996, Neil received the following distributions from its common stock investments:

November 6 - $30,000 cash dividend from B&K.

November 11 - $1,500 cash dividend from Amal.

December 26 - 3% common stock dividend from Amal. The closing price of this stock on a national exchange was $15 per share.

What amount of dividend revenue should Neil report for 1996?

    A. $1,500

    B. $4,200

    C. $31,500

    D. $34,200

The correct answer is (A). *(CPA 1191 I-44)*
  REQUIRED: The dividend revenue reported.
  DISCUSSION: The investment in B&K must be accounted for using the equity method. Thus, the cash dividend does not affect income. The $1,500 dividend from Amal is recognized as revenue because the investment is accounted for on the cost basis. Stock dividends are never recognized as income. Hence, the dividend revenue recognized is the $1,500 cash dividend from Amal.
  Answer (B) is incorrect because $4,200 includes the $2,700 (3% x 600 shares x $15) stock dividend. Answer (C) is incorrect because $31,500 includes the dividend from B&K. Answer (D) is incorrect because $34,200 equals the $2,700 stock dividend plus the $30,000 dividend from B&K.

55. If an investor accounts for an investment using the equity method and significant influence over the investee ceases to exist, the investor should

    A. Continue to use the equity method.

    B. Retroactively adjust the investment and income account back to the cost method.

    C. Cease using the equity method.

    D. Cease using the equity method and immediately recognize as expense all remaining excess of cost over fair market value of the investment.

The correct answer is (C). *(Publisher)*
  REQUIRED: The procedure when significant influence over an equity method investment ceases to exist.
  DISCUSSION: When significant influence over an equity-based investee ceases to exist (usually when the ownership of stock falls below 20%), the cost method rather than the equity method should be used. This accounting change should be recognized on a prospective basis only. No adjustment should be made to the investment account, and subsequent dividends received should be recorded as investment income.
  Answer (A) is incorrect because the cost rather than the equity method is appropriate. Answers (B) and (D) are incorrect because no retroactive adjustment is made.

Questions 55 and 56 are based on the following information. Boggs, Inc., paid $700,000 on January 1, 1996 for 100,000 shares of Mattly Corporation representing 30% of Mattly's outstanding common stock. The following computation was made by Boggs:

Purchase price	$700,000
30% equity in book value of Mattly's net assets	(500,000)
Excess cost over book value	$200,000

Because the book value of the identifiable net assets approximated the fair value, the excess cost over book value was attributed to goodwill and will be amortized over 20 years. Mattly reported net income for the year ended December 31, 1996 of $300,000. Mattly Corporation paid cash dividends of $100,000 on July 1, 1996.

56. If Boggs, Inc. exercised significant influence over Mattly Corporation and properly accounted for the long-term investment under the equity method, the amount of net investment revenue Boggs should report from its investment in Mattly is

A. $30,000

B. $60,000

C. $80,000

D. $90,000

The correct answer is (C). *(CMA 687 3-11)*

REQUIRED: The investment revenue reported under the equity method.

DISCUSSION: If Boggs exercises significant influence, the equity method of accounting should be used regardless of its percentage of ownership. Boggs' investment income is equal to the proportionate share of the declared income of Mattly minus the amortization of goodwill. The proportionate interest in the declared income is $90,000 ($300,000 x 30%). The amortization of goodwill is equal to $10,000 ($200,000 ÷ 20 years). Investment income should therefore be reported as $80,000 ($90,000 – $10,000).

Answer (A) is incorrect because $30,000 (30% x $100,000 of cash dividends) would be the net investment revenue if the cost method were used. Answer (B) is incorrect because $60,000 equals the proportionate share of net income minus the cash dividends. Answer (D) is incorrect because $90,000 results from failing to subtract $10,000 of amortization from the proportionate interest in income.

57. If Boggs, Inc. did not exercise significant influence over Mattly Corporation and properly accounted for the long-term investment under the cost method, the amount of net investment revenue Boggs should report from its investment in Mattly is

A. $20,000

B. $30,000

C. $60,000

D. $80,000

The correct answer is (B). *(CMA 687 3-12)*

REQUIRED: The investment revenue reported under the cost method.

DISCUSSION: If significant influence is not exercised, the cost method should be used. The proportionate ownership of the outstanding stock is not the determining factor. Under the cost method, investment revenue is equal to a proportionate interest in the dividends declared unless a liquidating dividend occurs. In this case, dividends ($100,000) are less than net income ($300,000), so the dividend is not liquidating. Investment revenue is thus $30,000 ($100,000 x 30%).

Answer (A) is incorrect because $20,000 results from subtracting $10,000 of amortization. Answer (C) is incorrect because $60,000 equals the proportionate share of net income minus the cash dividends. Answer (D) is incorrect because $80,000 is investment revenue reported under the equity method.

13.4 Cost Method

58. An investor uses the cost method to account for an investment in common stock. A portion of the dividends received this year were in excess of the investor's share of investee's earnings subsequent to the date of investment. The amount of dividend revenue that should be reported in the investor's income statement for this year is

A. Zero.

B. The total amount of dividends received this year.

C. The portion of the dividends received this year that were in excess of the investor's share of investee's earnings subsequent to the date of investment.

D. The portion of the dividends received this year that were not in excess of the investor's share of investee's earnings subsequent to the date of investment.

The correct answer is (D). *(CPA 1191 T-10)*
REQUIRED: The proper accounting for cash dividends in accordance with the cost method.
DISCUSSION: Under the cost method, dividends from an investee should be accounted for by the investor as dividend income unless a liquidating dividend is received. A liquidating dividend occurs when the total accumulated dividends received by the investor since the date of acquisition exceed the investor's proportionate share of the investee's net accumulated earnings during that time. A liquidating dividend is treated as a reduction in the carrying value of the investment rather than as dividend income. The portion of the dividends received that were not in excess of the investor's share of investee's earnings subsequent to the date of investment is reported as dividend revenue.
Answers (A), (B), and (C) are incorrect because dividend revenue should include the portion of the dividends received that are not liquidating dividends.

59. Pal Corp's 1996 dividend income included only part of the dividend received from its Ima Corp. investment. The balance of the dividend reduced Pal's carrying amount for its Ima investment. This reflects that Pal accounts for its Ima investment by the

A. Cost method, and only a portion of Ima's 1996 dividends represent earnings after Pal's acquisition.

B. Cost method, and its carrying amount exceeded the proportionate share of Ima's market value.

C. Equity method, and Ima incurred a loss in 1996.

D. Equity method, and its carrying amount exceeded the proportionate share of Ima's fair value.

The correct answer is (A). *(CPA 1192 T-30)*
REQUIRED: The reason the investor recognized only part of a dividend in income.
DISCUSSION: Under the cost method, dividends from an investee should be accounted for by the investor as dividend income unless a liquidating dividend is received. A liquidating dividend occurs when the total accumulated dividends received by the investor since the date of acquisition exceed the investor's proportionate share of the investee's net accumulated earnings during that time. A liquidating dividend is treated as a reduction in the carrying value of the investment rather than as dividend income. The portion of the dividends received that were not in excess of the investor's share of investee's earnings subsequent to the date of investment is reported as dividend revenue.
Answer (B) is incorrect because, under the cost method, the investee's market value is irrelevant. Answers (C) and (D) are incorrect because no dividend income is recognized under the equity method.

60. Monroe Corp. purchased 1,500 shares of the 10,000 outstanding shares of Cennedy Co. for $139,000 on January 1, 1995. During 1995, Cennedy declared income of $90,000 and paid dividends of $60,000. During 1996, Cennedy declared income of $40,000 and paid dividends of $60,000. At the end of 1996, Monroe's balance in its investment in Cennedy Co. stock account should be

A. $136,000

B. $139,000

C. $140,500

D. $157,000

The correct answer is (B). *(M. Richter)*
REQUIRED: The investment account balance 2 years after acquisition.
DISCUSSION: The 15% ownership (1,500 ÷ 10,000 shares) creates a presumption that significant influence cannot be exerted. Thus, Monroe should account for its investment on the cost basis. During 1995 and 1996, the net accumulated earnings ($90,000 + $40,000 = $130,000) of the investee are greater than the total dividends paid ($60,000 + $60,000 = $120,000). Consequently, no liquidating dividend was paid, and the carrying amount of the investment account should remain at the cost of the shares, or $139,000.
Answer (A) is incorrect because $136,000 assumes that the equity method was used for 1995. Answer (C) is incorrect because $140,500 assumes that the equity method was used for both years. Answer (D) is incorrect because $157,000 assumes that dividends were debited to the investment account.

61. Bort Co. purchased 2,000 shares of Crel Co. common stock on March 5, 1996 for $72,000. Bort received a $1,000 cash dividend on the Crel stock on July 15, 1996. Crel declared a 10% stock dividend on December 15, 1996 to shareholders of record as of December 31, 1996. The dividend was distributed on January 15, 1997. The market price of the stock was $38 on December 15, 1996, $40 on December 31, 1996, and $42 on January 15, 1997. What amount should Bort record as dividend revenue for the year ended December 31, 1996?

  A. $1,000

  B. $8,600

  C. $9,000

  D. $9,400

The correct answer is (A). *(CPA 592 I-43)*
  REQUIRED: The dividend revenue reported for the year.
  DISCUSSION: The $1,000 cash dividend is recognized as revenue for the year. Stock dividends are never recognized as income.
  Answer (B) is incorrect because $8,600 includes the stock dividend valued at $38 per share. Answer (C) is incorrect because $9,000 includes the stock dividend valued at $40 per share. Answer (D) is incorrect because $9,400 includes the stock dividend valued at $42 per share.

62. Information pertaining to dividends from Wray Corp.'s common stock investments for the year ended December 31, 1996 follows:

• On September 8, 1996, Wray received a $50,000 cash dividend from Seco, Inc. in which Wray owns a 30% interest. A majority of Wray's directors are also directors of Seco.

• On October 15, 1996, Wray received a $6,000 liquidating dividend from King Co. Wray owns a 5% interest in King Co.

• Wray owns a 2% interest in Bow Corp., which declared a $200,000 cash dividend on November 27, 1996 to shareholders of record on December 15, 1996, payable on January 5, 1997.

What amount should Wray report as dividend income in its income statement for the year ended December 31, 1996?

  A. $60,000

  B. $56,000

  C. $10,000

  D. $4,000

The correct answer is (D). *(CPA 1192 I-44)*
  REQUIRED: The dividend income reported in the income statement.
  DISCUSSION: Wray owns 30% of Seco, and a majority of its directors are also directors of Seco. Hence, Wray can exercise significant influence over Seco and should account for the investment using the equity method. Under the equity method, cash dividends are credited to the investment account, not dividend income. A liquidating dividend is also treated as a reduction in the carrying value of the investment, not dividend income. Wray owns 2% of Bow and is therefore presumed not to exert significant influence. Thus, the cost method should be used to account for the cash dividend from Bow. Under the cost method, dividends receivable should be debited and dividend income credited at the declaration date (11/27/96) for $4,000 (2% x $200,000).
  Answers (A), (B), and (C) are incorrect because neither the cash dividend from the equity-based investee nor the liquidating dividend is included in the determination of income.

63. Cobb Co. purchased 10,000 shares (2% ownership) of Roe Co. on February 12, 1996. Cobb received a stock dividend of 2,000 shares on March 31, 1996 when the carrying amount per share on Roe's books was $35 and the market value per share was $40. Roe paid a cash dividend of $1.50 per share on September 15, 1996. In Cobb's income statement for the year ended October 31, 1996, what amount should Cobb report as dividend income?

  A. $98,000

  B. $88,000

  C. $18,000

  D. $15,000

The correct answer is (C). *(CPA 1193 I-48)*
  REQUIRED: The amount of dividend income to be reported on the income statement.
  DISCUSSION: Because Cobb Co. owns only 2% of Roe Co., the investment should be accounted for on the cost basis. A stock dividend is not reported as dividend income under either the cost or equity method; therefore, the dividend income is $18,000 (12,000 shares x $1.50).
  Answer (A) is incorrect because $98,000 includes the value of the stock dividend at the market price. Answer (B) is incorrect because $88,000 includes the value of the stock dividend at the carrying amount. Answer (D) is incorrect because $15,000 does not include the cash dividend paid on the 2,000 shares received as a stock dividend.

64. Deed Co. owns 2% of Beck Cosmetic Retailers. A property dividend by Beck consisted of merchandise with a fair value lower than the listed retail price. Deed in turn gave the merchandise to its employees as a holiday bonus. How should Deed report the receipt and distribution of the merchandise in its income statement?

   A. At fair value for both dividend revenue and employee compensation expense.

   B. At listed retail price for both dividend revenue and employee compensation expense.

   C. At fair value for dividend revenue and listed retail price for employee compensation expense.

   D. By disclosure only.

The correct answer is (A). *(CPA 1192 T-20)*
   REQUIRED: The manner of reporting the receipt and distribution of a property dividend.
   DISCUSSION: According to APB 29, a nonmonetary asset received in a nonreciprocal transfer should be recorded at the fair value of the asset received. Dividend revenue should also be recognized at fair value. A transfer of a nonmonetary asset to a shareholder or other entity in a nonreciprocal transfer, for example, to employees as a bonus, should also be recorded at the fair value of the asset transferred.
   Answers (B), (C), and (D) are incorrect because both transactions should be reported at fair value in the income statement.

13.5 Impairment of a Loan

65. SFAS 114, *Accounting by Creditors for Impairment of a Loan*, requires recognition of an impairment when it is probable that a creditor will be unable to collect

	Contractual Principal Payments	Contractual Interest Payments
A.	Yes	No
B.	Yes	Yes
C.	No	Yes
D.	No	No

The correct answer is (B). *(Publisher)*
   REQUIRED: The payments the noncollection of which justify recognition of impairment of a loan.
   DISCUSSION: SFAS 114 requires a creditor to recognize impairment of a loan when it is probable that the creditor will not be able to collect all amounts due in accordance with the terms of the loan. All amounts include both principal and interest payments.
   Answers (A), (C), and (D) are incorrect because both contractual principal and interest payments are included.

66. Which of the following may be used to measure impairment of a loan?

  I. Observable market price
 II. Present value of future cash flows discounted at the loan's effective interest rate
III. Present value of future cash flows discounted at the loan's current market interest rate

   A. Both I and II.

   B. Both I and III.

   C. II only.

   D. III only.

The correct answer is (A). *(Publisher)*
   REQUIRED: The measure(s) of the impairment of a loan.
   DISCUSSION: A creditor shall measure impairment of a loan based on the present value of expected future cash flows discounted at the loan's effective rate. As a practical expedient, however, a creditor may use the loan's observable market price or the fair value of the collateral if the value of the loan is collateral dependent.
   Answers (B), (C), and (D) are incorrect because either an observable market price or the present value of future cash flows discounted at the loan's effective interest rate may be used.

13.6 Cash Surrender Value

67. On January 2, 1993, Beal, Inc. acquired a $70,000 whole-life insurance policy on its president. The annual premium is $2,000. The company is the owner and beneficiary. Beal charged officer's life insurance expense as follows:

1993	$2,000
1994	1,800
1995	1,500
1996	1,100
Total	$6,400

In Beal's December 31, 1996 balance sheet, the investment in cash surrender value should be

A. $0

B. $1,600

C. $6,400

D. $8,000

The correct answer is (B). *(CPA 1190 I-3)*
REQUIRED: The investment in cash surrender value.
DISCUSSION: Cash surrender value is the loan value or surrender value of a whole-life insurance policy. It is equal to the difference between the premiums paid and the life insurance expense recognized. Because the total of premiums paid is $8,000 (4 years x $2,000) and the total life insurance expense is $6,400, the investment in cash surrender value is $1,600. This amount is classified as a noncurrent asset on a classified balance sheet because management purchases life insurance policies for the life insurance aspect rather than as a short-term investment.
Answer (A) is incorrect because the excess of the premiums over the expenses is the cash surrender value. Answer (C) is incorrect because $6,400 is the total insurance expense for 4 years. Answer (D) is incorrect because $8,000 is the sum of the premiums for 4 years.

68. In 1991, Chain, Inc. purchased a $1,000,000 life insurance policy on its president, of which Chain is the beneficiary. Information regarding the policy for the year ended December 31, 1996 follows:

Cash surrender value, 1/1/96	$ 87,000
Cash surrender value, 12/31/96	108,000
Annual advance premium paid 1/1/96	40,000

During 1996, dividends of $6,000 were applied to increase the cash surrender value of the policy. What amount should Chain report as life insurance expense for 1996?

A. $40,000

B. $21,000

C. $19,000

D. $13,000

The correct answer is (C). *(CPA 1192 I-51)*
REQUIRED: The life insurance expense to be reported.
DISCUSSION: Life insurance expense is equal to the excess of the premiums paid over the increase in cash surrender value and dividends received. Since the dividends were applied to increase the cash surrender value, they were therefore not received. Hence, Chain's life insurance expense is $19,000.

Premium	$40,000
Minus:	
Increase in cash surrender value	
($108,000 – $87,000)	(21,000)
Life insurance expense	$19,000

Answer (A) is incorrect because $40,000 is the premium paid. Answer (B) is incorrect because $21,000 is the change in the cash surrender value. Answer (D) is incorrect because $13,000 results from subtracting the dividends applied.

69. An increase in the cash surrender value of a life insurance policy owned by a company would be recorded by

A. Decreasing annual insurance expense.

B. Increasing investment income.

C. Recording a memorandum entry only.

D. Decreasing a deferred charge.

The correct answer is (A). *(CPA 1194 F-46)*
REQUIRED: The proper recording of an increase.
DISCUSSION: The cash surrender value of the policy is an asset of the company. Thus, part of the premium paid is not expense. As the cash surrender value increases, the annual insurance expense decreases.
Answer (B) is incorrect because investment income is not affected by life insurance. Answers (C) and (D) are incorrect because, as the cash surrender value increases, the annual insurance expense decreases.

70. In 1996, Gar Corp. collected $300,000 as beneficiary of a key person life insurance policy carried on the life of Gar's controller, who had died in 1996. The life insurance proceeds are not subject to income tax. At the date of the controller's death, the policy's cash surrender value was $90,000. What amount should Gar report as revenue in its 1996 income statement?

A. $0

B. $90,000

C. $210,000

D. $300,000

The correct answer is (C). *(CPA 594 F-44)*

REQUIRED: The revenue reported from collection of life insurance.

DISCUSSION: Upon receipt of life insurance proceeds, cash is debited for the amount received. Cash surrender value is credited for the amount of the asset on the books, and the balancing credit is to insurance income (a revenue account). Hence, revenue equals $210,000 ($300,000 cash – $90,000 cash surrender value).

Answer (A) is incorrect because cash collected exceeded the asset. Answer (B) is incorrect because $90,000 is the cash surrender value. Answer (D) is incorrect because $300,000 equals the cash collected.

CHAPTER FOURTEEN
CURRENT LIABILITIES AND CONTINGENCIES

This chapter covers all liabilities and contingent liabilities except long-term liabilities, which are covered in Chapter 15. Also, Chapter 20, Income Tax Allocation, deals with related topics.

14.1 Current Liabilities

1. Brite Corp. had the following liabilities at December 31, 1996:

Accounts payable	$ 55,000
Unsecured notes, 8%, due 7/1/97	400,000
Accrued expenses	35,000
Contingent liability	450,000
Deferred income tax liability	25,000
Senior bonds, 7%, due 3/31/97	1,000,000

The contingent liability is an accrual for possible losses on a $1,000,000 lawsuit filed against Brite. Brite's legal counsel expects the suit to be settled in 1998 and has estimated that Brite will be liable for damages in the range of $450,000 to $750,000. The deferred income tax liability is not related to an asset for financial reporting and is expected to reverse in 1998. What amount should Brite report in its December 31, 1996 balance sheet for current liabilities?

A. $515,000

B. $940,000

C. $1,490,000

D. $1,515,000

The correct answer is (C). *(CPA 594 F-11)*

REQUIRED: The amount reported for current liabilities.

DISCUSSION: ARB 43, Chapter 3A, defines a current liability as an obligation that will be either liquidated using a current asset or replaced by another current liability. SFAS 78 amends ARB 43 to include the following as current liabilities: (1) obligations that, by their terms, are or will be due on demand within 1 year (or the operating cycle if longer) and (2) obligations that are or will be callable by the creditor within 1 year because of a violation of a debt covenant. Thus, the current liabilities are calculated as

Accounts payable	$ 55,000
Unsecured notes, 8%, due 7/1/97	400,000
Accrued expenses	35,000
Senior bonds, 7%, due 3/31/97	1,000,000
	$1,490,000

Answer (A) is incorrect because $515,000 excludes the senior bonds due within 1 year and includes the deferred income tax liability that will not reverse within 1 year. Whether a deferred tax asset or liability is current depends on the classification of the related asset or liability. If it is not related to an asset or liability, the expected reversal date of the temporary difference determines the classification. Answer (B) is incorrect because $940,000 includes the contingent liability not expected to be settled until 1998 and excludes the senior bonds. Answer (D) is incorrect because $1,515,000 includes the deferred income tax liability not expected to reverse until 1998.

2. Lyle, Inc. is preparing its financial statements for the year ended December 31, 1996. Accounts payable amounted to $360,000 before any necessary year-end adjustment related to the following:

- At December 31, 1996, Lyle has a $50,000 debit balance in its accounts payable to Ross, a supplier, resulting from a $50,000 advance payment for goods to be manufactured to Lyle's specifications.
- Checks in the amount of $100,000 were written to vendors and recorded on December 29, 1996. The checks were mailed on January 5, 1997.

What amount should Lyle report as accounts payable in its December 31, 1996 balance sheet?

A. $510,000

B. $410,000

C. $310,000

D. $210,000

The correct answer is (A). *(CPA 1193 I-30)*
REQUIRED: The amount of accounts payable reported after year-end adjustments.
DISCUSSION: The ending accounts payable balance should include amounts owed as of 12/31/96, on trade payables. Although Lyle wrote checks for $100,000 to various vendors, that amount should still be included in the accounts payable balance because the company had not surrendered control of the checks at year-end. The advance to the supplier was erroneously recorded as a reduction of (debit to) accounts payable. This amount should be recorded as a prepaid asset, and accounts payable should be credited (increased) by $50,000. Thus, accounts payable should be reported as $510,000 ($360,000 + $50,000 + $100,000).
Answer (B) is incorrect because $410,000 does not include the $100,000 in checks not yet mailed at year-end. Answer (C) is incorrect because $310,000 does not include the $100,000 in checks, and it reflects the subtraction, not the addition, of the $50,000 advance. Answer (D) is incorrect because $210,000 results from subtracting the advance payment and the checks.

3. On March 31, 1997, Dallas Co. received an advance payment of 60% of the sales price for special order goods to be manufactured and delivered within 5 months. At the same time, Dallas subcontracted for production of the special order goods at a price equal to 40% of the main contract price. What liabilities should be reported in Dallas' March 31, 1997 balance sheet?

| | Payables to |
Deferred Revenues	Subcontractor
A. None	None
B. 60% of main contract price	40% of main contract price
C. 60% of main contract price	None
D. None	40% of main contract price

The correct answer is (C). *(CPA 592 T-26)*
REQUIRED: The liabilities to be reported in the balance sheet.
DISCUSSION: The 60% advance payment is a deferred revenue (liability) because it has been realized but not earned. The entity has not substantially accomplished what it must do to be entitled to the benefits represented by the prepayment. The agreement with the subcontractor does not create a liability because the entity has no current obligation to transfer assets or provide services. That obligation will not arise until the subcontractor has performed.
Answer (A) is incorrect because the 60% prepayment should be credited to deferred revenue. Answer (B) is incorrect because Dallas has no liability to the subcontractor. Answer (D) is incorrect because the 60% prepayment should be credited to deferred revenue, and Dallas has no liability to the subcontractor.

4. Black Co. requires advance payments with special orders for machinery constructed to customer specifications. These advances are nonrefundable. Information for 1996 is as follows:

Customer advances--balance 12/31/95	$118,000
Advances received with orders in 1996	184,000
Advances applied to orders shipped in 1996	164,000
Advances applicable to orders canceled in 1996	50,000

In Black's December 31, 1996 balance sheet, what amount should be reported as a current liability for advances from customers?

A. $0

B. $88,000

C. $138,000

D. $148,000

The correct answer is (B). *(CPA 1194 F-25)*
REQUIRED: The current liability for advances.
DISCUSSION: The amount of $88,000 ($118,000 beginning balance + $184,000 advances received – $164,000 advances credited to revenue after shipment of orders – $50,000 for canceled orders) should be reported as a current liability for customer advances. Deposits or other advance payments are liabilities because they involve a probable future sacrifice of economic benefits arising from a current obligation. The advances applicable to canceled orders are not refundable. Thus, no future sacrifice of economic benefits is necessary.
Answer (A) is incorrect because deposits or other advance payments should be recognized as liabilities. Answer (C) is incorrect because $138,000 includes $50,000 applicable to orders canceled. Answer (D) is incorrect because $148,000 results from subtracting advances received and adding advances applied to shipments and advances for canceled orders.

5. Kent Co., a division of National Realty, Inc., maintains escrow accounts and pays real estate taxes for National's mortgage customers. Escrow funds are kept in interest-bearing accounts. Interest, minus a 10% service fee, is credited to the customer's account and used to reduce future escrow payments. Additional information follows:

Escrow accounts liability, 1/1/96	$ 700,000
Escrow payments received during 1996	1,580,000
Real estate taxes paid during 1996	1,720,000
Interest on escrow funds during 1996	50,000

What amount should Kent report as escrow accounts liability in its December 31, 1996 balance sheet?

- A. $510,000
- B. $515,000
- C. $605,000
- D. $610,000

The correct answer is (C). *(CPA 1193 I-32)*
REQUIRED: The amount of escrow accounts liability.
DISCUSSION: The liability at the beginning of the year was $700,000. Escrow payments of $1,580,000 were credited and taxes paid of $1,720,000 were debited to the account during the year. Furthermore, interest of $45,000 [$50,000 – (10% x $50,000) service fee] was credited. Thus, the year-end balance was $605,000 ($700,000 + $1,580,000 – $1,720,000 + $45,000).

Answer (A) is incorrect because $510,000 results from debiting $50,000 rather than crediting $45,000. Answer (B) is incorrect because $515,000 results from debiting $45,000 rather than crediting $45,000. Answer (D) is incorrect because $610,000 omits the adjustment for the service fee.

6. Hudson Hotel collects 15% in city sales taxes on room rentals, in addition to a $2 per room, per night, occupancy tax. Sales taxes for each month are due at the end of the following month, and occupancy taxes are due 15 days after the end of each calendar quarter. On January 3, 1997, Hudson paid its November 1996 sales taxes and its fourth quarter 1996 occupancy taxes. Additional information pertaining to Hudson's operations is

1996	Room Rentals	Room Nights
October	$100,000	1,100
November	110,000	1,200
December	150,000	1,800

What amounts should Hudson report as sales taxes payable and occupancy taxes payable in its December 31, 1996 balance sheet?

	Sales Taxes	Occupancy Taxes
A.	$39,000	$6,000
B.	$39,000	$8,200
C.	$54,000	$6,000
D.	$54,000	$8,200

The correct answer is (B). *(CPA 594 F-21)*
REQUIRED: The sales taxes payable and occupancy taxes payable.
DISCUSSION: Hudson presumably paid its October sales taxes during 1996, but it did not pay sales taxes for November and December and occupancy taxes for October, November, and December until 1997. Consequently, it should accrue a liability for sales taxes in the amount of $39,000 [15% x ($110,000 November rentals + $150,000 December rentals)] and a liability for occupancy taxes in the amount of $8,200 [$2 x (1,100 + 1,200 + 1,800) room nights].

Answer (A) is incorrect because $6,000 excludes October room nights. Answer (C) is incorrect because $54,000 includes October room rentals, and $6,000 excludes October room nights. Answer (D) is incorrect because $54,000 includes October room rentals.

7. On July 1, 1996, Ran County issued realty tax assessments for its fiscal year ended June 30, 1997. On September 1, 1996, Day Co. purchased a warehouse in Ran County. The purchase price was reduced by a credit for accrued realty taxes. Day did not record the entire year's real estate tax obligation, but instead records tax expenses at the end of each month by adjusting prepaid real estate taxes or real estate taxes payable, as appropriate. On November 1, 1996, Day paid the first of two equal installments of $12,000 for realty taxes. What amount of this payment should Day record as a debit to real estate taxes payable?

   A. $4,000

   B. $8,000

   C. $10,000

   D. $12,000

The correct answer is (B). *(CPA 1194 F-19)*
REQUIRED: The amount to be debited to real estate taxes payable.
DISCUSSION: The credit balance in real estate taxes payable at 11/1/96 is $8,000. This amount reflects accrued real estate taxes of $2,000 a month [(2 x $12,000) ÷ 12 months] for 4 months (July through October). This payable should be debited for $8,000 when the real estate taxes are paid.
Answer (A) is incorrect because the $4,000 includes real estate taxes for September and October only. Answer (C) is incorrect because $10,000 includes real estate taxes for November. Answer (D) is incorrect because $12,000 equals 6 months of real estate taxes.

8. Lime Co.'s payroll for the month ended January 31, 1997 is summarized as follows:

Total wages	$10,000
Federal income tax withheld	1,200

All wages paid were subject to FICA. FICA tax rates were 7% each for employee and employer. Lime remits payroll taxes on the 15th of the following month. In its financial statements for the month ended January 31, 1997, what amounts should Lime report as total payroll tax liability and as payroll tax expense?

	Liability	Expense
A.	$1,200	$1,400
B.	$1,900	$1,400
C.	$1,900	$ 700
D.	$2,600	$ 700

The correct answer is (D). *(CPA 1195 F-13)*
REQUIRED: The amounts reported as total payroll tax liability and as payroll tax expense.
DISCUSSION: The payroll liability is $2,600 ($1,200 federal income tax withheld + $700 employer's FICA + $700 employees' FICA). The payroll tax expense consists of the employer's share of FICA. The employees' share is considered a withholding, not an expense.
Answer (A) is incorrect because $1,200 does not include employer and employee shares of current FICA taxes, and $1,400 includes the employees' share of FICA taxes. Answer (B) is incorrect because $1,900 does not include $700 of FICA taxes, and $1,400 includes the employees' share of FICA taxes. Answer (C) is incorrect because $1,900 does not include $700 of FICA taxes.

9. Ryan Co. sells major household appliance service contracts for cash. The service contracts are for a 1-year, 2-year, or 3-year period. Cash receipts from contracts are credited to unearned service contract revenues. This account had a balance of $720,000 at December 31, 1996 before year-end adjustment. Service contract costs are charged as incurred to the service contract expense account, which had a balance of $180,000 at December 31, 1996. Outstanding service contracts at December 31, 1996 expire as follows:

During 1997	–	$150,000
During 1998	–.	225,000
During 1999	–	100,000

What amount should be reported as unearned service contract revenues in Ryan's December 31, 1996 balance sheet?

   A. $540,000

   B. $475,000

   C. $295,000

   D. $245,000

The correct answer is (B). *(CPA 1190 I-17)*
REQUIRED: The amount to be reported as unearned service contract revenues at year-end.
DISCUSSION: Unearned service contract revenues relate to outstanding contracts for which the agreed service has not yet been provided. Thus, the amount to be reported as unearned service contract revenues is the $475,000 ($150,000 + $225,000 + $100,000) of service contracts outstanding at 12/31/96.
Answer (A) is incorrect because $540,000 is the difference between the unearned service contract revenue before adjustment and the balance in the service contract expense account. Answer (C) is incorrect because $295,000 is the difference between the $180,000 balance in service contract expense and the $475,000 of unearned service contract revenue reported in the 12/31/96 balance sheet. Answer (D) is incorrect because $245,000 is the change in the unearned service contract revenue account ($720,000 – $475,000).

10. On January 3, 1996, Jannelle Company issued long-term bonds due January 3, 2001. The bond covenant includes a call provision that is effective if the firm's current ratio falls below 2:1. On June 30, 1996, the fiscal year-end for the company, its current ratio was 1.5:1. The bonds should be reported on the financial statements as a

A. Long-term debt because their maturity date is January 3, 2001.

B. Long-term debt if it is reasonably possible that Jannelle can cure the covenant violation before the end of any allowed grace period.

C. Current liability if the covenant violation is not cured.

D. Current liability, regardless of any action by the bondholder, because the company was in violation of the covenant on the balance sheet date.

The correct answer is (C). *(R.B. Posey)*

REQUIRED: The proper classification of callable obligations.

DISCUSSION: SFAS 78, *Classification of Obligations That Are Callable by the Creditor*, states that long-term obligations that are callable by the creditor because of the debtor's violation of the debt agreement at the balance sheet date shall be classified as current liabilities.

Answer (A) is incorrect because the violation of the debt agreement would allow the creditor to accelerate the maturity date. Answer (B) is incorrect because the debt should be classified as current unless it is probable that the violation will be cured within any grace period. Answer (D) is incorrect because a creditor's waiver of the right to demand repayment of the debt would allow Jannelle to classify the bonds as long-term.

11. According to SFAS 78, *Classification of Obligations That Are Callable by the Creditor*, long-term obligations that are or will become callable by the creditor because of the debtor's violation of a provision of the debt agreement at the balance sheet date should be classified as

A. Long-term liabilities.

B. Current liabilities unless the creditor has waived the right to demand repayment for more than 1 year from the balance sheet date.

C. Contingent liabilities until the violation is corrected.

D. Current liabilities unless it is reasonably possible that the violation will be corrected within the grace period.

The correct answer is (B). *(CMA 1287 3-29)*

REQUIRED: The proper classification of long-term debt callable by the creditor because of a violation of an agreement.

DISCUSSION: ARB 43, Chapter 3A, defines a current liability as an obligation that will be either liquidated using a current asset or replaced by another current liability. SFAS 78 amends ARB 43 to include as current liabilities (1) obligations that by their terms are or will be due on demand within 1 year (or the operating cycle, if longer) and (2) obligations that are or will be callable by the creditor within 1 year because of a violation of a debt covenant. An exception exists, however, if the creditor has waived or subsequently lost the right to demand repayment for more than 1 year (or the operating cycle, if longer) from the balance sheet date.

Answer (A) is incorrect because this kind of obligation should be classified as a current liability. Answer (C) is incorrect because the liability is not contingent. Answer (D) is incorrect because the obligation may be classified as noncurrent if it is probable that the violation will be corrected within the grace period.

14.2 Bonus and Profit Sharing

12. Ral Corp. has an incentive compensation plan under which a branch manager receives 10% of the branch's income after deduction of the bonus but before deduction of income tax. Branch income for 1996 before the bonus and income tax was $165,000. The tax rate was 30%. The 1996 bonus amounted to

   A. $11,907

   B. $15,000

   C. $16,500

   D. $18,000

The correct answer is (B). *(CPA 589 II-19)*
   REQUIRED: The bonus computed on pretax income after deduction of the bonus.
   DISCUSSION: The bonus is equal to 10% of the annual pretax income of $165,000 after the bonus has been deducted. Solving the equation given below, the bonus is equal to $15,000.

$$
\begin{aligned}
B &= .10(\$165,000 - B) \\
B &= \$16,500 - .1B \\
1.1B &= \$16,500 \\
B &= \$15,000
\end{aligned}
$$

   Answer (A) is incorrect because $11,907 is the bonus computed on after-tax income, assuming the bonus is deducted to determine taxable income. Answer (C) is incorrect because $16,500 is 10% of the branch income before deducting the bonus and income taxes. Answer (D) is incorrect because $18,000 is 10% of the sum of pretax, pre-bonus branch income plus the bonus.

13. Mann, Inc. has a bonus plan covering all employees. The total bonus is equal to 10% of Mann's preliminary (prebonus, pretax) income reduced by the income tax (computed on the preliminary income minus the bonus itself). Mann's preliminary income for the year is $200,000, and the income tax rate is 40%. How much is the bonus for the year?

   A. $12,000

   B. $12,500

   C. $18,818

   D. $20,000

The correct answer is (B). *(CPA 1185 I-53)*
   REQUIRED: The amount of a bonus computed on after-tax income before deducting the bonus.
   DISCUSSION: The problem requires setting up simultaneous equations because it has two unknowns, the bonus and the tax. Set the tax (T) equal to 40% of income of $200,000 minus the bonus. Set the bonus (B) equal to 10% of the $200,000 income minus taxes. Solve for T and then substitute the resulting value for T in the bonus equation.

$$
\begin{aligned}
T &= .4(\$200,000 - B) \\
T &= \$80,000 - .4B \\[4pt]
B &= .1(\$200,000 - T) \\
B &= \$20,000 - .1(\$80,000 - .4B) \\
B &= \$12,000 + .04B \\
.96B &= \$12,000 \\
B &= \$12,500 \text{ bonus}
\end{aligned}
$$

   Answer (A) is incorrect because $12,000 is 10% of the difference between preliminary income and 40% of preliminary income. Answer (C) is incorrect because $18,818 equals 10% of the difference between preliminary income and the bonus. Answer (D) is incorrect because $20,000 is 10% of preliminary income.

14.3 Unredeemed Coupons/Premiums

14. A department store sells gift certificates that may be redeemed for merchandise. Each certificate expires 3 years after issuance. The revenue from the gift certificates should be recognized

   A. Evenly over 3 years from the date of issuance.

   B. In the period the certificates are sold.

   C. In the period the certificates expire.

   D. In the period the certificates are redeemed or in the period they expire if they are allowed to lapse.

The correct answer is (D). *(CIA 1189 IV-29)*
   REQUIRED: The timing of revenue recognition for gift certificates.
   DISCUSSION: SFAC 5, *Recognition and Measurement in Financial Statements of Business Enterprises*, states that revenue should be recognized when realized or realizable and earned. Revenue from gift certificates is realized when the cash is received. It is earned when the certificates are redeemed or allowed to lapse. Thus, the criteria of being both realized and earned are satisfied when the certificates are redeemed or allowed to lapse.
   Answers (A), (B), and (C) are incorrect because the revenue from the certificates is not earned under these circumstances.

15. In June 1997, Northan Retailers sold refundable merchandise coupons. Northan received $10 for each coupon redeemable from July 1 to December 31, 1997 for merchandise with a retail price of $11. At June 30, 1997, how should Northan report these coupon transactions?

A. Unearned revenues at the merchandise's retail price.

B. Unearned revenues at the cash received amount.

C. Revenues at the merchandise's retail price.

D. Revenues at the cash received amount.

16. Regal Department Store sells gift certificates, redeemable for store merchandise, that expire 1 year after their issuance. Regal has the following information pertaining to its gift certificates sales and redemptions:

Unredeemed at 12/31/95	$ 75,000
1996 sales	250,000
1996 redemptions of prior-year sales	25,000
1996 redemptions of current-year sales	175,000

Regal's experience indicates that 10% of gift certificates sold will not be redeemed. In its December 31, 1996 balance sheet, what amount should Regal report as unearned revenue?

A. $125,000

B. $100,000

C. $75,000

D. $50,000

17. Dunn Trading Stamp Company records stamp service revenue and provides for the cost of redemptions in the year stamps are sold to licensees. Dunn's past experience indicates that only 80% of the stamps sold to licensees will be redeemed. Dunn's liability for stamp redemptions was $6,000,000 at December 31, 1995. Additional information for 1996 is as follows:

Stamp service revenue from stamps sold to licensees	$4,000,000
Cost of redemptions (stamps sold prior to 1/1/96)	2,750,000

If all the stamps sold in 1996 were presented for redemption in 1997, the redemption cost would be $2,250,000. What amount should Dunn report as a liability for stamp redemptions at December 31, 1996?

A. $7,800,000

B. $5,500,000

C. $5,050,000

D. $3,250,000

The correct answer is (B). *(CPA 1192 T-7)*

REQUIRED: The proper reporting of refundable merchandise coupons.

DISCUSSION: Revenue should not be recognized until it is realized or realizable and earned. Because the earning process is not complete until the coupons lapse or are redeemed, an unearned revenue (liability) account should be credited at the time of sale for the amount received.

Answer (A) is incorrect because the transaction is measured at the amount received, not the nominal retail price. Answers (C) and (D) are incorrect because revenue should not be recognized until it is realized or realizable and earned.

The correct answer is (D). *(CPA 1192 I-30)*

REQUIRED: The amount reported as unearned revenue at year-end.

DISCUSSION: Because the certificates expire after 1 year, all revenue from sales prior to 1996 has been earned. Hence, the unearned revenue balance for gift certificate sales at the end of 1996 relates solely to 1996 sales. Given 1996 sales of $250,000 and redemptions of $175,000, $75,000 of certificates are unredeemed at year-end. However, 10% of total certificates sold in 1996 (10% x $250,000 = $25,000) are not expected to be redeemed. Accordingly, unearned revenue is $50,000 ($75,000 – $25,000).

Answer (A) is incorrect because $125,000 is the sum of the beginning and ending balances. Answer (B) is incorrect because $100,000 assumes that none of the certificates reflected in the beginning balance have lapsed but that 10% of the certificates sold in 1996 are expected to lapse. Answer (C) is incorrect because $75,000 does not consider the 10% of certificates sold in 1996 that are estimated not to be redeemed.

The correct answer is (C). *(CPA 1190 I-28)*

REQUIRED: The reported liability for stamp redemptions at year-end.

DISCUSSION: The liability for stamp redemptions at the beginning of 1996 is given as $6,000,000. This liability would be increased in 1996 by $2,250,000 if all stamps sold in 1996 were presented for redemption. However, because only 80% are expected to be redeemed, the liability should be increased by $1,800,000 ($2,250,000 x 80%). The liability was decreased by the $2,750,000 attributable to the costs of redemptions. Thus, the liability for stamp redemptions at 12/31/96 is $5,050,000 ($6,000,000 + $1,800,000 – $2,750,000).

Answer (A) is incorrect because $7,800,000 omits the 1996 redemptions from the calculation. Answer (B) is incorrect because $5,500,000 assumes a 100% redemption rate. Answer (D) is incorrect because $3,250,000 omits the expected 1997 redemptions from the calculation.

18. Case Cereal Co. frequently distributes coupons to promote new products. On October 1, 1996, Case mailed 1,000,000 coupons for $.45 off each box of cereal purchased. Case expects 120,000 of these coupons to be redeemed before the December 31, 1996 expiration date. It takes 30 days from the redemption date for Case to receive the coupons from the retailers. Case reimburses the retailers an additional $.05 for each coupon redeemed. As of December 31, 1996, Case had paid retailers $25,000 related to these coupons and had 50,000 coupons on hand that had not been processed for payment. What amount should Case report as a liability for coupons in its December 31, 1996 balance sheet?

A. $35,000

B. $29,000

C. $25,000

D. $22,500

The correct answer is (A). *(CPA 1192 I-24)*
REQUIRED: The liability for coupons at year-end.
DISCUSSION: The company pays $.50 ($.45 + $.05) for the redemption of a coupon, and it expects 120,000 to be redeemed at a total cost of $60,000 (120,000 x $.50). Given that payments of $25,000 have been made, the liability at year-end must be $35,000 ($60,000 – $25,000). The cost associated with the unprocessed coupons on hand does not reduce the liability because payment for these coupons has not yet been made.

Answer (B) is incorrect because $29,000 ignores the additional $.05 per coupon paid to retailers. Answer (C) is incorrect because $25,000 is the cost of the coupons on hand that have not yet been processed for payment. Case expects to receive additional redeemed coupons for 30 days after the balance sheet date. Answer (D) is incorrect because $22,500 equals $.45 times 50,000 coupons.

19. In packages of its products, the Kent Food Company includes coupons that may be presented to grocers for discounts of certain products of Kent on or before a stated expiration date. The grocers are reimbursed when they send the coupons to Kent. In Kent's experience, 40% of such coupons are redeemed, and 1 month usually elapses between the date a grocer receives a coupon from a consumer and the date Kent receives it. During 1996, Kent issued two series of coupons as follows:

Issued on	Total Value	Consumer Expiration Date	Amount Disbursed as of 12/31/96
1/1/96	$100,000	6/30/96	$34,000
7/1/96	120,000	12/31/96	40,000

Kent's December 31, 1996 balance sheet should include a liability for unredeemed coupons of

A. $0

B. $8,000

C. $14,000

D. $48,000

The correct answer is (B). *(CPA 1188 I-25)*
REQUIRED: The year-end liability for unredeemed coupons.
DISCUSSION: Kent Food Company should report no liability for unredeemed coupons at December 31 with regard to the coupons issued on 1/1/96 because more than 1 month has elapsed since their expiration date. The total estimated liability for the coupons issued on 7/1/96 is equal to $48,000 (40% x $120,000 total face value of coupons issued) minus the $40,000 disbursed as of 12/31/96. Consequently, the liability is $8,000 ($48,000 – $40,000).

Answer (A) is incorrect because the amount disbursed was less than the total estimated liability. Answer (C) is incorrect because $14,000 assumes that less than 1 month has elapsed since the expiration date of the coupons issued on 1/1/96. Answer (D) is incorrect because $48,000 is the total estimated liability for the coupons issued on 7/1/96.

14.4 Warranties

20. A company sells a durable good to a customer on January 1, 1996, and the customer is automatically given a 1-year warranty. The customer also buys an extended warranty package, extending the coverage for an additional 2 years to the end of 1998. At the time of the original sale, the company expects warranty costs to be incurred evenly over the life of the warranty contracts. The customer has only one warranty claim during the 3-year period, and the claim occurs during 1997. The company will recognize revenue from the sale of the extended warranty

A. On January 1, 1996.

B. In years 1997 and 1998.

C. At the time of the claim in 1997.

D. December 31, 1998, when the warranty expires.

The correct answer is (B). *(CIA 1194 IV-24)*

REQUIRED: The recognition of revenue from the sale of an extended warranty.

DISCUSSION: Because warranty costs are expected to be incurred evenly over the life of the warranty contracts, the revenue should be recognized on the straight-line basis over the life of the extended warranty contract.

Answer (A) is incorrect because the recognition of revenue from the sale of the extended warranty is deferred until the extended warranty period begins. Answer (C) is incorrect because the revenue should be recognized evenly over the life of the contract. It is not related to the timing of the claims. Answer (D) is incorrect because revenue is recognized over the life of the warranty, not at expiration.

21. Vadis Co. sells appliances that include a 3-year warranty. Service calls under the warranty are performed by an independent mechanic under a contract with Vadis. Based on experience, warranty costs are estimated at $30 for each machine sold. When should Vadis recognize these warranty costs?

A. Evenly over the life of the warranty.

B. When the service calls are performed.

C. When payments are made to the mechanic.

D. When the machines are sold.

The correct answer is (D). *(CPA 1194 F-27)*

REQUIRED: The proper recording of warranty costs.

DISCUSSION: Under the accrual method, a provision for warranty costs is made when the related revenue is recognized. Revenue is recognized when the machines are sold, so warranty costs also should be recognized.

Answer (A) is incorrect because the accrual method matches the costs and the related revenues. Answer (B) is incorrect because, when the warranty costs can be reasonably estimated, the accrual method should be used. Recognizing the costs when the service calls are performed is the cash basis. Answer (C) is incorrect because recognizing costs when paid is the cash basis.

22. Product Engineering, Inc. sold 800,000 electronic can openers in 1996. Based on past experience, the company estimated that 10,000 of the 800,000 would prove to be defective and that 60% of these would be returned for replacement under the company's warranty. The cost to replace an electronic can opener is $6.00.

On January 1, 1996, the balance in the company's estimated liability for warranties account was $3,000. During 1996, 5,000 electronic can openers were replaced under the warranty. The estimated liability for warranties reported on December 31, 1996 should be

A. $6,000

B. $9,000

C. $36,000

D. $39,000

The correct answer is (B). *(O. Broome, Jr.)*

REQUIRED: The year-end estimated liability for warranties.

DISCUSSION: At the time of the sale of each electronic can opener, it is probable that a warranty liability has been incurred and its amount can be reasonably estimated. Consequently, a warranty expense should be recognized with a corresponding credit to an estimated liability for warranties account. As indicated below, the 1/1/96 balance in this account is $3,000. It was increased during 1996 by $36,000 (10,000 estimated defective can openers x 60% estimated replacement rate x $6 replacement fee). The account should be decreased by $30,000 (5,000 openers replaced x $6). Thus, the ending balance is $9,000.

Estimated Liability for Warranties

		$ 3,000	1/1/96
Replacements	$30,000	36,000	Warranty expense
		$ 9,000	12/31/96

Answer (A) is incorrect because $6,000 is the balance if you ignore the $3,000 balance already in the account. Answer (C) is incorrect because $36,000 is the estimated liability recorded when the can openers are sold. Answer (D) is incorrect because $39,000 is the balance in the estimated liability for warranties account before it is adjusted for the actual replacement costs incurred.

23. The selling price of a new company's units is $10,000 each. The buyers are provided with a 2-year warranty that is expected to cost the company $250 per unit in the year of the sale and $750 per unit in the year following the sale. The company sold 80 units in the first year of operation and 100 units in the second year. Actual payments for warranty claims were $10,000 and $65,000 in years one and two, respectively. The amount charged to warranty expense during the second year of operation would be

A. $25,000

B. $65,000

C. $85,000

D. $100,000

The correct answer is (D). *(CIA 596 IV-21)*
REQUIRED: The amount charged to warranty expense during the second year of operation.
DISCUSSION: Under the accrual method, the total estimated warranty costs are charged to operating expense in the year of sale. The total estimated warranty cost per unit is $1,000 ($250 + $750). In year two, 100 units were sold, so the warranty expense recognized is $100,000.
Answer (A) is incorrect because $25,000 is the expected amount of warranty claims for the first year of the warranty from second year sales. Answer (B) is incorrect because $65,000 is the actual amount of claims in the second year. Answer (C) is incorrect because $85,000 is the expected amount of warranty claims in the second year.

24. During 1995, Gum Co. introduced a new product carrying a 2-year warranty against defects. The estimated warranty costs related to dollar sales are 2% within 12 months following the sale and 4% in the second 12 months following the sale. Sales and actual warranty expenditures for the years ended December 31, 1995 and 1996 are as follows:

	Sales	Actual Warranty Expenditures
1995	$150,000	$2,250
1996	250,000	7,500
	$400,000	$9,750

What amount should Gum report as estimated warranty liability in its December 31, 1996 balance sheet?

A. $2,500

B. $3,250

C. $11,250

D. $14,250

The correct answer is (D). *(CPA 592 I-35)*
REQUIRED: The estimated warranty liability at the end of the second year.
DISCUSSION: Because this product is new, the beginning balance in the estimated warranty liability account at the beginning of 1995 is $0. For 1995, the estimated warranty costs related to dollar sales are 6% (2% + 4%) of sales, or $9,000 ($150,000 x 6%). For 1996, the estimated warranty costs are $15,000 ($250,000 x 6%). These amounts are charged to warranty expense and credited to the estimated warranty liability account. This liability account is debited for expenditures of $2,250 and $7,500 in 1995 and 1996, respectively. Hence, the estimated warranty liability at 12/31/96 is $14,250.

Estimated Warranty Liability			
		$ 0	1/1/95
1995 expenditures	$2,250	9,000	1995 expense
1996 expenditures	7,500	15,000	1996 expense
		$14,250	12/31/96

Answer (A) is incorrect because $2,500 is equal to 10% of 1996 sales. Answer (B) is incorrect because $3,250 is equal to 2% of 1995 sales plus 4% of 1996 sales less the $9,750 in actual expenses incurred. Answer (C) is incorrect because $11,250 is the sum of 1995's actual expenditures of $2,250 and the 1995 warranty expense of $9,000.

14.5 Product Financing Agreements

25. Zuber Corp. produced 1,000 units of Product X. It now sells these units for cash to Lewis Corp. and, in a related transaction, agrees to buy back the 1,000 units at a specified price at a future date. The price specified in the agreement is not subject to change based on future market fluctuations except for fluctuations resulting from finance and holding costs incurred by Lewis. In accounting for this situation, Zuber should

A. Record the sale in an ordinary manner and remove the inventory from the balance sheet.

B. Record the sale, remove the inventory from the balance sheet, and disclose the purchase commitment in the notes to the financial statements.

C. Continue to carry the inventory on the books and record a valuation account to be reported as a reduction to the inventory account on the balance sheet, rather than record a sale.

D. Record a liability and continue to carry the inventory on the books rather than record a sale.

The correct answer is (D). *(Publisher)*
REQUIRED: The proper accounting treatment of a sale of inventory coupled with a repurchase agreement.
DISCUSSION: The transaction is, in substance, a financing arrangement. In essence, the future reacquisition of the inventory is a return of collateral upon payment of a debt. Zuber should account for the transaction as if it were a financing arrangement, not record a sale. See SFAS 49, *Accounting for Product Financing Arrangements*.
Answers (A) and (B) are incorrect because each is appropriate for a sale. The Zuber-Lewis transactions are, in substance, a financing arrangement. Answer (C) is incorrect because the transaction must be accounted for by recording a liability and finance charges rather than by reducing inventory.

26. The Maxfield Corporation buys a product on behalf of the Pollock Corporation and, in a related transaction, the Pollock Corporation agrees to buy the product from Maxfield at a specified price at a specified date in the future. The Pollock Corporation should record an asset and a related obligation at the date that

A. The agreement is signed.

B. Maxfield acquires the product.

C. Maxfield ships the product to Pollock.

D. Pollock receives the product.

The correct answer is (B). *(Publisher)*
REQUIRED: The date on which a product financing arrangement should be recorded.
DISCUSSION: The transaction is essentially a financing arrangement because Pollock has acquired rights in the product without an immediate expenditure. Pollock should record the asset and the related liability when Maxfield acquires the product. Maxfield is acting for Pollock, and Pollock should treat the goods received by Maxfield as if Pollock itself had received them.
Answer (A) is incorrect because purchases are not ordinarily recorded until title to the goods passes.
Answers (C) and (D) are incorrect because Pollock should record the inventory and liability when Maxfield acquires the product, not later.

14.6 Refinancing of Short-Term Debt

27. At December 31, 1996, Cain, Inc. owed notes payable of $1,750,000, due on May 15, 1997. Cain expects to retire this debt with proceeds from the sale of 100,000 shares of its common stock. The stock was sold for $15 per share on March 10, 1997, prior to the issuance of the year-end financial statements. In Cain's December 31, 1996 balance sheet, what amount of the notes payable should be excluded from current liabilities?

A. $0

B. $250,000

C. $1,500,000

D. $1,750,000

The correct answer is (C). *(CPA 1191 I-21)*
REQUIRED: The amount of notes payable that should be excluded from current liabilities.
DISCUSSION: If an enterprise intends to refinance short-term obligations on a long-term basis and demonstrates an ability to consummate the refinancing, the obligation should be excluded from current liabilities and reclassified as noncurrent. The ability to consummate the refinancing may be demonstrated by a post-balance-sheet-date issuance of long-term obligations or equity securities. Thus, $1,500,000 (100,000 shares x $15) of the notes payable should be excluded from current liabilities and reclassified as noncurrent.
Answer (A) is incorrect because $1,500,000 should be excluded from current liabilities. Answer (B) is incorrect because $250,000 is the amount that should be classified as a current liability. Answer (D) is incorrect because $1,750,000 is the full amount of notes payable, which should be allocated between current and noncurrent liabilities.

28. Ames, Inc. has $1,000,000 of notes payable due June 15, 1997. At the financial statement date of December 31, 1996, Ames signed an agreement to borrow up to $1,000,000 to refinance the notes payable on a long-term basis. The financing agreement called for borrowings not to exceed 80% of the value of the collateral Ames was providing. At the date of issue of the December 31, 1996 financial statements, the value of the collateral was $1,200,000 and was not expected to fall below this amount during 1997. In its December 31, 1996 balance sheet, Ames should classify the notes payable as

	Short-term Obligations	Long-term Obligations
A.	$0	$1,000,000
B.	$40,000	$960,000
C.	$200,000	$800,000
D.	$1,000,000	$0

The correct answer is (B). *(CPA 591 I-35)*
REQUIRED: The proper classification of notes payable subject to a refinancing agreement.
DISCUSSION: The portion of debt scheduled to mature in the following fiscal year ordinarily should be classified as a current liability. However, if an enterprise intends to refinance short-term obligations on a long-term basis and demonstrates an ability to consummate the refinancing, the obligation should be excluded from current liabilities and classified as noncurrent. Ames has signed an agreement to borrow up to $1,000,000 to refinance the notes payable on a long-term basis, but the borrowings may not exceed 80% of the value of the collateral. Consequently, Ames has demonstrated an ability to refinance $960,000 ($1,200,000 collateral x 80% ceiling) of the notes payable. This amount should be classified as a long-term obligation. The remaining $40,000 ($1,000,000 – $960,000) should be reported as a short-term obligation.
Answer (A) is incorrect because Ames has not demonstrated an ability to refinance $40,000 of the notes payable. Answers (C) and (D) are incorrect because Ames has demonstrated an ability to refinance $960,000 of the notes payable.

29. Included in Lee Corp.'s liability account balances at December 31, 1996 were the following:

14% note payable issued October 1,
1996, maturing September 30, 1997 $125,000

16% note payable issued April 1, 1994,
   payable in six equal annual installments of $50,000 beginning
   April 1, 1995   200,000

Lee's December 31, 1996 financial statements were issued on March 31, 1997. On January 15, 1997, the entire $200,000 balance of the 16% note was refinanced by issuance of a long-term obligation payable in a lump sum. In addition, on March 10, 1997, Lee consummated a noncancelable agreement with the lender to refinance the 14%, $125,000 note on a long-term basis, on readily determinable terms that have not yet been implemented. Both parties are financially capable of honoring the agreement, and there have been no violations of the agreement's provisions. On the December 31, 1996 balance sheet, the amount of the notes payable that Lee should classify as short-term obligations is

   A. $175,000

   B. $125,000

   C. $50,000

   D. $0

The correct answer is (D). *(CPA 1190 I-11)*

REQUIRED: The amount that should be classified as short-term obligations.

DISCUSSION: If an enterprise intends to refinance short-term obligations on a long-term basis and demonstrates an ability to consummate the refinancing, the obligation should be excluded from current liabilities and reclassified as noncurrent. The ability to consummate the refinancing may be demonstrated by a post-balance-sheet-date issuance of long-term obligations or equity securities. Thus, the 16% note payable should be classified as noncurrent. The ability to refinance may also be shown by entering into a financing agreement that meets the following criteria: (1) The agreement does not expire within the longer of 1 year or the operating cycle; (2) it is noncancelable by the lender; (3) no violation of the agreement exists at the balance sheet date; and (4) the lender is financially capable of honoring the agreement. For this reason, the 14% note payable is also excluded from short-term obligations. The amount of the notes payable classified as short-term is therefore $0.

Answer (A) is incorrect because $175,000 is the sum of the installment payment of $50,000 due 4/1/96 and the $125,000 of the 14% note. Answer (B) is incorrect because $125,000 is the amount of the 14% note. Answer (C) is incorrect because $50,000 is the installment payment on the 16% note due 4/1/96.

30. On December 31, 1996, Largo, Inc. had a $750,000 note payable outstanding, due July 31, 1997. Largo borrowed the money to finance con-struction of a new plant. Largo planned to refinance the note by issuing long-term bonds. Because Largo temporarily had excess cash, it prepaid $250,000 of the note on January 12, 1997. In February 1997, Largo completed a $1,500,000 bond offering. Largo will use the bond offering proceeds to repay the note payable at its maturity and to pay construction costs during 1997. On March 3, 1997, Largo issued its 1996 financial statements. What amount of the note payable should Largo include in the current liabilities section of its December 31, 1996 balance sheet?

   A. $750,000

   B. $500,000

   C. $250,000

   D. $0

The correct answer is (C). *(CPA 593 I-2)*

REQUIRED: The amount that should be classified as short-term obligations.

DISCUSSION: The portion of debt scheduled to mature in the following fiscal year ordinarily should be classified as a current liability. However, if an enterprise intends to refinance short-term obligations on a long-term basis and demonstrates an ability to consummate the refinancing, the obligation should be excluded from current liabilities and classified as noncurrent. One method of demonstrating the ability to refinance is to issue long-term obligations or equity securities after the balance sheet date but before the financial statements are issued. Largo demonstrated an intention to refinance $500,000 of the note payable. Thus, the portion prepaid ($250,000) is a current liability, and the remaining $500,000 should be classified as noncurrent.

Answer (A) is incorrect because $750,000 includes the $500,000 that was refinanced. Answer (B) is incorrect because $500,000 is the amount that should be reclassified as noncurrent. Answer (D) is incorrect because $250,000 should be classified as a current liability.

14.7 Compensated Absences

31. At December 31, 1996, Taos Co. estimates that its employees have earned vacation pay of $100,000. Employees will receive their vacation pay in 1997. Should Taos accrue a liability at December 31, 1996 if the rights to this compensation accumulated over time or if the rights are vested?

	Accumulated	Vested
A.	Yes	No
B.	No	No
C.	Yes	Yes
D.	No	Yes

The correct answer is (C). *(CPA 1192 T-25)*
REQUIRED: The effect of accumulation and vesting on accrual of a liability for vacation pay.
DISCUSSION: SFAS 43, *Accounting for Compensated Absences*, requires an accrual for compensated services when the compensation relates to services previously provided, the benefits either vest or accumulate, and payment is both probable and reasonably estimable. The single exception is for sick pay benefits, which must be accrued only if the rights vest.
Answer (A) is incorrect because vesting meets one of the criteria for accrual of a liability. Answer (B) is incorrect because either vesting or accumulation meets one of the criteria for accrual of a liability. Answer (D) is incorrect because accumulation meets one of the criteria for accrual of a liability.

32. If the payment of employees' compensation for future absences is probable, the amount can be reasonably estimated, and the obligation relates to rights that vest, the compensation should be

A. Recognized when paid.

B. Accrued if attributable to employees' services whether or not already rendered.

C. Accrued if attributable to employees' services already rendered.

D. Accrued if attributable to employees' services not already rendered.

The correct answer is (C). *(CPA 1193 T-28)*
REQUIRED: The additional criterion to be met to accrue an expense for compensated absences.
DISCUSSION: SFAS 43 requires an accrual when four criteria are met: (1) The payment of compensation is probable, (2) the amount can be reasonably estimated, (3) the benefits either vest or accumulate, and (4) the compensation relates to employees' services that have already been rendered.
Answer (A) is incorrect because the cash basis is not appropriate for recognizing expenses related to compensated absences. Answers (B) and (D) are incorrect because the services must have been previously rendered.

33. SFAS 43, *Accounting for Compensated Absences*, establishes the requirements for employers to accrue a liability for employees' compensation for future absences. The item that would require accrual under the provisions of this statement is

A. Long-term disability pay.

B. Severance pay.

C. Postretirement benefits.

D. Vacation pay based on past service.

The correct answer is (D). *(CMA 1291 2-3)*
REQUIRED: The item that requires accrual under the provisions of SFAS 43.
DISCUSSION: SFAS 43 describes the accounting for compensated absences such as sick pay benefits, holidays, and vacations. The criteria for accrual are that the obligation arose from past services, the employees' rights vest or accumulate, payment is probable, and an amount can be reasonably estimated.
Answer (A) is incorrect because SFAS 43 does not apply to long-term disability pay, group insurance, or other long-term fringe benefits. Answer (B) is incorrect because SFAS 43 does not apply to severance or termination pay. Answer (C) is incorrect because SFAS 43 does not apply to postretirement benefits and deferred compensation.

34. On January 1, 1995, Baker Co. decided to grant its employees 10 vacation days and 5 sick days each year. Vacation days, but not sick days, may be carried over to the next year. However, sick pay benefits are vested. Each employee received payment for an average of 3 sick days in 1995. During 1995, each of Baker's six employees earned $100 per day and earned 10 vacation days. These vacation days were taken during 1996. What amount should Baker report for accrued compensated absence expense for the year ended December 31, 1995?

   A. $0

   B. $6,000

   C. $7,200

   D. $9,000

The correct answer is (C). *(CPA 1192 I-58)*
   REQUIRED: The accrued compensated absence expense.
   DISCUSSION: SFAS 43 requires an accrual for compensated services when the compensation relates to services previously provided, the benefits either vest or accumulate, and payment is both probable and reasonably estimable. The single exception is for sick pay benefits, which must be accrued only if the rights vest. Accordingly, Baker should report accrued compensated absence expense of $7,200 [(10 days x 6 employees x $100) vacation pay + (2 days x 6 employees x $100) sick pay].
   Answer (A) is incorrect because Baker must accrue accumulated vacation pay and vested sick pay benefits. Answer (B) is incorrect because $6,000 omits sick pay. Answer (D) is incorrect because $9,000 includes 5 days of sick pay per employee.

35. North Corp. has an employee benefit plan for compensated absences that gives employees 10 paid vacation days and 10 paid sick days. Both vacation and sick days can be carried over indefinitely. Employees can elect to receive payment in lieu of vacation days; however, no payment is given for sick days not taken. At December 31, 1996, North's unadjusted balance of liability for compensated absences was $21,000. North estimated that there were 150 vacation days and 75 sick days available at December 31, 1996. North's employees earn an average of $100 per day. In its December 31, 1996 balance sheet, what amount of liability for compensated absences is North required to report?

   A. $36,000

   B. $22,500

   C. $21,000

   D. $15,000

The correct answer is (D). *(CPA 593 I-30)*
   REQUIRED: The amount of liability for compensated absences.
   DISCUSSION: SFAS 43 requires accrual of vacation benefits earned but not yet taken. It does not require a liability to be accrued for future sick pay unless the rights are vested. Therefore, the estimated vacation days available at December 31, 1996 require a liability of $15,000 (150 days x $100).
   Answer (A) is incorrect because $36,000 is the sum of the $15,000 liability for compensated absences and the unadjusted balance of liability for compensated absences. Answer (B) is incorrect because the sick days should not be included in the liability for compensated absences. Answer (C) is incorrect because $21,000 is the unadjusted balance of liability for compensated absences.

14.8 Contingencies

36. According to SFAS 5, *Accounting for Contingencies*, a loss contingency should be accrued on a company's records only if it is

   A. Reasonably possible that a liability has been incurred and the amount of the loss is known.

   B. Probable that a liability has been incurred and the amount of the loss is unknown.

   C. Probable that a liability has been incurred and the amount of the loss can be reasonably estimated.

   D. Remotely probable that a liability has been incurred but the amount of the loss can be reasonably estimated.

The correct answer is (C). *(CMA 692 2-20)*
   REQUIRED: The circumstance under which a loss contingency should be accrued.
   DISCUSSION: Loss contingencies should be accrued when information available prior to issuance of financial statements indicates that it is probable that an asset has been impaired or a liability has been incurred, and the amount of loss can be reasonably estimated. Probable is defined as a condition in which future events are likely to occur.
   Answer (A) is incorrect because an event is reasonably possible if the chance of occurrence is more than remote but less than probable. Accrual requires that the event be probable. Answer (B) is incorrect because the amount of the loss must be capable of reasonable estimation. Answer (D) is incorrect because an event is remote if the chance of occurrence is slight.

37. At December 31, 1996, Date Co. awaits judgment on a lawsuit for a competitor's infringement of Date's patent. Legal counsel believes it is probable that Date will win the suit and indicated the most likely award together with a range of possible awards. How should the lawsuit be reported in Date's 1996 financial statements?

A. In note disclosure only.

B. By accrual for the most likely award.

C. By accrual for the lowest amount of the range of possible awards.

D. Neither in note disclosure nor by accrual.

The correct answer is (A). *(CPA 1193 T-21)*
REQUIRED: The proper treatment of a gain contingency.
DISCUSSION: SFAS 5 provides for recognition of a loss but not gain contingencies if certain criteria are met. Gain contingencies should be disclosed in a note but are not recognized until realized.

Answers (B) and (C) are incorrect because only losses may be accrued when the loss is probable and reasonably estimated. Answer (D) is incorrect because the gain contingency should be disclosed.

38. In 1995, a contract dispute between Dollis Co. and Brooks Co. was submitted to binding arbitration. In 1995, each party's attorney indicated privately that the probable award in Dollis' favor could be reasonably estimated. In 1996, the arbitrator decided in favor of Dollis. When should Dollis and Brooks recognize their respective gain and loss?

	Dollis' Gain	Brooks' Loss
A.	1995	1995
B.	1995	1996
C.	1996	1995
D.	1996	1996

The correct answer is (C). *(CPA 593 T-29)*
REQUIRED: The proper accounting for a contingent gain or loss that is probable and capable of reasonable estimation.
DISCUSSION: SFAS 5 requires that a contingent loss be accrued when two conditions are met: It is probable that at a balance sheet date an asset is overstated or a liability has been incurred, and the amount of the loss can be reasonably estimated. In accordance with SFAS 5, gain contingencies should not be recognized until they are realized. A gain contingency should be disclosed, but care should be taken to avoid misleading implications as to the likelihood of realization. Because the award in favor of Dollis is probable and can be reasonably estimated, a loss should be recognized in 1995 by Brooks. However, Dollis should not recognize the gain until 1996.

Answers (A), (B), and (D) are incorrect because Dollis should recognize a gain in 1996, and Brooks should recognize a loss in 1995.

39. A manufacturer of household appliances may incur a loss due to the discovery of a defect in one of its products. The occurrence of the loss is reasonably possible, and the resulting costs can be reasonably estimated. This possible loss should be

	Accrued	Disclosed in Footnotes
A.	Yes	No
B.	Yes	Yes
C.	No	Yes
D.	No	No

The correct answer is (C). *(CPA 591 T-16)*
REQUIRED: The proper accounting for a contingent loss that is reasonably possible and reasonably estimable.
DISCUSSION: SFAS 5 requires that a contingent loss be accrued when two conditions are met: It is probable that at a balance sheet date an asset is overstated or a liability has been incurred, and the amount of the loss can be reasonably estimated. If both conditions are not met, but the probability of the loss is at least reasonably possible, the amount of the loss must be disclosed. This loss is reasonably possible and reasonably estimable, and it therefore should be disclosed but not accrued as a liability. The financial statements should disclose the nature of the loss contingency and the amount or range of the possible loss. If an estimate cannot be made, the footnote should so state.

Answers (A), (B), and (D) are incorrect because the contingent loss should be disclosed but not accrued.

40. A company is currently being sued by a customer. A reasonable estimate can be made of the costs that would result from a ruling unfavorable to the company, and the amount involved is material. The company's managers, lawyers, and auditors agree that there is only a remote likelihood of an unfavorable ruling. This contingency

- A. Should be disclosed in a footnote.

- B. Should be disclosed as a parenthetical comment in the balance sheet.

- C. Need not be disclosed.

- D. Should be disclosed by an appropriation of retained earnings.

The correct answer is (C). *(Publisher)*
REQUIRED: The proper treatment of a loss contingency that is reasonably estimable but remote in probability.
DISCUSSION: Losses arising from litigation should be accrued if both probable and reasonably estimable, and should be disclosed if reasonably possible. Because the likelihood of this loss from litigation is remote, the contingent loss is required to be neither accrued nor disclosed.
Answers (A), (B), and (D) are incorrect because the contingent loss is required to be neither accrued nor disclosed.

41. During 1996, Leader Corp. sued Cape Co. for patent infringement. On December 31, 1996, Leader was awarded a $500,000 favorable judgment in the suit. On that date, Cape offered to settle out of court for $300,000 and not appeal the judgment. In February 1997, after the issuance of its 1996 financial statements, Leader agreed to the out-of-court settlement and received a certified check for $300,000. In its 1996 financial statements, how should Leader have reported these events?

- A. As a gain of $300,000.

- B. As a receivable and deferred credit of $300,000.

- C. As a disclosure in the notes to the financial statements only.

- D. It should not be reported in the financial statements.

The correct answer is (C). *(CPA 593 II-11)*
REQUIRED: The proper accounting for a favorable judgment subject to a settlement offer at the balance sheet date.
DISCUSSION: SFAS 5 requires that gain contingencies not be recognized until they are realized. Because the settlement did not occur until after the balance sheet date, and appeal was still possible, Leader should not record any revenue from the lawsuit in the 1996 income statement. This gain contingency should be disclosed; however, care should be taken to avoid misleading implications as to the likelihood of realization.
Answers (A) and (B) are incorrect because gain contingencies are not reflected in the accounts until realized. Answer (D) is incorrect because the contingency should be disclosed.

42. When reporting contingencies

- A. Guarantees of others' indebtedness are reported as a loss contingency only if the loss is considered imminent or highly probable.

- B. Disclosure of a loss contingency is to be made if there is a remote possibility that the loss has been incurred.

- C. Disclosure of a loss contingency must include a dollar estimate of the loss.

- D. A loss that is probable but not estimable must be disclosed with a notation that the amount of the loss cannot be estimated.

The correct answer is (D). *(CMA 693 2-14)*
REQUIRED: The true statement about reporting contingencies.
DISCUSSION: SFAS 5 prescribes the accounting for contingencies. Contingencies are divided into three categories: probable (likely to occur), reasonably possible, and remote. When contingent losses are probable and the amount can be reasonably estimated, the amount of the loss should be charged against income. If the amount cannot be reasonably estimated but the loss is at least reasonably possible, full disclosure should be made, including a statement that an estimate cannot be made.
Answer (A) is incorrect because SFAS 5 requires that a guarantee of another's indebtedness is to be disclosed even if the possibility of loss is remote. Answer (B) is incorrect because remote contingencies ordinarily need not be disclosed. Answer (C) is incorrect because disclosure need not include an amount when that amount cannot be reasonably estimated.

43. Management can estimate the amount of loss that will occur if a foreign government expropriates some company assets. If expropriation is reasonably possible, a loss contingency should be

A. Disclosed but not accrued as a liability.

B. Disclosed and accrued as a liability.

C. Accrued as a liability but not disclosed.

D. Neither accrued as a liability nor disclosed.

The correct answer is (A). *(CPA 1194 F-26)*
REQUIRED: The reporting of a loss contingency that is reasonably possible.
DISCUSSION: A contingent loss that is reasonably possible but not probable is disclosed but not accrued. The disclosure should describe the nature of the contingency and provide an estimate of the loss or range of loss or state that an estimate cannot be made (SFAS 5).
Answer (B) is incorrect because a contingent loss is accrued only if it is probable and reasonably estimable. Answers (C) and (D) are incorrect because, if a loss is reasonably possible, it is disclosed but not accrued.

44. On November 10, 1996, a Garry Corp. truck was in an accident with an auto driven by Dacey. On January 10, 1997, Garry received notice of a lawsuit seeking $800,000 in damages for personal injuries suffered by Dacey. Garry Corp.'s counsel believes it is reasonably possible that Dacey will be awarded an estimated amount in the range between $250,000 and $500,000 and that $400,000 is a better estimate of potential liability than any other amount. Garry's accounting year ends on December 31, and the 1996 financial statements were issued on March 6, 1997. What amount of loss should Garry accrue at December 31, 1996?

A. $0

B. $250,000

C. $400,000

D. $500,000

The correct answer is (A). *(CPA 1189 I-32)*
REQUIRED: The proper accounting for a contingent loss that is reasonably possible and can be estimated within a range.
DISCUSSION: SFAS 5 requires that a contingent loss be accrued when it is probable that, at a balance sheet date, an asset is overstated or a liability has been incurred and the amount of the loss can be reasonably estimated. If both conditions are not met but the probability of the loss is at least reasonably possible, the amount of the loss must be disclosed. This loss is reasonably possible and reasonably estimable. Hence, it should be disclosed but not accrued.
Answer (B) is incorrect because $250,000 is the amount that would be disclosed in a note if a better estimate did not exist. Answer (C) is incorrect because $400,000 is the amount that would be disclosed since it is the best estimate. It would not be accrued. Answer (D) is incorrect because $500,000 is the maximum amount of loss in the range, which would not be the amount used in a footnote disclosure.

45. On February 5, 1997, an employee filed a $2,000,000 lawsuit against Steel Co. for damages suffered when one of Steel's plants exploded on December 29, 1996. Steel's legal counsel expects the company will lose the lawsuit and estimates the loss to be between $500,000 and $1,000,000. The employee has offered to settle the lawsuit out of court for $900,000, but Steel will not agree to the settlement. In its December 31, 1996 balance sheet, what amount should Steel report as liability from lawsuit?

A. $2,000,000

B. $1,000,000

C. $900,000

D. $500,000

The correct answer is (D). *(CPA 593 I-33)*
REQUIRED: The contingent loss that should be accrued when a range of estimates is provided.
DISCUSSION: Because the loss is probable and can be reasonably estimated, it should be accrued if the amount is material. According to FASB Interpretation No. 14, *Reasonable Estimation of the Amount of a Loss*, if the estimate is stated within a given range, and no amount within that range appears to be a better estimate than any other, the minimum of the range should be accrued. Thus, Steel should report a $500,000 contingent liability.
Answers (A) and (B) are incorrect because the minimum of the range should be accrued. Answer (C) is incorrect because $900,000 is the proposed settlement amount.

46. In May 1993, Caso Co. filed suit against Wayne, Inc. seeking $1,900,000 damages for patent infringement. A court verdict in November 1996 awarded Caso $1,500,000 in damages, but Wayne's appeal is not expected to be decided before 1998. Caso's counsel believes it is probable that Caso will be successful against Wayne for an estimated amount in the range between $800,000 and $1,100,000, with $1,000,000 considered the most likely amount. What amount should Caso record as income from the lawsuit in the year ended December 31, 1996?

A. $0

B. $800,000

C. $1,000,000

D. $1,500,000

The correct answer is (A). *(CPA 593 II-7)*
REQUIRED: The amount of income recorded from the lawsuit.
DISCUSSION: SFAS 5 requires that gain contingencies not be recognized until they are realized. Because the appeal is not expected to be decided before 1998, Caso should not record any revenue from the lawsuit in the 1996 income statement. This gain contingency should be disclosed; however, care should be taken to avoid misleading implications as to the likelihood of realization.
Answers (B), (C), and (D) are incorrect because gains should not be recognized until they are realized.

47. Invern, Inc. has a self-insurance plan. Each year, retained earnings is appropriated for contingencies in an amount equal to insurance premiums saved minus recognized losses from lawsuits and other claims. As a result of a 1996 accident, Invern is a defendant in a lawsuit in which it will probably have to pay damages of $190,000. What are the effects of this lawsuit's probable outcome on Invern's 1996 financial statements?

A. An increase in expenses and no effect on liabilities.

B. An increase in both expenses and liabilities.

C. No effect on expenses and an increase in liabilities.

D. No effect on either expenses or liabilities.

The correct answer is (B). *(CPA 1192 T-17)*
REQUIRED: The effect on the financial statements of litigation with a probable unfavorable outcome.
DISCUSSION: A loss contingency is an existing condition, situation, or set of circumstances involving uncertainty as to the impairment of an asset's value or the incurrence of a liability as of the balance sheet date. Resolution of the uncertainty depends on the occurrence or nonoccurrence of one or more future events. A loss should be debited and either an asset valuation allowance or a liability credited when the loss contingency is both probable and reasonably estimable. Thus, the company should accrue a loss and a liability. Appropriations of retained earnings have no effect on these accounting treatments.
Answers (A), (C), and (D) are incorrect because the company should accrue a loss and a liability.

48. During 1995, Manfred Corp. guaranteed a supplier's $500,000 loan from a bank. On October 1, 1996, Manfred was notified that the supplier had defaulted on the loan and filed for bankruptcy protection. Counsel believes Manfred will probably have to pay between $250,000 and $450,000 under its guarantee. As a result of the supplier's bankruptcy, Manfred entered into a contract in December 1996 to retool its machines so that Manfred could accept parts from other suppliers. Retooling costs are estimated to be $300,000. What amount should Manfred report as a liability in its December 31, 1996 balance sheet?

A. $250,000

B. $450,000

C. $550,000

D. $750,000

The correct answer is (A). *(CPA 1192 I-31)*
REQUIRED: The amount reported as a liability.
DISCUSSION: SFAS 5 requires that a contingent loss be accrued when two conditions are met: It is probable that at a balance sheet date an asset is overstated or a liability has been incurred, and the amount of the loss can be reasonably estimated. According to FASB Interpretation No. 14, *Reasonable Estimation of the Amount of a Loss*, if the estimate is stated within a given range, and no amount within that range appears to be a better estimate than any other, the minimum of the range should be accrued. Hence, the minimum amount ($250,000) of the probable payment under the guarantee should be accrued as a liability. The retooling costs will be charged to the equipment account when incurred because they significantly improve the future service of the machines.
Answer (B) is incorrect because $450,000 is the maximum amount of the estimated range of loss. Answer (C) is incorrect because $550,000 includes the retooling costs. Answer (D) is incorrect because $750,000 equals the retooling costs plus the maximum amount of the estimated range of loss.

49. In January 1996, an explosion occurred at Sims Co.'s plant, causing damage to area properties. By March 10, 1996, no claims had yet been asserted against Sims. However, Sims' management and legal counsel concluded that it was reasonably possible that Sims would be held responsible for negligence and that $3,000,000 would be a reasonable estimate of the damages. Sims' $5,000,000 comprehensive public liability policy contains a $300,000 deductible clause. In Sims' December 31, 1995 financial statements, for which the auditor's field work was completed in April 1996, how should this casualty be reported?

A. As a footnote disclosing a possible liability of $3,000,000.

B. As an accrued liability of $300,000.

C. As a footnote disclosing a possible liability of $300,000.

D. No footnote disclosure or accrual is required for 1995 because the event occurred in 1996.

The correct answer is (C). *(CPA 592 I-36)*
REQUIRED: The proper accounting for a reasonably possible contingent loss covered under a liability policy.
DISCUSSION: A loss contingency involving an unasserted claim should be disclosed if it is considered probable that the claim will be asserted and at least reasonably possible that an unfavorable outcome will result. The amount of the loss to be disclosed equals the amount of the company's potential liability. The comprehensive public liability policy has a $300,000 deductible clause, and the policy is sufficient to cover the reasonable estimate of the liability. The company should therefore disclose in a footnote the possible loss of $300,000.
Answer (A) is incorrect because the possible loss to the company is limited to the $300,000 deductible. Answer (B) is incorrect because a reasonably possible loss should not be accrued. Answer (D) is incorrect because footnote disclosure is required to prevent the financial statements from being misleading even though no asset was impaired and no liability was incurred at the balance sheet date.

50. On December 20, an uninsured property damage loss was caused by a company car's being driven on company business by a company salesman. The company did not become aware of the loss until January 25, but the amount of the loss was reasonably estimable before the financial statements were issued. The company's December 31 financial statements should report an estimated loss as

A. A disclosure but not an accrual.

B. An accrual.

C. Neither an accrual nor a disclosure.

D. An appropriation of retained earnings.

The correct answer is (B). *(CPA 1183 T-18)*
REQUIRED: The manner of disclosure of a loss contingency.
DISCUSSION: A loss contingency is an existing condition, situation, or set of circumstances involving uncertainty as to the impairment of an asset's value or the incurrence of a liability as of the balance sheet date. Resolution of the uncertainty depends on the occurrence or nonoccurrence of one or more future events. A loss should be debited and either an asset valuation allowance or a liability credited when the loss contingency is both probable and reasonably estimable. The loss should be accrued even though the company was not aware of the contingency at the balance sheet date.
Answer (A) is incorrect because disclosure alone would suffice only if the loss had occurred after December 31. Answer (C) is incorrect because a loss that is both probable and reasonably estimable must always be disclosed. Accrual depends on the timing of the loss. Answer (D) is incorrect because the loss must be charged to income.

51. During January 1996, Haze Corp. won a litigation award for $15,000 that was tripled to $45,000 to include punitive damages. The defendant, who is financially stable, has appealed only the $30,000 punitive damages. Haze was awarded $50,000 in an unrelated suit it filed, which is being appealed by the defendant. Counsel is unable to estimate the outcome of these appeals. In its 1996 financial statements, Haze should report what amount of pretax gain?

A. $15,000

B. $45,000

C. $50,000

D. $95,000

The correct answer is (A). *(CPA 1192 II-53)*
REQUIRED: The amount of pretax gain from litigation.
DISCUSSION: In accordance with SFAS 5, gain contingencies should not be recognized until they are realized. A gain contingency should be disclosed, but care should be taken to avoid misleading implications as to the likelihood of realization. Consequently, the only litigation award to be recognized in income in 1996 is the $15,000 amount that has not been appealed. The other awards have not been realized because they have been appealed.
Answer (B) is incorrect because $45,000 includes the punitive damages that have been appealed. Answer (C) is incorrect because $50,000 is the amount of the award in the unrelated suit that has been appealed. Answer (D) is incorrect because $95,000 includes the punitive damages and the amount of the award in the unrelated suit. Both have been appealed.

CHAPTER FIFTEEN
LONG-TERM LIABILITIES

This chapter overlaps with Chapter 14, Current Liabilities and Contingencies, and Chapter 13, Investments in Debt and Equity Securities. For example, the definitions of bond types are also covered in Chapter 13, and the reclassification of short-term debt expected to be refinanced as long-term debt is treated in Chapter 14. The effective-interest method is mentioned frequently in connection with long-term liabilities. The term is used interchangeably with interest method, yield method, and compound interest method.

15.1 Bonds

1. The market price of a bond issued at a discount is the present value of its principal amount at the market (effective) rate of interest

A. Minus the present value of all future interest payments at the market (effective) rate of interest.

B. Minus the present value of all future interest payments at the rate of interest stated on the bond.

C. Plus the present value of all future interest payments at the market (effective) rate of interest.

D. Plus the present value of all future interest payments at the rate of interest stated on the bond.

The correct answer is (C). *(CPA 1191 T-35)*

REQUIRED: The market price of a bond issued at a discount.

DISCUSSION: The cash flows associated with a bond are the amount due at the end of the life of the bond (its face value) and the periodic payments. These cash flows must be allocated between principal and interest so that the interest reflects the prevailing market rate. Allocation is based on the present-value method. The sum of the present value of the amount due at the end of the bond's term plus the present value of the periodic interest payments, each discounted at the prevailing market rate, is the market value. The difference between the cash flows and the market value is interest. This difference should then be allocated to the interest periods during the life of the bond so that it is recognized at a constant rate (the interest method). This valuation method is applicable whether the bond is issued at a discount, a premium, or face value.

Answers (A), (B), and (D) are incorrect because the market price is the sum of the present values of the principal and interest payments discounted at the market rate.

2. Blue Corp.'s December 31, 1996 balance sheet contained the following items in the long-term liabilities section:

9¾% registered debentures, callable in 2007, due in 2012 $700,000

9½% collateral trust bonds, convertible into common stock beginning in 2005, due in 2015   600,000

10% subordinated debentures ($30,000 maturing annually beginning in 2002)   300,000

What is the total amount of Blue's term bonds?

  A. $600,000

  B. $700,000

  C. $1,000,000

  D. $1,300,000

The correct answer is (D). *(CPA 1192 I-39)*

REQUIRED: The total amount of term bonds.

DISCUSSION: Term bonds mature on a single date. Hence, the registered bonds and the collateral trust bonds are term bonds, a total of $1,300,000 ($700,000 + $600,000).

Answer (A) is incorrect because the registered bonds are also term bonds. Answer (B) is incorrect because the collateral trust bonds are also term bonds. Answer (C) is incorrect because the collateral trust bonds, not the subordinated debentures, are term bonds.

3. Hancock Co.'s December 31, 1996 balance sheet contained the following items in the long-term liabilities section:

Unsecured

9.375% registered bonds ($25,000 maturing annually beginning in 2000) $275,000

11.5% convertible bonds, callable beginning in 2005, due 2016   125,000

Secured

9.875% guaranty security bonds, due 2016 $250,000

10.0% commodity-backed bonds ($50,000 maturing annually beginning in 2001)   200,000

What are the total amounts of serial bonds and debenture bonds?

	Serial Bonds	Debenture Bonds
A.	$475,000	$400,000
B.	$475,000	$125,000
C.	$450,000	$400,000
D.	$200,000	$650,000

The correct answer is (A). *(CPA 591 I-47)*

REQUIRED: The total amounts of serial bonds and debenture bonds.

DISCUSSION: Serial bonds mature in installments at various dates. Debentures are unsecured bonds. The commodity-backed bonds and the registered bonds are serial bonds. They total $475,000 ($275,000 + $200,000). The registered bonds and the convertible bonds are debentures. They total $400,000 ($275,000 + $125,000).

Answer (B) is incorrect because the registered bonds are also debentures. Answer (C) is incorrect because the registered bonds, not the guaranty security bonds, are serial bonds. Answer (D) is incorrect because the registered bonds are serial bonds, and the guaranty security bonds are not debentures.

4. A bond issued on June 1, 1996 has interest payment dates of April 1 and October 1. Bond interest expense for the year ended December 31, 1996 is for a period of

  A. 7 months.

  B. 6 months.

  C. 4 months.

  D. 3 months.

The correct answer is (A). *(CPA 592 T-22)*

REQUIRED: The period for which interest is paid when a bond is issued between payment dates.

DISCUSSION: Interest expense should be recorded on a systematic and rational basis. The basis used is the passage of time. Because the period from June 1 to December 31 includes 7 months, 7 months of interest expense should be recorded for the year of issuance. The determination of interest expense is not dependent on the interest payment dates.

Answers (B), (C), and (D) are incorrect because the length of time outstanding determines the interest expense.

5. Unamortized debt discount should be reported on the balance sheet of the issuer as a

A. Direct deduction from the face amount of the debt.

B. Direct deduction from the present value of the debt.

C. Deferred charge.

D. Part of the issue costs.

The correct answer is (A). *(CPA 1173 T-7)*
REQUIRED: The issuer's balance sheet presentation of unamortized discount.
DISCUSSION: APB 21, *Interest on Receivables and Payables*, requires that bond discount appear as a direct deduction from the face amount of the bond payable to report the effective liability for the bonds. Hence, the bond liability is shown net of unamortized discount.
Answer (B) is incorrect because the face amount less the unamortized discount is equal to the present value (carrying value) of the bond. Answer (C) is incorrect because bond issue costs, not unamortized discount, appear as a deferred charge in the balance sheet. Answer (D) is incorrect because unamortized discount is segregated from issue costs.

6. The following information pertains to Camp Corp.'s issuance of bonds on July 1, 1996:

Face amount	$800,000
Term	10 years
Stated interest rate	6%
Interest payment dates	Annually on July 1
Yield	9%

	At 6%	At 9%
Present value of 1 for 10 periods	0.558	0.422
Future value of 1 for 10 periods	1.791	2.367
Present value of ordinary annuity of 1 for 10 periods	7.360	6.418

What should be the issue price for each $1,000 bond?

A. $1,000

B. $943

C. $864

D. $807

The correct answer is (D). *(CPA 592 I-30)*
REQUIRED: The issue price for each bond.
DISCUSSION: The issue price for each bond reflects the fair value. It equals the sum of the present values of the future cash flows (principal + interest). This amount is $807 {(.422 PV of 1 for 10 periods at 9% x $1,000 face amount) + [6.418 PV of an ordinary annuity for 10 periods at 9% x (6% x $1,000) interest]}.
Answer (A) is incorrect because $1,000 is the face amount. Answer (B) is incorrect because $943 is the result of discounting the interest payments at 9% and the face amount at 6%. Answer (C) is incorrect because $864 is the result of discounting the interest payments at 6% and the face amount at 9%.

7. On January 2, 1996, Nast Co. issued 8% bonds with a face amount of $1 million that mature on January 2, 2002. The bonds were issued to yield 12%, resulting in a discount of $150,000. Nast incorrectly used the straight-line method instead of the effective-interest method to amortize the discount. How is the carrying amount of the bonds affected by the error?

	At December 31, 1996	At January 2, 2002
A.	Overstated	Understated
B.	Overstated	No effect
C.	Understated	Overstated
D.	Understated	No effect

The correct answer is (B). *(CPA 595 F-20)*
REQUIRED: The effect of amortizing bond discount using the straight-line method.
DISCUSSION: The carrying amount of a bond issued at a discount equals its maturity value minus the unamortized discount. Under the effective-interest method, periodic interest expense equals the carrying amount times the effective (yield) rate. Discount amortization is the excess of interest expense over actual interest paid. When bonds are issued at a discount, the carrying amount increases over time as the discount is amortized, thereby increasing interest expense and the amount of amortization. Discount amortization under the straight-line method is a constant periodic amount. Thus, in the first year, straight-line amortization of the discount exceeds the amount determined under the interest method. The effect of the error is to overstate the carrying amount by this excess. At the due date of the bonds, however, the discount is fully amortized, and the carrying amount is the same under both methods.
Answers (A), (C), and (D) are incorrect because the error overstates the carrying amount at 12/31/96 but has no effect at 1/2/02.

8. During 1996, Lake Co. issued 3,000 of its 9%, $1,000 face value bonds at 101½. In connection with the sale of these bonds, Lake paid the following expenses:

Promotion costs	$ 20,000
Engraving and printing	25,000
Underwriters' commissions	200,000

What amount should Lake record as bond issue costs to be amortized over the term of the bonds?

A. $0

B. $220,000

C. $225,000

D. $245,000

The correct answer is (D). *(CPA 1192 I-37)*

REQUIRED: The amount to be recorded as bond issue costs.

DISCUSSION: Bond issue costs include printing costs, underwriters' commissions, attorney's fees, and promotion costs (including preparation of a prospectus). The issue costs to be amortized equal $245,000 ($20,000 promotion costs + $25,000 printing costs + $200,000 underwriters' commissions).

Answer (A) is incorrect because $245,000 of bond issue costs should be amortized. Answer (B) is incorrect because the $25,000 printing cost should be amortized. Answer (C) is incorrect because the $20,000 promotion costs should be amortized.

9. On May 1, 19X2 a company issued, at 103 plus accrued interest, 500 of its 12%, $1,000 bonds. The bonds are dated January 1, 19X2 and mature on January 1, 19X7. Interest is payable semiannually on January 1 and July 1. The journal entry to record the issuance of the bonds and the receipt of the cash proceeds is

A.	Cash	$515,000	
	Interest payable	20,000	
	Bonds payable		$500,000
	Premium on bonds payable		35,000

B.	Cash	$525,000	
	Bonds payable		$500,000
	Premium on bonds payable		15,000
	Interest payable		10,000

C.	Cash	$535,000	
	Bonds payable		$500,000
	Premium on bonds payable		15,000
	Interest payable		20,000

D.	Cash	$535,000	
	Bonds payable		$500,000
	Premium on bonds payable		35,000

The correct answer is (C). *(CIA 1186 IV-30)*

REQUIRED: The journal entry to record the issuance of a bond at a premium plus accrued interest.

DISCUSSION: The face amount of the 500 bonds is equal to $500,000 (500 x $1,000). The cash proceeds excluding interest from the issuance of the bonds are $515,000 (103% x $500,000). The $15,000 premium is the difference between the cash issuance proceeds and the face amount of the bonds. Because the bonds were issued between interest payment dates, the issuer is also entitled to receive accrued interest for the 4 months between the prior interest date and the issuance date. The accrued interest is $20,000 (500 bonds x $1,000 face value x 12% stated rate x 4/12). The issuing company will therefore receive $535,000 in cash ($515,000 + $20,000). The resulting journal entry includes a $535,000 debit to cash, a $500,000 credit to bonds payable, a $15,000 credit to premium, and a $20,000 credit to either interest payable or interest expense.

Answer (A) is incorrect because the bond premium is $15,000 ($500,000 x .03), and interest payable should be credited. Answer (B) is incorrect because interest payable should be $20,000 ($500,000 x .12 x 4/12). Answer (D) is incorrect because the premium on bonds payable should not include interest payable.

10. If the market rate of interest is <List A> the coupon rate when bonds are issued, then the bonds will sell in the market at a price <List B> the face value, and the issuing firm will record a <List C> on bonds payable.

	List A	List B	List C
A.	Equal to	Equal to	Premium
B.	Greater than	Greater than	Premium
C.	Greater than	Less than	Discount
D.	Less than	Greater than	Discount

The correct answer is (C). *(CIA 1195 IV-21)*

REQUIRED: The relationship of the market rate, the coupon rate, and the recording of a discount or premium.

DISCUSSION: If the market rate exceeds the coupon rate, the price of the bonds must decline to a level that equates the yield on the bonds with the market rate of interest. Accordingly, the bonds will be recorded by a debit to cash for the proceeds, a debit to discount on bonds payable, and a credit to bonds payable at face value.

Answer (A) is incorrect because, if the market rate equals the coupon rate, the bonds will sell at a premium or discount. Answer (B) is incorrect because, if the market rate exceeds the coupon rate, the bond issue will sell at a discount. Answer (D) is incorrect because, if the market rate is less than the coupon rate, the bonds will sell at a premium.

11. How is the carrying amount of a bond payable affected by amortization of the following?

	Discount	Premium
A.	Increase	Increase
B.	Decrease	Decrease
C.	Increase	Decrease
D.	Decrease	Increase

The correct answer is (C). *(CPA 1189 T-17)*

REQUIRED: The effect of discount and premium amortization on the carrying value of a bond payable.

DISCUSSION: The carrying value of a bond payable is equal to its maturity (face) amount plus any unamortized premium or minus any unamortized discount. Amortization results in a reduction of the discount or premium. Consequently, the carrying value of a bond is increased when discount is amortized and decreased when premium is amortized.

Answers (A), (B), and (D) are incorrect because the carrying amount of a bond payable is increased by the amortization of a discount and decreased by the amortization of a premium.

12. Able, Inc. had the following amounts of long-term debt outstanding at December 31, 1996:

14½% term note, due 1997	$ 3,000
11⅛% term note, due 2000	107,000
8% note, due in 11 equal annual principal payments, plus interest beginning December 31, 1997	110,000
7% guaranteed debentures, due 2001	100,000
Total	$320,000

Able's annual sinking-fund requirement on the guaranteed debentures is $4,000 per year. What amount should Able report as current maturities of long-term debt in its December 31, 1996 balance sheet?

- A. $4,000
- B. $7,000
- C. $10,000
- D. $13,000

The correct answer is (D). *(CPA 1192 I-5)*

REQUIRED: The amount to be reported as current maturities of long-term debt in the balance sheet.

DISCUSSION: A long-term liability that will become due within 1 year or the firm's operating cycle, whichever is longer, should be reclassified as a current liability, except when (1) the portion currently due will be refinanced on a long-term basis, (2) the assets that will be used to retire the currently due portion are classified as noncurrent assets, or (3) capital stock will be issued to retire the portion currently due. In this case, the obligations that should be reclassified as current are the $3,000 14½% term note due in 1997 and $10,000 of the 8% note (the payment is made to reduce principal in 11 equal payments) for a total of $13,000. None of the exceptions apply.

Answer (A) is incorrect because payments into a sinking fund are not considered payments made to retire debt, and $4,000 does not include the $10,000 8% and $3,000 14½% notes to be reclassified as current liabilities. Answer (B) is incorrect because payments into a sinking fund are not considered payments made to retire debt, and $10,000 of the 8% note must be reclassified as current. Answer (C) is incorrect because the 14½% note should be reclassified as a current liability.

13. Mann Corp.'s liability account balances at June 30, 1995 included a 10% note payable in the amount of $3,600,000. The note is dated October 1, 1994 and is payable in three equal annual payments of $1,200,000 plus interest. The first interest and principal payment was made on October 1, 1995. In Mann's June 30, 1996 balance sheet, what amount should be reported as accrued interest payable for this note?

- A. $270,000
- B. $180,000
- C. $90,000
- D. $60,000

The correct answer is (B). *(CPA 591 I-33)*

REQUIRED: The amount that should be reported as accrued interest payable.

DISCUSSION: Accrued interest on the note payable at the balance sheet date is the carrying value of the note multiplied by the interest rate on the note. Since the first payment was made 10/1/95, the carrying value of the note is $2,400,000 ($3,600,000 − $1,200,000). Also, interest has accrued for only 9 months since the first payment. As a result, accrued interest payable is $180,000 ($2,400,000 x 10% x 9/12).

Answer (A) is incorrect because the carrying value of the note should be reduced by the payment of $1,200,000 made on 10/1/95. Answer (C) is incorrect because the carrying value of the note should be reduced by the first payment of $1,200,000. Also, interest should be accrued for 9 months instead of 3. Answer (D) is incorrect because interest should be accrued for 9 months instead of 3.

14. On January 2, 1995, Gill Co. issued $2,000,000 of 10-year, 8% bonds at par. The bonds, dated January 1, 1995, pay interest semiannually on January 1 and July 1. Bond issue costs were $250,000. What amount of bond issue costs are unamortized at June 30, 1996?

A. $237,500

B. $225,000

C. $220,800

D. $212,500

The correct answer is (D). *(CPA 1193 I-34)*
REQUIRED: The amount to be recorded as unamortized bond issue costs.
DISCUSSION: Bond issue costs are customarily amortized using the straight-line method for the term of the bond. The amortization is $25,000 per year ($250,000 ÷ 10 years). Because the bond has been held for 18 months, $37,500 ($25,000 + $12,500) of issue costs has been amortized by 6/30/96. The unamortized issue costs are $212,500 ($250,000 – $37,500).
Answer (A) is incorrect because an additional full year of amortization should have been claimed. Answer (B) is incorrect because 6 more months of issue costs should have been amortized for the time between 1/1/96 through 6/30/96. Answer (C) is incorrect because $220,800 results from amortization using the interest method.

15. On January 1, 1989, Gilson Corporation issued one thousand of its 9%, $1,000 callable bonds for $1,030,000. The bonds are dated January 1, 1989 and mature on December 31, 2003. Interest is payable semiannually on January 1 and July 1. The bonds can be called by the issuer at 102 on any interest payment date after December 31, 1993. The unamortized bond premium was $14,000 at December 31, 1996, and the market price of the bonds was 99 on this date. In its December 31, 1996 balance sheet, at what amounts should Gilson report the carrying value of the bonds?

A. $1,020,000

B. $1,016,000

C. $1,014,000

D. $990,000

The correct answer is (C). *(CPA 1183 I-7)*
REQUIRED: The carrying value of bonds issued at a premium.
DISCUSSION: The face amount of the bonds is $1,000,000 (1,000 x $1,000), and unamortized premium is $14,000 (given). The carrying value is thus $1,014,000. The other data are irrelevant.
Answer (A) is incorrect because $1,020,000 is the amount to be paid if the bonds are called. Answer (B) is incorrect because $1,016,000 is the issue price minus the unamortized premium ($1,030,000 – $14,000). Answer (D) is incorrect because $990,000 is the market price.

16. A company issues 10-year bonds with a face value of $1,000,000, dated January 1, 1996 and bearing interest at an annual rate of 12% payable semiannually on January 1 and July 1. The full interest amount will be paid each due date. The market rate of interest on bonds of similar risk and maturity, with the same schedule of interest payments, is also 12%. If the bonds are issued on February 1, 1996, the amount the issuing company receives from the buyers of the bonds on that date is

A. $990,000

B. $1,000,000

C. $1,010,000

D. $1,020,000

The correct answer is (C). *(CIA 595 IV-19)*
REQUIRED: The amount received when bonds are issued subsequent to the date printed on the face of the bonds.
DISCUSSION: The amount the issuing company receives on 2/1/96 is the face value of the issue plus 1 month of accrued interest, or $1,010,000 {$1,000,000 + [($1,000,000 x 12%) ÷ 12]}.
Answer (A) is incorrect because $990,000 is the result if 1 month of accrued interest is deducted from, rather than added to, the amount received. Answer (B) is incorrect because the purchasers must pay for the accrued interest from the last interest date to the issue date. They will receive 6 months' interest on July 1 despite holding the bonds for 5 months. Answer (D) is incorrect because $1,020,000 results from adding 2 months of accrued interest to the face value.

Questions 17 and 18 are based on the following information. Marquette, Inc. issued $6,000,000 of 12% bonds on December 1, 1995, due on December 1, 2000, with interest payable each December 1 and June 1. The bonds were sold for $5,194,770 to yield 16%.

17. If the discount were amortized by the straight-line method, Marquette, Inc.'s interest expense for the fiscal year ended November 30, 1996 related to its $6,000,000 bond issue would be

A. $558,954

B. $623,372

C. $720,000

D. $881,046

The correct answer is (D). *(CMA 1290 2-11)*

REQUIRED: The interest expense under the straight-line amortization method.

DISCUSSION: Under the straight-line method, interest expense is the sum of the periodic cash flows plus the discount amortization. The periodic cash flows are equal to $720,000 ($6,000,000 face value x 12% coupon rate). The discount at the time of issuance was $805,230 ($6,000,000 face value – $5,194,770 issuance price). Because the term of the bonds is 5 years, amortization by the straight-line method each year will be $161,046 ($805,230 discount ÷ 5 years). Thus, interest expense is $881,046 ($720,000 + $161,046) for the fiscal year ended 11/30/96. Under the straight-line method, interest expense will be the same for each year in which the bonds are outstanding. Note that the straight-line method is allowable only when it does not differ materially from the interest method.

Answer (A) is incorrect because $558,954 results from subtracting the amortization of the discount. Answer (B) is incorrect because $623,372 equals the carrying amount of the bond multiplied by the coupon rate. Answer (C) is incorrect because $720,000 is interest payable.

18. If the discount were amortized by the effective-interest method, Marquette, Inc.'s interest expense for the fiscal year ended November 30, 1996 related to its $6,000,000 bond issue would be

A. $623,372

B. $720,000

C. $831,163

D. $835,610

The correct answer is (D). *(CMA 1290 2-12)*

REQUIRED: The interest expense for the first year under the effective-interest method.

DISCUSSION: Under the interest method, interest expense is equal to the carrying or book value of the bonds at the beginning of the interest period times the effective interest rate. The carrying value of the bonds at December 1, 1995 (the issuance date) was $5,194,770. The annual yield rate was 16%. Interest expense is therefore equal to $415,582 ($5,194,770 x 16% x 6/12) for the first 6 months of the year. For the same period, interest paid was $360,000 ($6,000,000 x 12% x 6/12). Hence, the semiannual discount amortization was $55,582 ($415,582 interest expense – $360,000 interest paid), and the carrying value of the bonds for the second 6-month period was $5,250,352 ($5,194,770 + $55,582). For this period, the semiannual interest expense was $420,028 ($5,250,352 x 16% x 6/12). Total interest expense for the year is equal to $835,610 ($415,582 + $420,028).

Answer (A) is incorrect because $623,372 is equal to the carrying amount of the bond multiplied by the coupon rate. Answer (B) is incorrect because $720,000 is interest payable. Answer (C) is incorrect because $831,163 results from calculating interest expense as if interest is payable annually.

19. On December 31, 1995, Arnold, Inc. issued $200,000 of 8% serial bonds, to be repaid in the amount of $40,000 each year. Interest is payable annually on December 31. The bonds were issued to yield 10% a year. The bond proceeds were $190,280 based on the present values at December 31, 1995 of the five annual payments:

Due Date	Amounts Due Principal	Interest	Present Value at 12/31/95
12/31/96	$40,000	$16,000	$ 50,900
12/31/97	40,000	12,800	43,610
12/31/98	40,000	9,600	37,250
12/31/99	40,000	6,400	31,690
12/31/00	40,000	3,200	26,830
			$190,280

Arnold amortizes the bond discount by the interest method. In its December 31, 1996 balance sheet, at what amount should Arnold report the carrying value of the bonds?

- A. $139,380
- B. $149,100
- C. $150,280
- D. $153,308

The correct answer is (D). *(CPA 1184 I-24)*
REQUIRED: The carrying value after year one of bonds issued at a discount.
DISCUSSION: The carrying value of the bonds for year one equals the proceeds of $190,280. Interest expense at the 10% effective rate is $19,028. Actual interest paid is $16,000, and discount amortization is $3,028 ($19,028 – $16,000). Thus, the discount remaining at year-end is $6,692 [($200,000 face value – $190,280 issue proceeds) – $3,028 discount amortization]. Given that $40,000 in principal is paid at year-end, the carrying value is $153,308 ($160,000 face value – $6,692 unamortized discount).
Answer (A) is incorrect because $139,380 is the carrying value of the bonds at 12/31/95 less the present value of the bonds due 12/31/96. Answer (B) is incorrect because $149,100 is the difference between the face amount of the bonds and the present value of the bonds due 12/31/96. Answer (C) is incorrect because $150,280 results from reducing the carrying amount at 12/31/95 by the payment due 12/31/96.

20. On July 1, 1996, Day Co. received $103,288 for $100,000 face amount, 12% bonds, a price that yields 10%. Interest expense for the 6 months ended December 31, 1996 should be

- A. $6,197
- B. $6,000
- C. $5,164
- D. $5,000

The correct answer is (C). *(CPA 591 I-55)*
REQUIRED: The amount of interest expense.
DISCUSSION: Under the interest method, interest expense for the 6 months since the bond was issued is equal to the carrying value of the bond multiplied by the effective interest rate for half a year. Thus, interest expense is $5,164 ($103,288 x 10% x 6/12).
Answer (A) is incorrect because $6,197 is equal to the carrying value multiplied by the coupon rate. Answer (B) is incorrect because $6,000 is equal to the face amount multiplied by the coupon rate. Answer (D) is incorrect because $5,000 is equal to the face amount multiplied by the yield rate.

21. On July 1, 1996, Lundy Company issued 500 of its 8%, $1,000 bonds for $438,000. The bonds were issued to yield 10%. The bonds are dated July 1, 1996 and mature on July 1, 2006. Interest is payable semiannually on January 1 and July 1. Using the interest method, how much of the bond discount should be amortized for the 6 months ended December 31, 1996?

- A. $3,800
- B. $3,100
- C. $2,480
- D. $1,900

The correct answer is (D). *(CPA 587 I-27)*
REQUIRED: The amount of bond discount to be amortized using the interest method.
DISCUSSION: Under the interest method, interest expense is equal to the carrying value of the bonds at the beginning of the interest period times the yield rate. Because interest is paid semiannually, the semiannual interest rate is equal to one-half of the annual rate. Interest expense is therefore $21,900 ($438,000 x 10% x 6/12). The periodic cash payment is $20,000 ($500,000 face value x 8% stated rate x 6/12). The $1,900 ($21,900 – $20,000) difference is the amount of discount to be amortized during this 6-month interest period.
Answer (A) is incorrect because $3,800 is the discount amortized for a full year. Answer (B) is incorrect because $3,100 is the difference between interest expense calculated at 10% and interest payable calculated at 10% for half a year. Answer (C) is incorrect because $2,480 is equal to the difference between interest expense calculated at 8% and interest payable calculated at 8% for half a year.

22. On January 1, 1996, Celt Corp. issued 9% bonds in the face amount of $1,000,000, which mature on January 1, 2006. The bonds were issued for $939,000 to yield 10%, resulting in a bond discount of $61,000. Celt uses the interest method of amortizing bond discount. Interest is payable annually on December 31. At December 31, 1996, Celt's unamortized bond discount should be

A. $51,000

B. $51,610

C. $52,000

D. $57,100

The correct answer is (D). *(CPA 1191 I-36)*
REQUIRED: The amount of unamortized bond discount at the end of the first year.
DISCUSSION: Under the interest method, interest expense is equal to the carrying value of the bonds at the beginning of the period times the market (yield) rate of interest. For the first year, interest expense is $93,900 ($939,000 carrying value x 10% yield rate). The periodic interest payment is $90,000 ($1,000,000 face value x 9% coupon rate). The $3,900 ($93,900 – $90,000) difference is the amount of bond discount to be amortized. Thus, the $61,000 unamortized bond discount at the beginning of the year should be reduced by $3,900 to a year-end balance of $57,100.

Answer (A) is incorrect because $51,000 results from reducing the discount by the face amount times the market (yield) rate less the interest payment. Answer (B) is incorrect because $51,610 results from reducing the discount by the difference between the carrying value times the yield less the carrying value times the coupon rate. Answer (C) is incorrect because the bond discount is reduced by the interest payment.

23. Webb Co. has outstanding a 7%, 10-year bond with a $100,000 face value. The bond was originally sold to yield 6% annual interest. Webb uses the effective-interest-rate method to amortize bond premium. On June 30, 1995, the carrying amount of the outstanding bond was $105,000. What amount of unamortized premium on the bond should Webb report in its June 30, 1996 balance sheet?

A. $1,050

B. $3,950

C. $4,300

D. $4,500

The correct answer is (C). *(CPA 1193 I-36)*
REQUIRED: The amount of unamortized premium.
DISCUSSION: Under the interest method, interest expense is equal to the carrying value of the bonds at the beginning of the interest period times the market (yield) rate of interest. Interest expense for the year ended 6/30/96 is $6,300 (6% x $105,000 carrying value), and the periodic interest payment is $7,000 (7% x $100,000). The difference ($7,000 – $6,300 = $700) is the amount of premium amortized. The unamortized premium is therefore $4,300 ($5,000 – $700).

Answer (A) is incorrect because $1,050 equals 18 months of interest payments. Answer (B) is incorrect because $3,950 equals the premium minus 18 months of interest payments. Answer (D) is incorrect because $4,500 assumes straight-line amortization and a 6/30/95 issue date.

24. On January 2, 1996, West Co. issued 9% bonds in the amount of $500,000, which mature on January 2, 2006. The bonds were issued for $469,500 to yield 10%. Interest is payable annually on December 31. West uses the interest method of amortizing bond discount. In its June 30, 1996 balance sheet, what amount should West report as bonds payable?

A. $469,500

B. $470,475

C. $471,025

D. $500,000

The correct answer is (B). *(CPA 1194 F-24)*
REQUIRED: The amount to be reported as bonds payable at an interim date.
DISCUSSION: Accrued interest expense is $23,475 ($469,500 x 10% x 6/12). Accrued interest payable is $22,500 ($500,000 x 9% x 6/12). The difference of $975 is the amount of discount amortization for the period. Bonds payable equal $470,475 ($469,500 + $975).

Answer (A) is incorrect because $469,500 is the issue price unadjusted for discount amortization. Answer (C) is incorrect because $471,025 reflects a full year's discount amortization. Answer (D) is incorrect because $500,000 is the face value of the bonds.

15.2 Convertible Bonds

> Questions 25 and 26 are based on the following information. On January 2, 1993, Chard Co. issued 10-year convertible bonds at 105. During 1996, these bonds were converted into common stock having an aggregate par value equal to the total face amount of the bonds. At conversion, the market price of Chard's common stock was 50% above its par value.

25. On January 2, 1993, cash proceeds from the issuance of the convertible bonds should be reported as

A. Contributed capital for the entire proceeds.

B. Contributed capital for the portion of the proceeds attributable to the conversion feature and as a liability for the balance.

C. A liability for the face amount of the bonds and contributed capital for the premium.

D. A liability for the entire proceeds.

The correct answer is (D). *(CPA 1190 T-29)*
REQUIRED: The proper accounting for cash proceeds received from the issuance of convertible bonds.
DISCUSSION: APB 14, *Convertible Debt and Debt Issued with Stock Purchase Warrants*, states that the entire proceeds from the issuance of convertible bonds should be reported as a liability until such time as the bonds are converted into stock.
Answers (A), (B), and (C) are incorrect because the cash proceeds from the issuance of the convertible bonds should be treated as a liability for the entire amount.

26. Depending on whether the book-value method or the market-value method was used, Chard should recognize gains or losses on conversion when using the

	Book-Value Method	Market-Value Method
A.	Either gain or loss	Gain
B.	Either gain or loss	Loss
C.	Neither gain nor loss	Loss
D.	Neither gain nor loss	Gain

The correct answer is (C). *(CPA 1190 T-30)*
REQUIRED: The accounting method(s) that recognizes gains or losses on the conversion of the convertible bonds.
DISCUSSION: Under the book-value method for recognizing the conversion of outstanding bonds payable to common stock, the stock issued is recorded at the carrying value of the bonds with no recognition of gain or loss. Under the market-value method, the stock is recorded at the market value of the stock (or of the bonds). A gain or loss is recognized equal to the difference between the market value recorded and the carrying value of the bonds payable. At the time of the conversion, Chard's common stock had an aggregate par value equal to the total face amount of the bonds, and the market price of the stock was 50% above its par value. Thus, a loss should have been recognized upon conversion in accordance with the market-value method. The total of the credits to shareholders' equity accounts exceeds the total of the debits to bonds payable and unamortized premium. The difference is the amount of the loss.
Answers (A), (B), and (D) are incorrect because, under the book-value method, no gain or loss is recognized at conversion. Under the market-value method, a loss would result in this situation.

27. What is the preferred method of handling unamortized discount, unamortized issue costs, and the costs of implementing a conversion of debt into common stock?

A. Expense them in the period bonds are converted.

B. Amortize them over the remaining life of the issue retired.

C. Amortize them over a period not to exceed 40 years.

D. Charge them to paid-in capital in excess of the par value of the stock issued.

The correct answer is (D). *(Publisher)*
REQUIRED: The preferred handling of unamortized discount, unamortized issue costs, and the costs of converting debt into common stock.
DISCUSSION: The conversion of debt into common stock is ordinarily based upon the book value of the debt at the time of issuance. Because the book value is based on all related accounts, the debit balances of unamortized bond discount, unamortized issue costs, and conversion costs should be considered reductions in the net carrying value at the time of conversion. Consequently, these items should be reflected as reductions in the paid-in capital in excess of par account.
Answers (A), (B), and (C) are incorrect because these amounts are not expensed. In effect, each reduces the amount at which the stock is issued.

28. On July 1, 1996, after recording interest and amortization, York Co. converted $1,000,000 of its 12% convertible bonds into 50,000 shares of $1 par value common stock. On the conversion date the carrying amount of the bonds was $1,300,000, the market value of the bonds was $1,400,000, and York's common stock was publicly trading at $30 per share. Using the book-value method, what amount of additional paid-in capital should York record as a result of the conversion?

A. $950,000

B. $1,250,000

C. $1,350,000

D. $1,500,000

The correct answer is (B). *(CPA 1193 I-37)*

REQUIRED: The amount of additional paid-in capital reported on the conversion of bonds when the book-value method is used.

DISCUSSION: Under the book-value method for recognizing the conversion of outstanding bonds payable to common stock, the stock issued is recorded at the carrying value of the bonds with no recognition of a gain or loss. Accordingly, the conversion should be recorded at $1,300,000. However, this amount must be allocated between common stock and additional paid-in capital. The common stock account is always valued at par value; therefore, $50,000 (50,000 shares x $1) will be credited to common stock and $1,250,000 to additional paid-in capital.

Answer (A) is incorrect because $950,000 equals the face value of the bonds minus the par value of the stock. Answer (C) is incorrect because $1,350,000 is the market value of the bonds less the par value of the stock. Answer (D) is incorrect because $1,500,000 is the market value of the stock.

29. According to SFAS 84, *Induced Conversions of Convertible Debt*, an issuer of a convertible security may attempt to induce prompt conversion of its convertible debt to equity securities by offering additional securities or other consideration as a sweetener. The additional consideration used to induce conversion should be reported as a(n)

A. Reduction of the paid-in capital recognized for the new equity securities.

B. Reduction of retained earnings.

C. Extraordinary item in the current income statement.

D. Expense of the current period, but not an extraordinary item.

The correct answer is (D). *(CMA 1290 2-25)*

REQUIRED: The proper treatment of a convertible debt sweetener.

DISCUSSION: A debtor may induce conversion of convertible debt by offering additional securities or other consideration to the holders of convertible debt. SFAS 84 requires that this convertible debt sweetener be recognized as an ordinary expense. It is equal to the fair value of the securities or other consideration transferred in excess of the fair value of the securities that would have been issued under the original conversion privilege.

Answers (A), (B), and (C) are incorrect because SFAS 84 requires the sweetener to be recognized as an ordinary expense.

30. Any gains or losses from the early extinguishment of convertible debt should be

A. Recognized in current income of the period of extinguishment.

B. Treated as an increase or decrease in paid-in capital.

C. Split between a portion that is an increase (decrease) in paid-in capital and a portion recognized in current income.

D. Amortized over the remaining original life of the extinguished convertible debt.

The correct answer is (A). *(Publisher)*

REQUIRED: The treatment of gains or losses from early extinguishment of convertible debt.

DISCUSSION: The accounting for the retirement of convertible debt and for ordinary debt is the same. APB 26, *Early Extinguishment of Debt*, states that a difference between the cash acquisition price of the debt and its net carrying amount should be recognized as income in the period of extinguishment. SFAS 4, *Reporting Gains and Losses from Extinguishment of Debt*, requires these gains or losses, whether or not from the purchase of convertible securities, to be aggregated, and if material, to be classified as an extraordinary item, net of tax effect.

Answers (B) and (C) are incorrect because the debt and equity features are treated as inseparable. The convertible debt should be accounted for as if it were ordinary debt. Answer (D) is incorrect because amortization was rejected by APB 26 in favor of current recognition in income of the full gain or loss.

15.3 Bonds and Warrants

31. How should the value of warrants attached to a debt security be accounted for?

- A. No value assigned.
- B. A separate portion of paid-in capital.
- C. An appropriation of retained earnings.
- D. A liability.

The correct answer is (A). *(CPA 581 T-9)*
REQUIRED: The accounting for the value of warrants attached to a debt security.
DISCUSSION: Assuming the warrants are not detachable and the debt security must be surrendered to exercise the warrants, the securities are substantially equivalent to convertible debt. Under APB 14, *Convertible Debt and Debt Issued with Stock Purchase Warrants*, no portion of the proceeds from the issuance should be accounted for as attributable to the conversion feature or the warrants.

Answer (B) is incorrect because the portion of the proceeds allocable to the warrants should be accounted for as paid-in capital only if the warrants are detachable. Answers (C) and (D) are incorrect because the value of the warrants should either not be recognized or be recognized as paid-in capital.

32. When bonds are issued with stock purchase warrants, a portion of the proceeds should be allocated to paid-in capital for bonds issued with

	Detachable Stock Purchase Warrants	Nondetachable Stock Purchase Warrants
A.	No	Yes
B.	No	No
C.	Yes	No
D.	Yes	Yes

The correct answer is (C). *(CPA 588 T-16)*
REQUIRED: The circumstances in which proceeds from the issuance of a bond should be allocated between the bond and stock warrants.
DISCUSSION: APB 14 requires the proceeds from debt securities issued with detachable warrants to be allocated between the debt securities and the warrants based on their relative fair values at the time of issuance. The portion allocated to the warrants should be accounted for as paid-in capital. However, when debt securities are issued with nondetachable warrants, no part of the proceeds should be allocated to the warrants.

Answers (A), (B), and (D) are incorrect because a portion of the proceeds should be allocated to paid-in capital for bonds with detachable stock purchase warrants, and no part of the proceeds should be allocated if the warrants are nondetachable.

33. Bonds with detachable stock warrants were issued by Flack Co. Immediately after issue the aggregate market value of the bonds and the warrants exceeds the proceeds. Is the portion of the proceeds allocated to the warrants less than their market value, and is that amount recorded as contributed capital?

	Less Than Warrants' Market Value	Contributed Capital
A.	No	Yes
B.	Yes	No
C.	Yes	Yes
D.	No	No

The correct answer is (C). *(CPA 1191 T-37)*
REQUIRED: The allocation of proceeds to detachable warrants and the recording of the allocation.
DISCUSSION: APB 14 requires the proceeds from debt securities issued with detachable warrants to be allocated between the debt securities and the warrants based on their relative fair values at the time of issuance. The portion allocated to the warrants should be accounted for as paid-in capital. Assuming that the market values of both the bonds and the warrants are known, and that the proceeds are less than their sum, the allocation process must result in crediting paid-in capital from stock warrants (stock warrants outstanding) for less than their market value. If the market value of the bonds is not known, the warrants will be credited at their market value.

Answer (A) is incorrect because the warrants will be credited at less than market value. Answer (B) is incorrect because the amount allocated to the warrants is credited to paid-in (contributed) capital. Answer (D) is incorrect because the warrants will be credited at less than market value, and the amount allocated to the warrants is credited to paid-in (contributed) capital.

34. On December 30, 1996, Fort, Inc. issued 1,000 of its 8%, 10-year, $1,000 face value bonds with detachable stock warrants at par. Each bond carried a detachable warrant for one share of Fort's common stock at a specified option price of $25 per share. Immediately after issuance, the market value of the bonds without the warrants was $1,080,000, and the market value of the warrants was $120,000. In its December 31, 1996 balance sheet, what amount should Fort report as bonds payable?

    A. $1,000,000

    B. $975,000

    C. $900,000

    D. $880,000

The correct answer is (C). *(CPA 1193 I-33)*
    REQUIRED: The amount reported for bonds payable with detachable stock warrants.
    DISCUSSION: The issue price of the bonds is allocated between the bonds and the detachable stock warrants based on their relative fair values. The market price of bonds without the warrants is $1,080,000, which is 90% [$1,080,000 ÷ ($1,080,000 + $120,000)] of the total fair value of the bonds without warrants plus the value of the warrants. Consequently, 90% of the issue price should be allocated to the bonds, and they should be reported at $900,000 (90% x $1,000,000) in the balance sheet.
    Answer (A) is incorrect because $1,000,000 equals the total proceeds. Answer (B) is incorrect because $975,000 is the result of deducting the option price of the stock from the total proceeds. Answer (D) is incorrect because $880,000 is the result of deducting the fair value of the warrants from the total proceeds.

35. Ray Corp. issued bonds with a face amount of $200,000. Each $1,000 bond contained detachable stock warrants for 100 shares of Ray's common stock. Total proceeds from the issue amounted to $240,000. The market value of each warrant was $2, and the market value of the bonds without the warrants was $196,000. The bonds were issued at a discount of

    A. $0

    B. $678

    C. $4,000

    D. $40,678

The correct answer is (B). *(CPA 591 II-5)*
    REQUIRED: The amount of the bond discount.
    DISCUSSION: The proceeds of bonds issued with detachable stock warrants must be allocated based on their relative fair values at the time of issuance. The fair values are $196,000 for the bonds and $40,000 for the warrants (200 bonds x 100 shares x 1 warrant per share x $2). Of the total proceeds of $240,000, $199,322 should be allocated to the bonds. Hence, bond discount is $678 ($200,000 face amount – $199,322 allocated proceeds).

$$\frac{\$196,000}{\$196,000 + \$40,000} \times \$240,000 = \$199,322$$

    Answer (A) is incorrect because the allocation to the bonds was less than their face value. Answer (C) is incorrect because $4,000 is the difference between the face value and the market value of the bonds. Answer (D) is incorrect because $40,678 is the amount allocated to the warrants.

36. On March 1, 1996, Evan Corp. issued $1,000,000 of 10%, nonconvertible bonds at 103. They were due on February 28, 2006. Each $1,000 bond was issued with 30 detachable stock warrants, each of which entitled the holder to purchase, for $50, one share of Evan common stock, par value $25. On March 1, 1996, the quoted market value of Evan's common stock was $20 per share, and the market value of each warrant was $4. What amount of the bond issue proceeds should Evan record as an increase in shareholders' equity?

    A. $120,000

    B. $90,000

    C. $30,000

    D. $0

The correct answer is (A). *(CPA 593 I-32)*
    REQUIRED: The amount of the proceeds from bonds issued with detachable stock warrants to be recorded as shareholders' equity.
    DISCUSSION: When bonds are issued with detachable stock warrants, the proceeds must be allocated between the warrants and the bonds on the basis of their relative fair values. When the fair value of the warrants but not the bonds is known, paid-in capital from stock warrants should be credited (increased) for the fair value of the warrants, with the remainder credited to the bonds. Evan issued 1,000 bonds ($1,000,000 ÷ 1,000); therefore, 30,000 warrants (1,000 bonds x 30 warrants) must also have been issued. Their fair value was $120,000 (30,000 warrants x $4), which is the amount of the credit to paid-in capital from stock warrants. The remainder of the proceeds [($1,000,000 x 103%) – $120,000 = $910,000] is allocated to bonds payable.
    Answer (B) is incorrect because $90,000 equals the discount on the bonds. Answer (C) is incorrect because $30,000 is the difference between the fair value of the warrants and the discount on the bonds. Answer (D) is incorrect because stock warrants outstanding (paid-in capital from stock warrants) is a shareholders' equity account.

37. Roaster Company issued bonds with detachable stock warrants. Each warrant granted an option to buy one share of $40 par value common stock for $75 per share. Five hundred warrants were originally issued, and $4,000 was appropriately credited to warrants. If 90% of these warrants are exercised when the market price of the common stock is $85 per share, how much should be credited to capital in excess of par on this transaction?

A. $19,350

B. $19,750

C. $23,850

D. $24,250

The correct answer is (A). *(CPA 575 I-8)*
REQUIRED: The credit to capital in excess of par upon exercise of 90% of the warrants.
DISCUSSION: If 90% of the warrants are exercised, 450 shares must be issued at $75 per share. The total debit to cash is $33,750. The debit to stock warrants outstanding reflects the exercise of 90% of $4,000 of warrants, or $3,600. The par value of the common stock issued is credited for $18,000 (450 shares x $40 par). The balance of $19,350 ($33,750 + $3,600 – $18,000) is credited to capital in excess of par. The transaction is based on the exercise price, not the fair value of the stock or warrants at the time of issuance.

Cash	$33,750	
Warrants	3,600	
Common stock at par		$18,000
Capital in excess of par		19,350

Answer (B) is incorrect because $19,750 results from assuming all of the warrants were exercised with the same amount of stock being issued. Answer (C) is incorrect because $23,850 results from issuing the stock for $85 per share instead of $75. Answer (D) is incorrect because $24,250 results from issuing the stock for $85 per share, instead of $75, and assuming all of the warrants were exercised with the same amount of stock being issued.

15.4 Extinguishment of Debt

38. An entity should not derecognize an existing liability under which of the following circumstances?

A. The entity exchanges convertible preferred stock for its outstanding debt securities. The debt securities are not canceled but are held as treasury bonds.

B. Because of financial difficulties being experienced by the entity, a creditor accepts a parcel of land as full satisfaction of an overdue loan. The value of the land is less than 50% of the loan balance.

C. The entity irrevocably places cash into a trust that will be used solely to satisfy scheduled principal and interest payments of a specific bond obligation. Because the trust investments will generate a higher return, the amount of cash is less than the carrying amount of the debt.

D. As part of the agreement to purchase a shopping center from the entity, the buyer assumes without recourse the mortgage for which the center serves as collateral.

The correct answer is (C). *(Publisher)*
REQUIRED: The circumstances under which an existing liability should not be derecognized.
DISCUSSION: SFAS 125, *Accounting for Transfers and Servicing of Financial Assets and Extinguishments of Liabilities*, prescribes the derecognition of a liability only if it has been extinguished. Extinguishment occurs when either (1) the debtor pays the creditor and is relieved of its obligation for the liability, or (2) the debtor is legally released from being the primary obligor under the liability, either judicially or by the creditor. SFAS 125, effective for extinguishments of liabilities occurring after December 31, 1996, prohibits the recognition of a gain or loss from an in-substance defeasance, previously permitted by SFAS 76, *Extinguishment of Debt*.
Answers (A), (B), and (D) are incorrect because they describe circumstance under which the debt is extinguished.

39. A gain or loss from the early extinguishment of debt, if material, should be

- A. Recognized in income before taxes in the period of extinguishment.

- B. Recognized as an extraordinary item in the period of extinguishment.

- C. Amortized over the life of the new issue.

- D. Amortized over the remaining original life of the extinguished issue.

The correct answer is (B). *(CPA 591 T-26)*
REQUIRED: The treatment of a gain or loss on the early extinguishment of debt.
DISCUSSION: A gain or loss from the early extinguishment of debt, if material, should be recognized as an extraordinary item in the period of extinguishment.
Answers (A), (C), and (D) are incorrect because a gain or loss from the early extinguishment of debt should be recognized as an extraordinary item in the period of extinguishment.

40. In open market transactions, Oak Corp. simultaneously sold its long-term investment in Maple Corp. bonds and purchased its own outstanding bonds. The broker remitted the net cash from the two transactions. Oak's gain on the purchase of its own bonds exceeded its loss on the sale of Maple's bonds. Oak should report the

- A. Net effect of the two transactions as an extraordinary gain.

- B. Net effect of the two transactions in income before extraordinary items.

- C. Effect of its own bond transaction gain in income before extraordinary items, and report the Maple bond transaction as an extraordinary loss.

- D. Effect of its own bond transaction as an extraordinary gain, and report the Maple bond transaction loss in income before extraordinary items.

The correct answer is (D). *(CPA 592 T-30)*
REQUIRED: The reporting of the sale of a long-term investment in bonds and an extinguishment of debt.
DISCUSSION: APB 26 requires that differences between the reacquisition prices and the net carrying amounts of extinguished debt be recognized currently as gains or losses in income of the period of extinguishment. SFAS 4 requires that such gains or losses be aggregated and, if material, classified as extraordinary items, net of related income tax effect. An exception is made for gains or losses from extinguishments of debt that satisfy sinking-fund requirements that must be met within 1 year. See SFAS 64. However, transactions are presumed to be ordinary and usual unless a pronouncement specifically states otherwise or the evidence clearly supports classification as extraordinary. The sale of securities is not clearly infrequent and unusual in the environment in which the entity operates. Thus, the loss on the sale of bonds should be reported in income before extraordinary items.
Answers (A) and (B) are incorrect because the items may not be netted. Answer (C) is incorrect because the extinguishment resulted in an extraordinary gain and the sale of securities in an ordinary loss.

41. Weald Co. took advantage of market conditions to refund debt. This was the fifth refunding operation carried out by Weald within the last 4 years. The excess of the carrying amount of the old debt over the amount paid to extinguish it should be reported as a(n)

- A. Deferred credit to be amortized over life of new debt.

- B. Part of continuing operations.

- C. Extraordinary gain, net of income taxes.

- D. Extraordinary loss, net of income taxes.

The correct answer is (C). *(CPA 593 T-18)*
REQUIRED: The proper accounting for the retirement of debt.
DISCUSSION: SFAS 4, *Reporting Gains and Losses from Extinguishment of Debt,* requires that gains and losses from early extinguishment be recognized in income in the year of extinguishment as an extraordinary item. Since the amount paid to extinguish the debt is less than the carrying amount, an extraordinary gain resulted.
Answers (A) and (B) are incorrect because gains and losses from early extinguishment of a debt should be treated as an extraordinary item. Answer (D) is incorrect because when the amount paid to extinguish a debt is less than the carrying amount of the debt, a gain, not a loss, results.

42. According to SFAS 4, *Reporting Gains and Losses from Extinguishment of Debt*, as amended, all of the following gains or losses from extinguishment of debt should be classified in the income statement as extraordinary items except those arising from

A. The extinguishment of debt at less than the net carrying amount.

B. The extinguishment of debt to satisfy sinking-fund requirements to be met within 1 year.

C. The extinguishment of debt by exchanging common shares of stock.

D. Refinancing existing debt with new debt.

The correct answer is (B). *(CMA 692 2-18)*
REQUIRED: The debt extinguishment not treated as an extraordinary item.
DISCUSSION: According to SFAS 64, *Extinguishment of Debt Made to Satisfy Sinking-Fund Requirements*, gains and losses from extinguishments of debt made to satisfy sinking-fund requirements that must be met within 1 year of the date of extinguishment should be treated as ordinary gains or losses. This classification is determined without regard to the means (cash or otherwise) of extinguishment.
Answer (A) is incorrect because extinguishment at less than the net carrying amount results in an extraordinary gain. Answer (C) is incorrect because extinguishments by means of exchanging common stock (other than as conversion privileges granted at the date of issuance of the debt) can result in an extraordinary gain or loss. Answer (D) is incorrect because refinancing old debt with new results in an extraordinary item.

43. E&S partnership purchased land for $500,000 on May 1, 1993, paying $100,000 cash and giving a $400,000 note payable to Big State Bank. E&S made three annual payments on the note totaling $179,000, which included interest of $89,000. E&S then defaulted on the note. Title to the land was transferred by E&S to Big State, which canceled the note, releasing the partnership from further liability. At the time of the default, the fair value of the land approximated the note balance. In E&S's 1996 income statement, the amount of the loss should be

A. $279,000

B. $221,000

C. $190,000

D. $100,000

The correct answer is (C). *(CPA 1191 I-57)*
REQUIRED: The amount of the loss after default on a note and repossession of the land.
DISCUSSION: The principal of the note had been reduced to $310,000 [$400,000 − ($179,000 total payments − $89,000 interest)] at the time of default. The resultant $190,000 loss is equal to the difference between the $500,000 carrying value (cost) of the land and the $310,000 carrying value of the note.
Answer (A) is incorrect because $279,000 results from subtracting the full amount of the payments ($179,000) in determining the remaining principal. Answer (B) is incorrect because $221,000 is the note payable balance after subtracting the $89,000 of interest. Answer (D) is incorrect because $100,000 is the amount of the initial payment.

44. Ray Finance, Inc. issued a 10-year, $100,000, 9% note on January 1, 1994. The note was issued to yield 10% for proceeds of $93,770. Interest is payable semiannually. The note is callable after 2 years at a price of $96,000. Due to a decline in the market rate to 8%, Ray retired the note on December 31, 1996. On that date, the carrying amount of the note was $94,582, and the discounted market rate was $105,280. What amount should Ray report as gain (loss) from retirement of the note for the year ended December 31, 1996?

A. $9,280

B. $4,000

C. $(2,230)

D. $(1,418)

The correct answer is (D). *(CPA 592 I-55)*
REQUIRED: The amount of gain (loss) from the retirement of a note.
DISCUSSION: The amount of gain or loss resulting from the extinguishment of debt is the difference between the amount paid less the carrying value of the note. Thus, a loss of $1,418 ($94,582 carrying value − $96,000 amount paid) results from the retirement.
Answer (A) is incorrect because $9,280 is the difference between the discounted market rate less the call price. Answer (B) is incorrect because $4,000 is the difference between the face amount of the note less the call price. Answer (C) is incorrect because $2,230 is the original issuing amount less the call price.

45. On July 31, 1996, Dome Co. issued $1 million of 10%, 15-year bonds at par and used a portion of the proceeds to call its 600 outstanding 11%, $1,000 face value bonds, due on July 31, 2006, at 102. On that date, unamortized bond premium relating to the 11% bonds was $65,000. In its 1996 income statement, what amount should Dome report as gain or loss, before income taxes, from retirement of bonds?

A. $53,000 gain.

B. $0

C. $(65,000) loss.

D. $(77,000) loss.

The correct answer is (A). *(CPA 1194 F-42)*
REQUIRED: The amount to be reported for the retirement of bonds.
DISCUSSION: The excess of the net carrying amount of the bonds over the reacquisition price is an extraordinary gain from extinguishment. The carrying amount of the bonds equals $665,000 ($600,000 face value + $65,000 unamortized premium). The reacquisition price is $612,000 (600 x $1,000 x 1.02). Thus, the gain from extinguishment is $53,000 ($665,000 – $612,000).
Answer (B) is incorrect because the excess of the carrying amount over the reacquisition cost is a gain. Answer (C) is incorrect because $65,000 is the unamortized premium. Answer (D) is incorrect because $77,000 equals the reacquisition price of $612,000, minus the face value of $600,000, plus $65,000 unamortized premium.

46. On June 2, 1991, Tory, Inc. issued $500,000 of 10%, 15-year bonds at par. Interest is payable semiannually on June 1 and December 1. Bond issue costs were $6,000. On June 2, 1996, Tory retired half of the bonds at 98. What is the net amount that Tory should use in computing the gain or loss on retirement of debt?

A. $250,000

B. $248,000

C. $247,000

D. $246,000

The correct answer is (B). *(CPA 1193 I-40)*
REQUIRED: The net amount used in computing the gain or loss on the retirement of debt.
DISCUSSION: The gain or loss on the retirement of debt is equal to the difference between the proceeds paid and the carrying value of the debt. The carrying value of the debt is equal to the face value plus any unamortized premium or minus any unamortized discount. In addition, any unamortized issue costs are considered in effect a reduction of the carrying value even though they are accounted for separately from the bond discount or premium. The amortization of the issue costs is $400 per year ($6,000 ÷ 15). Because accumulated amortization is $2,000 ($400 x 5), the unamortized issue costs are $4,000 ($6,000 – $2,000), of which 50% or $2,000 should be subtracted in determining the carrying value of the bonds retired. Consequently, the net carrying amount that should be used in computing the gain or loss on this early extinguishment of debt is $248,000 ($250,000 face amount – $2,000 unamortized deferred bond issue costs).
Answer (A) is incorrect because $250,000 is half of the par value. Answer (C) is incorrect because $247,000 is half of the par value minus half of the issue costs. Answer (D) is incorrect because $246,000 results from subtracting 100% of the unamortized issue costs.

47. On June 30, 1996, King Co. had outstanding 9%, $5,000,000 face value bonds maturing on June 30, 2001. Interest was payable semiannually every June 30 and December 31. On June 30, 1996, after amortization was recorded for the period, the unamortized bond premium and bond issue costs were $30,000 and $50,000, respectively. On that date, King acquired all its outstanding bonds on the open market at 98 and retired them. At June 30, 1996, what amount should King recognize as gain before income taxes on redemption of bonds?

A. $20,000

B. $80,000

C. $120,000

D. $180,000

The correct answer is (B). *(CPA 1192 I-47)*
REQUIRED: The amount of gain from the redemption of bonds.
DISCUSSION: The amount of gain or loss on the redemption of bonds is equal to the difference between the proceeds paid and the carrying value of the debt. The carrying value of the bonds is equal to the face amount plus unamortized bond premium less unamortized bond issue costs. Thus, the carrying value of the bonds is $4,980,000 (5,000,000 + 30,000 – 50,000). The $80,000 gain is the difference between the carrying value ($4,980,000) and the amount paid $4,900,000 ($5,000,000 x .98).
Answer (A) is incorrect because $20,000 results from subtracting the unamortized bond premium and bond issue costs from the face amount of the bond. Answer (C) is incorrect because the unamortized bond issue costs are added to the face value of the bond and bond premium is subtracted to find the carrying value. Answer (D) is incorrect because both the unamortized bond issue costs and bond premium are added to find the carrying value of the bond.

48. On January 2, 1997, Wright Corporation entered into an in-substance debt defeasance transaction by placing cash of $875,000 into an irrevocable trust. The trust assets are to be used solely for satisfying the interest and principal payments on Wright's 6%, $1,100,000, 30-year bond payable. Wright has not been legally released under the bond agreement, but the probability is remote that Wright will be required to place additional cash in the trust. On December 31, 1996, the bond's carrying amount was $1,050,000; its fair value was $800,000. Disregarding income taxes, what amount of extraordinary gain (loss) should Wright report in its 1997 income statement?

    A.   ($75,000)

    B. $0

    C. $175,000

    D. $225,000

The correct answer is (B). *(Publisher)*
    REQUIRED: The amount of extraordinary gain (loss) to be recognized on an in-substance defeasance.
    DISCUSSION: SFAS 125, effective for extinguishments of liabilities occurring after December 31, 1996, prohibits the recognition of a gain (loss) from an in-substance defeasance, previously permitted by SFAS 76, *Extinguishment of Debt*.
    Answers (A), (C), and (D) are incorrect because an in-substance defeasance does not result in the derecognition of a liability.

49. The extinguishment of debt denominated in U.S. dollars can occur when a debtor irrevocably places cash or other assets into a trust to be used solely for satisfying the future interest and principal payments of the specific debt. Which of the following is not a correct statement of a condition that must be met before the debt is treated as extinguished?

    A.   The trust is restricted to holding monetary assets.

    B.   The assets held by the trust are limited to obligations guaranteed by the U.S. government.

    C.   The assets held by the trust are limited to direct obligations of the U.S. government, states, or local governments.

    D.   The assets held by the trust provide cash flows that approximately coincide with the scheduled interest and principal payments of the debt to be extinguished.

The correct answer is (C). *(Publisher)*
    REQUIRED: The item that is not a condition for treating the debt as extinguished.
    DISCUSSION: According to SFAS 76, certain requirements regarding the nature of assets held by an irrevocable trust must be met before the debt is considered extinguished. The assets held must be essentially risk-free as to the amount, timing, and collection of interest and principal. The assets must be monetary and denominated in the currency in which the debt is payable. For debt denominated in U.S. dollars, only direct obligations of the U.S. government, obligations guaranteed by the U.S. government, and securities that are backed by U.S. government obligations as collateral may be held. Cash flows from the trust assets must approximately coincide, as to timing and amount, with the principal and interest payments on the debt.
    Answers (A), (B), and (D) are incorrect because each is a condition required by SFAS 76 for debt to be considered extinguished through placing assets in trust.

15.5 Refunding

50. Cole Corporation retired an issue of bonds before its maturity date through a direct exchange of securities. The best value for Cole to assign to the new issue of debt is the

A. Maturity value of the new issue.

B. Net carrying value of the old issue.

C. Present value of the new issue.

D. Maturity value of the old issue.

The correct answer is (C). *(CPA 574 T-38)*
REQUIRED: The best value to assign a new issue of debt used to retire an issue of bonds.
DISCUSSION: APB 26, *Early Extinguishment of Debt*, states that if an early extinguishment of debt is achieved by a direct exchange of new securities (a refunding), the reacquisition price is accounted for at the present value of the new securities.
Answers (A), (B), and (D) are incorrect because, under APB 26, *Early Extinguishment of Debt*, the present value of the new issue must be used.

51. Which of the following material gains on refunding of bonds payable should be recognized separately as an extraordinary gain?

	Direct Exchange of Old Bonds for New Bonds	Issuance of New Bonds; Proceeds Used to Retire Old Bonds
A.	Yes	No
B.	Yes	Yes
C.	No	Yes
D.	No	No

The correct answer is (B). *(CPA 1183 T-17)*
REQUIRED: The refunding gain(s) that should be recognized as extraordinary.
DISCUSSION: Regardless of whether the extinguishment is accomplished by a refunding or nonrefunding arrangement, SFAS 4 requires that the gains and losses from extinguishment be aggregated and, if material, classified as an extraordinary item, net of income tax effect. The entire gain or loss should be reported in the period of extinguishment. According to SFAS 64, *Extinguishments of Debt Made to Satisfy Sinking-Fund Requirements*, the only early extinguishment to which SFAS 4 does not apply is one made to satisfy sinking-fund requirements that an entity must meet within 1 year.
Answers (A), (C), and (D) are incorrect because, regardless of the arrangement, material gain from the refunding of bonds payable is reported as an extraordinary item.

52. A 15-year bond was issued in 1986 at a discount. During 1996, a 10-year bond was issued at face amount with the proceeds used to retire the 15-year bond at its face amount. The net effect of the 1996 bond transactions was to increase long-term liabilities by the excess of the 10-year bond's face amount over the 15-year bond's

A. Face amount.

B. Carrying amount.

C. Face amount minus the deferred loss on bond retirement.

D. Carrying amount minus the deferred loss on bond retirement.

The correct answer is (B). *(CPA 591 T-5)*
REQUIRED: The net effect of the bond transactions.
DISCUSSION: The 10-year bond was issued at its face amount, that is, at neither a premium nor a discount. Its face amount therefore equaled its proceeds, which were used to retire the 15-year bond at its face amount. The 15-year bond was carried at a discount (face amount − unamortized discount). Consequently, net long-term liabilities must have increased by the amount of the unamortized discount on the 15-year bond, which is the excess of the 10-year bond's face amount over the carrying value of the 15-year bond.
Answer (A) is incorrect because the face amount of the 10-year bond equaled the face amount of the 15-year bond. Answers (C) and (D) are incorrect because the loss on early extinguishment is not deferred.

15.6 Interest on Receivables and Payables

53. A company issued a noninterest-bearing note payable due in 1 year in exchange for land. Which of the following statements is correct concerning the accounting for the transaction?

A. The land should be recorded at the future value of the note, and interest should be imputed at the prevailing rate on similar notes.

B. No interest should be recognized on the note, and the land should be recorded at the present value of the note.

C. Interest on the note should be imputed at the prime rate and the land recorded at the discounted value of the note.

D. Interest on the note should be imputed at the prevailing rate for similar notes and the land recorded at present value of the note.

The correct answer is (D). *(CIA 1193 IV-44)*
REQUIRED: The proper accounting for a noninterest-bearing note.
DISCUSSION: If interest on a note is not stated, it is imputed by recording the note at the fair value of the property, goods, or services exchanged, or at the fair value of the note itself. If these values are not determinable, an interest rate must be imputed. APB 21 establishes certain guidelines for imputing an interest rate. The rate should be at least equal to that at which the debtor could obtain financing of a similar nature from other sources. Other considerations are the market rate for an exchange of the note, the prime or higher rate for notes discounted with banks in light of the credit standing of the maker, and the current rates for debt instruments with substantially identical terms and risks that are traded in open markets. Accordingly, if the fair value of the note or the land is not determinable, the transaction will be recorded at the present value of the note based on an imputed rate.
Answer (A) is incorrect because the land is recorded at present value. Answer (B) is incorrect because interest should be recognized on the note. Answer (C) is incorrect because the proper discount rate is the prevailing rate for similar notes, not the prime rate.

54. When it is necessary to impute interest in connection with a note receivable, the imputed rate should be

A. Influenced by the prevailing market rate for debt instruments with substantially identical terms and risks.

B. Two-thirds of the prime rate effective at the time the note is received.

C. Equal to the rate obtainable on government securities with comparable due dates.

D. The minimum rate allowed by the Internal Revenue Code.

The correct answer is (A). *(Publisher)*
REQUIRED: The correct statement concerning imputation of an interest rate in connection with a note receivable.
DISCUSSION: APB 21 establishes certain guidelines for selecting an interest rate. The rate should be at least equal to that at which the debtor could obtain financing of a similar nature from other sources. Other considerations are the market rate for an exchange of the note, the prime or higher rate for notes discounted with banks in light of the credit standing of the maker, and the current rates for debt instruments with substantially identical terms and risks that are traded in open markets.
Answers (B), (C), and (D) are incorrect because APB 21 does not specify any particular interest rate.

55. Ogden Corp. lends a supplier cash that is to be repaid 5 years hence with no stated interest. At the same time, a purchase contract is entered into for the supplier's products. Ogden will be required to recognize interest revenue in connection with the loan

   A. Under no circumstances.

   B. If the contract price is equal to the prevailing market rate.

   C. If the contract price is less than the prevailing market rate.

   D. If the contract price is more than the prevailing market rate.

The correct answer is (C). *(CPA 1173 T-9)*
   REQUIRED: The circumstances in which interest revenue will be recognized.
   DISCUSSION: Ordinarily, a note received solely for cash equal to its face amount is presumed to earn the stated rate of interest. However, if, in addition, some right or privilege has been exchanged, its value must be recognized in the accounts in accordance with APB 21. If the contract price is less than the market rate, Ogden's note receivable will be debited and cash credited for the amount of the loan. In addition, prepaid purchases (an asset) will be debited and discount on notes receivable will be credited for the difference between the amount lent and the present value of the note. Prepaid purchases will be treated as part of the cost of the products as they are purchased. Moreover, amortization of the discount will result in interest income under the effective-interest method over the life of the note.
   Answer (A) is incorrect because Ogden will recognize interest revenue if the supplier's contract price is below the market rate. Answers (B) and (D) are incorrect because, if the contract price is equal to or greater than the market rate, a loan with no stated interest would not be considered related to the purchase contract.

56. United Refinery Company, a refiner of peanut oil, lent $500,000 to James Barter, a peanut farmer, interest free for 5 years. The day after the loan agreement, Barter guaranteed that United Refinery could purchase up to 1,000,000 pounds of shucked peanuts per year for the next 6 years at a price 5¢ less per pound than the prevailing market price. Barter asked for nothing in return for this price concession. United should record the loan at

   A. Its face amount with no recognition of interest income over the 5-year period.

   B. A discount using the average cost of capital as the rate for imputing interest.

   C. Its face amount with interest income recognized each year in the amount of the price concession realized during that year.

   D. A discount equal to the expected value of the price concession granted.

The correct answer is (D). *(Publisher)*
   REQUIRED: The accounting for an interest-free loan related to an unstated right or privilege.
   DISCUSSION: Even though the price concession was not explicitly part of the loan agreement, the economic reality is that the noninterest-bearing loan is partial consideration for the purchase of products at lower than the prevailing market price. The expected value of the price concession should be the measure of the loan discount. It is the difference between the amount of the loan and the present value of the note. The discount should be recorded as a debit to prepaid purchases and a credit to discount on notes receivable. The prepaid asset will be written off as purchases are made (debit purchases, credit prepaid purchases) during the contract term. The discount should be amortized using the interest method as interest income over the 5-year life of the loan.
   Answer (A) is incorrect because APB 21 requires that the economic substance of the transaction be explicitly recognized in the accounts by recognizing the unstated right as an asset and a discount to the note receivable. Answer (B) is incorrect because the present value of the price concession should be used to discount the note. Answer (C) is incorrect because the discount on the note should be recognized as a direct deduction from the note receivable.

57. When a note receivable or a note payable has properly been recorded at its present value, any resulting discount should be disclosed in the financial statements

   A. As a separate asset or liability.

   B. As a deferred charge or credit.

   C. In a summary caption along with any related issue costs.

   D. As a direct deduction from the face amount of the note.

The correct answer is (D). *(Publisher)*
   REQUIRED: The proper financial statement disclosure of a discount related to a note receivable or payable.
   DISCUSSION: APB 21 states that discount or premium is not an asset or liability separable from the related note. A discount should therefore be reported in the balance sheet as a direct deduction from the face amount of the note.
   Answers (A), (B), and (C) are incorrect because the discount is disclosed as a direct adjustment to the face value of the note.

58. Which of the following is reported as interest expense?

    A. Pension cost interest.

    B. Postretirement healthcare benefits interest.

    C. Imputed interest on a noninterest-bearing note.

    D. Interest incurred to finance construction of machinery for an enterprise's own use.

The correct answer is (C). *(CPA 1193 T-33)*
    REQUIRED: The item reported as interest expense.
    DISCUSSION: When a noninterest-bearing note is exchanged for property, and neither the note nor the property has a clearly determinable exchange price, the present value of the note should be determined by discounting all future payments using an appropriately imputed interest rate. Periodic interest expense must be calculated and recognized in accordance with the effective-interest method.
    Answer (A) is incorrect because interest cost for a defined benefit pension plan is reported as a component of the net periodic pension cost. Answer (B) is incorrect because interest cost for a defined benefit postretirement plan is reported as a component of the net postretirement benefit cost. Answer (D) is incorrect because interest incurred to finance construction of machinery for an enterprise's own use is capitalized.

Questions 59 and 60 are based on the following information. House Publishers offered a contest in which the winner would receive $1 million, payable over 20 years. On December 31, 1996, House announced the winner of the contest and signed a note payable to the winner for $1 million, payable in $50,000 installments every January 2. Also on December 31, 1996, House purchased an annuity for $418,250 to provide the $950,000 prize monies remaining after the first $50,000 installment, which was paid on January 2, 1997.

---

59. In its December 31, 1996 balance sheet, what amount should House report as note payable-contest winner, net of current portion?

    A. $368,250

    B. $418,250

    C. $900,000

    D. $950,000

The correct answer is (B). *(CPA 1194 F-22)*
    REQUIRED: The amount of the note payable.
    DISCUSSION: Noninterest-bearing notes payable should be measured at their present value rather than their face value. Thus, House should report the note payable at $418,250 (the present value of the remaining payments).
    Answer (A) is incorrect because $368,250 includes a reduction of $50,000 for the first installment. Answer (C) is incorrect because $900,000 equals the face value of the note payable minus two installments. Answer (D) is incorrect because $950,000 equals the face value of the note payable minus the first installment.

---

60. In its 1996 income statement, what should House report as contest prize expense?

    A. $0

    B. $418,250

    C. $468,250

    D. $1,000,000

The correct answer is (C). *(CPA 1194 F-23)*
    REQUIRED: The contest prize expense.
    DISCUSSION: The contest prize expense equals $468,250 ($418,250 cost of the annuity + $50,000 first installment).
    Answer (A) is incorrect because $0 does not include the purchase of the annuity or the first installment as an expense in 1996. Answer (B) is incorrect because $418,250 does not include the $50,000 installment due in 1997. Answer (D) is incorrect because $1,000,000 is the face amount of the note.

61. On January 1, the Fulmar Company sold personal property to the Austin Company. The personal property had cost Fulmar $40,000. Fulmar frequently sells similar items of property for $44,000. Austin gave Fulmar a noninterest-bearing note payable in six equal annual installments of $10,000 with the first payment due beginning this December 31. Collection of the note is reasonably assured. A reasonable rate of interest for a note of this type is 10%. The present value of an annuity of $1 in arrears at 10% for six periods is 4.355. What amount of sales revenue from this transaction should be reported in Fulmar's income statement for the year of sale ended December 31?

    A. $10,000

    B. $40,000

    C. $43,550

    D. $44,000

The correct answer is (D). *(CPA 1176 I-10)*
   REQUIRED: The amount of sales revenue to be reported in the income statement of the recipient of a noninterest-bearing note.
   DISCUSSION: When a noninterest-bearing note is exchanged for property, the note, the sales price, and the cost of the property exchanged for the note should be recorded at the fair value of the property or at the market value of the note, whichever is more clearly determinable. Here, the $44,000 fair value of the property is clearly determinable because Fulmar frequently sells similar items for that amount. Consequently, $44,000 is the proper amount to be recorded as sales revenue from this transaction.
   Answer (A) is incorrect because $10,000 is the amount of the annual installment. Answer (B) is incorrect because $40,000 is the original cost of the property. Answer (C) is incorrect because $43,550 is the present value of the note, but the fair value of the property is more clearly determinable.

62. The Brown Company received a 2-year, $190,000 note on January 1, 1995 in exchange for property it sold to Gray Company. According to the terms of the note, interest of 5% is payable annually on January 1, 1996 and January 1, 1997, when the face amount is also due. There was no established exchange price for the property. The prevailing rate of interest for a note of this type was 12% at the beginning of 1995 and 14% at the beginning of 1996. What interest rates should be used to calculate the amount of interest revenue from this transaction for the years ended December 31, 1995 and 1996, respectively?

    A. 0% and 5%.

    B. 5% and 5%.

    C. 12% and 12%.

    D. 12% and 14%.

The correct answer is (C). *(CIA 1185 IV-15)*
   REQUIRED: The interest rates used to calculate interest revenue for successive years if the prevailing rate changes.
   DISCUSSION: When the nominal interest rate on a note is not equal to the prevailing market rate for this type of note, the face value of the note is not equal to its fair market value or present value. In this case, the present value of the note should be determined by discounting the $190,000 maturity value and the $9,500 annual interest payments using an appropriately imputed rate of interest. Given that 12% was the prevailing rate of interest for a note of that type at the issuance date, 12% should be used to determine both the fair market value and the interest revenue during the life of the note, regardless of fluctuations in prevailing interest rates.
   Answers (A), (B), and (D) are incorrect because the market rate of interest at the issuance date should be used to calculate the amount of interest revenue.

63. On January 1, 1996, Parke Company borrowed $360,000 from a major customer evidenced by a noninterest-bearing note due in 3 years. Parke agreed to supply the customer's inventory needs for the loan period at lower than market price. At the 12% imputed interest rate for this type of loan, the present value of the note is $255,000 at January 1, 1996. What amount of interest expense should be included in Parke's 1996 income statement?

A. $43,200

B. $35,000

C. $30,600

D. $0

The correct answer is (C). *(CPA 585 I-38)*

REQUIRED: The amount of interest expense recognized by the maker of a noninterest-bearing note.

DISCUSSION: A note issued solely for cash equal to its face amount is presumed to earn the stated rate of interest, even if that rate is zero. If, however, the parties have also exchanged stated or unstated rights or privileges, these must be recognized by determining the fair market value (present value) of the note based on an appropriate interest rate. Interest income or expense should be calculated and the discount amortized using the effective interest rate. Parke agreed to supply the customer's inventory needs for the loan period at lower than the market price. Hence, the note should be recorded at $255,000, with the remaining $105,000 ($360,000 – $255,000) recognized as a deferred adjustment to the market price. The interest expense is equal to the carrying amount of the note at the beginning of the interest period times the 12% imputed interest rate. The interest expense for 1996 should therefore be $30,600 ($255,000 carrying value x 12% imputed interest rate).

Answer (A) is incorrect because $43,200 results from applying the imputed interest rate to the face amount of the note instead of to the carrying value. Answer (B) is incorrect because $35,000 results from recognizing interest expense using the straight-line method. Answer (D) is incorrect because interest expense must be imputed on a noninterest-bearing note.

64. On September 1, 1995, Brok Co. issued a note payable to Federal Bank in the amount of $900,000, bearing interest at 12%, and payable in three equal annual principal payments of $300,000. On this date, the bank's prime rate was 11%. The first interest and principal payment was made on September 1, 1996. At December 31, 1996, Brok should record accrued interest payable of

A. $36,000

B. $33,000

C. $24,000

D. $22,000

The correct answer is (C). *(CPA 1193 I-31)*

REQUIRED: The amount to be recorded as accrued interest payable.

DISCUSSION: Under the interest method, accrued interest payable is equal to the face amount of the note at the beginning of the interest period, times the stated interest rate, times the portion of the interest period that is included within the accounting period. At 9/1/95, the face value of the note was $900,000. After the first $300,000 principal payment at 9/1/96, the face value of the note was $600,000 ($900,000 – $300,000). Accrued interest payable for the period 9/1/96 to 12/31/96 was thus $24,000 ($600,000 face value x 12% stated interest rate x 4/12). The prime rate is irrelevant to the calculation of accrued interest payable.

Answer (A) is incorrect because $36,000 was the accrued interest payable at 12/31/95. Answer (B) is incorrect because $33,000 would have been the accrued interest payable at 12/31/95 if the interest rate had been 11%. Answer (D) is incorrect because $22,000 would have been the accrued interest payable at 12/31/96 if the interest rate had been 11%.

65. On January 31, 1996, Beau Corp. issued $300,000 maturity value, 12% bonds for $300,000 cash. The bonds are dated December 31, 1995 and mature on December 31, 2005. Interest will be paid semiannually on June 30 and December 31. What amount of accrued interest payable should Beau report in its September 30, 1996 balance sheet?

A. $27,000

B. $24,000

C. $18,000

D. $9,000

The correct answer is (D). *(CPA 1193 I-29)*

REQUIRED: The amount of accrued interest payable that should be reported in the balance sheet.

DISCUSSION: Since interest is paid semiannually on June 30 and December 31, the amount of each payment is $18,000 [($300,000 x 12%) ÷ 2]. On June 30, $18,000 was paid. From 7/1 to 9/30/96 (3 months), interest accrued. Thus, $9,000 ($18,000 x 3/6) of accrued interest payable should be reported.

Answer (A) is incorrect because $27,000 includes the $18,000 already paid on June 30. Answer (B) is incorrect because $24,000 includes the $18,000 already paid on June 30 and erroneously records $6,000, which is the accrued interest for 2 months. Answer (C) is incorrect because $18,000 is the amount of the semiannual interest payable.

66. SFAS 47 specifies disclosure requirements for long-term obligations as a group. The FASB believed that a particular group of long-term obligations frequently was not disclosed adequately. Thus, this statement was specifically addressed to the group of items referred to as

A. Loss contingencies.

B. Unconditional purchase obligations.

C. Long-term borrowings.

D. Pension plans.

The correct answer is (B). *(CMA 683 3-15)*
REQUIRED: The long-term obligations covered by SFAS 47.
DISCUSSION: SFAS 47, *Disclosure of Long-Term Obligations*, requires that a company disclose commitments under unconditional purchase obligations that are associated with suppliers. Unconditional purchase obligations are commitments to transfer funds in the future for fixed or minimum amounts of goods or services at fixed or minimum prices.
Answer (A) is incorrect because loss contingencies are covered by SFAS 5, *Accounting for Contingencies*. Answer (C) is incorrect because long-term borrowings is a broad financial accounting topic for which there is no single authoritative pronouncement. Answer (D) is incorrect because pension plans are covered by SFAS 35, *Accounting and Reporting by Defined Benefit Pension Plans*; SFAS 87, *Employers' Accounting for Pensions*; and SFAS 88, *Employers' Accounting for Settlements and Curtailments of Defined Benefit Pension Plans and for Termination Benefits*.

67. SFAS 47, *Disclosure of Long-Term Obligations*, does not apply to an unconditional purchase obligation that is cancelable under which of the following conditions?

A. Upon the occurrence of a remote contingency.

B. With the permission of the other party.

C. If a replacement agreement is signed between the same parties.

D. Upon payment of a nominal penalty.

The correct answer is (D). *(Publisher)*
REQUIRED: The condition excluding unconditional purchase obligation coverage by SFAS 47.
DISCUSSION: SFAS 47 provides the standards of accounting for an unconditional purchase obligation that

1. Was negotiated as part of the financing arrangement for facilities that will provide contracted goods or services

2. Has a remaining term of more than 1 year

3. Is either noncancelable or cancelable only under specific terms

Excluded from these terms and from the provisions of SFAS 47 is a purchase obligation cancelable upon the payment of a nominal penalty.
Answers (A), (B), and (C) are incorrect because each is a condition indicating that the obligation is noncancelable in substance.

68. If an unconditional purchase obligation is not presented in the balance sheet, certain disclosures are required. A disclosure that is not required is

A. The nature and term of the obligation.

B. The variable components of the obligation.

C. The imputed interest necessary to reduce the unconditional purchase obligation to its present value.

D. The amounts purchased under the obligation for each period an income statement is presented.

The correct answer is (C). *(Publisher)*
REQUIRED: The item not required to be disclosed if an unconditional purchase obligation is not recognized in the balance sheet.
DISCUSSION: When an unconditional purchase obligation is not recorded in the balance sheet, SFAS 47 encourages, but does not require, the disclosure of the amount of imputed interest necessary to reduce the unconditional purchase obligation to its present value.
Answers (A), (B), and (D) are incorrect because each disclosure is explicitly required by SFAS 47 when an unconditional purchase obligation is not recorded in the balance sheet. SFAS 47 also requires disclosure of the amount of the fixed and determinable portion of the obligation in the aggregate as of the latest balance sheet date and the amounts due in each of the next 5 years.

69. When an entity discloses the imputed interest rate necessary to reduce an unconditional purchase obligation, not recorded in the balance sheet, to its present value, the interest rate disclosed should be which of the following?

A. If known by the purchaser, the effective initial interest rate of the debt that financed the facilities providing the contracted goods or services.

B. The purchaser's incremental borrowing rate.

C. The prime rate.

D. The current Aa bond interest rate.

The correct answer is (A). *(Publisher)*
REQUIRED: The interest rate to be used in determining the present value of an unconditional purchase obligation.
DISCUSSION: SFAS 47 encourages, but does not require, disclosure of the imputed interest rate. If known by the purchaser, the rate disclosed should be the initial effective interest rate of the debt that financed the facilities providing the contracted goods or services. If that rate cannot be determined by the purchaser, the purchaser's incremental borrowing rate should be used.
Answer (B) is incorrect because it is used only if the purchaser does not know the initial interest rate on the debt that financed the facilities providing the contracted goods or services. Answers (C) and (D) are incorrect because neither is discussed in SFAS 47.

70. Witt Corp. has outstanding at December 31, 1996 two long-term borrowings with annual sinking-fund requirements and maturities as follows:

	Sinking-Fund Requirements	Maturities
1997	$1,000,000	$ --
1998	1,500,000	2,000,000
1999	1,500,000	2,000,000
2000	2,000,000	2,500,000
2001	2,000,000	3,000,000
	$8,000,000	$9,500,000

In the notes to its December 31, 1996 balance sheet, how should Witt report the above data?

A. No disclosure is required.

B. Only sinking-fund payments totaling $8,000,000 for the next 5 years detailed by year need be disclosed.

C. Only maturities totaling $9,500,000 for the next 5 years detailed by year need be disclosed.

D. The combined aggregate of $17,500,000 of maturities and sinking-fund requirements detailed by year should be disclosed.

The correct answer is (D). *(CPA 1190 I-54)*
REQUIRED: The required footnote disclosure of sinking fund payments and maturities for long-term borrowings.
DISCUSSION: In addition to the disclosures required by other official pronouncements, SFAS 47 requires the disclosure of the following information for each of the 5 years following the date of the latest balance sheet presented: (1) the aggregate amount of payments for unconditional purchase obligations, (2) the aggregate amount of maturities and sinking-fund requirements for all long-term borrowings, and (3) the amount at which all issues of stock are redeemable at fixed or determinable prices on fixed or determinable dates. Thus, Witt Corp. should disclose in the notes to the December 31, 1996 balance sheet the combined aggregate of $17,500,000 ($8,000,000 + $9,500,000) of maturities and sinking-fund requirements detailed by year.
Answers (A), (B), and (C) are incorrect because the combined aggregate amount of maturities and sinking-fund payments for all borrowings must be disclosed.

15.7 Troubled Debt Restructurings by Debtors

71. SFAS 15, *Accounting by Debtors and Creditors for Troubled Debt Restructurings*, defined a troubled debt restructuring as one in which the

A. Fair value of cash, other assets, or an equity interest accepted by a creditor from a debtor in full satisfaction of its receivable at least equals the creditor's recorded investment in the receivable.

B. Creditor reduces the effective interest rate on the debt primarily to reflect a decrease in market interest rates in general.

C. Debtor issues, in exchange for its existing debt, new marketable debt having an effective interest rate that is at or near the current market interest rates for debt with similar maturity dates and stated interest rates issued by nontroubled debtors.

D. Creditor, for economic or legal reasons related to the debtor's financial difficulties, grants a concession to the debtor that it would not otherwise consider.

The correct answer is (D). *(CMA 1291 2-1)*
REQUIRED: The definition of a troubled debt restructuring under SFAS 15.
DISCUSSION: According to SFAS 15, a troubled debt restructuring occurs when the creditor, for economic or legal reasons related to the debtor's financial difficulties, grants a concession to the debtor that it would not otherwise consider. Troubled debt restructurings usually involve a continuation of debt with modified terms, a settlement at a value less than the amount of the debt owed, or a combination. The concession involved may be imposed by law or a court, or it may arise from an agreement between the creditor and the debtor. The creditor's purpose is to reduce the loss it would otherwise incur if it did not grant the concession.

Answers (A), (B), and (C) are incorrect because SFAS 15 lists these arrangements as examples of debt restructuring that do not qualify as troubled even if the debtor is having financial difficulties.

72. Which of the following situations that arise because of a debtor's financial difficulties and would not otherwise be acceptable to the creditor must be accounted for as a troubled debt restructuring?

A. Because of a court order, a creditor accepts as full satisfaction of its receivable a building the fair value of which equals the creditor's recorded investment in the receivable.

B. As part of a negotiated settlement, a creditor accepts as full satisfaction of its receivable a building the fair value of which equals the debtor's carrying amount of the payable.

C. Because of a court order, a creditor reduces the stated interest rate for the remaining original life of the debt.

D. As part of a negotiated settlement designed to maintain a relationship with a debtor, a creditor reduces the effective interest rate on debt outstanding to reflect the lower market interest rate currently applicable to debt of that risk class.

The correct answer is (C). *(Publisher)*
REQUIRED: The situation that must be accounted for as a troubled debt restructuring.
DISCUSSION: According to SFAS 15, *Accounting by Debtors and Creditors for Troubled Debt Restructurings*, a troubled debt restructuring occurs when the creditor, for economic or legal reasons related to the debtor's financial difficulties, grants a concession to the debtor that it would not otherwise consider. Troubled debt restructurings usually involve a continuation of debt with modified terms, a settlement at a value less than the amount of the debt owed, or a combination. A court order reducing a creditor's interest rate creates a troubled debt restructuring (assuming the reduction would not be otherwise acceptable to the creditor).

Answers (A) and (B) are incorrect because no troubled debt restructuring exists if the creditor receives full payment. Answer (D) is incorrect because, if the debtor could refund the debt at the lower market rate, the creditor is not making a substantive concession.

73. According to SFAS 15, *Accounting by Debtors and Creditors for Troubled Debt Restructurings*, all of the following disclosures are required by debtors involved in a troubled debt restructuring except disclosure of

- A. A description of the major changes in terms, major features of settlement, or both.

- B. The aggregate gain on restructuring and the related tax effect.

- C. The aggregate net gain or loss on transfer of assets.

- D. The gross interest revenue that would have been recorded in the period.

74. In 1991, May Corp. acquired land by paying $75,000 down and signing a note with a maturity value of $1,000,000. On the note's due date, December 31, 1996, May owed $40,000 of accrued interest and $1,000,000 principal on the note. May was in financial difficulty and was unable to make any payments. May and the bank agreed to amend the note as follows:

- The $40,000 of interest due on December 31, 1996 was forgiven.

- The principal of the note was reduced from $1,000,000 to $950,000 and the maturity date extended 1 year to December 31, 1997.

- May would be required to make one interest payment totaling $30,000 on December 31, 1997.

As a result of the troubled debt restructuring, May should report a gain, before taxes, in its 1996 income statement of

- A. $40,000
- B. $50,000
- C. $60,000
- D. $90,000

The correct answer is (D). *(CMA 692 2-24)*
REQUIRED: The disclosure that is not required of debtors following a troubled debt restructuring.
DISCUSSION: In addition to the items in (A) through (C), debtors must, in subsequent periods, disclose the extent to which contingent amounts are included in the carrying value of restructured payables. The gross interest revenue that would have been recorded in the period is not a required disclosure for debtors because interest revenue is applicable to receivables, not payables.
Answer (A) is incorrect because a description of the major changes in terms or major features of settlement must be disclosed. Answer (B) is incorrect because the aggregate gain on restructuring and the related tax effect must be disclosed. Answer (C) is incorrect because the gain or loss on transfer of assets must be disclosed.

The correct answer is (C). *(CPA 1191 I-52)*
REQUIRED: The amount of gain to be recognized from a troubled debt restructuring.
DISCUSSION: When a troubled debt restructuring is structured as a modification of terms, a debtor should recognize an extraordinary gain equal to the difference between the future undiscounted cash flows and the carrying value of the debt. Accordingly, May should report an extraordinary gain of $60,000 ($1,000,000 principal + $40,000 accrued interest – $950,000 new principal – $30,000 interest payment). In addition, the future payments of $980,000 ($950,000 + $30,000) should be recorded as further reductions of the debt. The result is that the debt will be reduced to $0 with no interest expense recognized.
Answer (A) is incorrect because $40,000 is the amount of interest forgiven. Answer (B) is incorrect because $50,000 is the reduction of the principal forgiven. Answer (D) is incorrect because $90,000 does not include the required interest payment of $30,000 in the calculation of the gain.

75. On October 15, 1995, Kam Corp. informed Finn Co. that Kam would be unable to repay its $100,000 note due on October 31 to Finn. Finn agreed to accept title to Kam's computer equipment in full settlement of the note. The equipment's carrying value was $80,000 and its fair value was $75,000. Kam's tax rate is 30%. What amounts should Kam report as ordinary gain (loss) and extraordinary gain for the year ended September 30, 1996?

	Ordinary Gain (Loss)	Extraordinary Gain
A.	$(5,000)	$17,500
B.	$0	$20,000
C.	$0	$14,000
D.	$20,000	$0

The correct answer is (A). *(CPA 1192 I-59)*
REQUIRED: The ordinary gain (loss) and extraordinary gain for the year.
DISCUSSION: A troubled debt restructuring may occur as an asset exchange, a modification of terms, or as a combination of these two methods. In this instance, the troubled debt restructuring is effected as an asset exchange. In such an exchange, the asset given up for the troubled debt must first be adjusted from its carrying amount to its fair value, with an ordinary gain or loss being recognized for the adjustment. Thus, the debtor should include an ordinary loss of $5,000 ($80,000 carrying amount of equipment – $75,000 fair value) in the measurement of net income for the period. The gain on the restructuring of the payable is then equal to the carrying amount of the payable minus the fair value of the asset transferred. This gain should be classified as an extraordinary item, net of tax effect, in the amount of $17,500 [($100,000 – $75,000) x (1.0 – 30%)].

Answers (B), (C), and (D) are incorrect because the debtor should recognize an ordinary loss equal to the difference between the carrying amount and the fair value of the asset and an extraordinary gain equal to the after-tax difference between the carrying amount of the payable and the fair value of the asset.

76. Franco Corporation owes Chester National Bank (CNB) on a 10-year, 15% note in the amount of $100,000, plus $30,000 accrued interest. Because of financial difficulty, Franco has been unable to make annual interest payments for the past 2 years, and the note is due today. Accordingly, CNB restructured Franco Corporation's debt as follows:

- The $30,000 of accrued interest was forgiven.

- Franco was given 3 more years to pay off the debt at 8% interest. Payments are to be made annually at year-end.

Franco would properly record the restructuring and the payment for the first year as

A. An increase in interest expense of $8,000, and an extraordinary gain of $2,000.

B. A decrease in accrued interest of $8,000.

C. A decrease in accrued interest of $8,000, and an extraordinary gain of $2,000.

D. A decrease in accrued interest of $30,000, and an extraordinary gain of $6,000.

The correct answer is (D). *(CMA 1289 3-6)*
REQUIRED: The entry for the restructuring of a debt if accrued interest is forgiven, the interest rate is lowered, and the payment period is extended.
DISCUSSION: According to SFAS 15, when modified terms of a restructured troubled debt provide for future undiscounted cash payments that are less than the carrying value of the debt, the debtor should record the difference as an extraordinary gain if it is material. Franco's future cash payments will total $124,000 after the restructuring ($100,000 of principal + 3 years of interest at $8,000 per year). Given a $130,000 carrying value ($100,000 principal + $30,000 interest), the result is an extraordinary gain of $6,000 ($130,000 – $124,000). Following a restructuring of this type, all future payments on the debt (principal and interest) are treated as reductions of the carrying value. Consequently, no interest expense is recorded in the years following a restructuring. The entry to recognize the restructuring and the extraordinary gain is

Note payable	$100,000	
Accrued interest	30,000	
Restructured note payable		$124,000
Extraordinary gain		6,000

The entry to record the first payment is to debit restructured note payable for $8,000 and credit cash for $8,000.

Answer (A) is incorrect because no interest expense is recognized on a restructuring, and the extraordinary gain is $6,000. Answer (B) is incorrect because accrued interest is reduced by $30,000 (the amount forgiven). Answer (C) is incorrect because accrued interest is reduced by $30,000, and the extraordinary gain is $6,000.

77. On December 31, 1996, X Corp. was indebted to Zyland Company on a $100,000, 10% note. Only interest had been paid to date, and the remaining life of the note was 2 years. Because X Corp. was in financial difficulties, the parties agreed that X Corp. would settle the debt on the following terms:

1. Settle one-half of the note by transferring land with a recorded value of $40,000 and a fair value of $45,000
2. Settle one-fourth of the note by transferring 1,000 shares of $1 par common stock with a fair market value of $15 per share
3. Modify the terms of the remaining one-fourth of the note by reducing the interest rate to 5% for the remaining 2 years and reducing the principal to $15,000

What total gains should X Corp. record in 1996 from this troubled debt restructuring?

	Ordinary	Extraordinary
A.	$15,000	$13,500
B.	$5,000	$23,500
C.	$5,000	$10,000
D.	$13,500	$15,000

The correct answer is (B). *(T. Miller)*
REQUIRED: The total gains recorded from a troubled debt restructuring.
DISCUSSION: SFAS 15 requires that a debtor recognize a gain upon restructuring a troubled debt. X Corp. should recognize an ordinary gain of $5,000 ($45,000 fair value − $40,000 cost) when recording the land at its fair value and an extraordinary gain of $5,000 when exchanging the land for a portion of the note worth $50,000 (50% x $100,000 face amount). An extraordinary gain of $10,000 should be recognized on the exchange of stock with a fair market value of $15,000 (1,000 shares x $15) for the portion of the note worth $25,000 (25% x $100,000 face amount). Accordingly, the carrying value of the balance of the note before the modification of its terms equals the remaining $25,000 principal of the original note. Since total cash payments after the restructuring will include principal of $15,000 and 2 years of interest equal to $1,500 [2 x (.05 x $15,000)], the difference between the $25,000 carrying value and the total cash payments of $16,500 is an extraordinary gain of $8,500. The total extraordinary gain is therefore $23,500 ($5,000 + $10,000 + $8,500). The total ordinary gain is $5,000.
Answers (A), (C), and (D) are incorrect because the ordinary gain is $5,000 and the extraordinary is $23,500.

78. An enterprise incurs legal fees amounting to $2,000 in granting an equity interest to a creditor in a troubled debt restructuring. In its financial statements, the enterprise should

A. Capitalize the $2,000 and amortize it over a period not to exceed 40 years.

B. Treat the $2,000 as an expense of the period.

C. Deduct the $2,000 from the $8,000 gain resulting from the restructuring of payables.

D. Reduce by $2,000 the amount that would otherwise be recorded for the equity interest.

The correct answer is (D). *(Publisher)*
REQUIRED: The debtor's accounting for legal fees incurred in granting an equity interest to a creditor in a troubled debt restructuring.
DISCUSSION: Under SFAS 15, legal fees and other direct costs that a debtor incurs in granting an equity interest to a creditor in a troubled debt restructuring reduce the amount otherwise recorded for the interest. Other direct costs a debtor incurs to effect a troubled debt restructuring are deducted in measuring the gain on the restructuring of the payables. If no such gain is recognized, these costs are expensed as they are incurred.
Answer (A) is incorrect because the legal fees should be applied to reduce the amount of the equity interest.
Answers (B) and (C) are incorrect because each represents the proper accounting treatment of direct debt restructuring costs incurred other than in granting an equity interest.

CHAPTER SIXTEEN
PENSIONS, OTHER POSTRETIREMENT BENEFITS
AND POSTEMPLOYMENT BENEFITS

The accounting for pensions by employers is covered in SFAS 87, *Employers' Accounting for Pensions*, and in SFAS 88, *Employers' Accounting for Settlements and Curtailments of Defined Benefit Pension Plans and for Termination Benefits*. The accounting by the plans themselves is covered in SFAS 35, *Accounting and Reporting by Defined Benefit Pension Plans*. The accounting for postretirement benefits other than pensions is covered in SFAS 106, *Employers' Accounting for Postretirement Benefits Other Than Pensions*. The accounting for postemployment benefits is covered in SFAS 112, *Employers' Accounting for Postemployment Benefits*.

16.1 Employers' Accounting for Pensions

1. SFAS 87, *Employers' Accounting for Pensions*, establishes financial accounting and reporting standards for an employer that offers pension benefits to its employees. The provisions of SFAS 87 are applicable to

A. Any arrangement that is similar in substance to a pension plan.

B. Any written arrangement that is similar in substance to a pension plan.

C. Any arrangement that is legally defined as a pension plan.

D. Any arrangement that provides pension benefits, life insurance benefits, and/or health insurance benefits to retirees.

The correct answer is (A). *(Publisher)*
REQUIRED: The arrangements to which the provisions of SFAS 87 are applicable.
DISCUSSION: The provisions of SFAS 87 are applicable to any arrangement that is similar in substance to a pension plan, regardless of form, the method of financing, or whether the plan is written or implied by the well-defined practice of paying postretirement benefits.
Answer (B) is incorrect because the arrangement may be written or implied. Answer (C) is incorrect because the provisions are applicable to any arrangement that is similar in substance to a pension plan. Answer (D) is incorrect because the provisions do not apply to a plan that provides only life insurance benefits and/or health insurance benefits to retirees.

2. The provisions of SFAS 87 are primarily applicable to a defined benefit pension plan. SFAS 87 is based on the fundamental assumption that a defined benefit pension plan is part of an employee's compensation incurred when the

A. Defined pension benefit becomes vested.

B. Defined pension benefit is paid.

C. Defined pension benefit becomes a legal obligation.

D. Employee's services are rendered.

The correct answer is (D). *(Publisher)*
REQUIRED: The fundamental consideration underlying SFAS 87.
DISCUSSION: SFAS 87 is based on the fundamental assumption that a defined benefit pension plan is part of an employee's compensation incurred when the services provided to the employer by the employee are rendered. The defined pension benefit is provided in the form of a deferred payment. It is not precisely determinable. It can only be estimated based on the plan benefit formula and relevant future events such as future compensation levels, mortality rates, ages at retirement, and vesting considerations.
Answers (A), (B), and (C) are incorrect because, under SFAS 87, a defined benefit pension plan is part of an employee's compensation received when the services provided to the employer by the employee are rendered.

3. Certain accounting treatments not ordinarily allowed under GAAP are allowed in accounting for pensions. Which of the following accounting treatments is generally allowed in accounting for defined benefit pension plans?

A. The tax basis of accounting.

B. The cash or modified cash basis of accounting.

C. The offsetting of assets and liabilities.

D. The immediate recognition of all costs.

The correct answer is (C). *(Publisher)*
REQUIRED: The accounting treatment ordinarily allowed under GAAP only for pension accounting.
DISCUSSION: SFAS 87 permits (1) the delayed recognition of certain events, (2) the reporting of a net cost, and (3) the offsetting of assets and liabilities. "Delayed recognition" means that certain changes in the pension obligation and in the value of the plan assets are not recognized as they occur. They are recognized on a systematic and gradual basis over subsequent accounting periods. "Net costs" means that various pension costs (service cost, interest, actuarial gains and losses, etc.) reflected in the income statement are reported as one expense. The "offsetting feature" means that the recognized values of the plan assets contributed to the plan are offset in the statement of financial position against the recognized liabilities.
Answers (A) and (B) are incorrect because SFAS 87 requires the accrual basis of accounting. Answer (D) is incorrect because delayed, rather than immediate, recognition is allowed for certain events.

4. According to SFAS 87, *Employers' Accounting for Pensions*, the projected benefit obligation is best described as the

A. Present value of benefits accrued to date based on future salary levels.

B. Present value of benefits accrued to date based on current salary levels.

C. Increase in retroactive benefits at the date of the amendment of the plan.

D. Amount of the adjustment necessary to reflect the difference between actual and estimated actuarial returns.

The correct answer is (A). *(CMA 1290 2-21)*
REQUIRED: The definition of the projected benefit obligation.
DISCUSSION: The projected benefit obligation (PBO) as of a date is equal to the actuarial present value of all benefits attributed by the pension benefit formula to employee service rendered prior to that date. The PBO is measured using assumptions as to future salary levels.
Answer (B) is incorrect because it defines the accumulated benefit obligation (ABO). Answer (C) is incorrect because it defines prior service costs. Answer (D) is incorrect because it defines the gain or loss component of net periodic pension cost.

5. The accumulated pension obligation of a company includes benefit obligations to <List A> employees at <List B> salary levels.

	List A	List B
A.	Vested	Current
B.	Vested	Future
C.	Vested and nonvested	Current
D.	Vested and nonvested	Future

The correct answer is (C). *(CIA 595 IV-16)*
REQUIRED: The nature of the ABO.
DISCUSSION: The accumulated benefit obligation is the present value of benefits accrued to date based on past and current compensation levels. Whether benefits are vested is irrelevant to the computation.
Answers (A), (B), and (D) are incorrect because the accumulated benefit obligation includes both vested and nonvested benefits and is calculated at current, not future, salary levels.

6. An employee's right to obtain pension benefits regardless of whether (s)he remains employed is known as his/her

    A. Prior service cost.

    B. Defined benefit plan.

    C. Vested interest.

    D. Minimum liability.

The correct answer is (C). *(CIA 1189 IV-44)*

REQUIRED: The term defined as the right to obtain pension benefits regardless of future employment.

DISCUSSION: Vested benefits (vested interest) are those earned pension benefits owed to an employee regardless of the employee's continued service. The employer's vested benefit obligation (VBO) is the actuarial present value of these vested benefits.

Answer (A) is incorrect because prior service cost relates to benefits for employee service provided prior to the adoption or amendment of a defined benefit pension plan. Answer (B) is incorrect because a defined benefit pension plan provides a defined pension benefit based on one or more factors, such as level of compensation, years of service, or age. Answer (D) is incorrect because a minimum liability must be recognized by a plan for the excess of the ABO over the fair value of the plan's assets.

7. Which of the following describes a fundamental aspect of pension accounting?

    A. Changes in pension assets and obligations are recognized immediately.

    B. The amount of pension benefits is not precisely determinable.

    C. Net periodic pension cost (NPPC) may be reported within maximum and minimum limits.

    D. When underfunding occurs, immediate recognition in the balance sheet and income statement is required.

The correct answer is (B). *(Publisher)*

REQUIRED: The statement of a fundamental aspect of pension accounting.

DISCUSSION: The total pension benefit to be provided in the form of deferred payments is not precisely determinable and can only be estimated based on the plan's benefit formula and relevant future events, many of which are not controllable by the employer. Such events include how long the employee and survivors live, years of service rendered, and levels of compensation.

Answer (A) is incorrect because certain changes in the pension obligation and in the value of the assets set aside to meet those obligations are not recognized as they occur. They are recognized on a systematic and gradual basis over subsequent accounting periods. All changes ultimately will be recognized except to the extent they may be offset by subsequent changes. Answer (C) is incorrect because SFAS 87 prescribes a standard method (not a range) for measuring NPPC. Answer (D) is incorrect because, although a liability must be recognized when the ABO exceeds plan assets, income statement recognition of the offsetting amount will be delayed.

8. Under SFAS 87, *Employers' Accounting for Pensions*, attribution of pension costs to periods of employee service for a defined benefit pension plan

    A. Is based on the plan's benefit formula.

    B. May be based on any acceptable actuarial cost method.

    C. Is determined as a level amount or as a level percentage of compensation.

    D. Should be based on a cost approach.

The correct answer is (A). *(Publisher)*

REQUIRED: The basis for attribution of pension costs.

DISCUSSION: SFAS 87 adopted a benefits approach based on the plan's benefit formula. Thus, SFAS 87 follows the traditional accounting practice of looking to the terms of the agreement as a basis for recording an exchange. According to the FASB, the benefits approach better reflects how the costs and liabilities are incurred.

Answer (B) is incorrect because the benefit formula, not any actuarial cost method, is the basis for attribution. Answer (C) is incorrect because the approach chosen by SFAS 87 recognizes the present value of the benefits earned during the period. Because the present value of a dollar of pension benefits increases as retirement nears, the cost recognized does not remain level. Answer (D) is incorrect because the cost is based on the benefits to be paid.

9. In measuring pension costs and pension obligations, certain significant assumptions must be made. Relative to these significant assumptions, the provisions of SFAS 87 require

   A. The assumptions to take into consideration a right of the employer to terminate the plan.

   B. The rate of return on plan assets to be based on the prime interest rate.

   C. Each significant assumption to reflect the best estimate solely with respect to that individual assumption.

   D. The measurements of the projected, accumulated, and vested benefit obligations to be based on the expected long-term rate of return on plan assets.

The correct answer is (C). *(Publisher)*
REQUIRED: The true statement about the pension cost and obligation assumptions required by SFAS 87.
DISCUSSION: SFAS 87 requires that each significant assumption used reflect the best estimate of the plan's future experience solely with respect to that individual assumption. This is called an explicit approach. SFAS 87 does not allow the implicit approach, which allows the combined use of assumptions that do not individually represent the best estimates of the plan's future experience but that result in an aggregate effect presumed to approximate that obtained by the explicit approach.
Answer (A) is incorrect because the assumptions should be based on the presumption that the plan will continue in effect unless contrary evidence exists. Answer (B) is incorrect because the expected long-term rate of return should be used. Answer (D) is incorrect because the PBO, ABO, and VBO should reflect the discount rate at which these pension benefit obligations could effectively be settled.

10. In the measurement of plan assets, SFAS 87 provides that

   A. Market-related value should be used for all purposes except determining asset gains and losses.

   B. All assets should be measured at cost.

   C. Plan assets that constitute plan investments should be measured at fair value for disclosure.

   D. Plan assets used in plan operations should be measured at market value.

The correct answer is (C). *(Publisher)*
REQUIRED: The true statement about the measurement of plan assets.
DISCUSSION: For disclosure and for determination of the minimum liability, plan investments are measured at their fair values. For calculating the expected return on plan assets and accounting for asset gains and losses, the market-related value is used. For measuring plan assets used in plan operations, e.g., an administrative building, cost less accumulated depreciation is the measurement base. Market-related value may be either fair value or a calculated value that recognizes changes in a fair value systematically and rationally over not more than 5 years, e.g., a 5-year moving average.
Answer (A) is incorrect because market-related value is used for calculating gains and losses. Answer (B) is incorrect because only plan assets used in operations should be measured at cost (less accumulated depreciation). Answer (D) is incorrect because plan assets used in operations should be measured at cost less accumulated depreciation.

11. Visor Co. maintains a defined benefit pension plan for its employees. The service cost component of Visor's net periodic pension cost is measured using the

   A. Unfunded accumulated benefit obligation.

   B. Unfunded vested benefit obligation.

   C. Projected benefit obligation.

   D. Expected return on plan assets.

The correct answer is (C). *(CPA 1193 T-30)*
REQUIRED: The item that is used to measure the service cost component of the net periodic pension cost.
DISCUSSION: The service cost is the actuarial present value of benefits attributed by the pension benefit formula to services rendered during the accounting period. The projected benefit obligation (PBO) as of a date is equal to the actuarial present value of all benefits attributed by the pension benefit formula to employee service rendered prior to that date. The PBO is measured using assumptions as to future salary levels.
Answer (A) is incorrect because the accumulated benefit obligation is based on current salaries without assumptions about future salaries. Answer (B) is incorrect because service cost includes nonvested benefits. Answer (D) is incorrect because the expected return on plan assets is not a cost.

12. SFAS 87, *Employers' Accounting for Pensions*, requires companies to recognize the actuarial present value of the increase in pension benefits payable to employees because of their services rendered during the current period as a component of periodic pension expense. This cost is the

A. Amortization of prior service costs.

B. Service cost.

C. Accumulated benefit obligation (ABO).

D. Projected benefit obligation (PBO).

The correct answer is (B). *(CMA 1292 2-22)*
REQUIRED: The term for the actuarial present value of the pension benefits attributable to employee services during the current period.
DISCUSSION: SFAS 87 defines service cost as the present value of the future benefits earned in the current period (as calculated according to the plan's benefit formula). This amount is usually calculated by the plan's actuary. Service cost is a component of net periodic pension cost. It is also a portion of the PBO.
Answer (A) is incorrect because amortization of prior service costs applies to benefits earned in earlier years that arise from amendment of a pension plan. Answer (C) is incorrect because the ABO is the same as the PBO except that it is limited to past and current compensation levels. Answer (D) is incorrect because the PBO is the actuarial present value of all future benefits attributed to past employee service at a moment in time. It is based on assumptions as to future compensation if the plan formula is based on future compensation.

13. Effective January 1, 1996, Flood Co. established a defined benefit pension plan with no retroactive benefits. The first of the required equal annual contributions was paid on December 31, 1996. A 10% discount rate was used to calculate service cost, and a 10% rate of return was assumed for plan assets. All information on covered employees for 1996 and 1997 is the same. How should the service cost for 1997 compare with 1996, and should the 1996 balance sheet report an accrued or a prepaid pension cost?

	Service Cost for 1997 Compared to 1996	Pension Cost Reported on the 1996 Balance Sheet
A.	Equal to	Accrued
B.	Equal to	Prepaid
C.	Greater than	Accrued
D.	Greater than	Prepaid

The correct answer is (D). *(CPA 1190 T-21)*
REQUIRED: The relationship of 1997 service cost to 1996 service cost and the proper balance sheet reporting of 1996 pension cost.
DISCUSSION: The service cost component of NPPC is equal to the actuarial present value of benefits attributed by the pension benefit formula to services rendered by employees during the accounting period. The service cost component is unaffected by the funded status of the plan. This defined benefit pension plan has no retroactive benefits, so the NPPC for 1996 will be equal to the service cost. Because the information on the covered employees for both 1996 and 1997 is the same, the actual pension benefits to be received upon retirement by the employees attributable to each of these years will also be the same. Thus, the service cost for 1996 will be less than the service cost for 1997 because the present value calculation of the same future benefits will be based on a discount period that is 1 year longer for 1996. Given that the company has decided to make equal annual contributions to the plan, and that the NPPC will be less in the earlier years than the later years, the amount of the contribution in 1996 will be greater than the net periodic pension cost in 1996 (that is, the plan will be overfunded). Hence, the 1996 balance sheet should report a prepaid pension cost.
Answers (A), (B), and (C) are incorrect because the service cost for 1997 is greater than that for 1996, and a prepaid pension cost should be reported on the 1996 balance sheet.

14. For a defined benefit pension plan, the discount rate used to calculate the projected benefit obligation is determined by the

	Expected Return on Plan Assets	Actual Return on Plan Assets
A.	Yes	Yes
B.	No	No
C.	Yes	No
D.	No	Yes

The correct answer is (B). *(CPA 591 T-37)*
REQUIRED: The basis for determining the discount rate used to calculate the projected benefit obligation.
DISCUSSION: Assumed discount rates are used to measure the PBO. They reflect the rates at which benefits can be settled. In estimating these rates, it is appropriate to consider current prices of annuity contracts that could be used to settle pension obligations as well as the rates on high-quality fixed investments (SFAS 87).
Answers (A), (C), and (D) are incorrect because neither the expected nor the actual return on plan assets determines the rate used to calculate the PBO.

15. Interest cost included in the net pension cost recognized for a period by an employer sponsoring a defined benefit pension plan represents the

    A.   Shortage between the expected and actual return on plan assets.

    B.   Increase in the projected benefit obligation resulting from the passage of time.

    C.   Increase in the fair value of plan assets resulting from the passage of time.

    D.   Amortization of the discount on unrecognized prior service costs.

The correct answer is (B). *(CPA 592 T-20)*
    REQUIRED: The definition of interest cost.
    DISCUSSION: The interest cost component of net periodic pension cost is defined as the increase in the PBO resulting from the passage of time. The PBO is a discounted amount of benefits to be paid. As the time to payment is reduced, the present value increases.
    Answers (A), (C), and (D) are incorrect because interest cost is calculated by applying an appropriate discount rate to the beginning balance of the PBO for the period.

16. Net periodic pension cost may include a gain or loss component. Gains and losses required to be amortized

    A.   Result only from experience different from that assumed.

    B.   Result only from changes in assumptions.

    C.   Do not include asset gains and losses not reflected in the market-related value of plan assets.

    D.   Only arise from unexpected changes in the projected benefit obligation.

The correct answer is (C). *(Publisher)*
    REQUIRED: The basis for determining unrealized gains and losses.
    DISCUSSION: Asset gains and losses are differences between the actual and expected return on plan assets. To the extent they are not reflected in the market-related value of plan assets (used to calculate the expected return), asset gains and losses are not subject to the required minimum amortization of gain or loss, which includes both realized and unrealized amounts.
    Answers (A) and (B) are incorrect because gains and losses result from both experience different from that assumed and from changes in assumptions. Answer (D) is incorrect because gains and losses include changes in the value of both the PBO and the plan assets.

17. Amortization of the unrecognized cumulative net gain or loss is a possible component of net periodic pension cost. Which of the following amortization policies is required?

    A.   If amortization is required, it will be over the average life expectancy of the plan's employee-participants.

    B.   SFAS 87 permits any systematic amortization method to be used provided the amortized amount does not exceed the prescribed minimum.

    C.   Amortization of a net unrecognized gain results in an increase in NPPC.

    D.   No amortization is required if the unrecognized net gain or loss falls within a corridor.

The correct answer is (D). *(G. Westmoreland)*
    REQUIRED: The required amortization of unrecognized net gain or loss.
    DISCUSSION: SFAS 87 adopts a corridor approach to reduce the volatility of the NPPC. The cumulative unrecognized net gain or loss (excluding asset gains and losses not reflected in the market-related value of plan assets) is subject to required amortization in NPPC only to the extent it exceeds 10% of the greater of the PBO or the market-related value of plan assets.
    Answer (A) is incorrect because, unless almost all participants are inactive, the amortization period is the average remaining service period of active employees expected to receive benefits under the plan. Answer (B) is incorrect because the amortized amount may be greater but not less than the minimum prescribed. Answer (C) is incorrect because gains decrease and losses increase NPPC.

18. On July 31, 1996, Tern Co. amended its single employee defined benefit pension plan by granting increased benefits for services provided prior to 1996. This prior service cost will be reflected in the financial statement(s) for

A. Years before 1996 only.

B. Year 1996 only.

C. Year 1996, and years before and following 1996.

D. Year 1996, and following years only.

The correct answer is (D). *(CPA 1192 T-26)*

REQUIRED: The year(s) in which prior service cost will be reflected in the financial statement(s).

DISCUSSION: The amortization of prior service cost should be recognized as a component of NPPC during the future service periods of those employees active at the date of the plan amendment who are expected to receive benefits under the plan. The cost of retroactive benefits is the increase in the PBO at the date of the amendment and should be amortized by assigning an equal amount to each future period of service of each employee active at the date of the amendment who is expected to receive benefits under the plan. However, to reduce the burden of these allocation computations, any alternative amortization approach (e.g., averaging) that more rapidly reduces the unrecognized prior service cost is acceptable provided it is applied consistently.

Answers (A) and (C) are incorrect because prior service cost is not recognized as a prior-period adjustment. Answer (B) is incorrect because prior service cost is allocated to future service periods on a systematic and rational basis.

19. A company that maintains a defined benefit pension plan for its employees reports an unfunded accrued pension cost. This cost represents the amount that the

A. Cumulative net pension cost accrued exceeds contributions to the plan.

B. Cumulative net pension cost accrued exceeds the vested benefit obligation.

C. Vested benefit obligation exceeds plan assets.

D. Vested benefit obligation exceeds contributions to the plan.

The correct answer is (A). *(CPA 1193 T-29)*

REQUIRED: The amount that the unfunded accrued pension cost represents in a defined benefit pension plan.

DISCUSSION: The prepaid/accrued pension cost account is an asset if it has a debit balance. It is a liability if it has a credit balance. The prepaid/accrued pension cost should be recognized as a liability if the cumulative net pension cost recognized exceeds the amounts the employer has contributed to the plan.

Answer (B) is incorrect because the VBO is not used to measure the extent of funding. Answers (C) and (D) are incorrect because unfunded accrued pension cost is defined in SFAS 86 as "cumulative net pension cost accrued in excess of the employer's contributions."

20. An employer sponsoring a defined benefit pension plan is subject to the minimum pension liability recognition requirement. An additional liability must be recorded equal to the unfunded

   A. Accumulated benefit obligation plus the previously recognized accrued pension cost.

   B. Accumulated benefit obligation less the previously recognized accrued pension cost.

   C. Projected benefit obligation plus the previously recognized accrued pension cost.

   D. Projected benefit obligation less the previously recognized accrued pension cost.

The correct answer is (B). *(CPA 1191 T-31)*
   REQUIRED: The amount of the additional minimum pension liability that must be recorded by an employer.
   DISCUSSION: An employer sponsoring a defined benefit pension plan is required to recognize an additional minimum pension liability if either (1) a portion of the ABO is unfunded and an asset has been recognized as prepaid pension cost, or (2) the existing liability (unfunded accrued pension cost) is less than the unfunded ABO. Thus, the additional liability equals the unfunded ABO plus prepaid pension cost or minus accrued pension cost.
   Answer (A) is incorrect because accrued pension cost is subtracted from, not added to, the ABO in order to calculate the additional minimum pension liability. Answers (C) and (D) are incorrect because the ABO, not the PBO, is used to calculate the additional minimum pension liability.

21. Which of the following defined benefit pension plan disclosures should be made in a company's financial statements?

   I. A description of the company's funding policies and types of assets held
  II. The amount of net periodic pension cost for the period
  III. The fair value of plan assets

   A. I and II.

   B. I, II, and III.

   C. II and III.

   D. I only.

The correct answer is (B). *(CPA 1191 T-30)*
   REQUIRED: The disclosure(s) about a defined benefit pension plan made in a company's statements.
   DISCUSSION: Under SFAS 87, an employer sponsoring a defined benefit pension plan should make various disclosures. A description of the plan should be given that includes employees covered, the type of benefit formula, the funding policy, the type of assets held and significant nonbenefit liabilities, and other significant matters affecting comparability. Net periodic pension cost should be presented showing separately service cost, interest cost, actual return on assets, and the net total of other components. Among the extensive disclosures required by SFAS 87 is a schedule that reconciles the funded status of the plan with amounts reported in the employer's statement of financial position. Separate disclosure is required of (1) the fair value of plan assets; (2) the PBO, with identification of the ABO and the vested benefit obligation (VBO); (3) unrecognized prior service cost; (4) unrecognized net gain or loss; (5) any remaining unrecognized transitional net obligation or net asset; (6) any additional minimum liability; and (7) net pension asset or liability recognized as the result of combining items 1 through 6.
   Answer (A) is incorrect because the fair value of plan assets must be disclosed. Answer (C) is incorrect because funding policies and types of assets must be disclosed. Answer (D) is incorrect because the fair value of plan assets and NPPC must be disclosed.

22. An employer sponsoring a defined benefit pension plan should disclose the

	Amount of Unrecognized Prior Service Cost	Projected Benefit Obligation
A.	Yes	Yes
B.	Yes	No
C.	No	No
D.	No	Yes

The correct answer is (A). *(CPA 589 T-35)*

REQUIRED: The disclosure required of an employer sponsoring a defined benefit pension plan.

DISCUSSION: Among the extensive disclosures required by SFAS 87 is a schedule that reconciles the funded status of the plan with amounts reported in the employer's statement of financial position. Separate disclosure is required of (1) the fair value of plan assets; (2) the PBO, with identification of the ABO and the vested benefit obligation (VBO); (3) unrecognized prior service cost; (4) unrecognized net gain or loss; (5) any remaining unrecognized transitional net obligation or net asset; (6) any additional minimum liability; and (7) net pension asset or liability recognized as the result of combining items 1 through 6.

Answers (B), (C), and (D) are incorrect because both the amount of unrecognized prior service cost and the projected benefit obligation should be disclosed in an employer-sponsored defined benefit pension plan.

23. Purchase of annuity contracts is a means of transferring the risk associated with a pension obligation from the employer to an insurer. To be treated as an annuity contract under SFAS 87, a contract

A. Must not be participating.

B. Must be unconditional and irrevocable.

C. Must be participating.

D. Must be eligible for inclusion in plan assets.

The correct answer is (B). *(Publisher)*

REQUIRED: The requirement for qualification as an annuity contract.

DISCUSSION: An annuity contract is a contract in which an insurance company unconditionally undertakes a legal obligation to provide specified pension benefits to specific individuals in return for a fixed consideration or premium. An annuity contract is irrevocable and involves the transfer of a significant risk from the employer to the insurance company.

Answers (A) and (C) are incorrect because, if the substance of a participating contract is that the employer remains subject to all or most of the risks and rewards associated with the obligations covered and the assets transferred to the insurer, the contract is not an annuity contract for purposes of SFAS 87. A participating annuity contract provides for the purchaser to participate (ordinarily by receipt of dividends) in the investment performance of the insurance company. Participation is neither a requirement for treatment as an annuity contract nor a disqualification. Answer (D) is incorrect because nonparticipating annuity contracts are excluded from plan assets, but, in the case of a participating contract, the excess of the cost of the participating contract over an equivalent nonparticipating contract (a participation right) is recognized as an asset. Benefits covered by both nonparticipating and qualifying participating annuity contracts are also excluded from both the PBO and the ABO.

24. The measurement date for pension plan assets and obligations is the

A. Beginning of the accounting period.

B. Date the actuary submits the information.

C. Date of the financial statements.

D. Date of the financial statements or a date not more than 3 months prior to that date.

The correct answer is (D). *(Publisher)*

REQUIRED: The measurement date for pension plan assets and obligations.

DISCUSSION: The measurement of plan assets and obligations required by SFAS 87 is as of the date of the financial statements or, if used consistently from year to year, a date not more than 3 months prior to the date of the financial statements. Data for measuring plan assets and obligations may be prepared by the actuary prior to these dates and projected forward to account for subsequent events.

Answers (A), (B), and (C) are incorrect because the measurement date for pension plan assets and obligations is either the date of the financial statements or a date not more than 3 months prior to that date (if used consistently).

25. If, in a business combination structured as a purchase, the acquired company sponsors a defined benefit pension plan, the acquiring company should

A. Recognize any previously existing unrecognized net gain or loss.

B. Assign part of the purchase price to the unrecognized prior service cost as an intangible asset.

C. Assign part of the purchase price to the excess of plan assets over the projected benefit obligation.

D. Recognize a previously existing unrecognized transition net asset or obligation of the plan.

The correct answer is (C). *(Publisher)*

REQUIRED: The acquiring company's accounting when the acquired company sponsors a pension plan.

DISCUSSION: In a business combination structured as a purchase, the acquiring company should recognize a pension liability if the PBO of the acquired company is in excess of that company's plan assets. Likewise, a pension asset should be recognized if plan assets exceed the PBO.

Answers (A), (B), and (D) are incorrect because, in a business combination accounted for as a purchase, unrecognized net gains and losses, prior service cost, and the transition net asset or obligation of the acquired company's defined benefit plan are eliminated by the assignment of part of the purchase price to a liability (excess of PBO over plan assets) or an asset (excess of plan assets over the PBO).

26. A pension plan that provides benefits in return for services rendered, provides an individual account for each participant, and specifies how contributions to the individual accounts are to be determined is a

A. Defined benefit pension plan.

B. Defined contribution plan.

C. Multiemployer plan.

D. Multiple-employer plan.

The correct answer is (B). *(Publisher)*

REQUIRED: The type of plan defined.

DISCUSSION: A defined contribution plan specifies how contributions to an individual's account are to be determined. The benefits a participant will receive depend solely on the amount contributed, the returns earned on investments of those contributions, and forfeitures of other participants' benefits that may be allocated to his/her account. The NPPC is the contribution called for in the particular accounting period.

Answer (A) is incorrect because a defined benefit pension plan is a plan that provides a defined pension benefit based on one or more factors. Answer (C) is incorrect because a multiemployer plan is a plan to which two or more unrelated employers contribute, usually pursuant to one or more collective bargaining agreements. Assets are not segregated and may be used to provide benefits to employees of any of the participating employers. Answer (D) is incorrect because a multiple-employer plan is a pension plan to which two or more unrelated employers contribute, usually to allow pooling of assets for investment purposes and to reduce administrative costs. Assets are segregated, and contributions may be based on benefit formulas that differ.

27. The following information pertains to Seda Co.'s pension plan:

Actuarial estimate of projected benefit obligation at 1/1/96	$72,000
Assumed discount rate	10%
Service cost for 1996	18,000
Pension benefits paid during 1996	15,000

If no change in actuarial estimates occurred during 1996, Seda's PBO at December 31, 1996 was

- A. $64,200
- B. $75,000
- C. $79,200
- D. $82,200

The correct answer is (D). *(CPA 1190 II-16)*

REQUIRED: The projected benefit obligation at the end of the year.

DISCUSSION: The ending balance of the PBO is the beginning balance plus the service cost and interest cost components, minus the benefits paid. The interest cost component is equal to the PBO's beginning balance times the discount rate.

Beginning PBO balance	$72,000
Service cost	18,000
Interest cost (10% x $72,000)	7,200
Benefits paid	(15,000)
Ending PBO balance	$82,200

Answer (A) is incorrect because it excludes the current year's service cost component. Answer (B) is incorrect because it excludes the interest cost component. Answer (C) is incorrect because it excludes both the service cost component and the benefits paid.

28. At the beginning of the year, the market-related value of the plan assets of Margie Company's defined benefit pension plan was $1,000,000. Margie uses a 5-year weighted-average method to determine market-related values. The company, however, had not previously experienced any asset gains and losses. The expected long-term rate of return on plan assets is 10%. The actual return during the year was $50,000. Contributions and benefits paid were $150,000 and $200,000, respectively. At year-end, the market-related value of Margie's plan assets is

- A. $1,140,000
- B. $1,040,000
- C. $1,000,000
- D. $950,000

The correct answer is (B). *(Publisher)*

REQUIRED: The market-related value of plan assets at year-end.

DISCUSSION: If market-related value is defined as fair value, the ending market-related value of the plan assets is the beginning value, plus the actual returns, plus the contributions, less the benefits paid. However, in this case, the company uses an alternative method to determine market-related value. This alternative includes 20% of the sum of the differences between the actual and the expected returns (asset gains and losses) over the last 5 years. The year-end market-related value is the beginning value, plus the expected return, plus the contributions, less the benefits paid, minus 20% of the difference between the actual return and the expected return for the current year only.

Beginning market-related value	$1,000,000
Expected return (10% x $1,000,000)	100,000
Contributions	150,000
Benefits paid	(200,000)
20% of $50,000 loss	(10,000)
Year-end market-related value	$1,040,000

Answer (A) is incorrect because it excludes the expected returns and benefits paid. Answer (C) is incorrect because it includes the entire loss. Answer (D) is incorrect because it excludes the expected return and 20% of the loss.

29. The following information pertains to Gali Co.'s defined benefit pension plan for 1996:

Fair value of plan assets, beginning of year	$350,000
Fair value of plan assets, end of year	525,000
Employer contributions	110,000
Benefits paid	85,000

In computing pension expense, what amount should Gali use as actual return on plan assets?

- A. $65,000
- B. $150,000
- C. $175,000
- D. $260,000

The correct answer is (B). *(CPA 595 F-39)*

REQUIRED: The actual return on plan assets.

DISCUSSION: The actual return on plan assets is based on the fair value of plan assets at the beginning and end of the accounting period adjusted for contributions and payments during the period. The actual return for Gali is $150,000 ($525,000 – $350,000 – $110,000 + $85,000).

Answer (A) is incorrect because $65,000 results when benefits paid to employees are not included. Answer (C) is incorrect because $175,000 is the change in the fair value of plan assets without adjustment for contributions or benefits paid. Answer (D) is incorrect because $260,000 does not deduct employer contributions.

30. The following information relates to the 1996 activity of the defined benefit pension plan of Twain Publishers, Ltd., a company whose stock is publicly traded:

Service cost	$120,000
Return on plan assets	30,000
Interest cost on pension benefit obligation	40,000
Amortization of actuarial loss	10,000
Amortization of prior service cost	5,000
Amortization of transition obligation	15,000

Twain's 1996 pension cost is

A. $120,000

B. $140,000

C. $150,000

D. $160,000

The correct answer is (D). *(A. Oddo)*

REQUIRED: The net periodic pension cost (NPPC) for the year.

DISCUSSION: Components of NPPC are service cost, interest cost, the expected return on plan assets, and amortization of any (1) unrecognized prior service cost, (2) net transition asset or obligation, or (3) unrecognized net gain (loss). Service cost; interest cost; and the amortization of actuarial loss, prior service cost, and a net transition obligation increase the net periodic pension cost. The expected return on plan assets decreases NPPC. As indicated below, NPPC for 1996 is $160,000.

Service cost	$120,000
Return on plan assets	(30,000)
Interest cost	40,000
Amortization of actuarial loss	10,000
Amortization of prior service cost	5,000
Amortization of transition obligation	15,000
Net periodic pension cost	$160,000

Answer (A) is incorrect because $120,000 includes only the service cost component. Answer (B) is incorrect because $140,000 excludes the amortization of prior service cost and the transition obligation. Answer (C) is incorrect because $150,000 excludes the amortization of the actuarial loss.

31. Janice, Inc. has a defined benefit pension plan. For the current year, the expected return on plan assets was $50,000. The actual return was $75,000. The increase in the projected benefit obligation was estimated to be $300,000. The amount of the projected benefit obligation determined at year-end reflected an increase of only $200,000. If no unrecognized net gain (loss) existed at the beginning of the year, the amount of net gain (loss) subject to required amortization for the current year is

A. $0

B. $(75,000)

C. $25,000

D. $125,000

The correct answer is (A). *(Publisher)*

REQUIRED: The amount of net gain (loss) subject to required amortization for the current year.

DISCUSSION: SFAS 87 does not require recognition of gains and losses as components of NPPC of the period in which they arise. The $25,000 asset gain ($75,000 actual return – $50,000 expected return) and the liability gain (the PBO at year-end was $100,000 less than estimated) are thus not required to be included in NPPC of the current year. The gain (loss) subject to amortization also does not include asset gains or losses not yet reflected in the market-related value of plan assets when market-related value is based on a moving average.

Answers (B), (C), and (D) are incorrect because SFAS 87 does not require recognition of gains and losses as components of NPPC of the period in which they arise. Also, gains (losses) subject to amortization do not include gains or losses not yet reflected in the market-related value of plan assets when it is based on a moving average.

32. The following information pertains to Kane Co.'s defined benefit pension plan:

Prepaid pension cost, January 1, 1996	$ 2,000
Service cost	19,000
Interest cost	38,000
Actual return on plan assets	22,000
Amortization of unrecognized prior service cost	52,000
Employer contributions	40,000

The fair value of plan assets exceeds the accumulated benefit obligation (ABO). In its December 31, 1996 balance sheet, what amount should Kane report as unfunded accrued pension cost?

- A. $45,000

- B. $49,000

- C. $67,000

- D. $87,000

The correct answer is (A). *(CPA 595 F-18)*

REQUIRED: The unfunded accrued pension cost.

DISCUSSION: The six possible components of net periodic pension cost (NPPC) are (1) service cost, (2) interest cost, (3) return on plan assets, (4) gain or loss to the extent recognized, (5) amortization of any unrecognized prior service cost, and (6) amortization of any transition amount. The NPPC is $87,000 ($19,000 service cost + $38,000 interest cost – $22,000 return on plan assets + $52,000 amortization of unrecognized prior service costs). The excess of the NPPC over contributions and prepaid pension cost is $45,000 ($87,000 – $40,000 – $2,000), which is the unfunded accrued pension cost. Because the fair value of plan assets exceeds the ABO, no additional liability should be recognized.

Answer (B) is incorrect because $49,000 results when prepaid pension cost is added instead of subtracted. Answer (C) is incorrect because $67,000 results when actual return on assets is not subtracted. Answer (D) is incorrect because $87,000 results when employer contributions and prepaid pension cost are not subtracted.

33. At end of the year, Penny Company's projected benefit obligation (PBO) was determined to be $1,500,000, which was $200,000 higher than had been expected. The market-related value of the defined benefit plan's assets was equal to its fair value of $1,250,000. No other gains and losses have occurred. If the average remaining service life is 20 years, the minimum required amortization of the unrecognized net gain (loss) in the next year will be

- A. $20,000

- B. $3,750

- C. $2,500

- D. $0

The correct answer is (C). *(Publisher)*

REQUIRED: The minimum required amortization of unrecognized net gain (loss) next year.

DISCUSSION: At a minimum, amortization of the cumulative unrecognized net gain or loss (excluding asset gains and losses not yet reflected in market-related value) must be included as a component of NPPC for a year if, as of the beginning of the year, that unrecognized gain or loss exceeds 10% of the greater of the PBO or the market-related value (MRV) of plan assets. At year-end, Penny's PBO was $200,000 greater than estimated (a $200,000 liability loss). Since no other gain or loss has occurred, the unrecognized net loss to be amortized beginning next year is $200,000. The corridor amount is $150,000 (10% of the greater of $1,500,000 PBO or $1,250,000 MRV of plan assets). The amount outside the corridor is $50,000 ($200,000 – $150,000), and the amount to be amortized is thus $2,500 ($50,000 ÷ 20 years of average remaining service life).

Answer (A) is incorrect because $20,000 is the result of using the full $200,000 liability loss without regard to the corridor amount and assumes an amortization period of 10 years instead of 20. Answer (B) is incorrect because $3,750 is the result of using $125,000 (10% x $1,250,000 plan assets) as the corridor amount instead of $150,000. Answer (D) is incorrect because $50,000 of the liability loss must be amortized over the average remaining service life beginning the year following the loss.

34. At the start of its current fiscal year, Emper Co. amended its defined benefit pension plan, resulting in an increase of $600,000 in the PBO. As of the date of the amendment, Emper had 50 employees. Ten employees are expected to leave at the end of each of the next 5 years (including the current year). The minimum amortization of prior service cost in the first year is

A. $80,000

B. $120,000

C. $160,000

D. $200,000

The correct answer is (D). *(Publisher)*
REQUIRED: The minimum amortization of prior service cost.
DISCUSSION: Prior service cost is amortized by assigning an equal amount to each future period of service of each employee active at the date of the plan amendment who is expected to receive benefits under the plan. If all or almost all of a plan's participants are inactive, the prior service cost is amortized based on the remaining life expectancy of the participants. An alternative amortization approach, such as a straight-line method, that recognizes the cost of retroactive amendments more quickly is also permitted if used consistently. For Emper, total service years rendered during the 5-year period is 150 (50 + 40 + 30 + 20 + 10). The amortization fraction for the first year is thus 50/150, and the minimum amortization is $200,000 ($600,000 x 50/150).
Answer (A) is incorrect because 50, not 20, must be used as the numerator of the amortization fraction. Answer (B) is incorrect because the use of straight-line amortization over 5 years does not recognize the cost of retroactive amendments more quickly, so the method described above must be used. Answer (C) is incorrect because 50, not 40, must be used as the numerator of the amortization fraction for the first year.

35. Webb Co. implemented a defined benefit pension plan for its employees on January 1, 1993. During 1993 and 1994, Webb's contributions fully funded the plan. The following data are provided for 1996 and 1995:

	1996 Estimated	1995 Actual
Projected benefit obligation, December 31	$750,000	$700,000
Accumulated benefit obligation, December 31	520,000	500,000
Plan assets at fair value, December 31	675,000	600,000
Projected benefit obligation in excess of plan assets	75,000	100,000
Pension expense	90,000	75,000
Employer's contribution	?	50,000

What amount should Webb contribute in order to report an accrued pension liability of $15,000 in its December 31, 1996 balance sheet?

A. $50,000

B. $60,000

C. $75,000

D. $100,000

The correct answer is (D). *(CPA 592 I-25)*
REQUIRED: The amount contributed to report an accrued pension liability.
DISCUSSION: The prepaid/accrued pension cost account is an asset if it has a debit balance. It is a liability if it has a credit balance. The prepaid/accrued pension cost should be recognized as a liability if the cumulative NPPC recognized exceeds the amounts the employer has contributed to the plan. No accrued/prepaid pension cost was recognized in 1993 or 1994 because the employer's contributions fully funded the plan. Accrued pension cost at the end of 1995 was $25,000 ($75,000 pension expense – $50,000 contribution). To reduce the accrued pension cost to $15,000 at the end of 1996 therefore requires overfunding of pension expense by $10,000. Hence, the contribution for 1996 should be $100,000 ($10,000 + $90,000 pension expense).
Answer (A) is incorrect because a contribution of $50,000 would result in an accrued liability of $65,000. Answer (B) is incorrect because a $60,000 contribution would result in an accrued liability of $55,000. Answer (C) is incorrect because a contribution of $75,000 would result in an accrued liability of $40,000.

36. On January 2, 1996, Loch Co. established a noncontributory defined benefit plan covering all employees and contributed $1,000,000 to the plan. At December 31, 1996, Loch determined that the 1996 service and interest costs for the plan were $620,000. The expected and the actual rate of return on plan assets for 1996 was 10%. There are no other components of Loch's pension expense. What amount should Loch report in its December 31, 1996 balance sheet as prepaid pension cost?

    A. $280,000

    B. $380,000

    C. $480,000

    D. $620,000

The correct answer is (C). *(CPA 1193 I-26)*
    REQUIRED: The amount of prepaid pension cost.
    DISCUSSION: Prepaid pension cost is recognized when the amount funded exceeds the amount recognized as net periodic pension cost. The net periodic pension cost is $520,000 [$620,000 service and interest costs – ($1,000,000 x 10% return on plan assets)]. Given that $1,000,000 was contributed, $480,000 is the prepaid pension cost ($1,000,000 – $520,000).
    Answer (A) is incorrect because $280,000 is the difference between the contributed amount and the service and interest costs with 10% of $1,000,000 subtracted from the difference. Answer (B) is incorrect because $380,000 is the difference between the contributed amount and the sum of the service and interest costs. Answer (D) is incorrect because $620,000 is the sum of the service and interest costs.

37. On January 1, 1996, East Corp. adopted a defined benefit pension plan. The plan's service cost of $75,000 was fully funded at the end of 1996. Prior service cost was funded by a contribution of $30,000 in 1996. Amortization of prior service cost was $12,000 for 1996. What is the amount of East's prepaid pension cost at December 31, 1996?

    A. $18,000

    B. $30,000

    C. $42,000

    D. $45,000

The correct answer is (A). *(CPA 593 I-28)*
    REQUIRED: The amount of prepaid pension cost at year-end.
    DISCUSSION: Prepaid pension cost is recognized when the amount funded exceeds the amount recognized as net periodic pension cost. For 1996, the initial year of the defined benefit pension plan, NPPC is equal to $87,000 ($75,000 service cost + $12,000 amortization of prior service cost). The plan's service cost was fully funded at the end of 1996. The plan's prior service cost was overfunded by $18,000 ($30,000 – $12,000). Consequently, East's prepaid pension cost in the year-end financial statements should be reported at $18,000.
    Answer (B) is incorrect because $30,000 is the contribution for prior service cost. Answer (C) is incorrect because $42,000 is the sum of prior service cost funding and amortization. Answer (D) is incorrect because $45,000 equals service cost funding minus prior service cost funding.

38. On June 1, 1994 Ward Corp. established a defined benefit pension plan for its employees. The following information was available at May 31, 1996:

Projected benefit obligation	$14,500,000
Accumulated benefit obligation	12,000,000
Unfunded accrued pension cost	200,000
Plan assets at fair market value	7,000,000
Unrecognized prior service cost	2,550,000

To report the proper pension liability in Ward's May 31, 1996 balance sheet, what is the amount of the adjustment required?

    A. $2,250,000

    B. $4,750,000

    C. $4,800,000

    D. $7,300,000

The correct answer is (C). *(CPA 1191 I-23)*
    REQUIRED: The amount of the adjustment required to reflect pension liability properly on the balance sheet.
    DISCUSSION: The minimum liability that must be recorded on the balance sheet is equal to the amount that the ABO exceeds the fair value of the plan assets plus (less) any unfunded prepaid (accrued) pension cost. Thus, the adjustment required would be $4,800,000 ($12,000,000 ABO – $7,000,000 fair value of plan assets – $200,000 unfunded accrued pension cost).
    Answer (A) is incorrect because the unfunded prior service cost is not included in the minimum liability. Answer (B) is incorrect because $4,750,000 results from calculating the additional liability based on the PBO and includes unrecognized prior service cost. Answer (D) is incorrect because $7,300,000 results from calculating the additional liability based on the PBO.

39. Payne, Inc. implemented a defined benefit pension plan for its employees on January 2, 1996. The following data are provided for 1996, as of December 31, 1996:

Accumulated benefit obligation	$103,000
Plan assets at fair value	78,000
Net periodic pension cost	90,000
Employer's contribution	70,000

What amount should Payne record as additional minimum pension liability at December 31, 1996?

A. $0

B. $5,000

C. $20,000

D. $45,000

The correct answer is (B). *(CPA 594 F-28)*
REQUIRED: The additional minimum pension liability.
DISCUSSION: SFAS 87 requires recognition of a liability that is at least equal to the unfunded ABO. For the net liability presented to equal the unfunded ABO, the company must recognize as a liability the difference between the ABO and the fair value of plan assets, plus any prepaid pension cost, or minus any accrued pension cost. Payne recognized an accrued pension cost of $20,000 ($90,000 NPPC – $70,000 contribution). Hence, the additional minimum pension liability should be $5,000 ($103,000 ABO – $78,000 fair value of plan assets – $20,000 accrued pension cost).
Answer (A) is incorrect because the full unfunded ABO has not been reflected in the accounts. Answer (C) is incorrect because $20,000 is the accrued pension cost. Answer (D) is incorrect because $45,000 equals the unfunded ABO plus the accrued pension cost.

Questions 40 and 41 are based on the following information.

The following information pertains to Hall Co.'s defined benefit pension plan at December 31, 1996:

Unfunded accumulated benefit obligation (ABO)	$25,000
Unrecognized prior service cost	12,000
Net periodic pension cost	8,000

Hall made no contributions to the pension plan during 1996.

---

40. At December 31, 1996, what amount should Hall record as additional pension liability?

A. $5,000

B. $13,000

C. $17,000

D. $25,000

The correct answer is (C). *(CPA 1195 F-14)*
REQUIRED: The additional pension liability.
DISCUSSION: An additional pension liability is recognized if the existing liability (unfunded accrued pension cost) is less than the unfunded ABO. No contributions were made in 1996, so the entire NPPC is unfunded and should be reported as accrued pension cost. The additional pension liability is equal to the unfunded ABO minus accrued pension cost, or $17,000 ($25,000 – $8,000).
Answer (A) is incorrect because $5,000 equals the unfunded ABO minus the prior service cost and the NPPC. Answer (B) is incorrect because $13,000 equals the unfunded ABO minus the prior service cost. Answer (D) is incorrect because $25,000 is the unfunded ABO.

41. In its December 31, 1996, statement of shareholders' equity, what amount should Hall report as excess of additional pension liability over unrecognized prior service cost?

A. $5,000

B. $13,000

C. $17,000

D. $25,000

The correct answer is (A). *(CPA 1195 F-15)*
REQUIRED: The excess of additional pension liability over unrecognized prior service cost.
DISCUSSION: An additional pension liability is recorded by a credit to a liability and a debit to an intangible asset. However, if the amount of the additional liability exceeds the unrecognized prior service cost, the excess is debited to a shareholders' equity account. The excess of the additional liability (calculated in the previous question) over unrecognized prior service cost is $5,000 ($17,000 – $12,000).
Answer (B) is incorrect because $13,000 is the excess of the minimum liability over unrecognized prior service cost. Answer (C) is incorrect because $17,000 is the additional liability. Answer (D) is incorrect because $25,000 is the unfunded ABO.

42. On January 1 of this year, Ring Co. acquired Red Co. in a business combination accounted for as a purchase. Red sponsors a single-employer defined benefit pension plan. At the date of the combination, the following data were available:

Projected benefit obligation	$5,000,000
Fair value of plan assets	4,000,000
Accumulated benefit obligation	4,500,000
Unrecognized net transition obligation	600,000
Unrecognized prior service cost	200,000
Prepaid pension cost	100,000

The allocation of the purchase price should be based on which of the following?

A. The only allocation related to the pension plan will be $100,000 for prepaid pension cost.

B. An allocation must be made to liabilities for the transition net obligation, prior service cost, and net loss.

C. A liability must be recognized for the excess of the projected benefit obligation over plan assets.

D. A liability must be recognized for the excess of the accumulated benefit obligation over plan assets.

The correct answer is (C). *(Publisher)*

REQUIRED: The proper allocation of the pension-plan-related portion of the purchase price in a business combination.

DISCUSSION: For business combinations accounted for as a purchase, when the acquired company sponsors a single-employer defined benefit plan, the acquiring company's allocation of the purchase price to the individual assets acquired and liabilities assumed must include recognition of a liability for a PBO in excess of plan assets or an asset for plan assets in excess of the PBO. Any previously existing unrecognized net gain or loss, prior service cost, or transition net obligation or asset is eliminated. Red's PBO exceeded plan assets, so Ring should recognize a liability of $1,000,000 ($5,000,000 – $4,000,000).

Answer (A) is incorrect because an allocation will be made to a liability account in order to recognize the amount that the PBO exceeds plan assets. Answer (B) is incorrect because the unrecognized transition net obligation, prior service cost, and any net gains or loss are eliminated. Answer (D) is incorrect because the difference between the PBO and plan assets is the amount of the liability that must be recorded, not the difference between the ABO and plan assets.

16.2 Disclosure and Reporting of Pensions

43. Which of the following is a provision of SFAS 35, *Accounting and Reporting by Defined Benefit Pension Plans*?

A. SFAS 35 establishes a requirement that defined benefit pension plans prepare and distribute financial statements.

B. SFAS 35 is not applicable to defined benefit pension plans that provide benefits on death, disability, or termination of employment in addition to pension benefits.

C. SFAS 35 applies only to defined benefit pension plans that are subject to the provisions of the Employee Retirement Income Security Act of 1974 (ERISA).

D. SFAS 35 applies to ongoing plans that provide pension benefits for the employees of one or more employers.

The correct answer is (D). *(Publisher)*

REQUIRED: The item that is an SFAS 35 provision about accounting and reporting by defined benefit pension plans.

DISCUSSION: SFAS 35 establishes the accounting and reporting requirements for defined benefit pension plans themselves, as opposed to SFAS 87's requirements for reporting in the employers' financial statements. A defined benefit pension plan specifies a determinable pension benefit, usually based on such factors as age, years of service, and salary.

Answer (A) is incorrect because SFAS 35 establishes standards of accounting and reporting for those defined benefit pension plans that issue financial statements. It does not require that such statements be prepared or distributed. Answers (B) and (C) are incorrect because SFAS 35 is applicable to all defined benefit pension plans. However, SFAS 75, *Deferral of the Effective Date of Certain Accounting Requirements for Pension Plans of State and Local Governmental Units*, defers indefinitely the applicability of SFAS 35 to pension plans of state and local governmental units.

44. SFAS 35 states that the primary objective of the financial statements of a pension plan is to provide financial information useful for assessing the plan's present and future ability to pay benefits when due. In order to accomplish that purpose, information about which of the following should be provided?

A. Plan resources.

B. Accumulated plan benefits of participants.

C. The results of transactions and events that affect the information regarding the plan resources and the accumulated plan benefits.

D. All of the answers are correct.

The correct answer is (D). *(Publisher)*

REQUIRED: The information required in the financial statements of a defined benefit pension plan.

DISCUSSION: The annual financial statements of a defined benefit pension plan should include information about each of the following:

1) The net assets available for benefits as of the end of the plan year (plan assets)
2) The changes in net assets during the year
3) The actuarial present value of accumulated plan benefits as of either the beginning or end of the plan year
4) The significant factors that affect the annual change in the actuarial present value of accumulated plan benefits

The information regarding the plan resources and the accumulated plan benefits must be presented as of the same date, and the changes therein must be presented for the same period.

Answers (A), (B), and (C) are incorrect because information about all three should be provided in the financial statements to be useful in assessing the plan's present and future ability to pay benefits when due. Therefore, the best answer is (D).

45. In addition to the required disclosures in the previous question, SFAS 35 requires a number of other disclosures to be made if applicable. Which of the following is usually not such a disclosure?

A. Identification of investments representing more than 5% of the net available assets.

B. Significant transactions between the plan and the sponsor, employer, or employee organizations.

C. The funding policy.

D. The income tax status.

The correct answer is (D). *(Publisher)*

REQUIRED: The item concerning pension plans not required to be disclosed per SFAS 35.

DISCUSSION: SFAS 35 requires disclosure of

1) The method of determining fair value of investments
2) The assumptions and methods underlying determination of the actuarial present value of accumulated plan benefits
3) A brief description of the plan agreement
4) Significant plan amendments during the year
5) The priority order of participants' claims
6) Benefits guaranteed by the pension plan
7) The funding policy
8) The tax status of the plan if favorable status has not been obtained or maintained
9) Identification of investments representing 5% or more of net assets
10) Significant transactions with any related party

The tax status disclosure is required only if a favorable letter of determination from the IRS has not been obtained or maintained. Because almost all pension plans obtain a favorable letter of determination prior to accumulating funds, the tax status is usually not a required disclosure.

Answers (A), (B), and (C) are incorrect because they are disclosures which are required by SFAS 35.

46. One of the requirements of SFAS 35 is that pension plans report the components of the change in net assets available for benefits. These components would not ordinarily include

A. Net appreciation and fair value for each significant class of investments.

B. Benefits paid to participants.

C. Contributions by the employer.

D. The change in the actuarial present value of accumulated plan benefits.

The correct answer is (D). *(Publisher)*
 REQUIRED: The item not a component of the change in net assets available for benefits of a pension plan.
 DISCUSSION: The change in the present value of accumulated plan benefits is not a component of the change in net assets available for benefits. It is a change in the estimated benefits that must be satisfied by the use of the available assets.
 Answers (A), (B), and (C) are incorrect because each is a component of the change in net assets available for benefits of a pension plan. Additional components are investment income (exclusive of appreciation of the fair value of investments), contributions from other sources, administrative expenses, and payments to insurance companies for beneficiaries.

16.3 Settlements and Curtailments of Pension Plans

47. In accounting for a settlement, SFAS 88, *Employers' Accounting for Settlements and Curtailments of Defined Benefit Pension Plans and for Termination Benefits*, provides that

A. The settlement gain (loss) is measured by the change in the projected benefit obligation as a result of the transaction.

B. The unrecognized transition net asset or obligation is included in the calculation of the maximum settlement gain or loss.

C. A transaction must eliminate significant risks related to the obligation and the assets involved to constitute a settlement.

D. The cost of a participation right reduces the maximum gain or loss subject to recognition in a settlement.

The correct answer is (C). *(Publisher)*
 REQUIRED: The prescribed accounting for settlements.
 DISCUSSION: A settlement is defined as an irrevocable action that relieves the employer (or the plan) of the primary responsibility for a PBO and eliminates significant risks related to the pension obligation and the assets used to effect the settlement.
 Answer (A) is incorrect because the maximum potential settlement gain or loss is the sum of any unrecognized net gain or loss plus any remaining transition net asset. The proportion of maximum gain or loss recognized in earnings equals the percentage reduction in the PBO. Answer (B) is incorrect because the transition net obligation is regarded as prior service cost, which is unaffected by a settlement. Answer (D) is incorrect because the cost of the right to participate in the investment and other experience of an insurer from which annuities have been purchased to settle a pension obligation reduces the maximum gain (but not loss).

48. SFAS 88 defines a curtailment as an event that significantly reduces the expected years of future service of present employees or eliminates for a significant number of employees the accrual of defined benefits for some or all of their future service. Which statement is descriptive of a curtailment?

A. It occurs only when a plan is terminated.

B. If the amount of net curtailment loss is less than or equal to the sum of the interest cost and service cost components of net periodic pension cost, recognition is not mandatory.

C. A curtailment gain resulting from a decrease in the projected benefit obligation is offset by any unrecognized transition net obligation.

D. It involves recognition of unamortized prior service cost.

The correct answer is (D). *(Publisher)*
 REQUIRED: The statement descriptive of a curtailment.
 DISCUSSION: A curtailment net gain or loss equals the combined amounts of (1) the unrecognized prior service cost associated with years of service no longer expected to be rendered and (2) the change in the PBO that does not represent a reversal of previously unrecognized net gains or losses. For this purpose, unrecognized prior service cost includes any remaining unrecognized transition net obligation.
 Answer (A) is incorrect because termination of a plan is not required for a curtailment. Answer (B) is incorrect because it is true of a settlement (not a curtailment) gain or loss. Recognition of a settlement gain or loss is required if the cost of all settlements in a year exceeds the sum of the interest cost and the service cost components. Answer (C) is incorrect because a curtailment gain is offset only by any unrecognized net loss.

49. Joe Company, with a final pay, noncontributory, defined benefit pension plan, settled its vested benefit obligation of $1,500,000 by purchasing participating annuity contracts for $1,650,000. Nonparticipating annuity contracts would have cost $1,500,000. The remaining unrecognized transition net asset is $180,000, the remaining unrecognized net loss since transition is $400,000, and the projected benefit obligation is $2,000,000. Prior service cost is $300,000. The settlement gain (loss) that should be recognized is

A. $135,000

B. $(165,000)

C. $(277,500)

D. $(390,000)

The correct answer is (B). *(Publisher)*

REQUIRED: The settlement gain (loss) that should be recognized.

DISCUSSION: The maximum settlement gain or loss is equal to the unrecognized net gain or loss arising subsequent to transition to SFAS 87 plus any remaining unrecognized net asset arising at transition. If the purchase of a participating annuity contract constitutes a settlement, the maximum gain is reduced by the cost of the participation rights, but the maximum loss is not adjusted. The maximum gain or loss is recognized if the entire PBO is settled. If only part is settled, a pro rata share of the maximum gain or loss is recognized equal to the percentage reduction in the PBO.

Unrecognized transition net asset	$ 180,000
Unrecognized net loss	(400,000)
Maximum loss	$(220,000)
Reduction % ($1,500,000 ÷ $2,000,000)	x .75
Settlement loss	$(165,000)

Answer (A) is incorrect because the $135,000 gain is the $180,000 unrecognized transition asset multiplied by the percentage reduction in the PBO. Answer (C) is incorrect because the loss should not be increased by the cost of the participation rights multiplied by the percentage reduction in the PBO. Answer (D) is incorrect because the prior service cost is not included in the calculation of settlement loss.

50. A curtailment has eliminated 50% of the estimated remaining future years of service of employees active at the date of the only amendment to Moe Co.'s defined benefit pension plan. The unrecognized prior service cost associated with that amendment is $200,000. The curtailment eliminated 60% of the estimated remaining future years of service of employees active at the date of transition to SFAS 87. The unrecognized transition net obligation is $300,000. The curtailment reduced the projected benefit obligation by $400,000. If the unrecognized net loss subsequent to transition is $100,000, the curtailment net gain (loss) is

A. $20,000

B. $120,000

C. $(180,000)

D. $200,000

The correct answer is (A). *(Publisher)*

REQUIRED: The curtailment net gain (loss).

DISCUSSION: The curtailment net gain or loss equals (1) the unrecognized prior service cost associated with years of service no longer expected to be rendered, plus (2) the change in the PBO that is not a reversal of previously unrecognized net gains or losses. For a curtailment, unrecognized prior service cost includes both the cost of retroactive plan amendments and any remaining unrecognized net obligation existing at the date of the initial transition to SFAS 87. The gain resulting from the decrease in the PBO is included to the extent it exceeds any remaining unrecognized net loss. Therefore, as indicated below, the curtailment net gain is $20,000.

Prior service cost (50% x $200,000)		$(100,000)
Transition net obligation		
(60% x $300,000)		(180,000)
PBO gain	$400,000	
Unrecognized net loss	(100,000)	
Curtailment gain		300,000
Curtailment net gain		$ 20,000

Answer (B) is incorrect because the gain must be reduced by 50% of the prior service cost. Answer (C) is incorrect because the curtailment loss must be increased by 50% of the prior service cost and reduced by the curtailment gain. Answer (D) is incorrect because the curtailment gain must also be reduced by 60% of the transition net obligation.

51. SFAS 88 defines termination benefits as benefits provided to employees in connection with their termination of employment. Termination benefits may be classified as either special termination benefits offered only for a short period of time or contractual termination benefits required by the terms of a pension plan only if a specified event occurs. The liability and loss arising from termination benefits should be recognized by an employer when the employees accept the offer and the amount can be reasonably estimated for

	Special Benefits	Contractual Benefits
A.	No	No
B.	No	Yes
C.	Yes	No
D.	Yes	Yes

52. On September 1, 1996, Howe Corp. offered special termination benefits to employees who had reached the early retirement age specified in the company's pension plan. The termination benefits consisted of lump-sum and periodic future payments. Additionally, the employees accepting the company offer receive the usual early retirement pension benefits. The offer expired on November 30, 1996. Actual or reasonably estimated amounts at December 31, 1996 relating to the employees accepting the offer are as follows:

- Lump-sum payments totaling $475,000 were made on January 1, 1997.
- Periodic payments of $60,000 annually for 3 years will begin January 1, 1998. The present value at December 31, 1996, of these payments was $155,000.
- Reduction of accrued pension costs at December 31, 1996 for the terminating employees was $45,000.

In its December 31, 1996 balance sheet, Howe should report a total liability for special termination benefits of

- A. $475,000
- B. $585,000
- C. $630,000
- D. $655,000

The correct answer is (C). *(Publisher)*
REQUIRED: The termination benefits that should be recognized by the employer when the employees accept the offer and the amount is reasonably estimable.
DISCUSSION: The liability and loss arising from special termination benefits should be recognized by an employer when the employees accept the offer and the amount can be reasonably estimated. The liability and loss arising from contractual termination benefits should be recognized when it is probable that employees will be entitled to benefits and the amount can be reasonably estimated.

Answers (A), (B), and (D) are incorrect because the liability and loss arising from special termination benefits should be recognized by an employer when the employees can accept the offer and the amount can be reasonably estimated. The liability and loss arising from contractual termination benefits should be recognized when it is probable that employees will be entitled to benefits and the amount can be reasonably estimated.

The correct answer is (C). *(CPA 588 I-29)*
REQUIRED: The total liability for special termination benefits to be reported in the 12/31/96 balance sheet.
DISCUSSION: The liability and expense arising from special termination benefits should be recognized by an employer when the employees accept the offer and the amount can be reasonably estimated. The amount should include the lump-sum payments and the present value of any future payments. Thus, Howe should report a total liability for special termination benefits of $630,000 ($475,000 lump-sum payments + $155,000 present value of future payments) in its 12/31/96 balance sheet.

Answer (A) is incorrect because $475,000 excludes the present value of the annual payments. Answer (B) is incorrect because the liability should not be reduced by the reduction of accrued pension costs. Answer (D) is incorrect because the present value of the annual payments of $155,000, not the full amount of $180,000, should be included in the calculation of the liability.

16.4 Employers' Accounting for Postretirement Benefits Other Than Pensions

53. SFAS 106 emphasizes an employer's accounting for a single-employer plan that defines other postretirement employee benefits (OPEB). OPEB, which are benefits other than pensions, are defined in terms of monetary amounts (e.g., a given dollar value of life insurance) or benefit coverage (e.g., amounts per day for hospitalization). The amount depends on such factors as the benefit formula, the life expectancy of the retiree and any beneficiaries and covered dependents, and the frequency and significance of events (e.g., illnesses) requiring payments. The basic elements of accounting for OPEB include

A. The expected postretirement benefit obligation (EPBO), which equals the accumulated postretirement benefit obligation (APBO) after the full eligibility date.

B. The APBO, which is the actuarial present value at a given date of the benefits projected to be earned after the full eligibility date.

C. Required recognition of a minimum liability for any excess of the EPBO over the APBO.

D. The projected benefit obligation (PBO) and the vested benefit obligation (VBO).

The correct answer is (A). *(Publisher)*
REQUIRED: The true statement about the elements of accounting for OPEB.
DISCUSSION: The EPBO for an employee is the actuarial present value at a given date of the OPEB expected to be paid. Its measurement depends on the anticipated amounts and timing of future benefits, the costs to be incurred to provide those benefits, and the extent the costs are shared by the employee and others (such as governmental programs). The APBO for an employee is the actuarial present value at a given date of the future benefits attributable to the employee's service as of that date. Unlike the calculation of the ABO described in SFAS 87, the determination of the APBO (as well as of the EPBO and service cost) implicitly includes the consideration of future salary progression to the extent the benefit formula defines benefits as a function of future compensation levels. The full eligibility date is reached when the employee has rendered all the services necessary to earn all of the benefits expected to be received by that employee. After the full eligibility date, the EPBO and APBO are equal. Prior to that date, the EPBO exceeds the APBO.
Answer (B) is incorrect because the full eligibility date is the date when an employee has earned all the benefits expected to be received. Answer (C) is incorrect because, unlike SFAS 87, SFAS 106 does not require recognition of a minimum liability. Answer (D) is incorrect because these terms relate to pension accounting only.

54. Which of the following components might be included in net periodic postretirement benefit cost (NPPBC) of an employer sponsoring a defined benefit health care plan?

	Amortization of Unrecognized Prior Service Cost	Interest Cost
A.	No	No
B.	Yes	No
C.	No	Yes
D.	Yes	Yes

The correct answer is (D). *(Publisher)*
REQUIRED: The true statement about the elements of NPPBC.
DISCUSSION: The six possible components of NPPBC are (1) service cost, (2) interest on the APBO, (3) return on plan assets, (4) amortization of unrecognized prior service cost, (5) amortization of the transition obligation or asset, and (6) the gain or loss component. The NPPBC is very similar to net periodic pension cost.
Answers (A), (B), and (C) are incorrect because both the amortization of unrecognized prior service cost and the interest cost should be included in the net periodic postretirement benefit cost of an employer sponsoring a defined benefit health care plan.

55. Twain Publishers, Ltd., a publicly traded company, sponsors both a pension plan and a postretirement plan providing other, nonpension benefits. The following information relates to the current year's activity of Twain's defined benefit postretirement plan:

Service cost	$240,000
Return on plan assets	60,000
Interest cost on accumulated benefit obligation	80,000
Amortization of actuarial loss	20,000
Amortization of prior service cost	10,000
Amortization of transition obligation	30,000

Twain's nonpension postretirement benefit cost is

A. $240,000

B. $280,000

C. $300,000

D. $320,000

The correct answer is (D). *(A. Oddo)*

REQUIRED: The net periodic postretirement benefit cost (NPPBC) for the year.

DISCUSSION: The components of the NPPBC are service cost, interest cost, the expected return on plan assets, and amortization of (1) any unrecognized prior service cost, (2) any transition asset or obligation, and (3) any unrecognized net gain (loss). Service cost; interest cost; and the amortization of actuarial loss, prior service cost, and a transition obligation increase the NPPBC. The expected return on plan assets decreases NPPBC. As indicated below, NPPBC for the year is $320,000.

Service cost	$240,000
Return on plan assets	(60,000)
Interest cost	80,000
Amortization of actuarial loss	20,000
Amortization of prior service cost	10,000
Amortization of transition obligation	30,000
Net periodic postretirement benefit cost	$320,000

Answer (A) is incorrect because $240,000 includes only the service cost component. Answer (B) is incorrect because $280,000 excludes the amortization of the prior service cost and the amortization of the transition obligation. Answer (C) is incorrect because $300,000 excludes the amortization of the actuarial loss from the calculation of NPPBC.

56. The service cost component of the NPPBC is

A. Included in the APBO but not in the EPBO.

B. The portion of the EPBO attributed to employee service for a period.

C. Included in the EPBO but not the APBO.

D. Measured using implicit and explicit actuarial assumptions and present value techniques.

The correct answer is (B). *(Publisher)*

REQUIRED: The definition of the service cost component of the NPPBC.

DISCUSSION: Service cost is defined as the actuarial present value of benefits attributed to services rendered by employees during the period. It is the portion of the EPBO attributed to service in the period and is not affected by the level of funding.

Answers (A) and (C) are incorrect because the service cost for the most recently completed period is included in the APBO as well as the EPBO. Answer (D) is incorrect because SFAS 106 requires the use of explicit assumptions, each of which is the best estimate of a particular event.

57. The interest cost component of the NPPBC is the

A. Increase in the EPBO because of the passage of time.

B. Increase in the APBO because of the passage of time.

C. Product of the market-related value of plan assets and the expected long-term rate of return on plan assets.

D. Change in the APBO during the period.

The correct answer is (B). *(Publisher)*

REQUIRED: The definition of the interest cost component of the NPPBC.

DISCUSSION: Interest cost reflects the change in the APBO during the period resulting solely from the passage of time. It equals the APBO at the beginning of the period times the assumed discount rate used in determining the present value of future cash outflows currently expected to be required to satisfy the obligation.

Answer (A) is incorrect because interest cost is a function of the APBO. Answer (C) is incorrect because it defines the expected return on plan assets. Answer (D) is incorrect because the change in the obligation reflects many factors, of which interest cost is one.

58. Prior service cost is defined as the cost of benefit improvements attributable to plan participants' prior service pursuant to a plan amendment or a plan initiation that provides benefits in exchange for plan participants' prior service. The general rule is that prior service cost should be recognized in NPPBC

A. By assigning an equal amount to each remaining year of service to the full eligibility date of each participant active at the amendment date who was not yet fully eligible for benefits.

B. In full in the accounting period in which the plan is amended.

C. By amortizing it over the remaining life expectancy of the participants.

D. In accordance with straight-line amortization over the average remaining years to full eligibility of the active participants.

The correct answer is (A). *(Publisher)*
REQUIRED: The general rule for recognition of prior service cost.
DISCUSSION: The effect of a plan amendment on a participant's EPBO should be attributed to each year of service in that individual's attribution period (ordinarily from the date of hire or a later date specified by the benefit formula to the full eligibility date). This period may include years of service already rendered. The cost of benefit improvements for years of service already rendered is the increase in the APBO as a result of an amendment and measured at the date of the amendment. The general rule is that equal amounts of this cost should be assigned to each remaining year of service to the full eligibility date for each active plan participant at the date of the amendment who was not yet fully eligible.

Answer (B) is incorrect because prior service cost is deemed to provide economic benefits to the employer in future periods. Thus, recognition in full in the year of the amendment is prohibited. Answer (C) is incorrect because this treatment is appropriate only if all or almost all of the participants are fully eligible. Answer (D) is incorrect because it describes a pragmatic exception to the general rule. An alternative, consistently applied amortization method that more rapidly reduces unrecognized prior service cost is permitted to reduce complexity and detail.

59. The gain or loss components of NPPBC (SFAS 106) and net periodic pension cost (SFAS 87) are calculated similarly. Moreover, under either pronouncement, an employer may use a systematic method of amortizing unrecognized net gain or loss other than the corridor approach described in each pronouncement. The alternative is allowable if it results in amortization at least equal to the minimum determined using that approach. Under SFAS 106, however, if an enterprise consistently recognizes gains and losses immediately,

A. Any net loss in excess of a net gain previously recognized first offsets any unrecognized prior service cost.

B. Any net gain in excess of a net loss previously recognized first offsets any unrecognized transition asset.

C. Any net loss in excess of a net gain previously recognized first offsets any unrecognized transition obligation.

D. Any net gain in excess of a net loss previously recognized first offsets any unrecognized transition obligation.

The correct answer is (D). *(Publisher)*
REQUIRED: The proper treatment of gains or losses recognized immediately.
DISCUSSION: Under either SFAS 87 or SFAS 106, gains and losses may be recognized immediately or delayed. But SFAS 106 also provides that immediately recognized gains (losses) that do not offset previously recognized losses (gains) must first reduce any unrecognized transition obligation (asset). The transition obligation (asset) represents an underlying unfunded (overfunded) APBO. The FASB believes that gains (losses) should not be recognized until the unfunded (overfunded) APBO is recognized.

Answers (A) and (C) are incorrect because a net loss in excess of a net gain previously recognized first offsets any unrecognized transition assets. Answer (B) is incorrect because a net gain in excess of a net loss previously recognized first offsets any unrecognized transaction obligation.

60. Employer Co. maintains a postretirement health care plan for its employees. Under the plan's terms, an excess of benefit payments over the sum of the employer's cost and the employees' contributions for a year will be recovered from increased employees' contributions in the subsequent year. However, for the current year only, Employer has decided not to adjust contributions. Employer should

    A. Delay recognition of the loss by using the corridor approach.

    B. Apply any systematic and rational delayed recognition approach to accounting for the loss.

    C. Immediately recognize the loss in income.

    D. Adjust the transition asset.

The correct answer is (C). *(Publisher)*
    REQUIRED: The treatment of a loss resulting from a temporary deviation from the plan.
    DISCUSSION: A gain or loss from a temporary deviation from the substantive plan is immediately recognized in income. No delayed recognition method is appropriate because the effect of a temporary deviation (1) is not deemed to provide future economic benefits and (2) relates to benefits already paid. If the deviation is other than temporary, that is, if the employer decides to continue to bear the burden of increased costs, the implication is that the substantive plan (the plan as understood by the parties as opposed to the extant written plan) has been amended. An amendment would require accounting for prior service cost.
    Answers (A), (B), and (D) are incorrect because a gain or loss from a temporary deviation from the substantive plan is immediately recognized in income.

61. Which of the following items of information should be disclosed by a company providing health care benefits to its retirees?

  I. The assumed health care cost trend rate used to measure the expected cost of benefits covered by the plan
  II. The accumulated postretirement benefit obligation

    A. I and II.

    B. I only.

    C. II only.

    D. Neither I nor II.

The correct answer is (A). *(CPA 593 T-30)*
    REQUIRED: The information that should be disclosed by a company providing health care benefits to its retirees.
    DISCUSSION: SFAS 106, *Employers' Accounting for Postretirement Benefits Other Than Pensions*, has a lengthy list of required disclosures, including

- The assumed health care cost trend rate(s) used to measure the expected cost of benefits covered by the plan (gross eligible charges) for the next year and a general description of the direction and pattern of change in the assumed trend rates thereafter, together with the ultimate trend rate(s) and when that rate is expected to be achieved.

- The accumulated postretirement benefit obligation, identifying separately the portion attributable to retirees, other fully eligible plan participants, and other active plan participants.

    Answers (B), (C), and (D) are incorrect because both I and II are required.

62. Bounty Co. provides postretirement health care benefits to employees who have completed at least 10 years service and are aged 55 years or older when retiring. Employees retiring from Bounty have a median age of 62, and no one has worked beyond age 65. Fletcher is hired at 48 years old. The attribution period for accruing Bounty's expected postretirement health care benefit obligation to Fletcher is during the period when Fletcher is aged

    A. 48 to 65.

    B. 48 to 58.

    C. 55 to 65.

    D. 55 to 62.

The correct answer is (B). *(CPA 1193 T-27)*
    REQUIRED: The attribution period for accruing the expected postretirement health care benefit obligation to an employee.
    DISCUSSION: The attribution period begins on the date of hire unless the plan's benefit formula grants credit for service only from a later date. The end of the period is the full eligibility date. If the exception does not apply, Fletcher's attribution is from age 48, the date of hire, to age 58, the date of full eligibility.
    Answers (A), (C), and (D) are incorrect because the attribution period is from the date of hire to the date of full eligibility.

16.5 Postemployment Benefits

63. SFAS 112, *Employers' Accounting for Postemployment Benefits*, establishes the accounting for

- A. Pension benefits provided to spouses of retired employees.
- B. Salary continuation benefits provided to employees on disability leave.
- C. Counseling benefits provided to employees nearing retirement age.
- D. Health care benefits provided to dependents of retired employees.

The correct answer is (B). *(Publisher)*
REQUIRED: The type of benefits accounted for under SFAS 112.
DISCUSSION: SFAS 112, *Employers' Accounting for Postemployment Benefits*, concerns accounting standards for employers who provide benefits to former or inactive employees, their beneficiaries, and their covered dependents after employment but before retirement. These benefits include, but are not limited to, salary continuation, supplemental unemployment benefits, severance benefits, disability-related benefits (including workers' compensation), job training and counseling, and continuation of benefits such as health care and life insurance coverage.
Answers (A) and (D) are incorrect because the former employees have retired and thus are not covered under SFAS 112. Answer (C) is incorrect because the employees are still employed.

64. If the payment of postemployment benefits is probable, the amount can be reasonably estimated, and the obligation relates to rights that vest or accumulate, employer's compensation for postemployment benefits should

- A. Be recognized when the benefits are paid.
- B. Be accrued at the date of the event giving rise to the payment of benefits.
- C. Be accrued if attributable to employees' services already rendered.
- D. Not be recognized.

The correct answer is (C). *(Publisher)*
REQUIRED: The treatment of postemployment benefits by the employer.
DISCUSSION: SFAS 112 requires employers to recognize the obligation to provide postemployment benefits if the obligation is attributable to employees' services already rendered, employees' rights accumulate or vest, payment is probable, and the amount of the benefits can be reasonably estimated.
Answers (A), (B), and (D) are incorrect because if the postemployment benefits are attributable to employees' services already rendered, payment is probable, the amount can be reasonably estimated, and the rights vest or accumulate, the obligation should be accrued.

65. At December 31, 1996, Cassill Corporation reasonably estimates that its obligations for postemployment benefits include

Severance pay	$120,000
Job training benefits	90,000

These benefits relate to employees' services already rendered, and payment is probable. The severance pay benefits vest; the job training benefits accumulate. In its December 31, 1996 balance sheet, Cassill should report a liability for postemployment benefits of

- A. $0
- B. $90,000
- C. $120,000
- D. $210,000

The correct answer is (D). *(Publisher)*
REQUIRED: The amount of liability that should be recorded for postemployment benefits.
DISCUSSION: According to SFAS 112, if postemployment benefits are attributable to employees' services already rendered, employees' rights accumulate or vest, payment is probable, and the amount of the benefits can be reasonably estimated, then the employer should recognize a liability for the obligation. Thus, the full amount of the severance pay and job training benefits of $210,000 ($120,000 + $90,000) should be reported as a liability.
Answers (A), (B), and (C) are incorrect because the full amount of both benefits should be included in the liability.

CHAPTER SEVENTEEN
LEASES

Leases have been the subject of more accounting pronouncements than any other financial accounting topic. In addition to the pronouncements listed below, leases have also been the subject of various FASB Technical Bulletins and many discussions by the Emerging Issues Task Force.

SFAS 13 - *Accounting for Leases*

22 - *Changes in the Provisions of Lease Agreements Resulting from Refundings of Tax-Exempt Debt*

23 - *Inception of the Lease*

27 - *Classification of Renewals or Extensions of Existing Sales-Type or Direct Financing Leases*

28 - *Accounting for Sales with Leasebacks*

29 - *Determining Contingent Rentals*

91 - *Accounting for Nonrefundable Fees and Costs Associated with Originating or Acquiring Loans and Initial Direct Costs of Leases*

98 - *Accounting for Leases: Sale-Leaseback Transactions Involving Real Estate, Sales-Type Leases of Real Estate, Definition of the Lease Term, Initial Costs of Direct Financing Leases*

FASB Interpretation No.

19 - *Lessee Guarantee of the Residual Value of Leased Property*

21 - *Accounting for Leases in a Business Combination*

23 - *Leases of Certain Property Owned by a Governmental Unit or Authority*

24 - *Leases Involving Only Part of a Building*

26 - *Accounting for Purchase of a Leased Asset by the Lessee During the Term of the Lease*

27 - *Accounting for a Loss on a Sublease*

17.1 Capital Leases

1. Leases should be classified by the lessee as either operating leases or capital leases. Which of the following statements best characterizes operating leases?

A. The rights and risks of ownership are transferred from the lessor to the lessee.

B. The lessee records leased property as an asset and the present value of the lease payments as a liability.

C. Operating leases transfer ownership to the lessee, contain a bargain purchase option, are for more than 75% of the leased asset's useful life, or have lease payments with a present value in excess of 90% of the value of the leased asset.

D. The lessor records lease revenue, asset depreciation, maintenance, etc., and the lessee records lease payments as rental expense.

The correct answer is (D). *(Publisher)*
REQUIRED: The true statement about operating leases.
DISCUSSION: Operating leases are transactions whereby lessees rent the right to use lessor assets without acquiring a substantial portion of the rights and risks of ownership of those assets.
Answer (A) is incorrect because, when the rights and risks of ownership are transferred from the lessor to the lessee, the transaction is a capital lease. Answer (B) is incorrect because it describes the proper accounting for a capital lease. Answer (C) is incorrect because satisfaction of any one of these four criteria requires the lease to be treated as a capital lease.

2. The present value of minimum lease payments should be used by the lessee in determining the amount of a lease liability under a lease classified by the lessee as a(n)

	Capital Lease	Operating Lease
A.	Yes	Yes
B.	Yes	No
C.	No	No
D.	No	Yes

The correct answer is (B). *(CPA 1189 T-16)*
REQUIRED: The lease for which the lessee's liability is based on the present value of the minimum lease payments.
DISCUSSION: SFAS 13, *Accounting for Leases*, states that the lessee must record a capital lease as an asset and an obligation at an amount equal to the present value of the minimum lease payments. Under an operating lease, the lessee records no liability except for rental expense accrued at the end of an accounting period. Such accrual would be at settlement value rather than present value.
Answer (A) is incorrect because an operating lease does not result in a lease liability for the lessee. Answer (C) is incorrect because the lease liability under a capital lease is the present value of minimum lease payments. Answer (D) is incorrect because the lease liability under a capital lease is the present value of minimum lease payments. Also, an operating lease does not result in a lease liability.

3. Generally accepted accounting principles require that certain lease agreements be accounted for as purchases. The theoretical basis for this treatment is that a lease of this type

A. Conveys substantially all of the benefits and risks incident to the ownership of property.

B. Is an example of form over substance.

C. Provides the use of the leased asset to the lessee for a limited period of time.

D. Must be recorded in accordance with the concept of cause and effect.

The correct answer is (A). *(CPA 1177 T-20)*
REQUIRED: The theoretical justification for capitalization of certain leases.
DISCUSSION: The provisions of SFAS 13 derive from the view that a lease transferring substantially all of the benefits and risks incident to the ownership of property should be accounted for as the acquisition of an asset and the incurrence of an obligation by the lessee. The lessor should account for the transaction as a sale or financing.
Answer (B) is incorrect because a lease is not a purchase in form, although transfer of substantially all of the benefits and risks of ownership make it similar to a purchase in substance. Answer (C) is incorrect because, although a lease is a contractual agreement covering the use of property for a specified time period, other aspects of the lease justify the capitalization treatment. Answer (D) is incorrect because the concept of cause and effect is not relevant to accounting for leases.

4. On January 1, 1996, Mollat Co. signed a 7-year lease for equipment having a 10-year economic life. The present value of the monthly lease payments equals 80% of the equipment's fair value. The lease agreement provides for neither a transfer of title to Mollat nor a bargain purchase option. In its 1996 income statement, Mollat should report

A. Rent expense equal to the 1996 lease payments.

B. Rent expense equal to the 1996 lease payments minus interest expense.

C. Lease amortization equal to one-tenth of the equipment's fair value.

D. Lease amortization equal to one-seventh of 80% of the equipment's fair value.

The correct answer is (A). *(CPA 592 T-34)*
REQUIRED: The income statement effect of the lease.
DISCUSSION: A lease is either a capital lease or an operating lease. A lease must be classified as a capital lease by a lessee if, at its inception, any one of four criteria is satisfied. Each of these criteria indicates that a substantial transfer of the rights and risks of ownership has occurred. The following are the four criteria: (1) The lease provides for the transfer of ownership of the leased property, (2) the lease contains a bargain purchase option, (3) the lease term is 75% or more of the estimated economic life of the leased property, or (4) the present value of the minimum lease payments (excluding executory costs) is at least 90% of the excess of the fair value of the leased property to the lessor at the inception of the lease less any related investment tax credit. Since none of these criteria are satisfied, the lease must be treated as an operating lease. Under an operating lease, the lessee recognizes periodic rental expense but records neither an asset nor a liability (except for accrued rental expense at the end of a period).
Answer (B) is incorrect because Mollat should not recognize interest expense on an operating lease. Answers (C) and (D) are incorrect because a capital lease requires amortization.

5. For a capital lease, the amount recorded initially by the lessee as a liability should normally

A. Exceed the total of the minimum lease payments.

B. Exceed the present value of the minimum lease payments at the beginning of the lease.

C. Equal the total of the minimum lease payments.

D. Equal the present value of the minimum lease payments at the beginning of the lease.

The correct answer is (D). *(CPA 592 T-33)*
REQUIRED: The amount recorded initially by the lessee as a liability.
DISCUSSION: SFAS 13 requires that the lessee record a capital lease as an asset and a liability at the present value of the minimum lease payments during the lease term. The discount rate is the lower of the lessor's implicit interest rate or the lessee's incremental borrowing rate of interest. The present value cannot exceed the fair value of the leased asset at the inception of the lease.
Answers (A) and (C) are incorrect because the amount recorded initially should be a present value. Hence, it will be less than the total of the minimum lease payments. Answer (B) is incorrect because the amount recorded initially should equal the present value of the minimum lease payments.

6. Jay's lease payments are made at the end of each period. Jay's liability for a capital lease would be reduced periodically by the

A. Minimum lease payment less the portion of the minimum lease payment allocable to interest.

B. Minimum lease payment plus the amortization of the related asset.

C. Minimum lease payment less the amortization of the related asset.

D. Minimum lease payment.

The correct answer is (A). *(CPA 1191 T-34)*
REQUIRED: The reduction of the liability for a capital lease after payments at the end of each period.
DISCUSSION: The lease liability consists of the present value of the minimum lease payments. The lease liability is reduced by the lease payment attributable to the lease liability. This amount is the lease payment less the interest component of the payment. Thus, the liability is decreased by the minimum lease payment each period less the portion of the payment allocable to interest.
Answers (B), (C), and (D) are incorrect because the lease liability is reduced by the minimum lease payment each period less the portion that is allocated to interest.

7. A 6-year capital lease expiring on December 31 specifies equal minimum annual lease payments. Part of this payment represents interest and part represents a reduction in the net lease liability. The portion of the minimum lease payment in the fifth year applicable to the reduction of the net lease liability should be

    A. Less than in the fourth year.

    B. More than in the fourth year.

    C. The same as in the sixth year.

    D. More than in the sixth year.

The correct answer is (B). *(CPA 1188 T-13)*

    REQUIRED: The trend of the change, if any, in the periodic reduction of the net lease liability.

    DISCUSSION: A lease payment has two components: interest expense and the portion applied to the reduction of the lease obligation. The effective interest method requires that the carrying value of the obligation at the beginning of each interest period be multiplied by the appropriate interest rate to determine the interest expense. The difference between the minimum lease payment and the interest expense is the amount of reduction in the carrying value of the lease obligation. Because the carrying value declines with each payment, interest expense in future years also declines, resulting in an increase in the amount applied to reduce the lease obligation. The fifth year's minimum lease payment will therefore result in a greater reduction in the liability than the fourth year's.

    Answers (A), (C), and (D) are incorrect because the carrying value of the lease liability declines with each payment, which reduces interest expense in future periods. As a result, more of the lease payment is applied to the lease liability in future years.

8. A lessee had a 10-year capital lease requiring equal annual payments. The reduction of the lease liability in year 2 should equal

    A. The current liability shown for the lease at the end of year 1.

    B. The current liability shown for the lease at the end of year 2.

    C. The reduction of the lease obligation in year 1.

    D. One-tenth of the original lease liability.

The correct answer is (A). *(CPA 590 T-11)*

    REQUIRED: The reduction of a capital lease liability in the second year.

    DISCUSSION: At the inception of a capital lease, a lessee should record a fixed asset and a lease obligation equal to the present value of the minimum lease payments. In a classified balance sheet, the lease liability must be allocated between the current and noncurrent portions. The current portion at a balance sheet date is the reduction of the lease liability in the forthcoming year.

    Answer (B) is incorrect because the current liability at the end of year 2 is equal to the reduction that will be recorded in year 3. Answers (C) and (D) are incorrect because the reduction of the lease liability will increase in each subsequent year.

9. A lease contains a bargain purchase option. In determining the lessee's capitalizable cost at the beginning of the lease term, the payment called for by the bargain purchase option is

    A. Not capitalized.

    B. Subtracted at its present value.

    C. Added at its exercise price.

    D. Added at its present value.

The correct answer is (D). *(CPA 584 T-12)*

    REQUIRED: The effect of a bargain purchase option on the lessee's capitalizable cost.

    DISCUSSION: The lessee must record a capital lease as an asset and an obligation at an amount equal to the present value of the minimum lease payments. A bargain purchase option is included in the minimum lease payments.

    Answers (A), (B), and (C) are incorrect because a bargain purchase option is an addition at the present value of the option.

10. On July 1, 1996 a company leased equipment under a 5-year, noncancelable, nonrenewable agreement. The company paid a consultant a commission of $3,000 for arranging the lease. The lessee incurred $900 in installation and $600 in pre-operational testing costs. The equipment has an expected life of 7 years. The lease does not contain a bargain purchase option, and at the expiration of the lease, the equipment reverts to the lessor. The fair value of the equipment is $300,000, and the present value of the future minimum lease payments is $280,000. At the inception of the lease, the company should classify this lease as a(n)

A.   Leveraged lease.

B.   Operating lease.

C.   Sale and leaseback.

D.   Capital lease.

The correct answer is (D). *(P. McBrayer)*
REQUIRED: The proper classification of a lease at its inception.
DISCUSSION: A lease must be classified as a capital lease by a lessee if, at its inception, any one of four criteria is satisfied. Each of these criteria indicates that a substantial transfer of the rights and risks of ownership has occurred. The following are the four criteria: (1) The lease provides for the transfer of ownership of the leased property, (2) the lease contains a bargain purchase option, (3) the lease term is 75% or more of the estimated economic life of the leased property, or (4) the present value of the minimum lease payments (excluding executory costs) is at least 90% of the excess of the fair value of the leased property to the lessor at the inception of the lease less any related investment tax credit. None of the first three criteria are satisfied. The fourth criterion is satisfied, however, because the $280,000 present value of the future minimum lease payments is greater than 90% of the $300,000 fair value of the equipment. Hence, this lease should be classified as a capital lease.

Answer (A) is incorrect because a leveraged lease involves financing the transaction with substantial leverage (i.e., nonrecourse debt). Answer (B) is incorrect because the lease qualifies as a capital lease. Answer (C) is incorrect because there is no sale to qualify as a sale-leaseback transaction.

11. On January 1, 1994 JCK Co. signed a contract for an 8-year lease of its equipment with a 10-year life. The present value of the 16 equal semiannual payments in advance equaled 85% of the equipment's fair value. The contract had no provision for JCK, the lessor, to give up legal ownership of the equipment. Should JCK recognize rent or interest revenue in 1996, and should the revenue recognized in 1996 be the same or smaller than the revenue recognized in 1995?

	1996 Revenues Recognized	1996 Amount Recognized Compared to 1995
A.	Rent	The same
B.	Rent	Smaller
C.	Interest	The same
D.	Interest	Smaller

The correct answer is (D). *(CPA 593 T-38)*
REQUIRED: The type of revenue recognized and the amount compared to the previous year.
DISCUSSION: A lease must be classified as a capital lease by a lessee if, at its inception, any one of four criteria is satisfied. One of the criteria is that the lease term be 75% or more of the estimated economic life of the leased property. Because the lease term is 80% (8 years ÷ 10 years) of the estimated life of the equipment, the lease is a capital lease. Whether the lessor treats the capital lease as a direct-financing or sales-type lease, it will recognize interest revenue. The amount declines over the lease term because the effective-interest method is used. As the carrying amount decreases, the interest component (applicable interest rate x carrying amount) of the periodic lease payment also decreases.

Answers (A), (B), and (C) are incorrect because the lessor should recognize interest revenue, the amount of which will decline over the lease term.

12. The terms of a 6-year, noncancelable lease include a guarantee by Lessee of Lessor's 7-year bank loan obtained to finance construction of the leased equipment, a termination penalty assuring that the lease will be renewed for 3 years following the expiration of the initial lease, and an option that allows Lessor to extend the lease for 3 years following the last renewal option exercised by Lessee. The lease term as defined by current authoritative literature is

A. 6 years.

B. 7 years.

C. 9 years.

D. 12 years.

The correct answer is (D). *(Publisher)*

REQUIRED: The number of years in the lease term.

DISCUSSION: SFAS 13, as amended by SFAS 98, states that the term of a lease includes not only the fixed noncancelable lease term but also (1) any periods covered by bargain renewal options, (2) any periods covered by ordinary renewal options preceding the date at which a bargain purchase option is exercisable, (3) any periods covered by ordinary renewal options during which a guarantee by the lessee of the lessor's debt or a loan from the lessee to the lessor related to the leased property is expected to be in effect, (4) any periods for which failure to renew the lease imposes a penalty on the lessee in an amount such that renewal appears to be reasonably assured, and (5) any periods representing renewals or extensions of the lease at the lessor's option. In no case can the lease term extend beyond the date a bargain purchase option becomes exercisable.

Here, the termination penalty covers the 3 years immediately following the initial 6-year lease term. The renewal option by Lessor at the end of the first 9 years covers an additional 3 years, resulting in a lease term of 12 years. The 7-year period of the bank loan is included in the 6-year term and the first 3-year renewal period.

Answer (A) is incorrect because 6 years includes only the fixed term. Answer (B) is incorrect because 7 years is the debt term. Answer (C) is incorrect because the lease term includes both the period that would result in a penalty to the lessee and the period that is at the option of the lessor.

13. At its inception, the lease term of Lease G is 65% of the estimated remaining economic life of the leased property. This lease contains a bargain purchase option. The lessee should record Lease G as

A. Neither an asset nor a liability.

B. An asset but not a liability.

C. An asset and a liability.

D. An expense.

The correct answer is (C). *(CPA 1185 T-5)*

REQUIRED: The proper classification of a lease containing a bargain purchase option.

DISCUSSION: A lease must be classified as a capital lease by a lessee if, at its inception, any one of four criteria is satisfied. Each of these criteria indicates that a substantial transfer of the rights and risks of ownership has occurred. One test is whether the lease contains a bargain purchase option, which is a provision that permits the lessee to purchase the leased property at a price significantly lower than the expected fair value of the property at the date the option becomes exercisable. A capital lease must be recorded by the lessee as both an asset and an obligation at an amount equal to the present value of the minimum lease payments.

Answers (A), (B), and (D) are incorrect because the lease qualifies as a capital lease due to the bargain purchase option. A capital lease should be recorded as both an asset and a liability at the present value of minimum lease payments.

14. On March 1, 1996 Rory Corp. became the lessee of new equipment under a noncancelable, 6-year lease. The total estimated economic life of this equipment is 10 years. The fair value of this equipment on March 1, 1996 was $100,000. The related investment tax credit retained, and expected to be realized, by the lessor is $10,000. The lease does not meet the criteria for classification as a capital lease with respect to transfer of ownership of the leased asset, the existence of a bargain purchase option, or the duration of the lease term. Nevertheless, Rory must classify this lease as a capital lease if, at the inception of the lease, the present value of the minimum lease payments (excluding executory costs) is equal to at least

   A. $67,500

   B. $81,000

   C. $90,000

   D. $99,000

The correct answer is (B). *(CPA 586 II-18)*
   REQUIRED: The present value of the minimum lease payments requiring classification of the lease as a capital lease.
   DISCUSSION: A lease must be classified as a capital lease by a lessee if, at its inception, any one of four criteria is satisfied. Each of these criteria indicates that a substantial transfer of the rights and risks of ownership has occurred. One test is whether the present value of the minimum lease payments (excluding executory costs to be paid by the lessor, such as maintenance, insurance, and taxes) is equal to or greater than 90% of the fair value of the leased property at the inception of the lease. For this test, however, the fair value must be reduced by any related investment tax credit retained, and expected to be realized, by the lessor. The threshold amount under the fair value test is therefore $81,000 [90% x ($100,000 – $10,000)].
   Answers (A), (C), and (D) are incorrect because the present value of the minimum lease payments must be equal to or greater than 90% of the fair value of the property reduced by the investment tax credit expected to be realized.

15. Lease A does not contain a bargain purchase option, but the lease term is equal to 90% of the estimated economic life of the leased property. Lease B does not transfer ownership of the property to the lessee by the end of the lease term, but the lease term is equal to 75% of the estimated economic life of the leased property. How should the lessee classify these leases?

	Lease A	Lease B
A.	Operating lease	Capital lease
B.	Operating lease	Operating lease
C.	Capital lease	Capital lease
D.	Capital lease	Operating lease

The correct answer is (C). *(CPA 1192 T-27)*
   REQUIRED: The proper classification of leases.
   DISCUSSION: For a lease to be classified as a capital lease by the lessee, any one of four criteria must be met. One of these criteria is that the lease term equal 75% or more of the estimated remaining economic life of the leased property. Both leases meet the 75% criterion and should be properly classified as capital leases.
   Answers (A), (B), and (D) are incorrect because both leases meet the 75% criterion for capitalization.

16. MacDunnell leased a new machine having an expected useful life of 30 years from Fiegull. Terms of the noncancelable, 25-year lease were that MacDunnell would gain title to the property upon payment of a sum equal to the fair value of the machine at the termination of the lease. MacDunnell accounted for the lease as a capital lease and recorded an asset and a liability in the financial records. The asset recorded under this lease should properly be amortized over

   A. 5 years (the period of actual ownership).

   B. 22.5 years (75% of the 30-year asset life).

   C. 25 years (the term of the lease).

   D. 30 years (the total asset life).

The correct answer is (C). *(Publisher)*
   REQUIRED: The proper amortization period for a lease with a purchase option.
   DISCUSSION: When a lease transfers ownership of the property to the lessee at the end of the lease or contains a bargain purchase option, the lessee will own the asset at the end of the lease. Hence, such a lease is capitalized and amortized over the expected useful life of the leased asset. If, instead, the lease meets either the 75% lease term test or the 90% fair value test, it will be accounted for as a capital lease and will be amortized over the lease term. Because the lease term is more than 75% of the expected useful life of the asset, the lease should be amortized over the lease term (25 years).
   Answer (A) is incorrect because the lessee's amortization period covers the entire period of the lease. Answer (B) is incorrect because, although it represents one of the four criteria for a capital lease, it does not reflect the proper amortization period. Answer (D) is incorrect because a lease is amortized over the expected useful life of the asset only when a bargain purchase option exists or ownership is automatically transferred at the end of the lease.

17. On January 1, 1995, West Co. entered into a 10-year lease for a manufacturing plant. The annual minimum lease payments are $100,000. In the notes to the December 31, 1996 financial statements, what amounts of subsequent years' lease payments should be disclosed?

	Amount for Appropriate Required Period	Aggregate Amount for the Period Thereafter
A.	$100,000	$0
B.	$300,000	$500,000
C.	$500,000	$300,000
D.	$500,000	$0

The correct answer is (C). *(CPA 1189 I-53)*
REQUIRED: The amounts of subsequent years' lease payments to be disclosed.
DISCUSSION: SFAS 13 requires that the future minimum lease payments as of the date of the latest balance sheet presented be disclosed in the aggregate and for each of the 5 succeeding fiscal years. This disclosure is required whether the lease is classified as a capital lease or as an operating lease.
Answer (A) is incorrect because the aggregate amount of the obligation is $800,000. This aggregate amount consists of the future payments for the next 5 years in the amount of $500,000, and the period thereafter in the amount of $300,000. Answer (B) is incorrect because the required disclosure period is 5 years, resulting in a required disclosure of $500,000. Answer (D) is incorrect because the total remaining obligation of $300,000 is disclosed in the aggregate in addition to the 5-year period.

18. Star Co. leases a building for its product showroom. The 10-year nonrenewable lease will expire on December 31, 2001. In January 1996, Star redecorated its showroom and made leasehold improvements of $48,000. The estimated useful life of the improvements is 8 years. Star uses the straight-line method of amortization. What amount of leasehold improvements, net of amortization, should Star report in its June 30, 1996 balance sheet?

A. $45,600

B. $45,000

C. $44,000

D. $43,200

The correct answer is (C). *(CPA 593 I-22)*
REQUIRED: The net amount of leasehold improvements reported in the balance sheet.
DISCUSSION: General improvements to leased property should be capitalized as leasehold improvements and amortized in accordance with the straight-line method over the shorter of their expected useful life or the lease term. Because the remaining lease term is less than the estimated life of the improvements, the cost should be amortized equally over 6 years. On 6/30/96, $44,000 {$48,000 − [($48,000 ÷ 6 years) x ½ year]} should be reported for net leasehold improvements.
Answer (A) is incorrect because $45,600 assumes the amortization period is 10 years. Answer (B) is incorrect because $45,000 assumes the amortization period is 8 years. Answer (D) is incorrect because $43,200 assumes that 1 year's amortization has been recorded and that the amortization period is 10 years.

19. On January 1, 1995, Bay Co. acquired a land lease for a 21-year period with no option to renew. The lease required Bay to construct a building in lieu of rent. The building, completed on January 1, 1996 at a cost of $840,000, will be depreciated using the straight-line method. At the end of the lease, the building's estimated fair value will be $420,000. What is the building's carrying amount in Bay's December 31, 1996 balance sheet?

A. $798,000

B. $800,000

C. $819,000

D. $820,000

The correct answer is (A). *(CPA 1191 I-16)*
REQUIRED: The building's carrying amount after 2 years.
DISCUSSION: General improvements to leased property should be capitalized as leasehold improvements and amortized in accordance with the straight-line method over the shorter of their expected useful life or the lease term. Given no renewal option, the amortization period is 20 years, the shorter of the expected useful life or the remaining lease term at the date of completion. The amortizable base is $840,000 even though the building will have a fair value of $420,000 at the end of the lease. The latter amount is not a salvage value because the building will become the lessor's property when the lease expires. Consequently, 1996 straight-line amortization is $42,000 ($840,000 ÷ 20 years), and the year-end carrying amount is $798,000 ($840,000 − $42,000).
Answer (B) is incorrect because $800,000 assumes a 21-year remaining lease term at 1/1/96. Answer (C) is incorrect because $819,000 assumes no amortization of an amount equal to the fair value at the end of the lease term. Answer (D) is incorrect because $820,000 assumes a 21-year remaining lease term at 1/1/96 and no amortization of an amount equal to the fair value at the end of the lease term.

20. Lessee Corporation has leased manufacturing equipment from Lessor Corporation in a transaction that is to be accounted for as a capital lease. Lessee has guaranteed Lessor a residual value for the equipment. How should this guarantee be reflected in the financial statements of Lessee?

A. The full amount of the residual guarantee should be capitalized as part of the cost of the equipment.

B. The present value of the residual guarantee should be capitalized as part of the cost of the equipment.

C. The guarantee will not be reflected in the body of the financial statements but should be disclosed in the footnotes.

D. The guarantee should not be reflected in the financial statements.

The correct answer is (B). *(CIA 1187 IV-36)*
REQUIRED: The effect of a guaranteed residual value on lessee accounting for a capital lease.
DISCUSSION: A guaranteed residual value is defined as the portion of the expected salvage value that is guaranteed by the lessee. This portion of the expected salvage value is included with the periodic rental payments in the definition of minimum lease payments. Because the leased asset should be recorded in an amount equal to the present value of the minimum lease payments, the guaranteed residual value is included in the capitalized cost of the equipment at an amount equal to its present value.
Answer (A) is incorrect because the present value should be capitalized as part of the cost of the equipment. Answers (C) and (D) are incorrect because the residual guarantee should be reflected in the body of the financial statements.

21. Beal, Inc. intends to lease a machine from Paul Corp. Beal's incremental borrowing rate is 14%. The prime rate of interest is 8%. Paul's implicit rate in the lease is 10%, which is known to Beal. Beal computes the present value of the minimum lease payments using

A. 8%

B. 10%

C. 12%

D. 14%

The correct answer is (B). *(CPA 589 I-44)*
REQUIRED: The discount rate used by the lessee in determining the present value of minimum lease payments.
DISCUSSION: According to SFAS 13, a lessee should compute the present value of the minimum lease payments using its incremental borrowing rate unless

1. The lessee knows the lessor's implicit rate.
2. The implicit rate is less than the lessee's incremental borrowing rate.

Since both conditions are met, Beal must use the 10% implicit rate.
Answer (A) is incorrect because 8% is the prime rate. Answer (C) is incorrect because 12% is the average of the implicit and incremental rates. Answer (D) is incorrect because 14% is the incremental rate, which is higher.

22. Which one of the following items is not part of the minimum lease payments recorded by the lessee?

A. The minimum rental payments called for by the lease.

B. A guarantee by the lessee of the lessor's debt.

C. Any guarantee the lessee is required to make at the end of the lease term regarding any deficiency from a specified minimum.

D. Any payment the lessee must make at the end of the lease term either to purchase the leased property or to satisfy a penalty for failure to renew the lease.

The correct answer is (B). *(CMA 681 3-16)*
REQUIRED: The item that is not a component of minimum lease payments.
DISCUSSION: The lease term includes not only the fixed, noncancelable term of the lease but also those years for which there is reasonable assurance that the lease will remain in effect. A guarantee by the lessee of the lessor's debt related to the leased property provides such assurance and thus may affect the term over which the minimum lease payments are calculated. Otherwise, such a guarantee does not affect the computation of minimum lease payments.
Answers (A), (C), and (D) are incorrect because each is an item included by the lessee in the computation of the minimum lease payments for a capital lease.

23. Equipment covered by a lease agreement is expected by the lessor to have a residual value at the end of the lease term of $20,000. As part of the lease agreement, the lessee guarantees a residual value of $12,000. In the case of excessive usage, the guaranteed residual value is $18,000. What is the amount of guaranteed residual value that should be included in the calculation of the minimum lease payments?

A. $0

B. $12,000

C. $18,000

D. $20,000

The correct answer is (B). *(Publisher)*

REQUIRED: The amount of guaranteed residual value to be included in minimum lease payments.

DISCUSSION: FASB Interpretation No. 19, *Lessee Guarantee of the Residual Value of Leased Property*, states that the amount of guaranteed residual value to be included in the determination of minimum lease payments is the determinable amount the lessee is required to make good, even if that amount is materially lower than the expected salvage value. Consequently, the $12,000 guarantee should be included. The additional guarantee of $6,000 ($18,000 – $12,000) is not included because it is contingent and thus nondeterminable.

Answer (A) is incorrect because the guaranteed residual value is included in the determination of minimum lease payments. Answer (C) is incorrect because the additional guarantee of $6,000 ($18,000 – $12,000) is not included because it is contingent and thus nondeterminable. Answer (D) is incorrect because the minimum lease payments include only the amount of residual value that is guaranteed.

24. Which of the following should be excluded by the lessee in determining minimum lease payments for a capital lease?

A. The guarantee of the residual value obtained by the lessee from a financially sound unrelated third party.

B. The minimum rental payments called for by the lease over the lease term.

C. The guarantee by the lessee of the residual value, excluding any residual deficiency attributable to excessive usage, of the leased property at the expiration of the lease term.

D. The payment that the lessee can be required to make upon failure to renew the lease at expiration of the lease term.

The correct answer is (A). *(Publisher)*

REQUIRED: The item excluded by the lessee in the computation of minimum lease payments for a capital lease.

DISCUSSION: FASB Interpretation No. 19 specifically excludes any guarantee of residual value made by a third party unrelated to the lessee from the determination of minimum lease payments. Furthermore, amounts paid as consideration for this third-party guarantee are treated as executory costs (along with insurance, maintenance, taxes, etc.) and are also excluded.

Answers (B), (C), and (D) are incorrect because each is an item included by the lessee in computing minimum lease payments for a capital lease.

25. On January 2, a clothing store entered into a lease with a shopping mall for space to be used as a retail store. Terms of the 5-year, noncancelable lease require monthly payments of $600 plus 1% of sales. Sales have been averaging $15,000 per month and are expected to remain constant or increase. What monthly amount(s) should be included in minimum lease payments?

A. Only the $150 payment based on expected sales.

B. Only the $600 monthly payment.

C. Both the $150 and $600 payments.

D. Neither the $150 nor $600 payments.

The correct answer is (B). *(Publisher)*

REQUIRED: The amount(s) to be included in minimum lease payments on a lease containing a contingent payment term.

DISCUSSION: SFAS 29, *Determining Contingent Rentals*, defines contingent rentals as lease payments based on a factor that does not exist or is not measurable at the inception of the lease. Future sales do not exist at the inception of the lease and meet the definition of a contingent rental.

SFAS 13 excludes contingent rentals from minimum lease payments. Because the $150 based on expected future sales is a contingent rental, only the $600 periodic payment is included in minimum lease payments.

Answer (A) is incorrect because the minimum lease payment includes only those payments that are measurable at the inception of the lease. Answer (C) is incorrect because the $150 payment is not measurable at the inception of the lease. Answer (D) is incorrect because the $600 payment is included in minimum lease payments because it is measurable.

26. On January 2, a 5-year lease for a major piece of equipment is signed. Terms of the lease require a fixed annual payment of $12,000 plus $100 for each 1% of a specific bank's prime interest rate. If the prime interest rate is 14% on January 2, is expected to rise to 16% by July 1, and is expected to average 10% for the life of the lease, the total minimum lease payments for the life of the lease should be

A. $60,000

B. $65,000

C. $67,000

D. $68,000

The correct answer is (C). *(Publisher)*

REQUIRED: The total minimum lease payments over the life of the lease.

DISCUSSION: SFAS 13 excludes contingent rentals from the definition of minimum lease payments. SFAS 29 defines contingent rentals as the changes in lease payments resulting from changes occurring subsequent to the inception of the lease. But lease payments that are based on a factor that exists and is measurable at the inception of the lease are not contingent rentals. Thus, total minimum lease payments for this piece of equipment should include the five annual payments of $12,000 per year ($60,000) plus $7,000, which is the sum of the five annual $1,400 payments. This amount is based on the prime interest rate (14%) existing at the inception of the lease ($100 x 14 = $1,400).

As the prime rate changes during the lease term, the corresponding increase or decrease of $100 for each 1% of the prime rate should be charged or credited to income as appropriate. Minimum lease payments, however, should not be adjusted.

Answer (A) is incorrect because $60,000 excludes the $7,000 ($100 x 14 x 5) measurable at the inception of the lease. Answer (B) is incorrect because $65,000 is based on the average expected prime rate of 10%. Answer (D) is incorrect because $68,000 is based on the 16% prime rate in July.

27. On December 29, 1996, Action Corp. signed a 7-year capital lease for an airplane to transport its sports team around the country. The airplane's fair value was $841,500. Action made the first annual lease payment of $153,000 on December 31, 1996. Action's incremental borrowing rate was 12%, and the interest rate implicit in the lease, which was known by Action, was 9%. The following are the rounded present value factors for an annuity due:

| 9% for 7 years | 5.5 |
| 12% for 7 years | 5.1 |

What amount should Action report as capital lease liability in its December 31, 1996 balance sheet?

A. $841,500

B. $780,300

C. $688,500

D. $627,300

The correct answer is (C). *(CPA 1192 I-33)*

REQUIRED: The amount that should be reported as a capital lease liability in the balance sheet.

DISCUSSION: The capital lease liability is recorded at the present value of minimum lease payments. The lease payments due should be discounted at the lesser of the borrower's incremental borrowing rate or the rate implicit in the lease if known by the borrower. In this situation, the lease should be recorded at the present value of minimum lease payments discounted at the implicit rate of 9% since it is known by the lessee. The amount is $841,500 ($153,000 x 5.5), which must then be reduced by the payment made at the inception of the lease of $153,000. The capital lease liability thus should be $688,500 ($841,500 – $153,000) in the December 31, 1996 balance sheet.

Answer (A) is incorrect because the liability must be reduced by the payment made at the inception of the lease. Answer (B) is incorrect because the present value of minimum lease payments should be discounted at 9% instead of 12%. Also, the liability should be reduced by the payment made at the inception of the lease. Answer (D) is incorrect because the lease liability should be recorded at 9% instead of 12%.

28. On January 1, 1996, Nori Mining Co. (lessee) entered into a 5-year lease for drilling equipment. Nori accounted for the acquisition as a capital lease for $120,000, which includes a $5,000 bargain purchase option. At the end of the lease, Nori expects to exercise the bargain purchase option. Nori estimates that the equipment's fair value will be $10,000 at the end of its 8-year life. Nori regularly uses straight-line depreciation on similar equipment. For the year ended December 31, 1996, what amount should Nori recognize as depreciation expense on the leased asset?

A. $13,750

B. $15,000

C. $23,000

D. $24,000

The correct answer is (A). *(CPA 1193 I-55)*

REQUIRED: The depreciation expense on a leased asset.

DISCUSSION: When a lease is capitalized because title passes to the lessee at the end of the lease term or because the lease contains a bargain purchase option, the depreciation period is the estimated economic life of the asset. The asset should be depreciated in accordance with the lessee's normal depreciation policy for owned assets. Nori regularly uses the straight-line method. Hence, depreciation expense is $13,750 [($120,000 leased asset – $10,000 salvage value) ÷ 8-year economic life].

Answer (B) is incorrect because $15,000 does not consider salvage value. Answer (C) is incorrect because $23,000 subtracts the bargain purchase option from the present value of the minimum lease payments, uses a 5-year life, and does not consider salvage value. Answer (D) is incorrect because $24,000 uses a 5-year life and does not consider salvage value.

29. Neal Corp. entered into a 9-year capital lease on a warehouse on December 31, 1996. Lease payments of $52,000, which include real estate taxes of $2,000, are due annually, beginning on December 31, 1997, and every December 31 thereafter. Neal does not know the interest rate implicit in the lease; Neal's incremental borrowing rate is 9%. The rounded present value of an ordinary annuity for 9 years at 9% is 5.6. What amount should Neal report as capitalized lease liability at December 31, 1996?

A. $280,000

B. $291,200

C. $450,000

D. $468,000

The correct answer is (A). *(CPA 1193 I-39)*

REQUIRED: The amount reported as capitalized lease liability.

DISCUSSION: For a capital lease, the present value of the minimum lease payments should be recorded at the inception date. The minimum lease payments exclude executory costs such as insurance, maintenance, and taxes. The capitalized lease liability is therefore $280,000 [($52,000 – $2,000) x 5.6].

Answer (B) is incorrect because $291,200 is based on a $52,000 annual payment. Answer (C) is incorrect because $450,000 is the total undiscounted amount of the minimum lease payments. Answer (D) is incorrect because $468,000 is the total undiscounted amount of the minimum lease payments plus real estate taxes.

30. Robbins, Inc. leased a machine from Ready Leasing Co. The lease qualifies as a capital lease and requires 10 annual payments of $10,000 beginning immediately. The lease specifies an interest rate of 12% and a purchase option of $10,000 at the end of the tenth year, even though the machine's estimated value on that date is $20,000. Robbins' incremental borrowing rate is 14%.

The present value of an annuity due of 1 at:
12% for 10 years is 6.328
14% for 10 years is 5.946

The present value of 1 at:
12% for 10 years is .322
14% for 10 years is .270

What amount should Robbins record as lease liability at the beginning of the lease term?

A. $62,160

B. $64,860

C. $66,500

D. $69,720

The correct answer is (C). *(CPA 592 I-34)*

REQUIRED: The amount that should be reported as a capital lease liability.

DISCUSSION: The capital lease liability should be recorded at the present value of the minimum lease payments. The lease liability should be calculated using the lesser of the implicit interest rate if known to the lessee or the incremental borrowing rate of the lessee. The minimum lease payments should include the present value of the bargain purchase option of $10,000 at 12% and the present value of an annuity due of $10,000 at 12% for 10 years. Therefore, the lease liability is equal to $66,500 [($10,000 x 6.328) + ($10,000 x .322)].

Answer (A) is incorrect because the present value of the bargain purchase option and the annual lease payments should be discounted at 12% instead of 14%. Answer (B) is incorrect because the value of the bargain purchase option is $10,000, not the estimated value at that date. Also, the discount rate for both the option and the annual payments should be 12% instead of 14%. Answer (D) is incorrect because the value of the bargain purchase option should be included in the present value of minimum lease payments, not the estimated value of the asset at the end of the lease.

31. KW Corporation leased equipment under a 4-year, noncancelable lease properly classified as a capital lease. The lease does not transfer ownership or contain a bargain purchase option. The equipment had an estimated economic life of 5 years and an estimated salvage value of $20,000. Terms of the lease included a guaranteed residual value of $50,000. If KW initially recorded the leased equipment at $240,000, the amount of depreciation that should be charged each year under the straight-line depreciation method is

A. $55,000

B. $47,500

C. $44,000

D. $38,000

The correct answer is (B). *(H.F. Bush)*

REQUIRED: The amount of depreciation to be recorded on a capital lease.

DISCUSSION: The lease does not transfer ownership or contain a bargain purchase option. Accordingly, the period of amortization should be the lease term. In accordance with the straight-line method, the depreciable base for this capital lease is equal to the $240,000 initially recorded value minus the $50,000 guaranteed residual value allocated equally over the 4-year lease term. Consequently, annual depreciation expense is $47,500 [($240,000 − $50,000) ÷ 4 years].

Answer (A) is incorrect because the guaranteed residual value, not the estimated salvage value, must be subtracted from the initially recorded value. Answer (C) is incorrect because the guaranteed residual value, not the estimated salvage value, must be subtracted from the initially recorded value, and the term of the lease, not the estimated economic life, is used as the denominator in the depreciation calculation. Answer (D) is incorrect because the term of the lease, not the estimated economic life, must be used as the denominator in the depreciation calculation.

32. Oak Co. leased equipment for its entire 9-year useful life, agreeing to pay $50,000 at the start of the lease term on December 31, 1995, and $50,000 annually on each December 31 for the next 8 years. The present value on December 31, 1995 of the nine lease payments over the lease term, using the rate implicit in the lease was $316,500. Oak knows that this rate is 10%. The December 31, 1995 present value of the lease payments using Oak's incremental borrowing rate of 12% was $298,500. Oak made a timely second lease payment. What amount should Oak report as capital lease liability in its December 31, 1996 balance sheet?

A. $350,000

B. $243,150

C. $228,320

D. $0

The correct answer is (B). *(CPA 1193 I-35)*

REQUIRED: The amount to be reported as a capital lease liability.

DISCUSSION: The lease is a capital lease because the lease term is at least 75% of the estimated economic life of the property. SFAS 13 requires that the lessee use the lower of the lessor's implicit interest rate (if known) or the lessee's incremental borrowing rate of interest. Oak knows the implicit rate; therefore, the present value of the minimum lease payments of this capital lease is $316,500, the amount based on the lessor's implicit rate. After the initial payment of $50,000, which contains no interest component, is deducted, the carrying value during 1996 is $266,500. Accordingly, the interest component of the next payment is $26,650 (10% implicit rate x $266,500), and the capital lease liability on 12/31/96 is $243,150 [$266,500 − ($50,000 − $26,650)].

Answer (A) is incorrect because $350,000 is the sum of the nine lease payments. Answer (C) is incorrect because $228,320 is based on a 12% rate. Answer (D) is incorrect because $0 is based on the assumption that the lease is an operating lease.

33. On January 1, 1996, Harrow Co. as lessee signed a 5-year noncancellable equipment lease with annual payments of $100,000 beginning December 31, 1996. Harrow treated this transaction as a capital lease. The five lease payments have a present value of $379,000 at January 1, 1996, based on interest of 10%. What amount should Harrow report as interest expense for the year ended December 31, 1996?

A. $37,900

B. $27,900

C. $24,200

D. $0

The correct answer is (A). *(CPA 1192 I-57)*

REQUIRED: The interest expense to be recognized in the first year of a capital lease.

DISCUSSION: The lease liability at the inception of the lease is $379,000. Under the effective-interest method, the lease liability balance (the carrying value) at the beginning of each year should be multiplied by the implicit interest rate to determine the interest expense for that year. Accordingly, the interest expense for the first year is $37,900 ($10% x $379,000).

Answer (B) is incorrect because $27,900 assumes the initial payment was made immediately. Answer (C) is incorrect because $24,200 is one-fifth of the total interest ($500,000 − $379,000). Answer (D) is incorrect because interest must be accrued.

34. On December 30, 1996, Rafferty Corp. leased equipment under a capital lease. Annual lease payments of $20,000 are due December 31 for 10 years. The equipment's useful life is 10 years, and the interest rate implicit in the lease is 10%. The capital lease obligation was recorded on December 30, 1996 at $135,000, and the first lease payment was made on that date. What amount should Rafferty include in current liabilities for this capital lease in its December 31, 1996 balance sheet?

- A. $6,500
- B. $8,500
- C. $11,500
- D. $20,000

The correct answer is (B). *(CPA 1192 I-4)*

REQUIRED: The current liability for the capital lease.

DISCUSSION: At the inception of a capital lease, a lessee should record a fixed asset and a lease obligation equal to the present value of the minimum lease payments. In a classified balance sheet, the lease liability must be allocated between the current and noncurrent portions. The current portion at a balance sheet date is the reduction of the lease liability in the forthcoming year. A periodic lease payment has two components: interest expense and the reduction of the lease obligation. Under the effective interest method, the appropriate interest rate is applied to the carrying value of the lease obligation at the beginning of the interest period to calculate interest expense. The portion of the minimum lease payment greater than the amount of interest expense is the reduction of the liability in the forthcoming year. At the beginning of 1997, the lease obligation is $115,000 ($135,000 – $20,000 initial payment). Thus, 1996 interest expense will be $11,500 (10% x $115,000), and the reduction of the liability when the next payment is made will be $8,500 ($20,000 – $11,500 interest).

Answer (A) is incorrect because $6,500 results from assuming that the carrying value of the lease in 1996 will be $135,000. Answer (C) is incorrect because $11,500 is the interest expense. Answer (D) is incorrect because $20,000 is the full payment due.

17.2 Direct Financing and Sales-Type Leases

35. What is the difference between a direct financing lease and a sales-type lease?

- A. Lessees usually depreciate direct financing leases over the term of the lease and sales-type leases over the useful life of the leased asset.

- B. The difference between the sum of all lease payments and the cost of the leased asset to the lessor is interest income for direct financing leases, and is part interest and part sales income for sales-type leases.

- C. The lease payments receivable on the books of a lessor are recorded at their present value for sales-type leases and at their gross value for direct financing leases.

- D. The lessor records the present value of the residual value of the leased asset for direct financing leases, but records the undiscounted (gross) residual value for sales-type leases.

The correct answer is (B). *(Publisher)*

REQUIRED: The difference between direct financing leases and sales-type leases.

DISCUSSION: Both direct financing and sales-type leases are accounted for by the lessee as capital leases. The difference between the two arises only for lessor accounting. In a direct financing lease, the difference between the gross investment and its cost or carrying amount is recorded as unearned interest revenue. No gross profit is recognized. In a sales-type lease, the same amount of unearned interest revenue will be recorded. However, a gross profit equal to the difference between the cost (plus initial direct costs – the present value of the unguaranteed residual value) and the sales price (present value of the minimum lease payments) is also recognized. The difference between a direct financing and a sales-type lease is that the cost used in accounting for a direct-financing lease is ordinarily the fair value. But the cost for a sales-type lease differs from the fair value.

Answer (A) is incorrect because lessees use the same depreciation methods for both kinds of leases. Answer (C) is incorrect because the receivable for the lease payments is recorded at gross on the books of the lessor for both the sales-type and direct financing leases. Answer (D) is incorrect because the undiscounted (gross) residual value is recorded by the lessor for both direct financing and sales-type leases. It is included as part of the gross investment, i.e., in lease payments receivable.

36. In a lease that is recorded as a sales-type lease by the lessor, interest revenue

A. Should be recognized in full as revenue at the lease's inception.

B. Should be recognized over the period of the lease using the straight-line method.

C. Should be recognized over the period of the lease using the effective-interest method.

D. Does not arise.

The correct answer is (C). *(CPA 1190 T-26)*
REQUIRED: The proper accounting for interest revenue in a sales-type lease.
DISCUSSION: SFAS 13 requires that the difference between the gross investment in the lease and the sum of the present values of the components of the gross investment be recorded as unearned income. This unearned income is amortized to income over the lease term using the effective-interest method, which produces a constant periodic rate of return on the net investment.
Answers (A), (B), and (D) are incorrect because the interest revenue should be recognized over the period of the lease using the effective-interest method.

37. For a direct financing lease, the gross investment (lease payments receivable) recorded by the lessor is equal to the

A. Present value of the minimum lease payments minus the unguaranteed residual value accruing to the lessor at the end of the lease term.

B. Lower of 90% of the present value of the minimum lease payments or the fair value of the leased asset.

C. Difference between the fair value of the leased asset and the unearned interest revenue.

D. Minimum lease payments plus the unguaranteed residual value accruing to the lessor at the end of the lease term.

The correct answer is (D). *(CMA 690 3-1)*
REQUIRED: The amount to be recorded as the gross investment in a direct financing lease.
DISCUSSION: The lessor should record as the gross investment in a direct financing lease the amount of the minimum lease payments (the periodic payments net of executory costs + any guaranteed residual value) plus any unguaranteed residual value. The net investment in the lease is equal to the gross investment, plus any unamortized initial direct costs, minus the unearned interest revenue.
Answers (A), (B), and (C) are incorrect because the gross investment in a direct financing lease equals the minimum lease payments plus any unguaranteed residual value.

38. Initial direct costs incurred by the lessor under a sales-type lease should be

A. Deferred and allocated over the economic life of the leased property.

B. Expensed in the period incurred.

C. Deferred and allocated over the term of the lease in proportion to the recognition of rental income.

D. Added to the gross investment in the lease and amortized over the term of the lease as a yield adjustment.

The correct answer is (B). *(CMA 690 3-2)*
REQUIRED: The accounting for initial direct costs in a sales-type lease.
DISCUSSION: SFAS 91, *Accounting for Nonrefundable Fees and Costs Associated with Originating or Acquiring Loans and Initial Direct Costs of Leases*, defines initial direct costs as having two components: (1) the lessor's external costs to originate a lease incurred in dealings with independent third parties and (2) the internal costs directly related to specified activities performed by the lessor for that lease. According to SFAS 13, in a sales-type lease, the cost, or carrying amount if different, plus any initial direct costs, minus the present value of any unguaranteed residual value, is charged against income in the same period that the present value of the minimum lease payments is credited to sales. The result is the recognition of a net profit or loss on the sales-type lease.
Answer (A) is incorrect because initial direct costs are considered an expense in the period of sale. Answers (C) and (D) are incorrect because they describe the proper treatment of initial direct costs in an operating lease and a direct financing lease, respectively.

39. Danco has agreed to lease equipment under a direct financing lease. As lessor, Danco has incurred a material amount of initial direct costs. What is the proper accounting for these initial direct costs by Danco?

A. Initial direct costs must be offset against unearned interest revenue so as to produce a constant periodic rate of return on the lease.

B. Initial direct costs must be capitalized as part of the net investment in the lease.

C. Initial direct costs must be capitalized as a deferred charge and written off at the end of the lease term.

D. Initial direct costs must be written off immediately.

The correct answer is (B). *(T.J. Phillips, Jr.)*
REQUIRED: The proper accounting for initial direct costs in a direct financing lease.
DISCUSSION: According to SFAS 98, *Accounting for Leases*, which amends certain relevant sections of SFAS 13 that were previously amended by SFAS 23 and SFAS 91, the initial direct costs of a direct financing lease "shall be amortized to income over the lease term so as to produce a constant periodic rate of return on the net investment in the lease." The net investment is the gross investment (minimum lease payments + any unguaranteed residual value), plus any unamortized initial direct costs, minus the unearned income. The unearned income equals the gross investment minus the cost or carrying amount, if different, of the leased property.
Answer (A) is incorrect because this treatment, which was prescribed by SFAS 17, *Accounting for Leases -- Initial Direct Costs*, was rescinded by SFAS 91. Answers (C) and (D) are incorrect because the initial direct costs should be capitalized as part of the net investment in the lease.

40. Glade Co. leases computer equipment to customers under direct financing leases. The equipment has no residual value at the end of the lease and the leases do not contain bargain purchase options. Glade wishes to earn 8% interest on a five-year lease of equipment with a fair value of $323,400. The present value of an annuity due of $1 at 8% for 5 years is 4.312. What is the total amount of interest revenue that Glade will earn over the life of the lease?

A. $51,600

B. $75,000

C. $129,360

D. $139,450

The correct answer is (A). *(CPA 1195 F-29)*
REQUIRED: The interest revenue earned over the life of a lease.
DISCUSSION: To earn 8% interest over the lease term, the annual payment must be $75,000 ($323,400 fair value at the inception of the lease ÷ 4.312 annuity factor). Given no residual value and no bargain purchase option, total lease payments will be $375,000 ($75,000 payment x 5 years). Because no profit is recognized on a direct financing lease, the fair value is presumably the carrying amount. The difference between the gross lease payments received and their present value is the total interest revenue of $51,600 ($375,000 – $323,400).
Answer (B) is incorrect because $75,000 is the annual lease payment. Answers (C) and (D) are incorrect because interest revenue equals the total lease payments of $375,000 minus the fair value of $323,400.

41. On August 1, Jones Corporation leased property to Smith Company for a 5-year period. The annual $20,000 lease payment is payable at the end of each year. The expected residual value at the end of the lease term is $10,000. Jones Company's implicit interest rate is 12%. The cost of the property to Jones was $50,000, which is the fair value at the lease date. The present value of an ordinary annuity of 1 for five periods is 3.605. The present value of 1 at the end of five periods is .567. At the inception of the lease, the recorded gross investment is

A. $110,000

B. $100,000

C. $72,100

D. $90,000

The correct answer is (A). *(J.O. Hall)*
REQUIRED: The amount to be recorded as gross investment at the inception of the lease.
DISCUSSION: For a direct financing or a sales-type lease, the lessor should record the gross investment in the lease at the undiscounted sum of the minimum lease payments (the total of the periodic payments and any guaranteed residual value, net of executory costs) and any unguaranteed residual value. Accordingly, the gross investment is the same regardless of whether any residual value is guaranteed. The five periodic payments of $20,000 equal $100,000. The expected residual value, including both guaranteed and unguaranteed portions, equals $10,000. Thus, the gross investment in this lease should be $110,000 ($100,000 + $10,000).
Answer (B) is incorrect because it fails to include the residual value in the gross investment. Answer (C) is incorrect because the annual lease payments should be recorded at their undiscounted value. Answer (D) is incorrect because the residual value is added to, not subtracted from, the undiscounted lease payments.

42. Assuming that the lease was a direct financing lease, what should be the interest entry in Anson's books on December 31 of the first year of the lease?

A. Cash $3,836
    Interest revenue $3,836

B. Unearned interest revenue $6,816
    Interest revenue $6,816

C. Cash $8,000
    Interest revenue $8,000

D. Cash $11,836
    Interest revenue $8,000
    Equipment   3,836

The correct answer is (B). *(CPA 577 II-2)*
REQUIRED: The interest income from a direct financing lease during the first year of the lease.
DISCUSSION: The annual $11,836 lease payment to Anson is payable at the beginning of each period. The first payment received from Scovil reduces Anson's lease investment by the full amount of the payment, leaving a carrying value of $68,164 ($80,000 – $11,836) at the beginning of the first year. Because the appropriate rate of return to Anson on this lease investment is 10%, interest earned in the first year is $6,816 (10% x $68,164). The difference between the gross investment and the lessor's cost or carrying amount, if different, of the leased property is reflected in the lessor's books as unearned interest income. Hence, the journal entry debit recognizing first-year interest income is to unearned interest revenue.
Answer (A) is incorrect because $3,836 is equal to the $11,836 rental payment minus $8,000 ($80,000 cost x 10%) and cash is received January 1. Answer (C) is incorrect because $8,000 is equal to the $80,000 cost unadjusted by the $11,836 initial payment x 10% and cash is received January 1. Answer (D) is incorrect because $8,000 is equal to the $80,000 cost unadjusted by the $11,836 initial payment x 10% and cash is received January 1, and equipment is not affected by the interest payment.

43. What is the initial journal entry by Anson Company to record the lease on January 1?

A. Leased asset $ 80,000
    Lease payment
      obligation $68,164
    Cash   11,836

B. Lease payments
    receivable $ 80,000
    Leased asset $80,000

C. Lease payments
    receivable $ 68,164
    Cash   11,836
    Leased asset $80,000

D. Cash $ 11,836
    Lease payments
    receivable   106,524
    Leased asset $80,000
    Unearned lease
      interest revenue   38,360

The correct answer is (D). *(Publisher)*
REQUIRED: The lessor's journal entry to record a direct financing lease.
DISCUSSION: For a direct financing lease, the lessor should record the total amount of the minimum lease payments, net of executory costs (10 x $11,836 = $118,360), plus any unguaranteed residual value ($0) as the gross investment in the lease (lease payments receivable). In this case, cash must also be debited and lease payments receivable credited for the first payment ($11,836) because the payments are made at the beginning of each year. The leased asset should be credited at its cost ($80,000), with the difference between the initial gross investment and cost ($118,360 – $80,000 = $38,360) recorded as unearned interest revenue.
Answer (A) is incorrect because it reflects the recording of the lease as a capital lease on the books of the lessee. Answers (B) and (C) are incorrect because the lease payments receivable are recorded at their gross value rather than at their present value.

44. The excess of the fair value of leased property at the inception of the lease over its cost or carrying amount should be classified by the lessor as

A. Unearned income from a sales-type lease.

B. Unearned income from a direct financing lease.

C. Manufacturer's or dealer's profit from a sales-type lease.

D. Manufacturer's or dealer's profit from a direct financing lease.

The correct answer is (C). *(CPA 1182 T-17)*

REQUIRED: The classification by the lessor of the excess of the fair value of leased property over its cost or carrying amount.

DISCUSSION: According to SFAS 13, in a sales-type lease, the cost, or carrying amount if different, plus any initial direct costs, minus the present value of any unguaranteed residual value, is charged against income in the same period that the present value of the minimum lease payments is credited to sales. The result is the recognition of a net profit or loss on the sales-type lease. Thus, by definition, a sales-type lease is one that gives rise to a manufacturer's or dealer's profit (or loss) because the fair value of the leased property at the inception of the lease (the present value of the minimum lease payments) differs from its cost or carrying value.

Answer (A) is incorrect because unearned income from a sales-type lease is equal to the difference between the gross investment and the present value of its components (minimum lease payments, which include any guaranteed residual value and are netted against executory costs, and the unguaranteed residual value). The net investment for a sales-type lease equals gross investment minus unearned income. Answers (B) and (D) are incorrect because the fair value and the cost or carrying value are the same in a direct financing lease.

45. Howe Co. leased equipment to Kew Corp. on January 2, 1996 for an 8-year period expiring December 31, 2003. Equal payments under the lease are $600,000 and are due on January 2 of each year. The first payment was made on January 2, 1996. The list selling price of the equipment is $3,520,000, and its carrying cost on Howe's books is $2,800,000. The lease is appropriately accounted for as a sales-type lease. The present value of the lease payments at an imputed interest rate of 12% (Howe's incremental borrowing rate) is $3,300,000. What amount of profit on the sale should Howe report for the year ended December 31, 1996?

A. $720,000

B. $500,000

C. $90,000

D. $0

The correct answer is (B). *(CPA 1193 I-44)*

REQUIRED: The amount of profit on a sales-type lease.

DISCUSSION: Howe Co., the lessor, should report a profit from a sales-type lease. The gross profit equals the difference between the sales price (present value of the minimum lease payments) and the cost. Consequently, the profit on the sale equals $500,000 ($3,300,000 – $2,800,000).

Answer (A) is incorrect because $720,000 is the result of using the list selling price instead of the present value of the lease payments. Answer (C) is incorrect because $90,000 is one-eighth of the difference between the list price and the cost. Answer (D) is incorrect because a profit of $500,000 should be reported.

46. ABC Manufacturing and Leasing Company leased a machine to XYZ Company on January 1. The lease meets the criteria for a sales-type lease. Title to the asset will automatically pass to the lessee at the end of the lease term. Other details are as follows:

Lease term	10 years
Useful life of the asset	10 years
Cost of the leased asset to the lessor	$55,000
Annual payment payable at the beginning of each year, beginning January 1	$10,000
Implicit interest rate	10%
Present value of an annuity due of $1 discounted for 10 years at 10%	$6.7590
Present value of $1 due in 10 years discounted at 10%	$.3855

The journal entry to record the inception of this lease on the lessor's books at January 1 would be

A. Leased machine $67,590
   Lease obligation $57,590
   Cash 10,000

B. Lease payments
   receivable $90,000
   Cash 10,000
   Cost of sales 55,000
   Inventory $55,000
   Unearned interest
   income--leases 45,000
   Sales 55,000

C. Lease payments
   receivable $90,000
   Cash 10,000
   Interest income $32,410
   Gross profit on
   sales-type lease 12,590
   Inventory 55,000

D. Lease payments
   receivable $90,000
   Cash 10,000
   Cost of sales 55,000
   Sales $67,590
   Inventory 55,000
   Unearned interest
   income--leases 32,410

The correct answer is (D). *(CIA 585 IV-22)*

REQUIRED: The lessor's journal entry at the inception of a sales-type lease.

DISCUSSION: For this sales-type lease, the lessor should record

1. As gross investment, the minimum lease payments

2. As unearned interest income, the difference between the gross investment in the lease and the present value of the minimum lease payments

3. As sales revenue, the present value of the minimum lease payments computed at the interest rate implicit in the lease

4. As cost of goods sold, the cost of the leased asset

Because the first payment is made at the inception of the lease, the payment structure is that of an annuity due. Sales revenue is therefore equal to the $10,000 periodic payment times the present value of an annuity due of $1 discounted for 10 years at 10% ($10,000 x 6.7590 = $67,590).

Given that cash is paid at the beginning of the year, the initial $10,000 cash debit immediately decreases the gross investment in the lease (lease payments receivable) from $100,000 to $90,000. The cost of the leased asset ($55,000) must also be charged to cost of sales and credited to inventory. Finally, at the inception of the lease, unearned interest income equals the difference between the gross investment and the sales price ($100,000 − $67,590 = $32,410).

Answer (A) is incorrect because it is the lessee's journal entry. Answer (B) is incorrect because the sale should be recorded at the present value of the minimum lease payments, and the unearned interest income should be recorded as the difference between the gross lease payments receivable and the present value of this gross investment. Answer (C) is incorrect because the lease should reflect both cost of goods sold and sales, not the netted gross profit on the sales-type lease.

47. Winn Co. manufactures equipment that is sold or leased. On December 31, 1996, Winn leased equipment to Bart for a 5-year period ending December 31, 2001, at which date ownership of the leased asset will be transferred to Bart. Equal periodic payments under the lease are $22,000 (including $2,000 of executory costs) and are due on December 31 of each year. The first payment was made on December 31, 1996. Collectibility of the remaining lease payments is reasonably assured, and Winn has no material cost uncertainties. The normal sales price of the equipment is $77,000, and cost is $60,000. For the year ended December 31, 1996, what amount of income should Winn realize from the lease transaction?

A. $17,000

B. $22,000

C. $23,000

D. $33,000

The correct answer is (A). *(CPA 1190 I-33)*
REQUIRED: The income to be recognized by the lessor from a lease transaction.
DISCUSSION: For a lessor to treat a lease as a capital lease, it must first meet one of four criteria. That ownership of the leased equipment transfers to the lessee at the end of the lease term is one of the four criteria. In addition, the lessor cannot treat the lease as a capital lease unless collectibility of the remaining lease payments is reasonably assured and there are no material cost uncertainties. These conditions are also met. Because the $77,000 fair value is greater than the $60,000 recorded cost of the equipment on the lessor's books, the lease should be accounted for as a sales-type lease. In a sales-type lease, two components of income may be recognized. These are the profit on the sale and interest income. The profit on the sale recorded at the inception of the lease is $17,000 ($77,000 normal sales price – $60,000 cost). At the inception of the lease, no interest income should be recorded. Thus, Winn should realize $17,000 of income from this lease transaction in 1996.
Answers (B), (C), and (D) are incorrect because under a sales-type lease only profit from the sale is recognized at the inception of the lease. Therefore, the amount of income recognized is $17,000 ($77,000 normal sales price – $60,000 cost).

48. On January 1, 1996, Jaffe Co. leased a machine to Pender Co. for 10 years, with $10,000 payments due at the beginning of each year effective at the inception of the lease. The machine cost Jaffe $55,000. The lease is appropriately accounted for as a sales-type lease by Jaffe. The present value of the 10 rent payments over the lease term discounted appropriately at 10% was $67,600. The estimated salvage value of the machine at the end of 10 years is equal to the disposal costs. How much interest revenue should Jaffe record from the lease for the year ended December 31, 1996?

A. $5,500

B. $5,760

C. $6,760

D. $7,020

The correct answer is (B). *(CPA 1189 I-38)*
REQUIRED: The interest income recognized by the lessor in the first year of a sales-type lease.
DISCUSSION: In accordance with the effective-interest method, the interest income is equal to the carrying value of the net investment in the lease at the beginning of the interest period multiplied by the interest rate used to calculate the present value of the lease payments. The present value of $67,600 is reduced by the $10,000 payment made at the inception of the lease, leaving a carrying value of $57,600. This balance multiplied by 10% yields $5,760 to be reflected as interest income for the first year of the lease.
Answer (A) is incorrect because interest income is calculated using the present value of the lease payments. The machine cost is irrelevant for this calculation.
Answer (C) is incorrect because the carrying value of the lease must first be reduced by the $10,000 payment at the inception of the lease. Answer (D) is incorrect because interest income is based on the carrying value of the lease multiplied by the discount rate. Therefore, the amount of interest income is $5,760 [($67,600 – $10,000) x 10%].

49. Benedict Company leased equipment to Mark, Inc. on January 1, 1995. The lease is for an 8-year period expiring December 31, 2002. The first of eight equal annual payments of $600,000 was made on January 1, 1995. Benedict had purchased the equipment on December 29, 1994 for $3,200,000. The lease is appropriately accounted for as a sales-type lease by Benedict. Assume that the present value at January 1, 1995 of all rent payments over the lease term discounted at a 10% interest rate was $3,520,000. What amount of interest income should Benedict record in 1996 (the second year of the lease period) as a result of the lease?

    A. $261,200

    B. $292,000

    C. $320,000

    D. $327,200

The correct answer is (A). *(CPA 1180 I-14)*
    REQUIRED: The interest income during the second year of a sales-type lease.
    DISCUSSION: The net investment to be recorded by the lessor at 1/1/95 is given as $3,520,000, the present value of the minimum lease payments discounted at 10%. The net investment is immediately reduced by the $600,000 lease payment on 1/1/95, resulting in a carrying value for 1995 of $2,920,000. Interest earned for the year 1995 at a rate of 10% ($2,920,000 x 10%) is $292,000. Thus, the $600,000 1/1/96 lease payment consists of the $292,000 interest component and a $308,000 reduction of the net investment. Since the 1996 net investment balance is $2,612,000 ($2,920,000 – $308,000), interest income for 1996 is $261,200 ($2,612,000 x 10%).
    Answer (B) is incorrect because the carrying value of the lease must be reduced by the payment on 1/1/96 for the amount applied to reducing the lease obligation. Answer (C) is incorrect because $320,000 is based on original cost of the leased asset. Answer (D) is incorrect because interest income is calculated by the carrying value of the lease multiplied by the discount rate. Therefore, the amount of interest income is $2,612,000 [($2,920,000 – $308,000) x 10%].

50. On the first day of its fiscal year, Lessor, Inc. leased certain property at an annual rental of $100,000 receivable at the beginning of each year for 10 years. The first payment was received immediately. The leased property is new, had cost $650,000, and has an estimated useful life of 13 years with no salvage value. Lessor's borrowing rate is 8%. The present value of an annuity of $1 payable at the beginning of the period at 8% for 10 years is 7.247. Lessor had no other costs associated with this lease. Lessor should have accounted for this lease as a sale but mistakenly treated the lease as an operating lease. What was the effect on net earnings during the first year of treating this lease as an operating lease rather than as a sale?

    A. No effect.

    B. Understated.

    C. Overstated.

    D. The effect depends on the method selected for income tax purposes.

The correct answer is (B). *(CPA 576 T-18)*
    REQUIRED: The effect of accounting for a lease as an operating rather than as a sales-type lease.
    DISCUSSION: Accounting for the lease as an operating lease during the first year generated $50,000 of income, the $100,000 lease payment minus $50,000 of depreciation ($650,000 ÷ 13).
    In a sales-type lease, the lessor recognizes two income components: profit on the sale and interest income. Total income from accounting for the lease as a sale would have been $124,676 ($74,700 + $49,976). The effect of the error on net earnings was therefore an understatement.

Net investment ($100,000 x 7.247)	$724,700
Book value	(650,000)
Profit on sale	$ 74,700
Net investment	$724,700
First lease payment	(100,000)
Lease balance	$624,700
Interest rate	x 8%
Interest income	$ 49,976

    Answers (A), (C), and (D) are incorrect because classifying the lease as an operating lease instead of a sales-type lease understates income by $74,676 ($124,676 – $50,000).

51. Which of the following disclosures is not required for lessors in direct financing and sales-type leases?

A. Future minimum lease payments for the next 5 years.

B. Initial direct costs for direct financing leases only.

C. Total contingent rentals for each period presented.

D. The gross amount of assets recorded under capital leases for each balance sheet presented.

The correct answer is (D). *(Publisher)*
   REQUIRED: The lessor disclosure not required for direct financing and sales-type leases.
   DISCUSSION: Disclosure of answer (D) is required of lessees. The required disclosures by lessors for sales-type and direct financing leases include

1. The components of the net investment in sales-type and direct financing leases as of the date of each balance sheet presented. This includes the future minimum lease payments to be received, the unguaranteed residual value, the amount of unearned income, and, for direct financing leases only, initial direct costs.

2. Future minimum lease payments to be received for each of the 5 succeeding fiscal years.

3. Total contingent rentals included in income for each period presented.

   Answers (A), (B), and (C) are incorrect because they are required disclosures by lessors for sales-type and direct financing leases.

17.3 Operating Leases

52. During January 1996, Vail Co. made long-term improvements to a recently leased building. The lease agreement provides for neither a transfer of title to Vail nor a bargain purchase option. The present value of the minimum lease payments equals 85% of the building's fair value, and the lease term equals 70% of the building's economic life. Should assets be recognized for the building and the leasehold improvements?

	Building	Leasehold Improvements
A.	Yes	Yes
B.	No	Yes
C.	Yes	No
D.	No	No

The correct answer is (B). *(CPA 1191 T-33)*
   REQUIRED: The item(s) for which an asset should be recognized.
   DISCUSSION: A lease must be classified as a capital lease by a lessee if, at its inception, any one of four criteria is satisfied. The four criteria are (1) the lease provides for the transfer of ownership of the leased property, (2) the lease contains a bargain purchase option, (3) the lease term is 75% or more of the estimated economic life of the leased property, or (4) the present value of the minimum lease payments (excluding executory costs) is at least 90% of the excess of the fair value of the leased property to the lessor at the inception of the lease. Since none of the criteria are satisfied, the lessee should not recognize a leased asset for the building. However, general improvements to leased property should be capitalized as leasehold improvements and amortized in accordance with the straight-line method over the shorter of their expected useful life or the lease term.
   Answers (A), (C), and (D) are incorrect because an asset should be recognized for the leasehold improvements but not the building.

53. On July 1, 1995, South Co. entered into a 10-year operating lease for a warehouse facility. The annual minimum lease payments are $100,000. In addition to the base rent, South pays a monthly allocation of the building's operating expenses, which amounted to $20,000 for the year ended June 30, 1996. In the notes to South's June 30, 1996 financial statements, what amounts of subsequent years' lease payments should be disclosed?

A. $100,000 per annum for each of the next 5 years and $500,000 in the aggregate.

B. $120,000 per annum for each of the next 5 years and $600,000 in the aggregate.

C. $100,000 per annum for each of the next 5 years and $900,000 in the aggregate.

D. $120,000 per annum for each of the next 5 years and $1,080,000 in the aggregate.

The correct answer is (C). *(CPA 1193 I-42)*
   REQUIRED: The amounts of subsequent years' lease payments to be disclosed.
   DISCUSSION: SFAS 13 requires that the future minimum lease payments as of the date of the latest balance sheet presented be disclosed in the aggregate and for each of the 5 succeeding fiscal years. This disclosure is required whether the lease is classified as a capital lease or as an operating lease. Thus, South should disclose that annual minimum lease payments are $100,000 for each of the next 5 years and that the aggregate is $900,000. The operating expenses are executory costs that are not included in the minimum lease payments.
   Answer (A) is incorrect because the aggregate is $900,000. Answer (B) is incorrect because the operating expenses should not be included and the aggregate amount is $900,000. Answer (D) is incorrect because the operating expenses should not be included.

54. On June 1, 1996, Oren Co. entered into a 5-year nonrenewable lease, commencing on that date, for office space and made the following payments to Cant Properties:

Bonus to obtain lease	$30,000
First month's rent	10,000
Last month's rent	10,000

In its income statement for the year ended June 30, 1996, what amount should Oren report as rent expense?

  A. $10,000

  B. $10,500

  C. $40,000

  D. $50,000

55. On January 1, 1996, Wren Company leased a building to Brill under an operating lease for 10 years at $50,000 per year, payable the first day of each lease year. Wren paid $15,000 to a real estate broker as a finder's fee. The annual depreciation on the building is $12,000. For 1996, Wren incurred insurance and property tax expenses totaling $9,000. Wren's net rental income for 1996 should be

  A. $27,500

  B. $29,000

  C. $35,000

  D. $36,500

The correct answer is (B). *(CPA 1193 I-59)*
REQUIRED: The amount to be reported as rent expense for an operating lease.
DISCUSSION: Rent expense is recognized as services are used. Payments which benefit the entire lease term should be amortized over the lease period. Therefore, the amount of rent expense as a result of this lease will include the rent payment for June and the amount of the bonus amortized for that period. Rent expense for June 1996 thus is $10,500 [$10,000 for the month's rent and $500 ($30,000 ÷ 5 x 1/12 amortization of the bonus)].
    Answer (A) is incorrect because the expense should include amortization of the bonus. Answer (C) is incorrect because the bonus should be amortized over the lease term benefited. Answer (D) is incorrect because the last month's rent payment should be deferred and expensed in the period it benefits. Also, the bonus should be amortized over the lease term.

The correct answer is (A). *(CPA 1190 I-37)*
REQUIRED: Net rental income that should be recorded for the first year.
DISCUSSION: Net rental income is equal to the $50,000 annual payment minus any expenses incurred during the year. These expenses include $12,000 of depreciation, $9,000 for insurance and property taxes, and $1,500 ($15,000 ÷ 10 years) amortization of the finder's fee. In an operating lease, a finder's fee is an initial direct cost that should be deferred and allocated over the lease term in proportion to the recognition of rental income. Accordingly, the net rental income for 1996 is $27,500.

Rental income	$50,000
Depreciation	(12,000)
Insurance and property tax expenses	(9,000)
Amortization	(1,500)
Net rental income	$27,500

    Answer (B) is incorrect because $29,000 excludes amortization of the finder's fee. Answer (C) is incorrect because $35,000 includes the entire finder's fee and excludes depreciation and the insurance and property tax expenses. Answer (D) is incorrect because $36,500 excludes the insurance and property tax expenses.

56. Kew Apparel, Inc. leases and operates a retail store. The following information relates to the lease for the year ended December 31, 1996:

- The store lease, an operating lease, calls for a base monthly rent of $1,500 due the first day of each month.
- Additional rent is computed at 6% of net sales over $300,000 up to $600,000 and 5% of net sales over $600,000, per calendar year.
- Net sales for 1996 were $900,000.
- Kew paid executory costs to the lessor for property taxes of $12,000 and insurance of $5,000.

For 1996, Kew's expenses relating to the store lease are

- A. $71,000
- B. $68,000
- C. $54,000
- D. $35,000

The correct answer is (B). *(CPA 1190 I-46)*
  REQUIRED: The lessee's expenses relating to a store lease.
  DISCUSSION: This lease is properly classified as an operating lease. The expenses for 1996 relating to this lease should include the fixed monthly rental payment, the contingent rental payments, and the executory costs. The 1996 expenses, as indicated below, amount to $68,000.

Monthly rent	$18,000	($1,500 x 12 months)
Additional rent	18,000	($600,000 – $300,000) × 6%
	15,000	($900,000 – $600,000) × 5%
Executory costs	12,000	(property taxes)
	5,000	(insurance)
Total expenses	$68,000	

Answer (A) is incorrect because $71,000 includes the contingent rent at 6%. Answer (C) is incorrect because $54,000 includes the contingent rent at 6% and excludes the executory costs. Answer (D) is incorrect because $35,000 excludes the contingent rent.

57. Lessor leased a new electronic widget tester to Lessee for a period of 10 years. At the termination of the noncancelable lease, Lessee has the right to purchase the machine for 20% of its fair value at that time. Lessee is a financially stable company, and there appears to be no question about the collectibility of future lease payments. The machine contains many technologically advanced components, and Lessor has guaranteed to repair any breakdown, no matter how minor, for the life of the lease plus an additional 10-year period. This unusual guarantee was offered by the Lessor to gain experience with the new machine in an actual use situation. The cost of meeting the terms of this guarantee cannot be reasonably estimated. According to current authoritative literature, Lessor should account for this lease as

- A.   A direct financing lease.
- B.   A leveraged lease.
- C.   An operating lease.
- D.   A sales-type lease.

The correct answer is (C). *(Publisher)*
  REQUIRED: The proper classification of the lease by the lessor.
  DISCUSSION: Lessors classify leases as operating, sales-type, or direct financing. If a lease meets any one of four criteria specified in SFAS 13, collectibility of payments from the lessee is reasonably predictable, and no important uncertainties surround the amount of unreimbursable costs yet to be incurred by the lessor under the lease, the lease is classified by the lessor as either a direct financing lease or a sales-type lease.

Because Lessee may purchase the machine for 20% of its fair value at the end of the lease, a bargain purchase option exists, which meets one of the four criteria specified in SFAS 13. However, the lessor has guaranteed all repairs for the next 20 years, so important uncertainties remain. Lessor must therefore classify the lease as an operating lease.

Answers (A), (B), and (D) are incorrect because the important uncertainties preclude treating the lease as either a direct financing lease or a sales-type lease. A leveraged lease is essentially a direct financing lease with special characteristics involving a third-party creditor.

58. On January 1, 1996, Glen Co. leased a building to Dix Corp. for a 10-year term at an annual rental of $50,000. At the inception of the lease, Glen received $200,000 covering the first 2 years' rent and a security deposit of $100,000. This deposit will not be returned to Dix upon expiration of the lease but will be applied to payment of rent for the last 2 years of the lease. What portions of the $200,000 should be shown as a current and a long-term liability, respectively, in Glen's December 31, 1996 balance sheet?

	Current Liability	Long-Term Liability
A.	$0	$200,000
B.	$50,000	$100,000
C.	$100,000	$100,000
D.	$100,000	$50,000

The correct answer is (B). *(CPA 1190 I-14)*
REQUIRED: The allocation of an advance payment between current and long-term.
DISCUSSION: Of the $200,000 received at the inception of the lease, $50,000 should be recognized as rental income for the year ended 12/31/96. At 12/31/96, the $50,000 attributable to rent for 1997 should be classified as a current liability, and the $100,000 applicable to the last 2 years of the lease should be classified as a long-term liability.
Answers (A), (C), and (D) are incorrect because $50,000 should be classified as current and $100,000 as long-term.

59. On December 1, 1996, Tell Co. leased office space for 5 years at a monthly rental of $60,000. On the same date, Tell paid the lessor the following amounts:

First month's rent	$ 60,000
Last month's rent	60,000
Security deposit (refundable at lease expiration)	80,000
Installation of new walls and offices	360,000

Tell's 1996 expense relating to utilization of the office space should be

A. $140,000

B. $120,000

C. $66,000

D. $60,000

The correct answer is (C). *(CPA 591 I-57)*
REQUIRED: The amount to be included as rent expense in relation to the lease.
DISCUSSION: Rent expense should be recognized as the services are used. Payments which benefit future periods should be deferred and recognized when incurred. Leasehold improvements (i.e., installation of new walls and offices) should be capitalized and amortized over the term of the lease. Therefore, the expense should include $60,000 rent for the first month of the lease and amortization of the leasehold improvement of $6,000 ($360,000/5 x 1/12). Total expense recognized should be $66,000 ($60,000 + $6,000).
Answer (A) is incorrect because $140,000 includes the security deposit and excludes amortization of the leasehold improvements. Answer (B) is incorrect because $120,000 includes the last month's rent and excludes amortization of the leasehold improvements. Answer (D) is incorrect because $60,000 excludes amortization of the leasehold improvements.

60. Wall Co. leased office premises to Fox, Inc. for a 5-year term beginning January 2, 1996. Under the terms of the operating lease, rent for the first year is $8,000 and rent for years 2 through 5 is $12,500 per annum. However, as an inducement to enter the lease, Wall granted Fox the first 6 months of the lease rent-free. In its December 31, 1996 income statement, what amount should Wall report as rental income?

A. $12,000

B. $11,600

C. $10,800

D. $8,000

The correct answer is (C). *(CPA 1193 I-50)*
REQUIRED: The rental revenue reported for the first year of an operating lease given a varying annual rental.
DISCUSSION: For an operating lease, rent is reported as income in accordance with the lease agreement. However, if rentals vary from a straight-line basis, the straight-line basis should be used unless another systematic and rational basis is more representative of the time pattern in which the use benefit from the property is reduced. No basis other than straight-line is more representative of the reduction in the use benefit of office space. Hence, Wall should report rental revenue of $10,800 {[($8,000 x 6/12) + (4 x $12,500)] ÷ 5 years}.
Answer (A) is incorrect because $12,000 equals the first year's rent payment plus 6 months of free rent. Answer (B) is incorrect because $11,600 does not adjust for the 6 months of free rent. Answer (D) is incorrect because $8,000 is equal to the first year's unadjusted rental payment.

61. Conn Corp. owns an office building and normally charges tenants $30 per square foot per year for office space. Because the occupancy rate is low, Conn agreed to lease 10,000 square feet to Hanson Co. at $12 per square foot for the first year of a 3-year operating lease. Rent for remaining years will be at the $30 rate. Hanson moved into the building on January 1, 1996 and paid the first year's rent in advance. What amount of rental revenue should Conn report from Hanson in its income statement for the year ended September 30, 1996?

A. $90,000

B. $120,000

C. $180,000

D. $240,000

The correct answer is (C). *(CPA 1192 I-45)*
REQUIRED: The amount of rent revenue to be included in the income statement.
DISCUSSION: In an operating lease, when payments differ from year to year, revenue is recognized by allocating the total amount of revenue to be received evenly over the lease term. At 9/30/96, the amount of revenue to be recognized is for 9 months. Thus, rent revenue is $180,000 {[$10,000 square feet x ($12 + $30 + $30)] x 9/36}.
Answer (A) is incorrect because $90,000 recognizes rent equal to the rental payments. Answer (B) is incorrect because $120,000 recognizes rent equal to rent payments for 12 months. Answer (D) is incorrect because $240,000 recognizes rent for 12 months.

62. On July 1, 1994, Gee, Inc. leased a delivery truck from Marr Corp. under a 3-year operating lease. Total rent for the term of the lease will be $36,000, payable as follows:

12 months at	$ 500 =	$ 6,000
12 months at	$ 750 =	9,000
12 months at	$1,750 =	21,000

All payments were made when due. In Marr's June 30, 1996 balance sheet, the accrued rent receivable should be reported as

A. $0

B. $9,000

C. $12,000

D. $21,000

The correct answer is (B). *(CPA 1191 I-11)*
REQUIRED: The amount to be included as rent receivable in the balance sheet.
DISCUSSION: For an operating lease, rent revenue is recognized in accordance with the straight-line method unless another systematic and rational basis is more representative of the benefits realized. Thus, monthly rent revenue of $1,000 [($6,000 + $9,000 + $21,000) ÷ 36 months] should be recognized. At 6/30/96 cumulative revenue recognized is $24,000 ($1,000 x 24 months). Since cumulative cash received is $15,000 ($6,000 + $9,000), an accrued receivable for the $9,000 ($24,000 – $15,000) difference should be recognized.
Answer (A) is incorrect because $9,000 is equal to rent received during the year ended 6/30/96. Answer (C) is incorrect because $12,000 is rent revenue recognized each year. Answer (D) is incorrect because $21,000 is equal to the rent payments to be received in the following fiscal year.

17.4 Sale-Leaseback Transactions

63. In a sale-leaseback transaction, the seller-lessee has retained the property. The gain on the sale should be recognized at the time of the sale-leaseback when the lease is classified as a(n)

	Capital Lease	Operating Lease
A.	Yes	Yes
B.	No	No
C.	No	Yes
D.	Yes	No

The correct answer is (B). *(CPA 1189 T-14)*
REQUIRED: The lease for which a gain on a sale-leaseback should be recognized at the time of the transaction.
DISCUSSION: A gain on the sale in a sale-leaseback transaction normally should be deferred and amortized in proportion to the amortization of the leased asset if the leaseback is classified as a capital lease. The amortization is in proportion to the gross rental payments expensed over the lease term if the leaseback is classified as an operating lease (SFAS 28, *Accounting for Sales with Leasebacks*). The gain on the sale is normally not recognized at the time of the sale-leaseback.
Answers (A), (C), and (D) are incorrect because the gain is normally deferred and amortized over the lease term.

64. Rig Co. sold its factory at a gain and simultaneously leased it back for 10 years. The factory's remaining economic life is 20 years. The lease was reported as an operating lease. At the time of sale, Rig should report the gain as

A. An extraordinary item, net of income tax.

B. An asset valuation allowance.

C. A separate component of shareholders' equity.

D. A deferred credit.

The correct answer is (D). *(CPA 592 T-32)*

REQUIRED: The proper treatment of a gain on a sale-leaseback.

DISCUSSION: A gain on the sale in a sale-leaseback normally should be deferred and amortized. When the seller-lessee classifies the lease arising from the sale-leaseback as an operating lease, no asset is shown on the balance sheet, and the deferral cannot be presented as a contra asset. Accordingly, the usual practice is to report the gain as a deferred credit.

Answer (A) is incorrect because the gain is ordinarily deferred. Answer (B) is incorrect because an asset valuation allowance would be reported if the lease qualified as a capital lease. Answer (C) is incorrect because the gain is usually reported as a deferred credit.

65. On December 31, 1996, Dirk Corp. sold Smith Co. two airplanes and simultaneously leased them back. Additional information pertaining to the sale-leasebacks follows:

	Plane #1	Plane #2
Sales price	$600,000	$1,000,000
Carrying amount, 12/31/96	$100,000	$550,000
Remaining useful life, 12/31/96	10 years	35 years
Lease term	8 years	3 years
Annual lease payments	$100,000	$200,000

In its December 31, 1996 balance sheet, what amount should Dirk report as deferred gain on these transactions?

A. $950,000

B. $500,000

C. $450,000

D. $0

The correct answer is (B). *(CPA 593 I-31)*

REQUIRED: The amount to be recorded as deferred revenue in a sale and leaseback.

DISCUSSION: The lease of plane #1 is a capital lease because its 8-year term exceeds 75% of the 10-year estimated remaining economic life of the plane. In a sale and leaseback transaction, any profit or loss on the sale is ordinarily required to be deferred and amortized in proportion to the amortization of the leased asset if the lease is a capital lease. The amortization is in proportion to the gross rental payments expensed over the lease term if the lease is an operating lease. At the inception of this lease, the $500,000 gain ($600,000 sales price – $100,000 carrying amount) should be reported as deferred revenue. The lease of plane #2 is an operating lease that falls under an exception provided by SFAS 28. When the seller-lessee relinquishes the right to substantially all of the remaining use of the property sold and retains only a minor portion of such use (in this case, less than 10% of the remaining useful life), the seller-lessee should account for the sale and the leaseback as separate transactions based upon their respective terms. Dirk should recognize the entire $450,000 gain ($1,000,000 sales price – $550,000 carrying amount). Thus, only the $500,000 gain from the sale of plane #1 is deferred.

Answer (A) is incorrect because $950,000 includes the gain on plane #2. Answer (C) is incorrect because $450,000 equals the gain on plane #2. Answer (D) is incorrect because the gain on plane #1 should be deferred.

66. On December 31, 1996, Ruhl Corp. sold equipment to Dorr and simultaneously leased it back for 3 years. The following data pertain to the transaction at this date:

Sales price	$220,000
Carrying amount	150,000
Present value of lease rentals ($2,000 for 36 months at 12%)	60,800
Estimated remaining useful life	10 years

At December 31, 1996 what amount should Ruhl report as deferred revenue from the sale of the equipment?

A. $0

B. $9,200

C. $60,800

D. $70,000

The correct answer is (C). *(CPA 588 I-32)*

REQUIRED: The amount to be reported as deferred revenue in a sale-leaseback.

DISCUSSION: In an ordinary sale and leaseback, any profit or loss on the sale is amortized over the life of the lease. But SFAS 28 provides for exceptions. One exception applies when a seller-lessee retains more than a minor part but less than substantially all of the use of the property through the leaseback. If the seller-lessee in this situation realizes a profit on the sale in excess of either (1) the present value of the minimum lease payments over the lease term if the leaseback is an operating lease, or (2) the recorded amount of the leased asset if the leaseback is classified as a capital lease, the "excess" profit on the sale is recognized at the date of the sale. "Substantially all" has essentially the same meaning as the "90% test" used in determining whether a lease is a capital or operating lease (the present value of the lease payments is 90% or more of the fair value of the leased property). "Minor" refers to a transfer of 10% or less of the use of the property in the lease.

For Ruhl Corp., the $60,800 present value of the lease rentals is greater than 10% and less than 90% of the fair value of the leased property as measured by the sales price. Thus, $9,200 in excess profit should be recognized.

Sales price	$220,000
Book value	(150,000)
Profit	$ 70,000
Minus PV of lease payments	(60,800)
Profit recognized	$ 9,200

The $60,800 remaining gain on the sale-leaseback should be amortized in proportion to the gross rentals expensed over the lease term because the leaseback is classified as an operating lease (none of the criteria for a capital lease is met). At 12/31/96, the date of the inception of the lease, the entire $60,800 should be reported in the balance sheet as deferred revenue from the sale of the equipment.

Answer (A) is incorrect because more than a minor part but less than substantially all of the use of the property has been retained. Therefore, only the excess profit is recognized immediately, and the remaining portion is deferred. Answer (B) is incorrect because $9,200 is the amount of profit that is recognized immediately, and $60,800 is deferred. Answer (D) is incorrect because $9,200 of the profit is recognized immediately, deferring the remaining $60,800 of revenue.

67. The following information pertains to a sale and leaseback of equipment by Mega Co. on December 31, 1996:

Sales price	$400,000
Carrying amount	$300,000
Monthly lease payment	$3,250
Present value of lease payments	$36,900
Estimated remaining life	25 years
Lease term	1 year
Implicit rate	12%

What amount of deferred gain on the sale should Mega report at December 31, 1996?

- A. $0
- B. $36,900
- C. $63,100
- D. $100,000

The correct answer is (A). *(CPA 592 I-31)*

REQUIRED: The amount of gain to defer resulting from a sale-leaseback transaction.

DISCUSSION: In a sale-leaseback transaction under SFAS 28, a seller will either defer all profits, recognize all profits, or recognize only excess profits. The rules for these recognition principles are based on the rights the seller retains in the property. If the seller-lessee retains substantially all rights in the property (greater than 90% of the present value of the lease payments or the useful life of the asset), then all profits and losses are deferred. If minor rights are retained (less than 10% of the present value of the lease payments or the useful life of the asset), then all profits and losses are recognized. If the rights retained are between these two thresholds, then only excess profits are recognized. In this situation, minor rights are retained so the entire gain of $100,000 ($400,000 sales price – $300,000 carrying amount) is recognized, and none is deferred.

Answer (B) is incorrect because $36,900 is the present value of the lease payments. Answer (C) is incorrect because $63,100 is the difference between the $100,000 gain and the present value of the minimum lease payments. Answer (D) is incorrect because $100,000 is the amount of gain recognized immediately.

68. On June 30, 1996, Lang Co. sold equipment with an estimated useful life of 11 years and immediately leased it back for 10 years. The equipment's carrying amount was $450,000; the sales price was $430,000; and the present value of the lease payments, which is equal to the fair value of the equipment, was $465,000. In its June 30, 1996 balance sheet, what amount should Lang report as deferred loss?

- A. $35,000
- B. $20,000
- C. $15,000
- D. $0

The correct answer is (B). *(CPA 1192 I-35)*

REQUIRED: The amount of deferred loss.

DISCUSSION: Any profit or loss on the sale in a sale-leaseback transaction is ordinarily deferred and amortized. Immediate recognition of the loss is permitted, however, when the fair value at the time of the transaction is less than the undepreciated cost (SFAS 28). Given a fair value of $465,000 and a carrying amount of $450,000, that exception does not apply. Consequently, the $20,000 ($450,000 – $430,000) excess of the carrying amount over the sales price should be deferred.

Answer (A) is incorrect because $35,000 is the excess of the fair value over the sales price. Answer (C) is incorrect because $15,000 is the excess of the fair value over the carrying amount. Answer (D) is incorrect because full recognition of the loss is not appropriate when the fair value is greater than the carrying amount.

17.5 Special Areas

69. A lease of property owned by a governmental unit or authority should be classified as an operating lease only if

   A. The leased property is governmental property that can be either closed or taken possession of by a governmental agency in accordance with the lease agreement or existing statutes or regulations.

   B. The leased property is nonmovable and is part of a larger facility.

   C. The lease has no provision for a transfer of ownership to the lessee.

   D. All of the answers are correct.

The correct answer is (D). *(Publisher)*
   REQUIRED: The condition(s) under which a lease of property from the government must be treated as an operating lease by a lessee.
   DISCUSSION: FASB Interpretation No. 23, *Leases of Certain Property Owned by a Governmental Unit or Authority*, requires that a lease meeting all of the conditions specified in (A), (B), and (C) be classified as an operating lease. In addition, the leased property or equivalent property in the same service area can be neither purchased nor leased from a nongovernmental source. If all of these conditions are not met, the general criteria for classifying leases are applicable.

70. The James Company is the lessee in a lease that involves only part of a building. In the process of determining the classification of this lease, management must determine if it has a basis for an objective determination of the fair value of the leased property. What evidence may be used to provide such a basis?

   A. Only data relating to recent sales of property similar to the leased property.

   B. Only data relating to recent sales of property similar to the leased property or an independent appraisal.

   C. Data relating to recent sales of property similar to the leased property or an independent appraisal or estimated replacement cost data.

   D. Data relating to recent sales of similar property, an independent appraisal, estimated cost information, or any valuation selected by the board of directors.

The correct answer is (C). *(Publisher)*
   REQUIRED: The evidence that may be used to provide an objective measure of the fair value of part of a building.
   DISCUSSION: FASB Interpretation No. 24, *Leases Involving Only Part of a Building*, states that other evidence, such as an independent appraisal or estimated replacement cost information, may be used as a basis for an objective determination of the fair value of part of a building even if no sales of similar property have occurred.
   Answers (A) and (B) are incorrect because other evidence, including both an independent appraisal and estimated replacement cost data, may be used. Answer (D) is incorrect because any valuation selected by the board of directors would not provide an objective determination of fair value.

71. Terms of a lease involving both land and a building include retention of ownership of both elements by the lessor at the end of the lease term. The fair value of the land is $250,000, and the fair value of the building is $500,000. Current authoritative literature requires that the minimum lease payments be allocated between the two elements

   A. In proportion to their fair values at the inception of the lease.

   B. In proportion to their expected fair values at the end of the lease term.

   C. First to the land element on the basis of its fair value at the inception of the lease with the remainder to the building element.

   D. First to the building element on the basis of its fair value at the inception of the lease with the remainder to the land element.

The correct answer is (C). *(Publisher)*
   REQUIRED: The correct allocation between the land and building included in a lease.
   DISCUSSION: Under SFAS 13, if a lease contains neither a bargain purchase option nor a term passing title to the lessee at the termination of the lease, and if the fair value of land in the lease involving both land and a building is 25% or more of the total fair value of the leased property at the inception of the lease, the minimum lease payments should be separated by determining the fair value of the land and applying the lessee's incremental borrowing rate to it to determine the annual minimum lease payments applicable to the land. The remaining minimum lease payments should be allocated to the building element.
   Answer (A) is incorrect because it describes proper allocation by the lessee when either a bargain purchase option exists or title to the property passes to the lessee at the termination of the lease. Answer (B) is incorrect because expected fair values at the expiration of the lease term are not a relevant consideration. Answer (D) is incorrect because the building should receive the residual allocation.

72. Which of the following statements describes the proper accounting when a lease includes equipment as well as land and a building?

A. The lessor may treat the lease as a single lease if the useful life of the assets approximates the lease term.

B. The lessor must account for the equipment as a separate lease but the lessee is not required to do so.

C. The lessee must account for the equipment as a separate lease but the lessor is not required to do so.

D. Both the lessee and lessor must account for the equipment as a separate lease.

73. Lessee has leased a new building and land from Lessor for 25 years. At the inception of the lease, the building and land have fair values of $200,000 and $25,000, respectively. The building has an expected economic life of 30 years. Which of the following statements is correct regarding the Lessee's treatment of the lease?

A. Lessee should treat the lease as a capital lease even though there is no bargain purchase option and no automatic transfer of ownership at the termination of the lease.

B. Lessee should treat the lease as a capital lease only if there is either a bargain purchase option or an automatic transfer of ownership at the termination of the lease.

C. Lessee should treat the lease as a capital lease provided that the land and building are recorded in separate asset accounts and accounted for separately.

D. Lessee should treat the lease as a capital lease only if Lessor treats the transaction as a leveraged lease.

The correct answer is (D). *(Publisher)*
REQUIRED: The accounting when a lease includes equipment, land, and a building.
DISCUSSION: If a lease involves equipment as well as land and a building (real estate), both the lessee and the lessor must first estimate the portion of the minimum lease payments that is applicable to the equipment element of the lease by whatever means are appropriate in the circumstances. The equipment portion of the lease is then classified and accounted for separately from the real estate portion.

Answers (A), (B), and (C) are incorrect because both the lessor and the lessee must account for the equipment portion of the lease separately from the real estate portion.

The correct answer is (A). *(Publisher)*
REQUIRED: The true statement regarding the lessee's accounting for a lease involving land and a building.
DISCUSSION: When the lease involves both land and a building, SFAS 13 provides for a special application of the four criteria for determining whether the lessee should treat the lease as a capital or an operating lease. If neither a bargain purchase option nor automatic transfer of ownership at the termination of the lease exists, but the fair value of the land is less than 25% of the total fair value of the leased property at the inception of the lease (as in this case), the land and building should be considered a single unit for purposes of applying the 75% lease term test and the 90% fair value test. Because the lease term in this question exceeds 75% of the estimated economic life of the building, the lease should be properly classified as a capital lease by the lessee. According to SFAS 98, *Accounting for Leases - Sale-Leaseback Transactions Involving Real Estate; Sales-Type Leases of Real Estate; Definition of the Lease Term; Initial Direct Costs of Direct Financing Leases*, if the collectibility of the lease payments is reasonably predictable and no important uncertainties surround the amount of unreimbursable costs, the lessor should account for the lease as a single unit as either a direct financing lease, a leveraged lease, or an operating lease. A lease involving real estate is classified as a sales-type lease only if it results in a manufacturer's or dealer's profit (or loss) and transfers ownership.

Answer (B) is incorrect because the four tests for capital leases apply to land and building leases as well as to leases of other assets. Answer (C) is incorrect because, when the fair value of the land is less than 25% of total fair value in a capital lease, the land and building should be capitalized and amortized as a single unit. Answer (D) is incorrect because classification of a lease as a leveraged lease is possible only by a lessor and has no bearing on lessee accounting.

74. Lessor Company agreed to sell Lessee Company an asset that Lessee Company currently is accounting for as a capital lease. At the time of the purchase, the following account balances were recorded:

Leased asset, net of amortization	$31,500
Lease obligation	33,500

At what amount should Lessee record this asset, given that the price paid to Lessor was $34,000?

    A. $31,500

    B. $32,000

    C. $33,500

    D. $34,000

The correct answer is (B). *(Publisher)*

REQUIRED: The amount at which a lessee should record the purchase of a leased asset during the lease term.

DISCUSSION: FASB Interpretation No. 26, *Accounting for Purchase of a Leased Asset by the Lessee During the Term of the Lease*, requires that the carrying value of the leased asset be adjusted for the difference, if any, between the purchase price and the carrying value of the lease obligation. Lessee Company should therefore record the asset at $32,000 ($31,500 + $34,000 – $33,500). If the leased asset is carried at an amount greater than the lease obligation, a loss may be recognized so that the purchased asset is not overvalued. For example, assuming the purchased asset had a fair value of $34,000, if the leased asset and obligation had been $33,500 and $31,500, respectively, a $2,000 loss would have been recognized (debit an asset for $34,000, a loss for $2,000, and the lease obligation for $31,500; credit the leased asset for $33,500 and cash for $34,000).

Answer (A) is incorrect because $31,500 is the carrying value of the leased asset. Answer (C) is incorrect because $33,500 is the carrying value of the lease obligation. Answer (D) is incorrect because $34,000 is the purchase price.

75. One criterion that must be met before the lease may be classified by the lessor as a sales-type lease or a direct financing lease is that "no important uncertainties surround the amount of unreimbursable costs yet to be incurred by the lessor under the lease." If the property covered by the lease is yet to be constructed by the lessor at the inception of the lease, this classification criterion should be applied at the date

    A. That marks the inception of the lease.

    B. That the construction of the property is completed.

    C. That the lessee takes possession of the property.

    D. That final payment is made to the contractor.

The correct answer is (B). *(Publisher)*

REQUIRED: The date at which a lessor should apply the cost uncertainties criterion when the property has not yet been constructed at the inception date.

DISCUSSION: The classification of a lease is determined at the date of its inception, which is the date of the lease agreement or commitment, if earlier. However, when property covered by a lease has yet to be constructed or has not been acquired by the lessor at the date of the lease agreement or commitment (the inception of the lease), SFAS 23, *Inception of the Lease*, states that the classification criterion regarding cost uncertainties is to be applied "at the date that construction of the property is completed or the property is acquired by the lessor."

Answer (A) is incorrect because, given that the property has yet to be constructed at the inception date, the determination regarding unreimbursable costs must await completion of the project. Answers (C) and (D) are incorrect because the application of the cost uncertainties criterion by the lessor should not be later than completion of construction.

76. The Henson Corporation is the lessor and the Lippert Corporation is the lessee in a lease agreement. The lease is for property that has not yet been acquired by the lessor. A preliminary lease agreement has been written and approved by both parties. Only two principal provisions are yet to be negotiated. The date considered to be the inception of this lease is

A. The date of the preliminary lease agreement.

B. The date that the property is acquired by the lessor.

C. The date that the remaining two principal provisions are agreed upon in writing.

D. The date that the lessee takes possession of the property.

The correct answer is (C). *(Publisher)*
REQUIRED: The inception date of a lease when the lease property has not yet been acquired by the lessor.
DISCUSSION: SFAS 23 defines the inception date for a lease that covers property not constructed or acquired by the lessor as the date of the lease agreement or any earlier commitment. The commitment must be in writing, must be signed by the interested parties, and must specifically set forth the principal lease provisions. If any of the principal provisions remains to be negotiated, the agreement does not meet the definition of a commitment.
Answers (A), (B), and (D) are incorrect because the inception date is defined as the date of a qualifying lease agreement or commitment, if earlier.

77. When the nature of a sublease transaction is such that the original lessee is not relieved of the primary obligation under the original lease, a loss (if it occurs) should be recognized by the original lessee under which of the following conditions?

A. Never.

B. Only if the sublease was entered into as part of the disposal of a segment of a business.

C. Under all circumstances.

D. Only when the sublease is a sales-type lease.

The correct answer is (C). *(Publisher)*
REQUIRED: The circumstances under which a loss on a sublease should be recognized.
DISCUSSION: In these circumstances, SFAS 13 "does not specifically require recognition of an indicated loss except for a sales-type loss on a sales-type sublease." However, according to FASB Interpretation No. 27, *Accounting for a Loss on a Sublease*, if the sublease is entered into as part of the disposal of a segment of a business, any gain or loss on the sublease must be recognized as part of the gain or loss on disposal. Moreover, FASB Technical Bulletin 79-15, *Accounting for Loss on a Sublease Not Involving the Disposal of a Segment*, requires recognition of a loss on operating and direct financing subleases in appropriate circumstances.
Answers (A), (B), and (D) are incorrect because the effect of the three pronouncements cited above is that a loss should be recognized whenever it occurs.

78. Under what conditions would a renewal or extension of either a sales-type or direct financing lease, that otherwise would qualify as a sales-type lease, be properly classified as a direct financing lease?

A. Under all conditions.

B. Under no conditions.

C. Under the condition that the renewal or extension occurs at or near the end of the lease term.

D. Under the condition that the renewal or extension does not occur at or near the end of the lease term.

The correct answer is (D). *(Publisher)*
REQUIRED: The condition(s) under which a renewal or extension should be classified as a direct financing lease.
DISCUSSION: SFAS 27, *Classification of Renewals or Extensions of Existing Sales-Type or Direct Financing Leases*, states that a renewal or extension of an existing sales-type or direct financing lease, that otherwise would qualify as a sales-type lease, should be classified as a direct financing lease unless the renewal or extension occurs at or near the end of the original lease term. At or near the end of the lease term is considered to mean the last few months of the existing lease.
Answers (A) and (B) are incorrect because the sales-type classification is only appropriate under certain conditions. Answer (C) is incorrect because, under this condition, the lease should be classified as a sales-type lease.

79. The City of Medford issued tax-exempt debt to construct a building that it leased to a company. The lease was capitalized by the lessee and treated as a direct financing lease by the lessor. Terms of the lease were such that the lease obligation was essentially the same as the tax-exempt debt. If the tax-exempt debt is advance refunded and the terms of the lease are changed to pass the perceived economic advantages of the refunding through to the lessee, which of the following statements is true?

A. If the advance refunding is treated as an early extinguishment of debt, both the lessor and the lessee should recognize a gain or loss.

B. Regardless of whether the advance refunding is treated as an early extinguishment of debt, both the lessor and the lessee should recognize a gain or loss.

C. If the advance refunding is treated as an early extinguishment of debt, only the lessee should recognize a gain or loss.

D. If the advance refunding is treated as an early extinguishment of debt, only the lessor should recognize a gain or loss.

The correct answer is (A). *(Publisher)*

REQUIRED: The correct statement about the effects of advance refunding of tax-exempt debt when the provisions of a lease are changed to pass the economic advantages of the refunding through to the lessee.

DISCUSSION: SFAS 22, *Changes in the Provisions of Lease Agreements Resulting from Refundings of Tax-Exempt Debt*, applies when an advance refunding of tax-exempt debt results in a revision of lease terms of a capital lease and the refunding is accounted for as an extinguishment of debt. In these circumstances, the lessee should adjust the lease obligation to the present value of the minimum lease payments under the revised lease using the effective interest rate applicable to the revised agreement. The lessee should also recognize any resulting gain or loss as a gain or loss on the extinguishment of debt (extraordinary).

The lessor should adjust the gross investment and the unearned interest income accounts to reflect as net investment the present value of the components of the gross investment, based on the interest rate applicable to the revised lease agreement, and should recognize the resulting adjustment as a gain or loss in the current period.

The criteria in SFAS 76, *Extinguishment of Debt*, determine whether the transaction qualifies as an extinguishment at the date of the advance refunding.

Answer (B) is incorrect because SFAS 22 states that, in these circumstances, any gain or loss should be recognized when the tax-exempt debt is considered to have been extinguished. Thus, if the advance refunding did not constitute an early extinguishment, no gain or loss should be recognized. Answers (C) and (D) are incorrect because both the lessor and the lessee should recognize a gain or loss.

80. Which of the following statements about leveraged leases is correct?

A. The lessee finances them largely by nonrecourse debt.

B. They are sales-type leases.

C. They provide depreciation expense, interest expense, and tax benefits to the lessee.

D. They provide for a creditor mortgage on the leased asset.

The correct answer is (D). *(Publisher)*

REQUIRED: The correct statement about leveraged leases.

DISCUSSION: A leveraged lease is in effect a direct financing lease in which the leased asset is financed by the lessor through a third-party long-term creditor. The third-party creditor's interest is secured either by a pledge of the lease payments or by a mortgage on the leased asset, and the debt is substantially nonrecourse as to the general credit of the lessor.

Answer (A) is incorrect because the lessor, not the lessee, finances the leased asset by nonrecourse debt. Answer (B) is incorrect because sales-type leases may not be accounted for as leveraged leases. Answer (C) is incorrect because the lessor, not the lessee, recognizes depreciation expense, interest expense, and tax benefits on a leveraged lease.

CHAPTER EIGHTEEN
SHAREHOLDERS' EQUITY

This chapter covers the material on corporations usually found in two chapters of most traditional intermediate textbooks. It also covers all aspects of shareholders' equity except earnings per share (EPS). EPS is covered in Chapter 19.

18.1 General

1. Which of the following is the primary element that distinguishes accounting for corporations from accounting for other legal forms of business organization (such as partnerships)?

A. The entity theory relates primarily to the other forms of business organization.

B. The corporation draws a sharper distinction in accounting for sources of capital.

C. In a corporation, retained earnings may be reduced only by the declaration of dividends.

D. Generally accepted accounting principles apply to corporations but have relatively little applicability to other forms of business organization.

The correct answer is (B). *(CPA 575 T-10)*
REQUIRED: The primary distinguishing feature of accounting for corporations.
DISCUSSION: The three primary forms of business organization are the corporation, the partnership, and the proprietorship. Of the three, only the corporation sharply differentiates between contributed ownership equity and ownership equity earned and retained in the business. Contributed capital is reflected in the various capital stock and additional paid-in capital (additional contributed capital) accounts. Earned capital is reflected in the retained earnings accounts.
Answer (A) is incorrect because the entity theory relates primarily to the corporation. It achieves a greater degree of separation from its owners than any other form of business enterprise. Answer (C) is incorrect because retained earnings may be reduced by numerous transactions, including a net operating loss. Answer (D) is incorrect because GAAP apply to all forms of business organization.

2. The issuance of shares of preferred stock to shareholders

A. Increases preferred stock outstanding.

B. Has no effect on preferred stock outstanding.

C. Increases preferred stock authorized.

D. Decreases preferred stock authorized.

The correct answer is (A). *(CPA 1186 T-20)*
REQUIRED: The effect of the issuance of shares of preferred stock to shareholders.
DISCUSSION: The charter (articles of incorporation) filed with the secretary of state of the state of incorporation indicates the classes of stock that may be issued and their authorized amounts in terms of shares and/or total dollar value. When authorized shares are issued, the effect is to increase the amount of that class of stock outstanding.
Answer (B) is incorrect because the effect of the issuance of shares is to increase the stock outstanding. Answers (C) and (D) are incorrect because the issuance of shares has no effect on the preferred stock authorized.

3. Beck Corp. issued 200,000 shares of common stock when it began operations in 1994 and issued an additional 100,000 shares in 1995. Beck also issued preferred stock convertible to 100,000 shares of common stock. In 1996, Beck purchased 75,000 shares of its common stock and held it in treasury. At December 31, 1996, how many shares of Beck's common stock were outstanding?

    A. 400,000

    B. 325,000

    C. 300,000

    D. 225,000

The correct answer is (D). *(CPA 593 II-2)*
    REQUIRED: The number of shares of outstanding common stock.
    DISCUSSION: Beck issued 200,000 shares of common stock in 1994 and 100,000 shares in 1995. The purchase of 75,000 shares of treasury stock decreased the number of shares of common stock outstanding in 1996 to 225,000 (200,000 + 100,000 – 75,000). The convertible preferred stock is not considered common stock.
    Answer (A) is incorrect because 400,000 includes the convertible preferred stock and the treasury stock. Answer (B) is incorrect because 325,000 includes the convertible preferred stock. Answer (C) is incorrect because 300,000 includes the treasury stock.

4. The preemptive right of shareholders is the right to

    A. Share equally in dividend distributions.

    B. Purchase shares of stock on a pro rata basis when new issues are offered for sale.

    C. Share in the distribution of assets on liquidation of the corporation.

    D. Participate in the management of the corporation.

The correct answer is (B). *(Publisher)*
    REQUIRED: The definition of the preemptive right of shareholders.
    DISCUSSION: The preemptive right refers to each shareholder's right to maintain proportionate ownership in the corporation if additional shares are offered for sale.
    Answers (A), (C), and (D) are incorrect because each is a shareholder right distinct from the preemptive right. Shareholders participate in management of the corporation by electing a board of directors and by voting on referendums presented by management and the directors.

5. On December 1, 1996, Line Corp. received a donation of 2,000 shares of its $5 par value common stock from a shareholder. On that date, the stock's market value was $35 per share. The stock was originally issued for $25 per share. By what amount would this donation cause total shareholders' equity to decrease?

    A. $70,000

    B. $50,000

    C. $10,000

    D. $0

The correct answer is (D). *(CPA 593 I-11)*
    REQUIRED: The decrease in shareholders' equity from receipt of a donation of the company's own stock.
    DISCUSSION: The receipt of a donation of a company's own stock is recorded at fair value as increases in both additional paid-in capital and treasury stock. Since these accounts offset, the net effect on shareholders' equity is $0.
    Answer (A) is incorrect because $70,000 records the effect equal to the current market price. Answer (B) is incorrect because $50,000 records the effect equal to the original issuance price. Answer (C) is incorrect because $10,000 records the effect equal to the par value.

6. East Co. issued 1,000 shares of its $5 par common stock to Howe as compensation for 1,000 hours of legal services performed. Howe usually bills $160 per hour for legal services. On the date of issuance, the stock was trading on a public exchange at $140 per share. By what amount should the additional paid-in capital account increase as a result of this transaction?

    A. $135,000

    B. $140,000

    C. $155,000

    D. $160,000

The correct answer is (A). *(CPA 1194 F-28)*
    REQUIRED: The increase in additional paid-in capital.
    DISCUSSION: When stock is issued for property or services, the transaction is recorded at the fair value of the stock or of the property or services received. In this case, the value of the stock is used because it is more definite. The $140,000 should be allocated as follows: $5,000 ($5 par x 1,000 shares) to common stock and $135,000 to additional paid-in capital.
    Answer (B) is incorrect because $5,000 should be allocated to common stock. Answers (C) and (D) are incorrect because the value of the stock should be used to record the transaction.

Questions 7 and 8 are based on the following information. Pugh Co. reported the following in its statement of shareholders' equity on January 1, 1996:

Common stock, $5 par value, authorized 200,000 shares, issued 100,000 shares	$ 500,000
Additional paid-in capital	1,500,000
Retained earnings	516,000
	$2,516,000
Minus treasury stock, at cost, 5,000 shares	40,000
Total shareholders' equity	$2,476,000

The following events occurred in 1996:

May 1 -- 1,000 shares of treasury stock were sold for $10,000.

July 9 -- 10,000 shares of previously unissued common stock sold for $12 per share.

October 1 -- The distribution of a 2-for-1 stock split resulted in the common stock's per-share par value being halved.

Pugh accounts for treasury stock under the cost method. Laws in the state of Pugh's incorporation protect shares held in treasury from dilution when stock dividends or stock splits are declared.

7. In Pugh's December 31, 1996 statement of shareholders' equity, the par value of the issued common stock should be

A. $550,000

B. $530,000

C. $275,000

D. $265,000

The correct answer is (A). *(CPA 591 I-19)*

REQUIRED: The par value of the issued common stock.

DISCUSSION: At the beginning of the year, 100,000 shares with a par value of $500,000 had been issued. These shares included the treasury stock (issued but not outstanding) accounted for at cost. Under the cost method, the par value recorded in the common stock account is unaffected by purchases and sales of treasury stock. On July 9, 10,000 shares of previously unissued common stock were sold. This transaction increased the aggregate par value to $550,000 (110,000 shares issued x $5). The 2-for-1 stock split reduced the par value per share by 50% but did not affect the aggregate par value of the issued stock.

Answer (B) is incorrect because $530,000 is the par value of the issued and outstanding shares. Answer (C) is incorrect because $275,000 is half the par value of the issued stock. Answer (D) is incorrect because $265,000 is half the par value of the issued and outstanding stock.

8. The number of outstanding common shares at December 31, 1996 should be

A. 222,000

B. 220,000

C. 212,000

D. 210,000

The correct answer is (C). *(CPA 591 I-20)*

REQUIRED: The number of outstanding common shares.

DISCUSSION: On January 1, 1996, 95,000 shares (100,000 issued – 5,000 treasury shares) were outstanding. The treasury stock sale and the issuance of previously unissued shares increased that amount to 106,000 shares (95,000 + 1,000 + 10,000). The stock split doubled the shares outstanding to 212,000 (2 x 106,000).

Answer (A) is incorrect because 222,000 assumes 100,000 shares were outstanding on January 1. Answer (B) is incorrect because 220,000 assumes 100,000 shares were outstanding on January 1 but omits the treasury stock sale. Answer (D) is incorrect because 210,000 omits the treasury stock sale.

9. Rudd Corp. had 700,000 shares of common stock authorized and 300,000 shares outstanding at December 31, 1995. The following events occurred during 1996:

January 31	Declared 10% stock dividend
June 30	Purchased 100,000 shares
August 1	Reissued 50,000 shares
November 30	Declared 2-for-1 stock split

At December 31, 1996, how many shares of common stock did Rudd have outstanding?

- A. 560,000
- B. 600,000
- C. 630,000
- D. 660,000

The correct answer is (A). *(CPA 593 II-1)*
REQUIRED: The number of outstanding shares of common stock.
DISCUSSION: Rudd had 300,000 shares outstanding at the beginning of the year. The 10% stock dividend (300,000 shares x 10% = 30,000) increased the shares outstanding to 330,000. The purchase reduced shares outstanding to 230,000. The reissuance increased these shares to 280,000. The 2-for-1 stock split increased shares outstanding to 560,000 (2 x 280,000).

Answer (B) is incorrect because 600,000 ignores all transactions except the stock split. Answer (C) is incorrect because 630,000 ignores the purchase and reissuance and assumes that the shares of the stock dividend were not split. Answer (D) is incorrect because 660,000 excludes the treasury stock purchase and the reissuance of 50,000 shares.

10. The December 31, 1996 condensed balance sheet of Adams and Gray, a partnership, follows:

Current assets	$140,000
Equipment (net)	130,000
	$270,000
Liabilities	$ 70,000
Adams and Gray, capital	200,000
	$270,000

Fair values at December 31, 1996 are as follows:

Current assets	$160,000
Equipment	210,000
Liabilities	70,000

On January 2, 1997, Adams and Gray was incorporated, with 5,000 shares of $10 par value common stock issued. How much should be credited to additional contributed capital?

- A. $320,000
- B. $300,000
- C. $250,000
- D. $200,000

The correct answer is (C). *(CPA 593 II-6)*
REQUIRED: The amount credited to additional contributed capital upon incorporation.
DISCUSSION: When assets of a partnership are contributed to a corporation in exchange for par value common stock, the contributed capital account should be credited for the fair value of the net assets. The fair value of the net assets equals $300,000 ($160,000 + $210,000 – $70,000). Of this amount, $50,000 (5,000 shares x $10 par value) should be credited to the capital stock account, with the remaining $250,000 credited to additional contributed capital.

Answer (A) is incorrect because $320,000 equals the total fair value of the assets minus the $50,000 allocated to capital stock. Answer (B) is incorrect because $300,000 is the fair value of the net assets. Answer (D) is incorrect because $200,000 is the partnership capital at its carrying amount.

11. On July 1, Rya Corporation issued 1,000 shares of its $10 par common and 2,000 shares of its $10 par convertible preferred stock for a lump sum of $40,000. At this date, Rya's common stock was selling for $18 per share and the convertible preferred stock for $13.50 per share. The amount of proceeds allocated to Rya's preferred stock should be

- A. $22,000
- B. $24,000
- C. $27,000
- D. $30,000

The correct answer is (B). *(CPA 592 II-1)*
REQUIRED: The proceeds to be allocated to preferred stock in a lump-sum issuance.
DISCUSSION: Given that the 1,000 shares of common stock and 2,000 shares of preferred stock were issued for a lump sum of $40,000, the proceeds should be allocated based on the relative fair values of the securities issued. The fair value of the common stock is $18,000 (1,000 shares x $18). The fair value of the preferred stock is $27,000 (2,000 shares x $13.50). Because 60% [$27,000 ÷ ($27,000 + $18,000)] of the total fair value is attributable to the preferred stock, $24,000 (60% x $40,000) of the proceeds should be allocated to this stock.

Answer (A) is incorrect because $22,000 equals the lump sum received minus the fair value of the common stock. Answer (C) is incorrect because $27,000 is the fair value of the preferred stock. Answer (D) is incorrect because $30,000 is the sum of the par values of the stock issued.

12. On July 1, 1996, Cove Corp., a closely held corporation, issued 6% bonds with a maturity value of $60,000, together with 1,000 shares of its $5 par value common stock, for a combined cash amount of $110,000. The market value of Cove's stock cannot be ascertained. If the bonds were issued separately, they would have sold for $40,000 on an 8% yield-to-maturity basis. What amount should Cove record for additional paid-in capital on the issuance of the stock?

A. $75,000

B. $65,000

C. $55,000

D. $45,000

The correct answer is (B). *(CPA 1192 II-44)*

REQUIRED: The amount allocated to additional paid-in capital.

DISCUSSION: The proceeds of the combined issuance of different classes of securities generally should be allocated based on the relative fair values of the securities. However, if the fair value of only one class of security is known, the proceeds should be first allocated to that class of security with the remainder allocated to the other class. Since the fair value of the stock is not known, the bonds should be recorded at their fair value ($40,000), with the remainder of the proceeds ($110,000 – $40,000 = $70,000) credited to common stock at par value ($5 x 1,000 shares = $5,000) and additional paid-in capital ($70,000 – $5,000 par = $65,000).

Answer (A) is incorrect because $75,000 results from adding the par value to the total allocable to the stock. Answer (C) is incorrect because $55,000 is based on an allocation of $60,000 to the stock. Answer (D) is incorrect because $45,000 is based on an allocation of $60,000 (maturity value) to the bonds.

13. When collectibility is reasonably assured, the excess of the subscription price over the stated value of no-par common stock subscribed should be recorded as

A. No-par common stock.

B. Additional paid-in capital when the subscription is recorded.

C. Additional paid-in capital when the subscription is collected.

D. Additional paid-in capital when the common stock is issued.

The correct answer is (B). *(CPA 1192 T-18)*

REQUIRED: The recording of the excess of the subscription price over the stated value of no-par common stock subscribed.

DISCUSSION: The accounting for subscriptions of no-par stock with a stated value is the same as for par value stock. When stock is subscribed, the corporation recognizes an obligation to issue stock, and the subscriber undertakes the legal obligation to pay for the shares subscribed. If collectibility of the subscription price is reasonably assured on the date the subscription is received, the issuing corporation should recognize the cash collected and a subscription receivable for the remainder. In addition, the common stock subscribed account should be credited for the stated value of the shares subscribed, with the excess of the subscription price over the stated value recognized as additional paid-in capital.

Answer (A) is incorrect because the credit is to additional paid-in capital. Answers (C) and (D) are incorrect because additional paid-in capital is credited when the subscription is recorded.

14. What is the entry to record issuance of stock after all monies have been received from a stock subscription, assuming an entry to record common stock authorized was made at the time of incorporation?

A. Common stock subscribed
Common stock

B. Common stock subscribed
Common stock
Paid-in capital in excess of par

C. Common stock subscribed
Unissued common stock

D. Stock subscriptions receivable
Common stock subscribed
Paid-in capital in excess of par

The correct answer is (C). *(Publisher)*

REQUIRED: The entry to record issuance of stock after all monies have been received from a stock subscription.

DISCUSSION: If unissued stock was debited (at par value) and authorized stock was credited (also at par) at the time of incorporation, no additional entry to the latter account is needed. Accordingly, common stock subscribed should be debited and unissued common stock should be credited when full payment for the shares has been received. The difference between the authorized stock and unissued stock accounts is the amount of issued stock.

Answer (A) is incorrect because it is the entry to record the issuance of fully paid, subscribed common stock if the authorized stock and unissued stock accounts are not used. Answer (B) is incorrect because paid-in capital in excess of par value is recorded at the time of the subscription rather than the time of issuance. Answer (D) is incorrect because it is the entry to record a stock subscription when no cash is received.

15. On December 1, 1996, shares of authorized common stock were issued on a subscription basis at a price in excess of par value. A total of 20% of the subscription price of each share was collected as a down payment on December 1, 1996, with the remaining 80% of the subscription price of each share due in 1997. Collectibility was reasonably assured. At December 31, 1996, the shareholders' equity section of the balance sheet should report additional paid-in capital for the excess of the sub-scription price over the par value of the shares of common stock subscribed and

A. Common stock issued for 20% of the par value of the shares of common stock subscribed.

B. Common stock issued for the par value of the shares of common stock subscribed.

C. Common stock subscribed for 80% of the par value of the shares of common stock subscribed.

D. Common stock subscribed for the par value of the shares of common stock subscribed.

The correct answer is (D). *(CPA 1188 T-17)*
   REQUIRED: The proper recording of subscribed stock in the shareholders' equity section.
   DISCUSSION: When stock is subscribed, the corpora-tion recognizes an obligation to issue stock, and the sub-scriber undertakes the legal obligation to pay for the shares subscribed. If collectibility of the subscription price is reasonably assured on the date the subscription is received, the issuing corporation should recognize the cash collected and a subscription receivable for the remainder. In addition, the common stock subscribed account should be credited for the par value of the shares subscribed, with the excess of the subscription price over the par value recognized as additional paid-in capital.
   Answers (A), (B), and (C) are incorrect because the shareholders' equity sections of the balance sheet should report the common stock subscribed account for the par value of the shares subscribed and additional paid-in capital for the excess of the subscription price over the par value.

16. If a subscriber to common stock defaults on the subscription and amounts already paid are forfeited, what is the journal entry in the books of the subscribed corporation?

A. Common stock subscribed
    Paid-in capital in excess of par value
        Stock subscriptions receivable
        Cash

B. Common stock subscribed
    Paid-in capital in excess of par value
        Stock subscriptions receivable
        Paid-in capital from stock
        subscription default

C. Paid-in capital in excess of par value
    Common stock
        Common stock subscribed
        Cash

D. Subscriptions receivable
    Common stock subscribed
    Paid-in capital in excess of par

The correct answer is (B). *(Publisher)*
   REQUIRED: The journal entry to record a default on a common stock subscription when the payments received are forfeited.
   DISCUSSION: When a subscriber defaults, the entry to record the subscription to common stock must be reversed. To the extent that payment has been received and is for-feited, paid-in capital from stock subscription default is credited for the amount forfeited.
   Answer (A) is incorrect because it is the entry for a common stock subscription default when amounts previously paid in are refunded to the subscriber. Answer (C) is incorrect because common stock cannot be debited if no stock has been issued by and returned to the corporation. Answer (D) is incorrect because it is the entry to record the stock subscription when no cash is received.

17. How should changes in the separate accounts included in shareholders' equity (in addition to retained earnings) be disclosed when both financial position and results of operations are presented?

    A.   The changes need not be specifically disclosed.

    B.   The changes should not be disclosed in the financial statements; rather, they must be disclosed in separate statements.

    C.   The changes may be disclosed in separate statements, on the face of the financial statements, or in notes thereto.

    D.   The changes should not be disclosed in separate statements; rather, they must be disclosed on the face of the financial statements or in notes thereto.

The correct answer is (C). *(Publisher)*
    REQUIRED: The correct disclosure of changes in the separate accounts included in shareholders' equity.
    DISCUSSION: APB 12, *Omnibus Opinion-1967*, states that, when both financial position and the results of operations are presented, disclosure of changes in the separate accounts included in shareholders' equity (in addition to retained earnings) is required to make the financial statements sufficiently informative. The disclosure may appear in separate statements, in the basic financial statements, or in notes thereto.
    Answer (A) is incorrect because APB 12 requires specific disclosure of the changes. Answers (B) and (D) are incorrect because the disclosure may be made in separate statements, in the basic financial statements, or in notes thereto.

18. At December 31, 1996, Eagle Corp. reported $1,750,000 of appropriated retained earnings for the construction of a new office building, which was completed in 1997 at a total cost of $1,500,000. In 1997, Eagle appropriated $1,200,000 of retained earnings for the construction of a new plant. Also, $2,000,000 of cash was restricted for the retirement of bonds due in 1998. In its 1997 balance sheet, Eagle should report what amount of appropriated retained earnings?

    A. $1,200,000

    B. $1,450,000

    C. $2,950,000

    D. $3,200,000

The correct answer is (A). *(CPA 593 II-5)*
    REQUIRED: The amount of appropriated retained earnings reported.
    DISCUSSION: Appropriating retained earnings is a formal way of marking a portion of retained earnings for other uses. A journal entry is used to reclassify retained earnings to appropriated retained earnings. When the appropriation is no longer necessary, the entry is reversed. The original appropriation of $1,750,000 in 1996 would have been reversed for that amount in 1997. The cash restriction is not included in appropriated retained earnings. If the amount is material, the restriction will require separate reporting of the cash item in the balance sheet, footnote disclosure, and reclassification as noncurrent. Thus, appropriated retained earnings at year-end 1997 should be reported at $1,200,000.
    Answer (B) is incorrect because $1,450,000 includes the previous year's excess of appropriated retained earnings over the actual cost. Answer (C) is incorrect because $2,950,000 includes the cash restriction and subtracts the previous year's excess of appropriated retained earnings over the actual cost. Answer (D) is incorrect because $3,200,000 includes the $2,000,000 restriction on cash for bond retirement.

19. Of the 125,000 shares of common stock issued by Vey Corp., 25,000 shares were held as treasury stock at December 31, 1995. During 1996, transactions involving Vey's common stock were as follows:

January 1 through October 31 -- 13,000 treasury shares were distributed to officers as part of a stock compensation plan.

November 1 -- A 3-for-1 stock split took effect.

December 1 -- Vey purchased 5,000 of its own shares to discourage an unfriendly takeover. These shares were not retired.

At December 31, 1996, how many of Vey's common stock were issued and outstanding?

	Shares Issued	Outstanding
A.	375,000	334,000
B.	375,000	324,000
C.	334,000	334,000
D.	324,000	324,000

The correct answer is (A). *(CPA 1191 II-1)*
REQUIRED: The number of shares issued and outstanding.
DISCUSSION: Given that 125,000 shares have been issued and that the stock has been split 3-for-1, the shares issued at year-end equal 375,000 (3 x 125,000). At the beginning of the year, 100,000 shares were outstanding (125,000 issued – 25,000 treasury shares). After 13,000 treasury shares were distributed, 113,000 shares were outstanding, an amount that increased to 339,000 (3 x 113,000) after the stock split. The purchase on December 1 reduced the shares outstanding to 334,000 (339,000 – 5,000).
Answer (B) is incorrect because 324,000 shares would be outstanding if the 5,000-share purchase had been made before the split. Answers (C) and (D) are incorrect because shares issued exceed shares outstanding.

20. On February 1, 1996, Hyde Corp., a newly formed company, had the following stock issued and outstanding:

• Common stock, no par, $1 stated value, 10,000 shares originally issued for $15 per share

• Preferred stock, $10 par value, 3,000 shares originally issued for $25 per share

Hyde's February 1, 1996 statement of shareholders' equity should report

	Common Stock	Preferred Stock	Additional Paid-in Capital
A.	$150,000	$30,000	$45,000
B.	$150,000	$75,000	$0
C.	$10,000	$75,000	$140,000
D.	$10,000	$30,000	$185,000

The correct answer is (D). *(CPA 593 I-6)*
REQUIRED: The amounts of common stock, preferred stock, and additional paid-in capital to be reported in the statement of shareholders' equity.
DISCUSSION: The common stock was issued for a total of $150,000 (10,000 shares x $15). Of this amount, $10,000 (10,000 shares x $1 stated value) should be allocated to the common stock, with the remaining $140,000 ($150,000 – $10,000) credited to additional paid-in capital. The preferred stock was issued for $75,000 (3,000 shares x $25), of which $30,000 (3,000 shares x $10 par value) should be allocated to the preferred stock and $45,000 ($75,000 – $30,000) to additional paid-in capital. In the February 1, 1996 statement of shareholders' equity, Hyde therefore should report $10,000 in the common stock account, $30,000 in the preferred stock account, and $185,000 ($140,000 + $45,000) as additional paid-in capital.
Answer (A) is incorrect because the excess of the issue price of the common stock over its stated value is credited to additional paid-in capital, not common stock. Answer (B) is incorrect because the excess of the issue price of the common stock over its stated value is credited to additional paid-in capital, not common stock, and the excess of the issue price of the preferred stock over its par value is credited to additional paid-in capital, not preferred stock. Answer (C) is incorrect because the excess of the issue price of the preferred stock over its par value is credited to additional paid-in capital, not preferred stock.

21. Atomic, Inc. completed a number of capital transactions during the year ended December 31 as follows:

An issue of 8% debentures was converted into common stock.

An issue of $2.50 preferred stock was called and retired.

A 10% common stock dividend was distributed on November 30.

Warrants for 200,000 shares of common stock were exercised on December 20.

For the year-end financial statements to be sufficiently informative, the most satisfactory method of presenting the effects of these events is

A. A formal retained earnings statement and general description in the notes to the financial statements.

B. A formal statement of changes in shareholders' equity that discloses changes in the various shareholders' equity accounts.

C. A detailed inclusion of each event or transaction in the statement of cash flows.

D. Comparative statements of income, financial position, and retained earnings for this year and last year.

The correct answer is (B). *(CMA 679 3-18)*
REQUIRED: The most satisfactory method of presenting the effects of the listed capital transactions.
DISCUSSION: When both financial position and results of operations are presented, APB 12 requires disclosure of changes in the accounts included in shareholders' equity (in addition to retained earnings). It also requires disclosure of the changes in the number of shares of equity securities during at least the most recent annual fiscal period and any subsequent interim periods presented. The required disclosure may be made in the basic financial statements, in notes thereto, or in a formal statement of changes in shareholders' equity (which is preferable).
Answer (A) is incorrect because a general description is inadequate. Answers (C) and (D) are incorrect because the disclosures made in the statements of cash flows, income, retained earnings, and financial position are insufficient.

22. During 1995, Brad Co. issued 5,000 shares of $100 par convertible preferred stock for $110 per share. One share of preferred stock can be converted into three shares of Brad's $25 par common stock at the option of the preferred shareholder. On December 31, 1996, when the market value of the common stock was $40 per share, all of the preferred stock was converted. What amount should Brad credit to common stock and to additional paid-in capital: common stock as a result of the conversion?

	Common Stock	Additional Paid-In Capital
A.	$375,000	$175,000
B.	$375,000	$225,000
C.	$500,000	$50,000
D.	$600,000	$0

The correct answer is (A). *(CPA 1194 F-29)*
REQUIRED: The amounts credited to common stock and additional paid-in capital.
DISCUSSION: Brad received $550,000 (5,000 x $110) for the preferred stock converted to common stock. The par value of the 15,000 shares (5,000 x 3) of common stock is $375,000 (15,000 x $25). The remaining $175,000 ($550,000 – $375,000) is credited to additional paid-in capital.
Answer (B) is incorrect because $175,000 is credited to additional paid-in capital ($550,000 – $375,000). Answer (C) is incorrect because $500,000 is the par value of the preferred stock, not the common stock. Answer (D) is incorrect because $600,000 equals the fair value of the common stock at the date of conversion.

23. At December 31, 1996, a corporation has the following account balances:

Common stock ($10 par, 50,000 shares issued)	$500,000
8% preferred stock ($50 par, 10,000 shares issued)	500,000
Paid-in capital in excess of par on common stock	640,000
Paid-in capital in excess of par on preferred stock	20,000
Retained earnings	600,000

The preferred stock is cumulative, nonparticipating, and has a call price of $55 per share. The journal entry to record the redemption of all preferred stock on January 2, 1997 pursuant to the call provision is

A.
Preferred stock	$500,000	
Paid-in capital in excess of par: preferred	20,000	
Discount on preferred stock	30,000	
Cash		$550,000

B.
Preferred stock	$500,000	
Paid-in capital in excess of par: preferred	20,000	
Loss on redemption of preferred stock	30,000	
Cash		$550,000

C.
Preferred stock	$500,000	
Loss on redemption of preferred stock	50,000	
Retained earnings	300,000	
Cash		$550,000
Paid-in capital in excess of par: preferred		300,000

D.
Preferred stock	$500,000	
Paid-in capital in excess of par: preferred	20,000	
Retained earnings	30,000	
Cash		$550,000

The correct answer is (D). *(CIA 1188 IV-36)*
REQUIRED: The journal entry to record the redemption of preferred stock pursuant to the call provision.
DISCUSSION: The exercise of the call provision resulted in the redemption of the 10,000 shares of preferred stock issued and outstanding at the call price of $550,000 (10,000 shares x $55 call price per share). To eliminate the carrying value of the preferred stock and recognize the cash paid in this transaction, the required journal entry is to debit preferred stock for $500,000, debit paid-in capital in excess of par: preferred for $20,000, and credit cash for $550,000. The difference of $30,000 ($550,000 cash – $520,000 carrying value of the preferred stock) is charged to retained earnings. No loss is reported because GAAP do not permit the recognition of a gain or loss on transactions involving a company's own stock.
Answers (A), (B), and (C) are incorrect because the $30,000 excess of cash paid over the carrying value of the redeemed stock should be debited to retained earnings. Answer (C) is incorrect because paid-in capital in excess of par: preferred should be debited for $20,000.

24. Company X effects self-insurance against loss from fire by appropriating an amount of retained earnings each year equal to the amount that would otherwise be paid out as fire insurance premiums. According to current accounting literature, the procedure used by Company X is

A. Prohibited for external reporting purposes.

B. Acceptable provided that fire losses are not charged against the appropriation.

C. Acceptable provided that fire losses are charged against the appropriation.

D. Acceptable if the amount is shown outside the shareholders' equity section of the balance sheet.

The correct answer is (B). *(Publisher)*
REQUIRED: The true statement about an appropriation of retained earnings to disclose self-insurance against fire loss.
DISCUSSION: SFAS 5, *Accounting for Contingencies*, permits no accrual of an expense prior to the occurrence of the event for which a company self-insures because the value of the property diminishes only if the event actually occurs. But an appropriation of retained earnings is acceptable to disclose the self-insurance policy if, when a fire loss occurs, the entry appropriating retained earnings is reversed, and the loss is charged against income of the period of loss and not against retained earnings.
Answer (A) is incorrect because an appropriation of retained earnings for self-insurance is permissible. Answer (C) is incorrect because fire losses may never be charged against the appropriation of retained earnings. Answer (D) is incorrect because the procedure is acceptable only if the appropriation is shown within the shareholders' equity section of the balance sheet.

25. United, Inc.'s unadjusted current assets section and shareholders' equity section of its December 31, 1996 balance sheet are as follows:

Current Assets

Cash	$ 60,000
Investments in trading securities (including $300,000 of United, Inc. common stock)	400,000
Trade accounts receivable	340,000
Inventories	148,000
Total	$948,000

Shareholders' Equity

Common stock	$2,224,000
Retained earnings (deficit)	(224,000)
Total	$2,000,000

The investments and inventories are reported at their costs, which approximate fair values. In its 1996 statement of shareholders' equity, United's total amount of equity at December 31, 1996 is

- A. $2,224,000
- B. $2,000,000
- C. $1,924,000
- D. $1,700,000

The correct answer is (D). *(CPA 592 I-1)*
REQUIRED: The total amount of equity.
DISCUSSION: The $300,000 of United, Inc. common stock is treasury stock that should be reported as a contra item in the shareholders' equity section, not as a current asset. Hence, total equity is $1,700,000 ($2,224,000 common stock – $224,000 deficit in retained earnings – $300,000 treasury stock).

Answer (A) is incorrect because $2,224,000 equals the common stock. Answer (B) is incorrect because $2,000,000 omits the treasury stock. Answer (C) is incorrect because $1,924,000 does not consider the deficit in retained earnings.

18.2 Cash and Property Dividends

26. George Corporation declared a cash dividend of $10,000 on January 17. This dividend was payable to shareholders of record on February 10, and payment was made on March 2. As a result of this cash dividend, working capital will increase (decrease) on

	January 17	February 10
A.	$0	$0
B.	$10,000	$0
C.	$(10,000)	$0
D.	$(10,000)	$10,000

The correct answer is (C). *(CPA 1181 II-18)*
REQUIRED: The effect of a cash dividend on working capital.
DISCUSSION: On January 17, the date of declaration, retained earnings is debited and dividends payable credited. The declaration decreases working capital because a current liability is increased. On February 10, the record date, no entry is made and there is no effect on working capital. On March 2, when payment is made, both a current liability (dividends payable) and a current asset (cash) are decreased, with no net effect on working capital.

Answers (A) and (B) are incorrect because the declaration of a dividend decreases working capital on the date of declaration because a current liability is increased. Answer (D) is incorrect because no entry is made on the record date.

27. East Corp., a calendar-year company, had sufficient retained earnings in 1996 as a basis for dividends but was temporarily short of cash. East declared a dividend of $100,000 on April 1, 1996 and issued promissory notes to its shareholders in lieu of cash. The notes, which were dated April 1, 1996, had a maturity date of March 31, 1997 and a 10% interest rate. How should East account for the scrip dividend and related interest?

A. Debit retained earnings for $110,000 on April 1, 1996.

B. Debit retained earnings for $110,000 on March 31, 1997.

C. Debit retained earnings for $100,000 on April 1, 1996 and debit interest expense for $10,000 on March 31, 1997.

D. Debit retained earnings for $100,000 on April 1, 1996 and debit interest expense for $7,500 on December 31, 1996.

The correct answer is (D). *(CPA 594 F-31)*
    REQUIRED: The accounting for a scrip dividend and its related interest.
    DISCUSSION: When a scrip dividend is declared, retained earnings should be debited and scrip dividends (or notes) payable should be credited for the amount of the dividend ($100,000) excluding interest. Interest accrued on the scrip dividend is recorded as a debit to interest expense up to the balance sheet date with a corresponding credit for interest payable. Thus, interest expense will be debited and interest payable credited for $7,500 (9/12 x $100,000 x 10%) on 12/31/96.
    Answer (A) is incorrect because interest expense is recognized on the balance sheet date and on the date of payment, not on the date of declaration. Answer (B) is incorrect because $7,500 of the $10,000 interest expense should be recognized at year-end, and retained earnings should be debited on the date of declaration. Answer (C) is incorrect because $7,500 of the $10,000 interest expense should be recognized at year-end.

28. A company declared a cash dividend on its common stock on December 15, 1996, payable on January 12, 1997. How would this dividend affect shareholders' equity on the following dates?

	December 15, 1996	December 31, 1996	January 12, 1997
A.	Decrease	No effect	Decrease
B.	Decrease	No effect	No effect
C.	No effect	Decrease	No effect
D.	No effect	No effect	Decrease

The correct answer is (B). *(CPA 591 T-17)*
    REQUIRED: The effect on retained earnings of a cash dividend.
    DISCUSSION: When cash dividends are declared, a liability to the shareholders is created because the dividends must be paid once they are declared. At the declaration date, retained earnings must be debited, resulting in a decrease in retained earnings. The effect is to decrease total shareholders' equity (assets – liabilities) because liabilities are increased with no corresponding increase in assets. At the balance sheet date, no entry is made and there is no effect on shareholders' equity. When the cash dividends are subsequently paid, the dividends payable account is debited and a cash account credited. Thus, at the payment date, shareholders' equity is also not affected.
    Answer (A) is incorrect because payment has no effect on shareholders' equity. Answer (C) is incorrect because declaration decreases shareholders' equity, but at year-end has no effect. Answer (D) is incorrect because declaration decreases shareholders' equity, but payment has no effect.

29. On January 2, 1996, Lake Mining Co.'s board of directors declared a cash dividend of $400,000 to shareholders of record on January 18, 1996, payable on February 10, 1996. The dividend is permissible under law in Lake's state of incorporation. Selected data from Lake's December 31, 1995 balance sheet are as follows:

Accumulated depletion	$100,000
Capital stock	500,000
Additional paid-in capital	150,000
Retained earnings	300,000

The $400,000 dividend includes a liquidating dividend of

A. $0

B. $100,000

C. $150,000

D. $300,000

The correct answer is (B). *(CPA 594 F-32)*
    REQUIRED: The amount of a liquidating dividend.
    DISCUSSION: Companies whose major activity is the exploitation of depletable resources may pay dividends in amounts up to the sum of retained earnings and accumulated depletion. However, any distribution by a corporation to its shareholders in excess of the dollar balance in the retained earnings account is considered a liquidating dividend and return of capital to the shareholders. Consequently, the liquidating dividend equals $100,000 ($400,000 dividend – $300,000 RE).
    Answer (A) is incorrect because the company paid a liquidating dividend. Answer (C) is incorrect because $150,000 is the additional paid-in capital. Answer (D) is incorrect because $300,000 equals retained earnings.

30. On December 1, Charles Company's board of directors declared a cash dividend of $1.00 per share on the 50,000 shares of common stock outstanding. The company also has 5,000 shares of treasury stock. Shareholders of record on December 15 are eligible for the dividend, which is to be paid on January 1. On December 1, the company should

A. Make no accounting entry.

B. Debit retained earnings for $50,000.

C. Debit retained earnings for $55,000.

D. Debit retained earnings for $50,000 and paid-in capital for $5,000.

The correct answer is (B). *(CMA 1292 2-7)*
REQUIRED: The proper journal entry on the declaration date of a dividend.
DISCUSSION: Dividends are recorded on their declaration date by a debit to retained earnings and a credit to dividends payable. The dividend is the amount payable to all shares outstanding. Treasury stock is not eligible for dividends because it is not outstanding. Thus, the December 1 entry is to debit retained earnings and credit dividends payable for $50,000 (50,000 x $1).
Answer (A) is incorrect because a liability should be recorded. Answer (C) is incorrect because the treasury stock is not eligible for a dividend. Answer (D) is incorrect because paid-in capital is not affected by the declaration of a dividend.

31. Arp Corp.'s outstanding capital stock at December 15, 1996 consisted of the following:

• 30,000 shares of 5% cumulative preferred stock, par value $10 per share, fully participating as to dividends. No dividends were in arrears.

• 200,000 shares of common stock, par value $1 per share.

On December 15, 1996, Arp declared dividends of $100,000. What was the amount of dividends payable to Arp's common shareholders?

A. $10,000

B. $34,000

C. $40,000

D. $60,000

The correct answer is (C). *(CPA 1191 II-5)*
REQUIRED: The amount of dividends payable to common shareholders.
DISCUSSION: The stated rate of dividends must be paid to preferred shareholders before any amount is paid to common shareholders. Because no dividends are in arrears, this amount is $15,000 (5% x $10 par x 30,000 shares). The preferred stock is also fully participating. The preferred will participate equally in the cash dividend after a 5% return is paid on the common. The basic return to common shareholders is $10,000 (5% x 200,000 shares x $1 par). The total of the basic distributions to the shareholders is $25,000 ($15,000 + $10,000). The remaining $75,000 ($100,000 – $25,000) of the total cash dividend will be shared by all shareholders in proportion to the par values of the shares outstanding.
The aggregate par value of the preferred is $300,000 ($10 par x 30,000 shares). The aggregate par value of the common is $200,000 ($1 par x 200,000 shares). The distribution will therefore be in the ratio of 3:2, and $45,000 ($75,000 x 60%) is the participating share of the preferred shareholders. The balance of $30,000 ($75,000 – $45,000) will be paid to the common shareholders. The total amount of dividends payable on the common stock is $40,000 ($10,000 + $30,000).
Answer (A) is incorrect because $10,000 is the basic return to common shareholders. Answer (B) is incorrect because $34,000 results from assuming that no basic return is paid to the common shareholders. Answer (D) is incorrect because $60,000 is the amount paid to the preferred shareholders.

32. At December 31, 1995 and 1996, Apex Co. had 3,000 shares of $100 par, 5% cumulative preferred stock outstanding. No dividends were in arrears as of December 31, 1994. Apex did not declare a dividend during 1995. During 1996, Apex paid a cash dividend of $10,000 on its preferred stock. Apex should report dividends in arrears in its 1996 financial statements as a(n)

A. Accrued liability of $15,000.

B. Disclosure of $15,000.

C. Accrued liability of $20,000.

D. Disclosure of $20,000.

The correct answer is (D). *(CPA 594 F-8)*
REQUIRED: The amount and means of reporting preferred dividends in arrears.
DISCUSSION: Dividends in arrears on preferred stock are not an obligation of the company and are not recognized in the financial statements. However, the aggregate and per-share amounts of arrearages in cumulative preferred dividends should be disclosed on the face of the balance sheet or in the notes (APB 10). The aggregate amount in arrears is $20,000 [(2 years x 5% x $100 par x 3,000 shares) – $10,000 paid in 1996].
Answers (A) and (C) are incorrect because dividends in arrears do not meet recognition criteria. Answer (B) is incorrect because $15,000 is the arrearage for 1 year.

Questions 33 and 34 are based on the following information. Frey, Inc. was organized on January 2 with the following capital structure:

10% cumulative preferred stock,
   par value $100 and liquidation
   value $105; authorized, issued,
   and outstanding 1,000 shares $100,000
Common stock, par value $25;
   authorized 100,000 shares; issued
   and outstanding 10,000 shares $250,000

Frey's net income for the first year ending December 31 was $450,000, but no dividends were declared.

33. How much was Frey's book value per preferred share at December 31?

- A. $100
- B. $105
- C. $110
- D. $115

The correct answer is (D). *(CPA 585 I-14)*
   REQUIRED: The book value of a share of preferred stock when dividends are in arrears.
   DISCUSSION: The book value per share of cumulative preferred stock is its liquidation value plus any dividends in arrears. Thus, Frey's book value per share of preferred stock is the $105 liquidation value plus $10 ($100 x 10%) of dividends in arrears, or $115.
   Answer (A) is incorrect because $100 is the par value of the preferred stock without the recognition of the liquidation value and the dividends in arrears. Answer (B) is incorrect because $105 is the liquidation value without recognition of the dividends in arrears. Answer (C) is incorrect because $110 is the par value of the stock, plus the dividends in arrears.

34. How much was Frey's book value per common share at December 31?

- A. $45.00
- B. $68.50
- C. $69.50
- D. $70.00

The correct answer is (B). *(CPA 585 I-15)*
   REQUIRED: The book value per common share when cumulative preferred dividends are in arrears.
   DISCUSSION: The preferred shareholders' equity is the liquidation value of the preferred shares plus the preferred dividends in arrears. As calculated in the previous question, Frey's book value per preferred share is $115. The book value of Frey's 1,000 shares of cumulative preferred stock is therefore $115,000 ($115 x 1,000 shares). The total book value of the company is $800,000 ($100,000 par value of preferred stock + $250,000 par value of common stock + retained earnings equal to $450,000 of net income). Hence, $685,000 ($800,000 – $115,000) is the book value of the common stock, and book value per common share is $68.50 ($685,000 ÷ 10,000 shares).
   Answer (A) is incorrect because $45.00 results from net income this year. Answer (C) is incorrect because $69.50 results from reducing the value of the company by the liquidation value without the dividends in arrears. Answer (D) is incorrect because $70.00 results from reducing the value of the company by the par value of the preferred stock instead of the liquidation value plus the dividends in arrears.

35. A property dividend should be recorded in retained earnings at the property's

    A. Market value at date of declaration.

    B. Market value at date of issuance (payment).

    C. Book value at date of declaration.

    D. Book value at date of issuance.

The correct answer is (A). *(CPA 593 T-2)*

    REQUIRED: The method of accounting for the value of property dividend.

    DISCUSSION: When a property dividend is declared, the property to be distributed should be restated at market value. Any gain or loss should be recognized. The declared dividend is then recorded as a debit to retained earnings and a credit to property dividends payable.

    Answer (B) is incorrect because the market value is determined as of the declaration date. Answers (C) and (D) are incorrect because market value at the date of declaration is used.

36. Instead of the usual cash dividend, Evie Corp. declared and distributed a property dividend from its overstocked merchandise. The excess of the merchandise's carrying amount over its fair value should be

    A. Ignored.

    B. Reported as a separately disclosed reduction of retained earnings.

    C. Reported as an extraordinary loss, net of income taxes.

    D. Reported as a reduction in income before extraordinary items.

The correct answer is (D). *(CPA 592 T-36)*

    REQUIRED: The method of accounting for the excess of the carrying amount of a property dividend over its fair value.

    DISCUSSION: APB 29, *Accounting for Nonmonetary Transactions*, requires that a nonreciprocal transfer of nonmonetary assets to owners other than one made "in a spinoff or other form of reorganization or liquidation or in a plan that is in substance the rescission of a prior business combination" be recorded at the fair value of the asset transferred on the declaration date. This property dividend qualifies as such a nonreciprocal transfer. Thus, a loss should be recognized on the disposition of the asset. This loss on merchandise is an operating item, not an extraordinary loss.

    Answers (A) and (B) are incorrect because accounting for the property dividend at fair value gives rise to a loss that should be reported in the income statement. Answer (C) is incorrect because the loss does not meet the criteria of an extraordinary item.

37. On June 27, 1996, Brite Co. distributed to its common shareholders 100,000 outstanding common shares of its investment in Quick, Inc., an unrelated party. The carrying amount on Brite's books of Quick's $1 par common stock was $2 per share. Immediately after the distribution, the market price of Quick's stock was $2.50 per share. In its income statement for the year ended June 30, 1996, what amount should Brite report as gain before income taxes on disposal of the stock?

    A. $250,000

    B. $200,000

    C. $50,000

    D. $0

The correct answer is (C). *(CPA 593 I-45)*

    REQUIRED: The amount to be reported as gain before income taxes on disposal of stock.

    DISCUSSION: When a property dividend is declared the property to be distributed should be restated from carrying amount to fair value, with the resultant gain or loss recognized. Brite thus should report a gain of $50,000 [100,000 shares x ($2.50 – $2.00)].

    Answer (A) is incorrect because $250,000 is the fair value of the property dividend. Answer (B) is incorrect because $200,000 is the book value of the property dividend. Answer (D) is incorrect because a $50,000 gain should be recognized.

18.3 Stock Dividends and Stock Splits

38. The following data are extracted from the shareholders' equity section of the balance sheet of DAN Corporation:

	12/31/95	12/31/96
Common stock ($2 par value)	$100,000	$102,000
Paid-in capital in excess of par	50,000	58,000
Retained earnings	100,000	104,600

During 1996, the corporation declared and paid cash dividends of $15,000 and also declared and issued a stock dividend. There were no other changes in stock issued and outstanding during 1996. Net income for 1996 was

A. $4,600

B. $19,600

C. $21,600

D. $29,600

The correct answer is (D). *(CIA 1182 IV-6)*
REQUIRED: The net income for 1996 after payment of cash and stock dividends.
DISCUSSION: The cash dividends reduced retained earnings by $15,000. The stock dividend reduced retained earnings by $10,000, as determined from the changes in the contributed capital accounts [($102,000 + $58,000) − ($100,000 − $50,000)]. Hence, as shown below, net income was $29,600.

Retained Earnings			
		$100,000	Beginning
Cash dividend	$15,000		
Stock dividend	10,000		
		29,600	Net income
		$104,600	Ending

Answer (A) is incorrect because $4,600 is the increase in retained earnings for the year. Answer (B) is incorrect because $19,600 results from not reducing retained earnings by the stock dividend. Answer (C) is incorrect because $21,600 results from reducing retained earnings for a $2,000 stock dividend.

39. When fractional share rights are issued as part of a stock dividend, the rights are often not exercised. The entry to record forfeiture of these rights is

A. Stock rights outstanding
   Paid-in capital from forfeiture
      of stock rights

B. Stock rights outstanding
   Common stock

C. Retained earnings
   Common stock

D. Stock rights outstanding
   Dividends payable

The correct answer is (A). *(Publisher)*
REQUIRED: The journal entry to record forfeiture of stock rights.
DISCUSSION: When fractional share rights are issued as part of a stock dividend, retained earnings is debited and the stock rights outstanding account is credited. If the stock rights are forfeited, stock rights outstanding should be debited and paid-in capital from forfeiture of stock rights credited.

Answer (B) is incorrect because it is the entry to record the issuance of common stock for stock rights. Answer (C) is incorrect because it is the entry to record the issuance of common stock dividends at par. Answer (D) is incorrect because it is an entry to convert outstanding stock rights to a liability.

40. The following information was abstracted from the accounts of the Oar Corp. at year-end:

Total income since incorporation	$840,000
Total cash dividends paid	260,000
Proceeds from sale of donated stock	90,000
Total value of stock dividends distributed	60,000
Excess of proceeds over cost of treasury stock sold	140,000

What should be the current balance of retained earnings?

A. $520,000

B. $580,000

C. $610,000

D. $670,000

The correct answer is (A). *(CPA 1180 II-6)*
REQUIRED: The current balance of retained earnings.
DISCUSSION: To compute the current balance, one must know which transactions affected retained earnings. Total income since incorporation ($840,000) increased retained earnings, whereas both the cash dividends and the stock dividends ($260,000 + $60,000) decreased it. Proceeds from the sale of the donated stock (assuming it was not Oar Corp. stock) would have already been included in income to the extent of gain or loss. Proceeds from the sale of donated stock (assuming it was Oar Corp. stock) would increase additional paid-in capital and not affect retained earnings. The excess of proceeds over the cost of treasury stock also does not affect retained earnings because gains on treasury stock transactions are credited to paid-in capital. The current balance of retained earnings is therefore equal to $520,000 ($840,000 – $260,000 – $60,000).
Answer (B) is incorrect because $580,000 results from not reducing retained earnings by the value of stock dividends distributed. Answer (C) is incorrect because $610,000 results from adding the proceeds from the sale of donated stock. Answer (D) is incorrect because $670,000 results from including the proceeds from the sale of donated stock and not subtracting the total value of the stock dividends distributed.

41. Ray Corp. declared a 5% stock dividend on its 10,000 issued and outstanding shares of $2 par value common stock, which had a fair value of $5 per share before the stock dividend was declared. This stock dividend was distributed 60 days after the declaration date. By what amount did Ray's current liabilities increase as a result of the stock dividend declaration?

A. $0

B. $500

C. $1,000

D. $2,500

The correct answer is (A). *(CPA 592 II-5)*
REQUIRED: The increase in current liabilities as a result of the stock dividend declaration.
DISCUSSION: Declaration of a small stock dividend is not accounted for as a liability but as a reclassification of shareholders' equity. The entry is to debit retained earnings for the fair value of the stock (5% x 10,000 shares x $5 fair value = $2,500), credit stock dividend distributable at par (5% x 10,000 shares x $2 = $1,000), and credit additional paid-in capital for the excess of fair over par value ($2,500 – $1,000 = $1,500).
Answers (B), (C), and (D) are incorrect because no liability is recognized.

42. A corporation issuing stock should charge retained earnings for the market value of the shares issued in a(n)

A. Employee stock bonus.

B. Pooling of interests.

C. 10% stock dividend.

D. 2-for-1 stock split.

The correct answer is (C). *(CPA 1192 T-22)*
REQUIRED: The basis for charging retained earnings when stock is issued.
DISCUSSION: ARB 43, Chapter 7B, states that a small stock dividend (one in which the number of shares issued is fewer than 20 to 25% of those outstanding) should be accounted for by debiting retained earnings for the fair value of the stock and crediting a capital stock account for the par or stated value. A difference between the fair value and the par or stated value is credited to an additional paid-in capital account. Hence, retained earnings decreases, but total shareholders' equity does not change.
Answer (A) is incorrect because an employee stock bonus is currently recorded at its intrinsic value. Answer (B) is incorrect because, in a pooling of interests, owners' equity amounts of the participating entities are combined at current book values. Answer (D) is incorrect because a stock split has no effect on the capital accounts.

43. The following stock dividends were declared and distributed by Sol Corp.:

Percentage of Common Shares Outstanding at Declaration Date	Fair Value	Par Value
10	$15,000	$10,000
28	40,000	30,800

What aggregate amount should be debited to retained earnings for these stock dividends?

   A. $40,800

   B. $45,800

   C. $50,000

   D. $55,000

The correct answer is (B). *(CPA 591 II-12)*
   REQUIRED: The aggregate amount debited to retained earnings.
   DISCUSSION: A small stock dividend (one in which the number of shares issued is fewer than 20 to 25% of those outstanding) is recorded as a debit to retained earnings for the fair value of the stock issued and a credit to the capital stock accounts. A large stock dividend is a split-up effected in the form of a stock dividend, that is, one greater than 20 to 25% of the outstanding shares. It requires a debit to retained earnings at least equal to the legal requirement in the state of incorporation (usually the par or stated value of the shares). Thus, the aggregate amount debited to retained earnings is $45,800 ($15,000 fair value of the 10% dividend + $30,800 par value of the 28% dividend).
   Answer (A) is incorrect because $40,800 includes the par value of the small stock dividend. Answer (C) is incorrect because $50,000 equals the fair value of the large stock dividend and the par value of the small stock dividend. Answer (D) is incorrect because $55,000 includes the fair value of the large stock dividend.

44. Unlike a stock split, a stock dividend requires a formal journal entry in the financial accounting records because stock

   A. Dividends increase the relative book value of an individual's stock holding.

   B. Splits increase the relative book value of an individual's stock holdings.

   C. Dividends are payable on the date they are declared.

   D. Dividends represent a transfer from retained earnings to capital stock.

The correct answer is (D). *(CIA 580 IV-8)*
   REQUIRED: The reason a stock dividend requires a formal journal entry and a stock split does not.
   DISCUSSION: ARB 43, Chapter 7B, states that the purpose of a stock dividend is to provide evidence to the shareholders of their interest in accumulated earnings without distribution of cash or other property.
   Answers (A) and (B) are incorrect because stock dividends and stock splits have no effect on total shareholders' equity or on the book value of an individual shareholder's investment. Answer (C) is incorrect because dividends, whether stock, cash, or property, are usually payable on a date different from the declaration date.

45. On December 31, 1995, the shareholders' equity section of Bergen, Inc. was as follows:

Common stock, par value $10;

authorized 30,000 shares;	
issued and outstanding 9,000 shares	$ 90,000
Additional paid-in capital	116,000
Retained earnings	146,000
Total shareholders' equity	$352,000

On March 31, 1996, Bergen declared a 10% stock dividend. Accordingly, 900 shares were issued when the fair market value was $16 per share. For the 3 months ended March 31, 1996, Bergen sustained a net loss of $32,000. The balance of Bergen's retained earnings as of March 31, 1996 should be

   A. $99,600

   B. $105,000

   C. $108,600

   D. $114,000

The correct answer is (A). *(CPA 585 I-18)*
   REQUIRED: The retained earnings balance after a stock dividend and incurring a net loss.
   DISCUSSION: When the number of shares issued is fewer than 20 to 25% of the outstanding stock, the issuance is considered a small stock dividend. Retained earnings should be debited for the fair value of the stock distributed as a small stock dividend. Thus, $14,400 (900 Bergen shares x $16 market value) should be debited to retained earnings. Retained earnings should also be decreased by the net loss of $32,000. Thus, the balance of Bergen's retained earnings as of March 31 is $99,600 ($146,000 beginning balance – $14,400 small stock dividend – $32,000 net loss).
   Answer (B) is incorrect because $105,000 results from reducing retained earnings by the par value of the stock dividend. Answer (C) is incorrect because $108,600 results from reducing retained earnings by the difference between the fair market value and the par value. Answer (D) is incorrect because $114,000 results from not reducing retained earnings for the small stock dividend.

Questions 46 and 47 are based on the following information. The format below was used by Gee, Inc. for its 1996 statement of owners' equity:

	Common Stock $1 par	Additional Paid-in Capital	Retained Earnings
Balance at 1/1/96	$90,000	$800,000	$175,000
Additions and deductions:			
100% stock dividend			
5% stock dividend	_____	_____	_____
Balance at 12/31/96			

When both the 100% and the 5% stock dividends were declared, Gee's common stock was selling for more than its $1 par value.

46. How would the 5% stock dividend affect the additional paid-in capital and retained earnings amounts reported in Gee's 1996 statement of owners' equity?

	Additional Paid-in Capital	Retained Earnings
A.	Increase	Decrease
B.	Increase	Increase
C.	No change	Decrease
D.	No change	Increase

The correct answer is (A). *(CPA 592 I-3)*

REQUIRED: The effect of a 5% stock dividend on additional paid-in capital and retained earnings.

DISCUSSION: ARB 43, Chapter 7B, states that a small stock dividend (one in which the number of shares issued is fewer than 20 to 25% of those outstanding) should be accounted for by debiting retained earnings for the fair value of the stock and crediting a capital stock account for the par or stated value. A difference between the fair value and the par or stated value is credited to an additional paid-in capital account. Hence, additional paid-in capital increases and retained earnings decreases.

Answers (B), (C), and (D) are incorrect because additional paid-in capital increases and retained earnings decreases.

47. How would the 100% stock dividend affect the additional paid-in capital and retained earnings amounts reported in Gee's 1996 statement of owners' equity?

	Additional Paid-in Capital	Retained Earnings
A.	Increase	Increase
B.	Increase	Decrease
C.	No change	Increase
D.	No change	Decrease

The correct answer is (D). *(CPA 592 I-2)*

REQUIRED: The effect of a 100% stock dividend on additional paid-in capital and retained earnings.

DISCUSSION: A large stock dividend (one greater than 20 to 25% of the outstanding shares) requires a debit to retained earnings at least equal to the legal requirement in the state of incorporation (usually the par or stated value of the shares). Thus, if retained earnings is debited for the par value of the shares, additional paid-in capital will be unaffected although retained earnings will decrease.

Answers (A), (B), and (C) are incorrect because additional paid-in capital will be unaffected although retained earnings will decrease.

48. Effective April 27, 1996, the shareholders of Dorr Corp. approved a 2-for-1 split of the company's common stock and an increase in authorized common shares from 100,000 shares (par value $20 per share) to 200,000 shares (par value $10 per share). Dorr's shareholders' equity accounts immediately before issuance of the stock split shares were as follows:

Common stock, par value $20; 100,000 shares authorized; 50,000 shares outstanding	$1,000,000
Additional paid-in capital ($3 per share on issuance of common stock)	150,000
Retained earnings	1,350,000

The stock split shares were issued on June 30, 1996. In Dorr's June 30, 1996 statement of shareholders' equity, the balances of additional paid-in capital and retained earnings are

	Additional Paid-in Capital	Retained Earnings
A.	$0	$500,000
B.	$150,000	$350,000
C.	$150,000	$1,350,000
D.	$1,150,000	$350,000

The correct answer is (C). *(CPA 589 I-13)*
REQUIRED: The effect of a 2-for-1 stock split on additional paid-in capital and retained earnings.
DISCUSSION: A 2-for-1 stock split is a nonreciprocal transfer of a company's own shares to its common shareholders generally for the purpose of reducing the unit market price of the shares. The purpose is to increase their marketability and broaden their distribution. The transaction described will increase the number of shares outstanding to 100,000 (50,000 shares x 2). The par value will be reduced to $10 ($20 ÷ 2), but the capital accounts will be unaffected. To effect a stock split, no formal entry is necessary because no capitalization of retained earnings occurs. Thus, additional paid-in capital ($150,000) and retained earnings ($1,350,000) will not change.
Answers (A), (B), and (D) are incorrect because a 2-for-1 stock split will affect only the number of shares outstanding and the par value. The capital accounts will remain unaffected in total.

18.4 Treasury Stock Transactions

49. Gains and losses on the purchase and resale of treasury stock may be reflected only in

A. Paid-in capital accounts.

B. Income, paid-in capital, and retained earnings accounts.

C. Retained earnings and paid-in capital accounts.

D. Income and retained earnings accounts.

The correct answer is (C). *(Publisher)*
REQUIRED: The accounts affected by gains and losses on treasury stock transactions.
DISCUSSION: Gains on treasury stock transactions must be credited to paid-in capital. Losses on treasury stock transactions may be charged to either retained earnings or paid-in capital, depending on the circumstances (APB 6, *Status of Accounting Research Bulletins*).
Answer (A) is incorrect because retained earnings may sometimes be charged for losses on treasury stock transactions. Answers (B) and (D) are incorrect because capital transactions in treasury stock do not affect income.

50. The acquisition of treasury stock will cause the number of shares outstanding to decrease if the treasury stock is accounted for by the

	Cost Method	Par Value Method
A.	Yes	No
B.	No	No
C.	Yes	Yes
D.	No	Yes

The correct answer is (C). *(CPA 590 T-13)*
REQUIRED: The effect of the acquisition of treasury stock on the number of shares outstanding.
DISCUSSION: When treasury stock is acquired, the effect will be to decrease the number of shares of common stock outstanding whether the treasury stock is accounted for by the cost method or the par value method.
Answers (A), (B), and (D) are incorrect because, when treasury stock is acquired, the number of shares outstanding will decrease under both the cost method and the par value method.

51. Treasury stock transactions may result in

A. Increases in the balance of retained earnings.

B. Increases or decreases in the amount of net income.

C. Decreases in the balance of retained earnings.

D. Increases or decreases in the amount of shares authorized to be issued.

The correct answer is (C). *(J.N. McKenna)*
REQUIRED: The effect of treasury stock transactions.
DISCUSSION: Under the par value method, when treasury shares are purchased for a price greater than the par value, retained earnings is debited for the excess of the purchase price over the par value if there is no existing paid-in capital from past treasury stock transactions or if the existing credit balance is insufficient to absorb the excess. Under the cost method, if the subsequent resale price of the treasury shares is less than the original acquisition price, it may be necessary to charge retained earnings for a portion or all of the excess of the original purchase price over the sales price.

Answer (A) is incorrect because equity credits from treasury stock transactions would affect paid-in capital accounts, not retained earnings. Answer (B) is incorrect because treasury stock transactions have no effect on net income. Answer (D) is incorrect because treasury stock transactions affect only the number of outstanding shares, not the authorized number.

52. In 1994, Fogg, Inc. issued $10 par value common stock for $25 per share. No other common stock transactions occurred until March 31, 1996, when Fogg acquired some of the issued shares for $20 per share and retired them. Which of the following statements correctly states an effect of this acquisition and retirement?

A. 1996 net income is decreased.

B. 1996 net income is increased.

C. Additional paid-in capital is decreased.

D. Retained earnings is increased.

The correct answer is (C). *(CPA 593 T-10)*
REQUIRED: The effect of the acquisition and retirement of a company's stock for less than the issue price.
DISCUSSION: When shares of common stock are reacquired and retired, contributed capital should be debited for the amount that was credited upon the issuance of the securities. In addition, because the acquisition of a company's own shares is an equity transaction, no gain or loss should be reflected in the determination of income. The entry is to debit common stock at par ($10 x number of shares) and additional paid-in capital [($25 – $10) x number of shares], and to credit additional paid-in capital from retirement of common stock [($25 – $20) x number of shares] and cash ($20 x number of shares). The effect is to decrease additional paid-in capital.

Answers (A) and (B) are incorrect because net income is not affected. Answer (D) is incorrect because retained earnings may not be increased because of treasury stock transactions.

53. Day Corp. holds 10,000 shares of its $10 par value common stock as treasury stock reacquired in 1994 for $120,000. On December 12, 1996, Day reissued all 10,000 shares for $190,000. Under the cost method of accounting for treasury stock, the reissuance resulted in a credit to

A. Capital stock of $100,000.

B. Retained earnings of $70,000.

C. Gain on sale of investments of $70,000.

D. Additional paid-in capital of $70,000.

The correct answer is (D). *(CPA 1188 I-44)*
REQUIRED: The effect of the reissuance of treasury stock accounted for under the cost method.
DISCUSSION: When treasury stock accounted for under the cost method is acquired, the treasury stock account is debited for the amount of the purchase price. If it is subsequently reissued for a price greater than its carrying value, the excess is credited to additional paid-in capital. For this transaction, the excess is $70,000 ($190,000 – $120,000).

Answer (A) is incorrect because the capital stock account is unaffected by purchases and subsequent resales of treasury stock accounted for by the cost method. Answers (B) and (C) are incorrect because gains on treasury stock transactions may not be credited to either income or retained earnings.

54. On December 31, 1996, Pack Corp.'s board of directors canceled 50,000 shares of $2.50 par value common stock held in treasury at an average cost of $13 per share. Before recording the cancellation of the treasury stock, Pack had the following balances in its shareholder's equity accounts:

Common stock	$540,000
Additional paid-in capital	750,000
Retained earnings	900,000
Treasury stock, at cost	650,000

In its balance sheet at December 31, 1996, Pack should report common stock outstanding of

A. $0

B. $250,000

C. $415,000

D. $540,000

The correct answer is (C). *(CPA 1192 II-50)*
REQUIRED: The common stock outstanding after cancellation of the treasury stock.
DISCUSSION: The treasury shares had an aggregate par value of $125,000 (50,000 shares x $2.50). Consequently, the common stock outstanding after their retirement is $415,000 ($540,000 par value of issued common stock – $125,000).
Answer (A) is incorrect because 166,000 shares ($415,000 ÷ $2.50) of common stock remain outstanding. Answer (B) is incorrect because $250,000 is the difference between retained earnings and the cost of the treasury stock. Answer (D) is incorrect because $540,000 is the par value of the issued shares prior to cancellation of the treasury stock.

55. Cross Corp. had outstanding 2,000 shares of 11% preferred stock, $50 par. On August 8, 1996, Cross redeemed and retired 25% of these shares for $22,500. On that date, Cross's additional paid-in capital from preferred stock totaled $30,000. To record this transaction, Cross should debit (credit) its capital accounts as follows:

	Preferred Stock	Additional Paid-in Capital	Retained Earnings
A.	$25,000	$ 7,500	$(10,000)
B.	$25,000	--	$ (2,500)
C.	$25,000	$(2,500)	--
D.	$22,500	--	--

The correct answer is (C). *(CPA 1192 II-42)*
REQUIRED: The accounting for redemption and retirement of preferred stock.
DISCUSSION: Under the cost method, the entry to record a treasury stock purchase is to debit treasury stock at cost ($22,500) and credit cash. The entry to retire this stock is to debit preferred stock at par [(25% x 2,000 shares) x $50 = $25,000], credit treasury stock at cost ($22,500), and credit additional paid-in capital from preferred stock ($2,500). No entry to retained earnings is necessary.
Answers (A) and (B) are incorrect because retained earnings is not affected. Answer (D) is incorrect because preferred stock is debited for the par value of the retired shares.

56. Holtrup Company had 100,000 shares of $4 par value common stock outstanding on June 12, 1996. On this date, Holtrup acquired 1,000 of its own shares as treasury stock at a cost of $12 per share. The acquisition was accounted for by the cost method. As a result of this treasury stock purchase,

A. Total assets and total shareholders' equity decreased.

B. Total assets and total shareholders' equity were unaffected.

C. Total assets, retained earnings, and total shareholders' equity decreased.

D. Total assets were unaffected, but retained earnings decreased.

The correct answer is (A). *(CMA 1288 4-22)*
REQUIRED: The effect on the balance sheet of an acquisition of treasury stock accounted for by the cost method.
DISCUSSION: Under the cost method, the acquisition of treasury stock is recorded as a debit to treasury stock and a credit to cash equal to the amount of the purchase price. This transaction results in a decrease in both total assets and total shareholders' equity.
Answer (B) is incorrect because both total assets and total shareholders' equity decrease. Answer (C) is incorrect because retained earnings are unaffected. Answer (D) is incorrect because total assets decrease and retained earnings are unaffected.

57. In 1996, Seda Corp. acquired 6,000 shares of its own $1 par value common stock at $18 per share. In 1997, Seda reissued 3,000 of these shares at $25 per share. Seda uses the cost method to account for its treasury stock transactions. What accounts and amounts should Seda credit in 1997 to record the reissuance of the 3,000 shares?

	Treasury Stock	Additional Paid-in Capital	Retained Earnings	Common Stock
A.	$54,000		$21,000	
B.	$54,000	$21,000		
C.		$72,000		$3,000
D.		$51,000	$21,000	$3,000

The correct answer is (B). *(CPA 1191 II-7)*

REQUIRED: The accounts and amounts to be credited when treasury stock is reissued.

DISCUSSION: Under the cost method, the treasury stock account should be debited for the purchase price. When this stock is subsequently reissued for an amount greater than its acquisition cost, the excess should be credited to additional paid-in capital. The 3,000 shares were purchased as treasury stock for $54,000 (3,000 shares x $18 per share). They were reissued for $75,000 (3,000 shares x $25 per share). Under the cost method, the carrying value of the 3,000 shares was $54,000. When these shares are reissued, the treasury stock account should be credited for $54,000, with the remaining $21,000 ($75,000 – $54,000) credited to additional paid-in capital.

Answer (A) is incorrect because additional paid-in capital, not retained earnings, should be credited. Answer (C) is incorrect because additional paid-in capital should be credited for $21,000 and treasury stock for $54,000. Common stock is unaffected. Answer (D) is incorrect because additional paid in capital should be credited for $21,000, and retained earnings and common stock are unaffected.

58. At its date of incorporation, Glean, Inc. issued 100,000 shares of its $10 par common stock at $11 per share. During the current year, Glean acquired 30,000 shares of its common stock at a price of $16 per share and accounted for them by the cost method. Subsequently, these shares were reissued at a price of $12 per share. Glean had made no other issuances or acquisitions of its own common stock. What effect does the reissuance of the stock have on the following accounts?

	Retained Earnings	Additional Paid-in Capital
A.	Decrease	Decrease
B.	No effect	Decrease
C.	Decrease	No effect
D.	No effect	No effect

The correct answer is (C). *(CPA 1190 T-33)*

REQUIRED: The effect of a reissuance of treasury stock on retained earnings and additional paid-in capital.

DISCUSSION: When shares are issued for an amount greater than their par value, the difference is credited to additional paid-in capital. Under the cost method, the treasury stock account should be debited for the price of reacquired shares. If the treasury stock is subsequently reissued for an amount less than its acquisition cost but greater than its original issuance price, the difference between the acquisition cost and the reissuance price should be recorded as a decrease in additional paid-in capital from treasury stock transactions. However, if this account has a $0 balance, retained earnings is decreased. Thus, Glean must debit cash for $360,000 ($12 reissuance price per share x 30,000 shares), debit (decrease) retained earnings for $120,000 [($16 cost per share – $12) x 30,000 shares], and credit treasury stock for $480,000 ($16 cost per share x 30,000 shares). As long as the reissuance price is greater than the original issuance price, additional paid-in capital will not be affected.

Answers (A), (B), and (D) are incorrect because, upon the reissuance of treasury stock, retained earnings will be decreased. Also, when the reissuance price is greater than the original issuance price, additional paid-in capital will not be affected.

59. Grid Corp. acquired some of its own common shares at a price greater than both their par value and original issue price but less than their book value. Grid uses the cost method of accounting for treasury stock. What is the impact of this acquisition on total shareholders' equity and the book value per common share?

	Total Share-holders' Equity	Book Value per Share
A.	Increase	Increase
B.	Increase	Decrease
C.	Decrease	Increase
D.	Decrease	Decrease

The correct answer is (C). *(CPA 1191 T-40)*
REQUIRED: The impact of the acquisition on total shareholders' equity and the book value per common share.
DISCUSSION: Under the cost method, the acquisition of treasury stock is recorded as a debit to treasury stock and a credit to cash equal to the amount of the purchase price. This transaction results in a decrease in both total assets and total shareholders' equity because treasury stock is a contra-equity account. Moreover, if the acquisition cost is less than book value, book value per share will increase.
Answers (A), (B), and (D) are incorrect because total shareholders' equity will decrease and book value per share will increase.

60. Posy Corp. acquired treasury shares at an amount greater than their par value but less than their original issue price. Compared with the cost method of accounting for treasury stock, does the par value method report a greater amount for additional paid-in capital and a greater amount for retained earnings?

	Additional Paid-in Capital	Retained Earnings
A.	Yes	Yes
B.	Yes	No
C.	No	No
D.	No	Yes

The correct answer is (C). *(CPA 1191 T-39)*
REQUIRED: The effect of the par value method on additional paid-in capital and retained earnings compared with that of the cost method.
DISCUSSION: Under the cost method, the purchase of treasury stock has no effect on additional paid-in capital and retained earnings. Under the par value method, given that the acquisition cost is greater than par but less than the original issue price, treasury stock is debited at par and cash is credited for the purchase price. Additional paid-in capital is debited and additional paid-in capital from treasury stock transactions is credited for the difference between par value and the purchase price. Hence, additional paid-in capital and retained earnings are not affected under either method.
Answers (A), (B), and (D) are incorrect because the par value method does not report a greater amount for additional paid-in capital or retained earnings.

61. On incorporation, Dee, Inc. issued common stock at a price in excess of its par value. No other stock transactions occurred except that treasury stock was acquired for an amount exceeding this issue price. If Dee uses the par value method of accounting for treasury stock appropriate for retired stock, what is the effect of the acquisition on the following?

	Net Common Stock	Additional Paid-in Capital	Retained Earnings
A.	No effect	Decrease	No effect
B.	Decrease	Decrease	Decrease
C.	Decrease	No effect	Decrease
D.	No effect	Decrease	Decrease

The correct answer is (B). *(CPA 591 T-18)*
REQUIRED: The effects of a purchase of treasury stock accounted for under the par value method.
DISCUSSION: Under the par value method, treasury stock is debited at par value, and the amount is reported as a reduction of common stock. The purchase also results in the removal of the additional paid-in capital associated with the original issue of the shares. Given that no other stock transactions occurred and that treasury stock was acquired for an amount exceeding the issue price, the balancing debit for the excess of the acquisition price over the issue price is to retained earnings. If additional paid-in capital from treasury stock transactions had been previously recorded, the balancing debit would be to that account but only to the extent of its credit balance. Thus, retained earnings is also decreased.
Answers (A), (C), and (D) are incorrect because net common stock, additional paid-in capital, and retained earnings are decreased.

62. Treasury stock was acquired for cash at a price in excess of its original issue price. The treasury stock was subsequently reissued for cash at a price in excess of its acquisition price. Assuming that the par value method of accounting for treasury stock transactions is used, what is the effect on total shareholders' equity of each of the following events?

	Acquisition of Treasury Stock	Reissuance of Treasury Stock
A.	Decrease	No effect
B.	Decrease	Increase
C.	Increase	Decrease
D.	No effect	No effect

18.5 Bankruptcies and Quasi-Reorganizations

63. Kent Co. filed a voluntary bankruptcy petition on August 15, 1996. The statement of affairs reflects the following amounts:

	Book Value	Estimated Current Value
Assets:		
Assets pledged with fully secured creditors	$ 300,000	$370,000
Assets pledged with partially secured creditors	180,000	120,000
Free assets	420,000	320,000
	$ 900,000	$810,000
Liabilities:		
Liabilities with priority	$ 70,000	
Fully secured creditors	260,000	
Partially secured creditors	200,000	
Unsecured creditors	540,000	
	$1,070,000	

Assume that the assets are converted to cash at the estimated current values and the business is liquidated. What amount of cash will be available to pay unsecured nonpriority claims?

A. $240,000

B. $280,000

C. $320,000

D. $360,000

The correct answer is (B). *(CPA 590 T-15)*
REQUIRED: The effect on total shareholders' equity of treasury stock transactions accounted for under the par value method.
DISCUSSION: The par value method treats the acquisition of treasury stock as a constructive retirement and its resale as a new issuance of stock. Thus, the acquisition of treasury stock will be reflected as a decrease in total shareholders' equity. The reissuance will be accounted for as an increase in total shareholders' equity.
Answers (A), (C), and (D) are incorrect because, under the par value method, acquisition of treasury stock is treated as a constructive retirement which will reduce total shareholders' equity. The reissuance of treasury stock is treated as a resale and will increase total shareholder's equity.

The correct answer is (D). *(CPA 1190 I-31)*
REQUIRED: The amount of cash available to pay unsecured nonpriority claims.
DISCUSSION: The liabilities to partially secured creditors total $200,000, and the assets pledged to secure these claims can be sold for $120,000. With respect to the $80,000 ($200,000 – $120,000) difference, these claimants have the status of general unsecured creditors. When converted to cash, the $370,000 of assets pledged with fully secured creditors and the $320,000 of free assets provide $690,000 to satisfy the $70,000 of liabilities with priority and the $260,000 of liabilities to fully secured creditors. Consequently, $360,000 ($690,000 – $70,000 – $260,000) is the amount of cash that will be available to pay unsecured nonpriority claims.
Answer (A) is incorrect because $240,000 results from reducing the remaining assets left to pay the unsecured nonpriority claims by the $120,000 that is paid to the partially secured creditors. Answer (B) is incorrect because $280,000 results from not treating the $80,000 ($200,000 – $120,000) remaining partially secured creditors claims as unsecured claims. Answer (C) is incorrect because $320,000 is the current value of the free assets.

64. Seco Corp. was forced into bankruptcy and is in the process of liquidating assets and paying claims. Unsecured claims will be paid at the rate of $.40 on the dollar. Hale holds a $30,000 noninterest-bearing note receivable from Seco collateralized by an asset with a book value of $35,000 and a liquidation value of $5,000. The amount to be realized by Hale on this note is

A. $5,000

B. $12,000

C. $15,000

D. $17,000

The correct answer is (C). *(CPA 591 II-14)*
REQUIRED: The total amount of cash to be realized from a partially unsecured claim.
DISCUSSION: Seco has a secured claim for the $5,000 liquidation value of the asset. The remaining $25,000 ($30,000 note – $5,000) is an unsecured claim. Given that unsecured claims will be paid at the rate of $.40 on the dollar, Seco will receive $10,000 ($25,000 x 40%) from its unsecured claim. The total amount to be realized is $15,000 ($5,000 + $10,000).
Answer (A) is incorrect because $5,000 is the amount of the secured claim. Answer (B) is incorrect because $12,000 results from treating the entire claim as unsecured, which would be paid $.40 on the dollar. Answer (D) is incorrect because $17,000 results from adding the $5,000 secured portion of the claim and the amount that would be paid if the entire amount were unsecured.

65. Kamy Corp. is in liquidation under Chapter 7 of the Federal Bankruptcy Code. The bankruptcy trustee has established a new set of books for the bankruptcy estate. After assuming custody of the estate, the trustee discovered an unrecorded invoice of $1,000 for machinery repairs performed before the bankruptcy filing. In addition, a truck with a carrying amount of $20,000 was sold for $12,000 cash. This truck was bought and paid for in the year before the bankruptcy. What amount should be debited to estate equity as a result of these transactions?

A. $0

B. $1,000

C. $8,000

D. $9,000

The correct answer is (D). *(CPA 592 II-10)*
REQUIRED: The amount debited to estate equity.
DISCUSSION: A trustee may continue to use the debtor's books or may open a new set. When a new set of books is opened, assets and liabilities are recorded at book value. Any unrecorded assets or liabilities discovered by the trustee as well as the estate's gains, losses, and liquidation expenses are entered in the estate equity account. Thus, the $1,000 of repairs (a liability and an expense) and the $8,000 loss on the sale of the truck are charges to estate equity, for a total of $9,000.
Answer (A) is incorrect because $9,000 should be charged to estate equity. Answer (B) is incorrect because $1,000 does not reflect the estate's loss on the sale of the truck. Answer (C) is incorrect because $8,000 does not reflect the unrecorded liability for repairs.

66. Wood Corp., a debtor-in-possession under Chapter 11 of the Federal Bankruptcy Code, granted an equity interest to a creditor in full settlement of a $28,000 debt owed to the creditor. At the date of this transaction, the equity interest had a fair value of $25,000. What amount should Wood recognize as an extraordinary gain on restructuring of debt?

A. $0

B. $3,000

C. $25,000

D. $28,000

The correct answer is (B). *(CPA 592 II-9)*
REQUIRED: The amount recognized as an extraordinary gain on restructuring of debt by a debtor that has granted an equity interest.
DISCUSSION: According to SFAS 15, a debtor that grants an equity interest in full settlement of a payable should account for the equity interest at fair value. The difference between the fair value of the equity interest and the carrying amount of the payable is an extraordinary gain. Consequently, Wood will recognize an extraordinary gain of $3,000 ($28,000 debt – $25,000 fair value of the equity interest).
Answer (A) is incorrect because an extraordinary gain should be recognized. Answer (C) is incorrect because $25,000 is the fair value of the equity interest. Answer (D) is incorrect because $28,000 is the carrying amount of the debt.

67. On December 30, 1996, Hale Corp. paid $400,000 cash and issued 80,000 shares of its $1 par value common stock to its unsecured creditors on a pro rata basis pursuant to a reorganization plan under Chapter 11 of the bankruptcy statutes. Hale owed these unsecured creditors a total of $1,200,000. Hale's common stock was trading at $1.25 per share on December 30, 1996. As a result of this transaction, Hale's total shareholder's equity had a net increase of

  A. $1,200,000

  B. $800,000

  C. $100,000

  D. $80,000

The correct answer is (B). *(CPA 593 II-18)*
  REQUIRED: The net increase in shareholder's equity immediately after the Chapter 11 reorganization.
  DISCUSSION: According to SFAS 15, a debtor that grants an equity interest in settlement of a payable should account for the equity interest at fair value. This will result in an increase in shareholders' equity of $100,000 (80,000 shares x $1.25). Because $400,000 in cash and a $100,000 equity interest are accepted as settlement of a $1,200,000 debt, a $700,000 ($1,200,000 – $400,000 – $100,000) extraordinary gain will also be recognized and result in an increase in shareholders' equity (retained earnings). Accordingly, the net increase in total shareholders' equity is $800,000 ($100,000 + $700,000).
  Answer (A) is incorrect because $1,200,000 is the amount of the debt. Answer (C) is incorrect because $100,000 is the increase in contributed capital. Answer (D) is incorrect because $80,000 is the increase in common stock.

68. The primary purpose of a quasi-reorganization is to give a corporation the opportunity to

  A. Obtain relief from its creditors.

  B. Revalue understated assets to their fair values.

  C. Eliminate a deficit in retained earnings.

  D. Distribute the stock of a newly created subsidiary to its shareholders in exchange for part of their stock in the corporation.

The correct answer is (C). *(CPA 1194 F-37)*
  REQUIRED: The purpose of a quasi-reorganization.
  DISCUSSION: A quasi-reorganization is undertaken to reduce a deficit in retained earnings to zero. The purpose is to permit the corporation to pay dividends in the near future.
  Answer (A) is incorrect because a quasi-reorganization is an accounting adjustment. It offers no relief from creditors. Answer (B) is incorrect because assets are usually written down to fair value. Answer (D) is incorrect because a quasi-reorganization does not entail an exchange of stock.

69. When a company goes through a quasi-reorganization, its balance sheet carrying amounts are stated at

  A. Original cost.

  B. Original book value.

  C. Replacement value.

  D. Fair value.

The correct answer is (D). *(CPA 1192 T-19)*
  REQUIRED: The amounts at which balance sheet accounts are stated after a quasi-reorganization.
  DISCUSSION: ARB 43, Chapter 7A, requires that quasi-reorganization be accomplished first by revaluing assets to fair values, a process that usually increases the deficit in retained earnings. Paid-in capital or its equivalent then must be available or must be created to provide a source of capital against which the deficit may be written off.
  Answers (A), (B), and (C) are incorrect because balance sheet amounts are stated at fair value.

Questions 70 and 71 are based on the following information. Gaston Co. has sustained heavy losses over a period of time. Conditions warrant that Gaston undergo a quasi-reorganization at December 31. Selected balance sheet items prior to the quasi-reorganization are as follows:

Inventory was recorded in the accounting records at December 31 at its market value of $6,000,000. Cost was $6,500,000.

Property, plant, and equipment was recorded in the accounting records at December 31 at $12,000,000, net of accumulated depreciation. The appraised value was $8,000,000.

Shareholders' equity on December 31 was as follows:

Common stock, par value $10 per share; authorized, issued and outstanding, 700,000 shares	$7,000,000
Capital in excess of par	1,600,000
Retained earnings (deficit)	(900,000)
	$7,700,000

Under the terms of the quasi-reorganization, the par value of the common stock is to be reduced from $10 per share to $5 per share.

---

70. Immediately after the quasi-reorganization has been accomplished, the total of shareholders' equity should be

A. $3,300,000

B. $3,500,000

C. $3,700,000

D. $4,200,000

The correct answer is (C). *(CPA 1180 II-17)*
REQUIRED: The total shareholders' equity immediately after the quasi-reorganization.
DISCUSSION: The first step in a quasi-reorganization is to revalue assets at their current fair values. The inventory is already recorded in the accounting records at its market value of $6,000,000. The property, plant, and equipment account should be reduced by $4,000,000 to reflect its appraised value. The corresponding debit will be to retained earnings, increasing the deficit to $4,900,000. To eliminate the deficit, enough capital in excess of par must be created to offset its full amount. This is accomplished by debiting the par value of the outstanding common stock and crediting capital in excess of par for $3,300,000 ($4,900,000 – $1,600,000). The final entry is a debit to capital in excess of par and a credit to retained earnings for $4,900,000.

These entries reduce total shareholders' equity to $3,700,000 ($7,700,000 – $4,000,000 revaluation of assets).

Answer (A) is incorrect because $3,300,000 is the amount that is credited to capital in excess of par to reduce the deficit in retained earnings. Answer (B) is incorrect because $3,500,000 is the combined difference between cost and fair market value for the inventory and property plant and equipment. Answer (D) is incorrect because $4,200,000 results when total retained earnings is reduced by the difference between cost and fair market value for the inventory and property plant and equipment.

---

71. Immediately after the quasi-reorganization has been accomplished, retained earnings (deficit) should be

A. $0

B. $(200,000)

C. $(4,400,000)

D. $(4,900,000)

The correct answer is (A). *(CPA 1180 II-18)*
REQUIRED: The amount in retained earnings after the quasi-reorganization.
DISCUSSION: Retained earnings should have a zero balance after the quasi-reorganization because the purpose of the procedure is to eliminate the deficit therein. Capital in excess of par may also have a zero balance, although that is not a requirement of the procedure.

Answers (B), (C), and (D) are incorrect because the main purpose of a quasi-reorganization is to eliminate any deficit in retained earnings.

72. In applying the quasi-reorganization to a consolidated entity,

A. The quasi-reorganization may be applied only to the parent company.

B. All losses should be written off against paid-in capital prior to charging retained earnings.

C. Paid-in capital cannot arise as a result of the transaction.

D. All consolidated retained earnings should be eliminated if any part of a loss is to be charged to paid-in capital.

The correct answer is (D). *(Publisher)*

REQUIRED: The correct statement about applying a quasi-reorganization to a consolidated entity.

DISCUSSION: Consistent with the treatment of an individual enterprise, all consolidated retained earnings should be eliminated in a quasi-reorganization of a consolidated entity by a charge to paid-in capital.

Answer (A) is incorrect because the procedure may be applied to the parent and/or some or all subsidiaries. Answer (B) is incorrect because losses are first written off to retained earnings. The retained earnings deficit is then written off to paid-in capital. Answer (C) is incorrect because, if the legal capital is reduced by more than the deficit, paid-in capital from quasi-reorganization arises.

18.6 Rights and Warrants

73. On November 2, 1995, Finsbury, Inc. issued warrants to its shareholders giving them the right to purchase additional $20 par value common shares at a price of $30. The shareholders exercised all warrants on March 1, 1996. The shares had market prices of $33, $35, and $40 on November 2, 1995, December 31, 1995, and March 1, 1996, respectively. What were the effects of the warrants on Finsbury's additional paid-in capital and net income?

	Additional Paid-in Capital	Net Income
A.	Increased in 1996	No effect
B.	Increased in 1995	No effect
C.	Increased in 1996	Decreased in 1995 and 1996
D.	Increased in 1995	Decreased in 1995 and 1996

The correct answer is (A). *(CPA 1193 T-15)*

REQUIRED: The effects on additional paid-in capital and net income when warrants are issued and exercised.

DISCUSSION: When stock rights and warrants are issued for no consideration, only a memorandum entry is made. Consequently, common stock and additional paid-in capital are not affected. However, when warrants are exercised and stock is issued, the issuing company will reflect the proceeds as an increase in common stock and additional paid-in capital. Consequently, Finsbury will increase additional paid-in capital in 1996 when stock is issued, but net income will not be affected.

Answer (B) is incorrect because only a memorandum entry is made in 1995. Answer (C) is incorrect because net income is not affected. Answer (D) is incorrect because only a memorandum entry is made in 1995, and net income is not affected.

74. Tem Co. issued rights to its existing shareholders without consideration. A shareholder received a right to buy one share for each 20 shares held. The exercise price was in excess of par value but less than the current market price. Retained earnings decreases when

	Rights Are Issued	Rights Are Exercised
A.	Yes	Yes
B.	Yes	No
C.	No	Yes
D.	No	No

The correct answer is (D). *(CPA 1191 T-38)*

REQUIRED: The effect on retained earnings when rights are issued and exercised.

DISCUSSION: When stock rights are issued for no consideration, only a memorandum entry is made. When stock rights are exercised and stock is issued, the issuing company will reflect the proceeds as an increase in common stock and additional paid-in capital. Thus, retained earnings will not be affected when rights are issued or exercised.

Answers (A), (B), and (C) are incorrect because retained earnings will not be affected when rights are issued or exercised.

75. Quoit, Inc. issued preferred stock with detachable common stock warrants. The issue price exceeded the sum of the warrants' fair value and the preferred stocks' par value. The preferred stocks' fair value was not determinable. What amount should be assigned to the warrants outstanding?

A. Total proceeds.

B. Excess of proceeds over the par value of the preferred stock.

C. The proportion of the proceeds that the warrants' fair value bears to the preferred stocks' par value.

D. The fair value of the warrants.

The correct answer is (D). *(CPA 593 T-13)*
REQUIRED: The amount assigned to outstanding warrants when the preferred stocks' fair value is not determinable.
DISCUSSION: When securities are issued with detachable stock warrants, the proceeds should generally be allocated between the securities and the warrants based on their relative fair values at issuance. However, If the fair value of only the warrants is known, the warrants should be recorded at fair value, with the remainder allocated to the securities.
Answer (A) is incorrect because the total proceeds need to be allocated between the warrants and the preferred stock. Answer (B) is incorrect because par value is not an appropriate basis for allocation. Answer (C) is incorrect because the fair value of the warrants is not related to the par value of the preferred stock.

76. On March 4, 1996, Evan Co. purchased 1,000 shares of LVC common stock at $80 per share. On September 26, 1996, Evan received 1,000 stock rights to purchase an additional 1,000 shares at $90 per share. The stock rights had an expiration date of February 1, 1997. On September 30, 1996, LVC's common stock had a market value, ex-rights, of $95 per share, and the stock rights had a market value of $5 each. What amount should Evan report on its September 30, 1996 balance sheet for investment in stock rights?

A. $4,000

B. $5,000

C. $10,000

D. $15,000

The correct answer is (A). *(CPA 1193 I-12)*
REQUIRED: The amount to be recorded for the investment in stock rights on the balance sheet.
DISCUSSION: The $80 original cost of each share of stock should be allocated between the stock and the stock right based on their relative fair values.

Stock:	[$95 ÷ ($95 + $5)] × $80 cost = $76
Right:	[$5 ÷ ($95 + $5)] × $80 cost = $4
	$80

Thus, the stock rights should be recorded at $4,000 (1,000 rights x $4) on the balance sheet.
Answer (B) is incorrect because $5,000 is the fair value of the rights. Answer (C) is incorrect because $10,000 is the difference between the cost of the 1,000 shares of stock and the exercise price for an additional 1,000 shares. Answer (D) is incorrect because $15,000 is the difference between the cost of the 1,000 shares of stock and their fair value.

77. In September 1991, Cal Corp. made a dividend distribution of one right for each of its 240,000 shares of outstanding common stock. Each right was exercisable for the purchase of 1/100 of a share of Cal's $50 variable rate preferred stock at an exercise price of $80 per share. On March 20, 1996, none of the rights had been exercised, and Cal redeemed them by paying each shareholder $0.10 per right. As a result of this redemption, Cal's shareholders' equity was reduced by

A. $240

B. $24,000

C. $48,000

D. $72,000

The correct answer is (B). *(CPA 1192 II-47)*
REQUIRED: The effect on shareholders' equity of the redemption of stock rights.
DISCUSSION: When rights are issued for no consideration, only a memorandum entry is made. Consequently, neither common stock nor additional paid-in capital is affected by the issuance of rights in a nonreciprocal transfer. The redemption of the rights reduces shareholders' equity by the amount of their cost (240,000 x $.10 = $24,000).
Answer (A) is incorrect because $240 equals $.10 times the number of shares (2,400) that could have been purchased. Answer (C) is incorrect because, if the rights were initially credited to paid-in capital at $72,000, or $.30 each [($80 exercise price − $50 par value) ÷ 100], and paid-in capital was reduced by the redemption price of $.10 each (240,000 x $.10 = $24,000), the balance remaining would be $48,000. Answer (D) is incorrect because $72,000 assumes a price per right of $.30 [($80 exercise price − $50 par value) ÷ 100].

78. On July 1, 1996, Vail Corp. issued rights to shareholders to subscribe to additional shares of its common stock. One right was issued for each share owned. A shareholder could purchase one additional share for 10 rights plus $15 cash. The rights expired on September 30, 1996. On July 1, 1996, the market price of a share with the right attached was $40, while the market price of one right alone was $2. Vail's shareholders' equity on June 30, 1996, comprised the following:

Common stock, $25 par value, 4,000 shares issued and outstanding	$100,000
Additional paid-in capital	60,000
Retained earnings	80,000

By what amount should Vail's retained earnings decrease as a result of issuance of the stock rights on July 1, 1996?

- A. $0
- B. $5,000
- C. $8,000
- D. $10,000

The correct answer is (A). *(CPA 592 II-8)*
REQUIRED: The effect on retained earnings when stock rights are issued.
DISCUSSION: When stock rights are issued for no consideration, only a memorandum entry is made. When stock rights are exercised and stock is issued, the issuing company will reflect the proceeds as an increase in common stock and additional paid-in capital. Thus, retained earnings will not be affected when rights are either issued or exercised.
Answers (B), (C), and (D) are incorrect because, when stock rights are issued, only a memorandum entry is made, having no effect on retained earnings.

18.7 Compensatory Stock Option Plans

79. SFAS 123, *Accounting for Stock-Based Compensation*, permits entities to account for their stock-based employee compensation plans in accordance with which of the following methods:

	Fair Value Based Method	Intrinsic Value Based Method
A.	Yes	Yes
B.	Yes	No
C.	No	Yes
D.	No	No

The correct answer is (A). *(Publisher)*
REQUIRED: The method prescribed for accounting for stock-based employee compensation plans.
DISCUSSION: SFAS 123 encourages entities to account for stock-based employee compensation plans in accordance with the fair value-based method prescribed by SFAS 123 but permits entities to continue accounting for these plans in accordance with the intrinsic value-based method prescribed by APB 25. However, entities electing to follow the intrinsic value-based method will be required to disclose pro forma net income and, if presented, earnings per share as if the fair value-based method had been applied.
Answers (B), (C), and (D) are incorrect because both methods are allowed.

80. The measurement date in accounting for stock issued to employees in compensatory stock option plans accounted for in accordance with the fair value method prescribed by SFAS 123 is

- A. The date on which options are granted to specified employees.
- B. The earliest date on which both the number of shares to be issued and the option price are known.
- C. The date on which the options are exercised by the employees.
- D. The date the corporation forgoes alternative use of the shares to be sold under option.

The correct answer is (A). *(Publisher)*
REQUIRED: The measurement date used to account for stock-based compensation plans accounted for in accordance with the fair value-based method prescribed by SFAS 123.
DISCUSSION: Under the fair value-based method prescribed by SFAS 123, compensation cost is measured at the grant date. This cost is based on the fair value of the award at that date and recognized over the service period, which generally is the vesting period.
Answers (B), (C), and (D) are incorrect because each may coincide with, but does not define, the measurement date.

81. The measurement date in accounting for stock issued to employees in compensatory stock option plans accounted for in accordance with the intrinsic value-based method prescribed by APB 25 is

A. The date on which options are granted to specified employees.

B. The earliest date on which both the number of shares to be issued and the option price are known.

C. The date on which the options are exercised by the employees.

D. The date the corporation forgoes alternative use of the shares to be sold under option.

The correct answer is (B). *(CPA 1175 T-24)*

REQUIRED: The measurement date used to account for stock issued to employees in compensatory stock option plans.

DISCUSSION: APB 25, *Accounting for Stock Issued to Employees*, defines the measurement date for determining compensation expense in stock option plans as the first date on which both the number of shares to which an employee is entitled and the option or purchase price, if any, are known. The date at which both criteria are met for most plans is usually the date of grant. The measurement date, however, may be later than the date of grant when a plan has variable terms; e.g., either the number of shares of stock or the option or purchase price depends on future events. The employee services need not have been rendered at the measurement date.

Answers (A), (C), and (D) are incorrect because each may coincide with, but does not define, the measurement date.

82. Junior stock is stock issued to certain employees that is subordinate to the employer's regular common stock but is convertible into the common stock if certain performance goals are achieved or if certain transactions occur. If the intrinsic value-based method prescribed by APB 25 is followed, at what date should compensation cost be measured for stock option, purchase, and award plans involving junior stock?

A. The date on which the plan is granted to employees.

B. The earliest date at which the junior stock is convertible into common stock.

C. The date on which the junior stock is converted into common stock.

D. The earliest date at which the number of shares of common stock to be received on conversion and the option or purchase price are both known.

The correct answer is (D). *(Publisher)*

REQUIRED: The measurement date for compensation cost for grants of junior stock.

DISCUSSION: FASB Interpretation No. 38, *Determining the Measurement Date for Stock Option, Purchase, and Award Plans Involving Junior Stock*, defines the measurement date as the earliest date at which both the number of shares of common stock that the employee will receive in exchange for the junior stock and the option or purchase price, if any, are known.

Answers (A), (B), and (C) are incorrect because each may coincide with, but does not define, the measurement date.

83. In a compensatory stock option plan accounted for in accordance with the intrinsic value-based method prescribed by APB 25 for which the grant, measurement, and exercise dates are all different, the stock options outstanding account should be reduced at the

A. Date of grant.

B. Measurement date.

C. Beginning of the service period.

D. Exercise date.

The correct answer is (D). *(CPA 593 T-14)*

REQUIRED: The date at which the stock options outstanding account should be reduced.

DISCUSSION: For a compensatory stock option plan, compensation costs should be recognized in the income statement of the period in which the services are rendered. When the measurement date is different from (later than) the grant date, the compensation expense in the periods prior to the measurement date should be based on the stock's quoted market price at the end of each period. When compensation expense is recognized, a corresponding credit should be made to a stock options outstanding account. At the time the stock options are exercised, this account should be debited (reduced).

Answers (A), (B), and (C) are incorrect because the stock options outstanding account is debited at the exercise date.

84. On January 2, 1996, Kine Co. granted Morgan, its president, compensatory stock options to buy 1,000 shares of Kine's $10 par common stock. The options call for a price of $20 per share and are exercisable for 3 years following the grant date. Morgan exercised the options on December 31, 1996. The market price of the stock was $50 on January 2, 1996 and $70 on December 31, 1996. If the intrinsic value-based method prescribed by APB 25 is followed, by what net amount should shareholders' equity increase as a result of the grant and exercise of the options?

A. $20,000

B. $30,000

C. $50,000

D. $70,000

The correct answer is (A). *(CPA 594 F-33)*

REQUIRED: The amount shareholders' equity increases as a result of the grant and exercise of a compensatory stock option.

DISCUSSION: The measurement date is January 2, 1996. At that date, the intrinsic value of the stock option is $30,000 [1,000 shares x ($50 market price – $20 option price)]. This $30,000 will be recorded as both compensation expense and stock options outstanding. The net effect on shareholders' equity is $0. When the options are exercised, the $20,000 (1,000 shares x $20 exercise price) cash received and the $30,000 stock options outstanding will be allocated to contributed capital as $10,000 common stock and $40,000 additional paid-in capital. The net effect on shareholders' equity will be a $20,000 increase.

Answer (B) is incorrect because $30,000 is the amount of compensation expense. Answer (C) is incorrect because $50,000 is the increase in the shareholders' equity without regard to the compensation expense. Answer (D) is incorrect because $70,000 results from calculating the increase in shareholders' equity using the stock price on the exercise date and excluding the decrease in retained earnings.

85. Compensatory stock options were granted to executives on May 1, 1993, with a measurement date of October 31, 1994, for services rendered during 1993, 1994, and 1995. The excess of the market value of the stock over the option price at the measurement date was reasonably estimimable at the date of grant. The stock options were exercised on June 30, 1996. Compensation expense accounted for in accordance with the intrinsic value-based method prescribed by APB 25 should be recognized in which of the following years?

	1993	1995
A.	Yes	No
B.	No	No
C.	Yes	Yes
D.	No	Yes

The correct answer is (C). *(CPA 1191 T-29)*

REQUIRED: The year(s), if any, in which compensation expense should be recognized.

DISCUSSION: For a compensatory stock option plan, compensation costs should be recognized in the income statement of the period in which the services are rendered. Given that the services to be compensated will be rendered in 1993, 1994, and 1995, compensation expense should be recognized in each of those years.

Answers (A), (B), and (D) are incorrect because compensation expense should be recognized in 1993, 1994, and 1995.

86. On January 2, 1996, Farm Co. granted an employee an option to purchase 1,000 shares of Farm's common stock at $40 per share. The option became exercisable on December 31, 1996, after the employee had completed 1 year of service, and was exercised on that date. The market prices of Farm's stock were as follows:

January 2, 1996	$50
December 31, 1996	65

If accounted for in accordance with the intrinsic value-based method prescribed by APB 25, what amount should Farm recognize as compensation expense for 1996?

A. $0

B. $10,000

C. $15,000

D. $25,000

The correct answer is (B). *(CPA 1194 F-33)*

REQUIRED: The amount to be recognized as compensation expense under a stock option plan.

DISCUSSION: Under APB 25, compensation expense is the excess of market price of the stock over the option price on the measurement date, which is the first date when both the number of shares an employee is entitled to and the purchase price are known. The measurement date is January 2, 1996. The compensation expense is $10,000 [1,000 shares x ($50 market price on 1/2/96 – $40 exercise price)].

Answer (A) is incorrect because compensation expense is recognized when the related services are performed. Answer (C) is incorrect because $15,000 is based on the difference between the market prices in January and December. Answer (D) is incorrect because $25,000 is based on the market price in December.

87. Wall Corp's employee stock purchase plan specifies the following:

- For every $1 withheld from employees' wages for the purchase of Wall's common stock, Wall contributes $2.

- The stock is purchased from Wall's treasury stock at market price on the date of purchase.

The following information pertains to the plan's 1996 transactions:

Employee withholdings for the year	$ 350,000
Market value of 150,000 shares issued	1,050,000
Carrying amount of treasury stock issued (cost)	900,000

Before payroll taxes, what amount should Wall recognize as expense in 1996 for the stock purchase plan if Wall accounts for its stock-based compensation plans in accordance with the intrinsic value-based method?

A. $1,050,000

B. $900,000

C. $700,000

D. $550,000

The correct answer is (C). *(CPA 1191 II-20)*
REQUIRED: The expense recognized for the stock purchase plan.
DISCUSSION: The plan is compensatory because, in effect, the company is offering a 662/3% discount (an employee pays $1 for each $3 of stock). According to APB 25, *Accounting for Stock Issued to Employees*, "Compensation for services that a corporation receives as consideration for stock issued through employee stock option, purchase, and award plans should be measured by the quoted market price of the stock minus the amount, if any, that the employee is required to pay." The 1996 expense is therefore $700,000 ($1,050,000 market price of shares issued – $350,000 wages withheld for stock purchases).
Answer (A) is incorrect because $1,050,000 is the market price. Answer (B) is incorrect because $900,000 is the carrying amount of the treasury stock. Answer (D) is incorrect because $550,000 equals the carrying amount of the treasury stock minus the employee withholdings.

88. Wolf Co.'s grant of 30,000 stock appreciation rights enables key employees to receive cash equal to the difference between $20 and the market price of the stock on the date each right is exercised. The service period is 1995 through 1997, and the rights are exercisable in 1998 and 1999. The market price of the stock was $25 and $28 at December 31, 1995 and 1996, respectively. What amount should Wolf report as the liability under the stock appreciation rights plan in its December 31, 1996 balance sheet if Wolf accounts for its stock-based compensation plans in accordance with the intrinsic value-based method?

A. $0

B. $100,000

C. $160,000

D. $240,000

The correct answer is (C). *(CPA 1191 I-22)*
REQUIRED: The liability under the stock appreciation rights plan.
DISCUSSION: Under FASB Interpretation 28, *Accounting for Stock Appreciation Rights and Other Variable Stock Option or Award Plans*, compensation equals the excess of the quoted market value over the value specified. The charge to expense is accrued over the service period. Accrued compensation is adjusted (but not below zero) in subsequent periods up to the measurement date for changes in the quoted market value, and the adjustment is reflected in income in the period of the change. Thus, the liability accrued after 2 years of the 3-year service period is $160,000 [30,000 rights x ($28 – $20 specified value) x 2/3].
Answer (A) is incorrect because a liability must be accrued. Answer (B) is incorrect because $100,000 is based on a $25 market price. Answer (D) is incorrect because $240,000 is the total compensation expense, but this amount must be allocated over the service period.

89. In connection with a stock option plan for the benefit of key employees, Ward Corp. intends to distribute treasury shares when the options are exercised. These shares were bought in 1995 at $42 per share. On January 1, 1996, Ward granted stock options for 10,000 shares at $38 per share as additional compensation for services to be rendered over the next 3 years. The options are exercisable during a 4-year period beginning January 1, 1998 by grantees still employed by Ward. Market price of Ward's stock was $47 per share at the grant date. No stock options were terminated during 1996. In Ward's December 31, 1996 income statement, what amount should be reported as compensation expense pertaining to the options if Ward accounts for its stock-based compensation plans in accordance with APB 25?

   A. $90,000

   B. $40,000

   C. $30,000

   D. $0

The correct answer is (C). *(CPA 591 I-51)*

REQUIRED: The compensation expense pertaining to the options reported in 1996.

DISCUSSION: Compensation should be measured by the quoted market price at the measurement date minus the amount the grantees are required to pay. The measurement date is the first date on which both the option price and the number of shares to be issued are known. The measurement date for Ward was 1/1/96. The total compensation to be reported is $90,000 [10,000 shares x ($47 market price on 1/1/96 – $38 option price)]. In the first year of the 3-year service period, $30,000 is recognized as compensation expense.

Answer (A) is incorrect because $90,000 is the total compensation to be reported over the 3-year period. Answer (B) is incorrect because $40,000 is the total compensation to be reported over the 3-year period if the cost of the treasury stock is used to measure the transaction. Answer (D) is incorrect because compensation should be recognized in 1996, the first year of the service period.

90. On June 1, 1995, Oak Corp. granted stock options to certain key employees as additional compensation. The options were for 1,000 shares of Oak's $2 par value common stock at an option price of $15 per share. Market price of this stock on June 1, 1995 was $20 per share. The options were exercisable beginning January 2, 1996, and expire on December 31, 1997. On April 1, 1996, when Oak's stock was trading at $21 per share, all the options were exercised. What amount of pretax compensation should Oak report in 1995 in connection with the options if Oak accounts for its stock-based compensation plans in accordance with APB 25?

   A. $6,000

   B. $5,000

   C. $2,500

   D. $2,000

The correct answer is (B). *(CPA 1192 II-56)*

REQUIRED: The amount of pretax compensation reported in 1995.

DISCUSSION: Under APB 25, "Compensation for services that a corporation receives as consideration for stock issued through employee stock option, purchase, and award plans should be measured by the quoted market price of the stock at the measurement date minus the amount, if any, that the employee is required to pay." The measurement date is the first date on which both the option price and the number of shares to be issued are known. The measurement date for Oak was June 1, 1995. The total compensation to be reported is $5,000 [1,000 shares x ($20 market price on 6/1/95 – $15 option price)]. Assuming that the options were granted as compensation for past and current service, the entire amount should be reported in 1995.

Answer (A) is incorrect because $6,000 assumes the measurement date was 4/1/96. Answer (C) is incorrect because $2,500 allocates the compensation over 2 years. Answer (D) is incorrect because $2,000 is based on a 3-year allocation and the market price on 4/1/96.

91. Pine Corp. is required to contribute, to an employee stock ownership plan (ESOP), 10% of its income after deduction for this contribution but before income tax. Pine's income before charges for the contribution and income tax was $75,000. The income tax rate is 30%. What amount should be accrued as a contribution to the ESOP?

A. $7,500

B. $6,818

C. $5,250

D. $4,907

The correct answer is (B). *(CPA 591 I-36)*
   REQUIRED: The amount accrued as a contribution to the ESOP.
   DISCUSSION: The contribution equals 10% of pretax income after deduction of the contribution. Hence, the contribution is $6,818.

$$C = 10\%(\$75,000 - C)$$
$$C = \$7,500 - .1C$$
$$1.1C = 7,500$$
$$C = \$6,818$$

Answer (A) is incorrect because $7,500 is 10% of pretax, precontribution income. Answer (C) is incorrect because $5,250 is 10% of after-tax net income determined without a deduction for the contribution. Answer (D) is incorrect because $4,907 assumes C = .10 ($75,000 − C − T) and T = .30 ($75,000 − C).

92. On January 1, 1996, Heath Corp. established an employee stock ownership plan (ESOP). Selected transactions relating to the ESOP during 1996 were as follows:

- On April 1, 1996, Heath contributed $45,000 cash and 3,000 shares of its $10 par value common stock to the ESOP. On this date, the market price of the stock was $18 a share.

- On October 1, 1996, the ESOP borrowed $100,000 from Union National Bank and acquired 6,000 shares of Heath's common stock in the open market at $17 a share. The note is for 1 year, bears interest at 10%, and is guaranteed by Heath.

- On December 15, 1996, the ESOP distributed 8,000 shares of Heath's common stock to employees of Heath in accordance with the plan formula. On this date, the market price of the stock was $20 a share.

In its 1996 income statement, what amount should Heath report as compensation expense relating to the ESOP?

A. $99,000

B. $155,000

C. $199,000

D. $259,000

The correct answer is (A). *(CPA 1189 I-56)*
   REQUIRED: The amount to be reported as compensation expense related to an ESOP.
   DISCUSSION: According to SOP 76-3, *Accounting Practices for Certain Employee Stock Ownership Plans*, the employer should recognize as compensation expense the amounts contributed or irrevocably committed as contributions for a given year. Thus, Heath should report $99,000 [$45,000 cash + (3,000 shares x $18 market price)] as compensation expense for 1996. The guarantee of the $100,000 note should be recognized as a liability and a reduction in shareholders' equity. The ESOP's distribution of shares does not affect the employer's accounting.
   Answer (B) is incorrect because $155,000 results from including only the $10 par value of the stock contributed to the ESOP and incorrectly including the 8,000 distributed to employees at par value. Answer (C) is incorrect because $199,000 results from treating the guarantee of the note as part of compensation expense. Answer (D) is incorrect because $259,000 results from including the 8,000 shares distributed from the ESOP as compensation expense at the market price of $20.

CHAPTER NINETEEN
EARNINGS PER SHARE

This chapter covers earnings per share (EPS) rules and calculations. Additional abbreviations used are

PEPS	--	Primary earnings per share
FDEPS	--	Fully diluted earnings per share
CSE	--	Common stock equivalents

The principal pronouncement is APB 15, *Earnings per Share*.

At December 1, 1996, the FASB had a Proposed Statement of Financial Accounting Standards, *Earnings per Share and Disclosure of Information about Capital Structure*, outstanding. If and when issued as a final statement, it will require publicly held entities to disclose earnings per share (EPS) amounts and all entities to disclose certain information about their capital structure. Per-share amounts will include a basic EPS (income available to common shareholders divided by the weighted number of common shares outstanding for the period) and a diluted EPS (similar to the fully diluted EPS required by APB 15).

19.1 Basic Concepts

1. With respect to the computation of earnings per share, which of the following would be most indicative of a simple capital structure?

A. Common stock, preferred stock, and convertible securities outstanding in lots of even thousands.

B. Earnings derived from one primary line of business.

C. Ownership interests consisting solely of common stock.

D. Equity represented materially by liquid assets.

The correct answer is (C). *(CPA 578 T-14)*

REQUIRED: The situation most indicative of a simple capital structure.

DISCUSSION: APB 15 defines a simple capital structure as one that contains only common stock or, if it contains potentially dilutive convertible securities, options, warrants, or other rights, one in which the aggregate dilutive effect upon conversion or exercise would not reduce EPS by 3% or more.

Answer (A) is incorrect because convertible securities in significant amounts could result in potential dilution of 3% or more. Whether securities have been issued in even thousands is not relevant. Answers (B) and (D) are incorrect because the characteristics of a simple capital structure are determined by the nature of shareholders' equity, not by the source of earnings or composition of assets.

2. In computing EPS, the equivalent number of shares of convertible preferred stock is added as an adjustment to the denominator (number of shares outstanding). If the preferred stock is preferred as to dividends, which amount should then be added as an adjustment to the numerator (earnings available to common shareholders)?

- A. Annual preferred dividend.

- B. Annual preferred dividend times (1 – the income tax rate).

- C. Annual preferred dividend times the income tax rate.

- D. Annual preferred dividend divided by the income tax rate.

The correct answer is (A). *(CPA 576 T-15)*
REQUIRED: The adjustment to the numerator for preferred dividends in the EPS computation.
DISCUSSION: If a capital structure has convertible preferred stock with a dilutive effect on EPS, the "if-converted" method is used. This method assumes the conversion of the preferred stock occurred at the beginning of the accounting period or at issuance, if later. The annual preferred dividend is accordingly added back to earnings available to common shareholders (the numerator of the EPS ratio).
Answers (B), (C), and (D) are incorrect because the tax rate is not a consideration. The preferred dividend is paid with after-tax dollars; i.e., preferred dividends are not tax deductible.

3. Earnings per share disclosures are required only for

- A. Companies with complex capital structures.

- B. Companies that change their capital structures during the reporting period.

- C. Public companies.

- D. Primary earnings.

The correct answer is (C). *(CMA 1286 3-17)*
REQUIRED: The circumstances under which EPS disclosures are required.
DISCUSSION: SFAS 21, *Suspension of the Reporting of EPS and Segment Information by Nonpublic Enterprises*, suspends the applicability of APB 15 to nonpublic companies. If EPS data are presented by these companies, however, they must comply with APB 15. EPS disclosures are thus required only for public companies.
Answer (A) is incorrect because public companies with either complex or simple capital structures must disclose EPS. Answer (B) is incorrect because whether companies change their capital structure during the reporting period is irrelevant to whether they must make EPS disclosures. Answer (D) is incorrect because both primary and fully diluted EPS must be disclosed by publicly held companies that have complex capital structures.

4. Both the numerator and the denominator of the EPS ratio may be affected by the existence of outstanding stock options and warrants. This result will occur if the number of shares of common stock obtainable from the exercise of the options and warrants is

- A. Less than 20% of the common stock outstanding.

- B. Equal to 20% of the common stock outstanding.

- C. More than 20% of the common stock outstanding, and the 20% limitation applicable to the shares assumed purchased under the treasury stock method is not reached.

- D. More than 20% of the common stock outstanding, and the 20% limitation applicable to the shares assumed purchased under the treasury stock method is exceeded.

The correct answer is (D). *(Publisher)*
REQUIRED: The condition under which both the numerator and the denominator would be affected by the existence of outstanding stock options and warrants.
DISCUSSION: When the number of shares obtainable from the exercise of all options and warrants exceeds 20% of the common stock outstanding at the end of the period, all options and warrants outstanding must be assumed to be exercised, whether they are individually dilutive or antidilutive. The proceeds from the assumed exercise are then used for an assumed purchase of up to 20% of the outstanding shares. Any excess proceeds are hypothetically used first to retire outstanding debt and then to purchase government securities. If the net effect of the assumed repurchase of shares, retirement of debt, and investment of remaining funds is dilutive, it should be included in the EPS calculation. Accordingly, to the extent that interest would be saved or earned, the numerator of the EPS ratio is affected. This change is in addition to the effect on the denominator of the assumed exercise of the options and repurchase of stock under the treasury stock method. The 20% rule described above is an exception to the principle that antidilutive securities are ignored in determining PEPS and FDEPS.
Answers (A), (B), and (C) are incorrect because none of these conditions would affect the numerator.

5. To what extent is treasury stock assumed to be acquired by a corporation applying the treasury stock method in earnings per share calculations?

A. To the maximum extent possible.

B. Up to 20% of earnings for the period being reported on.

C. None until all long-term debt has hypothetically been retired; then to the maximum extent possible.

D. Up to 20% of outstanding common stock.

The correct answer is (D). *(CPA 1175 T-8)*
REQUIRED: The maximum amount of treasury stock that may be assumed to be acquired when applying the treasury stock method.
DISCUSSION: The treasury stock method applies to EPS calculations for a capital structure that includes dilutive stock options and warrants. These securities are assumed to have been exercised and the proceeds used to purchase treasury stock up to a maximum of 20% of the outstanding common stock at the end of the period. Any remaining proceeds are assumed to be used first to retire short-term or long-term debt, and then to be invested in U.S. government securities or commercial paper.
Answer (A) is incorrect because the limit is 20%. Answer (B) is incorrect because earnings have no effect on the treasury stock computation. Answer (C) is incorrect because debt is assumed to be retired only after a hypothetical repurchase of 20% of the outstanding common stock.

6. The if-converted method of computing EPS data assumes conversion of convertible securities at the

A. Beginning of the earliest period reported (or at time of issuance, if later).

B. Beginning of the earliest period reported (regardless of time of issuance).

C. Middle of the earliest period reported (regardless of time of issuance).

D. Ending of the earliest period reported (regardless of time of issuance).

The correct answer is (A). *(CPA 1187 T-33)*
REQUIRED: The conversion assumption underlying the if-converted method.
DISCUSSION: The if-converted method of computing EPS assumes that convertible securities qualifying as CSE are included in the determination of PEPS and that all convertible securities are converted for the purpose of calculating FDEPS. Conversion is assumed to have occurred at the beginning of the earliest period reported or, if the security was issued at a later time, at the date of issuance.
Answers (B), (C), and (D) are incorrect because conversion is assumed at the beginning of the earliest period reported (or at the time of issuance, if later).

7. In computing earnings per share data, which of the following is true regarding the weighted average computation of shares outstanding?

A. Reacquired shares should be excluded from the date of their acquisition.

B. Reacquired shares should be excluded from the beginning of the period in which they were acquired.

C. Stock dividends and stock splits consummated after the close of the period do not affect the primary EPS computations, even though they may have been consummated before issuance of the financial statements.

D. The shares issued during the period as a result of a stock dividend are weighted according to the portion of the period for which they were actually outstanding.

The correct answer is (A). *(Publisher)*
REQUIRED: The correct statement concerning the computation of the weighted average of shares outstanding.
DISCUSSION: Reacquired shares, or treasury shares, no longer represent outstanding stock to the company as of the date of their repurchase. Thus, they should be excluded from the calculation of the weighted-average number of shares as of their reacquisition date.
Answer (B) is incorrect because, until the date of their repurchase, the shares represent outstanding ownership. Answer (C) is incorrect because stock dividends and stock splits occurring anytime before the issuance of the statements require retroactive adjustment of EPS for all periods presented. Answer (D) is incorrect because shares issued in a stock dividend are assumed to have been outstanding from the beginning of all periods presented.

8. In computing the loss per share of common stock, cumulative preferred dividends not earned should be

A. Deducted from the loss for the year.

B. Added to the loss for the year.

C. Deducted from income in the year paid.

D. Added to income in the year paid.

The correct answer is (B). *(CPA 1172 T-13)*
REQUIRED: The effect of unearned cumulative preferred dividends on the loss per share calculation.
DISCUSSION: When preferred stock is cumulative, the dividend, whether earned or not, should be deducted from net income or added to the loss for the year in computing earnings or loss, respectively, per share of common stock.

If the dividend is cumulative only if earned, no adjustment is necessary except to the extent of available income; that is, the preferred dividends accumulate only to the extent of net income. See APB 15, paragraph 50.

Answer (A) is incorrect because it has the effect of adding to the numerator and thus reducing loss per share. Answers (C) and (D) are incorrect because cumulative preferred dividends are a necessary adjustment for the year in which they accumulate regardless of when they are paid.

9. With regard to stock dividends and stock splits, current authoritative literature contains what general guideline for the computation of EPS?

A. If changes in common stock resulting from stock dividends, stock splits, or reverse splits have been consummated after the close of the period but before completion of the financial report, the per-share computations should be based on the new number of shares.

B. It is not necessary to give recognition to the effect on prior periods' computations of EPS for stock dividends or stock splits consummated in the current period.

C. Computations of EPS for prior periods must give recognition to changes in common shares due to stock splits, but not stock dividends, because stock dividends have such a small effect on EPS.

D. Footnote disclosure is necessary for anticipated stock dividends and stock splits and their effect on PEPS and FDEPS.

The correct answer is (A). *(Publisher)*
REQUIRED: The correct treatment of stock dividends and stock splits in the weighted-average number of shares calculation.
DISCUSSION: When a stock dividend, stock split, or reverse split occurs at any time before issuance of the financial statements, restatement of EPS is required for all periods presented. The purpose is to promote comparability of EPS data among reporting periods.

Answer (B) is incorrect because the effect of stock dividends and stock splits on prior-period earnings must be calculated, and EPS data should be restated for all periods presented in the financial statements. Answer (C) is incorrect because stock dividends and stock splits are treated the same, even in the case of a "small" stock dividend. Answer (D) is incorrect because a stock dividend or stock split is not accounted for or disclosed until it occurs.

10. In relation to the presentation of EPS data, APB 15 requires

A. Restatement of EPS data of a prior period if the earnings of the prior period have been restated by a prior-period adjustment.

B. Dual presentation of PEPS and FDEPS for the current period only.

C. The presentation of PEPS only for the results of operations of prior periods as presented in the financial statements.

D. That the effect of a restatement of prior-period earnings from a prior-period adjustment be disclosed in the current period, but not in EPS form.

The correct answer is (A). *(Publisher)*
REQUIRED: The financial statement presentation of EPS required under APB 15.
DISCUSSION: According to APB 15, when the results of operations of a prior period are restated in the financial statements, the EPS data for those prior periods must also be restated.

Answers (B) and (C) are incorrect because both PEPS and FDEPS must be disclosed for all periods presented if a corporation has a complex capital structure. Answer (D) is incorrect because APB 15 requires presentation of the effect of a prior-period adjustment on EPS for all prior periods affected by such restatement.

11. How are unpaid stock subscriptions handled in the computation of EPS?

- A. By use of the treasury stock method.
- B. They are not included until issued.
- C. By disclosure only.
- D. By use of the "if-converted" method.

The correct answer is (A). *(Publisher)*

REQUIRED: The way stock subscriptions are handled in EPS computations.

DISCUSSION: According to the Accounting Interpretations of APB 15, stock purchase contracts, stock subscriptions not paid, deferred compensation plans providing for issuance of common stock, and convertible securities allowing or requiring payment of cash at conversion are equivalent to stock options and warrants. They should be classified as CSE and ordinarily should be treated the same as stock options or warrants. For example, the unpaid balance of stock subscriptions is assumed to be proceeds used for treasury stock purchases. Thus, the treasury stock method is used to account for stock subscriptions not paid. Fully paid stock subscriptions, however, are deemed to be outstanding stock.

Answers (B) and (C) are incorrect because, if the stock subscriptions are dilutive, they must be included in the calculation of EPS. Answer (D) is incorrect because it describes the procedure applicable to convertible securities.

12. Earnings per share data should be reported on the face of the income statement for

	Income before Extraordinary Items	Cumulative Effect of a Change in Accounting Principle
A.	Yes	Yes
B.	Yes	No
C.	No	No
D.	No	Yes

The correct answer is (A). *(CPA 1191 T-16)*

REQUIRED: The EPS data that should be reported on the face of the income statement.

DISCUSSION: APB 15 requires that EPS data for income before extraordinary items and net income be reported on the face of the income statement. APB 20, *Accounting Changes*, requires that EPS data for the cumulative effect of a change in accounting principle be disclosed on the face of the income statement. APB 30, *Reporting the Results of Operations*, requires that EPS data for income from continuing operations be reported on the face of the income statement. Per-share data for the results of discontinued operations and gain or loss on disposal of a segment may be included on the face of the income statement or in a note.

Answers (B), (C), and (D) are incorrect because EPS data should be reported on the face of the income statement for income before extraordinary items and the cumulative effect of a change in accounting principle.

13. Current authoritative literature regarding earnings per share does not apply to which of the following?

- A. Corporations whose capital structures contain only common stock.
- B. Parent company financial statements accompanied by consolidated financial statements.
- C. Corporations whose capital structures contain both common stock and senior securities.
- D. Summaries of financial statements that purport to present the results of operations of publicly held corporations in conformity with generally accepted accounting principles.

The correct answer is (B). *(Publisher)*

REQUIRED: The type of capital structure or financial statement presentation to which EPS disclosure requirements do not apply.

DISCUSSION: APB 15 specifically exempts parent company financial statements accompanied by consolidated financial statements from these disclosure requirements.

Answers (A) and (C) are incorrect because, although the capital structure of a firm affects the presentation of EPS data, it does not affect the applicability of APB 15. Answer (D) is incorrect because EPS requirements specifically apply to financial summaries presented in accordance with GAAP. SFAS 21, *Suspension of the Reporting of Earnings per Share and Segment Information by Nonpublic Enterprises*, specifically exempts only nonpublicly held companies from presenting EPS data.

19.2 Weighted-Average Number of Shares

Questions 14 and 15 are based on the following information. Birch Corporation had net income for the year of $101,504 and a simple capital structure consisting of the following common shares outstanding:

Months Outstanding	Number of Shares
January - February	24,000
March - June	29,400
July - November	36,000
December	35,040
Total	124,440

14. Birch Corporation's earnings per share (rounded to the nearest cent) were

- A. $2.90
- B. $3.20
- C. $3.26
- D. $3.45

The correct answer is (B). *(CMA 1294 2-15)*
REQUIRED: The EPS for a company with a simple capital structure.
DISCUSSION: EPS equals net income divided by the weighted-average number of shares outstanding. The latter is calculated as follows:

$$24,000 \times (2 \div 12) = 4,000$$
$$29,400 \times (4 \div 12) = 9,800$$
$$36,000 \times (5 \div 12) = 15,000$$
$$35,040 \times (1 \div 12) = \underline{2,920}$$
$$31,720$$

Accordingly, EPS is $3.20 ($101,504 NI ÷ 31,720 shares). Answer (A) is incorrect because $2.90 is based on the shares outstanding at year-end. Answer (C) is incorrect because $3.26 is based on an unweighted average of the four levels of shares outstanding during the year. Answer (D) is incorrect because $3.45 is based on the shares outstanding March through June.

15. Assume Birch Corporation issued a 20% stock dividend on August 1st. In this case, earnings per share (rounded to the nearest cent) were

- A. $2.41
- B. $2.67
- C. $2.72
- D. $2.88

The correct answer is (B). *(CMA 1294 2-16)*
REQUIRED: The EPS after a stock dividend.
DISCUSSION: Under APB 15, stock dividends are assumed to have occurred at the beginning of the year. Thus, the weighted-average number of shares equals the amount before the dividend increased by 20%. EPS equals net income divided by the weighted-average number of shares outstanding. The latter is calculated as follows:

$$24,000 \times (2 \div 12) = 4,000$$
$$29,400 \times (4 \div 12) = 9,800$$
$$36,000 \times (5 \div 12) = 15,000$$
$$35,040 \times (1 \div 12) = \underline{2,920}$$
$$31,720$$

Increasing 31,720 by an additional 20% results in 38,064 shares after the dividend. Therefore, EPS is $2.67 ($101,504 ÷ 38,064).
Answer (A) is incorrect because $2.41 is based on the shares outstanding at year-end. Answer (C) is incorrect because $2.72 is based on an unweighted average of the four levels of shares outstanding during the year. Answer (D) is incorrect because $2.88 is based on the shares outstanding March through June.

16. A warrant may be exercised to purchase two shares of common stock by paying $100 cash or by tendering a $100 face value debenture of the issuer. Market prices are $45 per common share, $80 per debenture, and $12 per warrant. This warrant has an effective exercise price per share of obtainable common stock of

A. $50

B. $45

C. $40

D. $12

The correct answer is (C). *(CPA 572 II-31)*
REQUIRED: The effective exercise price per share of a warrant for two shares of common stock.
DISCUSSION: Two shares of common stock may be obtained by paying $100 in cash or tendering a $100 face value debenture with a fair market value of $80. Because the more favorable exercise of the warrant is the exchange of the debenture, such exchange is assumed to set the exercise price. This $80 exercise price allows the purchase of two shares, resulting in a $40-per-share exercise price. Neither the current market price of $45 per share nor the $12 price per warrant is relevant.
Answer (A) is incorrect because $50 is the per-share exercise price assuming the unfavorable $100 cash exercise price was taken. Answer (B) is incorrect because $45 is the market price per share and is irrelevant. Answer (D) is incorrect because $12 is the warrant price and is irrelevant.

17. Timp, Inc. had the following common stock balances and transactions during 1996:

1/1/96	Common stock outstanding	30,000
2/1/96	Issued a 10% common stock dividend	3,000
3/1/96	Issued common stock in a pooling of interests	9,000
7/1/96	Issued common stock for cash	8,000
12/31/96	Common stock outstanding	50,000

What was Timp's 1996 weighted-average shares outstanding?

A. 42,000

B. 44,250

C. 44,500

D. 46,000

The correct answer is (D). *(CPA 592 I-59)*
REQUIRED: The weighted-average shares outstanding given a stock dividend, issuance of stock in a pooling of interests, and an issuance of stock for cash.
DISCUSSION: Shares issued or retired during a period are customarily weighted by the fraction of the period they were outstanding. However, a stock dividend or split occurring at any time must be treated as though it occurred at the beginning of the earliest period presented for purposes of computing the weighted-average number of shares. Moreover, the issuance of shares required in a pooling of interests should also be treated as occurring at the beginning of the period. According to APB 15, the EPS computation after a pooling "should be based on the aggregate of the weighted-average outstanding shares of the constituent businesses, adjusted to equivalent shares of the surviving business for all periods presented." The weighted average of shares outstanding is therefore 46,000.

12/12 × 30,000 shares outstanding at 1/1	30,000
12/12 × 30,000 shares × 10% stock dividend	3,000
12/12 × 9,000 shares issued in pooling	9,000
6/12 × 8,000 shares issued for cash on 7/1	4,000
	46,000

Answer (A) is incorrect because 42,000 excludes the July 1 issuance. Answer (B) is incorrect because 44,250 treats the shares issued in the pooling as being outstanding only from March 1 and the stock dividend as outstanding only from February 1. Answer (C) is incorrect because 44,500 treats the shares issued in the pooling as being outstanding only from March 1.

18. Poe Co. had 300,000 shares of common stock issued and outstanding at December 31, 1995. No common stock was issued during 1996. On January 1, 1996, Poe issued 200,000 shares of nonconvertible preferred stock. During 1996, Poe declared and paid $75,000 of cash dividends on the common stock and $60,000 on the preferred stock. Net income for the year ended December 31, 1996 was $330,000. What should be Poe's 1996 earnings per common share?

    A. $1.10

    B. $0.90

    C. $0.85

    D. $0.65

The correct answer is (B). *(CPA 1190 I-52)*

  REQUIRED: The amount of earnings per common share.

  DISCUSSION: Earnings per common share is equal to the amount of earnings available to the common shareholders divided by the weighted-average number of shares of common stock outstanding during the year. To calculate earnings available to holders of common stock, dividends on cumulative preferred stock must be subtracted from net income whether or not the dividends were declared. Earnings per common share for 1996 thus amounted to $0.90.

$$\frac{\$330,000 - \$60,000}{300,000} = \$0.90$$

  Answer (A) is incorrect because $1.10 assumes no preferred dividends were declared. Answer (C) is incorrect because $0.85 assumes the common but not the preferred dividends were subtracted from the numerator. Answer (D) is incorrect because $0.65 assumes all dividends are subtracted from the numerator.

19. Newt Corp. had EPS of $12.00 for 1996, before taking any dilutive securities into consideration. No conversion or exercise of dilutive securities took place in 1996. However, possible conversion of convertible preferred stock, a common stock equivalent, would have reduced EPS to $11.90. The effect of possible exercise of common stock warrants would have reduced EPS by an additional $0.05. For 1996, what is the maximum amount that Newt may report as a single presentation of EPS?

    A. $12.00

    B. $11.95

    C. $11.90

    D. $11.85

The correct answer is (A). *(CPA 1186 II-18)*

  REQUIRED: The maximum amount that may be reported as a single presentation of EPS.

  DISCUSSION: When an enterprise has potentially dilutive securities outstanding in addition to its common stock, it must make a dual presentation of EPS unless the potential dilution is less than 3%. In that case, APB 15 describes the effect as immaterial and allows a single presentation. If all dilutive securities are considered, EPS would be $11.85 ($11.90 – $.05). Because this $.15 dilution ($12.00 – $11.85) is less than the $.36 ($12.00 x 3%) allowed, Newt Corp. may elect to make a single presentation of EPS in the amount of $12.00.

  Answers (B), (C), and (D) are incorrect because neither the effects of the preferred stock conversion nor the effects of the stock warrant exercise, alone or in conjunction, would be materially dilutive.

20. The following information pertains to Jet Corp.'s outstanding stock for 1996:

Common stock, $5 par value

Shares outstanding, 1/1/96	20,000
2-for-1 stock split, 4/1/96	20,000
Shares issued, 7/1/96	10,000

Preferred stock, $10 par value, 5% cumulative

Shares outstanding, 1/1/96	4,000

What are the number of shares Jet should use to calculate 1996 earnings per share?

A. 40,000

B. 45,000

C. 50,000

D. 54,000

The correct answer is (B). *(CPA 593 I-60)*

REQUIRED: The number of shares used to calculate EPS.

DISCUSSION: Earnings per common share is equal to the amount of earnings available to the common shareholders divided by the weighted-average number of shares of common stock outstanding during the year. When a stock dividend, stock split, or a reverse split occurs other than at the beginning of a year, a retroactive adjustment for the change in capital structure should be made as of the beginning of the earliest accounting period presented. Shares outstanding during the year must then be weighted by the number of months for which they were outstanding in calculating the weighted-average number of shares that is to be used in determining EPS. Hence, the new shares issued on 7/1/96 are included in year-end EPS at their weighted average of 5,000 shares [10,000 shares x (6 months ÷ 12 months)]. Preferred stock is not included. Consequently, the total shares used to calculate 1996 EPS equals 45,000 (20,000 shares outstanding at 1/1/96 + 20,000 stock-split shares + 5,000 shares issued 7/1/96).

Answer (A) is incorrect because 40,000 assumes that the stock split is not treated as though it occurred at the beginning of the period. Answer (C) is incorrect because 50,000 assumes that the shares issued on 7/1/96 were outstanding for 12 months. Answer (D) is incorrect because 54,000 includes the preferred stock and assumes that the shares issued on 7/1/96 were outstanding for 12 months.

Questions 21 through 24 are based on the following information. Sands, Inc. uses a calendar year for financial reporting. The company is authorized to issue 5,000,000 shares of $10 par common stock. At no time has Sands issued any potentially dilutive securities. A two-for-one stock split of Sands' common stock took place on March 31, 1996. Additional information is in the next column.

Number of common shares issued and outstanding at 12/31/93	1,000,000
Shares issued as a result of a 10% stock dividend on 9/30/94	100,000
Shares issued for cash on 3/31/95	1,000,000
Number of common shares issued and outstanding at 12/31/95	2,100,000

21. The weighted-average number of common shares used in computing earnings per common share for 1994 on the 1995 comparative income statement was

A. 1,100,000

B. 1,050,000

C. 1,025,000

D. 1,000,000

The correct answer is (A). *(CMA 1291 2-19)*

REQUIRED: The weighted-average number of shares used in the EPS computation for 1994 on the 1995 comparative income statement.

DISCUSSION: At the beginning of 1994, 1,000,000 shares were outstanding. Another 100,000 were issued as a result of a stock dividend on September 30. The dividend is assumed to have occurred at the beginning of the year. Accordingly, the number of shares outstanding throughout 1994 would have been 1,100,000. No stock dividends or stock splits occurred in 1995. Thus, the same 1,100,000 shares used in the EPS calculation on the 1994 income statement would be used to determine the 1994 EPS in the 1995 comparative statements.

Answer (B) is incorrect because 1,050,000 assumes the stock dividend affects shares outstanding for 6 months. Answer (C) is incorrect because 1,025,000 assumes the stock dividend affects shares outstanding for 3 months. Answer (D) is incorrect because 1,000,000 does not consider the stock dividend.

22. Refer to the information preceding question 21 on page 405. The weighted-average number of common shares used in computing earnings per common share for 1995 on the 1995 comparative income statement was

   A. 1,600,000

   B. 1,850,000

   C. 2,100,000

   D. 3,700,000

The correct answer is (B). *(CMA 1291 2-20)*

   REQUIRED: The weighted-average number of shares used in computing EPS for 1995 on the 1995 income statement.

   DISCUSSION: At the beginning of 1995, 1,100,000 shares were outstanding. This figure remained unchanged for 3 months until March 31 when an additional 1,000,000 shares were issued. Hence, for the last 9 months of the year, 2,100,000 shares were outstanding. Weighting the shares outstanding by the amount of time they were outstanding results in a weighted average of 1,850,000 shares {[(3/12) x 1,100,000] + [(9/12) x 2,100,000]}.

   Answer (A) is incorrect because the 1,000,000 shares issued on 3/31/95 are assumed to be outstanding for 6 months. Answer (C) is incorrect because the 1,000,000 shares issued on 3/31/95 are assumed to be outstanding for the entire year. Answer (D) is incorrect because 3,700,000 is the number of shares used in computing EPS for 1995 on the 1996 comparative income statement (see next question).

23. Refer to the information preceding question 21 on page 405. The weighted-average number of common shares to be used on computing earnings per common share for 1995 on the 1996 comparative income statement is

   A. 1,850,000

   B. 2,100,000

   C. 3,700,000

   D. 4,200,000

The correct answer is (C). *(CMA 1291 2-21)*

   REQUIRED: The weighted-average number of shares used in computing EPS for 1995 on the 1996 comparative income statement.

   DISCUSSION: A stock dividend or split occurring at any time must be treated as though it occurred at the beginning of the earliest period presented for purposes of computing the weighted-average number of shares. Thus, prior-period EPS figures presented for comparative purposes must be retroactively restated for the effects of a stock dividend or a stock split. The number of shares used in computing the 1995 EPS on the 1995 income statement was 1,850,000 (see previous question). However, because of the stock split on March 31, 1996, the number of shares doubled. Thus, the EPS calculation for 1995 on the 1996 comparative income statement should be based on 3,700,000 shares (2 x 1,850,000).

   Answer (A) is incorrect because 1,850,000 is the number of shares used in computing EPS for 1995 on the 1995 income statement. Answer (B) is incorrect because 2,100,000 ignores the 3/31/96 stock split. Answer (D) is incorrect because 4,200,000 is the number of shares used in computing EPS for 1996 on the 1996 comparative income statement (see next question).

24. Refer to the information preceding question 21 on page 405. The weighted-average number of common shares to be used in computing earnings per common share for 1996 on the 1996 comparative income statement is

   A. 2,100,000

   B. 3,150,000

   C. 3,675,000

   D. 4,200,000

The correct answer is (D). *(CMA 1291 2-22)*

   REQUIRED: The weighted-average number of shares used in computing EPS for 1996 on the 1996 comparative income statement.

   DISCUSSION: At the beginning of 1996, 2,100,000 shares were outstanding. Because of the March 31 two-for-one stock split, that number increased to 4,200,000. The stock split is assumed to have occurred on the first day of the year. Consequently, the number of shares outstanding throughout 1996 was 4,200,000.

   Answer (A) is incorrect because 2,100,000 ignores the 3/31/96 stock split. Answer (B) is incorrect because 3,150,000 assumes the stock split increases shares outstanding for 6 months. Answer (C) is incorrect because 3,675,000 assumes the stock split increases shares outstanding from the date the split occurred.

25. On January 31, 1996, Pack, Inc. split its common stock 2 for 1, and Young, Inc. issued a 5% stock dividend. Both companies issued their December 31, 1995 financial statements on March 1, 1996. Should Pack's 1995 earnings per share (EPS) take into consideration the stock split, and should Young's 1995 EPS take into consideration the stock dividend?

	Pack's 1995 EPS	Young's 1995 EPS
A.	Yes	No
B.	No	No
C.	Yes	Yes
D.	No	Yes

The correct answer is (C). *(CPA 1192 T-23)*
REQUIRED: The effect on EPS of a stock split and stock dividend occurring after the date of the financial statements but before their issuance.
DISCUSSION: When a stock dividend, stock split, or reverse split occurs at any time before issuance of the financial statements, restatement of EPS is required for all periods presented. The purpose is to promote comparability of EPS data among reporting periods.
Answers (A), (B), and (D) are incorrect because a stock dividend or stock split occurring after the date of the financial statements but before their issuance should be included in the EPS computation.

26. What is the correct treatment of stock compensation plans in EPS computations?

A. The numerator should be adjusted by the amount the employee must pay, the amount of measurable compensation not yet charged to expense, and the amount of windfall tax benefit.

B. The denominator should be adjusted only by the number of shares to be issued.

C. For PEPS, the average aggregate compensation and average market price for the period should be used to determine the dilutive effect.

D. For FDEPS, the year-end market price and the average aggregate compensation for the period should be used to determine the dilutive effect.

The correct answer is (C). *(Publisher)*
REQUIRED: The correct treatment of stock compensation plans in EPS calculations.
DISCUSSION: For PEPS, FASB Interpretation No. 31, *Treatment of Stock Compensation Plans in EPS Computations*, requires that the treasury stock calculation use the average aggregate compensation and the average market price for the period for purposes of computing the effect on the EPS denominator. The assumed exercise proceeds equal the sum of the amounts the employee must pay, the portion of the measurable compensation (market price-option price) that is ascribed to future services and not yet charged to expense, and any "windfall" tax benefit to be credited to capital. This sum is the assumed amount of funds available for the assumed repurchase of stock.
Answer (A) is incorrect because the numerator is usually not adjusted. Answer (B) is incorrect because the denominator is adjusted by the number of shares to be issued minus the number of shares assumed repurchased. Answer (D) is incorrect because, for FDEPS, the figures used are the more dilutive of (1) the average stock price or the year-end stock price and (2) the average aggregate compensation or the year-end aggregate compensation.

19.3 Primary Earnings per Share (PEPS)

27. When computing primary earnings per share, convertible securities that are common stock equivalents are

A. Ignored.

B. Recognized whether they are dilutive or antidilutive.

C. Recognized only if they are antidilutive.

D. Recognized only if they are dilutive.

The correct answer is (D). *(CPA 1193 T-16)*
REQUIRED: The true statement about the treatment of convertible securities that are CSE in computing PEPS.
DISCUSSION: APB 15 establishes a "no antidilution" rule. It states that PEPS calculations should not include CSE or other contingent issuances for any period in which their inclusion would increase EPS or decrease the loss per share.
Answer (A) is incorrect because convertible securities are not ignored. Answers (B) and (C) are incorrect because convertible securities are recognized only when they are dilutive.

28. The nature of primary earnings per share involving adjustment for stock options can be described as

    A. Historical because earnings are historical.

    B. Historical because it indicates the firm's valuation.

    C. Pro forma because it indicates potential changes in the number of shares.

    D. Pro forma because it indicates potential changes in earnings.

The correct answer is (C). *(CPA 577 T-28)*
    REQUIRED: The nature of the adjustment required for stock options in calculating PEPS.
    DISCUSSION: The denominator in the PEPS calculation is adjusted for the assumed exercise of outstanding stock options during the period if the exercise would have a dilutive effect on EPS. The change in the number of shares has not occurred and is only assumed, so the calculation is essentially pro forma.
    Answers (A) and (B) are incorrect because the conversion of stock options into common shares has not occurred, and the required adjustment is hypothetical. Answer (D) is incorrect because the assumed exercise of the options in calculating EPS usually affects only the denominator in the ratio.

29. In computing primary earnings per share, exercise of stock options or warrants is assumed to take place only if

    A. The average market price of the common stock for the year exceeds the ending market price.

    B. The exercise price of the options or warrants exceeds the market price of the common stock.

    C. The dilution is less than 3%.

    D. The common stock has been selling in excess of the exercise price for substantially all of the last 3 months preceding the end of a reporting period.

The correct answer is (D). *(D.B. Bradley)*
    REQUIRED: The factor determining whether options or warrants are assumed to be exercised in computing PEPS.
    DISCUSSION: The exercise of stock options or warrants should not be assumed until the common stock has been selling in excess of the exercise price for substantially all (at least 11 weeks) of the 3 consecutive months ending with the last month of a period to which EPS data relate. This test must be met only once. Thereafter, the computation is required for all succeeding quarters unless the options and warrants have an antidilutive effect in that quarter.
    Answer (A) is incorrect because the 3-month standard must first be met. If it is, the average market price is used to compute PEPS. Answer (B) is incorrect because market price must exceed the exercise price for the options and warrants to be dilutive. Answer (C) is incorrect because, if dilution is less than 3%, it is not material and the firm is assumed to have a simple capital structure.

30. In determining EPS in a complex capital structure, which of the following is a common stock equivalent?

	Nonconvertible Preferred Stock	Stock Option
A.	Yes	No
B.	Yes	Yes
C.	No	Yes
D.	No	No

The correct answer is (C). *(CPA 1186 T-32)*
    REQUIRED: The definition of a common stock equivalent.
    DISCUSSION: A CSE is a security that in form is not common stock but, because of the terms and circumstances under which it was issued, is in substance equivalent to common stock. Convertible preferred stock, convertible debt, participating securities and two-class common stocks, and contingent shares are within the definition if they meet certain criteria. Nonconvertible preferred stock is never a CSE. Stock options and warrants (and their equivalents) and stock purchase contracts are always CSE.
    Answers (A), (B), and (D) are incorrect because nonconvertible preferred stock is never a CSE, while a stock option is always a CSE.

31. Under the treasury stock method, PEPS data are computed as if options and warrants (outstanding for the entire year) were exercised at the

    A. End of the period and as if the funds obtained thereby were used to purchase common stock at the average market price during the period.

    B. Beginning of the period and as if the funds obtained thereby were used to purchase common stock at the average market price during the period.

    C. End of the period and as if the funds obtained thereby were used to purchase common stock at the current market price in effect at the end of the period.

    D. Beginning of the period and as if the funds obtained thereby were used to purchase common stock at the current market price in effect at the end of the period.

The correct answer is (B). *(Publisher)*
    REQUIRED: The proper application of the treasury stock method to the assumed exercise of options and warrants in the calculation of PEPS.
    DISCUSSION: The treasury stock method of accounting for options and warrants assumes the exercise of outstanding options and warrants at the beginning of the period or at time of issuance, if later. A further assumption is that the proceeds from the exercise were used to purchase common stock at the average market price during the period.
    Answer (A) is incorrect because the options and warrants are assumed to have been exercised at the beginning of the period. Answer (C) is incorrect because both the options and warrants are assumed to have been exercised at the beginning of the period. The current market price in effect at the end of the period is used in applying the treasury stock method in the calculation of FDEPS, not PEPS. Answer (D) is incorrect because the current market price in effect at the end of the period is used in applying the treasury stock method in the calculation of FDEPS, not PEPS.

32. A test to determine whether a convertible security is dilutive or antidilutive is to calculate EPS

    A. For the security alone.

    B. Without inclusion of the security.

    C. For the security alone and compare it to the EPS without inclusion of the security.

    D. For the security alone and compare it to EPS with inclusion of the security.

The correct answer is (C). *(Publisher)*
    REQUIRED: The method of determining whether a convertible security is dilutive or antidilutive.
    DISCUSSION: To ascertain whether its effect is dilutive or antidilutive, one should compute EPS without the security and then compute the EPS of the security itself. If the quotient of the change in the numerator and the change in the denominator is less than EPS excluding the security, the item is dilutive. For example, assuming that EPS without a hypothetical conversion of convertible preferred stock is $1.00, and that the quotient of the preferred dividend added back to the numerator and the shares potentially added to the denominator is $.90, the preferred stock is dilutive.
    Answers (A) and (B) are incorrect because both calculations are necessary to determine whether an item is dilutive. Answer (D) is incorrect because the comparison should be made with EPS that excludes the security.

33. In a primary earnings per share computation, the treasury stock method is used for options and warrants to reflect assumed reacquisition of common stock at the average market price during the period. If the exercise price of the options or warrants exceeds the average market price, the computation would

    A. Fairly present primary earnings per share on a prospective basis.

    B. Fairly present the maximum potential dilution of primary earnings per share on a prospective basis.

    C. Reflect the excess of the number of shares assumed issued over the number of shares assumed reacquired as the potential dilution of earnings per share.

    D. Be antidilutive.

The correct answer is (D). *(CPA 577 T-27)*
    REQUIRED: The effect on PEPS of an exercise price above the average market price for options and warrants.
    DISCUSSION: Using the treasury stock method, options and warrants are assumed to be exercised at the beginning of the period or at time of issuance, if later. The proceeds are then assumed to be used to reacquire common shares outstanding at the average market price for the period. The effect on the denominator in the PEPS calculation is the difference between the shares assumed to be issued and the treasury shares assumed to be acquired. If the exercise price exceeds the average market price, more shares would be purchased than issued. Because this would increase PEPS by decreasing the denominator, the effect would be antidilutive.
    Answers (A) and (B) are incorrect because, when the exercise price exceeds the average market price, the result is antidilutive. Answer (C) is incorrect because the number of shares reacquired would exceed the number issued.

34. In calculating annual primary or basic earnings per share, which of the following should not be considered?

   A. The weighted-average number of common shares outstanding.

   B. The amount of dividends declared on nonconvertible cumulative preferred shares.

   C. The amount of cash dividends declared on common shares.

   D. The number of common shares resulting from the assumed conversion of debentures outstanding.

The correct answer is (C). *(CIA 580 IV-24)*

REQUIRED: The information not included in the calculation of PEPS.

DISCUSSION: The numerator of the PEPS calculation represents the residual income for the period available to holders of common stock and dilutive CSE. A cash dividend on common stock has no effect on earnings available to common shareholders; i.e., earnings are included whether they are distributed or undistributed.

Answer (A) is incorrect because the weighted-average number of common shares outstanding is the denominator of the EPS calculation. Answer (B) is incorrect because the dividend on nonconvertible cumulative preferred stock, whether declared or not, must be deducted from net income to arrive at earnings available to common shareholders. Answer (D) is incorrect because the assumed conversion of debentures requires adjusting both the numerator (for interest, net of tax effect) and the denominator (for the shares assumed issued) of the EPS ratio.

35. SFAS 85, *Yield Test for Determining Whether a Convertible Security is a Common Stock Equivalent*, establishes that convertible securities are common stock equivalents if,

   A. At the time of issuance, they have an effective yield of less than 662/3% of the current average Aa corporate bond yield.

   B. At the time of issuance, they have a cash yield of less than 662/3% of the current average Aa corporate bond yield.

   C. At the time of issuance, they have a cash yield of less than 662/3% of the prime rate.

   D. At the balance sheet date, they have an effective yield of less than 662/3% of the current average Aa corporate bond yield.

The correct answer is (A). *(CMA 1291 2-10)*

REQUIRED: The test for establishing that a convertible security is a common stock equivalent.

DISCUSSION: If, at the time of its issuance, a convertible security is sold to have an effective yield of less than 2/3 (66.66%) of the current average Aa corporate bond yield, it is assumed that the main reason the investor bought the bond was its convertibility feature and that there is a high probability that it will be converted to common stock. Thus, it is considered a common stock equivalent.

Answers (B), (C), and (D) are incorrect because the effective yield on the issue date of the bond as compared to the current average Aa corporate bond yield is used to determine whether or not the bond is a CSE.

36. A company issued a new class of convertible preferred stock during 1986. At the date of issuance, the effective yield on the stock was 60% of the average Aa corporate bond yield. However, by the end of the year the effective yield was 90% of the average Aa corporate bond yield. At the end of the year, what type of classification should this security receive for computation of earnings per share?

   A. Long-term debt equivalent.

   B. Other potentially dilutive security.

   C. Convertible preferred stock.

   D. Common stock equivalent security.

The correct answer is (D). *(CPA 1177 T-22)*

REQUIRED: The treatment of a convertible security that, subsequent to issuance, fails to meet the effective yield test.

DISCUSSION: APB 15 requires that a convertible security classified as a CSE at the date of its issuance remain in that classification as long as it is outstanding. The preferred stock was a CSE at issuance because its effective yield was less than two-thirds of the average Aa corporate bond yield.

Answer (A) is incorrect because, for computation of EPS, stock is never classified as a debt equivalent. Answers (B) and (C) are incorrect because preferred stock must be classified as a CSE if it meets the effective yield test at issuance.

37. In determining primary earnings per share (PEPS), a common stock equivalent was found to be antidilutive in 1995 and dilutive in 1996. The common stock equivalent would be included in the computation for

	1995	1996
A.	Yes	Yes
B.	No	Yes
C.	No	No
D.	Yes	No

The correct answer is (B). *(CPA 587 T-32)*

REQUIRED: The circumstances under which a CSE is included in the determination of PEPS.

DISCUSSION: APB 15 states that PEPS is based on the weighted-average number of common shares outstanding during the period plus the common stock assumed to be outstanding so as to reflect the dilutive effect of CSE. Thus, in a period in which the effect of a common stock equivalent is antidilutive, it is not included in the determination of PEPS. It is included, however, in those periods in which its effect is dilutive.

Answers (A), (C), and (D) are incorrect because the CSE would not be included in determining PEPS in 1995, but would be included in 1996.

38. On June 30, 1995, Lomond, Inc. issued twenty $10,000, 7% bonds at par. Each bond was convertible into 200 shares of common stock. On January 1, 1996, 10,000 shares of common stock were outstanding. The bondholders converted all the bonds on July 1, 1996. On the bonds' issuance date, the average Aa corporate bond yield was 12%. During 1996, the average Aa corporate bond yield was 9%. The following amounts were reported in Lomond's income statement for the year ended December 31, 1996:

Revenues	$977,000
Operating expenses	920,000
Interest on bonds	7,000
Income before income tax	50,000
Income tax at 30%	15,000
Net income	$ 35,000

What amount should Lomond report as its 1996 primary earnings per share?

A. $2.50

B. $2.85

C. $3.00

D. $3.50

The correct answer is (B). *(CPA 592 I-60)*

REQUIRED: The PEPS given convertible bonds.

DISCUSSION: A convertible security meets the common stock equivalency test if its effective yield to the investor at issuance is less than two-thirds of the average Aa corporate bond yield. A dilutive security that meets this test is considered in the computation of both PEPS and FDEPS. The bonds are CSE because their effective yield (7% interest on bonds issued at par) is less than two-thirds of the 12% average Aa corporate bond yield on the date of issuance. The bonds are dilutive because their assumed conversion at the beginning of the year reduces PEPS. In accordance with the if-converted method, dilutive convertible bonds that are CSE are assumed to be converted into common stock at the beginning of the period or at the time of issuance, if later, for both PEPS and FDEPS. Given conversion, there would be no bonds upon which interest could have been paid. Interest is a deduction in arriving at net income. Accordingly, that interest savings, net of tax effect, should be added back to net income in the EPS computation. The numerator of the PEPS numerator is therefore $39,900 {$35,000 + [(1.0 – 30%) x $7,000 interest saved]}, the denominator is 14,000 shares [10,000 + (20 bonds x 200 shares)], and PEPS is $2.85 ($39,900 ÷ 14,000 shares).

Answer (A) is incorrect because $2.50 is based on a numerator of $35,000. Answer (C) is incorrect because $3.00 is based on a numerator of $42,000 (not net of tax). Answer (D) is incorrect because $3.50 is based on net income of $35,000 and 10,000 shares, that is, on the assumption that the bonds are not CSE.

39. Mann, Inc. had 300,000 shares of common stock issued and outstanding at December 31, 1995. On July 1, 1996, an additional 50,000 shares of common stock were issued for cash. Mann also had unexercised stock options to purchase 40,000 shares of common stock at $15 per share outstanding at the beginning and end of 1996. The average market price of Mann's common stock was $20 during 1996. What number of shares should be used in computing primary earnings per share for the year ended December 31, 1996?

A. 325,000

B. 335,000

C. 360,000

D. 365,000

The correct answer is (B). *(CPA 585 I-51)*

REQUIRED: The number of shares to be used in computing PEPS.

DISCUSSION: On July 1, 1996, 50,000 shares of common stock were issued. Hence, for the purpose of calculating Mann's weighted-average number of shares, 300,000 shares should be considered outstanding for the first 6 months and 350,000 shares for the second 6 months, a weighted average of 325,000 shares.

Stock options and warrants are CSE and are to be included in PEPS computations unless they are antidilutive. The options are assumed to be converted at the beginning of the period using the treasury stock method. This method assumes the options are exercised and the $600,000 proceeds (40,000 options x $15) are used to repurchase shares. In the PEPS computation, the assumed repurchase price is the average market price for the period ($20). Thus, 30,000 shares are assumed to be repurchased ($600,000 ÷ $20). The difference between the shares assumed to be issued and those repurchased (40,000 − 30,000 = 10,000) is added to the weighted average of shares of common stock outstanding to determine the PEPS denominator. Thus, 335,000 (325,000 + 10,000) shares should be used in computing PEPS for the year ending December 31, 1996.

Answer (A) is incorrect because 325,000 does not include the 10,000 shares includable due to the stock option. Answer (C) is incorrect because 360,000 includes the full 50,000 shares sold on July 1 instead of the weighted-average number of shares of 25,000. Answer (D) is incorrect because 365,000 includes the full 40,000 shares covered by the stock options instead of the amount computed under the treasury stock method.

40. During 1996, Moore Corp. had the following two classes of stock issued and outstanding for the entire year:

• 100,000 shares of common stock, $1 par.

• 1,000 shares of 4% preferred stock, $100 par, convertible share for share into common stock. This stock is not a common stock equivalent.

Moore's 1996 net income was $900,000, and its income tax rate for the year was 30%. In the computation of primary earnings per share for 1996, the amount to be used in the numerator is

A. $896,000

B. $898,800

C. $900,000

D. $901,200

The correct answer is (A). *(CPA 1188 I-50)*

REQUIRED: The numerator amount to be used in computing PEPS.

DISCUSSION: Primary earnings per share is equal to the amount of earnings available to common shareholders and to holders of CSE, divided by the weighted-average number of shares of common stock and CSE outstanding during the year. Because the preferred stock is not a CSE, the $4,000 (1,000 shares x 4% x $100 par) dividend on the preferred stock must be subtracted from the $900,000 of net income to determine the PEPS numerator ($900,000 − $4,000 = $896,000).

Answer (B) is incorrect because $898,800 includes a deduction for taxes on the amount of the preferred dividend rather than for the entire dividend. Answer (C) is incorrect because $900,000 results from treating the preferred stock as CSE. Answer (D) is incorrect because $901,200 includes an addition for taxes on the preferred dividend.

41. Weaver Company had 100,000 shares of common stock issued and outstanding at December 31, 1995. On July 1, 1996, Weaver issued a 10% stock dividend. Unexercised stock options to purchase 20,000 shares of common stock (adjusted for the 1996 stock dividend) at $20 per share were outstanding at the beginning and end of 1996. The average market price of Weaver's common stock (which was not affected by the stock dividend) was $25 per share during 1996. Net income for the year ended December 31, 1996 was $550,000. What should be Weaver's 1996 primary earnings per common share, rounded to the nearest penny?

A. $4.82

B. $5.00

C. $5.05

D. $5.24

The correct answer is (A). *(CPA 1180 I-10)*

REQUIRED: The PEPS for the year given a midyear stock dividend and unexercised stock options.

DISCUSSION: A stock dividend occurring at any time before issuance of the financial statements must be reflected as a retroactive adjustment to the capital structure at the beginning of the first period presented. Hence, the 110,000 shares outstanding after the stock dividend are deemed to have been outstanding during the entire year.

The options are CSE and are not antidilutive because the exercise price was less than the average market price. Accordingly, exercise of the options is assumed to have occurred at the beginning of the year at the exercise price of $20. Under the treasury stock method, the assumed proceeds of $400,000 (20,000 shares x $20) are used to repurchase 16,000 shares ($400,000 ÷ $25) at the average market price during the period. The difference between the 20,000 shares assumed to be issued and the 16,000 shares assumed to be repurchased increases the PEPS denominator from 110,000 shares to 114,000 shares. Thus, 1996 PEPS equals $4.82 ($550,000 income ÷ 114,000 shares).

Answer (B) is incorrect because $5.00 does not include the stock options in the calculation of shares outstanding for the year. Answer (C) is incorrect because $5.05 includes the shares issued on the stock dividend weighted-average basis. Answer (D) is incorrect because $5.24 includes the shares issued as the stock dividend on a weighted-average basis and does not include the stock options in the calculation of shares outstanding for the year.

42. Peters Corp.'s capital structure was as follows:

	December 31	
	1995	1996
Outstanding shares of stock:		
Common	110,000	110,000
Convertible preferred	10,000	10,000
8% convertible bonds	$1,000,000	$1,000,000

During 1996, Peters paid dividends of $3.00 per share on its preferred stock. The preferred shares are convertible into 20,000 shares of common stock and are considered common stock equivalents. The 8% bonds are convertible into 30,000 shares of common stock but are not considered common stock equivalents. Net income for 1996 was $850,000. Assume that the income tax rate is 30%. The primary earnings per share for 1996 is

A. $6.31

B. $6.54

C. $7.08

D. $7.45

The correct answer is (B). *(CPA 590 II-51)*

REQUIRED: The PEPS given outstanding convertible preferred stock classified as CSE and convertible bonds that are not CSE.

DISCUSSION: As CSE, the preferred stock must be considered in the computation of PEPS. The bonds are not CSE, and they are not considered. Because the convertible preferred shares are included in the calculation, the assumption is made that no dividends were paid to the preferred shareholders. The numerator for the PEPS calculation is thus equal to the $850,000 net income. The denominator is equal to 130,000 shares (110,000 common + 20,000 CSE). Consequently, primary earnings per share is $6.54 ($850,000 ÷ 130,000 shares).

Answer (A) is incorrect because $6.31 is based on a numerator of $820,000 ($850,000 net income – $30,000 preferred dividend). Answer (C) is incorrect because $7.08 is based on a denominator of 120,000 shares (110,000 common and 10,000 preferred). Answer (D) is incorrect because $7.45 is based on a denominator of 110,000 shares and a numerator of $820,000.

43. During all of 1996, Littlefield, Inc. had outstanding 100,000 shares of common stock and 5,000 shares of noncumulative, $7 preferred stock. Each share of the latter, which is classified as a common stock equivalent, is convertible into three shares of common. For 1996, Littlefield had $230,000 income from operations and $575,000 of extraordinary losses; no dividends were paid or declared. Littlefield should report 1996 primary earnings (loss) per share for income before extraordinary items and for net income (loss), respectively, of

A. $2.30 and $(3.45).

B. $2.00 and $(3.00).

C. $2.19 and $(3.29).

D. $2.26 and $(3.39).

The correct answer is (B). *(CPA 1172 II-8)*
REQUIRED: The primary earnings (loss) per share from operations and net income (loss) per share.
DISCUSSION: The noncumulative convertible preferred stock is a CSE. Hence, it is assumed to be converted into 15,000 (5,000 x 3) shares of common stock at the beginning of the period. The denominator for the PEPS calculation is therefore 115,000 shares. PEPS for income from operations before extraordinary items is $230,000 divided by 115,000 shares, or $2.00. Net loss equals the $230,000 income from operations minus the $575,000 extraordinary loss, or $345,000. This amount divided by the 115,000 shares results in a primary loss per share of $3.00.

The effect of including the CSE in the calculation of the net loss per share is antidilutive. However, given a CSE together with income from continuing operations and extraordinary items, one of the per-share amounts required to be disclosed on the face of the income statement may be diluted while others are increased. In that case, the CSE should be recognized for all EPS computations (APB 15 as amended by APB 30).

Answer (A) is incorrect because it excludes the convertible preferred stock from the calculation of shares outstanding for the year. Answer (C) is incorrect because each share of preferred stock is convertible into three shares of common stock. Answer (D) is incorrect because it calculates the number of shares outstanding as if three shares of preferred stock were convertible into one share of common stock.

44. The Brown Company was organized on January 1 and issued 10,000 shares of $10 par common stock. On July 1, Brown declared and issued a 10% common stock dividend. On October 1, an additional 2,000 shares of common stock were issued at par. Net income for the year ended December 31 was $12,650. Brown's primary earnings per share for the year ended December 31 was

A. $1.15

B. $1.27

C. $1.01

D. $1.10

The correct answer is (D). *(CMA 1277 3-8)*
REQUIRED: The PEPS given a stock dividend and an additional issue of common stock.
DISCUSSION: When a stock dividend is distributed by a company, the effect on the number of outstanding shares must be accounted for retroactively to the beginning of the period. Accordingly, the number of shares assumed to be outstanding for the first 9 months is 11,000. As a result of the October 1 issuance of 2,000 shares, 13,000 shares were outstanding for the last 3 months. The weighted-average number of shares outstanding is 11,500 shares [(11,000 x 9/12) + (13,000 x 3/12)]. Net income of $12,650 divided by 11,500 shares equals PEPS of $1.10.

Answer (A) is incorrect because $1.15 excludes the weighted-average number of shares issued during the year. Answer (B) is incorrect because $1.27 excludes shares issued under the stock dividend and the weighted-average number of shares issued during the year. Answer (C) is incorrect because $1.01 includes the shares issued during the year as if outstanding for the entire year and the stock dividend at their weighted average.

45. The Sunshine Corporation had 200,000 shares of common stock and 10,000 shares of noncumulative, $6 preferred stock outstanding during 1996. The preferred stock is classified as a common stock equivalent and is convertible at the rate of three shares of common per share of preferred. For 1996, the company had a $30,000 net loss from operations and declared no dividends. Sunshine should report 1996 primary loss per share of (rounded to the nearest cent)

   A. $(.13)

   B. $(.15)

   C. $(.39)

   D. $(.45)

The correct answer is (B). *(Publisher)*

   REQUIRED: The primary loss per share given preferred stock classified as CSE.

   DISCUSSION: The 10,000 shares of convertible noncumulative preferred stock are classified as CSE and should be included in the PEPS computation if they are dilutive. Since Sunshine had a net loss of $30,000 for 1996, the effect of including the CSE is antidilutive because an increase in the denominator without an offsetting increase in the numerator (the income available to common shareholders) decreases the loss per share. No change in the numerator would result given that no dividend was declared and that the stock is noncumulative. Consequently, primary loss per share is $(.15) [($30,000) ÷ 20,000].

   Answer (A) is incorrect because $(.13) includes the convertible preferred stock. Answer (C) is incorrect because $(.39) includes 200,000 shares of common stock as preferred stock convertible 3-for-1 into common stock (200,000 ÷ 3 = 66,666) and the 10,000 shares of preferred stock as common stock. Answer (D) is incorrect because $(.45) includes the 200,000 shares of common stock as preferred stock convertible 3-for-1 into common stock.

19.4 Fully Diluted Earnings per Share (FDEPS)

46. Which of the following items are included in computing fully diluted earnings per share but are not included in computing primary earnings per share?

   A.   Common shares issued during the year.

   B.   Convertible bonds (dilutive) that are not common stock equivalents.

   C.   Convertible bonds (nondilutive) that are common stock equivalents.

   D.   Stock warrants (dilutive).

The correct answer is (B). *(CPA 593 T-15)*

   REQUIRED: The items included in FDEPS but not PEPS.

   DISCUSSION: PEPS is based on the weighted-average number of common shares outstanding during the period plus common stock equivalents that have a dilutive effect. Thus, convertible debt must meet the common stock equivalency test and be dilutive to be included in the calculation of PEPS. FDEPS includes all potential dilution securities that have dilutive effect.

   Answer (A) is incorrect because common shares issued are included in the calculation of PEPS and FDEPS. Answer (C) is incorrect because nondilutive convertible bonds are usually excluded from the calculation of PEPS and FDEPS. Answer (D) is incorrect because stock options and warrants are included in the calculation of PEPS and FDEPS, if dilutive.

47. Murphy Corp. had 100,000 common shares outstanding on January 1, issued 60,000 shares on April 1 for cash, issued 160,000 shares on July 1 in a stock split, and had income applicable to common stock of $880,000 for the year ended December 31. Fully diluted earnings per common share for the calendar year (rounded to the nearest cent) would be

   A. $2.75

   B. $2.89

   C. $3.03

   D. $5.50

The correct answer is (C). *(Publisher)*

   REQUIRED: The FDEPS for the year given an additional issuance of stock and a stock split.

   DISCUSSION: The stock split requires a retroactive adjustment to the beginning of the year. Given that 160,000 shares were outstanding when the 160,000 additional shares were issued, the stock split was 2-for-1. Accordingly, 200,000 shares are deemed to have been outstanding January through March and 320,000 shares April through December. The weighted-average number of shares outstanding is 290,000 shares [(200,000 x 3/12) + (320,000 x 9/12)]. Thus, FDEPS is $3.03 ($880,000 income ÷ 290,000 shares).

   Answer (A) is incorrect because $2.75 is based on 320,000 shares. Answer (B) is incorrect because $2.89 is based on 305,000 shares. Answer (D) is incorrect because $5.50 is based on 160,000 shares.

48. In applying the treasury stock method of computing the dilutive effect of outstanding options or warrants for quarterly fully diluted earnings per share, when is it appropriate to use the ending market price of common stock as the assumed repurchase price?

A. Always.

B. Never.

C. When the ending market price is higher than the average market price and the exercise price.

D. When the ending market price is lower than the average market price and higher than the exercise price.

The correct answer is (C). *(CPA 1180 T-11)*
REQUIRED: The appropriate use of the end-of-period market price in applying the treasury stock method to options and warrants for quarterly FDEPS.
DISCUSSION: The higher of the ending market price and the average market price during the quarter is used to determine the number of hypothetically repurchased shares included in FDEPS. This price must be greater than the exercise price. Otherwise, the effect would be antidilutive. The use of the higher price results in maximum potential dilution.

Answers (A), (B), and (D) are incorrect because the ending price must be used in calculating FDEPS when it is higher than the average price.

49. At the beginning of the fiscal year, June 1, 1995, Boyd Corporation had 80,000 shares of common stock outstanding. Also outstanding was $200,000 of 8% convertible bonds that had been issued at $1,000 par. The bonds were convertible into 20,000 shares of common stock; however, no bonds were converted during the year. The company's tax rate is 34%, and the Aa bond interest rate has been 10%. Boyd's net income for the year was $107,000. The fully diluted earnings per share (rounded to the nearest cent) of Boyd common stock for the fiscal year ended May 31, 1996 was

A. $1.07

B. $1.18

C. $1.20

D. $1.23

The correct answer is (B). *(CMA 694 2-15)*
REQUIRED: The FDEPS given convertible bonds outstanding.
DISCUSSION: All potentially dilutive securities are included in the determination of FDEPS whether or not they qualify as CSE. Consequently, the denominator of the EPS calculation is 100,000 shares (80,000 common shares outstanding + 20,000 shares that could be issued if the bonds were converted as of the beginning of the year). The calculation of FDEPS assumes the conversion of the bonds at the beginning of the year, so the assumption is that no interest would be paid. Because bond interest was subtracted in determining net income, the FDEPS numerator should be increased by the interest paid (net of tax effect). This after-tax effect was a $10,560 reduction of net income [($8% x $200,000) x (1 – 34% tax rate)]. As indicated below, FDEPS is equal to $1.18 per share.

$$\frac{\$107,000 + \$10,560}{80,000 + 20,000} = \$1.18$$

Answer (A) is incorrect because $1.07 fails to adjust the numerator for the interest savings and extra taxes.
Answer (C) is incorrect because $1.20 uses the Aa bond rate of 10%, which is not relevant to the calculation of FDEPS.
Answer (D) is incorrect because $1.23 fails to consider the additional taxes that would have to be paid on the interest savings.

50. Jones Corp.'s capital structure was as follows:

	December 31	
	1996	1995
Outstanding shares of stock:		
Common	110,000	110,000
Convertible preferred	10,000	10,000
8% convertible bonds	$1,000,000	$1,000,000

During 1996, Jones paid dividends of $3.00 per share on its preferred stock. The preferred shares are convertible into 20,000 shares of common stock and are considered common stock equivalents. The 8% bonds are convertible into 30,000 shares of common stock but are not considered common stock equivalents. Net income for 1996 was $850,000. Assume that the income tax rate is 30%. The fully diluted earnings per share for 1996 is

A. $5.48

B. $5.66

C. $5.81

D. $6.26

The correct answer is (B). *(CPA 1189 I-54)*
REQUIRED: The FDEPS given outstanding convertible preferred shares are CSE and convertible bonds are not.
DISCUSSION: All potentially dilutive securities are included in the FDEPS calculation. Using the if-converted method, both the convertible preferred and the convertible bonds are assumed to have been converted into shares of common stock at the beginning of the year. The FDEPS denominator is therefore equal to 160,000 shares of common stock (110,000 outstanding at year-end + 20,000 from assumed conversion of preferred stock + 30,000 from assumed conversion of bonds). The if-converted method assumes the conversion of the preferred shares and the convertible bonds at the beginning of the year, so a secondary assumption is that neither the preferred dividend nor interest would be paid. Thus, the numerator of the FDEPS calculation will equal net income adjusted for the after-tax effect of bond interest but not preferred dividends. Bond interest net of tax effect was $56,000 [($1,000,000 x 8%) x (1 – 30% tax rate)]. This amount is added to net income. As indicated below, FDEPS is $5.66.

$$\frac{\$850,000 \ + \ \$56,000}{110,000 \ + \ 20,000 \ + \ 30,000} = \$5.66$$

Answer (A) is incorrect because $5.48 equals $876,000 divided by 160,000 shares. Answer (C) is incorrect because $5.81 equals $820,000 divided by 140,000 shares. Answer (D) is incorrect because $6.26 equals $876,000 divided by 140,000 shares.

51. The 1996 net income for the TelPas Co. is $50,000. During 1996, 10,000 shares of common stock and 1,000 warrants were outstanding. Each warrant gives the right to purchase one share of stock at $30 per share. If the average stock price for 1996 was $40, and the ending stock price was $50, what was fully diluted earnings per share?

A. $4.76

B. $4.81

C. $4.88

D. $5.00

The correct answer is (B). *(K. Putnam)*
REQUIRED: The FDEPS using the treasury stock method for outstanding stock options.
DISCUSSION: The treasury stock method of accounting for the dilutive effect of stock options and warrants assumes that they were exercised at the beginning of the period at the exercise price, with the proceeds being used to repurchase shares in the market. For FDEPS, the assumed repurchase price is the end-of-period price if it is higher than the average market price for the period. At the $50 end-of-period price, the proceeds of $30,000 (1,000 warrants x $30) could be used to purchase 600 shares ($30,000 ÷ $50). Assuming 1,000 shares were issued upon exercise of the warrants, the FDEPS denominator will be 10,400 shares (10,000 + 1,000 – 600). Hence, FDEPS is $4.81 ($50,000 net income ÷ 10,400 shares).

Answer (A) is incorrect because $4.76 results from averaging the number of shares available under the warrants. Answer (C) is incorrect because $4.88 results from using the average price of the shares for the year. Answer (D) is incorrect because $5.00 fails to include the stock warrants.

52. Ranchero Corporation has 300,000 shares of common stock outstanding. The only other securities outstanding are 10,000 shares of 9% cumulative preferred stock with detachable warrants (10 warrants per preferred share). Each warrant provides for the purchase of one share of common stock at $72. For 1996, net income was $1,600,000. During 1996, the average market price of common stock was $125. The price at December 31, 1996 was $120. What number of shares should be used to determine 1996 fully diluted earnings per share?

- A. 340,000
- B. 342,400
- C. 357,600
- D. 400,000

The correct answer is (B). *(L. Krueger)*

REQUIRED: The number of shares to be used to determine FDEPS.

DISCUSSION: The treasury stock method of accounting for the dilutive effect of stock options and warrants assumes they are exercised at the beginning of the period at the exercise price, with the proceeds being used to repurchase shares in the market. For FDEPS, the assumed repurchase price is the higher of the average market price and the end-of-period price. At the $125 average price, the $7,200,000 of proceeds (10,000 shares of preferred x 10 warrants per share x $72 exercise price) could be used to purchase 57,600 shares ($7,200,000 ÷ 125). Thus, the FDEPS denominator will be 342,400 shares (300,000 common shares outstanding + 100,000 assumed issued upon conversion – 57,600 assumed repurchased).

Answer (A) is incorrect because the 12/31/96 price of $120 is used. Answer (C) is incorrect because 357,600 includes the 57,600 shares assumed to be repurchased. Answer (D) is incorrect because 400,000 does not adjust for treasury stock assumed to have been purchased.

19.5 Primary and Fully Diluted Earnings per Share

53. In determining earnings per share, interest expense, net of applicable income taxes, on convertible debt that is both a common stock equivalent and dilutive should be

- A. Added back to net income for PEPS and ignored for FDEPS.
- B. Added back to net income for both PEPS and FDEPS.
- C. Deducted from net income for PEPS and ignored for FDEPS.
- D. Deducted from net income for both PEPS and FDEPS.

The correct answer is (B). *(CPA 591 T-29)*

REQUIRED: The correct treatment of after-tax interest on dilutive convertible debt that is a CSE.

DISCUSSION: In accordance with the if-converted method, dilutive convertible debt that is a CSE is assumed to be converted into common stock at the beginning of the period or at the time of issuance, if later, for both PEPS and FDEPS. Given conversion, there would be no debt upon which interest could have been paid. Interest is a deduction in arriving at net income. Accordingly, that interest savings, net of tax effect, should be added back to net income in the EPS computation.

Answers (A), (C), and (D) are incorrect because the interest, net of tax effect, should be added back for both PEPS and FDEPS.

54. When reporting both primary and fully diluted earnings per share,

- A. They should be presented with equal prominence on the face of the income statement.
- B. They need not be shown on the face of the income statement but must be disclosed in the notes to the financial statements.
- C. They need not be shown for any extraordinary items or the cumulative effect of an accounting principle change.
- D. The primary amounts are to be given prominence on the face of the income statement, and the fully diluted amounts may be disclosed in the notes to the financial statements.

The correct answer is (A). *(CMA 693 2-18)*

REQUIRED: The true statement about the reporting of both primary and fully diluted earnings per share (EPS).

DISCUSSION: APB 15 requires EPS information to be reported on the face of the income statement for both income before extraordinary items and net income. A separate EPS amount is also required for the cumulative effect of changes in accounting principle. Dual presentation of both primary and fully diluted EPS is required for companies with complex capital structures. All of these presentations are to be presented with equal prominence.

Answer (B) is incorrect because EPS must be presented on the face of the income statement. Answer (C) is incorrect because EPS must be presented for extraordinary items and the cumulative effect of a change in principle. Answer (D) is incorrect because both primary and fully diluted EPS are to be presented on the face of the income statement with equal prominence.

55. A company's convertible debt is both a common stock equivalent and dilutive in determining earnings per share. What would be the effect of consideration of the convertible debt in calculating

	Primary Earnings per Share	Fully Diluted Earnings per Share
A.	Decrease	Decrease
B.	Increase	No effect
C.	No effect	Decrease
D.	Decrease	Increase

The correct answer is (A). *(CPA 1189 T-28)*

REQUIRED: The effect of considering dilutive common stock equivalents in the calculation of PEPS and FDEPS.

DISCUSSION: APB 15 requires that securities classified as CSE be included in the computation of the number of common shares outstanding for both PEPS and FDEPS if the effect of the inclusion is dilutive. A dilutive effect decreases both PEPS and FDEPS.

Answers (B), (C), and (D) are incorrect because a dilutive effect decreases both PEPS and FDEPS.

Questions 56 and 57 are based on the following information. Howland Corporation had 60,000 shares of $10 par common stock and 10,000 shares of $100 par, 6%, cumulative, convertible preferred stock outstanding for the entire year ended November 30, 1996. The preferred stock, which was not in arrears at November 30, 1996, is not a common stock equivalent, and each share is convertible into four shares of common stock. Howland's net income for the year ended November 30, 1996 was $360,000.

---

56. The primary earnings per share of common stock that should be reported on Howland Corporation's Income Statement for the year ended November 30, 1996 is

A. $0.60

B. $3.60

C. $5.00

D. $6.00

The correct answer is (C). *(CMA 1293 2-22)*

REQUIRED: The primary earnings per share.

DISCUSSION: When there are no common stock equivalents, PEPS is calculated by dividing the net income available to common shareholders by the number of common shares outstanding. The portion of income attributable to common stock equals net income minus the preferred stock dividend requirement. The preferred dividend is $60,000 (10,000 shares x $100 par x 6%). PEPS is therefore $5 [($360,000 NI – $60,000 preferred dividend) ÷ 60,000 common shares].

Answer (A) is incorrect because $0.60 uses par value in the denominator instead of shares outstanding and does not adjust for preferred dividends. Answer (B) is incorrect because $3.60 includes the effect of the preferred stock. Answer (D) is incorrect because $6.00 fails to adjust net income for the preferred dividend.

57. The fully diluted earnings per share of common stock that should be reported on Howland Corporation's income statement for the year ended November 30, 1996 is

A. $0.60

B. $3.60

C. $5.00

D. $6.00

The correct answer is (B). *(CMA 1293 2-23)*

REQUIRED: The fully diluted earnings per share.

DISCUSSION: FDEPS reflects adjustments for all potentially dilutive securities, whether or not they are common stock equivalents. The convertible preferred stock is dilutive. Each of the 10,000 preferred shares is convertible into four shares of common stock. Adding these additional 40,000 shares to the 60,000 common shares currently outstanding increases the denominator to 100,000 shares. If the preferred stock were to be converted, there would be no preferred dividend requirement. Thus, all net income would be available to common shareholders. FDEPS is therefore $3.60 ($360,000 ÷ 100,000 shares).

Answer (A) is incorrect because $0.60 is the PEPS if par value, not shares outstanding, is used in the denominator and the preferred dividend is not subtracted from the numerator. Answer (C) is incorrect because $5 is PEPS. Answer (D) is incorrect because $6.00 is the PEPS with no adjustment for the preferred dividend.

Questions 58 and 59 are based on the following information. Jenna Corporation had 5,000 shares of common stock outstanding during the entire year. Stock options to purchase 2,000 shares at a price of $25 per share were also outstanding throughout the year. The market prices of Jenna's stock were as follows:

January 1	$25
December 31	$50
Average price	$40

58. Jenna had no other securities outstanding. According to APB 15, primary earnings per share should be based on how many shares?

A. 5,000

B. 6,000

C. 6,250

D. 7,000

The correct answer is (B). *(S. Byrd)*
   REQUIRED: The shares used in the PEPS calculation if stock options are outstanding during the entire year.
   DISCUSSION: Stock options are considered to be a CSE and are included in the PEPS calculation if they are dilutive. If the average price of Jenna's stock is greater than the option price, the options are dilutive, and the treasury stock method should be used. This method assumes that the options are exercised at the option price (2,000 shares x $25 = $50,000 proceeds). The proceeds are hypothetically used to repurchase shares at the average market price ($50,000 ÷ $40 = 1,250 shares). The net number of shares assumed to be issued (2,000 − 1,250 = 750) is normally added to the actual shares outstanding to arrive at the PEPS denominator. However, if the number of shares theoretically repurchased exceeds 20% of the shares actually outstanding at year-end, the number assumed repurchased is limited to 20%. Since 1,250 shares exceeds 1,000 shares (5,000 x 20%), the number of shares is limited to 1,000, and the PEPS denominator is 6,000 shares.
   Answer (A) is incorrect because 5,000 does not include the shares issued upon the assumed exercise of the stock warrants. Answer (C) is incorrect because 6,250 includes the shares assumed to be repurchased. Answer (D) is incorrect because 7,000 includes the number of shares assumed to be issued.

59. According to APB 15, fully diluted earnings per share should be based on how many shares?

A. 5,000 shares.

B. 6,000 shares.

C. 6,250 shares.

D. 7,000 shares.

The correct answer is (B). *(S. Byrd)*

REQUIRED: The shares used in the FDEPS calculation if stock options are outstanding during the entire year.

DISCUSSION: The higher of the average or year-end market price is used in the FDEPS calculation. Stock options, which are always considered to be CSE, are included in the FDEPS denominator if the higher of the average or the year-end market price (the assumed repurchase price under the treasury stock method) is greater than the option price. For Jenna, the only difference between FDEPS and PEPS is that the $50,000 (2,000 shares x $25) of hypothetical proceeds is divided by $50, not $40. Without regard to the 20% rule, the number of shares in the FDEPS denominator would therefore equal the 5,000 shares issued and outstanding, plus the 2,000 options outstanding, minus the 1,000 shares ($50,000 ÷ $50) assumed to be repurchased, or 6,000 shares. The number of shares repurchased under both PEPS and FDEPS is limited to 20% of the shares outstanding at the end of the period. However, no adjustment is needed in this instance because the number of shares assumed repurchased (1,000) equals 20% of the outstanding shares (20% x 5,000 = 1,000).

Answer (A) is incorrect because the shares issued upon the assumed exercise of the stock warrants are not included. Answer (C) is incorrect because the average price, not the year-end price, was used to calculate net shares issued. Also, the net shares issued, not the shares assumed repurchased, should be used to calculate shares outstanding for the year. Answer (D) is incorrect because the net number of shares assumed to be issued, not the total number of shares covered under the warrants, should be used to calculate shares outstanding for the year.

Questions 60 and 61 are based on the following information. J Co. had 10,000 shares of common stock outstanding throughout 1996. There was no potential dilution of earnings per share except as follows:

In 1995, J Co. agreed to issue 2,000 additional shares of its stock to the former shareholders of an acquired company if the acquired company's earnings for any of the 5 years 1996 through 2000 exceed $5,000. Results of operations for 1996 were

Net income of J Co.	$10,000
Net income of acquired company	4,000
Consolidated net income	$14,000

60. Primary earnings per share for 1996 on a consolidated basis would be

A. $14,000 ÷ 10,000 = $1.40

B. $14,000 ÷ 12,000 = $1.17

C. $15,000 ÷ 10,000 = $1.50

D. $15,000 ÷ 12,000 = $1.25

The correct answer is (A). *(CPA 1173 I-4)*
REQUIRED: The consolidated PEPS when contingent shares are outstanding and the conditions for issuance are not currently met.
DISCUSSION: APB 15 provides that when the conditions of a contingent issuance of common stock are not currently being met, the effect of the contingent issuance must be excluded from PEPS but included in FDEPS. Because the acquired company is not currently earning $5,000 per year, the contingent shares are disregarded. Accordingly, PEPS equals $1.40 ($14,000 consolidated net income ÷ 10,000 shares issued and outstanding).
Answers (B), (C), and (D) are incorrect because consolidated net income of $14,000 and 10,000 common shares outstanding are used to calculate PEPS.

61. The fully diluted earnings per share for 1996 on a consolidated basis would be

A. $14,000 ÷ 10,000 = $1.40

B. $14,000 ÷ 12,000 = $1.17

C. $15,000 ÷ 10,000 = $1.50

D. $15,000 ÷ 12,000 = $1.25

The correct answer is (D). *(CPA 1173 I-5)*
REQUIRED: The consolidated FDEPS given outstanding contingent shares when the conditions for issuance are not currently met.
DISCUSSION: When the issuance of common stock is contingent upon certain conditions (e.g., specified earnings), and those conditions are not being met, the dilutive effect on EPS is considered in FDEPS but not PEPS.
For FDEPS, the shares are assumed to be issued. The net income of the acquired company must then be adjusted upward to the contingency amount ($5,000). The denominator is also adjusted by adding the number of contingent shares. FDEPS is $1.25.

J Co. net income	$10,000
Plus: Acquired company contingency net income	5,000
Earnings for FDEPS	$15,000
Number of shares outstanding	10,000
Plus: Contingent shares	2,000
Number of shares for FDEPS	12,000

$$\frac{Earnings}{No.\ of\ shares} = \frac{\$15,000}{12,000} = \$1.25\ FDEPS$$

Answers (A), (B), and (C) are incorrect because FDEPS includes the effects of contingent issuances of stock and thus includes net income at the contingency amount and increases common stock outstanding by the amount of the contingent shares.

CHAPTER TWENTY
INCOME TAX ALLOCATION

The first module in this chapter covers the asset and liability method of interperiod tax allocation prescribed by SFAS 109. The second module concerns intraperiod tax allocation. The subject of Module 3 is the investment tax credit, for which the accounting is prescribed by APB 2 and APB 4. Even though the Tax Reform Act of 1986 repealed the ITC for fiscal years beginning after 1985, certain transitional rules allow some taxpayers to claim the credit for several more years. Reenactment of the ITC also remains a possibility.

20.1 Interperiod Tax Allocation - Asset and Liability Method

1. The provisions of SFAS 109, *Accounting for Income Taxes*, are applicable to

A. All foreign, state, and local taxes.

B. Domestic federal income taxes.

C. An enterprise's foreign operations accounted for by the cost method.

D. Financial statements of foreign enterprises required to pay U.S. federal income taxes.

The correct answer is (B). *(Publisher)*
REQUIRED: The applicability of SFAS 109.
DISCUSSION: The principles and requirements of SFAS 109 are applicable to domestic federal income taxes, i.e., the U.S. federal income taxes for U.S. enterprises.

Answer (A) is incorrect because the provisions of SFAS 109 are applicable only to foreign, federal, state, and local taxes that are based on income. Answer (C) is incorrect because the provisions are applicable only to an enterprise's domestic and foreign operations that are consolidated, combined, or accounted for by the equity method. Answer (D) is incorrect because the provisions are applicable to foreign enterprises for purposes of preparing financial statements in accordance with U.S. GAAP only.

2. In its 1996 income statement, Cere Co. reported income before income taxes of $300,000. Cere estimated that, because of permanent differences, taxable income for 1996 would be $280,000. During 1996, Cere made estimated tax payments of $50,000, which were debited to income tax expense. Cere is subject to a 30% tax rate. What amount should Cere report as income tax expense?

A. $34,000

B. $50,000

C. $84,000

D. $90,000

The correct answer is (C). *(CPA 1194 F-51)*
REQUIRED: The amount to be reported for income tax expense.
DISCUSSION: Income tax expense or benefit is the sum of current tax expense or benefit and deferred tax expense or benefit. A deferred tax expense or benefit is the change in an entity's deferred tax assets and liabilities. However, a permanent difference does not result in a change in a deferred tax asset or liability. Thus, income tax expense equals current income tax expense, which is the amount of taxes paid or payable for the year. Income taxes payable for 1996 equal $84,000 ($280,000 taxable income x 30%).

Answer (A) is incorrect because $34,000 equals the $84,000 of income taxes payable minus the $50,000 of income taxes paid. Answer (B) is incorrect because $50,000 equals income taxes paid, not the total current income tax expense. Answer (D) is incorrect because $90,000 is equal to the reported income of $300,000 times the tax rate.

3. SFAS 109, *Accounting for Income Taxes*, establishes standards of financial accounting and reporting for income taxes that are currently payable and for

- A. The tax consequences of revenues and expenses included in taxable income in a different year from the year in which they are recognized for financial reporting purposes.

- B. The method of accounting for the U.S. federal investment tax credit.

- C. The discounting of income taxes.

- D. The accounting for income taxes in general in interim periods.

The correct answer is (A). *(Publisher)*
REQUIRED: The applicability of SFAS 109.
DISCUSSION: SFAS 109 establishes standards of financial accounting and reporting for (1) income taxes currently payable; (2) the tax consequences of revenues, expenses, gains, and losses included in taxable income of an earlier or later year than the year in which they are recognized in income for financial reporting purposes; (3) other events that create differences between the tax bases of assets and liabilities and their amounts for financial reporting purposes; and (4) operating loss or tax credit carrybacks for refunds of taxes paid in prior years and carryforwards to reduce taxes payable in future years.
Answers (B) and (C) are incorrect because these issues are excluded from the scope of SFAS 109. Answer (D) is incorrect because, with certain exceptions, SFAS 109 does not address accounting for income taxes in interim periods. The exceptions relate to the recognition of tax benefits, the effects of enacted changes in tax law or rates, and changes in valuation allowance in interim periods.

4. Temporary differences arise when expenses are deductible for tax purposes

	After They Are Recognized in Financial Income	Before They Are Recognized in Financial Income
A.	No	No
B.	No	Yes
C.	Yes	Yes
D.	Yes	No

The correct answer is (C). *(CPA 1189 T-27)*
REQUIRED: The situations in which temporary differences arise.
DISCUSSION: A temporary difference exists when (1) the reported amount of an asset or liability in the financial statements differs from the tax basis of that asset or liability, and (2) the difference will result in taxable or deductible amounts in future years when the asset is recovered or the liability is settled at its reported amount. A temporary difference may also exist although it cannot be identified with a specific asset or liability recognized for financial reporting purposes. An example is a long-term contract accounted for by the percentage-of-completion method for financial reporting and the completed-contract method for tax purposes. Such a temporary difference must result from an event recognized in the financial statements and must also result in taxable or deductible amounts in future years based on the provisions of the tax laws. Temporary differences most commonly arise when either expenses or revenues are recognized for tax purposes either earlier or later than in the determination of financial income.
Answers (A), (B), and (D) are incorrect because temporary differences arise when expenses are deductible for tax purposes either before or after they are recognized in financial income.

5. For which of the following temporary differences is the recognition of a deferred tax liability or asset most likely not required by SFAS 109?

- A. A warranty liability covering 10 future years.

- B. Equipment whose depreciable life is twice its tax recovery life.

- C. The excess of the reported investment in a foreign subsidiary over the tax basis.

- D. A gain arising from an involuntary condemnation of a building.

The correct answer is (C). *(Publisher)*
REQUIRED: The temporary difference for which recognition of deferred taxes is usually not required.
DISCUSSION: In general, SFAS 109 requires that a deferred tax be recognized for all temporary differences. Certain of the areas addressed by APB 23, *Accounting for Income Taxes - Special Areas*, are exceptions. As amended by SFAS 109, APB 23 states that a deferred tax liability is not recognized for the excess of the reported amount of an investment in a foreign subsidiary over its tax basis that meets the indefinite reversal criteria stated in APB 23. Deferred tax liabilities or assets are also not recognized for leveraged leases, goodwill for which amortization is not permitted for tax purposes, and unallocated negative goodwill.
Answers (A), (B), and (D) are incorrect because each gives rise to a temporary difference for which a deferred tax liability or asset is recognized.

6. Among the items reported on Cord, Inc.'s income statement for the year ended December 31, 1996 were the following:

Amortization of goodwill	$10,000
Insurance premium on life of an officer, Cord is the owner and beneficiary	5,000

Neither is deductible for tax purposes. Temporary differences amount to

A. $0

B. $5,000

C. $10,000

D. $15,000

The correct answer is (A). *(CPA 589 I-42)*

REQUIRED: The amount of temporary differences.

DISCUSSION: Most temporary differences arise when (1) the reported amount of an asset or a liability in the financial statements differs from the tax basis of that asset or liability, and (2) the difference will result in taxable or deductible amounts in future years when the asset is recovered or the liability is settled at its reported amount. It is given that expenses for amortization of goodwill and payment of the premium for life insurance covering a key executive are recognized in the financial statements but are not deductible for tax purposes. Because neither will result in taxable or deductible amounts in future years, neither meets the definition of a temporary difference.

Answers (B), (C), and (D) are incorrect because neither expense is deductible for tax purposes.

7. West Corp. leased a building and received the $36,000 annual rental payment on June 15, 1996. The beginning of the lease was July 1, 1996. Rental income is taxable when received. West's tax rates are 30% for 1996 and 40% thereafter. West had no other permanent or temporary differences. West determined that no valuation allowance was needed. What amount of deferred tax asset should West report in its December 31, 1996 balance sheet?

A. $5,400

B. $7,200

C. $10,800

D. $14,400

The correct answer is (B). *(CPA 593 I-26)*

REQUIRED: The amount of deferred tax asset reported at year-end.

DISCUSSION: The $36,000 rental payment is taxable in full when received in 1996, but only $18,000 ($36,000 x 6/12) should be recognized in financial accounting income for the year. The result is a deductible temporary difference arising from the difference between the tax basis ($0) of the liability for unearned rent and its reported amount in the year-end balance sheet ($36,000 – $18,000 = $18,000). A deductible temporary difference results in a deferred tax asset. The income tax payable for 1996 based on the rental payment is $10,800 (30% tax rate for 1996 x $36,000), the deferred tax asset is $7,200 (40% enacted tax rate applicable after 1996 when the asset will be realized x $18,000 future deductible amount), and the income tax expense is $3,600 ($10,800 current tax expense – $7,200 deferred tax benefit). The deferred tax benefit equals the net change during the year in the enterprise's deferred tax liabilities and assets ($7,200 deferred tax asset recognized in 1996 – $0).

Answer (A) is incorrect because $5,400 is based on a 30% tax rate. Answer (C) is incorrect because $10,800 is income tax payable. Answer (D) is incorrect because $14,400 would be the income tax payable if the 40% tax rate applied in 1996.

8. Which one of the following temporary differences will result in a deferred tax asset?

A. Use of the straight-line depreciation method for financial statement purposes and the Modified Accelerated Cost Recovery System (MACRS) for income tax purposes.

B. Installment sale profits accounted for on the accrual basis for financial statement purposes and on a cash basis for income tax purposes.

C. Advance rental receipts accounted for on the accrual basis for financial statement purposes and on a cash basis for tax purposes.

D. Prepaid expenses accounted for on the accrual basis for financial statement purposes and on a cash basis for income tax purposes.

The correct answer is (C). *(CMA 696 2-9)*

REQUIRED: The temporary difference that will result in a deferred tax asset.

DISCUSSION: A deferred tax asset records the deferred tax consequences attributable to deductible temporary differences and carryforwards. Advance rental receipts accounted for on the accrual basis for financial statement purposes and on a cash basis for tax purposes would give rise to a deferred tax asset. The financial statements would show no income and no related tax expense because the rental payments apply to future periods. The tax return, however, would show the rent as income when the cash was received, and a tax would be due in the year of receipt. Because the tax is paid prior to recording the income for financial statement purposes, it represents an asset that will be recognized as an expense when income is finally recorded.

Answer (A) is incorrect because using accelerated depreciation on the tax return results in a deferred tax liability. Answer (B) is incorrect because recognizing installment income on the financial statements but not the tax return results in a taxable temporary difference. Answer (D) is incorrect because recognizing prepaid expenses earlier on the tax return than on the financial statements (a situation akin to the accelerated depreciation of fixed assets) gives rise to a deferred tax liability.

9. At the beginning of year 1, Cody Construction began work on a 3-year construction contract. This contract is accounted for by the percentage-of-completion method for financial accounting purposes and the completed-contract method for tax purposes. During year 1, Cody reported $800,000 of income from this contract. However, because of cost overruns incurred in year 2, Cody reported a $500,000 loss from this contract. According to SFAS 109, Cody's year 2 balance sheet should include a

	Deferred Tax Asset	Deferred Tax Liability
A.	Yes	Yes
B.	Yes	No
C.	No	No
D.	No	Yes

The correct answer is (D). *(CPA 1191 T-4)*
REQUIRED: The deferred tax account(s) to be recognized.
DISCUSSION: A deferred tax liability is recognized for the deferred tax consequences attributable to taxable temporary differences. A deferred tax asset is recognized for the deferred tax consequences attributable to deductible temporary differences. At the end of year 2, the cumulative effect of the difference in accounting for financial reporting and tax purposes is a $300,000 ($800,000 – $500,000) temporary difference. Because this $300,000 temporary difference will result in future taxable amounts, it is a taxable temporary difference for which a deferred tax liability is recognized.
Answer (A) is incorrect because a deferred tax asset is not recognized. Answer (B) is incorrect because a deferred tax liability, not an asset, is recognized. Answer (C) is incorrect because a deferred tax liability is recognized.

10. Rein, Inc. reported deferred tax assets and deferred tax liabilities at the end of both 1995 and 1996. According to SFAS 109, for the year ended in 1996, Rein should report deferred income tax expense or benefit equal to the

A. Sum of the net changes in deferred tax assets and deferred tax liabilities.

B. Decrease in the deferred tax assets.

C. Increase in the deferred tax liabilities.

D. Amount of the income tax liability plus the sum of the net changes in deferred tax assets and deferred tax liabilities.

The correct answer is (A). *(CPA 1192 T-41)*
REQUIRED: The method of determining deferred income tax expense or benefit.
DISCUSSION: The deferred tax expense or benefit recognized is the sum of the net changes in the deferred tax assets and deferred tax liabilities. The deferred income tax expense or benefit is aggregated with the income taxes currently payable or refundable to determine the amount of income tax expense or benefit for the year to be recorded in the income statement.
Answers (B) and (C) are incorrect because the deferred income tax expense or benefit is equal to the sum of the net changes in the deferred tax assets and deferred tax liabilities. Answer (D) is incorrect because this calculation determines the income tax expense or benefit for the year.

11. Because Jab Co. uses different methods to depreciate equipment for financial statement and income tax purposes, Jab has temporary differences that will reverse during the next year and add to taxable income. Deferred income taxes that are based on these temporary differences should be classified in Jab's balance sheet as a

A. Contra account to current assets.

B. Contra account to noncurrent assets.

C. Current liability.

D. Noncurrent liability.

The correct answer is (D). *(CPA 594 F-24)*
REQUIRED: The classification of deferred income taxes based on temporary differences.
DISCUSSION: These temporary differences arise from use of an accelerated depreciation method for tax purposes. Future taxable amounts reflecting the difference between the tax basis and the reported amount of the asset will result when the reported amount is recovered. Accordingly, Jab must recognize a deferred tax liability to record the tax consequences of these temporary differences. This liability is noncurrent because the related asset (equipment) is noncurrent.
Answers (A) and (B) are incorrect because a liability is not shown as an offset to assets. Answer (C) is incorrect because the classification of the deferred tax liability is determined by the classification of the asset to which it relates.

12. Thorn Co. applies SFAS 109, *Accounting for Income Taxes*. At the end of 1996, the tax effects of temporary differences were as follows:

	Deferred Tax Assets (Liabilities)	Related Asset Classification
Accelerated tax depreciation	($75,000)	Noncurrent asset
Additional costs in inventory for tax purposes	25,000 ($50,000)	Current asset

A valuation allowance was not considered necessary. Thorn anticipates that $10,000 of the deferred tax liability will reverse in 1997. In Thorn's December 31, 1996 balance sheet, what amount should Thorn report as noncurrent deferred tax liability?

- A. $40,000
- B. $50,000
- C. $65,000
- D. $75,000

The correct answer is (D). *(CPA 1194 F-6)*
REQUIRED: The amount of noncurrent deferred tax liability.
DISCUSSION: In a classified balance sheet, deferred tax assets and liabilities are separated into current and noncurrent amounts as stated in SFAS 37, *Balance Sheet Classification of Deferred Income Taxes*. Classification as current or noncurrent is based on the classification of the related asset or liability. Because the $75,000 deferred tax liability is related to a noncurrent asset, it should be classified as noncurrent.
Answer (A) is incorrect because $40,000 equals the $50,000 net deferred tax liability minus the $10,000 expected to reverse in 1997. Answer (B) is incorrect because $50,000 equals the net deferred tax liability. Answer (C) is incorrect because $65,000 equals the $75,000 noncurrent deferred tax liability minus the $10,000 expected to reverse in 1997.

13. Enterprises for which graduated tax rates are a significant factor measure a deferred tax liability or asset using the

- A. Alternative minimum tax rate.
- B. Average graduated tax rate.
- C. Marginal tax rate.
- D. Flat tax rate.

The correct answer is (B). *(Publisher)*
REQUIRED: The tax rate used to measure a deferred tax liability or asset if graduated rates are significant.
DISCUSSION: Enterprises for which graduated tax rates are significant measure a deferred tax liability or asset using the average graduated tax rate applicable to the amount of estimated annual taxable income in the periods in which the enterprise estimates that the deferred tax liability or asset will be settled or recovered.
Answer (A) is incorrect because the alternative minimum tax rate is considered only in the recognition of a deferred tax asset for an alternative minimum tax credit carryforward. Answer (C) is incorrect because the average graduated tax rate is used. Answer (D) is incorrect because the flat tax rate is used by enterprises for which graduated tax rates are not a significant factor.

14. SFAS 109, *Accounting for Income Taxes*, states that a deferred tax asset shall be reduced by a valuation allowance if it is

- A. Probable that some portion will not be realized.
- B. Reasonably possible that some portion will not be realized.
- C. More likely than not that some portion will not be realized.
- D. Likely that some portion will not be realized.

The correct answer is (C). *(Publisher)*
REQUIRED: The standard established by SFAS 109 for recognizing a valuation allowance for a deferred tax asset.
DISCUSSION: A deferred tax asset shall be reduced by a valuation allowance if the weight of the available evidence, both positive and negative, indicates that it is more likely than not (that is, the probability is greater than 50%) that some portion will not be realized. The allowance should suffice to reduce the deferred tax asset to the amount that is more likely than not to be realized.
Answers (A) and (D) are incorrect because the FASB specifically rejected the term probable (likely) as used in SFAS 5, *Accounting for Contingencies*. Answer (B) is incorrect because the FASB believes that the appropriate criterion is the one that produces results that are closest to the expected outcome. A reasonable possibility does not meet that standard.

15. The only temporary differences for a calendar-year firm arise from a major lease, which is capitalized for financial reporting purposes and treated as an operating lease for tax purposes. At December 31, the temporary difference amounts to $600,000, and the related deferred income tax asset account has a $240,000 debit balance. What portion of this deferred tax asset should be classified as noncurrent if the firm, in its next year, expects to deduct $480,000 for rental expense in its tax return and to expense a total of $420,000 as depreciation and interest related to the lease in the income statement?

A. $0

B. $180,000

C. $216,000

D. $240,000

The correct answer is (C). *(Publisher)*
REQUIRED: The balance of the December 31 noncurrent deferred income tax account.
DISCUSSION: SFAS 37, *Balance Sheet Classification of Deferred Income Taxes*, states that, when a temporary difference is not related to a specific asset or liability, the related deferred tax account should be classified based on the expected reversal date of the temporary difference.

The temporary difference arising from the lease is not related to a specific asset or liability because it is related to both the capitalized fixed asset and the lease obligation. The temporary difference is being reversed because the expected tax deduction for the next year is greater by $60,000 than the expected financial reporting expenses. Given that the $60,000 reversing difference expected in the next year is 10% ($60,000 ÷ $600,000) of the temporary difference at December 31, $24,000 (10% x $240,000) of the deferred tax balance at December 31 should be classified as current, and $216,000 (90% x $240,000) should be classified as noncurrent.

Answer (A) is incorrect because $216,000 should be classified as noncurrent deferred tax asset. Answer (B) is incorrect because $180,000 results from the difference between the temporary difference and the amount of expense for depreciation and interest for next year. Answer (D) is incorrect because $240,000 is the total deferred tax asset.

16. SFAS 109 requires that deferred tax assets be reduced by a valuation allowance if, based on the weight of the evidence, it is more likely than not that some portion or all of the deferred tax assets will not be realized. Which of the following kinds of evidence is considered in making this determination?

	Positive Evidence	Negative Evidence
A.	Yes	No
B.	Yes	Yes
C.	No	Yes
D.	No	No

The correct answer is (B). *(Publisher)*
REQUIRED: The evidence to be considered in determining whether a valuation allowance should be recognized.
DISCUSSION: In determining whether a valuation allowance is required to reduce deferred tax assets to the amount that is more likely than not to be realized, all available evidence should be considered. Available evidence includes both positive and negative evidence. In considering the relative impact of positive and negative evidence, the weight given to the potential effect of the evidence should be commensurate with the extent to which the evidence can be objectively verified. However, the more negative evidence in existence, the more positive evidence is necessary and the more difficult it is to support a conclusion that a valuation allowance is not necessary.

Answers (A), (C), and (D) are incorrect because all available evidence should be considered in determining whether a valuation allowance is required, including both positive and negative evidence.

17. When a change in the tax law or rates occurs, the effect of the change on a deferred tax liability or asset is

A. Not recognized.

B. Recognized as an adjustment as of the effective date of the change.

C. Recognized as an adjustment as of the enactment date of the change.

D. Recognized as a prior-period adjustment.

The correct answer is (C). *(Publisher)*
REQUIRED: The effect on a deferred tax liability or asset of a change in the tax law or rates.
DISCUSSION: When a change in the tax law or rates occurs, the effect of the change on a deferred tax liability or asset is recognized as an adjustment in the period that includes the enactment date of the change. The adjustment is allocated to income from continuing operations. It is not treated as an extraordinary item.

Answers (A), (B), and (D) are incorrect because when a change in tax law occurs, the effect of the change on deferred tax liability or asset is recognized as an adjustment in the period that includes the enactment date of the change.

18. On September 15, 1995, the county in which Spirit Company operates enacted changes in the county's tax law. These changes are to become effective on January 1, 1996. They will have a material effect on the deferred tax accounts that Spirit reported in accordance with SFAS 109. In which of the following interim and annual financial statements issued by Spirit should the effect of the changes in tax law initially be reported?

A. The interim financial statements for the 3-month period ending September 30, 1995.

B. The annual financial statements for the year ending December 31, 1995.

C. The interim financial statements for the 3-month period ending March 31, 1996.

D. The annual financial statements for the year ending December 31, 1996.

The correct answer is (A). *(Publisher)*
REQUIRED: The financial statements in which the effects of a change in tax law should initially be reported.
DISCUSSION: The effects of a change in tax law or rates initially should be included in income from continuing operations in the first financial statements issued for the period that includes the enactment date.
Answer (B) is incorrect because the effect should initially be reported in the first statements issued for the period that includes the enactment date. Answers (C) and (D) are incorrect because the periods covered include the effective date, not the enactment date.

19. In late summer, the K&S Partnership incorporated as a taxable entity. On September 7, the SPC Corporation, a taxable entity, changed its status to a partnership. In accordance with the provisions of SFAS 109, a deferred tax liability, based on temporary differences existing at the time of the change in the tax status of these enterprises, should

	K&S	SPC
A.	Not be recognized	Not be eliminated
B.	Be recognized	Not be eliminated
C.	Be recognized	Be eliminated
D.	Not be recognized	Be eliminated

The correct answer is (C). *(Publisher)*
REQUIRED: The effect on two enterprises of changes in tax status.
DISCUSSION: When an enterprise such as K&S changes its status from a nontaxable partnership to a taxable corporation, a deferred tax liability or asset should be recognized for taxable or deductible temporary differences or carryforwards existing at the date of the tax status change. When a company such as SPC changes its status from a taxable to a nontaxable enterprise, any existing deferred tax liability or asset should usually be eliminated at the date of the tax status change. The effect of either recognizing or eliminating a deferred tax liability or asset should be allocated to continuing operations. It should not be treated as an extraordinary item.
Answers (A), (B), and (D) are incorrect because when a nontaxable entity changes its status to a taxable entity, a deferred tax liability or asset should be recognized. Also, when a taxable entity changes it status to a nontaxable entity, any existing deferred tax assets or liabilities should be eliminated.

20. When an enterprise is acquired in a business combination that is properly accounted for as a purchase, a deferred tax liability or asset is recognized for the difference between the assigned value and the tax basis of

A. Goodwill for which amortization is not deductible.

B. A leveraged lease.

C. Inventory.

D. Unallocated negative goodwill.

The correct answer is (C). *(Publisher)*
REQUIRED: The effect on a deferred tax liability or asset of a purchase business combination.
DISCUSSION: SFAS 109 requires that a deferred tax liability or asset be recognized for differences between the assigned values and the tax bases of assets and liabilities recorded when an enterprise is acquired in a business combination properly accounted for as a purchase. The exceptions are for goodwill, unallocated negative goodwill, leveraged leases, and certain APB 23 differences. Accordingly, a difference between the assigned value and the tax basis of inventory results in recognition of a deferred tax liability or asset in these circumstances.
Answers (A), (B), and (D) are incorrect because deferred tax accounts are not recognized for these situations.

21. Which one of the following is correct regarding disclosure of income taxes, including deferred taxes?

A. The manner of reporting the tax benefit of an operating loss carryforward or carryback is determined by the source of the income or loss in the current year.

B. The manner of reporting the tax benefit of an operating loss carryforward or carryback is determined by the source of expected future income that will result in realization of a deferred tax asset for an operating loss carryforward from the current year.

C. The tax benefit of an operating loss carryforward or carryback is disclosed only in a note to the financial statements.

D. The tax benefit of an operating loss carryforward or carryback is a component of net tax expense and is not separately disclosed.

The correct answer is (A). *(CMA 693 2-26)*
REQUIRED: The correct statement about disclosures relating to income taxes.
DISCUSSION: Under SFAS 109, with certain exceptions, the tax benefit of an operating loss carryforward is reported in the same manner as the source of the income offset by the carryforward in the current year. Similarly, the tax benefit of an operating loss carryback is reported in the same manner as the source of the current-year loss.
Answer (B) is incorrect because the manner of reporting is controlled by the source of the income or loss in the current year. Answer (C) is incorrect because the tax benefit is recorded. Answer (D) is incorrect because operating loss carryforwards and carrybacks should be separately disclosed.

22. SFAS 109 prescribes which of the following disclosures?

A. The reconciliation of the reported amount of income tax expense attributable to continuing operations to income taxes currently payable.

B. The amounts and expiration dates of operating loss carryforwards for both financial reporting and tax purposes.

C. The amounts and expiration dates of tax credit carryforwards for financial reporting purposes only.

D. The reconciliation of the reported amount of income tax expense attributable to continuing operations to the amount of income tax expense that would result from applying domestic federal statutory tax rates to pretax income from continuing operations.

The correct answer is (D). *(Publisher)*
REQUIRED: The disclosure prescribed by SFAS 109.
DISCUSSION: SFAS 109 requires that the reported amount of income tax expense attributable to continuing operations for the year be reconciled to the amount of income tax expense that would result from applying domestic federal statutory tax rates to pretax income from continuing operations. Public enterprises must disclose the estimated amount and the nature of each significant reconciling item. Nonpublic enterprises must disclose the nature of significant reconciling items but may omit a numerical reconciliation.
Answer (A) is incorrect because the reconciliation is to the amount of income tax expense that would result from applying domestic federal statutory tax rates to pretax income from continuing operations. Answers (B) and (C) are incorrect because only the amounts and expiration dates of operating loss and tax credit carryforwards for tax purposes must be disclosed.

23. On December 31, 1996, Health Company reported a $150,000 warranty expense in its income statement. The expense was based on actual warranty costs of $30,000 in 1996 and expected warranty costs of $35,000 in 1997, $40,000 in 1998, and $45,000 in 1999. At December 31, 1996, deferred taxes should be based on a

A. $120,000 deductible temporary difference.

B. $150,000 deductible temporary difference.

C. $120,000 taxable temporary difference.

D. $150,000 taxable temporary difference.

The correct answer is (A). *(Publisher)*
REQUIRED: The taxable (deductible) temporary difference resulting from a warranty expense.
DISCUSSION: At year-end 1996, Health Company should report a $120,000 warranty liability in its balance sheet. The warranty liability is equal to the $150,000 warranty expense minus the $30,000 warranty cost actually incurred in 1996. Because warranty costs are not deductible until actually incurred, the tax basis of the warranty liability is $0. The result is a $120,000 temporary difference ($120,000 book basis – $0 tax basis). When the liability is settled through the actual incurrence of warranty costs, the amounts will be deductible. Thus, the temporary difference should be classified as a deductible temporary difference.
Answer (B) is incorrect because $150,000 equals the warranty expense, not the payable. Answer (C) is incorrect because warranty costs will result in a deductible amount. Answer (D) is incorrect because the warranty costs will result in a deductible amount, and the $30,000 actual warranty costs are currently deductible.

24. Stone Co. began operations in 1996 and reported $225,000 in income before income taxes for the year. Stone's 1996 tax depreciation exceeded its book depreciation by $25,000. Stone also had nondeductible book expenses of $10,000 related to permanent differences. Stone's tax rate for 1996 was 40%, and the enacted rate for years after 1996 is 35%. In its December 31, 1996 balance sheet, what amount of deferred income tax liability should Stone report?

A. $8,750

B. $10,000

C. $12,250

D. $14,000

The correct answer is (A). *(CPA 593 I-36)*
REQUIRED: The deferred income tax liability reported on the balance sheet.
DISCUSSION: In measuring a deferred tax liability or asset, the objective is to use the enacted tax rate(s) expected to apply to taxable income in the periods in which the deferred tax liability or asset is expected to be settled or realized. At 12/31/96, the only temporary difference is the $25,000 excess of tax depreciation over the book depreciation. This temporary difference will give rise to a $25,000 taxable amount in the years following 1996. Given the enacted tax rate of 35% applicable after 1996, the total tax consequence attributable to the taxable temporary difference (the deferred tax liability) is $8,750 ($25,000 x 35%).

Answer (B) is incorrect because the 35% tax rate applicable when the deferred tax liability is expected to be settled should be used. Answer (C) is incorrect because permanent differences do not create deferred tax liabilities. Answer (D) is incorrect because permanent differences do not create deferred tax liabilities, and the 35% tax rate applicable when the deferred tax liability is expected to be settled should be used.

25. Mobe Co. reported the following operating income (loss) for its first three years of operations:

1994	$ 300,000
1995	(700,000)
1996	1,200,000

For each year, there were no deferred income taxes, and Mobe's effective income tax rate was 30%. In its 1995 income tax return, Mobe elected to carry back the maximum amount of loss possible. In its 1996 income statement, what amount should Mobe report as total income tax expense?

A. $120,000

B. $150,000

C. $240,000

D. $360,000

The correct answer is (C). *(CPA 595 F-43)*
REQUIRED: The total income tax expense.
DISCUSSION: A net operating loss (NOL) can be carried back 3 years and forward 15 years. The taxpayer may also elect to carry the NOL forward only. Mobe elected to carry back the NOL. The carry back begins in 1994, the first year of operations. Mobe can apply only $300,000 of the NOL (the operating income for 1994) to 1994, and the remaining $400,000 of the NOL is carried forward to 1996. Given no deferred income taxes, Mobe recorded no deferred tax asset related to the NOL. Thus, total 1996 income tax expense (change in deferred tax accounts and the current tax paid or payable) equals the income tax paid or payable (taxable income x the effective tax rate) of $240,000 [($1,200,000 – $400,000 NOL carryforward) x 30%].

Answer (A) is incorrect because $120,000 is the tax saved. Answer (B) is incorrect because $150,000 is the income tax payable if the loss is carried forward only. Answer (D) is incorrect because $360,000 is the tax on $1,200,000.

26. Based on its current operating levels, Glucose Corporation estimates that its annual level of taxable income in the foreseeable future will be $200,000 annually. Enacted tax rates for the tax jurisdiction in which Glucose operates are 15% for the first $50,000 of taxable income, 25% for the next $50,000 of taxable income, and 35% for taxable income in excess of $100,000. Which tax rate should Glucose use to measure a deferred tax liability or asset in accordance with SFAS 109, *Accounting for Income Taxes?*

A. 15%

B. 25%

C. 27.5%

D. 35%

The correct answer is (C). *(Publisher)*
REQUIRED: The tax rate applicable to the measurement of a deferred tax liability or asset.
DISCUSSION: In measuring a deferred tax liability or asset, the objective is to use the enacted tax rate(s) expected to apply to taxable income in the periods in which the deferred tax liability or asset is expected to be settled or realized. If graduated tax rates are a significant factor for an enterprise, the applicable tax rate is the average graduated tax rate applicable to the amount of estimated future annual taxable income. As indicated, the applicable tax rate is 27.5%.

Taxable Income		Tax Rate		
$ 50,000	×	15%	=	$ 7,500
50,000	×	25%	=	12,500
100,000	×	35%	=	35,000
$200,000				$55,000

$55,000 ÷ $200,000 = 27.5%

Answer (A) is incorrect because 15% is the tax rate for the first $50,000 of income. Answer (B) is incorrect because 25% is the tax rate for income over $50,000 but less than $100,000. Answer (D) is incorrect because 35% is the tax rate for income over $100,000.

27. In its 1996 income statement, Noll Corp. reported depreciation of $400,000. Noll reported depreciation of $550,000 on its 1996 income tax return. The difference in depreciation is the only temporary difference, and it will reverse equally over the next 3 years. Assume that the enacted income tax rates are 35% for 1996, 30% for 1997, and 25% for 1998 and 1999. What amount should be included in the deferred income tax liability in Noll's December 31, 1996 balance sheet?

A. $37,500

B. $40,000

C. $45,000

D. $52,500

The correct answer is (B). *(CPA 1190 I-19)*
REQUIRED: The amount to be included in the deferred income tax liability at year-end.
DISCUSSION: At 12/31/96, the only temporary difference is the $150,000 ($550,000 – $400,000) excess of the tax depreciation over the book depreciation. This temporary difference will give rise to a $50,000 taxable amount in each of the years 1997 through 1999. Given the enacted tax rates of 30% in 1997 and 25% in 1998 and 1999, the total tax consequences are $40,000, which is the balance that should be reported in the deferred income tax liability at year-end.

Year	Taxable Amount	Enacted Tax Rates	Tax Consequences
1997	$50,000	30%	$15,000
1998	50,000	25%	12,500
1999	50,000	25%	12,500
			$40,000

Answer (A) is incorrect because $37,500 is based on a 25% tax rate. Answer (C) is incorrect because $45,000 is based on a 30% tax rate. Answer (D) is incorrect because $52,500 is based on a 35% tax rate.

28. Tower Corp. began operations on January 1, 1995. For financial reporting, Tower recognizes revenues from all sales under the accrual method. However, in its income tax returns, Tower reports qualifying sales under the installment method. Tower's gross profit on these installment sales under each method was as follows:

Year	Accrual Method	Installment Method
1995	$1,600,000	$ 600,000
1996	2,600,000	1,400,000

The income tax rate is 30% for 1995 and future years. There are no other temporary or permanent differences. In its December 31, 1996 balance sheet, what amount should Tower report as a liability for deferred income taxes?

A. $840,000

B. $660,000

C. $600,000

D. $360,000

The correct answer is (B). *(CPA 1192 I-32)*
REQUIRED: The deferred income tax liability resulting from sales under the installment and accrual method.
DISCUSSION: At year-end 1996, the only temporary difference is the $2,200,000 difference between the $4,200,000 ($1,600,00 + $2,600,000) profit recognized under the accrual method and the $2,000,000 ($600,000 + $1,400,000) profit recognized under the installment method. Since it will result in taxable amounts in future years when the installment amounts are collected, it is classified as a taxable temporary difference. Measured at the 30% applicable tax rate, it results in a $660,000 ($2,200,000 x 30%) deferred tax liability.
Answer (A) is incorrect because $840,000 assumes a $2,800,000 taxable temporary difference. Answer (C) is incorrect because $600,000 assumes a $2,000,000 taxable temporary difference. Answer (D) is incorrect because $360,000 assumes a $1,200,000 taxable temporary difference.

29. Taft Corp. uses the equity method to account for its 25% investment in Flame, Inc. During 1996, Taft received dividends of $30,000 from Flame and recorded $180,000 as its equity in the earnings of Flame. Additional information follows:

- All the undistributed earnings of Flame will be distributed as dividends in future periods.
- The dividends received from Flame are eligible for the 80% dividends received deduction.
- There are no other temporary differences.
- Enacted income tax rates are 30% for 1996 and thereafter.

In its December 31, 1996 balance sheet, what amount should Taft report for deferred income tax liability?

A. $9,000

B. $10,800

C. $45,000

D. $54,000

The correct answer is (A). *(CPA 593 I-35)*
REQUIRED: The deferred income tax liability reported on the balance sheet.
DISCUSSION: According to SFAS 109, the deferred tax liability constitutes the "deferred tax consequences attributable to taxable temporary differences. A deferred tax liability is measured using the applicable enacted tax rate and provisions of the enacted tax law." Taft's recognition of $180,000 of equity-based earnings creates a temporary difference that will result in taxable amounts in future periods when dividends are distributed. The deferred tax liability arising from this temporary difference is measured using the 30% enacted tax rate and the dividends received deduction. Accordingly, given that all the undistributed earnings will be distributed, a deferred tax liability of $9,000 [($180,000 equity – $30,000 dividends received) x 20% not deductible x 30% tax rate applicable after 1996] should be reported.
Answer (B) is incorrect because $10,800 equals 30% of 20% of the equity in the earnings of Flame. Answer (C) is incorrect because $45,000 is the net increase in Taft's investment in Flame account under the equity method multiplied by the 30% tax rate. Answer (D) is incorrect because $54,000 equals 30% of $180,000.

30. Black Co., organized on January 2, 1996, had pretax accounting income of $500,000 and taxable income of $800,000 for the year ended December 31, 1996. Black expected to maintain this level of taxable income in future years. The only temporary difference is for accrued product warranty costs expected to be paid as follows:

1997	$100,000
1998	50,000
1999	50,000
2000	100,000

The applicable enacted income tax rate is 30%. In Black's December 31, 1996 balance sheet, the deferred income tax asset and related valuation allowance should be

	Deferred Tax Asset	Valuation Allowance
A.	$0	$0
B.	$90,000	$90,000
C.	$90,000	$0
D.	$0	$90,000

The correct answer is (C). *(CPA 590 I-21)*
REQUIRED: The deferred tax asset and valuation allowance to be recognized at 12/31/96.
DISCUSSION: At 12/31/96, Black Company should report an accrued product warranty liability of $300,000. The result is a deductible temporary difference of $300,000 because the liability will be settled and related amounts will be tax deductible when the warranty costs are incurred. A deferred tax asset should be measured for deductible temporary differences using the applicable tax rate. Hence, Black Company should record a $90,000 ($300,000 x 30%) deferred tax asset. A valuation allowance should be used to reduce a deferred tax asset if, based on the weight of the available evidence, it is more likely than not that some portion will not be realized. In this case, however, Black Company had taxable income of $800,000 for 1996 and expects to maintain that level of taxable income in future years. The positive evidence therefore indicates that sufficient taxable income will be available for the future realization of the tax benefit of the existing deductible temporary differences. Given no negative evidence, a valuation allowance is not necessary.
Answer (A) is incorrect because a deferred tax asset should be recognized. Answer (B) is incorrect because a valuation allowance should not be recognized. Answer (D) is incorrect because a deferred tax asset but not a valuation allowance should be recognized.

31. In preparing its December 31, 1996 financial statements, Irene Corp. must determine the proper accounting treatment of a $180,000 loss carryforward available to offset future taxable income. There are no temporary differences. The applicable current and future income tax rate is 30%. Available evidence is not conclusive as to the future existence of sufficient taxable income to provide for the future realization of the tax benefit of the $180,000 loss carryforward. However, based on the available evidence, Irene believes that it is more likely than not that future taxable income will be available to provide for the future realization of $100,000 of this loss carryforward. In its 1996 statement of financial condition, Irene should recognize what amounts?

	Deferred Tax Asset	Valuation Allowance
A.	$0	$0
B.	$30,000	$0
C.	$54,000	$24,000
D.	$54,000	$30,000

The correct answer is (C). *(Publisher)*
REQUIRED: The amounts to be recognized as a deferred tax asset and related valuation allowance.
DISCUSSION: The applicable tax rate should be used to measure a deferred tax asset for an operating loss carryforward that is available to offset future taxable income. Irene should therefore recognize a $54,000 ($180,000 x 30%) deferred tax asset. A valuation allowance should be recognized to reduce the deferred tax asset if, based on the weight of the available evidence, it is more likely than not (the likelihood is more than 50%) that some portion or all of a deferred tax asset will not be realized. The valuation allowance should be equal to an amount necessary to reduce the deferred tax asset to the amount that is more likely than not to be realized. Based on the available evidence, Irene believes that it is more likely than not that the tax benefit of $100,000 of the operating loss will be realized. Thus, the company should recognize a $24,000 valuation allowance to reduce the $54,000 deferred tax asset to $30,000 ($100,000 x 30%), the amount of the deferred tax asset that is more likely than not to be realized.
Answer (A) is incorrect because a deferred tax asset equal to $54,000 should be recognized, and a valuation allowance should be recognized equal to $24,000 to reduce the deferred tax asset to $30,000. Answer (B) is incorrect because a deferred tax asset of $30,000 results from netting the valuation allowance against the deferred tax asset. Answer (D) is incorrect because $30,000 is the deferred tax asset, not the valuation allowance, after the two are netted.

Questions 32 and 33 are based on the following information. Venus Corp.'s worksheet for calculating current and deferred income taxes for 1996 follows:

	1996	1997	1998
Pretax income	$1,400		
Temporary differences:			
Depreciation	(800)	$(1,200)	$2,000
Warranty costs	400	(100)	(300)
Taxable income	$1,000	(1,300)	1,700
Loss carryback	(1,000)	1,000	
Loss carryforward		300	(300)
	$ 0	$ 0	$1,400
Enacted rate	30%	30%	25%
Deferred tax liability			
(asset)			
Current	$ (300)		
Noncurrent			$ 350

Venus had no prior deferred tax balances.

32. In its 1996 income statement, what amount should Venus report as current income tax expense?

A. $420

B. $350

C. $300

D. $0

33. In its 1996 income statement, what amount should Venus report as deferred income tax expense?

A. $350

B. $300

C. $120

D. $50

The correct answer is (C). *(CPA 593 I-55)*
REQUIRED: The current income tax expense.
DISCUSSION: Current tax expense is the amount of taxes paid or payable for the year. In 1996, Venus owes $300 ($1,000 taxable income x 30% tax rate).

Answer (A) is incorrect because $420 is the projected 1998 taxable income minus the loss carryforward, multiplied by the current (30%) tax rate. This amount is not owed in 1996. It is also pretax income of 1,400 x 30%. Answer (B) is incorrect because $350 is the projected 1998 taxable income minus the loss carryforward, multiplied by the 1998 (25%) tax rate. This amount is not owed in 1996. Answer (D) is incorrect because $0 is the income tax expense for 1997.

The correct answer is (D). *(CPA 593 I-56)*
REQUIRED: The deferred income tax expense.
DISCUSSION: The deferred tax expense or benefit recognized is the sum of the net changes in the deferred tax assets and deferred tax liabilities. The deferred income tax expense or benefit is aggregated with the income taxes currently payable or refundable to determine the amount of income tax expense or benefit for the year to be recorded in the income statement. Thus, deferred income tax expense is $50 ($350 increase in the deferred tax liability less the $300 increase in the deferred tax asset).

Answer (A) is incorrect because $350 is the deferred tax liability. Answer (B) is incorrect because $300 is the deferred tax asset. Answer (C) is incorrect because $120 assumes the noncurrent portion of the deferred tax amount is measured at a rate of 30% (i.e., 30% of $1,400 in 1998 = $420. $420 less the $300 deferred current asset). The entry to record 1996 tax including deferrals using the asset/liability method is

Current tax expense	$300	
Deferred tax expense	50	
Deferred current tax asset	300	
Deferred noncurrent tax liability		$350
Taxes payable		300

34. Leer Corp.'s pretax income in 1996 was $100,000. The temporary differences between amounts reported in the financial statements and the tax return are as follows:

Depreciation in the financial statements was $8,000 more than tax depreciation.

The equity method of accounting resulted in financial statement income of $35,000. A $25,000 dividend was received during the year, which is eligible for the 80% dividends received deduction (DRD).

Leer's effective income tax rate was 30% in 1996. In its 1996 income statement, Leer should report a current provision for income taxes of

   A. $26,400

   B. $23,400

   C. $21,900

   D. $18,600

The correct answer is (B). *(CPA 1191 I-48)*
   REQUIRED: The current provision for income taxes.
   DISCUSSION: Current tax expense is the amount of income taxes paid or payable for a year as determined by applying the provisions of the enacted tax law to the taxable income for that year. Pretax accounting income is given as $100,000. Financial statement depreciation exceeds tax depreciation by $8,000. Accounting income includes $35,000 of income determined in accordance with the equity method, but taxable income includes only $5,000 of this amount [$25,000 dividend received – (80% x $25,000) dividends-received deduction]. The reconciliation of pretax accounting income to taxable income is as follows:

Pretax accounting income	$100,000
Financial statement – tax depreciation	8,000
Equity-based income – taxable dividends	(30,000)
Taxable income	$ 78,000

Accordingly, the current provision for income taxes is $23,400 (30% applicable tax rate x $78,000).
   Answer (A) is incorrect because $26,400 is based on the assumption that taxable income includes equity-based income minus the 80% DRD. Answer (C) is incorrect because $21,900 assumes a 100% DRD. Answer (D) is incorrect because $18,600 results from subtracting, not adding, the excess financial statement depreciation.

35. The Grady Company acquired 100% of the Irwin Company for $1,000,000 in cash. The fair value of the identifiable net assets acquired is $600,000, and their tax basis is $450,000. Future recovery of the assets and settlement of the liabilities at their fair value will result in taxable and deductible amounts. If the enacted tax rate for the current year and all future years is 30%, the amount of goodwill to be recognized is

   A. $355,000

   B. $445,000

   C. $555,000

   D. $645,000

The correct answer is (B). *(Publisher)*
   REQUIRED: The goodwill in a purchase business combination given a difference between the tax basis and the assigned value of the identifiable net assets acquired.
   DISCUSSION: In accordance with SFAS 109, a deferred tax liability or asset is recognized for differences between the assigned values (fair values) and the tax bases of the assets and liabilities (except goodwill, unallocated negative goodwill, leveraged leases, and certain APB 23 differences) of an enterprise acquired in a purchase business combination. Because the difference between the assigned basis and the tax basis of the identifiable net assets acquired is $150,000 ($600,000 – $450,000), a net deferred tax liability of $45,000 ($150,000 x 30% tax rate) should be recognized. The assigned value other than goodwill is therefore $555,000 ($600,000 fair value of identifiable net assets acquired – $45,000 deferred tax liability). Goodwill of $445,000 ($1,000,000 purchase price – $555,000 assigned values) should be recorded.
   Answer (A) is incorrect because $355,000 results from adding, not subtracting, the deferred tax liability to the fair value of identifiable net assets. Answer (C) is incorrect because $555,000 results from calculating goodwill as the fair value of identifiable net assets less the deferred tax liability. Answer (D) is incorrect because $645,000 results from calculating goodwill as the fair value of identifiable net assets plus the deferred tax liability.

36. According to SFAS 109, *Accounting for Income Taxes*, which of the following items should affect current income tax expense for 1996?

A. Interest on a 1994 tax deficiency paid in 1996.

B. Penalty on a 1994 tax deficiency paid in 1996.

C. Change in income tax rate for 1996.

D. Change in income tax rate for 1997.

The correct answer is (C). *(CPA 592 T-10)*
REQUIRED: The item that affects current income tax expense for 1996.
DISCUSSION: Current tax expense is the amount of income taxes paid or payable for a year as determined by applying the provisions of the enacted tax law to the taxable income for that year.
Answers (A) and (B) are incorrect because interest and penalties on a prior-year tax deficiency do not affect current income tax expense. Answer (D) is incorrect because a change in income tax rate for 1997 would affect the deferred tax expense or benefit for 1996, assuming scheduled effects of a temporary difference will occur in 1997.

20.2 Intraperiod Tax Allocation

37. Intraperiod income tax allocation arises because

A. Items included in the determination of taxable income may be presented in different sections of the financial statements.

B. Income taxes must be allocated between current and future periods.

C. Certain revenues and expenses appear in the financial statements either before or after they are included in taxable income.

D. Certain revenues and expenses appear in the financial statements but are excluded from taxable income.

The correct answer is (A). *(CPA 1181 T-28)*
REQUIRED: The accounting reason for intraperiod allocation of income taxes.
DISCUSSION: To provide a fair presentation of the various components of the results of operations, SFAS 109 requires that income tax expense for the period be allocated among income from continuing operations, discontinued operations, extraordinary items, and items charged or credited directly to shareholders' equity.
Answer (B) is incorrect because it describes interperiod tax allocation. Answer (C) is incorrect because differences in the timing of revenues and expenses for financial statement and tax return purposes create the need for interperiod income tax allocation. Answer (D) is incorrect because revenues and expenses included in the financial statements but not in taxable income cause permanent differences between the financial statements and tax returns, but do not create a need for tax allocation.

38. Last year, before providing for taxes, Ajax Company had income from continuing operations of $930,000 and an extraordinary gain of $104,000. The current effective tax rate on continuing operations income was 40% and the total tax liability was $398,000 ignoring any temporary differences. The amount of the extraordinary gain net of tax effect was

A. $41,600

B. $62,400

C. $78,000

D. $104,000

The correct answer is (C). *(Publisher)*
REQUIRED: The amount of extraordinary gain net of the tax effect.
DISCUSSION: Given that the effective tax rate for continuing operations was 40%, the related tax expense was $372,000 ($930,000 x 40%). Because the total tax liability was $398,000, $26,000 ($398,000 – $372,000) was applicable to the extraordinary item. Accordingly, the extraordinary gain net of tax effect was $78,000 ($104,000 – $26,000).
Answer (A) is incorrect because $41,600 results from multiplying the extraordinary gain times the effective tax rate. Answer (B) is incorrect because $62,400 results from subtracting the extraordinary gain times the effective tax rate from the extraordinary gain. Answer (D) is incorrect because $104,000 results from not accounting for the tax effect.

20.3 Investment Tax Credit (ITC)

The Tax Reform Act of 1986 essentially repealed the use of investment tax credits (ITC) for tax (fiscal) years beginning after December 31, 1985. The financial accounting requirements, however, continue to be prescribed by APB 2 and APB 4 pending reenactment of the ITC.

39. For financial reporting purposes, it is considered generally acceptable to recognize benefits derived from the investment credit

A. Either over the life of the asset or in the year of acquisition.

B. Only as a reduction of income tax expense in the year of acquisition.

C. Only as a reduction in the cost of the asset.

D. Only over the life of the asset.

The correct answer is (A). *(Publisher)*
REQUIRED: The proper accounting for the investment tax credit (ITC).
DISCUSSION: APB 4, *Accounting for the Investment Credit*, states that both the deferral and the flow-through methods of accounting for the investment tax credit are generally acceptable. The deferral method spreads the benefit of the ITC over the life of the asset either by reducing the cost of the asset or by treating it as deferred income to be amortized over the life of the asset. The flow-through method recognizes the ITC in the year of investment.
Answers (B) and (D) are incorrect because neither is the only acceptable method for financial accounting purposes. Answer (C) is incorrect because a reduction of the asset cost is in effect recognizing the credit over the life of the asset by reduced annual depreciation. It is not the only acceptable method.

40. Andan Corporation purchased machinery that qualified for an investment tax credit of $10,000. This machinery is being depreciated over a 5-year period. Andan's taxable income and book income before income taxes was $250,000. Andan's effective income tax rate was 40%. If Andan accounts for the investment tax credit by the flow-through method, how much should Andan report in its income statement for income tax expense?

A. $90,000

B. $96,000

C. $98,000

D. $100,000

The correct answer is (A). *(CPA 1183 II-9)*
REQUIRED: The income tax expense given an ITC accounted for by the flow-through method.
DISCUSSION: The flow-through method recognizes the ITC in the year of investment. Tax expense before application of the ITC is $100,000 (.4 x $250,000). Tax expense after deducting the credit is $90,000 ($100,000 – $10,000). Taxes payable also would be equal to $90,000.
Answer (B) is incorrect because $96,000 results from deducting only 40% of the credit. Answer (C) is incorrect because $98,000 results from amortizing the $10,000 credit over 5 years and deducting that amount. Answer (D) is incorrect because $100,000 is the amount of tax expense before deducting the credit.

41. The Carine Company has a policy of deferring investment tax credits for accounting purposes. Investment tax credits of $100,000 were available on equipment that was purchased on January 1. The equipment has an estimated 10-year life. What is the amount of investment tax credits that should be credited to income for the calendar year?

A. $10,000

B. $14,286

C. $90,000

D. $100,000

The correct answer is (A). *(CPA 576 I-6)*
REQUIRED: The ITC using the deferral method.
DISCUSSION: Under the cost reduction or deferral method of accounting for ITC, the investment credits actually realized are deferred and amortized over the productive life of the acquired property.
Because Carine's $100,000 ITC is attributable to the purchase of equipment with a 10-year estimated useful life, 10% ($10,000) of the ITC should be credited to tax expense. The Tax Reform Act of 1986 has an effect on unused ITCs starting in 1987.
Answer (B) is incorrect because $14,286 results from amortizing the ITCs over 7 years. Answer (C) is incorrect because $90,000 is the amount of unused ITC. Answer (D) is incorrect because $100,000 results from expensing the entire credit in the current year.

CHAPTER TWENTY-ONE
ACCOUNTING CHANGES AND ERROR CORRECTIONS

This chapter covers two topics that are traditionally the subjects of separate chapters in intermediate texts. APB 20, *Accounting Changes*, specifies the treatment of accounting changes, and SFAS 16, *Prior Period Adjustments*, concerns prior-period adjustments.

21.1 General

1. At the time Hyman Corporation became a subsidiary of Duane Corporation, Hyman switched depreciation of its plant assets from the straight-line method to the sum-of-the-years'-digits method used by Duane. With respect to Hyman, this change was a

A. Change in an accounting estimate.

B. Correction of an error.

C. Change in accounting principle.

D. Change in the reporting entity.

The correct answer is (C). *(CPA 574 T-25)*

REQUIRED: The proper classification of the change in depreciation method.

DISCUSSION: A change from one generally accepted accounting principle to another is a change in accounting principle. The term "accounting principle" includes not only accounting principles and practices, but also the methods of applying them.

Answer (A) is incorrect because no change in an estimate used in the accounting process, e.g., the useful lives of assets, is mentioned. Answer (B) is incorrect because an error is an accounting mistake, such as in the application of an accounting principle. Answer (D) is incorrect because, as long as Hyman continues to report separately, its new status as a subsidiary does not constitute a change in the reporting entity.

2. Items reported as prior-period adjustments

A. Do not include the effect of a mistake in the application of accounting principles as this is accounted for as a change in accounting principle rather than as a prior-period adjustment.

B. Do not affect the presentation of prior-period comparative financial statements.

C. Do not require further disclosure in the body of the financial statements.

D. Are reflected as adjustments of the opening balance of the retained earnings of the earliest period presented.

The correct answer is (D). *(CMA 693 2-9)*

REQUIRED: The true statement about items reported as prior-period adjustments.

DISCUSSION: Prior-period adjustments are made for the correction of errors. According to SFAS 16, *Prior-period Adjustments*, the effects of errors on prior-period financial statements are reported as adjustments to beginning retained earnings for the earliest period presented in the retained earnings statement. Such errors do not affect the income statement for the current period.

Answer (A) is incorrect because accounting errors of any type are corrected by a prior-period adjustment. Answer (B) is incorrect because a prior-period adjustment will affect the presentation of prior-period comparative financial statements. Answer (C) is incorrect because prior-period adjustments should be fully disclosed in the notes or elsewhere in the financial statements.

3. A change in the periods benefited by a deferred cost because additional information has been obtained is

A. A correction of an error.

B. An accounting change that should be reported by restating the financial statements of all prior-periods presented.

C. An accounting change that should be reported in the period of change and future periods if the change affects both.

D. Not an accounting change.

The correct answer is (C). *(CPA 589 T-29)*

REQUIRED: The proper treatment of a change caused by additional information.

DISCUSSION: APB 20, *Accounting Changes*, states that accounting estimates change as new events occur, as more experience is acquired, or as additional information is obtained. A change in accounting estimate is accounted for on a prospective basis. Thus, a change in the periods benefited by a deferred cost because of additional information is an accounting change that should be reported in the period of change, as well as in future periods if the change affects them.

Answer (A) is incorrect because an accounting change based on new information is a change in estimate. Answer (B) is incorrect because a change in accounting estimate should be accounted for on a prospective basis. Answer (D) is incorrect because an accounting change is defined as a change in a principle, an estimate, or the reporting entity. This change is a change in estimate.

4. Pro forma effects on net income and earnings per share of retroactive application are usually reported on the face of the income statement for a

	Change in Accounting Entity	Change in Accounting Estimate
A.	Yes	Yes
B.	Yes	No
C.	No	No
D.	No	Yes

The correct answer is (C). *(CPA 1186 T-36)*

REQUIRED: The change(s) for which pro forma effects on net income and EPS of retroactive application should be reported.

DISCUSSION: Usually, the cumulative effect of a change from one generally accepted accounting principle to another should be reflected on the face of the income statement. In addition, pro forma effects on net income and EPS of retroactive application should be disclosed. A change in reporting entity, however, is a special type of change in accounting principle. It is reported by restating the financial statements of all prior-periods presented. The nature of, and the reason for, the change should be disclosed as well as the effects on income before extraordinary items, net income, and the related EPS amounts for all periods presented. Disclosure of pro forma effects is not required. A change in accounting estimate is accounted for on a prospective basis. Financial statements of previous periods are not restated. Accordingly, disclosure of pro forma effects, EPS data, and retroactive application also are not required.

Answers (A), (B), and (D) are incorrect because the pro forma effects on net income and EPS of retroactive application for both a change in accounting entity and a change in accounting estimate should not be reported on the face of the income statement.

5. The cumulative effect of changing to a new accounting principle on the amount of retained earnings at the beginning of the period in which the change is made should be included in net income of

	Future Periods	The Period of Change
A.	No	No
B.	Yes	No
C.	Yes	Yes
D.	No	Yes

The correct answer is (D). *(CPA 1188 T-32)*

REQUIRED: The proper reporting of a change in accounting principle.

DISCUSSION: With certain exceptions, a change from one acceptable method of accounting to another should be accounted for as the cumulative effect of a change in accounting principle. The cumulative effect should be recognized as a component of net income, net of tax effect, in the period of change. This amount should be presented between the captions extraordinary items and net income. The per-share amount of the cumulative effect should also be reported on the face of the income statement.

Answers (A), (B), and (C) are incorrect because the cumulative effect of a change in accounting principle should be included in net income in the period of change, not in future periods.

21.2 Changes in Accounting Principle

6. When reporting a change in accounting principle,

A. The change is recognized by including the cumulative effect of the change in the net income of the period of change for all but a few specific cases.

B. The change is recognized by retroactively adjusting the financial statements for all but a few specific cases.

C. The pro forma effects of retroactive application of the new principle upon income before extraordinary items and net income are not to be disclosed on the face of the income statement or in the notes to the financial statements.

D. The reporting requirements are the same as for reporting a change in accounting estimate.

The correct answer is (A). *(CMA 693 2-7)*
REQUIRED: The true statement about reporting a change in accounting principle.
DISCUSSION: In most situations, the cumulative effect of a change in accounting principle on the beginning balance of retained earnings for the period (net of the related tax effect) is included in the net income of the period of change. The cumulative effect is to be reported in a separate section of the income statement after extraordinary items. In a few specific cases, for example, a change from LIFO, a change from the completed-contract to the percentage-of-completion method (or vice versa), a change to or from the full-cost method used in the extractive industries, a change in the method of accounting for railroad track structures, or a change in the reporting entity, changes in principle require retroactive restatement of financial statements with full disclosure in the year of the change.

Answer (B) is incorrect because most changes are to be reported only in the year of change without retroactive restatement. Answer (C) is incorrect because these pro forma effects are required to be disclosed on the face of the income statement. Answer (D) is incorrect because a change in estimate is accounted for on a prospective basis, that is, reported in both the current and future periods.

7. The cumulative effect of changing to a new accounting principle should be recorded separately as a component of income after continuing operations for a change from the

A. Cash basis of accounting for vacation pay to the accrual basis.

B. Straight-line method of depreciation for previously recorded assets to the double-declining-balance method.

C. Presentation of statements of individual companies to their inclusion in consolidated statements.

D. Completed-contract method of accounting for long-term construction-type contracts to the percentage-of-completion method.

The correct answer is (B). *(CPA 1193 T-26)*
REQUIRED: The change in accounting principle that should be reported as a cumulative-effect-type change.
DISCUSSION: With certain exceptions, a change from one generally accepted method of accounting to another, such as a change in depreciation methods, should be reported as a cumulative-effect-type change in accounting principle. The cumulative effect on prior-periods' earnings should be reported separately, net of tax, as a component of net income after income from continuing operations, discontinued operations, and extraordinary items.

Answer (A) is incorrect because a change from an accounting principle that is not generally accepted to one that is, such as from the cash basis to the accrual basis for vacation pay, is a correction of an error that should be treated as a prior-period adjustment. Answer (C) is incorrect because a change to consolidated statements is a change in entity, that is, a special change in accounting principle that is represented as a restatement of prior-period statements. Answer (D) is incorrect because a change in the method of accounting for long-term construction-type contracts is a special change in accounting principle that is reported as a restatement of prior-period statements.

8. Is the cumulative effect of an inventory pricing change on prior years' earnings reported separately between extraordinary items and net income for a change from

	LIFO to Weighted Average?	FIFO to Weighted Average?
A.	Yes	Yes
B.	Yes	No
C.	No	No
D.	No	Yes

The correct answer is (D). *(CPA 591 T-34)*

REQUIRED: The inventory pricing change(s), if any, reported separately between extraordinary items and net income.

DISCUSSION: With certain exceptions (including a change from LIFO, a change in accounting for long-term construction contracts, a change to or from the full cost method in the extractive industries, and a change in the method of accounting for railroad track structures), a change in accounting principle should be reflected in income for the period of change. The cumulative effect of the change on beginning retained earnings should appear as a separate component after extraordinary items in the income statement. The exceptions, including a change from LIFO, however, should be accounted for by restatement of the financial statements of all prior-periods presented.

Answers (A), (B), and (C) are incorrect because a change from FIFO to weighted average is a cumulative-effect-type change, but the change from LIFO is a restatement.

9. SFAS 73, *Reporting a Change in Accounting for Railroad Track Structures*, amended APB 20 to specify the financial accounting treatment of a change from the retirement-replacement-betterment accounting method to the depreciation accounting method. This type of change should be reported

A. Retroactively.

B. Prospectively.

C. Currently.

D. Cumulatively.

The correct answer is (A). *(R.B. Posey)*

REQUIRED: The proper reporting of a change from RRB depreciation to depreciation accounting.

DISCUSSION: A change in accounting principle is normally accounted for by reporting the cumulative effect of the change on beginning retained earnings in the current year's income statement. SFAS 73 states that a change from RRB depreciation to depreciation accounting is one of the exceptions to the general rule. This change is to be reported by applying depreciation accounting retroactively and restating prior-year financial statements as if depreciation accounting had always been used.

Answer (B) is incorrect because the change is treated retroactively, not prospectively. Answers (C) and (D) are incorrect because each term describes the general rule.

10. Since the Moxley Manufacturing Corporation began business in 1985, it has included such indirect costs of manufacturing as factory janitorial expenses, depreciation of machinery, and insurance on the factory as elements of inventory costs. At the beginning of 1997, the company decided to begin expensing all insurance costs in the period in which they are incurred. To comply with current standards, the company must justify and disclose the reason for change. The reason that would be most appropriate is that the new principle

A. Constitutes an improvement in financial reporting.

B. Has been and continues to be the treatment used for tax purposes.

C. Is easier to apply because no assumptions about allocation must be made.

D. Is one used by the company for insurance costs other than those on factory-related activities.

The correct answer is (A). *(Publisher)*

REQUIRED: The most appropriate reason for making a change in accounting principle.

DISCUSSION: APB 20 establishes a presumption that, once adopted, an accounting principle should not be changed in accounting for events and transactions of a similar type. This presumption in favor of continuity may be overcome if the enterprise justifies the use of an alternative acceptable principle on the basis that it is preferable, i.e., that it constitutes an improvement in financial reporting. Preferability would automatically be established if a FASB standard created a new principle, expressed preference for a principle not being used, or rejected a principle being used.

Answers (B), (C), and (D) are incorrect because FASB Interpretation No. 1, *Accounting Changes Related to the Cost of Inventory*, states that preferability should be determined on the basis of whether the new principle constitutes an improvement in financial reporting. Other bases are not sufficient justification.

11. A company has changed its method of depreciation for all fixed assets acquired after the first day of the current fiscal year. All existing fixed assets acquired prior to this date will be depreciated using the original method. How should this change be reported in the current-year financial statements?

A. The cumulative effect of the change in method must be reflected in the current year's earnings statement immediately after extraordinary items and the reason(s) for the change in method disclosed in a footnote.

B. The financial statements must be restated to give effect to the change in the method of depreciation as if the new method were applied to all of the fixed assets as a group.

C. The financial statements must include a description of the nature of the change in method and its effect on earnings before extraordinary items, net earnings, and related per-share amounts.

D. No disclosure would be necessary in the current year because the change in method does not affect any depreciation taken on fixed assets in prior-periods.

The correct answer is (C). *(CPA 1177 T-3)*
REQUIRED: The proper reporting of a change in depreciation method in the current-year financial statements.
DISCUSSION: When a company has adopted a new accounting principle with respect to assets acquired in the year of change and thereafter but continues to use the old method for assets acquired prior to the year of change, APB 20 requires disclosure of the nature of the change and the effect on income before extraordinary items and net income of the period of the change, together with related per-share amounts. No cumulative-effect adjustment is made because the change in depreciation method does not apply to fixed assets acquired prior to the date of change.

Answers (A) and (B) are incorrect because a change in depreciation method for newly acquired assets is a change in accounting principle that requires neither a cumulative-effect adjustment nor restatement of prior-periods' statements. Answer (D) is incorrect because disclosure is required.

12. Goddard has used the FIFO method of inventory valuation since it began operations in 1993. Goddard decided to change to the weighted-average method for determining inventory costs at the beginning of 1996. The following schedule shows year-end inventory balances under the FIFO and weighted-average methods:

Year	FIFO	Weighted-Average
1993	$45,000	$54,000
1994	78,000	71,000
1995	83,000	78,000

What amount, before income taxes, should be reported in the 1996 income statement as the cumulative effect of the change in accounting principle?

A. $5,000 decrease.

B. $3,000 decrease.

C. $2,000 increase.

D. $0

The correct answer is (A). *(CPA 1191 I-56)*
REQUIRED: The cumulative income statement effect of changing from FIFO to weighted-average.
DISCUSSION: A change in accounting principle generally requires that the cumulative effect on prior-periods' earnings be reported separately in the income statement of the year of the change. In this case, the cumulative effect results from the decrease in beginning inventory. This change decreases net income for prior-periods by increasing aggregate cost of goods sold by $5,000 ($83,000 – $78,000). Thus, the cumulative effect of the change in accounting principle is a $5,000 decrease.

Answer (B) is incorrect because a $3,000 decrease results from netting the differences between FIFO and weighted-average for each year. Answer (C) is incorrect because a $2,000 increase results from netting the differences between FIFO and weighted average for 1993 and 1994. Answer (D) is incorrect because a cumulative effect of a change in accounting principle must be reported.

13. On January 2, 1996, to better reflect the variable use of its only machine, Holly, Inc. elected to change its method of depreciation from the straight-line method to the units-of-production method. The original cost of the machine on January 2, 1994 was $50,000, and its estimated life was 10 years. Holly estimates that the machine's total life is 50,000 machine hours. Machine hours usage was 8,500 during 1995 and 3,500 during 1994. Holly's income tax rate is 30%. Holly should report the accounting change in its 1996 financial statements as a(an)

A.   Cumulative effect of a change in accounting principle of $2,000 in its income statement.

B.   Adjustment to beginning retained earnings of $2,000.

C.   Cumulative effect of a change in accounting principle of $1,400 in its income statement.

D.   Adjustment to beginning retained earnings of $1,400.

The correct answer is (C). *(CPA 1193 I-4)*
REQUIRED: The reporting of an accounting change in the financial statements.
DISCUSSION: A change from one generally accepted accounting principle to another, such as a change in depreciation methods, ordinarily should be reported as a cumulative-effect change in the income statement. The depreciation under the straight-line method is $10,000 [2 x ($50,000 ÷ 10)]. Under the units-of-production method, the depreciation should be $8,500 in 1995 [($50,000 ÷ 50,000) x 8,500 hours used], and $3,500 in 1994. The total difference in accumulated depreciation is $2,000 ($12,000 – $10,000). After allowing for the reduction in tax expense of $600 ($2,000 x 30%), the cumulative effect of the change is to decrease net income by $1,400 ($2,000 – 600).

Answer (A) is incorrect because $2,000 is the difference between the two depreciation methods without considering the tax effects. Answers (B) and (D) are incorrect because the change is not recorded as a prior-period adjustment.

14. On January 1, 1994, Bray Company purchased for $240,000 a machine with a useful life of 10 years and no salvage value. The machine was depreciated by the double-declining-balance method (DDB), and the carrying amount of the machine was $153,600 on December 31, 1995. Bray changed retroactively to the straight-line method on January 1,1996. Bray can justify the change. What should be the depreciation expense on this machine for the year ended December 31, 1996?

A. $15,360

B. $19,200

C. $24,000

D. $30,720

The correct answer is (C). *(CPA 587 I-47)*
REQUIRED: The depreciation expense in the year of a change in accounting principle.
DISCUSSION: With few exceptions, when a change is made from one generally accepted accounting principle to another, APB 20 requires that, beginning in the year of the change, the financial statement amounts be calculated as if the new accounting method had always been used. The DDB method was used in 1994 and 1995, so a catch-up adjustment to the accumulated depreciation account at the beginning of 1996 is necessary. This adjustment equals the difference between DDB and straight-line depreciation. Under the DDB method, accumulated depreciation was $86,400 ($240,000 cost – $153,600 carrying amount). Under the straight-line method, accumulated depreciation would have been $48,000 [2 years x ($240,000 ÷ 10-year useful life)]. After the $38,400 ($86,400 – $48,000) adjustment, the accumulated depreciation balance would reflect the straight-line method for the first 2 years of this asset's existence. Following the adjustment, depreciation expense for 1996 and subsequent years should be $24,000 ($240,000 ÷ 10 years).

Answer (A) is incorrect because $15,360 is based upon the present carrying amount. Answer (B) is incorrect because $19,200 is based upon the present carrying value and remaining useful life. Answer (D) is incorrect because $30,720 is the result of continuing to depreciate the asset under the DDB method.

15. During 1996, Dale Corp. made the following accounting changes:

Method Used in 1995	Method Used in 1996	After-Tax Effect
Sum-of-the-years'-digits depreciation	Straight-line depreciation	$30,000
Weighted-average for inventory valuation	First-in, first-out for inventory valuation	98,000

What amount should be classified in 1996 as prior-period adjustments?

   A. $0

   B. $30,000

   C. $98,000

   D. $128,000

The correct answer is (A). *(CPA 1191 II-2)*
   REQUIRED: The amount classified as prior-period adjustments.
   DISCUSSION: A change from one generally accepted accounting principle to another, such as from SYD to straight-line depreciation or from weighted-average to FIFO inventory valuation, is generally accounted for as a cumulative-effect change that is included in the determination of income for the period of change. Consequently, neither change should be treated as a prior-period adjustment.
   Answer (B) is incorrect because $30,000 equals the after-tax effect in 1996 of the change from SYD to straight-line. Answer (C) is incorrect because $98,000 equals the after-tax effect in 1996 of the change from weighted-average to FIFO. Answer (D) is incorrect because $128,000 equals the after-tax effect in 1996 of the changes from SYD to straight-line and weighted-average to FIFO.

16. Milton Co. began operations on January 1, 1994. On January 1, 1996, Milton changed its inventory method from LIFO to FIFO for both financial and income tax reporting. If FIFO had been used in prior years, Milton's inventories would have been higher by $60,000 and $40,000 at December 31, 1996 and 1995, respectively. Milton has a 30% income tax rate. What amount should Milton report as the cumulative effect of this accounting change in its income statement for the year ended December 31, 1996?

   A. $0

   B. $14,000

   C. $28,000

   D. $42,000

The correct answer is (A). *(CPA 1192 I-60)*
   REQUIRED: The cumulative effect of the accounting change.
   DISCUSSION: A change from LIFO to any other method of inventory pricing is a special change in accounting principle that must be accounted for as a prior-period adjustment. The financial statements for all periods presented must be restated. Consequently, the change does not result in the recognition of the cumulative effect in income in the year of change.
   Answer (B) is incorrect because $14,000 is the after-tax effect of the differences between FIFO and LIFO at year-end 1996 and 1995, respectively. Answer (C) is incorrect because $28,000 is the after-tax effect of the difference between FIFO and LIFO at year-end 1995. Answer (D) is incorrect because $42,000 is the adjustment recorded directly as a change in retained earnings.

17. On January 1, 1991, Pell Corp. purchased a machine having an estimated useful life of 10 years and no salvage. The machine was depreciated by the double-declining-balance method for both financial statement and income tax reporting. On January 1, 1996, Pell changed to the straight-line method for financial statement reporting but not for income tax reporting. Accumulated depreciation at December 31, 1995 was $560,000. If the straight-line method had been used, the accumulated depreciation at December 31, 1995 would have been $420,000. Pell's enacted income tax rate for 1996 and thereafter is 30%. The amount shown in the 1996 income statement for the cumulative effect of changing to the straight-line method should be

   A. $98,000 debit.

   B. $98,000 credit.

   C. $140,000 credit.

   D. $140,000 debit.

The correct answer is (B). *(CPA 591 I-60)*
   REQUIRED: The amount shown in the income statement for the cumulative effect of changing to the straight-line method.
   DISCUSSION: The cumulative effect of the change on beginning retained earnings should be recorded as a separate component after extraordinary items in the income statement. It is the difference in depreciation expense accumulated under the DDB and straight-line methods, net of tax effect. Thus, the amount credited to reflect the lower straight-line expense is $98,000 [(1.0 − 30% tax rate) x ($560,000 DDB depreciation − $420,000 straight-line depreciation)]. A debit of $140,000 ($560,000 DDB − $420,000 straight-line) is made to accumulated depreciation. The balancing credit of $42,000 (30% x $140,000) is to a deferred tax liability account because the temporary difference created by the accounting change will result in future taxable amounts.
   Answer (A) is incorrect because the amount should be a credit. Answer (C) is incorrect because $140,000 is the pre-tax difference. Answer (D) is incorrect because $140,000 is the pretax difference, and the amount should be a credit.

18. On January 1, 1996, Poe Construction, Inc. changed to the percentage-of-completion method of income recognition for financial statement reporting but not for income tax reporting. Poe can justify this change in accounting principle. As of December 31, 1995, Poe compiled data showing that aggregate income under the completed-contract method was $700,000. If the percentage-of-completion method had been used, the accumulated income through December 31, 1995 would have been $880,000. Assuming an income tax rate of 40% for all years, the cumulative effect of this accounting change should be reported by Poe in the 1996

A. Retained earnings statement as a $180,000 credit adjustment to the beginning balance.

B. Income statement as a $180,000 credit.

C. Retained earnings statement as a $108,000 credit adjustment to the beginning balance.

D. Income statement as a $108,000 credit.

The correct answer is (C). *(CPA 586 I-58)*
REQUIRED: The method of reporting a change in the accounting for long-term, construction-type contracts.
DISCUSSION: A change in the method of accounting for long-term, construction-type contracts is a special change in accounting principle that must be accounted for as a prior-period adjustment. The financial statements for all prior periods presented must be restated. The adjustment should be made directly to the balance of beginning retained earnings. If Poe's new method of accounting (the percentage-of-completion method) had been used, accumulated net income for all prior years would have been $180,000 greater ($880,000 – $700,000). If net income had been greater during the prior-periods, the retained earnings at the end of those periods also would have been greater. Hence, Poe must credit the retained earnings balance for the after-tax effect of $108,000 [$180,000 x (1 – 40% tax rate)].
Answers (A) and (B) are incorrect because the restatement should be reflected net of taxes. Answers (B) and (D) are incorrect because the income statement is not affected.

19. Which of the following describes a change in reporting entity?

A. A company acquires a subsidiary that is to be accounted for as a purchase.

B. A manufacturing company expands its market from regional to nationwide.

C. A company acquires additional shares of an investee and changes from the equity method of accounting to consolidation of the subsidiary.

D. A business combination is made using the pooling-of-interests method.

The correct answer is (D). *(CPA 578 T-6)*
REQUIRED: The item that describes a change in reporting entity.
DISCUSSION: APB 20 describes the following as changes in the reporting entity: presenting consolidated or combined statements in place of statements of individual companies, changing the specific subsidiaries included in the group for which consolidated statements are presented, changing the companies included in combined statements, and effecting a business combination accounted for by the pooling-of-interests method.
Answers (A) and (C) are incorrect because only business combinations accounted for as poolings are considered changes in accounting entities. Answer (B) is incorrect because it is a change in scope of operations, not the entity.

20. Matt Co. included a foreign subsidiary in its 1996 consolidated financial statements. The subsidiary was acquired in 1990 and was excluded from previous consolidations. The change was caused by the elimination of foreign exchange controls. Including the subsidiary in the 1996 consolidated financial statements results in an accounting change that should be reported

A. By footnote disclosure only.

B. Currently and prospectively.

C. Currently with footnote disclosure of pro forma effects of retroactive application.

D. By restating the financial statements of all prior-periods presented.

The correct answer is (D). *(CPA 592 T-40)*
REQUIRED: The reporting of the change in the subsidiaries included in consolidated financial statements.
DISCUSSION: A change in the reporting entity requires retroactive treatment. Changing the specific subsidiaries included in the group for which consolidated statements are presented is a change in the reporting entity. The financial statements of all prior-periods presented must be restated for all periods presented.
Answers (A), (B), and (C) are incorrect because a change in the reporting entity requires retroactive treatment.

21.3 Changes in Accounting Estimates

21. How should the effect of a change in accounting estimate be accounted for?

- A. By restating amounts reported in financial statements of prior-periods.

- B. By reporting pro forma amounts for prior-periods.

- C. As a prior-period adjustment to beginning retained earnings.

- D. In the period of change and future periods if the change affects both.

The correct answer is (D). *(CPA 1194 F-54)*
REQUIRED: The accounting for the effect of a change in accounting estimate.
DISCUSSION: APB 20 requires that the effect of a change in accounting estimate be accounted for as a component of income from continuing operations in the period of change, if the change affects that period only, or in the period of change and future periods, if the change affects both. For a change in accounting estimate, neither the cumulative effect of a change in accounting principle nor the pro forma effect of retroactive application is reported.
Answers (A), (B), and (C) are incorrect because a change in accounting estimate is accounted for prospectively only.

22. For 1995, Pac Co. estimated its 2-year equipment warranty costs based on $100 per unit sold in 1995. Experience during 1996 indicated that the estimate should have been based on $110 per unit. The effect of this $10 difference from the estimate is reported

- A. In 1996 income from continuing operations.

- B. As an accounting change, net of tax, below 1996 income from continuing operations.

- C. As an accounting change requiring 1995 financial statements to be restated.

- D. As a correction of an error requiring 1995 financial statements to be restated.

The correct answer is (A). *(CPA 1193 T-23)*
REQUIRED: The proper accounting for a change in estimate.
DISCUSSION: APB 20 requires that the effect of a change in accounting estimate be accounted for in the period of change if the change affects that period only, or in the period of change and in future periods, if the change affects both. For a change in accounting estimate, neither the cumulative effect of a change in accounting principle nor the pro forma effect of retroactive application is reported. A change in the warranty costs is considered a change in estimate and not the correction of an error. Thus, it affects income from continuing operations.
Answer (B) is incorrect because a change in accounting estimate is reported as a component of income from continuing operations. Answer (C) is incorrect because a change in estimate is not reported retroactively. Answer (D) is incorrect because the change in estimate is not considered a correction of an error.

23. On July 1, 1993, Rey Corp. purchased computer equipment at a cost of $360,000. This equipment was estimated to have a 6-year life with no residual value and was depreciated by the straight-line method. On January 3, 1996, Rey determined that this equipment could no longer process data efficiently, that its value had been permanently impaired, and that $70,000 could be recovered over the remaining useful life of the equipment. What carrying amount should Rey report on its December 31, 1996 balance sheet for this equipment?

- A. $0

- B. $50,000

- C. $70,000

- D. $150,000

The correct answer is (B). *(CPA 1190 II-5)*
REQUIRED: The carrying amount 1 year after a change in estimate.
DISCUSSION: At 1/3/96, the carrying amount of the computer equipment should be written down to $70,000. This $70,000 is expected to be recovered over the 3½-year remaining useful life of the equipment. Under the straight-line method, the depreciation expense for the year ending 12/31/96 is $20,000 [($70,000 ÷ 42 months) x 12 months]. Thus, the carrying amount in the year-end balance sheet should be $50,000 ($70,000 – $20,000).
Answer (A) is incorrect because the computer should have a carrying value of $50,000. Answer (C) is incorrect because $20,000 of depreciation must be taken on the asset for 1996. Answer (D) is incorrect because the computer must be written down to $70,000 and depreciation taken on that amount. $150,000 would reflect continued depreciation based on the original assumptions.

24. Ali Company bought a machine on January 1, 1994 for $24,000, at which time it had an estimated useful life of 8 years, with no residual value. Straight-line depreciation is used for all of Ali's depreciable assets. On January 1, 1996, the machine's estimated useful life was determined to be only 6 years from the acquisition date. Accordingly, the appropriate accounting change was made in 1996. The direct effects of this change were limited to the effect on depreciation and the related provision for income tax. Ali's income tax rate was 40% in all the affected years. In Ali's 1996 financial statements, how much should be reported as the cumulative effect on prior years because of the change in the estimated useful life of the machine?

   A. $0

   B. $1,200

   C. $2,000

   D. $2,800

The correct answer is (A). *(CPA 1186 II-11)*
  REQUIRED: The proper accounting for a change in estimate.
  DISCUSSION: An adjustment arising from a revision in an asset's estimated useful life is a change in accounting estimate that should be accounted for on a prospective basis. The remaining depreciable base should be allocated over the revised remaining life with no adjustment to the depreciation accumulated at the time of the change. Because Ali should make no retroactive adjustment, the cumulative effect on prior years is $0. The remaining depreciable base of $18,000 ($24,000 cost – $6,000 accumulated depreciation based on a 6-year life) is allocated over the remaining expected life at $4,500 per year ($18,000 ÷ 4).
  Answers (B), (C), and (D) are incorrect because prior year's adjustment should not be made for a change in accounting estimate of the useful life of an asset.

25. On January 2, 1993, Union Co. purchased a machine for $264,000 and depreciated it by the straight-line method using an estimated useful life of 8 years with no salvage value. On January 2, 1996, Union determined that the machine had a useful life of 6 years from the date of acquisition and will have a salvage value of $24,000. An accounting change was made in 1996 to reflect the additional data. The accumulated depreciation for this machine should have a balance at December 31, 1996 of

   A. $179,000

   B. $160,000

   C. $154,000

   D. $146,000

The correct answer is (D). *(CPA 1193 I-60)*
  REQUIRED: The accumulated depreciation for a machine given changes in estimates.
  DISCUSSION: A change in estimated life is accounted for on a prospective basis. The new estimate affects the year of the change and subsequent years. For 1993 through 1995, the amount of depreciation was $33,000 per year ($264,000 ÷ 8). In 1996, the new estimates change annual depreciation to $47,000 [($264,000 – $99,000 accumulated depreciation – $24,000 expected salvage) ÷ 3 years remaining]. Thus, accumulated depreciation for 1996 is $146,000 ($99,000 + $47,000).
  Answer (A) is incorrect because $179,000 does not include accumulated depreciation in calculating depreciation for 1996. Answer (B) is incorrect because $160,000 would be the accumulated depreciation if the revised estimates had been used from the date of acquisition. Answer (C) is incorrect because $154,000 does not include salvage value in calculating depreciation for 1996.

26. Tone Company is the defendant in a lawsuit filed by Witt in 1995 disputing the validity of a copyright held by Tone. At December 31, 1995, Tone determined that Witt would probably be successful against Tone for an estimated amount of $400,000. Appropriately, a $400,000 loss was accrued by a charge to income for the year ended December 31, 1995. On December 15, 1996, Tone and Witt agreed to a settlement providing for a cash payment of $250,000 by Tone to Witt and the transfer of Tone's copyright to Witt. The carrying amount of the copyright on Tone's accounting records was $60,000 at December 15, 1996. What is the effect of the settlement on Tone's income before income tax in 1996?

   A. No effect.

   B. $60,000 decrease.

   C. $90,000 increase.

   D. $150,000 increase.

The correct answer is (C). *(CPA 587 I-35)*

   REQUIRED: The accounting for the effect of a settlement at an amount different from that previously accrued.

   DISCUSSION: In 1995, a $400,000 contingent loss and an accrued liability in the amount of $400,000 were properly recognized in accordance with SFAS 5. In 1996, the actual loss of $310,000 ($250,000 cash + $60,000 carrying amount of the copyright) was $90,000 less than the previously estimated amount. This new information should be treated as a change in estimate and accounted for in the period of change in accordance with APB 20. Consequently, the $90,000 difference will be credited to 1996 income as a recovery of a previously recognized loss.

   Answer (A) is incorrect because Tone's income before income tax will increase by $90,000. Answer (B) is incorrect because $60,000 is the carrying value of the copyright. Answer (D) is incorrect because a $150,000 increase does not include the carrying value of the copyright.

27. The effect of a change in accounting principle that is inseparable from the effect of a change in accounting estimate should be reported

   A. By restating the financial statements of all prior-periods presented.

   B. As a correction of an error.

   C. As a component of income from continuing operations, in the period of change and future periods if the change affects both.

   D. As a separate disclosure after income from continuing operations, in the period of change and future periods if the change affects both.

The correct answer is (C). *(CPA 1191 T-24)*

   REQUIRED: The reporting of the effect of a change in accounting principle that is inseparable from the effect of a change in accounting estimate.

   DISCUSSION: When the effect of a change in accounting principle is inseparable from the effect of a change in estimate, APB 20 requires that it be accounted for in the same manner as a change in estimate only. An example of such a change is the change from deferring and amortizing a cost to recording it as an expense when incurred because future benefits of the cost have become doubtful. Because the new method is adopted to recognize a change in estimated future benefits, the effect of the change in principle is inseparable from the change in estimate. APB 20 requires that the effect of a change in accounting estimate be accounted for as a component of income from continuing operations in the period of change if the change affects that period only, or in the period of change and in future periods, if the change affects both.

   Answer (A) is incorrect because prospective treatment is accorded to a change in principle inseparable from a change in estimate. Answer (B) is incorrect because a correction of an error is accounted for as a prior-period adjustment. Answer (D) is incorrect because the effect of a change in estimate is treated as a component of income from continuing operations.

28. Effective January 1, 1996, Younger Company adopted the accounting principle of expensing as incurred advertising and promotion costs. Previously, advertising and promotion costs applicable to future periods were recorded in prepaid expenses. Younger can justify the change, which was made for both financial statement and income tax reporting purposes. Younger's prepaid advertising and promotion costs totaled $500,000 at December 31, 1995. Assume that the income tax rate is 40% for 1995 and 1996. The adjustment for the effect of this change in accounting principle should result in a net charge against income in the 1996 income statement of

A. $0

B. $200,000

C. $300,000

D. $500,000

The correct answer is (C). *(CPA 1182 I-15)*
   REQUIRED: The adjustment for a change in accounting estimate that is inseparable from a change in accounting principle.
   DISCUSSION: Younger has effectively changed both its estimate of the future periods to which the prepaid advertising and promotion costs are applicable and its method of accounting for them. A change in accounting estimate that is recognized in whole or in part by a change in accounting principle should be reported as a change in accounting estimate. Younger's 12/31/95 prepaid advertising and promotion costs balance of $500,000 should be written off in 1996, the year in which the accounting change takes place. This write-off results in an after-tax charge against income of $300,000 [$500,000 x (1 – 40% tax rate)].
   Answer (A) is incorrect because $300,000 should be charged against income in 1996. Answer (B) is incorrect because $200,000 is the tax effect. Answer (D) is incorrect because $500,000 is the before-tax effect.

21.4 Corrections of Errors

29. The correction of an error in the financial statements of a prior-period should be reported, net of applicable income taxes, in the current

A. Retained earnings statement after net income but before dividends.

B. Retained earnings statement as an adjustment of the opening balance.

C. Income statement after income from continuing operations and before extraordinary items.

D. Income statement after income from continuing operations and after extraordinary items.

The correct answer is (B). *(CPA 1193 T-22)*
   REQUIRED: The proper recording of a prior-period adjustment (correction of an error).
   DISCUSSION: APB 9, *Reporting the Results of Operations*, as amended by SFAS 16, *Prior-period Adjustments*, requires that prior-period adjustments of single period statements be reported net of applicable income taxes as changes in the opening balance in the statement of retained earnings of the current period. In comparative financial statements, all prior-periods affected by the prior-period adjustment should be restated to reflect the adjustment.
   Answer (A) is incorrect because the correction of the error should be reported as an adjustment to beginning retained earnings. Answers (C) and (D) are incorrect because a prior-period adjustment is reported in the current retained earnings statement.

30. Which of the following errors could result in an overstatement of both current assets and shareholders' equity?

A. An understatement of accrued sales expenses.

B. Noncurrent note receivable principal is misclassified as a current asset.

C. Annual depreciation on manufacturing machinery is understated.

D. Holiday pay expense for administrative employees is misclassified as manufacturing overhead.

The correct answer is (D). *(CIA 593 T-17)*
   REQUIRED: The error that would result in an overstatement of both current assets and shareholders' equity.
   DISCUSSION: Thus, the classification of holiday pay expense as manufacturing overhead would overstate both current assets and shareholders' equity. Holiday pay expense for administrative employees should be expensed as incurred. By classifying the expense as manufacturing overhead, inventory (a current asset) is overstated. If this inventory was not sold in the period, ending inventory would be overstated and expenses for the period would be understated. The effect is to overstate current assets, net income, retained earnings, and shareholders' equity.
   Answer (A) is incorrect because an understatement of accrued sales would understate shareholders' equity, but would not affect current assets, only current liabilities. Answer (B) is incorrect because a misclassification of a noncurrent note receivable as a current asset would not affect shareholders' equity. Answer (C) is incorrect because an understatement of depreciation on equipment would not affect current assets.

31. At the end of 1995, Ritzcar Co. failed to accrue sales commissions earned during 1995 but paid in 1996. The error was not repeated in 1996. What was the effect of this error on 1995 ending working capital and on the 1996 ending retained earnings balance?

	1995 Ending Working Capital	1996 Ending Retained Earnings
A.	Overstated	Overstated
B.	No effect	Overstated
C.	No effect	No effect
D.	Overstated	No effect

The correct answer is (D). *(CPA 591 T-14)*

REQUIRED: The effect of failure to accrue sales commissions.

DISCUSSION: The 1995 ending working capital (current assets – current liabilities) is overstated because the error understates current liabilities. The 1996 ending retained earnings balance is unaffected because it is a cumulative amount. Whether the sales commission expense is recognized in 1995 when it should have been accrued or in 1996 when it was paid affects the net income amounts for 1995 and 1996 but not 1996 ending retained earnings.

Answer (A) is incorrect because 1996 ending retained earnings is unaffected. Answer (B) is incorrect because 1995 ending working capital is overstated, and 1996 ending retained earnings is unaffected. Answer (C) is incorrect because 1995 ending working capital is overstated.

32. The 1995 financial statements of Bice Company reported net income for the year ended December 31, 1995 of $2,000,000. On July 1, 1996, subsequent to the issuance of the 1995 financial statements, Bice changed from an accounting principle that is not generally accepted to one that is generally accepted. If the generally accepted accounting principle had been used in 1995, net income for the year ended December 31, 1995 would have been decreased by $1,000,000. On August 1, 1996, Bice discovered a mathematical error relating to its 1995 financial statements. If this error had been discovered in 1995, net income for the year ended December 31, 1995 would have been increased $500,000. What amount, if any, should be included in net income for the year ended December 31, 1996 because of the items noted above?

A. $0

B. $500,000 decrease

C. $500,000 increase

D. $1,000,000 decrease

The correct answer is (A). *(CPA 1177 I-1)*

REQUIRED: The amount that should be included in net income because of an accounting change and an accounting error.

DISCUSSION: APB 20 states that a change from an accounting principle that is not generally accepted to one that is generally accepted should be accounted for as the correction of an error. SFAS 16 requires that corrections of errors in financial statements of prior-periods be accounted for as prior-period adjustments and thus excluded from the determination of net income for the current period. Accordingly, the mathematical error and the change in accounting method have no effect on 1996 net income.

Answers (B), (C), and (D) are incorrect because current-period net income would not be affected by either the mathematical error or the change in accounting method.

33. An example of the correction of an error in previously issued financial statements is a change

A. From the completed-contract to the percentage-of-completion method of accounting for long-term construction-type contracts.

B. In the depletion rate based on new engineering studies of recoverable mineral resources.

C. From the sum-of-the-years'-digits to the straight-line method of depreciation for all plant assets.

D. From the installment basis of recording sales to the accrual basis when collection of the sales price has been and continues to be reasonably assured.

The correct answer is (D). *(CPA 573 T-10)*

REQUIRED: The example of the correction of an error in previously issued statements.

DISCUSSION: APB 20 defines a change from an accounting principle that is not generally accepted to one that is generally accepted as the correction of an accounting error. When collection of the sales price is reasonably assured, APB 10, *Omnibus Opinion-1966*, states that accounting under the accrual method is required. Accordingly, a change from the installment basis of recording sales to the accrual basis should be treated as the correction of an error.

Answers (A) and (C) are incorrect because each is a change from one generally accepted accounting principle to another. Answer (B) is incorrect because it is a change in accounting estimate.

34. Conn Co. reported a retained earnings balance of $400,000 at December 31, 1995. In August 1996, Conn determined that insurance premiums of $60,000 for the 3-year period beginning January 1, 1995 had been paid and fully expensed in 1995. Conn has a 30% income tax rate. What amount should Conn report as adjusted beginning retained earnings in its 1996 statement of retained earnings?

A. $420,000

B. $428,000

C. $440,000

D. $442,000

The correct answer is (B). *(CPA 1193 I-10)*
   REQUIRED: The adjusted beginning retained earnings after correction of an error.
   DISCUSSION: APB 9, as amended by SFAS 16, requires that prior-period adjustments be reflected net of applicable income taxes as changes in the opening balance in the statement of retained earnings. The $60,000 insurance prepayment in 1995 should have been expensed ratably over the 3-year period. Consequently, 1995 net income was understated by $40,000, net of tax effect, and $40,000 [$60,000 – ($60,000 ÷ 3)] should have been reported as a prepaid expense (an asset) at the beginning of 1996. The prior-period adjustment to the beginning balance of retained earnings is therefore a credit of $28,000 [$40,000 x (1.0 – .3 tax rate)]. The adjusted balance is $428,000 ($400,000 + $28,000).
   Answer (A) is incorrect because $420,000 is the sum of the beginning balance of retained earnings and the expense that should have been recognized in 1995. Answer (C) is incorrect because $440,000 does not consider the tax effect. Answer (D) is incorrect because $442,000 assumes that no insurance expense should have been recognized in 1995.

35. Foy Corp. failed to accrue warranty costs of $50,000 in its December 31, 1995 financial statements. In addition, a change from straight-line to accelerated depreciation made at the beginning of 1996 resulted in a cumulative effect of $30,000 on Foy's retained earnings. Both the $50,000 and the $30,000 are net of related income taxes. What amount should Foy report as prior-period adjustments in 1996?

A. $0

B. $30,000

C. $50,000

D. $80,000

The correct answer is (C). *(CPA 1194 F-55)*
   REQUIRED: The amount of prior-period adjustments.
   DISCUSSION: A prior-period adjustment is made to correct an error in the financial statements of a prior-period. Accordingly, the failure to accrue $50,000 of warranty costs requires a prior-period adjustment. The change in depreciation method is a change in accounting principle requiring a cumulative-effect adjustment. It should be included in the determination of net income for 1996, the year of change.
   Answer (A) is incorrect because the failure to accrue warranty costs requires a prior-period adjustment. Answers (B) and (D) are incorrect because the change in depreciation method is not treated as a prior-period adjustment.

36. On December 30, 1996, Astor Corp. sold merchandise for $75,000 to Day Co. The terms of the sale were net 30, FOB shipping point. The merchandise was shipped on December 31, 1996 and arrived at Day on January 5, 1997. Because of a clerical error, the sale was not recorded until January 1997, and the merchandise, sold at a 25% markup, was included in Astor's inventory at December 31, 1996. As a result, Astor's cost of goods sold for the year ended December 31, 1996 was

A. Understated by $75,000.

B. Understated by $60,000.

C. Understated by $15,000.

D. Correctly stated.

The correct answer is (B). *(CPA 1193 I-51)*
   REQUIRED: The cost of goods sold given delayed recording of a sale.
   DISCUSSION: Under the shipping terms, the sale should have been recognized on December 31, 1996 because title and risk of loss passed to the buyer on that date; that is, an earning process was complete. Astor should have debited a receivable and credited sales for $75,000, the net amount, on the date of shipment. Astor should also have debited cost of sales and credited inventory at cost on the same date. The error therefore understated cost of goods sold by $60,000 ($75,000 sales price ÷ 125% of cost).
   Answer (A) is incorrect because $75,000 is the selling price. Answer (C) is incorrect because $15,000 is the amount of the markup. Answer (D) is incorrect because cost of goods was understated by $60,000.

Questions 37 and 38 are based on the following information. On October 1, 1995, Fleur Retailers signed a 4-month, 16% note payable to finance the purchase of holiday merchandise. At that date, there was no direct method of pricing the merchandise, and the note's market rate of interest was 11%. Fleur recorded the purchase at the note's face amount. All of the merchandise was sold by December 1, 1995. Fleur's 1995 financial statements reported interest payable and interest expense on the note for 3 months at 16%. All amounts due on the note were paid February 1, 1996.

37. Fleur's 1995 cost of goods sold for the holiday merchandise was

A. Overstated by the difference between the note's face amount and the note's October 1, 1995 present value.

B. Overstated by the difference between the note's face amount and the note's October 1, 1995 present value plus 11% interest for 2 months.

C. Understated by the difference between the note's face amount and the note's October 1, 1995 present value.

D. Understated by the difference between the note's face amount and the note's October 1, 1995 present value plus 16% interest for 2 months.

The correct answer is (C). *(CPA 592 T-18)*
REQUIRED: The cost of goods sold.
DISCUSSION: The general presumption when a note is exchanged for property, goods, or services in an arm's-length transaction is that the rate of interest is fair and adequate. If the rate is not stated or the stated rate is unreasonable, the note and the property, goods, or services should be recorded at the fair value of the property, goods, or services or the market value of the note, whichever is more clearly determinable. In the absence of these values, the present value of the note should be used as the basis for recording both the note and the property, goods, or services. This present value is obtained by discounting all future payments on the note using the market rate of interest, in accordance with APB 21, *Interest on Receivables and Payables*. Because the imputed rate (11%) is less than the nominal rate (16%), the note (and the purchase) should be recorded at a premium. The face amount is the present value at the nominal rate. The face amount plus a premium is the present value at the (lower) market rate. Thus, recording the note and purchase at the face amount of the note understates the cost of the inventory sold.

Answers (A) and (B) are incorrect because the cost of goods sold was understated. Answer (D) is incorrect because the understatement was equal to the note's present value at 11% on the date of purchase minus the face amount (present value at the 16% nominal rate).

38. As a result of Fleur's accounting treatment of the note, interest, and merchandise, which of the following items was reported correctly?

	12/31/95 Retained Earnings	12/31/95 Interest Payable
A.	Yes	Yes
B.	No	No
C.	Yes	No
D.	No	Yes

The correct answer is (D). *(CPA 592 T-19)*
REQUIRED: The item correctly reported as a result of incorrectly recording a note payable.
DISCUSSION: If the note's rate is not stated, or the stated rate is unreasonable, the note and any related property, goods, or services should be recorded at the fair value of the property, goods, services, or the market value of the note, whichever is more clearly determinable. Since the note was recorded at its face amount, cost of goods sold was understated by the difference between the note's face amount and its present value. Interest expense should be calculated based on the present value of the note at the market rate of interest. Interest payable is the stated rate times the face amount, and amortization of premium or discount is the difference between the payable and interest expense. In this situation, interest expense and interest payable are both recorded at the stated rate multiplied by the face amount. Thus, retained earnings is misstated as a result of the error in calculating cost of goods sold and interest expense. Interest payable is correctly reported.

Answers (A), (B), and (C) are incorrect because retained earnings is misstated and interest payable is correctly stated.

39. For the past 3 years, Colbeth, Inc. has failed to accrue unpaid wages earned by workers during the last week of the year. The amounts omitted, which are considered material, were as follows:

December 31, 1994	$56,000
December 31, 1995	51,000
December 31, 1996	64,000

The entry on December 31, 1996 to correct for these omissions would include a

A. Credit to wage expense for $64,000.

B. Debit to wage expense for $51,000.

C. Debit to wage expense for $13,000.

D. Credit to retained earnings for $64,000.

The correct answer is (C). *(CMA 1293 2-10)*
REQUIRED: The entry to correct for failure to accrue wages.
DISCUSSION: Failing to record accrued wages is a self-correcting error. Expenses are understated in one year and overstated in the next, resulting in the correction of the error over the 2-year period. The 1994 error overstated 1994 earnings and understated 1995 earnings by $56,000. Consequently, no correction is necessary for the 1994 error. The 1995 error overstated 1995 earnings and understated 1996 earnings by $51,000. The 1996 error overstated 1996 earnings by $64,000. Thus, the net effect in 1996 of the 1995 and 1996 errors is a $13,000 ($64,000 – $51,000) overstatement. The correcting entry is to debit expense for $13,000, debit retained earnings for $51,000, and credit wages payable for $64,000.
Answer (A) is incorrect because $64,000 is the accrued wages payable, not the amount of the adjustment. Answer (B) is incorrect because $51,000 is the correct wage accrual for 1995. Answer (D) is incorrect because retained earnings should be debited for $51,000.

40. While preparing its 1996 financial statements, Dek Corp. discovered computational errors in its 1995 and 1994 depreciation expense. These errors resulted in overstatement of each year's income by $25,000, net of income taxes. The following amounts were reported in the previously issued financial statements:

	1995	1994
Retained earnings, 1/1	$700,000	$500,000
Net income	150,000	200,000
Retained earnings, 12/31	$850,000	$700,000

Dek's 1996 net income is correctly reported at $180,000. Which of the following amounts should be reported as prior-period adjustments and net income in Dek's 1996 and 1995 comparative financial statements?

	Year	Prior-Period Adjustment	Net Income
A.	1995	--	$150,000
	1996	$(50,000)	180,000
B.	1995	$(50,000)	$150,000
	1996	--	180,000
C.	1995	$(25,000)	$125,000
	1996	--	180,000
D.	1995	--	$125,000
	1996	--	180,000

The correct answer is (C). *(CPA 592 II-2)*
REQUIRED: The amounts that should be reported as prior-period adjustments and net income in comparative financial statements.
DISCUSSION: In the comparative financial statements presented for 1995 and 1996, the 1995 statements should be restated to reflect the adjustment. The beginning balance of retained earnings for 1995 should be adjusted to correct the $25,000 overstatement of after-tax income for 1994, a year for which financial statements are not presented. The statements for 1995 should be restated to reflect the correction of the error in 1995 net income. This amount will be correctly reported in the 1996 and 1995 financial statements as $125,000 ($150,000 in the previously issued 1995 statements – $25,000 overstatement). No adjustments to the 1996 financial statements are necessary.
Answer (A) is incorrect because restated 1995 net income is $125,000, and the prior-period adjustment is made to the beginning balance of retained earnings for 1995. Answer (B) is incorrect because restated 1995 net income is $125,000, and the adjustment to 1995 retained earnings is for $25,000 (the overstatement of 1994 net income). Answer (D) is incorrect because a $25,000 prior-period adjustment must be made in the 1995 statements.

41. The following information appeared on ECU, Inc.'s December 31 financial statements:

	1995	1996
Assets	$1,000,000	$1,200,000
Liabilities	750,000	800,000
Contributed capital	120,000	120,000
Dividends paid	100,000	60,000

In preparing its 1996 financial statements, ECU, Inc. discovered that it had misplaced a decimal in calculating depreciation for 1995. This error overstated 1995 depreciation by $10,000. In addition, changing technology had significantly shortened the useful life of ECU's computers. Based on this information, ECU determined that depreciation should be $30,000 higher in 1996 than was currently reflected in the 1996 financial statements. Assuming that no correcting or adjusting entries have been made and ignoring income taxes, how much should ECU report as 1996 net income?

A. $140,000

B. $170,000

C. $210,000

D. $230,000

The correct answer is (B). *(C. Hall)*

REQUIRED: The net income following a correction of an error and a change in estimate.

DISCUSSION: Retained earnings are equal to assets minus liabilities minus contributed capital. Thus, 1995 retained earnings equal $130,000 ($1,000,000 – $750,000 – $120,000). Retained earnings for 1996 equal $280,000 ($1,200,000 – $800,000 – $120,000). The error in 1995 depreciation overstated expense and therefore understated 1995 net income and 1995 retained earnings. To correct for this error, a prior-period adjustment to 1995 ending retained earnings (1996 beginning retained earnings) should be made. Corrected 1995 ending retained earnings equal $140,000 ($130,000 previously reported + $10,000 adjustment). Unadjusted 1996 net income is equal to the $140,000 increase in retained earnings ($280,000 – $140,000) plus the $60,000 dividends paid. Hence, unadjusted 1996 net income equals $200,000. The $30,000 increase in depreciation attributable to the change in the asset life is a change in estimate that should be reflected in 1996 net income. Consequently, the adjusted 1996 net income is $170,000 ($200,000 – $30,000).

Answer (A) is incorrect because the increase in retained earnings must be adjusted for dividends paid and the additional depreciation to arrive at net income. Answer (C) is incorrect because the prior-period error in calculating depreciation does not affect current-period net income, and the current-period additional depreciation must be subtracted to arrive at net income. Answer (D) is incorrect because the additional depreciation for the current period must be subtracted from, not added to, retained earnings.

42. In auditing your organization's records for 1996, the first year of operations, you discover the following errors were made at December 31, 1996:

Failed to accrue $50,000 interest expense.

Failed to record depreciation expense on office equipment of $80,000.

Failed to amortize prepaid rent expense of $100,000.

Failed to delay recognition of prepaid advertising expense of $60,000.

The net effect of the above errors was to overstate net income for 1996 by

A. $130,000

B. $170,000

C. $230,000

D. $290,000

The correct answer is (B). (CIA 593 IV-36)

REQUIRED: The effect of certain errors on net income.

DISCUSSION: The failure to accrue interest expense, record depreciation expense on office equipment, and amortize prepaid rent expense would overstate net income. Expensing the full amount of prepaid advertising instead of deferring recognition would understate net income. Thus, net income would be overstated by $170,000 ($50,000 + $80,000 + $100,000 – $60,000).

Answer (A) is incorrect because $130,000 includes only the interest expense and depreciation expense. Answer (C) is incorrect because $230,000 results from not subtracting the prepaid advertising expense. Answer (D) is incorrect because $290,000 results from adding prepaid advertising expense.

Questions 43 and 44 are based on the following information. An audit of a company has revealed the following four errors that have occurred but have not been corrected:

1. Inventory at December 31, 1995 - $40,000, Understated

2. Inventory at December 31, 1996 - $15,000, Overstated

3. Depreciation for 1995 - $7,000, Understated

4. Accrued expenses at December 31, 1996 - $10,000, Understated

43. The errors cause the reported net income for the year ending December 31, 1996 to be

A. Overstated by $72,000.

B. Overstated by $65,000.

C. Understated by $28,000.

D. Understated by $45,000.

The correct answer is (B). *(CIA 591 IV-45)*
REQUIRED: The effect of certain errors on net income.
DISCUSSION: Both the understatement of beginning inventory and the overstatement of ending inventory would understate cost of goods sold. The result would understate cost of goods sold and overstate net income by $55,000 ($40,000 + $15,000). The understatement of 1995's depreciation would have no effect on 1996's net income but would result in an overstatement of 1995 and 1996 retained earnings of $7,000. The understatement of accrued expenses would overstate net income by $10,000. Thus, net income is overstated by $65,000 ($40,000 + $15,000 + $10,000).

Answer (A) is incorrect because $72,000 results from including the $7,000 depreciation. Answer (C) is incorrect because a $28,000 understatement results from taking the difference between inventory errors ($40,000 – $15,000) and adding accrued expenses and subtracting depreciation expense. Answer (D) is incorrect because a $45,000 understatement results from adding beginning inventory and ending inventory and subtracting accrued expenses.

44. The errors cause the reported retained earnings at December 31, 1996 to be

A. Overstated by $65,000.

B. Overstated by $32,000.

C. Overstated by $25,000.

D. Understated by $18,000.

The correct answer is (B). *(CIA 591 IV-46)*
REQUIRED: The effect of errors on retained earnings.
DISCUSSION: The error in 12/31/95 inventory would understate income in 1995 (cost of goods sold would be overstated by $40,000) and overstate income in 1996 (cost of goods sold is understated by $40,000). The error in 12/31/96 inventory would understate cost of goods sold which would overstate net income in 1996 by $15,000. The understatement of depreciation of $7,000 would overstate 1995 net income. The understatement of accrued expenses would overstate income in 1996 by $10,000. The effect of these errors on net income would be reflected in retained earnings at 12/31/96. The result is an overstatement of retained earnings by $32,000 ($40,000 + $15,000 + $7,000 + $10,000 – $40,000).

Answer (A) is incorrect because an overstatement of $65,000 is the effect of the errors on 1996 net income. Answer (C) is incorrect because an overstatement of $25,000 results from taking into account only the ending inventory in 1996 and the accrued expenses. Answer (D) is incorrect because $18,000 results from subtracting, not adding, the effect of depreciation expense.

CHAPTER TWENTY-TWO
STATEMENT OF CASH FLOWS

SFAS 95, *Statement of Cash Flows*, replaces the statement of changes in financial position with a statement of cash flows. Several pronouncements have amended SFAS 95. These include SFAS 102, *Statement of Cash Flows - Exemption of Certain Enterprises and Classification of Cash Flows from Certain Securities Acquired for Resale*; SFAS 104, *Statement of Cash Flows - Net Reporting of Certain Cash Receipts and Cash Payments and Classification of Cash Flows from Hedging Transactions*; and SFAS 117, *Financial Statements of Not-for-Profit Organizations*.

22.1 Statement of Cash Flows -- General

1. A statement of cash flows is to be presented in general purpose external financial statements by which of the following?

    A. Publicly held business enterprises only.

    B. Privately held business enterprises only.

    C. All business enterprises.

    D. All business enterprises and not-for-profit organizations.

The correct answer is (D). *(Publisher)*
    REQUIRED: The entities required to present a statement of cash flows.
    DISCUSSION: SFAS 95 as amended by SFAS 117 requires a statement of cash flows as part of a full set of financial statements of all business entities (both publicly held and privately held) and not-for-profit organizations. Defined benefit pension plans, certain other employee benefit plans, and certain highly liquid investment companies, however, are exempted from this requirement by SFAS 102.
    Answers (A), (B), and (C) are incorrect because all business entities and not-for-profit organizations are required to present a statement of cash flows.

2. The primary purpose of a statement of cash flows of a business enterprise is to provide relevant information about

    A. Differences between net income and associated cash receipts and disbursements.

    B. An enterprise's ability to generate future positive net cash flows.

    C. The cash receipts and cash disbursements of an enterprise during a period.

    D. An enterprise's ability to meet cash operating needs.

The correct answer is (C). *(CPA 594 F-5)*
    REQUIRED: The primary purpose of a statement of cash flows.
    DISCUSSION: The primary purpose is to provide information about the cash receipts and cash payments during a period. This information helps investors, creditors, and other users to assess the enterprise's ability to generate net cash inflows, meet its obligations, pay dividends, and secure external financing. It also helps assess reasons for the differences between net income and net cash flow and the effects of cash and noncash financing and investing activities.
    Answers (A), (B), and (D) are incorrect because reconciling net income with cash flows, assessing the ability to generate cash flows, and assessing the ability to meet cash needs are secondary purposes.

3. A corporation issues a balance sheet and income statement for the current year and comparative income statements for each of the 2 previous years. Under SFAS 95, a statement of cash flows

    A. Should be issued for the current year only.

    B. Should be issued for the current and the previous year only.

    C. Should be issued for all 3 years.

    D. May be issued at the company's option for any or all of the 3 years.

The correct answer is (C). *(Publisher)*
    REQUIRED: The circumstances in which a statement of cash flows should be issued.
    DISCUSSION: When a business enterprise provides a set of financial statements that reports both financial position and results of operations, it must also present a statement of cash flows for each period for which the results of operations are provided.
    Answers (A) and (B) are incorrect because a statement of cash flows must be provided for all 3 years. Answer (D) is incorrect because the statement of cash flows is not optional in these circumstances.

4. Which of the following cash flows per share should be reported in a statement of cash flows?

    A. Primary cash flows per share only.

    B. Fully diluted cash flows per share only.

    C. Both primary and fully diluted cash flows per share.

    D. Cash flows per share should not be reported.

The correct answer is (D). *(CPA 592 T-8)*
    REQUIRED: The cash flows per share reported in a statement of cash flows.
    DISCUSSION: SFAS 95 proscribes reporting of a cash flow per share amount. Reporting a per-share amount might improperly imply that cash flow is an alternative to net income as a performance measure.
    Answers (A), (B), and (C) are incorrect because cash flows per share should not be reported.

5. Bay Manufacturing Co. purchased a 3-month U.S. Treasury bill. In preparing Bay's statement of cash flows, this purchase would

    A. Have no effect.

    B. Be treated as an outflow from financing activities.

    C. Be treated as an outflow from investing activities.

    D. Be treated as an outflow from lending activities.

The correct answer is (A). *(CPA 1191 T-22)*
    REQUIRED: The effect of purchasing a 3-month T-bill.
    DISCUSSION: SFAS 95 defines cash equivalents as short-term, highly liquid investments that are both readily convertible to known amounts of cash and so near their maturity that they present insignificant risk of changes in value because of changes in interest rates. Moreover, cash equivalents ordinarily include only investments with original maturities to the holder of 3 months or less. The T-bill is therefore a cash equivalent and has no effect on the statement of cash flows.
    Answers (B), (C), and (D) are incorrect because the transaction involves an exchange of cash for a cash equivalent and therefore has no effect.

6. At December 31, 1995, Kale Co. had the following balances in the accounts it maintains at First State Bank:

Checking account #101	$175,000
Checking account #201	(10,000)
Money market account	25,000
90-day certificate of deposit due 2/28/96	50,000
180-day certificate of deposit due 3/15/96	80,000

Kale classifies investments with original maturities of 3 months or less as cash equivalents. In its December 31, 1995 balance sheet, what amount should Kale report as cash and cash equivalents?

    A. $190,000

    B. $200,000

    C. $240,000

    D. $320,000

The correct answer is (C). *(CPA 594 F-13)*
    REQUIRED: The amount that should be reported in the balance sheet as cash and cash equivalents.
    DISCUSSION: Cash is an asset that must be readily available for use by the business. It normally consists of (1) coin and currency on hand, (2) demand deposits (checking accounts), (3) time deposits (savings accounts), and (4) near-cash assets (e.g., money market accounts). Cash equivalents usually are limited to investments with original maturities to the holding entity of 3 months or less. The original maturity is the date on which the obligation becomes due. As a result, cash and cash equivalents will be reported as $240,000 ($175,000 – $10,000 + $25,000 + $50,000).
    Answer (A) is incorrect because $190,000 excludes the 90-day CD. Answer (B) is incorrect because $200,000 excludes the 90-day CD and the checking account with a negative balance. Answer (D) is incorrect because $320,000 includes the 180-day CD.

7. The statement of cash flows may be presented in either a direct or an indirect (reconciliation) format. In which of these formats would cash collected from customers be presented as a gross amount?

	Direct	Indirect
A.	No	No
B.	No	Yes
C.	Yes	Yes
D.	Yes	No

The correct answer is (D). *(R. O'Keefe)*

REQUIRED: The format in which cash collected from customers would be presented as a gross amount.

DISCUSSION: The statement of cash flows may report cash flows from operating activities in either an indirect (reconciliation) or a direct format. The direct format reports the major classes of operating cash receipts and cash payments as gross amounts. The indirect presentation reconciles net income to the same amount of net cash flow from operations that would be determined in accordance with the direct method. To arrive at net operating cash flow, the indirect method adjusts net income by removing the effects of (1) all deferrals of past operating cash receipts and payments, (2) all accruals of expected future operating cash receipts and payments, (3) all financing and investing activities, and (4) all noncash operating transactions.

Answers (A), (B), and (C) are incorrect because only the direct method format for the statement of cash flows presents cash collected from customers as a gross amount.

8. In a statement of cash flows, which of the following items is reported as a cash outflow from financing activities?

I. Payments to retire mortgage notes
II. Interest payments on mortgage notes
III. Dividend payments

A. I, II, and III.

B. II and III.

C. I only.

D. I and III.

The correct answer is (D). *(CPA 591 T-31)*

REQUIRED: The cash outflows from financing activities.

DISCUSSION: Financing activities include issuance of stock, payment of dividends and other distributions to owners, treasury stock transactions, issuance of debt, receipt of donor-restricted resources to be used for long-term purposes, and repayment or other settlement of debt obligations. Thus, payment of the principal of a note and payment of dividends are outflows from financing activities.

Answers (A) and (B) are incorrect because interest payments are outflows from operating activities. Answer (C) is incorrect because dividend payments are outflows from financing activities.

9. Alp, Inc. had the following activities during 1996:

- Acquired 2,000 shares of stock in Maybel, Inc. for $26,000

- Sold an investment in Rate Motors for $35,000 when the carrying value was $33,000

- Acquired a $50,000, 4-year certificate of deposit from a bank. (During the year, interest of $3,750 was paid to Alp.)

- Collected dividends of $1,200 on stock investments

In Alp's 1996 statement of cash flows, net cash used in investing activities should be

A. $37,250

B. $38,050

C. $39,800

D. $41,000

The correct answer is (D). *(CPA 591 I-11)*

REQUIRED: The net cash used in investing activities.

DISCUSSION: Investing activities include the lending of money; the collection of those loans; and the acquisition, sale, or other disposal of (1) loans and other securities that are not cash equivalents and that have not been acquired specifically for resale and (2) property, plant, equipment, and other productive assets. Thus, the purchase of stock, sale of stock, and acquisition of a long-term certificate of deposit (not a cash equivalent) are investing activities. The receipts of interest and dividends are cash flows from operating activities. The net cash used in investing activities therefore equals $41,000 ($26,000 − $35,000 + $50,000).

Answer (A) is incorrect because $37,250 treats interest received as an investing cash inflow. Answer (B) is incorrect because $38,050 treats interest and dividends received as investing cash inflows and uses the carrying value of the investment sold. Answer (C) is incorrect because $39,800 treats dividends received as an investing cash inflow.

10. The following information was taken from the accounting records of Oak Corporation for the year ended December 31, 1996.

Proceeds from issuance of preferred stock F	$4,000,000
Dividends paid on preferred stock F	400,000
Bonds payable converted to common stock NC	2,000,000
Payment for purchase of machinery I	500,000
Proceeds from sale of plant building I	1,200,000
2% stock dividend on common stock NC	300,000
Gain on sale of plant building I	200,000

The net cash flows from investing and financing activities that should be presented on Oak's statement of cash flows for the year ended December 31, 1996 are, respectively

A. $700,000 and $3,600,000.

B. $700,000 and $3,900,000.

C. $900,000 and $3,900,000.

D. $900,000 and $3,600,000.

The correct answer is (A). *(CMA 1294 2-21)*
REQUIRED: The respective net cash flows from investing and financing activities.
DISCUSSION: Investing activities include the lending of money and the collecting of those loans, and the acquisition, sale, or other disposal of securities that are not cash equivalents and of productive assets that are expected to generate revenue over a long period of time. Financing activities include the issuance of stock, the payment of dividends, treasury stock transactions, the issuance of debt, the receipt of donor-restricted resources to be used for long-term purposes, and the repayment or other settlement of debt obligations. Investing activities include the purchase of machinery and the sale of a building. The net inflow from these activities is $700,000 ($1,200,000 – $500,000). Financing activities include the issuance of preferred stock and the payment of dividends. The net inflow is $3,600,000 ($4,000,000 – $400,000). The conversion of bonds into common stock and the stock dividend do not affect cash.
Answer (B) is incorrect because the stock dividend has no effect on cash flows from financing activities. Answers (C) and (D) are incorrect because the gain on the sale of the building is double counted in determining the net cash flow from investing activities.

11. On July 1, 1996, Dewey Co. signed a 20-year building lease that it reported as a capital lease. Dewey paid the monthly lease payments when due. How should Dewey report the effect of the lease payments in the financing activities section of its 1996 statement of cash flows?

A. An inflow equal to the present value of future lease payments at July 1, 1996, minus 1996 principal and interest payments.

B. An outflow equal to the 1996 principal and interest payments on the lease.

C. An outflow equal to the 1996 principal payments only.

D. The lease payments should not be reported in the financing activities section.

The correct answer is (C). *(CPA 1193 T-42)*
REQUIRED: The effect of lease payments on the financing activities section in the statement of cash flows.
DISCUSSION: Financing activities include the repayment or settlement of debt obligations. Financing activities do not include the payment of interest. Thus, the payment of principal is an outflow from financing activities. The payments for interest are operating cash flows.
Answer (A) is incorrect because payments made by a company are outflows. Answer (B) is incorrect because the interest payments should not be included as a financing activity. Answer (D) is incorrect because lease payments are considered cash outflows from financing activities.

12. In preparing the statement of cash flows, if the payment of cash dividends was omitted, then the net cash provided by <List A> activities will be <List B>.

	List A	List B
A.	Operating	Understated
B.	Investing	Understated
C.	Investing	Overstated
D.	Financing	Overstated

The correct answer is (D). *(CIA 595 IV-6)*
REQUIRED: The effect of omitting payment of cash dividends.
DISCUSSION: Cash flows from financing activities include (1) obtaining resources from owners and providing them with a return on and of their investment, (2) borrowing from and repaying creditors, and (3) receiving restricted resources that by donor stipulation must be used for long-term purposes. This category of cash flows will be overstated if the use of cash to pay dividends to equity holders is omitted from the statement of cash flows.
Answer (A) is incorrect because cash flows from operating activities ordinarily arise from transactions that enter into the determination of net income. Cash dividends do not affect the cash flows from operating activities. Answers (B) and (C) are incorrect because cash flows from investing activities arise from making and collecting loans and acquiring and disposing of investments (both debt and equity) and property, plant, and equipment. Cash dividends do not affect the cash flows from investing activities.

13. Which of the following related cash transactions should be disclosed as gross amounts of cash receipts and cash payments rather than as net amounts?

A. The purchase and sale of fixed assets.

B. Changes in cash and cash equivalents.

C. The purchase and sale of federal funds.

D. The receipts and payments from demand deposits.

The correct answer is (A). *(Publisher)*

REQUIRED: The related receipts and payments that should be classified as gross amounts.

DISCUSSION: In general, cash inflows and cash outflows from operating, investing, and financing activities should be reported separately at gross amounts in a statement of cash flows. In certain instances, however, the net amount of related cash receipts and cash payments may provide sufficient information about particular classes of cash flows. For example, SFAS 104 permits banks, saving institutions, and credit unions to report net amounts for (1) the placement and withdrawal of deposits with other financial institutions, (2) the acceptance and repayment of time deposits, and (3) the making of loans to customers and the collection of principal.

Answers (B), (C), and (D) are incorrect because they represent classes of related cash flows that may be presented as net amounts.

14. Fara Co. reported bonds payable of $47,000 at December 31, 1995, and $50,000 at December 31, 1996. During 1996, Fara issued $20,000 of bonds payable in exchange for equipment. There was no amortization of bond premium or discount during the year. What amount should Fara report in its 1996 statement of cash flows for redemption of bonds payable?

A. $3,000

B. $17,000

C. $20,000

D. $23,000

The correct answer is (B). *(CPA 594 F-50)*

REQUIRED: The amount reported in the statement of cash flows for redemption of bonds payable.

DISCUSSION: Assuming no amortization of premium or discount, the net amount of bonds payable reported was affected solely by the issuance of bonds for equipment and the redemption of bonds. Given that $20,000 of bonds were issued and that the amount reported increased by only $3,000, $17,000 of bonds must have been redeemed. This amount should be reported in the statement of cash flows as a cash outflow from a financing activity.

Answer (A) is incorrect because $3,000 equals the increase in bonds payable. Answer (C) is incorrect because $20,000 is the amount of bonds issued. Answer (D) is incorrect because $23,000 is the sum of the bonds issued and the increase in bonds payable.

22.2 Operating Activities -- Indirect Presentation

15. How should a gain from the sale of used equipment for cash be reported in a statement of cash flows using the indirect method?

A. In investment activities as a reduction of the cash inflow from the sale.

B. In investment activities as a cash outflow.

C. In operating activities as a deduction from income.

D. In operating activities as an addition to income.

The correct answer is (C). *(CPA 593 T-33)*

REQUIRED: The presentation of a gain on the sale of used equipment in a statement of cash flows (indirect method).

DISCUSSION: Cash received from the sale of equipment is ordinarily classified in a statement of cash flows as a cash inflow from an investing activity. The cash inflow is equal to the carrying value of the equipment plus any gain or minus any loss realized. Because the gain will be included in the determination of income from continuing operations, it must be subtracted from the net income figure presented in the statement of cash flows (indirect method) in the reconciliation of net income to net cash flow from operating activities. The purpose of the adjustment is to remove the effect of the gain from both net income and the cash inflows from operating activities. In the cash flows from investing activities section, the amount reported is the sum of the gain and the carrying value of the equipment.

Answers (A), (B), and (D) are incorrect because the gain should be reported in the statement of cash flows in operating activities as a deduction from income.

16. In the indirect presentation of cash flows from operating activities, net income of a business enterprise is adjusted for noncash revenues, gains, expenses, and losses to determine the cash flows from operating activities. A reconciliation of net cash flows from operating activities to net income

A. Must be reported in the statement of cash flows.

B. Must be presented separately in a related disclosure.

C. May be either reported in the statement of cash flows or presented separately in a related disclosure.

D. Need not be presented.

The correct answer is (C). *(Publisher)*
REQUIRED: The proper reporting of a reconciliation of net cash flows from operating activities to net income.
DISCUSSION: When an indirect presentation of net cash flows from operating activities is made, a reconciliation with net income must be provided for all noncash revenues, gains, expenses, and losses. This reconciliation may be either reported in the statement of cash flows or provided separately in related disclosures, with the statement of cash flows presenting only the net cash flows from operating activities.
Answer (A) is incorrect because the reconciliation may be presented in a related disclosure. Answer (B) is incorrect because the reconciliation may be reported in the statement of cash flows. Answer (D) is incorrect because a reconciliation must be reported in an indirect presentation of the statement of cash flows.

17. If the indirect method is used to present the statement of cash flows of a business enterprise, depreciation expense is

A. Presented as an addition to net income in the operating section of the statement.

B. Presented as a deduction from net income in the operating section of the statement.

C. Reported as a cash outflow in the investing section of the statement.

D. Not disclosed on the statement.

The correct answer is (A). *(R. Derstine)*
REQUIRED: The correct presentation of depreciation when the indirect method is used.
DISCUSSION: In an indirect presentation of net cash flows from operating activities, the statement of cash flows should begin with net income adjusted for certain items including those recognized in the determination of income that did not affect cash during the period. The recognition of depreciation expense reduces net income without directly affecting cash. Thus, depreciation must be added back to net income in the determination of cash flows from operating activities.
Answer (B) is incorrect because depreciation is an addition to net income. Answer (C) is incorrect because depreciation is not a cash flow. Answer (D) is incorrect because depreciation is disclosed as an adjustment to net income.

18. When using the indirect method to prepare the statement of cash flows, the amortization of goodwill should be presented as a(n)

A. Cash flow from investing activities.

B. Cash flow from financing activities.

C. Deduction from net income.

D. Addition to net income.

The correct answer is (D). *(CMA 1294 2-18)*
REQUIRED: The treatment of goodwill amortization in a statement of cash flows based on the indirect method.
DISCUSSION: The statement of cash flows may report operating activities in the form of either an indirect or a direct presentation. The indirect presentation removes from net income the effects of past deferrals of past operating cash flows, all accruals of expected future operating cash flows, and net income items not affecting operating cash flows. The result is net operating cash flow. Goodwill amortization is a noncash expense and should be added to net income.
Answers (A) and (B) are incorrect because goodwill amortization is not a cash flow, and it is not an investing or financing activity. Answer (C) is incorrect because goodwill amortization is added to net income.

19. The net income for Cypress Inc. was $3,000,000 for the year ended December 31, 1996. Additional information is as follows:

Depreciation on fixed assets	$1,500,000
Gain from cash sale of land	200,000
Increase in accounts payable	300,000
Dividends paid on preferred stock	400,000

The net cash provided by operating activities in the statement of cash flows for the year ended December 31, 1996 should be

   A. $4,200,000

   B. $4,500,000

   C. $4,600,000

   D. $4,800,000

The correct answer is (C). *(CMA 1294 2-20)*
   REQUIRED: The net cash provided by operations.
   DISCUSSION: The statement of cash flows may be in the form of an indirect or a direct presentation. The indirect presentation removes from net income the effects of all deferrals of past operating cash flows, all accruals of expected future operating cash flows, and net income items not affecting operating cash flows. The result is net operating cash flow. Depreciation is an expense not directly affecting cash flows that should be added back to net income. The increase in accounts payable is added to net income because it indicates that an expense has been recorded but not paid. The gain on the sale of land is an inflow from an investing, not an operating, activity and should be subtracted from net income. The dividends paid on preferred stock do not affect net income or net cash flow from operating activities and do not require an adjustment. Thus, net cash flow from operations is $4,600,000 ($3,000,000 + $1,500,000 – $200,000 + $300,000).
   Answer (A) is incorrect because $4,200,000 equals net income, plus depreciation, minus the increase in accounts payable. Answer (B) is incorrect because $4,500,000 equals net income, plus depreciation. Answer (D) is incorrect because $4,800,000 equals net income, plus depreciation, plus the increase in accounts payable.

20. Kresley Co. has provided the following 1996 current account balances for the preparation of the annual statement of cash flows:

	January 1	December 1
Accounts receivable	$11,500	$14,500
Allowance for uncollectible		
accounts	400	500
Prepaid rent expense	6,200	4,100
Accounts payable	9,700	11,200

Kresley's 1996 net income is $75,000. Net cash provided by operating activities in the statement of cash flows should be

   A. $72,700

   B. $74,300

   C. $75,500

   D. $75,700

The correct answer is (D). *(CPA 591 I-9)*
   REQUIRED: The net cash provided by operating activities.
   DISCUSSION: Net income should be adjusted for the effects of items properly included in the determination of net income but having either a different effect or no effect on net operating cash flow. The increase in gross accounts receivable should be subtracted from net income. The increase indicates that sales exceeded cash received. The increase in the allowance for uncollectible accounts should be added to net income. This amount reflects a noncash expense. The decrease in prepaid rent expense should be added to net income. The cash was disbursed in a prior period, but the expense was recognized currently as a noncash item. The increase in accounts payable indicates that liabilities and related expenses were recognized without cash outlays. Thus, the change in this account should be added to net income. The net cash provided by operating activities is $75,700 ($75,000 NI – $3,000 change in A/R + $100 change in allowance + $2,100 decrease in prepaid rent + $1,500 increase in A/P).
   Answer (A) is incorrect because $72,700 results from subtracting the increase in accounts payable. Answer (B) is incorrect because $74,300 results from adding the change in accounts receivable and subtracting the changes in the other balances. Answer (C) is incorrect because $75,500 results from subtracting the change in the allowance.

21. In a statement of cash flows (indirect method) of a business enterprise, an increase in inventories should be presented as

   A.   An outflow of cash.

   B.   An inflow and outflow of cash.

   C.   An addition to income from continuing operations.

   D.   A deduction from income from continuing operations.

The correct answer is (D). *(CPA 587 T-28)*

REQUIRED: The presentation of an increase in inventories in a statement of cash flows (indirect method).

DISCUSSION: The objective of a statement of cash flows is to explain the cash receipts and cash disbursements of an entity during an accounting period. In a statement of cash flows in which operating activities are presented on an indirect or reconciliation basis, cash flows from operating activities are determined by adjusting net income (which includes income from continuing operations) to remove the effects of all (1) deferrals of past operating cash receipts and payments, (2) accruals of expected future operating cash receipts and payments, (3) all investing or financing activities, and (4) noncash operating transactions. Cost of goods sold is included in the determination of net income. Cash paid to suppliers, however, should be the amount included in determining net cash flows from operating activities. To adjust net income to cash flow from operating activities for the difference between cost of goods sold and cash paid to suppliers, a two-step adjustment is necessary. The first step is to adjust net income for the change in the inventory account. This step adjusts for the difference between cost of goods sold and purchases. The second step is to adjust for the changes in the accounts payable account. This step adjusts for the difference between purchases and the amounts disbursed to suppliers. An increase in inventories indicates that purchases were greater than cost of goods sold. Thus, as part of the first step, an increase in inventories should be presented in a statement of cash flows (indirect method) as a deduction from net income.

Answers (A), (B), and (C) are incorrect because an increase in inventory should be presented as a deduction from income from continuing operations under the indirect method.

22. Would the following be added back to net income of a business enterprise when reporting operating activities' cash flows by the indirect method?

	Excess of Treasury Stock Acquisition Cost over Sales Proceeds (Cost Method)	Bond Discount Amortization
A.	Yes	Yes
B.	No	No
C.	No	Yes
D.	Yes	No

The correct answer is (C). *(CPA 1191 T-21)*

REQUIRED: The item(s) added back to net income when reporting operating activities' cash flows by the indirect method.

DISCUSSION: Bond discount amortization is a noncash component of interest expense. Since the amortization decreases net income, it is added back in the reconciliation of net income to net operating cash flow. Treasury stock transactions involve cash flows that do not affect net income. They are also classified as financing activities, not operating activities.

Answer (A) is incorrect because cash flows from treasury stock transactions do not affect net income. Answer (B) is incorrect because the bond discount amortization should be added to net income. Answer (D) is incorrect because the bond discount amortization should be added to net income, and cash flows from treasury stock transactions do not affect net income.

Questions 23 and 24 are based on the following information. Karr, Inc. reported net income of $300,000 for 1996. Changes occurred in several balance sheet accounts as follows:

Equipment	$25,000 increase
Accumulated depreciation	40,000 increase
Note payable	30,000 increase

Additional information:

- During 1996, Karr sold equipment costing $25,000, with accumulated depreciation of $12,000, for a gain of $5,000.

- In December 1996, Karr purchased equipment costing $50,000 with $20,000 cash and a 12% note payable of $30,000.

- Depreciation expense for the year was $52,000.

23. In Karr's 1996 statement of cash flows, net cash provided by operating activities should be

- A. $340,000
- B. $347,000
- C. $352,000
- D. $357,000

The correct answer is (B). *(CPA 1193 I-6)*
REQUIRED: The net cash provided by operating activities in the statement of cash flows.
DISCUSSION: Net income should be adjusted for the effects of items included in the determination of net income that have no effect on net cash provided by operating activities. Depreciation is included in the determination of net income but has no cash effect. Thus, depreciation should be added to net income. The sale of equipment resulted in a gain included in the determination of net income, but the cash effect is classified as an inflow from an investing activity. Thus, the gain should be subtracted from net income. The cash outflow for the purchase of equipment is from an investing activity and has no effect on net income. Hence, it requires no adjustment. Thus, the net cash provided by operating activities is $347,000 ($300,000 NI + $52,000 depreciation – $5,000 gain).

Answer (A) is incorrect because $340,000 reflects addition of the accumulated depreciation. Answer (C) is incorrect because $352,000 results from not deducting the gain. Answer (D) is incorrect because $357,000 results from adding the gain.

24. In Karr's 1996 statement of cash flows, net cash used in investing activities should be

- A. $2,000
- B. $12,000
- C. $18,000
- D. $20,000

The correct answer is (A). *(CPA 1193 I-7)*
REQUIRED: The net cash used in investing activities.
DISCUSSION: Cash flows from investing activities include the cash inflow from the sale of equipment and the cash outflow from the purchase of equipment. The issuance of a note payable as part of the acquisition price of equipment is classified as a noncash financing and investing activity. The cash inflow from the sale of equipment (carrying value + gain) is $18,000 [($25,000 – $12,000) + $5,000]. The cash outflow from the purchase of equipment is $20,000 cash. Thus, net cash used is $2,000 ($20,000 – $18,000).

Answer (B) is incorrect because $12,000 assumes a $30,000 cash payment for the equipment. Answer (C) is incorrect because $18,000 is the cash inflow from the sale of equipment. Answer (D) is incorrect because $20,000 is the cash outflow from the purchase of equipment.

25. The comparative balance sheet for a company that had net income of $150,000 for the year ended December 31, 1996 and paid $125,000 of dividends during 1996 is as follows:

	12/31/96	12/31/95
Cash	$150,000	$180,000
Accounts receivable	200,000	220,000
Total assets	$350,000	$400,000
Payables	$ 80,000	$160,000
Capital stock	130,000	125,000
Retained earnings	140,000	115,000
Total	$350,000	$400,000

The amount of net cash provided by operating activities during 1996 was

- A. $70,000
- B. $90,000
- C. $150,000
- D. $210,000

The correct answer is (B). *(CIA 596 IV-10)*
REQUIRED: The amount of net cash provided by operating activities during 1995.
DISCUSSION: Net income is adjusted to determine the net cash provided by operations. The payment of cash dividends is a cash flow from a financing activity. Hence, it is not a reconciling item. However, the decrease in accounts receivable ($220,000 – $200,000 = $20,000) during the period represents a cash inflow (collections of pre-1995 receivables) not reflected in 1995 net income. Moreover, the decrease in payables ($160,000 –$80,000 = $80,000) indicates a cash outflow (payment of pre-1995 liabilities) that also is not reflected in 1995 net income. Accordingly, net cash provided by operations was $90,000 ($150,000 + $20,000 – $80,000).
Answer (A) is incorrect because $70,000 fails to add to net income the reduction in accounts receivable. Answer (C) is incorrect because $150,000 is net income. Answer (D) is incorrect because $210,000 subtracts the reduction in receivables and adds the reduction in payables.

26. In its statement of cash flows issued for the year ending June 30, Prince Company reported a net cash inflow from operating activities of $123,000. The following adjustments were included in the supplementary schedule reconciling cash flow from operating activities with net income:

Depreciation	$38,000
Increase in net accounts receivable	31,000
Decrease in inventory	27,000
Increase in accounts payable	48,000
Increase in interest payable	12,000

Net income is

- A. $29,000
- B. $41,000
- C. $79,000
- D. $217,000

The correct answer is (A). *(Publisher)*
REQUIRED: The net income given cash flow from operating activities and reconciling adjustments.
DISCUSSION: To derive net income from net cash inflow from operating activities, various adjustments are necessary. The depreciation of $38,000 should be subtracted because it is a noncash item included in the determination of net income. The increase in net accounts receivable of $31,000 should be added because it signifies that sales revenue was greater than the cash collections from customers. The increase in accounts payable should be subtracted because it indicates that purchases were $48,000 greater than cash disbursements to suppliers. The second step of the transformation from cash paid to suppliers to cost of goods sold is to subtract the decrease in inventory. This change means that cost of goods sold was $27,000 greater than purchases. The $12,000 increase in interest payable should also be subtracted because it indicates that interest expense was greater than the cash paid to the lenders. Thus, the net adjustment to net cash inflow from operating activities is –$94,000 (–$38,000 + $31,000 – $27,000 – $48,000 – $12,000). Net income is $29,000 ($123,000 net cash inflow – $94,000 net adjustment).
Answer (B) is incorrect because the increase in interest payable is not subtracted. Answer (C) is incorrect because depreciation and the increase in interest payable are not subtracted. Answer (D) is incorrect because depreciation, the increase in accounts payable, the decrease in inventory, and the increase in interest payable should be subtracted, and the increase in net accounts receivable should be added.

27. Lance Corp.'s statement of cash flows for the year ended September 30, 1996 was prepared using the indirect method and included the following:

Net income	$60,000
Noncash adjustments:	
Depreciation expense	9,000
Increase in accounts receivable	(5,000)
Decrease in inventory	40,000
Decrease in accounts payable	(12,000)
Net cash flows from operating activities	$92,000

Lance reported revenues from customers of $75,000 in its 1996 income statement. What amount of cash did Lance receive from its customers during the year ended September 30, 1996?

- A. $80,000
- B. $70,000
- C. $65,000
- D. $55,000

The correct answer is (B). *(CPA 1192 I-42)*
REQUIRED: The cash collected from customers.
DISCUSSION: Collections from customers equal sales revenue minus the increase in accounts receivable, or $70,000 ($75,000 – $5,000).
Answer (A) is incorrect because $80,000 adds the increase in accounts receivable. Answers (C) and (D) are incorrect because the only adjustment to the $75,000 of revenue from customers is for the $5,000 increase in accounts receivable.

22.3 Operating Activities -- Direct Presentation

28. In a statement of cash flows of a business enterprise, which of the following would increase reported cash flows from operating activities using the direct method? (Ignore income tax considerations.)

- A. Dividends received from investments.
- B. Gain on sale of equipment.
- C. Gain on early retirement of bonds.
- D. Change from straight-line to accelerated depreciation.

The correct answer is (A). *(CPA 592 T-7)*
REQUIRED: The item that would increase reported cash flows from operating activities using the direct method.
DISCUSSION: Operating activities are transactions and other events not classified as investing and financing activities. In general, the cash effects of operating activities (other than gains and losses) enter into the determination of income from continuing operations. Thus, cash receipts from dividends is an operating activity.
Answer (B) is incorrect because the sale of equipment is an investing activity. Answer (C) is incorrect because an early retirement of bonds is a financing activity. Answer (D) is incorrect because a change in accounting principle is a noncash event.

29. Lane Company acquired copyrights from authors, in some cases paying advance royalties and in others paying royalties within 30 days of year-end. Lane reported royalty expense of $375,000 for the year ended December 31, 1996. The following data are included in Lane's balance sheet:

	1995	1996
Prepaid royalties	$60,000	$50,000
Royalties payable	75,000	90,000

In its 1996 statement of cash flows, Lane should report cash disbursements for royalty payments of

- A. $350,000
- B. $370,000
- C. $380,000
- D. $400,000

The correct answer is (A). *(CPA 586 I-55)*
REQUIRED: The cash disbursements for royalty payments.
DISCUSSION: A decrease in a prepaid royalties asset account implies that royalty expense was greater than the related cash disbursements. Similarly, an increase in a royalties payable liability account indicates that royalties expense exceeded cash disbursements. Royalty expense therefore exceeds the amount of cash disbursements for royalty payments by the amount of the decrease in the prepaid royalties account plus the increase in the royalties payable account. Thus, Lane's 1996 cash disbursements for royalty payments total $350,000 ($375,000 royalty expense – $10,000 decrease in prepaid royalties – $15,000 increase in royalties payable).
Answer (B) is incorrect because the $10,000 decrease in prepaid royalties should be subtracted, not added.
Answer (C) is incorrect because the $15,000 increase in royalties payable should be subtracted from royalty expense, not added. Answer (D) is incorrect because the decrease in prepaid royalties and the increase in royalties payable should be subtracted, not added.

30. The Ayres Corporation owns extensive rental property. For some of this property, rent is paid in advance. For other property, rent is paid following the end of the year. In the income statement for the year ended December 31, 1996, Ayres reported $140,000 in rental income. The following data are included in Ayres' December 31 balance sheet:

	1996	1995
Rent receivable	$95,000	$120,000
Deferred rent income	40,000	50,000

In its statement of cash flows for the year ended December 31, 1996, Ayres should report cash receipts from rental properties totaling

A. $105,000

B. $125,000

C. $155,000

D. $175,000

The correct answer is (C). *(K.M. Boze)*
REQUIRED: The amount of total rental cash receipts.
DISCUSSION: No write-offs of rent receivables are mentioned. Consequently, a decrease in the rent receivable asset account implies that Ayres collected more in cash receipts from rental customers than it recognized as rental income in 1996. In contrast, a decrease in the deferred rent income liability account signifies that Ayres recognized more rental income than it received in cash payments. To determine cash receipts from rental properties, the rental income of $140,000 should be increased by the $25,000 change in the rent receivable account and decreased by the $10,000 reduction in the deferred rent income account. Cash receipts from rental properties were therefore $155,000.

Answer (A) is incorrect because the $25,000 decrease in rent receivable should be added to rental income, not subtracted. Answer (B) is incorrect because the $25,000 decrease in rent receivable should be added to rental income, not subtracted, and the $10,000 decrease in deferred rental income should be subtracted, not added. Answer (D) is incorrect because the $10,000 decrease in deferred rental income should be subtracted from rental income, not added.

31. The following information was taken from the 1996 financial statements of Planet Corp.:

Accounts receivable, January 1, 1996	$ 21,600
Accounts receivable, December 31, 1996	30,400
Sales on account and cash sales	438,000
Uncollectible accounts	1,000

No accounts receivable were written off or recovered during the year. If the direct method is used in the 1996 statement of cash flows, Planet should report cash collected from customers as

A. $447,800

B. $446,800

C. $429,200

D. $428,200

The correct answer is (C). *(CPA 591 I-8)*
REQUIRED: The cash collected from customers.
DISCUSSION: Collections from customers equal sales revenue adjusted for the change in gross accounts receivable and write-offs and recoveries. Because no accounts receivable were written off or recovered during the year, no adjustment for these transactions is needed. Accounts receivable increased by $8,800 ($30,400 – $21,600), which represents an excess of revenue recognized over cash received. Planet thus should report cash collected from customers of $429,200 ($438,000 – $8,800).

Answer (A) is incorrect because $447,800 results from adding the increase in accounts receivable and the uncollectible accounts balance. Answer (B) is incorrect because $446,800 results from adding the increase in accounts receivable. Answer (D) is incorrect because $428,200 results from subtracting the uncollectible accounts balance.

32. Rory Co.'s prepaid insurance was $50,000 at December 31, 1996 and $25,000 at December 31, 1995. Insurance expense was $20,000 for 1996 and $15,000 for 1995. What amount of cash disbursements for insurance should be reported in Rory's 1996 net cash flows from operating activities presented on a direct basis?

A. $55,000

B. $45,000

C. $30,000

D. $20,000

The correct answer is (B). *(CPA 1190 II-17)*

REQUIRED: The amount to be reported as cash disbursements for insurance.

DISCUSSION: Cash disbursements for insurance is equal to the $50,000 ending balance, plus the $20,000 expensed in 1996, minus the $25,000 beginning balance. As indicated below, cash disbursements for insurance are equal to $45,000.

	Prepaid Insurance		
12/31/95	$25,000		
Disbursement	45,000	$20,000	Expense
12/31/96	$50,000		

Answer (A) is incorrect because $55,000 is the sum of the $50,000 12/31/96 balance and the $5,000 difference between the 1996 and 1995 expense accounts. Answer (C) is incorrect because $30,000 is the sum of the $25,000 12/31/95 balance and the $5,000 difference between the 1996 and 1995 expense accounts. Answer (D) is incorrect because $20,000 is the insurance expense for 1996.

33. Duke Co. reported cost of goods sold of $270,000 for 1996. Additional information is as follows:

	December 31	January 1
Inventory	$60,000	$45,000
Accounts payable	26,000	39,000

If Duke uses the direct method, what amount should Duke report as cash paid to suppliers in its 1996 statement of cash flows?

A. $242,000

B. $268,000

C. $272,000

D. $298,000

The correct answer is (D). *(CPA 1193 I-9)*

REQUIRED: The amount reported as cash paid to suppliers in the statement of cash flows.

DISCUSSION: To reconcile cost of goods sold to cash paid to suppliers, a two-step adjustment is needed. First, determine purchases by adding the increase in inventory to cost of goods. Second, determine cash paid for goods sold by adding the decrease in accounts payable to purchases. Thus, cash paid for goods sold equals $298,000 [$270,000 + ($60,000 − $45,000) + ($39,000 − $26,000)].

Answer (A) is incorrect because $242,000 results from subtracting the changes in inventory and accounts payable. Answer (B) is incorrect because $268,000 results from subtracting the change in inventory. Answer (C) is incorrect because $272,000 results from subtracting the change in accounts payable.

34. The following balances were reported by Mall Co. at December 31, 1996 and 1995:

	12/31/96	12/31/95
Inventory	$260,000	$290,000
Accounts payable	75,000	50,000

Mall paid suppliers $490,000 during the year ended December 31, 1996. What amount should Mall report for cost of goods sold in 1996?

A. $545,000

B. $495,000

C. $485,000

D. $435,000

The correct answer is (A). *(CPA 592 I-47)*

REQUIRED: The cost of goods sold.

DISCUSSION: If trade accounts increased by $25,000, purchases must have been $25,000 higher than the disbursements for purchases. Purchases thus are $515,000 ($490,000 + $25,000). The decrease in merchandise inventory indicates that cost of goods sold must have been $30,000 higher than purchases. Hence, CGS equals $545,000 ($515,000 + $30,000).

Answer (B) is incorrect because $495,000 results from subtracting the increase in accounts payable. Answer (C) is incorrect because $485,000 results from subtracting the decrease in inventory. Answer (D) is incorrect because $435,000 results from subtracting the decrease in inventory and the increase in accounts payable.

Questions 35 through 38 are based on the following information. Flax Corp. uses the direct method to prepare its statement of cash flows. Flax's trial balances at December 31, 1996 and 1995 are as follows:

| | December 31 | |
	1996	1995
Debits		
Cash	$ 35,000	$ 32.000
Accounts receivable	33,000	30,000
Inventory	31,000	47,000
Property, plant, & equipment	100,000	95,000
Unamortized bond discount	4,500	5,000
Cost of goods sold	250,000	380,000
Selling expenses	141,500	172,000
General and administrative expenses	137,000	151,300
Interest expense	4,300	2,600
Income tax expense	20,400	61,200
	$756,700	$976,100
Credits		
Allowance for uncollectible accounts	$ 1,300	$ 1,100
Accumulated depreciation	16,500	15,000
Trade accounts payable	25,000	17,500
Income taxes payable	21,000	27,100
Deferred income taxes	5,300	4,600
8% callable bonds payable	45,000	20,000
Common stock	50,000	40,000
Additional paid-in capital	9,100	7,500
Retained earnings	44,700	64,600
Sales	538,800	778,700
	$756,700	$976,100

- Flax purchased $5,000 in equipment during 1996.

- Flax allocated one-third of its depreciation expense to selling expenses and the remainder to general and administrative expenses.

35. What amounts should Flax report in its statement of cash flows for the year ended December 31, 1996 for cash collected from customers?

A. $541,800

B. $541,600

C. $536,000

D. $535,800

The correct answer is (D). *(CPA 1192 I-9)*
   REQUIRED: The cash collected from customers.
   DISCUSSION: Collections from customers equal sales minus the increase in gross accounts receivable, or $535,800 ($538,800 – $33,000 + $30,000).
   Answer (A) is incorrect because $541,800 results from adding the increase in receivables. Answer (B) is incorrect because $541,600 results from adding the increase in receivables and subtracting the increase in the allowance for uncollectible accounts, that is, from adding net accounts receivable. Answer (C) is incorrect because $536,000 results from subtracting net accounts receivable.

36. What amounts should Flax report in its statement of cash flows for the year ended December 31, 1996 for cash paid for interest?

A. $4,800

B. $4,300

C. $3,800

D. $1,700

The correct answer is (C). *(CPA 1192 I-11)*
REQUIRED: The cash paid for interest.
DISCUSSION: Interest expense is $4,300. This amount includes $500 of discount amortization, a noncash item. Hence, the cash paid for interest was $3,800 ($4,300 – $500).
Answer (A) is incorrect because $4,800 results from adding the amortized discount. Answer (B) is incorrect because $4,300 is the total interest expense. Answer (D) is incorrect because $1,700 is the increase in interest expense.

37. What amounts should Flax report in its statement of cash flows for the year ended December 31, 1996 for cash paid for income taxes?

A. $25,800

B. $20,400

C. $19,700

D. $15,000

The correct answer is (A). *(CPA 1192 I-12)*
REQUIRED: The cash paid for income taxes.
DISCUSSION: To reconcile income tax expense to cash paid for income taxes, a two-step adjustment is needed. The first step is to add the decrease in income taxes payable. The second step is to subtract the increase in deferred income taxes. Hence, cash paid for income taxes equals $25,800 [$20,400 + ($27,100 – $21,000) – ($5,300 – $4,600)].
Answer (B) is incorrect because $20,400 is income tax expense. Answer (C) is incorrect because $19,700 equals income tax expense minus the increase in deferred income taxes. Answer (D) is incorrect because $15,000 results from subtracting the decrease in income taxes payable and adding the increase in deferred taxes payable.

38. What amounts should Flax report in its statement of cash flows for the year ended December 31, 1996 for cash paid for selling expenses?

A. $142,000

B. $141,500

C. $141,000

D. $140,000

The correct answer is (C). *(CPA 1192 I-13)*
REQUIRED: The cash paid for selling expenses.
DISCUSSION: Cash paid for selling expenses equals selling expenses minus the depreciation allocated to selling expenses. Total depreciation expense equals the $1,500 ($16,500 – $15,000) change in accumulated depreciation. Thus, cash paid for selling expenses equals $141,000 ($141,500 1996 expense – $1,500 1996 depreciation x 331/3% allocated to selling).
Answer (A) is incorrect because $142,000 results from adding the depreciation allocated to selling expenses. Answer (B) is incorrect because $141,500 equals the selling expenses for 1996. Answer (D) is incorrect because $140,000 results from subtracting 100% of depreciation expense from selling expenses.

CHAPTER TWENTY-THREE
ACCOUNTING FOR CHANGING PRICES

The accounting valuation method primarily used in basic financial statements presented in accordance with generally accepted accounting principles is based on the effects of historical transactions measured in terms of historical cost (historical cost/nominal dollar).

In SFAS 33, *Financial Reporting and Changing Prices*, the FASB required large public enterprises to supplement their basic financial statements with footnote disclosure of certain current cost/constant purchasing power and historical cost/constant purchasing power information. SFAS 33 was issued as an experiment in requiring supplemental information on the effects of inflation and changes in specific prices.

In the 5 years following the issuance of SFAS 33, the FASB reviewed the results of the experiment. Based on that review, the board concluded that further supplemental disclosures should be encouraged but not required. It therefore issued SFAS 89, *Financial Reporting and Changing Prices*, which superseded SFAS 33 and its subsequent amendments. These amendments were included in the following pronouncements:

SFAS 39 - *Financial Reporting and Changing Prices: Specialized Assets -- Mining and Oil and Gas*

SFAS 40 - *Financial Reporting and Changing Prices: Specialized Assets -- Timberlands and Growing Timber*

SFAS 41 - *Financial Reporting and Changing Prices: Specialized Assets -- Income-Producing Real Estate*

SFAS 46 - *Financial Reporting and Changing Prices: Motion Picture Films*

SFAS 54 - *Financial Reporting and Changing Prices: Investment Companies*

SFAS 69 - *Disclosures about Oil and Gas Producing Activities (paragraphs 35-38 and footnote 10)*

SFAS 70 - *Financial Reporting and Changing Prices: Foreign Currency Translation*

SFAS 82 - *Financial Reporting and Changing Prices: Elimination of Certain Disclosures*

FASB Technical Bulletin 81-4 - *Classification as Monetary or Nonmonetary Items*

SFAS 89 thus eliminates the requirement that supplementary information on the effects of changing prices be presented. However, SFAS 89 encourages companies to experiment with such disclosures and provides guidance for their measurement and presentation.

23.1 General

1. Which of the following is a method of accounting based on measures of current cost or lower recoverable amount in units of currency having the same general purchasing power?

- A. Historical cost/constant purchasing power accounting.
- B. Historical cost/nominal dollar accounting.
- C. Current cost/constant purchasing power accounting.
- D. Current cost/nominal dollar accounting.

The correct answer is (C). *(CPA 583 T-7)*
REQUIRED: The method of accounting based on measures of current cost or lower recoverable amount in units of the same general purchasing power.
DISCUSSION: Current cost accounting attempts to present an enterprise's assets and liabilities on the basis of current worth (current cost or lower recoverable amount). Constant purchasing power accounting reports financial statement elements in units of currency with the same general purchasing power.
Answers (A) and (B) are incorrect because, in historical cost accounting, items are measured and reported at their historical prices. Answers (B) and (D) are incorrect because, under nominal dollar accounting, dollars are not restated into units with the same general purchasing power.

2. Financial statements that are presented assuming a stable monetary unit are

- A. General price-level financial statements.
- B. Nominal dollar financial statements.
- C. Current value financial statements.
- D. Fair value financial statements.

The correct answer is (B). *(CPA 580 T-27)*
REQUIRED: The financial statements that assume a stable monetary unit.
DISCUSSION: Nominal dollar financial statements assume that the unit of measure does not fluctuate in value significantly. Although this assumption has the virtues of simplicity and objectivity, it produces figures in the financial statements that do not reflect inflation.
Answer (A) is incorrect because general price-level statements recognize that monetary units change in value and require price-level adjustments. Answers (C) and (D) are incorrect because current fair value takes into account the effect of specific price-level indexes.

3. Which of the following items is included in the 5-year summary of selected financial data recommended by SFAS 89, *Financial Reporting and Changing Prices*?

- A. Net income.
- B. Income from continuing operations on a current cost basis.
- C. Purchasing power gain or loss on net nonmonetary items.
- D. Cash dividends paid per common share.

The correct answer is (B). *(Publisher)*
REQUIRED: The item included in the 5-year summary of selected financial data.
DISCUSSION: SFAS 89 recommends that an enterprise disclose the following information for each of the 5 most recent years:

a) Net sales and other operating revenues.
b) Income from continuing operations on a current cost basis.
c) Purchasing power gain or loss on net monetary items.
d) Increase or decrease in the current cost or lower recoverable amount of inventory and property, plant, and equipment, net of inflation.
e) The aggregate foreign currency translation adjustment on a current cost basis (if applicable).
f) Net assets at year-end on a current cost basis.
g) Income per common share from continuing operations on a current cost basis.
h) Cash dividends declared per common share.
i) Market price per common share at year-end.

Answers (A), (C), and (D) are incorrect because SFAS 89 does not recommend that an enterprise disclose net income, purchasing power gain or loss on net nonmonetary items, and cash dividends paid per common share.

4. SFAS 89, *Financial Reporting and Changing Prices*, recommends that the information presented in the 5-year summary of selected financial data be stated in terms of

A. Beginning-of-the-year units of constant purchasing power.

B. Average-for-the-year units of constant purchasing power.

C. Nominal units of money.

D. Dollars equivalent in purchasing power to dollars used in calculating the current period Consumer Price Index for All Urban Consumers.

The correct answer is (B). *(Publisher)*

REQUIRED: The unit of measure used to state the selected financial data included in the 5-year summary.

DISCUSSION: SFAS 89 recommends that the information presented in the 5-year summary be stated in average-for-the-year units of constant purchasing power, in end-of-year units of constant purchasing power, or in dollars having a purchasing power equal to that of the dollars of the base period used by the Bureau of Labor Statistics in calculating the Consumer Price Index for All Urban Consumers.

Answers (A), (C), and (D) are incorrect because SFAS 89 does not recommend that information presented in the 5-year summary be stated in beginning-of-the-year units of constant purchasing power, in nominal units of money, or in dollars equivalent in purchasing power to dollars used in calculating the current period Consumer Price Index for All Urban Consumers.

5. SFAS 89 recommends that a 5-year summary of certain selected financial data be presented. If the current year income from continuing operations on a current cost/constant purchasing power basis differs significantly from income from continuing operations in the primary financial statements, an enterprise should also disclose

A. All components of income from continuing operations for the current year on a current cost basis.

B. All components of net income for the current year on a current cost basis.

C. Certain components of income from continuing operations for the current year on a current cost basis.

D. All operating expenses for the current year on a current cost basis.

The correct answer is (C). *(Publisher)*

REQUIRED: The information for the current year that should be disclosed when income from continuing operations on a current cost/constant purchasing power basis differs from that reported in the primary financial statements.

DISCUSSION: When income from continuing operations on a current cost/constant purchasing power basis differs significantly from income from continuing operations reported in the primary financial statements, SFAS 89 recommends that certain components of income from continuing operations for the current year be disclosed on a current cost basis. The information may be presented in a statement format, in a reconciliation format, or in notes to the 5-year summary. Whichever format is used, the presentation should disclose or allow the reader to determine the difference between the amount in the primary statements and the current cost amount of the following: cost of goods sold, depreciation, depletion, and amortization expense.

Answers (A), (B), and (D) are incorrect because SFAS 89 recommends that only certain components of income from continuing operations for the current year be disclosed on a current cost basis.

6. A company that wishes to disclose information about the effect of changing prices in accordance with SFAS 89, *Financial Reporting and Changing Prices*, should report this information in

A. The body of the financial statements.

B. The notes to the financial statements.

C. Supplementary information to the financial statements.

D. Management's report to shareholders.

The correct answer is (C). *(CPA 1194 F-4)*

REQUIRED: The reporting of the effect of changing prices.

DISCUSSION: SFAS 89 encourages, but does not require, disclosure of supplementary current cost/constant purchasing power information.

Answers (A) and (B) are incorrect because voluntary disclosures about the effects of changing prices should not be reported in the body of, or the notes to, the financial statements. Answer (D) is incorrect because information about the effect of changing prices is meaningful to users of financial statements other than shareholders.

23.2 Current Cost

7. Deecee Co. adjusted its historical cost income statement by applying specific price indexes to its depreciation expense and cost of goods sold. Deecee's adjusted income statement is prepared according to

A. Fair value accounting.

B. General purchasing power accounting.

C. Current cost accounting.

D. Current cost/general purchasing power accounting.

The correct answer is (C). *(CPA 1193 T-2)*
REQUIRED: The basis of accounting that applies specific price indexes to historical cost items.
DISCUSSION: According to SFAS 89, current cost is the estimated cost of acquiring the service potential provided by an asset, adjusted for depreciation, etc. An enterprise that chooses to report supplementary information on the effects of changing prices should disclose income from continuing operations on a current cost basis. This basis measures cost of goods sold at current cost or lower recoverable amount at the date of sale or at the date resources are used on, or committed to, a specific contract. Depreciation is measured on the basis of the average current cost of the assets' service potential or lower recoverable amount during the period of use.

Answer (A) is incorrect because fair value accounting presents the current fair values of assets and the changes in those values with or without separate identification of the effects of general price-level changes. Current cost is one possible estimate of current fair value. Exit value and capitalization of net cash inflows are other possible estimates. Answers (B) and (D) are incorrect because general (constant) purchasing power accounting reports financial statement elements in units of currency with the same general purchasing power. Thus, it applies a general price index.

8. At December 31, 1996, Jannis Corp. owned two assets as follows:

	Equipment	Inventory
Current cost	$100,000	$80,000
Recoverable amount	95,000	90,000

Jannis voluntarily disclosed supplementary information about current cost at December 31, 1996. In such a disclosure, at what amount would Jannis report total assets?

A. $175,000

B. $180,000

C. $185,000

D. $190,000

The correct answer is (A). *(CPA 1188 I-52)*
REQUIRED: The amount at which supplementary information about the current cost of equipment and inventory should be reported.
DISCUSSION: According to SFAS 89, inventory is measured at current cost or lower recoverable amount at the measurement date. Property, plant, and equipment are measured at the current cost or lower recoverable amount of the remaining service potential at the measurement date. Thus, the equipment should be reported at $95,000 and the inventory at $80,000, a total of $175,000.

Answer (B) is incorrect because $180,000 results from using the current cost for equipment instead of the recoverable amount. Answer (C) is incorrect because $185,000 results from using the recoverable amount for inventory instead of current cost. Answer (D) is incorrect because $190,000 results from using the current cost for equipment and recoverable amount for inventory.

9. Manhof Co. prepares supplementary reports on income from continuing operations on a current cost basis in accordance with SFAS 89, *Financial Reporting and Changing Prices*. How should Manhof compute cost of goods sold on a current cost basis?

A. Number of units sold times average current cost of units during the year.

B. Number of units sold times current cost of units at year-end.

C. Number of units sold times current cost of units at the beginning of the year.

D. Beginning inventory at current cost, plus cost of goods purchased, minus ending inventory at current cost.

The correct answer is (A). *(CPA 1192 T-40)*
REQUIRED: The method of computing cost of goods sold on a current cost basis.
DISCUSSION: If an enterprise provides supplementary information about the effects of changing prices in accordance with SFAS 89 and operating income on a current cost/constant purchasing power basis differs significantly from that reported in the primary statements, it should, among other items, disclose the difference between the cost of goods sold in the primary financial statements and the current cost amount. SFAS 89 calculates the latter by multiplying the units sold during the period by the average of the unit current cost or lower recoverable amounts at the beginning and end of the period.
Answers (B), (C), and (D) are incorrect because SFAS 89 calculates the cost of goods sold on a current cost basis as the number of units sold times average current cost of units during the year.

10. The following information pertains to each unit of merchandise purchased for resale by Vend Co.:

March 1, 1996

Purchase price	$8
Selling price	$12
Price level index	110

December 31, 1996

Replacement cost	$10
Selling price	$15
Price level index	121

Under current cost accounting, what is the amount of Vend's holding gain on each unit of this merchandise?

A. $0

B. $0.80

C. $1.20

D. $2.00

The correct answer is (D). *(CPA 592 II-13)*
REQUIRED: The holding gain on each unit under current cost accounting.
DISCUSSION: SFAS 89, *Financial Reporting and Changing Prices*, defines the current cost of inventory as the current cost of purchasing the goods or the current cost of the resources needed to produce the goods (including an allowance for the current overhead costs according to the allocation bases used under GAAP), whichever is applicable in the circumstances. Thus, the current cost at 12/31 was the $10 replacement cost, and the holding gain, calculated without restatement into units of constant purchasing power, is $2.00 ($10 – $8 historical cost).
Answer (A) is incorrect because a holding gain occurred. Replacement cost exceeds historical cost. Answer (B) is incorrect because $0.80 is the adjustment necessary to inflate the 3/1 unit purchase price to the 12/31 price level. Answer (C) is incorrect because $1.20 equals the difference between replacement cost and the historical cost if the latter is restated into units of constant purchasing power to reflect the 12/31 price level.

11. Compared with historical cost income from continuing operations, which of the following conditions increases Pollard's current cost income from continuing operations?

   A. Current cost of equipment is greater than historical cost.

   B. Current cost of land is greater than historical cost.

   C. Current cost of cost of goods sold is less than historical cost.

   D. Ending net monetary assets are less than beginning net monetary assets.

The correct answer is (C). *(CPA 592 T-4)*

REQUIRED: The condition that increases current cost income from continuing operations compared with historical cost income.

DISCUSSION: Revenues reflect current cost when they are earned. Thus, they are stated at current cost in the historical cost income statement. Expenses, such as cost of goods sold, however, will vary because the current cost and historical cost of nonmonetary items, such as inventory, differ over time. If the current cost or lower recoverable amount is less than the historical cost, the effect is that current cost of goods sold is lower than historical cost of goods sold. Hence, current cost operating income (sales – CGS – operating expenses) will be greater than historical cost operating income.

Answers (A) and (B) are incorrect because holding gains (excess of current cost over the historical cost) are not included in current cost operating income. They are added to that amount in the determination of current cost net income. Answer (D) is incorrect because the income statement effects of a change during the period in the amount of net monetary assets are the same under the historical cost and current cost bases. The reason is that monetary items are already stated at current cost in the historical cost financial statements.

12. Could current cost financial statements report holding gains for goods sold during the period and holding gains on inventory at the end of the period?

	Goods Sold	Inventory
A.	Yes	Yes
B.	Yes	No
C.	No	Yes
D.	No	No

The correct answer is (A). *(CPA 591 T-2)*

REQUIRED: The true statement as to whether current cost financial statements may report holding gains for goods sold during the period and holding gains on inventory at the end of the period.

DISCUSSION: According to SFAS 89, the change in the current cost amounts of inventory and property, plant, and equipment is the difference between the measures of the assets at their entry dates for the year (beginning of the year or dates of acquisition) and their exit dates (end of the year or dates of use, sale, or commitment to a specific contract). A change in the current cost of inventory is reflected in the current cost income statement. A holding gain for inventory is the excess of the current cost at the exit date over the current cost at the entry date. Consequently, a realized holding gain is recognized when inventory is sold, and an unrealized holding gain is recognized on inventory held at the end of the period.

Answers (B), (C), and (D) are incorrect because current cost financial statements may report holding gains for goods sold during the period and holding gains on inventory at the end of the period.

	Historical Costs	Units Purchased	Units Sold
Questions 13 and 14 are based on the following information. Rice Wholesaling Corp. accounts for inventory on a FIFO basis. There were 8,000 units in inventory on January 1. Costs were incurred and goods purchased during the year as presented in the next column.			
1st quarter	$ 410,000	7,000	7,500
2nd quarter	550,000	8,500	7,300
3rd quarter	425,000	6,500	8,200
4th quarter	630,000	9,000	7,000
	$2,015,000	31,000	30,000

Rice estimates that the current cost per unit of inventory was $57 at January 1 and $71 at December 31.

13. In Rice's voluntary supplementary information restated into current cost, the December 31 inventory should be reported at

A. $576,000

B. $585,000

C. $630,000

D. $639,000

The correct answer is (D). *(CPA 1187 I-54)*

REQUIRED: The current cost of the year-end inventory.

DISCUSSION: SFAS 89 states that the current cost amounts of inventory should be measured at current cost or lower recoverable amount at the measurement date. At December 31, the current cost per unit is $71. Because 9,000 units are in the ending inventory (8,000 BI + 31,000 units purchased – 30,000 units sold), the current cost of the ending inventory is $639,000 (9,000 units x $71).

Answer (A) is incorrect because $576,000 results from applying the average of current cost from the beginning- and end-of-year costs. Answer (B) is incorrect because $585,000 results from multiplying ending inventory times $65 (the average purchase price for the year). Answer (C) is incorrect because $630,000 is the cost of purchases during the fourth quarter.

14. In Rice's voluntary supplementary information restated into current cost, the cost of goods sold for the year is

A. $1,920,000

B. $1,944,000

C. $2,100,000

D. $2,130,000

The correct answer is (A). *(CPA 1187 I-55)*

REQUIRED: The cost of goods sold restated into current cost.

DISCUSSION: To restate cost of goods sold into current cost, the number of units sold (30,000) is multiplied by the average current cost per unit. The average current cost per unit is $64 [($57 + $71) ÷ 2]. The current cost of goods sold is therefore $1,920,000 (30,000 units x $64).

Answer (B) is incorrect because $1,944,000 results from calculating cost of goods sold using an average cost of $64.80. Answer (C) is incorrect because $2,100,000 results from calculating cost of goods sold using an average cost of $70 (the cost per unit during the fourth quarter). Answer (D) is incorrect because $2,130,000 results from using an average current cost of $71 (the current cost at December 31).

15. Details of Poe Corp.'s plant assets at December 31, 1996 are as follows:

Year Acquired	Percentage Depreciated	Historical Cost	Estimated Current Cost
1994	30	$200,000	$280,000
1995	20	60,000	76,000
1996	10	80,000	88,000

Poe uses straight-line depreciation at 10% per annum. A full year's depreciation is charged in the year of acquisition. There were no disposals of plant assets. In Poe's voluntary supplementary information restated into current cost, the net current cost (after accumulated depreciation) of the plant assets at December 31, 1996 should be

A. $364,000

B. $336,000

C. $260,000

D. $232,000

The correct answer is (B). *(CPA 587 I-57)*

REQUIRED: The net current cost of the plant assets after accumulated depreciation.

DISCUSSION: The net current cost of plant assets is equal to the estimated current cost of the assets minus the depreciation to date. Depreciation is based on the average current cost of an asset's service potential or lower recoverable amount during the period of use. The net current cost calculated below is thus equal to $336,000.

	Current Cost	Depreciation	Current Cost Depreciation
1994	$280,000	30%	$ 84,000
1995	76,000	20%	15,200
1996	88,000	10%	8,800
	$444,000		$108,000

$444,000 – $108,000 = $336,000

Answer (A) is incorrect because depreciation incorrectly calculated using historical cost for depreciation [($200,000 x 30%) + ($60,000 x 20%) + ($80,000 x 10%)] is deducted from current cost ($444,000 – $80,000). Answer (C) is incorrect because depreciation incorrectly calculated using historical cost for depreciation is deducted from the historical cost ($340,000 – $80,000). Answer (D) is incorrect because depreciation correctly calculated using current cost ($108,000) is incorrectly deducted from the historical cost ($340,000 – $108,000).

16. Kerr Company purchased a machine for $115,000 on January 1, the company's first day of operations. At the end of the year, the current cost of the machine was $125,000. The machine has no salvage value, has a 5-year life, and is depreciated by the straight-line method. For the first year of operations, the amount of the current cost depreciation expense that would appear in supplementary current cost financial statements is

A. $14,000

B. $23,000

C. $24,000

D. $25,000

The correct answer is (C). *(CPA 1186 I-60)*

REQUIRED: The depreciation expense for the year on the current cost basis using the straight-line method.

DISCUSSION: Depreciation, depletion, and amortization expense of property, plant, and equipment should be measured on the basis of the average current cost or lower recoverable amount during the period of use. The average current cost for Kerr Company's machine is $120,000 [($115,000 + $125,000) ÷ 2]. Based on the straight-line depreciation method over a 5-year expected useful life with no salvage value, the depreciation expense determined on a current cost basis is $24,000 ($120,000 ÷ 5).

Answer (A) is incorrect because $14,000 results when the difference between the end of the year current cost and the purchase price is subtracted from the current cost depreciation expense. Answer (B) is incorrect because the historical cost of the machine is used ($115,000 ÷ 5). Answer (D) is incorrect because the current cost of the machine is used ($125,000 ÷ 5).

23.3 Constant Purchasing Power

17. In its financial statements, Hila Co. discloses supplemental information on the effects of changing prices in accordance with SFAS 89, *Financial Reporting and Changing Prices*. Hila computed the increase in current cost of inventory as follows:

Increase in current cost (nominal dollars)	$15,000
Increase in current cost (constant dollars)	$12,000

What amount should Hila disclose as the inflation component of the increase in current cost of inventories?

    A. $3,000

    B. $12,000

    C. $15,000

    D. $27,000

The correct answer is (A). *(CPA 594 F-58)*

REQUIRED: The inflation component of the increase in current cost of inventories.

DISCUSSION: If supplemental information on the effects of changing prices is presented in accordance with SFAS 89, the change in current cost amounts of inventory and property, plant, and equipment is reported both before and after eliminating the effects of general inflation. The inflation component of the increase in current cost (the change attributable to general price-level changes) is the difference between the nominal dollar and constant dollar measures, or $3,000 ($15,000 – $12,000).

Answer (B) is incorrect because $12,000 is the increase in current cost stated in constant dollars. Answer (C) is incorrect because $15,000 is the increase in current cost stated in nominal dollars. Answer (D) is incorrect because $27,000 is the sum of the increase in current cost stated in constant dollars plus the increase in current cost stated in nominal dollars.

18. A method of accounting based on measures of historical prices in dollars, each of which has the same general purchasing power, is

    A. Current cost/constant purchasing power accounting.

    B. Current cost/nominal dollar accounting.

    C. Historical cost/constant purchasing power accounting.

    D. Historical cost/nominal dollar accounting.

The correct answer is (C). *(CPA 582 T-36)*

REQUIRED: The method of accounting based on measures of historical prices in dollars, each of which has the same general purchasing power.

DISCUSSION: In historical cost/constant purchasing power accounting, the historical cost principle is retained, but the unit of measure is restated to reflect changes in the general purchasing power of the dollar.

Answers (A) and (B) are incorrect because current cost accounting is based on measures of current cost or lower recoverable amount. Answers (B) and (D) are incorrect because nominal dollar accounting is based on measures of dollars unadjusted for changes in general purchasing power.

19. During a period of inflation in which an asset account remains constant, which of the following occurs?

    A. A purchasing power gain, if the item is a monetary asset.

    B. A purchasing power gain, if the item is a nonmonetary asset.

    C. A purchasing power loss, if the item is a monetary asset.

    D. A purchasing power loss, if the item is a nonmonetary asset.

The correct answer is (C). *(CPA 594 F-59)*

REQUIRED: The effect of an asset account's remaining constant during a period of inflation.

DISCUSSION: A monetary asset is "money or a claim to receive a sum of money the amount of which is fixed or determinable without reference to future prices of specific goods or services" (SFAS 89). A purchasing power gain or loss is determined by restating in units of constant purchasing power the opening and closing balances of, and transactions in, a monetary item. If the balance of a monetary asset has remained constant in nominal dollars despite a decline in the general purchasing power of money, the ending balance will reflect less purchasing power than the beginning balance, that is, a purchasing power loss.

Answers (A), (B), and (D) are incorrect because a purchasing power loss on a monetary asset has occurred.

20. When computing purchasing power gain or loss on net monetary items, which of the following accounts is classified as nonmonetary?

   A. Accumulated depreciation of equipment.

   B. Advances to unconsolidated subsidiaries.

   C. Allowance for doubtful accounts.

   D. Unamortized premium on bonds payable.

The correct answer is (A). *(CPA 1193 T-1)*
   REQUIRED: The item classified as nonmonetary in historical cost/constant purchasing power accounting.
   DISCUSSION: A monetary asset is either money or a claim to receive a sum of money the amount of which is fixed or determinable without reference to future prices of specific goods or services. A monetary liability is an obligation to pay a sum of money the amount of which is fixed or determinable without reference to future prices of specific goods and services. Equipment and the related accumulated depreciation account are an asset and a contra asset, respectively, the value of which will change in relationship to future prices of specific goods and services. Hence, accumulated depreciation is a nonmonetary item.
   Answers (B), (C), and (D) are incorrect because advances to unconsolidated subsidiaries, the allowance for doubtful accounts, and unamortized premium on bonds payable are within the definition of either a monetary asset or a monetary liability.

21. When computing information on a historical cost/constant purchasing power basis, which of the following is classified as nonmonetary?

   A. Cash surrender value of life insurance.

   B. Long-term receivables.

   C. Allowance for doubtful accounts.

   D. Inventories, other than inventories used on contracts.

The correct answer is (D). *(CPA 1181 T-7)*
   REQUIRED: The item classified as nonmonetary on a historical cost/constant purchasing power basis.
   DISCUSSION: Nonmonetary assets include goods held primarily for resale or assets held primarily for direct use in providing services to the enterprise. SFAS 89 classifies inventories as nonmonetary, with the exception of inventories used on contracts. They are effectively rights to receive fixed sums of money if the future cash receipts on the contracts will not vary with future changes in specific prices.
   Answers (A), (B), and (C) are incorrect because SFAS 89 specifically classifies each as a monetary item.

22. In the context of general price-level adjustments, which of the following is a nonmonetary item?

   A. Receivables under capitalized leases.

   B. Obligations under capitalized leases.

   C. Goodwill.

   D. Unamortized discount on bonds payable.

The correct answer is (C). *(CPA 576 T-16)*
   REQUIRED: The nonmonetary item in the context of general price-level adjustments.
   DISCUSSION: SFAS 89 specifically states that nonmonetary items include residual rights such as goodwill and equity interests.
   Answers (A), (B), and (D) are incorrect because each involves fixed dollar amounts that will not vary with fluctuations in the future prices of specific goods or services.

23. When computing information on the historical cost/constant purchasing power basis, which of the following is classified as monetary?

   A. Equity investment in unconsolidated subsidiaries.

   B. Obligations under warranties.

   C. Unamortized discount on bonds payable.

   D. Deferred investment tax credits.

The correct answer is (C). *(CPA 1183 T-4)*
   REQUIRED: The item treated as monetary in historical cost/constant purchasing power accounting.
   DISCUSSION: SFAS 89 defines a monetary item as one that is fixed in amount by contract or otherwise. Because an unamortized discount on bonds payable is inseparable from the debt (a monetary item) to which it relates, the discount is a monetary item.
   Answers (A), (B), and (D) are incorrect because each is a nonmonetary item.

24. All of the following are monetary liabilities except

A. Bonds payable that are due in 1997.

B. Accounts payable.

C. Unearned subscription revenue.

D. A note payable due in 6 months.

The correct answer is (C). *(CMA 681 3-15)*

REQUIRED: The item that is not a monetary liability.

DISCUSSION: Monetary liabilities are obligations to pay sums of money that are fixed or determinable without reference to future prices of specific goods or services. Unearned subscription revenue is not a monetary liability because it is deferred revenue, which involves an obligation to furnish goods or services in the future that may vary in cost (price).

Answers (A), (B), and (D) are incorrect because each is payable in a fixed amount.

25. The following assets were among those that appeared on Baird Co.'s books at the end of the year:

Demand bank deposits	$650,000
Net long-term receivables	400,000
Patents and trademarks	150,000

In preparing constant dollar financial statements, how much should Baird classify as monetary assets?

A. $1,200,000

B. $1,050,000

C. $800,000

D. $650,000

The correct answer is (B). *(CPA 590 II-50)*

REQUIRED: The amount that should be classified as monetary assets.

DISCUSSION: Monetary assets are either cash or a claim to receive a sum of cash the amount of which is fixed or determinable without reference to future prices of specific goods or services. The value of nonmonetary assets will change in relationship to future prices of specific goods and services. The demand bank deposits of $650,000 and the long-term receivables of $400,000 meet the criteria for monetary assets. The patents and trademarks satisfy the definition of nonmonetary assets. Thus, Baird should classify $1,050,000 ($650,000 + $400,000) as monetary assets.

Answer (A) is incorrect because $1,200,000 results from including the patents and trademarks as monetary assets. Answer (C) is incorrect because $800,000 results from not including the net long-term receivables and including the patents and trademarks as monetary assets. Answer (D) is incorrect because $650,000 results from not including the net long-term receivables as a monetary asset.

26. The following schedule lists the average Consumer Price Index for All Urban Consumers of the indicated year:

1994	100
1995	125
1996	150

Carl Corporation's plant and equipment data at December 31, 1996 follow:

Date Acquired	Percentage Depreciated	Historical Cost
1994	30	$30,000
1995	20	20,000
1996	10	10,000
		$60,000

Depreciation is calculated at 10% per annum, straight-line. A full year's depreciation is charged in the year of acquisition. No disposals occurred in 1996. What amount of depreciation expense should be included in the income statement adjusted for general inflation (historical cost/constant purchasing power accounting)?

A. $6,000

B. $7,200

C. $7,900

D. $9,000

The correct answer is (C). *(CPA 581 II-1)*

REQUIRED: The amount of depreciation expense after adjustment for general inflation on the historical cost/constant purchasing power basis.

DISCUSSION: The historical cost of each asset must be restated in terms of constant purchasing power. This adjustment is achieved by multiplying each asset's historical cost by a fraction with a numerator equal to the current consumer price index and a denominator equal to the price index for the year of acquisition. As shown below, the total constant purchasing power cost of the plant and equipment is $79,000. Given straight-line depreciation at 10% per year, the historical cost/constant purchasing power depreciation expense is $7,900.

1994 (150 ÷ 100) × $30,000 =	$45,000
1995 (150 ÷ 125) × $20,000 =	24,000
1996 (150 ÷ 150) × $10,000 =	10,000
Constant purchasing power cost	$79,000
	× 10%
Constant purchasing power depreciation	$ 7,900

Answer (A) is incorrect because the historical cost without any adjustments for general inflation is used to calculate depreciation expense ($60,000 x 10%). Answer (B) is incorrect because the plant and equipment accounts are adjusted using the 1995 average CPI [$60,000 x (150 ÷ 125) x 10%]. Answer (D) is incorrect because the plant and equipment accounts are adjusted using the 1996 average CPI [$60,000 x (150 ÷ 100) x 10%].

27. Loy Corp. purchased a machine in 1994 when the average Consumer Price Index (CPI) was 180. The average CPI was 190 for 1995 and 200 for 1996. Loy prepares supplementary constant dollar statements (adjusted for changing prices). Depreciation on this machine is $200,000 a year. In Loy's supplementary constant purchasing power statements for 1996, the amount of depreciation expense should be stated as

A. $180,000

B. $190,000

C. $210,526

D. $222,222

The correct answer is (D). *(CPA 583 II-15)*

REQUIRED: The amount of depreciation expense in the supplementary constant purchasing power statement.

DISCUSSION: Given that the machine was purchased when the CPI was 180 and the CPI for 1996 is 200, the adjustment to depreciation for the change in the general price level involves multiplying the historical cost depreciation of $200,000 by a fraction with a numerator equal to the 1996 CPI and a denominator equal to the 1994 CPI (200 ÷ 180). Loy's price-level-adjusted depreciation expense is therefore $222,222.

Answer (A) is incorrect because the 1994 index is incorrectly used in the numerator, and the 1996 index is incorrectly used in the denominator [(180 ÷ 200) x $200,000]. Answer (B) is incorrect because the 1995 CPI is incorrectly used in the numerator, and the 1996 CPI is incorrectly used in the denominator [(190 ÷ 200) x $200,000]. Answer (C) is incorrect because the 1995 CPI is incorrectly used in the denominator [(200 ÷ 190) x $200,000].

28. The following data summarize a company's fixed asset acquisitions:

Year	Cost of Acquisitions	Price Index
1981	$1,000	200 ÷ 80
1991	1,000	200 ÷ 150
1996	1,000	200 ÷ 200

The total of these assets in constant purchasing power at the end of 1996 is

A. C$4,833

B. C$2,000

C. C$650

D. C$3,300

The correct answer is (A). *(CIA 583 IV-14)*

REQUIRED: The total fixed assets in constant purchasing power at the end of the current period.

DISCUSSION: In historical cost/constant purchasing power accounting, the historical cost principle is retained, but the unit of measure is restated to reflect changes in the general purchasing power of the monetary unit. Thus, each asset should be restated using the price index in effect at the time of acquisition. The 1981 acquisition should be valued at $2,500 [(200 ÷ 80) x $1,000], the 1991 acquisition at $1,333 [(200 ÷ 150) x $1,000], and the 1996 acquisition at $1,000 [(200 ÷ 200) x $1,000]. The total in constant purchasing power is C$4,833 ($2,500 + $1,333 + $1,000).

Answers (B), (C), and (D) are incorrect because the total of the assets in constant purchasing power is $4,833 as calculated above.

29. Lewis Company was formed on January 1, 1995. Selected balances from the historical cost balance sheet at December 31, 1996 follow:

Land (purchased in 1995) $120,000
Investment in nonconvertible bonds
   (purchased in 1995, and expected
   to be held to maturity)   60,000
Long-term debt   80,000

The average Consumer Price Index was 100 for 1995 and 110 for 1996. In a supplementary constant purchasing power balance sheet (adjusted for changing prices) at December 31, 1996, these selected account balances should be shown at

	Land	Investment	Long-term Debt
A.	$120,000	$60,000	$88,000
B.	$120,000	$66,000	$88,000
C.	$132,000	$60,000	$80,000
D.	$132,000	$66,000	$80,000

30. A corporation has gathered the following data in order to compute the purchasing power gain or loss to be included in its supplementary information for the year ended December 31, 1996:

	Amount in Nominal Dollars	
	December 31 1995	December 31 1996
Net monetary assets	$800,000	$943,000

	Index Number
Consumer Price Index at December 31, 1995	200
Consumer Price Index at December 31, 1996	230
Average Consumer Price Index for 1996	220

The purchasing power gain or loss on net monetary items (expressed in average-for-the-year dollars for 1996) should be reported at what amount for the year ended December 31, 1996?

A. $121,000 purchasing power loss.

B. $121,000 purchasing power gain.

C. $126,500 purchasing power loss.

D. $126,500 purchasing power gain.

The correct answer is (C). *(CPA 1185 I-51)*
REQUIRED: The amounts at which selected account balances should be shown in a supplementary constant purchasing power balance sheet.
DISCUSSION: Monetary items by their nature are already stated in terms of constant purchasing power. Nonmonetary items, on the other hand, require restatement. Monetary items are those that involve claims or obligations that are fixed in monetary terms. Nonmonetary items are those the valuations of which will change as the general price level fluctuates. The investment in nonconvertible bonds and the long-term debt are fixed claims and obligations. Accordingly, only the land should be restated in terms of constant purchasing power. The $120,000 historical cost is multiplied by a fraction with a numerator equal to the 1996 CPI of 110 and a denominator equal to the 1995 CPI of 100. Land should therefore appear in the supplementary constant purchasing power balance sheet at $132,000 ($120,000 x 110 ÷ 100), whereas the investment in nonconvertible bonds and the long-term debt should be recorded at their face values of $60,000 and $80,000, respectively.

Answers (A) and (B) are incorrect because long-term debt is a monetary item and should not be adjusted. Also, land is a nonmonetary account that should be adjusted.
Answers (B) and (D) are incorrect because the investment in nonconvertible bonds is a monetary account and should not be adjusted.

The correct answer is (A). *(CIA 1190 IV-39)*
REQUIRED: The amount to be reported as purchasing power gain or loss on net monetary items.
DISCUSSION: Purchasing power gain or loss expressed in average constant monetary units equals the beginning net monetary position restated to average constant monetary units, plus the actual change in the net monetary position during the year expressed in average constant monetary units, minus the ending net monetary position restated to average constant monetary units. The restatement to average constant monetary units requires multiplying the nominal dollar amount by a fraction with a numerator equal to the average CPI (220) and the denominator equal to the CPI at the date of the recording of the net monetary assets. For December 31, 1995, the denominator is 200. For the $943,000 December 31, 1996 balance, the denominator is 230. For the $143,000 difference between the beginning and ending balances, the denominator is 220, based on the assumption this change occurred evenly throughout the year. As indicated below, a purchasing power loss (inflation is unfavorable to holders of monetary assets) of $121,000 results.

Nominal Dollars	Adjustment Fraction	Constant Dollars
$ 800,000	220 ÷ 200	$ 880,000
+143,000	220 ÷ 220	+143,000
– 943,000	220 ÷ 230	– 902,000
Purchasing power loss		$ 121,000

Answers (B) and (D) are incorrect because there is a purchasing power loss. Answers (C) and (D) are incorrect because purchasing power loss is equal to $121,000.

31. Cartwright Corporation prepared the following data needed to compute the purchasing power gain or loss on net monetary items for inclusion in its supplementary information for the year ended December 31, 1996:

	Amount in Nominal Dollars	
	December 31, 1995	December 31, 1996
Monetary assets	$ 600,000	$1,000,000
Monetary liabilities	1,566,000	2,449,000
Net monetary liabilities	966,000	1,449,000
Assumed Consumer Price Index numbers:		
At December 31, 1995	210	
At December 31, 1996	230	
Average for 1996	220	

Cartwright's purchasing power gain or loss (expressed in average 1996 constant purchasing power) on net monetary items for the year ended December 31, 1996 should be

A. $109,000 gain.

B. $109,000 loss.

C. $111,000 gain.

D. $111,000 loss.

The correct answer is (A). *(CPA 1181 I-6)*

REQUIRED: The purchasing power gain or loss on net monetary items expressed in average constant purchasing power.

DISCUSSION: Purchasing power gain or loss expressed in average constant monetary units equals the beginning net monetary position restated to average constant monetary units, plus the actual change in the net monetary position during the year, minus the ending net monetary position restated to average constant monetary units. The actual changes are assumed to be in average dollars for the year. The beginning balance is the 1995 net liability of $966,000. The ending balance is the 1996 net liability of $1,449,000. The change is $483,000 ($1,449,000 − $966,000). Restatement requires multiplying by a fraction with a numerator equal to the average CPI (220). The denominator is either the CPI at the beginning of the year (210) or the end of the year (230), as appropriate. Cartwright's purchasing power gain (inflation favors debtors) is therefore $109,000.

	Nominal $$	Index	Avg. 1996 Constant $$
12/31/95	$ 966,000 × (220 ÷ 210) =		$1,012,000
1996 actual increase	483,000		483,000
			$1,495,000
12/31/96	1,449,000 × (220 ÷ 230) =		(1,386,000)
Purchasing power gain			$ 109,000

Answer (B) is incorrect because Cartwright has a purchasing power gain. Answers (C) and (D) are incorrect because $111,000 is the loss that results from switching the denominators of the fractions used to adjust the beginning and ending balances.

Questions 32 and 33 are based on the following corporate information.

	Historical Cost	Current Replacement Cost
Inventory (as of 1/1)	$100,000	$120,000
Inventory (as of 12/31)	120,000	180,000
Cost of sales (as of date of sale)	200,000	220,000
Purchases (as of date of purchase)	220,000	220,000

The corporation follows the LIFO method of inventory. The beginning inventory was all acquired when the general price-level index was 100 (1/1 of last year). The general price-level index at various dates was as follows:

1/1:	120
12/31:	150
This year's average:	125

Assume that sales and purchases were made evenly throughout the year (that is, use this year's average index if any adjustments of those items are necessary).

32. What is the difference between ending inventory at historical cost adjusted for inflation and at replacement cost?

A. $0

B. $30,000

C. $60,000

D. $6,000

The correct answer is (D). *(CIA 583 IV-36)*

REQUIRED: The difference between ending inventory at historical cost adjusted for inflation and at replacement cost.

DISCUSSION: The ending inventory at replacement cost is given as $180,000. The ending LIFO inventory at historical cost is given as $120,000, including a $100,000 component acquired when the price-level index was 100 and a $20,000 component acquired when the average index was 125. To adjust for inflation, the $100,000 component should be multiplied by the ratio of the 12/31 index (150) divided by last year's 1/1 index (100). The product is $150,000. The $20,000 component was acquired evenly throughout this year and should be multiplied by the ratio of the 12/31 index (150) divided by the average index for this year (125), giving a product of $24,000. The price-level-adjusted ending inventory value is thus $174,000 ($150,000 + $24,000), which is $6,000 less than replacement cost.

Answer (A) is incorrect because the ending inventory adjusted for inflation {[$100,000 x (150 ÷ 100)] + [$20,000 x (150 ÷ 125)]} is less than the current replacement cost ($180,000). Answer (B) is incorrect because the ending inventory balance is used and is incorrectly adjusted with the ending index (150) divided by the beginning index (120) [$120,000 x (150 ÷ 120)]. Answer (C) is incorrect because historical cost of inventory is not adjusted for inflation.

33. The cost of sales at historical cost adjusted for inflation is

A. $200,000

B. $220,000

C. $240,000

D. $264,000

The correct answer is (C). *(CIA 583 IV-37)*

REQUIRED: The cost of sales at historical cost adjusted for inflation.

DISCUSSION: Purchases for this year exceeded sales. Given a LIFO flow assumption, sales are deemed to have come entirely from purchases. Accordingly, the adjustment for inflation should use the average index for this year. The $200,000 historical cost of sales should be multiplied by the ratio of the 12/31 price-level index (150) divided by the average index for this year (125), giving an adjusted cost of sales of $240,000.

Answer (A) is incorrect because $200,000 is not adjusted for inflation. Answer (B) is incorrect because $220,000 is the cost of sales at current replacement cost. Answer (D) is incorrect because $264,000 is equal to the purchases adjusted by the beginning index (120) divided by last year's beginning index (100).

CHAPTER TWENTY-FOUR
FINANCIAL STATEMENT DISCLOSURES

This chapter covers the four subjects listed above. The disclosure requirements for all other financial reporting topics are covered in the appropriate chapters throughout this book. APB 22, *Disclosure of Accounting Policies*, may also apply to these topics. Development stage enterprises, related party disclosures, and financial instrument disclosures are distinct from other financial statement disclosure issues and are not discussed elsewhere.

24.1 Disclosure of Accounting Policies

1. The specific accounting policies and methods considered to be appropriate by management and used for reporting purposes

   A. Should be disclosed parenthetically in the tabular portion of the financial statements.

   B. Should be disclosed in a separate summary of significant accounting policies preceding the notes to the financial statements or in the initial note to the financial statements.

   C. Should be disclosed in management's discussion of operations.

   D. Need not be disclosed unless they are at variance with generally accepted accounting principles.

The correct answer is (B). *(CMA 1286 3-15)*
REQUIRED: The most appropriate statement concerning disclosure of accounting policies.
DISCUSSION: APB 22 requires that all significant accounting policies of a reporting entity be disclosed as an integral part of its financial statements. APB 22 expresses a preference for including a summary of accounting policies in a separate section preceding the footnotes or in the initial note. Disclosure should encompass those principles and methods that involve a selection from existing acceptable alternatives, those methods peculiar to the industry in which the entity operates, and any unusual or innovative applications of GAAP.
Answers (A) and (C) are incorrect because necessary disclosures should precede the notes to the financial statements or appear in the initial note. Answer (D) is incorrect because accounting policies and methods must be disclosed.

2. When it is appropriate to issue one of the basic financial statements without the others, disclosure of the pertinent accounting policies is

   A. Not required.

   B. Not required if a complete set of financial statements has not or will not be issued separately.

   C. Required only for an annual financial statement.

   D. Usually required.

The correct answer is (D). *(Publisher)*
REQUIRED: The most appropriate statement about disclosure of accounting policies when only one financial statement is issued.
DISCUSSION: When it is appropriate to issue one or more of the basic financial statements without the others, purporting to present fairly the information given in accordance with GAAP, the statements should also include disclosure of the pertinent accounting policies.
Answers (A), (B), and (C) are incorrect because pertinent accounting policies must be disclosed regardless of whether a complete set of statements is issued separately or whether the statement is for an annual or interim period.

3. Disclosure of accounting policies is not necessary when

A. Selection of an accounting principle or method has been made from existing acceptable alternatives.

B. The accounting principles and methods used by an entity are peculiar to the entity's industry, provided that such principles and methods are predominantly followed in that industry.

C. Unaudited financial statements are issued as of a date between annual reporting dates and the reporting entity has not changed its accounting policies since the end of its preceding fiscal year.

D. An entity makes unusual or innovative applications of GAAP.

The correct answer is (C). *(Publisher)*
REQUIRED: The situation in which disclosure of accounting policies is not necessary.
DISCUSSION: APB 22 does not require disclosure of accounting policies in unaudited interim financial statements when the reporting entity has not changed its policies since the end of the preceding fiscal year. Users of such interim statements will presumably consult the disclosure concerning significant accounting policies in the statements issued at the close of the preceding fiscal year.
Answers (A), (B), and (D) are incorrect because each represents a need for disclosure of accounting policies explicitly recognized by APB 22.

4. Which of the following information should be disclosed in the summary of significant accounting policies?

A. Refinancing of debt subsequent to the balance sheet date.

B. Guarantees of indebtedness of others.

C. Criteria for determining which investments are treated as cash equivalents.

D. Adequacy of pension plan assets relative to vested benefits.

The correct answer is (C). *(CPA 1194 F-59)*
REQUIRED: The disclosure of the summary of significant accounting policies.
DISCUSSION: APB 22 requires that all significant accounting policies be disclosed as an integral part of the financial statements. SFAS 95 amends APB 22 to require disclosure of the policy for determining which investments are treated as cash equivalents.
Answers (A), (B), and (D) are incorrect because the refinancing of debt subsequent to the balance sheet date, guarantees of the indebtedness of others, and the adequacy of pension plan benefits are not accounting policies but are items disclosed in the footnotes.

5. The accounting profession has adopted various standards to be followed when reporting inventory in the financial statements. All of the following are required to be reported in the financial statements or disclosed in notes to the financial statements except for

A. Inventory detail, such as raw materials, work-in-process, and finished goods.

B. Significant financing agreements, such as product financing arrangements and pledging of inventories.

C. The method used in determining cost.

D. Unrealized profit on inventories.

The correct answer is (D). *(CMA 695 2-23)*
REQUIRED: The item not a required disclosure about inventory.
DISCUSSION: APB 22 requires disclosure of accounting policies in a separate summary of significant policies or as the first footnote to the financial statements. The disclosure should specify accounting principles adopted and the method of applying those principles. Examples include inventory valuation methods; inventory details, such as the mix of finished goods, work-in-progress, and raw materials; methods used in determining costs; and any significant financing agreements, such as leases, related party transactions, product financing arrangements, firm purchase commitments, pledging of inventories, and involuntary liquidation of LIFO layers. Unrealized profit on inventories is not reported because the company usually has no assurance that the inventories will be sold.
Answers (A), (B), and (C) are incorrect because inventory details, financing agreements, and cost determinants should be disclosed in the footnotes.

6. Which of the following information should be included in Melay, Inc.'s 1996 summary of significant accounting policies?

A. Property, plant, and equipment is recorded at cost with depreciation computed principally by the straight-line method.

B. During 1996, the Delay Segment was sold.

C. Business segment 1996 sales are Alay $1M, Belay $2M, and Celay $3M.

D. Future common share dividends are expected to approximate 60% of earnings.

The correct answer is (A). *(CPA 1193 T-19)*
REQUIRED: The item properly disclosed in the summary of significant accounting policies.
DISCUSSION: APB 22 explicitly lists certain items as commonly required disclosures in a summary of significant accounting policies. These items include the basis of consolidation, depreciation methods, amortization of intangibles, inventory pricing, recognition of profit on long-term construction-type contracts, and recognition of revenue from franchising and leasing operations. Hence, the summary of significant accounting policies should include information about property, plant, and equipment depreciated by the straight-line method.
Answer (B) is incorrect because the sale of a segment is a transaction, not an accounting principle. It is reflected in the discontinued operations section on the income statement. Answer (C) is incorrect because specific segment information does not constitute an accounting policy. An accounting policy is a specific principle or a method of applying it. Answer (D) is incorrect because future dividend policy is not an accounting policy.

7. Which of the following should be disclosed in the summary of significant accounting policies?

	Composition of Inventories	Maturity Dates of Long-Term Debt
A.	Yes	Yes
B.	Yes	No
C.	No	No
D.	No	Yes

The correct answer is (C). *(CPA 589 T-28)*
REQUIRED: The item(s) properly disclosed in the summary of significant accounting policies.
DISCUSSION: APB 22 explicitly lists certain items as commonly required disclosures in a summary of significant accounting policies. These items include the basis of consolidation, depreciation methods, amortization of intangibles, inventory pricing, recognition of profit on long-term construction-type contracts, and recognition of revenue from franchising and leasing operations. APB 22 also recognizes that financial statement disclosure of accounting policies should not duplicate details presented elsewhere in the financial statements. Details about the composition of inventories and the maturity dates of long-term debts are disclosed elsewhere in the financial statements. Hence, the summary of significant accounting policies should refer to these details but need not duplicate them.
Answers (A), (B), and (D) are incorrect because neither the composition of inventories nor the maturity dates of long-term debt should be disclosed in the summary of significant accounting policies.

8. APB 22, *Disclosure of Accounting Policies*, recommends that, when financial statements are issued, a statement identifying the accounting policies adopted by the reporting entity be presented as part of the financial statements. All of the following are required to be disclosed with respect to accounting policies except the

A. Depreciation methods used for plant assets.

B. Accounting for long-term construction contracts.

C. Estimated lives of depreciable assets.

D. Principles of consolidation.

The correct answer is (C). *(CMA 695 2-30)*
REQUIRED: The item not a required disclosure by APB 22.
DISCUSSION: APB 22 requires disclosure of accounting policies in a separate summary of significant accounting policies or in the initial footnote to the financial statements. The disclosures should identify the principles followed and the methods of applying them that materially affect the statements. Moreover, the disclosures should encompass principles and methods involving a selection from acceptable alternatives, accounting principles peculiar to a particular industry, and innovative or unusual applications of GAAP. However, the disclosures should not repeat details presented elsewhere, e.g., the estimated lives of depreciable assets.
Answers (A), (B), and (D) are incorrect because examples of required disclosures include depreciation and amortization methods, means of accounting for long-term construction contracts, and basis of consolidation.

9. The summary of significant accounting policies should disclose the

A. Pro forma effect of retroactive application of an accounting change.

B. Basis of profit recognition on long-term construction contracts.

C. Adequacy of pension plan assets in relation to vested benefits.

D. Future minimum lease payments in the aggregate and for each of the 5 succeeding fiscal years.

The correct answer is (B). *(CPA 591 T-32)*
REQUIRED: The item disclosed in the summary of significant accounting policies.
DISCUSSION: APB 22 explicitly lists certain items as commonly required disclosures in a summary of significant accounting policies. These items include the basis of consolidation, depreciation methods, amortization of intangibles, inventory pricing, recognition of profit on long-term construction-type contracts, and recognition of revenue from franchising and leasing operations.
Answer (A) is incorrect because APB 20, *Accounting Changes*, states that the pro forma effect of retroactive application of an accounting change should be shown on the face of the income statement. Answer (C) is incorrect because the adequacy of pension plan assets in relation to vested benefits is not a disclosure required by SFAS 87, *Employers' Accounting for Pensions*. Answer (D) is incorrect because the future minimum lease payments in the aggregate and for each of the 5 succeeding fiscal years should be disclosed in the notes, but not in the summary of significant accounting policies.

10. A footnote must be included in the financial statements commenting on normal transactions concerning each of the following except

A. Assets acquired by lease.

B. Trade accounts receivable.

C. Pension plans.

D. Employee stock options.

The correct answer is (B). *(CPA 1178 T-44)*
REQUIRED: The subject not requiring a footnote commenting on normal transactions.
DISCUSSION: Trade accounts receivable that arise in the ordinary course of business are not specialized or unusual and accordingly do not require disclosure. In addition, no official pronouncement requires footnote comment on normal transactions in trade accounts receivable.
Answer (A) is incorrect because SFAS 13, *Accounting for Leases*, requires footnote disclosure of certain transactions involving assets acquired by lease. Answer (C) is incorrect because SFAS 87 requires footnote disclosure regarding certain transactions relating to pension plans. Answer (D) is incorrect because Chapter 13b of ARB 43 requires footnote disclosure of data related to employee stock options.

24.2 Development Stage Enterprises

11. A company is considered to be in the development stage if

A. 12 months of operations have not been completed.

B. Planned principal operations have commenced but have not yet begun to produce significant revenue.

C. The entity has not previously shown a profit from operations.

D. The entity has not obtained 50% of the initial planned activity level.

The correct answer is (B). *(Publisher)*
REQUIRED: The statement that describes the development stage of a company.
DISCUSSION: An enterprise is considered to be in the development stage if planned principal operations have not yet commenced or if they have not yet begun to generate significant revenue.
Answer (A) is incorrect because the development stage has no time limit. Answer (C) is incorrect because amounts of profit or loss do not define the development stage. Answer (D) is incorrect because the development stage is not defined by a level of planned activity.

12. A statement of cash flows for a development stage enterprise

    A. Is the same as that of an established operating enterprise and, in addition, shows cumulative amounts from the enterprise's inception.

    B. Shows only cumulative amounts from the enterprise's inception.

    C. Is the same as that of an established operating enterprise, but does not show cumulative amounts from the enterprise's inception.

    D. Is not presented.

The correct answer is (A). *(CPA 1192 T-44)*
    REQUIRED: The true statement about a statement of cash flows for a development stage enterprise.
    DISCUSSION: Development stage enterprises must present financial statements in conformity with GAAP together with certain additional information accumulated since the firm's inception. Cumulative net losses must be disclosed in the shareholders' equity section of the balance sheet, cumulative amounts of revenue and expense in the income statement, cumulative amounts of cash inflows and outflows in the statement of cash flows, and information about each issuance of stock in the statement of shareholders' equity.
    Answer (B) is incorrect because the statement of cash flows must also conform with GAAP applicable to established enterprises. Answer (C) is incorrect because the statement of cash flows must also show cumulative amounts from the enterprise's inception. Answer (D) is incorrect because a statement of cash flows is required as part of a full set of financial statements.

13. Current authoritative literature requires an enterprise to disclose that it had been in the development stage until the

    A. Planned principal operations have commenced.

    B. Planned principal operations have commenced to generate revenue.

    C. Planned principal operations have commenced to generate significant revenue.

    D. Second fiscal year in which an enterprise is no longer considered to be in the development stage.

The correct answer is (D). *(Publisher)*
    REQUIRED: The time when an enterprise no longer must disclose that it had been in a development stage.
    DISCUSSION: During the development stage, an enterprise's financial statements should be identified as those of a development stage enterprise, the nature of the development stage activities should be disclosed, and certain additional information should be included in the financial statements. When the development stage has been completed, the financial statements for the first fiscal year thereafter must disclose that, in prior years, the enterprise had been in the development stage. No further disclosure is required. The development stage is considered to be complete when significant revenue is generated from the planned principal operations.
    Answers (A), (B), and (C) are incorrect because an enterprise is required to disclose that it had been in the development stage until the second year after the development stage is completed.

14. Financial reporting by a development stage enterprise differs from financial reporting for an established operating enterprise in regard to footnote disclosures

    A. Only.

    B. And expense recognition principles only.

    C. And revenue recognition principles only.

    D. And revenue and expense recognition principles.

The correct answer is (A). *(CPA 592 T-49)*
    REQUIRED: The way in which financial reporting by a development stage enterprise differs from financial reporting for an established operating enterprise.
    DISCUSSION: Development stage enterprises must present financial statements in conformity with GAAP together with certain additional information accumulated since the firm's inception. Cumulative net losses must be disclosed in the shareholders' equity section of the balance sheet, cumulative amounts of revenue and expense in the income statement, cumulative amounts of cash inflows and outflows in the statement of cash flows, and information about each issuance of stock in the statement of shareholders' equity.
    Answers (B), (C), and (D) are incorrect because development stage and established enterprises apply the same revenue and expense recognition principles.

15. Lex Corp. was a development stage enterprise from October 10, 1994 (inception) through December 31, 1995. The year ended December 31, 1996 was the first year in which Lex qualified as an established operating enterprise. The following are among the costs incurred by Lex:

	For the Period 10/10/94 - 12/31/95	For the Year Ended 12/31/96
Leasehold improvements, equipment, and furniture	$1,000,000	$ 300,000
Security deposits	60,000	30,000
Research and development	750,000	900,000
Laboratory operations	175,000	550,000
General and administrative	225,000	685,000
Depreciation	25,000	115,000
	$2,235,000	$2,580,000

From its inception through the period ended December 31, 1996, what is the total amount of costs incurred by Lex that should be charged to operations?

A. $3,425,000

B. $2,250,000

C. $1,775,000

D. $1,350,000

The correct answer is (A). *(CPA 1190 I-58)*
REQUIRED: The total amount of costs that a development stage enterprise should charge to operations.
DISCUSSION: SFAS 7, *Accounting and Reporting by Development Stage Enterprises*, requires development stage enterprises to use the same GAAP as established operating enterprises. An established operating enterprise would have capitalized the entire $1,300,000 of leasehold improvements, equipment, and furniture, as well as the $90,000 of security deposits. Consequently, Lex Corp., a development stage enterprise, should also capitalize these costs. An established operating enterprise would have expensed the $1,650,000 of research and development costs, the $725,000 of laboratory operations costs, the $910,000 of general and administrative costs, and the $140,000 of depreciation. Lex Corp. should also expense these costs. The total to be expensed by Lex therefore equals $3,425,000 ($1,650,000 + $725,000 + $910,000 + $140,000).
Answer (B) is incorrect because $2,250,000 equals costs incurred in 1996 minus security deposits and leasehold improvements, equipment, and furniture. Answer (C) is incorrect because $1,775,000 excludes R&D costs. Answer (D) is incorrect because $1,350,000 equals costs incurred during the development stage, minus leasehold improvements, equipment, and furniture, plus 1996 depreciation.

16. Tanker Oil Co., a developmental stage enterprise, incurred the following costs during its first year of operations:

Legal fees for incorporation and other related matters	$55,000
Underwriters' fees for initial stock offering	40,000
Exploration costs and purchases of mineral rights	60,000

Tanker had no revenue during its first year of operation. What amount may Tanker capitalize as organizational costs?

A. $155,000

B. $100,000

C. $95,000

D. $55,000

The correct answer is (D). *(CPA 593 II-14)*
REQUIRED: The amount of organizational costs to be capitalized.
DISCUSSION: Organizational costs incurred in the formation of a business entity should be capitalized and amortized over the period of their expected useful life, not to exceed 40 years. These costs include incorporation fees, attorneys' fees, and various promotional costs. Initial stock issue costs should be treated as a reduction in the proceeds. Exploration costs and purchases of mineral rights may be capitalized but not as organizational costs. Thus, Tanker should capitalize $55,000 of organizational costs.
Answer (A) is incorrect because $155,000 includes the exploration costs and the underwriters' fees. Answer (B) is incorrect because $100,000 includes the exploration costs. Answer (C) is incorrect because $95,000 includes the underwriters' fees.

24.3 Related Party Disclosures

17. Related party transactions include transactions between the enterprise and

    A. The principal owners, management, and any of their relatives.

    B. Affiliates.

    C. Trusts for the benefit of employees whether or not the trustee is independent of management.

    D. Beneficial owners of at least 5% of the voting interests of the entity.

The correct answer is (B). *(Publisher)*
    REQUIRED: The parties to related party transactions.
    DISCUSSION: According to SFAS 57, *Related Party Disclosures*, related party transactions include transactions between

1. A parent and its subsidiaries.
2. Subsidiaries of a common parent.
3. An enterprise and employee trusts managed by or under the trusteeship of the enterprise's management.
4. An enterprise and its principal owners, management, or members of their immediate families.
5. Affiliates.
6. An enterprise and its equity-based investees.
7. An enterprise and any other entity if one party can significantly influence the other to the extent that one party may be prevented from fully pursuing its own interests.
8. Parties all of which can be significantly influenced by another party.

    Answer (A) is incorrect because only immediate family members of the principal owners and management are considered related parties. Answer (C) is incorrect because employee benefit trusts that are not managed by the entity are not related parties. Answer (D) is incorrect because only those owners of record or known beneficial owners of more than 10% of the voting interests of the entity are related parties.

18. The Financial Accounting Standards Board has provided guidance on disclosures of transactions between related parties, for example, transactions between subsidiaries of a common parent. SFAS 57, *Related Party Disclosures*, requires all of the following disclosures except

    A. The nature of the relationship involved.

    B. A description of the transactions for each period an income statement is presented.

    C. The dollar amounts of transactions for each period an income statement is presented.

    D. The effect on the cash flow statement for each period a cash flow statement is presented.

The correct answer is (D). *(CMA 1290 2-24)*
    REQUIRED: The disclosure not required for related party transactions.
    DISCUSSION: SFAS 57 requires disclosure of (1) the nature of the relationship involved; (2) a description of the transactions for each period an income statement is presented and such other information as is deemed necessary to an understanding of the effects of the transactions; (3) the dollar amounts of transactions for each period an income statement is presented and the effects of any change in the method of establishing their terms; (4) amounts due from or to related parties as of the date of each balance sheet, including the terms of settlement; and (5) certain tax information required by SFAS 109 if the enterprise is part of a group that files a consolidated tax return. SFAS 57 does not require disclosure of the effect on the cash flow statement for each period a cash flow statement is presented.
    Answers (A), (B), and (C) are incorrect because each disclosure is required by SFAS 57.

19. For purposes of SFAS 57, *Related Party Disclosures*, principal owners are

    A. Parties that, directly or indirectly, through one or more intermediaries, control, are controlled by, or are under common control with an enterprise.

    B. Owners of record or known beneficial owners of more than 10% of the voting interests of that enterprise.

    C. Owners of record or known beneficial owners of more than 30% of the voting interests of that enterprise.

    D. Persons who are responsible for achieving the objectives of the enterprise and who have the authority to establish policies and make decisions by which those objectives are pursued.

The correct answer is (B). *(Publisher)*
    REQUIRED: The definition of a principal owner for the purpose of disclosing related party transactions.
    DISCUSSION: SFAS 57 defines principal owners as owners of record or known beneficial owners of more than 10% of the voting interests of the enterprise.
    Answer (A) is incorrect because it states the definition of an affiliate. Answer (C) is incorrect because the threshold percentage of ownership is 10%, not 30%. Answer (D) is incorrect because it defines management.

20. SFAS 57 requires the disclosure of certain related party transactions. Which of the following is not a related party transaction?

    A. The JMC Company borrowed money from the CMK Company at the prevailing market rate of interest. Both companies are subsidiaries of the RCJ Corporation.

    B. The DWH Corporation established a profit-sharing trust fund administered by an independently owned bank located in the same community. The trustees invested part of the trust fund in DWH Corporation's outstanding bonds.

    C. The Dierks Company provided management services to its subsidiary without charge.

    D. The Simmons Company lent $25,000 to the son of the company's president at the prevailing market rate of interest.

The correct answer is (B). *(Publisher)*
    REQUIRED: The transaction that is not between related parties.
    DISCUSSION: Related parties include

1. A parent and its subsidiaries.
2. Subsidiaries of a common parent.
3. An enterprise and employee trusts managed by or under the trusteeship of the enterprise's management.
4. An enterprise and its principal owners, management, or members of their immediate families.
5. Affiliates.
6. An enterprise and its equity-based investees.
7. An enterprise and any other entity if one party can significantly influence the other to the extent that one party may be prevented from fully pursuing its own interests.
8. Parties all of which can be significantly influenced by another party.

If a trust fund established to benefit employees is administered by an independent party (the bank), the investment of trust assets in the bonds of the reporting enterprise is not a transaction between related parties.
    Answer (A) is incorrect because transactions between subsidiaries of a common parent are considered related party transactions even if they were consummated at arm's length and at prevailing market interest rates. Answer (C) is incorrect because transactions between a parent and subsidiary are considered related party transactions even if they are not recorded when they occur. Answer (D) is incorrect because a transaction between a reporting enterprise and a member of the immediate family of one of its policy makers is a related party transaction.

21. The material transaction between related parties that must be disclosed in financial statements is the

A. Compensation arrangement between a company and its president.

B. Intercompany loan between a parent company and its consolidated subsidiary.

C. Intercompany loan between a parent company and its unconsolidated subsidiary.

D. Expense allowance provided by a company to its chief executive officer.

The correct answer is (C). *(Publisher)*

REQUIRED: The transaction between related parties that must be disclosed.

DISCUSSION: SFAS 57 requires the disclosure of material related party transactions other than compensation arrangements, expense allowances, and other similar items in the ordinary course of business. Related party transactions that are eliminated in the preparation of consolidated or combined financial statements also are not required to be disclosed in those financial statements. An intercompany loan between a parent and an unconsolidated subsidiary would not be eliminated, so the transaction would have to be disclosed.

Answer (A) is incorrect because a compensation agreement in the ordinary course of business need not be disclosed. Answer (B) is incorrect because transactions that will be eliminated in the preparation of consolidated statements need not be disclosed. Answer (D) is incorrect because expense allowances in the ordinary course of business need not be disclosed.

22. The disclosure of certain related party transactions is considered useful to financial statement users in formulating their investment and credit decisions. Which of the following statements about related party transactions is true?

A. A reporting company need only disclose that it is the subsidiary of another company when transactions have taken place between it and its parent.

B. Representations about transactions between related parties may not imply that they were equivalent to arm's-length transactions.

C. Transactions between related parties are not considered to be related party transactions unless they are given accounting recognition.

D. Transactions between related parties cannot ordinarily be presumed to be carried out on an arm's-length basis.

The correct answer is (D). *(Publisher)*

REQUIRED: The true statement about related party transactions.

DISCUSSION: Transactions reflected in financial statements are usually presumed to have been consummated between independent parties on an arm's-length basis. When transactions occur between related parties, the required conditions of competitive, free-market dealings may not be present, and this general presumption is not applicable.

Answer (A) is incorrect because, even if there were no transactions between the enterprises, disclosure of the control relationship is required when common ownership or management control could result in financial position or operating results of a reporting enterprise materially different from those obtainable if the enterprises were independent. Answer (B) is incorrect because such representations may be made if they can be substantiated. Answer (C) is incorrect because accounting recognition is not a requirement of a related party transaction.

23. Dean Co. acquired 100% of Morey Corp. prior to 1996. During 1996, the individual companies included in their financial statements the following:

	Dean	Morey
Officers' salaries	$ 75,000	$50,000
Officers' expenses	20,000	10,000
Loans to officers	125,000	50,000
Intercompany sales	150,000	--

What amount should be reported as related party disclosures in the notes to Dean's 1996 consolidated financial statements?

A. $150,000

B. $155,000

C. $175,000

D. $330,000

The correct answer is (C). *(CPA 1190 I-53)*

REQUIRED: The amount to be reported as related party disclosures.

DISCUSSION: SFAS 57 requires the disclosure of material related party transactions other than compensation arrangements, expense allowances, and other similar items in the ordinary course of business. Related party transactions that are eliminated in the preparation of consolidated or combined financial statements also are not required to be disclosed in those financial statements. Accordingly, the compensation arrangements (officers' salaries and expenses) and the intercompany sales, which will be eliminated in the consolidated financial statements, need not be disclosed. However, other transactions between an enterprise and its management, such as borrowings and lendings, must be disclosed. Dean should therefore report as related party disclosures the $175,000 ($125,000 + $50,000) of loans to officers.

Answer (A) is incorrect because $150,000 equals the intercompany sales. Answer (B) is incorrect because $155,000 equals the officers' salaries and officers' expenses. Answer (D) is incorrect because $330,000 equals the officers' salaries and officers' expenses plus the loans to officers.

24. If the reporting enterprise and another enterprise are under common ownership or management control, what is the criterion for disclosure of the control relationship?

A. The existence of that control could result in financial position or operating results of the reporting enterprise significantly different from those that would have been obtained if the enterprises were autonomous.

B. Related party transactions have taken place.

C. Related party transactions have taken place that might not have been the same if they had occurred at arm's length.

D. One or more of the enterprises involved is publicly held.

The correct answer is (A). *(Publisher)*

REQUIRED: The basis for disclosing the relationship between commonly owned or controlled entities.

DISCUSSION: When common ownership or management control could result in financial position or operating results of the reporting enterprise significantly different from those that would have been obtained if common control did not exist, that control relationship should be disclosed even if there were no transactions between the commonly controlled enterprises.

Answers (B) and (C) are incorrect because the control relationship must be disclosed regardless of whether related party transactions occurred or were at arm's length. Answer (D) is incorrect because no distinction is made between public and nonpublic companies with respect to related party disclosures.

24.4 Financial Instrument Disclosures

25. SFAS 105, *Disclosure of Information about Financial Instruments with Off-Balance-Sheet Risk and Financial Instruments with Concentrations of Credit Risk*, requires the disclosure of information about the extent, nature, and terms of financial instruments with off-balance-sheet credit or market risk and about concentrations of credit risk for all financial instruments. Which of the following is defined as a financial instrument?

    A. Merchandise inventory.

    B. Deferred subscriptions revenue.

    C. A note payable in U.S. Treasury bonds.

    D. A warranty payable.

The correct answer is (C). *(Publisher)*
    REQUIRED: The item meeting the definition of a financial instrument.
    DISCUSSION: SFAS 105 defines a financial instrument as cash, evidence of an ownership interest in an entity, or a contract that both (1) imposes on one entity a contractual obligation (A) to deliver cash or another financial instrument to a second entity or (B) to exchange financial instruments on potentially unfavorable terms with the second entity, and (2) conveys to that second entity a contractual right (A) to receive cash or another financial instrument from the first entity or (B) to exchange other financial instruments on potentially favorable terms with the first entity. A note payable in U.S. Treasury bonds gives the holder the contractual right to receive and imposes on the issuer the contractual obligation to deliver bonds that are themselves financial instruments. Thus, given that one entity has a contractual obligation to deliver a financial instrument and the second entity has a contractual right to receive a financial instrument, the note payable in U.S. Treasury bonds meets the definition of a financial instrument.
    Answer (A) is incorrect because, although the sale of inventory could result in the receipt of cash, the holder of the inventory has no current contractual right to receive cash. Answers (B) and (D) are incorrect because these obligations will result in the delivery of goods or services.

26. SFAS 105 defines the risk of accounting loss from a financial instrument that arises from the failure of another party to perform according to the terms of a contract as

    A. Credit risk.

    B. Market risk.

    C. The risk of physical loss.

    D. Inherent risk.

The correct answer is (A). *(Publisher)*
    REQUIRED: The risk of accounting loss from a financial instrument that arises from a party's breach of a contract.
    DISCUSSION: Credit risk is the risk of accounting loss from a financial instrument because of the possibility that a loss may occur from the failure of another party to perform according to the terms of a contract.
    Answer (B) is incorrect because market risk arises from the possibility that future changes in market prices may make a financial instrument less valuable or more onerous. Answer (C) is incorrect because physical loss has nothing to do with the contractual performance of another party. Answer (D) is incorrect because inherent risk is the risk intrinsic to a particular item or account.

27. All of the following must be disclosed regarding financial instruments with off-balance-sheet risk of accounting loss except the

- A. Accounting loss incurred if any party to the instrument failed completely to perform, and the collateral proved to be of no value.

- B. Face or contract amount.

- C. Instrument's nature and terms, including credit risk, market risk, cash requirements, and related accounting policies.

- D. Amount by which earnings per share would change if the accounting loss were to occur.

The correct answer is (D). *(CMA 693 2-20)*

REQUIRED: The item not a required disclosure for financial instruments with off-balance-sheet risk of accounting loss.

DISCUSSION: SFAS 105 specifies the disclosure requirements for all entities with regard to the extent, nature, and terms of financial instruments with off-balance-sheet risk of accounting loss. An entity must also disclose the credit risk of financial instruments with off-balance-sheet credit risk and significant concentrations of credit risk for all financial instruments. The amount by which EPS will be affected if such loss were to occur is not required to be disclosed.

Answer (A) is incorrect because, in the financial statements or in a note, an entity must disclose accounting loss incurred if any party to the instrument failed completely to perform, and the collateral proved to be of no value. Answer (B) is incorrect because the nature, extent, and terms of financial instruments with off-balance-sheet risk, including the face or contract amount, must be disclosed. Answer (C) is incorrect because disclosure of the nature and terms should include, at a minimum, discussion of credit and market risk, cash requirements, and the related accounting policy.

28. Disclosure of information about significant concentrations of credit risk is required for

- A. All financial instruments.

- B. Financial instruments with off-balance-sheet credit risk only.

- C. Financial instruments with off-balance-sheet market risk only.

- D. Financial instruments with off-balance-sheet risk of accounting loss only.

The correct answer is (A). *(CPA 595 F-4)*

REQUIRED: The financial instruments for which disclosure of significant concentrations of credit risk is required.

DISCUSSION: SFAS 105 requires the disclosure of information about the extent, nature, and terms of financial instruments with off-balance-sheet credit or market risk and about concentrations of credit risk for all financial instruments.

Answers (B), (C), and (D) are incorrect because disclosure of significant concentrations of credit risk is required for all financial instruments.

CHAPTER TWENTY-FIVE
LONG-TERM CONTRACTS, CONSIGNMENTS, AND INSTALLMENT SALES

The topics of long-term contracts, consignments, and installment sales would usually appear in a chapter on revenue recognition in an intermediate text. Related matters are covered elsewhere in this book, such as franchise accounting in Chapter 12, Intangible Assets; specialized industry accounting in Chapter 34, Specialized Industry Accounting; and general revenue recognition issues in Chapter 4, Basic Concepts.

25.1 Long-Term Construction Contracts

1. A building contractor has a contract to construct a large building. It is estimated that the building will take 2 years to complete. Progress billings will be sent to the customer at quarterly intervals. Which of the following describes the preferable point for revenue recognition for this contract?

    A. After the contract is signed.

    B. As progress is made toward completion of the contract.

    C. As cash is received.

    D. When the contract is completed.

The correct answer is (B). *(CIA 1193 IV-28)*

REQUIRED: The moment when revenue should be recognized.

DISCUSSION: There are two methods used for revenue recognition for long-term construction contracts: the percentage-of-completion method and the completed-contract method. Under the percentage-of-completion method, revenues and gross profit are recognized each period based upon the progress of the construction. The presumption is that the percentage-of-completion approach is the better method and that the completed-contract method should be used only when the percentage-of-completion method is inappropriate.

Answer (A) is incorrect because revenue is not earned until progress has been made toward completion. Answer (C) is incorrect because an accrual method, such as the percentage-of-completion method, should be used. Answer (D) is incorrect because the completed-contract method should be used only if conditions for using the percentage-of-completion method cannot be met.

2. A construction company's projects extend over several years, and collection of receivables is reasonably certain. Each project has a firm contract price, reliable estimates of the extent of progress and cost to finish, and a contract that is specific as to the rights and obligations of all parties. The contractor and the buyer are expected to fulfill their contractual obligations on each project. The method that the company should use to account for construction revenue is

A. Installment sales.

B. Percentage-of-completion.

C. Completed-contract.

D. Point-of-sale.

The correct answer is (B). *(CIA 1185 IV-13)*

REQUIRED: The method appropriate to account for construction revenue.

DISCUSSION: SFAC 5, *Recognition and Measurement in Financial Statements of Business Enterprises*, states that revenue should be recognized when it is both realized or realizable and earned. If a project is contracted for before production and is long in relation to reporting periods, revenues may be recognized by a percentage-of-completion method as they are earned (as production occurs), provided reasonable estimates of results at completion and reliable measures of progress are available. This method results in information that is more relevant and representationally faithful than that based on waiting for delivery, completion of the project, or payment.

Answer (A) is incorrect because the installment method is appropriate if collectibility is doubtful. Answer (C) is incorrect because the completed-contract method is appropriate if reasonable estimates of results at completion and reliable measures of progress are not available. Answer (D) is incorrect because the point-of-sale method is appropriate when the product or merchandise is delivered or services are rendered directly to customers.

3. How should the balances of progress billings and construction in progress be shown at reporting dates prior to the completion of a long-term contract?

A. Progress billings as deferred income, construction in progress as a deferred expense.

B. Progress billings as income, construction in progress as inventory.

C. Net, as a current asset if debit balance and current liability if credit balance.

D. Net, as income from construction if credit balance, and loss from construction if debit balance.

The correct answer is (C). *(CPA 1178 T-40)*

REQUIRED: The proper balance sheet presentation of progress billings and construction in progress.

DISCUSSION: ARB 45, *Long-Term Construction-Type Contracts*, requires that the difference between construction in progress (costs and recognized income) and progress billings to date be shown as a current asset if construction in progress exceeds total billings, and as a current liability if billings exceed construction in progress.

Answers (A) and (B) are incorrect because progress billings and construction in progress should be netted for balance sheet presentation as a current asset or liability. Answer (D) is incorrect because neither income nor loss results from progress billings.

4. The calculation of the income recognized in the third year of a 5-year construction contract accounted for using the percentage-of-completion method includes the ratio of

A. Total costs incurred to date to total estimated costs.

B. Total costs incurred to date to total billings to date.

C. Costs incurred in year 3 to total estimated costs.

D. Costs incurred in year 3 to total billings to date.

The correct answer is (A). *(CPA 1193 T-38)*

REQUIRED: The ratio used in the calculation of income recognized for a construction contract using the percentage-of-completion method.

DISCUSSION: According to ARB 45, the percentage-of-completion method provides for the recognition of income based on the relationship between costs incurred to date and estimated total costs for completion of the contract. The amount of income recognized in the third year of a 5-year contract is calculated as follows: The total anticipated income (based on the latest available estimated costs) is multiplied by the ratio of costs incurred to date to the latest available total estimated costs, and the product is reduced by previously recognized income.

Answer (B) is incorrect because the ratio of total costs incurred to date to total billings to date is not relevant. Answer (C) is incorrect because total costs incurred must be used. Answer (D) is incorrect because neither the issuance nor the collection of billings results in income recognition.

5. A company used the percentage-of-completion method of accounting for a 4-year construction contract. Which of the following items should be used to calculate the income recognized in the second year?

	Income Previously Recognized	Progress Billings to Date
A.	Yes	Yes
B.	No	Yes
C.	Yes	No
D.	No	No

The correct answer is (C). *(CPA 1192 T-8)*

REQUIRED: The item(s) used in computing income in the second year using the percentage-of-completion method.

DISCUSSION: The percentage-of-completion method provides for the recognition of income based on the relationship between the costs incurred to date and estimated total costs for the completion of the contract. The amount of income (based on the latest available estimated costs) recognized in the second year of a 4-year contract is calculated as follows: The total anticipated income is multiplied by the ratio of the costs incurred to date to the total estimated costs, and the product is reduced by previously recognized income. Income previously recognized is therefore used to calculate income to be recognized in the second year. However, progress billings to date have no effect on the amount of income to be recognized in the second year.

Answers (A), (B), and (D) are incorrect because income previously recognized is used to calculate the income recognized. Progress billings to date are not.

6. A company uses the percentage-of-completion method to account for a 4-year construction contract. Which of the following should be used in the calculation of the income recognized in the first year?

	Progress Billings	Collections on Progress Billings
A.	Yes	Yes
B.	Yes	No
C.	No	No
D.	No	Yes

The correct answer is (C). *(CPA 1188 T-22)*

REQUIRED: The effect that progress billings and collections have on the determination of earnings.

DISCUSSION: Under GAAP, revenue should be recognized when it is realized or realizable and earned. For long-term construction contracts, these criteria are met in accordance with either the percentage-of-completion or the completed-contract method. Neither the issuance of a progress billing (debit accounts receivable, credit progress billings) nor the collection of cash (debit cash, credit accounts receivable) results in recognition of income.

Answers (A), (B), and (D) are incorrect because neither progress billings nor collections on progress billings should be used to calculate income.

7. Lake Construction Company has consistently used the percentage-of-completion method of recognizing income. During 1995, Lake entered into a fixed-price contract to construct an office building for $10,000,000. Information relating to the contract is as follows:

	December 31	
	1995	1996
Percentage of completion	20%	60%
Estimated total costs at completion	$7,500,000	$8,000,000
Income recognized (cumulative)	500,000	1,200,000

Contract costs incurred during 1996 were

A. $3,200,000

B. $3,300,000

C. $3,500,000

D. $4,800,000

The correct answer is (B). *(CPA 1187 I-21)*

REQUIRED: The contract cost incurred during the second year of a long-term contract.

DISCUSSION: If the percentage of completion is based on the relationship of the cumulative costs incurred to date to estimated total costs at completion, the cumulative amount incurred at 12/31/95 was $1,500,000 (20% x $7,500,000). At 12/31/96, the cumulative amount incurred was $4,800,000 (60% x $8,000,000). The difference of $3,300,000 ($4,800,000 – $1,500,000) equals contract costs incurred during 1989.

Answer (A) is incorrect because $3,200,000 equals the $8,000,000 estimated total costs multiplied by the 40% (60% – 20%) change in the percentages of completion. Answer (C) is incorrect because $3,500,000 equals the $10,000,000 contract price multiplied by the 40% change in the percentage of completion minus the $500,000 income recognized in 1995. Answer (D) is incorrect because $4,800,000 equals the $8,000,000 estimated total costs multiplied by the 60% percentage of completion.

8. Barr Corp. started a long-term construction project in 1996. The following data relate to this project:

Contract price	$4,200,000
Costs incurred in 1996	1,750,000
Estimated costs to complete	1,750,000
Progress billings	900,000
Collections on progress billings	800,000

The project is accounted for by the percentage-of-completion method of accounting. In Barr's 1996 income statement, what amount of gross profit should be reported for this project?

A. $350,000

B. $150,000

C. $133,333

D. $100,000

The correct answer is (A). *(CPA 591 I-49)*

REQUIRED: The gross profit for the first year of a long-term construction contract.

DISCUSSION: In 1996, one-half of the estimated costs of this construction project were incurred [$1,750,000 ÷ ($1,750,000 + $1,750,000)]. The company should therefore recognize one-half of the estimated profit in 1996. At year-end, the estimated profit is $700,000, equal to the contract price minus total estimated costs [$4,200,000 – ($1,750,000 + $1,750,000)]. In 1996, $350,000 should be recognized as gross profit ($700,000 x ½).

Answers (B), (C), and (D) are incorrect because gross profit should be recognized based on the amount of estimated costs incurred to complete the project compared to the amount of estimated total costs to complete the project.

9. State Co. recognizes construction revenue and expenses using the percentage-of-completion method. During 1995, a single long-term project was begun, which continued through 1996. Information on the project follows:

	1995	1996
Accounts receivable from construction contract	$100,000	$300,000
Construction expenses	105,000	192,000
Construction in progress	122,000	364,000
Partial billings on contract	100,000	420,000

Profit recognized from the long-term construction contract in 1996 should be

A. $50,000

B. $108,000

C. $120,000

D. $228,000

The correct answer is (A). *(CPA 1191 I-40)*

REQUIRED: The profit recognized from the long-term construction contract.

DISCUSSION: Construction in progress includes profit recognized and costs incurred. Costs incurred through 1996 equal $297,000 ($105,000 + $192,000). Hence, profit recognized in 1995 and 1996 is $67,000 ($364,000 construction in progress – $297,000 cumulative costs). Because profit was recognized in 1995 ($122,000 construction in progress – $105,000 of costs), $50,000 ($67,000 – $17,000) should be recognized in 1996.

Answer (B) is incorrect because $108,000 equals the 1996 accounts receivable minus 1996 costs. Answer (C) is incorrect because $120,000 equals 1996 billings minus 1996 accounts receivable. Answer (D) is incorrect because $228,000 equals 1996 billings minus 1996 costs.

10. Hansen Construction, Inc. has consistently used the percentage-of-completion method of recognizing income. During 1996, Hansen started work on a $3,000,000 fixed-price construction contract. The accounting records disclosed the following data for the year ended December 31, 1996:

Costs incurred	$ 930,000
Estimated costs to complete	2,170,000
Progress billings	1,100,000
Collections	700,000

How much loss should Hansen have recognized in 1996?

A. $230,000

B. $100,000

C. $30,000

D. $0

The correct answer is (B). *(CPA 585 I-23)*

REQUIRED: The loss to be recorded in the first year of a long-term construction contract.

DISCUSSION: The total of the costs incurred in 1996 plus estimated costs to complete is $3,100,000 ($930,000 + $2,170,000). Because this sum exceeds the $3,000,000 fixed-price construction contract amount, a $100,000 loss should be recognized.

Answer (A) is incorrect because $230,000 is the difference between the costs incurred and the collections ($930,000 – $700,000). Answer (C) is incorrect because $30,000 is the ratio of estimated costs incurred to total costs applied to the loss that should be recognized [$930,000 ÷ ($930,000 + $2,170,000) x $100,000 = $30,000.] Answer (D) is incorrect because a loss is recognized in the period in which it occurs.

11. Long Corp. began construction work under a 3-year contract this year. The contract price is $800,000. Long uses the percentage-of-completion method for financial accounting purposes. The income to be recognized each year is based on the proportion of costs incurred to total estimated costs for completing the contract. The following financial statement presentations relate to this contract at December 31 of the first year:

Balance Sheet

Accounts receivable- construction contract billings		$15,000
Construction in progress	$50,000	
Minus contract billings	(47,000)	
Costs of uncompleted contract in excess of billings		3,000

Income Statement

Income (before tax) on the contract recognized in year 1	$10,000

How much cash was collected in the first year on this contract?

A. $15,000

B. $32,000

C. $35,000

D. $47,000

The correct answer is (B). *(CPA 575 I-13)*
REQUIRED: The cash collections in the first year on a contract accounted for under the percentage-of-completion method.
DISCUSSION: Billings on a construction contract are debited to a receivable and credited to a cumulative contract billings account. Collections are debited to cash and credited to the receivable. The billings account, however, will not be reduced until it is closed at the end of the contract. Consequently, the difference between the billings and receivable accounts is the amount collected. For Long Corp., collections equal $32,000 ($47,000 contract billings – $15,000 accounts receivable).
Answer (A) is incorrect because $15,000 is the accounts receivable balance for the contract billings. Answer (C) is incorrect because $35,000 is the difference between construction in progress and the accounts receivable balance. Answer (D) is incorrect because $47,000 is the amount of contract billings.

12. During 1996, Tidal Co. began construction on a project scheduled for completion in 1998. At December 31, 1996, an overall loss was anticipated at contract completion. What would be the effect of the project on 1996 operating income under the percentage-of-completion method and the completed-contract method?

	Percentage-of- Completion	Completed-Contract
A.	No effect	No effect
B.	No effect	Decrease
C.	Decrease	No effect
D.	Decrease	Decrease

The correct answer is (D). *(CPA 1191 T-5)*
REQUIRED: The effect of the project on 1996 operating income under the percentage-of-completion method and the completed-contract method.
DISCUSSION: When the current estimate of total contract costs indicates a loss, an immediate provision for the entire loss should be made regardless of method. Thus, under either method, 1996 operating income is decreased by the projected loss.
Answers (A), (B), and (C) are incorrect because, under either method, 1996 operating income is decreased by the projected loss.

Questions 13 and 14 are based on the following information. Data pertaining to Pell Co.'s construction jobs, which commenced during 1996 are as follows:

	Project 1	Project 2
Contract price	$420,000	$300,000
Costs incurred during 1996	240,000	280,000
Estimated costs to complete	120,000	40,000
Billed to customers during 1996	150,000	270,000
Received from customers during 1996	90,000	250,000

13. If Pell used the completed-contract method, what amount of gross profit (loss) would Pell report in its 1996 income statement?

A. $(20,000)

B. $0

C. $340,000

D. $420,000

The correct answer is (A). *(CPA 593 I-38)*
REQUIRED: The amount of gross profit (loss) reported in the income statement under the completed-contract method.
DISCUSSION: Under the completed-contract method, profit is recognized when the contract is completed. Neither project will be completed by the end of 1996. Hence, no profit is recognized for Project 1 even though estimated data predict a profit of $60,000 ($420,000 contract price – $240,000 costs incurred – $120,000 additional estimated costs). However, when the current estimate of total contract costs indicates a loss, an immediate provision for the entire loss should be made regardless of the method of accounting used. Thus, a $20,000 loss ($300,000 contract price – $280,000 costs incurred – $40,000 additional estimated costs) will be reported for Project 2.
Answer (B) is incorrect because estimated losses must be recognized. Answers (C) and (D) are incorrect because profit is not recognized until the contract is completed.

14. If Pell used the percentage-of-completion method, what amount of gross profit (loss) would Pell report in its 1996 income statement?

A. $(20,000)

B. $20,000

C. $22,500

D. $40,000

The correct answer is (B). *(CPA 593 I-39)*
REQUIRED: The amount of gross profit (loss) reported in the income statement using the percentage-of-completion method.
DISCUSSION: Percentages of completion are based on the ratio of cumulative costs incurred to date to the total estimated costs. At the end of 1996, Project 1 is 66⅔% complete [$240,000 ÷ ($240,000 + $120,000)], and Project 2 is 87.5% complete [$280,000 ÷ ($280,000 + $40,000)]. Each project's percentage of completion is multiplied by its expected total profit. Accordingly, Pell recognizes $40,000 [(66⅔% x ($420,000 contract price – $240,000 costs incurred – $120,000 additional estimated costs)] of profit for Project 1. However, Project 2 estimates indicate a loss of $20,000 ($300,000 – $280,000 – $40,000). Because the full amount of a loss is reported immediately irrespective of the accounting method used, a gross profit of $20,000 [$40,000 Project 1 + $(20,000) Project 2] is recognized.
Answer (A) is incorrect because $(20,000) does not include the profit from Project 1. Answer (C) is incorrect because the entire loss projected for Project 2 is reported. Answer (D) is incorrect because $40,000 excludes the loss on Project 2.

15. Haft Construction Co. has consistently used the percentage-of-completion method. On January 10, 1995, Haft began work on a $3,000,000 construction contract. At the inception date, the estimated cost of construction was $2,250,000. The following data relate to the progress of the contract:

Income recognized at 12/31/95	$ 300,000
Costs incurred 1/10/95 through 12/31/96	1,800,000
Estimated cost to complete at 12/31/96	600,000

In its income statement for the year ended December 31, 1996, what amount of gross profit should Haft report?

A. $450,000

B. $300,000

C. $262,500

D. $150,000

The correct answer is (D). *(CPA 593 I-41)*

REQUIRED: The amount of gross profit reported using the percentage-of-completion method.

DISCUSSION: The percentage-of-completion method provides for the recognition of income based on the relationship between the costs incurred to date and estimated total costs for the completion of the contract. The total anticipated income is multiplied by the ratio of the costs incurred to date to the total estimated costs, and the product is reduced by previously recognized income. The percentage-of-completion at 12/31/96 is 75% [$1,800,000 ÷ ($1,800,000 + $600,000)]. The total anticipated income is $600,000 ($3,000,000 contract price – $2,400,000 expected total costs). Consequently, a profit of $150,000 [(75% x $600,000 total profit) – $300,000 previously recognized income] is recognized for 1996.

Answer (A) is incorrect because the current year's profit equals the cumulative income minus the previously recognized profit. Answer (B) is incorrect because $300,000 is the previously recognized profit. Answer (C) is incorrect because $262,500 assumes the total estimated profit is $750,000 ($3,000,000 price – $2,250,000 originally estimated total cost).

16. A company uses the completed-contract method to account for a long-term construction contract. Revenue is recognized when recorded progress billings

	Are Collected	Exceed Recorded Costs
A.	Yes	Yes
B.	No	No
C.	Yes	No
D.	No	Yes

The correct answer is (B). *(CPA 592 T-44)*

REQUIRED: The effect of the completed-contract method on revenue recognition.

DISCUSSION: Under the completed-contract method of accounting for long-term construction contracts, recorded progress billings have no effect on the recognition of income.

Answers (A), (C), and (D) are incorrect because under the completed-contract method, progress billings are recorded when issued and removed at the completion of the contract.

17. A company uses the completed-contract method to account for a 4-year construction contract that is currently in its third year. Progress billings were recorded and collected in the third year. Based on events occurring in the third year, a loss is now anticipated on the contract. When will the effect of each of the following be reported in the company's income statement?

	Third-Year Progress Billings	Anticipated Loss
A.	Not third year	Third year
B.	Not third year	Fourth year
C.	Third year	Third year
D.	Third year	Fourth year

The correct answer is (A). *(CPA 589 T-13)*

REQUIRED: The effect of progress billings and an anticipated loss on the company's income statement.

DISCUSSION: Under the completed-contract method, the gross profit on the contract should be recognized upon the completion of the contract. If a loss is anticipated, however, the loss should be recognized immediately. Under GAAP, the entries to record progress billings and their collection do not affect the recognition of profit or loss. Thus, the third-year progress billings have no effect on the income statement, but the loss anticipated in the third year should be recognized in full in that year.

Answers (B), (C), and (D) are incorrect because, under the completed-contract method, progress billings have no effect on the recognition of income, and an anticipated loss should be recognized in the year it occurs.

25.2 Installment Sales

18. Cash collection is a critical event for income recognition in the

	Cost-Recovery Method	Installment Method
A.	No	No
B.	Yes	Yes
C.	No	Yes
D.	Yes	No

The correct answer is (B). *(CPA 1193 T-39)*
REQUIRED: The method(s), if any, under which cash collection is important for recognizing income.
DISCUSSION: When receivables are collected over an extended period and no reasonable basis exists for estimating the degree of collectibility, the installment method or the cost-recovery method of accounting may be used. Under the installment method, gross profit recognized during each period of the term of an installment receivable is equal to the gross profit ratio on the installment sales for the period in which the receivable is recognized multiplied by the amount of cash collected on that receivable during the period. The cost-recovery method recognizes profit only after collections exceed the cost of the item sold, that is, when the full cost has been recovered. Subsequent amounts collected are treated entirely as realized gross profit.
Answers (A), (C), and (D) are incorrect because cash collections are critical to both the cost-recovery and the installment method.

19. Pie Co. uses the installment sales method to recognize revenue. Customers pay the installment notes in 24 equal monthly amounts, which include 12% interest. What is the balance of an installment note receivable 6 months after the sale?

A. 75% of the original sales price.

B. Less than 75% of the original sales price.

C. The present value of the remaining monthly payments discounted at 12%.

D. Less than the present value of the remaining monthly payments discounted at 12%.

The correct answer is (C). *(CPA 1192 T-9)*
REQUIRED: The balance of an installment note 6 months after sale.
DISCUSSION: The balance of an installment note receivable equals the unpaid principal. The difference between the gross receivable and the unpaid principal equals interest. Thus, the balance of the note is equal to the present value of the remaining payments discounted at the contract interest rate.
Answers (A) and (B) are incorrect because the balance will be greater than 75% of the price. Because early payments contain a greater interest component than later payments, the sum of the principal components of the first six payments will be less than 25% of the price. Answer (D) is incorrect because the principal balance equals the present value of the remaining payments.

20. On January 2, 1996, Yardley Co. sold a plant to Ivory, Inc. for $1,500,000. On that date, the plant's carrying cost was $1,000,000. Ivory gave Yardley $300,000 cash and a $1,200,000 note, payable in four annual installments of $300,000 plus 12% interest. Ivory made the first principal and interest payment of $444,000 on December 31, 1996. Yardley uses the installment method of revenue recognition. In its 1996 income statement, what amount of realized gross profit should Yardley report?

A. $344,000

B. $200,000

C. $148,000

D. $100,000

The correct answer is (B). *(CPA 593 I-42)*
REQUIRED: The amount of realized profit under the installment method of revenue recognition.
DISCUSSION: The installment method recognizes income on a sale as the related receivable is collected. The amount recognized each period is the gross profit ratio (gross profit ÷ selling price) multiplied by the cash collected. In addition, interest income must be accounted for separately from the gross profit on the sale. The cash collected is the $300,000 paid to Yardley on 1/2/96, plus the $300,000 principal paid on 12/31/96. The gross profit is $500,000 ($1,500,000 − $1,000,000), and the gross profit ratio is 33 1/3% ($500,000 ÷ $1,500,000). Thus, the amount of realized profit is $200,000 ($600,000 x 33 1/3%).
Answer (A) is incorrect because $344,000 includes the interest income of $144,000 ($1,200,000 x 12%). Answer (C) is incorrect because $148,000 equals the gross profit ratio applied to the total payment of interest and principal (33 1/3% x $444,000). Answer (D) is incorrect because $100,000 is equal to the gross profit ratio applied to $300,000.

21. Dolce Co., which began operations on January 1, 1995, appropriately uses the installment method of accounting to record revenues. The following information is available for the years ended December 31, 1995 and 1996:

	1995	1996
Sales	$1,000,000	$2,000,000
Gross profit realized on sales made in:		
1995	150,000	90,000
1996	--	200,000
Gross profit percentages	30%	40%

What amount of installment accounts receivable should Dolce report in its December 31, 1996, balance sheet?

- A. $1,100,000
- B. $1,300,000
- C. $1,700,000
- D. $1,900,000

The correct answer is (C). *(CPA 592 I-21)*

REQUIRED: The amount of installment accounts receivable.

DISCUSSION: Because gross profit realized equals the gross profit percentage times cash collected. Cash collected may be calculated by dividing gross profit realized by the gross profit percentage. Hence, cash collected on 1995 sales was $800,000 [($150,000 + $90,000) ÷ 30%], and cash collected on 1996 sales was $500,000 ($200,000 ÷ 40%). Since installment accounts receivable equals sales minus collections, the remaining balance of installment receivables is $1,700,000 ($1,000,000 + $2,000,000 − $800,000 − $500,000).

Answer (A) is incorrect because $1,100,000 equals total gross profit (both realized and unrealized) for 1995 and 1996. Answer (B) is incorrect because $1,300,000 is total cash collected. Answer (D) is incorrect because $1,900,000 equals total sales minus total gross profit for 1995 and 1996.

22. Luge Co., which began operations on January 2, 1996, appropriately uses the installment sales method of accounting. The following information is available for 1996:

Installment accounts receivable, December 31, 1996	$800,000
Deferred gross profit, December 31, 1996 (before recognition of realized gross profit for 1996)	560,000
Gross profit on sales	40%

For the year ended December 31, 1996, cash collections and realized gross profit on sales should be

	Cash Collections	Realized Gross Profit
A.	$480,000	$320,000
B.	$480,000	$240,000
C.	$600,000	$320,000
D.	$600,000	$240,000

The correct answer is (D). *(CPA 1193 I-16)*

REQUIRED: The amount of cash collections and realized gross profit under the installment sales method.

DISCUSSION: Under the installment method, the periodic recognition of income over the term of the installment receivable is equal to the gross profit margin on the sale multiplied by the amount of cash collected. Given that 1996 was the first year of operations for Luge, the $560,000 of total deferred gross profit before recognition of realized gross profit represents 40% of all sales. Hence, sales during the year were $1,400,000 ($560,000 ÷ 40%). The $800,000 in accounts receivable at year-end is the difference between total sales and cash collections; therefore, cash collections must have been $600,000 ($1,400,000 − $800,000). Because gross profit is recognized in proportion to cash collections, the realized gross profit for the year is equal to $240,000 ($600,000 cash collections x 40% gross margin).

Answer (A) is incorrect because $320,000 is the deferred gross profit after recognition of the realized gross profit, and $480,000 equals year-end installment receivables minus the deferred gross profit. Answer (B) is incorrect because $480,000 equals year-end installment receivables minus the deferred gross profit. Answer (C) is incorrect because $320,000 is the deferred gross profit after recognition of the realized gross profit.

23. On January 1, 1995, Blake Co. sold a used machine to Cooper, Inc. for $525,000. On this date, the machine had a depreciated cost of $367,500. Cooper paid $75,000 cash on January 1, 1995 and signed a $450,000 note bearing interest at 10%. The note was payable in three annual installments of $150,000 beginning January 1, 1996. Blake appropriately accounted for the sale under the installment method. Cooper made a timely payment of the first installment on January 1, 1996 of $195,000, which included interest of $45,000 to date of payment. At December 31, 1996, Blake has deferred gross profit of

A. $105,000

B. $99,000

C. $90,000

D. $76,500

The correct answer is (C). *(CPA 1193 I-45)*
REQUIRED: The deferred gross profit.
DISCUSSION: The deferred gross profit balance at the end of the year is equal to the amount of installment sales for which cash has not been collected times the gross profit margin. The uncollected amount of installment sales is $300,000 ($525,000 price – $75,000 downpayment – $150,000 installment payment). The gross profit margin is 30% [($525,000 price – $367,500 carrying amount) ÷ $525,000]. Hence, the deferred gross profit is $90,000 (30% x $300,000).

Answer (A) is incorrect because $105,000 is equal to the $150,000 first installment payment minus the $45,000 interest. Answer (B) is incorrect because $99,000 includes 30% of the interest that will be due on January 1, 1997. Answer (D) is incorrect because $76,500 results from deducting the interest paid as part of the first installment from the balance of the installment receivable.

24. Gant Co., which began operations on January 1, 1996, appropriately uses the installment method of accounting. The following information pertains to Gant's operations for the year 1996:

Installment sales	$1,000,000
Regular sales	600,000
Cost of installment sales	500,000
Cost of regular sales	300,000
General and administrative expenses	100,000
Collections on installment sales	200,000

The balance in the deferred gross profit account in Gant's December 31, 1996 balance sheet should be

A. $200,000

B. $320,000

C. $400,000

D. $500,000

The correct answer is (C). *(CPA 1192 I-28)*
REQUIRED: The deferred gross profit at the end of the first year of operations.
DISCUSSION: The installment method results in periodic recognition of income as collections on installment sales are made. Income recognized equals the cash collected multiplied by the gross profit margin on the installment sale that gave rise to the receivable. The ending balance in the deferred gross profit account equals the year-end balance of installment accounts receivable times the gross profit margin on the installment sales. The installment accounts receivable have a year-end balance of $800,000 ($1,000,000 installment sales – $200,000 collections on installment sales). The gross profit margin is equal to the installment sales minus their cost, divided by the installment sales. As indicated below, the gross profit margin on 1996 installment sales is 50%. At 12/31/96, Gant should record a deferred gross profit of $400,000 ($800,000 x 50%).

$$\frac{\$1,000,000 - \$500,000}{\$1,000,000} = 50\% \text{ gross profit margin}$$

Answer (A) is incorrect because $200,000 equals collections on installment sales. Answer (B) is incorrect because $320,000 results from including the general and administrative expenses in the cost of installment sales. Answer (D) is incorrect because $500,000 is the total of deferred and recognized gross profit.

25. When assets that have been sold and accounted for by the installment method are subsequently repossessed and returned to inventory, they should be recorded on the books at

A. Selling price.

B. The amount of the installment receivable less associated deferred gross profit.

C. Net realizable value.

D. Net realizable value minus normal profit.

The correct answer is (D). *(Publisher)*
   REQUIRED: The recorded amount of repossessed assets accounted for by the installment method.
   DISCUSSION: Repossessed assets returned to inventory should usually be recorded at their net realizable value minus normal profit. Net realizable value is the selling price minus costs of completion, reconditioning, and reselling. Sales profit should be recognized upon resale.
   Answer (A) is incorrect because, if repossessed goods are recorded at selling price, a loss would occur upon resale if reconditioning or selling costs were incurred. Answer (B) is incorrect because the installment receivable minus the associated deferred gross profit is usually not equal to the net realizable value of the asset. Answer (C) is incorrect because recording at net realizable value precludes recognition of profit upon resale.

26. Wren Co. sells equipment on installment contracts. Which of the following statements best justifies Wren's use of the cost-recovery method of revenue recognition to account for these installment sales?

A. The sales contract provides that title to the equipment passes to the purchaser only when all payments have been made.

B. No cash payments are due until one year from the date of sale.

C. Sales are subject to a high rate of return.

D. There is no reasonable basis for estimating collectibility.

The correct answer is (D). *(CPA 594 F-41)*
   REQUIRED: The best justification for the cost-recovery method.
   DISCUSSION: APB 10 states that revenues ordinarily should be accounted for when a transaction is completed, with appropriate provision for uncollectible accounts. However, when there is no reasonable basis for estimating the degree of collectibility, either the installment method or the cost-recovery method may be used. The cost-recovery method recognizes profit only after collections exceed the cost of the item sold.
   Answer (A) is incorrect because passage of title is not a recognition criterion. Answers (B) and (C) are incorrect because neither a delayed due date nor a high rate of return necessarily indicates that collectibility cannot be reasonably estimated.

27. Several of Fox, Inc.'s customers are having cash flow problems. Information pertaining to these customers for the years ended March 31, 1995 and 1996 follows:

	3/31/95	3/31/96
Sales	$10,000	$15,000
Cost of sales	8,000	9,000
Cash collections		
on 1995 sales	7,000	3,000
on 1996 sales	--	12,000

If the cost-recovery method is used, what amount would Fox report as gross profit from sales to these customers for the year ended March 31, 1996?

A. $2,000

B. $3,000

C. $5,000

D. $15,000

The correct answer is (C). *(CPA 1192 I-43)*
   REQUIRED: The gross profit from sales if the cost-recovery method is used.
   DISCUSSION: The cost-recovery method recognizes profit only after collections exceed the cost of the item sold, that is, when the full cost has been recovered. Subsequent amounts collected are treated entirely as realized gross profit. The sum of collections in excess of costs to be recognized as gross profit is $5,000 [($3,000 of 1996 collections on 1995 sales + $7,000 of 1995 collections on 1995 sales − $8,000 cost) + ($12,000 of collections on 1996 sales − $9,000 cost)].
   Answer (A) is incorrect because $2,000 excludes the profit on 1996 sales. Answer (B) is incorrect because $3,000 excludes the profit on 1995 sales. Answer (D) is incorrect because $15,000 equals 1996 sales.

28. The following information pertains to a sale of real estate by Ryan Co. to Sud Co. on December 31, 1995:

Carrying amount		$2,000,000
Sales price:		
Cash	$ 300,000	
Purchase money		
mortgage	2,700,000	3,000,000

The mortgage is payable in nine annual installments of $300,000 beginning December 31, 1996, plus interest of 10%. The December 31, 1996 installment was paid as scheduled, together with interest of $270,000. Ryan uses the cost-recovery method to account for the sale. What amount of income should Ryan recognize in 1996 from the real estate sale and its financing?

A. $570,000

B. $370,000

C. $270,000

D. $0

The correct answer is (D). *(CPA 591 I-50)*
  REQUIRED: The income recognized under the cost-recovery method.
  DISCUSSION: The cost-recovery method recognizes profit only after collections exceed the cost of the item sold, that is, when the full cost has been recovered. As of 12/31/96, only $600,000 of the $2,000,000 cost has been recovered. Consequently, no income should be recognized.
  Answers (A), (B), and (C) are incorrect because no income should be recognized.

25.3 Consignments

29. In accounting for sales on consignment, sales revenue and the related cost of goods sold should be recognized by the

A. Consignor when the goods are shipped to the consignee.

B. Consignee when the goods are shipped to the third party.

C. Consignor when notification is received that the consignee has sold the goods.

D. Consignee when cash is received from the customer.

The correct answer is (C). *(CIA 589 IV-27)*
  REQUIRED: The basis for recognition of sales revenue and related cost of goods sold for goods on consignment.
  DISCUSSION: Under a consignment sales arrangement, the consignor ships merchandise to the consignee who acts as agent for the consignor in selling the goods. The goods are in the physical possession of the consignee but remain the property of the consignor and are included in the consignor's inventory count. Sales revenue and the related cost of goods sold from these consigned goods should be recognized by the consignor only when the merchandise is sold and delivered to the ultimate customer. Accordingly, recognition occurs when notification is received that the consignee has sold the goods.
  Answer (A) is incorrect because, at the date of shipment, the goods are still the property of the consignor.
  Answers (B) and (D) are incorrect because the consignee does not recognize sales revenue or cost of goods sold for these goods. The consignee recognizes commission revenue only when the goods are sold and delivered to the third party.

30. The following information was derived from the 1996 accounting records of Clem Co.:

	Clem's Central Warehouse	Clem's Goods Held by Consignees
Beginning inventory	$110,000	$12,000
Purchases	480,000	60,000
Freight-in	10,000	
Transportation to consignees		5,000
Freight-out	30,000	8,000
Ending inventory	145,000	20,000

Clem's 1996 cost of sales was

A. $455,000

B. $485,000

C. $507,000

D. $512,000

The correct answer is (D). *(CPA 1190 II-8)*

REQUIRED: The total cost of sales for goods sold from a central warehouse and by consignees.

DISCUSSION: Cost of sales is equal to the cost of goods available for sale minus the ending inventory. Cost of goods available for sale is equal to beginning inventory, plus purchases, plus additional costs (such as freight-in and transportation to consignees) that are necessary to prepare the inventory for sale. As indicated below, the cost of sales for the inventory items held in the central warehouse is $455,000. The cost of sales for the inventory held by consignees is $57,000. Hence, total 1996 cost of sales equals $512,000 ($455,000 + $57,000). Freight-out is a selling cost and therefore not included in the determination of cost of sales.

Central Warehouse Inventory			
1/1/96	$110,000	$455,000	Cost of sales
Purchases	480,000		
Freight-in	10,000		
12/31/96	$145,000		

Consigned Inventory			
1/1/96	$12,000	$57,000	Cost of sales
Purchases	60,000		
Transportation	5,000		
12/31/96	$20,000		

Answer (A) is incorrect because $455,000 is the cost of sales for the central warehouse inventory. Answer (B) is incorrect because $485,000 is the cost of sales for the central warehouse inventory assuming freight-out is included as a cost of sales. Answer (C) is incorrect because $507,000 is Clem's 1996 cost of sales minus the cost of transportation to consignees ($512,000 – $5,000).

31. Southgate Co. paid the in-transit insurance premium for consignment goods shipped to Hendon Co., the consignee. In addition, Southgate advanced part of the commissions that will be due when Hendon sells the goods. Should Southgate include the in-transit insurance premium and the advanced commissions in inventory costs?

	Insurance Premium	Advanced Commissions
A.	Yes	Yes
B.	No	No
C.	Yes	No
D.	No	Yes

The correct answer is (C). *(CPA 592 T-23)*

REQUIRED: The item(s) included in a consignor's inventory costs.

DISCUSSION: Inventoriable costs include all costs of making the inventory ready for sale. Costs incurred by a consignor on the transfer of goods to a consignee are costs necessary to the sale of the inventory. Consequently, they are inventoriable. Thus, the in-transit insurance premium is inventoried. The advanced commissions constitute a receivable or prepaid expense, not an element of inventory cost.

Answer (A) is incorrect because the advanced commissions are not an element of inventory cost. Answer (B) is incorrect because the in-transit insurance premium is inventoried. Answer (D) is incorrect because the in-transit insurance premium is inventoried, but the advanced commissions are not an element of inventory cost.

Questions 32 and 33 are based on the following information. Turner China Corporation sells all of its china on a consignment basis. The consignees receive reimbursement of expenses plus a sales commission of 10% of retail value. During the current year, Turner shipped 11,800 units with a cost of $24 per unit and a retail value of $44 per unit to the Newbrite China Gallery. Freight paid by Turner on these shipments totaled $26,600. Newbrite reported that it sold 9,500 units and incurred expenses relating to the sold units, exclusive of commissions, in the amount of $19,200. Newbrite remitted cash for the units sold minus commissions and expenses.

32. The cash collected during the year by Turner China Corporation from Newbrite China Gallery is

A. $208,800

B. $357,000

C. $186,000

D. $398,800

The correct answer is (B). *(CMA 1294 2-9)*

REQUIRED: The cash collected by the consignor.

DISCUSSION: The consignor will receive cash equal to the sales price of the units sold, minus expenses of $19,200, minus a 10% sales commission. The units sold for $418,000 ($44 x 9,500). Cash collected equaled $357,000 [$418,000 – (10% x $418,000) – $19,200].

Answer (A) is incorrect because $208,800 is based on the cost of $24 per unit, not the retail selling price, and ignores the sales commissions. Answer (C) is incorrect because $186,000 is based on the cost of $24 per unit, not the retail selling price of $44. Answer (D) is incorrect because $398,800 omits the 10% sales commission.

33. Turner China Corporation's profit before taxes from consignment sales made by Newbrite China Gallery for the current year is

A. $129,000

B. $138,280

C. $102,400

D. $163,400

The correct answer is (C). *(CMA 1294 2-10)*

REQUIRED: The consignor's profit before taxes.

DISCUSSION: The consignor will receive cash equal to the sales price of the units sold, minus expenses of $19,200, minus a 10% sales commission. The units sold for $418,000 ($44 x 9,500). Cash collected equaled $357,000 [$418,000 – (10% x $418,000) – $19,200]. Thus, pretax profit is $102,400 [$357,000 – $26,600 freight costs – ($24 unit cost x 9,500)].

Answer (A) is incorrect because $129,000 ignores the freight costs of $26,600. Answer (B) is incorrect because $138,280 assumes 11,800 units were sold. Answer (D) is incorrect because $163,400 does not include commissions and other expenses related to the units sold in the calculation.

34. On October 1, the Ajax Company consigned 100 television sets to M & R Retailers, Inc. Each television set had a cost of $150. Freight on the shipment was paid by Ajax in the amount of $200. On December 1, M & R submitted an "account sales" stating that it had sold 60 sets, and it remitted the $12,840 balance due. The remittance was net of the following deductions from the sales price of the televisions sold:

Commission	20% of sales price
Advertising	$500
Delivery and installation charges	100

What was the total sales price of the television sets sold by M & R?

A. $13,440

B. $15,000

C. $16,800

D. $17,000

The correct answer is (C). *(CPA 579 II-6)*

REQUIRED: The total sales price of the consigned goods sold during the period.

DISCUSSION: Because the television sets are on consignment from Ajax, M & R should make no accounting entry to record their receipt. The inventory should remain on the books of Ajax. A consignment-in account is used by M & R to record both reimbursable expenses in connection with the consignment and sales of the consigned goods.

Assuming the advertising and delivery and installation charges are expenses of Ajax, they are debits to consignment-in (reimbursable cash outlays). Moreover, the commission of 20% of the sales price due M & R should be debited to the account. The solution for sales is given below:

Consignment-In			
Adv.	$500	X	Sales
Del. & inst.	100		
Commission	.2 X		
Remit to Ajax	$12,840		

$$\$500 + \$100 + .2\,X + \$12,840 = X$$
$$\$13,440 = X - .2\,X$$
$$\$13,440 = .8\,X$$
$$\$16,800 = X$$

Answer (A) is incorrect because $13,440 is the total sales price if the amount of commission is excluded. Answer (B) is incorrect because $15,000 is the amount of consigned television sets multiplied by the cost per set (100 x $150). Answer (D) is incorrect because $17,000 is the total sales price plus the freight costs paid by Ajax ($16,800 + $200).

35. Jel Co., a consignee, paid the freight costs for goods shipped from Dale Co., a consignor. These freight costs are to be deducted from Jel's payment to Dale when the consignment goods are sold. Until Jel sells the goods, the freight costs should be included in Jel's

A. Cost of goods sold.

B. Freight-out costs.

C. Selling expenses.

D. Accounts receivable.

The correct answer is (D). *(CPA 1192 T-12)*

REQUIRED: The consignee's classification of freight costs paid by the consignee on behalf of the consignor.

DISCUSSION: The consignee should debit consignment-in for the freight costs. Consignment-in is a receivable/payable account used by consignees. It represents the amount payable to the consignor if it has a credit balance. If it has a debit balance, it reflects the amount receivable from the consignor. Before consigned goods are sold, expenditures chargeable to the consignor are recorded in the consignment-in account as a receivable. After the consigned goods are sold, the consignee's net liability to the consignor is reflected in the account.

Answers (A), (B), and (C) are incorrect because the freight costs constitute a receivable.

36. Mare Co.'s December 31, 1996 balance sheet reported the following current assets:

Cash	$ 70,000
Accounts receivable	120,000
Inventories	60,000
Total	$250,000

An analysis of the accounts disclosed that accounts receivable consisted of the following:

Trade accounts	$ 96,000
Allowance for uncollectible accounts	(2,000)
Selling price of Mare's unsold goods out on consignment, at 130% of cost, not included in Mare's ending inventory	26,000
Total	$120,000

At December 31, 1996, the total of Mare's current assets is

A. $224,000

B. $230,000

C. $244,000

D. $270,000

The correct answer is (C). *(CPA 1194 F-11)*

REQUIRED: The amount of total current assets to be reported at year-end.

DISCUSSION: Under a consignment sales agreement, the goods are in the physical possession of the consignee but remain the property of the consignor and are included in the consignor's inventory. Thus, unsold consigned goods should be included in inventory at cost ($26,000 ÷ 130% = $20,000), not in receivables at their sale price. Current assets should therefore be $244,000 ($70,000 cash + $94,000 net receivables + $80,000 inventory).

Answer (A) is incorrect because $224,000 does not include the cost of the consigned goods in inventory. Answer (B) is incorrect because $230,000 results from subtracting the cost of the consigned goods from the total reported current assets. Answer (D) is incorrect because $270,000 results from adding the cost of the consigned goods to the total reported current assets.

37. Stone Co. had the following consignment transactions during December 1996:

Inventory shipped on consignment to Beta Co.	$18,000
Freight paid by Stone	900
Inventory received on consignment from Alpha Co.	12,000
Freight paid by Alpha	500

No sales of consigned goods were made through December 31, 1996. Stone's December 31, 1996 balance sheet should include consigned inventory at

A. $12,000

B. $12,500

C. $18,000

D. $18,900

The correct answer is (D). *(CPA 592 I-17)*

REQUIRED: The recognition of inventory for consignment sales.

DISCUSSION: In a consignment, the consignor ships merchandise to the consignee, who acts as agent for the consignor in selling the goods. The goods are in the physical possession of the consignee but remain the physical property of the consignor and are included in the consignor's inventory. Costs incurred by a consignor on the transfer of goods to a consignee are inventoriable. Therefore, Stone's inventory account should include $18,900 equal to the $18,000 inventory shipped to Beta on consignment and the $900 associated freight charges.

Answer (A) is incorrect because $12,000 is the inventory received from Alpha, which is not the property of Stone. Answer (B) is incorrect because $12,500 is the inventory received from Alpha and the associated freight charges. Answer (C) is incorrect because $18,000 does not include the $900 freight cost.

38. On December 1, 1996, Alt Department Store received 505 sweaters on consignment from Todd. Todd's cost for the sweaters was $80 each, and they were priced to sell at $100. Alt's commission on consigned goods is 10%. At December 31, 1996, five sweaters remained. In its December 31, 1996 balance sheet, what amount should Alt report as payable for consigned goods?

A. $49,000

B. $45,400

C. $45,000

D. $40,400

The correct answer is (C). *(CPA 593 I-29)*

REQUIRED: The payable reported by the consignee for consigned goods.

DISCUSSION: Consignment-in is a receivable/payable account used by consignees. It is the amount payable to the consignor if it has a credit balance. The amount of the payable equals total sales minus 10% commission on the goods sold, or $45,000 [($100 x 500) sales – 10% x ($100 x 500)].

Answer (A) is incorrect because $49,000 equals sales minus 10% of the gross margin on sales. Answer (B) is incorrect because $45,400 equals the cost of 505 sweaters, plus the commissions on the 500 sweaters sold. Answer (D) is incorrect because $40,400 is the cost of 505 sweaters.

CHAPTER TWENTY-SIX
STATEMENT ANALYSIS

This chapter emphasizes ratio analysis, which is the subject of a separate chapter or major section in most intermediate texts. Ratio analysis is frequently covered in conjunction with other topics. Most ratios, such as debt-to-equity, are self-explanatory.

26.1 General

1. A useful tool in financial statement analysis is the common-size financial statement. What does this tool enable the financial analyst to do?

A. Evaluate financial statements of companies within a given industry of approximately the same value.

B. Determine which companies in the same industry are at approximately the same stage of development.

C. Compare the mix of assets, liabilities, capital, revenue, and expenses within a company over time or between companies within a given industry without respect to relative size.

D. Ascertain the relative potential of companies of similar size in different industries.

The correct answer is (C). *(CPA 578 T-40)*
REQUIRED: The purposes of a common-size financial statement.
DISCUSSION: A common-size financial statement presents the items in a financial statement as percentages of a common base. The items in a balance sheet are usually stated in percentages of total assets. The items in the income statement are usually expressed as a percentage of sales. Thus, comparisons among firms in the same industry are made possible despite differences in size. Comparison of firms in different industries has drawbacks because the optimum mix of assets, liabilities, etc., will vary from industry to industry.
Answer (A) is incorrect because common-size statements are designed to permit comparison of different-sized companies. Answers (B) and (D) are incorrect because common-size statements do not reveal the stage of development of a company and are not as useful for comparing companies in different industries.

2. Of the several methods of financial analysis, the most basic and widely used is fundamental analysis, which values a common stock based upon

A. All available information concerning the company in relation to similar companies.

B. Daily volume of trading and price changes.

C. The stock's risk relative to its rate of return.

D. The relationship of past stock prices and earnings.

The correct answer is (A). *(Publisher)*
REQUIRED: The description of fundamental analysis.
DISCUSSION: Fundamental analysis is based on the assumption that the inherent worth of a security can be determined by consideration of the facts. An investor will then make buy and sell decisions based on the relation of the inherent worth to the market price of the security. Ratio analysis is a form of fundamental analysis.
Answer (B) is incorrect because it describes technical analysis. Answer (C) is incorrect because it describes capital market analysis (based on the efficient market hypothesis). Answer (D) is incorrect because it describes linear regression analysis.

3. In capital market analysis, the nonsystematic risk

- A. Is correlated with qualitative aspects of the underlying entity.
- B. Is correlated with quantitative aspects of the underlying entity.
- C. Cannot easily be overcome by individual investors.
- D. Is considered random.

The correct answer is (D). *(Publisher)*
REQUIRED: The correct statement about nonsystematic risk in capital market analysis.
DISCUSSION: Nonsystematic risk is considered individual to a firm and therefore random. In capital market theory, nonsystematic risk can largely be avoided through investment in diversified securities.
Answers (A) and (B) are incorrect because nonsystematic risk cannot be correlated with any variable, whether qualitative or quantitative. Answer (C) is incorrect because it can be overcome through diversification.

4. In financial statement analysis, the expression of all financial statement figures as a percentage of base-year figures is called

- A. Horizontal common-size analysis.
- B. Vertical common-size analysis.
- C. Cross-sectional analysis.
- D. Ratio analysis.

The correct answer is (A). *(CMA 688 4-17)*
REQUIRED: The financial statement analysis based on the expression of financial statement figures as a percentage of base-year figures.
DISCUSSION: Horizontal common-size analysis is a percentage analysis technique in which financial data from two or more accounting periods are expressed in terms of a single designated base. Percentage analysis is a technique used to highlight trends in individual line items or accounts of financial statements.
Answer (B) is incorrect because, in vertical analysis, all of the line items or accounts in a particular financial statement are presented as a percentage of a single designated line item or account in that financial statement. Answer (C) is incorrect because cross-sectional analysis is a technique that is not time related. Answer (D) is incorrect because ratio analysis is an analysis technique that deals with the relationship between two or more line items or accounts in the financial statements.

5. The relationship of the total debt to the total equity of a corporation is a measure of

- A. Liquidity.
- B. Profitability.
- C. Creditor risk.
- D. Solvency.

The correct answer is (C). *(CMA 688 4-21)*
REQUIRED: The information provided by the debt to equity ratio.
DISCUSSION: The ratio of total debt to total equity is a measure of risk to creditors. It helps in the evaluation of a company's relative reliance on debt and equity financing (leverage).
Answers (A) and (D) are incorrect because liquidity and solvency measures describe the ability of a company to meet its short-term obligations. Answer (B) is incorrect because profitability ratios measure the relative success of a firm in earning a return on its assets, sales, equity, etc.

6. What type of ratio is earnings per share?

- A. Profitability ratio.
- B. Activity ratio.
- C. Liquidity ratio.
- D. Leverage ratio.

The correct answer is (A). *(Publisher)*
REQUIRED: The proper classification of the earnings-per-share ratio.
DISCUSSION: Earnings per share is a profitability ratio. It measures the level of profitability of the firm on a per-share basis.
Answer (B) is incorrect because activity ratios measure management's efficiency in using specific resources. Answer (C) is incorrect because liquidity ratios indicate the ability of a company to meet short-term obligations. Answer (D) is incorrect because leverage or equity ratios concern the relationship of debt to equity and measure the impact of the debt on profitability and risk.

7. Are the following ratios useful in assessing the liquidity position of a company?

	Defensive-Interval Ratio	Return on Shareholders' Equity
A.	Yes	Yes
B.	Yes	No
C.	No	Yes
D.	No	No

The correct answer is (B). *(CPA 1190 T-10)*

REQUIRED: The ratio(s) useful in assessing the liquidity position of a company.

DISCUSSION: The defensive-interval ratio is equal to defensive assets divided by average daily expenditures for operations. Defensive assets include cash, short-term marketable securities, and net short-term receivables. This ratio provides information about a company's ability to survive in the absence of external cash flows. It is therefore useful in assessing liquidity (the ability to meet obligations as they mature). In contrast, return on shareholders' equity is equal to net income minus preferred dividends, divided by average common shareholders' equity. Return on shareholders' equity provides information about the profitability of the firm. It does not provide information that is useful in assessing liquidity.

Answers (A), (C), and (D) are incorrect because the defensive-interval ratio but not the return on shareholders' equity is useful in assessing the liquidity position.

26.2 Quick (Acid Test) Ratio

8. Which of the following ratios is(are) useful in assessing a company's ability to meet currently maturing or short-term obligations?

	Acid Test Ratio	Debt-to-Equity Ratio
A.	No	No
B.	No	Yes
C.	Yes	Yes
D.	Yes	No

The correct answer is (D). *(CPA 589 T-37)*

REQUIRED: The ratio(s) useful in assessing a company's ability to meet currently maturing obligations.

DISCUSSION: Liquidity ratios measure the ability of a company to meet its short-term obligations. A commonly used liquidity ratio is the acid test or quick ratio, which equals the sum of the quick assets (net accounts receivable, trading securities, and cash) divided by current liabilities. The debt-to-equity ratio is a leverage ratio. Leverage ratios measure the impact of debt on profitability and risk.

Answers (A), (B), and (C) are incorrect because the acid test ratio but not the debt-to-equity ratio is useful in assessing a company's ability to meet currently maturing or short-term obligations.

9. How is the average inventory used in the calculation of each of the following?

	Acid Test (Quick) Ratio	Inventory Turnover Rate
A.	Numerator	Numerator
B.	Numerator	Denominator
C.	Not used	Denominator
D.	Not used	Numerator

The correct answer is (C). *(CPA 590 T-38)*

REQUIRED: The use of average inventories in the acid test (quick) ratio and the inventory turnover ratio.

DISCUSSION: Assets included in the numerator of the acid test (quick) ratio include cash, trading securities, and net accounts receivable. The inventory turnover rate is equal to cost of goods sold divided by average inventory. Thus, average inventory is included in the denominator of the inventory turnover rate but is not used in the acid test ratio.

Answers (A), (B), and (D) are incorrect because average inventory is not used to calculate the acid test ratio, but it is the denominator of the inventory turnover rate.

10. Selected financial data from Drew Company are

	As of December 31, 1996
Cash	$ 75,000
Accounts receivable (net)	225,000
Merchandise inventory	270,000
Trading securities	40,000
Land and building (net)	500,000
Mortgage payable-current portion	30,000
Accounts payable and accrued liabilities	120,000
Short-term notes payable	50,000

	Year Ended December 31, 1996
Sales	$1,500,000
Cost of goods sold	900,000

Drew's quick (acid test) ratio as of December 31, 1996 is

  A. 3.6 to 1.

  B. 3.1 to 1.

  C. 2.0 to 1.

  D. 1.7 to 1.

The correct answer is (D). *(CPA 587 I-54)*
  REQUIRED: The company's quick (acid test) ratio.
  DISCUSSION: The quick or acid test ratio is a measure of the firm's ability to pay its maturing liabilities in the short run. It is defined as quick assets divided by current liabilities. Quick assets are current monetary assets, such as cash, trading securities, and net accounts receivable. Drew Company's quick assets equal $340,000 ($75,000 + $225,000 + $40,000). The current liabilities equal $200,000 ($30,000 + $120,000 + $50,000). Dividing the $340,000 of quick assets by the $200,000 of current liabilities results in a quick (acid test) ratio of 1.7 to 1.
  Answer (A) is incorrect because 3.6 to 1 includes inventory in the quick assets and does not include the current portion of the mortgage payable in the current liabilities. Answer (B) is incorrect because 3.1 (rounded) to 1 includes inventory in the current monetary assets. Answer (C) is incorrect because 2.0 to 1 does not include the current portion of the mortgage payable in the current liabilities.

11. Given an acid test ratio of 2.0, current assets of $5,000, and inventory of $2,000, the value of current liabilities is

  A. $1,500

  B. $2,500

  C. $3,500

  D. $6,000

The correct answer is (A). *(CIA 590 IV-47)*
  REQUIRED: The value of current liabilities given the acid test ratio, current assets, and inventory.
  DISCUSSION: The acid test or quick ratio equals the ratio of the quick assets (cash, net accounts receivable, and trading securities) divided by current liabilities. Current assets equal the quick assets plus inventory and prepaid expenses. This question assumes that the entity has no prepaid expenses. Given current assets of $5,000, inventory of $2,000, and no prepaid expenses, the quick assets must be $3,000. Because the acid test ratio is 2.0, the quick assets are double the current liabilities. Current liabilities therefore are equal to $1,500 ($3,000 quick assets ÷ 2.0).
  Answer (B) is incorrect because $2,500 results from dividing the current assets by 2.0. Current assets include inventory, which should not be included in the calculation of the acid test ratio. Answer (C) is incorrect because $3,500 results from adding inventory to current assets rather than subtracting it. Answer (D) is incorrect because $6,000 results from multiplying the quick assets by 2 instead of dividing by 2.

26.3 Current Ratio and Net Working Capital

12. At December 30, 1996, Vida Co. had cash of $200,000, a current ratio of 1.5:1, and a quick ratio of .5:1. On December 31, 1996, all cash was used to reduce accounts payable. How did these cash payments affect the ratios?

	Current Ratio	Quick Ratio
A.	Increased	Decreased
B.	Increased	No effect
C.	Decreased	Increased
D.	Decreased	No effect

The correct answer is (A). *(CPA 594 F-60)*
REQUIRED: The effect of the cash payments on the current and quick ratios.
DISCUSSION: The current ratio (1.5) equals current assets (cash, net accounts receivable, trading securities, certain available-for-sale and held-to-maturity securities, inventory, prepaid expenses) divided by current liabilities (accounts payable, etc.). If a ratio is greater than 1.0, equal decreases in the numerator and denominator (debit accounts payable and credit cash for $200,000) increase the ratio. The quick ratio (.5) equals quick assets (cash, trading securities, net accounts receivable) divided by current liabilities. If a ratio is less than 1.0, equal decreases in the numerator and denominator (debit accounts payable and credit cash for $200,000) decrease the ratio.
Answers (B), (C), and (D) are incorrect because the current ratio increased and the quick ratio decreased.

13. Information from Guard Company's year-end financial statements is as follows:

	1995	1996
Current assets	$2,000,000	$2,100,000
Current liabilities	1,000,000	900,000
Shareholders' equity	2,500,000	2,700,000
Net sales	8,300,000	8,800,000
Cost of goods sold	6,200,000	6,400,000
Operating income	500,000	550,000

What is the current ratio at December 31, 1996?

- A. 1.20 to 1.
- B. 2.25 to 1.
- C. 2.33 to 1.
- D. 7.33 to 1.

The correct answer is (C). *(CPA 1178 I-10)*
REQUIRED: The current ratio at the end of the second year.
DISCUSSION: The current ratio equals current assets divided by current liabilities. For 1996, the current ratio equals $2,100,000 divided by $900,000, or 2.33. The other information is irrelevant.
Answers (A), (B), and (D) are incorrect because the current ratio equals current assets divided by current liabilities.

14. In comparing the current ratios of two companies, why is it invalid to assume that the company with the higher current ratio is the better company?

- A. The current ratio includes assets other than cash.
- B. A high current ratio may indicate inadequate inventory on hand.
- C. A high current ratio may indicate inefficient use of various assets and liabilities.
- D. The two companies may define working capital in different terms.

The correct answer is (C). *(CPA 578 T-42)*
REQUIRED: The reason comparison of firms' current ratios does not indicate the better company.
DISCUSSION: The current ratio measures only the ratio of current assets to current liabilities. It does not measure the efficiency of handling the individual current asset accounts. A high ratio may indicate, for example, slow collection of accounts receivable, holding of excess inventory, or retention of more cash than needed for the cash flow requirements of the firm. A higher current ratio may indeed indicate the weaker and less efficient company.
Answer (A) is incorrect because the composition of the assets in the current ratio does not, by itself, indicate whether a higher or lower ratio is preferable. Answer (B) is incorrect because a high ratio more likely indicates excess inventory on hand. Answer (D) is incorrect because working capital is always defined as the excess of current assets over current liabilities.

15. Zenk Co. wrote off obsolete inventory of $100,000 during 1996. What was the effect of this write-off on Zenk's ratio analysis?

A. Decrease in current ratio but not in quick ratio.

B. Decrease in quick ratio but not in current ratio.

C. Increase in current ratio but not in quick ratio.

D. Increase in quick ratio but not in current ratio.

The correct answer is (A). *(CPA 592 II-18)*
   REQUIRED: The effect of writing off obsolete inventory.
   DISCUSSION: The entry is to debit a loss and credit inventory, an asset that is included in the numerator of the current but not the quick ratio. Hence the write-off decreases the current but not the quick ratio.
   Answers (B), (C), and (D) are incorrect because the write-off decreases the current but not the quick ratio.

16. Heath Co.'s current ratio is 4:1. Which of the following transactions would normally increase its current ratio?

A. Purchasing inventory on account.

B. Selling inventory on account.

C. Collecting an account receivable.

D. Purchasing machinery for cash.

The correct answer is (B). *(CPA 1192 T-38)*
   REQUIRED: The transaction that would increase a current ratio.
   DISCUSSION: The current ratio is equal to current assets divided by current liabilities. Given that Heath Co. has a current ratio of 4:1, an increase in current assets or decrease in current liabilities would cause this ratio to increase. If the company sold merchandise on open account that earned a normal gross margin, receivables would be increased at the time of recording the sales revenue in an amount greater than the decrease in inventory from recording the cost of goods sold. The effect would be an increase in the current assets and no change in the current liabilities. Thus, the current ratio would be increased.
   Answer (A) is incorrect because the purchase of inventory on open account increases current assets and current liabilities by the same amount. Equal increases in the numerator and denominator of a fraction that exceeds one decrease the fraction. Answer (C) is incorrect because collecting an account receivable decreases one current asset and increases another by the same amount. Answer (D) is incorrect because purchasing machinery for cash decreases a current asset and increases a noncurrent asset, thereby decreasing the ratio.

17. Gil Corp. has current assets of $90,000 and current liabilities of $180,000. Which of the following transactions would improve Gil's current ratio?

A. Refinancing a $30,000 long-term mortgage with a short-term note.

B. Purchasing $50,000 of merchandise inventory with a short-term account payable.

C. Paying $20,000 of short-term accounts payable.

D. Collecting $10,000 of short-term accounts receivable.

The correct answer is (B). *(CPA 1191 II-19)*
   REQUIRED: The transaction that improves the current ratio.
   DISCUSSION: If a current ratio is less than 1.0, a transaction that results in equal increases in the numerator and denominator will improve the ratio. Gil's current ratio is .5 ($90,000 ÷ $180,000). Debiting inventory and crediting accounts payable increases the ratio to .61 ($140,000 ÷ $230,000).
   Answer (A) is incorrect because refinancing a $30,000 long-term mortgage with a short-term note results in an increase in the denominator and no change in the numerator. Answer (C) is incorrect because decreasing the denominator and the numerator by the same amount decreases a current ratio that is lower than 1.0. Answer (D) is incorrect because collecting $10,000 of short-term accounts receivable has no effect on the amount of the numerator or denominator.

18. A company has a current ratio of 2.0. This ratio will decrease if the company

   A. Receives a 5% stock dividend on one of its marketable securities.

   B. Pays a large account payable that had been a current liability.

   C. Borrows cash on a 6-month note.

   D. Sells merchandise for more than cost and records the sale using the perpetual inventory method.

The correct answer is (C). *(CPA 576 T-12)*

REQUIRED: The transaction reducing a positive current ratio.

DISCUSSION: If a current ratio is greater than 1.0, an equal increase in current assets and current liabilities, such as the borrowing of cash on a short-term basis, decreases the ratio.

Answer (A) is incorrect because stock dividends do not affect the carrying value of the securities. Answer (B) is incorrect because paying a current liability decreases current assets and liabilities equally, thereby increasing the ratio. Answer (D) is incorrect because it increases the numerator with no effect on the denominator, which causes the ratio to increase.

19. Rice Inc. uses the allowance method to account for uncollectible accounts. An account receivable that was previously determined to be uncollectible and written off was collected during May. The effect of the collection on Rice's current ratio and total working capital is

	Current Ratio	Working Capital
A.	None	None
B.	Increase	Increase
C.	Decrease	Decrease
D.	None	Increase

The correct answer is (A). *(CMA 690 4-11)*

REQUIRED: The effect of the collection of a previously written off account receivable on the current ratio and total working capital.

DISCUSSION: The current ratio is the ratio of current assets to current liabilities. Working capital is equal to the difference between current assets and current liabilities. When an account receivable is written off, the allowance for uncollectible accounts and the gross receivables are decreased by the same amount. Thus, there is no effect on net accounts receivable. When an account receivable that was previously determined to be uncollectible and written off is collected, the amounts previously written off must be reestablished (debit accounts receivable, credit the allowance). This entry also has no net effect on net accounts receivable. The collection is then recorded as an equal increase in cash and a decrease in accounts receivable. The changes in these accounts are equal, so net current assets is unchanged. Because the net amount of current assets remains the same, neither the current ratio nor working capital is affected.

Answers (B), (C), and (D) are incorrect because the net amount of current assets remains the same so neither the current ratio nor working capital is affected.

20. If a company converted a short-term note payable into a long-term note payable, this transaction would

   A. Decrease only working capital.

   B. Decrease both working capital and the current ratio.

   C. Increase only working capital.

   D. Increase both working capital and the current ratio.

The correct answer is (D). *(CPA 572 T-2)*

REQUIRED: The effect of converting a short-term note to a long-term note.

DISCUSSION: Converting a short-term note to a long-term note would reduce current liabilities but not current assets. Thus, the transaction would increase both working capital and the current ratio.

Answer (A) is incorrect because a reduction in current liabilities increases working capital. Answer (B) is incorrect because a reduction in current liabilities with no change in current assets increases both working capital and the current ratio. Answer (C) is incorrect because a decrease in current liabilities increases the current ratio as well as working capital.

Questions 21 and 22 are based on the following information. Calculation of ratios and the determination of other factors are considered important in analysis of financial statements. Prior to the independent events described below, the corporation concerned had current and quick ratios in excess of one to one and reported a net income (as opposed to a loss) for the period just ended. Income tax effects are to be ignored. The corporation had only one class of shares outstanding.

21. The effect of recording a 100% stock dividend would be to

A. Decrease the current ratio, decrease working capital, and decrease book value per share.

B. Leave inventory turnover unaffected, decrease working capital, and decrease book value per share.

C. Leave working capital unaffected, decrease earnings per share, and decrease book value per share.

D. Leave working capital unaffected, decrease earnings per share, and decrease the debt-to-equity ratio.

The correct answer is (C). *(CPA 1174 T-4)*
REQUIRED: The effect of recording a 100% stock dividend.
DISCUSSION: A 100% stock dividend is a stock split that would usually involve an increase in shares outstanding with no increase in the capital stock account. Thus, the par or stated value of the shares is adjusted so that the total is unchanged. It has no effect on assets, liabilities, working capital, or total shareholders' equity. EPS and book value per share decline because more shares are outstanding.
Answers (A), (B), and (D) are incorrect because the current ratio, the working capital, and the debt-to-equity ratio are unaffected.

22. Recording the payment (as distinguished from the declaration) of a cash dividend the declaration of which was already recorded will

A. Increase the current ratio but have no effect on working capital.

B. Decrease both the current ratio and working capital.

C. Increase both the current ratio and working capital.

D. Have no effect on the current ratio or earnings per share.

The correct answer is (A). *(CPA 1174 T-5)*
REQUIRED: The effect of the payment of a cash dividend.
DISCUSSION: The payment of a previously declared cash dividend reduces current assets and current liabilities equally. An equal reduction in current assets and current liabilities causes an increase in a positive (greater than 1.0) current ratio.
Answers (B), (C), and (D) are incorrect because the current ratio is increased, but neither working capital nor EPS is affected by the dividend payment.

26.4 Receivable and Inventory Ratios

23. The following information is available from Timber Corp.'s financial records for 1996:

Sales	
Net credit sales	$500,000
Net cash sales	250,000
	$750,000

Accounts Receivable	
Balance, January 1, 1996	$ 75,000
Balance, December 31, 1996	50,000

How many times did Timber's accounts receivable turn over in 1996?

A. 15

B. 12

C. 10

D. 8

The correct answer is (D). *(CPA 1188 I-49)*
REQUIRED: The accounts receivable turnover.
DISCUSSION: The accounts receivable turnover is equal to net credit sales divided by the average accounts receivable. Net credit sales is $500,000. The average accounts receivable is $62,500 [($75,000 + $50,000) ÷ 2]. Accounts receivable turnover is 8 ($500,000 ÷ $62,500).
Answer (A) is incorrect because 15 results from dividing total sales by ending accounts receivable. Answer (B) is incorrect because 12 results from dividing total sales by average accounts receivable. Answer (C) is incorrect because 10 results from dividing net credit sales by ending accounts receivable.

24. During 1996, Rand Co. purchased $960,000 of inventory. The cost of goods sold for 1996 was $900,000, and the ending inventory at December 31, 1996 was $180,000. What was the inventory turnover for 1996?

A. 6.4

B. 6.0

C. 7.2

D. 5.0

The correct answer is (B). *(CPA 1190 I-57)*

REQUIRED: The inventory turnover given cost of sales, purchases, and ending inventory.

DISCUSSION: Inventory turnover is equal to cost of goods sold divided by the average inventory. Average inventory is equal to the average of beginning inventory and ending inventory [(BI+EI) ÷ 2]. As calculated below, beginning inventory is equal to $120,000. Average inventory is therefore equal to $150,000 [($120,000 + $180,000) ÷ 2]. Inventory turnover is 6.0 ($900,000 cost of goods sold ÷ $150,000 average inventory).

Cost of goods sold	$ 900,000
Ending inventory	180,000
Goods available	$1,080,000
Purchases	(960,000)
Beginning inventory	$ 120,000

Answer (A) is incorrect because 6.4 equals purchases divided by average inventory. Answer (C) is incorrect because 7.2 results from dividing goods available for sale by average inventory. Answer (D) is incorrect because 5.0 results from dividing cost of goods sold by ending inventory.

25. Selected data from Sheridan Corporation's year-end financial statements are presented below. The difference between average and ending inventory is immaterial.

Current ratio	2.0
Quick ratio	1.5
Current liabilities	$120,000
Inventory turnover (based on cost of goods sold)	8 times
Gross profit margin	40%

Sheridan's net sales for the year were

A. $800,000

B. $480,000

C. $1,200,000

D. $240,000

The correct answer is (A). *(CMA 1293 2-14)*

REQUIRED: The net sales for the year.

DISCUSSION: Net sales can be calculated indirectly from the inventory turnover ratio and the other ratios given. If the current ratio is 2.0 and current liabilities are $120,000, current assets must be $240,000 (2.0 x $120,000). Similarly, if the quick ratio is 1.5, the total quick assets must be $180,000 (1.5 x $120,000). The major difference between quick assets and current assets is that inventory is not included in the definition of quick assets. Consequently, ending inventory must be $60,000 ($240,000 – $180,000). The inventory turnover ratio (CGS ÷ average inventory) is 8. Thus, cost of goods sold must be 8 times average inventory, or $480,000, given no material difference between average and ending inventory. If the gross profit margin is 40%, the cost of goods sold percentage is 60%, cost of goods sold equals 60% of sales, and sales must be $800,000 ($480,000 ÷ 60%).

Answer (B) is incorrect because $480,000 is cost of goods sold. Answer (C) is incorrect because $1,200,000 is based on a 60% gross profit margin. Answer (D) is incorrect because $240,000 equals current assets.

26. On December 31, 1996, Northpark Co. collected a receivable due from a major customer. Which of the following ratios would be increased by this transaction?

A. Inventory turnover ratio.

B. Receivable turnover ratio.

C. Current ratio.

D. Quick ratio.

The correct answer is (B). *(CPA 592 T-48)*

REQUIRED: The ratio increased by collection of a receivable.

DISCUSSION: The accounts receivable turnover is equal to net credit sales divided by the average accounts receivable. Collection of a receivable decreases the denominator and increases the ratio.

Answer (A) is incorrect because the inventory turnover ratio equals the cost of goods sold divided by the average inventory. Collection of a receivable does not affect it. Answers (C) and (D) are incorrect because a decrease in a receivable and an equal increase in cash have no effect on the current ratio or the quick ratio.

27. Which one of the following inventory cost flow assumptions will result in a higher inventory turnover ratio in an inflationary economy?

A. FIFO.

B. LIFO.

C. Weighted average.

D. Specific identification.

The correct answer is (B). *(CMA 688 4-16)*

REQUIRED: The cost flow assumption that will result in a higher inventory turnover ratio in an inflationary economy.

DISCUSSION: The inventory turnover ratio equals the cost of goods sold divided by the average inventory. LIFO assumes that the last goods purchased are the first goods sold and that the oldest goods purchased remain in inventory. The result is a higher cost of goods sold and a lower average inventory than under other inventory cost flow assumptions if prices are rising. Because cost of goods sold (the numerator) will be higher and average inventory (the denominator) will be lower than under other inventory cost flow assumptions, LIFO produces the highest inventory turnover ratio.

Answers (A), (C), and (D) are incorrect because, when prices are rising, LIFO results in a higher cost of goods sold and a lower average inventory than under other inventory cost flow assumptions.

28. If a company decides to change from the first-in, first-out (FIFO) inventory method to the last-in, first-out (LIFO) method during a period of rising prices, its

A. Current ratio will be reduced.

B. Inventory turnover ratio will be reduced.

C. Cash flow will be decreased.

D. Debt-to-equity ratio will be decreased.

The correct answer is (A). *(CMA 692 2-27)*

REQUIRED: The effect of changing from FIFO to LIFO during a period of rising prices.

DISCUSSION: Changing from FIFO to LIFO during a period of rising prices will result in a lower inventory valuation and a higher cost of goods sold. Thus, the current ratio will be reduced because current assets are lower under LIFO.

Answer (B) is incorrect because inventory turnover will increase. Cost of goods sold (the numerator) will increase, and the average inventory (the denominator) will decline. Answer (C) is incorrect because cash flow will be unchanged except for the tax savings from switching to LIFO. The tax savings will result in increased cash flow. Answer (D) is incorrect because the debt-to-equity ratio will increase. Assets and equity will be lower, but debt will be unchanged.

29. Which of the following ratios should be used in evaluating the effectiveness with which the company uses its assets?

	Receivables Turnover	Dividend Payout Ratio
A.	Yes	Yes
B.	No	No
C.	Yes	No
D.	No	Yes

The correct answer is (C). *(CPA 1189 T-37)*

REQUIRED: The ratios that should be used in evaluating the effectiveness with which assets are used by a company.

DISCUSSION: The receivables turnover is equal to net credit sales divided by average accounts receivable, which is an estimate of the number of times a year that receivables are collected. It may indicate the quality of receivables and the success of collection efforts. Accordingly, this ratio is a measure of the effectiveness with which a company uses its assets. In contrast, the dividend payout ratio is equal to the declared cash dividends divided by income available to common shareholders (net income – preferred dividends). It measures the extent to which a company distributes its assets and may be useful to investors desiring regular income from equity securities. However, the payout ratio does not reflect the efficiency and effectiveness of management.

Answers (A), (B), and (D) are incorrect because the receivables turnover but not the dividend payout ratio is useful in evaluating the effectiveness with which the company uses its assets.

30. Utica Company's net accounts receivable were $250,000 at December 31, 1995 and $300,000 at December 31, 1996. Net cash sales for 1996 were $100,000. The accounts receivable turnover for 1996 was 5.0. What were Utica's total net sales for 1996?

A. $1,475,000

B. $1,500,000

C. $1,600,000

D. $2,750,000

The correct answer is (A). *(CPA 1180 I-5)*
REQUIRED: The net sales given accounts receivable, net cash sales, and the accounts receivable turnover.
DISCUSSION: Total sales equal cash sales plus credit sales. Utica's cash sales were $100,000. Credit sales may be determined from the accounts receivable turnover formula, which equals net credit sales divided by average accounts receivable. Net credit sales are equal to 5.0 times average receivables [($250,000 + $300,000) ÷ 2], or $1,375,000. Total sales were equal to $1,475,000 ($1,375,000 + $100,000).
Answer (B) is incorrect because $1,500,000 equals ending accounts receivable multiplied by the accounts receivable turnover ratio. Answer (C) is incorrect because $1,600,000 equals ending accounts receivable multiplied by the accounts receivable turnover ratio plus cash sales. Answer (D) is incorrect because $2,750,000 equals beginning accounts receivable plus ending accounts receivable multiplied by the accounts receivable turnover ratio.

31. Selected information from the accounting records of Dalton Manufacturing Company follows:

Net sales	$1,800,000
Cost of goods sold	1,200,000
Inventories at January 1	336,000
Inventories at December 31	288,000

Assuming there are 300 working days per year, what is the number of days' sales in average inventories for the year?

A. 78

B. 72

C. 52

D. 48

The correct answer is (A). *(CPA 1183 I-18)*
REQUIRED: The number of days' sales in average inventories.
DISCUSSION: The number of days' sales in average inventories equals the number of working days in the year (300) divided by the inventory turnover ratio (CGS ÷ average inventory). CGS is given as $1,200,000, and average inventory is $312,000 [($336,000 + $288,000) ÷ 2]. The number of days' sales in average inventories is therefore 78 [300 ÷ ($1,200,000 ÷ $312,000)].
Answer (B) is incorrect because 72 results from using ending inventory rather than average inventory in the inventory turnover ratio. Answer (C) is incorrect because 52 results from using net sales rather than cost of goods sold in the inventory turnover ratio. Answer (D) is incorrect because 48 results from using net sales and ending inventory rather than cost of goods sold and average inventory in the inventory turnover ratio.

32. In a comparison of 1996 with 1995, Neir Co.'s inventory turnover ratio increased substantially although sales and inventory amounts were essentially unchanged. Which of the following statements explains the increased inventory turnover ratio?

A. Cost of goods sold decreased.

B. Accounts receivable turnover increased.

C. Total asset turnover increased.

D. Gross profit percentage decreased.

The correct answer is (D). *(CPA 1193 T-20)*
REQUIRED: The statement that explains the increased inventory turnover ratio.
DISCUSSION: The inventory turnover ratio is equal to cost of goods sold divided by average inventory. If inventory is unchanged, an increase in cost of goods sold increases the inventory turnover ratio. A decrease in the gross profit percentage [(sales – cost of goods sold) ÷ sales] signifies an increase in cost of goods sold given that the amount of sales is constant.
Answer (A) is incorrect because a decrease in cost of goods sold results in a decrease in the inventory turnover ratio. Answer (B) is incorrect because the accounts receivable turnover does not affect the inventory turnover ratio. Answer (C) is incorrect because total asset turnover does not affect the inventory turnover ratio.

33. Selected information from the accounting records of the Vigor Company is as follows:

Net A/R at December 31, 1995	$ 900,000
Net A/R at December 31, 1996	$1,000,000
Accounts receivable turnover	5 to 1
Inventories at December 31, 1995	$1,100,000
Inventories at December 31, 1996	$1,200,000
Inventory turnover	4 to 1

What was Vigor's gross margin for 1996?

   A. $150,000

   B. $200,000

   C. $300,000

   D. $400,000

The correct answer is (A). *(CPA 1177 I-7)*

REQUIRED: The gross margin for 1996 given inventory, receivables, and the related turnover ratios.

DISCUSSION: Gross margin is net sales minus cost of goods sold. Net sales may be calculated from the accounts receivable turnover ratio, which is net sales divided by average receivables. The average accounts receivable is $950,000 [($900,000 + $1,000,000) ÷ 2]. Sales equal average receivables multiplied by the related turnover ratio, or $4,750,000 (5 x $950,000).

Cost of goods sold may be calculated from the inventory turnover ratio, which is cost of goods sold divided by average inventory. Average inventory is $1,150,000 [($1,100,000 + $1,200,000) ÷ 2]. Cost of goods sold equals average inventory multiplied by the inventory turnover ratio, or $4,600,000 (4 x $1,150,000). Thus, the gross margin is $150,000 ($4,750,000 net sales – $4,600,000 cost of goods sold).

Answer (B) is incorrect because $200,000 results from subtracting the ending inventory times the inventory turnover from the ending accounts receivable times the accounts receivable turnover. Answer (C) is incorrect because $300,000 results from subtracting the sum of the beginning and ending inventories times the inventory turnover from the sum of the beginning and ending accounts receivable times the accounts receivable turnover. Answer (D) is incorrect because $400,000 results from subtracting the sum of the beginning and ending accounts receivable from the sum of the beginning and ending inventories.

34. Using the data presented below, calculate the cost of sales for the Beta Corporation for 1996.

Current ratio	3.5
Acid test ratio	3.0
Current liabilities 12/31/96	$600,000
Inventory 12/31/95	$500,000
Inventory turnover	8.0

   A. $1,600,000

   B. $2,400,000

   C. $3,200,000

   D. $6,400,000

The correct answer is (C). *(CMA 688 4-12)*

REQUIRED: The cost of sales given various ratios, ending liabilities, and beginning inventory.

DISCUSSION: Inventory turnover equals cost of sales divided by average inventory. The turnover ratio and the beginning inventory are known. If ending inventory can be determined, average inventory and cost of sales can also be calculated. The relationship among the current ratio, acid test ratio, and current liabilities facilitates this calculation. The current ratio is the ratio of current assets to current liabilities. Thus, Beta's current assets are 3.5 times its current liabilities. Given that current liabilities at year-end are $600,000, current assets at year-end must be $2,100,000 (3.5 x $600,000). The acid test ratio is equal to the ratio of the sum of cash, net accounts receivable, and short-term marketable securities to current liabilities. Accordingly, Beta's quick assets are 3.0 times its current liabilities. If current liabilities at year-end are $600,000, the quick assets are $1,800,000 (3.0 x $600,000). The difference between current assets and quick assets is equal to inventory (assuming no prepaid expenses are included in current assets). Because current assets at year-end are $2,100,000 and quick assets are $1,800,000, ending inventory must be $300,000. Average inventory is equal to $400,000 [($500,000 beginning inventory + $300,000 ending inventory) ÷ 2]. An inventory turnover (cost of sales ÷ average inventory) of 8.0 indicates that cost of sales is 8.0 times average inventory. Cost of sales is therefore equal to $3,200,000 (8.0 x $400,000).

Answers (A), (B), and (D) are incorrect because cost of sales equals average inventory times inventory turnover.

35. The following computations were made from Clay Co.'s 1996 books:

Number of days' sales in inventory	61
Number of days' sales in trade accounts receivable	33

What was the number of days in Clay's 1996 operating cycle?

A. 33

B. 47

C. 61

D. 94

The correct answer is (D). *(CPA 592 II-16)*
REQUIRED: The number of days in the operating cycle.
DISCUSSION: The operating cycle is the time needed to turn cash into inventory, inventory into receivables, and receivables back into cash. It is equal to the sum of the number of days' sales in inventory and the number of days' sales in receivables. The number of Clay Co.'s days' sales in inventory is given as 61 days. The number of days' sales in receivables is given as 33 days. Hence, the number of days in the operating cycle is 94 (61 + 33).

Answer (A) is incorrect because 33 is the number of days' sales in receivables. Answer (B) is incorrect because 47 equals the sum of the number of days' sales in inventory and the number of days' sales in receivables divided by 2. Answer (C) is incorrect because 61 is the number of days' sales in inventory.

26.5 Equity Ratios

36. Boe's Corp.'s shareholders' equity at December 31, 1996, was as follows:

6% noncumulative preferred stock, $100 par (liquidation value $105 per share)	$100,000
Common stock, $10 par	300,000
Retained earnings	95,000

At December 31, 1996, Boe's book value per common share was

A. $13.17

B. $13.00

C. $12.97

D. $12.80

The correct answer is (B). *(CPA 1192 II-43)*
REQUIRED: The book value per share of common stock at year-end.
DISCUSSION: The preferred stock is noncumulative, so the equity of the preferred shareholders equals the liquidation value. The liquidation value is $105,000 ($105 per share x 1,000 shares). Given total shareholders' equity of $495,000 ($100,000 + $300,000 + $95,000), common shareholders' equity is $390,000 ($495,000 – $105,000). Therefore, book value per share of common stock equals $13.00 ($390,000 ÷ 30,000 shares).

Answer (A) is incorrect because $13.17 equals the sum of common stock and retained earnings divided by the shares outstanding of common stock. Answer (C) is incorrect because $12.97 equals the sum of common stock and retained earnings, minus the preferred stock dividend, divided by the number of common stock shares outstanding. Answer (D) is incorrect because $12.80 results from deducting the preferred stock dividend from common shareholders' equity and dividing by the number of common shares outstanding.

37. The following data pertain to Cowl, Inc., for the year ended December 31, 1996:

Net sales	$ 600,000
Net income	150,000
Total assets, January 1, 1996	2,000,000
Total assets, December 31, 1996	3,000,000

What was Cowl's rate of return on assets for 1996?

A. 5%

B. 6%

C. 20%

D. 24%

The correct answer is (B). *(CPA 1195 F-60)*
REQUIRED: The rate of return on assets.
DISCUSSION: Return on assets equals net income divided by average total assets, or 6% ($150,000 ÷ $2,500,000).

Answer (A) is incorrect because 5% results from using ending total assets instead of the average total assets. Answer (C) is incorrect because 20% results from dividing net sales by ending total assets. Answer (D) is incorrect because 24% results from dividing net sales by average total assets.

38. Hoyt Corp.'s current balance sheet reports the following shareholders' equity:

5% cumulative preferred stock, par value $100 per share; 2,500 shares issued and outstanding	$250,000
Common stock, par value $3.50 per share; 100,000 shares issued and outstanding	350,000
Additional paid-in capital in excess of par value of common stock	125,000
Retained earnings	300,000

Dividends in arrears on the preferred stock amount to $25,000. If Hoyt were to be liquidated, the preferred shareholders would receive par value plus a premium of $50,000. The book value per share of common stock is

    A. $7.75

    B. $7.50

    C. $7.25

    D. $7.00

The correct answer is (D). *(CPA 1191 II-3)*
REQUIRED: The book value per share of common stock upon liquidation.
DISCUSSION: Since the preferred stock is cumulative, the liquidation value of the preferred stock equals the par value, plus the premium, plus the dividends in arrears. Liquidation value equals $325,000 ($250,000 + $50,000 + $25,000). Given total shareholders' equity of $1,025,000 ($250,000 + $350,000 + $125,000 + $300,000), common shareholders' equity is $700,000 ($1,025,000 − $325,000). Therefore, book value per share of common stock equals $7.00 ($700,000 ÷ 100,000 shares outstanding).
Answer (A) is incorrect because $7.75 does not include the dividends in arrears or the premium. Answer (B) is incorrect because $7.50 does not include the premium. Answer (C) is incorrect because $7.25 does not include the dividends in arrears.

39. Return on investment may be calculated by multiplying total asset turnover by

    A. Average collection period.

    B. Profit margin.

    C. Debt ratio.

    D. Fixed-charge coverage.

The correct answer is (B). *(CIA 586 IV-24)*
REQUIRED: The method of calculating return on investment.
DISCUSSION: Return on investment is equal to profit divided by the average total assets. Asset turnover is equal to net sales divided by average total assets. Profit margin is equal to the profit divided by net sales. Thus, multiplying the asset turnover by the profit margin results in the cancellation of net sales from both ratios, leaving a ratio composed of profit in the numerator and average total assets in the denominator, which equals return on investment.
Answers (A), (C), and (D) are incorrect because return on investment cannot be determined using these ratios.

40. What would be the effect on book value per share and earnings per share if the corporation purchased its own shares in the open market at a price greater than book value per share?

    A. No effect on book value per share but increase earnings per share.

    B. Increase both book value per share and earnings per share.

    C. Decrease both book value per share and earnings per share.

    D. Decrease book value per share and increase earnings per share.

The correct answer is (D). *(CPA 1174 T-6)*
REQUIRED: The effect of a treasury stock purchase for more than book value on book value per share and EPS.
DISCUSSION: When treasury stock is purchased, the number of shares of stock outstanding is decreased, causing an increase in EPS. When the price paid is greater than the existing book value per share, the book value per share of the remaining stock outstanding is decreased.
Answers (A) and (B) are incorrect because a treasury stock purchase for more than book value decreases book value per share of the remaining stock outstanding. Answer (C) is incorrect because a treasury stock purchase increases earnings per share.

41. If Company A has a higher rate of return on assets than Company B, this could be because Company A has a <List A> profit margin on sales, or a <List B> asset turnover ratio, or both.

	List A	List B
A.	Higher	Higher
B.	Higher	Lower
C.	Lower	Higher
D.	Lower	Lower

The correct answer is (A). *(CIA 1194 IV-14)*

REQUIRED: The reason for a higher rate of return on assets.

DISCUSSION: The return on assets equals the product of the profit margin and the asset turnover.

Return on assets = Profit margin × Asset turnover

$$\frac{Net\ income}{Assets} = \frac{Net\ income}{Sales} \times \frac{Sales}{Assets}$$

If one company has a higher return on assets than another, it may have a higher profit margin, a higher asset turnover, or both.

Answers (B), (C), and (D) are incorrect because a higher profit margin on sales or a higher asset turnover ratio may explain a higher return on assets.

42. Selected information for Irvington Company is as follows:

	December 31, 1995	1996
Preferred stock, 8%, par $100, nonconvertible, noncumulative	$125,000	$125,000
Common stock	300,000	400,000
Retained earnings	75,000	185,000
Dividends paid on preferred stock for year ended	10,000	10,000
Net income for year ended	60,000	120,000

Irvington's return on common shareholders' equity, rounded to the nearest percentage point, for 1996 is

A. 17%

B. 19%

C. 23%

D. 25%

The correct answer is (C). *(CPA 1180 I-7)*

REQUIRED: The return on common shareholders' equity for the year.

DISCUSSION: Return on common shareholders' equity is equal to the earnings available to common shareholders divided by the average common shareholders' equity. Earnings available to common equals net income ($120,000) minus preferred dividends (8% x $125,000 = $10,000), that is, $110,000. Average shareholders' equity is equal to the average of beginning and ending equity, or $480,000 [($375,000 + $585,000) ÷ 2]. Thus, return on common shareholders' equity equals 23% ($110,000 ÷ $480,000).

Answer (A) is incorrect because 17% results from dividing net income for 1996 by total shareholders' equity. Answer (B) is incorrect because 19% results from dividing earnings available to common shareholders by ending common shareholders' equity. Answer (D) is incorrect because 25% results from dividing net income for 1996 by average common shareholders' equity without subtracting the preferred dividends from net income.

43. Stock options are frequently provided to officers of companies. Stock options that are exercised improve

A. The debt-to-equity ratio.

B. Earnings per share.

C. The ownership interest of existing shareholders.

D. The total asset turnover.

The correct answer is (A). *(CMA 679 4-13)*

REQUIRED: The effect of exercising stock options.

DISCUSSION: Exercising stock options improves (decreases) the debt-to-equity ratio because equity is increased with no effect on debt. When stock options are issued, common stock and paid-in capital are credited and cash is debited.

Answer (B) is incorrect because EPS decreases when the number of shares outstanding increases. Answer (C) is incorrect because stock options exercised increase the number of shares outstanding, thereby diluting the existing ownership interest. Answer (D) is incorrect because asset turnover equals net sales divided by average assets. The exercise of stock options increases assets, thereby decreasing the ratio.

44. Barr Co. has total debt of $420,000 and shareholders' equity of $700,000. Barr is seeking capital to fund an expansion. Barr is planning to issue an additional $300,000 in common stock and is negotiating with a bank to borrow additional funds. The bank is requiring a debt-to-equity ratio of .75. What is the maximum additional amount Barr will be able to borrow?

A. $225,000

B. $330,000

C. $525,000

D. $750,000

The correct answer is (B). *(CPA 1195 F-59)*
REQUIRED: The maximum additional borrowing allowed to satisfy a specific debt-to-equity ratio.
DISCUSSION: Barr will have $1 million ($700,000 + $300,000) in total shareholders' equity. The debt-to-equity restriction allows up to $750,000 ($1,000,000 x .75) in debt. Barr already has $420,000 in debt, so the additional borrowing cannot exceed $330,000 ($750,000 – $420,000).
Answer (A) is incorrect because $225,000 results from multiplying the $300,000 of additional common stock by the debt-to-equity ratio. Answer (C) is incorrect because $525,000 equals the $700,000 of shareholders' equity times the debt-to-equity ratio. Answer (D) is incorrect because $750,000 is the total debt allowed.

45. A company has 100,000 outstanding common shares with a market value of $20 per share. Dividends of $2 per share were paid in the current year, and the company has a dividend payout ratio of 40%. The price-to-earnings (P-E) ratio of the company is

A. 2.5

B. 4

C. 10

D. 50

The correct answer is (B). *(CIA 1195 IV-32)*
REQUIRED: The P-E ratio.
DISCUSSION: The P-E ratio equals the share price divided by EPS. If the dividends per share equaled $2 and the dividend payout ratio was 40%, EPS must have been $5 ($2 ÷ .4). Accordingly, the P-E ratio is 4 ($20 share price ÷ $5 EPS).
Answer (A) is incorrect because 2.5 equals EPS divided by dividends per share. Answer (C) is incorrect because 10 equals share price divided by dividends per share. Answer (D) is incorrect because 50 equals price per share divided by the dividend payout percentage.

46. Information concerning Hamilton's common stock is presented below for the fiscal year ended May 31, 1996.

Common shares outstanding	750,000
Stated value per share	$15.00
Market price per share	45.00
1995 dividends paid per share	4.50
1996 dividends paid per share	7.50
Primary earning per share	11.25
Fully diluted earnings per share	9.00

The price-earnings ratio for Hamilton's common stock is

A. 3.0 times.

B. 4.0 times.

C. 5.0 times.

D. 6.0 times.

The correct answer is (C). *(CMA 692 2-26)*
REQUIRED: The price-earnings ratio for the common stock.
DISCUSSION: The price-earnings ratio is calculated by dividing the current market price of the stock by the earnings per share. Fully diluted earnings per share is used if disclosed. Thus, Hamilton's price-earnings ratio is 5.0 ($45 market price ÷ $9 FDEPS).
Answer (A) is incorrect because the 3.0 figure is based on the stated value per share in the denominator. Answer (B) is incorrect because 4.0 is based on the primary earnings per share in the denominator. Answer (D) is incorrect because 6.0 is derived by using 1996 dividends per share in the denominator.

47. Smith Company had net income of $5,300,000 and earnings per share on common stock of $2.50. Included in the net income was $500,000 of bond interest expense related to its long-term debt. The income tax rate was 50%. Dividends on preferred stock were $300,000. The dividend-payout ratio on common stock was 40%. What were the dividends on common stock?

   A. $1,800,000

   B. $1,900,000

   C. $2,000,000

   D. $2,120,000

The correct answer is (C). *(CPA 580 I-13)*
  REQUIRED: The dividends on common stock given the dividend-payout ratio.
  DISCUSSION: The dividend-payout ratio is equal to the dividends on common stock divided by the earnings available to common. If earnings available to common were $5,000,000 ($5,300,000 net income – $300,000 preferred dividends) and the payout ratio was 40%, the dividends on common were $2,000,000.
  Answers (A), (B), and (D) are incorrect because the dividends on common stock are determined by multiplying the earnings available to common shareholders by the dividend-payout ratio.

48. How are the following used in the calculation of the dividend payout ratio for a company with only common stock outstanding?

	Dividends Per Share	Earnings Per Share	Book Value Per Share
A.	Denominator	Numerator	Not used
B.	Denominator	Not used	Numerator
C.	Numerator	Denominator	Not used
D.	Numerator	Not used	Denominator

The correct answer is (C). *(CPA 1182 T-40)*
  REQUIRED: The components of the dividend payout ratio.
  DISCUSSION: In the absence of preferred stock, the dividend payout ratio may be stated as the dividends per share (numerator) divided by the earnings per share (denominator).
  Answer (A) is incorrect because dividends per share is the numerator and earnings per share is the denominator in the dividend payout ratio. Answer (B) is incorrect because dividends per share is the numerator, earnings per share is the denominator, and book value per share is not used in the dividend payout ratio. Answer (D) is incorrect because earnings per share is the denominator and book value per share is not used in the dividend payout ratio.

49. A drop in the market price of a firm's common stock will immediately affect its

   A. Return on equity.

   B. Dividend-payout ratio.

   C. Debt-to-net-worth ratio.

   D. Dividend yield.

The correct answer is (D). *(CMA 685 4-16)*
  REQUIRED: The effect of a drop in the market price of a firm's common stock.
  DISCUSSION: Dividend yield equals dividends per common share divided by the market price per common share. Hence, a drop in the market price of the stock will affect this ratio.
  Answers (A), (B), and (C) are incorrect because these ratios are based on book values in their calculation rather than the market price of the common stock.

50. The ratio of earnings before interest and taxes to total interest expense is a measure of

   A. Liquidity.

   B. Risk.

   C. Activity.

   D. Profitability.

The correct answer is (B). *(CPA 574 T-9)*
  REQUIRED: The function of the times-interest-earned ratio.
  DISCUSSION: The ratio of earnings before interest and taxes to total interest expense is the times-interest-earned ratio. This ratio assists a creditor in estimating risk by measuring a firm's ability to pay interest expense.
  Answer (A) is incorrect because the current (liquidity) ratio measures the ability to pay short-term liabilities out of current assets. Answer (C) is incorrect because turnover ratios measure a firm's activity. Answer (D) is incorrect because EPS measures return to owners.

Questions 51 and 52 are based on the following
information. Selected financial data of Apex
Corporation for the year ended December 31,
1996 are as follows. Common stock dividends
were $120,000.

Operating income	$900,000
Interest expense	(100,000)
Income before income tax	$800,000
Income tax expense	(320,000)
Net income	$480,000
Preferred stock dividends	(200,000)
Net income available to common shareholders	$280,000

51. The times-interest-earned ratio is

A. 2.8 to 1.

B. 4.8 to 1.

C. 8.0 to 1.

D. 9.0 to 1.

The correct answer is (D). *(CPA 1186 I-56)*
REQUIRED: The times-interest-earned ratio.
DISCUSSION: The times-interest-earned ratio is a
measure of the firm's ability to pay interest on debt. It equals
the sum of net income, interest expense, and taxes divided
by the amount of interest. Taxes are added back to the
numerator because the ability to pay interest is not affected
by the taxes to be paid in the future. That is, if all available
income were used to pay interest, the entity would have no
tax liability. Thus, times-interest-earned ratio is 9.0 to 1.

$$\frac{\$480,000 \ + \ \$100,000 \ + \ \$320,000}{\$100,000} \ = \ 9.0$$

Answer (A) is incorrect because 2.8 to 1 results from
dividing net income available to common shareholders by
interest expense. Answer (B) is incorrect because 4.8 to 1
results from dividing net income by interest expense.
Answer (C) is incorrect because 8.0 to 1 results from dividing
income before income tax by interest expense.

52. The times-preferred-dividend-earned ratio is

A. 1.4 to 1.

B. 1.7 to 1.

C. 2.4 to 1.

D. 4.0 to 1.

The correct answer is (C). *(CPA 1186 I-57)*
REQUIRED: The times-preferred-dividend-earned ratio.
DISCUSSION: The times-preferred-dividend-earned ratio
is a measure of the company's ability to pay preferred
dividends. It equals net income divided by preferred
dividends. Preferred dividends are not added back to net
income in the numerator because they are not deducted in
arriving at net income. Income taxes are also not added
back to net income in the numerator because preferred
dividends are not tax deductible and are paid only after
senior claims to income, such as interest and taxes, have
been satisfied. Apex's times-preferred-dividend-earned ratio
is 2.4 to 1 ($480,000 net income ÷ $200,000 preferred
dividends).
Answers (A), (B), and (D) are incorrect because the
times-preferred-dividend-earned ratio equals net income
divided by preferred dividends.

26.6 Questions on More Than One Ratio

Questions 53 and 54 are based on the following information. Selected data pertaining to Lore Co. for the calendar year 1996 is as follows:

Net cash sales	$ 3,000
Cost of goods sold	18,000
Inventory at beginning of year	6,000
Purchases	24,000
Accounts receivable at beginning of year	20,000
Accounts receivable at end of year	22,000

53. The accounts receivable turnover for 1996 was 5.0 times. What were Lore's 1996 net credit sales?

A. $105,000

B. $107,000

C. $110,000

D. $210,000

The correct answer is (A). *(CPA 595 F-58)*
REQUIRED: The net credit sales.
DISCUSSION: Credit sales may be determined from the accounts receivable turnover formula (credit sales ÷ average accounts receivable). Credit sales are equal to 5.0 times average receivables [($20,000 + $22,000) ÷ 2], or $105,000.

Answer (B) is incorrect because $107,000 equals ending accounts receivable multiplied by the accounts receivable turnover ratio, minus cash sales. Answer (C) is incorrect because $110,000 equals ending accounts receivable multiplied by the accounts receivable turnover ratio. Answer (D) is incorrect because $210,000 equals beginning accounts receivable plus ending accounts receivable, multiplied by the accounts receivable turnover ratio.

54. What was the inventory turnover for 1996?

A. 1.2 times.

B. 1.5 times.

C. 2.0 times.

D. 3.0 times.

The correct answer is (C). *(CPA 595 F-59)*
REQUIRED: The inventory turnover ratio.
DISCUSSION: Inventory turnover is equal to cost of goods sold divided by average inventory. Ending inventory equals beginning inventory, plus purchases, minus cost of goods sold, or $12,000 ($6,000 + $24,000 – $18,000). Average inventory is $9,000 [($6,000 + $12,000) ÷ 2]. Inventory turnover is 2.0 times ($18,000 cost of goods sold ÷ $9,000 average inventory).

Answer (A) is incorrect because 1.2 times uses the average of beginning inventory and purchases. Answer (B) is incorrect because 1.5 times uses ending inventory instead of average inventory. Answer (D) is incorrect because 3.0 times uses beginning inventory instead of average inventory.

Questions 55 through 57 are based on the following information. The following inventory and sales data are available for the current year for Volpone Company. Volpone uses a 365-day year when computing ratios.

	November 30, 1996	November 30, 1995
Net credit sales	$6,205,000	
Gross receivables	350,000	320,000
Inventory	960,000	780,000
Cost of goods sold	4,380,000	

55. Volpone Company's average number of days to collect accounts receivable for the current year is

A. 18.82 days.

B. 19.43 days.

C. 19.71 days.

D. 20.59 days.

The correct answer is (C). *(CMA 1294 2-22)*
REQUIRED: The average collection period.
DISCUSSION: The average collection period equals 365 days divided by the receivables turnover (net credit sales ÷ average accounts receivable). Turnover is 18.52 times {$6,205,000 sales ÷ [($350,000 + $320,000) ÷ 2]}. Hence, the average collection period is 19.71 days (365 ÷ 18.52).

Answer (A) is incorrect because 18.82 days is based on receivables of $320,000. Answer (B) is incorrect because 19.43 days is based on a 360-day year. Answer (D) is incorrect because 20.59 days is based on receivables of $350,000.

56. Volpone Company's average number of days to sell inventory for the current year is

A. 51.18 days.

B. 65.00 days.

C. 71.51 days.

D. 72.50 days.

The correct answer is (D). *(CMA 1294 2-23)*
REQUIRED: The average days to sell inventory.
DISCUSSION: The average number of days to sell inventory equals 365 days divided by the inventory turnover (cost of goods sold ÷ average inventory). Thus, turnover is 5.0345 times {$4,380,000 CGS ÷ [($960,000 + $780,000) ÷ 2]}. The average number of days to sell inventory is 72.5 days (365 ÷ 5.0345).

Answer (A) is incorrect because 51.18 days is based on sales, not cost of sales. Sales are recorded at retail prices. Answer (B) is incorrect because 65.00 days is based on the beginning inventory. Answer (C) is incorrect because 71.51 days is based on a 360-day year, not a 365-day year.

57. Volpone Company's operating cycle for the current year is

A. 70.61 days.

B. 93.09 days.

C. 92.21 days.

D. 99.71 days.

The correct answer is (C). *(CMA 1294 2-24)*
REQUIRED: The length of the firm's operating cycle.
DISCUSSION: The operating cycle is the length of time it takes a company to complete normal operating activities. Thus, the operating cycle is a cash-to-cash cycle equivalent to the average time that inventory is held plus the average time that receivables are held. Volpone holds its inventory 72.50 days [365 days ÷ ($4,380,000 CGS ÷ $870,000 average inventory)] and its receivables 19.71 days [365 days ÷ ($6,205,000 sales ÷ $335,000 average receivables)]. Its operating cycle is 92.21 days (72.50 + 19.71).

Answer (A) is incorrect because the inventory alone is held for 72.50 days. Answer (B) is incorrect because 93.09 days is based on the ending receivables balance.
Answer (D) is incorrect because 99.71 days is based on the ending inventory.

Questions 58 and 59 are based on the following information. CPZ Enterprises had the following account information.

Accounts receivable	$200,000
Accounts payable	80,000
Bonds payable, due in 10 years	300,000
Cash	100,000
Interest payable, due in 3 months	10,000
Inventory	400,000
Land	250,000
Notes payable, due in 6 months	50,000
Prepaid expenses	40,000

The company has an operating cycle of 5 months.

58. The current ratio for CPZ Enterprises is

A. 1.68

B. 2.14

C. 5.00

D. 5.29

The correct answer is (D). *(CMA 695 2-1)*

REQUIRED: The current ratio.

DISCUSSION: The current ratio equals current assets divided by current liabilities. This company's current assets consist of accounts receivable, cash, inventory, and prepaid expenses, which total $740,000 ($200,00 + $100,000 + $400,000 + $40,000). The current liabilities consist of accounts payable, interest payable, and notes payable, which total $140,000 ($80,000 + $10,000 + $50,000). Thus, the current ratio is 5.29 ($740,000 ÷ $140,000).

Answer (A) is incorrect because 1.68 treats bonds payable as a current liability. Answer (B) is incorrect because 2.14 is the quick ratio. Answer (C) is incorrect because 5.00 excludes prepaid expenses from current assets.

59. What is the company's acid test (quick) ratio?

A. 0.68

B. 1.68

C. 2.14

D. 2.31

The correct answer is (C). *(CMA 695 2-2)*

REQUIRED: The acid test (quick) ratio.

DISCUSSION: The acid test, or quick, ratio equals quick assets divided by current liabilities. Quick assets consist of cash ($100,000) and accounts receivable ($200,000), for a total of $300,000. The current liabilities consist of accounts payable, interest payable, and notes payable, for a total of $140,000 ($80,000 + $10,000 + $50,000). Hence, the quick ratio is 2.14 ($300,000 ÷ $140,000).

Answer (A) is incorrect because 0.68 equals the quick assets divided by the sum of the current liabilities and the bonds payable. Answer (B) is incorrect because 1.68 equals current assets divided by the sum of current liabilities and the bonds payable. Answer (D) is incorrect because 2.31 omits interest payable from the current liabilities.

Questions 60 through 62 are based on the
following information. A company reports the
following account balances at year-end:

Account	Balance
Long-term debt	$200,000
Cash	50,000
Net sales	600,000
Fixed assets (net)	320,000
Tax expense	67,500
Inventory	25,000
Common stock	100,000
Interest expense	20,000
Administrative expense	35,000
Retained earnings	150,000
Accounts payable	65,000
Accounts receivable	120,000
Cost of goods sold	400,000
Depreciation expense	10,000

Additional Information:

The opening balance of common stock was
$100,000.

The opening balance of retained earnings was
$82,500.

The company had 10,000 common shares
outstanding all year.

No dividends were paid during the year.

60. For the year just ended, the company has times-interest-earned of

A. 3.375 times.

B. 6.75 times.

C. 7.75 times.

D. 9.5 times.

The correct answer is (C). *(CIA 594 IV-12)*
    REQUIRED: The times-interest-earned ratio (TIE).
    DISCUSSION: The TIE ratio is a leverage ratio. It emphasizes the company's ability to pay interest expense. The ratio equals income before interest and taxes divided by interest.

$$= \frac{(Sales - CGS - Administrative\ expense - Depreciation)}{(Interest\ expense)}$$

$$= \frac{\$600,000 - \$400,000 - \$35,000 - \$10,000}{\$20,000}$$

$$= 7.75\ times$$

    Answer (A) is incorrect because 3.375 times results from including in the numerator deductions for taxes and interest. Answer (B) is incorrect because 6.75 times results from including in the numerator a deduction for interest. Answer (D) is incorrect because 9.5 times results from failing to deduct the administrative expenses from the numerator.

61. At year-end, the company has a book value per share, to the nearest cent, of

   A. $10.00

   B. $15.00

   C. $21.63

   D. $25.00

The correct answer is (D). *(CIA 594 IV-13)*

   REQUIRED: The book value per share at year-end.

   DISCUSSION: Book value per share, based on balance sheet amounts, measures the per-share amount that would be received if the company were liquidated. The ratio is calculated as common shareholders' equity divided by the number of outstanding shares.

$$= \frac{Common\ stock\ +\ Retained\ earnings}{Outstanding\ shares}$$

$$= \frac{\$100,000\ +\ \$150,000}{10,000\ shares}$$

$$= \underline{\$25}$$

   Answer (A) is incorrect because $10.00 excludes retained earnings from the numerator. Answer (B) is incorrect because $15.00 excludes common stock from the numerator. Answer (C) is incorrect because $21.63 is based on average shareholder equity.

62. For the year just ended, the company had a rate of return on common equity, rounded to two decimals, of

   A. 31.21%

   B. 58.06%

   C. 67.50%

   D. 71.68%

The correct answer is (A). *(CIA 594 IV-14)*

   REQUIRED: The rate of return on common equity for the year just ended.

   DISCUSSION: Rate of return on common equity, a profitability ratio, measures the rate of return on investment. The ratio equals net income divided by average shareholders' equity.

$$= \frac{Sales\ -\ CGS\ -\ Adm.\ exp.\ -\ Deprec.\ -\ Interest\ -\ Tax}{(Beginning\ equity\ +\ Ending\ equity)\ \div\ 2}$$

$$= \frac{\begin{array}{c}\$600,000\ -\ \$400,000\ -\ \$35,000\ -\\ \$10,000\ -\ \$20,000\ -\ \$67,500\end{array}}{(\$182,500\ +\ 250,000)\ \div\ 2}$$

$$= \frac{\$67,500}{216,250}$$

$$= 31.21\%$$

   Answer (B) is incorrect because 58.06% excludes common stock from the denominator. Answer (C) is incorrect because 67.50% excludes retained earnings from the denominator. Answer (D) is incorrect because 71.68% excludes interest expense and tax expense from the numerator.

Questions 63 through 69 are based on the following information. Depoole Company is a manufacturer of industrial products and employs a calendar year for financial reporting purposes. These questions present several of Depoole's transactions during the year. Assume that total quick assets exceeded total current liabilities both before and after each transaction described. Further assume that Depoole has positive profits during the year and a credit balance throughout the year in its retained earnings account.

63. Payment of a trade account payable of $64,500 would

   A. Increase the current ratio, but the quick ratio would not be affected.

   B. Increase the quick ratio, but the current ratio would not be affected.

   C. Increase both the current and quick ratios.

   D. Decrease both the current and quick ratios.

The correct answer is (C). *(CMA 1280 4-1)*
   REQUIRED: The effect of paying a trade account payable on the current and quick ratios.
   DISCUSSION: Given that the quick assets exceed current liabilities, both the current and quick ratios exceed one because the numerator of the current ratio includes other current assets in addition to the quick assets of cash, net accounts receivable, and short-term marketable securities. An equal reduction in the numerator and the denominator, such as a payment of a trade payable, will cause each ratio to increase.
   Answers (A), (B), and (D) are incorrect because both the current ratio and the quick ratio would increase.

64. The purchase of raw materials for $85,000 on open account would

   A. Increase the current ratio.

   B. Decrease the current ratio.

   C. Increase net working capital.

   D. Decrease net working capital.

The correct answer is (B). *(CMA 1280 4-2)*
   REQUIRED: The effect of a credit purchase of raw materials on the current ratio and/or working capital.
   DISCUSSION: The purchase increases both the numerator and denominator of the current ratio by adding inventory to the numerator and payables to the denominator. Because the ratio before the purchase was greater than one, the ratio is decreased.
   Answer (A) is incorrect because the current ratio is decreased. Answers (C) and (D) are incorrect because the purchase of raw materials on account has no effect on working capital (current assets and current liabilities change by the same amount).

65. The collection of a current accounts receivable of $29,000 would

   A. Increase the current ratio.

   B. Decrease the current ratio and the quick ratio.

   C. Increase the quick ratio.

   D. Not affect the current or quick ratios.

The correct answer is (D). *(CMA 1280 4-3)*
   REQUIRED: The effect of collection of a current account receivable on the current and/or quick ratios.
   DISCUSSION: Collecting current accounts receivable has no effect on either the current ratio or the quick ratio because current assets, quick assets, and current liabilities are unchanged by the collection.
   Answers (A), (B), and (C) are incorrect because collecting current accounts receivable does not change current assets, quick assets, or current liabilities, which means the current and quick ratios are not changed.

66. Obsolete inventory of $125,000 was written off during the year. This transaction

   A. Decreased the quick ratio.

   B. Increased the quick ratio.

   C. Increased net working capital.

   D. Decreased the current ratio.

The correct answer is (D). *(CMA 1280 4-4)*
   REQUIRED: The effect of writing off obsolete inventory.
   DISCUSSION: Writing off obsolete inventory reduced current assets but not quick assets (cash, receivables, and marketable securities). Thus, the current ratio was reduced, and the quick ratio was unaffected.
   Answers (A) and (B) are incorrect because the quick ratio was not affected. Answer (C) is incorrect because working capital was decreased.

67. The issuance of new shares in a five-for-one split of common stock

   A. Decreases the book value per share of common stock.

   B. Increases the book value per share of common stock.

   C. Increases total shareholders' equity.

   D. Decreases total shareholders' equity.

The correct answer is (A). *(CMA 1280 4-5)*
   REQUIRED: The effect of a five-for-one split of common stock.
   DISCUSSION: Given that five times as many shares of stock are outstanding, the book value per share of common stock is one-fifth of the former value after the split.
   Answer (B) is incorrect because the book value per share is decreased. Answers (C) and (D) are incorrect because the stock split does not change the amount of shareholders' equity.

68. The issuance of serial bonds in exchange for an office building, with the first installment of the bonds due late this year,

   A. Decreases net working capital.

   B. Decreases the current ratio.

   C. Decreases the quick ratio.

   D. Affects all of the above as indicated.

The correct answer is (D). *(CMA 1280 4-6)*
   REQUIRED: The effect of issuing serial bonds with the first installment due late this year.
   DISCUSSION: The first installment is a current liability; thus the amount of current liabilities increases with no corresponding increase in current assets. The effect is to decrease working capital, the current ratio, and the quick ratio.
   Answer (A) is incorrect because the bond issuance would also decrease the current ratio and the quick ratio.
   Answer (B) is incorrect because the bond issuance would also decrease net working capital and the quick ratio.
   Answer (C) is incorrect because the bond issuance would also decrease net working capital and the quick ratio.

69. The early liquidation of a long-term note with cash affects the

   A. Current ratio to a greater degree than the quick ratio.

   B. Quick ratio to a greater degree than the current ratio.

   C. Current and quick ratio to the same degree.

   D. Current ratio but not the quick ratio.

The correct answer is (B). *(CMA 1280 4-7)*
   REQUIRED: The effect of an early liquidation of a long-term note with cash.
   DISCUSSION: The numerators of the quick and current ratios are decreased when cash is expended. Early payment of a long-term liability has no effect on the denominator (current liabilities). Since the numerator of the quick ratio, which includes cash, net receivables, and marketable securities, is less than the numerator of the current ratio, which includes all current assets, the quick ratio is affected to a greater degree.
   Answers (A), (C), and (D) are incorrect because the quick ratio is affected to a greater degree than the current ratio.

Questions 70 through 72 are based on the following information. The selected data below pertain to a company at December 31, 1996:

Quick assets	$208,000
Acid test ratio	2.6 to 1
Current ratio	3.5 to 1
Net sales for 1996	$1,800,000
Cost of sales for 1996	$990,000
Average total assets for 1996	$1,200,000

70. The company's current liabilities at December 31, 1996 amount to

A. $59,429

B. $80,000

C. $134,857

D. $187,200

The correct answer is (B). *(CIA 1190 IV-40)*
REQUIRED: Current liabilities at year-end.
DISCUSSION: The acid test ratio is equal to quick assets divided by current liabilities. Thus, current liabilities equal the $208,000 of quick assets divided by the 2.6 acid test ratio. Hence, current liabilities equal $80,000.
Answers (A), (C), and (D) are incorrect because the current liabilities at year-end are determined using the quick assets total and the acid test ratio: Current liabilities equal the quick assets divided by the acid test ratio.

71. The company's inventory balance at December 31, 1996, is

A. $72,000

B. $187,200

C. $231,111

D. $282,857

The correct answer is (A). *(CIA 1190 IV-41)*
REQUIRED: The inventory balance at year-end.
DISCUSSION: Inventory is equal to the difference between current assets and quick assets (assuming no prepaid expenses are included in current assets). The current ratio is equal to current assets divided by current liabilities. Accordingly, multiplying the current liabilities of $80,000 (determined in the previous question) by the current ratio of 3.5 gives current assets of $280,000. Subtracting the $208,000 of quick assets from the $280,000 of current assets results in an inventory balance of $72,000.
Answers (B), (C), and (D) are incorrect because inventory equals the difference between current assets and quick assets (assuming no prepaid expenses). Multiplying the current liabilities by the current ratio gives the current assets. Subtracting the quick assets from the current assets gives the inventory balance.

72. The company's asset turnover for 1996 is

A. .675

B. .825

C. 1.21

D. 1.50

The correct answer is (D). *(CIA 1190 IV-42)*
REQUIRED: The asset turnover for the year.
DISCUSSION: Asset turnover equals $1,800,000 of net sales divided by $1,200,000 of average total assets. The asset turnover for 1996 is therefore equal to 1.5.
Answers (A), (B), and (C) are incorrect because asset turnover equals net sales divided by average total assets.

CHAPTER TWENTY-SEVEN
PARTNERSHIP ACCOUNTING

Partnerships generally account for their profits (losses) in the same way as any other profit-oriented entity except for the accounts reflecting ownership of the entity. The partners' capital accounts take the place of capital stock and other related accounts.

27.1 Organization

1. A partnership is

A. Any association of two or more persons or entities.

B. An association of two or more persons to carry on, as co-owners, a business for a profit.

C. A separate legal entity for most legal purposes.

D. An entity created by following statutory requirements.

The correct answer is (B). *(Publisher)*
REQUIRED: The definition of a partnership.
DISCUSSION: A partnership, as defined by the Uniform Partnership Act, is an association of two or more persons to carry on, as co-owners, a business for a profit.
Answer (A) is incorrect because a partnership must be a profit-oriented business arrangement among co-owners. Answer (C) is incorrect because a partnership is viewed for most legal purposes as a group of individuals rather than a separate entity. Answer (D) is incorrect because no statutory requirements need be met to create a general partnership. A partnership may arise regardless of the intent of the parties when an arrangement satisfies the definition. However, specific statutory requirements must be followed to create a limited partnership.

2. When property other than cash is invested in a partnership, at what amount should the noncash property be credited to the contributing partner's capital account?

A. Fair value at the date of contribution.

B. Contributing partner's original cost.

C. Assessed valuation for property tax purposes.

D. Contributing partner's tax basis.

The correct answer is (A). *(CPA 594 F-35)*
REQUIRED: The credit to the contributing partner's capital account when noncash assets are invested.
DISCUSSION: The capital account should be credited for the current fair value of the assets at the date of the contribution. This approach is consistent with APB 29, which states that "in general, accounting for nonmonetary transactions should be based on the fair values of the assets (or services) involved." APB 21 specifically applies this principle to nonmonetary assets received in nonreciprocal transfers.
Answers (B), (C), and (D) are incorrect because fair value best reflects the economic substance of the transaction.

3. Roberts and Smith drafted a partnership agreement that lists the following assets contributed at the partnership's formation:

	Contributed by	
	Roberts	Smith
Cash	$20,000	$30,000
Inventory	--	15,000
Building	--	40,000
Furniture and equipment	15,000	--

The building is subject to a mortgage of $10,000, which the partnership has assumed. The partnership agreement also specifies that profits and losses are to be distributed evenly. What amounts should be recorded as capital for Roberts and Smith at the formation of the partnership?

	Roberts	Smith
A.	$35,000	$85,000
B.	$35,000	$75,000
C.	$55,000	$55,000
D.	$60,000	$60,000

The correct answer is (B). *(CPA 593 II-13)*
REQUIRED: The capital balances of partners at the formation of the partnership.
DISCUSSION: The balances should reflect the fair values of the assets contributed. The building should be valued net of the mortgage. Hence, the capital balances for Roberts and Smith are $35,000 ($20,000 + $15,000) and $75,000 ($30,000 + $15,000 + $40,000 – $10,000), respectively.
Answer (A) is incorrect because the building should be included net of the mortgage. Answer (C) is incorrect because the partners did not agree to divide capital equally. Answer (D) is incorrect because the partners did not agree to divide capital equally, and the building should be included net of the mortgage.

4. Partnership capital and drawing accounts are similar to the corporate

A. Paid-in capital, retained earnings, and dividends accounts.

B. Retained earnings account.

C. Paid-in capital and retained earnings accounts.

D. Preferred and common stock accounts.

The correct answer is (A). *(Publisher)*
REQUIRED: The corporate accounts similar to partnership capital and drawing accounts.
DISCUSSION: Partnership capital accounts make up the residual equity section of the partnership balance sheet. For corporations, the residual equity section consists of paid-in capital and retained earnings accounts. Partnership drawing accounts and corporate dividends accounts are nominal accounts that are closed to partnership capital and corporate retained earnings, respectively, at the end of each period.
Answers (B) and (C) are incorrect because drawing accounts are comparable to dividends accounts. Answer (D) is incorrect because drawing accounts are not like preferred and common stock accounts.

27.2 Distribution of Income

5. If the partnership agreement does not specify how income is to be allocated, profit and loss should be allocated

A. Equally.

B. In proportion to the weighted average of capital invested during the period.

C. Equitably so that partners are compensated for the time and effort expended on behalf of the partnership.

D. In accordance with an established ratio.

The correct answer is (A). *(Publisher)*
REQUIRED: The profit and loss allocation among partners absent a provision in the partnership agreement.
DISCUSSION: Common law and the Uniform Partnership Act both provide that profit and loss are to be distributed equally among partners unless the articles of copartnership provide otherwise. The equal distribution should be based on the number of partners rather than in proportion to the partners' capital balances.
Answers (B), (C), and (D) are incorrect because each may be a basis for allocation only if it is provided in the partnership agreement.

6. Closing entries of a partnership include entries to

A. Close the profit and loss and dividends declared accounts to retained earnings.

B. Close income and expense accounts to the profit and loss account and then to close the profit and loss and drawing accounts to the capital accounts.

C. Record distribution of cash to the partners.

D. Eliminate the capital accounts and record the distribution of assets to partners to effect the partnership termination and liquidation.

The correct answer is (B). *(Publisher)*
   REQUIRED: The entries required to close a partnership.
   DISCUSSION: Closing entries of a partnership are similar to those of any other enterprise. The income and expense accounts are closed to the P&L account (income summary). The P&L and drawing accounts are then closed to the partner capital accounts. The drawing account is similar to the corporate dividends account.
   Answer (A) is incorrect because the dividends declared and retained earnings accounts relate to corporations, not to partnerships. Answer (C) is incorrect because the distribution of cash to partners may occur at any time during the year and is not part of the year-end closing process. Answer (D) is incorrect because closing entries record the elimination of balances in the nominal accounts, not the termination and liquidation of the partnership.

7. During 1996, Young and Zinc maintained average capital balances in their partnership of $160,000 and $100,000, respectively. The partners receive 10% interest on average capital balances, and residual profit or loss is divided equally. Partnership profit before interest was $4,000. By what amount should Zinc's capital account change for the year?

A. $1,000 decrease.

B. $2,000 increase.

C. $11,000 decrease.

D. $12,000 increase.

The correct answer is (A). *(CPA 1195 F-23)*
   REQUIRED: The change in a partner's capital account.
   DISCUSSION: The partners are to receive 10% interest and then split the residual profit or loss. Because interest exceeds partnership profit before interest, the residual loss is $22,000 {[10% x ($160,000 + $100,000)] – $4,000}. Zinc's account is increased by $10,000 (10% x $100,000) and decreased by $11,000 (50% x $22,000 loss), a net decrease of $1,000.
   Answer (B) is incorrect because $2,000 is 50% of the partnership profit before interest. Answer (C) is incorrect because an $11,000 decrease does not include the $10,000 of interest owed to Zinc. Answer (D) is incorrect because a $12,000 increase equals 10% of capital plus 50% of the partnership profit before interest.

8. The partnership agreement of Reid and Simm provides that interest at 10% per year is to be credited to each partner on the basis of weighted-average capital balances. A summary of Simm's capital account for the year ended December 31, 1996 is as follows:

Balance, January 1	$140,000
Additional investment, July 1	40,000
Withdrawal, August 1	(15,000)
Balance, December 31	165,000

What amount of interest should be credited to Simm's capital account for 1996?

A. $14,000

B. $15,375

C. $16,500

D. $18,000

The correct answer is (B). *(CPA 591 II-3)*
   REQUIRED: The amount of interest credited to Simm's capital account.
   DISCUSSION: Simm's balance was $140,000 for 6 months, $180,000 for 1 month, and $165,000 for 5 months. Consequently, the weighted-average balance was $153,750, as shown below, and interest was $15,375 (10% x $153,750).

$$(6/12) \times \$140,000 = \$\ 70,000$$
$$(1/12) \times \$180,000 = \ \ 15,000$$
$$(5/12) \times \$165,000 = \ \underline{\ 68,750}$$
$$\underline{\$153,750}$$

Answer (A) is incorrect because $14,000 is based on the beginning balance. Answer (C) is incorrect because $16,500 is based on the year-end balance. Answer (D) is incorrect because $18,000 is based on the July 1 balance.

9. Yefim Geller and Maia Harden formed a partnership on January 2 and agreed to share profits 90% and 10%, respectively. Geller contributed capital of $25,000. Harden contributed no capital but has a specialized expertise and manages the firm full time. There were no withdrawals during the year. The partnership agreement provides that capital accounts are to be credited annually with interest at 5% of beginning capital; Harden is to be paid a salary of $1,000 a month; Harden is to receive a bonus of 20% of income calculated before deducting her salary, the bonus, and interest on both capital accounts; and bonus, interest, and Harden's salary are to be considered partnership expenses. The partnership annual income statement follows:

Revenues	$96,450
Expenses (including salary, interest, and bonus)	(49,700)
Net income	$46,750

What is Harden's bonus?

   A. $11,688

   B. $12,000

   C. $14,687

   D. $15,000

The correct answer is (D). *(CPA 575 I-11)*
REQUIRED: The amount of a bonus calculated as a percentage of income before salary and interest.
DISCUSSION: The bonus payable to Harden is equal to 20% of the income before deduction of her salary and interest on both capital accounts. Net income after deduction of salary, interest, and the bonus is $46,750. The solution requires adding back salary ($1,000 x 12 months), interest (.05 x $25,000), and the bonus (B) to the net income. The bonus (B) equals 20% of the sum of these items.

$$B = .2(\$46,750 + \$12,000 + \$1,250 + B)$$
$$B = .2(\$60,000 + B)$$
$$B = \$12,000 + .2B$$
$$.8B = \$12,000$$
$$B = \$15,000$$

Answer (A) is incorrect because $11,688 results from omitting salary and interest from the bonus computation. Answer (B) is incorrect because $12,000 is the amount of the salary. Answer (C) is incorrect because $14,687 results from omitting interest from the bonus computation.

Questions 10 and 11 are based on the following information. The Cor-Eng Partnership was formed on January 2, 1996. Under the partnership agreement, each partner has an equal initial capital balance accounted for under the goodwill method. Partnership net income or loss is allocated 60% to Cor and 40% to Eng. To form the partnership, Cor originally contributed assets costing $30,000 with a fair value of $60,000 on January 2, 1996, and Eng contributed $20,000 in cash. Drawings by the partners during 1996 totaled $3,000 by Cor and $9,000 by Eng. Cor-Eng's 1996 net income was $25,000.

10. Eng's initial capital balance in Cor-Eng is

A. $20,000

B. $25,000

C. $40,000

D. $60,000

The correct answer is (D). *(CPA 1192 II-48)*

REQUIRED: The initial capital balance credited to Eng based on the goodwill method.

DISCUSSION: If $60,000 (the fair value of Cor's original contribution) is 50% of the partnership capital, the total initial capital is $120,000, and goodwill of $40,000 should be recognized ($120,000 – $60,000 – $20,000 cash contributed by Eng). Thus, Eng's initial capital is $60,000.

Answer (A) is incorrect because $20,000 is Eng's initial cash contribution. Answer (B) is incorrect because $25,000 equals 50% of the cost of assets contributed by Cor plus the cash contributed by Eng. Answer (C) is incorrect because $40,000 is the goodwill recorded.

11. Cor's share of Cor-Eng's 1996 net income is

A. $15,000

B. $12,500

C. $12,000

D. $7,800

The correct answer is (A). *(CPA 1192 II-49)*

REQUIRED: The share of partnership net income allocable to Cor.

DISCUSSION: The partnership net income or loss is allocated 60% to Cor and 40% to Eng. Consequently, Cor's share is $15,000 (60% x $25,000).

Answer (B) is incorrect because $12,500 assumes an even division of net income. Answer (C) is incorrect because $12,000 equals Cor's share of net income minus Cor's drawings. Answer (D) is incorrect because $7,800 equals 60% of the excess of net income over total drawings.

12. Albert and Bernard are partners who share profits and losses in the ratio of 6:4, respectively. Albert's salary is $20,000 and Bernard's is $10,000. The partners also are paid interest on their average capital balances. In 1996, Albert received $10,000 of interest and Bernard $4,000. The profit and loss allocation is determined after deductions for the salary and interest payments. If Bernard's share of partnership income was $40,000 in 1996, what was the total partnership income?

A. $65,000

B. $95,000

C. $100,000

D. $109,000

The correct answer is (D). *(P. Lockett)*

REQUIRED: The partnership income given the distribution of income to one partner.

DISCUSSION: Given that Bernard's share of partnership income was $40,000, his share of residual income must have been $26,000 ($40,000 – $10,000 salary – $4,000 interest on his average capital balance). This amount represents 40% of the residual income, so total residual income was $65,000 ($26,000 ÷ 40%). Consequently, Albert's share of residual income was $39,000 (60% x $65,000). Moreover, Albert's share of partnership income was equal to $69,000 ($10,000 interest + $20,000 salary + $39,000 residual income). Total partnership income was therefore $109,000 ($69,000 + $40,000).

Answer (A) is incorrect because $65,000 was the residual income. Answer (B) is incorrect because $95,000 was the sum of residual income and salaries. Answer (C) is incorrect because $100,000 was the residual income assuming Bernard's share of residual income was $40,000.

13. The partnership agreement of Axel, Berg & Cobb provides for the year-end allocation of net income in the following order:

- First, Axel is to receive 10% of net income up to $100,000 and 20% over $100,000.
- Second, Berg and Cobb are each to receive 5% of the remaining income over $150,000.
- The balance of income is to be allocated equally among the three partners.

The partnership's 1996 net income was $250,000 before any allocations to partners. What amount should be allocated to Axel?

- A. $101,000
- B. $106,667
- C. $108,000
- D. $110,000

The correct answer is (C). *(CPA 1191 II-11)*
REQUIRED: The amount of partnership net income allocated to Axel.
DISCUSSION: Axel initially receives $40,000 {(10% x $100,000) + [20% x ($250,000 − $100,000)]}. The remaining income is $210,000 ($250,000 − $40,000). Of this amount, Berg and Cobb each receive $3,000 [5% x ($210,000 − $150,000)], a total of $6,000. The balance is allocated equally [($250,000 − $40,000 − $6,000) ÷ 3 = $68,000]. Thus, Axel receives a total of $108,000 ($40,000 + $68,000).
Answer (A) is incorrect because $101,000 omits the 10% of net income up to $100,000 paid to Axel. Answer (B) is incorrect because $106,667 assumes, in the calculation of amounts paid to Berg and Cobb, that the remaining income over $150,000 is $100,000. Answer (D) is incorrect because $110,000 omits the 5% of remaining income over $150,000 paid to both Berg and Cobb.

14. The Flat and Iron partnership agreement provides for Flat to receive a 20% bonus on profits before the bonus. Remaining profits and losses are divided between Flat and Iron in the ratio of 2 to 3, respectively. Which partner has a greater advantage when the partnership has a profit or when it has a loss?

	Profit	Loss
A.	Flat	Iron
B.	Flat	Flat
C.	Iron	Flat
D.	Iron	Iron

The correct answer is (B). *(CPA 1191 T-15)*
REQUIRED: The partner with a greater advantage when the partnership has a profit or when it has a loss.
DISCUSSION: When the partnership has a loss, Iron is allocated 60% and Flat 40%. Hence, Flat has the advantage when the partnership has a loss. When the partnership has a profit, Flat receives 20% plus 40% of the remaining 80%, a total of 52% [20% + (40% x 80%)]. Thus, Flat also has the advantage in this situation.
Answers (A), (C), and (D) are incorrect because Flat has the advantage in the case of either a profit or a loss.

15. Beck, the active partner in Beck & Cris, receives an annual bonus of 25% of partnership net income after deducting the bonus. For the year ended December 31, 1996, partnership net income before the bonus amounted to $300,000. Beck's 1996 bonus should be

- A. $56,250
- B. $60,000
- C. $75,000
- D. $100,000

The correct answer is (B). *(CPA 1189 II-20)*
REQUIRED: The amount of a bonus defined as a percentage of income after deduction of the bonus.
DISCUSSION: Calculating the bonus requires formulating an equation with one unknown. The bonus (B) is equal to 25% of net income ($300,000) minus the bonus.

$$
\begin{aligned}
B &= .25(NI − B) \\
B &= .25(\$300,000 − B) \\
B &= \$75,000 − .25B \\
1.25B &= \$75,000 \\
B &= \$60,000
\end{aligned}
$$

Answer (A) is incorrect because $56,250 is the result of taking 25% of $300,000, subtracting that amount from $300,000, and then multiplying the remainder by 25%. Answer (C) is incorrect because $75,000 is 25% of the net income before the bonus. Answer (D) is incorrect because $100,000 is 25% of the sum of net income plus the bonus.

27.3 Admission of New Partners

16. Abel and Carr formed a partnership and agreed to divide initial capital equally, even though Abel contributed $100,000 and Carr contributed $84,000 in identifiable assets. Under the bonus approach to adjust the capital accounts, Carr's unidentifiable asset should be debited for

- A. $46,000

- B. $16,000

- C. $8,000

- D. $0

The correct answer is (D). *(CPA 591 II-1)*

REQUIRED: The unidentifiable asset debited under the bonus approach.

DISCUSSION: The goodwill and the bonus methods are two means of adjusting for differences between the book value and the fair value of partnership net assets. When new partners are admitted under the goodwill method, assets are revalued. Under the bonus method, assets are not revalued. Instead, adjustments are made to partnership capital accounts. Consequently, total partnership capital differs between the two methods, and an unidentifiable asset may be debited under the goodwill but not the bonus method.

Answer (A) is incorrect because $46,000 is 50% of the balance in each partner's capital account under the bonus method. Answer (B) is incorrect because $16,000 is the unidentifiable asset recognized under the goodwill method. Answer (C) is incorrect because $8,000 is the amount transferred from Abel's capital account to Carr's capital account under the bonus method.

17. In the Adel-Brick partnership, Adel and Brick had a capital ratio of 3:1 and a profit and loss ratio of 2:1, respectively. The bonus method was used to record Colter's admittance as a new partner. What ratio would be used to allocate, to Adel and Brick, the excess of Colter's contribution over the amount credited to Colter's capital account?

- A. Adel and Brick's new relative capital ratio.

- B. Adel and Brick's new relative profit and loss ratio.

- C. Adel and Brick's old capital ratio.

- D. Adel and Brick's old profit and loss ratio.

The correct answer is (D). *(CPA 592 T-35)*

REQUIRED: The ratio used to allocate to the original partners the excess of the new partner's contribution over the amount credited to his/her capital account.

DISCUSSION: The bonus method makes no changes in existing asset accounts. Capital accounts of existing partners are adjusted in accordance with the old profit and loss ratio to reflect the bonus. The entry will be to debit cash (or the fair value of the property) contributed and to credit Colter's capital account for a lesser amount. The excess will be credited in the ratio of 2:1 to the original partners' capital balances.

Answers (A), (B), and (C) are incorrect because the bonus to the original partners should be allocated based on the old profit and loss ratio.

18. If a new partner acquires a partnership interest directly from the partners rather than from the partnership itself,

- A. No entry is required.

- B. The partnership assets must be revalued.

- C. The existing partners' capital accounts should be reduced and the new partner's account increased.

- D. The partnership has undergone a quasi-reorganization.

The correct answer is (C). *(Publisher)*

REQUIRED: The true statement about the acquisition of a partnership interest directly from the partners.

DISCUSSION: When an incoming partner deals directly with existing partners, no exchange takes place between the partnership and the new partner. The only accounts that need to be adjusted are the existing partners' capital accounts. Accordingly, the capital interest acquired by the new partner must be credited to his/her capital account with corresponding debits to the capital accounts of the other partners.

Answer (A) is incorrect because the new partner's equity in the partnership capital must be recorded. Answer (B) is incorrect because only the capital accounts need to be adjusted. Answer (D) is incorrect because quasi-reorganizations relate to corporations, not to partnerships.

19. Kern and Pate are partners with capital balances of $60,000 and $20,000, respectively. Profits and losses are divided in the ratio of 60:40. Kern and Pate decided to form a new partnership with Grant, who invested land valued at $15,000 for a 20% capital interest in the new partnership. Grant's cost of the land was $12,000. The partnership elected to use the bonus method to record the admission of Grant into the partnership. Grant's capital account should be credited for

A. $12,000

B. $15,000

C. $16,000

D. $19,000

The correct answer is (D). *(CPA 593 II-19)*
REQUIRED: The amount to be credited to a new partner's capital account.
DISCUSSION: This transaction is to be accounted for under the bonus method. The incoming partner invests $15,000 fair value of land for a 20% interest in the capital of the new partnership. Hence, the incoming partner's capital account should be credited for 20% of the total capital following the investment. The total capital following the investment by the new partner equals $95,000 ($60,000 + $20,000 + $15,000). Because 20% of this amount is $19,000, Grant's capital account should be credited for $19,000.
   Answer (A) is incorrect because $12,000 is the cost of the land. Answer (B) is incorrect because $15,000 is the fair value of the land. Answer (C) is incorrect because $16,000 equals 20% of the capital of the original partners.

20. William desires to purchase a one-fourth capital and profit and loss interest in the partnership of Eli, George, and Dick. The three partners agree to sell William 25% of their respective capital and profit and loss interests in exchange for a total payment of $40,000. The capital accounts and the respective percentage interests in profits and losses immediately before the sale to William follow:

	Capital Accounts	Percentage Interests in Profits and Losses
Eli	$ 80,000	60%
George	40,000	30
Dick	20,000	10
Total	$140,000	100%

All other assets and liabilities are fairly valued and implied goodwill is to be recorded prior to the acquisition by William. Immediately after William's acquisition, what should be the capital balances of Eli, George, and Dick, respectively?

A. $60,000; $30,000; $15,000

B. $69,000; $34,500; $16,500

C. $77,000; $38,500; $19,500

D. $92,000; $46,000; $22,000

The correct answer is (B). *(CPA 1175 II-2)*
REQUIRED: The capital balances of the original partners after sale of an interest and the recording of implied goodwill.
DISCUSSION: Assuming that all other assets and liabilities are fairly valued, the purchase of a 25% interest for $40,000 suggests that the value of the partnership is $160,000. The book value is $140,000, so goodwill of $20,000 must be allocated among the original partners prior to the sale in accordance with their agreed profit and loss ratio. The first journal entry to record the transaction consists of a debit to goodwill for $20,000 and credits to the respective capital accounts of the original partners according to their profit and loss ratio. The second journal entry includes a credit of $40,000 to William's capital account and debits to the accounts of Eli, George, and Dick to reflect a sale of 25% of their respective interests.

	Eli	George	Dick
Beginning capital	$80,000	$40,000	$20,000
Goodwill	12,000	6,000	2,000
	$92,000	$46,000	$22,000
Minus 25%	(23,000)	(11,500)	(5,500)
Ending capital	$69,000	$34,500	$16,500

   Answer (A) is incorrect because $60,000, $30,000, and $15,000 are 75% of the beginning balances of Eli, George, and Dick, respectively. These amounts do not include goodwill. Answer (C) is incorrect because ending balances of $77,000, $38,500, and $19,500 for Eli, George, and Dick, respectively, reflect total debits of $25,000, not $40,000. Answer (D) is incorrect because the ending capital balances should include a deduction for the 25% interest sold.

21. If E is the total capital of a partnership before the admission of a new partner, F is the total capital of the partnership after the admission of the new partner, G is the amount of the new partner's investment, and H is the amount of capital credited to the new partner, then there is

A. Goodwill to the new partner if F > (E + G) and H < G.

B. Goodwill to the old partners if F = E + G and H > G.

C. A bonus to the new partner if F = E + G and H > G.

D. Neither bonus nor goodwill if F > (E + G) and H > G.

The correct answer is (C). *(CPA 573 T-18)*
   REQUIRED: The true statement concerning the allocation of a bonus or goodwill.
   DISCUSSION: If the new partnership capital is equal to the sum of the old partnership capital and the new partner's contribution, and the new partner is credited with an amount of capital in excess of his/her contribution, a bonus must have been credited to the new partner.
   Answer (A) is incorrect because, if the new capital is greater than the old capital plus the new partner's investment, goodwill must have been recorded. However, if the new partner's capital is less than his/her contribution, a bonus must have been allocated to the old partners. A bonus and goodwill would not be recorded in the same transaction. Answer (B) is incorrect because, if the new capital is equal to the sum of the old capital and the new partner's contribution, no goodwill could have been recorded. Answer (D) is incorrect because, if the new capital exceeds the sum of the old capital and the new partner's contribution, goodwill must have been recorded.

22. Whit and Wes have a partnership with capital balances of $50,000 and $70,000, respectively. They wish to admit Alice into the partnership partly because of the prestige that she will bring to the partnership. If Alice purchases a one-fourth interest in capital and future profit and loss for $25,000, her capital account should reflect assigned goodwill in what amount?

A. $10,000

B. $11,250

C. $15,000

D. $25,000

The correct answer is (C). *(Publisher)*
   REQUIRED: The goodwill assigned to a new partner.
   DISCUSSION: The partnership capital is $120,000 prior to the admission of Alice, and she is to receive 25% of the capital for her contribution of cash and goodwill. Thus, $120,000 equals 75% of the new capital after her admission. The total capital will therefore be $160,000 ($120,000 ÷ .75), and Alice's capital account will be credited for $40,000. Because she contributed only $25,000 in cash, a debit to goodwill of $15,000 also is required.
   Answer (A) is incorrect because $10,000 is the difference between the cash contribution and the goodwill assigned. Answer (B) is incorrect because $11,250 equals 25% of the capital excluding goodwill, minus the cash contribution. Answer (D) is incorrect because $25,000 equals the cash contribution.

23. The capital accounts of the partnership of Newton, Sharman, and Jackson are presented below with their respective profit and loss ratios:

Newton	$139,200	1/2
Sharman	208,800	1/3
Jackson	96,000	1/6

Sidney was admitted to the partnership when he purchased, for $132,000, a proportionate interest from Newton and Sharman in the net assets and profits of the partnership. As a result, Sidney acquired a one-fifth interest in the net assets and profits of the firm. Assuming implied goodwill is not to be recorded, what is the combined gain realized by Newton and Sharman upon the sale of a portion of their interests in the partnership to Sidney?

A. $0

B. $43,200

C. $62,400

D. $88,800

The correct answer is (B). *(CPA 578 II-2)*
   REQUIRED: The combined gain realized by the sellers of a partnership interest if no goodwill is recorded.
   DISCUSSION: The problem is simpler than it appears at first glance because it states that Sidney acquired a net one-fifth interest in the firm directly from Newton and Sharman and no goodwill is to be recorded. In other words, this was a transaction between partners. The book value of the partnership is $444,000, one-fifth of which is $88,800. The difference between the selling price of $132,000 and the book value of a one-fifth interest is $43,200, the amount of the combined gain.
   Answer (A) is incorrect because the selling price exceeded book value. Hence, the partners realized a gain. Answer (C) is incorrect because $62,400 assumes that 20% of the book value of the combined interests of Newton and Sharman was sold, not 20% of the total book value. Answer (D) is incorrect because $88,800 is 20% of the book value of the firm.

Questions 24 and 25 are based on the following information. Presented below is the condensed balance sheet for the partnership of Lever, Polen, and Quint, who share profits and losses in the ratio of 4:3:3, respectively.

Cash	$ 90,000	Accounts payable	$210,000
Other assets	830,000	Quint, loan	30,000
Lever, loan	20,000	Lever, capital	310,000
	$940,000	Polen, capital	200,000
		Quint, capital	190,000
			$940,000

24. Assume that the assets and liabilities are fairly valued on the balance sheet and that the partnership decides to admit Fahn as a new partner with a 20% interest. No goodwill or bonus is to be recorded. How much should Fahn contribute in cash or other assets?

A. $140,000

B. $142,000

C. $175,000

D. $177,500

The correct answer is (C). *(CPA 1185 II-10)*
REQUIRED: The amount to be contributed by a new partner when neither goodwill nor bonus is to be recorded.
DISCUSSION: The book value of the partnership is the sum of the capital accounts of Lever, Polen, and Quint, i.e., $700,000. If Fahn is to have a 20% interest without recording goodwill or bonus, the current sum of the capital accounts will be equal to 80% of the book value after the admission of Fahn. Dividing the original book value of $700,000 by 80% yields the new book value after Fahn's admission ($875,000). The difference between the respective book values is the amount the new partner must contribute.

New partnership ($700,000 ÷ 80%)	$875,000
Old partnership	(700,000)
Fahn's contribution	$175,000

Answer (A) is incorrect because $140,000 equals 20% of the $700,000 book value. Answer (B) is incorrect because $142,000 equals 20% of the $700,000 book value plus the $10,000 excess of the Quint payable over the Lever receivable. Answer (D) is incorrect because $177,500 assumes that the $10,000 excess of the Quint payable over the Lever receivable is added to the sum of the existing capital accounts before being divided by 80%.

25. Assume that, instead of admitting a new partner, the partners decide to liquidate. How much of the available cash should be distributed to Lever if the other assets are sold for $700,000?

A. $230,000

B. $238,000

C. $258,000

D. $310,000

The correct answer is (B). *(CPA 1185 II-11)*
REQUIRED: The amount Lever should receive upon liquidation.
DISCUSSION: The $130,000 loss ($830,000 of other assets sold for $700,000) must be distributed to the capital accounts according to the profit-loss ratio of 4:3:3. Thus, $52,000 of loss ($130,000 x 40%) must be allocated to Lever's capital balance, which will reduce it from $310,000 to $258,000. Lever will receive $238,000 after the $20,000 loan is deducted.

Answer (A) is incorrect because $230,000 assumes that the receivable from Lever is added to the total loss to be allocated. Answer (C) is incorrect because $258,000 does not allow for the deduction of the receivable from Lever. Answer (D) is incorrect because $310,000 was Lever's original balance.

26. Max Blau and Harry Rubi are partners who share profits and losses in the ratio of 6:4, respectively. On May 1, 1996, their respective capital accounts were as follows:

Blau	$60,000
Rubi	50,000

On that date, Joe Lind was admitted as a partner with a one-third interest in capital and profits for an investment of $40,000. The new partnership began with total capital of $150,000. Immediately after Lind's admission, Blau's capital should be

A. $50,000

B. $54,000

C. $56,667

D. $60,000

The correct answer is (B). *(CPA 1189 II-19)*
REQUIRED: The capital balance of an existing partner following the admission of a new partner.
DISCUSSION: Following the entrance of Lind, the partnership began with total capital of $150,000. Lind received a one-third interest; therefore, his capital balance must be credited for $50,000 ($150,000 x 1/3). But Lind contributed only $40,000, so the $10,000 difference ($50,000 − $40,000) must be allocated to the existing partners in the ratio of 6:4. The result will be debits to the capital accounts of Blau and Rubi of $6,000 ($10,000 x 60%) and $4,000 ($10,000 x 40%), respectively. Consequently, immediately after Lind's admission, Blau's capital is $54,000 ($60,000 − $6,000).
Answer (A) is incorrect because $50,000 is Lind's capital balance. Answer (C) is incorrect because $56,667 assumes Blau's balance was reduced by one-third of the difference between Lind's balance and his contribution. Answer (D) is incorrect because $60,000 was Blau's original capital balance.

27. Dunn and Grey are partners with capital account balances of $60,000 and $90,000, respectively. They agree to admit Zorn as a partner with a one-third interest in capital and profits, for an investment of $100,000, after revaluing the assets of Dunn and Grey. Goodwill to the original partners should be

A. $0

B. $33,333

C. $50,000

D. $66,667

The correct answer is (C). *(CPA 591 II-2)*
REQUIRED: The goodwill to the original partners.
DISCUSSION: If a one-third interest is worth an investment of $100,000, the value of the partnership must be $300,000 ($100,000 ÷ 33 1/3%). The total of the existing capital balances and Zorn's investment is $250,000 ($60,000 + $90,000 + $100,000). Thus, goodwill is $50,000 ($300,000 − $250,000). The entry will be to debit cash (or property at fair value) for $100,000 and goodwill for $50,000, and to credit Zorn's capital balance for $100,000 and the capital balances of Dunn and Grey for a total of $50,000.
Answer (A) is incorrect because goodwill should be recognized and credited to the capital balances of Dunn and Grey. Answer (B) is incorrect because $33,333 is one-third of the new partner's investment. Answer (D) is incorrect because $66,667 is two-thirds of the new partner's investment.

28. Presented below is the condensed balance sheet of the partnership of Kane, Clark, and Lane, who share profits and losses in the ratio of 6:3:1, respectively:

Cash	$ 85,000
Other assets	415,000
	$500,000
Liabilities	$ 80,000
Kane, capital	252,000
Clark, capital	126,000
Lane, capital	42,000
	$500,000

Assume that the partners agree to sell to Bayer 20% of their respective capital and profit and loss interests for a total payment of $90,000. The payment by Bayer is to be made directly to the individual partners. The partners agree that implied goodwill is to be recorded prior to the acquisition by Bayer. What are the capital balances of Kane, Clark, and Lane, respectively, after the acquisition by Bayer?

A. $198,000; $99,000; $33,000

B. $201,600; $100,800; $33,600

C. $216,000; $108,000; $36,000

D. $270,000; $135,000; $45,000

The correct answer is (C). *(CPA 580 II-9)*
REQUIRED: The capital balances of the original partners after recording goodwill and selling an interest to a new partner.
DISCUSSION: If Bayer is to purchase a 20% interest in the partnership for $90,000, the partnership is estimated to be worth $450,000 ($90,000 ÷ 20%). But the sum of the original capital balances is only $420,000. Since goodwill is to be recognized prior to the purchase, $30,000 must be allocated to the capital accounts of the original partners. This amount will be shared in the profit and loss ratio of 6:3:1. The final step is to debit the capital accounts of the original partners for 20% of their respective interests and to credit the new partner's account for $90,000.

	Kane	Clark	Lane	Bayer
Beginning capital	$252	$126	$42	
Goodwill	18	9	3	
	$270	$135	$45	
Minus 20% sold	(54)	(27)	(9)	$90
Ending capital	$216	$108	$36	$90

Answer (A) is incorrect because $198,000, $99,000, and $33,000 equal the balances of Kane, Clark, and Lane, respectively, if $90,000 is allocated according to the profit-and-loss ratio from the partners' original balances to Bayer's account. Answer (B) is incorrect because $201,600, $100,800, and $33,600 are the original partners' balances if no goodwill is recognized and 20% of the original balances (20% x $420,000 = $84,000) is deemed to have been sold. Answer (D) is incorrect because $270,000, $135,000, and $45,000 are the original partners' balances after allocation of goodwill but before deduction of the interest sold.

27.4 Retirement of Partners

29. When Mill retired from the partnership of Mill, Yale, and Lear, the final settlement of Mill's interest exceeded Mill's capital balance. Under the bonus method, the excess

A. Was recorded as goodwill.

B. Was recorded as an expense.

C. Reduced the capital balances of Yale and Lear.

D. Had no effect on the capital balances of Yale and Lear.

The correct answer is (C). *(CPA 1194 F-35)*
REQUIRED: The treatment of the excess of the settlement of a partner's interest over the capital balance.
DISCUSSION: The bonus method reduces the capital accounts of the other partners because the bonus, that is, the excess of settlement value over the retiring partner's capital balance, is deemed to be paid to the withdrawing partner by the remaining partners.
Answer (A) is incorrect because goodwill is not recorded under the bonus method. Answers (B) and (D) are incorrect because the excess reduces the capital accounts; it is not an expense.

30. James Dixon, a partner in an accounting firm, decided to withdraw from the partnership. Dixon's share of the partnership profits and losses was 20%. Upon withdrawing from the partnership, he was paid $74,000 in final settlement of his interest. The total of the partners' capital accounts before recognition of partnership goodwill prior to Dixon's withdrawal was $210,000. After his withdrawal, the remaining partners' capital accounts, excluding their share of goodwill, totaled $160,000. The total agreed upon goodwill of the firm was

A. $120,000

B. $160,000

C. $210,000

D. $250,000

The correct answer is (A). *(CPA 580 II-4)*

REQUIRED: The amount of goodwill agreed upon prior to Dixon's withdrawal.

DISCUSSION: The balance in Dixon's account prior to recognition of goodwill was $50,000 ($210,000 – $160,000). Given that he was paid $74,000 upon withdrawing, Dixon's account must have been credited with $24,000 in goodwill. If his share of partnership profits and losses was 20%, the total agreed upon goodwill equals $120,000 ($24,000 ÷ 20%).

Answer (B) is incorrect because $160,000 was the sum of the remaining partners' capital balances exclusive of goodwill. Answer (C) is incorrect because $210,000 was the sum of the partners' capital balances prior to Dixon's withdrawal. Answer (D) is incorrect because $250,000 assumes that Dixon was assigned $50,000 of goodwill.

31. On June 30, 1996, the condensed balance sheet for the partnership of Jeannette Eddy, Nelson Fox, and Jacob Grimm, together with their respective profit and loss sharing percentages, was as follows:

Assets, net of liabilities	$320,000
Eddy, capital (50%)	$160,000
Fox, capital (30%)	96,000
Grimm, capital (20%)	64,000
	$320,000

Eddy decided to retire from the partnership and by mutual agreement is to be paid $180,000 out of partnership funds for her interest. Total goodwill implicit in the agreement is to be recorded. After Eddy's retirement, what are the capital balances of the other partners?

	Fox	Grimm
A.	$84,000	$56,000
B.	$102,000	$68,000
C.	$108,000	$72,000
D.	$120,000	$80,000

The correct answer is (C). *(CPA 1188 I-26)*

REQUIRED: The capital balances of the remaining partners following the retirement of a partner.

DISCUSSION: The $180,000 paid to Eddy represents Eddy's 50% interest in the partnership. The total value of the partnership is therefore $360,000 ($180,000 ÷ 50%), and the goodwill implicit in the retirement agreement is $40,000 ($360,000 total value – $320,000 net assets prior to the recording of goodwill). This $40,000 should be allocated 50% ($20,000) to Eddy, 30% ($12,000) to Fox, and 20% ($8,000) to Grimm. Fox's capital balance following the recording of goodwill is $108,000 ($96,000 + $12,000), and Grimm's is $72,000 ($64,000 + $8,000).

Answer (A) is incorrect because it assumes no goodwill is recognized, and the additional $20,000 paid to Eddy is deducted from the balances of Fox and Grimm in the ratio of 3:2. Answer (B) is incorrect because $20,000, not $10,000, of goodwill should be allocated to Fox and Grimm. Answer (D) is incorrect because the entire amount of goodwill should not be allocated to Fox and Grimm.

27.5 Liquidation of Partnerships

32. Prior to partnership liquidation, a schedule of possible losses is frequently prepared to determine the amount of cash that may be safely distributed to the partners. The schedule of possible losses

A. Consists of each partner's capital account plus loan balance, divided by that partner's P&L sharing ratio.

B. Shows the successive losses necessary to eliminate the capital accounts of partners (assuming no contribution of personal assets by the partners).

C. Indicates the distribution of successive amounts of available cash to each partner.

D. Assumes contribution of personal assets by partners unless there is a substantial presumption of personal insolvency by the partners.

The correct answer is (B). *(Publisher)*
REQUIRED: The true statement about a schedule of possible losses.
DISCUSSION: A schedule of possible losses presents a series of incremental losses to indicate the amount of loss in a liquidation that will eliminate each partner's capital account. The presumption is that losses or partners' capital deficits will not be repaid by individual partners. The schedule is used to determine the amount of cash that may be safely distributed to the individual partners without potential impairment of the rights of any party.
Answer (A) is incorrect because it describes the computation that determines the order in which partners' capital accounts will be eliminated by losses, not the amounts thereof. Answer (C) is incorrect because it describes a cash distribution schedule. Answer (D) is incorrect because the presumption (for the schedule) is that losses or deficits will not be repaid by individual partners.

33. Quinn, Rob, Sam, and Tod are partners sharing profits and losses equally. The partnership is insolvent and is to be liquidated. The status of the partnership and each partner is as follows:

	Partnership Capital Balance	Personal Assets (Exclusive of Partnership Interest)	Personal Liabilities (Exclusive of Partnership Interest)
Quinn	$ 15,000	$100,000	$40,000
Rob	10,000	30,000	60,000
Sam	(20,000)	80,000	5,000
Tod	(30,000)	1,000	28,000
	$(25,000)		

Assuming the Uniform Partnership Act applies, the partnership creditors

A. Must first seek recovery against Sam because he is solvent personally and has a negative capital balance.

B. Will not be paid in full regardless of how they proceed legally because the partnership assets are less than the partnership liabilities.

C. Will have to share Rob's interest in the partnership on a pro rata basis with his personal creditors.

D. Have first claim to the partnership assets before any partner's personal creditors have rights to the partnership assets.

The correct answer is (D). *(CPA 575 T-6)*
REQUIRED: The rights of partnership creditors under the Uniform Partnership Act.
DISCUSSION: The Uniform Partnership Act follows the legal concept of marshaling of assets. Accordingly, the assets of the partnership are made available first to the partnership creditors. Only after their claims are fully satisfied will the personal creditors of the partners be able to proceed against partnership assets. Similarly, the personal creditors of each general partner have first claim to the personal assets of that general partner. The Bankruptcy Reform Act of 1978, however, altered the marshaling of assets concept with regard to the personal assets of a bankrupt partner when the partnership is also bankrupt. The trustee of a bankrupt partnership shares pro rata with the other general unsecured creditors of a bankrupt general partner.
Answer (A) is incorrect because, after exhausting the partnership assets, the creditors must seek recovery against all partners in one legal proceeding; i.e., the partners are jointly liable. Answer (B) is incorrect because the partnership creditors ultimately have recourse to the personal assets of all the general partners. Answer (C) is incorrect because, under the UPA, the partnership creditors have first claim to the partnership assets.

34. The following condensed balance sheet is presented for the partnership of Axel, Barr, and Cain, who share profits and losses in the ratic of 4:3:3, respectively:

Cash	$100,000
Other assets	300,000
Total	$400,000
Liabilities	$150,000
Axel, capital	40,000
Barr, capital	180,000
Cain, capital	30,000
Total	$400,000

The partners agreed to dissolve the partnership after selling the other assets for $200,000. Upon dissolution of the partnership, Axel should have received

A. $0

B. $40,000

C. $60,000

D. $70,000

The correct answer is (A). *(CPA 589 II-5)*

REQUIRED: The amount Axel should receive upon liquidation.

DISCUSSION: When the other assets with a carrying value of $300,000 were sold for $200,000, a loss of $100,000 resulted. When this loss is distributed in the ratio of 4:3:3 to the capital balances, Axel's and Cain's capital balances are eliminated. Thus, upon dissolution of the partnership, neither Axel nor Cain will receive any cash. Of the $300,000 available ($100,000 cash on hand + $200,000 proceeds from the sale of other assets), $150,000 will be distributed to creditors (liabilities) and $150,000 to Barr.

	Axel	Barr	Cain
Beginning capital	$40,000	$180,000	$30,000
Loss on sale	(40,000)	(30,000)	(30,000)
Distribution of cash	$ 0	$150,000	$ 0

Answer (B) is incorrect because $40,000 is the beginning balance in Axel's capital account. Answer (C) is incorrect because $60,000 assumes that Axel is due 40% of the $150,000 available to distribute to partners. Answer (D) is incorrect because $70,000 is the sum of the capital balances of Axel and Cain.

35. On January 1, the partners of Cobb, Davis, and Eddy, who share profits and losses in the ratio of 5:3:2, respectively, decided to liquidate their partnership. On this date, the partnership condensed balance sheet was as follows:

Assets

Cash	$ 50,000
Other assets	250,000
	$300,000

Liabilities and Capital

Liabilities	$ 60,000
Cobb, capital	80,000
Davis, capital	90,000
Eddy, capital	70,000
	$300,000

On January 15, the first cash sale of other assets with a carrying amount of $150,000 realized $120,000. Safe installment payments to the partners were made the same date. How much cash should be distributed to each partner?

	Cobb	Davis	Eddy
A.	$15,000	$51,000	$44,000
B.	$40,000	$45,000	$35,000
C.	$55,000	$33,000	$22,000
D.	$60,000	$36,000	$24,000

The correct answer is (A). *(CPA 587 I-33)*

REQUIRED: The safe installment payments to partners after the initial sale of assets.

DISCUSSION: When the liquidation of a partnership proceeds over time, a conservative approach must be taken to the distribution of assets (cash) to partners. This conservative approach incorporates three steps. In the first step, a gain or loss realized from the actual sale of assets ($120,000 – $150,000 = $30,000 loss) is allocated to the partners' capital accounts in accordance with the profit and loss ratio. In the second step, remaining assets are assumed to have a fair market value of $0, which results in an assumed loss equal to their carrying value. For this partnership, an assumed loss of $100,000 ($250,000 of other assets – $150,000 of other assets sold) results. This assumed loss is also allocated to the partners' accounts in accordance with the profit and loss ratio. The third step is taken only if at least one of the partners' capital accounts has a deficit balance. If a deficit results, the conservative approach requires allocation of the deficit to the remaining partners' accounts. This step is not necessary in this example. The final balances in the partnership accounts equal the amounts of cash that may be distributed in a safe installment payment schedule.

	Cobb	Davis	Eddy
Beginning capital	$80,000	$90,000	$70,000
Realized loss ($30,000)	(15,000)	(9,000)	(6,000)
Assumed loss ($100,000)	(50,000)	(30,000)	(20,000)
Resulting capital	$15,000	$51,000	$44,000

Answer (B) is incorrect because a maximum of $110,000 in cash can be distributed given available cash of $170,000 and liabilities of $60,000. Answer (C) is incorrect because $55,000, $33,000, and $22,000 are equal to 50%, 30%, and 20%, respectively, of the excess of the total cash available over the liabilities. Answer (D) is incorrect because $60,000, $36,000, and $24,000 are equal to 50%, 30%, and 20%, respectively, of the $120,000 of cash realized from the sale of other assets.

36. The following condensed balance sheet is presented for the partnership of Smith and Jones, who share profits and losses in the ratio of 60:40, respectively:

Other assets	$450,000
Smith, loan	20,000
	$470,000
Accounts payable	$120,000
Smith, capital	195,000
Jones, capital	155,000
	$470,000

The partners have decided to liquidate. If the other assets are sold for $385,000, what amount of the available cash should be distributed to Smith?

A. $136,000

B. $156,000

C. $159,000

D. $195,000

The correct answer is (A). *(CPA 594 F-37)*
REQUIRED: The amount of cash to be distributed to a partner.
DISCUSSION: When the partnership sells the other assets, it must recognize a loss of $65,000 ($450,000 – $385,000). This loss must be allocated to the partners based on their loss ratio of 60:40. Thus, Smith's capital account is reduced to $156,000 [$195,000 – (60% x $65,000)] and Jones' to $129,000 [$155,000 – (40% x $65,000)]. The accounts payable are then paid, leaving assets of $265,000. Finally, the balance of the loan is subtracted from Smith's capital account balance, and each partner receives the balance in his/her capital account. Thus, Smith should receive $136,000 in cash ($156,000 – $20,000).
Answer (B) is incorrect because $156,000 results from not subtracting the loan from Smith's capital account.
Answer (C) is incorrect because $159,000 equals 60% of the assets remaining after the liabilities have been settled.
Answer (D) is incorrect because $195,000 equals Smith's unadjusted capital balance.

Questions 37 and 38 are based on the following information. December 31 balance sheet accounts of the Dan, Jim, and Mary partnership follow:

Cash	$ 20,000
Inventory	120,000
Plant assets - net	300,000
Accounts payable	170,000
Dan, capital	100,000
Jim, capital	90,000
Mary, capital	80,000

The partners' profit and loss percentages are Dan, 50%; Jim, 30%; and Mary, 20%.

On January 1 of the next year, the partners decide to liquidate the partnership. They agree that all cash should be distributed as soon as it becomes available during the liquidation process. They also agree that a cash predistribution plan is necessary to facilitate the distribution of cash.

37. The predistribution plan should be based on relative vulnerability to losses. For the Dan, Jim, and Mary partnership, the relative vulnerability should show that

A. Dan is the most vulnerable.

B. Dan is the least vulnerable.

C. Jim is the most vulnerable.

D. Jim is the least vulnerable.

The correct answer is (A). *(Publisher)*
REQUIRED: The true statement about relative vulnerability.
DISCUSSION: A cash predistribution plan is based on the partners' relative vulnerability to losses under the assumption that a partner would not repay a deficit capital balance. This vulnerability is determined by projecting the loss that, in accordance with the profit-loss ratio, would eliminate each partner's account. Because Dan would be allocated 50% of each loss, a projected loss of $200,000 ($100,000 capital balance ÷ 50%) would eliminate his account. Projected losses of $300,000 ($90,000 ÷ 30%) and $400,000 ($80,000 ÷ 20%) would eliminate Jim's and Mary's balances, respectively. Accordingly, Dan is the most vulnerable because his capital balance would be eliminated by the smallest projected loss.
Answers (B) and (C) are incorrect because Dan is the most vulnerable. Answer (D) is incorrect because Mary is the least vulnerable.

38. If cash of $220,000, including the $20,000 cash on hand, becomes available, it should be distributed in accordance with the cash predistribution plan. How much should be distributed to the creditors and partners respectively?

	Creditors	Dan	Jim	Mary
A.	$170,000	$25,000	$15,000	$10,000
B.	$170,000	$0	$26,000	$24,000
C.	$170,000	$10,000	$32,000	$8,000
D.	$170,000	$0	$18,000	$32,000

The correct answer is (D). *(Publisher)*

REQUIRED: The distribution of cash to partners and creditors using a cash predistribution plan.

DISCUSSION: To prepare a cash predistribution plan, the smallest projected loss that will eliminate the partner most vulnerable to losses is allocated in the profit-loss ratio. Then, based on the newly calculated capital balances, the projected loss that will eliminate the next most vulnerable partner is allocated. The projected loss and its allocation are based on a profit-loss ration adjusted for the previous elimination of more vulnerable partners.

Once projected losses to eliminate all partners are calculated, the plan sets forth a distribution of cash that prevents an overpayment to an insolvent partner. Liabilities to outside creditors must be satisfied before cash is distributed to the partners.

After satisfying the accounts payable of $170,000, $50,000 remains to be distributed to partners. The first $20,000 is to be distributed to Mary. Of the remaining $30,000, 60% ($18,000) will be distributed to Jim and 40% ($12,000) to Mary. The $50,000 should therefore be distributed $0 to Dan, $18,000 to Jim, and $32,000 to Mary.

Cash Distribution Plan

Projected Loss	Dan-50%	Jim-30%	Mary-20%
	$100,000	$90,000	$80,000
$200,000	(100,000)	(60,000)	(40,000)
	$ -0-	$30,000	$40,000
$ 50,000		(30,000)	(20,000)
		$ -0-	$20,000
$ 20,000			(20,000)
			$ -0-

Cash Distribution	Creditors	Dan	Jim	Mary
First $170,000	100%			
Next 20,000				100%
Next 50,000			60%	40%
Then		50%	30%	20%

Answer (A) is incorrect because a 5:3:2 distribution is appropriate only for amounts in excess of $240,000. Answers (B) and (C) are incorrect because the first $170,000 must go to creditors, the next $20,000 must go to Mary, and the remaining $30,000 should be distributed to Jim and Mary in the ratio of 3:2.

CHAPTER TWENTY-EIGHT
BUSINESS COMBINATIONS, CONSOLIDATIONS, AND BRANCH ACCOUNTING

This chapter emphasizes business combinations that are accomplished by a stock investment in one or more subsidiary (combining) companies by a parent (surviving) company. This arrangement requires consolidated working papers to be prepared for each set of consolidated financial statements. The alternative is to record the assets and liabilities of the acquired (combining) corporation(s) on the books of the parent (surviving) company. This latter approach requires the combining (consolidation) of the assets and liabilities to be undertaken only one time, at the date of the business combination.

At December 1, 1996, the FASB had a Proposed Statement of Financial Accounting Standards, *Consolidated Financial Statements: Policy and Procedures*, outstanding. If and when issued as a final statement, it will redefine the circumstances under which entities should be included in consolidated financial statements. It also will materially affect certain valuations reported in the consolidated financial statements.

The chapter also emphasizes the two different methods of accounting for a business combination: the pooling method and the purchase method. In addition, a combined purchase and pooling module is used to differentiate purchase and pooling accounting.

Branch accounting is covered since it is closely related to business combinations in that the same kinds of intercompany accounts exist on the home-office and branch books.

28.1 Basic Concepts

1. A business combination may be legally structured as a merger, a consolidation, or an investment in stock (also known as an acquisition). Which of the following describes a business combination that is legally structured as a merger?

A. The surviving company is one of the two combining companies.

B. The surviving company is neither of the two combining companies.

C. An investor-investee relationship is established.

D. A parent-subsidiary relationship is established.

The correct answer is (A). *(Publisher)*

REQUIRED: The characteristic of a business combination legally structured as a merger.

DISCUSSION: In a business combination legally structured as a merger, the assets and liabilities of one of the combining companies are transferred to the books of the other combining company (the surviving company). The surviving company continues to exist as a separate legal entity. The nonsurviving company ceases to exist as a separate entity. Its stock is canceled, and its books are closed.

Answer (B) is incorrect because it describes a consolidation, in which a new firm is formed to account for the assets and liabilities of the combining companies. Answers (C) and (D) are incorrect because they describe an investment in stock. A parent-subsidiary relationship exists when the investor company holds more than 50% of the outstanding stock of the investee company.

2. Business combinations are accomplished either through a direct acquisition of assets and liabilities by a surviving corporation or by stock investments in one or more companies. A parent-subsidiary relationship always arises from a

A. Tax-free reorganization.

B. Vertical combination.

C. Horizontal combination.

D. Greater than 50% stock investment in another company.

The correct answer is (D). *(Publisher)*
REQUIRED: The situation creating a parent-subsidiary relationship.
DISCUSSION: A parent-subsidiary relationship arises from an effective investment in the stock of another enterprise in excess of 50%. The financial statements for the two companies ordinarily should be presented on a consolidated basis. To the extent the corporation is not wholly owned, a minority interest is presented.
Answer (A) is incorrect because a tax-free reorganization may or may not be a combination, and it may or may not result in a parent-subsidiary relationship. Answers (B) and (C) are incorrect because vertical and horizontal combinations may also be accomplished by a merger or a consolidation, in which case the combining companies become one. A vertical combination combines a supplier and customer. A horizontal combination combines competitors.

3. A business combination legally structured as a merger has one set of books and accounting records (the surviving company's) to account for the combined (consolidated) operations. On the other hand, if the combination is accomplished by a stock investment, each of the combining companies continues to maintain its individual books and accounting records. For a stock investment, the books and accounting records of the consolidated organization are usually

A. Maintained by the parent separately from the surviving company's books.

B. Prepared in worksheet form each time consolidated statements are prepared.

C. Maintained by each organization in the same manner that branch-home office accounting is accomplished.

D. Maintained by the subsidiary corporation.

The correct answer is (B). *(Publisher)*
REQUIRED: The true statement about the books and accounting records of a consolidated entity created by a stock investment.
DISCUSSION: No formal books are kept and no formal journal entries are prepared for a consolidated entity created by a stock investment. When consolidated financial statements are prepared, the normal procedure is to start with the output of the formal accounting systems of the parent and the subsidiary and, on a worksheet only, prepare the informal (worksheet) adjusting and elimination entries necessary to prepare the consolidated financial statements. These consolidating adjusting entries must be cumulative because previous worksheet entries were not recorded in the accounts of either the parent or the subsidiary.
Answers (A), (C), and (D) are incorrect because a separate (formal) set of accounting records is usually not maintained for a consolidated entity.

4. Mill Corp. acquired Vore Corp. in a business combination. At the acquisition date, Vore's plant and equipment had a carrying amount of $750,000 and a fair value of $875,000. What amount should the combined entity report for Vore's plant and equipment under each of the following methods at the date of acquisition?

	Pooling of Interests	Purchase
A.	$750,000	$875,000
B.	$750,000	$750,000
C.	$875,000	$875,000
D.	$875,000	$750,000

The correct answer is (A). *(CPA 1191 II-17)*
REQUIRED: The treatment of plant and equipment under different methods of accounting for a business combination.
DISCUSSION: Under the pooling-of-interests method of accounting for a business combination, assets and liabilities are recorded by the combined entity at their carrying (book) value.
Under the purchase method, the fair values of assets and liabilities acquired in the transaction should be used to record values in the surviving company's books.
Answers (B), (C), and (D) are incorrect because a pooling is recorded at book value and a purchase at fair value.

5. Which of the following statements is supportive of the pooling-of-interests method in accounting for a business combination?

    A.   Bargaining between the parties is based on current values for assets and liabilities.

    B.   Shareholder groups remain intact but combine.

    C.   Goodwill is ordinarily a part of any acquisition.

    D.   A portion of the total cost is assigned to individual assets acquired on the basis of their fair value.

The correct answer is (B). *(CPA 1193 T-13)*
    REQUIRED: The statement that supports the pooling-of-interests method in a business combination.
    DISCUSSION: One of the 12 requirements for the pooling-of-interests method is that the ratio of ownership among individual shareholders remains the same. Hence, the shareholder groups remain intact but combine.
    Answer (A) is incorrect because book values are used to account for a pooling. Answer (C) is incorrect because goodwill is recorded when the purchase method is used. Answer (D) is incorrect because book values are used to record assets.

6. When a parent-subsidiary relationship exists, consolidated financial statements are prepared in recognition of the accounting concept of

    A.   Reliability.

    B.   Materiality.

    C.   Legal entity.

    D.   Economic entity.

The correct answer is (D). *(CPA 593 T-5)*
    REQUIRED: The accounting concept recognized in consolidated financial statements.
    DISCUSSION: Consolidated financial statements should reflect the economic activities of a business enterprise measured without regard to the boundaries of the legal entity. Accounting information pertains to a business enterprise, the boundaries of which are not necessarily those of the legal entity. For instance, a parent and subsidiary are legally separate but are treated as a single business enterprise in consolidated statements.
    Answer (A) is incorrect because reliability reflects the quality of information assuring that it is reasonably free from error and bias and faithfully represents what it purports to represent. Answer (B) is incorrect because materiality requires reporting of information that has a value significant enough to affect decisions of those using the financial statements. Answer (C) is incorrect because the boundaries of the legal entity are disregarded in the preparation of consolidated financial statements.

7. Which of the following is a potential abuse that can arise when a business combination is accounted for as a pooling of interests?

    A.   Assets of the investee may be overvalued when the price paid by the investor is allocated among specific assets.

    B.   Liabilities may be undervalued when the price paid by the investor is allocated to the specific liabilities.

    C.   An undue amount of cost may be assigned to goodwill, thus potentially allowing for an overstatement of pooled earnings.

    D.   Earnings of the pooled entity may be increased because of the combination only and not as a result of efficient operations.

The correct answer is (D). *(CPA 580 T-14)*
    REQUIRED: The potential abuse from accounting for a business combination as a pooling of interests.
    DISCUSSION: Because a pooling of interests is accounted for as a combining of ownership interests rather than an acquisition, the net income of the pooled entity must be restated to include the income of all of the constituent companies. There is no accounting recognition of the value of the stock exchanged, so earnings of the pooled entity would increase even if the combination were economically inefficient.
    Answers (A) and (B) are incorrect because the pooling-of-interests method does not allocate fair values among specific assets and/or liabilities but combines the assets and liabilities at their book values. Answer (C) is incorrect because the pooling-of-interests method does not give rise to goodwill recognition.

8. If a business combination is accounted for as a pooling of interests, which one of the following items does not need to be disclosed in notes to the financial statements?

    A. Details of an increase or decrease in retained earnings from changing the fiscal year of a combining company.

    B. Details of the results of operations of the previously separate companies, for the period before the combination is consummated, that are included in the current combined net income.

    C. Description and number of shares of stock issued in the business combination.

    D. Description of the plan for amortization of goodwill resulting from the combination.

The correct answer is (D). *(Publisher)*
    REQUIRED: The financial statement disclosure not required in a pooling of interests.
    DISCUSSION: In a pooling of interests, the assets and liabilities of the combining companies are brought together at their book values. Accordingly, recognition or disclosure of goodwill is not appropriate.
    Answer (A) is incorrect because, if the pooling of interests results in changing the fiscal year of a combining company, details of any changes must be disclosed in shareholders' equity for the period excluded from the reported results of operations. Answer (B) is incorrect because a combined corporation should disclose the revenue, extraordinary items, and net income of each separate company from the beginning of the period to the date the combination is consummated in notes to financial statements. Answer (C) is incorrect because details of the stock issued in a business combination must be disclosed.

9. When a business combination occurs that is accounted for by the purchase method, what pro forma data should be disclosed as supplemental information in the financial statements of the acquiring company?

    A. Contingent payments, options, or commitments specified in the acquisition agreement.

    B. If comparative statements are presented, the results of operations for all periods reported as though the companies had combined at the beginning of the earliest period.

    C. If comparative financial statements are presented, the results of operations for the immediately preceding period as though the companies had combined at the beginning of that period.

    D. The period for which the results of operations of the acquired company are included on the income statement of the acquiring corporation.

The correct answer is (C). *(Publisher)*
    REQUIRED: The pro forma disclosure required.
    DISCUSSION: APB 16, *Business Combinations*, requires pro forma disclosure of the results of operations (1) for the current period, as though the companies had combined at the beginning of the period, and (2) for the immediately preceding period, if comparative financial statements are presented. SFAS 79, *Elimination of Certain Disclosures for Business Combinations by Nonpublic Enterprises*, eliminates these pro forma disclosures for nonpublic entities.
    Answers (A) and (D) are incorrect because each is a required disclosure of actual data. Answer (B) is incorrect because disclosure is required only for the immediately preceding period.

10. Penn, Inc., a manufacturing company, owns 75% of the common stock of Sell, Inc., an investment company. Sell owns 60% of the common stock of Vane, Inc., an insurance company. In Penn's consolidated financial statements, should consolidation accounting or equity method accounting be used for Sell and Vane?

    A. Consolidation used for Sell and equity method used for Vane.

    B. Consolidation used for both Sell and Vane.

    C. Equity method used for Sell and consolidation used for Vane.

    D. Equity method used for both Sell and Vane.

The correct answer is (B). *(CPA 1192 T-31)*
    REQUIRED: The method of accounting used by a company that has a direct controlling interest in one entity and an indirect interest in another.
    DISCUSSION: SFAS 94, *Consolidation of All Majority-Owned Subsidiaries*, amended ARB 51, *Consolidated Financial Statements*, to require that all companies in which a parent has a controlling financial interest through direct or indirect ownership of a majority voting interest be consolidated. Exceptions are allowed when control is likely to be temporary or does not rest with the majority owner. Penn has direct control of Sell and indirect control of Vane and should consolidate both.
    Answers (A), (C), and (D) are incorrect because Penn should consolidate both Sell and Vane.

11. Consolidated financial statements are typically prepared when one company has a controlling financial interest in another unless

A.   The subsidiary is a finance company.

B.   The fiscal year-ends of the two companies are more than 3 months apart.

C.   Such control is likely to be temporary.

D.   The two companies are in unrelated industries, such as manufacturing and real estate.

The correct answer is (C). *(CPA 594 F-7)*
REQUIRED: The exception to consolidation.
DISCUSSION: SFAS 94 requires consolidation of all majority-owned subsidiaries unless control is temporary or does not rest with the majority owner.

Answers (A), (B), and (D) are incorrect because the nature of the subsidiary's business, a difference in fiscal periods, and whether the parent and subsidiary are in related industries are irrelevant under SFAS 94.

12. A 70%-owned subsidiary company declares and pays a cash dividend. What effect does the dividend have on the retained earnings and minority interest balances in the parent company's consolidated balance sheet?

A.   No effect on either retained earnings or minority interest.

B.   No effect on retained earnings and a decrease in minority interest.

C.   Decreases in both retained earnings and minority interest.

D.   A decrease in retained earnings and no effect on minority interest.

The correct answer is (B). *(CPA 1192 T-34)*
REQUIRED: The effect on retained earnings and minority interest balances in the parent company's consolidated balance sheet after a subsidiary's payment of a cash dividend.
DISCUSSION: The parent's investment in subsidiary account and its proportionate share of the subsidiary's shareholders' equity accounts, which include retained earnings, are eliminated in a consolidation. The remainder of the subsidiary's shareholders' equity is reported separately as the minority interest. Thus, consolidated retained earnings is essentially the parent's retained earnings at year-end. The subsidiary's cash dividend reduces its retained earnings balance and therefore the minority interest but not the parent's.

Answers (A), (C), and (D) are incorrect because cash dividends from a subsidiary have no effect on retained earnings but decrease the minority interest.

13. When a parent company sells part of the stock it holds in a subsidiary, it should account for the difference at the time of sale between the selling price and the carrying amount of the stock sold as which of the following?

A.   A gain or loss.

B.   A direct adjustment to paid-in capital.

C.   A direct adjustment to retained earnings.

D.   Either a gain or loss or a direct adjustment to paid-in capital.

The correct answer is (A). *(Publisher)*
REQUIRED: The proper treatment of the difference between the selling price and the carrying value in a sale of stock by a parent company.
DISCUSSION: When an investor sells part of the stock it holds in an investee, APB 18, *Equity Method for Investments in Common Stock*, requires that the difference at the time of the sale between the selling price and the carrying value of the stock sold be accounted for as a gain or loss. This principle also applies to the sale of a subsidiary's stock by a parent.

Answers (B), (C), and (D) are incorrect because the difference should be accounted for as a gain or loss.

14. Combined statements may be used to present the results of operations of

	Companies under Common Management	Commonly Controlled Companies
A.	No	Yes
B.	Yes	No
C.	No	No
D.	Yes	Yes

The correct answer is (D). *(CPA 593 T-8)*
REQUIRED: The condition(s) in which combined financial statements are appropriate.
DISCUSSION: ARB 51 states that combined (as distinguished from consolidated) statements of commonly controlled companies may be more meaningful than their separate statements. For example, combined statements may be used (1) to combine the statements of several companies with related operations when one individual owns a controlling interest in them, (2) to present financial position and results of operations of a group of unconsolidated subsidiaries, or (3) to combine the statements of companies under common management.

Answers (A), (B), and (C) are incorrect because common management or common control justifies use of combined statements.

15. At December 31, 1996, Spud Corp. owned 80% of Jenkins Corp.'s common stock and 90% of Thompson Corp.'s common stock. Jenkins' 1996 net income was $100,000 and Thompson's 1996 net income was $200,000. Thompson and Jenkins had no intercompany ownership or transactions during 1996. Combined 1996 financial statements are being prepared for Thompson and Jenkins in contemplation of their sale to an outside party. In the combined income statement, combined net income should be reported at

A. $210,000

B. $260,000

C. $280,000

D. $300,000

The correct answer is (D). *(CPA 1188 I-58)*
REQUIRED: The combined net income.
DISCUSSION: Combined financial statements are appropriate when a relationship such as common management or common ownership exists for two or more companies not subject to consolidation. In similar fashion to consolidated net income, combined net income should be recorded at the total of the net income reported by the combined companies, adjusted for any intercompany profits or losses. In the combined income statement issued for Jenkins Corp. and Thompson Corp., net income should be reported at $300,000 ($100,000 + $200,000).

Answer (A) is incorrect because $210,000 is 70% of the combined net income. Answer (B) is incorrect because $260,000 equals 80% of the net income of Jenkins and 90% of the net income of Thompson. Answer (C) is incorrect because $280,000 equals 80% of the net income of Jenkins and 100% of Thompson's net income.

28.2 Criteria for Pooling

16. APB Opinion No. 16, *Business Combinations*, contains conditions that must be met in order for the pooling-of-interests method of accounting to be used. Which one of the following is not a condition that must be met to use the pooling-of-interests method to record a business combination?

A. No constituent company may have more than a 10% ownership of the outstanding voting common stock of another constituent company.

B. At least 90% of the combinee's outstanding voting common stock must be exchanged for the combinor's majority voting common stock.

C. No additional capital stock must be contingently issuable to former shareholders of a combinee after a combination has been initiated.

D. A majority of the officers of the combinee company must also be officers in the combined enterprise after the combination.

The correct answer is (D). *(CMA 1291 2-7)*
REQUIRED: The item not a condition that must be met for the pooling-of-interests method to be used.
DISCUSSION: According to APB 16, the 12 conditions are grouped into three categories:

Combining Companies

1. Each combining company is autonomous.
2. Each company is independent of the others.

Combining Interests

1. A combination is a single transaction or is completed within 1 year of initiation.
2. An issuance is made solely of common stock for at least 90% of the outstanding voting common stock of the other company.
3. No change in stockholders' equities is made in contemplation of the combination.
4. No reacquisition of more than a normal number of shares prior to the combination occurs.
5. The ratio of ownership among individual stockholders remains the same.
6. Voting rights of stockholders are not restricted.
7. No contingent stock issuances, payments, etc., exist after the combination is consummated.

Absence of Planned Transactions

1. There are no plans to retire any of the common stock issued in the combination.
2. No special arrangements exist to benefit former stockholders.
3. There is no intention to dispose of significant assets, except duplicate facilities or excess capacity, for 2 years.

Thus, APB 16 has no provision regarding the officers of the combined companies.

Answer (A) is incorrect because APB 16 limits common ownership of the constituent companies. Answer (B) is incorrect because APB 16 states that at least 90% of the combinee's outstanding voting common stock must be exchanged for the combinor's majority voting common stock. Answer (C) is incorrect because APB 16 states that no additional capital stock must be contingently issuable to former shareholders of a combinee after a combination has been initiated.

17. The disclosures required for a business combination concluded in the current year and accounted for as a pooling of interests include all of the following except

    A. A description of the stock transaction along with the number of shares of stock issued in the combination.

    B. The names and descriptions of the enterprises combined, except an enterprise whose name is carried forward to the combined enterprise.

    C. The names of the finance companies cooperating in or providing funds to the acquiring company to facilitate the acquisition.

    D. Detailed operational results of the previously separate enterprises for the period before the combination that are included in the current combined net income.

The correct answer is (C). *(CMA 693 2-11)*
    REQUIRED: The item not a required disclosure for a pooling of interests concluded during the current year.
    DISCUSSION: Under APB 16, the disclosures made in the statements for the year in which a pooling of interests occurred should include the items in answers (A), (B), and (D) as well as the method of accounting for the combination, descriptions of the nature of the adjustments of net assets required for the combining companies to adopt the same accounting principles and of the effects on net income previously reported, and reconciliations of revenue and earnings previously reported by the company that issued stock in the combination with the combined amounts in the current statements. There is no requirement under APB 16 to provide the names of the finance companies cooperating in or providing funds to the acquiring company to facilitate the acquisition.
    Answer (A) is incorrect because a description of the stock transaction should be disclosed in the consolidated financial statements. Answer (B) is incorrect because the names and descriptions of the combining enterprises should be disclosed in the consolidated financial statements. Answer (D) is incorrect because financial statements of prior periods should be reported for the pooled entities.

18. For the past several years, M.F.S. Company has invested in the common stock of Annabelle Company. M.F.S. currently owns approximately 13% of the total of Annabelle's outstanding voting common stock. Recently, managements of the two companies have discussed a possible combination of the two entities. If they do decide to combine, the resulting combination should be accounted for as a

    A. Pooling of interests.

    B. Purchase.

    C. Part purchase, part pooling.

    D. Joint venture.

The correct answer is (B). *(Publisher)*
    REQUIRED: The accounting for a business combination, given 13% ownership of one combining entity by the other.
    DISCUSSION: If a business combination meets 12 conditions, it should be accounted for under the pooling-of-interests method. If any one of these conditions is not met, however, the purchase method must be used. One condition is that the combining companies may hold as intercorporate investments no more than 10% of the outstanding voting common stock of any combining company as of the dates of initiation and consummation of the combination. M.F.S. already owns 13% of Annabelle, and the combination will not meet this ownership test.
    Answer (A) is incorrect because the ownership test is not met. Answer (C) is incorrect because accounting for a business combination as part purchase and part pooling is not allowed. Answer (D) is incorrect because a business combination cannot be accounted for as a joint venture.

19. In order to report a business combination as a pooling of interests, the minimum amount of an investee's common stock that must be acquired during the combination period in exchange for the investor's common stock is

    A. 51%

    B. 80%

    C. 90%

    D. 100%

The correct answer is (C). *(CPA 590 T-32)*
    REQUIRED: The minimum investment for a business combination to qualify as a pooling of interests.
    DISCUSSION: One of the 12 conditions to be satisfied before a business combination is eligible for the pooling-of-interests method is that a corporation offer and issue only common stock in exchange for substantially all (90% or more) of the outstanding voting common stock of another company. The measurement date is the date the business combination is consummated.
    Answers (A), (B), and (D) are incorrect because the applicable percentage is 90%.

20. Dan Corporation offered to exchange two shares of Dan common stock for each share of Boone Company common stock. On the initiation date, Dan held 3,000 shares of Boone common and Boone held 500 shares of Dan common. In later cash transactions, Dan purchased 2,000 shares of Boone common and Boone purchased 2,500 shares of Dan common. At all times, the number of common shares outstanding was 1,000,000 for Dan and 100,000 for Boone. After consummation, Dan held 100,000 Boone common shares. How many shares are considered exchanged in determining whether this combination should be accounted for by the pooling-of-interests method?

A.   100,000

B.   95,000

C.   93,500

D.   92,000

The correct answer is (C). *(CPA 572 II-28)*

REQUIRED: The number of a combining company's shares assumed exchanged in determining whether the pooling method is appropriate.

DISCUSSION: The 100,000 shares actually held at the date of consummation must be reduced by the Boone shares owned by Dan at the date of initiation (3,000) and the shares purchased by Dan subsequent to the date of initiation but before the date of consummation (2,000). Also, the 500 shares of Dan owned by Boone at the initiation date and the 2,500 shares of Dan purchased during the period between initiation and consummation must be converted to equivalent shares of Boone and excluded.

Given that Dan exchanged two shares for one share of Boone, each share of Dan owned by Boone is equivalent to 1/2 share of Boone owned by Dan. To convert Boone's 3,000 shares of Dan into an equivalent of Boone owned by Dan, divide by 2.

Boone outstanding shares	100,000
Deduct: Boone shares owned by Dan	(3,000)
Boone shares purchased by Dan	(2,000)
Equivalent Boone shares	
Owned by Boone (500 ÷ 2)	(250)
Purchased by Boone (2,500 ÷ 2)	(1,250)
Boone shares assumed exchanged	93,500

Answer (A) is incorrect because 100,000 is the amount of Boone shares held, not exchanged. Answer (B) is incorrect because 95,000 does not exclude the Boone equivalent of the Dan shares held by Boone. Answer (D) is incorrect because 92,000 assumes that one share of Dan equals one share of Boone.

21. Which of the following conditions would cause a business combination to be accounted for by the purchase method?

A.   The combined corporation intends to dispose of duplicate facilities within 1 year of the combination.

B.   Cash is to be used to acquire 2% of the outstanding stock of one of the combining companies.

C.   After the combination is consummated, one of the combining companies will be a subsidiary of another combining company.

D.   Before the combination is consummated, one of the combining companies holds 15% of the outstanding stock of another of the combining companies.

The correct answer is (D). *(CPA 1192 T-32)*

REQUIRED: The condition that would cause a business combination to be accounted for by the purchase method.

DISCUSSION: If a business combination meets 12 conditions, it should be accounted for under the pooling-of-interests method. If any one of these conditions is not met, however, the purchase method must be used. One condition is that the combining companies may hold as intercorporate investments no more than 10% of the outstanding voting common stock of any combining company as of the dates of initiation and consummation of the combination.

Answer (A) is incorrect because pooling is not permissible unless there is no intention to dispose of significant assets, except duplicate facilities or excess capacity, for 2 years. Answer (B) is incorrect because pooling may be used. The condition that one corporation offer and issue common stock in exchange for substantially all of the outstanding voting common stock of another company is met when 90% or more is considered to be exchanged. Answer (C) is incorrect because pooling is applicable to the parent-subsidiary relationship.

28.3 Pooling Accounting--Implementation

22. Kiwi, Inc.'s planned combination with Mori Co. on January 1, 1996 can be structured as either a purchase or a pooling of interests. In a purchase, Kiwi would acquire Mori's identifiable net assets for more than their book values. These book values approximate fair values. Mori's assets consist of current assets and depreciable noncurrent assets. Ignoring costs required to effect the combination and income tax expense, how would the combined entity's 1996 net income under purchase accounting compare with that under pooling-of-interests accounting?

- A. Less than pooling.
- B. Equal to pooling.
- C. Greater than pooling.
- D. Not determinable from information given.

The correct answer is (A). *(CPA 594 F-51)*
REQUIRED: The comparison of purchase accounting and pooling accounting net income.
DISCUSSION: Because this combination occurred on the first day of the calendar and fiscal year, the combined results of operations will include the results of operations for all of 1996 for both companies regardless of the method of accounting chosen. However, purchase accounting will yield a lower net income than pooling accounting. The former method records depreciable assets acquired at more than their amounts on Mori's books. Hence, depreciation charges will be higher and net income lower under purchase accounting.
Answers (B), (C), and (D) are incorrect because purchase accounting net income is lower.

23. When a parent corporation acquires a new subsidiary and the pooling-of-interests method is used to account for the combination, the retained earnings balance of the combined entity immediately after acquisition is normally equal to

- A. The retained earnings balance of the parent company immediately prior to the acquisition.
- B. The sum of the retained earnings balances of the combining companies.
- C. The sum of the retained earnings balances of the combining companies plus the amount of the goodwill originating from the business combination.
- D. The retained earnings balance of the parent company immediately prior to acquisition plus the amount of goodwill originating from the business combination.

The correct answer is (B). *(CIA 591 IV-42)*
REQUIRED: The retained earnings balance after a pooling of interests.
DISCUSSION: In a pooling of interests, the retained earnings balance of the surviving entity should be equal to the total of retained earnings of the combining entities except in certain circumstances, such as when an allocation of retained earnings was made to contributed capital or when intercompany transactions must be eliminated.
Answer (A) is incorrect because the retained earnings of the subsidiary should be included. Answer (C) is incorrect because no goodwill is recognized in a pooling of interests. Answer (D) is incorrect because the subsidiary's retained earnings should be included, and goodwill is not recognized in a pooling of interests.

24. A business combination is accounted for as a pooling of interests. Costs of furnishing information to shareholders related to effecting the business combination should be

- A. Deducted directly from retained earnings of the combined corporation.
- B. Deducted in determining net income of the combined corporation for the period in which the costs were incurred.
- C. Capitalized but not amortized.
- D. Capitalized and subsequently amortized over a period not exceeding 40 years.

The correct answer is (B). *(CPA 1191 T-12)*
REQUIRED: The accounting treatment for costs of furnishing information to shareholders about a business combination.
DISCUSSION: APB 16 states that all costs incurred to effect a business combination accounted for as a pooling of interests should be treated as expenses of the combined entity.
Answers (A), (C), and (D) are incorrect because the costs incurred should be treated as expenses of the combined entity.

25. Chun Corporation issued voting common stock in exchange for 90% of the outstanding voting common stock of Key Company. The combination was accounted for by the pooling-of-interests method. If Chun later issued voting common stock, which had a fair value of $100,000 and a par value of $1,000, for the remaining 10% of the Key common stock, which had a stated value of $5,000, Chun Corporation's consolidated assets would increase by

A. $100,000

B. $5,000

C. $1,000

D. $0

The correct answer is (A). *(CPA 572 II-27)*
REQUIRED: The effect on consolidated assets of an acquisition of additional common stock subsequent to a business combination.
DISCUSSION: According to APB 16, a business combination accounted for as a pooling can occur only once between entities. It must be effected in one transaction or completed within 1 year in accordance with a specific plan. Any subsequent acquisition of common shares is treated as the purchase of an asset and recorded at fair value. Since Chun issued common stock having a fair value of $100,000, the transaction would increase consolidated assets by that amount.
Answer (B) is incorrect because $5,000 is the stated value of the Key stock. Answer (C) is incorrect because $1,000 is the par value of the Chun stock. Answer (D) is incorrect because the transaction is treated as a purchase and recorded at its fair value of $100,000.

Questions 26 through 28 are based on the following information. On June 30, 1996, Post, Inc. issued 630,000 shares of its $5 par common stock, for which it received 180,000 shares (90%) of Shaw Corp.'s $10 par common stock, in a business combination appropriately accounted for as a pooling of interests. The shareholders' equities immediately before the combination were

	Post	Shaw
Common stock	$ 6,500,000	$2,000,000
Additional paid-in capital	4,400,000	1,600,000
Retained earnings	6,100,000	5,400,000
	$17,000,000	$9,000,000

Both corporations continued to operate as separate businesses, maintaining accounting records with years ending December 31. For 1996, net income and dividends paid from separate company operations were

	Post	Shaw
Net Income		
6 months ended 6/30/96	$1,000,000	$300,000
6 months ended 12/31/96	1,100,000	500,000
Dividends Paid		
April 1, 1996	1,300,000	--
October 1, 1996	--	350,000

---

26. In the June 30, 1996 consolidated balance sheet, common stock should be reported at

A. $9,650,000

B. $9,450,000

C. $8,500,000

D. $8,300,000

The correct answer is (A). *(CPA 588 I-13)*
REQUIRED: The common stock that should be reported in a consolidated balance sheet at the date of a pooling.
DISCUSSION: In a pooling of interests, the capital stock of the surviving corporation must equal the par or stated value of outstanding shares of that entity. Post common stock outstanding prior to the pooling was $6,500,000. The additional shares issued to effect the pooling should be recorded at $3,150,000 (630,000 shares x $5 par). The $9,650,000 ($6,500,000 + $3,150,000) recorded as common stock on Post's books is equal to the common stock reported in the consolidated balance sheet dated June 30, 1996.
Answer (B) is incorrect because $9,450,000 equals Post's common stock prior to the pooling, plus the shares issued, minus 10% of Shaw's common stock. Answer (C) is incorrect because $8,500,000 is the sum of the common stock of Post and Shaw before the combination. Answer (D) is incorrect because $8,300,000 equals the sum of Post's common stock and 90% of Shaw's common stock before the combination.

27. In the June 30, 1996 consolidated balance sheet, additional paid-in capital should be reported at

    A. $4,400,000

    B. $4,490,000

    C. $5,840,000

    D. $6,000,000

The correct answer is (B). *(CPA 588 I-14)*

  REQUIRED: The additional paid-in capital recorded in a consolidated balance sheet at the date of a pooling.

  DISCUSSION: In a pooling of interests, the contributed capital of the surviving company must equal the contributed capital of the combining entities. Post's contributed capital is equal to $10,900,000 ($6,500,000 common stock + $4,400,000 additional paid-in capital). Shaw's contributed capital is $3,240,000 [90% x ($2,000,000 common stock + $1,600,000 contributed capital)]. Total contributed capital therefore equals $14,140,000 ($10,900,000 + $3,240,000). As discussed in the previous question, $9,650,000 should be allocated to common stock. The remaining $4,490,000 ($14,140,000 – $9,650,000) should be allocated to additional paid-in capital in the June 30, 1996 consolidated balance sheet.

  Answer (A) is incorrect because $4,400,000 is Post's additional paid-in capital before the pooling. Answer (C) is incorrect because $5,840,000 is the sum of Post's additional paid-in capital before the pooling and 90% of Shaw's. Answer (D) is incorrect because $6,000,000 equals the sum of Post's and Shaw's additional paid-in capital before the pooling.

28. In the June 30, 1996 consolidated balance sheet, retained earnings should be reported at

    A. $6,100,000

    B. $9,660,000

    C. $10,960,000

    D. $11,500,000

The correct answer is (C). *(CPA 588 I-15)*

  REQUIRED: The retained earnings reported in a consolidated balance sheet at the date of a pooling.

  DISCUSSION: In a pooling of interests, the contributed capital of the surviving entity should be equal to the total of the contributed capital for the combining entities. The retained earnings for the surviving entity should also be equal to the total of the retained earnings of the combining entities except in certain circumstances, e.g., when an allocation of retained earnings was made to contributed capital or the effects of intercompany transactions must be eliminated. Given that 90% of Shaw Corp. is included in the pooling, $4,860,000 ($5,400,000 retained earnings x 90%) should be combined with the $6,100,000 of retained earnings of Post resulting in consolidated retained earnings of $10,960,000.

  Answer (A) is incorrect because $6,100,000 is Post's retained earnings before the pooling. Answer (B) is incorrect because $9,660,000 deducts the dividends paid by Post for the 6 months prior to the combination. Answer (D) is incorrect because $11,500,000 assumes no minority interest.

29. The business combination of Jax Company -- the issuing company -- and the Bell Corporation was consummated on March 14. At the initiation date, Jax held 1,000 shares of Bell. If the combination were accounted for as a pooling of interests, the 1,000 shares of Bell held by Jax would be accounted for as

    A. Retired stock.

    B. 1,000 shares of treasury stock.

    C. (1,000 divided by the exchange rate) shares of treasury stock.

    D. (1,000 times the exchange rate) shares of treasury stock.

The correct answer is (A). *(CPA 573 I-6)*

  REQUIRED: The treatment of stock of a combining company held by the issuing company in a business combination accounted for under the pooling-of-interests method.

  DISCUSSION: APB 16 requires that an investment in a combining company by the surviving entity at the date of initiation of a combination be treated as stock retired as part of the business combination.

  Answer (B) is incorrect because the stock is considered retired rather than treasury stock. Answers (C) and (D) are incorrect because either dividing by or multiplying by the exchange rate is not appropriate in this calculation.

30. On September 30, 1996, Payne, Inc. exchanged some of its shares for all of the common stock of Salem, Inc. in a business combination accounted for as a pooling of interests. Salem continued as a wholly owned subsidiary of Payne. How should Salem's January 1, 1996 retained earnings and income for January 1 to September 30 be reported in 1996 consolidated statements?

	1/1/96 Retained Earnings	Income for 1/1 to 9/30/96
A.	Added to consolidated retained earnings	Added to consolidated income
B.	Added to consolidated retained earnings	Excluded from consolidated income
C.	Added to consolidated additional paid-in capital	Added to consolidated income
D.	Added to consolidated additional paid-in capital	Excluded from consolidated income

The correct answer is (A). *(CPA 1192 T-35)*
REQUIRED: The treatment of the subsidiary's beginning retained earnings and income in the year of a pooling.
DISCUSSION: In a pooling of interests, the contributed capital of the surviving entity should be equal to the total of the contributed capital for the combining entities. The retained earnings for the surviving entity should also be equal to the total of the retained earnings of the combining entities except in certain circumstances, e.g., when an allocation of retained earnings was made to contributed capital or the effects of intercompany transactions must be eliminated. In the year of a business combination appropriately accounted for as a pooling of interests, consolidated income should be recorded as the combined net income of the entities involved regardless of when the combination occurred during the year (assuming no intercompany transactions).
Answers (B), (C), and (D) are incorrect because 1/1/96 retained earnings and income for 1/1 to 9/30/96 are added to the consolidated amounts.

31. On January 1, 1997, Neal Co. issued 100,000 shares of its $10 par value common stock in exchange for all of Frey Inc.'s outstanding stock. This business combination was accounted for as a pooling of interests. The fair value of Neal's common stock on December 31, 1996 was $19 per share. The carrying amounts and fair values of Frey's assets and liabilities on December 31, 1996 were as follows:

	Carrying Amount	Fair Value
Cash	$ 240,000	$ 240,000
Receivables	270,000	270,000
Inventory	435,000	405,000
Property, plant and equipment	1,305,000	1,440,000
Liabilities	(525,000)	(525,000)
Net assets	$1,725,000	$1,830,000

What is the amount of goodwill resulting from the business combination?

A. $175,000

B. $105,000

C. $70,000

D. $0

The correct answer is (D). *(CPA 1191 I-20)*
REQUIRED: The amount of goodwill resulting from the business combination.
DISCUSSION: In a pooling of interests, the assets and liabilities of the combining companies are recorded at their book values. Accordingly, recognition or disclosure of goodwill is not appropriate.
Answer (A) is incorrect because $175,000 is the difference between the carrying amount of Frey's net assets and the fair value of the stock issued by Neal. Answer (B) is incorrect because $105,000 is the difference between the carrying amount of Frey's net assets and its fair value. Answer (C) is incorrect because $70,000 would be the amount of goodwill if the combination were accounted for as a purchase.

28.4 Purchase Accounting--Valuation

32. On January 1, 1996, Prim, Inc. acquired all the outstanding common shares of Scarp, Inc. for cash equal to the book value of the stock. The carrying amounts of Scarp's assets and liabilities approximated their fair values, except that the carrying amount of its building was more than fair value. In preparing Prim's 1996 consolidated income statement, which of the following adjustments would be made?

A. Depreciation expense would be decreased, and goodwill amortization would be recognized.

B. Depreciation expense would be increased, and goodwill amortization would be recognized.

C. Depreciation expense would be decreased, and no goodwill amortization would be recognized.

D. Depreciation expense would be increased, and no goodwill amortization would be recognized.

The correct answer is (A). *(CPA 1192 T-33)*
REQUIRED: The adjustments made in preparing the consolidated income statement.
DISCUSSION: APB 16 requires that a business combination be accounted for as a purchase when cash is used to effect the combination. Under purchase accounting, assets acquired and liabilities assumed should be recorded at their fair values. The differences between fair values and book bases will be allocated to income when related expenses are incurred. The effect of recording the building at fair value in the consolidated balance sheet instead of its higher carrying amount on Scarp's books will be to decrease future depreciation. The excess of the cost over fair value of the net identifiable assets acquired will be recognized as goodwill, an amount that will be amortized over its expected useful life, not to exceed 40 years.
Answers (B), (C), and (D) are incorrect because depreciation will decrease and goodwill will be amortized.

33. PDX Corp. acquired 100% of the outstanding common stock of Sea Corp. in a purchase transaction. The cost of the acquisition exceeded the fair value of the identifiable assets and assumed liabilities. The general guidelines for assigning amounts to the inventories acquired provide for

A. Raw materials to be valued at original cost.

B. Work-in-process to be valued at the estimated selling prices of finished goods, minus both costs to complete and costs of disposal.

C. Finished goods to be valued at replacement cost.

D. Finished goods to be valued at estimated selling prices, minus both costs of disposal and a reasonable profit allowance.

The correct answer is (D). *(CPA 593 T-7)*
REQUIRED: The proper accounting for inventories when the cost of the acquisition exceeds the fair value of the identifiable net assets acquired.
DISCUSSION: APB 16 states general guides for assigning amounts to the individual assets acquired and liabilities assumed in a business combination accounted for as a purchase. Finished goods and merchandise should be assigned amounts equal to estimated selling prices minus the sum of (1) costs of disposal and (2) a reasonable profit allowance for the selling effort of the acquiring corporation.
Answer (A) is incorrect because raw materials should be valued at current replacement cost. Answer (B) is incorrect because work-in-process should be valued at estimated selling prices of finished goods minus the sum of (1) costs to complete, (2) costs of disposal, and (3) a reasonable profit allowance for the completing and selling effort of the acquiring corporation based on profit for similar finished goods. Answer (C) is incorrect because finished goods are valued at estimated selling prices minus the sum of (1) costs of disposal and (2) a reasonable profit allowance.

34. Say Co. purchased Ivy Co. at a cost that resulted in recognition of goodwill having an expected 10-year benefit period. However, Say plans to make additional expenditures to maintain goodwill for a total of 40 years. What costs should be capitalized and over how many years should they be amortized?

	Costs Capitalized	Amortization Period
A.	Acquisition costs only	10 years
B.	Acquisition costs only	40 years
C.	Acquisition and maintenance costs	10 years
D.	Acquisition and maintenance costs	40 years

The correct answer is (A). *(CPA 1191 T-13)*

REQUIRED: The costs to be capitalized and the amortization period.

DISCUSSION: APB 16, *Business Combinations*, requires that the cost of goodwill from a business combination accounted for as a purchase be capitalized and amortized over its estimated useful life. In contrast, the cost of developing, maintaining, or restoring intangible assets that are inherent in a continuing business and related to an enterprise as a whole should be expensed as incurred.

Answer (B) is incorrect because the goodwill acquired externally should be amortized over its 10-year benefit period. Answer (C) is incorrect because the costs of maintaining goodwill should be expensed as incurred. Answer (D) is incorrect because the goodwill acquired externally should be amortized over its 10-year benefit period and the costs of maintaining goodwill should be expensed as incurred.

35. Pride, Inc. owns 80% of Simba, Inc.'s outstanding common stock. Simba, in turn, owns 10% of Pride's outstanding common stock. What percentage of the common stock cash dividends declared by the individual companies should be reported as dividends declared in the consolidated financial statements?

	Dividends Declared by Pride	Dividends Declared by Simba
A.	90%	0%
B.	90%	20%
C.	100%	0%
D.	100%	20%

The correct answer is (A). *(CPA 1191 T-9)*

REQUIRED: The percentage of common stock cash dividends declared by the individual companies that should be reported as dividends declared in the consolidated financial statements.

DISCUSSION: Because the parent owns 80% of the subsidiary and the subsidiary owns 10% of the parent, 80% of the dividends declared by the subsidiary and 10% of the dividends declared by the parent are not transferred outside of the consolidated entity. These amounts are eliminated as intercompany transactions. Consequently, 90% of the parent's and 20% of the subsidiary's dividend payments are to third parties. The 90% declared by the parent will be reported as dividends declared under the parent company theory of consolidation. The 20% declared by the subsidiary is treated as a reduction of the minority interest in the consolidated financial statements, not as consolidated dividends declared.

Answers (B), (C), and (D) are incorrect because 90% of the parent's dividends and 0% of the subsidiary's are treated as consolidated dividends declared.

36. On November 30, 1996, Parlor, Inc. purchased for cash at $15 per share all 250,000 shares of the outstanding common stock of Shaw Co. At November 30, 1996, Shaw's balance sheet showed a carrying amount of net assets of $3,000,000. At that date, the fair value of Shaw's property, plant, and equipment exceeded its carrying amount by $400,000. In its November 30, 1996 consolidated balance sheet, what amount should Parlor report as goodwill?

A. $750,000

B. $400,000

C. $350,000

D. $0

The correct answer is (C). *(CPA 593 I-25)*

REQUIRED: The goodwill to be recorded at the date of the business combination.

DISCUSSION: In a business combination accounted for as a purchase, the excess of the purchase price over the fair value of the identifiable net assets acquired equals goodwill. Thus, goodwill is $350,000 [($15 x 250,000 shares) – $3,000,000 carrying amount – $400,000 additional fair value of PPE].

Answer (A) is incorrect because $750,000 equals the excess of the price over the carrying amount. Answer (B) is incorrect because $400,000 is the fair value in excess of the carrying amount of the identifiable net assets. Answer (D) is incorrect because goodwill should be recognized. The price exceeds the fair value of the identifiable net assets acquired.

37. On August 31, 1996, Wood Corp. issued 100,000 shares of its $20 par value common stock for the net assets of Pine, Inc., in a business combination accounted for by the purchase method. The market value of Wood's common stock on August 31 was $36 per share. Wood paid a fee of $160,000 to the consultant who arranged this acquisition. Costs of registering and issuing the equity securities amounted to $80,000. No goodwill was involved in the purchase. What amount should Wood capitalize as the cost of acquiring Pine's net assets?

A. $3,600,000

B. $3,680,000

C. $3,760,000

D. $3,840,000

The correct answer is (C). *(CPA 591 II-13)*
REQUIRED: The amount capitalized as the cost of acquiring the net assets.
DISCUSSION: Three types of costs may be incurred in effecting a business combination: direct costs of acquisition, costs of registering and issuing equity securities, and indirect and general expenses. Direct costs, such as finders' and consultants' fees, should be included in the determination of the cost of the company acquired. Costs of registering and issuing equity securities should be treated as a reduction in the otherwise determinable fair value of the securities. Indirect and general expenses should be included in the determination of net income when incurred.

An asset acquired by issuing stock is recorded at the fair value of the asset. However, the fair value of securities is normally more clearly evident than the fair value of an acquired company. Hence, the quoted piece of the equity securities issued to effect the combination may be used to approximate the fair value of the acquired company. The investment should be debited for $3,760,000 [(100,000 shares x $36) + $160,000 consultant's fee], and additional paid-in capital should be debited for $80,000 (the registration and issuance costs). The credits are to common stock for $2,000,000 ($20 x 100,000 shares), additional paid-in capital for $1,600,000 [($36 – $20 par) x 100,000 shares], and cash for $240,000 ($160,000 + $80,000).

Answer (A) is incorrect because $3,600,000 ignores the other costs of the combination. Answer (B) is incorrect because $3,680,000 treats the registration and issuance costs as a reduction of the investment instead of paid-in capital. Answer (D) is incorrect because $3,840,000 treats the registration and issuance costs as an addition to the investment instead of as a reduction of paid-in capital.

38. Penn Corp. paid $300,000 for the outstanding common stock of Star Co. At that time, Star had the following condensed balance sheet:

	Carrying Amounts
Current assets	$ 40,000
Plant and equipment, net	380,000
Liabilities	200,000
Shareholders' equity	220,000

The fair value of the plant and equipment was $60,000 more than its recorded carrying amount. The fair values and carrying amounts were equal for all other assets and liabilities. What amount of goodwill, related to Star's acquisition, should Penn report in its consolidated balance sheet?

A. $20,000

B. $40,000

C. $60,000

D. $80,000

The correct answer is (A). *(CPA 593 II-8)*
REQUIRED: The amount of goodwill reported in the consolidated balance sheet.
DISCUSSION: APB 16 requires that a business combination be accounted for as a purchase when cash is used to effect the combination. Under purchase accounting, assets acquired and liabilities assumed should be recorded at their fair values. Any excess of cost over the fair value of the identifiable net assets acquired is recorded as goodwill. After adjusting the net plant and equipment, and assuming other items are stated at fair value, the fair value of the identifiable net assets is $280,000 [$40,000 current assets + ($380,000 + $60,000) plant and equipment – $200,000 liabilities]. Hence, goodwill is $20,000 ($300,000 cost – $280,000).

Answer (B) is incorrect because $40,000 is the amount of current assets. Answer (C) is incorrect because $60,000 is the amount plant and equipment is undervalued. Answer (D) is incorrect because $80,000 is the difference between the $300,000 cost and the $220,000 book value of the net assets.

Questions 39 and 40 are based on the following information. On January 1, 1996, Ritt Corp. purchased 80% of Shaw Corp.'s $10 par common stock for $975,000. On this date, the carrying amount of Shaw's net assets was $1,000,000. The fair values of Shaw's identifiable assets and liabilities were the same as their carrying amounts except for plant assets (net), which were $100,000 in excess of the carrying amount. For the year ended December 31, 1996, Shaw had net income of $190,000 and paid cash dividends totaling $125,000.

39. In the January 1, 1996 consolidated balance sheet, goodwill should be reported at

A. $0

B. $75,000

C. $95,000

D. $175,000

The correct answer is (C). *(CPA 589 I-55)*
  REQUIRED: The goodwill to be recorded in a consolidated balance sheet at the date of the business combination.
  DISCUSSION: In a business combination accounted for as a purchase, the excess of the purchase price over the sum of the fair values of the identifiable assets and liabilities is goodwill. As indicated below, the fair value of 80% of the identifiable net assets is $880,000. Goodwill is therefore $95,000.

Purchase price	$975,000
Fair value of identifiable net assets:	
Carrying value: $1,000,000 x 80%	(800,000)
Undervalued plant: $100,000 x 80%	(80,000)
Goodwill	$ 95,000

  Answer (A) is incorrect because the price exceeds the fair value of the identifiable net assets acquired. Hence, goodwill should be recognized. Answer (B) is incorrect because $75,000 assumes that 100% of the undervaluation is included in Ritt's 80% interest. Answer (D) is incorrect because $175,000 assumes that carrying value equals fair value.

40. In the December 31, 1996 consolidated balance sheet, the minority interest should be reported at

A. $200,000

B. $213,000

C. $220,000

D. $233,000

The correct answer is (B). *(CPA 589 I-56)*
  REQUIRED: The minority interest to be reported in the consolidated balance sheet at year-end.
  DISCUSSION: The minority interest is equal to the 20% (100% – 80%) interest in Shaw not held by Ritt (the parent). Whereas the parent's interest reflects the fair value of the net assets acquired at the date of purchase, the minority interest should be recorded at the carrying values recorded on the subsidiary's books. As indicated below, the minority interest to be reported in the year-end balance sheet equals 20% of the shareholders' interest (net assets) at the beginning of the year, plus 20% of the net income, minus 20% of the dividends. Thus, the minority interest should be reported at $213,000.

	20% Minority Interest
Shareholders' equity at 1/1/96	$200,000
Net income (20% x $190,000)	38,000
Dividends (20% x $125,000)	(25,000)
Minority interest at 12/31/96	$213,000

  Answer (A) is incorrect because $200,000 was the minority interest at 1/1/96. Answer (C) is incorrect because $220,000 is the minority interest measured at fair value at 1/1/96. Answer (D) is incorrect because $233,000 is the minority interest measured at fair value at 1/1/96, plus its share of net income, minus its share of dividends.

41. The Action Corporation issued nonvoting preferred stock with a fair value of $4,000,000 in exchange for all of the outstanding common stock of Master Corporation. On the date of the exchange, Master had tangible net assets with a book value of $2,000,000 and a fair value of $2,500,000. In addition, Action issued preferred stock valued at $400,000 to an individual as a finder's fee in arranging the transaction. As a result of this transaction, Action should record an increase in net assets of

A. $2,000,000
B. $2,500,000
C. $2,900,000
D. $4,400,000

The correct answer is (D). *(CPA 1180 II-13)*
REQUIRED: The initial recorded value of net assets acquired in a business combination accounted for using the purchase method.
DISCUSSION: In applying the purchase method of accounting for a business combination, the cost to the purchasing entity of acquiring another entity is the amount of cash or the fair value of other assets given up in the transaction. In addition, any direct fees paid related to the combination are added to the consideration given.
The fair value of the preferred stock given up in the transaction is $4,000,000, and the fair value of the finder's fee paid is $400,000. Accordingly, Action should recognize an increase in net assets at the date of the combination of $4,400,000 ($4,000,000 + $400,000).
Answer (A) is incorrect because $2,000,000 is the book value of Master's net assets. Answer (B) is incorrect because $2,500,000 is the fair value of Master's tangible net assets. Answer (C) is incorrect because $2,900,000 equals the fair value of Master's tangible net assets plus the finder's fee.

42. In a business combination accounted for as a purchase, the appraisal value of the identifiable assets acquired exceeds the acquisition price. The excess appraisal value should be reported as a

A. Deferred credit.
B. Reduction of the values assigned to current assets and a deferred credit for any unallocated portion.
C. Reduction of the values assigned to noncurrent assets and a deferred credit for any unallocated portion.
D. Pro rata reduction of the values assigned to current and noncurrent assets.

The correct answer is (C). *(CPA 590 T-33)*
REQUIRED: The accounting for a bargain purchase business combination.
DISCUSSION: In a business combination accounted for using the purchase method, any excess of the fair value of the identifiable net assets acquired over the cost of the purchase must be allocated to noncurrent assets other than long-term investments in marketable securities based on their relative fair values. Any excess remaining after noncurrent assets are adjusted to zero is a deferred credit to be amortized over the period benefited but not exceeding 40 years.
Answer (A) is incorrect because a deferred credit is established only after the noncurrent assets other than long-term investments in marketable securities are reduced to zero. Answers (B) and (D) are incorrect because the excess appraisal value reduces noncurrent but not current assets.

43. Needle Corporation purchased for cash at $10 per share all 100,000 shares of the outstanding common stock of Thread Company. The total appraised value of the identifiable assets minus liabilities of Thread was $1,400,000 on the date of purchase, including the appraised value of Thread's property, plant, and equipment (its only noncurrent asset) of $250,000. The consolidated balance sheet of Needle Corporation and its wholly owned subsidiary should reflect

A. A deferred credit (negative goodwill) of $150,000.
B. Goodwill of $150,000.
C. A deferred credit (negative goodwill) of $400,000.
D. Goodwill of $400,000.

The correct answer is (A). *(CPA 580 I-2)*
REQUIRED: The accounting treatment of the excess of fair value over cost resulting from a bargain purchase.
DISCUSSION: When the fair value of the identifiable net assets acquired exceeds the cost in a business combination accounted for as a purchase, the excess (negative goodwill) must first be allocated to the value of noncurrent assets, except long-term investments in marketable securities. Any remaining excess must be recorded as a deferred credit and amortized over a period not exceeding 40 years.
The amount of negative goodwill acquired in this transaction is $400,000 ($1,400,000 appraised value – $1,000,000 cash paid). Because Thread's noncurrent assets total $250,000, the excess of $150,000 ($400,000 – $250,000) remaining after allocation is recognized as a deferred credit.
Answers (B) and (D) are incorrect because negative goodwill results when fair value exceeds the cost. Answer (C) is incorrect because $250,000 of the $400,000 is allocated to noncurrent assets.

44. An entire acquired company is sold. The unamortized cost of the goodwill recognized in the acquisition should be

A. Included in the cost of the assets sold.

B. Charged to retained earnings of the current period.

C. Expensed in the period sold.

D. Charged to retained earnings of prior periods.

The correct answer is (A). *(Publisher)*
REQUIRED: The accounting for unamortized goodwill when an acquired company is sold.
DISCUSSION: Unamortized goodwill on the books of a consolidated entity related to the company whose purchase gave rise to the goodwill must be added to the carrying value of the assets when the related assets are sold to determine any gain or loss on the disposition.
Answers (B), (C), and (D) are incorrect because goodwill directly related to the underlying assets sold is not properly chargeable to retained earnings or income.

45. Included in the assets of an acquired subsidiary that was accounted for as a purchase are a patent that was internally developed, equipment used in research and development (R&D) that has alternative use, and equipment used in R&D that has no alternative use. FASB Interpretation No. 4, *Applicability of SFAS 2 to Business Combinations Accounted for by the Purchase Method*, requires that the purchase price be allocated to these three asset categories based on their fair values at the date of the business combination. Which statement is correct concerning the subsequent accounting for these three asset types?

A. The value assigned to all three assets should be immediately expensed as R&D expense.

B. The value assigned to the two types of equipment to be used in R&D should be expensed immediately as R&D expense.

C. The value assigned only to the equipment to be used in R&D that has no alternative use should be immediately expensed as R&D expense.

D. The value assigned to the equipment to be used in R&D that has an alternative use should be expensed immediately as R&D expense.

The correct answer is (C). *(Publisher)*
REQUIRED: The proper accounting for R&D costs arising from a business combination accounted for as a purchase.
DISCUSSION: FASB Interpretation No. 4 requires the allocation of the purchase price to all identifiable assets, whether tangible or intangible. FASB Interpretation No. 4 further requires that the cost assigned to assets that are to be used in a particular R&D project and that have no alternative future use be charged to R&D expense at the date of the consummation of the combination.
Answers (A), (B), and (D) are incorrect because only the R&D equipment with no alternative future use should be charged to R&D expense. The patent and the R&D equipment with alternative uses should be capitalized.

46. Company B has properly treated as expense $200,000 of research and development costs that resulted in a patent. When Company A acquired Company B in a transaction accounted for by the purchase method, it was determined that the patent had a value of $500,000. Which of the following statements is true?

A. On the books of Company A, the patent should have a value of $200,000 because that was the cost to produce it.

B. The cost of the patent on the books of Company A should be $500,000.

C. The cost of the patent on the books of Company A should be the same as on the books of Company B.

D. The cost of the patent on the books of Company A should be represented by the legal costs involved in the patent process.

The correct answer is (B). *(Publisher)*
REQUIRED: The accounting for the fair value of an asset not recorded in the books of the acquired company at the date of a business combination accounted for as a purchase.
DISCUSSION: In applying the purchase method of accounting for a business combination, the fair values of all identifiable assets and liabilities must be determined and recorded regardless of whether they are recorded in the books of the acquired company. The $500,000 value of the patent must therefore be recorded in the books of Company A at the date of the combination, even though it was previously expensed by Company B.
Answers (A), (C), and (D) are incorrect because purchase accounting in a business combination requires use of fair values in recording the net assets of the acquired company.

47. Which of the following statements is true about a lease held by a subsidiary acquired in a business combination accounted for as a purchase?

A. The classification of a lease in accordance with the criteria of SFAS 13 should be based on the value assigned to the lease at the date of the business combination.

B. The provisions of a lease that are modified in connection with the business combination should be disregarded in the classification of the lease.

C. The lease should be accounted for by the combined enterprise in the same manner that it was accounted for (both classification and valuation) by the subsidiary.

D. The valuation of the lease asset and obligation should be based on their fair market values as of the date of the business combination.

The correct answer is (D). *(Publisher)*
    REQUIRED: The true statement about the accounting for a lease of a subsidiary acquired in a business combination accounted for as a purchase.
    DISCUSSION: FASB Interpretation No. 21, *Accounting for Leases in a Business Combination*, requires that the amounts assigned to lease assets and lease liabilities assumed at the date of the business combination be allocated based on their fair values as of the date the combination is accounted for as a purchase.
    Answers (A) and (B) are incorrect because the classification of a lease should be changed only if the provisions of the lease are modified in the business combination. The modified lease should then be classified by the combined enterprise in accordance with the criteria in SFAS 13, *Accounting for Leases*. Answer (C) is incorrect because the valuation should be changed to fair value, but the classification should not be changed unless the lease is modified in the business combination.

28.5 Purchase Accounting--Implementation

48. How would the retained earnings of a subsidiary acquired in a business combination usually be treated in a consolidated balance sheet prepared immediately after the acquisition?

A. Excluded for both a purchase and a pooling of interests.

B. Excluded for a pooling of interests but included for a purchase.

C. Included for both a purchase and a pooling of interests.

D. Included for a pooling of interests but excluded for a purchase.

The correct answer is (D). *(CPA 1182 T-2)*
    REQUIRED: The treatment of retained earnings of a subsidiary in a consolidated balance sheet prepared immediately after the business combination.
    DISCUSSION: A pooling is viewed as a combining of ownership interests. Hence, the assets, liabilities, and owners' equity (including retained earnings) of a subsidiary acquired in a business combination are included at book value in a consolidated balance sheet. A purchase is viewed as an acquisition of net assets. Thus, only the fair value of the net assets of a subsidiary is included in a consolidated balance sheet prepared using the purchase method. The shareholders' equity, including retained earnings, is excluded.
    Answers (A), (B), and (C) are incorrect because the retained earnings of a subsidiary are included for a pooling but excluded for a purchase.

Questions 49 through 53 are based on the following information. Polk Corp. and Strass Corp. condensed balance sheets on January 1, 1996 are presented in the opposite column.

On January 2, 1996, Polk borrowed $60,000 and used the proceeds to purchase 90% of the outstanding common shares of Strass. Ten equal principal and interest payments begin December 30, 1996. The excess cost of the investment over Strass's book value of acquired net assets should be allocated 60% to inventory and 40% to goodwill.

	Polk	Strass
Current assets	$ 70,000	$20,000
Noncurrent assets	90,000	40,000
Total assets	$160,000	$60,000
Current liabilities	$ 30,000	$10,000
Long-term debt	50,000	--
Shareholders' equity	80,000	50,000
Total liabilities and shareholders' equity	$160,000	$60,000

49. On Polk's January 2, 1996 consolidated balance sheet, current assets should be

A. $99,000

B. $96,000

C. $90,000

D. $79,000

The correct answer is (A). *(CPA 1188 I-2)*
REQUIRED: The current assets to be reported in a consolidated balance sheet at the date of the combination.
DISCUSSION: Because Polk used cash to effect the combination, the transaction should be treated as a purchase. Polk's 90% interest in the carrying value of the net assets of Strass equals $45,000 [($60,000 assets – $10,000 liabilities) x 90%]. The excess cost of the investment over the book value of the acquired net assets is $15,000 ($60,000 price – $45,000). Of this amount, $9,000 ($15,000 x 60%) should be allocated to inventory and the remaining $6,000 ($15,000 x 40%) to goodwill. ARB 51 requires that 100% of the net assets of a subsidiary be included in the consolidated financial statements. Thus, the amount of current assets to be reported in the consolidated balance sheet should be $99,000 ($70,000 current assets of Polk + $20,000 current assets of Strass + $9,000 allocation to inventory).
Answer (B) is incorrect because $96,000 assumes an allocation of $6,000 to inventory. Answer (C) is incorrect because $90,000 ignores the excess cost of the investment. Answer (D) is incorrect because $79,000 excludes Strass's current assets.

50. On Polk's January 2, 1996 consolidated balance sheet, noncurrent assets should be

A. $130,000

B. $134,000

C. $136,000

D. $140,000

The correct answer is (C). *(CPA 1188 I-3)*
REQUIRED: The noncurrent assets reported in the consolidated balance sheet at the date of the combination.
DISCUSSION: The noncurrent assets should be recorded at $136,000 ($90,000 noncurrent assets of Polk + $40,000 noncurrent assets of Strass + $6,000 allocation to goodwill computed in the preceding question).
Answer (A) is incorrect because $130,000 ignores goodwill. Answer (B) is incorrect because $134,000 assumes that a 100% interest was acquired and that goodwill was therefore $4,000 [($60,000 – $50,000) x 40%]. Answer (D) is incorrect because $140,000 assumes that a 100% interest was acquired and that goodwill was $10,000.

51. On Polk's January 2, 1996 consolidated balance sheet, current liabilities should be

A. $50,000

B. $46,000

C. $40,000

D. $30,000

The correct answer is (B). *(CPA 1188 I-4)*

REQUIRED: The current liabilities to be reported in the consolidated balance sheet at the date of the combination.

DISCUSSION: The total current liabilities include the $30,000 of current liabilities on Polk's books, the $10,000 on Strass's books, and the $6,000 ($60,000 debt ÷ 10 equal annual principal payments) that will be due and payable on December 30, 1996. Thus, current liabilities should be recorded at $46,000.

Answer (A) is incorrect because $50,000 is the pre-existing long-term debt. Answer (C) is incorrect because $40,000 ignores the new borrowing. Answer (D) is incorrect because $30,000 is the amount of Polk's preexisting current liabilities.

52. On Polk's January 2, 1996 consolidated balance sheet, noncurrent liabilities, including the minority interest, should be

A. $115,000

B. $109,000

C. $104,000

D. $55,000

The correct answer is (B). *(CPA 1188 I-5)*

REQUIRED: The noncurrent liabilities, including the minority interest, that should be recorded in a consolidated balance sheet at the date of the business combination.

DISCUSSION: The noncurrent liabilities include the $50,000 in long-term debt on Polk's books on January 1, 1996, the $54,000 ($60,000 total debt − $6,000 current portion) noncurrent portion of the debt used to effect the business combination, and the minority interest. The minority interest is equal to $5,000 ($50,000 shareholders' equity of the acquired company x 10% minority interest). Accordingly, the noncurrent liabilities, including the minority interest, total $109,000.

Answer (A) is incorrect because $115,000 assumes the entire new borrowing is a noncurrent liability. Answer (C) is incorrect because $104,000 omits the minority interest. Answer (D) is incorrect because $55,000 ignores the new borrowing.

53. On Polk's January 2, 1996 consolidated balance sheet, shareholders' equity should be

A. $80,000

B. $85,000

C. $90,000

D. $130,000

The correct answer is (A). *(CPA 1188 I-6)*

REQUIRED: The shareholders' equity that should be reported in the consolidated balance sheet at the date of a business combination effected as a purchase.

DISCUSSION: This business combination was accounted for as a purchase, and the minority interest was treated as part of noncurrent liabilities. Thus, the shareholders' equity section of the current parent company balance sheet is the same as the shareholders' equity section of the consolidated balance sheet. Consequently, shareholders' equity is $80,000.

Answer (B) is incorrect because $85,000 equals Polk's shareholders' equity plus the minority interest. Answer (C) is incorrect because $90,000 equals the total liabilities of the two companies at 1/1/96. Answer (D) is incorrect because $130,000 is the sum of the shareholders' equity amounts for Polk and Strass at 1/1/96.

Questions 54 through 58 are based on the following information. The separate condensed balance sheets and income statements of Purl Corp. and its wholly owned subsidiary, Scott Corp., are as follows:

BALANCE SHEETS
December 31, 1996

	Purl	Scott
Assets		
Current assets		
Cash	$ 80,000	$ 60,000
Accounts receivable (net)	140,000	25,000
Inventories	90,000	50,000
Total current assets	310,000	135,000
Property, plant, and equipment (net)	625,000	280,000
Investment in Scott (equity method)	390,000	--
Total assets	$1,325,000	$415,000
Liabilities and Shareholders' Equity		
Current liabilities		
Accounts payable	$ 160,000	$ 95,000
Accrued liabilities	110,000	30,000
Total current liabilities	270,000	125,000
Shareholders' equity		
Common share ($10 par)	300,000	50,000
Additional paid-in capital		10,000
Retained earnings	755,000	230,000
Total shareholders' equity	$1,055,000	$290,000
Total liabilities and shareholders' equity	$1,325,000	$415,000

INCOME STATEMENTS
For the Year Ended December 31, 1996

	Purl	Scott
Sales	$2,000,000	$750,000
Cost of goods sold	1,540,000	500,000
Gross margin	460,000	250,000
Operating expenses	260,000	150,000
Operating income	200,000	100,000
Equity in earnings of Scott	60,000	--
Income before income taxes	260,000	100,000
Provision for income taxes	60,000	30,000
Net income	$ 200,000	$ 70,000

Additional Information:

• On January 1, 1996, Purl purchased for $360,000 all of Scott's $10 par, voting common stock. On January 1, 1996, the fair value of Scott's assets and liabilities equaled their carrying amount of $410,000 and $160,000, respectively, except that the fair values of certain items identifiable in Scott's inventory were $10,000 more than their carrying amounts. These items were still on hand at December 31, 1996. Purl's policy is to amortize intangible assets over a 10-year period, unless a definite life is ascertainable.

• During 1996, Purl and Scott paid cash dividends of $100,000 and $30,000, respectively. For tax purposes, Purl receives the 100% exclusion for dividends received from Scott.

• There were no intercompany transactions, except for Purl's receipt of dividends from Scott and Purl's recording of its share of Scott's earnings.

• Both Purl and Scott paid income taxes at the rate of 30%.

---

54. In the December 31, 1996 consolidated financial statements of Purl and its subsidiary, total assets should be

A. $1,740,000

B. $1,450,000

C. $1,350,000

D. $1,325,000

The correct answer is (B). *(CPA 591 I-14)*

REQUIRED: The consolidated total assets.

DISCUSSION: All of a subsidiary's assets should be included in a consolidated balance sheet after elimination of intercompany transactions. Since the only intercompany transaction in 1996 was the dividend payment, no adjustment for intercompany transactions is needed. The amount of total assets is determined as follows:

Total assets (12/31/96)		
($1,325,000 + $415,000)		$1,740,000
Minus: Investment in Scott		(390,000)
Add: Increase in inventory and unamortized goodwill:		
Cost of investment	$360,000	
Shareholders' equity acquired ($410,000 – $160,000)	(250,000)	
Excess	$110,000	
Applied to inventory	(10,000)	10,000
Goodwill	$100,000	
Goodwill amortization ($100,000 ÷ 10)	(10,000)	90,000
		$1,450,000

Answer (A) is incorrect because $1,740,000 is the unadjusted sum of the assets of Purl and Scott. Answer (C) is incorrect because $1,350,000 is not adjusted for the fair value of inventory and for goodwill. Answer (D) is incorrect because $1,325,000 equals the parent's total assets.

55. In the December 31, 1996 consolidated financial statements of Purl and its subsidiary, total current assets should be

A. $455,000

B. $445,000

C. $310,000

D. $135,000

The correct answer is (A). *(CPA 591 I-13)*

REQUIRED: The consolidated total current assets.

DISCUSSION: In a purchase business combination, the excess of the purchase price over the subsidiary's shareholders' equity is allocated to specific assets and/or liabilities. Any remaining excess is treated as goodwill. As stated, $10,000 was allocated to inventory items that were still on hand at year-end. Hence, total current assets at year-end equals $455,000 ($310,000 Purl current assets + $135,000 Scott current assets + $10,000 excess fair value attributable to inventory).

Answer (B) is incorrect because $445,000 does not reflect the fair value of the inventory. Answer (C) is incorrect because $310,000 equals the parent's current assets. Answer (D) is incorrect because $135,000 equals the unadjusted current assets of the subsidiary.

56. In the December 31, 1996 consolidated financial statements of Purl and its subsidiary, total retained earnings should be?

A. $985,000

B. $825,000

C. $795,000

D. $755,000

The correct answer is (D). *(CPA 591 I-15)*

REQUIRED: The consolidated total retained earnings.

DISCUSSION: Purl acquired Scott in a purchase transaction and properly accounts for the investment using the equity method. Thus, Purl's $755,000 of retained earnings equals consolidated retained earnings.

Answer (A) is incorrect because $985,000 includes the subsidiary's retained earnings. Answer (B) is incorrect because $825,000 includes the subsidiary's net income, an amount already reflected in the parent's retained earnings under the equity method. Answer (C) is incorrect because $795,000 includes the subsidiary's net income minus the dividends paid, an amount already accounted for using the equity method.

57. In the December 31, 1996 consolidated financial statements of Purl and its subsidiary, net income should be

A. $270,000

B. $200,000

C. $190,000

D. $170,000

The correct answer is (B). *(CPA 591 I-16)*

REQUIRED: The consolidated net income.

DISCUSSION: The equity in the earnings of the subsidiary recorded on the parent's income statement is recorded in accordance with the equity method. Thus, the parent's $200,000 of net income equals consolidated net income.

Answer (A) is incorrect because $270,000 equals the sum of the net incomes of Purl and Scott. Answer (C) is incorrect because $190,000 equals Purl's net income minus goodwill amortization, an expense already included in the determination of net income. Answer (D) is incorrect because $170,000 equals Purl's net income minus the dividend payment, which does not affect equity-based net income.

58. In the December 31, 1996 consolidated financial statements of Purl and its subsidiary, goodwill amortization expense should be

A. $20,000

B. $10,000

C. $6,000

D. $0

The correct answer is (B). *(CPA 591 I-17)*

REQUIRED: The goodwill amortization expense.

DISCUSSION: Goodwill or the excess of the cost of the investment over the fair value of the identifiable net assets acquired is $100,000 ($360,000 – $250,000 carrying value – $10,000 additional fair value of inventory). Purl's policy is to amortize intangible assets over 10 years. Accordingly, the amortization expense is $10,000 ($100,000 ÷ 10).

Answer (A) is incorrect because $20,000 equals net income divided by 10 years. Answer (C) is incorrect because $6,000 equals equity in Scott's earnings divided by 10 years. Answer (D) is incorrect because $0 assumes no goodwill was recognized.

Questions 59 through 62 are based on the following information. December 31, 1996 balance sheet items of the Star Company are presented in the opposite column on both a historical cost and a fair value basis.

	Historical Cost	Fair Value
Current assets	$250,000	$300,000
Fixed assets	350,000	500,000
Liabilities	100,000	100,000
Capital stock, $5 par	150,000	
Additional paid-in capital	150,000	700,000
Retained earnings	200,000	

59. On January 2, 1997, Planet Company issued 25,000 shares of its $10 par value stock in exchange for all of the outstanding shares of Star Company in a business combination that did not meet the criteria for pooling. If the market price of Planet's stock was $40 at the date of acquisition, which entry records Planet's investment in its new subsidiary?

A. Investment in subsidiary $500,000
   Capital stock $250,000
   Paid-in capital 250,000

B. Investment in subsidiary $1,000,000
   Capital stock $250,000
   Paid-in capital 750,000

C. Investment in subsidiary $500,000
   Capital stock $250,000
   Paid-in capital 50,000
   Retained earnings 200,000

D. Current assets $300,000
   Fixed assets 500,000
   Goodwill 300,000
   Liabilities $100,000
   Capital stock 250,000
   Paid-in capital 750,000

The correct answer is (B). *(Publisher)*
REQUIRED: The journal entry to record a stock investment accounted for as a purchase.
DISCUSSION: To account for a stock investment in a subsidiary accounted for as a purchase, the investment in subsidiary account should be debited for the $1,000,000 fair value of the stock issued (25,000 shares x $40). The capital stock account should be credited for $250,000 (25,000 shares x $10 par), and the remaining $750,000 should be credited to additional paid-in capital.
Answer (A) is incorrect because fair value, not carrying value, is the appropriate value to be used in a purchase. Answer (C) is incorrect because it reflects a pooling of interests. Answer (D) is incorrect because it reflects a merger rather than a stock investment.

60. Assume that, in addition to the issuance of 25,000 shares of stock on January 2, 1997, the purchase agreement provides for the contingent issuance of 5,000 shares of Planet's stock to the previous shareholders of Star in 1996 if a certain level of earnings is attained. If the required level of earnings is attained and the 5,000 additional shares are issued when the market price of Planet's shares is $45, the journal entry to reflect this transaction is which of the following?

A. No entry is necessary.

B. Investment in subsidiary $225,000
   Capital stock $225,000

C. Investment in subsidiary $225,000
   Capital stock $ 50,000
   Paid-in capital 175,000

D. Investment in subsidiary $200,000
   Capital stock $ 50,000
   Paid-in capital 150,000

The correct answer is (C). *(Publisher)*
REQUIRED: The journal entry to reflect a contingent issuance of shares based on earnings.
DISCUSSION: APB 16 states that, when a contingency based on earnings is resolved and additional consideration such as stock is issued, the acquiring corporation should record the current fair value of the stock issued as an additional cost of the acquired company. This additional cost should usually be reflected as goodwill and amortized over the remaining life of the asset. Thus, Planet should debit investment in subsidiary for an additional $225,000 (5,000 shares x $45). The capital stock account should be credited for $50,000 (5,000 shares x $10), and additional paid-in capital should be credited for the $175,000 remainder ($225,000 – $50,000).
Answer (A) is incorrect because an entry is necessary. Answer (B) is incorrect because the $225,000 must be allocated between capital stock and additional paid-in capital. Answer (D) is incorrect because the current fair value of the stock issued should be used, rather than the $40 fair value at the date of the original acquisition.

61. Assume that, in addition to the issuance of 25,000 shares of stock on January 2, 1997, the purchase agreement provides for the contingent issuance of additional shares necessary to pay a $1,000,000 purchase price if the market price of Planet's stock is not equal to $40 on December 31, 1997. If the market price of Planet's shares is $25 on December 31, 1997, which of the following entries is necessary to reflect the issuance of the contingent shares?

  A. No entry is necessary.

  B. Paid-in capital $150,000
       Capital stock $150,000

  C. Investment in subsidiary $375,000
       Capital stock $150,000
       Paid-in capital   225,000

  D. Investment in subsidiary $150,000
       Capital stock $150,000

62. Assume that, in addition to the assets and liabilities among Star Company's December 31, 1996 balance sheet items, Star has brought suit against a competitor for an infringement of a patent. If sufficient evidence exists to indicate that settlement of the lawsuit in the amount of $75,000 is probable, the allocation of the $1,000,000 purchase price (25,000 shares x $40) should include goodwill of

  A. $0

  B. $225,000

  C. $375,000

  D. $425,000

The correct answer is (B). *(Publisher)*
  REQUIRED: The journal entry to reflect the issuance of shares to resolve a contingency based on valuation of the acquiring company's stock.
  DISCUSSION: APB 16 states that the cost of an acquired company recorded at the date of acquisition represents the entire payment, including any contingent issuance of securities based on security prices. For any additional shares distributed at a later date, the acquiring corporation should reduce the fair value previously allocated to the shares of stock issued. In this situation, Planet must issue an additional 15,000 shares of $10 par stock at a market price of $25; i.e., a total of 40,000 shares must be issued to pay the $1,000,000 purchase price. Thus, $400,000 (40,000 shares x $10 par) must be allocated to the capital stock account and $600,000 to additional paid-in capital. To adjust the existing capital stock balance of $250,000 and the paid-in capital balance of $750,000, the paid-in capital account must be debited and capital stock credited for $150,000.
  Answer (A) is incorrect because an entry is necessary. Answers (C) and (D) are incorrect because the cost of the acquired company is not changed, so an adjustment to the investment account is unnecessary.

The correct answer is (B). *(Publisher)*
  REQUIRED: The determination of goodwill when a preacquisition contingency exists.
  DISCUSSION: According to SFAS 38, *Accounting for Preacquisition Contingencies of Purchased Enterprises*, if the contingency is settled during the allocation period or if during this period information is obtained indicating it is probable an asset existed, a liability had been incurred, or an asset had been impaired at the date of the combination, and the amount of the asset or liability affected can be reasonably estimated, the preacquisition contingency must be included in the allocation of the purchase price based on that fair value. The fair value of the identifiable net assets is $775,000 ($300,000 current assets + $500,000 noncurrent assets – $100,000 liabilities + $75,000 contingent settlement). The excess of the $1,000,000 cost over the $775,000 fair value of the net identifiable assets is $225,000 of goodwill.
  Answer (A) is incorrect because goodwill must be recognized when cost exceeds fair value of the net identifiable assets. Answer (C) is incorrect because $375,000 assumes that a contingent liability has been incurred by Star. Answer (D) is incorrect because $425,000 is based on historical costs, not fair values.

63. Beni Corp. purchased 100% of Carr Corp.'s outstanding capital stock for $430,000 cash. Immediately before the purchase, the balance sheets of both corporations reported the following:

	Beni	Carr
Assets	$2,000,000	$750,000
Liabilities	$ 750,000	$400,000
Common stock	1,000,000	310,000
Retained earnings	250,000	40,000
Liabilities and shareholder's equity	$2,000,000	$750,000

At the date of purchase, the fair value of Carr's assets was $50,000 more than the aggregate carrying amounts. In the consolidated balance sheet prepared immediately after the purchase, the consolidated shareholders' equity should amount to

A. $1,680,000

B. $1,650,000

C. $1,600,000

D. $1,250,000

The correct answer is (D). *(CPA 1191 II-10)*

REQUIRED: The consolidated shareholders' equity after the purchase.

DISCUSSION: A purchase is viewed as an acquisition of net assets. Thus, only the fair value of the net assets of a subsidiary is included in a consolidated balance sheet prepared using the purchase method. The shareholders' equity, including retained earnings, is excluded. Thus, the shareholders' equity section of the current parent company balance sheet is the same as the shareholders' equity section of the consolidated balance sheet. Consequently, shareholders' equity is $1,250,000 ($1,000,000 common stock + 250,000 RE).

Answer (A) is incorrect because $1,680,000 is the sum of the shareholders' equity of Beni plus the cash price. Answer (B) is incorrect because $1,650,000 is the sum of the shareholders' equity of Beni and Carr plus the excess fair value of Carr's assets. Answer (C) is incorrect because $1,600,000 is the sum of the shareholders' equity of Beni and Carr.

64. On July 1, the Prime Company acquired 90% of the Simple Company for cash in an amount equal to the carrying value of the net assets on Simple Company's books. During the year, Simple Company, a nonseasonal company, declared net income of $400,000, and it paid dividends of $50,000 on June 30 and December 31. The preferred presentation of the year-end consolidated income statement should contain which of the following amounts?

A. Minority income of $10,000.

B. Minority income of $20,000.

C. Preacquisition earnings of $180,000.

D. Preacquisition earnings of $200,000.

The correct answer is (C). *(Publisher)*

REQUIRED: The amount arising from a midyear purchase contained in a consolidated income statement.

DISCUSSION: ARB 51, *Consolidated Financial Statements*, states that, when a subsidiary is purchased during the year, the preferred method of presenting the results of operations is to include the subsidiary's operations in the consolidated income statement as though it had been acquired at the beginning of the year and to deduct from the total earnings the preacquisition earnings. The minority interest income for the entire year is also deducted. Preacquisition or purchased earnings are earnings of a subsidiary earned prior to the date of the acquisition of the subsidiary by the parent. These earnings are included in determining the purchase price. The minority income equals the year-end minority interest multiplied by the subsidiary's income for the annual period. Because the purchase of Simple Company occurred at midyear, the minority interest was 10% at year-end, and the subsidiary is nonseasonal, the preacquisition earnings are $180,000 [50% x ($400,000 total income − $40,000 minority interest income)].

Answers (A) and (B) are incorrect because minority income deducted is $40,000 (10% year-end minority interest x $400,000 annual net income). Answer (D) is incorrect because the preacquisition earnings do not include the minority income earned prior to the date of the acquisition.

65. SFAS 38, *Accounting for Preacquisition Contingencies of Purchased Enterprises*, defines a preacquisition contingency as a contingency of an enterprise acquired in a business combination accounted for by the purchase method that is in existence before the end of the allocation period. The allocation period is defined as the period required to identify and quantify the assets acquired and the liabilities assumed. A preacquisition contingency will be excluded from the allocation of the purchase price if it involves an infringement of patent lawsuit brought

A. Against the acquired company that is settled before the consummation of the business combination.

B. By the acquired company against a competitor that is settled before the consummation of the business combination.

C. By the acquired company against a competitor for which information obtained prior to the end of the allocation period indicates that it is probable that the lawsuit will be favorably settled for an amount that is reasonably estimable.

D. By the acquired company against a competitor for which information obtained prior to the end of the allocation period indicates that it is reasonably possible that the lawsuit will be favorably settled for an amount that is reasonably estimable.

The correct answer is (D). *(Publisher)*
REQUIRED: The preacquisition contingency to which part of the purchase price would not be allocated in a combination accounted for by the purchase method.
DISCUSSION: SFAS 38 states that a preacquisition contingency may be a contingent asset, a contingent liability, or a contingent impairment of an asset. The preacquisition contingency, other than the potential tax benefit of a loss carryforward, must be included in the allocation of the purchase price if the contingency is settled during the period required to identify and quantify the assets acquired and the liabilities assumed, or if information obtained during this period indicates that it is probable the contingency will be satisfied and the amount of the asset or liability is reasonably estimable. However, if these conditions are not met, the preacquisition contingency should not be included in the allocation of the purchase price. Accordingly, a reasonably possible preacquisition contingency concerning the patent infringement lawsuit should be included in the determination of net income in the period in which settlement is reached.
Answers (A), (B), and (C) are incorrect because each reflects preacquisition contingencies that meet the criteria of SFAS 38 for inclusion in the allocation of the purchase price.

66. SFAS 72, *Accounting for Certain Acquisitions of Banking or Thrift Institutions*, is applicable to business combinations in which the fair value of liabilities assumed exceeds the fair value of the identifiable assets acquired in the acquisition by a banking or thrift institution. In such an acquisition, the identifiable intangible asset (goodwill) that is recognized in the business combination should be amortized over

A. Its expected useful life using the straight-line method.

B. Its expected useful life, not exceeding 40 years, using the straight-line method.

C. Its expected useful life, not exceeding 40 years, using the interest method.

D. A period no longer than that over which the discount on the long-term interest-bearing assets acquired is to be recognized as interest income, not to exceed 40 years, using the interest method.

The correct answer is (D). *(Publisher)*
REQUIRED: The proper method of accounting for goodwill acquired in certain acquisitions of banking or thrift institutions.
DISCUSSION: According to SFAS 72, in certain business combinations of banking or thrift institutions, when the fair value of liabilities assumed exceeds the fair value of identifiable assets acquired, the unidentifiable intangible asset (goodwill) recognized should usually be amortized by the interest method, over a period no longer than that over which the discount on the long-term interest-bearing assets acquired is to be recognized as interest income. In no case, however, should the period of amortization exceed 40 years. In other words, low-rate interest-bearing assets may have been discounted to fair value by applying current (higher) interest rates, and the fair value of the liabilities assumed may then exceed the fair value of the assets acquired. In that case, the unidentifiable intangible asset (goodwill) and the discount on the identifiable assets will be amortized to income using the interest method over the same period, that is, the estimated remaining life of the long-term interest-bearing assets acquired.
Answer (A) is incorrect because the 40-year limit applies to the amortization of all goodwill recognized. Answers (B) and (C) are incorrect because the expected useful life of the goodwill is not the relevant consideration.

67. In connection with an acquisition by a banking or thrift institution, a regulatory authority may provide assistance by agreeing to pay amounts by which future interest received or receivable on the interest-bearing assets acquired is less than the interest cost of carrying those assets for a period by a stated margin. Which of the following statements relative to such a case is true?

A. The projected assistance must be included in the determination of the fair value of the interest-bearing assets acquired.

B. The carrying amount of interest-bearing assets must be adjusted as the projected assistance is received.

C. The actual assistance must be reported in the income of the period in which it is received.

D. The projected assistance must be included in the determination of the fair value of interest-bearing assets, except those assets that the enterprise intends to sell all or a portion of.

The correct answer is (A). *(Publisher)*
REQUIRED: The true statement about regulatory-assisted business combinations by banking or thrift institutions.
DISCUSSION: SFAS 72, *Accounting for Certain Acquisitions of Banking or Thrift Institutions,* is applicable when a regulatory authority provides assistance to a business combination by a banking or thrift institution in the form of amounts by which future interest receivable on the interest-bearing assets acquired is less than the interest cost of carrying those assets for a period by a stated margin. The projected assistance, computed as of the date of acquisition and based on the interest rate margin existing at that date, must be considered as additional interest on the assets acquired in determining their fair value for purposes of applying the purchase method of accounting.
Answer (B) is incorrect because the interest-bearing assets must be valued at the date of the business combination and not adjusted for subsequent changes in the estimated amount of assistance to be received. Answer (C) is incorrect because the actual assistance should be reported in the period in which it is accrued. Answer (D) is incorrect because, for those interest-bearing assets acquired that the acquiring enterprise intends to sell, projected assistance must be included in the determination of fair value to the degree those assets are not stated at amounts in excess of their current market values.

68. Sorrento Company repurchased 10,000 shares of its outstanding stock for $600,000 on December 31. Sorrento's owners' equity sections immediately before and immediately after this treasury stock transaction are presented below.

	Before	After
Capital stock, $10 par	$1,000,000	$1,000,000
Additional paid-in capital	1,500,000	1,500,000
Retained earnings	2,500,000	2,500,000
Treasury stock	-0-	(600,000)
Total owners' equity	$5,000,000	$4,400,000

Assume that Sorrento repurchased this stock from the general public. By what amount should Palermo Company, which holds 75,000 shares of the outstanding stock of Sorrento, adjust its investment in subsidiary account because of Sorrento's treasury stock transaction?

A. $0

B. $83,333 debit.

C. $83,333 credit.

D. $366,667 debit.

The correct answer is (C). *(Publisher)*
REQUIRED: The investment in subsidiary account adjustment to reflect the repurchase of shares by the subsidiary from the minority interest.
DISCUSSION: Immediately before this treasury stock transaction, the parent's interest in the subsidiary was 75% (75,000 shares held ÷ 100,000 shares outstanding). Immediately after the transaction, it was 831/3% (75,000 shares held ÷ 90,000 shares outstanding). The parent's proportionate interest in the total recorded owners' equity of the subsidiary decreased from $3,750,000 (75% x $5,000,000) to $3,666,667 (831/3% x $4,400,000). Thus, the investment account should be credited (decreased) by $83,333 ($3,750,000 – $3,666,667). The carrying value of the investment account is not needed to calculate the adjustment because the adjustment relates only to the parent's proportionate interest in the subsidiary's owners' equity.
Answer (A) is incorrect because the investment account should be adjusted for the change in the parent's proportionate interest. Answer (B) is incorrect because the $83,333 decrease should be credited, not debited. Answer (D) is incorrect because $3,666,667 is the parent's proportionate interest in the subsidiary.

Questions 69 and 70 are based on the following information. Suwannee Company issued 20,000 additional shares of its common stock for $1,600,000. Suwannee Company's owners' equity sections immediately before and immediately after this issuance of stock transaction are presented below.

	Before	After
Capital stock, $10 par	$1,000,000	$1,200,000
Additional paid-in capital	2,500,000	3,900,000
Retained earnings	3,900,000	3,900,000
Total owners' equity	$7,400,000	$9,000,000

69. Assume that Suwannee Company issued this stock to the general public. By what amount should Palatka Corporation, the owner of 80,000 of the outstanding shares of Suwannee Company, adjust its investment in subsidiary account because of the issuance of stock by Suwannee Company?

A. $0

B. $80,000 debit.

C. $80,000 credit.

D. $1,280,000 debit.

70. Assume that Suwannee Company issued the stock to Palatka Corporation, whose ownership interest thereby increased from 80,000 shares to 100,000 shares. If the carrying value of the identifiable assets of Suwannee is equal to their fair value at the time the additional shares are issued, the goodwill indicated in the purchase of the additional shares equals

A. $0

B. $20,000

C. $320,000

D. $1,580,000

The correct answer is (B). *(Publisher)*
REQUIRED: The investment in subsidiary account adjustment to reflect the issuance of stock by a subsidiary to the general public.
DISCUSSION: Immediately prior to the issuance of the additional shares of stock by Suwannee Company, Palatka's ownership interest was 80% (80,000 shares held ÷ 100,000 shares outstanding). Its proportionate interest in the subsidiary's recorded owners' equity was $5,920,000 (80% x $7,400,000). Immediately after the issuance of the shares, Palatka's ownership interest was 662/3% (80,000 shares held ÷ 120,000 shares outstanding), and its proportionate ownership interest was $6,000,000 (662/3% x $9,000,000). Thus, its investment in subsidiary account should be debited (increased) for the $80,000 difference ($6,000,000 after – $5,920,000 before). The corresponding credit is to paid-in capital.
Answer (A) is incorrect because the investment in subsidiary account should be adjusted for the change in the parent's proportionate interest. Answer (C) is incorrect because the increase should be debited. Answer (D) is incorrect because $1,280,000 assumes that the ownership percentage remained at 80%.

The correct answer is (B). *(Publisher)*
REQUIRED: The determination of goodwill when the parent purchases additional stock issued by the subsidiary.
DISCUSSION: Prior to the issuance of the new securities, the parent company owned 80% of the outstanding stock of the subsidiary, resulting in a proportionate ownership in the subsidiary's recorded owners' equity of $5,920,000. Following the issuance of the 20,000 shares, the parent holds an 831/3% interest (100,000 shares held ÷ 120,000 shares outstanding), resulting in a proportionate ownership interest in the subsidiary's owners' equity of $7,500,000 (831/3% x $9,000,000). The difference is $1,580,000 ($7,500,000 – $5,920,000). Hence, goodwill of $20,000 results ($1,600,000 price paid – $1,580,000).
Answer (A) is incorrect because goodwill must be recognized. The purchase price exceeded the fair value of the identifiable net assets acquired. Answer (C) is incorrect because $320,000 assumes the ownership percentage did not change. Answer (D) is incorrect because $1,580,000 is the increase in the proportionate interest.

Questions 71 through 74 are based on the following information. Akron, Inc. owns 80% of the capital stock of Benson Co. and 70% of the capital stock of Cashin, Inc. Benson Co. owns 15% of the capital stock of Cashin, Inc. Cashin, Inc., in turn, owns 25% of the capital stock of Akron, Inc. These ownership interrelationships are illustrated in the following diagram:

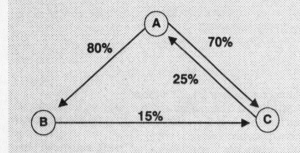

Net income before adjusting for interests in intercompany net income for each corporation follows:

Akron, Inc. $190,000
Benson Co.   170,000
Cashin, Inc.   230,000

Ignore all income tax considerations.

A = Akron's consolidated net income, i.e., its net income plus its share of Benson and Cashin.

B = Benson's consolidated net income, i.e., its net income plus its share of the consolidated net income of Cashin.

C = Cashin's consolidated net income, i.e., its net income plus its share of the consolidated net income of Akron.

---

71. The equation, in a set of simultaneous equations, that computes A is

A. A = .75($190,000 + .8B + .7C)

B. A = $190,000 + .8B + .7C

C. A = .75($190,000) + .8($170,000) + .7($230,000)

D. A = .75($190,000) + .8B + .7C

The correct answer is (B). *(CPA 573 I-27)*
REQUIRED: The equation that computes Akron's consolidated net income.
DISCUSSION: Akron's consolidated net income is its net income of $190,000, plus 80% of Benson's consolidated net income, plus 70% of Cashin's consolidated net income.
Answers (A), (C), and (D) are incorrect because there is no reduction in Akron's consolidated net income for the ownership by Cashin from a consolidated point of view.

72. The equation, in a set of simultaneous equations, that computes B is

A. B = $170,000 + .15C − .75A

B. B = $170,000 + .15C

C. B = .2($170,000) + .15($230,000)

D. B = .2($170,000) + .15C

The correct answer is (B). *(CPA 573 I-28)*
REQUIRED: The equation that computes Benson's consolidated net income.
DISCUSSION: Benson's consolidated net income is its net income plus 15% of Cashin's consolidated net income.
Answer (A) is incorrect because being Akron's subsidiary does not affect Benson's consolidated net income. Answers (C) and (D) are incorrect because Benson's consolidated income includes its entire net income, not only its minority shareholders' share. Answer (C) is also incorrect because Benson includes its share of Cashin's consolidated net income, not only its share of Cashin's net income.

73. Cashin's minority interest in consolidated net income is

A. .15($130,000)

B. $230,000 + .25A

C. .15($230,000) + .25A

D. .15C

The correct answer is (D). *(CPA 573 I-29)*
REQUIRED: The share of consolidated net income attributable to Cashin's minority interest.
DISCUSSION: From a consolidated point of view, 15% of Cashin is held outside the consolidated entity because 70% of Cashin is owned by Akron and 15% by Benson.
Answer (A) is incorrect because Cashin's consolidated net income is $230,000 plus 25% of Akron's consolidated net income. Answer (B) is incorrect because Cashin's minority interest is only 15% (not 100%) of Cashin's consolidated net income. Answer (C) is incorrect because the second term (.25A) of the expression should also be multiplied by 15%.

74. Benson's minority interest in consolidated net income is

A. $34,000

B. $45,755

C. $58,774

D. $161,824

The correct answer is (B). *(CPA 573 I-30)*

REQUIRED: The share of consolidated net income attributable to Benson's minority interest.

DISCUSSION: The minority interest in Benson's income is 20% (100% – 80% owned by Akron), which may be computed by solving a set of simultaneous equations. Each of the first three equations below represents the consolidated net income of one of the three companies. Equations (4), (5), and (6) provide the algebraic solution for Cashin's consolidated net income. Equation (7) is Benson's consolidated income. Equation (8) is Benson's minority interest in consolidated net income.

(1) $A = \$190,000 + .8B + .7C$
(2) $B = \$170,000 + .15C$
(3) $C = \$230,000 + .25A$
(4) $-A = \$920,000 - 4C$
(5) $0 = \$1,110,000 + .8B - 3.3C$
(6) $0 = \$1,110,000 + \$136,000 + .12C - 3.3C$
     $3.18C = \$1,246,000$
     $C = \$391,824$
(7) $B = \$170,000 + .15(\$391,824) = \$228,774$
(8) $.20B = \$45,755$

Answer (A) is incorrect because $34,000 is 20% of Benson's unadjusted net income. Answer (C) is incorrect because $58,774 equals the minority interest in Cashin's net income. Answer (D) is incorrect because $161,824 equals Cashin's share of Akron's consolidated net income.

75. Sub Company had net assets according to its books of $1,000,000 on January 1, 1996. On the same date, Parr Company owned 9,000 of the 12,000 outstanding shares of Sub's only class of stock, and its investment in Sub Company account had a balance of $795,000. If, on January 1, 1996, Sub repurchased 2,000 shares from Parr for $200,000, the gain on the sale of the stock recognized by Parr was

A. $3,000

B. $7,000

C. $10,000

D. $23,333

The correct answer is (B). *(Publisher)*

REQUIRED: The gain on a purchase of treasury stock by a subsidiary from its parent.

DISCUSSION: The gain recognized by the parent will equal the difference between the amount received and the credit to the investment account. The latter has two components: (1) the decrease in the parent's equity in the net assets of the subsidiary and (2) the reduction in the unamortized differential (investment balance – equity in the subsidiary's net assets) attributable to the decrease in the percentage of ownership. Prior to the treasury stock transaction, Parr's equity in Sub's net assets was $750,000 [$1,000,000 x (9,000 shares ÷ 12,000 total shares)]. Hence, the unamortized differential was $45,000 ($795,000 investment balance – $750,000 interest in net assets). Parr's equity in Sub after the treasury stock transaction was $560,000 [(7,000 shares ÷ 10,000 total shares) x $800,000], and the decrease in the equity was therefore $190,000 ($750,000 – $560,000). Given a reduction in percentage stock ownership from 75% (9,000 ÷ 12,000) to 70% (7,000 ÷ 10,000), the reduction in the unamortized differential was $3,000 {[(75% – 70%) ÷ 75%] x $45,000}. Accordingly, the total decrease in the investment account was $193,000 ($190,000 + $3,000), and Parr realized a gain of $7,000 ($200,000 proceeds – $193,000 credit to the investment account). The journal entry in Parr's books was

Cash	$200,000	
Investment in Sub Company		$193,000
Gain on sale		7,000

Answer (A) is incorrect because $3,000 is the reduction in the unamortized differential. Answer (C) is incorrect because $10,000 ignores the reduction in the unamortized differential. Answer (D) is incorrect because $23,333 assumes that the investment balance is reduced by approximately 22.22% (2,000 shares ÷ 9,000 shares).

28.6 Intercompany Transactions

76. Wright Corp. has several subsidiaries that are included in its consolidated financial statement. In its December 31, 1996 trial balance, Wright had the following intercompany balances before eliminations:

	Debit	Credit
Current receivable due from Main Co.	$ 32,000	
Noncurrent receivable from Main	114,000	
Cash advance to Corn Corp.	6,000	
Cash advance from King Co.		$ 15,000
Intercompany payable to King		101,000

In its December 31, 1996 consolidated balance sheet, what amount should Wright report as intercompany receivables?

- A. $152,000
- B. $146,000
- C. $36,000
- D. $0

The correct answer is (D). *(CPA 593 I-14)*

REQUIRED: The intercompany receivables reported in a consolidated balance sheet.

DISCUSSION: In a consolidated balance sheet, reciprocal balances, such as receivables and payables, between a parent and a consolidated subsidiary should be eliminated in their entirety regardless of the portion of the subsidiary's stock held by the parent. Thus, Wright should report $0 as intercompany receivables.

Answers (A), (B), and (C) are incorrect because the effects of intercompany transactions should be completely eliminated in consolidated financial statements.

77. At December 31, 1996, Grey, Inc. owned 90% of Winn Corp., a consolidated subsidiary, and 20% of Carr Corp., an investee over which Grey cannot exercise significant influence. On the same date, Grey had receivables of $300,000 from Winn and $200,000 from Carr. In its December 31, 1996 consolidated balance sheet, Grey should report accounts receivable from affiliates of

- A. $500,000
- B. $340,000
- C. $230,000
- D. $200,000

The correct answer is (D). *(CPA 590 I-11)*

REQUIRED: The accounts receivable from a consolidated subsidiary and a cost-basis investee.

DISCUSSION: In a consolidated balance sheet, reciprocal balances, such as receivables and payables, between a parent and a consolidated subsidiary should be eliminated completely regardless of the portion of the subsidiary's stock held by the parent. Hence, the $300,000 receivable from Winn should be eliminated in its entirety. Because Grey cannot exercise significant influence over Carr, even though it holds 20% of the outstanding shares, this investment should be accounted for on the cost basis. Receivables owed by a cost-basis investee should be reported on the consolidated balance sheet. Grey should therefore report $200,000 in accounts receivable from affiliates.

Answer (A) is incorrect because the $300,000 receivable from Winn should be eliminated. Answer (B) is incorrect because $340,000 includes the receivable from Winn and 20% of the receivable from Carr. Answer (C) is incorrect because $230,000 includes 10% of the receivable from the consolidated subsidiary.

78. Shep Co. has a receivable from its parent, Pep Co. Should this receivable be separately reported in Shep's balance sheet and in Pep's consolidated balance sheet?

	Shep's Balance Sheet	Pep's Consolidated Balance Sheet
A.	Yes	No
B.	Yes	Yes
C.	No	No
D.	No	Yes

The correct answer is (A). *(CPA 591 T-21)*

REQUIRED: The treatment of an intercompany receivable in the balance sheet of a subsidiary and in the consolidated balance sheet.

DISCUSSION: In a consolidated balance sheet, reciprocal balances, such as receivables and payables, between a parent and a consolidated subsidiary should be eliminated in their entirety regardless of the portion of the subsidiary's stock held by the parent. However, intercompany transactions should not be eliminated from the separate financial statements of the entities.

Answers (B), (C), and (D) are incorrect because the receivable should be eliminated from the consolidated statements but not from the subsidiary's balance sheet.

79. Mr. and Mrs. Dart own a majority of the outstanding capital stock of Wall Corp., Black Co., and West, Inc. During 1996, Wall advanced cash to Black and West in the amount of $50,000 and $80,000, respectively. West advanced $70,000 in cash to Black. At December 31, 1996, none of the advances were repaid. In the combined December 31, 1996 balance sheet of these companies, what amount would be reported as receivables from affiliates?

A. $200,000

B. $130,000

C. $60,000

D. $0

The correct answer is (D). *(CPA 1191 I-10)*
REQUIRED: The amount to be reported in the combined balance sheet as receivables from affiliates.
DISCUSSION: Consolidated financial statements are presented when one corporation (the parent) owns the majority of the outstanding stock of another corporation (a subsidiary). Combined financial statements are issued when a relationship such as common ownership or common management exists for two or more corporations. Intercompany transactions and profits or losses are eliminated from combined statements as in consolidated statements. Consequently, the receivables among the combined entities should be eliminated.
Answer (A) is incorrect because $200,000 is the total of the amounts advanced by the affiliated entities to each other. Answer (B) is incorrect because $130,000 is the sum of the advances made by Wall. Answer (C) is incorrect because $60,000 is the sum of the advances made by Wall minus the advance made by Black.

80. Perez, Inc. owns 80% of Senior, Inc. During 1996, Perez sold goods with a 40% gross profit to Senior. Senior sold all of these goods in 1996. For 1996 consolidated financial statements, how should the summation of Perez and Senior income statement items be adjusted?

A. Sales and cost of goods sold should be reduced by the intercompany sales.

B. Sales and cost of goods sold should be reduced by 80% of the intercompany sales.

C. Net income should be reduced by 80% of the gross profit on intercompany sales.

D. No adjustment is necessary.

The correct answer is (A). *(CPA 1193 T-11)*
REQUIRED: The adjustment, if any, to prepare consolidated financial statements given a sale by the parent to the subsidiary.
DISCUSSION: Given that all of the goods were sold, no adjustment is necessary for intercompany profit in ending inventory. Accordingly, the parent's cost should be included in consolidated cost of goods sold, and the price received by the subsidiary should be included in consolidated sales. The required adjustment is to eliminate the sale recorded by the parent and the cost of goods sold recorded by the subsidiary.
Answer (B) is incorrect because the elimination is made without regard to the minority interest. Answer (C) is incorrect because no profit should be eliminated. All of the goods sold to Senior have been resold. Answer (D) is incorrect because sales and cost of sales should be reduced.

81. Parker Corp. owns 80% of Smith, Inc.'s common stock. During 1996, Parker sold Smith $250,000 of inventory on the same terms as sales made to third parties. Smith sold all of the inventory purchased from Parker in 1996. The following information pertains to Smith and Parker's sales for 1996:

	Parker	Smith
Sales	$1,000,000	$700,000
Cost of sales	400,000	350,000
	$ 600,000	$350,000

What amount should Parker report as cost of sales in its 1996 consolidated income statement?

A. $750,000

B. $680,000

C. $500,000

D. $430,000

The correct answer is (C). *(CPA 592 I-11)*
REQUIRED: The cost of sales in the consolidated income statement.
DISCUSSION: Given that Smith purchased inventory from Parker for $250,000 and sold all of it during the year, $250,000 must be eliminated from consolidated cost of goods sold. Hence, the cost of sales in the consolidated income statement is $500,000 [($400,000 + $350,000) − $250,000].
Answer (A) is incorrect because $750,000 is the total of the amounts reported separately by Parker and Smith. Answer (B) is incorrect because $680,000 equals Parker's CGS plus 80% of Smith's. Answer (D) is incorrect because $430,000 equals Parker's CGS plus 80% of Smith's, minus $250,000.

Questions 82 and 83 are based on the following information. Scroll, Inc., a wholly owned subsidiary of Pirn, Inc., began operations on January 1, 1996. The following information is from the condensed 1996 income statements of Pirn and Scroll:

	Pirn	Scroll
Sales to Scroll	$100,000	$ --
Sales to others	400,000	300,000
	500,000	300,000
Cost of goods sold:		
Acquired from Pirn	--	80,000
Acquired from others	350,000	190,000
Gross profit	150,000	30,000
Depreciation	40,000	10,000
Other expenses	60,000	15,000
Income from operations	50,000	5,000
Gain on sale of equipment to Scroll	12,000	--
Income before income taxes	$ 38,000	$ 5,000

Additional Information

- Sales by Pirn to Scroll are made on the same terms as those made to third parties.

- Equipment purchased by Scroll from Pirn for $36,000 on January 1, 1996 is depreciated using the straight-line method over 4 years.

82. In Pirn's December 31, 1996 consolidating worksheet, how much intercompany profit should be eliminated from Scroll's inventory?

A. $30,000

B. $20,000

C. $10,000

D. $6,000

The correct answer is (D). *(CPA 592 I-8)*
REQUIRED: The intercompany profit eliminated from Scroll's inventory.
DISCUSSION: Sales by Pirn to Scroll totaled $100,000, and Scroll reported related CGS of $80,000. Thus, the remaining inventory of these items must have been $20,000. Since Pirn's gross profit rate was 30% ($150,000 gross profit ÷ $500,000 sales), the intercompany profit eliminated from Scroll's inventory should be $6,000 (30% x $20,000).
Answer (A) is incorrect because $30,000 is Scroll's total gross profit. Answer (B) is incorrect because $20,000 is the intercompany inventory. Answer (C) is incorrect because $10,000 equals the total gross profit minus the inventory obtained from Pirn.

83. What amount should be reported as depreciation expense in Pirn's 1996 consolidated income statement?

A. $50,000

B. $47,000

C. $44,000

D. $41,000

The correct answer is (B). *(CPA 592 I-9)*
REQUIRED: The depreciation expense in the consolidated income statement.
DISCUSSION: The depreciation attributable to the gain on sale of equipment to Scroll should be eliminated. Thus, the depreciation expense in the consolidated income statement should be $47,000 [($40,000 Pirn depreciation + $10,000 Scroll depreciation) – ($12,000 ÷ 4 years)].
Answer (A) is incorrect because $50,000 does not eliminate the effect of the gain. Answer (C) is incorrect because $44,000 equals total depreciation minus the inventory profit. Answer (D) is incorrect because $41,000 equals total depreciation minus the inventory profit and the effect of the gain.

84. Clark Co. had the following transactions with affiliated parties during 1996:

- Sales of $50,000 to Dean, Inc., with $20,000 gross profit. Dean had $15,000 of this inventory on hand at year-end. Clark owns a 15% interest in Dean and does not exert significant influence.

- Purchases of raw materials totaling $240,000 from Kent Corp., a wholly owned subsidiary. Kent's gross profit on the sale was $48,000. Clark had $60,000 of this inventory remaining on December 31, 1996.

Before eliminating entries, Clark had consolidated current assets of $320,000. What amount should Clark report in its December 31, 1996 consolidated balance sheet for current assets?

A. $320,000

B. $314,000

C. $308,000

D. $302,000

The correct answer is (C). *(CPA 593 I-9)*
REQUIRED: The amount reported on the consolidated balance sheet for current assets.
DISCUSSION: When an investor buys inventory from a cost-basis investee, no adjustment for intercompany profit is made. Thus, no adjustment is made to the inventory purchased from Dean. When a parent buys inventory from a subsidiary, the inventory on the consolidated balance sheet must be adjusted to remove any intercompany profit. Hence, the inventory must be reduced by the pro rata share of intercompany profit made on the sale by Kent. The reduction is $12,000 [($60,000 EI ÷ $240,000 purchases) x $48,000 gross profit]. Thus, current assets equal $308,000 ($320,000 – $12,000).
Answer (A) is incorrect because $320,000 does not eliminate intercompany transactions. Answer (B) is incorrect because $314,000 does not eliminate the effect of the transactions with Kent but deducts the gross profit included in the inventory held by Dean. Answer (D) is incorrect because $302,000 treats the sales between Clark and Dean as an intercompany transaction.

85. Ahm Corp. owns 90% of Bee Corp.'s common stock and 80% of Cee Corp.'s common stock. The remaining common shares of Bee and Cee are owned by their respective employees. Bee sells exclusively to Cee, Cee buys exclusively from Bee, and Cee sells exclusively to unrelated companies. Selected 1996 information for Bee and Cee follows:

	Bee Corp.	Cee Corp.
Sales	$130,000	$91,000
Cost of sales	100,000	65,000
Beginning inventory	None	None
Ending inventory	None	65,000

What amount should be reported as gross profit in Bee and Cee's combined income statement for the year ended December 31, 1996?

A. $26,000

B. $41,000

C. $47,800

D. $56,000

The correct answer is (B). *(CPA 592 II-20)*
REQUIRED: The gross profit in the combined income statement.
DISCUSSION: Cee buys exclusively from Bee. Thus, Cee's cost of sales equals the sales price charged by Bee, which represented a 30% [($130,000 – $100,000) ÷ $100,000] markup on the cost to the combined entity. Consequently, the gross profit of the combined entity on sales to unrelated companies should include Bee's markup as well as Cee's gross profit. Because Bee's sales were 130% of its cost, the cost to the entity of Cee's sales was $50,000 ($65,000 cost of sales ÷ 130%). The gross profit in the combined income statement was therefore $41,000 ($91,000 – $50,000).
Answer (A) is incorrect because $26,000 was Cee's gross profit. Answer (C) is incorrect because $47,800 is the sum of 90% of Bee's and 80% of Cee's gross profits. Answer (D) is incorrect because $56,000 is the sum of Bee's and Cee's gross profits.

86. Port Inc. owns 100% of Salem Inc. On January 1, 1996, Port sold Salem delivery equipment at a gain. Port had owned the equipment for 2 years and used a 5-year straight-line depreciation rate with no residual value. Salem is using a 3-year straight-line depreciation rate with no residual value for the equipment. In the consolidated income statement, Salem's recorded depreciation expense on the equipment for 1996 will be decreased by

A. 20% of the gain on sale.

B. 33 1/3% of the gain on sale.

C. 50% of the gain on sale.

D. 100% of the gain on sale.

The correct answer is (B). *(CPA 593 T-4)*
REQUIRED: The consolidated depreciation expense on equipment sold by a parent to a subsidiary.
DISCUSSION: The effects of intercompany transactions should be eliminated. Consequently, the equipment and the related depreciation expense should be reported at amounts that exclude the gain on the sale to Salem. Given that the equipment was held by Port for 2 of its 5 years of estimated useful life, that it has no salvage value, and that Salem is depreciating it over 3 years, Salem recognizes as depreciation expense in its separate 1996 statements 33 1/3% of the acquisition cost, which equals the gain recognized by Port plus Port's carrying amount. Thus, 33 1/3% of the gain is included in the 1996 depreciation expense recorded on the equipment and should be eliminated.
Answer (A) is incorrect because 20% assumes a 5-year life. Answer (C) is incorrect because 50% assumes a 2-year life. Answer (D) is incorrect because 100% assumes a 1-year life.

87. On January 1, 1996, Poe Corp. sold a machine for $900,000 to Saxe Corp., its wholly owned subsidiary. Poe paid $1,100,000 for this machine, which had accumulated depreciation of $250,000. Poe estimated a $100,000 salvage value and depreciated the machine on the straight-line method over 20 years, a policy that Saxe continued. In Poe's December 31, 1996 consolidated balance sheet, this machine should be included in cost and accumulated depreciation as

	Cost	Accumulated Depreciation
A.	$1,100,000	$300,000
B.	$1,100,000	$290,000
C.	$900,000	$40,000
D.	$850,000	$42,500

The correct answer is (A). *(CPA 591 I-7)*
REQUIRED: The cost and accumulated depreciation in the consolidated balance sheet.
DISCUSSION: The effect of the intercompany transaction should be eliminated. Thus, the machine should be carried at cost ($1,100,000) minus accumulated depreciation of $300,000 {$250,000 + [($1,100,0000 – $100,000) ÷ 20]}.
Answer (B) is incorrect because $290,000 assumes that 1996 depreciation is based on a $900,000 cost, $100,000 salvage value, and a remaining 20-year life. Answer (C) is incorrect because $900,000 is the sales price, and $40,000 is the depreciation based on a $900,000 cost, $100,000 salvage value, and a remaining 20-year life. Answer (D) is incorrect because $850,000 was the carrying value at the time of sale, and $42,500 would be the depreciation in Saxe's separate financial statements assuming the $850,000 cost, a 20-year life, and no salvage value.

88. At January 1, Seacoast Company, an 80%-owned subsidiary of Plantation Corporation, had $1,000,000 face value of 14% bonds outstanding. They had been issued at face value. Market conditions at January 1 provided a 10% yield rate when Plantation purchased these bonds in the open market for $1,100,000. Which of the following amounts should be included in a consolidated income statement for the year?

A. Bond interest expense of $140,000.

B. Bond interest revenue of $110,000.

C. Constructive loss of $100,000.

D. Constructive loss of $80,000.

The correct answer is (C). *(Publisher)*
REQUIRED: The amount of an intercompany bond transaction in consolidated net income.
DISCUSSION: Because a consolidated financial statement should include both Plantation and Seacoast as a single (consolidated) reporting entity, the purchase of the $1,000,000 outstanding bonds of Seacoast by Plantation for $1,100,000 was in substance a retirement of debt for $100,000 more than the debt's carrying value. This transaction should be reflected in the consolidated income statement as a constructive loss (extraordinary) from the retirement of debt in the amount of $100,000.
Answers (A) and (B) are incorrect because each represents the intercompany interest reflected on the subsidiary's and parent's books that must be eliminated in the consolidated financial statements. Answer (D) is incorrect because ARB 51 requires an adjustment for the total loss, not just the parent's share.

89. Wagner, a holder of a $1,000,000 Palmer, Inc. bond, collected the interest due on March 31, 1996, and then sold the bond to Seal, Inc. for $975,000. On that date, Palmer, a 75% owner of Seal, had a $1,075,000 carrying amount for this bond. What was the effect of Seal's purchase of Palmer's bond on the retained earnings and minority interest amounts reported in Palmer's March 31, 1996 consolidated balance sheet?

	Retained Earnings	Minority Interest
A.	$100,000 increase	$0
B.	$75,000 increase	$25,000 increase
C.	$0	$25,000 increase
D.	$0	$100,000 increase

The correct answer is (A). *(CPA 592 I-4)*
REQUIRED: The effect of the purchase by the subsidiary of the parent's debt.
DISCUSSION: The purchase was in substance a retirement of debt by the consolidated entity for less than its carrying amount. The transaction resulted in a constructive gain (extraordinary) of $100,000 ($1,075,000 carrying amount − $975,000 price) and therefore a $100,000 increase in consolidated retained earnings. The minority interest was unaffected. The minority interest is based on the subsidiary's book values adjusted for subsidiary income and dividends. This transaction did not result in gain or loss for Seal.
Answer (B) is incorrect because the gain is not allocated. Answers (C) and (D) are incorrect because retained earnings is increased by $100,000, but the minority interest is not affected.

90. During 1996, Pard Corp. sold goods to its 80%-owned subsidiary, Seed Corp. At December 31, 1996, one-half of these goods were included in Seed's ending inventory. Reported 1996 selling expenses were $1,100,000 and $400,000 for Pard and Seed, respectively. Pard's selling expenses included $50,000 in freight-out costs for goods sold to Seed. What amount of selling expenses should be reported in Pard's 1996 consolidated income statement?

A. $1,500,000
B. $1,480,000
C. $1,475,000
D. $1,450,000

The correct answer is (D). *(CPA 1191 I-53)*
REQUIRED: The selling expenses reported in the consolidated income statement.
DISCUSSION: The effects of intercompany transactions should be eliminated from consolidated financial statements in their entirety regardless of the parent's percentage of ownership. Consequently, consolidated selling expense is $1,450,000 ($1,100,000 + $400,000 − $50,000 of freight-out incurred on a sale by Pard to Seed). Seed's inventory balance is not relevant to this calculation because selling expenses, including freight-out, are not inventoried.
Answer (A) is incorrect because $1,500,000 assumes no elimination of the effects of the intercompany transaction. Answer (B) is incorrect because $1,480,000 assumes that the selling expense eliminated is related to the inventory held by Seed and that a minority interest in the remainder (20% x $25,000) is also not eliminated. Answer (C) is incorrect because $1,475,000 assumes that the selling expense eliminated is related to the inventory held by Seed.

28.7 Purchase and Pooling Compared

91. A subsidiary may be acquired by issuing common stock in a pooling-of-interests transaction or by paying cash in a purchase transaction. Which of the following items is reported in the consolidated financial statements at the same amount regardless of the accounting method used?

A. Minority interest.
B. Goodwill.
C. Retained earnings.
D. Capital stock.

The correct answer is (A). *(CPA 582 T-12)*
REQUIRED: The item having the same value under both the pooling-of-interests and the purchase methods of accounting.
DISCUSSION: When a stock investment includes more than 50% but less than 100% of the outstanding stock of a company, a minority interest exists. The computation of that minority interest is identical under both the pooling-of-interests and the purchase methods.
Answer (B) is incorrect because the pooling-of-interests method does not allow the recognition of goodwill. Answer (C) is incorrect because retained earnings is reported differently in a pooling of interests than in a purchase. Answer (D) is incorrect because capital stock is reported differently in a pooling of interests than in a purchase.

92. Poe, Inc. acquired 100% of Shaw Co. in a business combination on September 30, 1996. During 1996, Poe declared quarterly dividends of $25,000, and Shaw declared quarterly dividends of $10,000. Under each of the following methods of accounting for the business combination, what amount should be reported as dividends declared in the December 31, 1996 consolidated statement of retained earnings?

	Purchase	Pooling of Interests
A.	$100,000	$130,000
B.	$100,000	$140,000
C.	$130,000	$130,000
D.	$130,000	$140,000

The correct answer is (A). *(CPA 595 F-54)*

REQUIRED: The dividends declared to be reported under the purchase and pooling methods.

DISCUSSION: Under the purchase method, no part of the shareholders' equity of the acquired company is carried forward after the combination. Thus, only the $100,000 of dividends declared by Poe will be included in the statement of retained earnings. Under the pooling-of-interests method, the retained earnings balances of the combining companies at the time of the combination are carried forward. Accordingly, the dividends declared by Shaw prior to the combination date plus the dividends declared by Poe ($100,000 + $30,000 = $130,000) will be reported in the consolidated statement of retained earnings.

Answer (B) is incorrect because $140,000 includes the $10,000 dividend declared by Shaw after the combination date. Answer (C) is incorrect because only the dividends declared by Poe are reported under the purchase method. Answer (D) is incorrect because $130,000 is the amount declared under the pooling-of-interests method, and $140,000 includes the dividends declared by Shaw after the combination date.

93. A business combination occurs in the middle of the year. Results of operations for the year of combination include the combined results of operations of the separate companies for the entire year if the business combination is a

	Purchase	Pooling of Interests
A.	Yes	Yes
B.	Yes	No
C.	No	No
D.	No	Yes

The correct answer is (D). *(CPA 594 F-52)*

REQUIRED: The accounting for combined operating results if a business combination occurs in midyear.

DISCUSSION: In a business combination accounted for as a pooling, the results of operations for the year of combination include the combined results of operations of the separate companies for the entire year. For a purchase, the combined results include the results of operations of the acquired company only from the date of acquisition to the end of the year.

Answers (A), (B), and (C) are incorrect because results are combined for the full year under pooling but not purchase accounting.

94. Cedar Co.'s planned combination with Birch Co. on January 1, 1996 can be structured as either a purchase or a pooling of interests. In a purchase, Cedar would acquire Birch's identifiable net assets for less than their book values. These book values approximate fair values. Birch's assets consist of current assets and depreciable noncurrent assets. How would the combined entity's 1996 net income and operating cash flows under purchase accounting compare to those under pooling-of-interests accounting? Ignore costs required to effect the combination and income tax expense.

	Purchase Accounting Net Income	Purchase Accounting Operating Cash Flows
A.	Equal to pooling	Greater than pooling
B.	Equal to pooling	Equal to pooling
C.	Greater than pooling	Greater than pooling
D.	Greater than pooling	Equal to pooling

The correct answer is (D). *(CPA 1191 T-11)*

REQUIRED: The comparison of net income and operating cash flows under purchase accounting and the pooling-of-interests method.

DISCUSSION: Cedar would acquire Birch's identifiable net assets for less than their book values and these book values approximate fair values. If the combination was structured as a purchase, negative goodwill would result. This negative goodwill must first be allocated against Birch's depreciable noncurrent assets with any remainder recognized as a deferred credit. The resulting decrease in depreciation expense and amortization of any deferred credit would increase purchase accounting net income to an amount greater than Birch's reported net income. Since pooling accounting net income is equal to this reported net income, purchase net income would be greater than pooling net income. In contrast, since the business combination occurred at the beginning of the year, cash flows would be the same under both purchase and pooling.

Answers (A), (B), and (C) are incorrect because cash flows will be the same, but purchase accounting net income will be greater.

Questions 95 and 96 are based on the following information. Costs incurred in completing a business combination are listed below.

Direct acquisition expenses	$120,000
Indirect acquisition expenses	60,000
Costs to register and issue stock	40,000

95. Assuming that this business combination is appropriately accounted for as purchase, the amount charged to expenses of business combination account should be

A. $40,000

B. $60,000

C. $100,000

D. $120,000

The correct answer is (B). *(CMA 1286 4-22)*
REQUIRED: The treatment of business combination costs in a purchase.
DISCUSSION: Three types of costs may be incurred in effecting a business combination: direct costs of acquisition, costs of registering and issuing equity securities, and indirect and general expenses. Direct costs, such as finders' and consultants' fees, should be included in the determination of the cost of the company acquired. Costs of registering and issuing equity securities should be treated as a reduction of the proceeds from the issuance of the securities. Indirect and general costs should be expensed. Thus, assuming this business combination is appropriately accounted for as a purchase, only the $60,000 in indirect acquisition expenses should be charged to the expenses of the business combination.
Answer (A) is incorrect because $40,000 equals the costs to register and issue stock, which reduce the proceeds from the issuance of the securities. Answer (C) is incorrect because $100,000 includes the costs to register and issue stock. Answer (D) is incorrect because $120,000 equals direct acquisition costs, which are included in the cost of the company acquired.

96. Assuming that this business combination is appropriately accounted for as a pooling of interests, the amount charged to the expenses of business combination account should be

A. $40,000

B. $60,000

C. $100,000

D. $220,000

The correct answer is (D). *(CMA 1286 4-23)*
REQUIRED: The treatment of business combination costs in a pooling of interests.
DISCUSSION: APB 16 requires all costs incurred to effect a business combination accounted for as a pooling of interests to be expensed in the period in which the costs are incurred. Accordingly, if this business combination is appropriately accounted for as a pooling of interests, the amount to be charged to the expenses of the business combination should be $220,000 ($120,000 + $60,000 + $40,000).
Answer (A) is incorrect because $40,000 excludes the direct and indirect acquisition expenses. Answer (B) is incorrect because $60,000 excludes the direct expenses of acquisition and the registration and issuance costs. Answer (C) is incorrect because $100,000 excludes the direct acquisition expenses.

Questions 97 and 98 are based on the following information. On June 30, 1992, Pane Corp. exchanged 150,000 shares of its $20 par value common stock for all of Sky Corp.'s common stock. At that date, the fair value of Pane's common stock issued was equal to the book value of Sky's net assets. Both corporations continued to operate as separate businesses, maintaining accounting records with years ending December 31. Information from separate company operations follows:

	Pane	Sky
Retained earnings - 12/31/95	$3,200,000	$925,000
Net income - 6 months ended 6/30/96	800,000	275,000
Dividends paid - 3/25/96	750,000	--

97. If the business combination is accounted for as a pooling of interests, what amount of retained earnings would Pane report in its June 30, 1996 consolidated balance sheet?

A. $5,200,000

B. $4,450,000

C. $3,525,000

D. $3,250,000

The correct answer is (B). *(CPA 593 I-7)*
REQUIRED: The retained earnings at the date of acquisition after a pooling of interests.
DISCUSSION: In a pooling of interests, the contributed capital of the surviving entity should be equal to the total of the contributed capital for the combining entities. The retained earnings for the surviving entity should also be equal to the total of the retained earnings of the combining entities except in certain circumstances, e.g., when an allocation of retained earnings was made to contributed capital or the effects of intercompany transactions must be eliminated. Since these circumstances are not present, the total of the retained earnings of the combining companies on June 30, 1996 is $4,450,000 ($3,200,000 Pane's RE at 12/31/95 + $800,000 Pane's NI at 6/30/96 + $925,000 Sky's RE at 12/31/95 + $275,000 Sky's NI at 6/30/96 – $750,000 dividends paid by Pane on 3/25/96).
Answer (A) is incorrect because $5,200,000 includes the dividends paid by Pane. Answer (C) is incorrect because $3,525,000 does not include Sky's beginning retained earnings. Answer (D) is incorrect because $3,250,000 equals Pane's separate retained earnings on June 30, 1996.

98. If the business combination is accounted for as a purchase, what amount of retained earnings would Pane report in its June 30, 1996 consolidated balance sheet?

A. $5,200,000

B. $4,450,000

C. $3,525,000

D. $3,250,000

The correct answer is (D). *(CPA 593 I-8)*
REQUIRED: The retained earnings at the date of a business combination accounted for as a purchase.
DISCUSSION: A purchase is viewed as an acquisition of net assets. Thus, only the fair value of the net assets of a subsidiary is included in a consolidated balance sheet prepared using the purchase method. The shareholders' equity, including retained earnings, is excluded. Pane's separate retained earnings is therefore equal to the amount in the consolidated balance sheet, i.e., $3,250,000 ($3,200,000 beginning RE + $800,000 NI – $750,000 dividends).
Answer (A) is incorrect because $5,200,000 includes Sky's retained earnings at 6/30/96 and does not deduct the dividends paid. Answer (B) is incorrect because $4,450,000 equals the consolidated retained earnings if the combination is accounted for as a pooling. Answer (C) is incorrect because $3,525,000 includes Sky's net income through 6/30/96.

Questions 99 and 100 are based on the following information. Rolan Corporation issued 10,000 shares of common stock in exchange for all of Sandin Corporation's outstanding stock on January 1. Rolan's common stock had a market price of $60 per share on January 1. The market price of Sandin's stock was not readily ascertainable. Condensed balance sheets of Rolan and Sandin immediately prior to the combination are as indicated below.

	Rolan	Sandin
Total assets	$1,000,000	$500,000
Liabilities	$ 300,000	$150,000
Common stock ($10 par)	200,000	100,000
Retained earnings	500,000	250,000
Total equities	$1,000,000	$500,000

99. Assuming that the combination of Rolan and Sandin qualifies as a purchase, Rolan's investment in Sandin's stock will be stated in Rolan's balance sheet immediately after the combination in the amount of

A. $100,000

B. $350,000

C. $500,000

D. $600,000

The correct answer is (D). *(CPA 1181 II-36)*
REQUIRED: The recorded value of the purchased entity's net assets using the purchase method of accounting.
DISCUSSION: In accounting for a business combination by the purchase method, the cost to the purchasing entity is measured by the amount of cash disbursed or the fair value of other assets distributed. Given that Rolan issued 10,000 shares of common stock with a fair value of $60 per share to effect the purchase, the total cost is $600,000, the amount to be recorded as Rolan's investment in Sandin.
Answer (A) is incorrect because $100,000 equals the par value of the stock issued. Answer (B) is incorrect because $350,000 equals the book value of Sandin's net assets. Answer (C) is incorrect because $500,000 equals the fair value of the stock issued minus its par value.

100. Assuming that the combination of Rolan and Sandin qualifies as a pooling of interests, rather than as a purchase, what should be reported as retained earnings in the consolidated balance sheet immediately after the combination?

A. $500,000

B. $600,000

C. $750,000

D. $850,000

The correct answer is (C). *(CPA 1181 II-37)*
REQUIRED: The consolidated retained earnings after a business combination accounted for as a pooling of interests.
DISCUSSION: The surviving entity has $300,000 in common stock, the sum of $200,000 initially outstanding and $100,000 issued to effect the combination ($10 par x 10,000 shares). Because this amount does not exceed the $300,000 sum of the common stock accounts of the combining entities ($200,000 + $100,000), the retained earnings of the separate entities will be recorded as stated. The consolidated balance sheet will report retained earnings of $750,000 ($500,000 + $250,000).
Answer (A) is incorrect because $500,000 equals Rolan's separate retained earnings. Answer (B) is incorrect because $600,000 equals the fair value of the issued shares. Answer (D) is incorrect because $850,000 equals the combined retained earnings plus the par value of the issued shares.

Questions 101 and 102 are based on the following information. On December 31, 1996, Saxe Corporation was merged into Poe Corporation. In the business combination, Poe issued 200,000 shares of its $10 par common stock, with a market price of $18 a share, for all of Saxe's common stock. The shareholders' equity section of each company's balance sheet immediately before the combination was as presented in the next column:

	Poe	Saxe
Common stock	$3,000,000	$1,500,000
Additional paid-in capital	1,300,000	150,000
Retained earnings	2,500,000	850,000
	$6,800,000	$2,500,000

101. Assume that the merger qualifies for treatment as a purchase. In the December 31, 1996 consolidated balance sheet, additional paid-in capital should be reported at

A. $950,000

B. $1,300,000

C. $1,450,000

D. $2,900,000

The correct answer is (D). *(CPA 1189 I-10)*
REQUIRED: The additional paid-in capital to be reported in the consolidated balance sheet assuming a purchase.
DISCUSSION: A business combination accounted for as a purchase is treated as an acquisition. To effect the acquisition, the 200,000 shares were issued for $3,600,000 (200,000 shares x $18 market price per share). Of this amount, $2,000,000 (200,000 shares x $10 par) should be allocated to the common stock of Poe, with the remaining $1,600,000 ($3,600,000 – $2,000,000) allocated to additional paid-in capital. The additional paid-in capital recorded on Poe's (the parent company's) books is $2,900,000 ($1,300,000 + $1,600,000). This balance is also reported on the 1996 consolidated balance sheet.
Answer (A) is incorrect because $950,000 is the additional paid-in capital reported under the pooling-of-interests method. Answer (B) is incorrect because $1,300,000 is the amount reported by Poe immediately before the combination. Answer (C) is incorrect because $1,450,000 is the sum of the amounts reported by Poe and Saxe immediately before the combination.

102. Assume that the merger qualifies for treatment as a pooling of interests. In the December 31, 1996 consolidated balance sheet, additional paid-in capital should be reported at

A. $950,000

B. $1,300,000

C. $1,450,000

D. $2,900,000

The correct answer is (A). *(CPA 1189 I-11)*
REQUIRED: The additional paid-in capital to be reported in the consolidated balance sheet for a merger qualifying as a pooling of interests.
DISCUSSION: If the transaction is accounted for as a pooling of interests, the contributed capital for the combined entity is equal to the sum of the contributed capital for the combining entities. Poe's contributed capital is $4,300,000 ($3,000,000 common stock + $1,300,000 additional paid-in capital). Saxe's contributed capital is $1,650,000 ($1,500,000 common stock + $150,000 additional paid-in capital). Contributed capital for the consolidated entity is therefore equal to $5,950,000. Of this total, $3,000,000 should be allocated to the common stock account for the Poe stock outstanding prior to the combination. An additional $2,000,000 (200,000 shares x $10 par value) should be allocated to common stock because of the issuance of stock to effect the combination. The remaining $950,000 ($5,950,000 total contributed capital – $5,000,000 total common stock) is allocated to additional paid-in capital for Poe as the parent and for the consolidated entity.
Answer (B) is incorrect because $1,300,000 is the amount reported by Poe immediately before the combination. Answer (C) is incorrect because $1,450,000 is the sum of the amounts reported by Poe and Saxe immediately before the combination. Answer (D) is incorrect because $2,900,000 is the additional paid-in capital reported under the purchase method.

28.8 Branch Accounting

103. An enterprise uses a branch accounting system in which it establishes separate formal accounting systems for its home office operations and its branch office operations. Which of the following statements about this arrangement is false?

A. The home office account on the books of a branch office represents the equity interest of the home office in the net assets of the branch.

B. The branch office account on the books of the home office represents the equity interest of the branch office in the net assets of the home office.

C. The home office and branch office accounts are reciprocal accounts that must be eliminated in the preparation of the enterprise's financial statements that are presented in accordance with GAAP.

D. Unrealized profit from internal transfers between the home office and a branch must be eliminated in the preparation of the enterprise's financial statements that are presented in accordance with GAAP.

The correct answer is (B). *(Publisher)*
REQUIRED: The false statement about branch accounting.
DISCUSSION: In branch accounting, the branch office account on the books of the home office represents the investment by the home office in the net assets of the branch, not the branch's equity in the home office.
Answers (A), (C), and (D) are incorrect because each is a true statement about branch accounting.

104. Allen Corporation bills its branch office for shipments of goods at a 20% markup on cost and records the billed prices in its shipments to branch account. During the first year of operation of the branch, Allen sent merchandise to the branch at a billed price of $24,000 (cost $20,000). Some of the goods were returned as spoiled (billed price $600). Branch cost of goods sold for the period totaled $13,800. Assuming no losses of inventory items, by how much should Allen adjust the reported income of the branch?

A. $1,800

B. $2,300

C. $2,760

D. $4,000

The correct answer is (B). *(J.R. Barnhart)*
REQUIRED: The year-end adjustment to branch income.
DISCUSSION: Cost of goods sold as reported by the branch includes the 20% markup of $2,300 [$13,800 – ($13,800 ÷ 120%)]. Allen should adjust the reported branch income and the balance in shipments to its branch account for the amount of the billed markup realized during the year. The home office entry at year-end when the shipments to branch account has been credited at billed cost is first to debit the shipments to branch account (reducing it to cost) and to credit an unrealized profit in branch inventories account for the markup on the shipments. The second part of the entry is to debit the unrealized profit account and credit branch income for the amount of the markup realized on branch sales to outside entities ($2,300, as calculated above).
Answer (A) is incorrect because $1,800 equals the markup included in branch cost of goods sold minus the cost to the company of the goods returned. Answer (C) is incorrect because $2,760 equals 20% of branch cost of goods sold. Answer (D) is incorrect because $4,000 equals the total markup on goods sent to the branch.

105. The following information pertains to shipments of merchandise from Home Office to Branch during 1996:

Home Office's cost of merchandise	$160,000
Intracompany billing	200,000
Sales by Branch	250,000
Unsold merchandise at Branch on December 31, 1996	20,000

In the combined income statement of Home Office and Branch for the year ended December 31, 1996, what amount of the above transactions should be included in sales?

A. $250,000

B. $230,000

C. $200,000

D. $180,000

The correct answer is (A). *(CPA 1192 II-60)*
REQUIRED: The sales reported on the combined income statement.
DISCUSSION: ARB 51 states that intercompany balances and transactions should be eliminated. The only sales to be recognized in the income statement are Branch's sales to outside parties.
Answer (B) is incorrect because $230,000 equals sales minus year-end inventory. Answer (C) is incorrect because $200,000 equals intraoffice billing. Answer (D) is incorrect because $180,000 equals intraoffice billing minus year-end inventory.

106. Which represents the proper journal entry for a periodic inventory system that should be made on the books of the home office when goods that cost the home office $100,000 to manufacture are shipped to a branch at a transfer price of $125,000 and the billed price is not recorded in the shipments to branch account?

A.	Branch office	$100,000	
	Shipments to branch		$100,000
B.	Branch office	$125,000	
	Shipments to branch		$125,000
C.	Branch office	$125,000	
	Shipments to branch		$100,000
	Unrealized profit		25,000
D.	Shipments to branch	$100,000	
	Unrealized profit	25,000	
	Shipments from home office		$125,000

The correct answer is (C). *(Publisher)*
REQUIRED: The home office journal entry to reflect merchandise shipments at cost plus a markup.
DISCUSSION: When goods are shipped from a home office to a branch at a transfer price that reflects original cost plus a markup, the branch must record the shipment at the transfer price. The home office most often reflects the shipments to branch at original cost. To maintain a reciprocal relationship between the home office and the branch office accounts, an unrealized profit in branch inventories account reflects the markup.
Answers (A) and (B) are incorrect because neither reflects the unrealized profit. Answer (A) is incorrect because the branch office should be recorded at $125,000. Answer (B) is incorrect because the shipments to branch should be recorded at the original cost of $100,000. Answer (D) is incorrect because it is the work sheet entry necessary to eliminate this intercompany transaction in the preparation of the financial statements.

107. Which represents the proper journal entry for a periodic inventory system that should be made on the books of the branch when goods that cost the home office $100,000 to manufacture are shipped to the branch at a price of $125,000?

A.	Shipments from home office	$100,000	
	Home office		$100,000
B.	Shipments from home office	$125,000	
	Home office		$125,000
C.	Shipments from home office	$125,000	
	Unrealized profit		$ 25,000
	Home office		100,000
D.	Shipments to branch	$100,000	
	Unrealized profit	25,000	
	Shipments from home office		$125,000

The correct answer is (B). *(Publisher)*
REQUIRED: The journal entry on the branch books to reflect the receipt of merchandise shipments at a transfer price that reflects cost plus a markup.
DISCUSSION: In a periodic system, when merchandise is received by a branch from the home office, the merchandise should be reflected as a shipment from the home office in the amount of the transfer price, with a corresponding entry to the home office account to indicate the equity of the home office in the net assets of the branch.
Answer (A) is incorrect because the shipments should be reflected at the transfer price. Answer (C) is incorrect because the home office equity should be reflected at the transfer price. Answer (D) is incorrect because it is the worksheet entry used to eliminate this intercompany transaction in the preparation of the enterprise's financial statements.

CHAPTER TWENTY-NINE
INTERIM STATEMENTS

Interim reports cover periods of less than 1 year. The applicable accounting principles are ordinarily the same as those for annual statements, but some modifications are necessary so that interim statements may relate more closely to the results of operations for the annual period.

29.1 Basic Concepts

1. In considering interim financial reporting, how did the Accounting Principles Board conclude that such reporting should be viewed?

A. As a "special" type of reporting that need not follow generally accepted accounting principles.

B. As useful only if activity is evenly spread throughout the year so that estimates are unnecessary.

C. As reporting for a basic accounting period.

D. As reporting for an integral part of an annual period.

The correct answer is (D). *(CPA 1176 T-18)*
REQUIRED: The APB's view of interim financial reporting.
DISCUSSION: APB 28, *Interim Financial Reporting*, views each interim period primarily as an integral part of an annual period. Ordinarily, the results for an interim period should be based on the same accounting principles the enterprise uses in preparing annual statements. Certain principles and practices used for annual reporting, however, may require modification at interim dates so that interim reports may relate more closely to the results of operations for the annual period.
Answer (A) is incorrect because interim reporting is not a "special" type of reporting, and GAAP should be followed. Answer (B) is incorrect because interim reports may be useful for seasonal and unevenly spread activities. Answer (C) is incorrect because the APB rejected the view that the interim period is a discrete accounting period.

2. A tennis and racquetball club offers membership privileges for a 3-year period under the following arrangements:

1) The applicant pays the entire $1,600 membership fee in eight quarterly installments during the first 2 years of the contract period.

2) The applicant is entitled to unlimited use of the tennis and racquetball facilities during the 3-year contract period.

Based on experience, the club is able to reasonably estimate uncollectible receivables. The club prepares quarterly financial statements. In which accounting period(s) should the club recognize the membership fee as revenue for financial statement reporting?

    A. In the quarter that the membership contract is signed.

    B. Evenly over the eight quarters in which the installment payments are to be received.

    C. In the quarter that the membership period terminates.

    D. Evenly over the 12-quarter membership period.

The correct answer is (D). *(CIA 1187 IV-25)*
    REQUIRED: The accounting period in which revenue should be recognized.
    DISCUSSION: In general, APB 28 states that the results for an interim period should be based on the same accounting principles that the enterprise uses in preparing annual statements. SFAC 5 states that revenue should be recognized when it is realized or realizable and earned. For revenue associated with membership privileges, the earning process is completed in proportion to the amount of the membership period elapsed. This principle is applicable in both annual and interim periods. Thus, the $1,600 membership fee should be allocated evenly over the 12-quarter membership period.
    Answers (A), (B), and (C) are incorrect because the membership revenue should be prorated evenly over the membership period.

3. Which of the following statements is a correct description of the disclosure requirements when a publicly traded company that regularly reports interim information to its security holders does not issue a separate fourth quarter interim report?

    A. Such omission is not permitted if the company is publicly traded.

    B. A note to the annual financial statements must include certain disclosures concerning the fourth interim period that are more limited than those required in a separate fourth quarter report.

    C. All three prior interim reports must be revised and reissued if the aggregate effect of year-end adjustments is material to the results of the fourth quarter.

    D. Current year-to-date interim data must be disclosed.

The correct answer is (B). *(Publisher)*
    REQUIRED: The true statement about disclosures for a company that does not issue a separate fourth quarter interim report.
    DISCUSSION: When interim financial data are not reported separately for the fourth quarter, certain disclosures required by APB 28 must be made in a footnote to the annual financial statements. These disclosures are less extensive than the minimum information required when a publicly traded company chooses to report at interim dates (see the next question). The disclosures must include disposals of segments; extraordinary, unusual, or infrequent items; and the aggregate effect of material year-end adjustments. Moreover, if an accounting change is made in the fourth quarter, the appropriate disclosures about accounting changes required by APB 28 and SFAS 3, *Reporting Accounting Changes in Interim Statements*, should also be included in the note.
    Answer (A) is incorrect because APB 28 specifically permits disclosure of fourth quarter data in a footnote to the annual statements. Answer (C) is incorrect because APB 28 does not require restatement or revision of prior interim reports, even if year-end adjustments are necessary. Answer (D) is incorrect because the current year-to-date interim data are the annual statements themselves.

4. Interim reporting disclosures should include all of the following except

    A. Primary and fully diluted earnings per share.

    B. Significant changes in estimates or provisions for income tax.

    C. Changes in accounting principles or estimates.

    D. Changes in investment policy.

The correct answer is (D). *(CMA 685 4-32)*
    REQUIRED: The interim financial reporting disclosures not required by APB 28.
    DISCUSSION: APB 28 does not require presentation of interim income statements, statements of financial position, or statements of cash flows. Nor does it require disclosure of changes in investment policy. Although interim financial statements may be presented, minimum disclosures required when a publicly held company does issue a financial summary of interim operations include

1) Sales or gross revenues, provision for income taxes, extraordinary items, cumulative effect of changes in accounting principles, and net income.
2) Primary and fully diluted EPS.
3) Seasonal revenues, costs, or expenses.
4) Significant changes in estimates or provisions for income taxes.
5) Disposal of a segment and extraordinary, unusual, or infrequent items.
6) Contingent items.
7) Changes in accounting principles or estimates.
8) Significant cash flows.

    Answers (A), (B), and (C) are incorrect because disclosures required by APB 28 include PEPS, FDEPS, changes in estimates and principles, and estimates or provisions for income tax.

5. How should material seasonal variations in revenue be reflected in interim financial statements?

    A. The seasonal variation should be disclosed by showing pro forma financial statements for subsequent interim periods within the fiscal year.

    B. Because the total revenue pattern of the current annual period is not known with certainty, any statements about seasonal patterns may be misleading and must be omitted from interim statements.

    C. Footnote disclosure should warn the statement reader that revenues are subject to seasonal variation, but no supplemental schedules of past seasonality should be shown.

    D. The seasonal nature should be disclosed. Revenue information for 12-month periods ended at the interim date may be disclosed.

The correct answer is (D). *(Publisher)*
    REQUIRED: The proper method of reflecting material seasonal variations in revenue in interim financial statements.
    DISCUSSION: If they issue interim data, APB 28 makes certain disclosures mandatory for businesses that have material seasonal fluctuations. Such disclosures safeguard the user of the statements from being misled into believing that interim results from such businesses are fairly representative of annual results. Businesses must disclose the seasonal nature of their activities and should consider supplementing interim reports with information for the 12-month period that ended at the interim date for the current and preceding years.
    Answer (A) is incorrect because the disclosure requirement may be met by providing financial data for prior, not subsequent, interim periods within the fiscal year. Answer (B) is incorrect because businesses must disclose the seasonal nature of their activities. Answer (C) is incorrect because supplemental schedules with information for the 12-month period ending at the interim date for the current and preceding years are proper disclosures.

6. For interim financial reporting, an extraordinary gain occurring in the second quarter should be

   A. Recognized ratably over the last three quarters.

   B. Recognized ratably over all four quarters, with the first quarter being restated.

   C. Recognized in the second quarter.

   D. Disclosed by footnote only in the second quarter.

The correct answer is (C). *(CPA 1190 T-7)*
   REQUIRED: The appropriate recognition of an extraordinary gain in an interim report.
   DISCUSSION: Extraordinary items are material gains or losses that are unusual in nature and infrequent in occurrence within the environment in which the business operates. APB 28 requires that extraordinary items be disclosed separately and included in the determination of net income for the interim period in which they occur. Gains and losses similar to those that would not be deferred at year-end should not be deferred to later interim periods of the same year. Hence, the extraordinary gain should not be prorated.
   Answers (A) and (B) are incorrect because the gain should be recognized in the quarter in which it occurs. Answer (D) is incorrect because the gain should be recognized in income. Disclosure in footnotes is not sufficient.

7. Advertising costs may be accrued or deferred to provide an appropriate expense in each period for

	Interim Financial Reporting	Year-end Financial Reporting
A.	Yes	No
B.	Yes	Yes
C.	No	No
D.	No	Yes

The correct answer is (B). *(CPA 590 T-34)*
   REQUIRED: The type(s) of reporting in which advertising costs may be accrued or deferred.
   DISCUSSION: Advertising costs should be allocated on a systematic and rational basis to the accounting periods to which these costs relate. Thus, the accrual or deferral of advertising costs is appropriate for both interim and year-end financial reporting if their benefits clearly apply to more than one period. Moreover, if a cost that would be fully expensed in an annual report benefits more than one interim period, it may be allocated to those interim periods.
   Answers (A), (C), and (D) are incorrect because advertising costs may be accrued or deferred for interim or year-end financial reporting.

8. On March 15, 1996, Krol Company paid property taxes of $180,000 on its factory building for calendar year 1996. On April 1, 1996, Krol made $300,000 in unanticipated repairs to its plant equipment. The repairs will benefit operations for the remainder of the calendar year. What total amount of these expenses should be included in Krol's quarterly income statement for the 3 months ended June 30, 1996?

   A. $75,000

   B. $145,000

   C. $195,000

   D. $345,000

The correct answer is (B). *(CPA 1192 II-52)*
   REQUIRED: The proper accounting for payments of property taxes and major repair costs in a quarterly income statement.
   DISCUSSION: The benefit from the payment of the property taxes relates to all four quarters of 1996 and should be prorated at $45,000 ($180,000 ÷ 4) per quarter. The benefit from the unanticipated repairs to plant equipment relates to the second, third, and fourth quarters. It should be spread evenly over these quarters at $100,000 ($300,000 ÷ 3) per quarter. The total amount of expenses that should be included in the quarterly income statement for the 3 months ended June 30, 1996 is therefore $145,000.
   Answer (A) is incorrect because $75,000 results from not prorating the property taxes and from prorating the repair cost over all four quarters. Answer (C) is incorrect because $195,000 assumes that the entire repair cost is allocated to the first two quarters. Answer (D) is incorrect because $345,000 results from not allocating the repair expense.

9. Vilo Corp. has estimated that total depreciation expense for the year ending December 31, 1996 will amount to $60,000 and that 1996 year-end bonuses to employees will total $120,000. In Vilo's interim income statement for the 6 months ended June 30, 1996, what is the total amount of expense relating to these two items that should be reported?

A. $0

B. $30,000

C. $90,000

D. $180,000

The correct answer is (C). *(CPA 589 II-12)*
REQUIRED: The amount of expenses related to depreciation and year-end bonuses that should be reported in the 6-month income statement.
DISCUSSION: APB 28 states that costs and expenses other than product costs should be either charged to income in interim periods as incurred or allocated among interim periods based on the benefits received. The depreciation and the bonuses to employees clearly provide benefits throughout the year, and they should be allocated ratably to all interim periods. In the interim income statement for the 6 months ended June 30, 1996, the total amount of expense that should be recorded is $90,000 [($180,000 ÷ 12 months) x 6 months].
Answer (A) is incorrect because depreciation and bonus expenses should be allocated ratably. Answer (B) is incorrect because $30,000 excludes the allocation of bonuses. Answer (D) is incorrect because $180,000 allocates the expenses entirely to the 6-month interim period ending 6/30/96.

10. In August 1996, Ella Company spent $150,000 on an advertising campaign for subscriptions to the magazine it sells on getting ready for the skiing season. There are only two issues: one in October and one in November. The magazine is sold only on a subscription basis, and the subscriptions started in October 1996. Assuming Ella's fiscal year ends on March 31, 1997, what amount of expense should be included in Ella's quarterly income statement for the 3 months ended December 31, 1996 as a result of this expenditure?

A. $37,500

B. $50,000

C. $75,000

D. $150,000

The correct answer is (D). *(CPA 1179 I-11)*
REQUIRED: The amount of advertising expense included in the third quarter's income statement.
DISCUSSION: Even if payments are received in advance, subscription revenue may be recognized only when it has been realized and earned. Because the magazine is published only during October and November, recognition of subscription revenue and related expenses is appropriate only during that quarter. Accordingly, the entire advertising expense of $150,000 should be recognized in that period.
Answer (A) is incorrect because $37,500 results from allocating the $150,000 expense ratably to four quarters. Answer (B) is incorrect because $50,000 results from allocating 1/3 of the $150,000 expense. Answer (C) is incorrect because $75,000 results from allocating 1/2 of the $150,000 expense.

11. On June 30, 1996, Mill Corp. incurred a $100,000 net loss from disposal of a business segment. Also, on June 30, 1996, Mill paid $40,000 for property taxes assessed for the calendar year 1996. What amount of the foregoing items should be included in the determination of Mill's net income or loss for the 6-month interim period ended June 30, 1996?

A. $140,000

B. $120,000

C. $90,000

D. $70,000

The correct answer is (B). *(CPA 592 II-12)*

REQUIRED: The amount of property taxes and loss from disposal of a business segment that should be included in the determination of net income or loss for the interim period.

DISCUSSION: Costs other than product costs, such as rent, interest, or property taxes, that will clearly benefit two or more interim periods should be allocated among those periods based on estimates of time expired, the benefit received, or the activity associated with each period. Thus, Mill should allocate $20,000 (6/12 x $40,000) of the property taxes to the 6-month interim period ended 6/30/96. Gains and losses that arise in an interim period that are similar to gains and losses that would not be deferred at year-end should not be deferred to later interim periods within the same fiscal year. Consequently, gains or losses from disposal of a segment should not be prorated over the balance of the fiscal year, and the loss on disposal of a segment ($100,000) should be recognized in full for the interim period ended 6/30/96. The total included in the interim income statement for the two items is therefore $120,000 ($20,000 + $100,000).

Answer (A) is incorrect because $140,000 reflects a failure to prorate the property taxes. Answer (C) is incorrect because $90,000 reflects proration of the loss on disposal of a segment and the full amount of the property taxes. Answer (D) is incorrect because $70,000 reflects proration of the loss on disposal of a segment.

12. Kell Corp.'s $95,000 net income for the quarter ended September 30, 1996 included the following after-tax items:

- A $60,000 extraordinary gain, realized on April 30, 1996, was allocated equally to the second, third, and fourth quarters of 1996.
- A $16,000 cumulative-effect loss resulting from a change in inventory valuation method was recognized on August 2, 1996.

In addition, Kell paid $48,000 on February 1, 1996 for 1996 calendar-year property taxes. Of this amount, $12,000 was allocated to the third quarter of 1996. For the quarter ended September 30, 1996, Kell should report net income of

A. $91,000

B. $103,000

C. $111,000

D. $115,000

The correct answer is (A). *(CPA 1191 II-13)*

REQUIRED: The net income reported for the quarter.

DISCUSSION: APB 28 requires that extraordinary items be disclosed separately and included in the determination of net income for the interim period in which they occur. Gains and losses similar to those that would not be deferred at year-end should not be deferred to later interim periods of the same year. Hence, the extraordinary gain should not be prorated. SFAS 3, *Reporting Accounting Changes in Interim Financial Statements*, covers cumulative-effect type accounting changes. If an accounting change occurs in other than the first quarter of the enterprise's fiscal year, the proper treatment is to calculate the cumulative effect on retained earnings at the beginning of the year and include it in restated net income presented in the first quarter financial statements. In addition, all previously issued interim financial statements of the current year must be restated to reflect the new accounting method. The property taxes were properly allocated among the four quarters of the fiscal year. Thus, after adjustment for the foregoing items, third quarter net income is $91,000 [$95,000 – ($60,000 ÷ 3) + $16,000].

Answer (B) is incorrect because $103,000 results from adding back the allocation of property tax expense. Answer (C) is incorrect because $111,000 does not adjust for the extraordinary gain. Answer (D) is incorrect because $115,000 equals $95,000 of net income plus one-third of the extraordinary gain.

29.2 Inventory

13. Which of the following reporting practices is permissible for interim financial reporting?

A. Use of the gross profit method for interim inventory pricing.

B. Use of the direct costing method for determining manufacturing inventories.

C. Deferral of unplanned variances under a standard cost system until year-end.

D. Deferral of inventory market declines until year-end.

The correct answer is (A). *(CPA 1175 T-27)*
REQUIRED: The inventory reporting practice permissible in interim financial reporting.
DISCUSSION: Certain accounting principles and practices followed for annual reporting purposes may be modified for interim reporting. For example, the gross profit method may be used for estimating cost of goods sold and inventory because a physical inventory count at the interim date may not be feasible.
Answer (B) is incorrect because the direct costing method is never permissible for financial reporting. Answer (C) is incorrect because only variances that are planned and expected to be absorbed by the end of the annual period may be deferred. Answer (D) is incorrect because only market declines that can reasonably be expected to be restored within the fiscal year may be deferred.

14. A store uses the gross profit method to estimate inventory and cost of goods sold for interim reporting purposes. Past experience indicates that the average gross profit rate is 25% of sales. The following data relate to the month of March:

Inventory cost, March 1	$25,000
Purchases during the month at cost	67,000
Sales	84,000
Sales returns	3,000

Based on the data above, what is the estimated ending inventory at March 31?

A. $20,250

B. $21,000

C. $29,000

D. $31,250

The correct answer is (D). *(CIA 1185 IV-14)*
REQUIRED: The estimated ending inventory under the gross profit method.
DISCUSSION: In accordance with the gross profit method, cost of goods sold is estimated by multiplying the net sales figure by one minus the gross profit rate. In this example, the estimate of cost of goods sold is $60,750 [($84,000 sales − $3,000 sales returns) x (1 − .25)]. As indicated below, subtracting the estimated cost of goods sold from the goods available for sale results in an estimated ending inventory at March 31 of $31,250.

Beginning inventory	$25,000
March purchases	67,000
Goods available for sale	$92,000
Estimated CGS	(60,750)
Estimated ending inventory	$31,250

Answer (A) is incorrect because $20,250 is the gross profit. Answer (B) is incorrect because purchases are subtracted from beginning inventory, and cost of goods sold ($84,000 x 75% = 63,000) is not adjusted for sales returns and is added to beginning inventory (25,000 − 67,000 + 63,000 = 21,000). Answer (C) is incorrect because cost of goods sold is not adjusted for sales returns.

15. Because of a decline in market price in the second quarter, Petal Co. incurred an inventory loss. The market price is expected to return to previous levels by the end of the year. At the end of the year, the decline had not reversed. When should the loss be reported in Petal's interim income statements?

A. Ratably over the second, third, and fourth quarters.

B. Ratably over the third and fourth quarters.

C. In the second quarter only.

D. In the fourth quarter only.

The correct answer is (D). *(CPA 593 T-21)*
REQUIRED: The true statement about reporting inventory at interim dates when a market decline expected to reverse by year-end does not.
DISCUSSION: A market decline reasonably expected to be restored within the fiscal year may be deferred at an interim reporting date because no loss is anticipated for the year. Inventory losses from nontemporary market declines, however, must be recognized at the interim reporting date. Consequently, Petal would not have reported the market decline until it determined at the end of the fourth quarter that the expected reversal would not occur.
Answers (A), (B), and (C) are incorrect because, during the second quarter, the decline in market value was expected to reverse, and the decline was not deemed other than temporary until the end of the fourth quarter.

16. An inventory loss from a market price decline occurred in the first quarter. The loss was not expected to be restored in the fiscal year. However, in the third quarter the inventory had a market price recovery that exceeded the market decline that occurred in the first quarter. For interim financial reporting, the dollar amount of net inventory should

- A. Decrease in the first quarter by the amount of the market price decline and increase in the third quarter by the amount of the market price recovery.

- B. Decrease in the first quarter by the amount of the market price decline and increase in the third quarter by the amount of decrease in the first quarter.

- C. Decrease in the first quarter by the amount of the market price decline and not be affected in the third quarter.

- D. Not be affected in either the first quarter or the third quarter.

The correct answer is (B). *(CPA 1192 T-16)*
REQUIRED: The proper interim financial reporting of a market decline and subsequent recovery.
DISCUSSION: APB 28 requires that a market price decline in inventory be recognized in the interim period in which it occurs unless it is expected to be temporary, i.e., unless the decline is expected to be restored by the end of the fiscal year. Because this loss was not expected to be restored in the fiscal year, the company should report the dollar amount of the market price decline as a loss in the first quarter. When a market price recovery occurs in an interim period, it should be treated as a change in estimate. The market price recovery recognized in the third quarter is limited, however, to the extent of losses previously recognized. Accordingly, the inventory should be written up to its original cost.
Answer (A) is incorrect because the recovery recognized in the third quarter is limited to the amount of the losses previously recognized. Answers (C) and (D) are incorrect because the first quarter loss and the third quarter recovery would be offsetting.

17. An inventory loss from a permanent market decline of $360,000 occurred in May 1996. Cox Co. appropriately recorded this loss in May 1996 after its March 31, 1996 quarterly report was issued. What amount of inventory loss should be reported in Cox's quarterly income statement for the 3 months ended June 30, 1996?

- A. $0

- B. $90,000

- C. $180,000

- D. $360,000

The correct answer is (D). *(CPA 590 II-43)*
REQUIRED: The permanent inventory loss from a market decline reported in a quarterly income statement.
DISCUSSION: APB 28 requires that an inventory loss from market decline not be deferred beyond the interim period in which it occurs, unless it is expected to be recovered within the fiscal year. The $360,000 market decline occurring in the quarter ended 6/30/96 is not considered temporary. Hence, it should be recognized in full in that quarter.
Answer (A) is incorrect because the decline should be recognized in full in the quarter ended 6/30/96. Answer (B) is incorrect because $90,000 assumes proration over four quarters. Answer (C) is incorrect because $180,000 assumes proration over two quarters.

18. When a standard cost system of accounting is used to determine costs for valuation of inventory in interim financial statements,

- A. Unanticipated variances should be spread prospectively to the remaining interim periods in the current annual reporting period.

- B. Unplanned variances should be recognized in the interim period in which they are incurred.

- C. Unplanned volume variances should be retroactively allocated to prior interim periods in the current annual reporting period if they occur after the first quarter.

- D. Unplanned variances should be deferred to the fourth quarter and recognized as a component of year-end adjustments.

The correct answer is (B). *(Publisher)*
REQUIRED: The true statement about interim reporting of unplanned variances when using standard costs.
DISCUSSION: APB 28 allows planned standard cost variances to be deferred if they are expected to be absorbed in subsequent interim periods of a year. Unplanned or unanticipated variances, however, should be recognized in the interim period in which they are incurred.
Answers (A) and (D) are incorrect because unplanned or unanticipated variances should be expensed in the interim period in which they are incurred. Answer (C) is incorrect because an unplanned volume variance is not a basis for a retroactive restatement.

19. A company that uses the last-in, first-out (LIFO) method of inventory pricing at an interim reporting date has encountered a partial liquidation of the base-period inventory level. The decline is considered temporary, and the partial liquidation will be replaced prior to year-end. The amount shown as inventory at the interim reporting date should

A. Not give effect to the LIFO liquidation, and cost of sales for the interim reporting period should include the expected cost of replacement of the liquidated LIFO base.

B. Be shown at the actual level, and cost of sales for the interim reporting period should reflect the decrease in LIFO base-period inventory level.

C. Not give effect to the LIFO liquidation, and cost of sales for the interim reporting period should reflect the decrease in the LIFO base-period inventory level.

D. Be shown at the actual level, and the decrease in inventory level should not be reflected in the cost of sales for the interim reporting period.

29.3 Cumulative-Effect Type Changes

20. If a cumulative-effect type accounting change is made in other than the first period of an enterprise's fiscal year, the cumulative effect of the change should be

A. Included in net income of the period of change.

B. Reported as an adjustment of prior years' financial statements.

C. Excluded from net income of the period of change.

D. Reported as an extraordinary item in the period of change.

The correct answer is (A). *(CPA 1177 T-9)*
REQUIRED: The true statement about inventory valuation at an interim reporting date when a temporary LIFO liquidation has occurred.
DISCUSSION: The situation presented is one in which interim financial reporting departs from the customary practice of annual financial reporting. Given that the partial liquidation of the base-period inventory is only temporary and will be replaced within the fiscal year, APB 28 states that the partial liquidation need not be given effect in the interim financial statements, and the cost of sales for the interim period should include the expected cost of replacement of the liquidated base.
Answers (B), (C), and (D) are incorrect because no effect should be given to the LIFO liquidation. The cost of sales should reflect the expected cost of replacement, not the decrease in the base-period inventory level.

The correct answer is (C). *(Publisher)*
REQUIRED: The proper treatment of the cumulative effect of an accounting change made in other than the first period of the fiscal year.
DISCUSSION: SFAS 3, *Reporting Accounting Changes in Interim Financial Statements*, covers cumulative-effect type accounting changes. If an accounting change occurs in other than the first quarter of the enterprise's fiscal year, the proper treatment is to calculate the cumulative effect on retained earnings at the beginning of the year and include it in restated net income presented in the first quarter financial statements. In addition, all previously issued interim financial statements of the current year must be restated to reflect the new accounting method.
Answer (A) is incorrect because the cumulative effect of the change on beginning retained earnings for the year is included in restated net income for the first interim period. Answer (B) is incorrect because no prior annual period adjustment is permitted in this circumstance. Answer (D) is incorrect because the cumulative effect is reported neither as an ordinary nor an extraordinary item in the period of change.

21. A company has changed from the straight-line to the declining-balance depreciation method for all depreciable assets during the second interim period of the entity's fiscal year. In the interim report provided for that period,

A. Net income of the first interim period need not be restated.

B. No cumulative effect of the change is to be included in the net income of the second period.

C. Justification for the change need not be disclosed because such disclosure will normally be included in the annual report.

D. No disclosure is required for effects on any interim period of prior fiscal years unless financial information for such period is being presented.

The correct answer is (B). *(Publisher)*
REQUIRED: The proper treatment of a cumulative-effect type accounting change occurring in the second quarter.
DISCUSSION: The change in depreciation methods is a change in accounting principle that should be accounted for as a cumulative-effect type change. If the change is not made in the first quarter, the first quarter statements should be restated to include the cumulative effect on beginning retained earnings as a separate component of restated first quarter net income. The net income of the second period will reflect the new method without including the cumulative effect.
Answer (A) is incorrect because net income of the first interim period must be restated. Answer (C) is incorrect because disclosure of the nature and justification of the accounting change should be made in both the annual and the interim financial reports. Answer (D) is incorrect because APB 28 requires that disclosure in the period of change be made of amounts of income for the same interim period of the immediately preceding fiscal year. This information includes actual and pro forma amounts of income from continuing operations, net income, and related per-share amounts.

22. The following information is applicable to an accounting change made in the second quarter of the year from the straight-line method of depreciation to an accelerated method of depreciation. The effect of the change is limited to the effects on depreciation and the related income tax provisions (a 40% tax rate).

Period	Net Income on the Basis of Straight-Line Depreciation	Gross Effect of Change	Gross Effect Minus Income Taxes
Prior to			
1st Qtr	$6,262,000	$300,000	$180,000
1st Qtr	1,032,400	60,000	36,000
2nd Qtr	1,282,400	60,000	36,000
3rd Qtr	1,298,600	90,000	54,000
4th Qtr	1,164,800	120,000	72,000

Net income for the first quarter should be restated as

A. $816,400

B. $1,032,400

C. $1,248,400

D. $996,400

The correct answer is (A). *(Publisher)*
REQUIRED: The restated net income for the first quarter resulting from a cumulative-effect type accounting change made in the second quarter.
DISCUSSION: According to SFAS 3, the cumulative-effect of an accounting change on retained earnings at the beginning of the fiscal year should be included in restated net income of the first period of the year in which the change is made (assuming the change is made in other than the first interim period). Income for all other prechange quarters should also be restated to reflect the new accounting method. Given that the change was made in the second quarter, the income for the first quarter should be restated to include the cumulative effect net of taxes of $180,000 and the depreciation effect net of taxes of $36,000. Because a change to an accelerated method increases depreciation, this adjustment of $216,000 should be deducted from the $1,032,400 first quarter net income to produce a restated net income of $816,400.
Answer (B) is incorrect because the first quarter net income was not adjusted for the change. Answer (C) is incorrect because an accelerated method of depreciation would decrease, not increase, net income. Answer (D) is incorrect because $180,000 should be deducted from the first quarter's net income.

23. When a firm makes a cumulative-effect type accounting change in an interim period, certain disclosures are required in the interim report. These include the effect of the change on income from continuing operations, net income, and related EPS figures for the interim period in which the change is made and for each prechange interim period of that fiscal year. In addition, these same disclosures are required to be made in

A. Year-to-date statements.

B. 12-month-to-date statements.

C. Both year-to-date statements and 12-month-to-date statements.

D. Neither year-to-date statements nor 12-month-to-date statements.

The correct answer is (C). *(Publisher)*
REQUIRED: The required disclosures in interim financial reports for cumulative-effect type accounting changes.
DISCUSSION: Both year-to-date and 12-month-to-date statements should provide the same types of disclosures as the interim reports for the period of change. See SFAS 3.
Answer (A) is incorrect because the same disclosure must also be made in 12-month-to-date statements. Answer (B) is incorrect because the same disclosures must also be made in year-to-date statements. Answer (D) is incorrect because the disclosures are required for both year-to-date statements and 12-month-to-date statements.

24. When a firm experiences a cumulative-effect type accounting change (other than a change to LIFO) during an interim period, which of the following items need not be disclosed in the interim financial reports?

A. The effect of the change on interim net income per share.

B. The nature of and justification for the change to the newly adopted accounting principle.

C. The effect of the change on interim income for each of the prior years not presented.

D. The effect of the change on interim income from continuing operations.

The correct answer is (C). *(Publisher)*
REQUIRED: The item that need not be disclosed in the interim reports when a firm experiences a cumulative-effect type accounting change other than to LIFO.
DISCUSSION: According to SFAS 3, if no financial information for interim periods of prior fiscal years is being presented, disclosure should be made in the period of change of actual and pro forma amounts of income from continuing operations, net income, and related per-share amounts for the preceding year's interim period that corresponds to the interim period in which the change is made.
Answers (A), (B), and (D) are incorrect because each describes a disclosure that is required in these circumstances.

25. If a company adopts a change to the LIFO method of inventory pricing during an interim period, which one of the following must be disclosed?

A. The net income, on a pro forma basis, for the interim period in which the change is made.

B. The cumulative effect of the change upon retained earnings.

C. The effect of the change on net income for the interim period in which the change is made.

D. The per-share income from continuing operations, on a pro forma basis, for any interim periods of prior years for which financial information is presented.

The correct answer is (C). *(Publisher)*
REQUIRED: The necessary disclosure when a company adopts a change to LIFO during an interim period.
DISCUSSION: A change in accounting principle to the LIFO method is usually based on the assumption that the ending inventory of the previous year based on the previous inventory method equals the beginning LIFO inventory for the current year. Thus, neither the pro forma amounts nor the cumulative effect of the change on retained earnings at the beginning of the fiscal year in which the change is made can be calculated. In these situations, the disclosures required by SFAS 3 should be made (except the pro forma amounts for interim periods of prior fiscal years). These disclosures include the effect of the change on net income for the interim period of change.
Answers (A), (B), and (D) are incorrect because the cumulative effect of the change upon retained earnings and pro forma amounts are generally not determined.

26. When a publicly traded company makes an accounting change in the fourth quarter, it must

- A. Issue a separate fourth quarter financial statement explaining the change and make the other disclosures required by SFAS 3.

- B. Make the required disclosures in a separate footnote to the annual financial statements if a fourth quarter financial statement is not issued.

- C. Either issue a separate interim statement or, in the annual financial statements, label a separate footnote Accounting Change in the Fourth Quarter.

- D. Not make a special disclosure because APB 20 requires the disclosure to be made on an annual basis.

The correct answer is (B). *(Publisher)*
REQUIRED: The requirement for disclosing an accounting change in the fourth quarter.
DISCUSSION: When a publicly traded company makes an accounting change in the last quarter, full disclosure must be made in a separate footnote to the annual financial statements in the absence of separate fourth quarter statements or disclosure in the annual report to security holders (SFAS 3).

Answer (A) is incorrect because fourth quarter statements are not required if disclosures are made in a separate footnote to the annual financial statements. Answer (C) is incorrect because the footnote need not be labeled Accounting Change in the Fourth Quarter. Answer (D) is incorrect because separate disclosure with respect to the effect on interim statements must be made, either in an interim report in the annual report or in a footnote to the annual statements.

29.4 Annual Effective Tax Rate

27. For interim financial reporting, a company's income tax provision for the second quarter should be determined using the

- A. Statutory tax rate for the year.

- B. Effective tax rate expected to be applicable for the full year as estimated at the end of the first quarter.

- C. Effective tax rate expected to be applicable for the full year as estimated at the end of the second quarter.

- D. Effective tax rate expected to be applicable for the second quarter.

The correct answer is (C). *(CPA 1193 T-31)*
REQUIRED: The tax rate used to determine the interim income tax provision.
DISCUSSION: APB 28 requires that, at the end of each interim period, an enterprise make its best estimate of the effective tax rate expected to be applicable for the full fiscal year. That rate should be used in providing for income taxes on a current year-to-date basis.

Answers (A), (B), and (D) are incorrect because the quarterly tax provision should be based on the rate expected to be applicable for the full year as determined at the end of the quarter.

28. For interim financial reporting, the computation of a company's second quarter provision for income taxes uses an effective tax rate expected to be applicable for the full fiscal year. The effective tax rate should reflect anticipated

	Foreign Tax Rates	Available Tax Planning Alternatives
A.	No	Yes
B.	No	No
C.	Yes	No
D.	Yes	Yes

The correct answer is (D). *(CPA 1189 T-35)*
REQUIRED: The factors used to estimate the annual effective tax rate for interim statements.
DISCUSSION: The estimated effective annual tax rate should be based upon the statutory rate adjusted for the current year's expected conditions. These conditions include anticipated investment tax credits, foreign tax rates, percentage depletion, capital gain rates, and other tax planning alternatives.

Answers (A), (B), and (C) are incorrect because the effective tax rate should reflect anticipated foreign tax rates and available tax planning alternatives.

29. The computation of a company's third quarter provision for income taxes should be based upon earnings

 A. For the quarter at an expected annual effective income tax rate.

 B. For the quarter at the statutory rate.

 C. To date at an expected annual effective income tax rate, minus prior quarters' provisions.

 D. To date at the statutory rate, minus prior quarters' provisions.

The correct answer is (C). *(CPA 1180 T-16)*
 REQUIRED: The correct computation of a third quarter provision for income taxes.
 DISCUSSION: According to FASB Interpretation No. 18, the income tax provision for an interim period should be calculated by applying the estimated annual effective tax rate to the ordinary earnings for the year to date and then deducting the prior interim periods' income tax provisions.
 Answer (A) is incorrect because the calculation must apply the expected annual effective income tax rate to the cumulative ordinary earnings for the year to date, and then deduct prior quarters' tax provisions. Answers (B) and (D) are incorrect because the company must use an estimated annual effective income tax rate.

30. In interim financial statements, tax expense (benefit) for extraordinary items and discontinued operations is shown net of tax just as in annual statements. The tax expense (benefit) is computed

 A. By applying the estimated annual tax rate of the company to the particular item.

 B. As the difference between the tax on income including the other items and the tax on income excluding the other items.

 C. At the statutory rate on both extraordinary items and discontinued operations.

 D. At the estimated tax rate for the particular interim period in which the extraordinary item or discontinued item occurred.

The correct answer is (B). *(Publisher)*
 REQUIRED: The method of computing the income tax expense (benefit) for extraordinary items and discontinued operations in interim financial statements.
 DISCUSSION: Under FASB Interpretation No. 18, the income tax expense (benefit) for extraordinary items and discontinued operations is determined based on an incremental calculation. It is the difference between the tax on the interim period ordinary income and the total tax on the sum of ordinary income and the other items.
 Answers (A), (C), and (D) are incorrect because the tax effect (benefit) for extraordinary items and discontinued operations is based on an incremental calculation.

31. During the first quarter of 1996, Tech Co. had income before taxes of $200,000, and its effective income tax rate was 15%. Tech's 1995 effective annual income tax rate was 30%, but Tech expects its 1996 effective annual income tax rate to be 25%. In its first quarter interim income statement, what amount of income tax expense should Tech report?

 A. $0

 B. $30,000

 C. $50,000

 D. $60,000

The correct answer is (C). *(CPA 593 II-17)*
 REQUIRED: The provision for income taxes for the first interim period.
 DISCUSSION: According to APB 28, "At the end of each interim period the company should make its best estimate of the effective tax rate expected to be applicable for the full fiscal year. The rate so determined should be used in providing for income taxes on a current year-to-date basis." Tech's ordinary income before taxes for the first quarter is $200,000, and the estimated annual effective tax rate for 1996 is 25%. The provision for income taxes for the first interim period is therefore $50,000 (25% x $200,000).
 Answer (A) is incorrect because $0 excludes any income tax expense. Answer (B) is incorrect because $30,000 uses Tech's quarterly effective income tax rate. Answer (D) is incorrect because $60,000 uses Tech's 1995 effective annual income tax rate.

32. The following information was used in preparing quarterly income statements during the first half of 19X6:

Quarter	Income Before Income Taxes	Estimated Effective Annual Income Tax Rate
1	$80,000	45%
2	70,000	45%

For the third quarter of 19X6, income before income taxes was $50,000, and the estimated effective annual income tax rate was 40%. The income statement for the third quarter of 19X6 should include a provision for income taxes of

A. $12,500

B. $17,500

C. $20,000

D. $22,500

The correct answer is (A). *(CIA 1186 IV-32)*
REQUIRED: The provision for income taxes in the interim income statement for the third quarter.
DISCUSSION: According to FASB Interpretation No. 18, the tax provision for the third quarter is calculated by multiplying the estimated annual effective tax rate determined at the end of the third quarter times the cumulative year-to-date ordinary income and then subtracting the cumulative tax provision for the first two quarters. At the end of the third quarter, the year-to-date ordinary income is $200,000 ($80,000 + $70,000 + $50,000), and the cumulative tax provision is $80,000 ($200,000 x 40%). Because the cumulative tax provision at the end of the second quarter was $67,500 [($80,000 + $70,000) x 45%], $12,500 ($80,000 – $67,500) should be reported as a provision for income taxes for the third quarter.
Answer (B) is incorrect because $17,500 adds the estimated income tax of $50,000 at 40% to the cumulative tax provision and then subtracts $150,000 (80,000 + 70,000) x 40%. Answer (C) is incorrect because $20,000 is the third-quarter effective annual income tax rate multiplied by income before taxes (40% x $50,000). Answer (D) is incorrect because $22,500 is the second-quarter effective annual income tax rate multiplied by income before taxes (45% x $50,000).

33. Ross Corporation expects to sustain an operating loss of $100,000 for the full year ending December 31. Ross operates entirely in one jurisdiction where the tax rate is 40%. Tax credits for the year total $10,000. No permanent differences are expected. Realization of the full tax benefit of the expected operating loss and of the anticipated tax credits is assured beyond any reasonable doubt because they will be carried back. For the quarter ended March 31, Ross reports an operating loss of $20,000. How much of a tax benefit should Ross report for the interim period ended March 31?

A. $0

B. $8,000

C. $10,000

D. $12,500

The correct answer is (C). *(CPA 583 II-17)*
REQUIRED: The tax benefit to be reported for an interim period.
DISCUSSION: The current effective tax rate is based on the statutory rate adjusted for the current year's expected conditions, e.g., tax credits. The interim period tax benefit for the first quarter is the estimated annual effective tax rate applied to the loss for the quarter (because the full benefit of the operating loss and tax credits will be realized). The tax benefit of the annual operating loss is $40,000 (40% tax rate x $100,000). The total tax benefit is therefore $50,000 ($40,000 + $10,000 tax credit), and the annual effective tax rate is 50% ($50,000 benefit ÷ $100,000 loss). The quarterly loss was $20,000; thus the quarterly tax benefit is $10,000 (50% x $20,000).
Answer (A) is incorrect because a tax benefit should be realized. Answer (B) is incorrect because $8,000 is the operating loss multiplied by the statutory tax rate. Answer (D) is incorrect because $12,500 is the operating loss multiplied by the tax rate ($20,000 x 40%) plus the tax credits multiplied by the average of the annual effective tax rate and the regular tax rate.

29.5 Prior Interim Period Adjustments

34. During the third quarter of 1996, the accountant at the JEK Company discovered that a machine purchased January 2, 1994 for $60,000 had been erroneously charged against first quarter net income in 1994. The machine should have been depreciated at a rate of $1,000 per month. The correction of this error should include

A. A charge of $33,000 to income before taxes of the third quarter of 1996.

B. An adjustment of $24,000 to the previously declared income before taxes of the first quarter of 1996.

C. An adjustment of $27,000 to the previously declared income before taxes of the first quarter of 1996.

D. An adjustment of $3,000 to the previously declared income before taxes of the first quarter of 1996.

The correct answer is (D). *(Publisher)*
REQUIRED: The proper treatment of an accounting error.
DISCUSSION: An error was committed when the full cost of the asset was expensed in the period of acquisition. Instead, the cost should have been capitalized and the asset depreciated over its useful life. The correction of this error should be accounted for as a prior-period adjustment. Ignoring tax effects, this requires an entry to beginning retained earnings for the year to correct the understatement of income (and of retained earnings) that resulted from the error. If comparative statements are issued, a restatement of prior-period financial statements is also necessary. The previously reported income of the first quarter of 1996 (as well as that for the second quarter) should be restated to reflect the $3,000 ($1,000 x 3 months) depreciation that should have been taken on the asset during that period.
Answers (A), (B), and (C) are incorrect because the adjustment should be $3,000 applied to the previously declared income before taxes of the first quarter of 1996.

35. On June 15, 1996, a court of law found the SPC Corporation, a calendar-year company, guilty of patent infringement and awarded damages of $5,000,000 to the plaintiff. Of this amount, $2,000,000 related to each of the years 1994 and 1995; $500,000 related to each of the two quarters of 1996. No provision for loss had been recorded previously. If the applicable tax rate is 40%, this event should result in a

A. Charge of $3,000,000 to income reported for the second quarter of 1996.

B. Restatement of the previously reported net income for the first quarter of 1996 to include a charge of $300,000.

C. Restatement of the previously reported net income for the first quarter of 1996 to include a charge of $2,700,000.

D. Restatement of the previously reported net income for the first quarter of 1996 to include a charge of $3,000,000.

The correct answer is (C). *(Publisher)*
REQUIRED: The proper treatment of the settlement of litigation related to a prior interim period and prior fiscal years.
DISCUSSION: According to SFAS 16, *Prior Period Adjustments*, if an item of profit or loss that relates to settlement of litigation occurs in other than the first interim period of the fiscal year and all or a part of the item meets the criteria for an adjustment related to prior interim periods of that fiscal year, the financial statements for the prior interim periods should be restated to include their allocable portions of the adjustment. The portion of the adjustment directly related to prior fiscal years should also be included in the determination of net income of the first interim period of the current fiscal year. The settlement in this case occurred in the second quarter; thus the first quarter should be restated for the $500,000 directly related to first-quarter operations and the $4,000,000 directly related to prior years' operations. The restated net income for the first quarter of 1996 should therefore include a $2,700,000 adjustment ($4,500,000 – the tax savings of $1,800,000).
Answers (A), (B), and (D) are incorrect because a restatement of the previously reported net income for the first quarter is required for $2,700,000.

36. On September 30, 1996, the XYZ Corporation, a calendar-year company, reached an agreement with the Internal Revenue Service. The company agreed to pay additional income taxes of $2,000,000 that directly related to a loss claimed in the third quarter of 1994. In accordance with current authoritative literature, this transaction should be recorded as a

A. Component of the net income reported for the third quarter of 1996.

B. Restatement of the net income previously reported for the first quarter of 1996.

C. Restatement of the beginning retained earnings previously reported for the third quarter of 1996.

D. Restatement of the beginning retained earnings previously reported for the first quarter of 1996.

The correct answer is (A). *(Publisher)*
REQUIRED: The proper recording of an income tax settlement reached in the third quarter of 1996 relating to the third quarter of 1994.
DISCUSSION: SFAS 16 may require a prior interim period adjustment for an adjustment or settlement of litigation, income taxes (except for the effects of retroactive tax legislation), renegotiation proceedings, and utility revenue under rate-making processes. All or part of the adjustment or settlement must relate specifically to a prior interim period of the current year, its effect must be material, and the amount must have become reasonably estimable only in the current interim period. XYZ's transaction does not qualify as a prior interim period adjustment because no portion of the item is related to prior interim periods of the current fiscal year. Thus, the tax settlement liability should be included in net income in the third quarter of 1996.
Answers (B) and (C) are incorrect because the item does not qualify for treatment as a prior interim period adjustment in the current fiscal year. Answer (D) is incorrect because a tax settlement related to a prior fiscal year is not treated as a prior-period adjustment.

37. On June 1, 1996, the Fat Corporation, a calendar-year company, settled a patent infringement lawsuit. The court awarded Fat $3,000,000 in damages. Of this amount, $1,000,000 related to each of the years 1994 and 1995, and $500,000 related to each of the first two quarters in 1996. The applicable tax rate is 40%. What effect does the settlement have on the net income of the second quarter of 1996?

A. $200,000

B. $300,000

C. $600,000

D. $1,800,000

The correct answer is (B). *(Publisher)*
REQUIRED: The effect of a patent lawsuit settlement on second quarter net income.
DISCUSSION: Under SFAS 16, if an item of profit related to settlement of litigation occurs in other than the first interim period of the fiscal year (here, the second quarter of a calendar-year company), and all or part of the item of profit meets the criteria for an adjustment related to a prior interim period of the current fiscal year, the portion of the item allocable to the current interim period should be included in the determination of net income for that period. Prior interim periods should be restated to include their allocable portions of the adjustment. Accordingly, $500,000 of the settlement should be included in the determination of net income for the second quarter. Given a tax rate of 40%, the settlement increases net income of the second quarter by $300,000.
Answer (A) is incorrect because $200,000 is the amount of the income tax. Answer (C) is incorrect because $600,000 is the adjustment to be made to each year (1995 and 1994). Answer (D) is incorrect because the income should not be recognized entirely in 1996.

CHAPTER THIRTY
SEGMENT REPORTING

Disclosure of disaggregated information is required in annual financial statements of public enterprises by SFAS 14, *Financial Reporting for Segments of a Business Enterprise*, as amended by SFAS 18, *Financial Reporting for Segments of a Business Enterprise--Interim Financial Statements*; SFAS 21, *Suspension of the Reporting of Earnings per Share and Segment Information by Nonpublic Enterprises*; and SFAS 24, *Reporting Segment Information in Financial Statements That Are Presented in Another Enterprise's Financial Report*. The disaggregated information to be disclosed may include information about the enterprise's operations in different industries, its foreign operations, its export sales, and/or its major customers.

At December 1, 1996, the FASB had a Proposed Statement of Financial Accounting Standards, *Reporting Disaggregated Information about a Business Enterprise*, outstanding. If and when issued as a final statement, it will require public business enterprises to report disaggregated information based on management's organization of the enterprise. The information disclosed will include certain information about the enterprise's products and services, the geographic areas in which the enterprise operates, and its major customers.

30.1 Industry Segments

1. Current authoritative pronouncements require the disclosure of segment information when certain criteria are met. Which of the following reflects the type of financial statement and the type of firm for which this disclosure is required?

A. Annual financial statements of publicly held companies.

B. Annual financial statements for both publicly held and nonpublicly held companies.

C. Annual and interim financial statements for publicly held companies.

D. Annual and interim financial statements for both publicly held and nonpublicly held companies.

The correct answer is (A). *(Publisher)*

REQUIRED: The financial statements and firms required to disclose segment information.

DISCUSSION: SFAS 14 required that segment information be provided in both interim and annual financial statements for public and nonpublic companies. SFAS 18, *Financial Reporting for Segments of a Business Enterprise--Interim Financial Statements*, later eliminated the requirement for interim financial statements. SFAS 21, *Suspension of the Reporting of Earnings per Share and Segment Information by Nonpublic Enterprises*, eliminated the requirement for nonpublicly held companies. Thus, segment information must now be disclosed only in the annual financial statements of publicly held companies.

Answers (B), (C), and (D) are incorrect because interim financial statements need no longer disclose segment information, and segment disclosure requirements no longer apply to nonpublicly held companies.

2. An industry segment is defined as

A. A business activity listed in the SIC (Standard Industrial Classification).

B. A component of an enterprise engaged in providing a product or service or a group of related products and services primarily to unaffiliated customers for a profit.

C. A business activity listed in the ESIC (Enterprise Standard Industrial Classification).

D. An activity center coinciding with a profit center for individual goods and services or groups of goods and services.

The correct answer is (B). *(Publisher)*
REQUIRED: The definition of an industry segment.
DISCUSSION: A segment is a component of an enterprise providing products or services primarily to unaffiliated customers for a profit. This definition precludes internal processing points from being treated as segments. The requirement that sales be primarily to unaffiliated customers usually creates a horizontal division rather than a division of vertically integrated operations.

Answers (A) and (C) are incorrect because the SIC and the ESIC define classification categories of goods and services. Answer (D) is incorrect because, although profit centers within an enterprise may help identify segments, industry segments are defined in terms of goods and services produced.

3. Diversified Company, Inc. is in the process of defining industry segments for the purpose of determining proper financial reporting for segments of the enterprise. Which of the following is correct?

A. The Standard Industrial Classification must be used as authority in classifying business activities into segments.

B. The Enterprise Standard Industrial Classification must be used as authority in classifying business activities into segments.

C. Industry segments must be clearly separated into domestic and foreign classifications. Segments may not be determined on a worldwide basis.

D. No single set of characteristics is universally applicable in determining the industry segments of all enterprises.

The correct answer is (D). *(Publisher)*
REQUIRED: The true statement regarding the definition of industry segments.
DISCUSSION: SFAS 14 states that, although several systems have been developed for classifying business activities, no single set of characteristics is universally applicable in determining the industry segments of all enterprises, nor is any single characteristic determinative in all cases. Determination of industry segments must depend, to a considerable extent, on the judgment of the management of the enterprise.

Answers (A) and (B) are incorrect because, although SIC and ESIC are systems for classifying business activities, SFAS 14 has determined that, for purposes of its requirements, neither, by itself, is universally suitable to determine industry segments. Answer (C) is incorrect because industry segments should be determined on a worldwide basis to the extent practicable. Separating industry segments into domestic and foreign operations should occur only when segment reporting on a worldwide basis is impracticable.

4. A reportable business segment must disclose

A. Amortized expenses.

B. Total liabilities.

C. Income taxes on operating profits.

D. Extraordinary items.

The correct answer is (A). *(CMA 1288 4-25)*
REQUIRED: The item required to be disclosed by a reportable business segment.
DISCUSSION: SFAS 14 requires a reportable business segment to disclose the following information: revenue information that separately discloses sales to unaffiliated customers and sales or transfers to other industry segments; operating profit or loss; carrying amounts of identifiable assets; the aggregate amount of depreciation, depletion, and amortized expenses; the effects on operating profit of changes in accounting principles; capital expenditures; and certain information about vertically integrated equity-method investees.

Answers (B), (C), and (D) are incorrect because they are not disclosures required by SFAS 14.

5. YIV Inc. is a multidivisional corporation that makes both intersegment sales and sales to unaffiliated customers. YIV should report segment financial information for each division meeting which one of the following criteria?

    A. Segment operating profit or loss is 10% or more of consolidated profit or loss.

    B. Segment operating profit or loss is 10% or more of combined operating profit or loss of all company segments.

    C. Segment revenue is 10% or more of combined revenue of all the company segments.

    D. Segment revenue is 10% or more of consolidated revenue.

The correct answer is (C). *(CPA 590 T-36)*
    REQUIRED: The criterion used to identify the industry segments as reportable segments.
    DISCUSSION: An industry segment is classified as a reportable segment when it is significant to the enterprise. An industry segment is considered significant if it satisfies one or more of three tests: Its revenue (including sales to both affiliated and unaffiliated customers) is equal to at least 10% of the combined revenue (including sales to both affiliated and unaffiliated customers) of all the enterprise's industry segments; its identifiable assets are equal to at least 10% of the combined identifiable assets of all its industry segments; and the absolute amount of its operating profit or operating loss is equal to at least 10% of the greater, in absolute amount, of the combined operating profit of all segments that did not incur an operating loss or the combined loss of all segments that did incur an operating loss.
    Answers (A), (B), and (D) are incorrect because they are not specified as tests by SFAS 14.

6. An enterprise determines that it must report segment data in annual reports for the year ended December 31. Which of the following is not an acceptable way of reporting segment information?

    A. Within the body of the financial statements, with appropriate explanatory disclosures in the footnotes.

    B. Entirely in the footnotes to the financial statements.

    C. As a special report issued separately from the financial statements.

    D. In a separate schedule that is included as an integral part of the financial statements.

The correct answer is (C). *(Publisher)*
    REQUIRED: The unacceptable method of presenting required segment information.
    DISCUSSION: SFAS 14 permits segment information disclosure by means of a separate schedule that is included as an integral part of the financial statements. If, in a report to shareholders, that schedule is located on a page that is not clearly a part of the financial statements, the schedules should be referenced in the financial statement as an integral part thereof. Reporting in a special report issued separately from the financial statement does not meet the requirements of SFAS 14.
    Answers (A), (B), and (D) are incorrect because each is one of the three acceptable methods of presentation.

7. Which of the following is not a consideration in segment reporting for diversified enterprises?

    A. Allocation of joint costs.

    B. Transfer pricing.

    C. Defining the segments.

    D. Consolidation policy.

The correct answer is (D). *(CPA 577 T-21)*
    REQUIRED: The factor not considered in segment reporting.
    DISCUSSION: The information required to be reported by SFAS 14 is a disaggregation of the consolidated financial information. SFAS 14 uses the term "consolidated financial information" to mean aggregate information relating to an enterprise as a whole whether or not the enterprise has consolidated subsidiaries. Consolidation policy (i.e., which subsidiaries are included in the consolidated statements) is thus not a factor in the disaggregation required for segment reporting.
    Answers (A), (B), and (C) are incorrect because each is a relevant consideration in segment reporting for diversified enterprises.

8. SFAS 24, *Reporting Segment Information in Financial Statements That Are Presented in Another Enterprise's Financial Report*, requires segment data disclosures in which of the following financial statements presented in financial reports that contain consolidated financial statements?

- A. Financial statements of an unconsolidated subsidiary that are presented in a financial report of a nonpublic enterprise.

- B. Financial statements of a consolidated subsidiary that are presented in a financial report of a public entity.

- C. Financial statements of a foreign investee that is not a subsidiary of the primary reporting enterprise, unless the separately issued financial statements of the foreign investee are prepared in accordance with GAAP.

- D. Financial statements of an unconsolidated investee that are presented in a financial report of a public entity.

The correct answer is (D). *(Publisher)*
REQUIRED: The financial statements in which disclosure of segment information is required when those financial statements are contained in a financial report that contains consolidated financial statements.
DISCUSSION: SFAS 24 requires the disclosure of segment information in the complete financial statements presented for a parent company, subsidiary, corporate joint venture, or 50%-or-less-owned investee when those statements are contained in a financial report that contains consolidated financial statements, unless one of the exceptions described in answers (A), (B), or (C) occurs.
Answer (A) is incorrect because SFAS 21 provides an exception for nonpublic entities. Answer (B) is incorrect because an exception exists if the financial statements are also consolidated or combined and segment data are presented for the consolidated statements. Answer (C) is incorrect because an exception also exists for a foreign investee that is not a subsidiary of the primary reporting enterprise if the investee does not present the disclosure of segment information in its separately issued financial statements.

9. According to current authoritative literature, enterprises with vertically integrated operations

- A. Are exempt from industry segment reporting requirements.

- B. Are not required to disaggregate vertically integrated operations for industry segment reporting purposes.

- C. Must disaggregate vertically integrated operations for industry segment reporting purposes.

- D. Must disaggregate domestic vertically integrated operations for industry segment reporting purposes but are not required to disaggregate foreign integrated operations.

The correct answer is (B). *(Publisher)*
REQUIRED: The true statement regarding segment reporting for vertically integrated operations.
DISCUSSION: SFAS 14 defines an industry segment in terms of products or services sold primarily to unaffiliated customers; thus, it does not require the disaggregation of vertically integrated operations of an enterprise.
Answer (A) is incorrect because, although vertically integrated operations need not be disaggregated, they are not exempt from segment reporting requirements. Answer (C) is incorrect because SFAS 14 states that vertically integrated operations need not be disaggregated. Answer (D) is incorrect because domestic and foreign vertically integrated operations are not distinguished for segment reporting purposes.

10. Selected data for a segment of a business enterprise are to be separately reported in accordance with SFAS 14 when the revenue of the segment exceeds 10% of the

- A. Combined net income of all segments reporting profits.

- B. Total revenue obtained in transactions with outsiders.

- C. Total revenue of all the enterprise's industry segments.

- D. Total combined revenue of all segments reporting profits.

The correct answer is (C). *(CPA 1180 T-28)*
REQUIRED: The revenue test for selecting reportable segments.
DISCUSSION: An industry segment is a reportable segment if it satisfies one or more of three tests. One test is whether its revenue is 10% or more of the combined revenue of all the enterprise's industry segments.
Answers (A) and (D) are incorrect because whether a segment reported a profit is not a factor in the revenue test. Answer (B) is incorrect because the test for revenue applies both to sales to unaffiliated customers and to intersegment sales or transfers.

11. In financial reporting for segments of a business enterprise, the revenue of a segment should include

    A. Intersegment billings for the cost of shared facilities.

    B. Intersegment sales of services similar to those sold to unaffiliated customers.

    C. Equity in income from unconsolidated subsidiaries.

    D. Extraordinary items.

The correct answer is (B). *(CPA 588 T-37)*
    REQUIRED: The amounts to be included in the revenue of a segment.
    DISCUSSION: The revenue of an industry segment includes both sales to unaffiliated customers and intersegment sales or transfers, if any, of products and services similar to those sold to unaffiliated customers. Revenue also includes interest from sources outside the enterprise and interest earned on intersegment trade receivables if the asset on which the interest is earned is included among the industry segment's identifiable assets.
    Answers (A), (C), and (D) are incorrect because they are not included in the definition of revenue by SFAS 14.

12. In financial reporting of segment data, which of the following would be used to determine a segment's operating income?

    A. Gain or loss on discontinued operations.

    B. General corporate expense.

    C. Sales to other segments.

    D. Income tax expense.

The correct answer is (C). *(CPA 593 T-36)*
    REQUIRED: The item used to determine a segment's operating income.
    DISCUSSION: Operating profit or loss is defined by SFAS 14 as revenue (both from sales to unaffiliated customers and from intersegment sales or transfers) minus all operating expenses (expenses relating to both revenue from sales to unaffiliated customers and revenue from intersegment sales or transfers). SFAS 14 further excludes the following from the determination of operating profit or loss: revenue earned at the corporate level and not derived from the operations of any industry segment; general corporate expenses; interest expense; domestic and foreign income taxes; equity in income or loss from unconsolidated subsidiaries and other unconsolidated and consolidated investees; gain or loss on discontinued operations; extraordinary items; minority interests; and the cumulative effect of a change in accounting principles.
    Answer (A) is incorrect because gain or loss on discontinued operations is excluded by SFAS 14. Answer (B) is incorrect because general corporate expense is excluded by SFAS 14. Answer (D) is incorrect because income tax expense is excluded by SFAS 14.

13. The following information pertains to revenue earned by Timm Co.'s industry segments for the year ended December 31, 1996:

Segment	Sales to Unaffiliated Customers	Intersegment Sales	Total Revenue
Alo	$ 5,000	$ 3,000	$ 8,000
Bix	8,000	4,000	12,000
Cee	4,000	--	4,000
Dil	43,000	16,000	59,000
Combined	60,000	$23,000	83,000
Elimination	--	(23,000)	(23,000)
Consolidated	$60,000	--	$60,000

In conformity with the revenue test, Timm's reportable segments were

    A. Only Dil.

    B. Only Bix and Dil.

    C. Only Alo, Bix, and Dil.

    D. Alo, Bix, Cee, and Dil.

The correct answer is (B). *(CPA 591 II-11)*
    REQUIRED: The reportable segments in conformity with the revenue test.
    DISCUSSION: For the purpose of identifying reportable segments, SFAS 14 defines revenue to include sales to unaffiliated customers and intersegment sales. In accordance with the revenue test, a reportable industry segment has revenue equal to 10% or more of the total combined revenue of all of the enterprise's industry segments. Given combined revenue of $83,000, only Bix ($12,000) and Dil ($59,000) qualify because their revenues are at least $8,300 (10% x $83,000).
    Answers (A), (C), and (D) are incorrect because only Bix and Dil qualify.

Questions 14 and 15 are based on the following information.

	Revenue Test (dollars in thousands)		
	Wholesale Segment	Retail Segment	Finance Segment
Sales -- unaffiliated customers	$2,100	$850	$ 0
Sales -- intersegment	400	100	0
Loan interest income -- intersegment	0	80	350
Loan interest income -- unaffiliated	0	150	50
Income -- equity-based investees	0	200	0

14. Determine the amount of revenue for each of the three segments that would be used to identify the reportable industry segments in accordance with the revenue test specified by SFAS 14.

	Wholesale	Retail	Finance
A.	$2,100	$850	$0
B.	$2,500	$950	$0
C.	$2,500	$1,100	$400
D.	$2,500	$1,380	$400

The correct answer is (C). *(Publisher)*

REQUIRED: The revenue for each segment used to determine whether the segment is reportable.

DISCUSSION: For the purpose of identifying reportable segments, SFAS 14 defines revenue to include sales to unaffiliated customers and intersegment sales, interest revenue from unaffiliated enterprises, and interest from intersegment trade receivables when the asset on which the interest is earned is included in the identifiable assets of the segment. However, interest on intersegment loans and advances is excluded unless the segment is primarily financial in nature. Also excluded is income from equity-based investees. Thus, revenues for the wholesale segment are $2,500 ($2,100 + $400); for the retail segment, $1,100 ($850 + $100 + $150); and for the finance segment, $400 ($350 + $50).

Answer (A) is incorrect because it includes sales only to unaffiliated customers. Answer (B) is incorrect because it includes sales only to unaffiliated and affiliated customers. Answer (D) is incorrect because it fails to exclude intersegment interest income for nonfinancial segments and equity-based income.

15. Which of the three segments would be identified as a reportable industry segment in accordance with the revenue test?

A. Wholesale and retail segments.

B. Wholesale and finance segments.

C. Retail and finance segments.

D. Wholesale, retail, and finance segments.

The correct answer is (D). *(Publisher)*

REQUIRED: The reportable segments in accordance with the revenue test.

DISCUSSION: In accordance with the revenue test, a reportable industry segment has combined revenue equal to 10% or more of the total combined revenue of all of the enterprise's industry segments. All three are reportable segments because the revenue of each equals or exceeds the test criterion of $400 ($4,000 x 10%).

Segment	Revenue
Wholesale	$2,500
Retail	1,100
Finance	400
	$4,000

Answers (A), (B), and (C) are incorrect because all three segments meet the revenue test criterion.

16. The profitability information that should be reported for each reportable segment of a business enterprise includes

    A. An operating profit or loss figure consisting of segment revenue minus traceable costs and allocated common costs.

    B. An operating profit or loss figure consisting of segment revenue minus traceable costs but not allocated common costs.

    C. An operating profit or loss figure consisting of segment revenue minus allocated common costs but not traceable costs.

    D. Segment revenue only.

The correct answer is (A). *(CPA 583 T-44)*

REQUIRED: The profitability information required for segment reporting.

DISCUSSION: Operating profit or loss for each reportable segment must be presented in annual financial statements. Operating profit or loss is defined by SFAS 14 as segment revenue minus all operating expenses. Operating expenses include traceable costs relating to segment revenue both from sales to unaffiliated customers and from intersegment sales or transfers. Operating expenses that are not directly traceable to an industry segment should be allocated among those industry segments for the benefit of which the expenses were incurred (allocated common costs).

Answers (B) and (C) are incorrect because both traceable costs and allocated common costs are reductions in revenue when reporting profitability information. Answer (D) is incorrect because both revenue and profitability data should be presented for all reportable segments.

17. In financial reporting for segments of a business enterprise, the operating profit or loss of a manufacturing segment includes a portion of

	General Corporate Expenses	Indirect Operating Expenses
A.	Yes	Yes
B.	Yes	No
C.	No	Yes
D.	No	No

The correct answer is (C). *(CPA 1194 F-60)*

REQUIRED: The item(s), if any, included in a segment's operating profit or loss.

DISCUSSION: Operating profit or loss is defined by SFAS 14 as revenue (both from sales to unaffiliated customers and from intersegment sales or transfers) minus all operating expenses (expenses relating to both revenue from sales to unaffiliated customers and revenue from intersegment sales or transfers). SFAS 14 excludes general corporate expenses from the determination of operating profit or loss of an industry segment.

Answers (A), (B), and (D) are incorrect because operating profit or loss of a manufacturing segment includes a portion of indirect operating expenses but not general corporate expenses.

18. Hyde Corp. has three manufacturing divisions, each of which has been determined to be a reportable segment. Common costs are appropriately allocated on the basis of each division's sales in relation to Hyde's aggregate sales. In 1996, Clay division had sales of $3,000,000, which was 25% of Hyde's total sales, and had traceable operating costs of $1,900,000. In 1996, Hyde incurred operating costs of $500,000 that were not directly traceable to any of the divisions. In addition, Hyde incurred interest expense of $300,000 in 1996. In reporting segment information, what amount should be shown as Clay's operating profit for 1996?

    A. $875,000

    B. $900,000

    C. $975,000

    D. $1,100,000

The correct answer is (C). *(CPA 590 II-54)*

REQUIRED: The amount to be shown as operating profit for a manufacturing division.

DISCUSSION: As indicated below, the operating profit for Clay division is calculated by subtracting the $1,900,000 traceable costs and the $125,000 ($500,000 x 25%) of the allocated common costs from the division's sales of $3,000,000. The operating profit for the division is $975,000.

Sales	$ 3,000,000
Traceable costs	(1,900,000)
Common costs (25% allocation)	(125,000)
Operating profit	$ 975,000

Answer (A) is incorrect because $875,000 results from reducing Clay's operating profit by one-third of Hyde's interest expense of $300,000. Answer (B) is incorrect because $900,000 results from subtracting 25% of the interest expense from Clay's operating profit. Answer (D) is incorrect because $1,100,000 fails to consider the allocated common costs when computing operating profit.

19. Taft Corp. discloses supplemental industry segment information. The following information is available for 1996:

Segment	Sales	Traceable Operating Expenses
A	$1,000,000	$ 600,000
B	800,000	500,000
C	600,000	350,000
	$2,400,000	$1,450,000

Additional 1996 expenses, not included above, are as follows:

Indirect operating expenses	$360,000
General corporate expenses	240,000

Appropriate common expenses are allocated to segments based on the ratio of a segment's sales to total sales. Segment C's 1996 operating profit was

A. $100,000

B. $130,000

C. $160,000

D. $250,000

The correct answer is (C). *(CPA 593 II-12)*
REQUIRED: The operating profit for a segment if common costs are allocated according to the ratio of segment sales to total sales.
DISCUSSION: To determine operating profit, both traceable costs and nontraceable (indirect) costs that can be allocated on a reasonable basis must be subtracted from operating revenue. Accordingly, 25% of Taft's indirect operating costs should be allocated to Segment C on the basis of the ratio of Segment C's sales to total sales ($600,000 ÷ $2,400,000). The general corporate expenses are excluded from the calculation of the operating profit of a segment. As indicated below, Segment C's operating profit is $160,000.

	Segment C
Sales	$ 600,000
Traceable costs	(350,000)
Indirect expenses ($360,000 x 25%)	(90,000)
Operating profit	$160,000

Answer (A) is incorrect because $100,000 results from subtracting 25% of the general corporate expenses.
Answer (B) is incorrect because $130,000 results from subtracting 33 1/3% of indirect operating expenses.
Answer (D) is incorrect because $250,000 equals sales minus traceable costs.

20. Company M operates in four industries. Which of the following industry segments should be identified as a reportable segment under the operating profit or loss test?

Segment	Operating Profit (Loss)
S	$ 90,000
T	(100,000)
U	910,000
V	(420,000)

A. Segment U only.

B. Segments U and V.

C. Segments T, U, and V.

D. Segments S, T, U, and V.

The correct answer is (C). *(Publisher)*
REQUIRED: The reportable segments under the operating profit or loss test.
DISCUSSION: Under SFAS 14, an industry segment is identified as a reportable segment if it meets the profit or loss test (among others). If the absolute amount of the operating profit or loss equals at least 10% of the greater, in absolute amount, of (1) the combined operating profit of all segments not reporting an operating loss or (2) the combined operating loss of all segments reporting an operating loss, the segment is reportable.
Segments T, U, and V are reportable segments. As shown below, the sum of the operating profits of S and U ($1,000,000) is greater than the sum of the operating losses of T and V ($520,000). Consequently, the test criterion is $100,000 (10% x $1,000,000).

Segment	Operating Profit	Operating Loss
S	$ 90,000	$ 0
T	0	100,000
U	910,000	0
V	0	420,000
	$1,000,000	$520,000

Answers (A), (B), and (D) are incorrect because Segments T, U, and V each meet the operating profit or loss test, while Segment S does not.

Questions 21 and 22 are based on the following information.

	Operating Profit or Loss Test (dollars in thousands)		
	Wholesale Segment	Retail Segment	Finance Segment
Operating revenue	$2,500	$1,100	$400
Cost of sales--unaffiliated	900	400	0
Cost of sales--intersegment	300	200	0
Interest expense--unaffiliated	50	40	200
Interest expense--intersegment	10	20	100
Other operating expenses	800	100	50
Tax expense	220	170	25

21. Determine the amount of operating profit or loss for each segment that should be used to identify which is a reportable segment in accordance with the operating profit or loss test specified by SFAS 14.

	Wholesale	Retail	Finance
A.	$500	$400	$350
B.	$500	$400	$50
C.	$440	$340	$50
D.	$220	$170	$25

The correct answer is (B). *(Publisher)*
REQUIRED: The amount of each segment's operating profit or loss to be used to identify whether the segment is a reportable segment.
DISCUSSION: SFAS 14 defines operating profit or loss as operating revenue minus all operating expenses. Operating revenue includes that from intersegment sales, so the cost of intersegment sales is deducted. Excluded from the definition of operating expenses are general corporate expenses, income taxes, and all interest expense (except for financial segments). Also excluded are income or loss from equity-based investees, significant unusual or nonrecurring gains or losses, discontinued operations, extraordinary items, the cumulative effect of a change in accounting principle, and minority interests.

The operating profit for the wholesale segment is equal to $500 ($2,500 – $900 – $300 – $800); for the retail segment, $400 ($1,100 – $400 – $200 – $100); and for the financial segment, $50 ($400 – $200 – $100 – $50).

Answers (A), (C), and (D) are incorrect because the determination of operating profit or loss excludes interest expense for nonfinancial segments and income tax expense. The cost of intersegment sales must be included, as operating revenue includes intersegment sales.

22. Assuming there are no other industry segments in this enterprise, which of the three segments should be identified as a reportable segment in accordance with the operating profit or loss test?

	Wholesale	Retail	Finance
A.	Yes	Yes	No
B.	Yes	No	Yes
C.	No	Yes	Yes
D.	Yes	Yes	Yes

The correct answer is (A). *(Publisher)*
REQUIRED: The reportable segments under the operating profit or loss test.
DISCUSSION: In accordance with the operating profit or loss test, a reportable industry segment has an absolute operating profit or loss equal to at least 10% of the greater, in absolute amount, of (1) the combined operating profit of all segments not reporting an operating loss or (2) the combined operating loss of all segments not reporting an operating profit. The revenue of both the wholesale and the retail segments exceeds the test criterion of $95 ($950 x 10%), so these segments are reportable segments.

Segment	Operating Profit
Wholesale	$500
Retail	400
Finance	50
	$950

Answers (B), (C), and (D) are incorrect because the wholesale and retail segments meet the 10% operating profit or loss test criterion, but the finance segment does not.

23. Cott Co.'s four business segments have revenues and identifiable assets expressed as percentages of Cott's total revenues and total assets as follows:

	Revenues	Assets
Ebon	64%	66%
Fair	14%	18%
Gel	14%	4%
Hak	8%	12%
	100%	100%

Which of these business segments are deemed to be reportable segments?

A. Ebon only.

B. Ebon and Fair only.

C. Ebon, Fair, and Gel only.

D. Ebon, Fair, Gel, and Hak.

The correct answer is (D). *(CPA 1192 T-36)*
REQUIRED: The segment(s) deemed to be reportable.
DISCUSSION: An industry segment is a reportable segment if it satisfies one or more of three tests. One test is whether its revenue is 10% or more of the combined revenue of all the enterprise's industry segments. According to the identifiable assets test, an industry segment with identifiable assets equal to 10% or more of the combined identifiable assets of all industry segments is a reportable segment. Ebon, Fair, and Gel meet the revenue test, and Ebon, Fair, and Hak meet the identifiable assets test.
Answers (A), (B), and (C) are incorrect because all four segments meet at least one of the tests.

24. Correy Corp. and its divisions are engaged solely in manufacturing operations. The following data (consistent with prior years' data) pertain to the industries in which operations were conducted for the year ended December 31, 1996:

Industry	Total Revenue	Operating Profit	Identifiable Assets at 12/31/96
A	$10,000,000	$1,750,000	$20,000,000
B	8,000,000	1,400,000	17,500,000
C	6,000,000	1,200,000	12,500,000
D	3,000,000	550,000	7,500,000
E	4,250,000	675,000	7,000,000
F	1,500,000	225,000	3,000,000
	$32,750,000	$5,800,000	$67,500,000

In its segment information for 1996, how many reportable segments does Correy have?

A. Three.

B. Four.

C. Five.

D. Six.

The correct answer is (C). *(CPA 590 II-56)*
REQUIRED: The number of reportable segments.
DISCUSSION: Four segments (A, B, C, and E) have segment revenue equal to or greater than 10% of the $32,750,000 total revenue. These four segments also have segment operating profit equal to or greater than 10% of the $5,800,000 total operating profit. Five segments (A, B, C, D, and E) have identifiable assets greater than 10% of the $67,500,000 total identifiable assets. Because a segment is reportable if it meets one or more of the three tests established by SFAS 14, Correy Corp. has five reportable segments for 1996.
Answers (A), (B), and (D) are incorrect because a segment must meet one of three tests to be considered a reportable segment.

Questions 25 and 26 are based on the following information.

Identifiable Asset Test (dollars in thousands)

	Wholesale Segment	Retail Segment	Finance Segment	General Segment
Loans and receivables--unaffiliated	$ 400	$200	$200	$ 0
Loans and advances--intersegment	200	100	750	0
Other current assets	600	50	100	0
Plant assets	2,500	150	50	0
Investments--intersegment	600	200	0	0
General corporate assets				250

25. Determine the appropriate amount of identifiable assets of the three industry segments.

	Wholesale	Retail	Finance
A.	$3,500	$400	$1,100
B.	$3,500	$400	$350
C.	$4,100	$600	$1,100
D.	$4,300	$700	$1,100

The correct answer is (A). *(Publisher)*
REQUIRED: The amount of each segment's identifiable assets.
DISCUSSION: Identifiable assets include tangible and intangible assets either used exclusively by the industry segment or constituting an allocated portion of assets jointly used by two or more segments. Excluded from the definition are general corporate assets; investments in unconsolidated subsidiaries and other equity-method investments; and intersegment loans, advances, and investments. Intersegment loans and advances should be included as identifiable assets for finance segments only.

For the wholesale segment, the identifiable assets equal $3,500 ($400 + $600 + $2,500); for the retail segment, $400 ($200 + $50 + 150); and for the finance segment, $1,100 ($200 + $750 + $100 + $50).

Answers (B), (C), and (D) are incorrect because only the finance segment includes intersegment loans and advances among the identifiable assets. General corporate assets and intersegment investments should be excluded by all segments.

26. Which segments should be identified as reportable industry segments in accordance with the identifiable assets test?

	Wholesale	Retail	Finance
A.	Yes	Yes	No
B.	Yes	No	Yes
C.	No	Yes	Yes
D.	Yes	Yes	Yes

The correct answer is (B). *(Publisher)*
REQUIRED: The reportable segments under the identifiable assets test.
DISCUSSION: According to the identifiable assets test, an industry segment with identifiable assets equal to 10% or more of the combined identifiable assets of all industry segments is a reportable segment. General corporate assets are excluded from total identifiable assets of all reportable segments. Both the wholesale and the finance segments exceed the test criterion of $500 ($5,000 x 10%) and should be identified as reportable segments.

Segment	Identifiable Assets
Wholesale	$3,500
Retail	400
Finance	1,100
	$5,000

Answers (A), (C), and (D) are incorrect because both the wholesale and financial segments meet the 10% identifiable assets test criterion, and the retail segment does not.

27. Which of the following materiality tests is required to determine whether the industry segments of an enterprise that have been identified as reportable industry segments represent a substantial portion of the total operations of the enterprise?

A. The combined revenue of all reportable segments equals or exceeds 75% of the combined revenue of all industry segments.

B. The combined revenue from sales to unaffiliated customers by all reportable segments equals or exceeds 75% of the combined revenue of all industry segments.

C. The combined revenue from sales to unaffiliated customers by all reportable segments equals or exceeds 75% of the combined revenue from sales to unaffiliated customers by all industry segments.

D. The combined revenue of all reportable segments equals or exceeds 75% of the combined revenue from sales to unaffiliated customers by all industry segments.

The correct answer is (C). *(Publisher)*
REQUIRED: The test for determining whether the reportable segments represent a substantial portion of the enterprise's total operations.
DISCUSSION: SFAS 14 requires that the reportable segments represent a substantial portion of the enterprise's total operations. To determine materiality, the combined revenue from sales to unaffiliated customers by all reportable segments must equal or exceed 75% of the combined revenue from sales to unaffiliated customers by all industry segments. The test should be applied separately for each fiscal year for which financial statements are presented. When the test criterion is not met, additional segments must be identified as reportable until the criterion is met. Segments may have to be combined to meet one of the 10% tests.
Answers (A), (B), and (D) are incorrect because the comparison is based upon revenue from sales to unaffiliated customers by both reportable segments and the entire enterprise.

28. Which of the following statements about financial reporting for segments of a business enterprise is true?

A. The practical limit for the number of industry segments for which an enterprise reports information is 12.

B. The reportable industry segments of an enterprise should represent at least 50% of the combined revenue from sales to unaffiliated customers by all industry segments.

C. The reportable industry segments of an enterprise shall represent at least 75% of the combined revenue from sales to both affiliated and unaffiliated customers by all industry segments.

D. An industry segment is a component of an enterprise that is engaged in providing a product or service primarily to unaffiliated customers for a profit.

The correct answer is (D). *(Publisher)*
REQUIRED: The true statement regarding industry segment reporting requirements.
DISCUSSION: For purposes of SFAS 14, an industry segment is defined as a component of an enterprise engaged in providing a product or service, or a group of related products and services, primarily to unaffiliated customers (customers outside the enterprise) for a profit.
Answer (A) is incorrect because a practical limit is not precisely defined by SFAS 14. However, consideration should be given to limit the number of reportable segments to about 10. Answer (B) is incorrect because SFAS 14 states that the combined revenue of sales to unaffiliated customers by all reportable segments should constitute at least 75% of the combined revenue from sales by all industry segments to unaffiliated customers. Answer (C) is incorrect because the 75% test involves the computation of sales to unaffiliated customers only.

29. When an enterprise operates exclusively in a single industry or a dominant portion of an enterprise's operations are within a single industry segment, the only disclosure required by SFAS 14 is the identification of the industry. For an industry segment to be classified as dominant, which of the following tests must be met?

A. The revenue, operating profit or loss, and identifiable assets of the segment at least equal 90% of the related totals for all industry segments, and no other industry segment meets any of the 10% tests.

B. The revenue, operating profit or loss, and identifiable assets of the segment exceed 90% of the related totals for all industry segments, and no other industry segment meets any of the 10% tests.

C. The revenue, operating profit or loss, and identifiable assets of the segment equal or exceed 75% of the related totals for all industry segments.

D. The revenue, operating profit or loss, and identifiable assets of the segment exceed 90% of at least two of the related totals for all industry segments.

The correct answer is (B). *(Publisher)*
REQUIRED: The test for determining whether an industry segment is dominant.
DISCUSSION: SFAS 14 requires only the disclosure of the particular industry when an enterprise operates exclusively in a single industry or when the revenue, operating profit or loss, and identifiable assets of one of its industry segments exceed 90% of the related combined totals for all industry segments, and no other industry segment meets any of the 10% tests.
Answers (A), (C), and (D) are incorrect because the dominant industry segment must account for more than 90% of the totals in the test categories, and no other segment can meet any of the 10% tests.

30.2 Foreign Operations and Export Sales

30. The disclosure of information about an enterprise's foreign operations is required if either of two conditions is met. Which of the following statements contains one of the prescribed conditions?

A. Revenue generated by foreign operations from sales to both affiliated and unaffiliated customers is 10% or more of the combined revenue generated by domestic and foreign operations from sales to both affiliated and unaffiliated customers.

B. Revenue generated by foreign operations from sales to both affiliated and unaffiliated customers is 10% or more of consolidated revenue.

C. Identifiable assets of the foreign operations are 10% or more of the combined identifiable assets of domestic and foreign operations.

D. Identifiable assets of the foreign operations are 10% or more of the consolidated total assets.

The correct answer is (D). *(Publisher)*
REQUIRED: The condition requiring disclosure of information about foreign operations.
DISCUSSION: If either of two conditions specified by SFAS 14 is met, an enterprise must disclose certain information about its foreign operations. The two conditions are (1) revenue generated by the enterprise's foreign operations from sales to unaffiliated customers is 10% or more of consolidated revenue, and (2) the value of identifiable assets of the enterprise's foreign operations is 10% or more of consolidated total assets. The definitions of revenue and identifiable assets are the same as for segment reporting.
Answers (A) and (B) are incorrect because the revenue test involves comparison of consolidated revenue with revenue generated by the foreign operations from sales to unaffiliated customers. Answer (C) is incorrect because the asset test compares identifiable assets of the foreign operations with consolidated total assets.

31. What information should a public company present about revenues from foreign operations?

A. Disclose separately the amount of sales to unaffiliated customers and the amount of intracompany sales between geographic areas.

B. Disclose as a combined amount sales to unaffiliated customers and intracompany sales between geographic areas.

C. Disclose separately the amount of sales to unaffiliated customers but not the amount of intracompany sales between geographic areas.

D. No disclosure of revenues from foreign operations need be reported.

The correct answer is (A). *(CPA 1193 T-17)*
   REQUIRED: The information that should be presented about revenues from foreign operations.
   DISCUSSION: In its annual financial statements, a public company with foreign operations must disclose certain information for each foreign operation that meets one of two criteria: (1) Revenue from unaffiliated customers is 10% or more of consolidated revenue, and (2) the value of identifiable assets of the enterprise's foreign operations is 10% or more of consolidated total assets. SFAS 14 requires the separate disclosure of sales to unaffiliated customers and the amount of intracompany sales between geographic areas.
   Answer (B) is incorrect because the amounts should be disclosed separately. Answer (C) is incorrect because intracompany sales must also be disclosed. Answer (D) is incorrect because a disclosure is required if one of two criteria is met.

Questions 32 and 33 are based on the following information. This information is about the revenue of General Consolidated Company (in $000).

	Domestic Operations	Foreign Geographic Areas A	B	C	Eliminations	Consolidated
Sales to unaffiliated customers	$24,000	$1,000	$3,000	$2,000		$30,000
Sales to affiliated customers	3,000			1,000	$(4,000)	
Total revenue	$27,000	$1,000	$3,000	$3,000	$(4,000)	$30,000

---

32. For the purpose of determining whether a foreign geographic area is significant, thereby requiring separate disclosure, the revenue of that geographic area must equal or exceed 10% of which of the following amounts?

A. $6,000,000

B. $7,000,000

C. $30,000,000

D. $34,000,000

The correct answer is (C). *(Publisher)*
   REQUIRED: The amount to be used in applying the revenue test for foreign operations disclosure requirements.
   DISCUSSION: SFAS 14 requires that if one of two tests concerning foreign operations is met, certain financial information about such foreign operations must be disclosed in the financial statements. One of the two tests is whether revenue generated by the foreign operations from sales to unaffiliated customers is 10% or more of consolidated revenue as reported in the income statement. Consolidated revenue given as $30,000,000 should be used in applying the test for required disclosure.
   Answers (A), (B), and (D) are incorrect because the revenue test for foreign operations disclosure is based upon consolidated revenue, which is given as $30,000,000.

33. On the basis of the revenue test, disclosure of information about foreign operations of the General Consolidated Company should be presented in which of the following ways?

A. Separately for domestic operations and geographic area B; in the aggregate for areas A and C.

B. Separately for domestic operations; in the aggregate for foreign operations.

C. Separately for domestic operations and for each foreign geographic area.

D. No disclosure is required.

The correct answer is (A). *(Publisher)*
   REQUIRED: The required disclosure for foreign operations based on the revenue test.
   DISCUSSION: If an enterprise's foreign operations are conducted in two or more geographic areas, information required by SFAS 14 should be presented separately for each significant foreign geographic area and in the aggregate for all others. Only foreign area B is significant. Its sales to unaffiliated customers of $3,000,000 meet the revenue test (10% x $30,000,000 consolidated revenue). Foreign operation B should thus be disclosed separately, and areas A and C should be presented in the aggregate.
   Answer (B) is incorrect because foreign operations should not be aggregated. Area B meets the revenue test. Answer (C) is incorrect because separate disclosure for each foreign geographic area is not necessary. Areas A and C do not meet the revenue test. Answer (D) is incorrect because SFAS 14 specifically requires disclosure of significant foreign operations.

Questions 34 and 35 are based on the following information. This information is about the asset structure of the Ajax Consolidated Company (in $000).

| | Domestic Operations | Foreign Geographic Areas | | | Eliminations | Consolidated |
		A	B	C		
Identifiable assets	$40,000	$ 7,000	$8,000	$5,000		$60,000
Investment in affiliates	6,000	4,000				10,000
General corporate assets	5,000					5,000
Intercompany loans	3,000			2,000	$(5,000)	
Total assets	$54,000	$11,000	$8,000	$7,000	$(5,000)	$75,000

34. For the purpose of determining whether a foreign geographic area is significant, thereby requiring separate disclosure, the identifiable assets of that geographic area must equal or exceed 10% of which of the following amounts?

A. $60,000,000

B. $70,000,000

C. $75,000,000

D. $80,000,000

The correct answer is (C). *(Publisher)*
REQUIRED: The amount to be used in applying the identifiable asset test for determining foreign operations disclosure requirements.
DISCUSSION: Certain information about foreign operations must be presented for an enterprise if either of two tests is met, one of which is that identifiable assets of the enterprise's foreign operations are 10% or more of consolidated total assets. Consolidated total assets are given as $75,000,000, and any foreign geographic area with identifiable assets equal to or greater than 10% of $75,000,000 requires separate disclosure per SFAS 14.
Answers (A), (B), and (D) are incorrect because total identifiable consolidated assets of $75,000,000 are used to determine foreign operations disclosure requirements under the identifiable assets test.

35. On the basis of the identifiable asset test, how should disclosure of information about foreign operations of the Ajax Consolidated Company be presented?

A. Separately for domestic operations and geographic area B; in the aggregate for areas A and C.

B. Separately for domestic operations; in the aggregate for foreign operations.

C. Separately for domestic operations and for each foreign geographic area.

D. No disclosure is required.

The correct answer is (A). *(Publisher)*
REQUIRED: The required disclosure based on the identifiable asset test for foreign operations.
DISCUSSION: If an enterprise's foreign operations are conducted in two or more geographic areas, an operation meeting either the identifiable asset test or the revenue test must be presented separately from other foreign operations and domestic operations. Domestic operations and geographic area B should be presented separately because area B's identifiable assets of $8,000,000 are greater than $7,500,000 (10% x $75,000,000 consolidated total assets). Foreign geographic areas A and C may be aggregated since neither meets the 10% of assets test.
Answer (B) is incorrect because foreign area B must be segregated. It meets the 10% of identifiable assets test. Answer (C) is incorrect because A and C may be aggregated. Neither meets the asset test. Answer (D) is incorrect because SFAS 14 requires disclosure of significant foreign operations.

36. Disclosure of information about export sales is required

    A. Only if the enterprise also is required to report information about its operations in different industries.

    B. Only if the enterprise also is required to report information about foreign operations.

    C. If the amount of export sales from an enterprise's home country to unaffiliated customers in foreign countries is 10% or more of its consolidated sales.

    D. If the amount of export sales from an enterprise's domestic and foreign operations is 10% or more of its consolidated sales.

The correct answer is (C). *(Publisher)*
    REQUIRED: The true statement regarding export sales reporting requirements.
    DISCUSSION: With respect to an enterprise's domestic operations, if the amount of export sales from the enterprise's home country to unaffiliated customers in foreign countries is 10% or more of the total consolidated sales revenue, the export sales amount must be separately reported, both in the aggregate and by such geographic areas as are considered appropriate in the circumstances. This disclosure requirement is independent of industry segment and foreign operations disclosure requirements (SFAS 14).
    Answers (A) and (B) are incorrect because export sales disclosure requirements apply even when the enterprise is not required to report information about foreign operations or its operations in different industries. Answer (D) is incorrect because the export sales disclosure requirement is for an enterprise's domestic operations only.

37. If domestic operation sales to customers in foreign countries are required to be disclosed, the disclosures should include the

    A. Amount of export sales in the aggregate and by geographic area as appropriate if either industry segment or foreign operations data are required to be disclosed.

    B. Aggregate revenue, operating profit (loss), and amount of identifiable assets related to export sales.

    C. Amount of export sales in the aggregate and by geographic area as appropriate.

    D. The same data as required for industry segments except on an export basis.

The correct answer is (C). *(Publisher)*
    REQUIRED: The disclosures required for export sales.
    DISCUSSION: When the amount of export sales from an enterprise's home country to unaffiliated customers in foreign countries is 10% or more of total revenue from sales to unaffiliated customers as reported in a consolidated income statement, SFAS 14 requires the aggregate amount of export revenue and amounts by geographic area, as appropriate, to be disclosed.
    Answer (A) is incorrect because the disclosure of export sales information is necessary whether or not other segment information disclosures are required. Answers (B) and (D) are incorrect because only the revenues in the aggregate and by geographic area, as appropriate, are required.

30.3 Major Customers

38. The disclosure of information about major customers is required when the amount of sales to a single customer is 10% or more of the revenue of an enterprise. Which of the following must be disclosed?

    A. The identity of the major customer.

    B. The percent of total revenue derived from the major customer.

    C. The industry segment or segments making the sale.

    D. The geographic area or areas from which the sales were made.

The correct answer is (C). *(Publisher)*
    REQUIRED: The required disclosure for sales to major customers.
    DISCUSSION: If 10% or more of the revenue of an enterprise is derived from sales to any single customer, that fact and the amount of revenue from each such customer (without disclosing the identity of the customer) must be disclosed according to SFAS 14. The identity of the industry segment or segments making the sales must also be disclosed.
    Answers (A), (B), and (D) are incorrect because none states a disclosure required by SFAS 14.

39. Grum Corp., a publicly owned corporation, is subject to the requirements for segment reporting. In its income statement for the year ended December 31, 1996, Grum reported revenues of $50,000,000, operating expenses of $47,000,000, and net income of $3,000,000. Operating expenses include payroll costs of $15,000,000. Grum's combined identifiable assets of all industry segments on December 31, 1996 were $40,000,000. In its 1996 financial statements, Grum should disclose major customer data if sales to any single customer amount to at least

A. $300,000

B. $1,500,000

C. $4,000,000

D. $5,000,000

The correct answer is (D). *(CPA 1192 II-54)*
REQUIRED: The sales level requiring disclosure of major customer data.
DISCUSSION: If 10% or more of the revenue of an enterprise is derived from sales to any single customer, that fact and the amount of revenue from each such customer (without disclosing the identity of the customer) must be disclosed according to SFAS 14. The identity of the industry segment or segments making the sales must also be disclosed. Hence, sales to a single customer of $5,000,000 (10% x $50,000,000 total revenue) will necessitate disclosure of major customer data.
Answer (A) is incorrect because $300,000 is 10% of net income. Answer (B) is incorrect because $1,500,000 is 10% of payroll costs. Answer (C) is incorrect because $4,000,000 is 10% of combined identifiable assets of all industry segments.

40. For each of the following groups of customers, purchases amounted to 10% or more of the revenue of a publicly held company. For which of these groups must the company disclose information about major customers?

A. Federal governmental agencies, 6%; state governmental agencies, 4%.

B. French governmental agencies, 6%; German governmental agencies, 4%.

C. Parent company, 6%; subsidiary of parent company, 4%.

D. Federal governmental agencies, 6%; foreign governmental agencies, 4%.

The correct answer is (C). *(Publisher)*
REQUIRED: The set of circumstances requiring disclosure about major customers.
DISCUSSION: For purposes of SFAS 14, a group of customers under common control must be regarded as a single customer in determining whether 10% or more of the revenue of an enterprise is derived from sales to any single customer. A parent and a subsidiary are under common control, and they should be regarded as a single customer. Major customer disclosure is required in situation (C) because total combined revenue is 10% (6% + 4%).
Answers (A), (B), and (D) are incorrect because, according to SFAS 30, each governmental unit is to be treated as a separate customer in applying the 10% revenue test.

41. Listed below are the most recent year's sales to the three largest customers of the Prevost Company, a publicly held firm.

Federal government	$2,500,000
State of Iowa	2,000,000
State of Indiana	1,500,000

If Prevost's total revenue amounts to $22,000,000, Prevost should disclose the total amount of sales to major customers as which of the following amounts?

A. $0

B. $2,500,000

C. $4,500,000

D. $6,000,000

The correct answer is (B). *(Publisher)*
REQUIRED: The total amount of sales to major customers required to be separately reported.
DISCUSSION: An enterprise should disclose information about the extent of the enterprise's reliance on its major customers. If 10% or more of the revenue of an enterprise is derived from sales to any single customer, that fact, the identity of the industry segment or segments making the sale, and the amount of revenue from such customer must be disclosed. A single customer includes a group of entities under common control, the federal government, a state government, a local government, or a foreign government. Total revenue for Prevost is $22,000,000. Thus, Prevost should disclose the amount of sales to any major customer from whom sales revenue totals $2,200,000 (10% x $22,000,000). Because the year's sales to the federal government totaled $2,500,000, such disclosure must be made (but not necessarily identifying the customer).
Answers (A), (C), and (D) are incorrect because only sales to the federal government meet or exceed the 10% of total revenues test.

CHAPTER THIRTY-ONE
FOREIGN EXCHANGE
TRANSACTIONS AND TRANSLATION

This chapter concerns translation of foreign currency financial statements for the purpose of accounting for a consolidation, a combination, or an equity-based investment. It also applies to accounting for transactions of a reporting enterprise in currencies other than its functional currency, e.g., sales to foreign customers denominated in a foreign currency. Accounting for hedging transactions is also covered. The basic authoritative pronouncement is SFAS 52, *Foreign Currency Translation*.

At December 1, 1996, the FASB had a Proposed Statement of Financial Accounting Standards, *Accounting for Derivatives and Similar Financial Instruments and for Hedging Activities*, outstanding. If and when issued as a final statement, it will require all entities to account for changes in the fair value of a derivative based on whether the derivative was designated as a hedge and, if designated as a hedge, the type of hedge.

31.1 Foreign Currency Financial Statements

1. The economic effects of a change in foreign exchange rates on a relatively self-contained and integrated operation within a foreign country relate to the net investment by the reporting enterprise in that operation. Consequently, translation adjustments that arise from the consolidation of that operation

A. Affect cash flows but should not be reflected in income.

B. Affect cash flows and should be reflected in income.

C. Do not affect cash flows and should not be reflected in income.

D. Do not affect cash flows but should be reflected in income.

The correct answer is (C). *(Publisher)*

REQUIRED: The true statement about translation adjustments arising from consolidation of a self-contained foreign operation with its U.S. parent/investor.

DISCUSSION: SFAS 52, *Foreign Currency Translation*, concludes that foreign currency translation adjustments for a foreign operation that is relatively self-contained and integrated within its environment do not affect cash flows of the reporting enterprise and should be excluded from net income. When an operation is relatively self-contained, the cash generated and expended by the entity is normally in the currency of the foreign country, and that currency is deemed to be the operation's functional currency.

Answers (A) and (B) are incorrect because, when an operation is relatively self-contained, it is presumed that translation adjustments do not affect cash flows. Answers (B) and (D) are incorrect because translation adjustments should be included as a separate component of consolidated owners' equity, not recognized in income.

2. The financial results and relationships of foreign subsidiaries that are presented in the consolidated financial statements of a U.S.-based parent company should be measured in accordance with the

A. Functional currency translation method.

B. Current/noncurrent translation method.

C. Monetary/nonmonetary translation method.

D. Temporal translation method.

The correct answer is (A). *(Publisher)*
REQUIRED: The method used to convert foreign subsidiary financial statements for consolidation purposes.
DISCUSSION: According to SFAS 52, the functional currency translation approach is appropriate for use in accounting for and reporting the financial results and relationships of foreign subsidiaries in consolidated statements. It involves identifying the functional currency of the entity (the currency of the primary economic environment in which the entity operates), measuring all elements of the financial statements in the functional currency, and using a current exchange rate for translation from the functional currency to the reporting currency.
Answers (B), (C), and (D) are incorrect because the functional currency translation method is prescribed by SFAS 52.

3. The financial statements of a foreign subsidiary are to be measured by use of the subsidiary's functional currency. The functional currency of an entity is defined as the currency of the

A. Parent company.

B. United States.

C. Primary economic environment in which the entity operates.

D. Geographic location in which the entity's headquarters are located.

The correct answer is (C). *(CIA 593 IV-41)*
REQUIRED: The definition of the functional currency of an entity.
DISCUSSION: An entity's functional currency is the currency of the primary economic environment in which the entity operates; normally, that is the currency of the environment in which an entity primarily generates and expends cash.
Answer (A) is incorrect because the currency of the parent may or may not be the functional currency of the foreign subsidiary. Answer (B) is incorrect because the U.S. dollar may or may not be the functional currency of a foreign subsidiary. Answer (D) is incorrect because a foreign entity's functional currency might not be the currency of the country in which the entity is located.

4. SFAS 52, *Foreign Currency Translation*, provides specific guidelines for translating foreign currency financial statements. The translation process begins with a determination of whether a foreign affiliate's functional currency is also its local reporting currency. Which one of the following factors indicates that a foreign affiliate's functional currency is the U.S. dollar?

A. Cash flows are primarily in foreign currency and do not affect parent's cash flows.

B. Financing is primarily obtained from local foreign sources and from the affiliate's operations.

C. Sales prices are responsive to short-term changes in exchange rates and worldwide competition.

D. Labor, materials, and other costs consist primarily of local costs to the foreign affiliate.

The correct answer is (C). *(CMA 692 2-15)*
REQUIRED: The factor indicating that a foreign affiliate's functional currency is the U.S. dollar.
DISCUSSION: The functional currency is the currency of the primary economic environment in which an entity operates. It is normally the currency of the environment in which an entity primarily generates and expends cash. If a U.S. company's foreign affiliate's sales prices are responsive to short-term changes in exchange rates and worldwide competition, its functional currency is likely to be the U.S. dollar.
Answer (A) is incorrect because cash flows that are primarily in a foreign currency indicate that the foreign currency is the functional currency. Answer (B) is incorrect because, when financing is obtained primarily from foreign sources and operations, the foreign currency is likely to be the functional currency. Answer (D) is incorrect because, when costs are primarily paid in the foreign country, the foreign currency is likely to be the functional currency.

5. The financial results of three foreign subsidiaries are included along with those of a U.S. parent company in consolidated financial statements. The subsidiaries are distinct and separable from the parent and from each other. If the four operations are conducted in four different economic environments, how many different functional currencies are necessary to measure these operations?

A. One.

B. Two.

C. Three.

D. Four.

The correct answer is (D). *(Publisher)*
REQUIRED: The number of functional currencies involved in measuring the financial activities of a parent and three distinct subsidiaries operating in different environments.
DISCUSSION: The activities of an entity must be measured in terms of the currency of the primary economic environment in which the entity operates, that is, the functional currency. Because the four operations (parent and three subsidiaries) are distinct and separable from each other and are conducted in four different economic environments, each entity will use a different functional currency to measure its operations.
Answers (A), (B), and (C) are incorrect because each of the four operations has its own functional currency.

6. Which of the following is not an integral part of the functional currency translation approach?

A. The functional currency of each foreign operation must be identified.

B. All elements of the financial statements of a foreign operation must be measured in the functional currency.

C. If the functional currency of a foreign operation differs from the reporting currency, translation using the current exchange rate method is required.

D. The gain or loss arising from translation must be included in the determination of the current period's income.

The correct answer is (D). *(Publisher)*
REQUIRED: The item that is not an element of the functional currency translation approach.
DISCUSSION: According to SFAS 52, a gain or loss arising from translation from the functional currency into the reporting currency is not reflected in the current period's income. Translation adjustments are reported separately and accumulated as a component of owners' equity.
Answers (A), (B), and (C) are incorrect because each is an integral part of the functional currency translation approach.

7. Certain balance sheet accounts of a foreign subsidiary of Rowan, Inc., on December 31, 1996, have been translated into U.S. dollars as follows:

	Translated at	
	Current Rates	Historical Rates
Note receivable, long-term	$240,000	$200,000
Prepaid rent	85,000	80,000
Patent	150,000	170,000
	$475,000	$450,000

The subsidiary's functional currency is the currency of the country in which it is located. What total amount should be included in Rowan's December 31, 1996 consolidated balance sheet for the above accounts?

A. $450,000

B. $455,000

C. $475,000

D. $495,000

The correct answer is (C). *(CPA 590 II-44)*
REQUIRED: The total translated amount to be included in the consolidated balance sheet.
DISCUSSION: When the currency used to prepare a foreign entity's financial statements is its functional currency, SFAS 52 specifies that the current rate method be used to translate the foreign entity's financial statements into the reporting currency. This method applies the current exchange rate at the balance sheet date to assets and liabilities and historical rates to shareholders' equity. The translation gains and losses arising from applying this method are taken directly to owners' equity in the consolidated statements and are not reflected in income. Because Rowan's listed assets should be translated at current rates, $475,000 is the total amount that should be included in the consolidated balance sheet.
Answer (A) is incorrect because $450,000 reflects translation at historical rates. Answer (B) is incorrect because the note and patent are translated at historical rates. Answer (D) is incorrect because the patent is translated at historical rates.

8. If an entity's books of accounts are not maintained in its functional currency, SFAS 52, *Foreign Currency Translation*, requires remeasurement into the functional currency prior to the translation process. An item that should be remeasured by use of the current exchange rate is

A. An investment in bonds to be held until maturity.

B. A plant asset and the associated accumulated depreciation.

C. A patent and the associated accumulated amortization.

D. The revenue from a long-term construction contract.

The correct answer is (A). *(CMA 692 2-16)*
REQUIRED: The item that should be remeasured into the functional currency using the current exchange rate.
DISCUSSION: The current rate should be used for all items except common nonmonetary balance sheet accounts and their related revenues, expenses, gains, and losses, which are remeasured at historical rates. Thus, most monetary items, such as an investment in bonds, are remeasured at the current exchange rate.
Answer (B) is incorrect because plant assets are remeasured at historical rates. Answer (C) is incorrect because a patent is remeasured at historical rates. Answer (D) is incorrect because the revenue from a long-term construction contract is one of the exceptions for which the current rate is not to be used.

9. If all assets and liabilities of a firm's foreign subsidiary are translated into the parent's currency at the current exchange rate (the rate in effect at the date of the balance sheet), the extent of the parent firm's translation gain or loss is based on the subsidiary's

A. Current assets minus current liabilities.

B. Total assets minus total liabilities.

C. Monetary assets minus monetary liabilities.

D. Operating cash flows.

The correct answer is (B). *(CIA 583 IV-11)*
REQUIRED: The basis for the parent's translation gain or loss if all assets and liabilities of the foreign subsidiary are translated at the current exchange rate.
DISCUSSION: When the functional currency of a foreign subsidiary is the local (foreign) currency, translation of all assets and liabilities is required at the current rate as of the balance sheet date.
Answers (A), (C), and (D) are incorrect because translation of net assets (total assets – total liabilities) is required.

10. A wholly owned subsidiary of Ward, Inc. has certain expense accounts for the year ended December 31, 1996 stated in local currency units (LCU) as follows:

	LCU
Depreciation of equipment (related assets purchased Jan. 1, 1994)	120,000
Provision for doubtful accounts	80,000
Rent	200,000

The exchange rates at various dates are as follows:

	Dollar Equivalent of 1 LCU
December 31, 1996	$.40
Average for year ended 12/31/96	.44
January 1, 1994	.50

Assume that the LCU is the subsidiary's functional currency and that the charges to the expense accounts occurred approximately evenly during the year. What total dollar amount should be included in Ward's 1996 consolidated income statement to reflect these expenses?

A. $160,000

B. $168,000

C. $176,000

D. $183,200

The correct answer is (C). *(CPA 585 I-41)*
REQUIRED: The amount of expenses in the consolidated income statement.
DISCUSSION: When the local currency of the subsidiary is the functional currency, translation into the reporting currency is necessary. Assets and liabilities are translated at the exchange rate at the balance sheet date, and revenues, expenses, gains, and losses are usually translated at average rates for the period. Thus, the $400,000 in total expenses should be translated at the average exchange rate of $.44, resulting in expenses reflected in the consolidated income statement of $176,000 ($400,000 x $.44).
Answer (A) is incorrect because the average exchange rate, not the current year-end rate, should be used. Answers (B) and (D) are incorrect because the average exchange rate, not a combination of rates, should be used.

11. A foreign subsidiary's functional currency is its local currency, which has not experienced significant inflation. The weighted-average exchange rate for the current year is the appropriate exchange rate for translating

	Wages Expense	Sales to Customers
A.	Yes	No
B.	Yes	Yes
C.	No	Yes
D.	No	No

The correct answer is (B). *(CPA 592 T-39)*
REQUIRED: The item(s) translated at the weighted-average exchange rate for the current year.
DISCUSSION: When an entity's local currency is the functional currency and this currency has not experienced significant inflation, translation into the reporting currency of all elements of the financial statements must be at a current exchange rate. Assets and liabilities are translated at the exchange rate at the balance sheet date. Revenues (e.g., sales), expenses (e.g., wages), gains, and losses should be translated at the rates in effect when they were recognized. However, translation at a weighted-average rate for the period is permitted.
Answers (A), (C), and (D) are incorrect because wages expense and sales to customers are appropriately translated using the weighted-average exchange rate for the current year.

12. Which of the following should be reported as a shareholders' equity contra account?

A. Discount on convertible bonds that are common stock equivalents.

B. Premium on convertible bonds that are common stock equivalents.

C. Cumulative foreign exchange translation loss.

D. Organization costs.

The correct answer is (C). *(CPA 1193 T-14)*
REQUIRED: The account that should be reported as a shareholders' equity contra account.
DISCUSSION: When the currency used to prepare a foreign entity's financial statements is its functional currency, SFAS 52 specifies that the current rate method be used to translate the foreign entity's financial statements into the reporting currency. The translation gains and losses arising from applying this method are taken directly to owners' equity in the consolidated statements and are not reflected in income. They are reported separately and accumulated in a separate component of equity. A cumulative foreign exchange translation loss is a debit item and is therefore reported as a shareholders' equity contra account.
Answer (A) is incorrect because a discount on bonds is a contra account to bonds payable in the liability section of the balance sheet. Answer (B) is incorrect because premium on bonds is a contra account to bonds payable in the liability section. Answer (D) is incorrect because organizational costs are intangible assets.

13. Park Co.'s wholly owned subsidiary, Schnell Corp., maintains its accounting records in German marks. Because all of Schnell's branch offices are in Switzerland, its functional currency is the Swiss franc. Remeasurement of Schnell's 1996 financial statements resulted in a $7,600 gain, and translation of its financial statements resulted in an $8,100 gain. What amount should Park report as a foreign exchange gain in its income statement for the year ended December 31, 1996?

A. $0

B. $7,600

C. $8,100

D. $15,700

The correct answer is (B). *(CPA 595 F-31)*
REQUIRED: The gain reported as a result of translation and remeasurement.
DISCUSSION: The financial statements must be remeasured into the functional currency (Swiss francs) using the temporal method and then translated into the reporting currency (U.S. dollar) using the current rate method. The $7,600 gain arising from remeasurement should be reported as part of continuing operations. The $8,100 translation gain should be taken directly to the shareholders' equity section of the consolidated statements. Translation gains are not reflected in income.
Answer (A) is incorrect because the gain on remeasurement should be reported in the income statement. Answers (C) and (D) are incorrect because the $8,100 translation gain is not reported in the income statement.

14. SFAS 52, *Foreign Currency Translation*, requires the current rate of exchange to be used for remeasuring certain balance sheet items and the historical rate of exchange for other balance sheet items. An item that should be remeasured using the historical exchange rate is

A. Accounts and notes receivable.

B. Accounts and notes payable.

C. Taxes payable.

D. Prepaid expenses.

The correct answer is (D). *(CMA 685 3-33)*
REQUIRED: The item that should be remeasured using the historical exchange rate.
DISCUSSION: Financial statements are remeasured using the temporal rate method. In general, this method adjusts monetary items at the current rate and nonmonetary items at the historical rate. Prepaid expenses, a nonmonetary item, should be remeasured using the historical rate.
Answers (A), (B), and (C) are incorrect because they are monetary items. Thus, they should be remeasured using the current rate of exchange.

15. A wholly owned foreign subsidiary of Union Corporation has certain expense accounts for the year ended December 31, 1996 stated in local currency units (LCU) as follows:

	LCU
Amortization of patent (related patent acquired January 1, 1994)	40,000
Provision for doubtful accounts	60,000
Rent	100,000

The exchange rates at various dates are as follows:

	Dollar Equivalent of 1 LCU
December 31, 1996	$.20
Average for the year ended December 31, 1996	.22
January 1, 1994	.25

The subsidiary's operations were an extension of the parent company's operations. What total dollar amount should be included in Union's income statement to reflect the above expenses for the year ended December 31, 1996?

A. $40,000

B. $42,000

C. $44,000

D. $45,200

The correct answer is (D). *(CPA 1180 I-11)*
REQUIRED: The dollar amount of remeasured expenses of a foreign subsidiary whose operations are an extension of the parent's.
DISCUSSION: Given that the foreign subsidiary's operations are an extension of the parent company's, the functional currency of the subsidiary is considered to be the U.S. dollar. Thus, remeasurement from the local currency to the U.S. dollar is required for financial statement purposes.
Nonmonetary balance sheet items and related revenues and expenses (e.g., cost of sales, depreciation, and amortization) should be remeasured using historical rates to produce the same results as if those items had been initially recorded in the functional currency (U.S. dollar). Accordingly, the amortization of patent expense (LCU = 40,000) should be remeasured at the rate of exchange in effect at the date the patent was acquired, $.25. Monetary and current value items should be remeasured at a current rate. Hence, provision for doubtful accounts and rent should be remeasured at the average 1996 exchange rate of $.22, which is the customary approximation of the current rate used to remeasure expenses not related to nonmonetary items.

Patent amortization	40,000 × $.25 =	$10,000
Provision for doubtful accounts	60,000 × $.22 =	13,200
Rent	100,000 × $.22 =	22,000
Total remeasured expenses		$45,200

Answer (A) is incorrect because $40,000 results from applying the year-end exchange rate to the total expenses. Answer (B) is incorrect because $42,000 results from applying the average rate to the patent and the year-end rate to the rent. Answer (C) is incorrect because $44,000 results from applying the average rate to the total expenses.

16. A foreign subsidiary of a U.S. parent reports its financial statements in its local currency although its functional currency is the U.S. dollar. In the consolidated financial statements, all of the following accounts of the subsidiary are remeasured into the functional currency at the historical rate except

A. Marketable securities carried at cost.

B. Inventories carried at market.

C. Property, plant, and equipment.

D. Goodwill.

The correct answer is (B). *(J.W. Mantooth)*
REQUIRED: The account that is not remeasured at the historical rate.
DISCUSSION: When a foreign subsidiary's functional currency is the U.S. dollar, all accounts of that subsidiary reported in a foreign currency must be remeasured as if they had been recorded in the U.S. dollar. Nonmonetary balance sheet items and related revenue, expense, gain, and loss accounts are remeasured at the historical rate. Monetary accounts are remeasured at the current rate. Inventories carried at market value are classified as monetary assets and should therefore be remeasured at the current rate.
Answers (A), (C), and (D) are incorrect because they are listed by SFAS 52 as accounts to be remeasured using historical exchange rates.

17. When remeasuring foreign currency financial statements into the functional currency, which of the following items would be remeasured using historical exchange rates?

A. Inventories carried at cost.

B. Equity securities reported at fair values.

C. Bonds payable.

D. Accrued liabilities.

The correct answer is (A). *(CPA 1193 T-36)*
REQUIRED: The item that would be remeasured using historical exchange rates.
DISCUSSION: SFAS 52 requires the current rate of exchange to be used for remeasuring certain balance sheet items and the historical rate of exchange for other balance sheet items. Nonmonetary balance sheet items and related revenue, expense, gain, and loss accounts are remeasured at the historical rate. Monetary accounts are remeasured at the current rate. Inventories valued at cost are nonmonetary items and are measured at historical rates.

Answers (B), (C), and (D) are incorrect because equity securities reported at fair values, bonds payable, and accrued liabilities are monetary items valued at the current rate.

18. The Brinjac Company owns a foreign subsidiary. Included among the subsidiary's liabilities for the year just ended are 400,000 LCU of revenue received in advance, recorded when $.50 was the dollar equivalent per LCU, and a deferred tax liability for 187,500 LCU, recognized when $.40 was the dollar equivalent per LCU. The rate of exchange in effect at year-end was $.35 per LCU. If the accounting is in accordance with SFAS 52 and SFAS 109 and the dollar is the functional currency, what total should be included for these two liabilities on Brinjac's consolidated balance sheet at year-end?

A. $205,625

B. $215,000

C. $265,625

D. $275,000

The correct answer is (D). *(C.J. Skender)*
REQUIRED: The total of two liability accounts of a foreign subsidiary in the consolidated statements if the functional currency is the U.S. dollar.
DISCUSSION: When a foreign entity's functional currency is the U.S. dollar, the financial statements of the entity recorded in a foreign currency must be remeasured in terms of the U.S. dollar. In accordance with SFAS 52, revenue received in advance (deferred income) is considered a nonmonetary balance sheet item and is translated at the applicable historical rate (400,000 LCU x $.50/LCU = $200,000). Deferred charges and credits (except policy acquisition costs for life insurance companies) are also remeasured at historical exchange rates. Deferred taxes were formerly not subject to this rule, but SFAS 109 amended SFAS 52 to eliminate the exception. Consequently, the deferred tax liability (a deferred credit) should be remeasured at the historical rate (187,500 LCU x $.40/LCU) = $75,000). The total for these liabilities is therefore $275,000 ($200,000 + $75,000).

Answer (A) is incorrect because $205,625 results from applying the year-end rate to the total liabilities. Answer (B) is incorrect because the historical, not current, rate should be used to remeasure the deferred income. Answer (C) is incorrect because the historical rate is used to remeasure nonmonetary balance sheet items, including deferred tax assets and liabilities.

19. For the purpose of remeasuring financial statements of a foreign entity into the functional currency, a highly inflationary economy is considered to be one that has a(n)

A. Inflation rate of 100% or more per year for a 3-year period.

B. Inflation rate 100% greater than that of the reporting currency for a 3-year period.

C. Inflation rate of 100% per year for 3 out of 5 years.

D. Cumulative inflation rate of 100% or more over a 3-year period.

The correct answer is (D). *(J. Bruno)*
REQUIRED: The test for a highly inflationary economy applied to a foreign economic environment.
DISCUSSION: The financial statements of a foreign entity in a highly inflationary economy should be remeasured into the reporting currency; that is, the reporting currency should be treated as if it were the functional currency. SFAS 52 defines a highly inflationary economy as one that has cumulative inflation of approximately 100% or more over a 3-year period.

Answers (A), (B), and (C) are incorrect because the cumulative inflation rate is used to determine highly inflationary economies.

20. The Dease Company owns a foreign subsidiary with 3,600,000 local currency units (LCU) of property, plant, and equipment before accumulated depreciation on December 31, 1996. The subsidiary's functional currency is the U.S. dollar. Of this amount, 2,400,000 LCU were acquired in 1989 when the rate of exchange was 1.6 LCU to $1, and 1,200,000 LCU were acquired in 1992 when the rate of exchange was 1.8 LCU to $1. The rate of exchange in effect at December 31, 1996 was 2 LCU to $1. The weighted average of exchange rates in effect during 1996 was 1.92 LCU to $1. Assuming that the property, plant, and equipment are depreciated using the straight-line method over a 10-year period with no salvage value, how much depreciation expense relating to the foreign subsidiary's property, plant, and equipment should be charged in Dease's income statement for 1996 if SFAS 52 is followed?

A. $180,000

B. $187,500

C. $200,000

D. $216,667

The correct answer is (D). *(CPA 1176 I-1)*
REQUIRED: The amount of remeasured depreciation expense recognized in consolidating a foreign subsidiary whose functional currency is the U.S. dollar.
DISCUSSION: Given that the subsidiary's functional currency is the U.S. dollar, the financial statements of the subsidiary must be remeasured in terms of the dollar. Nonmonetary assets and the related revenues and expenses should be remeasured based on the historical rates in effect at the dates of the transactions. Depreciation expense relates to the property, plant, and equipment (nonmonetary assets), so the rate of exchange in effect when these fixed assets were acquired should be used in remeasuring depreciation expense for the period.
Because 2,400,000 LCU of fixed assets were acquired when the rate of exchange was 1.6, depreciation expense can be remeasured by multiplying the LCU depreciation by 1/1.6, resulting in $150,000 of remeasured depreciation expense [(2,400,000 ÷ 10) x $1/1.6]. Depreciation related to the asset that cost 1,200,000 LCU is $66,667 in remeasured terms [(1,200,000 ÷ 10) x $1/1.8]. Total depreciation expense equals $216,667 ($150,000 + $66,667).
Answer (A) is incorrect because $180,000 results from applying the current (year-end) rate to the total depreciation expense. Answer (B) is incorrect because $187,500 results from applying the average rate to the total depreciation expense. Answer (C) is incorrect because the rate prevailing at the time the assets were acquired should be used for each group of assets.

21. When the foreign operations are conducted in a highly inflationary economy, at what exchange rates should the following balance sheet accounts in foreign statements be remeasured into U.S. dollars?

	Equipment	Accumulated Depreciation of Equipment
A.	Current	Current
B.	Current	Average for year
C.	Historical	Current
D.	Historical	Historical

The correct answer is (D). *(CPA 1181 T-27)*
REQUIRED: The proper exchange rates used for balance sheet items of a foreign operation in a highly inflationary economy.
DISCUSSION: When a foreign entity operates in an environment that is highly inflationary (approximately 100% or more inflation over a 3-year period), SFAS 52 requires that financial statements be remeasured into the reporting currency; that is, the reporting currency is treated as if it were the functional currency. A nonmonetary asset, such as equipment, and its related expense or revenue items are remeasured at applicable historical rates. The results should be the same as if those items had initially been recorded in the currency (the U.S. dollar) into which they are being remeasured.
Answers (A), (B), and (C) are incorrect because nonmonetary assets and related expenses are remeasured at historical rates.

22. A widely diversified U.S. corporation sold portions of three wholly owned foreign subsidiaries in the same year. The functional currency of each subsidiary was the currency of the country in which it was located. The percentage sold and the amount of the translation adjustment component of equity attributable to each subsidiary at the time of sale follow:

	% Sold	Translation Adjustment Component
Sub A	100%	$90,000 credit
Sub B	50%	40,000 debit
Sub C	10%	25,000 debit

What total amount of the translation adjustment component should be reported as part of the gain on sale of the three subsidiaries?

A. $90,000 credit.

B. $70,000 net credit.

C. $67,500 net credit.

D. $0

The correct answer is (C). *(Publisher)*
REQUIRED: The total translation adjustment component of equity included in the gain on the sale of subsidiaries.
DISCUSSION: FASB Interpretation No. 37, *Accounting for Translation Adjustments upon Sale of Part of an Investment in a Foreign Entity*, clarifies SFAS 52. A pro rata portion of the accumulated translation adjustment component of equity attributable to an investment shall be recognized in measuring the gain or loss on the sale of all or part of a company's interest in a foreign entity. Here, the total amount to be reported is a $67,500 net credit [(100% x $90,000) − (50% x $40,000) − (10% x $25,000)].

Answer (A) is incorrect because a $90,000 credit fails to consider Subs B and C. Answer (B) is incorrect because a $70,000 net credit fails to consider Sub C. Answer (D) is incorrect because a translation adjustment component is recognized as part of the gain on the sale of the subsidiaries.

31.2 Foreign Currency Transactions

23. On October 1, 1996, Velec Co., a U.S. company, contracted to purchase foreign goods requiring payment in francs 1 month after the receipt of the goods at Velec's factory. Title to the goods passed on December 15, 1996. The goods were still in transit on December 31, 1996. Exchange rates were one dollar to 22 francs, 20 francs, and 21 francs on October 1, December 15, and December 31, 1996, respectively. Velec should account for the exchange rate fluctuation in 1996 as

A. A loss included in net income before extraordinary items.

B. A gain included in net income before extraordinary items.

C. An extraordinary gain.

D. An extraordinary loss.

The correct answer is (B). *(CPA 593 T-34)*
REQUIRED: The classification of a gain or loss due to exchange rate fluctuations.
DISCUSSION: SFAS 52 requires that a receivable or payable denominated in a foreign currency be adjusted to its current exchange rate at each balance sheet date. The transaction gain or loss arising from this adjustment should ordinarily be reflected in current income. Because title passed on December 15, the liability fixed in francs should have been recorded on that date at the 20-franc exchange rate. The increase to 21 francs per dollar at year-end decreases the dollar value of the liability and results in an exchange gain. Such a gain is ordinarily treated as a component of income from continuing operations.

Answer (A) is incorrect because the strengthening of the dollar resulted in a gain. Answers (C) and (D) are incorrect because an extraordinary item is infrequent and unusual in nature. Exchange rates change frequently.

24. On October 1, 1996, Mild Co., a U.S. company, purchased machinery from Grund, a German company, with payment due on April 1, 1997. If Mild's 1996 operating income included no foreign exchange transaction gain or loss, the transaction could have

A. Resulted in an extraordinary gain.

B. Been denominated in U.S. dollars.

C. Caused a foreign currency gain to be reported as a contra account against machinery.

D. Caused a foreign currency translation gain to be reported as a separate component of shareholders' equity.

The correct answer is (B). *(CPA 1193 T-35)*
REQUIRED: The reason no foreign currency transaction gain or loss occurred when a U.S. company purchased machinery from a German company.
DISCUSSION: A foreign currency transaction gives rise to a receivable or a payable, fixed in terms of the amount of foreign currency. A change in the exchange rate between the functional currency and the currency in which the transaction is denominated is a gain or loss that ordinarily should be included as a component of income from continuing operations in the period in which the exchange rate changes. If Mild Co.'s functional currency is the U.S. dollar and the transaction was denominated in U.S. dollars, the transaction is a foreign transaction, not a foreign currency transaction. Thus, no foreign currency transaction gain or loss occurred.
Answer (A) is incorrect because foreign currency transaction gains and losses are ordinarily treated as operating items. Answer (C) is incorrect because foreign currency transaction gains and losses are included in the determination of net income. Answer (D) is incorrect because foreign currency transaction gains and losses are included in the determination of net income.

25. SFAS 52 states that transaction gains and losses have direct cash flow effects when foreign-denominated monetary assets are settled in amounts greater or less than the functional currency equivalent of the original transactions. These transaction gains and losses should be reflected in income

A. At the date the transaction originated.

B. On a retroactive basis.

C. In the period the exchange rate changes.

D. Only at the year-end balance sheet date.

The correct answer is (C). *(CMA 1291 2-5)*
REQUIRED: The time when foreign currency transaction gains and losses should be reflected in income.
DISCUSSION: A foreign currency transaction is one whose terms are denominated in a currency other than the entity's functional currency. When a foreign currency transaction gives rise to a receivable or a payable that is fixed in terms of the amount of foreign currency to be received or paid, a change in the exchange rate between the functional currency and the currency in which the transaction is denominated results in a gain or loss that ordinarily should be included as a component of income from continuing operations in the period in which the exchange rate changes.
Answer (A) is incorrect because the extent of any gain or loss cannot be known at the date of the original transaction. Answer (B) is incorrect because retroactive recognition is not permitted. Answer (D) is incorrect because gains and losses are to be recognized in the period of the rate change.

26. The functional currency of Nash, Inc.'s subsidiary is the French franc. Nash borrowed French francs as a partial hedge of its investment in the subsidiary. In preparing consolidated financial statements, Nash's translation loss on its investment in the subsidiary exceeded its exchange gain on the borrowing. How should the effects of the loss and gain be reported in Nash's consolidated financial statements?

A. The translation loss minus the exchange gain is reported separately in the shareholders' equity section of the balance sheet.

B. The translation loss minus the exchange gain is reported in the income statement.

C. The translation loss is reported separately in the shareholders' equity section of the balance sheet, and the exchange gain is reported in the income statement.

D. The translation loss is reported in the income statement, and the exchange gain is reported separately in the shareholders' equity section of the balance sheet.

The correct answer is (A). *(CPA 592 T-38)*
REQUIRED: The reporting of the translation loss and exchange gain.
DISCUSSION: Translation adjustments are gains and losses from translating financial statements from the functional to the reporting currency. They should be reported separately and accumulated as a separate component of shareholders' equity. They are not included in the determination of net income. When a foreign currency transaction gives rise to a receivable or a payable, fixed in terms of the amount of foreign currency, a change in the exchange rate between the functional currency and the currency in which the transaction is denominated is a gain or loss that ordinarily should be included as a component of income from continuing operations in the period in which the exchange rate changes. However, a gain or loss on a foreign currency transaction that hedges a net investment in a foreign entity is not included in the determination of net income but is reported in the same manner as a translation adjustment. Thus, the translation loss and the exchange gain should be accumulated in a separate component of equity.
Answers (B), (C), and (D) are incorrect because the translation loss and the exchange gain are accumulated in a separate component of equity, not in the income statement.

27. Shore Co. records its transactions in U.S. dollars. A sale of goods resulted in a receivable denominated in Japanese yen, and a purchase of goods resulted in a payable denominated in French francs. Shore recorded a foreign exchange gain on collection of the receivable and an exchange loss on settlement of the payable. The exchange rates are expressed as so many units of foreign currency to one dollar. Did the number of foreign currency units exchangeable for a dollar increase or decrease between the contract and settlement dates?

	Yen Exchangeable for $1	Francs Exchangeable for $1
A.	Increase	Increase
B.	Decrease	Decrease
C.	Decrease	Increase
D.	Increase	Decrease

The correct answer is (B). *(CPA 1191 T-18)*
REQUIRED: The movements in exchange rates.
DISCUSSION: When a foreign currency transaction gives rise to a receivable or a payable, fixed in terms of the amount of foreign currency, a change in the exchange rate between the functional currency and the currency in which the transaction is denominated is a gain or loss that ordinarily should be included as a component of income from continuing operations in the period in which the exchange rate changes. A gain on a receivable denominated in a foreign currency results when the fixed amount of the foreign currency can be exchanged for a greater number of dollars at the date of collection, that is, when the number of foreign currency units exchangeable for a dollar decreases. A loss on a payable denominated in a foreign currency results when the number of dollars needed to purchase the fixed amount of the foreign currency increases, that is, when the number of foreign currency units exchangeable for a dollar decreases.
Answers (A), (C), and (D) are incorrect because a gain on a foreign currency receivable and a loss on a foreign currency payable result when the dollar weakens.

28. Ball Corp. had the following foreign currency transactions during 1996:

• Merchandise was purchased from a foreign supplier on January 20, 1996 for the U.S. dollar equivalent of $90,000. The invoice was paid on March 20, 1996 at the U.S. dollar equivalent of $96,000.

• On July 1, 1996, Ball borrowed the U.S. dollar equivalent of $500,000 evidenced by a note that was payable in the lender's local currency on July 1, 1998. On December 31, 1996, the U.S. dollar equivalents of the principal amount and accrued interest were $520,000 and $26,000, respectively. Interest on the note is 10% per annum.

In Ball's 1996 income statement, what amount should be included as foreign exchange loss?

A. $0

B. $6,000

C. $21,000

D. $27,000

The correct answer is (D). *(CPA 1190 I-43)*
REQUIRED: The amount to be included as foreign exchange loss.
DISCUSSION: When a foreign currency transaction gives rise to a receivable or a payable that is fixed in terms of the foreign currency, a change in the exchange rate between the functional currency and the currency in which the transaction is denominated is a gain or loss that ordinarily should be included as a component of income from continuing operations in the period in which the exchange rate changes. In the 1996 income statement, the foreign exchange loss should include the $6,000 difference between the $90,000 initially recorded as a payable and the $96,000 payment amount, the $20,000 difference between the $500,000 equivalent amount of the principal of the note on December 31 and its $520,000 equivalent on July 1, and the $1,000 difference between the $26,000 equivalent of the interest accrued and the $25,000 ($500,000 x 10% x 6/12) interest on the initially recorded amount of the loan. The foreign exchange loss therefore equals $27,000 ($6,000 + $20,000 + $1,000).
Answer (A) is incorrect because the loss must be recognized. Answer (B) is incorrect because the differences in principal and interest on the $500,000 note are excluded. Answer (C) is incorrect because $21,000 excludes the $6,000 difference in the recording and payment for the foreign purchase.

29. On September 1, 1995, Cano & Co., a U.S. corporation, sold merchandise to a foreign firm for 250,000 francs. Terms of the sale require payment in francs on February 1, 1996. On September 1, 1995, the spot exchange rate was $0.20 per franc. On December 31, 1995, Cano's year-end, the spot rate was $0.19, but the rate increased to $0.22 by February 1, 1996, when payment was received. How much should Cano report as foreign exchange gain or loss in its 1996 income statement?

A. $0

B. $2,500 loss.

C. $5,000 gain.

D. $7,500 gain.

The correct answer is (D). *(CPA 1191 I-46)*
REQUIRED: The foreign exchange gain or loss in the 1996 income statement.
DISCUSSION: A receivable or payable denominated in a foreign currency should be recorded at the current exchange rate and then adjusted to the current exchange rate at each balance sheet date. That adjustment is a foreign currency transaction gain or loss that is ordinarily included in the determination of net income for the period of change. Furthermore, a gain or loss measured from the transaction date or the most recent intervening balance sheet date is recognized when the transaction is settled. Accordingly, Cano should recognize a foreign currency transaction gain of $7,500 [($0.22 – $0.19) x 250,000 francs receivable] in 1996.
Answer (A) is incorrect because the exchange rate changed between the balance sheet date and the settlement date. Answer (B) is incorrect because a $2,500 loss was incurred in 1995. Answer (C) is incorrect because $5,000 is the net transaction gain.

30. Hunt Co. purchased merchandise for £300,000 from a vendor in London on November 30, 1996. Payment in British pounds was due on January 30, 1997. The exchange rates to purchase one pound were as follows:

	November 30, 1996	December 31, 1996
Spot-rate	$1.65	$1.62
30-day rate	1.64	1.59
60-day rate	1.63	1.56

In its December 31, 1996 income statement, what amount should Hunt report as foreign exchange gain?

A. $12,000

B. $9,000

C. $6,000

D. $0

31. Fay Corp. had a realized foreign exchange loss of $15,000 for the year ended December 31, 1996 and must also determine whether the following items will require year-end adjustment:

- Fay had an $8,000 loss resulting from the translation of the accounts of its wholly owned foreign subsidiary for the year ended December 31, 1996.

- Fay had an account payable to an unrelated foreign supplier payable in the supplier's local currency. The U.S. dollar equivalent of the payable was $64,000 on the October 31, 1996 invoice date and $60,000 on December 31, 1996. The invoice is payable on January 30, 1997.

In Fay's 1996 consolidated income statement, what amount should be included as foreign exchange loss?

A. $11,000

B. $15,000

C. $19,000

D. $23,000

The correct answer is (B). *(CPA 1197 I-49)*
REQUIRED: The amount of foreign exchange gain to be reported in the income statement.
DISCUSSION: Under SFAS 52, gains and losses from fluctuations in the exchange rate are ordinarily reflected in income when the rate changes. The exchange gain is the difference between the spot rate on the date the transaction originates and the spot rate at year-end. Hence, the exchange gain for Hunt Co. is $9,000 [($1.65 – $1.62) x £300,000].
Answer (A) is incorrect because $12,000 is the result of using the 60-day rate on 11/30/96 and the 30-day rate on 12/31/96. Answer (C) is incorrect because $6,000 results from using the 30-day rate on 11/30/96 and the spot rate on 12/31/96. Answer (D) is incorrect because a gain should be recorded.

The correct answer is (A). *(CPA 590 I-52)*
REQUIRED: The amount to be included as foreign exchange loss.
DISCUSSION: SFAS 52 requires that translation adjustments (gains and losses) be reported separately as a component of shareholders' equity. Translation adjustments are therefore not included in the determination of income. SFAS 52 further requires that a receivable or payable denominated in a foreign currency be recorded at the date of the transaction at the current rate of exchange. This receivable or payable must then be adjusted to its current value at each balance sheet date. The gain or loss from this adjustment is included in the determination of current income. Accordingly, the $4,000 ($64,000 – $60,000) gain adjustment arising from the foreign currency transaction should be included along with the realized foreign exchange loss of $15,000 in the 1996 consolidated income statement. The amount to be reported is an $11,000 ($15,000 loss – $4,000 gain) foreign exchange loss.
Answer (B) is incorrect because $15,000 excludes the $4,000 gain. Answer (C) is incorrect because the gain was added to, rather than subtracted from, the loss. Answer (D) is incorrect because the translation loss is added to the loss, and the exchange gain is not included.

32. A foreign exchange contract may be a speculation, a hedge of a net investment, a hedge of an identifiable future commitment, or a hedge of an exposed net asset or net liability position. Which of the following describes an exposed net asset position?

A. A future sale of a foreign currency that is not a hedging transaction.

B. The excess of assets denominated in a foreign currency over liabilities that are denominated in that foreign currency.

C. The excess of liabilities denominated in a foreign currency over the assets that are denominated in that foreign currency.

D. A contract to sell goods in the future payable in a foreign currency.

The correct answer is (B). *(Publisher)*
REQUIRED: The definition of an exposed net asset position.
DISCUSSION: An exposed net asset position is the excess of assets (primarily receivables) that are denominated in a foreign currency over the liabilities that are denominated in that same currency. Denominated means that payment will be made or received in the foreign currency.
Answer (A) is incorrect because it is the definition of a speculation. Answer (C) is incorrect because it is the definition of an exposed net liability position. Answer (D) is incorrect because it is the definition of an identifiable future commitment.

33. For which kind of forward foreign exchange contracts are both the receivable and the liability recorded at the forward exchange rate?

A. Speculative forward contract.

B. Hedge of a net investment.

C. Hedge of an identifiable foreign currency commitment.

D. Hedge of an exposed liability position.

The correct answer is (A). *(Publisher)*
REQUIRED: The kind of forward foreign exchange contract for which both the receivable and the liability are recorded at the forward exchange rate.
DISCUSSION: A speculative forward contract is a contract that does not hedge any exposure to foreign currency fluctuations; it creates the exposure. Both the receivable from the broker and the liability to the broker are recorded at the forward exchange rate existing at the date of the contract. The receivable or liability denominated in the foreign currency is adjusted to reflect the forward rate at each ensuing balance sheet date and at the date of settlement, with a corresponding recognition of exchange gain or loss.
Answers (B), (C), and (D) are incorrect because the receivable or payable denominated in dollars is recorded at the forward exchange rate, and the payable or receivable denominated in foreign exchange units is recorded at the spot rate. The difference is recorded as a discount or premium.

34. The premium or discount on a forward exchange contract is calculated using the difference between the

A. Spot rate at the balance sheet date and the spot rate at the date of inception of the forward contract.

B. Spot rate at the balance sheet date and the spot rate last used to measure a gain or loss on that contract for an earlier period.

C. Spot rate at the date of inception of the forward contract and the spot rate last used to measure a gain or loss on that contract for an earlier period.

D. Contracted forward rate and the spot rate at the date of inception of the contract.

The correct answer is (D). *(CMA 1288 3-29)*
REQUIRED: The calculation of the premium or discount on a foreign exchange contract.
DISCUSSION: A difference between the contract rate and the spot rate at the date of a forward exchange contract's inception is a discount or premium on the forward contract. A discount or premium should be accounted for separately from the gain or loss on the contract and should be included in net income over the life of the contract. An exception to this amortization requirement is a hedge of an identifiable foreign currency commitment. In this case, the discount or premium related to the commitment period may be included in the related foreign currency transaction when recorded.
Answers (A), (B), and (C) are incorrect because a premium or discount is calculated as the difference between the contracted forward rate and the spot rate at the date of inception of the contract.

35. On September 1, 1996, Brady Corp. entered into a foreign exchange contract for speculative purposes by purchasing 50,000 deutsche marks for delivery in 60 days. The rates to exchange $1 for 1 deutsche mark follow:

	9/1/96	9/30/96
Spot rate	.75	.70
30-day forward rate	.73	.72
60-day forward rate	.74	.73

In its September 30, 1996 income statement, what amount should Brady report as foreign exchange loss?

A. $2,500

B. $1,500

C. $1,000

D. $500

The correct answer is (C). *(CPA 593 I-46)*

REQUIRED: The foreign exchange loss on a speculative forward contract.

DISCUSSION: A forward contract that is speculative is valued at forward rates during the contract, and exchange gains and losses occur as a result of a change in the futures rates. The journal entry on September 1 is based on the 60-day forward rate. The entry is to debit a receivable from and credit a liability to the broker for $37,000 (50,000 marks x $0.74). The journal entry at Brady's fiscal year-end is to debit a loss and credit the liability to the broker for $1,000 [50,000 marks x ($0.74 – $0.72 30-day rate)].

Answer (A) is incorrect because $2,500 is based on the change in spot rates. Answer (B) is incorrect because $1,500 is based on the difference between the 30-day rate on September 1 and the spot rate on September 30. Answer (D) is incorrect because $500 is based on the change in either the 30-day or the 60-day rates.

Questions 36 through 39 are based on information. Presented below is information concerning exchange rates for local currency units (LCU) on selected dates.

	11/1/96	12/31/96	1/31/97
Spot rate	$.50	$.54	$.51
30-day future rate	.49	.52	.49
60-day future rate	.48	.51	.48
90-day future rate	.48	.50	.47

---

36. On November 1, 1996, the Ring Company, a calendar-year enterprise, speculated in LCU by selling 80,000 LCU for delivery in 90 days. What amounts of exchange gain or loss from this transaction should be included in net income determined for 1996 and 1997?

	1996	1997
A.	$3,200 loss	$2,400 gain
B.	$4,800 loss	$2,400 gain
C.	$3,200 loss	$800 gain
D.	$3,200 gain	$800 loss

The correct answer is (C). *(Publisher)*

REQUIRED: The exchange gains or losses in 1996 and 1997 resulting from a speculative forward exchange contract.

DISCUSSION: A forward contract that is speculative is valued at forward rates during the contract, and exchange gains and losses occur as a result of a change in the futures rates.

At the inception of the contract, a receivable in dollars and a corresponding liability in LCU for $38,400 are recorded at the 90-day forward rate for LCU of $.48. On 12/31/96, the contract has 30 days until settlement, and the forward rate for 30-day futures on 12/31/96 is $.52. Hence, the LCU liability must be adjusted to $41,600 (80,000 LCU x $.52), and an exchange loss of $3,200 must be reflected in income for 1996 ($41,600 – $38,400).

On 1/31/97, when the contract is settled, the exchange rate (spot rate) is $.51. Because the LCU liability is currently on Ring Company's books at $41,600 and the amount of cash needed to settle the contract is only $40,800 (80,000 LCU x $.51), an exchange gain of $800 is recorded on this date.

Answers (A), (B), and (D) are incorrect because the loss in 1996 is computed using the 90-day and 30-day future rates. The 1997 gain is computed using the 30-day future and spot rates.

Questions 37 through 39 are based on the information preceding Q. 36 on page 653.

37. On November 1, 1996, the Ring Company purchased merchandise for immediate delivery from the Sawall Company for 100,000 LCU. At the same time, this net liability position was hedged with the purchase of 100,000 LCU for delivery in 60 days when payment to the Sawall Company was due. What amount of exchange gain or loss from this transaction should be included in the determination of 1996 net income for the Ring Company?

A. $0

B. $2,000 loss.

C. $2,000 gain.

D. $4,000 loss.

The correct answer is (A). *(Publisher)*
REQUIRED: The amount of gain or loss from a forward exchange contract that hedges a net liability position.
DISCUSSION: When a foreign currency forward exchange contract is intended and is effective as an economic hedge against an exposed net asset or net liability position (e.g., an outstanding receivable or liability), any exchange gain or loss on the forward contract will offset any exchange gain or loss on the exposed net asset or net liability position. Thus, no exchange gain or loss will result.
Any discount or premium that arises at the time of the purchase of the 100,000 LCU will be amortized to income over the 60-day life of the contract.
Answers (B), (C), and (D) are incorrect because any gain or loss on the forward contract will offset any gain or loss on the exposed position.

38. If 25% of the merchandise purchased from the Sawall Company remains unsold at year-end, at what amount should this inventory be carried in Ring Company's December 31, 1996 balance sheet?

A. $12,000

B. $12,500

C. $13,500

D. $25,000

The correct answer is (B). *(Publisher)*
REQUIRED: The cost of inventory purchased in a hedged foreign currency transaction.
DISCUSSION: On 11/1/96, Ring Company should record its purchase from the Sawall Company at the spot rate of $.50 for a total purchase cost of $50,000 (100,000 LCU x $.50). This debit to purchases remains unchanged even if the foreign currency rate changes in the future. The remaining inventory at 12/31/96 is therefore carried at 25% of the initial purchase price, or $12,500 (25% x $50,000).
Answers (A), (C), and (D) are incorrect because ending inventory is valued using the spot rate at the date of purchase.

39. On November 1, 1996, the Ring Company sold 60,000 LCU for delivery in 90 days to hedge an identifiable future commitment to deliver merchandise to the Ross Company on January 31, 1997 at a fixed selling price of 60,000 LCU. What amount of sales revenue from this transaction should be reflected in the 1997 financial statements of the Ring Company?

A. $28,800

B. $30,000

C. $30,600

D. $60,000

The correct answer is (A). *(Publisher)*
REQUIRED: The amount of sales revenue resulting from a fully hedged foreign currency sales transaction.
DISCUSSION: An identifiable future commitment is a commitment for a future sale or purchase that will be denominated in a foreign currency. SFAS 52 provides for a gain or loss on a forward contract that is considered a hedge of an identifiable foreign currency commitment to be deferred and included in the measurement of the related foreign currency transaction (the purchase or sale). Similarly, any discount or premium arising from the transaction intended as a hedge of the foreign currency commitment may be included in the measurement basis of the related foreign currency transaction when recorded.
The result of the hedge is that sales revenue is fixed at the date of sale at the forward rate even though the sale itself will not be recorded until a future date. Thus, for Ring Company, sales revenue is $28,800 (60,000 LCU x $.48).
Answers (B), (C), and (D) are incorrect because sales revenue should be recorded at the 90-day spot rate on 11/1/96.

CHAPTER THIRTY-TWO
STATE AND LOCAL GOVERNMENTAL ACCOUNTING

Governmental accounting (for state and local governments) is also known as fund accounting. Three categories of funds, seven major fund types, and two account groups are used in state and local governmental accounting.

The categories are governmental funds, proprietary funds, and fiduciary funds. Governmental funds include the general fund and the special revenue, capital projects, and debt service funds. The proprietary funds include enterprise and internal service funds. The fiduciary funds are trust and agency funds.

The two account groups are for general fixed assets and general long-term debts.

The special assessment fund type (formerly treated as a governmental fund) may no longer be used in general purpose financial reporting. It is used for compliance reporting only.

The Governmental Accounting Standards Board is the authoritative body that issues pronouncements on generally accepted accounting principles for state and local governments. GASB Statement 1, *Authoritative Status of NCGA Pronouncements and AICPA Industry Audit Guides*, issued in 1984, states that all National Council on Governmental Accounting (NCGA) pronouncements in effect and the currently effective accounting and financial reporting guidance contained in the AICPA Industry Audit Guide, *Audits of State and Local Governmental Units*, are continued in force until and unless changed by a subsequent GASB pronouncement. In 1986, the AICPA revised and reissued *Audits of State and Local Governmental Units* as an Audit and Accounting Guide.

The most recent comprehensive statement on generally accepted accounting principles for state and local governments is NCGA Statement 1, *Governmental Accounting and Financial Reporting Principles*.

Chapter 33, Nonprofit Accounting, covers not-for-profit accounting other than governmental accounting. It includes coverage of pronouncements relevant to colleges and universities, health care providers, voluntary health and welfare organizations, and other nonprofit organizations.

32.1   General

1. The primary authoritative body for determining the measurement focus and basis of accounting standards for governmental fund operating statements is the

- A.   Governmental Accounting Standards Board (GASB).

- B.   National Council on Governmental Accounting (NCGA).

- C.   Governmental Accounting and Auditing Committee of the AICPA (GAAC).

- D.   Financial Accounting Standards Board (FASB).

The correct answer is (A). *(CPA 591 T-51)*
REQUIRED: The authoritative body that issues pronouncements on GAAP for state and local governments.
DISCUSSION: The Governmental Accounting Standards Board (GASB) is the authoritative body that determines the measurement focus and basis of accounting for state and local governments. GASB Statement 1, *Authoritative Status of NCGA Pronouncements and AICPA Industry Audit Guides*, issued in 1984, stated that all NCGA pronouncements in effect and the currently effective accounting and financial reporting guidance contained in the AICPA Industry Audit Guide are continued in force until and unless changed by a subsequent GASB pronouncement.
Answer (B) is incorrect because the National Council on Governmental Accounting (NCGA) was a predecessor committee to the GASB. Answer (C) is incorrect because the Government Accounting and Auditing Committee of the AICPA (GAAC) is not currently an active and functioning committee of the AICPA. Answer (D) is incorrect because the Financial Accounting Standards Board (FASB) is the primary authoritative standard-setting board for private sector accounting.

2. The primary emphasis in accounting and reporting for governmental funds is on

- A.   Flow of financial resources.

- B.   Income determination.

- C.   Capital maintenance.

- D.   Transfers relating to proprietary activities.

The correct answer is (A). *(CPA 594 TMG-51)*
REQUIRED: The primary emphasis in accounting and reporting for governmental funds.
DISCUSSION: Governmental fund accounting focuses on the flow of financial resources since the objective of the entity is the availability of resources for the accomplishment of certain goals and activities without regard to profitability.
Answer (B) is incorrect because governmental funds do not focus on profitability. Answer (C) is incorrect because capital maintenance focuses on maintaining resources rather than expending resources. Governmental funds focus on the flow of financial resources and not on earnings. Answer (D) is incorrect because proprietary activities are the primary emphasis of proprietary funds.

3. Governmental financial reporting should provide information to assist users in which situation(s)?

I.   Making social and political decisions

II. Assessing whether current-year citizens received services but shifted part of the payment burden to future-year citizens

- A.   I only.

- B.   II only.

- C.   Both I and II.

- D.   Neither I nor II.

The correct answer is (C). *(CPA 595 TMG-52)*
REQUIRED: The use(s) of governmental reporting.
DISCUSSION: GASB Concepts Statement 1 states, "Financial reporting by state and local governments is used in making economic, social, and political decisions and in assessing accountability." It also states that "interperiod equity is a significant part of accountability and is fundamental to public administration." Thus, "financial reporting should help users assess whether current-year revenues are sufficient to pay for the services provided that year and whether future taxpayers will be required to assume burdens for services previously provided."
Answers (A), (B), and (D) are incorrect because governmental financial reporting provides information for both purposes.

4. Thornton County is required under state law to report its financial statements on a basis that conflicts with generally accepted governmental accounting principles. On which basis of accounting should Thornton County's financial statements be prepared?

A. Generally accepted governmental accounting basis only.

B. State basis only.

C. State basis with supplemental disclosure of generally accepted governmental accounting reconciliation schedules.

D. Generally accepted governmental accounting basis with supplemental supporting schedules as necessary to report compliance with state law.

The correct answer is (D). *(J.P. Trebby)*

REQUIRED: The proper presentation of county financial statements when state law conflicts with GAAP.

DISCUSSION: Certain state laws and regulatory requirements conflict with generally accepted accounting and financial reporting practices. When such a conflict exists, the governmental entity should prepare basic financial statements conforming with GAAP and also present supporting schedules as necessary to clearly report upon compliance with legal responsibilities.

Answer (A) is incorrect because the financial statements should include supplemental supporting schedules to comply with state law. Answers (B) and (C) are incorrect because the financial statements should be prepared in accordance with GAAP.

5. Which event(s) is (are) supportive of interperiod equity as a financial reporting objective of a governmental unit?

I. A balanced budget is adopted.

II. Residual equity transfers out equal residual equity transfers in.

A. I only.

B. II only.

C. Both I and II.

D. Neither I nor II.

The correct answer is (A). *(CPA 1195 TMG-59)*

REQUIRED: The event(s), if any, supportive of the interperiod equity financial reporting objective.

DISCUSSION: Under the interperiod equity concept, the objective of a governmental unit should be to equate spending during a period with the resources provided. A balanced budget conforms to the interperiod equity assumption because it is a plan of expenditures to be made and of the financial resources to be used to pay for them. Residual equity transfers are nonrecurring or nonroutine transfers of equity between funds. Transfers in and out of a fund are typically not related.

Answers (B), (C), and (D) are incorrect because interperiod equity relates to adoption of a balanced budget, not to residual equity transfers.

6. A local governmental unit could use which of the following types of funds?

	Fiduciary	Proprietary
A.	Yes	No
B.	Yes	Yes
C.	No	Yes
D.	No	No

The correct answer is (B). *(CPA 1187 T-59)*

REQUIRED: The types of funds that could be used by a local governmental unit.

DISCUSSION: Three broad categories and seven generic fund types can be used by a state or local governmental unit for general purpose financial statements.

1) Governmental - general, special revenue, debt service, and capital projects funds
2) Proprietary - internal service and enterprise funds
3) Fiduciary - trust and agency funds

GASB Statement 6, *Accounting and Financial Reporting for Special Assessments*, restricts the use of special assessment funds to internal and compliance reporting. Special assessment funds are no longer used in general purpose financial statements.

Answers (A), (C), and (D) are incorrect because a local governmental unit can use both fiduciary and proprietary funds.

7. The general purpose financial statements of a state government

A. May not be issued separately from the comprehensive annual financial report.

B. Are composed of the combined financial statements and related notes.

C. Are synonymous with the comprehensive annual financial report.

D. Contain more detailed information regarding the state government's finances than is contained in the comprehensive annual financial report.

The correct answer is (B). *(CPA 594 TMG-53)*
REQUIRED: The nature of the general purpose financial statements of a state government.
DISCUSSION: There are two types of annual reports that a state government can issue: the general purpose financial statements and the comprehensive annual financial report. The general purpose financial statements (GPFS) include the minimum disclosures required by GAAP and are comprised of the combined statements and related notes of the state government. The comprehensive annual financial report (CAFR) is a more detailed document which contains the general purpose financial statements as well as other statements and schedules.
Answer (A) is incorrect because the GPFS may be issued separately from the CAFR. Answer (C) is incorrect because the CAFR includes information not present in the GPFS. Answer (D) is incorrect because the CAFR contains more detailed information than the GPFS.

8. In a government's comprehensive annual financial report (CAFR), account groups are included in which of the following combined financial statements?

	Balance Sheet	Statement of Revenues, Expenditures, and Changes in Fund Balances
A.	Yes	No
B.	No	Yes
C.	Yes	Yes
D.	No	No

The correct answer is (A). *(CPA 591 T-59)*
REQUIRED: The financial statements that include account groups.
DISCUSSION: The account groups are for general fixed assets and general long-term debt (liabilities) and there are no fund flows or revenues to consider. Thus, only a combined balance sheet is required for account groups.
Answers (B) and (C) are incorrect because account groups do not reflect revenues or expenditures and, hence, require no reports to indicate changes in fund balances. Answer (D) is incorrect because account groups do require a combined balance sheet.

9. In preparing combined financial statements for a governmental entity, interfund receivables and payables should be

A. Reported as reservations of fund balance.

B. Reported as additions to or reductions from the unrestricted fund balance.

C. Reported as amounts due to and due from other funds.

D. Eliminated.

The correct answer is (C). *(CPA 595 TMG-53)*
REQUIRED: The reporting of interfund receivables and payables in combined financial statements.
DISCUSSION: In combined financial statements for a governmental unit, interfund receivables and payables are not eliminated. They should be reported as amounts due to and due from other funds. Because each fund is a separate fiscal and accounting entity, these amounts should be reflected in the fund accounts and financial statements.
Answers (A), (B), and (D) are incorrect because interfund receivables and payables should be reported as amounts due to and due from other funds in combined financial statements.

10. Which of the following statements is correct concerning a governmental entity's combined statement of cash flows?

   A. Cash flows from capital financing activities are reported separately from cash flows from noncapital financing activities.

   B. The statement format is the same as that of a business enterprise's statement of cash flows.

   C. Cash flows from operating activities may not be reported using the indirect method.

   D. The statement format includes columns for the general, governmental, and proprietary fund types.

The correct answer is (A). *(CPA 593 T-58)*
   REQUIRED: The correct characteristic of a governmental unit's combined statement of cash flows.
   DISCUSSION: The categories are increase (decrease) in cash and cash equivalents; cash flows from noncapital financing activities; cash flows from capital and related financing activities; cash flows from investing activities; reconciliation of operating income (loss) to net cash provided by (used in) operating activities; and noncash investing, capital, and financing activities.
   Answer (B) is incorrect because the categories of cash transactions are different, and there are separate columns for enterprise funds, internal service funds, and nonexpendable trust funds, and a totals column showing the previous year's figures. Answer (C) is incorrect because either method is acceptable, although GASB Statement No. 11 encourages the use of the direct method. Answer (D) is incorrect because only proprietary fund types (and nonexpendable trust funds) are required to issue a combined statement of cash flows.

11. If a city legally adopts its annual general fund budget on the modified accrual basis of accounting, its estimated revenues should be

   A. Reported on the modified accrual basis of accounting in the general fund statement of revenues, expenditures, and changes in fund balance -- budget and actual.

   B. Converted to the cash basis of accounting and reported in the general fund statement of revenues, expenditures, and other changes in fund balance -- budget and actual.

   C. Reported as current assets in the general fund balance sheet.

   D. Reported as noncurrent assets in the general fund balance sheet.

The correct answer is (A). *(CPA 1191 T-52)*
   REQUIRED: The proper reporting of estimated revenues for a general fund budget.
   DISCUSSION: GASB Cod. Section 2400.102 requires a combined statement of revenues, expenditures, and changes in fund balances -- budget and actual for general funds and special revenue funds, and for other similar governmental funds for which an annual budget has been adopted.
   Answer (B) is incorrect because governmental accounting is never converted to the cash basis of accounting. Answers (C) and (D) are incorrect because estimated revenues are not assets and, hence, are not reported on the annual balance sheet.

12. Under the modified accrual basis of accounting for a governmental unit, revenues that are measurable should be recognized in the accounting period in which they are

   A. Earned.

   B. Available.

   C. Budgeted.

   D. Collected.

The correct answer is (B). *(CPA 592 T-57)*
   REQUIRED: The timing of revenue recognition for measurable revenues under the modified accrual basis of accounting.
   DISCUSSION: Under the accrual basis of accounting, revenue should be recognized when realized or realizable and earned. Under the modified accrual basis of accounting, revenues are recognized in the period in which they become available and measurable.
   Answer (A) is incorrect because the full accrual basis recognizes revenues when they are earned. Answers (C) and (D) are incorrect because neither is a criterion for recognition under either the accrual or the modified accrual basis.

13. One feature of state and local government accounting and financial reporting is that fixed assets used for general government activities

A. Generally are not expected to contribute to the generation of revenues.

B. Do not depreciate as a result of such use.

C. Are acquired only when direct contribution to revenues is expected.

D. Should not be maintained at the same level as those of businesses so that current financial resources can be used for other government services.

The correct answer is (A). *(CPA 1191 T-51)*
REQUIRED: The correct feature of governmental accounting relating to fixed assets.
DISCUSSION: General government activities are accounted for in the governmental funds. The focus of these funds is spending, rather than the generation of revenue. Since fixed assets used for general government activities are not expendable, they are not capitalized in the governmental funds. They are accounted for in the general fixed assets account group.
Answer (B) is incorrect because depreciation may be accumulated in the general fixed asset account group. Answer (C) is incorrect because the generation of revenue is not the focus of governmental funds. Answer (D) is incorrect because fixed assets of a governmental unit, whether they are general fixed assets or fund fixed assets, should be maintained for both management and accountability purposes.

32.2 Governmental Funds

14. At December 31, 1996, the following balances were due from the state government to Clare City's various funds:

Capital projects	$300,000
Trust and agency	100,000
Enterprise	80,000

In Clare's December 31, 1996 combined balance sheet for all fund types and account groups, what amount should be classified under governmental funds?

A. $100,000

B. $180,000

C. $300,000

D. $480,000

The correct answer is (C). *(CPA 592 II-29)*
REQUIRED: The amount due from state government to be classified as governmental funds.
DISCUSSION: Capital projects funds are governmental funds. The other funds are proprietary funds.
Answer (A) is incorrect because $100,000 is reached by assuming that the trust and agency fund should be classified as a governmental fund-type. Answer (B) is incorrect because $180,000 is reached by assuming that trust and agency funds and enterprise funds are accounted for as governmental funds. Answer (D) is incorrect because $480,000 is reached by assuming that all the funds listed are governmental funds.

15. Park City uses encumbrance accounting and formally integrates its budget into the general fund's accounting records.

For the year ending July 31, 1996, the following budget was adopted:

Estimated revenues	$30,000,000
Appropriations	27,000,000
Estimated transfer to debt service fund	900,000

When Park's budget is adopted and recorded, Park's budgetary fund balance would be a

A. $3,000,000 credit balance.

B. $3,000,000 debit balance.

C. $2,100,000 credit balance.

D. $2,100,000 debit balance.

The correct answer is (C). *(CPA 592 II-23)*
REQUIRED: The budgetary fund balance when a budget is adopted and recorded.
DISCUSSION: The initial entry to record the budget consists of a $30,000,000 debit to estimated revenues, a $27,000,000 credit to appropriations, and a $900,000 credit to estimated transfer to debt service fund; the $2,100,000 residual is credited to fund balance.
Answer (A) is incorrect because the $900,000 estimated transfer to debt service fund must be credited. Answers (B) and (D) are incorrect because the estimated revenues should be debited.

16. In 1996, New City issued purchase orders and contracts of $850,000 that were chargeable against 1996 budgeted appropriations of $1,000,000. The journal entry to record the issuance of the purchase orders and contracts should include a

A. Credit to vouchers payable of $1,000,000.

B. Credit to reserve for encumbrances of $850,000.

C. Debit to expenditures of $1,000,000.

D. Debit to appropriations of $850,000.

The correct answer is (B). *(CPA 1194 TMG-18)*
REQUIRED: The entry for issuance of purchase orders and contracts.
DISCUSSION: When a purchase order is approved or a contract is signed, an estimated liability is recorded in the encumbrance account for the amount of the purchase order. The entry is a debit to encumbrances and a credit to reserve for encumbrances.
Answers (A) and (C) are incorrect because expenditures will be debited and vouchers payable credited for $850,000 when the liability has been incurred. Answer (D) is incorrect because appropriations is debited when the budgetary accounts are closed.

17. When a snowplow purchased by a governmental unit is received, it should be recorded in the general fund as a(n)

A. Encumbrance.

B. Expenditure.

C. Fixed asset.

D. Appropriation.

The correct answer is (B). *(CPA 1194 TMG-9)*
REQUIRED: The effect of receipt of goods.
DISCUSSION: When previously ordered goods are received, the entry includes a debit to expenditures for the actual amount to be paid. An expenditure is recognized when a liability is incurred, that is, when an executory contract is complete or virtually complete.
Answer (A) is incorrect because an encumbrance is recorded to account for the purchase commitment. Answer (C) is incorrect because fixed assets are not accounted for in the general fund. Answer (D) is incorrect because appropriations are accounted for when recording the budget.

18. Which of the following amounts are included in a general fund's encumbrance account?

I. Outstanding vouchers payable amounts

II. Outstanding purchase order amounts

III. Excess of the amount of a purchase order over the actual expenditure for that order

A. I only.

B. I and III.

C. II only.

D. II and III.

The correct answer is (C). *(CPA 591 T-53)*
REQUIRED: The amounts included in a general fund's encumbrance account.
DISCUSSION: The encumbrance account is debited when goods are approved to be purchased, and a purchase order is prepared. When the goods are actually received, the encumbrance account is credited. Therefore, the encumbrance account includes only those amounts that represent outstanding purchase orders.
Answers (A) and (B) are incorrect because the encumbrance account does not include voucher payable amounts, only outstanding purchase order amounts. Answer (D) is incorrect because excesses of the actual expenditure over the purchase order are recorded in the expenditure control account.

19. Gold County received goods that had been approved for purchase but for which payment had not yet been made. Should the accounts listed below be increased?

	Encumbrances	Expenditures
A.	No	No
B.	No	Yes
C.	Yes	No
D.	Yes	Yes

The correct answer is (B). *(CPA 1191 T-53)*
REQUIRED: The effect of receipt of previously ordered goods on the encumbrances and expenditures accounts.
DISCUSSION: The encumbrances account will be decreased when previously ordered goods have been received. Expenditures and vouchers payable will be increased for the actual amount to be paid for the goods.
Answer (A) is incorrect because the expenditures control account is increased upon receipt of goods previously ordered. Answer (C) is incorrect because the encumbrances account is decreased and the expenditures account is increased at the time goods are received. Answer (D) is incorrect because the encumbrances account is decreased when the goods are received.

20. For the budgetary year ending December 31, 1996, Maple City's general fund expects the following inflows of resources:

Property taxes, licenses, and fines	$9,000,000
Proceeds of debt issue	5,000,000
Interfund transfers for debt service	1,000,000

In the budgetary entry, what amount should Maple record for estimated revenues?

- A. $9,000,000
- B. $10,000,000
- C. $14,000,000
- D. $15,000,000

The correct answer is (A). *(CPA 1193 II-3)*

REQUIRED: The amount to be recorded as estimated revenues.

DISCUSSION: When preparing the annual budget, estimated revenues generally include taxes, licenses, permits, fines, and forfeits. Estimated revenues do not include the proceeds of debt issues. They also do not include estimated interfund transfers to the debt service fund. Thus, Maple's estimated revenues would be $9,000,000.

Answer (B) is incorrect because $10,000,000 incorrectly includes the interfund transfers. Answer (C) is incorrect because $14,000,000 incorrectly includes the debt issue proceeds. Answer (D) is incorrect because $15,000,000 incorrectly includes the debt issue proceeds and interfund transfers.

21. During its fiscal year ended June 30, 1996, Cliff City issued purchase orders totaling $5,000,000, which were properly charged to encumbrances at that time. Cliff received goods and related invoices at the encumbered amounts totaling $4,500,000 before year-end. The remaining goods of $500,000 were not received until after year-end. Cliff paid $4,200,000 of the invoices received during the year. What amount of Cliff's encumbrances were outstanding at June 30, 1996?

- A. $0
- B. $300,000
- C. $500,000
- D. $800,000

The correct answer is (C). *(CPA 1193 II-4)*

REQUIRED: The amount of encumbrances outstanding.

DISCUSSION: In fund accounting, when a commitment is made to expend monies, encumbrances are debited and reserve for encumbrances is credited. When the goods are received, this entry is reversed. Since goods totaling $500,000 were not received at year-end, encumbrances outstanding total $500,000 ($5,000,000 – $4,500,000).

Answer (A) is incorrect because not all of the goods related to the encumbrance amounts were received during the year. Answer (B) is incorrect because $300,000 is the excess of goods received over amount actually paid on the invoices during the year. Answer (D) is incorrect because $800,000 is the excess of total encumbrances over the amount paid on the invoices.

22. Elm City issued a purchase order for supplies with an estimated cost of $5,000. When the supplies were received, the accompanying invoice indicated an actual price of $4,950. What amount should Elm have debited (credited) to the reserve for encumbrances after the supplies and invoice were received?

- A. $(50)
- B. $50
- C. $4,950
- D. $5,000

The correct answer is (D). *(CPA 1193 II-5)*

REQUIRED: The debit (credit) to the reserve for encumbrances after the supplies and invoice were received.

DISCUSSION: Expenditures are actual decreases in net financial resources. They are recognized in the governmental funds when fund liabilities are incurred, if measurable. When supplies are received by, or services are rendered to, a governmental unit, a journal entry is made to debit the expenditures control and to credit vouchers payable. In addition, a previously recorded encumbrance must be reversed by debiting the fund balance reserved for encumbrances and crediting encumbrances control. Since the original budgetary entry is reversed, reserve for encumbrances must be debited for the previously recognized estimated cost of $5,000.

Answer (A) is incorrect because reserve for encumbrances is debited, not credited, for the original estimated cost. Answer (B) is incorrect because $50 is the difference between the estimated and actual price. Answer (C) is incorrect because $4,950 is the actual, not the estimated price.

23. When Rolan County adopted its budget for the year ending June 30, 1996, $20,000,000 was recorded for estimated revenues control. Actual revenues for the year ended June 30, 1996 amounted to $17,000,000. In closing the budgetary accounts at June 30, 1996,

A. Revenues control should be debited for $3,000,000.

B. Estimated revenues control should be debited for $3,000,000.

C. Revenues control should be credited for $20,000,000.

D. Estimated revenues control should be credited for $20,000,000.

The correct answer is (D). *(CPA 1190 II-57)*
REQUIRED: The journal entry to close estimated revenues control and revenues control.
DISCUSSION: Estimated revenues control is a budgetary account recognized upon the adoption of the budget. Revenues control is a nominal account in which revenues are recorded when they meet the criteria of being available and measurable. At year-end, both accounts are closed to fund balance. The journal entry to close estimated revenues control and actual revenues to fund balance is

Revenues control	$17,000,000	
Fund balance	3,000,000	
Estimated revenues control		$20,000,000

Answers (A), (B), and (C) are incorrect because revenues control should be debited for $17,000,000; fund balance should be debited for $3,000,000; and estimated revenues control should be credited for $20,000,000.

24. Which of the following fund types used by a government most likely would have a fund balance reserved for inventory of supplies?

A. General.

B. Internal service.

C. Nonexpendable trust.

D. Capital projects.

The correct answer is (A). *(CPA 1190 T-52)*
REQUIRED: The fund type most likely to have a fund balance reserved for inventory of supplies.
DISCUSSION: Governmental units normally record the purchases of supplies inventory in the general fund. In accounting for supplies, the expenditure account may be charged (debited) when the materials and supplies are purchased or when they are consumed. Under either method, the inventory of supplies remaining at year-end must be recorded on the balance sheet as an asset. In addition, because resources have already been expended to acquire these supplies, a fund balance reserved for inventory of supplies must be established (credited) to indicate the unavailability of resources in this amount for other expenditures.
Answers (B) and (C) are incorrect because the focus of these funds is on capital maintenance, not spending. Therefore, designation of the fund balance as reserved is not relevant. Answer (D) is incorrect because supplies are not generally recognized as an asset of a capital project fund.

25. A budgetary fund balance reserved for encumbrances in excess of a balance of encumbrances indicates

A. An excess of vouchers payable over encumbrances.

B. An excess of purchase orders over invoices received.

C. An excess of appropriations over encumbrances.

D. A recording error.

The correct answer is (D). *(CPA 1193 T-52)*
REQUIRED: The reason the reserve for encumbrances balance would exceed the encumbrance balance.
DISCUSSION: The entry to record an encumbrance is a debit to encumbrances and a credit to reserve for encumbrances. Thus, reserve for encumbrances should never exceed encumbrances. If it does, a recording error must exist.
Answers (A), (B), and (C) are incorrect because reserve for encumbrances should never exceed encumbrances.

26. The budget of a governmental unit, for which the appropriations exceed the estimated revenues, was adopted and recorded in the general ledger at the beginning of the year. During the year, expenditures and encumbrances were less than appropriations, whereas revenues equaled estimated revenues. The budgetary fund balance account is

A. Credited at the beginning of the year and debited at the end of the year.

B. Credited at the beginning of the year and not changed at the end of the year.

C. Debited at the beginning of the year and credited at the end of the year.

D. Debited at the beginning of the year and not changed at the end of the year.

The correct answer is (C). *(CPA 591 T-52)*

REQUIRED: The proper treatment of the budgetary fund balance account when appropriations exceed estimated revenues and actual expenditures are less than appropriations.

DISCUSSION: When estimated revenues are anticipated to exceed appropriations, the fund balance will carry a credit balance. When appropriations are expected to exceed estimated revenues, the fund balance must carry a debit balance. At year-end, the fund balance is updated to its actual balance, and because actual expenditures did not exceed appropriations, there are no further debits to fund balance.

Answer (A) is incorrect because a debit to fund balance at year-end would mean that actual expenditures had exceeded appropriations, and fund balance had decreased further. Answer (B) is incorrect because fund balance is always updated at year-end. Further, a credit to fund balance at the beginning of the year reflects an excess of estimated revenue over appropriations. Answer (D) is incorrect because fund balance is always updated at year-end.

27. Expenditures of a governmental unit for insurance extending over more than one accounting period

A. Must be accounted for as expenditures of the period of acquisition.

B. Must be accounted for as expenditures of the periods subsequent to acquisition.

C. Must be allocated between or among accounting periods.

D. May be allocated between or among accounting periods or may be accounted for as expenditures of the period of acquisition.

The correct answer is (D). *(CPA 1194 TMG-15)*

REQUIRED: The proper treatment of expenditures extending over more than one period.

DISCUSSION: Under current GAAP, prepaid insurance may be reported by either the purchase method or the consumption method. Under the purchase method, an expenditure is reported when the policy is purchased. Under the consumption method, an expenditure is reported when the asset is consumed.

Answers (A), (B), and (C) are incorrect because, under current GAAP, prepaid insurance may be either allocated among the periods used or expensed in the period of acquisition.

28. The following information pertains to Park Township's general fund at December 31, 1996:

Total assets, including $200,000 of cash $1,000,000
Total liabilities   600,000
Reserved for encumbrances   100,000

Appropriations do not lapse at year-end. At December 31, 1996, what amount should Park report as unreserved fund balance in its general fund balance sheet?

A. $200,000

B. $300,000

C. $400,000

D. $500,000

The correct answer is (B). *(CPA 1193 II-20)*

REQUIRED: The amount to be reported as unreserved fund balance.

DISCUSSION: The amount in the unreserved fund balance is equal to the amount of assets available to finance expenditures of the current and/or succeeding year. The fund balance is $400,000 ($1,000,000 assets − $600,000 liabilities). Since $100,000 is reserved for encumbrances, the unreserved fund balance is $300,000 ($400,000 − $100,000).

Answer (A) is incorrect because $200,000 is the amount of cash available. Answer (C) is incorrect because $400,000 incorrectly includes the reserve for encumbrances. Answer (D) is incorrect because $500,000 is net assets (assets minus liabilities) plus the reserve for encumbrances.

29. During the year, a city's electric utility, which is operated as an enterprise fund, rendered billings for electricity supplied to the general fund. Which of the following accounts should be debited by the general fund?

    A. Appropriations.

    B. Expenditures.

    C. Due to electric utility enterprise fund.

    D. Other financing uses -- operating transfers-out.

The correct answer is (B). *(CPA 1194 TMG-16)*

REQUIRED: The account debited by the general fund for a transfer between funds.

DISCUSSION: Enterprise funds are used to account for operations similar to those of private businesses. This rendition of services by the enterprise fund to the general fund is a quasi-external transaction. The entry is to debit expenditures control and credit due to enterprise fund.

Answer (A) is incorrect because appropriations is debited when the budgetary accounts are closed. Answer (C) is incorrect because due to enterprise fund should be credited. Answer (D) is incorrect because this transaction is a quasi-external transaction, not an operating transfer.

30. Which of the following funds of a governmental unit recognizes revenues in the accounting period in which they become available and measurable?

	General Fund	Enterprise Fund
A.	Yes	No
B.	No	Yes
C.	Yes	Yes
D.	No	No

The correct answer is (A). *(CPA 593 T-55)*

REQUIRED: The criteria for revenue recognition for general and enterprise funds.

DISCUSSION: The general fund is accounted for on a modified accrual basis. This basis of accounting recognizes revenues in the period in which they are measurable and available. The enterprise fund, a proprietary fund-type, is accounted for under the full accrual basis. This basis of accounting recognizes revenues in the accounting period in which they are realized and earned.

Answer (B) is incorrect because the opposite situation is true. Answer (C) is incorrect because the enterprise fund recognizes revenues when they are realized and earned. Answer (D) is incorrect because the general fund recognizes revenues when they are available and measurable.

31. On December 31, 1996, Elm Village paid a contractor $4,500,000 for the total cost of a new Village Hall built in 1996 on Village-owned land. Financing for the capital project was provided by a $3,000,000 general obligation bond issue sold at face amount on December 31, 1996, with the remaining $1,500,000 transferred from the general fund. What account and amount should be reported in Elm's 1996 financial statements for the general fund?

    A. Other financing sources control $4,500,000

    B. Expenditures control $4,500,000

    C. Other financing sources control $3,000,000

    D. Other financing uses control $1,500,000

The correct answer is (D). *(CPA 1190 II-42)*

REQUIRED: The account and amount to be reported in the financial statements for the general fund.

DISCUSSION: Transfers between funds are either residual equity transfers or operating transfers. Residual equity transfers are defined as nonrecurring or nonroutine transfers of equity between funds. All transfers that are not residual equity transfers are classified as operating transfers. The $1,500,000 transferred from the general fund to the capital projects fund is an operating transfer. The accounting for state and local governments requires that operating transfers be reported as other financing sources by the fund receiving the transfer and other financing uses by the fund making the transfer. The bond issue proceeds and the cost of construction will be accounted for in the capital projects fund. The debt will be recorded in the general long-term debt account group. Accordingly, the general fund should record only the operating transfer out. The appropriate entry is to debit other financing uses control for $1,500,000 and credit a liability. The capital projects fund should credit other financing sources for $1,500,000 and debit a receivable.

Answer (A) is incorrect because other financing sources control is used to record transfers into a fund. Further, the $3,000,000 from the bond issue was not transferred in or out of the general fund. Answer (B) is incorrect because the sum paid to the contractor would be reflected in the capital projects fund. Answer (C) is incorrect because other financing sources control is used to record transfers into a fund. In addition, the $3,000,000 from the bond issue was not transferred in or out of the general fund.

32. Cal City maintains several major fund types. The following were among Cal's cash receipts during 1996:

Unrestricted state grant	$1,000,000
Interest on bank accounts held for employees' pension plan	200,000

What amount of these cash receipts should be accounted for in Cal's general fund?

A. $1,200,000

B. $1,000,000

C. $200,000

D. $0

The correct answer is (B). *(CPA 1193 II-8)*

REQUIRED: The amount of cash receipts to be accounted for in the general fund.

DISCUSSION: The general fund is used to account for all transactions of a governmental unit that are not accounted for in another fund. The interest is accounted for in a pension trust fund. Thus, the general fund accounts for only the $1,000,000 grant.

Answer (A) is incorrect because $1,200,000 incorrectly includes the interest. Answer (C) is incorrect because $200,000 incorrectly includes the interest and excludes the unrestricted state grant. Answer (D) is incorrect because $0 excludes the unrestricted state grant.

33. When a capital lease of a governmental unit represents the acquisition of a general fixed asset, the acquisition should be reflected as

A. An expenditure but not as an other financing source.

B. An other financing source but not as an expenditure.

C. Both an expenditure and an other financing source.

D. Neither an expenditure nor an other financing source.

The correct answer is (C). *(CPA 1194 TMG-10)*

REQUIRED: The accounting treatment of general fixed assets acquired by capital lease.

DISCUSSION: General fixed assets that are acquired by capital lease are recorded in the same manner as fixed assets acquired by outright purchase. The principal amount of the lease is initially debited as an expenditure, and "other financing sources -- capital lease" is credited.

Answers (A), (B), and (D) are incorrect because both an expenditure and an other financing source account are affected.

34. In which situation(s) should property taxes due to a governmental unit be recorded as deferred revenue?

I. Property taxes receivable are recognized in advance of the year for which they are levied.

II. Property taxes receivable are collected in advance of the year in which they are levied.

A. I only.

B. Both I and II.

C. II only.

D. Neither I nor II.

The correct answer is (B). *(CPA 1194 TMG-17)*

REQUIRED: The situation(s) when taxes due should be recorded as deferred revenue.

DISCUSSION: A property tax assessment is made to finance the budget of a specific period. Hence, the revenue produced should be recognized in the period for which the assessment was levied, provided it meets the criteria of being available and measurable. Under government accounting standards, when property taxes are recognized or collected in advance, they should be recorded as deferred revenue. They are not recognized as revenue until the year for which they are levied.

Answers (A), (C), and (D) are incorrect because property taxes recognized or collected in advance should be initially recorded as deferred revenue.

35. Lake County received the following proceeds that are legally restricted to expenditure for specified purposes:

Levies on affected property owners to install sidewalks	$500,000
Gasoline taxes to finance road repairs	900,000

What amount should be accounted for in Lake's special revenue funds?

A. $1,400,000

B. $900,000

C. $500,000

D. $0

The correct answer is (B). *(CPA 592 II-27)*

REQUIRED: The amount to be recorded in Lake County's special revenue funds.

DISCUSSION: The levy on affected property owners for sidewalks is an example of a special assessment. According to GASB rules, special assessments for construction activity may be accounted for in a capital projects fund. The gasoline taxes are special revenues received from the state government to be expended on a specific purpose and are properly recorded in the special revenue funds.

Answer (A) is incorrect because $1,400,000 is based on the assumption that both of the revenue sources are to be recorded in special revenue funds. Answer (C) is incorrect because special assessment levies are accounted for in a capital projects fund. Answer (D) is incorrect because $0 is based on the assumption that neither revenue source is accounted for in special revenue funds.

36. Revenues that are legally restricted to expenditures for specified purposes should be accounted for in special revenue funds, including

- A. Accumulation of resources for payment of general long-term debt principal and interest.
- B. Pension trust fund revenues.
- C. Gasoline taxes to finance road repairs.
- D. Proprietary fund revenues.

The correct answer is (C). *(CPA 590 T-56)*
REQUIRED: The revenues legally restricted to expenditures for specified purposes that should be accounted for in special revenue funds.
DISCUSSION: A special revenue fund is used to account for the proceeds of specific revenue sources (other than expendable trusts or for major capital projects) that are legally restricted to expenditure for certain specified purposes. Gasoline taxes levied to finance road repair are revenues legally restricted to expenditures for specified purposes that should be accounted for in special revenue funds.
Answer (A) is incorrect because these resources are accounted for in the debt service fund. Answer (B) is incorrect because pension trust fund revenues are accounted for in the pension trust fund. Answer (D) is incorrect because proprietary fund revenues are accounted for in either enterprise or internal service funds.

37. The following information pertains to Grove City's interfund receivables and payables at December 31, 1996:

Due to special revenue fund from
general fund $10,000
Due to agency fund from special revenue
fund   4,000

In Grove's special revenue fund balance sheet at December 31, 1996, how should these interfund amounts be reported?

- A. As an asset of $6,000.
- B. As a liability of $6,000.
- C. As an asset of $4,000 and a liability of $10,000.
- D. As an asset of $10,000 and a liability of $4,000.

The correct answer is (D). *(CPA 1193 II-9)*
REQUIRED: The proper reporting of interfund amounts in the special revenue fund balance sheet.
DISCUSSION: In a special revenue fund balance sheet, funds due "to" the special revenue fund are receivables (assets), and funds due to another fund "from" the special revenue fund are payables (liabilities). Thus, Grove would report a $10,000 asset and a $4,000 liability in the special revenue fund balance sheet.
Answer (A) is incorrect because, in a special revenue fund balance sheet, assets are not reported net of liabilities. Answer (B) is incorrect because $6,000 is the amount of net assets. Answer (C) is incorrect because "due to special revenue fund" is a receivable (asset) and "due from special revenue fund" is a payable (liability).

38. Which of the following funds of a governmental unit uses the modified accrual basis of accounting?

- A. Internal service funds.
- B. Enterprise funds.
- C. Special revenue funds.
- D. Nonexpendable trust funds.

The correct answer is (C). *(CPA 1193 T-54)*
REQUIRED: The fund for which the modified accrual basis of accounting is appropriate.
DISCUSSION: Governmental accounting and financial reporting standards require the use of the modified accrual basis for all governmental funds and for expendable trust funds. Agency funds also account on this basis. The accrual basis is used for proprietary funds, nonexpendable trusts, and pension trust funds. Special revenue funds are governmental funds; thus they use the modified accrual basis.
Answers (A), (B), and (D) are incorrect because internal service funds, enterprise funds, and nonexpendable trust funds use the accrual basis.

39. Should a special revenue fund with a legally adopted budget maintain its accounts on an accrual basis and integrate budgetary accounts into its accounting system?

	Maintain an Accrual Basis	Integrate Budgetary Accounts
A.	Yes	Yes
B.	Yes	No
C.	No	Yes
D.	No	No

The correct answer is (C). *(CPA 1190 T-53)*
REQUIRED: The proper accounting by a special revenue fund with a legally adopted budget.
DISCUSSION: Governmental accounting and financial reporting standards require the use of the modified accrual basis for all governmental funds, for expendable trust funds, and for the assets and liabilities of agency funds. Since a special revenue fund is a governmental fund, it should maintain its accounts on the modified accrual basis.
According to the GASB standards, the integration of budgetary accounts into the formal accounting system is a management control technique used to assist in controlling expenditures and enforcing revenue provisions. The extent to which the budgetary accounts should be integrated varies among governmental fund types and according to the nature of fund transactions. However, integration is considered essential in the general, special revenue, and other annually budgeted governmental funds with numerous types of revenues, expenditures, and transfers. Formal integration is also essential in controlling expendable trust funds that are similar to special revenue funds. Thus, a special revenue fund with a legally adopted budget should integrate its budgetary accounts into its accounting system.
Answers (A) and (B) are incorrect because special revenue funds are maintained on the modified accrual basis. Answer (D) is incorrect because the special revenue fund with a legally adopted budget should integrate its budgetary accounts into its accounting system.

40. Kew City received a $15,000,000 federal grant to finance the construction of a center for rehabilitation of drug addicts. The proceeds of this grant should be accounted for in the

A. Special revenue funds.

B. General fund.

C. Capital projects funds.

D. Trust funds.

The correct answer is (C). *(CPA 1190 II-47)*
REQUIRED: The fund used to account for a federal grant earmarked to finance the construction of a center for rehabilitation of drug addicts.
DISCUSSION: The capital projects fund is used to account for the receipt and disbursement of resources restricted to acquisition of major capital facilities (other than those financed by proprietary and trust funds) through purchase or construction.
Answers (A) and (B) are incorrect because these funds do not record resources to be used for major capital facilities. Answer (D) is incorrect because a grant for a drug rehabilitation center would not be accounted for in a trust fund. A trust fund accounts for assets held by a governmental entity in the capacity of a trustee.

41. Financing for the renovation of Fir City's municipal park, begun and completed during 1996, came from the following sources:

Grant from state government	$400,000
Proceeds from general obligation bond issue	500,000
Transfer from Fir's general fund	100,000

In its 1996 capital projects fund operating statement, Fir should report these amounts as

	Revenues	Other Financing Sources
A.	$1,000,000	$0
B.	$900,000	$100,000
C.	$400,000	$600,000
D.	$0	$1,000,000

The correct answer is (C). *(CPA 1193 II-11)*
REQUIRED: The amounts to be reported in the capital projects fund operating statement.
DISCUSSION: In a capital projects fund operating statement, revenues include grants and interest earned. Other financing sources include proceeds from bonds and operating transfers in. Thus, Fir would report revenues of $400,000 and other financing sources of $600,000 ($500,000 + $100,000) in its capital projects fund operating statements.
Answer (A) is incorrect because the proceeds from the bond issue and the transfer from the general fund should be reported under other financing sources. Answer (B) is incorrect because the proceeds from bond issue should be reported under other financing sources. Answer (D) is incorrect because the grant should be reported under revenues.

42. Grove Township issued $50,000 of bond anticipation notes at face amount in 1996 and placed the proceeds in its capital projects fund. All legal steps were taken to refinance the notes, but Grove was unable to consummate refinancing. In the capital projects fund, what account should be credited to record the $50,000 proceeds?

A. Other financing sources control.

B. Revenues control.

C. Deferred revenues.

D. Bond anticipation notes payable.

The correct answer is (D). *(CPA 590 II-10)*
REQUIRED: The account to be credited to record the $50,000 proceeds from bond anticipation notes.
DISCUSSION: Bond anticipation notes of governmental funds should be reported in the general long-term debt account group if all legal steps have been taken to refinance the bond anticipation notes and the intent is supported by an ability to consummate the refinancing on a long-term basis. If both criteria are not met, the bond anticipation notes should be reported as a fund liability in the fund in which the proceeds are recorded. Thus, because Grove was unable to consummate the refinancing, the proceeds should be recorded as a bond anticipation note payable in the capital projects fund.
Answers (A), (B), and (C) are incorrect because the bond anticipation notes should be recorded in the capital projects fund as bond anticipation notes payable.

43. In 1995, Menton City received $5,000,000 of bond proceeds to be used for capital projects. Of this amount, $1,000,000 was expended in 1995. Expenditures for the $4,000,000 balance were expected to be incurred in 1996. These bond proceeds should be recorded in capital projects funds in the amount of

A. $5,000,000 in 1995.

B. $5,000,000 in 1996.

C. $1,000,000 in 1995 and $4,000,000 in 1996.

D. $1,000,000 in 1995 and in the general fund for $4,000,000 in 1995.

The correct answer is (A). *(CPA 1187 II-48)*
REQUIRED: The date(s) bond proceeds should be recorded in a capital projects fund.
DISCUSSION: A capital projects fund is a governmental fund for which revenues and expenditures should be recognized on the modified accrual basis. On this basis, revenues should be recognized in the accounting period in which they become available and measurable. Expenditures should be recognized in the accounting period in which the fund liability is incurred. Thus, the entire $5,000,000 of bond proceeds should be recorded in the capital projects fund when it was received in 1995.
Answers (B), (C), and (D) are incorrect because the $5,000,000 in bond proceeds should be recognized in 1995 when the revenues are available and measurable.

44. In what fund type should the proceeds from special assessment bonds issued to finance construction of sidewalks in a new subdivision be reported?

A. Agency fund.

B. Special revenue fund.

C. Enterprise fund.

D. Capital projects fund.

The correct answer is (D). *(CPA 1192 T-55)*
REQUIRED: The fund type used to account for special assessment bond proceeds used to finance construction of sidewalks.
DISCUSSION: The purpose of a capital projects fund is to account for major construction or acquisition projects. Construction of sidewalks in a new subdivision is properly considered a capital project. Thus, the bond proceeds should be accounted for in a capital project fund. However, since the bonds are not general obligation bonds, the liability should be recorded in a debt service fund rather than the general long-term debt account group.
Answers (A), (B), and (C) are incorrect because proceeds from special assessment bonds issued to finance a construction project should be accounted for in a capital projects fund.

45. A public school district should recognize revenue from property taxes levied for its debt service fund when

    A. Bonds to be retired by the levy are due and payable.

    B. Assessed valuations of property subject to the levy are known.

    C. Funds from the levy are measurable and available to the district.

    D. Proceeds from collection of the levy are deposited in the district's bank account.

The correct answer is (C). *(CPA 593 T-56)*
    REQUIRED: The timing of revenue recognition for a school district's tax levy.
    DISCUSSION: A school district is a governmental unit with the power to levy taxes. Debt service funds are governmental funds and, thus, are accounted for on the modified accrual basis. This basis of accounting provides that revenues be recognized when they are measurable and available.
    Answers (A), (B), and (D) are incorrect because tax revenues are recognized when they are measurable and available.

46. Tott City's serial bonds are serviced through a debt service fund with cash provided by the general fund. In a debt service fund's statements, how are cash receipts and cash payments reported?

	Cash Receipts	Cash Payments
A.	Revenues	Expenditures
B.	Revenues	Operating transfers
C.	Operating transfers	Expenditures
D.	Operating transfers	Operating transfers

The correct answer is (C). *(CPA 591 T-54)*
    REQUIRED: The proper reporting of cash receipts and cash payments in a debt service fund's financial statements.
    DISCUSSION: Cash receipts of a debt service fund (DSF) must be transferred in from other funds, as a DSF has no revenue-raising attributes of its own. Cash payments made to retire principal and interest payments of serial bonds are recorded as expenditures of the governmental unit's resources.
    Answers (A) and (B) are incorrect because transfers to a debt service fund are not considered revenues. These funds have already been recorded as revenues to the general fund. In addition, cash payments from a debt service fund to retire principal and interest are properly considered expenditures. Answer (D) is incorrect because cash payments are considered expenditures.

47. In which of the following fund types of a city government are revenues and expenditures recognized on the same basis of accounting as the general fund?

    A. Nonexpendable trust.

    B. Internal service.

    C. Enterprise.

    D. Debt service.

The correct answer is (D). *(CPA 1191 T-54)*
    REQUIRED: The fund that recognizes revenues and expenditures in the same manner as the general fund.
    DISCUSSION: The debt service fund is the only fund listed that is classified as a governmental fund. The other funds are classified as proprietary fund types. Governmental fund types use the modified accrual basis, and proprietary fund types use the full accrual basis.
    Answer (A) is incorrect because a nonexpendable trust fund is accounted for in a manner similar to that of proprietary funds. Answers (B) and (C) are incorrect because the internal service and enterprise funds are proprietary funds and use full accrual.

48. Wood City, which is legally obligated to maintain a debt service fund, issued the following general obligation bonds on July 1, 1996:

Term of bonds	10 years
Face amount	$1,000,000
Issue price	101
Stated interest rate	6%

Interest is payable January 1 and July 1. What amount of bond premium should be amortized in Wood's debt service fund for the year ended December 31, 1996?

    A. $1,000

    B. $500

    C. $250

    D. $0

The correct answer is (D). *(CPA 1193 II-6)*
    REQUIRED: The amount of bond premium amortized in the debt service fund.
    DISCUSSION: The debt service fund of a governmental unit is a governmental fund used to account for the accumulation of resources for, and the payment of, general long-term debt principal and interest. Since the focus is on spending, there is no amortization of premium.
    Answers (A), (B), and (C) are incorrect because there is no amortization of bond premium in the debt service fund.

49. In connection with Albury Township's long-term debt, the following cash accumulations are available to cover payment of principal and interest on

Bonds for financing of water
  treatment plant construction $1,000,000
General long-term obligations   400,000

The amount of these cash accumulations that should be accounted for in Albury's debt service funds is

A. $0

B. $400,000

C. $1,000,000

D. $1,400,000

The correct answer is (B). *(CPA 1188 II-45)*
  REQUIRED: The amount of cash accumulations to be accounted for in debt service funds.
  DISCUSSION: A debt service fund is used to account for revenue raised to pay the principal and interest of general obligation long-term debt issued by a governmental unit. Water treatment plants and other utilities are customarily accounted for in enterprise funds because they tend to be financed and operated in the same manner as private businesses. Cash accumulations to cover payment of principal and interest on enterprise fund obligations are accounted for in the enterprise fund itself. Hence, only the $400,000 of general long-term obligations should be accounted for in the debt service funds.
  Answer (A) is incorrect because the amount accumulated for payment of the general long-term obligations is properly accounted for in the debt service fund. Answer (C) is incorrect because the amount accumulated for the bonds should be accounted for in the water/utility enterprise fund. Answer (D) is incorrect because $1,400,000 includes the bonds for the water/utility fund project.

50. Dale City is accumulating financial resources that are legally restricted to payments of general long-term debt principal and interest maturing in future years. At December 31, 1996, $5,000,000 has been accumulated for principal payments, and $300,000 has been accumulated for interest payments. These restricted funds should be accounted for in the

	Debt Service Fund	General Fund
A.	$0	$5,300,000
B.	$300,000	$5,000,000
C.	$5,000,000	$300,000
D.	$5,300,000	$0

The correct answer is (D). *(CPA 592 II-36)*
  REQUIRED: The proper fund in which to account for funds reserved for principal and interest.
  DISCUSSION: Debt service funds are created to accumulate financial resources for repayment of principal and interest of long-term general obligation debt. The general fund does not become involved with this process, except perhaps to make operating transfers to the debt service fund.
  Answer (A) is incorrect because it incorrectly assumes that the general fund handles the accumulation of principal and interest to repay long-term debt. Answer (B) is incorrect because it incorrectly assumes that the general fund handles principal accumulations and that the debt service fund handles interest accumulations. Answer (C) is incorrect because this answer incorrectly assumes that the debt service fund handles accumulations of principal and that the general fund handles accumulation of interest on long-term debt.

51. A major exception to the general rule of expenditure accrual for governmental units relates to unmatured

	Principal of General Long-Term Debt	Interest on General Long-Term Debt
A.	Yes	Yes
B.	Yes	No
C.	No	Yes
D.	No	No

The correct answer is (A). *(CPA 1194 TMG-14)*
  REQUIRED: The major exception to the general rule of expenditure accrual for governmental units.
  DISCUSSION: According to the modified accrual basis of accounting, expenditures are recognized when liabilities are incurred. For general debt service, however, principal and interest expenditures ordinarily are recognized when payments on the debt are due.
  Answers (B), (C), and (D) are incorrect because both the principal and interest of general long-term debt are recognized when due, not when incurred.

52. Old equipment, which is recorded in the general fixed asset account group, is sold for less than its carrying amount. The sale reduces the investments in general fixed assets' balance by the

- A. Difference between the cost of the equipment and the sales price.
- B. Difference between the carrying amount of the equipment and the sales price.
- C. Selling price of the equipment.
- D. Carrying amount of the equipment.

The correct answer is (D). *(CPA 591 T-56)*
REQUIRED: The amount at which equipment sold at a loss is removed from the books.
DISCUSSION: When an asset recorded in the general fixed asset account group is sold, the asset and any accumulated depreciation are removed from the books at their carrying amounts. The price received for the equipment is recorded as revenue normally in the general fund.
Answers (A), (B), and (C) are incorrect because the investments in general fixed assets are reduced by the carrying amount of the equipment sold.

53. Fixed assets should be accounted for in the general fixed assets account group for the

	Enterprise Fund	Special Revenue Fund
A.	Yes	No
B.	Yes	Yes
C.	No	Yes
D.	No	No

The correct answer is (C). *(CPA 1189 T-56)*
REQUIRED: The fund(s) whose fixed assets are accounted for in the general fixed assets account group.
DISCUSSION: The general fixed assets group of accounts is a self-balancing group of accounts that lists the governmental unit's fixed assets, i.e., those used in operations accounted for by the governmental funds and not by the proprietary and trust funds, and their sources. Accordingly, when assets are purchased by the special revenue fund (a governmental fund) an expenditure is debited to the fund, and the asset and its source are recorded in the general fixed assets group of accounts. Fixed assets acquired by an enterprise fund (a proprietary fund) are accounted for in the fund, not in the general fixed assets account group.
Answers (A) and (B) are incorrect because fixed assets purchased by an enterprise fund are accounted for in the fund, not in the general fixed assets account group. Answers (A) and (D) are incorrect because assets purchased by a special revenue fund are accounted for in the general fixed assets account group.

54. Fixed assets donated to a governmental unit should be recorded

- A. As a memorandum entry only.
- B. At the donor's carrying amount.
- C. At estimated fair value when received.
- D. At the lower of donor's carrying amount or estimated fair value when received.

The correct answer is (C). *(CPA 590 T-59)*
REQUIRED: The proper recording of fixed assets donated to a governmental unit.
DISCUSSION: Fixed assets donated to a governmental unit should be recorded in the general fixed assets account group at estimated fair value when received.
Answer (A) is incorrect because the receipt of a donated fixed asset should be recorded. Answers (B) and (D) are incorrect because the donated asset should be recorded at its estimated fair value when received.

55. If a primary government's general fund has an equity interest in a joint venture, all or a portion of this equity interest should be reported in the

- A. General fixed assets account group.
- B. Trust fund.
- C. Agency fund.
- D. Internal service fund.

The correct answer is (A). *(CPA 1194 TMG-5)*
REQUIRED: The reporting of a general fund's equity interest in a joint venture.
DISCUSSION: According to SGAS 14, an equity interest in a joint venture ordinarily does not meet the definition of a financial resource. Hence, the net investment should not be reported in a governmental fund, e.g., the general fund. All or a portion of the equity interest should be reported in the GFAAG. The GFAAG accounts for all fixed assets not accounted for in proprietary or trust funds.
Answers (B), (C), and (D) are incorrect because fixed assets are reported in the GFAAG if they are not accounted for in proprietary or trust funds.

56. The following are Boa City's fixed assets:

Fixed assets used in proprietary fund activities	$1,000,000
Fixed assets used in governmental-type trust funds	1,800,000
All other fixed assets	9,000,000

What aggregate amount should Boa account for in the general fixed assets account group?

A. $9,000,000

B. $10,000,000

C. $10,800,000

D. $11,800,000

The correct answer is (A). *(CPA 592 II-33)*

REQUIRED: The amount to be recorded in the general fixed assets account group.

DISCUSSION: Fixed assets that relate to proprietary fund activities should be recorded in proprietary funds. Fixed assets used in trust funds are accounted for in that trust fund. All other fixed assets are general fixed assets that should be recorded in the general fixed assets account group.

Answer (B) is incorrect because $10,000,000 assumes that the proprietary fund fixed assets are recorded in the general fixed assets account group. Answer (C) is incorrect because $10,800,000 assumes that trust fund fixed assets are recorded in the general fixed assets account group. Answer (D) is incorrect because $11,800,000 assumes that all fixed assets should be recorded in the general fixed assets account group.

57. Which of the following accounts would be included in the fund equity section of the combined balance sheet of a governmental unit for the general fixed assets account group?

	Investment in General Fixed Assets	Fund Balance Reserved for Encumbrances
A.	Yes	Yes
B.	Yes	No
C.	No	No
D.	No	Yes

The correct answer is (B). *(CPA 587 T-56)*

REQUIRED: The account to be included in the combined balance sheet for the general fixed assets account group.

DISCUSSION: General fixed assets are not financial resources available for expenditure but items for which financial resources have been used and for which accountability should be maintained. The general fixed assets account group is not a fund because it has no fiscal responsibility. It is used as a management control over, and an accountability listing of, a government's general fixed assets, not those assets used in commercial-type activities or held in trust. This listing is balanced by accounts that show the sources by which the assets were financed. One such account is the investment in general fixed assets account. The fund balance reserved for encumbrances is not appropriate because the general fixed assets account group is not a fund.

Answers (A), (C), and (D) are incorrect because the investment in general fixed assets account would be included in the combined balance sheet, but the fund balance reserved for encumbrances would not since the general fixed assets account group is not a fund.

58. Dodd Village received a gift of a new fire engine from a local civic group. The fair value of this fire engine was $400,000. The entry to be made in the general fixed assets account group for this gift is

		Debit	Credit
A.	Memorandum entry only	--	--
B.	General fund assets	$400,000	
	Private gifts		$400,000
C.	Investment in general fixed assets	$400,000	
	Gift revenue		$400,000
D.	Machinery & equipment	$400,000	
	Investment in general fixed assets from private gifts		$400,000

The correct answer is (D). *(CPA 1193 II-16)*

REQUIRED: The entry to be made in the general fixed assets account group for this gift.

DISCUSSION: When general fixed assets are acquired, through gift, purchase, or otherwise, the asset is debited and investment in general fixed assets is credited indicating the source from which the asset was provided. In this case, the source is private gifts.

Answer (A) is incorrect because a journal entry is required. Answers (B) and (C) are incorrect because the individual asset (machinery and equipment) is recorded along with investment in general fixed assets.

59. The recording of accumulated depreciation in the general fixed assets account group is

A. Never allowed.

B. Dependent on materiality.

C. Optional.

D. Mandatory.

The correct answer is (C). *(CPA 1193 T-57)*
REQUIRED: The correct statement about depreciation relative to the general fixed assets group of accounts.
DISCUSSION: Fixed assets recorded in the general fixed assets group of accounts are the fixed assets used in operations accounted for in the governmental funds. Depreciation of general fixed assets may not be recorded in the accounts of governmental funds. Depreciation of general fixed assets, however, may be recorded in cost accounting systems or calculated for cost finding analysis. The recording of accumulated depreciation in the general fixed assets account group is optional (even though depreciation expense is not recorded in any fund or the fixed assets group).
Answer (A) is incorrect because depreciation, rather than accumulated depreciation, may not be recorded in the accounts of governmental funds. Answer (B) is incorrect because materiality is not relevant to the issue concerning accumulated depreciation. Answer (D) is incorrect because recording accumulated depreciation is optional, not mandatory.

60. On June 28, 1996, Silver City's debt service fund received funds for the future repayment of bond principal. As a consequence, the long-term debt account group reported

A. An increase in the amount available in debt service funds and an increase in the fund balance.

B. An increase in the amount available in debt service funds and an increase in the amount to be provided for bonds.

C. An increase in the amount available in debt service funds and a decrease in the amount to be provided for bonds.

D. No changes in any amount until the bond principal is actually paid.

The correct answer is (C). *(CPA 1191 T-56)*
REQUIRED: The effect of receipt of funds for debt service on the general long-term account group.
DISCUSSION: The receipt of funds for the future repayment of bond principal by the debt service fund also requires recognition in the long-term debt account group. The receipt is recorded by debiting (increasing) the amount available in debt service funds and crediting (decreasing) the amount to be provided for payment of bonds account.
Answer (A) is incorrect because the long-term debt account group has no fund balance. Answer (B) is incorrect because an increase in the amount to be provided for bonds would mean that less funds were available. Answer (D) is incorrect because accounting recognition of the amount available is required.

61. Unmatured general obligation bonds payable of a governmental unit should be reported in the liability section of the

A. General fund.

B. Capital projects fund.

C. General long-term debt account group.

D. Debt service fund.

The correct answer is (C). *(CPA 589 T-56)*
REQUIRED: The proper accounting for unmatured general obligation bonds payable of a governmental unit.
DISCUSSION: The general long-term debt group of accounts lists general obligation liabilities as credits and amounts available (for repayment) or amounts to be provided (for repayment) as debits. When the bonds are issued, amount to be provided is debited. As monies are set aside in the debt service fund for repayment of the principal, amount available is debited and amount to be provided is credited.
Answers (A), (B), and (D) are incorrect because general obligation liabilities of the governmental unit are accounted for in the general long-term debt account group. Such debt is not recorded in the governmental funds themselves.

62. The following obligations were among those reported by Fern Village at December 31, 1996:

Vendor financing with a term of 10 months when incurred, in connection with a capital asset acquisition that is not part of a long-term financing plan	$ 150,000
Long-term bonds for financing of capital asset acquisition	3,000,000
Bond anticipation notes due in 6 months, issued as part of a long-term financing plan for capital purposes	400,000

What aggregate amount should Fern report as general long-term debt at December 31, 1996?

 A. $3,000,000

 B. $3,150,000

 C. $3,400,000

 D. $3,550,000

The correct answer is (C). *(CPA 592 II-34)*
 REQUIRED: The amount to be reported as general long-term debt for 1996.
 DISCUSSION: Both the bond anticipation notes and the long-term bonds are general obligation debts of Fern Village. Therefore, they are properly recorded in the general long-term debt account group. The vendor financing is not a long-term lease and should be recorded as an expenditure as payments are incurred.
 Answer (A) is incorrect because $3,000,000 is based on the assumption that the bond anticipation notes are not long-term; however, they are issued as part of a long-term financing plan and, therefore, should be included as long-term debt. Answer (B) is incorrect because $3,150,000 is based on the assumption that the vendor financing is a long-term liability and that the bond anticipation notes are not long-term. Answer (D) is incorrect because $3,550,000 is based on the assumption that the vendor financing should be included as long-term debt.

63. The debt service transactions of a special assessment bond issue for which the government is not obligated in any manner should be reported in the

 A. Agency fund.

 B. Enterprise fund.

 C. Special revenue fund.

 D. Long-term debt account group.

The correct answer is (A). *(CPA 1193 T-56)*
 REQUIRED: The proper reporting of debt service transactions of a special assessment bond issue for which the government is not obligated.
 DISCUSSION: The debt service transactions of a special assessment issue for which the government is not obligated in any manner should be reported in an agency fund rather than a debt service fund. This reflects that the government's duties are limited to acting as an agent for the assessed property owners and the bondholders.
 Answer (B) is incorrect because an enterprise fund is a proprietary fund used to account for for-profit operations. Answer (C) is incorrect because a special revenue fund is a governmental fund used to account for the proceeds of specific revenue sources that are legally restricted and expended for a specific purpose. Answer (D) is incorrect because the government is not obligated for this special assessment bond issue.

64. Flac City recorded a 20-year building rental agreement as a capital lease. The building lease asset was reported in the general fixed asset account group. Where should the lease liability be reported in Flac's combined balance sheet?

 A. General long-term debt account group.

 B. Debt service fund.

 C. General fund.

 D. A lease liability should not be reported.

The correct answer is (A). *(CPA 1193 T-59)*
 REQUIRED: The proper reporting of a lease liability in the combined balance sheet.
 DISCUSSION: General obligation debt of a governmental entity is reported in the general long-term debt account group.
 Answer (B) is incorrect because the debt service fund is used to account for the general accumulation of resources for, and the payment of, general long-term debt principal and interest. Answer (C) is incorrect because the general fund does not record long-term debt. Answer (D) is incorrect because the capital lease liability is recorded similarly to other long-term debt of governmental funds.

65. The portion of special assessment debt maturing in 5 years, to be repaid from general resources of the government, should be reported in the

- A.   General fund.
- B.   General long-term debt account group.
- C.   Agency fund.
- D.   Capital projects fund.

The correct answer is (B). *(CPA 1194 TMG-13)*
   REQUIRED: The reporting of special assessment debt maturing in 5 years.
   DISCUSSION: The GLTDAG maintains accounting records for all unmatured general long-term liabilities of the governmental unit with the exception of long-term liabilities related to proprietary funds and trust funds. The debt recorded in the GLTDAG includes long-term special assessment debt on which the governmental unit is obligated in some manner.
   Answers (A), (C), and (D) are incorrect because the GLTDAG accounts for all unmatured general long-term debt except that of proprietary and trust funds.

32.3 Proprietary Funds

66. The following equity balances are among those maintained by Cole City:

Enterprise funds	$1,000,000
Internal service funds	400,000

Cole's proprietary equity balances amount to

- A. $1,400,000
- B. $1,000,000
- C. $400,000
- D. $0

The correct answer is (A). *(CPA 1193 II-12)*
   REQUIRED: The amount of proprietary equity balances.
   DISCUSSION: Proprietary funds include enterprise funds and internal service funds. Thus, the proprietary equity balances equal $1,400,000 ($1,000,000 + $400,000).
   Answer (B) is incorrect because $1,000,000 excludes the equity balance of the internal service funds. Answer (C) is incorrect because $400,000 excludes the equity balance of the enterprise funds. Answer (D) is incorrect because $0 excludes the equity balances of the enterprise funds and the internal service funds.

67. Which event(s) should be included in a statement of cash flows for a governmental entity?

I.   Cash inflow from issuing bonds to finance city hall construction

II.   Cash outflow from a city utility representing payments in lieu of property taxes

- A.   I only.
- B.   II only.
- C.   Both I and II.
- D.   Neither I nor II.

The correct answer is (B). *(CPA 1195 TMG-63)*
   REQUIRED: The event(s), if any, included in a statement of cash flows for a governmental entity.
   DISCUSSION: A combined statement of cash flows is required to be presented for all proprietary funds, nonexpendable trust funds, and other governmental entities that use proprietary fund accounting. A city utility is accounted for using a proprietary fund, whereas city hall construction is accounted for using a capital projects fund (a governmental fund).
   Answers (A), (C), and (D) are incorrect because the cash inflow from issuing bonds to finance city hall construction would not be included in a statement of cash flows, but the cash outflow from a city utility representing payments in lieu of property taxes would be.

68. With regard to the statement of cash flows for a governmental unit's enterprise fund, items generally presented as cash equivalents are

	2-month Treasury Bills	3-month Certificates of Deposit
A.	No	No
B.	No	Yes
C.	Yes	Yes
D.	Yes	No

The correct answer is (C). *(CPA 1193 T-58)*
   REQUIRED: The items generally presented as cash equivalents.
   DISCUSSION: Cash equivalents are highly liquid investments, readily convertible to known amounts of cash with an original time to maturity at acquisition of 3 months or less. The T-bills and CDs both meet these criteria and are presented as cash equivalents.
   Answers (A), (B), and (D) are incorrect because both the 2-month T-bill and the 3-month CD are cash equivalents.

69. Which of the following does not affect an internal service fund's net income?

    A. Depreciation expense on its fixed assets.

    B. Operating transfers in.

    C. Operating transfers out.

    D. Residual equity transfers.

The correct answer is (D). *(CPA 1193 T-55)*

REQUIRED: The transaction not affecting an internal service fund's net income.

DISCUSSION: Residual equity transfers are nonrecurring or nonroutine transfers of equity between funds. Since only equity is transferred, an internal service fund's net income is not affected.

Answer (A) is incorrect because depreciation expense decreases net income. Answer (B) is incorrect because operating transfers in increase net income. Answer (C) is incorrect because operating transfers out decrease net income.

70. Bay Creek's municipal motor pool maintains all city-owned vehicles and charges the various departments for the cost of rendering those services. In which of the following funds should Bay account for the cost of such maintenance?

    A. General fund.

    B. Internal service fund.

    C. Special revenue fund.

    D. Special assessment fund.

The correct answer is (B). *(CPA 593 II-32)*

REQUIRED: The correct fund in which to account for the cost of vehicle maintenance provided by the motor pool department to other governmental units.

DISCUSSION: An internal service fund is used when one governmental entity provides billable services to other governmental units that would result in revenues, expenses, or expenditures if one of the parties were outside of the governmental unit.

Answer (A) is incorrect because the general fund is used to account for transactions not accounted for in other governmental funds. Answer (C) is incorrect because the special revenue fund is used to account for certain restricted categories of revenue. Answer (D) is incorrect because the special assessment fund is an internal fund used to account for the proceeds of special assessment bonds pledged with special assessment tax levies.

71. Gem City's internal service fund received a residual equity transfer of $50,000 cash from the general fund. This $50,000 transfer should be reported in Gem's internal service fund as a credit to

    A. Revenues.

    B. Other financing sources.

    C. Accounts payable.

    D. Contributed capital.

The correct answer is (D). *(CPA 592 II-31)*

REQUIRED: The correct account to which a residual equity transfer in should be recorded in the internal service fund.

DISCUSSION: A residual equity transfer in would be credited to the contributed capital account.

Answer (A) is incorrect because the sum of money transferred in had already been recorded as revenue in the general fund. Answer (B) is incorrect because operating transfers, not equity transfers, are considered other financing sources of a fund. Answer (C) is incorrect because the transfer is a permanent transfer that does not have to be repaid.

72. Through an internal service fund, New County operates a centralized data processing center to provide services to New's other governmental units. In 1996, this internal service fund billed New's parks and recreation fund $150,000 for data processing services. What account should New's internal service fund credit to record this $150,000 billing to the parks and recreation fund?

    A. Data processing department expenses.

    B. Intergovernmental transfers.

    C. Interfund exchanges.

    D. Operating revenues control.

The correct answer is (D). *(CPA 1193 II-13)*

REQUIRED: The account to be credited by an internal service fund to record a billing to other governmental units.

DISCUSSION: This kind of transaction is a quasi-external transaction. It is an internal transaction for which a revenue, an expenditure, or an expense is recorded. Billings issued for services rendered by an internal service data processing center to other governmental units should be recorded as a debit to a receivable account and a credit to an operating revenues control account.

Answer (A) is incorrect because the services provided should be recorded as a revenue, not a decrease in an expense. Answers (B) and (C) are incorrect because service provided by an internal service fund should be accounted for as a quasi-external transaction giving rise to the recording of revenues.

73. An enterprise fund is used when the governing body requires that

I. Accounting for the financing of an agency's services to other government departments be on a cost-reimbursement basis.

II. User charges cover the costs of general public services.

III. Net income information be provided for an activity.

A. I only.

B. I and II.

C. I and III.

D. II and III.

The correct answer is (D). *(CPA 1191 T-55)*
REQUIRED: The condition(s) under which an enterprise fund is used.
DISCUSSION: An enterprise fund is used when a government provides a service to the public on a user-charge basis.
Answers (A), (B), and (C) are incorrect because an internal service fund is used when accounting for the financing of an agency's services to other government departments on a cost-reimbursement basis.

74. Cy City's Municipal Solid Waste Landfill Enterprise Fund was established when a new landfill was opened January 3, 1996. The landfill is expected to close December 31, 2015. Cy's 1996 expenses would include a portion of which of the year 2016 expected disbursements?

I. Cost of a final cover to be applied to the landfill

II. Cost of equipment to be installed to monitor methane gas buildup

A. I only.

B. II only.

C. Both I and II.

D. Neither I nor II.

The correct answer is (C). *(CPA 595 TMG-55)*
REQUIRED: The accounting for municipal solid waste landfill (MSWLF) closure and postclosure care costs.
DISCUSSION: SGAS 18 states that owners and operators of MSWLF sites must incur a variety of costs to protect the environment during the period of operation and during the postclosure period. Certain costs result in disbursements near or after the date that the MSWLF stops accepting solid waste and during the postclosure period. The costs of final cover and of gas monitoring systems are included in the estimated total current closure and postclosure care costs. A proprietary fund (e.g., an enterprise fund) should recognize a portion of the estimated total current cost as an expense and a liability in each period that the MSWLF accepts solid waste.
Answers (A), (B), and (D) are incorrect because portions of the costs of final cover and of gas monitoring systems are included in 1996 expenses.

75. The following transactions were among those reported by Corfe City's electric utility enterprise fund for 1996:

Capital contributed by subdividers	$ 900,000
Cash received from customer households	2,700,000
Proceeds from sale of revenue bonds	4,500,000

In the electric utility enterprise fund's statement of cash flows for the year ended December 31, 1996, what amount should be reported as cash flows from capital and related financing activities?

A. $4,500,000

B. $5,400,000

C. $7,200,000

D. $8,100,000

The correct answer is (B). *(CPA 1194 TMG-21)*
REQUIRED: The amount reported as cash flows from capital and related financing activities.
DISCUSSION: Cash flows should be classified as operating, noncapital financing, capital and related financing, or investing. Operating activities include producing and delivering goods and providing services. Thus, cash from customer households is a revenue item reported under cash flows from operating activities. Capital and related financing activities include acquiring and disposing of capital assets, borrowing and repaying money related to capital asset transactions, etc. Assuming the sale of revenue bonds and the capital contributions by subdividers are for the acquisition or improvement of capital assets, the amount to report under capital and related financing activities is $5,400,000 ($900,000 + $4,500,000).
Answer (A) is incorrect because $4,500,000 omits the capital contributed by subdividers. Answer (C) is incorrect because $7,200,000 includes customer fees revenue and omits capital contributed by subdividers. Answer (D) is incorrect because $8,100,000 includes customer fees.

76. Fixed assets of an enterprise fund should be accounted for in the

- A. Enterprise fund, but no depreciation on the fixed assets should be recorded.

- B. Enterprise fund, and depreciation on the fixed assets should be recorded.

- C. General fixed assets account group, but no depreciation on the fixed assets should be recorded.

- D. General fixed assets account group, and depreciation on the fixed assets should be recorded.

The correct answer is (B). *(CPA 589 T-55)*
    REQUIRED: The proper accounting for fixed assets of an enterprise fund.
    DISCUSSION: Governmental accounting and reporting standards require that proprietary funds (enterprise and internal service funds) account for their operations on the accrual basis. Fixed assets are therefore carried on the books of proprietary funds, and depreciation expense is recognized.
    Answers (A) and (C) are incorrect because depreciation on fixed assets should be recorded. The enterprise fund accounts for depreciation on the same basis as a business enterprise. Answers (C) and (D) are incorrect because general fixed assets should be accounted for in the enterprise fund itself.

77. A state government had the following activities:

I. State-operated lottery	$10,000,000
II. State-operated hospital	3,000,000

Which of the above activities should be accounted for in an enterprise fund?

- A. Neither I nor II.

- B. I only.

- C. II only.

- D. Both I and II.

The correct answer is (D). *(CPA 1194 TMG-22)*
    REQUIRED: The activities to be accounted for in the enterprise fund.
    DISCUSSION: Enterprise funds are used to account for the activities of a state or local governmental agency that provides goods or services primarily to the public on a user-charge basis. A state-operated hospital and a state-operated lottery qualify as enterprise fund activities.
    Answers (A), (B), and (C) are incorrect because a state-run hospital and a state-run lottery are services provided to the public on a user-charge basis.

32.4 Fiduciary Funds

78. The following fund types used by Cliff City had total assets at December 31, 1996 as follows:

Special revenue funds	$100,000
Agency funds	150,000
Trust funds	200,000

Total fiduciary fund assets amounted to

- A. $200,000

- B. $300,000

- C. $350,000

- D. $450,000

The correct answer is (C). *(CPA 1188 II-48)*
    REQUIRED: The total fiduciary fund assets.
    DISCUSSION: Fiduciary funds are used to account for assets that are held by governmental units in a trustee capacity or as an agent for individuals, private organizations, other governmental units, and/or other funds. Fiduciary funds include trust funds and agency funds. Trust funds include expendable trust funds, nonexpendable trust funds, and pension trust funds. The total fiduciary fund assets include the $150,000 agency funds and the $200,000 trust funds, a total of $350,000.
    Answer (A) is incorrect because $200,000 excludes agency funds. Answer (B) is incorrect because $300,000 includes special revenue funds but not agency funds. Answer (D) is incorrect because $450,000 includes special revenue funds.

79. Fish Road property owners in Sea County are responsible for special assessment debt that arose from a storm sewer project. If the property owners default, Sea has no obligation regarding debt service, although it does bill property owners for assessments and uses the monies it collects to pay debt holders. What fund type should Sea use to account for these collection and servicing activities?

A. Agency.

B. Debt service.

C. Expendable trust funds.

D. Capital projects.

The correct answer is (A). *(CPA 1195 TMG-64)*
REQUIRED: The reporting of debt service transactions of a special assessment issue.
DISCUSSION: "The debt service transactions of a special assessment issue for which the government is not obligated in any manner should be reported in an agency fund rather than a debt service fund, to reflect that the government's duties are limited to acting as an agent for the assessed property owners and the bondholders" (SGAS 6).
Answers (B), (C), and (D) are incorrect because the debt service transactions of a special assessment issue for which the government is not obligated are specifically assigned to agency funds.

80. Stone Corp. donated investments to Pine City and stipulated that the income from the investments be used to acquire art for the city's museum. Which of the following funds should be used to account for the investments?

A. Endowment fund.

B. Special revenue fund.

C. Expendable trust fund.

D. Nonexpendable trust fund.

The correct answer is (D). *(CPA 593 II-39)*
REQUIRED: The correct fund in which to record donated investments.
DISCUSSION: Nonexpendable trust funds are used when a donor donates assets to a governmental unit and requires that the principal be kept intact and that the earnings be used for a specified governmental activity. The income earned from the corpus of the trust is often transferred to an expendable trust fund.
Answer (A) is incorrect because endowment funds are accounts typically used in accounting for hospitals, colleges and universities, and other nonprofit entities--not in governmental accounting. If used in governmental, an endowment fund is an account contained within the non-expendable trust funds. Answer (B) is incorrect because the investments donated by Stone Corp. represent an asset accounted for in a trust fund. Answer (C) is incorrect because an expendable trust fund is used to account for expendable amounts.

81. River City has a defined contribution pension plan. How should River report the pension plan in its financial statements?

A. Amortize any transition asset over the estimated number of years of current employees' service.

B. Disclose in the notes to the financial statements the amount of the pension benefit obligation and the net assets available for benefits.

C. Identify in the notes to the financial statements the types of employees covered and the employer's and employees' obligations to contribute to the fund.

D. Accrue a liability for benefits earned but not paid to fund participants.

The correct answer is (C). *(CPA 1192 T-58)*
REQUIRED: The method for reporting a defined contribution pension plan.
DISCUSSION: GASB Statement 5, *Disclosure of Pension Information by Public Employee Retirement Systems and State and Local Government Employers*, requires that a defined contribution pension plan report a plan description and a summary of significant accounting policies and plan asset matters. The plan description should include the types of employees covered and current membership, a brief statement about plan provisions and eligibility requirements, employer and employee obligations to contribute, and the authority under which those obligations are established.
Answer (A) is incorrect because no transition asset arises under a defined contribution plan. Answer (B) is incorrect because a pension benefit obligation arises under a defined benefit pension plan. Answer (D) is incorrect because, under a defined contribution plan, the government employer's obligation is for contributions, not benefits.

82. Glen County uses governmental fund accounting and is the administrator of a multiple-jurisdiction deferred compensation plan covering both its own employees and those of other governments participating in the plan. This plan is an eligible deferred compensation plan under the U.S. Internal Revenue Code and Income Tax Regulations. Glen has legal access to the plan's $40,000,000 in assets, comprising $2,000,000 pertaining to Glen and $38,000,000 pertaining to the other participating governments. In Glen's balance sheet, what amount should be reported in an agency fund for plan assets and as a corresponding liability?

A. $0

B. $2,000,000

C. $38,000,000

D. $40,000,000

The correct answer is (D). *(CPA 592 II-32)*
REQUIRED: The correct amount of deferred compensation plan assets and liability to record in the balance sheet.
DISCUSSION: When a government administers an eligible deferred compensation plan that is funded, it should be recorded in an agency fund in the total amount of plan assets to which it has access. In addition, a corresponding liability should be recorded that is limited to the amount of the plan's assets. It does not matter that funds are held on behalf of other governments; these amounts are properly reportable in an agency fund.
Answer (A) is incorrect because the government must report as an asset the amount of plan assets to which it has access, and a corresponding liability must be recorded. Answer (B) is incorrect because $2,000,000 is based on the assumption that only Glen's portion of the plan assets must be reported. Answer (C) is incorrect because $38,000,000 is based on the assumption that only the portion of assets applicable to the other governments must be reported. All such assets to which a government has access must be reported.

83. Maple City's public employee retirement system (PERS) reported the following account balances at June 30, 1996:

Reserve for employer's contributions	$5,000,000
Actuarial deficiency in reserve for employer's contributions	300,000
Reserve for employees' contributions	9,000,000

Maple's PERS fund balance at June 30, 1996, should be

A. $5,000,000

B. $5,300,000

C. $14,000,000

D. $14,300,000

The correct answer is (D). *(CPA 592 II-22)*
REQUIRED: The PERS fund balance.
DISCUSSION: Governmental accounting and reporting standards require that the three account balances be included in the fund balance.
Answer (A) is incorrect because $5,000,000 does not include the reserve for employees' contributions or the actuarial deficiency in reserve for employer's contributions. Answer (B) is incorrect because $5,300,000 does not include the reserve for employees' contributions. Answer (C) is incorrect because $14,000,000 does not include the actuarial deficiency in reserve for employer's contributions.

84. Arlen City's fiduciary funds contained the following cash balances at December 31, 1996:

Under the Forfeiture Act--cash confiscated from illegal activities; disbursements used only for law enforcement activities	$300,000
Sales taxes collected by Arlen to be distributed to other governmental units	500,000

What amount of cash should Arlen report in its expendable trust funds at December 31, 1996?

A. $0

B. $300,000

C. $500,000

D. $800,000

The correct answer is (B). *(CPA 1193 II-14)*
REQUIRED: The amount of cash to be reported in the expendable trust funds.
DISCUSSION: In an expendable trust fund, the government agrees to accept resources and to spend them in ways specified by the donor. Because the confiscated cash can be used only for law enforcement activities, it must be reported in the expendable trust fund. The sales tax collected is to be distributed to other governmental units and is accounted for in an agency fund.
Answer (A) is incorrect because $0 excludes the confiscated cash. Answer (C) is incorrect because $500,000 includes the sales taxes and excludes the confiscated cash. Answer (D) is incorrect because $800,000 includes the sales taxes.

32.5 Multifund Governmental Transactions

Questions 85 through 87 are based on the following information. On March 2, 1996, Finch City issued 10-year general obligation bonds at face amount, with interest payable March 1 and September 1. The proceeds were to be used to finance the construction of a civic center over the period April 1, 1996, to March 31, 1997. During the fiscal year ended June 30, 1996, no resources were provided to the debt service fund for the payment of principal and interest.

85. On June 30, 1996, Finch's debt service fund should include interest payable on the general obligation bonds for

A. 0 months.

B. 3 months.

C. 4 months.

D. 6 months.

The correct answer is (A). *(CPA 1190 T-54)*
    REQUIRED: The interest payable on general obligation bonds to be recorded in the debt service fund balance sheet at fiscal year-end.
    DISCUSSION: Accrual of interest payable at year-end is not permitted in a debt service fund unless the resources to pay the interest have been accrued or received in the debt service fund and the debt service payment is due early in the next year. Thus, no interest payable should be recorded in the year-end debt service fund balance sheet.
    Answers (B), (C), and (D) are incorrect because no resources were provided to the debt service fund during the fiscal year. Therefore, no interest payable should be recorded in the debt service fund balance sheet.

86. Proceeds from the general obligation bonds should be recorded in the

A. General fund.

B. Capital projects fund.

C. General long-term debt account group.

D. Debt service fund.

The correct answer is (B). *(CPA 1190 T-55)*
    REQUIRED: The fund in which the proceeds from general obligation bonds should be recorded.
    DISCUSSION: Proceeds to be used to finance the construction of a civic center should be credited to bond proceeds (other financing sources) in the capital projects fund. The debt should also be recorded in the general long-term debt account group.
    Answers (A) and (D) are incorrect because bond proceeds to be used to finance a capital project should be recorded in the capital projects fund. Answer (C) is incorrect because the bond liability should be recorded in the general long-term debt account group.

87. On June 30, 1996, Finch's combined balance sheet should report the construction in progress for the civic center in the

	Capital Projects Fund	General Fixed Assets Account Group
A.	Yes	Yes
B.	Yes	No
C.	No	No
D.	No	Yes

The correct answer is (D). *(CPA 1190 T-57)*
    REQUIRED: The proper recording of the construction in progress in the year-end combined balance sheet.
    DISCUSSION: Expenditures related to the construction project should be recorded in the capital projects fund. The construction in progress and ultimately the completed asset should be recorded in the general fixed assets account group.
    Answer (A) is incorrect because expenditures are reported in the capital projects fund. Answer (B) is incorrect because both the completed and the in-progress assets are reported in the GFAAG, not the capital projects fund. Answer (C) is incorrect because both the completed and the in-progress assets are recorded in the GFAAG.

88. Lisa County issued $5,000,000 of general obligation bonds at 101 to finance a capital project. The $50,000 premium was to be used for payment of principal and interest. This transaction should be accounted for in the

A. Capital projects funds, debt service funds, and the general long-term debt account group.

B. Capital projects funds and debt service funds only.

C. Debt service funds and the general long-term debt account group only.

D. Debt service funds only.

The correct answer is (A). *(CPA 1190 II-48)*
REQUIRED: The funds and account group affected by the issuance of general obligation bonds at a premium to be used to finance a capital project.
DISCUSSION: The $5,000,000 in bond proceeds to be used to finance the capital project should be credited to bond proceeds (other financing sources) in a capital projects fund. The $50,000 premium to be used for payment of principal and interest should be recorded in the debt service fund. The $5,000,000 of general obligation bonds should be recorded at par value in the general long-term debt account group.
Answers (B), (C), and (D) are incorrect because the transaction should be accounted for in the capital projects fund, the debt service funds, and the general long-term debt account group.

Questions 88 and 89 are based on the following information. Leyland City, during the year ended December 31, received a state grant of $500,000 to finance the purchase of buses and an additional grant of $100,000 to aid in the financing of bus operations for the year. Only $300,000 of the capital grant was used for the purchase of buses, but the entire operating grant of $100,000 was spent during the year.

---

89. If Leyland's bus transportation system is accounted for as part of the city's general fund, how much should Leyland report as grant revenues for the year ended December 31?

A. $100,000

B. $300,000

C. $400,000

D. $500,000

The correct answer is (C). *(CPA 582 II-32)*
REQUIRED: The grant revenue for a bus system accounted for by a general fund.
DISCUSSION: NCGA Statement 2, *Grant, Entitlement, and Shared Revenue Accounting and Reporting by State and Local Governments*, states that grants, entitlements, and shared revenues should be recognized as revenue according to the modified accrual basis of accounting when they become both measurable and available. For grants, expenditure is the prime factor for determining eligibility, and revenue should be recognized when the expenditure is made. Thus, grant revenues of $400,000 should be reported by Leyland because it expended $400,000 of grant monies during the year.
Answer (A) is incorrect because $100,000 does not include the $300,000 used to purchase buses. Answer (B) is incorrect because $300,000 does not include the $100,000 used to finance bus operations. Answer (D) is incorrect because the grant revenues should be recognized when the expenditure is made.

90. If Leyland's bus transportation system is accounted for as an enterprise fund, how much should Leyland report as grant revenues for the year ended December 31?

A. $100,000

B. $300,000

C. $400,000

D. $500,000

The correct answer is (A). *(CPA 582 II-33)*
REQUIRED: The amount of grant revenues if enterprise fund accounting is used.
DISCUSSION: The concept of matching grant revenue with related expenditures applies not only to governmental funds but also to enterprise funds. Because an enterprise fund accounts for fixed assets as would a business operated for profit, the $300,000 in grant expenditures for the purchase of buses would be a capital item, not an expense. Accordingly, grant revenue of only $100,000 should be reported.
Answers (B), (C), and (D) are incorrect because grant revenue of $100,000 would be recognized. The $300,000 expenditure would be treated as a capital item not an expense.

CHAPTER THIRTY-THREE
NONPROFIT ACCOUNTING

This chapter addresses certain pronouncements that specifically address the accounting and reporting by nonbusiness, not-for-profit organizations and health care organizations (including not-for-profit and for-profit) that are nongovernmental. These pronouncements include SFAC 4, *Objectives of Financial Reporting by Nonbusiness Organizations*, SFAS 93, *Recognition of Depreciation by Not-for-Profit Organizations*, SFAS 116, *Accounting for Contributions Received and Contributions Made*, SFAS 117, *Financial Statements of Not-for-Profit Organizations*, SFAS 124, *Accounting for Certain Investments Held by Not-for-Profit Organizations*, the AICPA Audit and Accounting Guide, *Not-for-Profit Organizations* (June 1, 1996), and the AICPA Audit and Accounting Guide, *Health Care Organizations* (June 1, 1996).

These FASB and AICPA pronouncements have changed and standardized not-for-profit accounting to require presentation of statements of financial position, activities, and cash flows. Revenues are reported in a statement of activities as increases in unrestricted, temporarily restricted, or permanently restricted net assets, and expenses decrease unrestricted net assets. Net assets in the statement of financial position are reported as unrestricted, temporarily restricted, and permanently restricted. Fund accounting may be used for internal accounting purposes but is not required or encouraged for external reporting purposes.

No specialized industry accounting or financial reporting principles are presented for different types of not-for-profit organizations, such as voluntary health and welfare organizations or educational institutions. However, accounting by health care organizations retains some distinctive features. Previously, various fund accounting schemes were employed for the various not-for-profit entities. Now, all not-for-profit organizations must follow SFAS 117, which requires generic financial statements similar to those of business enterprises. Health care financial reporting is also largely standardized for all entities, whether they are for profit, not-for-profit, or governmental.

The accounting and reporting for governmental organizations is addressed in Chapter 32, State and Local Governmental Accounting.

33.1 Nonbusiness Organizations

1. Which of the following is ordinarily not considered one of the major distinguishing characteristics of nonbusiness organizations?

    A. Significant amounts of resources are provided by donors in nonreciprocal transactions.

    B. There is an absence of defined, transferable ownership interests.

    C. Performance indicators similar to a business enterprise's profit are readily available.

    D. The primary operating purpose is not to provide goods or services at a profit.

The correct answer is (C). *(Publisher)*

    REQUIRED: The statement not ordinarily considered a major characteristic of nonbusiness organizations.

    DISCUSSION: SFAC 4, Objectives of Financial Reporting by Nonbusiness Organizations, states that the objectives of financial reporting are derived from the common interests of those who provide the resources to nonbusiness organizations. Such organizations ordinarily have no single indicator of performance comparable to a business enterprise's profit. Thus, nonbusiness organization performance is usually evaluated in terms of management stewardship.

    Answers (A), (B), and (D) are incorrect because SFAC 4 specifically gives each as a distinguishing characteristic of nonbusiness organizations.

2. Which of the following is a characteristic of nonbusiness organizations?

    A. Noneconomic reasons seldom underlie the decision to provide resources to nonbusiness enterprises.

    B. Business and nonbusiness organizations usually obtain resources in the same way.

    C. Both nonbusiness and business organizations use scarce resources in the production and distribution of goods and services.

    D. The operating environment of nonbusiness organizations ordinarily differs from that of business organizations.

The correct answer is (C). *(Publisher)*

    REQUIRED: The characteristic of nonbusiness organizations.

    DISCUSSION: The operating environments of nonbusiness and business organizations are similar in many ways. Both produce and distribute goods and services using scarce resources.

    Answer (A) is incorrect because many noneconomic factors affect decisions to provide resources to nonbusiness enterprises. Answer (B) is incorrect because business organizations obtain resources by providing goods and services. Many nonbusiness organizations obtain resources from contributors and are accountable to the providers of those resources or to their representatives. Answer (D) is incorrect because the operating environments of nonbusiness and business organizations are similar.

3. Financial reporting by nonbusiness organizations should provide information useful in

    A. Making resource allocation decisions.

    B. Assessing services and the ability to continue to provide services.

    C. Assessing management stewardship and performance.

    D. All of the answers are correct.

The correct answer is (D). *(Publisher)*

    REQUIRED: The objective(s) of financial reporting by nonbusiness organizations.

    DISCUSSION: Answers (A) through (C) are included among the basic objectives of financial reporting for nonbusiness organizations stated in SFAC 4. Additional objectives are to provide information about the liquidity of the organization, economic resources, obligations, net resources, and changes in them, including managers' explanations and interpretations.

    Answers (A), (B), and (C) are incorrect because financial reporting by nonbusiness organizations should provide information useful in making resource allocation decisions, assessing services and the ability to continue to provide services, and assessing management stewardship and performance.

4. Typical users of financial reports of nonbusiness organizations include which of the following?

    A. Resource providers.

    B. Constituents.

    C. Governing and oversight bodies.

    D. All of the answers are correct.

The correct answer is (D). *(Publisher)*

    REQUIRED: The typical users of financial reports prepared by nonbusiness organizations.

    DISCUSSION: In addition to those users listed in answers (A) through (C), others potentially interested in the financial information provided by nonbusiness organizations include managers, organization members, taxpayers, contributors, grantors, lenders, suppliers, creditors, employees, directors and trustees, service beneficiaries, financial analysts and advisers, brokers, underwriters, lawyers, economists, taxing authorities, regulatory authorities, legislators, the financial press, labor unions, trade associations, researchers, teachers, and students.

    Answers (A), (B), and (C) are incorrect because resource providers, constituents, and governing and oversight bodies are typical users.

33.2 Not-for-Profit Organizations

5. SFAS 117, *Financial Statements of Not-for-Profit Organizations*, establishes standards for general-purpose external financial statements issued by not-for-profit organizations. A complete set of financial statements should include

    A. Statements of financial position as of the beginning and end of the reporting period, a statement of cash flows, and a statement of activities.

    B. A statement of financial position as of the end of the reporting period, a statement of cash flows prepared on the direct basis, and a statement of activities.

    C. A statement of financial position as of the end of the reporting period, a statement of cash flows, and a statement of activities.

    D. Statements of financial position as of the beginning and end of the reporting period, comparative statements of cash flows, and comparative statements of activities.

The correct answer is (C). *(Publisher)*

    REQUIRED: The statements included in a complete set of financial statements of not-for-profit organizations.

    DISCUSSION: SFAS 117 states that "a complete set of financial statements of a not-for-profit organization shall include a statement of financial position as of the end of the reporting period, a statement of activities and a statement of cash flows for the reporting period, and accompanying notes to financial statements."

    Answer (A) is incorrect because the statement of financial position should be as of the end of the reporting period. Answer (B) is incorrect because SFAS 117 does not specify how the statement of cash flows is to be prepared. Answer (D) is incorrect because the statement of financial position should be as of the end of the reporting period, and comparative statements are not required.

6. SFAS 117, *Financial Statements of Not-for-Profit Organizations*, focuses on

    A. Basic information for the organization as a whole.

    B. Standardization of funds nomenclature.

    C. Inherent differences of not-for-profit organizations that affect reporting presentations.

    D. Distinctions between current fund and non-current fund presentations.

The correct answer is (A). *(CPA 1194 TMG-30)*

    REQUIRED: The focus of SFAS 117.

    DISCUSSION: SFAS 117 is intended to promote the relevance, understandability, and comparability of financial statements issued by not-for-profit organizations by requiring that certain basic information be reported. The focus of the financial statements required by SFAS 117 is on the not-for-profit organization as a whole.

    Answers (B), (C), and (D) are incorrect because, according to SFAS 117, the focus is on the not-for-profit organization as a whole and on reporting assets, liabilities, and net assets; changes in net assets; flows of economic resources; cash flows, borrowing and repayment of borrowing, and other factors affecting liquidity; and service efforts.

7. In a statement of financial position, a not-for-profit organization should report amounts for which of the following classes of net assets?

I. Unrestricted
II. Temporarily restricted
III. Permanently restricted

    A. I, II, and III.

    B. I and II only.

    C. I and III only.

    D. II and III only.

The correct answer is (A). *(Publisher)*
REQUIRED: The classes of net assets reported in a statement of financial position of a not-for-profit organization.
DISCUSSION: SFAS 117, *Financial Statements of Not-for-Profit Organizations*, requires a not-for-profit organization to report amounts for all three classes: permanently restricted net assets, temporarily restricted net assets, and unrestricted net assets. Information regarding the nature and amounts of permanently or temporarily restricted net assets should be provided by reporting amounts on the face of the statement or by including details in the notes to financial statements.
Answers (B), (C), and (D) are incorrect because a not-for-profit organization should report amounts for all three classes.

8. In its statement of activities, a not-for-profit organization may report expenses as decreases in which of the following classes of net assets?

	Unrestricted	Permanently Restricted	Temporarily Restricted
A.	Yes	Yes	No
B.	Yes	No	Yes
C.	Yes	No	No
D.	Yes	Yes	Yes

The correct answer is (C). *(Publisher)*
REQUIRED: The reporting of expenses in a not-for-profit organization's statement of activities.
DISCUSSION: In a statement of activities, revenues and expenses ordinarily should be reported as gross amounts. Revenues may be reported as increases in either unrestricted or restricted (temporarily or permanently) net assets. Expenses ordinarily should be reported as decreases in unrestricted net assets. However, investment revenues, reported as increases in unrestricted or restricted net assets, may be reported net of related fees such as custodial fees and investment advisory fees provided that these fees are disclosed either on the face of the statement or in the related notes.
Answers (A), (B), and (D) are incorrect because not-for-profit organizations should report expenses as decreases in unrestricted net assets. Expenses do not decrease permanently and temporarily restricted net assets.

9. For which of the following assets held by a religious organization should depreciation be recognized in the organization's general purpose external financial statements?

    A. The house of worship.

    B. A priceless painting.

    C. A nationally recognized historical treasure.

    D. Land used for a building site.

The correct answer is (A). *(Publisher)*
REQUIRED: The asset held by a nonprofit organization for which depreciation should be recognized.
DISCUSSION: SFAS 93, *Recognition of Depreciation by Not-for-Profit Organizations*, requires all nonprofit organizations to recognize the cost of using up long-lived tangible assets (depreciation) in their general purpose external financial statements. Hence, a building used for religious activity is ordinarily depreciable.
Answers (B) and (C) are incorrect because depreciation does not have to be recognized for certain works of art and historical treasures whose economic benefit or service potential is used up so slowly that their estimated useful lives are extraordinarily long. Answer (D) is incorrect because land is normally not depreciated by any organization.

10. The League, a not-for-profit organization, received the following pledges:

Unrestricted	$200,000
Restricted for capital additions	150,000

All pledges are legally enforceable and are expected to be received in the upcoming year. The League's experience indicates that 10% of all pledges prove to be uncollectible. What amount may the League report as a reasonable estimate of the fair value of pledges receivable?

    A. $135,000

    B. $180,000

    C. $315,000

    D. $350,000

The correct answer is (C). *(CPA 593 II-35)*

REQUIRED: The amount to report as a reasonable estimate of the fair value of pledges receivable.

DISCUSSION: SFAS 116, *Accounting for Contributions Received and Contributions Made*, requires not-for-profit organizations to recognize unconditional promises to give at fair value. The present value of estimated future cash flows is an appropriate measure of fair value. However, unconditional promises to give expected to be collected in less than 1 year may be recognized at net realizable value. The League may therefore report net pledges receivable of $315,000 [($200,000 + $150,000) x (1 – 10%)].

Answer (A) is incorrect because $135,000 is based on the assumption that only the pledges "restricted for capital additions" are reported as receivables, net of 10% of the amount. Answer (B) is incorrect because $180,000 is based on the assumption that only the unrestricted pledges are reported, net of 10% of that amount. Answer (D) is incorrect because pledges receivable expected to be collected in less than 1 year may be reported at net realizable value.

11. In Yew Co.'s 1996 annual report, Yew described its social awareness expenditures during the year as follows:

The Company contributed $250,000 in cash to youth and educational programs. The Company also gave $140,000 to health and human-service organizations, of which $80,000 was contributed by employees through payroll deductions. In addition, consistent with the Company's commitment to the environment, the Company spent $100,000 to redesign product packaging.

What amount of the above should be included in Yew's income statement as charitable contributions expense?

    A. $310,000

    B. $390,000

    C. $410,000

    D. $490,000

The correct answer is (A). *(CPA 1193 I-53)*

REQUIRED: The amount of charitable contribution expense included in the income statement.

DISCUSSION: The company cannot deduct a charitable expense for money donated by employees. In addition, the redesign of a product's package cannot be considered a charitable expense. Accordingly, the charitable contribution expense is $310,000 ($250,000 + $140,000 –$80,000).

Answer (B) is incorrect because $390,000 includes the employees' charitable contribution. Answer (C) is incorrect because $410,000 includes the redesign costs. Answer (D) is incorrect because $490,000 includes the employees' charitable contribution and the redesign costs.

12. On December 30, 1996, Leigh Museum, a not-for-profit organization, received a $7,000,000 donation of Day Co. shares with donor-stipulated requirements as follows:

- Shares valued at $5,000,000 are to be sold with the proceeds used to erect a public viewing building.
- Shares valued at $2,000,000 are to be retained, with the dividends used to support current operations.

As a consequence of the receipt of the Day shares, how much should Leigh report as temporarily restricted net assets on its 1996 statement of financial position?

    A. $0

    B. $2,000,000

    C. $5,000,000

    D. $7,000,000

The correct answer is (C). *(CPA 595 TMG-57)*

REQUIRED: The amount to report as temporarily restricted net assets.

DISCUSSION: A temporary restriction permits the donee organization to "expend the donated assets as specified and is satisfied either by the passage of time or by actions of the organization" (SFAS 116). The shares valued at $5,000,000 meet this definition because they are to be sold and used for a specified project. A permanent restriction requires that the "resources be maintained permanently but permits the organization to use up or expend part or all of the income derived" (SFAS 116). The $2,000,000 stock donation meets this definition and should be reported as permanently restricted net assets. Leigh should report $5,000,000 as temporarily restricted net assets.

Answer (A) is incorrect because the shares valued at $5,000,000 are only temporarily restricted. Answer (B) is incorrect because the shares valued at $2,000,000 are permanently restricted, and the shares valued at $5,000,000 have temporary restrictions. Answer (D) is incorrect because only the shares valued at $5,000,000 have temporary restrictions.

13. The Jones family lost its home in a fire. On December 25, 1996, a philanthropist sent money to the Amer Benevolent Society to purchase furniture for the Jones family. The resource provider did not explicitly grant Amer the unilateral power to redirect the use of the assets. During January 1997, Amer purchased this furniture for the Jones family. Amer, a not-for-profit organization, should report the receipt of the money in its 1996 financial statements as a(n)

A. Unrestricted contribution.

B. Temporarily restricted contribution.

C. Permanently restricted contribution.

D. Liability.

The correct answer is (D). *(CPA 595 TMG-58)*
   REQUIRED: The reporting of a transfer to an NPO with a direction that the assets be used to aid a specific beneficiary.
   DISCUSSION: FASB Interpretation No. 42, *Accounting for Transfers of Assets in Which a Not-for-Profit Organization is Granted Variance Power*, clarifies SFAS 116. SFAS 116 applies to contributions but not to agency transactions. According to the Interpretation, the resource provider must explicitly grant the recipient variance power, that is, the unilateral power to redirect the use of the assets away from the specified beneficiary. Because Amer was not explicitly granted variance power, it is an agent, trustee, or intermediary. Thus, the transfer should be accounted for as a liability, not a contribution.
   Answers (A), (B), and (C) are incorrect because, absent variance power, the transfer should be accounted for as a liability.

14. The Pel Museum, a not-for-profit organization, received a contribution of historical artifacts. It need not recognize the contribution if the artifacts are to be sold and the proceeds used to

A. Support general museum activities.

B. Acquire other items for collections.

C. Repair existing collections.

D. Purchase buildings to house collections.

The correct answer is (B). *(CPA 595 TMG-59)*
   REQUIRED: The circumstance under which a contribution of artifacts to be sold need not be recognized.
   DISCUSSION: Contributions of such items as art works and historical treasures need not be capitalized and recognized as revenues if they are added to collections that are (1) subject to a policy that requires the proceeds of sale of collection items to be used to acquire other collection items; (2) protected, kept unencumbered, cared for, and preserved; and (3) held for public exhibition, education, or research for public service purposes rather than financial gain (SFAS 116).
   Answers (A), (C), and (D) are incorrect because, if the proceeds are used to support general museum activities, repair existing collections, or purchase buildings to house collections, the contribution must be recognized.

15. SFAS 116, *Accounting for Contributions Received and Contributions Made*, requires not-for-profit organizations to report receipts of contributions as

	Unrestricted Support	Restricted Support
A.	No	No
B.	No	Yes
C.	Yes	No
D.	Yes	Yes

The correct answer is (D). *(Publisher)*
   REQUIRED: The classification of contributions received by not-for-profit organizations.
   DISCUSSION: SFAS 116 requires that contributions received by not-for-profit organizations be reported as restricted support or unrestricted support. Contributions with donor-imposed restrictions are reported as restricted support. Restricted support increases permanently restricted net assets or temporarily restricted net assets. Contributions without donor-imposed restrictions are reported as unrestricted support.
   Answers (A), (B), and (C) are incorrect because not-for-profit organizations must record contributions as unrestricted support or restricted support.

16. SFAS 116 requires not-for-profit organizations to recognize a conditional promise to give when

A. The promise is received.

B. The promise is received in writing.

C. The conditions are met.

D. It is reasonably possible that the conditions will be met.

The correct answer is (C). *(Publisher)*
   REQUIRED: The timing of recognition of a conditional promise to give.
   DISCUSSION: A conditional promise to give is one that depends on the occurrence of a specified future, uncertain event to establish the promisor's obligation. It is recognized when the conditions are substantially met, i.e., when the conditional promise becomes unconditional. If the possibility is remote that the condition will not be met, the recognition criterion is satisfied.
   Answers (A) and (B) are incorrect because receipt of the promise is not sufficient for recognition of a contribution. Answer (D) is incorrect because the possibility that the condition will not be met must be remote before a contribution is recognized.

Questions 17 through 19 are based on the following information. On June 30, 1996, the Orange County Retraining Organization, a not-for-profit organization, received a building and the land on which it was constructed as a gift from Tyler Corporation. The building is intended to support the organization's education and training mission or any other purpose consistent with the organization's mission. Immediately prior to the contribution, the fair values of the building and land had been appraised as $350,000 and $150,000, respectively. Carrying values on Tyler's books at June 30, 1996 were $290,000 and $75,000, respectively.

17. If the Orange County Retraining Organization does not have a policy of implying time restrictions on gifts of long-lived assets, the gift should be recorded by the organization as

	Unrestricted Support	Restricted Support
A.	$150,000	$350,000
B.	$500,000	$0
C.	$0	$500,000
D.	$75,000	$290,000

The correct answer is (B). *(Publisher)*
REQUIRED: The amount at which a contribution of long-lived assets should be recorded by the donee.
DISCUSSION: The terms of this contribution allow the long-lived assets to be used for any purpose consistent with the NPO's mission. It does not have a policy of implying time restrictions on gifts of long-lived assets. Thus, the building and land on which it was constructed should be recorded at fair value as assets and unrestricted support.
Answers (A), (C), and (D) are incorrect because both the building and land should be recorded at fair value as unrestricted support.

18. If the Orange County Retraining Organization has a policy of implying time restrictions on gifts of long-lived assets, the gift should be recorded by the organization as

	Unrestricted Support	Restricted Support
A.	$150,000	$350,000
B.	$500,000	$0
C.	$0	$500,000
D.	$75,000	$290,000

The correct answer is (C). *(Publisher)*
REQUIRED: The amount at which a contribution of long-lived assets should be recorded by the donee.
DISCUSSION: The terms of this gift allow the long-lived assets to be used for any purpose consistent with the NPO mission. In the absence of a policy implying time restrictions on gifts of long-lived assets, the contribution would be recorded as unrestricted support. However, given that the Orange County Retraining Organization has a policy of implying a time restriction, the building and land on which it was constructed should be recorded at fair value as assets and restricted support. The restriction will expire over the expected useful life of the building.
Answers (A), (B), and (D) are incorrect because both the building and the land should be recorded at fair value as restricted support.

19. Tyler Corporation should record its contribution of the building and land as a

A. $365,000 reduction in contributed capital.

B. $500,000 reduction in contributed capital.

C. $365,000 expense.

D. $500,000 expense.

The correct answer is (D). *(Publisher)*
REQUIRED: The amount at which a contribution of long-lived assets should be recorded by the donor.
DISCUSSION: Contributions made should be recognized as expenses in the period made. They should be measured at the fair value of the assets contributed.
Answers (A), (B), and (C) are incorrect because the contribution should be recorded as an expense and measured at the fair value of the assets contributed.

20. Kids are Wonderful Foundation, a not-for-profit agency, receives free electricity on a continuous basis from a local utility company. The utility company's contribution is made subject to cancellation by the donor. Kids are Wonderful should account for this contribution as a(n)

A. Unrestricted revenue only.

B. Restricted revenue only.

C. Unrestricted revenue and an expense.

D. Restricted revenue and an expense.

The correct answer is (C). *(Publisher)*
   REQUIRED: The amount at which a contribution of electricity should be recorded by the donee.
   DISCUSSION: SFAS 116 defines a contribution of utilities, such as electricity, as a contribution of other assets, not a contribution of services. A simultaneous receipt and use of utilities should be recognized as both an unrestricted revenue and expense in the period of receipt and use. The revenue and expense should be measured at estimated fair value. This estimate can be obtained from the rate schedule used by the utility company to determine rates charged to a similar customer.
   Answers (A), (B), and (D) are incorrect because the simultaneous receipt of use of electricity should be recorded as an unrestricted revenue and expense in the period of receipt and use.

21. At December 31, 1996, Childwelfare Society, a not-for-profit organization, holds an investment in common stock of one publicly traded entity and an investment in debt securities of another. The not-for-profit organization holds the common stock as a long-term investment, and has the intent and the ability to hold the debt securities until maturity.

	Investment in Common Stock	Investment in Debt Securities
Original cost	$50,000	$35,000
Amortized cost		$28,000
Fair value	$63,000	$40,000

In the December 31, 1996 statement of financial position, Childwelfare Society should value these investments as

	Investment in Common Stock	Investment in Debt Securities
A.	$50,000	$28,000
B.	$50,000	$40,000
C.	$63,000	$28,000
D.	$63,000	$40,000

The correct answer is (D). *(Publisher)*
   REQUIRED: The amount to be recorded by a not-for-profit organization for investments in equity and debt securities.
   DISCUSSION: SFAS 124, *Accounting for Certain Investments Held by Not-for-Profit Organizations*, requires not-for-profit entities to measure investments in equity securities with readily determinable fair values and all investments in debt securities at fair value in the statement of financial position.
   Answers (A), (B), and (C) are incorrect because these investments should be measured at fair value.

Questions 22 through 26 are based on the following information. Early in 1996, a not-for-profit organization (NPO) received a $2,000,000 gift from a wealthy benefactor. This benefactor specified that the gift be invested in perpetuity with income restricted to provide speaker fees for a lecture series named for the benefactor. The NPO is permitted to choose suitable investments and is responsible for all other costs associated with initiating and administering this series. Neither the donor's stipulation nor the law addresses gains and losses on this permanent endowment. In 1996, the investments purchased with the gift earned $50,000 in dividend income. The fair value of the investments increased by $120,000.

22. The $2,000,000 gift should be recorded in the 1996 statement of activity as an increase in

   A. Unrestricted net assets.

   B. Temporarily restricted net assets.

   C. Permanently restricted net assets.

   D. Either unrestricted or temporarily restricted net assets.

The correct answer is (C). *(Publisher)*
   REQUIRED: The classification of a gift to be invested in perpetuity.
   DISCUSSION: A donor-imposed restriction limits the use of contributed assets. This gift is unconditional in the sense that no condition is imposed on the transfer, but it includes a permanent restriction on the use of the assets. Under SFAS 117, the gift should therefore be classified as an increase in permanently restricted net assets.
   Answers (A), (B), and (D) are incorrect because the donor stipulated that the gift be invested in perpetuity, a permanent restriction.

23. Three presentations in the lecture series were held in 1996. The speaker fees for the three presentations amounted to $90,000. The not-for-profit organization used the $50,000 dividend income to cover part of the total fees. Because the board of directors did not wish to sell part of the investments, the organization used $40,000 in unrestricted resources to pay the remainder of the speaker fees. In the 1996 statement of activity, the $50,000 of dividend revenue should be recorded as an increase in

   A. Unrestricted net assets.

   B. Temporarily restricted net assets.

   C. Permanently restricted net assets.

   D. Either unrestricted or temporarily restricted net assets.

The correct answer is (D). *(Publisher)*
   REQUIRED: The classification of expended dividend income generated from investments held in perpetuity.
   DISCUSSION: SFASs 117 and 124 require that income from donor-restricted permanent endowments be classified as an increase in temporarily restricted or permanently restricted net assets if the donor restricts its use. However, if the donor-imposed restrictions are met in the same reporting period as the gains and investment income are recognized, the gains and income may be reported as increases in unrestricted net assets, provided that the organization has a similar policy for reporting contributions received, reports on a consistent basis from period to period, and adequately discloses its accounting policy. The temporary restriction on the $50,000 of investment income was met by expenditure in 1996, the year the gain and income were recognized. Thus, the dividend revenue may be classified as an increase in either unrestricted or temporarily restricted net assets, depending on the NPO's accounting policy.
   Answers (A), (B), and (C) are incorrect because investment income may be reported as an increase in either unrestricted or temporarily restricted net assets in these circumstances.

24. Refer to the information preceding question 22 on page 693. The NPO's accounting policy is to record increases in net assets, for which a donor-imposed restriction is met in the same accounting period as gains and investment income are recognized, as increases in unrestricted net assets. In the 1996 statement of activity, the $120,000 unrealized gain should be recorded as

A. A $40,000 increase in unrestricted net assets and an $80,000 increase in temporarily restricted net assets.

B. A $120,000 increase in unrestricted net assets.

C. A $120,000 increase in temporarily restricted net assets.

D. A $120,000 increase in permanently restricted net assets.

The correct answer is (B). *(Publisher)*
REQUIRED: The classification of unrealized gain from investments held in perpetuity.
DISCUSSION: SFASs 117 and 124 permit the recognition of gains and investment income as increases in unrestricted net assets if the donor-imposed restrictions are met in the same reporting period as the gains and investment income are recognized, provided that the organization has a similar policy for reporting contributions received, reports on a consistent basis from period to period, and adequately discloses its accounting policy. The temporary restriction on the income was met by expenditure in 1996, the year the income and the gain were recognized. Thus, consistent with its policy, the NPO should treat the gain as an increase in unrestricted net assets. Given that the donor of the endowment allows the NPO to choose suitable investments and that no permanent restriction is imposed on the gain by the donor or by the law, the classification of the gain is the same as that of the income.
Answers (A), (C), and (D) are incorrect because the NPO's policy is to report the gain as an increase in unrestricted net assets if the donor restriction is met in the period the gain and income are recognized.

25. Refer to the information preceding question 22 on page 693. If the lecture series were not scheduled to begin until 1997, the $50,000 dividend income would be recorded in the 1996 statement of activity as an increase in

A. Unrestricted net assets.

B. Temporarily restricted net assets.

C. Permanently restricted net assets.

D. Either unrestricted or temporarily restricted net assets.

The correct answer is (B). *(Publisher)*
REQUIRED: The classification of unexpended dividend income generated from investments held in perpetuity.
DISCUSSION: SFAS 117 requires that gains and investment income from donor-restricted permanent endowments be classified as increases in temporarily restricted net assets if the donor restricts the use of these resources to a specific purpose that either expires with the passage of time or can be met by actions of the organization. The restriction is temporary because it will expire when the income is expended in a future period.
Answers (A), (C), and (D) are incorrect because the donor-imposed restriction is temporary. It will expire when the income is expended. Moreover, the income cannot be classified as unrestricted because recognition and the expiration of the restriction do not occur in the same period.

26. Refer to the information preceding question 22 on page 693. The $120,000 unrealized gain should be recorded in the 1996 statement of activity as an increase in

A. Unrestricted net assets.

B. Temporarily restricted net assets.

C. Permanently restricted net assets.

D. Either unrestricted or temporarily restricted net assets.

The correct answer is (B). *(Publisher)*
REQUIRED: The classification of an unrealized gain on investments held in perpetuity.
DISCUSSION: Given that the NPO has the discretion to choose suitable investments (as opposed to holding specific securities in perpetuity), the gain is not permanently restricted absent a donor stipulation or a legal requirement. Rather, the gain has the same classification as the income. The latter is temporarily restricted because it is to be expended in a future period. Hence, the gain is also temporarily restricted.
Answers (A), (C), and (D) are incorrect because the income and the gain are temporarily restricted.

27. Following the destruction of its house of worship by fire, a religious organization held a rebuilding party. Part of the labor was donated by professional carpenters. The remainder was donated by members of the organization. Capitalization is required for the value of the services provided by

A. The professional carpenters only.

B. The members only.

C. The professional carpenters and the members.

D. Neither the professional carpenters nor the members.

The correct answer is (C). *(Publisher)*
REQUIRED: The contributed services to be capitalized.
DISCUSSION: Contributions of services by the professional carpenters should be capitalized. Under SFAS 116, the contributions of services requiring specialized skills, such as those of carpenters, electricians, etc., should be recognized if they are provided by individuals possessing those skills and would typically need to be purchased if not provided by donation. SFAS 116 also requires that donated services creating or enhancing nonfinancial assets be recognized even though specialized skills are not involved. Because the members' labor helped rebuild the church, their contributions of services also should be capitalized.
Answers (A), (B), and (D) are incorrect because the church members' donated labor and the services of the professional carpenters should be capitalized.

28. Cura Foundation, a voluntary health and welfare organization supported by contributions from the general public, included the following costs in its statement of functional expenses for the year:

Fund-raising	$500,000
Administrative (including data processing)	300,000
Research	100,000

Cura's functional expenses for program services included

A. $900,000

B. $500,000

C. $300,000

D. $100,000

The correct answer is (D). *(CPA 584 II-46)*
REQUIRED: The amount of functional expenses for program services incurred by a VHWO.
DISCUSSION: An NPO's statement of activities or notes thereto should classify expenses by function. The major functional classes include program services and supporting services. Management and general expenses, along with fund-raising expenses, are classified in the supporting services category. Program services expenses are those directly related to the administration of programs. Of the costs given, only the research costs ($100,000) are program services expenses.
Answer (A) is incorrect because $900,000 includes $500,000 of fund-raising expenses and $300,000 of administrative expenses, which should be included in supporting services expenses. Answer (B) is incorrect because $500,000 of fund-raising expenses should be classified as supporting services expenses. Answer (C) is incorrect because $300,000 of administrative expenses should be classified as supporting services expenses.

29. When a nonprofit organization combines fund-raising efforts with educational materials or program services, the total combined costs incurred are

A. Reported as program services expenses.

B. Allocated between fund-raising and program services expenses using an appropriate allocation basis.

C. Reported as fund-raising costs.

D. Reported as management and general expenses.

The correct answer is (B). *(CPA 593 T-60)*
REQUIRED: The correct accounting treatment of combined fund-raising and educational materials or program services costs.
DISCUSSION: When fund-raising costs are combined with program services costs or educational materials, the total of these combined services should be systematically and rationally allocated between the programs and fund-raising.
Answers (A) and (C) are incorrect because costs that do not completely relate to one category should be allocated. Answer (D) is incorrect because the costs must be allocated to the proper programs to which they relate.

30. For the fall semester of 1996, Ames University assessed its students $3,000,000 for tuition and fees. The net amount realized was only $2,500,000 because scholarships of $400,000 were granted to students and tuition remissions of $100,000 were allowed to faculty members' children attending Ames. What amount should Ames report for the period as revenues for tuition and fees?

    A. $2,500,000

    B. $2,600,000

    C. $2,900,000

    D. $3,000,000

The correct answer is (D). *(CPA 593 II-33)*

REQUIRED: The amount reported as revenues for tuition and fees.

DISCUSSION: In accounting for tuition and fees for colleges and universities, the full amount of the tuition assessed is reported as revenue. Tuition waivers, scholarships, and like items are recorded as expenses if given in exchange transactions. Refunds are handled by merely debiting revenues and crediting cash, so tuition is automatically reported net of refunds.

Answer (A) is incorrect because $2,500,000 assumes that only net tuition is recorded. Answer (B) is incorrect because $2,600,000 assumes that scholarships are deducted before recording tuition revenues. Answer (C) is incorrect because $2,900,000 assumes that tuition remissions are deducted before recording tuition revenues.

31. Rega Foundation is a voluntary welfare organization funded by contributions from the general public. During 1996, unrestricted pledges of $600,000 were received, of which it was estimated that $72,000 would be uncollectible. By the end of 1996, $480,000 of the pledges had been collected, and it was expected that an additional $48,000 of these pledges would be collected in 1997, with the balance to be written off as uncollectible. Donors did not specify any periods during which the donations were to be used. Also during 1996, Rega sold a computer for $18,000. Its cost was $21,000, and its book value was $15,000. Rega made the correct entry to record the gain on the sale.

What amount should Rega include as unrestricted support in 1996 for contributions?

    A. $480,000

    B. $528,000

    C. $531,000

    D. $600,000

The correct answer is (B). *(CPA 589 II-36)*

REQUIRED: The net contributions.

DISCUSSION: Because donors placed no restrictions on the pledges, none of them will be considered restricted support. Moreover, the pledge receivables are expected to be collected within 1 year and should be reported at their net realizable value. Amounts estimated as uncollectible should be deducted from pledges received, and an allowance for uncollectible pledges account should be established. Accordingly, unrestricted support from contributions equaled the net realizable value of $528,000 ($480,000 + $48,000).

Answer (A) is incorrect because $480,000 assumes that unrestricted support is recorded on a cash basis. Answer (C) is incorrect because $531,000 assumes that the gain from the sale of the computer is added to unrestricted support. The gain is considered separately under the revenue category in the statement of activities. Answer (D) is incorrect because $600,000 assumes that pledge receivables are reported on a gross basis.

32. Midtown Church received a donation of equity securities with readily determinable fair values from a church member. The securities had appreciated in value after they were purchased by the donor, and they continued to appreciate through the end of Midtown's fiscal year. At what amount should Midtown report its investment in donated securities in its year-end balance sheet?

    A. Donor's cost.

    B. Fair value at the date of receipt.

    C. Fair value at the balance sheet date.

    D. Fair value at either the date of receipt or the balance sheet date.

The correct answer is (C). *(CPA 593 II-38)*

REQUIRED: The valuation of donated equity securities.

DISCUSSION: In its statement of financial position, a not-for-profit organization should measure the following investments at fair value: (1) equity securities with readily determinable fair values and (2) debt securities. Thus, the total change in the fair value of the donated securities from the date of receipt to the balance sheet date must be reported in the statement of activities (SFAS 124).

Answers (A), (B), and (D) are incorrect because all investments to which SFAS 124 applies are reported at fair value.

33. Cancer Educators, a not-for-profit organization, incurred costs of $10,000 in its combined program services and fund-raising activities. Which of the following cost allocations might Cancer report in its statement of activities?

	Program Services	Fund-Raising	General Services
A.	$0	$0	$10,000
B.	$0	$6,000	$4,000
C.	$6,000	$4,000	$0
D.	$10,000	$0	$0

The correct answer is (C). *(CPA 1194 TMG-26)*
REQUIRED: The allocation of costs for combined functions.
DISCUSSION: NPOs must provide information about expenses reported by functional classification. The $10,000 of costs should therefore be divided between program services and fund-raising.
Answers (A), (B), and (D) are incorrect because the costs resulted from program services and fund-raising. The entire $10,000 should be allocated between those classifications.

34. Environs, a community foundation, incurred $10,000 in management and general expenses during 1996. In Environs' statement of activities for the year ended December 31, 1996, the $10,000 should be reported as

A. A direct reduction of fund balance.

B. Part of supporting services.

C. Part of program services.

D. A contra account to offset revenue.

The correct answer is (B). *(CPA 592 II-40)*
REQUIRED: The expense classification for management and general expenses in the statement of activities.
DISCUSSION: Two functional categories of expenses for an NPO are program services expenses and supporting services expenses. Supporting services expenses, which do not relate to the primary mission of the organization, may be further subdivided into (1) management and general expenses, (2) fund-raising expenses, and (3) membership development costs.
Answer (A) is incorrect because a direct reduction of fund balance would be the result of a transfer or a refund to a donor. Moreover, fund accounting information is not required to be externally reported. Answer (C) is incorrect because program services expenses relate directly to the primary mission of the NPO. Answer (D) is incorrect because only costs directly related to a certain source of support, such as a special event or estimated uncollectible pledges, may be offset against revenue.

35. The following expenditures were made by Green Services, a society for the protection of the environment:

Printing of the annual report	$12,000
Unsolicited merchandise sent to encourage contributions	25,000
Cost of an audit performed by a CPA firm	3,000

What amount should be classified as fund-raising costs in the society's statement of activities?

A. $37,000

B. $28,000

C. $25,000

D. $0

The correct answer is (C). *(CPA 593 II-24)*
REQUIRED: The amount to be reported as fund-raising costs in the activity statement.
DISCUSSION: There are two major classifications of expenses for an NPO: program service expenses and supporting services expenses. Program service expenses relate directly to the primary purpose or mission of the organization. Supporting services expenses are further classified as management and general expenses, fund-raising expenses, and membership development costs. The only fund-raising-related cost here is clearly the unsolicited merchandise sent to encourage contributions.
Answer (A) is incorrect because $37,000 classifies all of the expenses as fund-raising expenses when, in fact, only the unsolicited merchandise is related to fund-raising. Answer (B) is incorrect because the cost of an audit is a management-related expense. Answer (D) is incorrect because this answer assumes that none of the expenses listed are related to fund-raising when, in fact, the unsolicited merchandise is a fund-raising expense.

36. Lane Foundation received a permanent endowment of $500,000 in 1995 from Gant Enterprises. The endowment assets were invested in publicly traded securities, and Lane is permitted to choose suitable investments. Gant did not specify how gains and losses from dispositions of endowment assets were to be treated. No restrictions were placed on the use of dividends received and interest earned on fund resources. In 1996, Lane realized gains of $50,000 on sales of fund investments and received total interest and dividends of $40,000 on fund securities. What amount of these capital gains, interest, and dividends increases unrestricted net assets?

- A. $0
- B. $40,000
- C. $50,000
- D. $90,000

The correct answer is (D). *(CPA 1188 II-51)*
REQUIRED: The amount of capital gains, interest, and dividends that increases unrestricted net assets.
DISCUSSION: Absent an explicit donor stipulation or law to the contrary, assuming the donee is allowed to choose suitable investments, income and gains or losses on a donor-restricted endowment fund's assets are changes in unrestricted net assets. Thus, the increase in unrestricted net assets is $90,000 ($50,000 gains + $40,000 interest and dividends).
Answer (A) is incorrect because $0 assumes the income and gains are restricted. Answer (B) is incorrect because $40,000 assumes the gains are restricted. Answer (C) is incorrect because $50,000 assumes the income is restricted.

37. On January 2, 1996, a nonprofit botanical society received a gift of an exhaustible fixed asset with an estimated useful life of 10 years and no salvage value. The donor's cost of this asset was $20,000, and its fair value at the date of the gift was $30,000. What amount of depreciation of this asset should the society recognize in its 1996 financial statements?

- A. $3,000
- B. $2,500
- C. $2,000
- D. $0

The correct answer is (A). *(CPA 1188 II-60)*
REQUIRED: The amount of depreciation to be recognized in the financial statements.
DISCUSSION: SFAS 93 requires not-for-profit organizations to recognize depreciation in the statement of activities. Moreover, contributions are recorded at their fair value when received. Assuming the straight-line method is used, the amount of depreciation that the nonprofit botanical society should recognize is $3,000 [($30,000 fair value – $0 salvage value) ÷ 10 years].
Answers (B), (C), and (D) are incorrect because depreciation on a straight-line basis for this asset would result in a $3,000 per year charge to depreciation. SFAS 93 requires all not-for-profit organizations to recognize depreciation in their statements of activity.

38. In 1995, a nonprofit trade association enrolled five new member companies, each of which was obligated to pay nonrefundable initiation fees of $1,000. These fees were receivable by the association in 1996. Three of the new members paid the initiation fees in 1996, and the other two new members paid their initiation fees in 1997. Annual dues (excluding initiation fees) received by the association from all of its members have always covered the organization's costs of services provided to its members. It can be reasonably expected that future dues will cover all costs of the organization's future services to members. Average membership duration is 10 years because of mergers, attrition, and economic factors. What amount of initiation fees from these five new members should the association recognize as revenue in 1996?

- A. $5,000
- B. $3,000
- C. $500
- D. $0

The correct answer is (A). *(CPA 1188 II-59)*
REQUIRED: The amount of initiation fees to be reported as revenue.
DISCUSSION: Membership dues received or receivable in exchange transactions that relate to several accounting periods should be allocated and recognized as revenue in those periods. Nonrefundable initiation and life membership fees are recognized as revenue when they are receivable if future dues and fees can be reasonably expected to cover the costs of the organization's services. Otherwise, they are amortized to future periods. Hence, given that future dues are expected to cover the organization's costs, the $5,000 in nonrefundable initiation fees should be recognized as revenue when assessed and reported as such in the 1996 statement of activities.
Answers (B), (C), and (D) are incorrect because the full amount of nonrefundable initiation fees that are receivable in 1996 are recognized as revenue, provided that future dues and fees can be reasonably expected to cover costs of the organization's services.

39. In July 1995, Ross irrevocably donated $200,000 cash to be invested and held in trust by a church. Ross stipulated that the revenue generated from this gift be paid to Ross during Ross's lifetime. After Ross dies, the principal is to be used by the church for any purpose chosen by its governing body. The church received interest of $16,000 on the $200,000 for the year ended June 30, 1996, and the interest was remitted to Ross. In the church's June 30, 1996, annual financial statements

A. $200,000 should be reported as revenue.

B. $184,000 should be reported as revenue.

C. $16,000 should be reported as revenue.

D. The gift and its terms should be disclosed only in notes to the financial statements.

The correct answer is (A). *(CPA 590 II-11)*
REQUIRED: The proper accounting for a split-interest agreement.
DISCUSSION: An NPO should report an irrevocable split-interest agreement. Assets under the control of the NPO are recorded at fair value at the time of initial recognition, and the contribution is recognized as revenue. Because the NPO has a remainder interest, it should not recognize revenue from receipt of the income of the trust. Thus, the NPO should recognize revenue of $200,000 (the presumed fair value of the contributed cash).
Answer (B) is incorrect because the contribution is not reduced by the income paid to the donor. Answer (C) is incorrect because the income paid to the donor is not revenue of the NPO. Answer (D) is incorrect because the contribution should be recognized at fair value.

40. Maple Church has cash available for investments from contributions with different restrictions. Maple's policy is to maximize its financial resources. How may Maple pool its investments?

A. Maple may not pool its investments.

B. Maple may pool all investments but must equitably allocate realized and unrealized gains and losses among participants.

C. Maple may pool only unrestricted investments but must equitably allocate realized and unrealized gains and losses among participating funds.

D. Maple may pool only restricted investments but must equitably allocate realized and unrealized gains and losses among participating funds.

The correct answer is (B). *(CPA 593 II-40)*
REQUIRED: The true statement about pooling of investments by an NPO.
DISCUSSION: Investment pools, including investments from contributions with different restrictions, are created for portfolio management. Ownership interests are assigned (ordinarily in terms of units) to the pool categories (participants) based on the market value of the cash and securities obtained from each participant. Current market value also determines the units allocated to additional assets placed in the pool and to value withdrawals. Investment income, realized gains and losses, and recognized unrealized gains and losses are allocated based on the units assigned.
Answer (A) is incorrect because pooling of investments is allowed to obtain investment flexibility and reduce risk. Answers (C) and (D) are incorrect because no prohibition exists as to the types of investments that may be pooled.

Questions 41 through 43 are based on the following information. United Together, a labor union, had the following receipts and expenses for the year ended December 31, 1996:

Receipts:		Expenses:	
Per capita dues	$680,000	Labor negotiations	$500,000
Initiation fees	90,000	Fund-raising	100,000
Sales of organizational supplies	60,000	Membership development	50,000
Gift restricted by		Administrative and general	200,000
donor for loan purposes			
for 10 years	30,000	
Gift restricted by		
donor for loan purposes		
in perpetuity	25,000	

Additional information: The union's constitution provides that 10% of the per capita dues are designated for the Strike Insurance Fund to be distributed for strike relief at the discretion of the union's executive board.

41. In United Together's statement of activities for the year ended December 31, 1996, what amount should be reported as revenue?

A. $795,000

B. $830,000

C. $825,000

D. $885,000

The correct answer is (D). *(CPA 1190 II-58)*

REQUIRED: The amount classified as revenue.

DISCUSSION: NPOs generate resources through contributions, exchange transactions, and agency transactions. Revenues are recognized on contributions and exchange transactions. Contributions of resources by donors result from nonreciprocal transactions. Thus, revenue includes not only the resources provided as membership dues, initiation fees, sales revenue, investment income, gains and losses on the disposal of fixed assets and investments, and fees for services rendered but also the contributions received as restricted support. United Together should recognize $885,000 ($680,000 dues + $90,000 initiation fees + $60,000 sales + $30,000 gift + $25,000 gift) of revenue in 1996.

Answer (A) is incorrect because the initiation fees of $90,000 should be included as revenue. Answer (B) is incorrect because the revenue should include the amounts for gifts. Answer (C) is incorrect because the amount for sales of organizational supplies should be included as revenue.

42. In United Together's statement of activities for the year ended December 31, 1996, what amount should be reported under the classification of program services expenses?

A. $850,000

B. $600,000

C. $550,000

D. $500,000

The correct answer is (D). *(CPA 1190 II-59)*

REQUIRED: The amount to be reported under the classification of program services.

DISCUSSION: Program services include the expenses that relate directly to the primary missions of the NPO. These expenses include both the direct expenses clearly identified with the program and a systematic and rational allocation of indirect costs. Because the $500,000 labor negotiation expenses are the only expenses that relate directly to the primary mission of the labor union, $500,000 should be reported in the statement of activities under the classification of program services.

Answer (A) is incorrect because fund-raising, membership development, and administrative costs relate to supporting services. Answer (B) is incorrect because the fund-raising amount should be supporting services expenses. Answer (C) is incorrect because the expenses for membership development are supporting services expenses.

43. In United Together's statement of activities for the year ended December 31, 1996, what amount should be reported under the classification of restricted support?

A. $55,000

B. $30,000

C. $25,000

D. $0

The correct answer is (A). *(CPA 1190 II-60)*

REQUIRED: The amount of restricted support.

DISCUSSION: Contributions with donor-imposed restrictions, whether temporary or permanent, are reported as restricted support. Restricted support increases temporarily or permanently restricted net assets. Thus, $55,000 ($30,000 temporarily restricted gift + $25,000 permanently restricted gift) should be reported as restricted support.

Answer (B) is incorrect because $30,000 omits the non-expendable gift in perpetuity. Answer (C) is incorrect because $25,000 omits the nonexpendable gift for loan purposes that is donor-restricted for 10 years. Answer (D) is incorrect because both donor-restricted gifts are capital additions.

33.3 Health Care Organizations

44. Monies from educational programs of a hospital normally are included in

A. Ancillary service revenue.

B. Patient service revenue.

C. Nonoperating gains.

D. Other revenue.

The correct answer is (D). *(CPA 1189 T-59)*

REQUIRED: The classification of monies derived from educational programs of a hospital.

DISCUSSION: Revenues of a hospital are classified as patient service revenue and other revenue. Other revenue includes the usual ongoing operating revenues derived by hospitals from sources other than patient care and services. Major sources of other revenue are student tuition and fees and revenue recognized upon expenditure of donor restricted gifts, grants, or subsidies for specific purposes such as research and education. Thus, the monies received from an educational program conducted by a hospital should be classified as other revenue.

Answer (A) is incorrect because ancillary service revenue is included under patient service revenues. Answer (B) is incorrect because educational program revenue is not directly related to patient care and is, therefore, not includable in patient service revenues. Answer (C) is incorrect because nonoperating gains typically arise from activities such as sales of investments or fixed assets, or investment income.

45. Which of the following should normally be considered ongoing or central transactions for a not-for-profit hospital?

I. Room and board fees from patients
II. Recovery room fees

A. Neither I nor II.

B. Both I and II.

C. II only.

D. I only.

The correct answer is (B). *(CPA 1195 TMG-75)*

REQUIRED: The item(s), if any, that are ongoing or central transactions for a not-for-profit hospital.

DISCUSSION: Revenues arise from an entity's ongoing major or central operations. Revenue from health care services includes inpatient and outpatient services provided directly to patients for their medical care. The resulting revenues derive from furnishing room and board and nursing services. Health care service revenues are also earned by the operating room, recovery room, labor and delivery room, and other ancillary departments that give patient care.

Answer (A), (C), and (D) are incorrect because room and board fees from patients and recovery room fees are ongoing or central transactions.

46. Valley's community hospital normally includes proceeds from the sale of cafeteria meals in

A. Deductions from dietary service expenses.

B. Ancillary service revenues.

C. Patient service revenues.

D. Other revenues.

The correct answer is (D). *(CPA 594 TMG-60)*
REQUIRED: The classification of revenue from cafeteria meals.
DISCUSSION: Other revenues are derived from services other than providing health care services or coverage to patients, residents, or enrollees. This category includes proceeds from sale of cafeteria meals and guest trays to employees, medical staff, and visitors.
Answer (A) is incorrect because revenues from cafeteria sales are accounted for separately and not as a component of any related expenses. Answer (B) is incorrect because "ancillary service revenues" is not a proper classification for hospital revenues. Answer (C) is incorrect because patient service revenues are health care services revenues.

47. Palma Hospital's patient service revenue for services provided in 1996 at established rates amounted to $8,000,000 on the accrual basis. For internal reporting, Palma uses the discharge method. Under this method, patient service revenue is recognized only when patients are discharged, with no recognition given to revenue accruing for services to patients not yet discharged. Patient service revenue at established rates using the discharge method amounted to $7,000,000 for 1996. According to generally accepted accounting principles, Palma should report patient service revenue for 1996 of

A. Either $8,000,000 or $7,000,000, at the option of the hospital.

B. $8,000,000

C. $7,500,000

D. $7,000,000

The correct answer is (B). *(CPA 1187 II-46)*
REQUIRED: The amount of patient service revenue to be reported.
DISCUSSION: The general principle is that gross service revenue is recorded on the accrual basis at the health care organization's established rates, regardless of whether it expects to collect the full amount. Contractual and other adjustments are also recorded on the accrual basis and subtracted from gross service revenue to arrive at net service revenue. Charity care is excluded from service revenue for financial reporting purposes. Thus, the discharge method currently used by Palma Hospital for internal reporting is not acceptable under GAAP. In its general purpose external financial statements, Palma should report $8,000,000 of patient service revenue based on established rates.
Answers (A) and (D) are incorrect because the $7,000,000 resulting from the discharge method is not acceptable under GAAP. Answer (C) is incorrect because $7,500,000 is the average of the $8,000,000 accrual basis amount and the $7,000,000 discharge method amount.

48. Under Cura Hospital's established rate structure, health care services revenues of $9,000,000 would have been earned for the year ended December 31, 1996. However, only $6,750,000 was collected because of charity allowances of $1,500,000 and discounts of $750,000 to third-party payors. For the year ended December 31, 1996, what amount should Cura report as net health care services revenues in the statement of operations?

A. $6,750,000

B. $7,500,000

C. $8,250,000

D. $9,000,000

The correct answer is (A). *(CPA 1188 II-56)*
REQUIRED: The health care services revenues reported in the statement of operations.
DISCUSSION: Gross health care services revenues do not include charity care, which is disclosed separately in the notes to the financial statements. Moreover, such revenues are reported in the financial statements net of contractual and other adjustments. Thus, health care services revenues are recorded in the accounting records at the gross amount (excluding charity care) of $7,500,000 but reported in the financial statements at the net realizable value of $6,750,000.
Answer (B) is incorrect because $7,500,000 equals gross revenues. Answer (C) is incorrect because $8,250,000 assumes that charity allowances are included in gross and net revenues. Answer (D) is incorrect because charity care is excluded from gross revenue, and contractual adjustments are subtracted to arrive at net revenue.

49. In April 1996, Delta Hospital purchased medicines from Field Pharmaceutical Co. at a cost of $5,000. However, Field notified Delta that the invoice was being canceled and that the medicines were being donated to Delta. Delta should record this donation of medicines as

A. A memorandum entry only.

B. A $5,000 credit to nonoperating expenses.

C. A $5,000 credit to operating expenses.

D. Other operating revenue of $5,000.

The correct answer is (D). *(CPA 595 TMG-60)*
REQUIRED: The accounting for a donation of medicine.
DISCUSSION: Contributions of noncash assets that are not long-lived are reported at fair value in the statement of operations. Donated medicines, office supplies, and other materials that normally would be purchased by a hospital should be credited at fair value as other revenue because they directly relate to the hospital's ongoing major operations but are not derived from services directly provided to patients.
Answer (A) is incorrect because donated assets should be recorded at their fair value when received. Answers (B) and (C) are incorrect because this donation should be credited to another revenue account or a gain account.

50. In health care accounting, restricted net assets are

A. Not available unless the directors remove the restrictions.

B. Restricted as to use only for board-designated purposes.

C. Not available for current operating use; however, the income generated is available for current operating use.

D. Restricted as to use by the donor, grantor, or other source of the resources.

The correct answer is (D). *(CPA 593 II-29)*
REQUIRED: The correct definition of restricted net assets.
DISCUSSION: In health care organization accounting, the term "restricted" is used to describe resources that have been restricted as to their use by the donors or grantors of those resources. Temporarily restricted net assets are those donor-restricted net assets that can be used by the not-for-profit organization for their specified purpose once the donor's restriction is met. Permanently restricted net assets (for example, endowment funds) are those with donor restrictions that do not expire with the passage of time and cannot be removed by any actions taken by the entity.
Answer (A) is incorrect because donor restrictions are not removable by the board. Temporary restrictions expire by passage of time or by actions by the entity consistent with the donor's restrictions. Answer (B) is incorrect because board-designated restrictions are board-removable. Answer (C) is incorrect because income generated by restricted net assets can be restricted for specific purposes.

51. Which of the following normally would be included in the health care revenues of a hospital?

	Revenues from Educational Programs	Unrestricted Gifts
A.	No	No
B.	No	Yes
C.	Yes	No
D.	Yes	Yes

The correct answer is (C). *(CPA 1194 TMG-28)*
REQUIRED: The health care revenues of a hospital.
DISCUSSION: Health care services revenues are derived from services other than health care provided to patients and residents. Other revenues may include cafeteria sales, tuition from educational programs, donated medicine, and office space rentals. However, contributions, either unrestricted or for a specific purpose, are treated as gains unless fund-raising is an ongoing major activity of the hospital. They are recognized at fair value.
Answers (A), (B), and (D) are incorrect because revenues from educational programs are other revenues, but unrestricted gifts are usually gains.

52. An organization of high school seniors performs services for patients at Leer Hospital. These students are volunteers and perform services that the hospital would not otherwise provide, such as wheeling patients in the park and reading to patients. They donated 5,000 hours of service to Leer in 1996. At a minimum wage rate, these services would amount to $18,750, while it is estimated that the fair value of these services was $25,000. In Leer's 1996 statement of activities, what amount should be reported as nonoperating revenue?

- A. $25,000
- B. $18,750
- C. $6,250
- D. $0

The correct answer is (D). *(CPA 1188 II-57)*
REQUIRED: The nonoperating revenue to record for services by volunteers.
DISCUSSION: Contributed services are recognized if they (a) create or enhance nonfinancial assets or (b) require special skills, are provided by persons possessing those skills, and would ordinarily be purchased if not provided by donation. Hence, the hospital should report no revenue. Nonfinancial assets are not involved, and no special skills, such as those of professionals or craftsmen, are required.
Answers (A), (B), and (C) are incorrect because the volunteered services do not meet the criteria for revenue recognition of contributions.

53. General purpose external financial reporting by a health care organization requires presentation of

- A.   Fund group information by a not-for-profit organization.
- B.   A statement of operations.
- C.   A separate statement of changes in equity or net assets.
- D.   A performance indicator only by for-profit entities.

The correct answer is (B). *(Publisher)*
REQUIRED: The true statement about external reporting by a health care organization.
DISCUSSION: The basic financial statements of a health care organization include a balance sheet, a statement of operations, a statement of changes in equity or net assets, and a statement of cash flows.
Answer (A) is incorrect because fund accounting may be used for internal purposes but is not required or encouraged for external reporting. Answer (C) is incorrect because the statement of changes in equity or net assets may be combined with the statement of operations. Answer (D) is incorrect because the statement of operations of all HCOs, including NPOs, should report a performance indicator and other changes in net assets.

CHAPTER THIRTY-FOUR
SPECIALIZED INDUSTRY ACCOUNTING

This chapter concerns the specialized industry topics not covered elsewhere in this study manual for which authoritative pronouncements exist. The questions are designed to present an overview of the subject matter, including identification of major issues.

A few extremely specialized pronouncements are not covered, e.g., SFAS 44, *Accounting for Intangible Assets of Motor Carriers.*

34.1 Personal Financial Statements

1. Personal financial statements should report assets and liabilities at

A. Estimated current values at the date of the financial statements and, as additional information, at historical cost.

B. Estimated current values at the date of the financial statements.

C. Historical cost and, as additional information, at estimated current values at the date of the financial statements.

D. Historical cost.

The correct answer is (B). *(CPA 1193 T-44)*
REQUIRED: The valuation basis for assets and liabilities in personal financial statements.
DISCUSSION: SOP 82-1, *Accounting and Financial Reporting for Personal Financial Statements*, requires personal financial statements to present assets at their estimated current values and liabilities at their estimated current amounts at the date of the statement. The estimated current value of an asset is defined as the amount at which the asset could be exchanged between informed and willing sellers and buyers, neither of whom is compelled to buy or sell. Estimated current amounts of liabilities are defined as the lower of either the amount of future cash to be paid discounted at the interest rate implicit in the transaction in which the debt was incurred or the amount at which the debt could currently be discharged.
Answers (A) and (C) are incorrect because the historical cost of assets and liabilities does not have to be reported. Answer (D) is incorrect because estimated current values should be used.

2. Personal financial statements should include which of the following statements?

	Financial Condition	Changes in Net Worth	Cash Flows
A.	No	Yes	Yes
B.	Yes	No	No
C.	Yes	Yes	No
D.	Yes	Yes	Yes

The correct answer is (C). *(CPA 1189 T-39)*
REQUIRED: The basic financial statements that should be included in personal financial statements.
DISCUSSION: SOP 82-1 requires that personal financial statements include at least a statement of financial condition. SOP 82-1 further recommends, but does not require, a statement of changes in net worth and comparative financial statements. A personal statement of cash flows, however, is neither required nor recommended.
Answers (A), (B), and (D) are incorrect because statements of financial condition and changes in net worth, but not of cash flows, should be included.

3. Smith owns several works of art. At what amount should these artworks be reported in Smith's personal financial statements?

   A. Original cost.

   B. Insured amount.

   C. Smith's estimate.

   D. Appraised value.

The correct answer is (D). *(CPA 1192 T-43)*
   REQUIRED: The amount at which works of art should be reported in personal financial statements.
   DISCUSSION: SOP 82-1 requires that assets be presented at their estimated current values in a personal statement of financial condition. Current value may be based on discounted cash flow, market price, appraisal value, or other basis, depending on the asset. Appraisal value is appropriate for works of art.
   Answers (A), (B), and (C) are incorrect because appraisal value is appropriate for works of art.

4. The following information pertains to an insurance policy that Barton owns on his life:

Face amount	$100,000
Accumulated premiums paid up to	
December 31, 1996	8,000
Cash value at December 31, 1996	12,000
Policy loan	3,000

In Barton's personal statement of financial condition at December 31, 1996, what amount should be reported for the investment in life insurance?

   A. $97,000

   B. $12,000

   C. $9,000

   D. $8,000

The correct answer is (C). *(CPA 1192 II-59)*
   REQUIRED: The amount reported for the investment in life insurance.
   DISCUSSION: SOP 82-1 requires that a life insurance policy be reported at its cash value minus any loans against it. Accordingly, the amount reported should be $9,000 ($12,000 – $3,000).
   Answer (A) is incorrect because $97,000 equals the face value of the policy minus the loan. Answer (B) is incorrect because $12,000 equals the cash value. Answer (D) is incorrect because $8,000 equals the premiums paid.

5. Moran is preparing a personal statement of financial condition as of April 30, 1996. Included in Moran's assets are the following:

- 50% of the voting stock of Crow Corp. A shareholders' agreement restricts the sale of the stock and, under certain circumstances, requires Crow to repurchase the stock based on carrying amounts of net assets plus an agreed amount for goodwill. At April 30, 1996, the buyout value of this stock is $337,500. Moran's tax basis for the stock is $215,000.

- Jewelry with a fair value aggregating $35,000 based on an independent appraisal on April 30, 1996 for insurance purposes. This jewelry was acquired by purchase and gift over a 10-year period and has a total tax basis of $20,000.

At what total amount should the Crow stock and jewelry be reported in Moran's April 30, 1996 personal statement of financial condition?

   A. $372,500

   B. $357,500

   C. $250,000

   D. $235,000

The correct answer is (A). *(CPA 591 II-8)*
   REQUIRED: The amount at which stock and jewelry should be reported in a personal statement of financial condition.
   DISCUSSION: SOP 82-1 requires that all assets be reported at estimated current value. An interest in a closely held business is an asset and should be shown at its estimated current value. The buyout value is a better representation of the current value of the Crow stock than the tax basis. The appraisal value is the appropriate basis for reporting the jewelry. Thus, the stock and jewelry should be reported at $372,500 ($337,500 + $35,000).
   Answer (B) is incorrect because $357,500 includes the jewelry's tax basis rather than fair value. The tax basis is used only when the jewelry is sold to determine taxable profit. Answer (C) is incorrect because $250,000 includes the stock at its tax basis. Answer (D) is incorrect because $235,000 reports both assets at their tax bases.

6. Jen has been employed by Komp, Inc. since February 1, 1996. Jen is covered by Komp's Section 401(k) deferred compensation plan. Jen's contributions have been 10% of salaries. Komp has made matching contributions of 5%. Jen's salaries were $21,000 in 1996, $23,000 in 1997, and $26,000 in 1998. Employer contributions vest after an employee completes 3 years of continuous employment. The balance in Jen's 401(k) account was $11,900 at December 31, 1998, which included earnings of $1,200 on Jen's contributions. What amount should be reported for Jen's vested interest in the 401(k) plan in Jen's December 31, 1998 personal statement of financial condition?

   A. $11,900

   B. $8,200

   C. $7,000

   D. $1,200

The correct answer is (B). *(CPA 1192 II-58)*
   REQUIRED: The amount reported for the vested interest in the 401(k) plan in the personal statement of financial condition.
   DISCUSSION: Jen's contributions equaled $7,000 [10% x ($21,000 + $23,000 + $26,000)], and earnings on those contributions were $1,200, a total of $8,200. The remainder of the balance in the 401(k) account consists of employer contributions that have not yet vested. Jen should report the employee contributions and earnings thereon but not the nonvested employer contributions. The latter do not constitute nonforfeitable rights to receive future sums.
   Answer (A) is incorrect because $11,900 includes the nonvested employer contributions. Answer (C) is incorrect because $7,000 excludes earnings on the employee contributions. Answer (D) is incorrect because $1,200 excludes the employee contributions.

7. At December 31, 1996, Ryan had the following noncancellable personal commitments:

- Pledge to be paid to County Welfare Home 30 days after volunteers paint the walls and ceiling of the Home's recreation room $ 5,000
- Pledge to be paid to City Hospital on the recovery of Ryan's comatose sister   25,000

What amount should be included in liabilities in Ryan's personal statement of financial condition at December 31, 1996?

   A. $0

   B. $5,000

   C. $25,000

   D. $30,000

The correct answer is (A). *(CPA 1191 II-15)*
   REQUIRED: The amount included in liabilities for noncancelable personal commitments.
   DISCUSSION: SOP 82-1 requires that noncancelable commitments to pay future sums be presented at their estimated current amounts as liabilities in personal financial statements if they (1) are for fixed or determinable amounts, (2) are not contingent on another's life expectancy or the occurrence of a particular event such as disability or death, and (3) do not require the future performance of service by another. Consequently, neither of Ryan's commitments qualifies for inclusion.
   Answer (B) is incorrect because the pledge to the County Welfare Home requires the future performance of service by another. Answer (C) is incorrect because the pledge to City Hospital is contingent on another's life expectancy. Answer (D) is incorrect because neither pledge qualifies for inclusion.

8. Shea, a calendar-year taxpayer, is preparing a personal statement of financial condition as of April 30, 1996. Shea's 1995 income tax liability was paid in full on April 15, 1996. Shea's tax on income earned from January through April 1996 is estimated at $30,000. In addition, $25,000 is estimated for income tax on the differences between the estimated current values of Shea's assets and the current amounts of liabilities and their tax bases at April 30, 1996. No withholdings or payments have been made towards the 1996 income tax liability. In Shea's statement of financial condition at April 30, 1996, what is the total of the amount or amounts that should be reported for income taxes?

   A. $0

   B. $25,000

   C. $30,000

   D. $55,000

The correct answer is (D). *(CPA 592 II-19)*
   REQUIRED: The total of the amount(s) that should be reported for income taxes.
   DISCUSSION: No amount should be reported for 1995 taxes because the 1995 liability was paid in full. Shea should report estimated income taxes for amounts earned through April 1996 and for the differences between the estimated current values of assets and the estimated current amounts of liabilities and their tax bases, a sum of $55,000.
   Answer (A) is incorrect because Shea must report estimated income taxes. Answer (B) is incorrect because $25,000 excludes the estimated income taxes on 1996 income earned to date. Answer (C) is incorrect because $30,000 excludes estimated income taxes for the differences between the estimated current values of assets and the estimated current amounts of liabilities and their tax bases.

9. On December 31, 1996, Shane is a fully vested participant in a company-sponsored pension plan. According to the plan's administrator, Shane has at that date the nonforfeitable right to receive a lump sum of $100,000 on December 28, 1997. The discounted amount of $100,000 is $90,000 at December 31, 1996. The right is not contingent on Shane's life expectancy and requires no future performance on Shane's part. In Shane's December 31, 1996 personal statement of financial condition, the vested interest in the pension plan should be reported at

A. $0

B. $90,000

C. $95,000

D. $100,000

The correct answer is (B). *(CPA 1188 I-59)*

REQUIRED: The amount at which the vested interest in a pension plan should be reported in a personal statement of financial condition.

DISCUSSION: SOP 82-1 requires that noncancelable rights to receive future sums be presented at their estimated current value as assets in personal financial statements if they (1) are for fixed or determinable amounts; (2) are not contingent on the holder's life expectancy or the occurrence of a particular event, such as disability or death; and (3) do not require the future performance of service by the holder. The fully vested rights in the company-sponsored pension plan therefore should be reported at their current value, which is equal to the $90,000 discounted amount.

Answer (A) is incorrect because the current value of the right should be reported. Answer (C) is incorrect because $95,000 is the average of the discounted and nondiscounted amounts. Answer (D) is incorrect because $100,000 is the undiscounted amount.

10. Ely had the following personal investments at December 31, 1996:

• Realty held as a limited business activity not conducted in a separate business entity. Mortgage payments were made with funds from sources unrelated to the realty. The cost of this realty was $500,000, and the related mortgage payable was $100,000 at December 31, 1996.

• Sole proprietorship marketable as a going concern. Its cost was $900,000, and it had related accounts payable of $80,000 at December 31, 1996.

The costs of both investments equal estimated current values. The balances of liabilities equal their estimated current amounts. How should the foregoing information be reported in Ely's statement of financial condition at December 31, 1996?

		Assets	Liabilities
A.	Investment in real estate	$400,000	
	Investment in sole proprietorship	820,000	
B.	Investment in real estate	$500,000	
	Investment in sole proprietorship	820,000	
	Mortgage payable		$100,000
C.	Investment in real estate	$500,000	
	Investment in sole proprietorship	900,000	
	Mortgage payable		$100,000
	Accounts payable		80,000
D.	Investments	$1,400,000	
	Accounts and mortgage payable		$180,000

The correct answer is (B). *(CPA 1191 II-14)*

REQUIRED: The reporting of personal investments.

DISCUSSION: For an investment in a limited business activity not conducted in a separate business entity (such as an investment in real estate and a related mortgage), SOP 82-1 requires that the assets and liabilities not be presented as a net amount. Instead, they should be presented as separate assets at their estimated current values and separate liabilities at their estimated current amounts. This presentation is particularly important if a large portion of the liabilities may be satisfied with funds from sources unrelated to the investments. SOP 82-1 requires that a business interest constituting a large part of an individual's total assets be presented in a personal statement of financial condition as a single amount equal to the estimated current value of the business interest. This investment should be disclosed separately from other investments if the entity is marketable as a going concern. Thus, the realty and the related mortgage should be presented as separate amounts at $500,000 and $100,000, respectively, and the sole proprietorship should be disclosed separately as a single amount equal to $820,000 ($900,000 – $80,000).

Answer (A) is incorrect because the realty and the related mortgage should be presented as separate amounts. Answer (C) is incorrect because the sole proprietorship should be disclosed separately as a single amount. Answer (D) is incorrect because the realty and the related mortgage should be presented as separate amounts, and the sole proprietorship should be disclosed separately as a single amount.

34.2 Prospective Financial Statements

The questions in this sideheading are based on the AICPA Guide for Prospective Financial Statements.
NOTE: References in the Guide to a statement of changes in financial position or to changes in financial position should be read in the light of the requirement of SFAS 95 that a complete set of the basic financial statements include a statement of cash flows.

11. Prospective financial information is any financial information about the future. Prospective financial information represents financial position, results of operations, and changes in cash flows. Prospective financial statements include which of the following?

A. Financial forecasts and pro forma financial statements.

B. Financial forecasts and financial projections.

C. Financial projections and pro forma financial statements.

D. Financial forecasts and partial presentations.

The correct answer is (B). *(Publisher)*
REQUIRED: The types of information defined as prospective financial statements.
DISCUSSION: Prospective financial statements consist of either financial forecasts or financial projections, including the summaries of significant assumptions and accounting policies. Financial forecasts are prospective financial statements that present, to the best of the responsible party's knowledge and belief, an entity's expected financial position, results of operations, and changes in cash flows. Financial projections are prospective financial statements that present, to the best of the responsible party's knowledge and belief given one or more hypothetical assumptions, an entity's expected financial position, results of operations, and changes in cash flows.
Answers (A) and (C) are incorrect because pro forma financial statements demonstrate the effect of a future or hypothetical transaction on financial statements of a past period as if the transaction had been consummated during the period covered by those statements. Thus, pro forma financial statements are not prospective. Answer (D) is incorrect because a partial presentation omits one or more items of financial data required of prospective financial statements.

12. Financial forecasts and financial projections preferably should be in the format of the historical financial statements that would be issued for the future period(s) covered if the responsible party and potential users do not have an agreement specifying another format. Financial forecasts and financial projections may take the form of complete basic financial statements or may be limited to a presentation of certain minimum items. Which of the following is not one of the minimum items?

A. Net income.

B. Discontinued operations or extraordinary items, if any.

C. Significant changes in cash flows.

D. Statement of financial position.

The correct answer is (D). *(Publisher)*
REQUIRED: The item not required in prospective financial statements.
DISCUSSION: Prospective financial statements may be limited to certain minimum items of financial data (when such items would be presented for historical financial statements for the period). These are (1) sales or gross revenue, (2) gross profit or cost of sales, (3) unusual or infrequently occurring items, (4) provision for income taxes, (5) discontinued operations or extraordinary items, (6) income from continuing operations, (7) net income, (8) primary and fully diluted earnings per share, and (9) significant changes in cash flows.
The following disclosures should also accompany prospective financial statements, whatever their form: (1) a description of what the responsible party intends the prospective financial statements to present, a statement that the assumptions are based on the responsible party's judgment at the time the prospective information was prepared, and a caveat that the prospective results may not be achieved; (2) a summary of significant assumptions; and (3) a summary of significant accounting policies.
Answers (A), (B), and (C) are incorrect because they are all required items when prospective financial statements are presented in a limited form.

13. The AICPA Guide for Prospective Financial Statements authorizes the use of prospective financial statements in certain instances. Which of the following best describes an authorized use?

   A.   Financial forecasts expressed as a single point estimate are appropriate for general use; financial forecasts expressed as a range are appropriate only for limited use.

   B.   Financial projections expressed as a single point estimate are appropriate for general use; financial projections expressed as a range are appropriate only for limited use.

   C.   Financial forecasts expressed as either a single point estimate or a range are appropriate only for limited use.

   D.   Financial forecasts expressed as either a single point estimate or a range are appropriate for general use.

The correct answer is (D). *(Publisher)*
   REQUIRED: The use(s) appropriate for financial forecasts or financial projections.
   DISCUSSION: Prospective financial statements are designated as for general use or limited use. General use refers to use by persons with whom the responsible party is not negotiating directly. Limited use refers to use by the responsible party alone or by the responsible party and third parties with whom the responsible party is negotiating directly. Financial forecasts expressed as either a single point estimate or a range are appropriate for either of these uses. A financial projection, however, expressed as either a single point estimate or a range, is appropriate only for limited use, unless the projection (1) is used to supplement a financial forecast and (2) is for a period also covered by the forecast.
   Answers (A) and (C) are incorrect because financial forecasts expressed as either a single point estimate or a range are appropriate for general use. Answer (B) is incorrect because a financial projection is appropriate for limited use only unless it supplements a financial forecast.

14. Certain items are basic to the entity's operations and serve as a foundation for prospective financial statements. Which is the best term for these significant matters?

   A.   Key factors.

   B.   Assumptions.

   C.   Hypothetical assumptions.

   D.   Responsible parties.

The correct answer is (A). *(Publisher)*
   REQUIRED: The term for the items basic to an entity's operations.
   DISCUSSION: Key factors are the significant matters on which an entity's future results are expected to depend, i.e., the basis for the assumptions underlying the prospective financial statements. They encompass matters affecting the entity's sales, service, production, and financing activities.
   Answer (B) is incorrect because an assumption reflects conditions the responsible party expects to exist in the future. Answer (C) is incorrect because a hypothetical assumption represents a condition or course of action that is not necessarily expected to occur but is consistent with the purpose of a projection. Answer (D) is incorrect because it refers to the person(s) (usually management) responsible for establishing the assumptions underlying the prospective financial statements.

15. Which of the following statements best describes the use of appropriate accounting principles in the preparation of prospective financial statements?

   A.   The accounting principles used in prospective financial statements should always be the same as those used in the historical financial statements.

   B.   Accounting changes should be reflected in financial projections only if the responsible party expects to make the change in the historical statements for that period.

   C.   A basis of accounting used in prospective financial statements may differ from that used in the historical financial statements.

   D.   Accounting changes reflected in prospective financial statements should be recorded as a cumulative-effect type of change.

The correct answer is (C). *(Publisher)*
   REQUIRED: The statement that best describes the appropriate use of accounting principles in prospective financial statements.
   DISCUSSION: Occasionally, a basis of accounting used in a financial forecast or financial projection may differ from that used in the historical financial statements for that period; e.g., a cash-basis statement may be prepared rather than an accrual-basis statement. When a different basis of accounting is used, it should be reconciled to results that would be obtained using the basis of accounting found in the historical financial statements.
   Answer (A) is incorrect because a different basis of accounting may occasionally be used. Answer (B) is incorrect because an accounting change may be reflected in a financial projection for analytical purposes, even if there is no intention of actually changing the method of accounting. Answer (D) is incorrect because accounting changes reflected in prospective financial statements should be reflected on the same basis as in historical financial statements, which may or may not be cumulative.

16. In a financial forecast, the disclosures concerning the assumptions underlying the forecast ordinarily should include all except

- A. Assumptions for which there is a reasonable possibility of the occurrence of a variation that may significantly affect the forecasted results.

- B. Assumptions about anticipated conditions that are expected to be significantly different from current conditions that are not otherwise reasonably apparent.

- C. Assumptions implicit in the forecast that have enormous potential impact on the forecast, such as conditions of peace, absence of natural disasters, etc.

- D. Other matters deemed important to the forecast or to its interpretation.

The correct answer is (C). *(Publisher)*
REQUIRED: The assumptions not requiring disclosure in a financial forecast.
DISCUSSION: Assumptions are considered by the AICPA Guide for Prospective Financial Statements to be the single most important ingredient of a financial forecast and, at a minimum, should include the assumptions described in answers (A), (B), and (D). Basic assumptions, implicit in a forecast, that have enormous potential impact, such as conditions of peace, absence of natural disasters, and the like, need be disclosed only when there is a reasonable probability that the current conditions will not prevail.
Answers (A), (B), and (D) are incorrect because each should be included as a disclosure.

34.3 Futures Contracts

17. A change in the market value of a futures contract is recognized in income in the period in which the change takes place if the contract qualifies as a hedge of

- A. An existing asset.

- B. A firm commitment.

- C. An asset that is reported at fair value.

- D. An existing liability.

The correct answer is (C). *(Publisher)*
REQUIRED: The circumstance in which a change in the market value of a futures contract is recognized in income.
DISCUSSION: SFAS 80, *Accounting for Futures Contracts*, requires that a change in the market value of a futures contract be recognized in income in the period in which the change occurs if the contract either does not qualify as a hedge of an existing asset, liability, or firm commitment, or does qualify as a hedge of an item reported at fair value.
Answers (A) and (D) are incorrect because the change is recognized as an adjustment of the carrying value of the account. Answer (B) is incorrect because the change is included in the measurement of the transaction that satisfies the commitment.

18. On December 1, 1995, the Merlin Corporation purchased ten March 1996 futures contracts at $3.00 per bushel in a transaction that qualified as a hedge of its anticipated need for 50,000 bushels of grain at the beginning of March 1996. Each contract is for 5,000 bushels. The market price per bushel is $2.90 at year-end, $2.95 on February 1, 1996, and $3.05 on March 1, 1996, when 50,000 bushels of grain were purchased. At what amount should the March 1, 1996 purchase be recorded?

- A. $150,000 if the futures contracts qualify as a hedge.

- B. $150,000 if the futures contracts do not qualify as a hedge.

- C. $152,500 if the futures contracts qualify as a hedge.

- D. $152,500 whether or not the futures contracts qualify as a hedge.

The correct answer is (A). *(Publisher)*
REQUIRED: The amount at which the purchase should be recorded.
DISCUSSION: A futures contract qualifies as a hedge if the item to be hedged exposes the enterprise to price or interest rate risk and if the contract reduces that risk and is designated as a hedge. SFAS 80 requires that a change in the market value of a futures contract that qualifies as a hedge of a firm commitment be included in the measurement of the transaction that satisfies the commitment. Similar treatment may also be accorded to a futures contract hedging a transaction that an enterprise expects, but is not obligated, to carry out. This treatment is appropriate if it is probable that the anticipated transaction will occur and its significant characteristics and expected terms are identified. Thus, the net change in the market value of the futures contracts of $2,500 [50,000 bushels x ($3.00 – $3.05)] reduces the purchase price of the grain from $152,500 to $150,000.
Answer (B) is incorrect because, if the futures contracts do not qualify as a hedge, Merlin should record the purchase on March 1, 1996 at $152,500 ($3.05 x 50,000 bushels). Answers (C) and (D) are incorrect because the purchase is recorded at $150,000 if the futures contracts qualify as a hedge.

34.4 Regulated Industries

19. Which of the following is a true statement about enterprises with regulated operations to which SFAS 71, *Accounting for the Effects of Certain Types of Regulation*, applies?

A. Profit on sales to regulated affiliates normally should be eliminated in general purpose financial statements.

B. In all circumstances, the amount of interest that should be capitalized on a construction project should be calculated in accordance with SFAS 34, *Capitalization of Interest Cost*.

C. Refunds to customers required by a regulator should be recorded as liabilities only in the period in which they must be refunded.

D. Rate actions of a regulator may result in the required capitalization of an incurred cost that would be charged to expense by a nonregulated enterprise.

The correct answer is (D). *(Publisher)*
REQUIRED: The true statement about the required accounting for an enterprise with regulated operations to which SFAS 71 applies.
DISCUSSION: If rate actions of a regulator are such that reasonable assurance is provided of the existence of an asset, an enterprise subject to the provisions of SFAS 71 should capitalize the cost incurred even though a nonregulated enterprise normally would charge it to expense.
Answer (A) is incorrect because profit on sales to regulated affiliates should not be eliminated if the sales price is reasonable and if it is probable that, through the rate-making process, future revenues approximately equal to the sales price will result from the use of the products by the regulated affiliates. Answer (B) is incorrect because SFAS 34 does not apply when a regulator requires the capitalization of financing costs on a construction project that is financed partially by borrowings and partially by equity. Answer (C) is incorrect because, if a regulator requires refunds to customers, a liability should be recorded when it is both probable and reasonably estimable.

20. The basic question addressed by SFAS 71 is whether accounting prescribed by regulatory authorities should be considered in and of itself generally accepted for purposes of financial reporting by rate-regulated enterprises. Which of the following statements best describes the authoritative position taken relative to this basic issue?

A. Accounting prescribed by regulatory authorities in and of itself is considered generally accepted for purposes of financial reporting by rate-regulated enterprises.

B. GAAP as currently prescribed for nonrate-regulated enterprises are equally appropriate for rate-regulated enterprises.

C. Certain differences should exist between the application of GAAP as currently prescribed for nonrate-regulated enterprises and rate-regulated enterprises.

D. GAAP as currently prescribed for nonrate-regulated enterprises are not applicable to rate-regulated enterprises.

The correct answer is (C). *(Publisher)*
REQUIRED: The authoritative position on the application of GAAP to rate-regulated enterprises.
DISCUSSION: SFAS 71 states that accounting prescribed by regulatory agencies should not be considered generally accepted in and of itself. The board concluded that differences should exist between the application of generally accepted accounting principles as currently prescribed for nonrate-regulated enterprises and rate-regulated enterprises. Thus, SFAS 71 applies GAAP in the regulatory environment.
Answer (A) is incorrect because SFAS 71 states that accounting prescribed by regulatory agencies should not be considered GAAP in and of itself. Answer (B) is incorrect because GAAP for nonrate-regulated enterprises are not always appropriate for rate-regulated enterprises. Answer (D) is incorrect because GAAP, as currently presented for nonrate-regulated enterprises, are appropriate for rate-regulated enterprises under many circumstances.

21. SFAS 71 is applicable to the general purpose external financial statements of an enterprise with regulated operations that meet certain specified criteria. Which of the following is not one of the criteria that must be met?

A. The enterprise's rates for regulated services or products are established by, or are subject to, approval by an independent third-party regulator.

B. The enterprise's rates for regulated services or products are established by, or are subject to, a contractual arrangement with a governmental agency.

C. The regulated rates are designed to recover the specific enterprise's costs of providing the regulated services or products.

D. Reasonable assurance must exist that the regulated environment and its economic effect will continue to exist.

The correct answer is (B). *(Publisher)*
REQUIRED: The criterion not required to be met for SFAS 71 to be applicable.
DISCUSSION: SFAS 71 requires the existence of an independent third-party regulator. This criterion is intended to exclude contractual arrangements in which the government or another party that could be viewed as the regulator is a party to a contract and is the principal customer of the enterprise. If an enterprise's regulated operations cease meeting these criteria for any reason, SFAS 101, *Regulated Enterprises--Accounting for the Discontinuation of Application of FASB Statement No. 71*, requires that the enterprise discontinue the application of SFAS 71.
Answers (A), (C), and (D) are incorrect because each is one of the three criteria that must be met for SFAS 71 to be applicable to the operations of the enterprise.

22. A major difference between nonregulated and regulated enterprises is the ability of a regulatory action to create a future economic benefit that in substance is an asset. Which of the following actions relative to the rate-making process results in the creation of a future economic benefit that should be recognized as an asset by a regulated entity?

A. A regulator provides current rates intended to recover costs that are expected to be incurred in the future, with the understanding that, if the costs are not incurred, future rates will be reduced.

B. A regulator requires that a gain or other reduction of net allowable costs be passed on to customers over future periods.

C. A regulator allows future rates to be increased by the amount of the excess cost of reacquired debt over the debt's net carrying value.

D. A regulator allows a regulated enterprise to bill for requested rate increases before the regulator has ruled on the request.

The correct answer is (C). *(Publisher)*
REQUIRED: The action by a regulator that results in the recognition of an asset through the creation of a future economic benefit.
DISCUSSION: If debt is reacquired for an amount in excess of its net carrying value and the regulator allows an increase in future rates to provide for this difference, reasonable assurance is considered to have been given of the existence of a future economic benefit that should be recognized as an asset.
Answers (A), (B), and (D) are incorrect because the regulator's action in each instance would give rise to the creation and recognition of a liability under SFAS 71, not a benefit.

23. Plumblee Electric has reached a decision to discontinue construction on a partially completed generating plant. Based on previous action by the rate-making board, Plumblee believes that recovery of certain of the construction costs incurred plus a full return on investment for these costs will be allowed. Based on this information, Plumblee should

A. Write off the construction costs incurred immediately.

B. Amortize the construction costs incurred over the normal recovery period.

C. Write down the construction costs incurred to an amount equal to the allowable costs.

D. Write down the construction costs incurred to the present value of the future revenues expected to be provided.

The correct answer is (C). *(Publisher)*
REQUIRED: The accounting for a plant abandonment by a regulated enterprise.
DISCUSSION: SFAS 90, *Regulated Enterprises - Accounting for Abandonments and Disallowances of Plant Costs*, states that when it becomes probable that an operating asset, or an asset under construction, will be abandoned, its cost shall be removed from construction work-in-process or plant-in-service. Any disallowance of all or part of the cost of the abandoned plant that is probable and reasonably estimable shall be recognized as a loss. If a full return on investment is likely to be provided by the regulator, the carrying basis of the recorded asset shall be similarly reduced, and the remainder of the cost shall be reported as a separate new asset. The amount of the allowable cost shall then be amortized in the same manner as that used for rate-making purposes.
Answer (A) is incorrect because an immediate write-off is not appropriate. Answer (B) is incorrect because only the allowable construction costs should be amortized over the normal recovery period. Answer (D) is incorrect because a write-down of the construction costs incurred to the present value of the future revenues expected to be provided is appropriate when a partial return or no return on investment is likely to be provided.

24. When a utility completes a new plant, conventional rate-making procedures usually establish rates to provide recovery of the current operating costs of the plant, depreciation, interest, and shareholder earnings on the investment. However, if regulatory agencies defer recovery of part of these costs because of the significantly increased cost of the new plant, the deferred cost to be recovered under a phase-in plan can be capitalized if certain specified criteria are met. For plants that were completed, or on which substantial physical construction was performed, before January 1, 1988, which of the following criteria must be met before all allowable costs deferred for future recovery may be capitalized for financial reporting?

A. It is probable that the regulator will agree to the plan.

B. The plan specifies the timing of recovery of all deferred allowable costs.

C. All allowable costs deferred under the plan are scheduled for recovery within 40 years.

D. The percentage increase in rates under the plan is the same for each future year.

The correct answer is (B). *(Publisher)*
REQUIRED: The criterion used to determine whether capitalization is appropriate.
DISCUSSION: According to SFAS 92, *Regulated Enterprises - Accounting for Phase-in Plans*, if a phase-in plan is ordered by a regulatory body in connection with a plant that either was completed before January 1, 1988 or on which substantial physical construction was performed before that date, certain criteria must be met before all allowable costs deferred by the regulator under the phase-in plan may be capitalized for financial reporting as a separate asset. One of the criteria is that the plan must specify the timing of recovery of all allowable costs that will be deferred.
Answer (A) is incorrect because the regulator must have agreed to the plan. Answer (C) is incorrect because the recovery period must be within 10 years of the date when deferrals begin. Answer (D) is incorrect because the percentage increase in rates scheduled under the plan for each future year may not be greater than the percentage increase scheduled for each immediately preceding year.

34.5 Oil and Gas

25. An oil company using the successful-efforts method drilled two wells. The first, a dry hole, cost $50,000. The second cost $100,000 and had estimated recoverable reserves of 25,000 barrels, of which 10,000 were sold this year. What will be the total expense for the year related to the exploration and production from these two wells?

A. $40,000

B. $60,000

C. $90,000

D. $150,000

The correct answer is (C). *(CIA 592 IV-37)*

REQUIRED: The total expense for the year related to the exploration and production from these two wells using the successful-efforts method.

DISCUSSION: Under the successful-efforts method, exploration costs are capitalized and subsequently amortized for the cost of finding recoverable oil and gas. This method expenses costs of unsuccessful efforts in the year incurred. The alternative is the full-cost method, under which all of the costs of acquiring, exploring, and developing oil and gas properties in very large geographical areas are capitalized and subsequently amortized, whether the costs are related to successful or unsuccessful projects. The successful-efforts method capitalizes the $100,000 cost of the second well, expenses the $50,000 cost of the first well, and amortizes an amount of the capitalized cost of the second well that is proportionate to the oil produced. Amortization for the year equals $40,000 [$100,000 capitalized cost x (10,000 barrels sold ÷ 25,000 barrels of resources)]. Consequently, the total expense is $90,000 ($50,000 + $40,000).

Answer (A) is incorrect because $40,000 is amortization for the year. Answer (B) is incorrect because $60,000 is based on the full-cost method [(10,000 ÷ 25,000) x ($100,000 + $50,000)]. Answer (D) is incorrect because $150,000 equals the cost of both wells.

26. An oil company has acquired the right to use 2,000 acres of land to explore for oil. The lease cost is $50,000; the related exploration costs for a discovered oil deposit on the property are $200,000; and intangible development costs in erecting and drilling the well are $750,000. It is estimated that the well will provide approximately 1,000,000 barrels of oil. If 200,000 barrels are withdrawn and sold in the first year, and the successful-efforts approach is used, the amount to be reported for depletion for that first year is

A. $50,000

B. $150,000

C. $200,000

D. $1,000,000

The correct answer is (C). *(CPA 1192 IV-34)*

REQUIRED: The amount to be reported for depletion for the first year under the successful-efforts method.

DISCUSSION: Under the successful-efforts method, exploration costs are capitalized and subsequently amortized for the cost of finding recoverable oil and gas. This method expenses costs of unsuccessful efforts in the year incurred. The alternative is the full-cost method, under which all of the costs of acquiring, exploring, and developing oil and gas properties in very large geographical areas are capitalized and subsequently amortized, whether the costs are related to successful or unsuccessful projects. The costs of natural resources include (1) acquisition cost of the deposit, (2) exploration costs, and (3) development costs. These costs are spread evenly over the estimated recoverable units in the deposit to calculate the estimated cost of the units removed from the well during the period. The depletion cost for the first year is $1,000,000 ($50,000 + $200,000 + $750,000). Thus, unit depletion cost is $1 ($1,000,000 ÷ 1,000,000 barrels), and total depletion for the first year is $200,000 ($1 x 200,000 barrels).

Answer (A) is incorrect because $50,000 omits the $750,000 intangible development costs from the depletion base. Answer (B) is incorrect because $150,000 omits the $50,000 cost of the lease and the $200,000 related exploration costs from the depletion base. Answer (D) is incorrect because $1,000,000 is based on the assumption that all costs are expensed immediately.

27. SFAS 19, *Financial Accounting and Reporting by Oil and Gas Producing Companies*, required the successful-efforts method of accounting. SFAS 25, *Suspension of Certain Accounting Requirements for Oil and Gas Producing Companies*, amended SFAS 19 to permit the full-cost accounting method as well as the successful-efforts method. Why was SFAS 25 issued?

A. The oil and gas industry refused to abide by SFAS 19.

B. The SEC indicated its continued acceptance of the full-cost method.

C. Political pressures from the oil and gas industry forced the FASB to reverse its position.

D. Congress threatened legislation to permit continued use of full costing.

The correct answer is (B). *(Publisher)*
REQUIRED: The reason SFAS 25 was issued to amend SFAS 19.
DISCUSSION: Prior to SFAS 19, both the full-cost and successful-efforts methods were acceptable ways to account for the exploration and development activities of oil- and gas-producing companies. SFAS 19 indicated that only the successful-efforts method was acceptable. SFAS 25 reinstated full cost because the SEC manifested its continued acceptance of this method through Accounting Series Release 253.
Answers (A), (C), and (D) are incorrect because the SEC's action forced the FASB to issue SFAS 25, although answers (A), (C), and (D) contributed to the SEC's decision.

28. SFAS 69, *Disclosures about Oil and Gas Producing Activities*, requires publicly traded companies with significant oil and gas activities to disclose certain supplemental information in complete sets of annual financial statements. The disclosures include

A. Proved oil and gas reserve quantities and standardized measure of discounted future net cash flows relating to them.

B. Capitalized costs relating to oil- and gas-producing activities and costs incurred in oil and gas property acquisition, exploration, and development activities.

C. Results of operations for oil- and gas-producing activities.

D. All of the answers are correct.

The correct answer is (D). *(Publisher)*
REQUIRED: The disclosure(s) required by SFAS 69 regarding oil and gas activities.
DISCUSSION: Each of the listed disclosures is required by SFAS 69. Most important to SFAS 69 is the requirement of disclosure of a standardized measure of discounted future net cash flows relating to proved oil and gas quantities. This disclosure reflects the value-based approach that the SEC encouraged the FASB to develop.
Answers (A), (B), and (C) are incorrect because SFAS 69 requires disclosures about proved reserves, capitalized costs, and results of operations.

29. According to SFAS 69, the standard measure of discounted future net cash flows relating to proved oil and gas reserve quantities should include consideration of which of the following?

A. Future cash inflows based on year-end prices applied to the proved year-end reserves.

B. Development and production costs based on year-end costs.

C. Future income tax based on applying year-end statutory tax rates.

D. All of the answers are correct.

The correct answer is (D). *(Publisher)*
REQUIRED: The factor(s) included in the determination of discounted future net cash flows of oil and gas reserves.
DISCUSSION: SFAS 69 requires disclosure of a standardized measure of discounted future net cash flows relating to an enterprise's interests in both proved oil and gas reserves and oil and gas subject to purchase under long-term supply agreements and contracts for oil- and gas-producing properties. Each of the factors listed in (A) through (C) should be considered. Additionally, the future cash flows should be discounted at 10% per year.
Answers (A), (B), and (C) are incorrect because the factors included in determining discounted future net cash flows of oil and gas reserves include future cash inflows, development and production costs, and future taxes.

30. SFAS 69 requires publicly traded companies to have significant oil- and gas-producing activities before the disclosure requirements come into effect. Activity is significant if

A. Revenue from oil- and gas-producing activities related to unaffiliated customers and internal operations is 25% of total sales to unaffiliated customers and internal operations.

B. Revenue from oil- and gas-producing activities related to unaffiliated customers and internal operations is 20% of total sales to unaffiliated customers and internal operations.

C. The amount of revenue, operating results, or identifiable assets meets the criteria for a segment established in SFAS 14, *Financial Reporting for Segments of a Business Enterprise*.

D. Revenue, current or prospective, is of probable interest to financial statement users as defined by management.

The correct answer is (C). *(Publisher)*

REQUIRED: The definition of significant oil- and gas-producing activities in SFAS 69.

DISCUSSION: Under SFAS 69, oil- and gas-producing activities are considered significant if, in general, the activities satisfy the criteria in SFAS 14 that define a reportable industry segment.

Answers (A) and (B) are incorrect because the criteria include operating results and identifiable assets, as well as revenue. Also, the amounts must be at or above the 10% level rather than 20% or 25%. Answer (D) is incorrect because the decision is not left to management but is based on the relative level of oil- and gas-producing revenue, operating results, or identifiable assets.

31. FASB Interpretation No. 36, *Accounting for Exploratory Wells in Progress at the End of a Period*, provides a clarification of SFAS 19's requirement that the costs of exploratory wells that do not locate proved oil and gas reserves be charged to expense. Which of the following statements reflects the proper accounting treatment?

A. The costs incurred for exploratory wells in progress at the end of the reporting period should be expensed unless it is probable at the end of the reporting period that proved reserves will be discovered.

B. The cost of all exploratory wells in progress at the end of the period should be expensed.

C. The costs of all exploratory wells in progress at the end of the year should be deferred.

D. The costs of exploratory wells in progress at the end of the period that are completed without finding proved reserves before the financial statements are issued should be expensed in the period for which the statements are issued.

The correct answer is (D). *(Publisher)*

REQUIRED: The proper accounting for exploratory wells in progress at year-end.

DISCUSSION: FASB Interpretation No. 36 states that the costs of exploratory wells in progress at year-end should be expensed if the wells are determined to be unsuccessful (i.e., determined not to have proved reserves) before the financial statements for that period are issued.

Answer (A) is incorrect because it cannot be deemed probable that proved reserves exist until they are located. Answer (B) is incorrect because the cost of exploratory wells may be deferred under the full-cost approach if they are successful, i.e., when proved reserves have been found. Answer (C) is incorrect because the costs of exploratory wells should be expensed in the period for which the statements are issued if the wells have been completed without locating proved reserves prior to the issuance of the statements.

32. SFAS 19 and SFAS 25 define proved, proved developed, and proved undeveloped oil and gas reserves. Proved oil and gas reserves are defined as quantities of oil and gas

A. Expected to be recovered from new wells on undrilled acreage or from existing wells when a relatively major expenditure is required for completion.

B. Expected to be recoverable in future years from known reservoirs under existing economic and operating conditions.

C. In a single reservoir or multiple reservoirs grouped or related to the same geological condition.

D. Expected to be recovered through existing wells developed with existing equipment and operating methods, including those available under improved recovery techniques.

The correct answer is (B). *(Publisher)*
REQUIRED: The definition of proved oil and gas reserves.
DISCUSSION: Proved reserves are those expected to be recoverable in future years from known reservoirs under existing economic and operating conditions.
Answer (A) is incorrect because it defines proved undeveloped reserves. Answer (C) is incorrect because it defines a field. Answer (D) is incorrect because it defines proved developed reserves.

34.6 Record and Music Industry, Cable TV, Motion Pictures, and Broadcasters

33. SFAS 50, *Financial Reporting in the Record and Music Industry*, establishes standards of financial reporting for licensors and licensees. A licensor may recognize income when

A. The licensor has delivered the usable rights to the licensee and collectibility of the license fee is reasonably assured.

B. Payment of the licensing fee by the licensee is guaranteed by a third party.

C. The licensor has delivered the usable rights to the licensee and has no remaining significant obligations pursuant to a noncancelable contract, and collection is reasonably assured.

D. A minimum guarantee is paid in advance.

The correct answer is (C). *(Publisher)*
REQUIRED: The requirement(s) for recognition of income by the licensor of record and music masters and copyrights.
DISCUSSION: A licensing agreement may, in substance, be an outright sale. A licensor may recognize income if the licensor has signed a noncancelable contract, has agreed to a fixed fee, and has delivered the rights to the licensee with the right to use them; if no significant obligations remain; and if collection is reasonably assured. The earning process is then complete.
Answer (A) is incorrect because, in addition, the licensor must have signed a noncancelable contract and have no remaining significant obligations. Answer (B) is incorrect because there is no third-party guarantee requirement, and assurance of collection does not mean the earning process is complete. Answer (D) is incorrect because minimum guarantees that are received in advance should be recorded initially as a liability and recognized as revenue when the license fee is earned under the agreement.

34. According to SFAS 50, the licensee accounts for minimum guarantees paid in advance as

A. Expense in the year paid.

B. An asset and charged to expense in accord with the license agreement.

C. An asset if the record master is estimated to be profitable in the future based upon the performer's past performance and current popularity.

D. An advance royalty to the artist if it is probable that the advance will be recoverable from future royalties earned by the artist.

The correct answer is (B). *(Publisher)*
REQUIRED: The accounting by licensees of record and music copyrights for advance payments to licensors.
DISCUSSION: Advance payments by a licensee to a licensor should be capitalized as an asset and charged to expense according to the terms of the license agreement, unless all or a portion of the guarantee appears nonrecoverable. In that event, the amount should be expensed.
Answer (A) is incorrect because the advance payment is usually deferred as an asset and amortized. Answer (C) is incorrect because it describes the accounting for record masters by the licensor, not minimum guarantees by the licensee. Answer (D) is incorrect because it states the proper accounting by licensors for advance royalties paid to artists.

35. SFAS 51, *Financial Reporting by Cable Television Companies*, prescribes accounting by cable TV companies during the prematurity period. This period begins with the first subscriber revenue and ends when a predetermined subscriber level is reached, when no additional investment for the cable TV plant is required, or when the first major construction period is completed. During the prematurity period,

A. Costs of cable television plant, including materials, direct labor, and construction overhead, are capitalized.

B. Subscriber-related costs and general administrative expenses should be capitalized.

C. Programming costs and other system costs should be capitalized in full.

D. Depreciation should not be recognized.

The correct answer is (A). *(Publisher)*

REQUIRED: The accounting procedure applicable to the prematurity period of a cable TV company.

DISCUSSION: During the prematurity period, SFAS 51 requires that the cost of the cable television plant, including materials, direct labor, and overhead, be capitalized in full.

Answer (B) is incorrect because subscriber-related costs and general administrative expenses should be expensed during, as well as after, the prematurity period. Answers (C) and (D) are incorrect because programming and other system costs and depreciation are expensed according to the relationship of the current level of subscription revenue to the amount expected at the end of the prematurity stage.

36. According to SFAS 51, the initial hookup revenue of cable television companies should be

A. Deferred and amortized to income over the estimated average period that subscribers are expected to remain connected to the system.

B. Recognized as revenue immediately to the extent direct selling costs are incurred, with the remainder deferred and amortized.

C. Recognized as revenue upon receipt.

D. Recognized as revenue systematically and rationally over a period of not less than 5 and not more than 10 years.

The correct answer is (B). *(Publisher)*

REQUIRED: The proper accounting for cable television company initial hookup revenue.

DISCUSSION: Initial hookup revenue is recognized as revenue to the extent that direct selling costs are incurred. Direct selling costs include commissions, salespersons' compensation, local advertising, document processing, etc. Any remaining initial hookup revenue should be deferred and amortized over the estimated average period that subscribers are expected to remain connected to the system.

Answer (A) is incorrect because all or part of hookup revenue is used to offset direct selling costs. Answers (C) and (D) are incorrect because hookup revenue is deferred and amortized to the extent it exceeds direct selling costs.

37. Initial subscriber installation costs for cable television service, including materials, labor, and overhead, should be

A. Expensed as incurred.

B. Expensed in the periods that initial hookup revenue is recognized.

C. Capitalized and depreciated.

D. Capitalized and expensed at the point that reconnection fees are earned.

The correct answer is (C). *(Publisher)*

REQUIRED: The accounting for initial subscriber installation costs.

DISCUSSION: Initial subscriber installation costs should be capitalized and depreciated over a period not to exceed the expected useful life of the cable TV plant. The costs of subsequent disconnecting and reconnecting are expensed as incurred.

Answer (A) is incorrect because initial installation costs are capitalized. Answers (B) and (D) are incorrect because capitalization and depreciation are required.

38. SFAS 53, *Financial Reporting by Producers and Distributors of Motion Picture Films*, sets forth the criteria to recognize revenues and expenses of producers and distributors of motion picture films. Revenues should be recognized

- A. On the dates of exhibition for percentage and flat-fee engagements.

- B. When an agreement has been reached and nonrefundable guarantees have been received.

- C. When the license fee of each film is known, the cost of each film is known or determinable, and the collectibility of the full license fee is reasonably assured.

- D. When the film has been accepted by the licensee and is ready for showing.

The correct answer is (A). *(Publisher)*
REQUIRED: The timing of revenue recognition by motion picture producers and distributors.
DISCUSSION: Motion picture distribution rights are usually licensed to movie theaters for a percentage of box office receipts or for a flat fee. The revenue is earned and should be recognized as the movies are exhibited.

Answer (B) is incorrect because, when nonrefundable guarantees are prepaid, the licensor should record them as deferred revenue and recognize them on the dates of exhibition. Answers (C) and (D) are incorrect because each is incomplete. Together, they define when revenue recognition should occur for the sale of rights relative to films licensed to television.

39. For films licensed to television, SFAS 53 recognizes revenue from a licensing agreement when

- A. The license fee for each film is known and its cost is known or reasonably determinable.

- B. The collectibility of the full license fee is reasonably assured.

- C. The film has been accepted by the licensee and is available for a first showing or telecast.

- D. All of the answers are correct.

The correct answer is (D). *(Publisher)*
REQUIRED: The timing of revenue recognition for film licensing agreements with television.
DISCUSSION: Licensing revenue should be recognized by a licensor when the license period begins and all of the criteria in (A) through (C) have been met. The earning process is then complete.

Answers (A), (B), and (C) are incorrect because the criteria for recognition of licensing revenue include knowledge of the fee per film and the cost, reasonable assurance of collectibility, acceptance of the film by the licensee, and its availability for its first use.

40. According to SFAS 53, the costs to produce a film are

- A. Expensed as incurred.

- B. Capitalized and amortized over a period not to exceed 5 years.

- C. Capitalized and amortized so that gross revenues from a single film yield a constant rate of gross profit.

- D. Capitalized and expensed in the period revenue is first recognized from licensing the film to movie theaters or television.

The correct answer is (C). *(Publisher)*
REQUIRED: The proper treatment of film production costs.
DISCUSSION: Film production costs should be capitalized and amortized in accordance with the individual-film-forecast-computation method. This method amortizes a film's cost in the ratio of gross revenues to anticipated gross revenues. Thus, the gross revenues from the single film yield a constant rate of gross profit. Amortization should begin when the film is released.

Answers (A) and (D) are incorrect because the films are amortized over their expected revenue-generating life rather than expensed in any one period. Answer (B) is incorrect because the amount of amortization in any period should be in proportion to the gross revenue received in that period.

41. Exploitation costs to promote films are frequently incurred during the final production phase and during the release periods of films in both primary and secondary markets. They include costs of film prints, advertising expense, rents, salaries, and other distribution expenses. Exploitation costs should be

- A. Expensed as incurred.
- B. Capitalized if they clearly benefit future periods.
- C. Capitalized only if they are going to be reimbursed.
- D. Capitalized for local advertising but expensed for national advertising.

The correct answer is (B). *(Publisher)*
REQUIRED: The proper accounting for exploitation costs incurred by producers of films.
DISCUSSION: Exploitation costs are advertising costs that may be capitalized if they clearly benefit future periods. They should be amortized in the same manner as film production costs, as discussed in the explanation to the previous question.
Answer (A) is incorrect because exploitation costs should be expensed as incurred only if they do not clearly benefit future periods or if they benefit only local areas. Answer (C) is incorrect because movie producers are not reimbursed for advertising expense. Answer (D) is incorrect because exploitation costs are normally capitalized when incurred on a national basis and expensed when incurred for a local market.

42. Broadcasters frequently barter unsold advertising time for products or services. According to SFAS 63, *Financial Reporting by Broadcasters*, barter revenue should be recognized when

- A. The barter agreement is signed.
- B. The commercials are broadcast.
- C. The merchandise or services are received or used.
- D. An enforceable contract is entered into to sell the products or services.

The correct answer is (B). *(Publisher)*
REQUIRED: The timing of recognition by broadcasters of barter revenue.
DISCUSSION: Barter revenue should be recognized in appropriate amounts when the commercials are broadcast. The amounts should be reported at the estimated fair value of the product or service received in accordance with APB 29, *Accounting for Nonmonetary Transactions*.
Answer (A) is incorrect because the revenue has not been earned until the commercials are broadcast. Answer (C) is incorrect because an asset should be recognized if the commercials are broadcast before the merchandise or services are received. A liability should be recognized if the merchandise or services are received before the commercials are broadcast. Answer (D) is incorrect because the merchandise or services need not be resold for revenue to be recognized.

43. When a broadcaster enters into a license agreement for program material, the broadcaster should report

- A. An asset and a liability for the rights acquired and obligations incurred when the agreement is reached.
- B. An asset and a liability when the cost of each program is known or determinable, the program material has been accepted, and the program is available for viewing or telecast.
- C. The related assets and liability as current if the license period expires within 1 year and as noncurrent if the license period expires in more than 1 year.
- D. An asset and a liability but only for the present value of future payments in accordance with the procedures set forth in APB 21.

The correct answer is (B). *(Publisher)*
REQUIRED: The proper accounting by the broadcaster for a license agreement for program material.
DISCUSSION: Broadcasters (licensees) should report the rights acquired and obligations incurred under a license agreement when the license period begins and when

1. The cost of each program is known or determinable.
2. The program material has been accepted by the licensee.
3. The program is available for viewing or telecast.

Answer (A) is incorrect because the license period must have begun and the three criteria specified in SFAS 63 must be met. Answer (C) is incorrect because the asset should be allocated in the balance sheet between current and noncurrent based on the time of usage, and the liability should be allocated between current and noncurrent based on payment terms. Answer (D) is incorrect because SFAS 63 permits the asset and liability to be valued at either the present value or the gross amount of the liability.

44. Network affiliation agreements of a broadcaster should be reported as

A. Intangible assets.

B. Expenses when incurred.

C. Deferred charges in shareholders' equity.

D. Deferred network program advertising.

The correct answer is (A). *(Publisher)*
REQUIRED: The reporting of network affiliation agreements in the financial statements of a broadcaster.
DISCUSSION: Network affiliation agreements are intangible assets that should be accounted for in accordance with APB 17, *Intangible Assets*.
Answer (B) is incorrect because intangible assets must be amortized rather than expensed when incurred. Answer (C) is incorrect because intangible assets are an asset rather than a contra shareholders' equity item. Answer (D) is incorrect because it is a nonsense term.

34.7 Investment Companies, Municipal Bond Funds, Insurance Enterprises, Title Plants, Mortgage Bankers

45. SOP 77-1, *Financial Accounting and Reporting by Investment Companies*, reaffirms that investment companies should report their securities portfolios at fair value. In the case of short-term investment (money market) instruments, market value is usually approximated by valuing the short-term instruments at which of the following?

A. Original cost plus amortized discount or accrued interest.

B. Quoted sales prices.

C. Bid and asked prices.

D. Appraisals by market makers.

The correct answer is (A). *(Publisher)*
REQUIRED: The method used to approximate fair value for money market instruments that mature within a short time.
DISCUSSION: The original cost of short-term money market instruments plus amortized discount or accrued interest is normally used to approximate fair value. In the case of unusual events such as the impairment of the credit standing of the issuer or changes in interest rates, cost plus amortized discount or accrued interest might not approximate the value of the short-term money market instruments.
Answers (B), (C), and (D) are incorrect because, in unusual cases, the investments should be valued on the basis of quoted sales prices, bid and asked prices, or fair value based on appraisals furnished by market makers.

46. SOP 79-1, *Accounting for Municipal Bond Funds*, amends the AICPA Industry Audit Guide, *Audits of Investment Companies*, to include consideration of tax-exempt municipal bond funds. A tax-exempt municipal bond fund invests principally in debt instruments that are obligations of local governments the interest on which is exempt from federal income tax. Of the following instruments issued by a local government for which the interest is tax-exempt, which one is not usually classified as a municipal bond?

A. Revenue bond.

B. General obligation bond.

C. Industrial development bond.

D. Tax anticipation note.

The correct answer is (D). *(Publisher)*
REQUIRED: The tax-exempt instrument issued by a local government that is usually not classified as a bond.
DISCUSSION: A municipal bond is usually a long-term obligation issued to obtain funds for a variety of public purposes. Municipal notes are obligations of a local government that ordinarily mature in less than 3 years and are not classified as bonds. They are designated as tax anticipation, revenue anticipation, or bond anticipation notes because they are redeemable upon receipt of the anticipated taxes, revenue, or refinancing from the proceeds of municipal bonds.
Answers (A) and (B) are incorrect because each is one of the two principal classifications of municipal bonds. Revenue bonds are payable from revenues derived from a particular source. General obligation bonds represent the issuing government's unqualified pledge based on its ability to service the principal and interest when due. Answer (C) is incorrect because industrial development bonds (issued by or on behalf of public authorities to obtain funds to privately finance industrial or commercial facilities) may be classified as municipal bonds if the interest paid is exempt from federal income tax.

47. SFAS 60, *Accounting and Reporting by Insurance Enterprises*, sets forth specialized accounting principles and practices for insurance enterprises other than mutual life insurance companies, assessment enterprises, and fraternal benefit societies. With respect to short-term insurance contracts (primarily property and liability insurance contracts),

A. Claim costs are expensed when paid.

B. Premiums are recognized as revenue over the contract period in proportion to the amount of insurance protection provided.

C. Claim costs for claims relating to insured events that have occurred but have not yet been reported are not expensed until reported.

D. If premiums are subject to adjustment as in retroactively rated policies, the premium should ordinarily be accounted for by the cost-recovery method or the deposit method.

The correct answer is (B). *(Publisher)*
REQUIRED: The correct statement about accounting for short-term insurance contracts.
DISCUSSION: Premiums for short-term contracts are recognized as revenue over the period of the contract in proportion to the amount of insurance protection provided.
Answer (A) is incorrect because claim costs are expensed when the insured events occur, not when the claims are settled. Answer (C) is incorrect because claim costs expense should include estimates of insured events that have occurred but have not yet been reported. Answer (D) is incorrect because only if the ultimate premium cannot be easily estimated, which is unusual, should the cost-recovery or deposit method be used. Normally, the ultimate premium is reasonably estimable and is recognized as revenue over the contract period.

48. With respect to insurance companies, which of the following statements is correct concerning the accounting for the valuation of investments?

A. Common and redeemable preferred stocks are reported at market, and bonds are reported at amortized cost.

B. Mortgage loans are reported at outstanding principal or amortized cost.

C. Real estate is reported at depreciated cost.

D. All of the answers are correct.

The correct answer is (D). *(Publisher)*
REQUIRED: The correct statement(s) concerning the valuation of investments by insurance enterprises.
DISCUSSION: Each of the statements is correct according to SFAS 60. Each describes the appropriate basis of accounting for the respective investment assets.
Answers (A), (B), and (C) are incorrect because insurance companies value stock at market, bonds at amortized cost, mortgages at outstanding principal or amortized cost, and realty at depreciated cost.

49. SFAS 97, *Accounting and Reporting by Insurance Enterprises for Certain Long-Duration Contracts and for Realized Gains and Losses from the Sale of Investments*, establishes standards of financial accounting and reporting for investment contracts, limited-payment contracts, and universal life-type contracts. Under SFAS 97,

A. Investment contracts issued by an insurance enterprise shall be accounted for as insurance contracts.

B. The collection of premiums on a limited-payment contract represents the completion of an earning process.

C. Premiums collected on universal life-type contracts shall be reported as revenue in the statement of earnings.

D. Premiums from long-duration contracts, such as whole-life contracts, shall be recognized as revenue when due from policyholders.

The correct answer is (D). *(Publisher)*
REQUIRED: The accounting provision established by SFAS 97.
DISCUSSION: SFAS 60, *Accounting and Reporting by Insurance Enterprises*, was amended by SFAS 97 to require that premiums from long-duration contracts, such as whole-life contracts, guaranteed renewable term life contracts, and title insurance contracts, be recognized as revenue when due from policyholders.
Answer (A) is incorrect because investment contracts, as defined by SFAS 97, do not incorporate significant insurance risk and shall not be accounted for as insurance contracts. Answer (B) is incorrect because the collection of premiums does not represent the completion of an earning process. Any gross premium (the premium charged for an insurance contract) exceeding the net premium (the part of the gross premium required to provide for benefits and expenses) is deferred and recognized in income in a constant relationship with insurance in force (life insurance) or with expected future payments (annuity contracts). Answer (C) is incorrect because the collection of premiums on universal life-type contracts shall not be recorded as revenue. Revenue is based on amounts assessed against policyholders and is ordinarily reported in the period of assessment.

50. SFAS 61, *Accounting for Title Plant*, applies to title insurance enterprises. It defines title plant as including

A. Indexed and cataloged information concerning ownership and encumbrances on parcels of the land in a geographic area.

B. Information relating to persons having an interest in real estate.

C. Maps and plots, copies of prior title insurance contracts, and other documents and records.

D. All of the answers are correct.

The correct answer is (D). *(Publisher)*
REQUIRED: The components of a title plant as defined in SFAS 61.
DISCUSSION: A title plant constitutes a historical record of all matters affecting title to parcels of land in a particular geographic area. It includes all of the items in (A) through (C). Updated on a daily or other frequent basis, title plants are maintained for the number of years required by regulation and for the minimum information period considered necessary to issue title insurance policies efficiently. Title plant does not include the building, furniture, fixtures, etc., of the title insurance firm.
Answers (A), (B), and (C) are incorrect because title plant includes information about ownership and encumbrances, persons having an interest in real estate, and various documents and records.

51. SFAS 61 applies to title insurance enterprises, title abstract enterprises, and title agents that use a title plant in their operations. Which is the false statement about accounting for title plants?

A. The costs of a title plant should not be depreciated.

B. The costs of maintaining a title plant and doing title searches should be expensed as incurred.

C. The cost incurred to construct a title plant should be capitalized.

D. Costs subsequent to initial operations to convert to another information retrieval system should be capitalized but not depreciated.

The correct answer is (D). *(Publisher)*
REQUIRED: The false statement about accounting for title plants.
DISCUSSION: The costs of title plants should be capitalized as they are developed. After completion, they should not be depreciated. All the costs of updating (maintaining) the title plant and doing title searches should be expensed as incurred. Costs of subsequent modernization of the information retrieval system or conversion to another retrieval system should be capitalized and expensed systematically and rationally (i.e., depreciated).
Answers (A) and (C) are incorrect because title plant costs are capitalized but not depreciated. Answer (B) is incorrect because costs of updating and title searches are expensed as incurred.

52. SFAS 65, *Accounting for Certain Mortgage Banking Activities*, as amended by SFAS 91, *Accounting for Nonrefundable Fees and Costs Associated with Originating or Acquiring Loans and Initial Direct Costs of Leases*, establishes accounting and reporting standards for the mortgage banking industry. Which of the following is an appropriate method of accounting for this industry?

A. Loan origination fees related to loans held for investment are recognized as revenue when the loans are consummated.

B. Direct loan origination costs related to loans held for investment are recognized as revenue when the loans are consummated.

C. Fees for services performed by third parties and loan placement fees are recognized as revenue over the life of the loan.

D. Loan origination fees related to loans held for resale are deferred until the related loan is sold.

The correct answer is (D). *(Publisher)*
REQUIRED: The accounting prescribed for the mortgage banking industry.
DISCUSSION: SFAS 65 as amended by SFAS 91 states that if a loan is held for resale, loan origination fees and the direct loan origination costs specified in SFAS 91 are deferred until the related loan is sold.
Answers (A) and (B) are incorrect because, if the loan is held for investment, loan origination fees and the direct loan origination costs specified in SFAS 91 are deferred and recognized as an adjustment of yield by the interest method. Answer (C) is incorrect because fees for services performed by third parties and loan placement fees are recognized as revenue when all significant services have been performed.

53. SFAS 91 is an attempt to standardize the accounting by financial institutions for nonrefundable loan origination fees and direct loan origination costs. The adjustment for these items is recognized in accordance with which of the following methods?

A. Straight-line method.

B. Sum-of-the-years'-digits method.

C. Interest method.

D. Double-declining-balance method.

The correct answer is (C). *(P.E. Bayes)*
REQUIRED: The method used to amortize loan origination fees and direct loan origination costs.
DISCUSSION: Loan origination fees and direct loan origination costs are deferred and recognized over the life of the related loan as an adjustment of yield. Such fees and costs for a given loan are offset, and only the net amount is deferred and amortized. The net amount of fees or costs that is required to be recognized as an adjustment of yield over the life of the related loan is normally recognized by the interest method.
Answers (A), (B), and (D) are incorrect because the interest method is required.

34.8 Real Estate

54. For which of the following forms of investment in real estate or real estate development projects by two or more entities may the cost basis of accounting be more appropriate for the investor than the equity basis?

A. An undivided interest that is subject to joint control by the owners.

B. A corporate joint venture.

C. A noncontrolling interest in a general partnership.

D. A controlling interest in a limited partnership.

The correct answer is (A). *(Publisher)*
REQUIRED: The form of investment in real estate or real estate development projects that ordinarily may be accounted for by an investor on the cost basis.
DISCUSSION: SOP 78-9, *Accounting for Investments in Real Estate Ventures*, states that an undivided interest that is subject to joint control by both the owners and a noncontrolling interest in a limited partnership may, if the investment is minor, be more appropriately accounted for on the cost basis than the equity basis.
Answers (B), (C), and (D) are incorrect because each should ordinarily be accounted for either on the equity basis or as a subsidiary.

55. Which of the following valuation bases is appropriate for recording property acquired by a real estate investment trust (REIT) in a troubled debt restructuring?

A. Carrying value of the debtor.

B. Fair value as if the property had been acquired for cash.

C. Net realizable value.

D. Price level adjusted value.

The correct answer is (B). *(Publisher)*
REQUIRED: The value at which property acquired by a REIT in a troubled debt restructuring should be recorded.
DISCUSSION: SOP 78-2, *Accounting Practices of Real Estate Investment Trusts*, states that property acquired by a REIT as the creditor in a troubled debt restructuring should be recorded as if the property had been acquired for cash at its fair value.
Answers (A) and (D) are incorrect because neither has theoretical support in any transaction. Answer (C) is incorrect because an entry value rather than an exit value is deemed appropriate by SOP 78-2.

56. A commitment fee is defined, in general, as any fee paid by a potential borrower to a potential lender for a promise to lend money in the future. For a REIT, the recognition of income from commitment fees should be in accordance with which of the following?

A. Immediate recognition.

B. Deferral and amortization over the commitment period.

C. Deferral and amortization over the loan period.

D. Deferral and amortization over the combined commitment and loan periods.

The correct answer is (D). *(Publisher)*
REQUIRED: The basis for the recognition by a REIT of income from commitment fees.
DISCUSSION: SOP 75-2, *Accounting Practices of Real Estate Investment Trusts*, requires that income from commitment fees be recognized by a REIT by deferral and amortization over the combined commitment and loan periods.
Answers (A), (B), and (C) are incorrect because none of these alternatives is permitted by SOP 75-2.

57. For a real estate investment trust, the method for determining a provision for loan losses should be based on which of the following?

    A. An evaluation of the individual loans and foreclosed properties.

    B. The percentages of loan balances outstanding.

    C. A percentage of income.

    D. Actual loan defaults.

The correct answer is (A). *(Publisher)*
    REQUIRED: The basis for determining a provision for loan losses of REITs.
    DISCUSSION: The allowance for losses of REITs should be based on an evaluation of the recoverability of individual loans and properties. Consideration should be given to the circumstances at the time of the evaluation and to reasonable probabilistic estimates of future economic conditions and other relevant information (SOP 75-2).
    Answers (B), (C), and (D) are incorrect because methods other than the evaluation of the individual loans and foreclosed properties are not permitted.

58. SOP 75-2 states that the recognition of interest revenue by a REIT should be discontinued when it is no longer reasonable to expect that the revenue will be received. Which of the following conditions establishes a presumption that interest revenue will not be received?

    A. The borrower is in default.

    B. The payments of principal or interest are past due.

    C. The creditworthiness of the borrower is in doubt because of pending or actual bankruptcy.

    D. All of the answers are correct.

The correct answer is (D). *(Publisher)*
    REQUIRED: The condition(s) establishing a presumption that interest revenue will not be received.
    DISCUSSION: The borrower's default or bankruptcy or overdue payments should each be regarded as a condition that establishes a presumption that revenue will not be received and that recognition of interest revenue should be discontinued. Other considerations that establish this presumption are that the loan has been renegotiated, foreclosure procedures have been or are expected to be initiated, and cost overruns and/or delays in construction cast doubt on the economic viability of the project.
    Answers (A), (B), and (C) are incorrect because the presumption is established when the borrower is in default, payments are overdue, or the borrower is bankrupt.

59. SFAS 67, *Accounting for Costs and Initial Rental Operations of Real Estate Projects*, requires that certain costs be capitalized as part of the cost of a real estate project. Which of the following costs is not capitalized?

    A. Payment to obtain an option to acquire real property.

    B. Property taxes and insurance during the construction period.

    C. Indirect project costs that relate to several real estate projects.

    D. Incremental costs from incidental operations in excess of incremental revenues.

The correct answer is (D). *(Publisher)*
    REQUIRED: The cost that should not be capitalized as part of the cost of a real estate project.
    DISCUSSION: SFAS 67 states that incremental revenue from incidental operations in excess of incremental costs (e.g., profits from an adjacent golf course) should be accounted for as a reduction of the capitalized project costs. However, incremental costs in excess of incremental revenues should not be capitalized. They should be expensed because the incidental operations did not reduce the cost of developing the property for its intended use.
    Answers (A), (B), and (C) are incorrect because SFAS 67 requires each to be capitalized as part of the cost of a real estate project.

60. According to SFAS 67, preacquisition costs such as payments to obtain an option to acquire real property should be capitalized. Other costs related to real property that are incurred before the enterprise acquires the property should be capitalized if certain conditions are met. Which of the following is not one of the conditions required to be met before other preacquisition costs are capitalized?

A. The costs are directly identifiable with a specific property.

B. The costs would be capitalized if the property had already been acquired.

C. Acquisition of an option to acquire the property is probable.

D. Acquisition of the property is reasonably possible.

The correct answer is (D). *(Publisher)*
REQUIRED: The condition that is not required to be met before preacquisition costs are capitalized as part of the cost of a real estate project.
DISCUSSION: The reasonable possibility that a real estate property may be acquired is not sufficient. One of the conditions required by SFAS 67 is that acquisition of the property or of an option to acquire the property be probable.
Answers (A), (B), and (C) are incorrect because each is required by SFAS 67 for capitalization of preacquisition costs.

61. Which of the following statements about costs incurred to sell and rent real estate projects is true?

A. All costs incurred to sell real estate projects should be expensed as incurred.

B. All costs incurred to rent real estate projects should be expensed as incurred.

C. A real estate project is considered substantially completed and held available for occupancy no later than 1 year from the cessation of major construction activities.

D. A real estate project for which portions are under construction and other portions are substantially completed and held available for occupancy should be accounted for as a single project.

The correct answer is (C). *(Publisher)*
REQUIRED: The correct statement about costs incurred to sell and rent real estate projects.
DISCUSSION: SFAS 67 states that a real estate project should be considered substantially completed and held available for occupancy upon completion of tenant improvements by the developer, but no later than 1 year from the cessation of major construction activity. When the project is substantially complete, costs are expensed as they accrue and previously capitalized costs should be amortized.
Answer (A) is incorrect because costs incurred to sell real estate projects should be capitalized if they are incurred for tangible assets used directly throughout the selling period to aid in the sale of the project. Answer (B) is incorrect because costs incurred to rent a real estate project should be capitalized if they directly relate to the rental of the real estate project and their recovery is reasonably expected.
Answer (D) is incorrect because costs related to a rental project for which some portions are substantially completed and others are still under construction should be allocated to each portion, which then should be treated as separate projects.

62. According to SFAS 67, *Accounting for Costs and Initial Rental Operations of Real Estate Projects*, allocation of capitalized costs to the components of a real estate project may not be done on the basis of

A. Relative fair value before construction.

B. Relative sales value.

C. Land area.

D. An equal amount to each component.

The correct answer is (D). *(CMA 685 3-35)*
REQUIRED: The inappropriate basis for allocation of the capitalized cost to the components of a real estate project.
DISCUSSION: SFAS 67 states that the preferable method of allocating capitalized costs of a real estate project to its individual components is specific identification. If specific identification is not practicable, however, land costs should be allocated based on the relative fair values of the individual land parcels before construction, and construction costs should be allocated to the individual units on the basis of the relative sales value of each unit. Furthermore, if allocation based on relative value is also not practicable, the capitalized cost should be allocated based on an area method such as square footage or other value method appropriate under the circumstances.
Answers (A), (B), and (C) are incorrect because each may be used as a basis of allocation in certain circumstances.

63. SFAS 66, *Accounting for Sales of Real Estate*, defines a retail land sales project as a homogeneous, reasonably contiguous area of land that may, for development and marketing, be subdivided in accordance with a master plan. Which of the following statements is true about the recognition of profit for sales transactions within a retail land sales project?

    A. A single method of recognizing profit will be determined and used without change for all sales transactions within a project.

    B. A single method of recognizing profit that will be changed when certain conditions are met for the entire project should be applied to all sales transactions within a project.

    C. The full accrual method of recognizing profit should be applied to all sales transactions within a project.

    D. The installment method of recognizing profit should be applied to all sales transactions within a project.

The correct answer is (B). *(Publisher)*
    REQUIRED: The correct statement about the recognition of profit on sales transactions within a retail land sales project.
    DISCUSSION: SFAS 66 requires that a single method be used to recognize profit from all sales transactions within a retail land sales project. However, when certain conditions change for the entire project, the method of recognizing profit should be changed to reflect the new conditions.
    Answer (A) is incorrect because the single method should be changed to reflect changed conditions. Answers (C) and (D) are incorrect because certain criteria specified in SFAS 66 must be met before the installment method can be used, and still more criteria must be met before the full accrual method can be used in a retail land sales project.

64. For a particular retail land development project, the Reliable Company requires at least a 25% down payment. The period of cancellation with refund for this project has expired on the lots sold, and the receivables from the sale are not subject to subordination to new loans on the property. Under what additional condition should the full accrual basis of accounting for the profit be used to account for the sales transactions?

    A. The seller is financially capable.

    B. The development is practical.

    C. Progress has been made on improvements.

    D. The development has been completed.

The correct answer is (D). *(Publisher)*
    REQUIRED: The additional condition that must be met before the full accrual method may be used to account for a retail land sale.
    DISCUSSION: SFAS 66 requires that the full accrual method of accounting be applied to a retail land sale if all of the following conditions are met:

1. The period of cancellation with refund has expired.
2. Cumulative payments equal or exceed 10% of the contract sales price.
3. The receivables are collectible.
4. The receivables are not subject to subordination.
5. The development is complete.

A down payment of at least 20% is considered an acceptable indication of the collectibility of receivables. Because all other conditions are met, the full accrual method should be used if the development has been completed.
    Answer (A) is incorrect because this condition, in addition to the first two of the five conditions listed above, indicates that the installment method should be used. Answers (B) and (C) are incorrect because these conditions, together with the first four of the five conditions listed above, indicate that the percentage-of-completion method should be used.

65. Which method of recognizing profit should be applied to all sales transactions within a retail land sales project if the period of cancellation with refund has expired for the project, the cumulative payments are at least equal to 10% of the sales price, the receivables are collectible and are not subject to subordination, there has been progress on improvements, and the development is practical?

A. The full accrual method.

B. The percentage-of-completion method.

C. The installment method.

D. The deposit method.

The correct answer is (B). *(Publisher)*
REQUIRED: The accounting method that should be applied given the conditions listed.
DISCUSSION: SFAS 66 requires that the percentage-of-completion method of accounting be applied to sales transactions within a retail land sales project if all of the following criteria are met:

1. The period of cancellation with refund has expired.
2. Cumulative payments equal or exceed 10% of the contract sales price.
3. The receivables are collectible.
4. The receivables are not subject to subordination.
5. There has been progress on improvements.
6. The development is practical.

Answer (A) is incorrect because the full accrual method should be used if, in addition to the first four criteria, the development has been completed. Answer (C) is incorrect because the installment method should be used if, in addition to the first two criteria, the seller is financially capable. Answer (D) is incorrect because the deposit method should be used when the necessary criteria for the other three methods are not met.

66. Which of the following methods should be used to account for retail land sales when (1) the period of cancellation with refund has expired, (2) the cumulative payments of principal and interest equal at least 10% of the contract sales price, and (3) the seller is financially capable?

A. Full accrual.

B. Percentage-of-completion.

C. Installment.

D. Deposit.

The correct answer is (C). *(Publisher)*
REQUIRED: The accounting method for the described retail land sales.
DISCUSSION: SFAS 66 requires that the installment method of accounting be applied to a retail land sales transaction for which the period of cancellation with refund has expired, the cumulative payments equal or exceed 10% of the contract sales price, and the seller is financially capable.

Answers (A) and (B) are incorrect because each method is appropriate only when conditions have been met in addition to those required for the installment method. Answer (D) is incorrect because the deposit method should be used only when the criteria for all the other methods have not been met.

67. According to SFAS 66, which of the following conditions does not indicate that a sale has been consummated in a real estate sales transaction other than a retail land sale?

A. The parties are bound by the terms of a contract.

B. All consideration has been exchanged.

C. Any permanent financing for which the seller is responsible has been arranged.

D. An agreement to sell is signed.

The correct answer is (D). *(Publisher)*
REQUIRED: The condition that is not indicative of the consummation of a real estate sale.
DISCUSSION: In addition to the conditions listed in (A) through (C), SFAS 66 requires that all conditions precedent to closing must have been performed. The four conditions required are usually met at the time of closing or after closing, not when an agreement to sell is signed or at a preclosing.

Answers (A), (B), and (C) are incorrect because the consummation of a real estate sale occurs when the parties are bound, consideration has been exchanged, and permanent financing has been arranged.

68. SFAS 66 requires that profit be recognized in full on real estate sales transactions other than retail land sales, provided that the profit is determinable and the earning process is virtually complete. Which of the following criteria must be met before the full accrual method may be used to recognize profit on real estate sales transactions other than retail land sales?

A. The sale is consummated.

B. The buyer demonstrates a commitment to pay for the property.

C. The seller's receivable is not subject to future subordination.

D. All of the answers are correct.

The correct answer is (D). *(Publisher)*

REQUIRED: The condition(s) that must be met before the full accrual method of accounting for profit may be used for a nonretail land sale.

DISCUSSION: SFAS 66 requires that the sale be consummated, the buyer demonstrate a commitment to pay, and the seller's receivable not be subordinated. In addition, the seller must not have a substantial continuing involvement with the property.

Answers (A), (B), and (C) are incorrect because consummation of the sale, demonstration of the buyer's commitment to pay, and the priority of the seller's receivable are conditions for use of the full accrual method.

69. One of the conditions required by SFAS 66 before the full accrual method of accounting for nonretail real estate sales may be used is that the buyer's initial and continuing investments are adequate to demonstrate a commitment to pay for the property. In measuring the adequacy of a buyer's initial investment, which of the following payments should be included in the determination of the initial investment?

A. Payments by the buyer to third parties to reduce existing indebtedness on the property.

B. A permanent loan commitment by an independent third party to replace a loan made by the seller.

C. Payments by the buyer to third parties for improvements to the property.

D. Funds that have been or will be lent, refunded, or directly or indirectly provided to the buyer by the seller.

The correct answer is (A). *(Publisher)*

REQUIRED: The consideration that should be included in the determination of the buyer's initial investment.

DISCUSSION: SFAS 66 states that the buyer's initial investment should include only the following:

1. Cash paid as a down payment.
2. The buyer's notes supported by irrevocable letters of credit from an independent, established lending institution.
3. Amounts paid by the buyer that are part of the sales value.
4. Payments by the buyer to third parties to reduce existing indebtedness on the property.

Answers (B), (C), and (D) are incorrect because each is explicitly excluded by SFAS 66 from the determination of the buyer's initial investment.

70. If a real estate sale is not a retail land sale, the seller has transferred substantially all of the risks and rewards of ownership, and the buyer's initial or continuing investment does not qualify for the full accrual method, but the recovery of the cost of the property is reasonably assured if the buyer defaults, which method of accounting should be used?

A. Deposit method or cost-recovery method.

B. Installment method or cost-recovery method.

C. Deposit method or installment method.

D. Installment method only.

The correct answer is (B). *(Publisher)*

REQUIRED: The appropriate accounting method(s) for real estate sales when recovery of the cost of the property is reasonably assured.

DISCUSSION: For real estate sales other than retail land sales, SFAS 66 states that if the buyer's initial investment does not meet the criteria for the accrual method, but recovery of the cost of the property is reasonably assured if the buyer defaults, the installment method should be used. The cost-recovery method may also be used to account for nonretail sales of real estate for which the installment method would be appropriate.

Answer (A) is incorrect because the deposit method is appropriate only when recovery of the cost of the property is not reasonably assured if the buyer defaults. Answer (C) is incorrect because the deposit and installment methods are never appropriate for the same transaction. Answer (D) is incorrect because the cost-recovery method may also be used when the installment method is appropriate.

APPENDIX A
MODULE CROSS-REFERENCES TO INTERMEDIATE AND ADVANCED FINANCIAL ACCOUNTING TEXTBOOKS

The next 9 pages contain the tables of contents of current intermediate and advanced financial accounting textbooks with cross-references to the related modules or chapters in this study manual. The books are listed in alphabetical order by the first author. As you study a particular chapter in your intermediate or advanced textbook, you can easily determine which module(s) to study in this manual. You should review all questions in the module.

INTERMEDIATE ACCOUNTING TEXTBOOKS

Chasteen, Flaherty, O'Connor, *Intermediate Accounting,* Fourth Edition, Random House, 1992.

Dyckman, Dukes, Davis, *Intermediate Accounting*, Third Edition, Richard D. Irwin, 1995.

Kieso and Weygandt, *Intermediate Accounting,* Eighth Edition, John Wiley & Sons, Inc., 1996.

Mosich, *Intermediate Accounting*, Revised Sixth Edition, McGraw-Hill, Inc., 1989.

Nikolai and Bazley, *Intermediate Accounting,* Seventh Edition, South-Western Publishing Company, 1997.

Smith and Skousen, *Intermediate Accounting,* Twelfth Edition, South-Western Publishing Co., 1995.

Williams, Stanga, Holder, *Intermediate Accounting,* Fifth Edition, The Dryden Press, 1995.

ADVANCED ACCOUNTING TEXTBOOKS

Baker, Lembke, King, *Advanced Financial Accounting,* Third Edition, McGraw-Hill, Inc., 1996.

Beams, *Advanced Accounting,* Sixth Edition, Prentice-Hall, Inc., 1995.

Boatsman, Griffin, Vickrey, Williams, *Advanced Accounting,* Seventh Edition, Richard D. Irwin, 1994.

Engler and Bernstein, *Advanced Accounting,* Third Edition, Richard D. Irwin, 1995.

Fischer, Taylor, *Advanced Accounting,* Sixth Edition, South-Western Publishing Co., 1995.

Haried, Imdieke, Smith, *Advanced Accounting,* Sixth Edition, John Wiley & Sons, Inc., 1994.

Hoyle, *Advanced Accounting*, Fourth Edition, Richard D. Irwin, 1994.

Huefner and Largay, *Advanced Financial Accounting,* Third Edition, The Dryden Press, 1992.

Jensen, Coffman, Stephens, Burns, *Advanced Accounting,* Third Edition, McGraw-Hill, 1994.

Larsen, *Modern Advanced Accounting,* Seventh Edition, McGraw-Hill, Inc., 1997.

Pahler and Mori, *Advanced Accounting: Concepts and Practice,* Fifth Edition, The Dryden Press, 1994.

INTERMEDIATE ACCOUNTING TEXTBOOKS

Chasteen, Flaherty, O'Connor, *Intermediate Accounting*, Fourth Edition, Random House, 1992.

Chapter 1 - Financial Accounting and Reporting: An Introduction and Historical Development - 4.1
Chapter 2 - Financial Accounting and Reporting: A Theoretical Structure - 4.2
Chapter 3 - Accounting Process: Error Analysis and Correction - 5.1-5.3
Chapter 4 - The Income Statement - Ch. 6, Ch. 18
Chapter 5 - The Balance Sheet - 8.1-8.3
Chapter 6 - The Statement of Cash Flows - 22.1-22.4
Chapter 7 - Revenue Recognition and Income Determination - 4.3-4.4
Chapter 8 - Short-Term Monetary Items: Cash, Receivables, and Current Liabilities - 8.3, 8.4-8.8
Chapter 9 - Inventory Valuation: Determining Cost and Using Cost Flow Assumptions - 9.1-9.9
Chapter 10 - Inventory Valuation: Departures From Historical Cost and Methods of Estimating Inventory Cost - 9.1-9.9
Chapter 11 - Plant Assets and Intangibles: Acquisition and Subsequent Expenditures - Ch. 10
Chapter 12 - Plant Assets and Intangibles: Depreciation, Depletion, Amortization and Disposition - Ch. 11
Chapter 13 - Financial Instruments: Investments and Equity Securities - 13.1-13.5
Chapter 14 - Financial Instruments: Debt Securities - 13.1-15.5
Chapter 15 - Leases - 17.1-17.5
Chapter 16 - Pensions - 16.1-16.4
Chapter 17 - Income Taxes - 20.1-20.4
Chapter 18 - Stockholders' Equity - 18.1-18.7
Chapter 19 - Earnings Per Share - 22.1-22.3
Chapter 20 - Accounting for Price Changes - 23.1-23.4

Dyckman, Dukes, Davis, *Intermediate Accounting*, Third Edition, Richard D. Irwin, 1995.

Part I - Foundation and Review
    Chapter 1 - The Environment of Accounting - 4.1
    Chapter 2 - The FASB's Conceptual Framework of Accounting - 4.2
    Chapter 3 - Review: The Accounting Information Processing System - Ch. 5
    Chapter 4 - Review: The Income Statement and the Retained Earnings Statement - 6.1-6.5
    Chapter 5 - Review: The Balance Sheet and the Statement of Cash Flows - 8.1-8.3, 22.1-22.4
    Chapter 6 - Interest: Concepts of Future and Present Value - Ch. 7
Part II - Asset Recognition and Measurement
    Chapter 7 - Revenue and Expense Recognition - 4.3-4.4
    Chapter 8 - Cash and Receivables - 8.3, 8.5-8.6
    Chapter 9 - Inventory: Basic Valuation Methods - Ch. 9
    Chapter 10 - Inventory: Alternative Valuation Methods - Ch. 9
    Chapter 11 - Operational Assets: Acquisition, Disposal, and Exchange - Ch. 10
    Chapter 12 - Operational Assets: Depreciation and Impairment - Ch. 11
    Chapter 13 - Intangible Assets and Natural Resources - Ch. 12
    Chapter 14 - Investments in Debt and Equity Securities - Ch. 13
Part III - Liabilities
    Chapter 15 - Short-Term Liabilities - Ch. 14
    Chapter 16 - Long-Term Liabilities - 15.1-15.7
    Chapter 17 - Accounting for Income Taxes - 20.1-20.4
    Chapter 18 - Accounting for Leases - 17.1-17.5
    Chapter 19 - Accounting for Pensions - 16.1-16.4
Part IV - Owners' Equity
    Chapter 20 - Corporations: Contributed Capital - Ch. 18
    Chapter 21 - Corporations: Retained Earnings and Stock Options - Ch. 18
    Chapter 22 - Earnings per Share - Ch. 19
Part V - Special Topics
    Chapter 23 - Statement of Cash Flows - Ch. 22
    Chapter 24 - Accounting Changes and Error Corrections - Ch. 21
    Chapter 25 - Special Topics: Segment Reporting, Interim Reporting, and Disclosures - Ch.'s 29 & 30

Kieso and Weygandt, *Intermediate Accounting,* Eighth Edition, John Wiley & Sons, Inc., 1996.

Mosich, *Intermediate Accounting*, Revised Sixth Edition, McGraw-Hill, Inc., 1989.

Nikolai and Bazley, *Intermediate Accounting,* **Seventh Edition, South-Western Publishing Company, 1997.**

Part 1 - Financial Reporting: Concepts, Financial Statements, and Related Disclosures
    Chapter 1 - The Environment of Financial Reporting - 4.1-4.4
    Chapter 2 - Financial Reporting: Its Conceptual Framework - 4.1-4.4
    Chapter 3 - The Balance Sheet and Statement of Changes in Stockholders' Equity - 8.1-8.3, 18.1-18.7
    Chapter 4 - The Income Statement and Statement of Cash Flows - Ch. 6, Ch. 18, 22.1-22.4
    Chapter 5 - Additional Aspects of Financial Reporting and Financial Analysis
Part 2 - Financial Reporting: Asset Measurement and Income Determination
    Chapter 6 - Cash Receivables - 8.3-8.5
    Chapter 7 - Inventories: Cost Measurement and Flow Assumptions - 9.1-9.3, 9.7, 9.8
    Chapter 8 - Inventories: Special Valuation Issues - 9.4-9.6, 9.9
    Chapter 9 - Property, Plant, and Equipment: Acquisition and Disposal - 10.1-10.5
    Chapter 10 - Depreciation and Depletion - 11.1-11.3
    Chapter 11 - Intangibles - 12.1-12.6
Part 3 - Financial Reporting: Valuation of Liabilities and Investments
    Chapter 12 - Current Liabilities and Contingencies - 14.1-14.8
    Chapter 13 - Long-Term Liabilities and Receivables - 15.1-15.7
    Chapter 14 - Investments - 13.1-13.5
Part 4 - Financial Reporting: Stockholders' Equity
    Chapter 15 - Contributed Capital - 18.1
    Chapter 16 - Earnings Per Share and Retained Earnings - 19.1-19.5
Part 5 - Financial Reporting: Special Topics
    Chapter 17 - Income Recognition and Measurement of Net Assets - 4.4, 25.1-25.3
    Chapter 18 - Accounting for Income Taxes - 20.1-20.4
    Chapter 19 - Accounting for Postemployment Benefits - 16.1-16.4
    Chapter 20 - Accounting for Leases - 17.1-17.5
    Chapter 21 - The Statement of Cash Flows - 22.1-22.3
    Chapter 22 - Accounting Changes and Errors - 21.1-21.4

Smith and Skousen, *Intermediate Accounting,* **Twelfth Edition, South-Western Publishing Co., 1995.**

Part One - Overview of Accounting and Its Theoretical Foundation
    Chapter 1 - Financial Reporting and the Accounting Profession - 4.1-4.4
    Chapter 2 - A Conceptual Framework of Accounting - 4.1-4.4
    Chapter 3 - Review of the Accounting Process - 5.1-5.3
    Chapter 4 - The Income Statement - 6.1-6.5
    Chapter 5 - The Balance Sheet - 22.1-22.4
    Chapter 6 - The Statement of Cash Flows - Ch. 22
    Chapter 7 - Time Value of Money - 7.1-7.3
Part Two - Components of Financial Statements
    Chapter 8 - Cash and Receivables - 8.3-8.5
    Chapter 9 - Inventories: Cost Allocation and Valuation - Ch. 9
    Chapter 10 - Inventories: Estimation and Noncost Procedures - Ch. 9
    Chapter 11 - Noncurrent Operating Assets: Acquisition - 10.1-10.5
    Chapter 12 - Noncurrent Operating Assets: Utilization and Retirement - 11.1-11.3
    Chapter 13 - Liabilities: Current and Contingent - 14.1-14.8
    Chapter 14 - Long-Term Debt - 15.1-15.7
    Chapter 15 - Owners' Equity: Contributed Capital - 18.1, 18.4, 18.5
    Chapter 16 - Owners' Equity: Retained Earnings - 18.2, 18.3, 18.6, 18.7
    Chapter 17 - Investments in Debt and Equity Instruments - Ch. 13
Part Three - Special Problems in Income Determination
    Chapter 18 - Complexities in Revenue Recognition - 4.3, 25.1-25.3
    Chapter 19 - Accounting for Leases - 17.1-17.5
    Chapter 20 - Accounting for Income Taxes - 20.1-20.4
    Chapter 21 - Accounting for Pensions and Other Postretirement Benefits - 16.1-16.4
    Chapter 22 - Accounting Changes and Error Corrections - 29.1-29.5
Part Four - Other Dimensions of Financial Reporting
    Chapter 23 - Earnings Per Share - 22.1-22.3
    Chapter 24 - Reporting the Impact of Changing Prices - Domestic and Foreign - 23.1-23.4
    Chapter 25 - Financial Reporting and Analysis - 26.1-26.6

Williams, Stanga, Holder, *Intermediate Accounting,* Fifth Edition, The Dryden Press, 1995.

Part 1 - Theoretical Foundation for Financial Reporting
    Chapter 1 - The Financial Accounting Environment - 4.1
    Chapter 2 - Financial Accounting Theory - 4.2
    Chapter 3 - Nature and Measurement of the Elements of Financial Statements - 4.2, 4.3, 4.4
    Chapter 4 - Basic Financial Statements - 6.1, 8.1, 8.2
Part 2 - Tools of Accounting
    Chapter 5 - The Accounting Cycle - 5.1, 5.2, 5.3
    Chapter 6 - Compound Interest Concepts - 7.1-7.3
Part 3 - Asset Accounting
    Chapter 7 - Cash and Receivables - 8.3, 8.6-8.8
    Chapter 8 - Inventories: Basic Valuation Methods - 9.1-9.9
    Chapter 9 - Inventories: Additional Valuation Methods - 9.1-9.9
    Chapter 10 - Investments and Funds - 13.1-13.5
    Chapter 11 - Property, Plant, and Equipment: Acquisition and Disposal - 10.1-10.5
    Chapter 12 - Property, Plant, and Equipment: Depreciation, Depletion, and Special Problems - 11.1-11.3
    Chapter 13 - Intangible Assets - 12.1-12.6
Part 4 - Liability and Stockholders' Equity Accounting
    Chapter 14 - Current and Contingent Liabilities - 14.1-14.8
    Chapter 15 - Long-Term Debt - 15.1-15.7
    Chapter 16 - Stockholders' Equity: Corporate Formation and Contributed Capital - 18.1-18.7
    Chapter 17 - Stockholders' Equity: Operations, Earnings, Dividends, and Other Issues - 18.1-18.7
    Chapter 18 - Earnings Per Share - 19.1-19.5
Part 5 - Additional Financial Reporting Issues
    Chapter 19 - Financial Reporting of Income Taxes - 20.1-20.4
    Chapter 20 - Accounting Changes and Corrections of Errors - 21.1-21.4
    Chapter 21 - Revenue Measurement and Income Presentation - 4.3, 6.1-6.5
    Chapter 22 - Reporting Cash Flow Information - 22.1-22.4
    Chapter 23 - Accounting for Leases - 17.1-17.5
    Chapter 24 - Accounting for Retirement Benefits - 16.1-16.4
    Chapter 25 - Additional Disclosure Issues and Financial Analysis - 24.1-24.4, 26.1-26.6
    Chapter 26 - Financial Reporting and Changing Prices - 23.1-23.4

ADVANCED ACCOUNTING TEXTBOOKS

Baker, Lembke, King, *Advanced Financial Accounting,* Third Edition, McGraw-Hill, Inc., 1996.

Chapter 1 - Corporate Expansion and Accounting for Business Combinations - 28.1
Chapter 2 - Reporting Intercorporate Investments in Common Stock - 28.1-28.7
Chapter 3 - The Reporting Entity and Consolidated Financial Statements - 28.1-28.7
Chapter 4 - Consolidation as of the Date of Acquisition - 28.5
Chapter 5 - Consolidation Following Acquisition - 28.5
Chapter 6 - Intercorporate Transfers: Noncurrent Assets - 28.6
Chapter 7 - Intercompany Inventory Transactions - 28.6
Chapter 8 - Intercompany Indebtedness - 28.6
Chapter 9 - Consolidation Ownership Issues - 28.7
Chapter 10 - Additional Consolidation Reporting Issues - 28.7
Chapter 11 - Accounting for Branch Operations - 28.8
Chapter 12 - Multinational Accounting: Foreign Currency Transactions - 31.2
Chapter 13 - Multinational Accounting: Translation of Foreign Entity Statements - 31.1
Chapter 14 - Segment and Interim Reporting - 29.1-29.5, 30.1-30.3
Chapter 15 - SEC Reporting
Chapter 16 - Partnerships: Formation, Operation, and Changes of Membership - 27.1-27.4
Chapter 17 - Partnerships: Liquidations - 27.5
Chapter 18 - Governmental Entities: Introduction and General Fund Accounting - 32.1
Chapter 19 - Governmental Entities: Special Funds and Account Groups - 32.2-32.5
Chapter 20 - Not-For-Profit Entities: Colleges and Universities - 33.2
Chapter 21 - Not-For-Profit Entities: Health Care Providers, Voluntary Health and Welfare Organizations, and Other
             Entities - 33.3-33.5
Chapter 22 - Corporations in Financial Difficulty - 18.5

Beams, *Advanced Accounting*, Sixth Edition, Prentice-Hall, Inc., 1995.

Chapter 1 - Business Combinations - 28.1
Chapter 2 - Stock Investments - Investor Accounting and Reporting - 13.4, 13.5
Chapter 3 - An Introduction to Consolidated Financial Statements - 28.1
Chapter 4 - Consolidation Techniques and Procedures - 13.4, 13.5
Chapter 5 - Intercompany Profit Transactions -- Inventories - 28.6
Chapter 6 - Intercompany Profit Transactions -- Plant Assets - 28.6
Chapter 7 - Intercompany Profit Transactions -- Bonds - 28.6
Chapter 8 - Consolidations - Changes in Ownership Interests - 28.5
Chapter 9 - Indirect and Mutual Holdings - 28.5
Chapter 10 - Subsidiary Preferred Stock, Consolidated Earnings Per Share, and Consolidated Income Taxation
Chapter 11 - Consolidation Theories, Push Down Accounting, and Corporate Joint Ventures
Chapter 12 - Accounting for Branch Operations - 28.8
Chapter 13 - Foreign Currency Concepts and Transactions - 31.2
Chapter 14 - Foreign Currency Financial Statements - 31.1
Chapter 15 - Segment and Interim Financial Reporting - 29.1-29.5, 30.1-30.3
Chapter 16 - Partnerships -- Formation, Operations, and Changes in Ownership Interests - 27.1-27.4
Chapter 17 - Dissolution and Liquidation of a Partnership - 27.5
Chapter 18 - Corporate Liquidations, Reorganizations, and Debt Restructurings for Financially Distressed
          Corporations - 15.7
Chapter 19 - Accounting for State and Local Governmental Units - Part I - 32.1-32.5
Chapter 20 - Accounting for State and Local Governmental Units - Part II - 32.1-32.5
Chapter 21 - Voluntary Health and Welfare Organizations, Health Care Entities, and Colleges and Universities -
          33.1-33.5
Appendix A - SEC Influence on Accounting
Appendix B - Estates and Trusts

Boatsman, Griffin, Vickrey, Williams, *Advanced Accounting*, Seventh Edition, Richard D. Irwin, 1994.

Unit I - Accounting for Combined Corporate Entities
    Chapter 1 - Economic and Accounting Issues in Business Combinations - Ch. 28
    Chapter 2 - Fundamentals of Consolidated Statements - Ch. 28
    Chapter 3 - Issues in Purchase Combinations - Ch. 28
    Chapter 4 - Additional Measurement and Reporting Issues - Ch. 28
    Chapter 5 - Accounting for Corporate Restructurings and Alternative Organizational Forms - Ch. 28
Unit II - Consolidated Statements: An Expanded Analysis
    Chapter 6 - Consolidated Statements -- Unconfirmed Profits on Inventory Transfers - Ch. 28
    Chapter 7 - Consolidated Statements -- Unconfirmed Profits on Intercompany Transfers and Other Assets - Ch. 28
    Chapter 8 - Consolidated Statements -- Preference Interests - Ch. 28
    Chapter 9 - Consolidated Statements -- Changes in Parent Companies' Ownership Percents - Ch. 28
    Chapter 10 - Consolidated Statements -- Special Ownership Configurations - Ch. 28
    Chapter 11 - Branch Accounting; Segmental and Interim Reporting - 28.8, Ch. 29, Ch. 30
Unit III - Accounting for International Operations
    Chapter 12 - Foreign Currency Transactions - 31.2
    Chapter 13 - Foreign Currency Translation - 31.1
    Chapter 14 - Additional Topics in International Financial Reporting
Unit IV - Accounting for Partnerships
    Chapter 15 - Formation and Operations of Partnerships - 27.1-27.2
    Chapter 16 - Realignment of Partnership Ownership Structure - 27.3-27.4
    Chapter 17 - Partnership Liquidation - 27.5
Unit V - Fiduciary and Institutional Accounting
    Chapter 18 - Accounting for Estates and Trusts
    Chapter 19 - Financial Distress: Dissolution, Liquidation and Other Alternatives - 18.5
    Chapter 20 - Accounting for State, County, and Municipal Governmental Units -- General Funds - 32.1
    Chapter 21 - Accounting for State, County, and Municipal Governmental Units -- Other Funds and Account Groups -
          32.2-32.5
    Chapter 22 - Accounting for Colleges and Universities, Hospitals, and Other Nonprofit Organizations - Ch. 33

Engler and Bernstein, *Advanced Accounting,* Third Edition, Richard D. Irwin, 1995.

Chapter 1 - Environmental Issues in Financial Reporting - 28.8
Chapter 2 - Business Combinations -- 28.1-28.3
Chapter 3 - Consolidated Statements -- Date of Acquisition - 28.5
Chapter 4 - Consolidated Statements -- Subsequent to Date of Acquisition - 28.5
Chapter 5 - Consolidated Statements -- Intercompany Profits on Inventories - 28.6
Chapter 6 - Consolidated Statements -- Intercompany Profit on Plant Asset Transfers and Other Matters Related to
          Consolidated Statements - 28.6
Chapter 7 - Consolidated Statements -- Transactions in Intercompany Bonds and Preferred Stock - 28.6
Chapter 8 - Consolidated Statements -- Changes in Parent's Percentage of Ownership of Subsidiary's Stock - 28.3
Chapter 9 - Consolidated Statements -- Complex Affiliation Structures - 28.5
Chapter 10 - Branch Accounting and Alternatives to the Equity Method - 31.1, 31.2
Chapter 11 - Accounting for Foreign Transactions - 31.1, 31.2
Chapter 12 - Accounting for Foreign Currency Translation
Chapter 13 - Segment Reporting by Diversified Enterprises and Interim Financial Reporting - 30.1-30.3
Chapter 14 - Accounting for Estates and Trusts
Chapter 15 - Corporate Reorganizations and Liquidations - 18.5
Chapter 16 - Partnerships -- Formation, Operation, and Changes in Ownership - 27.1-27.4
Chapter 17 - Partnerships -- Liquidation and Dissolution - 27.5
Chapter 18 - Accounting for State and Local Governments -- Basic Concepts and the General Fund - 32.1
Chapter 19 - Accounting for State and Local Governments -- Other Funds and Account Groups - 32.2-32.5
Chapter 20 - Accounting for Colleges and Hospitals - 33.2, 33.3
Chapter 21 - Accounting for Voluntary Health and Welfare Organizations and Other Not-for-Profit Organizations -
          33.4, 33.5

Fischer, Taylor, *Advanced Accounting,* Sixth Edition, South-Western Publishing Co., 1995.

Part 1 - Combined Corporate Entities and Consolidations
    Chapter 1 - Introduction to Business Combinations - 28.1
    Chapter 2 - Consolidated Statements at the Date of Acquisition - 28.3-28.5
    Chapter 3 - Consolidated Statements Subsequent to Acquisition - 28.3-28.5
    Chapter 4 - Intercompany Transactions: Merchandise, Plant Assets, and Notes - 28.6
    Chapter 5 - Intercompany Transactions: Bonds and Leases - 28.6
    Chapter 6 - Cash Flow, EPS, Taxation, and Unconsolidated Investments
    Chapter 7 - Special Issues in Accounting for an Investment in a Subsidiary - 28.7
    Chapter 8 - Subsidiary Equity Transactions; Indirect and Mutual Holdings - 28.5
Part 2 - Multinational Accounting
    Chapter 9 - The International Accounting Environment
    Chapter 10 - Foreign Currency Transactions - Ch. 31
    Chapter 11 - Translation of Foreign Financial Statements - Ch. 31
Part 3 - Special Reporting Concerns
    Chapter 12 - Interim Reporting and Segmental Data - Ch. 29, Ch. 30
    Chapter 13 - The Disclosure of Earnings Per Share
Part 4 - Partnerships
    Chapter 14 - Partnerships: Characteristics, Formation, and Accounting for Activities - 27.1, 27.2
    Chapter 15 - Partnerships: Ownership Changes and Liquidation - 27.3-27.5
Part 5 - Government and Not-For-Profit Accounting
    Chapter 16 - Governmental Accounting: The General Fund and the Account Groups - 32.1
    Chapter 17 - Governmental Accounting: Other Governmental Funds, Proprietary Funds, and Fiduciary Funds -32.2-
          32.5
    Chapter 18 - Accounting for Not-For-Profit: Public and Private Universities - 33.1-33.3
    Chapter 19 - Accounting for Not-for-Profit: Health Care Providers and Voluntary Health and Welfare Organizations -
          33.4
Part 6 - Fiduciary Accounting
    Chapter 20 - Estates and Trusts: Their Nature and the Accountant's Role
    Chapter 21 - Debt Restructuring, Corporate Reorganizations and Liquidations - 18.5

Haried, Imdieke, Smith, *Advanced Accounting,* **Sixth Edition, John Wiley & Sons, Inc., 1994.**

Chapter 1 - Business Combinations - 28.1
Chapter 2 - Consolidated Financial Statements - Date of Acquisition - 28.1
Chapter 3 - Consolidated Financial Statements after Acquisition - 13.4, 13.5, 28.1
Chapter 4 - Assignment, Depreciation, and Amortization of the Difference between Cost and Book Value - 28.4
Chapter 5 - Elimination of Unrealized Profit in Intercompany Sales of Inventory - 28.6
Chapter 6 - Elimination of Unrealized Profit on Intercompany Sales of Property and Equipment - 28.6
Chapter 7 - Deferred Income Tax Consequences in Business Combinations and Consolidated Financial Statements
Chapter 8 - Changes in Ownership Interest - 28.5
Chapter 9 - Indirect Ownership and Reciprocal Stockholdings - 28.5
Chapter 10 - Consolidated Financial Statements -- Miscellaneous Topics - Ch. 28
Chapter 11 - Pooling of Interests and Alternative Concepts of Consolidated Financial Statements - 28.2-28.3
Chapter 12 - The Equity Method of Reporting Investments in Common Stock - 13.4
Chapter 13 - Accounting for Home Office and Branch Activities - 28.8
Chapter 14 - Accounting for Foreign Currency Transactions - Ch. 31
Chapter 15 - The Translation of Financial Statements of Foreign Affiliates - Ch. 31
Chapter 16 - Reporting for Segments and Interim Financial Periods - Ch. 29, Ch. 30
Chapter 17 - Insolvency -- Liquidation and Reorganization - 15.7
Chapter 18 - Partnerships: Formation, Operation, and Ownership Changes - 27.1-27.4
Chapter 19 - Partnership Liquidation - 27.5
Chapter 20 - Introduction to Fund Accounting - 32.1
Chapter 21 - Introduction to Accounting for State and Local Governmental Units - Ch. 32
Chapter 22 - Introduction to Accounting for Nongovernment Nonbusiness Organizations - Ch. 33
Chapter 23 - Accounting for Estates and Trusts
Chapter 24 - Accounting for Installment Sales and Consignment Transactions - 25.1-25.3

Hoyle, *Advanced Accounting,* **Fourth Edition, Richard D. Irwin, 1994.**

Chapter 1 - The Equity Method of Accounting for Investments - 13.3
Chapter 2 - Consolidation of Financial Information - Ch. 28
Chapter 3 - Consolidations -- Subsequent to the Date of Acquisition - Ch. 28
Chapter 4 - Consolidated Financial Statements and Outside Ownership - Ch. 28
Chapter 5 - Consolidated Financial Statements -- Intercompany Asset Transactions - 28.6
Chapter 6 - Intercompany Debt and Other Consolidation Issues - 28.6
Chapter 7 - Consolidated Financial Statements -- Ownership Patterns and Income Taxes - Ch. 28
Chapter 8 - Branch and Consignment Accounting - 28.8
Chapter 9 - Foreign Currency Translation and Remeasurement - Ch. 31
Chapter 10 - International Accounting Standards/National Accounting Standards
Chapter 11 - Segment Reporting - Ch. 30
Chapter 12 - Accounting for Legal Reorganizations and Liquidations - 18.5
Chapter 13 - Partnerships: Formation and Operation - 27.1-27.3
Chapter 14 - Partnerships: Termination and Liquidation - 27.4-27.5
Chapter 15 - Accounting for State and Local Governments (Part One) - Ch. 32
Chapter 16 - Accounting for State and Local Governments (Part Two) - Ch. 32
Chapter 17 - Accounting for Not-for-Profit Organizations: Colleges and Universities - 33.2
Chapter 18 - Accounting for Not-for-Profit Organizations: Health Care Entities and Voluntary Health and Welfare
           Organizations - 33.3-33.4
Chapter 19 - Accounting for Estates and Trusts
Chapter 20 - Financial Reporting and the Securities and Exchange Commission

Huefner and Largay, *Advanced Financial Accounting,* Third Edition, The Dryden Press, 1992.

Part One - Mergers, Acquisitions, and Consolidated Statements
    Chapter 1 - Business Combinations: Mergers and Acquisitions - Ch. 28
    Chapter 2 - Introduction to Consolidation: The Balance Sheet - Ch. 28
    Chapter 3 - Consolidation after Date of Acquisition - Ch. 28
    Chapter 4 - Conceptual Issues and Consolidated Financial Reporting - Ch. 28
    Chapter 5 - Consolidated Financial Statements: Intercompany Transactions 1 - Ch. 28
    Chapter 6 - Consolidated Financial Statements: Intercompany Transactions 2 - Ch. 28
    Chapter 7 - Consolidated Financial Statements: Special Topics - Ch. 28
Part Two - International Operations and Financial Instruments
    Chapter 8 - Translating Foreign Currency Financial Statements - Ch. 31
    Chapter 9 - Accounting for Foreign Currency Transactions - Ch. 31
    Chapter 10 - Financial Instruments: Futures Contracts, Options, and Financial Swaps - 34.3
Part Three - Special Topics in Corporate Reporting
    Chapter 11 - Mergers and Acquisitions: Leveraged Buyouts, Takeover Defenses, and Tax Effects
    Chapter 12 - Branch Accounting and Segment Reporting - 28.8, Ch. 30
    Chapter 13 - The SEC and its Role in Financial Reporting
    Chapter 14 - Bankruptcy, Reorganization, and Troubled Debt - 15.7
Part Four - Governmental and Not-for-Profit Entities
    Chapter 15 - Accounting and Reporting for Routine Activities of Local Government - Ch. 32
    Chapter 16 - Accounting and Reporting for Nonroutine Activities of Local Government - Ch. 32
    Chapter 17 - Accounting and Reporting by Not-for-Profit Organizations - Ch. 33
Part Five - Simple Entities
    Chapter 18 - Personal Financial Statements and Estates of Individuals - 34.1
    Chapter 19 - Partnerships: Formation, Operation, and Expansion - Ch. 27
    Chapter 20 - Partnerships: Contraction, Termination, and Liquidation - Ch. 27

Jensen, Coffman, Stephens, Burns, *Advanced Accounting*, Third Edition, McGraw-Hill, 1994.

Part 1 - Business Combinations and Consolidation
    Chapter 1 - Business Combinations - 28.1
    Chapter 2 - Acquisitions of Stock and Date-of-Acquisition Consolidation - 28.3-28.5
    Chapter 3 - The Equity Method and Postacquisition Consolidation - 28.4-28.5
    Chapter 4 - Intercompany Merchandise Transfers - 28.6
    Chapter 5 - Intercompany Plant Asset Transfers - 28.6
    Chapter 6 - Intercompany Debt Transactions - 28.6
    Chapter 7 - Intercompany Stock Transactions - 28.6
    Chapter 8 - Additional Topics in Consolidation - Ch. 28
    Chapter 9 - Reporting Disaggregated Financial Information - Ch. 30
    Chapter 10 - Researching Accounting Principles - Ch. 4
    Chapter 11 - Corporate Reorganization and Liquidation
Part 2 - Multinational Companies
    Chapter 12 - Restatement of Foreign Financial Statements - 31.1
    Chapter 13 - Foreign Currency Transactions - 31.2
Part 3 - Partnerships and Branches
    Chapter 14 - Partnerships: Formation, Operations, and Ownership Changes - 27.1-27.3
    Chapter 15 - Partnerships: Liquidations - 27.4-27.5
    Chapter 16 - Accounting for Branches - 28.8
Part 4 - Governmental and Nonprofit Entities
    Chapter 17 - Accounting for Governments: Fundamentals and the General Fund - 32.1-32.2
    Chapter 18 - Accounting for Governments: Specific Purpose Funds, Account Groups, and Annual Financial
                Reporting - 31.2-32.5
    Chapter 19 - Accounting for Nonprofit Organizations - 33.1-33.5

Larsen, *Modern Advanced Accounting,* Seventh Edition, McGraw-Hill, Inc., 1997.

Chapter 1 - Ethical Issues in Advanced Accounting
Partnerships
Chapter 2 - Partnerships: Organization and Operation - 27.1-27.4
Chapter 3 - Partnership Liquidation and Incorporation; Joint Ventures - 27.5
Chapter 4 - Accounting for Branches; Combined Financial Statements - 28.8
Business Combinations and Consolidated Financial Statements
Chapter 5 - Business Combinations and Consolidated Financial Statements - 28.1
Chapter 6 - Consolidated Financial Statements: On Date of Purchase-Type Business Combinations - 28.5
Chapter 7 - Consolidated Financial Statements: Subsequent to Date of Purchase-Type Business Combinations - 28.5
Chapter 8 - Consolidated Financial Statements: Pooling-Type Business Combinations - 28.3, 28.4
Chapter 9 - Consolidated Financial Statements: Intercompany Profits (Gains) and Losses - 28.6
Chapter 10 - Consolidated Financial Statements: Income Taxes, Cash Flows, and Installment Acquisitions - 28.5
Chapter 11 - Consolidated Financial Statements: Special Problems - 28.7
Accounting for Nonbusiness Organizations
Chapter 12 - Governmental Entities: General Fund - 32.1
Chapter 13 - Governmental Entities: Other Governmental Funds and Account Groups - 32.2-32.5
Chapter 14 - Governmental Entities: Proprietary Funds, Fiduciary Funds, and Comprehensive Annual Financial Reports - 32.3-32.4
Chapter 15 - Nonprofit Organizations - 33.5
Accounting for Fiduciaries
Chapter 16 - Bankruptcy: Liquidation and Reorganization - 18.5
Chapter 17 - Estates and Trusts
International Accounting Issues
Chapter 18 - International Accounting Standards; Accounting for Foreign Currency Transactions - 31.2
Chapter 19 - Translation of Foreign Currency Financial Statements - 31.1
Chapter 20 - Segments; Interim Reports; Reporting for the SEC - Ch. 30

Pahler and Mori, *Advanced Accounting: Concepts and Practice,* Fifth Edition, The Dryden Press, 1994.

Part I - Consolidated Financial Statements: Fundamentals
Chapter 1 - Internal Expansion: Acct. for Wholly Owned Created Subsidiaries -- At Date of Creation - Ch. 28
Chapter 2 - Internal Expansion: Acct. for Wholly Owned Created Subsidiaries -- Subseq. to Date of Creation - Ch. 28
Chapter 3 - Introduction to Business Combinations - 28.1
Chapter 4 - The Purchase Method of Accounting -- Wholly Owned Subsidiaries - Ch. 28
Chapter 5 - The Purchase Method of Accounting -- Partially Owned Subsidiaries and Block Acquisitions - 28.5
Chapter 6 - The Pooling of Interests Method of Accounting - 28.3, 28.4
Chapter 7 - New Basis of Accounting
Part II - Consolidated Financial Statements: Specialized Subjects
Chapter 8 - Intercompany Transactions: Overall Discussion and Intercompany Inventory Transfers - 28.6
Chapter 9 - Intercompany Fixed Assets Transfers - 28.6
Chapter 10 - Intercompany Bond Holdings - 28.6
Chapter 11 - Changes in Parent's Ownership Interest and Subsidiary with Preferred Stock - Ch. 28
Chapter 12 - Indirect and Reciprocal Holdings - 28.5
Chapter 13 - Income Taxes, Earnings Per Share, and Consolidated Statement of Cash Flows - Ch. 28
Part III - Foreign Transactions and Foreign Operations
Chapter 14 - Reporting Disaggregated Information - Ch. 30
Chapter 15 - Translation of Foreign Currency Transactions - 31.1
Chapter 16 - Translation of Foreign Currency Financial Statements: Concepts - 31.1
Chapter 17 - Foreign Currency Translation: Practice - 31.1
Chapter 18 - Foreign Currency Translation: Evaluating the Validity of the Functional Currency Concept - 31.1
Part IV - Miscellaneous Corporate Reporting Topics
Chapter 19 - Interim Reporting - 29.1-29.5
Chapter 20 - Securities and Exchange Commission Reporting
Chapter 21 - Troubled Debt Restructurings, Bankruptcy Reorganizations, and Liquidations - 15.7, 18.5
Part V - Government and Nonprofit Organizations
Chapter 22 - Governmental Accounting: Basic Principles and the General Fund - 32.1
Chapter 23 - Governmental Accounting: The Special-Purpose Funds and Account Groups - 32.2-32.5
Chapter 24 - Accounting for Nonprofit Organizations - 33.1-33.5
Chapter 25 - Accounting for Private Nonprofit Organizations: New FASB Standards on Contributions and Financial Statements - Ch. 33
Part VI - Partnerships and Estates and Trusts
Chapter 26 - Partnerships: Formation and Operation - 27.1, 27.2
Chapter 27 - Partnerships: Changes in Ownership - 27.3, 27.4
Chapter 28 - Partnerships: Liquidations - 27.5
Chapter 29 - Estates and Trusts

INDEX

SUCCESSFUL
CAREERS IN
ACCOUNTING
BEGIN WITH
THE GLEIM SERIES OF OBJECTIVE
QUESTIONS AND EXPLANATIONS · · ·

The New Gleim
CPA Review Series

*...AND ARE
ACCELERATED
WITH*

- AUDITING & SYSTEMS
- BUSINESS LAW/LEGAL STUDIES
- FEDERAL TAX
- FINANCIAL ACCOUNTING
- MANAGERIAL ACCOUNTING

CONTENT:

- Each book contains about 2,000 multiple-choice questions and can be used in two or more classes.
  - The questions are organized into *modules* (study units) with learning concepts progressing from basic to complex.
  - Each question has an explanation of the correct answer **PLUS** explanations of why each incorrect answer is wrong.
- Exhaustive **cross-references** are presented for all related textbooks, so that you can easily determine which group of questions pertains to a given chapter in your textbook.

PURPOSE:

- To provide *programmed learning* so that you absorb important information more efficiently, more quickly, and more permanently.
- To support other accounting texts by providing questions and answer explanations so that you can test your knowledge before taking exams.
- To give you practice for CIA, CMA, and CPA exams.
- To demonstrate to you the **standards** to which you will be held as a professional accountant.
- To provide complete coverage of all topics, enabling you to improve your college test scores and prepare for certification exams later.

CPA Review (illustrated above), *CIA Review,* and *CMA Review* are each multivolume, comprehensive study programs designed to prepare you to pass the CPA (Certified Public Accountant), CIA (Certified Internal Auditor), and CMA (Certified Management Accountant) exams. *CFM Review* (Corporate Financial Management) is also available.

Each set of books contains structured, point-by-point outlines of all material tested, and clear and concise phraseology to help you understand and remember the concepts. They also explain the respective certification programs, introduce you to examination preparation and grading procedures, and help you organize your examination strategy. Thousands of past exam questions (with our answer explanations) complement the outlines to provide you with a complete and effective study package.

Now available on 3.5" DD diskettes: **CIA, CMA/CFM,** and **CPA Test Prep** interactive software. Each diskette covers one section of each exam with over 1,000 recent questions and explanations.

Gleim Publications, Inc. • P.O. Box 12848 • Gainesville, FL 32604 • (800) 87-GLEIM
(352) 375-0772   FAX: (352) 375-6940   E-MAIL: admin@gleim.com   Internet: www.gleim.com
Telephone Hours: 8:00 a.m. - 7:00 p.m., Mon. - Fri. and 9:00 a.m. - 2:00 p.m., Sat. Eastern Time
Please have your VISA/MasterCard ready

"THE GLEIM SERIES" OBJECTIVE QUESTION AND EXPLANATION BOOKS

AUDITING & SYSTEMS .... (704 pages • 1,784 questions) .... $16.95 $_____
BUSINESS LAW/LEGAL STUDIES ...... (736 pages • 1,788 questions) $16.95
FEDERAL TAX .... (800 pages • 2,524 questions) .... $16.95   _____
FINANCIAL ACCOUNTING .... (768 pages • 1,756 questions) .... $16.95   _____
MANAGERIAL ACCOUNTING .... (752 pages • 1,290 questions) .... $16.95   _____

CIA REVIEW *(7th Edition)*
VOLUME I: Outlines & Study Guides .... $27.95 $_____
VOLUME II: Problems & Solutions .... $27.95   _____

CIA TEST PREP Software (@ $35.00 each part) ☐ Part I ☐ Part II ☐ Part III ☐ Part IV   _____

CMA REVIEW *(7th Edition)*
VOLUME I: Outlines & Study Guides .... $27.95 $_____
VOLUME II: Problems & Solutions .... $27.95   _____

CMA TEST PREP Software (@ $25.00 each part) ☐ Part 1 ☐ Part 2 ☐ Part 3 ☐ Part 4   _____

CFM REVIEW *(1st Edition)* .... $22.95   _____

CFM TEST PREP Software (Part 2CFM only) .... $35.00   _____

CPA REVIEW *(1996-1997 Edition)*

	Books*	Audiotapes	CPA Test Prep Software	
Auditing	☐ @ $24.50	☐ @ $75.00	☐ @ $35.00	$_____
Business Law	☐ @ $24.50	☐ @ $75.00	☐ @ $35.00	_____
TAX-MAN-GOV	☐ @ $24.50	☐ @ $75.00	☐ @ $35.00	_____
Financial	☐ @ $24.50	☐ @ $75.00	☐ @ $35.00	_____

A System for Success (112 pp.) .... ☐ FREE with your order of any Gleim CPA Review book

*Contain outlines, examples, questions, and answer explanations.

The Complete Gleim System (save 15%) .... $457.00 _____
    (5 books, 4 audio cassette albums (41 tapes), and 4 CPA Test Prep diskettes)

Shipping (nonrefundable): **1 item = $3; 2 items = $4; 3 items = $5; 4 or more items = $6** ... _____

Add applicable sales tax for shipments within Florida. .... _____

Fax or write for prices/instructions for shipments outside the 48 contiguous states.   **TOTAL $_____**

1. We process and ship orders daily, generally one day after receipt of your order.

2. Please PHOTOCOPY this order form for use by others.

3. No CODs. All orders from individuals must be prepaid. Library and company orders may be purchased on account. Shipping and a handling charge will be added to the invoice, and to telephone orders.

4. Gleim Publications, Inc. guarantees the immediate refund of all resalable texts if returned within 30 days. Applies only to books purchased direct from Gleim Publications, Inc. Refunds or credit are not offered on software and audiotapes. Our shipping charge is nonrefundable.

NAME (please print) _____

ADDRESS _____ Apt. _____
        (street address required for UPS)

_____

CITY _____ STATE _____ ZIP _____

____ MC/VISA ____ Check/M.O.   Daytime
                                Telephone (_____)_____

MC/VISA _____ - _____ - _____ - _____

Exp. ____/____   Signature _____
    Mo. / Yr.

118F

Printed 12/96. Prices subject to change without notice.

☞ Visit our home page on the Internet at www.gleim.com.

Please forward your suggestions, corrections, and comments concerning typographical errors, etc., to **Irvin N. Gleim • c/o Gleim Publications, Inc. • P.O. Box 12848 • University Station • Gainesville, Florida • 32604**. Please include your name and address so we can properly thank you for your interest.

1. _____

2. _____

3. _____

4. _____

5. _____

6. _____

7. _____

8. _____

9. _____

10. _____

11. _____

12. _____

☞ For updates and other important information, visit our home page (www.gleim.com).

13. _____

14. _____

15. _____

16. _____

17. _____

18. _____

19. _____

20. _____

21. _____

22. _____

Name: _____

Address: _____

City/State/Zip: _____

Telephone: Home: _____   Work: _____   FAX: _____

E-mail: _____